VIRTUE POLITICS

VIRTUE
POLITICS

SOULCRAFT AND STATECRAFT
IN RENAISSANCE ITALY

James Hankins

THE BELKNAP PRESS OF HARVARD UNIVERSITY PRESS

CAMBRIDGE, MASSACHUSETTS

LONDON, ENGLAND

First Harvard University Press paperback edition, 2023
First printing

Design by Dean Bornstein

Library of Congress Cataloging-in-Publication Data

Names: Hankins, James, author.
Title: Virtue politics : soulcraft and statecraft in Renaissance Italy / James Hankins.
Description: Cambridge, Massachusetts : The Belknap Press of
Harvard University Press, 2019. | Includes bibliographical references and index.
Identifiers: LCCN 2019034187 | ISBN 9780674237551 (cloth) | ISBN 9780674278738 (pbk.)
Subjects: LCSH: Social ethics—Italy—History. | Philosophy, Renaissance. |
Ethics, Renaissance. | Common good. | Virtue. | Public interest—Italy—History.
Classification: LCC HM665 .H36 2019 | DDC 170—dc23
LC record available at https://lccn.loc.gov/2019034187

In memory of Virginia Brown, 1940–2009
femina doctissima
uxor carissima
S.T.T.L.

CONTENTS

PREFACE

In the cold winter of 2010 I had the honor and pleasure of delivering the Carlyle Lectures in the History of Political Thought at the University of Oxford. I decided to use the occasion to pull together various reflections and contentions about Italian humanist political thought I had elaborated over the previous fifteen years. My aim was to see whether, suitably developed, they might add up to something like a fresh interpretation of that neglected literature. The book that has at length emerged, though quite different from the lectures as delivered, continues to orbit around the questions I attempted to address on that occasion, and if the answers given to those questions have changed, this is in no small part owing to the stimulus provided by Oxford's extraordinary community of scholars during my residence at All Souls College that winter and again in 2014. Though portions of the book have been presented to many academic audiences from Rome to Munich and from Berkeley to Shanghai, the project as a whole is in essence unchanged from the one delivered in lecture form in the Examination Schools on High Street during Hilary term of 2010.

That project is to describe, effectively (I believe) for the first time, a new kind of political education, and indeed a new way of thinking about political questions, invented and promoted by the Italian humanists in the century and a half from Petrarch to Machiavelli. Claims to originality, whether for oneself or for one's objects of study, always set off alarms among scholars, and the sound of knives being sharpened activates one's instinct to limit and qualify. Nevertheless, I intend to persist in the claim to originality that I hope the book as a whole will justify. The claim that any significant phenomenon can be uncovered in the Western tradition at this stage in the history of scholarship, especially in a period as intensely studied as the Renaissance, is bound to be suspect on its face. But if a neglected tradition is to be discovered anywhere, it seems to me, the likeliest place to find it is among a group of sources that have remained largely unread and difficult of access. The political writings of the humanists, despite specialized study of certain texts, are still, I would contend, relatively unexplored and not well understood as expressions of a movement of moral and civic reform.[1] Even today, especially in the world of Anglophone scholarship, humanist political literature has had the reputation of being theoretically impoverished.[2] It is often dismissed as "mere rhetoric" (in the modern sense of empty verbosity) and derivative, consisting of dull mosaics of classical quotation deployed in the service of flattering princes.

Scholarly humility requires us, however, to recognize that this all-too-typical dismissal of six or seven generations' worth of Renaissance intellectual life might have something to do with certain imperfections in our own point of view. The special *déformation* of modern historians of political thought—our own suspicion of power and propaganda, our battered but still formative myth of progress—hardly equips us to appreciate the humanist cult of eloquence and a type of reforming zeal that worked by idealizing the past. At the same time, a narrow focus on certain attractive themes within Renaissance political thought has, in my view, led to imbalance and distortion in the evaluation of humanist political writing in general. The connection between humanism and republican liberty, as explored by the great Renaissance historians Hans Baron and Eugenio Garin in the 1950s and '60s and again, more broadly, in luminous works by J. G. A. Pocock and Quentin Skinner and their followers from the 1970s onward, has stimulated wide interest in what is called "civic humanism" or "the republican tradition" from the Middle Ages down to the time of the American Revolution and beyond. The tendency to focus on republican liberty, usually combined with anachronistic understandings of what a republic might be, has left in shadow large tracts of humanist political reflection. There are, for instance, rich veins of humanist literature that discuss such themes as the morality of war, empire, and interstate relations generally; cosmopolitanism and the pitfalls (or advantages) of nativism; the proper role of wealth and the wealthy in politics; how rulers may secure obedience without coercion; the dependence of laws and constitutions on the moral character of rulers and the causes of political corruption; the justification for social hierarchies; the moral reform of elites; the theory of deliberation; the role of honor and piety in knitting together the social fabric; and how to diagnose, prevent, and reform the human impulse to tyranny. All these are themes that have been marginalized by a narrative that focuses narrowly on ideas of liberty found in the Renaissance oligarchies we are pleased to honor with the name "republics." Inattention to the wider goals of the movement leads to distortions even when attending to texts that discuss liberty. Scholars tend to dig up the relatively few mentions of republican liberty in the hope of excavating modern understandings of freedom—freedom as a natural right for instance—while failing to notice that for most Renaissance humanists, freedom was a moral achievement, the fruit of virtue, and was prevented from collapse into license only by good character.

Another form of blindness comes from a tendency to base generalizations on the same restricted group of easily accessible texts. These are most often treatises and other works of formal theory that boast titles promising to deal with political subjects. In the Anglophone world especially, the small group of sources studied tend to be works in Italian or works that have been translated (often badly) from Latin. Many scholars have chosen to ignore that, during what Christopher Celenza calls "the long quattrocento," Latin texts were not only far more numerous, but far more prestigious than works written in vernaculars.[3] Longer works in Latin, like Francesco Patrizi's twin treatises on republican and royal education, are sometimes culled for specific themes, but they are less often studied in the round as intellectual projects. And there are whole genres of Renaissance Latin literature that have been overlooked by historians of political thought. Aside from a couple of famous speeches by Leonardo Bruni on republican liberty, the vast collections of humanist oratory, rich in political themes, have hardly been explored; the subtle constitutional analyses in antiquarian writings, such as Biondo Flavio's three books on Roman republican institutions in the *Roma Triumphans,* have remained unread; reflections on politics and international relations found in historical works have received little attention; the commentary literature on texts central to humanist political thought such as Aristotle's *Politics* and *Ethics,* Cicero's *De officiis,* Livy, and Sallust escapes study; epic, lyric, and occasional poetry as well as satire, comedy, and tragedy have been more or less completely ignored. Humanist correspondence is studded with long, semi-public letters, such as Petrarch's letters to the Emperor Charles IV, full of advice fortified by passionate study of ancient political philosophy, but these have typically been studied from a narrowly biographical perspective, if at all. Orations, treatises, letters, prefaces, and dialogues dealing with education, history, biography, descriptive geography, marriage, and household management often bear crucially on political issues, but these have only rarely been recognized as sources for the history of political thought. The humanists were reformers actively engaged in educating and advising elites, and they used every means at their disposal, every genre of literature, every form of art and culture to fill the ears of their audience with their principal message: that cities needed to be governed by well-educated men and women of high character, possessed of practical wisdom, and informed by the study of ancient literature and moral philosophy.

Even more serious than inattention to so-called informal sources of political thought is the general neglect of sources available only in manuscript. The heroic researches of the great Renaissance scholar Paul Oskar Kristeller from the 1930s through the 1990s disclosed to view the enormous body of unpublished Renaissance Latin texts in general and exposed (or should have exposed) as false the common view that any text of importance must have made it into print.[4] This assumption is quite erroneous for the early Renaissance, and there is certainly no guarantee that the authors and texts printed in the last quarter of the fifteenth century were necessarily the ones that were most popular and influential in the fourteenth and early fifteenth centuries. As specialists are well aware, it is a fallacy to believe that there was no publication before the printing press was invented. In fact the world's manuscript depositories still boast tens of thousands of humanistic manuscripts produced by professional scribes for a literate audience, particularly in the period from the 1420s to the 1470s. Individual works by famous writers such as Leonardo Bruni circulated, in some cases, in hundreds of manuscripts that reached every corner of Europe well before the print revolution organized more formal markets for political literature.

There is, to be sure, one great exception to this general pattern of neglect: Machiavelli. Machiavelli's works in all genres have been studied almost to a fault, and stimulating books continue to be published every year about this inexhaustibly fascinating figure. Yet the books that are written, despite the current emphasis on context, are often written in substantial ignorance of the humanist literature about politics that preceded him and to which he was often responding. This situation has led to a serious distortion in wider perceptions about the Renaissance. Since Machiavelli is the only Renaissance author studied in most courses on the history of political thought, he has come to stand proxy for the political thought of the Renaissance almost in the way, two generations ago, Aquinas was taken as the archetypal representative of medieval scholasticism. One goal of this book is to make the case that the common equation of Machiavelli with Renaissance political thought should be resisted. While Machiavelli does indeed develop in an extreme form several strands within Renaissance political thought, he is in most respects highly atypical of humanist thought and in fact challenges it on many levels. Neither the Renaissance nor Machiavelli can be understood if Machiavelli is taken to be typical of the Renaissance.

A comprehensive history of Italian humanist political thought that would survey all the hitherto neglected sources and compensate for the blind spots and distortions of the current literature would certainly be desirable, but that is not the book I have been able to write. My goal in this volume is more modest. I have sought to present the political ideas of the humanists as the expression of a movement of thought and action, similar in its physiognomy if not in its content to the movement of the *philosophes* of the Enlightenment. It was a movement that was stimulated by a crisis of legitimacy in late medieval Italy and by widespread disgust with its political and religious leadership. Its adherents were men who had wide experience—often bitter, personal experience—with tyranny. They knew that oligarchs and even popular governments could be as tyrannical as princes. Their movement was largely in agreement about its goals: to rebuild Europe's depleted reserves of good character, true piety, and practical wisdom. They also agreed widely about means: the revival of classical antiquity, which the humanists presented as an inspiring pageant, rich in examples of noble conduct, eloquent speech, selfless dedication to country, and inner moral strength, nourished by philosophy and uncorrupt Christianity. The humanist movement yearned after greatness, moral and political. Its most pressing historical questions were how ancient Rome had achieved her vast and enduring empire, and whether it was possible to bring that greatness to life again under modern conditions. This led to the question of whether it was the Roman Republic or the Principate that should be emulated; and, once the humanists had learned Greek, it provoked the further question of whether Rome was the only possible ancient model to emulate, or whether Athens or Sparta, or even the Persia of Xenophon's Cyrus, held lessons for contemporary statesmen.

The interpretation of Italian humanism as a movement of moral and political reform presented in this book is not, it must be allowed, the view of the movement that is current among specialists in Renaissance studies today. In recent historical scholarship it has become customary to present humanism as a movement principally concerned with language and style; engaged in the recovery and elaboration of ancient literary genres, methods, and textual practices; and preoccupied with antiquarian and philological questions. This interpretation in my view represents a confusion of ends with means, and reflects the priorities and sympathies of modern scholars more than it does the fundamental values and goals of the humanist movement. The foregrounding in modern scholarship of Lorenzo Valla and Angelo Poliziano, both known primarily for their philological work, is symptomatic of this outlook. I do not of course maintain that the humanists were not concerned, indeed obsessed, with correct texts and correct Latinity. Since they were professional writers, speakers, and teachers, such matters were bound to be among their central concerns as well as sources of prestige among their peers. Nor am I claiming that their work as students of texts and language is unworthy of study. That would be an odd sort of claim from someone who has spent the last forty years of his life doing just that. But no important intellectual movement lasting for centuries and numbering many thousands of adherents can ever acquire a purchase on the collective imagination without appealing to some larger common purposes and values and creating structures within which individuals can pursue meaningful activity. The early scholastics created such values, goals, and structures, as (for example) did the *philosophes* of the Enlightenment and *mutatis mutandis* the early Progressive movement in America. The humanist movement, beginning with Petrarch, did so too. It is these values, goals, and structures that I believe have been neglected or badly understood in the modern literature, and it is the project of this book to recover them.

In presenting portions of this book to various academic audiences over the last seven years, I have sometimes met with a different sort of objection to my understanding of humanist reformers. My critics will grant, since the textual evidence is overwhelming, that humanists talked incessantly about virtue, nobility, and wisdom and the urgent need for the recovery and study of antiquity. There might even be a few humanists, they admit, who believed what they were saying, perhaps a Petrarch or an Erasmus. But for most humanists such "virtue talk" was merely gestural; it was a fashion, copied from ancient sources, adopted to give one's own writings a patina of antiquity; it was a social convention adopted to lay claim to membership in an elite. You urged the young to improve their character or heaped praise on your prince or patron because that was what you were expected to do. No one believed the prince you were praising actually possessed the virtues and wisdom with which you were crediting him. Such advice was self-serving too, since in selling the humanities the humanists were selling their own wares. Moreover, when one looks at what actually went on in humanist schools, the argument continues, reconstructing their practices from surviving schoolbooks or annotated copies of the classics used by schoolmasters, one finds a moral vacuum: total concentration on grammar and syntax and the identification of names and places; utter neglect of any moral or political lessons to be found in the ancient authors. Furthermore, the spectacular misbehavior of many humanists and the elites they trained in the humanities showed that such men evinced little personal concern for virtue and displayed no more wisdom than others among their contemporaries.[5]

This sort of objection misses the point of my argument. Leave aside the question whether any modern historian is able to discern the motives, in all their undoubted complexity, of historical actors living many hundreds of years in the past, or to make reliable generalizations about them. We can make informed guesses, but we can never know. Grant even that many humanists may never have thought deeply about the goals and underlying values of the inherited practices in which they were engaged. This is surely a common feature of all intellectual movements; there are always leaders and followers, visionaries and epigones, as well as parasites and camp followers. To take a parallel case, probably few scholastics after the first generations were actuated by the same splendid vision that drove Irnerius, Gratian, and Abelard to create rational unity and harmony from the cacophony of inherited authorities and to impose divine order on the chaotic societies and the souls of medieval Christians. When humanists thought about their own movement, as Patrick Baker has recently shown, they saw themselves as cultivating eloquence, and through eloquence, civilization.[6] So much is certainly true and certainly illuminating. But the humanists' self-image does not necessarily reveal the deeper goals, values, and structures of the movement. Their belief in the exemplary value of antiquity, their assumption that improving human character through classical education was possible and necessary, their conviction that contemporary states needed the stores of prudence preserved in the experience of the past, were, like the modern belief in progress and science, too obvious, too much taken for granted, to require incessant restatement. And (again like the belief in progress and science) to articulate those underlying assumptions too insistently could have risked calling into question institutions and practices constitutive of individual and social identity. Self-consciousness was therefore difficult and self-criticism a kind of cultural sedition. That sort of consciousness only came later in European civilization, in writers like Machiavelli, Francis Bacon, and Hobbes.

The objection that humanist schoolmasters did not concern themselves—as far as we can tell from representative case studies of schoolroom practice—is easier to answer, and leads to a serious point concerning humanist culture beyond the schoolroom. The modern scholars who began in the later 1980s and '90s to emphasize the evidence of the schoolroom were making the claim that the high educational ideals set forth in humanist treatises on education and taken as pro-grammatic by earlier generations of scholars, were not exemplified by actual schoolroom practice during the Renaissance. The suggestion was that humanist educators were guilty of a certain hypocrisy or at least false advertising when they claimed that their methods would produce exceptional human beings.[7] This criti-cism, I believe, is unfair. It is hardly surprising that Renaissance schoolmasters spent most of their time teaching language and not ethics or politics. They were not leading seminars on Great Books. Their pupils needed to learn Latin before they could learn anything else, and learning Latin at a high level is hard. We would not say to educators who devised pre-medical programs for undergradu-ates today that their programs were ineffectual or constituted false advertising because the students were learning biochemistry and mastering details of cell structure, nucleic acids, and gluconeogenesis but never learning how to live a healthy life. To be a doctor one has to understand biochemistry; to be a person of high character and practical wisdom who can contribute to a human community one needs to be able to study the humanities. Or so the humanists thought.[8]

Moreover, learning to read difficult texts and write and speak in Latin was a foundation, or as the humanists would say, a doorway.[9] Once you passed through the doorway you would find Livy and Sallust, Cicero and Demosthenes, Plato and Aristotle waiting to engage you in conversation.[10] It was the lifelong compan-ionship of the ancients that was supposed to do you good, not the mastery of ir-regular verbs. Real education did not end with grammar school. It was supposed to go on for your entire life. As Cicero wrote in the *Pro Archia*—a speech which became a kind of manifesto for humanists—it was supposed to enrich and inform your entire life.[11] The concept of *institutio* for the humanists did not only mean learning to read old books in school. It meant absorbing the moral and intellec-tual formation human beings needed to live successfully in civilized societies. It included manners *(mores)* learned informally in the family and the school. It in-cluded the customs of the community, practices like those associated with mar-riage, with taking meals together, with showing reverence for elders, with other ritual forms, and with military service.[12] As Machiavelli later learned from Poly-bius and Dionysius of Halicarnassus, the formation of societies via religion, cus-toms, and manners was at least as important to the moral health of a state than legal codes or constitutions. Moral and intellectual excellence could also be sup-ported by what I call "the virtuous environment": physical spaces recalling in their architecture and decoration the nobler world of the ancient Greeks and

Romans, even soundscapes filled with "classical" music.[13] Humanists and the artists inspired by them created a whole culture designed to reshape the soul. And if we look for proof that *humanitas* in its wider sense produced men capable of profound moral and spiritual reflection, it is surely enough to mention the names of Francesco Petrarch, Leonardo Bruni, Lorenzo Valla, Giovanni Pontano, Marsilio Ficino, Francesco Guicciardini, and yes, Niccolò Machiavelli—all men whose education began in the humanist schoolroom but did not end there.

My focus in this book is on humanist writings that bear on political thought, but one lesson we have rightly learned from Hans Baron and Quentin Skinner is that political texts can never and should never be treated in abstraction from the political struggles and social realities that shaped them. We need to be constantly aware of what modern social and political historians have taught us about the lived experience of these frightened and fractious little towns under their often brutal princes and corrupt oligarchs. Using neutral, analytic terminology, where appropriate, is important. For example, in order to avoid the ambiguities of the term *respublica* in the Renaissance, as discussed in Chapter 3, I use the term "oligarchy" throughout to indicate regimes under the control of small groups of men. The term is meant to be descriptive rather than evaluative. It is not intended to signal disapproval, as it does for example in Aristotle's *Politics,* where it is a pejorative term meaning a regime conducted in the interests of the few rather than the many, a corruption of aristocracy, or rule by wealthy men lacking in virtue. I find persuasive the view of Pareto that all government by nature is and must always be oligarchical, the rule of few over many. For a modern scholar to engage in cheerleading in favor of republican as opposed to monarchical regimes strikes me as anachronistic and likely to mislead.[14] The modern West prides itself on its liberal democratic values, and rightly so, and it is certainly understandable that historians have hungered to understand the genesis of those values in the past. But the sort of "tunnel history" (as J. H. Hexter called it decades ago) devoted to archeologizing a "republican tradition" inevitably distorts the very different moral perceptions and categories of historical actors. The Renaissance humanists as a rule were not so ingenuous as to believe that the regimes we call republican were *eo ipso* enlightened and monarchical ones tyrannical; most of them thought pure popular regimes were dangerously unstable and unwise; most thought that the men labeled as tyrants by jurists sometimes made better rulers than those who held legitimate titles to rule. Bartolus' view, widely shared, was that most governments were bad some of the time, and that prudence dictated one take a realistic estimate of the possibilities for improvement before advocating radical regime change, especially any change that involved giving power to ordinary people, usually referred to (tellingly) as the *plebs* or the *vulgus.* Most humanists were conservative, in other words, and even the most enlightened (from our point of view) wanted careful limits on popular power and devices to ensure that the *optimates,* the best men, the great and the good, would predominate in the councils of government. It is impossible to conduct a poll, of course, but if such a poll could be taken, it would likely find that the majority of educated people in the late medieval world preferred monarchy to oligarchy; certainly most political theorists did. We will misunderstand the relatively few humanist voices that defended popular government if we fail to understand that the rhetorical situation they found themselves in was overwhelmingly hostile to their beliefs.

A similar danger of anachronism is involved in the use of the words "humanism" and "humanist." I have decided after some hesitation to go on using these problematic terms, but it should be understood that "humanism" was not a contemporary term, and "humanist" in Renaissance Latin and Italian usage had a much narrower denotation than in modern usage. By the end of the fifteenth century the word *humanista* was sometimes used in university slang to indicate a teacher of the *studia humanitatis,* that is, ancient literature and philosophy, but the commonest terms used for the figures we call "humanists" in the fifteenth century were *literati, oratores, viri docti, studiosi, eruditi* and—interestingly, in view of the word's later history—*philosophi.*[15] In the fourteenth century Petrarch and Boccaccio often used *poetae* for the kind of men most interested in ancient culture and the artistic use of language. The terms *studiosi* and *docti* are sometimes clarified by the addition of words indicating the objects of study: *bonae litterae, optimae* or *bonae artes, honestissimae artes, studia eloquentiae, studia humanitatis.* These terms were meant to exclude the professional study of law, medicine, or theology, though it was recognized (and applauded) that many lawyers, doctors, and theologians could have interests in the humanities as well. Contemporaries were also conscious of a difference between those who had a professional interest in the language arts—chiefly schoolteachers, university professors of humane subjects, secretaries and chancellors of public men and public bodies, diplomats and court poets—and those who were their auditors, readers, patrons, and employers. From the mid-quattrocento onward there was a further penumbra of humanism, as doctors, lawyers, philosophers, and theologians began using the methods and sources made popular by the humanists. The terms "humanist" and "humanism" are less likely to mislead now than formerly, thanks to the work of Paul Oskar Kristeller, who carefully distinguished Renaissance humanism from its nineteenth- and twentieth-century namesake.[16] The danger for scholars today is more likely to be a tendency to reify a phenomenon that displayed important local variations, or to attribute a stable identity to groups of writers whose interests, aims, and methods developed dynamically over time. As Ronald Witt has shown, the humanist movement had deep roots in the literary culture of the Middle Ages, a culture that defined itself in part by its long rivalry with the legal culture of medieval Italy.[17] That rivalry continued to shape the political thinking of humanists in the Renaissance, as we shall see, and to define the fresh approach to political problems I explore in Chapter 2. In the case of political thought, the reification of humanism in modern scholarship has often taken the form of regarding it as "republican" in its essence, a characterization that is far from accurate.[18] It is one of the goals of this book to show that what was common to humanist political literature was a commitment, not not to a particular regime type or to "republican liberty," but rather to a reform project that was in a certain sense *supra partes,* directed at political elites in general, whatever regime they served.

The plan of this book is as follows. It begins in Chapter 1 with an account of the origins of Renaissance humanism in the work of Petrarch, particularly as it bears on political thought. In Chapter 2, I present an overview of humanist virtue politics, describing in broad terms the assumptions about politics common to most humanists. One argument of this book is that Italian humanist political thought has an underlying unity that transcends partisan commitments to particular forms of government or constitutions, and Chapter 2 is where that argument is principally laid out. To put this another way, while in the ancient world an emphasis on virtue and reason is normally associated with anti-democratic politics, in the Renaissance, I contend, virtue politics is compatible with different regime types, including popular regimes, and this feature is one of its strengths as an approach to political reform. Whereas the central question of ancient political theory (according, at least, to some modern interpreters) is, What is the best regime?, for the humanists constitutional form was far less important than the character of rulers.[19] Hence in this chapter I try also to explain why humanist political thought represents a distinctive way of thinking about politics, focusing as it does on improving the character of rulers and political elites rather than re-designing regimes and reforming institutions. The third chapter discusses humanist ideas of the state, in particular what the humanists meant by the term "republic"; it also explains why all humanist political thought, whether written by humanists in the service of oligarchies or of princes, could be described as "republican," and why "civic humanism" is not necessarily an ideological product of popular regimes. The fourth chapter discusses humanist concepts of tyranny, arguing that in general they represent a rejection of the Ciceronian and Roman-law understanding of tyranny in favor of what I call a "Greek" conception, at once more realistic and more focused on questions of moral psychology.

In the following twelve chapters I present the political thought of nine key humanist thinkers and show how they exemplify the principles of virtue politics, despite their very different political commitments. These thinkers endorsed a variety of regime types and represented a broad spectrum of opinion on a range of topics, including foreign relations and warfare (Chapters 8 and 9). They did not form a school elaborating the vision of a single thinker, like Marxists or Confucians, but drew on a common and constantly expanding reservoir of ancient sources—continually enriched with sources newly translated from Greek—to assemble distinctive versions of virtue politics. It is another aim of this book to trace the enrichment of Western political thought via this "second wave" in the reception of Greek texts. Chapter 14 discusses how George of Trebizond's passionate rejection of Platonic political thought led him to anticipate modern ideas about political liberalism and cosmopolitanism. Chapters 15–17 discuss how humanist political thinkers responded to new Greek sources made available by humanist scholars, in particular those describing the Spartan regime, those containing expositions of non-Aristotelian regime theory, and those presenting classical and Hellenistic theories of ideal kingship. Chapter 16 reveals a growing awareness among humanists that the fundamental project of virtue politics—reforming the character of political leaders or *principes*—would ultimately require corroboration from laws and institutions. Chapters 16 and 17 together show how humanist writings prepared the ground for early modern debates about constitutionalism and absolutism. I end with three chapters on Machiavelli, both to defend my contention that Machiavelli's politics is atypical of humanist political thought, being hostile to the basic principles of virtue politics, and also to bring into sharper relief the distinctive character of humanist thinking on politics in general. In the conclusion I discuss parallels between virtue politics and the Confucian political tradition as a strategy for assessing the former's viability as an approach to politics and its significance in the global history of political thought.

SOCRATES. So that is what the skilled and good orator will look to whenever he applies to people's souls whatever speeches he makes.... He will always give his attention to how justice may come to exist in the souls of his fellow citizens and injustice be gotten rid of, how self control may come to exist there and lack of discipline be gotten rid of, and how the rest of virtue may come into being there and evil may depart.

Shouldn't we then attempt to care for the city and its citizens with the aim of making the citizens themselves as good as possible? For without this, ... it does no good to provide any other service, if the intentions of those who are likely to make a great deal of money or take a position of rule over people or some other position of power aren't admirable and good.

Plato, Gorgias 504e, 514a (tr. Zeyl)

The end of political expertise is dedicated above all to making the citizens be of a certain quality, i.e. good, and doers of fine things.... The true political expert will have worked at virtue more than anything, for what he wants is to make the members of the citizen body good, and obedient to the laws.

Aristotle, Ethics 1.9, 1.13 (tr. Rowe)

The happy state may be shown to be that which is best and which acts rightly, and it cannot act rightly without doing right actions, and neither individual nor state can do right actions without virtue and wisdom. Thus the courage, justice, and wisdom of a state have the same form and nature as the qualities which give the individual who possesses them the nature of just, wise or temperate.

Aristotle, Politics 8.1 (tr. Jowett-Barnes)

Virtue is only achieved by an educated and well-taught mind.

Seneca, Moral Letters 90.46

Take the opposite course. Do not apply yourself to learning for the sake of appearance and show, nor in order to hide vain inaction behind an impressive name, but in order to take charge of public affairs more steadily amid the trials of fortune.

Tacitus, Histories 4.5

A CIVILIZATION IN CRISIS

Who can doubt that Rome would instantly rise up again,
if she would only begin to know herself?

PETRARCH, *FAMILIARES* 6.3 (TR. FANTHAM)

A New "Paideuma" and the Birth of the Humanities

The humanism of the Italian Renaissance was born from a profound sense of loss and longing. It arose from a new kind of historical awareness shared by literary men—men newly conscious of vanished glories and present humiliations. Rome and Italy had once ruled over a vast empire, the greatest and longest lived (they believed) the world had ever known. Absorbing the best of what the Greeks had to offer, Italians had built an extraordinary civilization based on military virtue, a common law, and a common language. Rome's imperial rule had collected the diverse cultures of the Mediterranean around a single core, imposing peace and promoting commercial prosperity while banishing war to the empire's margins. Its traditions and moral values were passed down from generation to generation by literati who had created a superb instrument, the Latin language, capable of order, beauty, and eloquence, able to move the heart and the mind, to compel clashing wills to work in harmony without resort to violence. It was the primary tool of Roman civilization.

The humanists of the fourteenth century remembered the glory of Rome because of literary monuments that had been preserved through ages of barbarism, written with ink on dried animal skins: histories, poetry, oratory, letters, and philosophical dialogues. They could also see Rome's greatness with their eyes. Like hobbits wandering through Middle-earth, they saw the relics of an older and higher civilization lying all about them. In Rome and other cities of Italy, houses and churches huddled at the feet of huge, half-ruined monuments: amphitheaters, baths, and temples, arches commemorating great victories, and forums with their public buildings. They still used the Romans' well-made roads, built over a thousand years before, and they could see rising above them the immense aqueducts that had brought water to vast populations. From time to time they would dig up statuary, carven gems, coins, funerary monuments, architectural fragments, inscriptions, and other ancient relics, "silently expressing old mortality," testifying to a world of wealth and artistic skill that no longer existed.

The memory of Rome, to be sure, had never died in the long centuries since the collapse of the Western empire in the sixth century after Christ. Rome's literary monuments had been continually copied and studied in monasteries and cathedral schools during the medieval centuries. When a new civilization emerged in Western Europe in the twelfth century, it had access, directly via Latin or through Arabic intermediaries, to enough written sources surviving from antiquity to enable Europe to become a third-order civilization, building on the achievements of Greece and Rome. The study of Rome's law codes and jurisprudence was revived early in the twelfth century and had become the basis of legal education in the medieval universities by the thirteenth. Greek medicine had come back to the West via the Muslim cultures of the southern Mediterranean. Logic and natural philosophy, particularly as presented in the works of Aristotle, freshly translated into Latin, became the backbone of the arts curriculum in scholastic institutions throughout Europe.

Yet in Italy during the fourteenth century there was a profound change in the way Europeans evaluated the civilizations of the past. The fundamental character of this change cannot be fully appreciated without taking a wider look at the dynamic relationship, formed over many centuries, between Christianity and the culture it inherited from Graeco-Roman antiquity. To analyze this relationship, and especially to distinguish medieval humanisms from Renaissance humanism, it will be helpful, I believe, to make use of an unfamiliar term, "paideuma," adapted from the ethnologist Leo Frobenius.[1] As I use the term (idiosyncratically to be sure) in this book, it refers to an intentional form of elite culture that seeks power within a society with the aim of altering the moral attitudes and behaviors of society's members, especially its leadership class.[2] It may aim at a moral revolution in Kwame Anthony Appiah's sense.[3] Those who participate in a paideuma, as adherents of a reform movement for example, share its diagnosis of personal or social ills, a common set of values, and a common set of prescriptions to restore individual or social health. A paideuma will typically produce a *paideia,* a set of social technologies designed to alter minds and hearts, which constitute its soulcraft. *Paideia*—which in this book I will call *institutio,* using the humanists' Latin equivalent—in order to compass its ends, designs, adapts, or revives formal educational routines but also customs, rituals, the plastic arts, music, theater, and oratory. Participants in a paideuma may seek to alter the structure of professional, political, or economic incentives that regulate status and rewards so as to encourage the desired moral changes. When a paideuma comes to dominate a society, especially its elites, it may transform itself into a "comprehensive doctrine" in John Rawls's sense.[4]

A key issue in evaluating a paideuma is the way it relates to subaltern or rival paideumata within the larger society—its toleration of pluralism to use modern terms. The character of a given paideuma may encourage those who inhabit it, when given power, to become oppressive, militant, or fanatical, while other paideumata may be capable of condominium with multiple conceptions of the good life. To use terms from the sociology of religion, some paideumata are exclusivist, while others are inclusive or pluralist; some justify the use of violence and indoctrination to achieve their ends, while others restrict themselves to education and the arts of persuasion.[5] A paideuma may also alter its character in the course of its historical development and relate differently, at different times and places, to what may be called (with apologies for the coinage) exopaideumic elements in the circumambient society. Examples of paideumata that have varied their habits of condominium over time and space might include particular expressions or dispositions of Confucianism, Buddhism, Islam, socialism, liberalism, and Christianity.

The dominant paideumata of late antiquity and the Middle Ages in the West were of course tightly linked to the Christian faith tradition. Christianity, though historically capable of being turned into an intolerant comprehensive doctrine—during the early modern Wars of Religion for example—had in practice, over the centuries, adopted a variety of stances to non-Christian elements in the ancient world, or inherited from the ancient world after its demise.[6] These included the literary and philosophical disciplines cultivated by the educated elites of Greece and Rome, designed in part to sustain the social and political order of those societies. In the long history of Christianity since its founder, Christian attitudes to pagan civic culture had undergone a number of transformations.[7] Christ himself and St. Paul the Apostle had prescribed total rejection of pagan culture within the church—separatism—while insisting on the legitimacy of non-Christian political authorities and the Christian's duty to obey them. In the pre-Constantinian period, pagan high culture was often held in deep suspicion, bordering sometimes on paranoia. The African church father Tertullian (c. 155–240 AD), for example, famously wrote that "the patriarchs of philosophy are the patriarchs of heresy."

Other early Christian writers such as Origen and Lactantius made wide use of the pagan literary and philosophical heritage while claiming that Christian belief had superseded it. When Christianity achieved what Christians saw as a "stunning, supernatural victory"[8] over the pagan gods in the fourth century, becoming the official and exclusive religion of the Roman Empire, the attitude to pagan culture changed again. At first it was triumphalist, determined to make Rome fully Christian and thus bring into being the perfect Third Age. This entailed stamping out the remaining pockets of Graeco-Roman *paideia,* which the more fanatical saw as indissolubly linked with pagan religion and the worship of demons.

Later Christian thinkers like St. Augustine, Cassiodorus, and Pope St. Gregory the Great recognized a space for the licit use of Graeco-Roman literary and philosophical disciplines, so long as their study was strictly subordinated to the ends of salvation.[9] The narrowed and repurposed *paideia* or *institutio* produced by this compromise was known in Western Christendom as the liberal arts. They were organized into a cycle of seven disciplines by Martianus Capella, a contemporary of St. Augustine, and were defined as "secular," belonging to the present age. They were meant as temporary aids to Christians in their pilgrimage toward the next life. With the emergence of Christendom at the end of antiquity and the triumph of ascetic ideals, political, cultural, and religious authorities merged, enforcing yet another change of attitude, one that degraded still further the prestige of the Graeco-Roman inheritance.[10]

In the High Middle Ages, however, the great spiritual movement we call scholasticism opened Europe up afresh to non-Christian sources of knowledge. The paideuma of the scholastics revealed a vast ambition to create bodies of legal reasoning and systems of thought that would serve the ends of lay and ecclesiastical government, bringing order to a chaotic world. Scholastic culture drew on pagan, Jewish, Muslim, and Christian authorities, especially Aristotle and the corpus of Roman law codified under the Christian emperor Justinian, imposing logical and lawyerly ways of thought on many generations of minds from the twelfth century forward.[11] The seven liberal arts as codified in late antiquity were eventually palimpsested beneath the new scholastic disciplines and lost their coherence and distinctive raison d'être.

The humanists of the Italian Renaissance, led by Petrarch, brought into being a new Christian paideuma, different from the one dominant in the scholastic era. The new paideuma aimed at nothing less than a comprehensive revival of the lost Graeco-Roman literary and philosophical culture as it had existed in the ancient

Mediterranean. In the context of Christianity's long mistrust of pagan culture and its uneasy, piecemeal attempts to adapt pagan disciplines to Christian use without—as St. Basil of Caesarea put it—"surrendering the rudder of our minds," the change was nothing short of astonishing. The rest of this chapter explains why Petrarch and his followers came to believe that a new, more unreserved, indeed passionate embrace of the pagan civilizations of the past was necessary in order to prevent the collapse of Christendom. It shows why they believed that a new *institutio,* whose foundation was what they called the *studia humanitatis*—the humanities— was necessary to repair the damage inflicted on human nature by the fall of Rome and the loss of ancient civilization.[12]

The new paideuma was the product of a civilizational crisis of great magnitude that shook confidence in medieval culture and undermined the legitimacy of key institutions. In its general outlines the crisis is well known. Every student of medieval history will have learned about the collapse in the power and authority of the Holy Roman Empire and the Papacy; the "Babylonian captivity" of the Church and the Great Schism; and the self-assertion of kings, princes, and cities against the enfeebled universal authorities of the High Middle Ages. Every student of medieval Italy will have learned of the devolution of northern Italy into warring tyrannies, bringing to an end most of the popular communes that had flourished in the thirteenth century. They will have read about the effects of the Hundred Years' War and the marauding bands of mercenaries that tormented Italy for decades; the bankruptcy of Europe's nascent financial system in the 1340s; the rising challenge of the Ottoman Turks on Europe's eastern borders; recurrent famines and other natural disasters; and above all the calamity of the Black Death, the terrifying plague that wiped out as much as a third of Europe's population and remained endemic in Europe for centuries after its initial outbreak in 1347–1349.

The effects of this civilizational crisis on European and especially Italian mentalities, however, is less well understood. Certain fruits of the crisis, such as those stemming from the Black Death or from political attacks on ecclesiastical monarchy, have been studied in detail, but a broader grasp of how Europe's intellectual and moral leaders understood and coped with the multiplying crises of the times is harder to acquire.[13] To achieve some sense of how the wider crisis was experienced and interpreted by contemporaries, however, we can turn to Francesco Petrarca, or Petrarch as he is called in English. Petrarch is a key actor in the story told in this volume, as he was the real founder of Renaissance humanism, the most reflective and articulate man of his time. His works—especially his vast correspondence, revealing a network of contacts throughout Europe with men of middling and high station, lay and clerical, ranging over the half century before his death in 1374—throw off a brilliant light that illuminates for us the devastation of his times.

One long letter, written near the end of his life to a childhood friend, Guido Sette, is especially revealing. Petrarch opens the letter by revisiting wistfully the pleasant scenes of his early education in southern France and the great university town of Bologna, "Bologna the Fat," once the happiest place on earth. He then shares with Guido his conviction that the Christian world had been rapidly coming apart during his lifetime and was tumbling toward its destruction. He doesn't want to be an irritable and complaining old man, Petrarch says, the classic figure described by Horace as the encomiast of times past, the *laudator temporis acti*. But being as objective as he could be, judging "not from listening or reading but from experience at first hand," the conclusion is inescapable: things have gotten worse, much worse. "Is the mind so blunted that it does not recognize that everything is changed and disfigured?" The lovely town of Carpentras where they had learned their letters has become the seat of a provincial courthouse, "or more correctly a house of demons." Like all the towns of his youth that had once lain open to the countryside, it was now surrounded by walls to protect it from marauding soldiers. At Bologna, once celebrated for its great legal minds, the great queen Ignorance had set up her throne, and all had surrendered to her. That happy, prosperous city, where as a student he could wander in and out freely, day and night, was now an armed camp ruled by a tyrant. Avignon, to which he returned after his student days in Bologna, a place that "should have been religion's highest citadel," had become a squalid, debauched, and venal place, where (quoting Livy on Hannibal) there was "nothing true or sacred, no fear of God, no scruple." The "new house" of the popes, once secure and unarmed, protected by respect for the Apostolic See, had been "reduced to extreme misery by an army of brigands." The city was now infested with tax collectors, desperately raising funds to build ever-stronger fortifications. Even in his rural retreat in nearby Vaucluse there were now thieves, wandering brigands, and prowling wolves. Gascony, where as a young man he had spent a blessed summer that still shone in his memory, was now a military camp. His youthful desire to see the world had led him, once upon a time, to visit the flourishing regions of northern France, the homeland of chivalry. But now they were in ashes, destroyed by cruel and loutish English soldiers, who, astonishingly to Petrarch's mind, had even taken captive the great king of the French. And Paris—ah, Paris!—

> where is that city of Paris which, although always inferior to its fame and owing much to the fictions of its residents, was undoubtedly once a great place? Where are the hordes of students, the excitement of its university, the riches of citizens, the amusements of them all? It is not the clash of argument that is heard there but of warfare; you see heaps not of books but of weapons, no syllogisms, no disputations, but night watches and battering rams that echo as they are driven against the walls. The shouting and enthusiasm of hunters is suspended; the walls are full of bustle, the woods are silent, and men are scarcely safe in the towns themselves; the calm which seemed to have found a sanctuary in that place has given way and utterly departed; nowhere is there so little freedom from anxiety, nowhere so many dangers.

Everywhere the story was the same. Naples had spiraled quickly into decline after the glorious days of King Robert. Petrarch's native land of Florence had added factional struggle to fires, wars, and plagues; Milan, Pavia, Venice, Pisa, and Siena were no longer what they had been. Rome had once had some "noble sparks" glittering among its ruins in the time of Cola di Rienzo, but these were now turned to ashes. When he was young, military men had marched to recover Jerusalem from the Muslims, driven by crusading zeal; in recent decades, roving armies of mercenaries, the so-called free companies or companies of adventure, went from city to city, threatening fellow Christians with fire and sword. The chivalry of Europe had degenerated into bands of savage animals, motivated only by lust and greed.[14]

The theme of decline had been a common one in Petrarch's writings ever since the time of the Black Death. In a letter of 1352 to his friend and disciple Stefano Colonna, he gave the young man a depressing world tour. Everywhere you looked, from Spain to Jerusalem, from France to Sicily, there was war, tyranny, plague, and moral collapse. In a collection of letters written anonymously, known as the *Sine nomine,* Petrarch cried out in anger and bitterness against the venality, sensual depravity, and moral paralysis of the Holy See and the papal curia. In a passage of his *De vita solitaria* (1346 / 1372) Petrarch gave a somber review of the history of Christendom: how in antiquity the faith had flooded the whole world, even passing beyond the borders of the Roman Empire, but in later centuries had receded under pressure from the Muslim conquests. He recalled the sad story of the Crusades, how initial successes had more recently given way to failure, owing above all to the lack of commitment from cowardly, weak, and selfish Christian princes, among whom he included the pope, the Holy Roman Emperor, and the emperor of the Greeks in Byzantium.

The Causes of the Crisis

It was Petrarch's analysis of the causes that underlay Christendom's collapse that first opened to view his vision of a path to political reform, which grew into that of the humanist movement of the Renaissance as a whole. In the letter to Guido Sette mentioned above, he concedes to hypothetical critics that all times have had their vicissitudes, that nature and the stars play a role, and that only God knows the true causes behind historical change. The sufferings of Christendom must surely in some part be understood as God's punishment for wickedness. But of the causes of decline that can be seen by us, he has no doubt that

> many explanations of this change lie in men themselves and, if anyone probes more deeply, perhaps all its causes lie in mankind, but some are manifest and others not. Certainly, since piety and truth and loyalty and peace are in exile, while impiety, falsehood, treachery, discord and warfare are ruling and raging over the whole earth, and since impious bands of brigands wander as they choose like proper armies and lay waste and plunder whatever is in their path, and neither cities nor kings have the strength to resist them, or again, since morals are polluted, studies are perverted and manners disfigured, it is obvious that the evil is completely and exclusively rooted in human beings.[15]

For Petrarch the chief reason for the moral decline of Italy, and therefore of the whole Latin West, lay in the moral effects of barbarism. Italians had forgotten their past greatness, lost the arts of war and peace, and even corrupted the Latin language that was their lifeline, their one link to the glory of Rome. They had ceased to be human, falling below the level of beasts. Late in life, in a letter to his disciple Boccaccio, who had urged him to scale back his literary labors and preserve his health, Petrarch gave vent to the bitterness and rage he felt, damning his ignorant contemporaries for their meanness and lack of spirit:

> But if your opinion makes you urge this on me, because you think me greedy for a long life, you are much deceived. How could I want to live on surrounded by the corrupt mores of our time, which it grieves me greatly to have reached,

and, to say nothing of worse offenses, the grotesque and obscene behavior of
the most frivolous men, about whom I often complain in writing and speech,
although I cannot find strength to express fully in words my grief and indig-
nation? They are called Italians and live in Italy, but do everything to appear
barbarians—if only they *were* barbarians, to free my eyes and those of true
Italians from so shameful a sight! May Almighty God damn them, living or
dead, for whom it was not enough to have lost through their own cowardice
the virtues and glory of their ancestors, or all the arts of war and peace, unless
in their folly they should also dishonor their ancestral speech and character;
in fact I do not so much bless our fathers who departed from this world in
good time, but even judge the blind to be blessed for not seeing those things.[16]

The changed character of barbarized men, the loss of the civil virtues, the loss
of true piety, the perversion of language and education—these then are the deeper
causes of Christendom's decline. Yet to what authorities could contemporaries appeal who hoped for reform? Not to the Church or the Empire in their current
condition. To the law? The inheritance of Roman law was of no use if there was
no one to enforce it. Half a century before, Dante had exclaimed:

Ahi serva Italia, di dolore ostello
nave sanza nocchiere in gran tempesta . . .
Che val perché ti racconciasse il freno
Iustiniano, se la sella è vòta?

Ah, Italy, you slave, abode of misery,
pilotless ship in a great tempest tossed . . .
If there is no one in your saddle, what good
was it for Justinian to have repaired your harness?[17]

Could they appeal to current cultural and intellectual authorities, then? Hardly.
It was Petrarch's judgment that if the downward cycle of history should ever be
reversed and the West recover its ancient vigor and high purpose, so great a revolution of affairs could not come about by relying on the existing educational institutions of Europe. The mere thought was laughable.

In particular, modern jurists in the law schools would not be able to help. In
antiquity—as Petrarch wrote to a young man who was worried about the moral
effects of going to law school—study of the law had been a noble calling. It had

reached its high point in the age of Cicero, when it was combined with eloquence and the power to persuade men to pursue the good. In that age law was "a citadel of many-sided learning and celestial eloquence."[18] From the top of its moral cycle the study of the law had descended to a condition, still noble, in the early and late empire, when it "succeeded simply through the bare knowledge of the law and flourished with excellence." This was the period of the great Roman jurists, whose wisdom was preserved in Justinian's *Institutes*.[19] But now—well, today the situation was far different. A further descent from the heights of Cicero's time had occurred, "but a much greater descent than the first." Legal study had plummeted to the point where it was now merely *loquax ignorantia,* a talkative ignorance. And it was sure to plunge further still, though that was hard to imagine:

> [The jurists of our time] either do not understand or distort the laws recorded by our ancestors with such seriousness of mind or agility of intellect, and they dishonor justice, cultivated by our ancestors with so much passion. What a marketable piece of merchandise they have made of [the law]! Their tongue, their hand and mind and breath and glory and honor, their time and pledge of friendship, finally absolutely everything is for sale, and at no more cost than is fair. What a disproportion between the old and the new times or manners! The men of old armed justice with sacred laws while these men prostitute it, disarmed and stripped bare; truth was valued among the men of old, but fraud among the moderns; the men of old gave trusty and unshakable replies to the nations, the moderns nourish their lawsuits with tricks and petty cheating, and long to become immortal by the very tricks they are called upon to demolish with the spearhead of the law. Need I waste more words on this subject? Whoever of these has been the readier to drag the resisting and unwilling law to match his whim has fulfilled the service of a legal adviser and earned the reputation of a learned man; but if any rare person, far from these wiles, were to seize the right path of bare truth, apart from having no share in profit and influence, he would suffer the ill repute of being a simple and foolish fellow.

Anyone who tried to be a true jurist in the present age would only be mocked as naive. But it was not just that the modern study of the law was hopelessly mired in ignorance and venality, nearing the bottom of its historical cycle, with no recovery in sight. The deeper problem was that contemporary life was too dependent on an impoverished notion of legality, on mere observance of rules. The idea that law by itself, backed by the force of government, was enough to bring order and justice to society was fundamentally mistaken. The laws themselves might be good—at least those not made by tyrants—but they were always abused by wicked men, who were always greater in number than the good, just as gold and iron are good in themselves but might be abused by the greedy and the cruel: "The chief element in human actions is the intention of the agent, and it makes a great difference with what motive you tackle an undertaking. And it is not the undertaking itself but your mind *(mens)* which deserves praise or blame; that is what turns good actions into an evil and what seems evil into a good thing." What is fundamental, what needs to change if law is to be effective and society reformed is our *mens*—a word that means not only mind but also one's fundamental disposition, purpose, or self-understanding. But how was that to change? How could wickedness be overcome and a good mind, character, virtue be instilled?

Petrarch's fullest answer to that question comes in one of his invectives, entitled, characteristically, *On His Own Ignorance and That of Many Others* (1367 / 1371), sent to a younger humanist named Donato Albanzani.[20] Albanzani had been scandalized to hear that his revered teacher Petrarch had been "tried" in an informal court by four Venetian "friends," secretly envious of his fame, who had charged him with ignorance. His apologia—which (as so often with Petrarch) began as a letter and became a book—broadened out into a defense of humanistic studies and an attack on the educational value of scholastic philosophy. To cut him down to size Petrarch's so-called friends had attacked the kind of learning he pursued, priding themselves on their own mastery of natural philosophy, derived mostly from medieval translations of Aristotle. Petrarch's defense aimed, among other things, to show that the philosophical studies of contemporary universities, like their legal studies, were morally empty, even destructive of good morals. His friends were filled with smug self-satisfaction because they could repeat a jumble of dubious facts about the natural world, but they showed no interest in the only studies, the humanities, that could help produce in them what should be their principal concerns as men: happiness and virtue. In the view of his friendly enemies, by contrast, Petrarch was an ignoramus because he lacked knowledge of the most prestigious kind of philosophy in the late medieval world, Aristotle's natural science. Hence the four friends had declared him "a good man without learning."

Petrarch in response affirms that true goodness comes from God and not from Aristotle, and that learning without guidance from divine wisdom is worthless, a learned ignorance. His conceited opponents think piety is foolishness, but the wise know it is wisdom itself. Their kind of learning makes men more ignorant and ruins their character by giving them an arrogant overconfidence in their knowledge. They relied far too much on the authority of "their god, Aristotle," who was only human and made mistakes, even great mistakes. Their subservience to their god made them Aristotelians, not really philosophers, not lovers of the truth wherever it was to be found, and certainly not Christians. In fact, part of the reason why his critics cling to their famous pagan name is that its *auctoritas* gives them license to laugh in secret at the Christian faith. In public they bracket questions of faith when discussing philosophy. "Isn't this the same as seeking what is true while despising the Truth?" The impiety of university-trained philosophers is another element in the present crisis of Christendom, and it stems ultimately from too-great reliance on pagan philosophy in matters of divinity. When applied to divine matters, Greek philosophy appears to offer illumination but is in fact dangerous, like honey mixed with poison.

Aristotle cannot be our guide to the highest and deepest questions. Among the great mistakes Aristotle made was his doctrine of happiness, which was fatally flawed because it failed to understand the need for faith and immortality. Like other philosophers, Aristotle falsely believed human reason could find blessedness on its own. Such saving knowledge is beyond human reason. A philosophy appropriate to human beings would not pretend it has just come down from the assembly of the gods (as Cicero joked) but would concern itself instead with the world of humanity. If we look for an understanding of divine things, we will find far more of it, in fact, in the writings of the orator Cicero—the great humanist authority—than in Aristotle. Yet even Cicero cannot be used as an infallible guide to divinity. All philosophers have to be judged by "the coherence and consistency of their thought," and when it comes to divinity all pagan philosophers will be found wanting by the light of Christian truth. Human philosophy should rightly restrict itself to the world of men. Its best use was as an aid to the *studia humanitatis;* a merely human, unredeemed philosophy such as that of the ancient Greeks was a treacherous handmaid of the *studia divinitatis.* The Christian humanist should follow the example of Socrates, whose skepticism about the scientific speculations of Anaxagoras led him to summon philosophy down from the heavens and establish it, as Cicero reported, "in cities and the household, compelling it to inquire into our way of life and our mores, and into things good and evil."[21] This brand of "Socratic philosophy," as it came to be called in the quattrocento— skeptical about pagan theology but eager to exploit the wisdom of the ancients to reform the sublunar human world, including the world of politics—would become paradigmatic for humanists down to the time of Ficino and beyond.[22]

The problem with scholastic philosophy is not just that it flies up beyond the range of human reason. Its real defect is that it does not make us any better, even when it deals with a properly human subject such as ethics. Petrarch claims to have heard scholastic lectures on Aristotle's ethical books, but they left him cold:

> I see how brilliantly he defines and distinguishes virtue, and how shrewdly he analyzes it together with the properties of vice and virtue. Having learned this, I know slightly more than I did before. But my mind is the same as it was; my will is the same; and I am the same *(idem tamen est animus qui fuerat, voluntasque eadem, idem ego)*. For it is one thing to know, and another to love; one thing to understand, and another to will. I don't deny that he teaches us the nature of virtue. But reading him offers us none of those exhortations, or only a very few, that goad and inflame our minds to love virtue and hate vice.
>
> Anyone looking for such exhortations will find them in our Latin authors, especially in Cicero and Seneca, and, surprisingly, in Horace, a poet coarse in style but very pleasant for his maxims. What good is there in knowing what virtue is, if this knowledge doesn't make us love it? What point is there in knowing vice, if this knowledge doesn't make us shun it? By heaven, if the will is corrupt, an idle and irresolute mind will take the wrong path when it discovers the difficulty of the virtues and the alluring ease of the vices. We should not be surprised if Aristotle barely arouses and excites our minds to virtue, for he mocked Socrates, the father of moral philosophy, as "a peddler of morality."[23]

What is needed is authors who will change us for the better, who have eloquence, who can move the human will:

> By contrast, everyone who has read our Latin authors knows that they touch and pierce our vitals with the sharp, burning barbs of their eloquence. By these the sluggish are aroused, the frigid are inflamed, the drowsy are awakened, the weak are strengthened, the prostrate are raised, and the earthbound are lifted up toward lofty thoughts and noble desires. Then earthly matters seem squalid, and the sight of vices inspires great loathing. Virtue in turn is revealed to our inner eyes; and its beauty—what Plato calls "the face of the good made visible"—engenders a wonderful love of both wisdom and virtue.[24]

Petrarch knows that true goodness comes from Christ, but "the [ancient Latin] writers I have mentioned offer much encouragement and much assistance," as St. Augustine himself attested in the *Confessions*. There the great doctor of the ancient church described how reading Cicero's *Hortensius* had turned his will from the outward pursuit of pleasure and success inward, toward philosophy and truth, and thus ultimately toward the true God. The right use of pagan literature and philosophy was to put us on the path to moral seriousness and true piety. Our wills must be changed, and for that we need to listen to authors steeped in both ancient wisdom and in the ancient arts of persuasion:

> Although our ultimate goal does not lie in virtue, where the philosophers placed it, yet the straight path toward our goal passes through the virtues, and not through virtues that are merely known, I say, but loved. Thus the true moral philosophers and valuable teachers of virtues are those whose first and last purpose is to make their students and readers good. They not only teach the definitions of virtue and vice, haranguing us about virtue's splendor and vice's drabness. They also instill in our breasts both love and zeal for what is good, and hatred and abhorrence of evil.[25]

What would be needed, then, to bring Europe out of its moral crisis; to revive virtue, nobility, and true religion; and to reverse the cycle of history and revive the greatness of Rome is a fundamental reconstruction of the forms of culture used to educate and form its citizens, a new *institutio*. The education offered by medieval universities offered no resources for moral reform; it was part of the problem. Political institutions had not failed because laws and institutions were bad, but because they were interpreted and enforced by bad men. The way forward was not to reform governments, but governors. As later humanists would put it, paraphrasing Thucydides (7.77.7), "Men, not walls, make the city."

The Reform of Christian Culture

Petrarch himself never went so far as to try to organize a movement for the reform of European civilization. That was not his way. His contribution lay in the realm of ideas, in the articulation of a new paideuma. His might have been the motto of the Dominican Order, *Contemplata aliis tradere* (Hand on to others the fruits of contemplation). After his disappointing experience in the 1340s as an advocate for the revolution of Cola di Rienzo, a man of high inspiration but flawed character,

Petrarch realized that the work of reconstructing European culture, if it were possible at all, would be a more laborious, long-term task than either he or Cola had ever imagined. It would not, at least initially, take the form of a political revolution. Once he had proclaimed with youthful confidence, "Who can doubt that Rome would instantly rise up again, if she would only begin to know herself?"[26] Once he had dreamed that Cola's revolution would catch fire throughout Italy and restore Rome to her leadership of the world. That had not happened, and Petrarch, based in Avignon, had a privileged seat from which to observe the hard and crooked timber of humanity that prevented reform. The Black Death, coming on the heels of Cola's failure, was God's judgment on human wickedness and only emphasized for Petrarch that any hope for the future would have to begin in the human heart.

In his final decades Petrarch led an increasingly solitary life, in part because so many of his friends had died of plague. One of his chief goals became *traditio,* searching out, copying, and preserving what had been left to Italy of its ancient literary monuments and passing them down to future, possibly better times. He often despaired of his own times and questioned whether there was any escape for Christendom from its miseries and from God's deserved punishment. He sometimes gave advice to the readers of his moral works that sounds like political defeatism or worse, especially when taken out of context. In one work, a series of moral dialogues, he addressed the issue of what to do when faced with an evil lord. To a representative of an imaginary people oppressed by tyranny, Petrarch's "voice of reason" counsels patience, penitence, endurance:

> The natural evil of tyranny should not be aggravated by impatience, nor violently subdued, since you yourself brought on this force. Seldom, indeed, arises a tyrant in a community without the fault of the people. . . . Since all power, be it for the tribulation of the good or the punishment of the wicked, comes from God, it is proper that you consider yourself subject to the power of God, not the power of man. If God's representative seems cruel, your patience may possibly make him more gentle. There is hardly a mind so ferocious that it would not be tempered by obedience and submissiveness. In short, anything that oppresses is either to be suffered or to be ignored.[27]

Petrarch's attitude here seems utterly passive, reflecting the counsel of the Apostle Paul in Romans 13.[28] He is far more conservative than the scholastic William of Ockham, who endorsed resistance to tyranny in extreme cases, or even St. Thomas

Aquinas, who allowed that one has no duty in conscience to obey laws made by tyrants that contravene Divine Law.[29] But Petrarch's reflection on Paul does not end with his counsel to endure tyrants. Tyrants may not be resisted, but it may be possible to do something to change the people whose faults have enabled tyranny.

Still, Petrarch's political activities in the end belied his professions of pessimism and counsels of patience. He took up residence near but (crucially, to his mind) not actually *in* the courts of several northern Italian princes in succession, in Parma, Milan, and Padua—men that some of his contemporaries labelled as tyrants. He found himself able to express carefully phrased admiration for these princes and hoped he might influence them for the better. He continued to press both the pope and the emperor to return to Rome, the true capital of Christendom; he called for the popes to reform the Holy See and for the Emperor Charles IV to march down from Germany and reassert his authority over the fractious Italian cities with their oligarchs and tyrants. Charles would find, once he tried, that the task of conquest would be easy: if Cola di Rienzo, an obscure plebeian, had been able to accomplish so much in so short a time, if he had been able to make the corrupt governments of Italy quake with fear at the mere echo of the Roman name, what might not Charles, a true Roman emperor, accomplish?[30] And if Rome were once more the home of a reformed Roman pope and a powerful Roman emperor imposing peace on the nations, the conditions for a renewal of Christendom would exist again, and—who knows?—the cycle of history might begin to climb upward again. It might even reach another peak such as Rome enjoyed in the times of Augustus, the Roman emperor Petrarch most admired, under whose rule God had chosen to send his Son into the world.

Petrarch, indeed, never ceased to hold out hope for a return of the Golden Age. In a letter to the people of Rome written in October 1352 urging them to intervene in the trial of Cola di Rienzo and praising Cola for having revived a great issue—the restoration of the Roman Empire to Roman people, an issue "asleep and buried for many centuries"—he proclaimed that such a restoration was "the single avenue to the reformation of their public standing and to the beginning of a Golden Age."[31] Around the same time, in one of his *Metrical Epistles* sent to his Florentine follower Francesco Nelli, he described himself as living in a dark middle age located between ancient times and the happier times that might perhaps lie in the future:

Aut prius aut multo decuit post tempore nasci;
Nam fuit, et fortassis erit, felicius evum.

Grace it was to have been born earlier or much later;
for there was, and perhaps shall be, a happier age.[32]

In 1366, in a trumpet-call of a letter to Urban VI, he informed the pope that Christ, to start a new Golden Age, desired to summon his Church, which he had long allowed to wander owing to the fault of mankind, "back to the ancient seats that were its own and to the original condition of the faith."[33] Petrarch's dream was the same one he had revealed to the Holy Roman Emperor Charles IV: a new Golden Age emanating from the city of Rome, combining a return to the primitive church with a new, universal *imperium Romanorum.* Here was the idea of the Renaissance and Reformation *in nuce;* powerful ideas have a way of becoming prophecies. Petrarch's greatest work of Latin poetry, the epic *Africa,* begun in his youth and left unfinished at his death, has a startling prophecy near its end. There Petrarch addresses his own poem, personified, expressing the hope that, despite the storms and turmoil that surrounded its author in the present age, presided over by a cruel Jove, the *Africa* itself will nevertheless live on into better times:

> But if you, as is my wish
> and ardent hope, shall live on after me,
> a more propitious age will come again:
> this Lethean stupor surely can't endure
> forever. Our posterity, perchance,
> when the dark clouds are lifted, may enjoy
> once more the radiance the ancients knew.[34]

One day there will come a renaissance of poetry and learning and all the Muses:

> Then shall you see on Helicon's green slope
> new growth arise, the sacred laurel bear
> new leaves, and talents will spring up renewed,
> and gentle spirits, in whose hearts the zeal
> for learning will be joined with the old love
> for all the Muses, will come forth again.[35]

His late moral writings too show that Petrarch's oft-expressed despair at the state of Christendom was shot through with hope and zeal for political reform. He stressed over and over again that humanistic studies were the key to the most critical task, reforming the character of Europe's leaders. Princes who were not themselves lettered should accept counsel from literati. He set an example of such counsel in a letter-treatise (1352) to Niccola Acciaiuoli, grand seneschal of the king of Naples, telling him how to advise his sovereign in the arts of government. This "mirror of princes" was among Petrarch's most widely circulated works, both in Latin and Italian translation.[36]

> So let him show himself teachable in good disciplines, and let him read and listen to the achievements of our ancestors and be a keen and passionate observer and imitator of illustrious examples. . . . Let him know that he has been given as many teachers of life and as many leaders and guides towards glory as the distinguished names that have gone before him; sometimes examples inflame noble spirits as much as rewards, and words no less than statues; it is a source of joy to compare oneself to much-praised names, and the emulation which competes in virtue is noble.[37]

In his "ethical masterpiece" and most popular Latin work, entitled *On Remedies for Fortune Fair and Foul* (1354 / 1367) and dedicated to his close friend and benefactor, Azzo da Correggio, onetime lord of Parma—another "tyrant"—he explains how only virtue, acquired through the study of wise and eloquent authors, could overcome the blows of fortune. Men of action need to find space in their busy lives for philosophy. We need to live with the ancients and converse with them. But since Azzo had no time for deep perusal of the Latin authors, Petrarch's *Remedies* would provide him with a breviary of ancient wisdom in the form of 254 short dialogues on what today would be called "life questions": how to deal morally with the challenges of life such as ill health, poverty, being hated, being envied, having a bad lord, exile, betrayal, the loss of lordship, the burden of too many children. Even more dangerous to one's moral health, according to Petrarch, was success in life, so he instructed his readers how to respond to good health, status, wealth, a good lord, appointment to a magistracy, and so forth. The *Remedies* was, in other words, a kind of humanistic self-help book.[38] Petrarch's goal was to do for Azzo what Seneca had done for his brother Gallio: digest the opinions of the philosophers, abstract from their useless debates and quarrels, and reshape their teachings into a practical guide to the moral life.

The other great project of his mature years was a collection of classical biographies, the *De viris illustribus,* a work which also may be said to have had a political purpose in the widest sense. It was begun during his years in Vaucluse, perhaps around 1338, in parallel with the *Africa,* but was abandoned for a time after the death of King Robert of Naples, the original dedicatee. Work on it resumed again in 1351 / 1353 during his last residence at Vaucluse, then was abandoned, then was taken up again at the urging of Petrarch's last great patron, Francesco da Carrara, lord of Padua. In his preface to Francesco, Petrarch described his mode of collecting information, his principle of selection, and his motives. He had collected material from many authors but had not bothered himself with "the rash and useless task" some scholars impose on themselves of reconciling their authorities, thus weighing down their work with empty controversies, cloudy divagations or insoluble knots. Not being a *pacificator historicorum,* he would instead cut briefly to the facts, guided by the principle of usefulness *(commoditas),* which meant studying the virtues and vices of great men: "In my work may be sought only deeds that can be attributed to virtue and its opposite, for this, unless I am mistaken, is the fruitful end and purpose of historians, to treat only of acts that readers should imitate or avoid. Whoever presumes to wander beyond these borders, let him be aware that he is straying in foreign territory, and let him return instantly, unless from time to time he should seek out pleasant diversions to entertain his readers."[39]

Petrarch, no stranger to digression, is forced to admit that he too sometimes reports amusing anecdotes about the lives of illustrious men and quotes their grave or witty sayings. Nevertheless, the moral purpose of history is his guiding star. History is properly a school of prudence; its goal is to make human beings better, and by so doing to reform states and revive the greatness of ancient Rome.

The Humanist Movement Takes Shape

Petrarch was not the first humanist of Italy, if by humanist we mean someone who read and imitated the classical authors with the aim of reviving and continuing the literary traditions of antiquity. As Ronald Witt has shown, Petrarch belonged to the third generation within the late medieval tradition of Italian humanism that began in the thirteenth century with Lovato Lovati of Padua.[40] Nevertheless, it is still right to call him the father of *Renaissance* humanism, since it was he who created the new paideuma that opened Christian culture anew to the lost civilizations of the ancient world. It was he who deepened the admiration for ancient authors that had long existed in medieval culture into a kind of *Sehnsucht,* a longing for the restoration of lost qualities of mind, for the return of ancient virtue. It was he who turned the new paideuma that was the fruit of that longing into an *institutio*—a way of forming the mind, oriented above all to the acquisition of virtue, wisdom, and eloquence. Thanks to his fame, charisma, and the example offered by his devoted life of letters, he was able, like a magnet, to collect and focus the scattered impulses to renewal inherited from his predecessors and fire younger generations with a new sense of purpose.[41] His disciples and followers eventually formed a network of literati who devoted themselves to recovering classical antiquity, reviving its literary and philosophical traditions, setting up new schools of literature with new goals, and establishing new opportunities for public oratory. The literary cultures of medieval Europe, long overshadowed by the prestige of scholasticism, began in Italy to compete with university studies on a more equal basis, charged with a fresh and more powerful justification for their studies.[42] Newly energized, Italian literary culture was able to replicate the kind of appeal Petrarch had enjoyed in the great courts of France and Italy, and by so doing transformed itself into the culture of a social and political elite. The classical became identified with the noble—in the humanist sense of nobility, to which we shall return in the next chapter.

By the beginning of the fifteenth century the movement was well on its way to being established in schools, princely courts, the chanceries of republics and high ecclesiastical officials, and even in universities, the citadels of scholasticism.[43] Humanists had found themselves roles as teachers, diplomats, court poets, and chancery officials—language specialists in other words. The *studia humanitatis* had cohered into a group of disciplines, a distinct kind of *institutio,* with a clear goal: conferring personal distinction and promoting moral and intellectual reform among political elites.[44] By the early quattrocento the case had successfully been made that political elites in signories and republics needed a humanistic education. Opportunities for humanists to address the public in formal speeches had multiplied.[45] Classical quotations increasingly appear in the records of political meetings.[46] Petrarch's hostility to legalism had become an article of humanist faith, and his criticism of the Church had mutated into a kind of low-level anti-clericalism, always muffled by the circumstance that many humanists, including Petrarch himself, enjoyed or hoped to enjoy the patronage of the Church.[47] Thanks to their alliance with political elites, ancient literary texts were being taught in universities. In Italy universities were civic institutions, run by boards of citizens, and therefore far less autonomous, far less insulated from the civic community than the privileged corporate universities of northern Europe. This made it easier to introduce humanistic subjects and lecturers into the curriculum of universities, first in

the form of entertaining feast-day lectures open to the public, then as more serious courses on standard humanist authors.[48]

By the early quattrocento the humanists had won considerable territory in their
ongoing struggle against the empire of scholasticism. Here again Petrarch's example
was decisive. His criticism of the hermetic language of both lawyers and scholastic
philosophers became a cultural meme, and clarity of speech became a permanent
aspiration of the new *institutio.* Language was to be used to communicate with all
educated persons, especially those outside one's academic specialty, and this meant
that clarity was to be prized above all. As Petrarch had said, "The highest proof of
intelligence and knowledge was clarity."[49] Clarity as humanists understood it was
in a sense manufactured, since they defined clarity in Latin by the linguistic standards of Cicero and other classical writers, and to understand and mimic that language required many years of study in a humanist school. One could say that the
humanists merely redrew the line of exclusion. The scholastics excluded non-
professionals; the humanists excluded the non-Latinate, as for them, knowledge
of Latin defined the educated elite. Still, the humanists had a point. They aspired
to build political communities led by educated people, and the leaders of those
communities ought to be able to address their fellow citizens as equals in council,
using lucid arguments. They should not take refuge in legal mysteries understood
only by specialists. Antiquity, again, was the guide. The humanist idol Cicero had
been able to advocate courses of action to his fellow Roman citizens in their
common speech, however artfully arranged, while the legal profession, even in antiquity, preferred to wrap itself in a jargon understood only by itself.[50] Clarity and
precision of speech thus became a fundamental value of modern Latin literature
(or Neo-Latin), and later of the vernacular literatures that the humanist movement
sought to reshape in the likeness of Latin.

But it was not enough that language be clear. It also had to be persuasive. The
new humanist watchword was *eloquentia,* which meant "speaking out" and
"speaking with courage and conviction," as well as eloquence in our sense. It was
not a mere set of rules. The aspiration to eloquence went well beyond mastering
the decorative art of rhetoric as taught by scholastic grammarians. The humanist
movement sought to wrest rhetoric away from the law schools, where students were
taught how to write letters and argue: the *ars dictaminis* and the *ars aregandi.* Humanists had nothing but contempt for the handbooks written in dog-Latin used
to teach medieval notaries and lawyers their trade. They wanted to reclaim the

public sphere from the charmless tongues of lawyers and use their own command of language to accomplish their political goals.[51] In their eyes the acquisition of eloquence was a moral discipline intended to persuade and forge consensus in states; the man who acquired eloquence had acquired an indispensable tool of political leadership.[52] The new humanist *orator,* a word that in Renaissance Latin could also mean "ambassador" or "spokesman," would, like Cicero, denounce tyranny and corruption and preserve the republic from its enemies. Being able to speak your mind with power and beauty made you fully human and able to contribute more fully to the human community.

The humanists also found that eloquence and beauty of speech could be a source of pleasure, and that pleasure was an effective tool in promoting their studies to prospective students. They liked to repeat the advice of Horace from the *Ars poetica* that it was the poet's task both to delight and instruct:

> Poets want either to profit or delight
> or to say things both worthy and pleasant for life. . . .
> The man who mixes the useful with the sweet,
> delighting the reader and instructing him too
> wins every vote.[53]

Law, by contrast, was ridiculed as "the yawning science," the *scientia oscitans,* and the young making that choice of study were reminded that years of crushing boredom lay ahead.[54] Since a surprising number of humanists were law school dropouts—the list begins with Petrarch, Boccaccio, and Leonardo Bruni—they knew whereof they spoke.

By the second half of the fifteenth century the humanists' assault on scholastic jargon had evolved to the point where they were demanding eloquence in university teaching, in writing about natural philosophy, and even in law. Ermolao Barbaro, the great humanist expert on natural philosophy, declared that the belief one could be a natural philosopher or a jurist without eloquence was a *persuasio exitialis et monstrosa,* a destructive and monstrous opinion. In the preface (dated 1480) to his translation of Themistius' paraphrase of Aristotle's *Physics,* dedicated to the Neapolitan humanist Antonio de Ferraris (known as Galateo), Barbaro notes that many people believe it is impossible to teach natural philosophy, the science of law, or mathematics in good Latin, and thus come to believe that these sciences are incompatible with humane letters. Scholastic philosophers and jurists are content to babble in their subhuman argot and achieve great reputations by doing so. But there is nothing more pernicious in the state *(respublica)* than this conviction, nothing more useless, foul and worthless in all of life than this depravity and perversion of education. I would add more facts and testimony to make the point but I don't want to belabor the obvious. I will say this, that what the common people believe—that philosophers are tiny little men unsuited to government—has no other source than the fact that most of them devote themselves to a single specialty, despising and ignoring the rest. They abjure eloquence, that is, civilized refinement, and neglect history, that is, the master and commander of the good and blessed life, from which all our usages proceed and from which all experience concerning public administration and policy is brought to life. When such men are sent out as ambassadors, when they sit down as judges to judge cases, when they are asked their views in the Senate, it's no wonder if sometimes they arouse laughter among onlookers when they blurt out foolish, crazy and extreme statements, when their talk is as crude as it is imprudent. By Hercules, no kind of men is to be seen so averse to common sense, of such twisted and corrupt judgement, than the men who go in for philosophy and the study of law without the studying humane letters. But let's put these people aside—please!—as more in need of physical than verbal chastisement.[55]

Barbaro alerts us to another, extraordinary acquisition of Renaissance humanists: their eager appropriation of ancient Greek philosophy. In the *De ignorantia* Petrarch had added to his indictment of scholastic Aristotelians the charge that their translations had defaced the works of Aristotle thanks to their ignorant and clumsy word-for-word renderings. He asserted on the authority of Cicero that Aristotle had in fact been among the most eloquent of the ancients.[56] The humanists, beginning with Leonardo Bruni, made new, more eloquent versions of Aristotle by adopting the revolutionary new method of translation *ad sententiam* (or *ad sensum*)—translation according to sense. This new method too was inspired by the ancients, above all Cicero.[57] The goal of eloquent or artistic translation was not simply to make ancient philosophy more accessible and pleasant to read, but to recover the moral power of the author.[58] Bruni made Aristotle into a humanist author—and an extremely popular one by his own account—by retranslating the moral philosophy of Aristotle: the *Nicomachean Ethics* (1418, dedicated to Pope Martin V), the pseudo-Aristotelian *Economics* (1421, dedicated to Cosimo de'Medici), and the *Politics* (1437, dedicated to Pope Eugene IV).[59] Numerous other "eloquent" humanist translations of Aristotle continued to be made throughout the fifteenth and sixteenth centuries.

But Aristotle was only the beginning. Petrarch in the *De ignorantia* had blamed the scholastics for their fixation on Aristotle and recommended the study of other ancient Greek philosophers, especially Plato, whom Cicero and all antiquity had regarded as superior to Aristotle: *A maioribus Plato, a pluribus Aristoteles laudatus est.* The majority of men may now praise Aristotle but greater ones, the ancients, praised Plato. Petrarch's followers took up the challenge, and in the following centuries Italy and eventually Europe witnessed the unfolding of a vast civilizational project, shared among thousands of translators and publishers in many countries, to translate all the surviving monuments of Greek philosophy into Latin.[60] Their mastery of Greek philosophy gave humanists an enormous advantage in the competition with scholastics for the accolade of *sapiens*. It gave them a moral advantage as well, for the humanists discovered in the Greek philosophers a rich debate about the proper relationship between law and virtue, a debate that (in broad terms) gave the primacy to virtue.[61] As will be seen in the next chapter, a core element of the humanists' mission was to teach virtue via instruction in classical authors. The study of Greek philosophy was to become a central witness supporting the claims of humanist educators and literati to high moral purpose, for the great philosophers of antiquity imbued humanist studies with sublime contemplative wisdom.[62] Meanwhile, humanists continued to denigrate legal education and scholastic philosophy as indifferent to piety and motivated principally by the desire for wealth and status.

Some humanists, remarkably, went so far as to credit Greek philosophy with having invented civility itself, the moral consciousness that allowed civilization to flourish. In an oration in praise of the humanities addressed to the humanist pope Pius II, Bartolomeo Platina, later the biographer of the popes and the second librarian of the Vatican Library, even showed a kind of dim and partial awareness of the moral revolution Karl Jaspers named the Axial Age. Relying in part on the newly translated histories of Herodotus and Diodorus Siculus, Platina wrote,

> It is my considered opinion that the human race would have at one time been on the road to destroying itself with its own violence had not Socrates, that interpreter and messenger of the Divine Mind, transferred from the gods to mankind the precepts of living well. Before Socrates, immortal gods! how life was lived on the earth, how feral, how cruel, how aggressive it was! There was no religion, no piety, no forgiveness, no mercy practiced among the men who lived at that time. Held in honor were the strong men who all too commonly committed slaughter, plunder, fires, and rape; to such men

were offered empires, kingdoms, and magistracies, as we find written in the chronicles of our ancestors about the early kings. Ninus, we read, the first to be seduced into universal empire, added foreign peoples to his empire by violence and arms. Following him, Astiages, Cyrus, Xerxes, and the rest of the barbarian kings invaded not only Asia but even part of Europe with such violence and rage that they entirely wiped out great cities, despoiled provinces, and destroyed whole peoples *(nationes everterint)*. Around the very same time in both in Europe and Africa monsters of this kind came to rule over men, as we read of Mezentius and Cacus in Italy, Capaneus in Greece, and Geryon in Spain.

But when there began to be philosophical discussions in cities, debating the nature of life and morality, then finally men expelled the tyrants, founded laws and rights, and set out rewards and punishments for good and evil persons, so that the former were set aflame for virtue and the latter deterred from vice. Thanks to philosophy cities grew, kingdoms were enlarged, small republics rose to conditions of the highest international prestige, while empires, as Sallust says, improved their moral standing.[63]

Greek philosophy here threatens almost to take the place of religion as a social glue, but the humanists, however anti-clerical they could be at times, were as a rule careful not to challenge the primacy of the Christian religion in the spiritual realm. It was of incalculable importance, indeed, to the success of the movement that Petrarch was able to convince his contemporaries that the study of pagan authors did not represent a threat to Christian faith, as had often been charged in the past. Indeed, it could even serve as kind of preparation for the gospel, a training in virtue and wisdom that might open hearts to true piety.[64] Like the ancient Israelites in Exodus, they could licitly despoil the Egyptians of their vessels of gold and silver, "designing them for a better use," as St. Augustine taught.[65] In this life, humane studies offered a way to reform and ennoble individuals, states, and societies.

In this respect, and despite his hostility to scholasticism, Petrarch took advantage of the theoretical divide that had opened up in the medieval university between the realms of the sacred and the secular. The distinction between the natural and supernatural ends of man was no invention of St. Thomas Aquinas but was inscribed in the way studies had evolved in medieval universities after the twelfth century, with separate faculties for philosophy and theology as well as for civil and canon law. The distinction was clear to the jurists themselves, as Petrarch's law professor at Bologna, the famous decretalist Giovanni d'Andrea, made clear in his commentary on the *Liber Sextus:*

> Now the subject matter of the science of canon law is man as oriented not only to the common good, but to God. . . . [Civil laws are corrected by canon law only when the soul is endangered]: in a matter which does not concern danger to the soul, the laws are to be preserved in their proper court, and canon law in its court. For the Pope cannot abrogate laws related to secular justice except in matters concerning danger to the soul, since the powers are distinct, that is to say, the ecclesiastical power is distinct from the secular.[66]

The secular as understood by medieval society was not the opposite of religious, as it is for moderns, but the opposite of eternal. The secular is what belongs to this age, to the *saeculum* before the end of time, when time will be rolled up into eternity, *in saeculum saeculorum.*[67]

The distinction between temporal goods and eternal goods was fundamental for late medieval society. For Petrarch it was thus natural to distinguish between what belongs to our time and is oriented to the temporary ends of this life, and what belongs to the realm of eternity, where immortal human souls are destined for hell and punishment, or heaven and the enjoyment of God. Understood in this sense, there was no need for conflict, at least on the face of it, between humane studies and Christianity. The *studia humanitatis* had to do with the edification of human beings in this life and the reform of human states and societies. The next life could be left in the care of priests, and ultimate questions could be bracketed for treatment by theologians. Human fame could be offered as the reward of virtue so long as it was understood that fame was a good that might endure beyond the grave, but not forever; it was not an eternal good.[68] Christianity did not abolish pre-Christian culture but gave it a new, transcendent orientation.

The early humanists of the generations immediately after Petrarch continued to present their movement as restricted to the reform of human nature insofar as it was oriented to the ends of this life. In the quattrocento the situation would change, and in some milieux, such as Sigismondo Malatesta's Rimini, the paganism of the ancients could become an alternative in the realm of imagination. It is not that humanists were tempted to sacrifice milk-white bulls on the steps of the Tempio Malatestiano but rather that it became possible to enact, at least in literary play, pagan values incompatible with Christianity.[69] Yet most humanists continued to see humanistic studies as compatible with Christian belief, even mutually reinforcing.

A key moment came in 1403 when Leonardo Bruni translated the letter *Ad adolescentes* (To Young Men) by St. Basil of Caesarea, a Greek church father of the fourth century. The text was an answer to a humanist's prayer and soon became far and away the most popular patristic text of the Renaissance.[70] It made the argument that humanistic studies would not only help students in the secular duties of life but would prepare their souls for Christian teachings. St. Basil urged young men just finishing their first training in grammar to go on and devote themselves to classical literature. They should not be discouraged by the philistine attitude of some of their fellow Christians but should recognize the extraordinary value of pagan literature. Not that everything in those authors could be approved: students should take only what was useful to them as Christian members of society. They should avoid acquiring a pagan spirit; they should not "surrender the rudder of [their] minds" to the pagan authors. They should be discriminating, like bees who take only what they need from the best flowers. The present life is nearly worthless compared to the life to come, but at their age they were unable to appreciate the full wisdom of Christ, rooted in eternity. Just as those who intended to be soldiers must start with physical exercises that may seem to have nothing to do with fighting, so were the young to be exercised in "the poets and historians and orators" and other writers who could improve their minds. Like fullers preparing cloth to receive its eventual color, the classical authors prepared us with *tou kalou doxa,* a correct opinion of the Good, before the heavenly Dyer fixes in us the true colors of faith. Moses acquired the learning of the Egyptians before becoming leader of the Israelites, as Daniel in Babylon learned the lore of the Chaldaeans.

In particular his young men should take the lessons pertaining to virtue from pagan poets, orators, and philosophers, whose eloquence will imprint those lessons deeply upon their tender minds. "All the poetry of Homer is praise of virtue." By closing the gap between being and seeming, virtue prevents the souls of young men from being torn into factions; it makes them harmonious and strong. Philosophy releases us from the prison of the body's passions. To be worthy of the prize of eternal life we must do our allotted tasks in this life well, and study of pagan classical authors will help the young Christian keep his soul in tune while performing his earthly duties and awaiting the fuller light that will come as he approaches his heavenly reward.

The division of responsibilities between the *studia humanitatis* and the *studia divinitatis* applied to politics as well. Francesco Patrizi of Siena, the great humanist authority on politics, made a strong distinction between "divine magistrates," meaning the bishops and clergy, and "human magistrates." Divine magistrates had charge of "sacred cult, ceremonies, mysteries and sacrifices"; their role was to lead the people to true religion and eradicate empty superstition. Laws and institutions would be of no effect without the support of divine teachings, authorized by Best and Greatest God. In primordial societies divine authority was combined with royal authority, but in Christian times divine and human powers were distinct. "We who follow in the ancient ways depart in no way from true religion, but we should heed the words of priests. They are of divine inspiration and instruct us in holiness and immortality." Human magistrates had their own sphere of action. "Human magistrates are those who bear the public persona, are in charge of the state, and pass legal judgements." Their expertise was different. In addition to training in the humanistic disciplines they should have an excellent understanding of the city's laws, customs, and ancestral ways, and should know how to observe justice and equity in all things. Human magistracies should be modeled on ancient exemplars, particularly those of the Romans.[71]

Only later in the fifteenth century did humanists become more ambitious to use the resources of ancient wisdom to reform theology and religion. But the "secular" or this-worldly orientation of humanistic studies remained fundamental. The distinction between studies human and divine was reinforced by the cultivation of classicizing Latin, a discourse which filtered out much of contemporary reality.[72] This helps account for why the institutional Church and Christian doctrine (as opposed to generalized virtues of "piety" and "religion") make so few appearances in the political literature of the humanists by comparison with that of the scholastics. It is no doubt the case that some considerable number of later Italian humanists were indifferent or lukewarm in their religion—especially the generation that experienced the Great Schism (1378–1417)—but the existence of well-understood boundaries between literary and religious studies protected the humanities from effective criticism for several generations.[73]

Bartolomeo Platina illuminates how humanists understood those boundaries in the mid-quattrocento. In the same oration to Pius II mentioned earlier, he praises "the pursuit of the good arts and of that form of erudition we call *humanitas*." Without the humanities, he says, even the contemplative life that sets aside earthly things would be impoverished. But the real focus of the humanities is the present life:

> But come, let's put aside that form of life that is hidden away and remote from all human action, loved and embraced by those who reckon that the highest good is located only in the contemplation of the universe. It is allowable to take on a civil frame of mind and a middling way of life, and we could certainly not be kept within bounds in this life—so many are the attractions of vice—unless we were aided by learning, that learning in particular by whose help, we believe, civil life is held together. Through that learning we grasp the path to modesty, temperance, justice and courage—virtues on which human life and political life depend—so that if these were to be taken from the community, I don't see what difference there could be between man and beast. The latter are moved only by their appetites, while it is proper to a cultured and well-educated human being to be motivated by reason and the will.[74]

Once the humanities were well established in Italy, as they were by the mid-fifteenth century, the boundaries between human and divine studies would be renegotiated. The generations between Lorenzo Valla and Erasmus found a new, specifically religious role for the humanities, although the old boundaries could still be invoked, and often were—not least by those opposing the cultural imperialism of the humanities, as their influence began to spread into law, medicine, and theology, the citadels of scholasticism.[75] Humanist literati continued to expand their reforming ambitions in the realm of politics down to the end of the fifteenth century, when the French invasions threw into doubt their claim to be instilling virtue in rising generations.[76] In the quattrocento, faith in the reforming power of humane studies remained strong. Statesmen of the period trained in humane disciplines believed they could build republics of virtue approximating in this life the eternal city of the next. As the Venetian patrician Lauro Quirini put it in the peroration of his humanist utopia, the *De republica* (c. 1449):

> In this way, when good and noble men shall emerge and shall embrace the most holy chorus of the virtues, acquiring prudence to advise the city well, self-control that they may not be corrupted by lusts, justice that the whole city might glow like the rays of the sun, and shall preserve its liberty inviolate and unshaken, casting aside avarice and sloth and the intestine discord that

corrupts cities like poison, dwelling in peace and tranquility—for they shall enter no war without divine sanction—then our city shall thrive, happy and blessed, like unto that most holy and eternal city which is to come.[77]

Petrarch's new paideuma, his powerful reordering of cultural and educational goals, implied a turn from what had been the principal guides to human life in the scholastic Middle Ages—law and theology—to history, literature, philosophy, and the study of language and eloquence. He rejected the basic tool of scholasticism, the *quaestio,* a technique for harmonizing conflict among authorities developed in the twelfth century to provide rational solutions to concrete moral and religious issues. It encouraged a legalistic, ahistorical form of analysis and was designed to sharpen the thinking of professional administrators. To be sure, the scholastic tradition continued in the West and, after a relatively dry period in the late fourteenth century, would become creative again in the fifteenth and sixteenth, enjoying its own Renaissance in quattrocento Italy.[78] Relics of it could still be found in the nineteenth century. What Petrarch and his followers established was an alternative *institutio,* with a new and ever-expanding source base, new textual practices (many of them revived from classical antiquity), and above all a new moral purpose: restoring civilization by restoring to human beings their full humanity. That new purpose was to affect profoundly the way politics and political reform were understood in the Renaissance.

CHAPTER 2

VIRTUE POLITICS

Obedience and Legitimacy

Why should citizens obey their government? Many people today might answer, "So that I am not arrested and fined or imprisoned." They obey because they fear the government's power. Since the Axial Period in antiquity all civilizations have recognized, however, that such an answer is both morally and practically inadequate. No state can last long that relies entirely on force or the threat of force to exact obedience. As the example of the global "color revolutions" vividly demonstrates, when the actions of a state begin to be perceived as mere tyranny, when force is not seen as legitimate, the government of that state is in trouble. If enough people start to disobey, the government will fall and more credible sources of legitimacy will be sought. Appeals will inevitably be made to the good of all as opposed to the interests of the part, to use the language Aristotle gave us 2,500 years ago.

Maintaining legitimacy is a perennial challenge for all governments, but it becomes especially acute when governments need to impose themselves on new subject populations or when societies are riven by factionalism. After your soldiers have defeated their enemies and subdued a territory, how can a form of rule be established that will be accepted by the subject population as legitimate? In societies where ruling elites lack legitimacy, how can it be created or restored? How can a reforming government stop abuses of power, how can it motivate wealthy and powerful citizens to prefer the common good to their own private goods? How can a society replace a regime that has grown morally corrupt or illegitimate?

These were fundamental problems faced by Renaissance humanists in their struggle to deal with the new political world that had grown out of the civilizational crisis of the fourteenth century. Their world was now dominated by two basic forms of power, monarchy and oligarchy. Both were plagued with problems of legitimacy.[1] Italy in the fifteenth century was divided into five major states—Venice, Milan, Florence, the Papal State, and the Kingdom of Naples—and a host of smaller city-states and signories. Four large Italian city-states were republics: Venice, Florence, Lucca, and Siena. The other states were monarchical, ruled by princes. Humanists used the word *princeps,* or prince, to translate *signore,* lord, precisely to elide the issue of the legitimacy, since few Renaissance princes could boast unquestioned legitimacy in the received legal sense. *Princeps* was a morally convenient term that covered both manifest tyrants and lords whose titles to rule were less in question. In the plural, *principes* usually referred to the "leading men," or members of the political elite. In any case, enjoying the formal title "king" or "pope" made only a small difference. The popes of the quattrocento were continually challenged in their authority, territorial claims, and prerogatives by church councils and anti-popes, and by lay rulers like the kings of France and Naples. The Kingdom of Naples, called the *Regno,* a regional state in the Italian *Mezzogiorno,* was claimed by two rival dynasties, the houses of Aragon and of Anjou, who conducted ideological war to delegitimate each other as well as conventional wars.[2] The numerous Italian city-states in north and central Italy that in the thirteenth century had been ruled by popular communes—themselves hardly free of problems of legitimacy—had been replaced in the fourteenth by *signori* who held power at swordpoint or by oligarchies dominated behind the scenes by wealthy merchants. Humanists tended to be too complacent about city-states governed by warlords, but having absorbed the prejudices of ancient literary culture about trade and commerce, they were often disgusted by the spectacle of merchants in power.

Since humanist political thinkers were not academic theorists but teachers and advisors of statesmen—even sometimes themselves statesmen, like Giovanni Pontano, prime minister of the king of Naples—they tended to confront problems of legitimacy as practical men. The inherited juristic language of legitimacy they tended to dismiss as an intellectual tool of lawyers and as such inadequate.[3] In any case, in states like Milan, where *signori* claimed *plenitudo potestatis* to make new law, law itself seemed to lack legitimacy.[4] Writers like Bartolomeo Platina, Francesco Patrizi of Siena, and Giovanni Pontano tended to see the problem of legitimacy from a broader and more psychological perspective, as a problem of willing obedience. This does not mean, however, that they lacked concern for the problem of just government. For such writers, with their orientation to virtue, the problem was how to promote justice in the heart of rulers and how to instill in the ruled a respect for justice. They were the same problems Plato had confronted in the *Laws.*[5] Like Plato, they did not think obedience could be secured merely by writing down laws and institutions that conformed to abstract principles of justice. Human justice began in the soul, and a way had to be found of engraving laws in the souls of both rulers and ruled. Justice was not a right or an entitlement, as most people believe today, but a personal commitment to give fellow citizens what they deserved, even citizens poorer or weaker than oneself. It was a virtue—an excellent character trait informed by practical wisdom—and without it there could be no willing compliance with authority.

Obedience to a ruler can be secured in three ways: by making obedience expedient through fear of punishment; by appealing to material interests through the provision of benefits; or by appeal to justice, which entails convincing the ruled that their rulers deserve to be obeyed. Merely expedient obedience is a sign of tyranny, as all humanists agreed; terror and silence were effects of tyrannical power. The provision of benefits—what modern theorists call "performance legitimacy"— is hard to manage in a way that escapes charges of clientelism or partisanship. Statesmen normally are supported in power by some groups and not others, and such support inevitably comes at the cost of differential bestowal of benefits. Yet as the humanists learned from Seneca's *De beneficiis,* it was possible, especially for monarchs, to confer benefits in laudable ways by rewarding those who deserved reward. Rulers whose rule brings general prosperity, as the history of the post-1989 Chinese government shows, have a strong hedge against challenges to their legitimacy. In the Renaissance, princes might be seen to confer benefits on a country by successfully defending it, or by conquest of foreign territory, or simply by providing peace and order. Such benefits were often celebrated by humanists in speeches meant to contribute to the legitimacy of regimes. But by and large humanists agreed with ancient political philosophers that the best way to secure obedience was through just rule. They simply had their own approach to achieving just rule, one that differed sharply from the lawyerly and coercive approach that had dominated Europe for centuries.

In the West in modern times liberal democrats believe that governments, in the words of the American Declaration of Independence, "derive their just powers from the consent of the governed" via an implied or explicit social contract. Consent is assumed to be just because the will of the governed, the people, is held to be good; or failing that, because it is thought better for the largest number of people to secure their interests through electoral majorities, so long as minorities are not tyrannized.[6] This elaborate ideological construct, from a humanist point of view, would be unhappily legalistic in its contractual aspect and its reliance on rights secured by law, though not on that account necessarily hostile to considerations of virtue.[7] It is, however, a relatively recent invention, foreign to premodern ways of thinking about legitimacy.

Roman law, the dominant ideological tool of Western governments before modern times, recognized three primary forms of legitimation. One was divine right. Indeed, the Christian emperor Justinian began the *Digest* of Roman law by claiming that his rule of the Roman Empire, transmitted to him by the Celestial Majesty, was conducted *deo auctore,* with God's authority.[8] Christian emperors and kings in the West continued to appropriate Justinian's appeal to divine authority down to modern times. But that did not mean that an emperor's power was unlimited, since he was constrained by the need to respect his own laws if they were to be effective.[9] He was constrained too by a second form of legitimation, *inveterata consuetudo,* or timeless custom, whose ultimate sanction came from the people. As the ancient jurist Julian explained in the same text, "Long-standing custom not undeservingly is observed in place of law, and this is the *ius* [justice or legality] which is said to be established by custom; for since the laws themselves constrain us precisely because they are received by judgement of the people, it is right that custom too, which the people approve without any writing, shall restrain everyone."[10]

Custom was the way of our ancestors, the *mos maiorum,* and to change it was a threat to political identity; to affirm and protect it therefore could be a source of political legitimacy. It is closely linked with the third form of legitimacy recognized in Roman (and later canon) law: popular consent. The classic text was also found in the *Digest:* "What pleases the ruler has the force of law, since by the *lex regia,* which was made concerning the emperor's rule, the people conferred on him all of its power to rule."[11] Thus by the *lex regia* the imperial office was in principle considered elective, even in the late empire, though the preponderance of legal opinion long held that the people were unable to reclaim their authority once it had been granted to an emperor. In practice, acclamation by the people of Rome in the ceremony of imperial investiture was a well-managed affair. Nevertheless the seed of the *lex regia* could be and was developed in the later Middle Ages into a theory of popular consent or even popular sovereignty.[12] Already in the fourteenth century Marsilius of Padua stated in an extreme form the doctrine that political legitimacy had its source in the people: "All coercive power comes from the people."[13] William of Ockham's position was more measured: political power, the right to coerce, comes both from God *and* from the people, and the community can choose to depose a ruler should he become a tyrant.[14]

Scholastic theologians in the Aristotelian tradition such as Thomas Aquinas or Giles of Rome had access to a different way of thinking about the justification of political power, and this brings us a step closer to the humanists. Aristotle saw political power as well justified when exercised on behalf of the whole political community for that community's common good, especially when it enabled each member to live the best kind of life possible. Regimes that violated this principle were by definition unjust. He appreciated the role of law and good magistrates in enabling the virtues; the virtues for him were descriptions of the best patterns of behavior, leading to happiness for states as well as individuals. By the same token he taught that laws had to be made and, as far as possible, administered by the wise and virtuous if regimes were to avoid eventual corruption. All societies had a natural hierarchy distinguishing the wiser and better citizens from their moral inferiors, and the better should always rule the worse as the soul rules the body. For Aristotle the nature of the virtues and the form of the best polity were inferred a posteriori, from experience and careful collection, collation and analysis of comparative data; through this process access was gained to nature's intentions, which were assumed to be benign.

None of the scholastics, however, were fully Aristotelian in their political theories since they universally accepted that God was the source of law and that law could be known a priori through right reason.[15] This meant that the natural law would be experienced as binding (as the Stoic Seneca taught). To choose the virtuous course was to obey a command of reason and not, as for Aristotle, to follow a mere counsel of prudence directed toward developing habits of human excellence. In the case of Aquinas, political theory was oriented chiefly toward the question of how to make moral choices for the community as a whole and what counted as the best constitution. Aquinas was more concerned to establish limits on political power than grounds for obeying it. When the tyrant promulgated laws that violated natural law and commanded unjust actions, "it is tyrant rather than the subject who is morally guilty of sedition."[16] His disciple Giles of Rome, the most influential scholastic thinker on politics, developed in his popular treatise *De regimine principis* (1277 / 1280) a neo-Aristotelian theory designed in part to improve the quality of rulership via the acquisition of virtues moral and theological.[17] The prince's virtues are not, however, made the basis of his legitimacy.[18] In Giles' *Commentary on the Sentences,* by contrast, he follows Augustine in his discussion of the origins of political authority among human beings after the Fall. Since all post-lapsarian rule for Giles is morally flawed, legitimacy is reduced to voluntary obedience and can only be established in terms of benefits a ruler provides to the ruled. The condition of legitimacy, in other words, is the approbation of the subject.[19] In other writings he defends a (narrowly limited) theory of consent with respect to the election of the pope, while in his more famous treatise *De ecclesiastica potestate* (1302) he sets forth the most expansive view of papal power to be found in medieval political literature, a power that depends immediately on divine providential choice of the pope as the holder of *plenitudo potestatis.*

The humanist attitude to political right represents a new approach to the problem of obedience, inspired by classical antiquity, and differs strikingly from the juristic, theological, and scholastic Aristotelian theories of legitimacy characteristic of the medieval centuries.[20] Insofar as it appeals to a notion of right or desert we may classify it as a form of moral legitimacy. Rejecting expediency and material interests as inadequate grounds for obedience, it appeals to the virtues and practical wisdom of rulers, the true cornerstone of legitimate government. The focus on virtue allowed the humanists to sidestep traditional issues involving the sources of papal and imperial power, *plenitudo potestatis,* and the best constitution. Humanist "virtue politics," as I call it in this book, is not so much a theory as it is a project for political and civilizational renewal. It is a program for the reform of Christendom's social, political, and religious leadership, to instill in it the charism of worldly virtue and spur it to action with the silver trumpet of eloquence.

Virtue Politics

The expression "virtue politics," as those familiar with modern philosophical ethics will recognize, is meant to recall the term "virtue ethics." The latter is an approach to moral philosophy, usually said to descend from Aristotle, that has been revived in the modern academy by philosophers such as Elizabeth Anscombe, Bernard Williams, Alasdair MacIntyre, and Julia Annas.[21] In contrast to the other two leading approaches to normative ethics in the modern world—deontology and utilitarianism—virtue ethics emphasizes the need to develop, through reflection and practice, excellent patterns of conduct (the virtues) so as to achieve the human good and human flourishing (*eudaimonia,* or happiness). It thus distinguishes itself from other ethical theories that are more concerned with (1) defining norms of practical action, or duties, based on maxims common to all rational beings, as in Kant; or (2) elaborating rules to be followed by a subject who judges the moral value of actions primarily by their consequences, that is, their capacity to maximize goodness, as in the case of the utilitarians. "Virtue politics," by analogy with virtue ethics, focuses on improving the character and wisdom of the ruling class with a view to bringing about a happy and flourishing commonwealth. It sees the political legitimacy of the state as tightly linked with the virtue of rulers and especially their practice of justice, defined as a preference for the common good over private goods—their "other-directedness" as a modern might put it.

The issue of legitimacy is a key one in humanist texts. Not the legitimation of rulers via law and institutional routines, which was rarely discussed by humanists, but moral legitimacy. For humanists what gives rulers legitimacy are personal qualities of character and intellect that win trust, obedience, and love from the ruled.[22] Political legitimacy for them does not come from divine sanction or from hereditary right or from the constitutional form of the polity or from the express consent of the governed. What ultimately makes a regime legitimate is *power well exercised,* what may be called legitimacy of exercise, a species of moral legitimacy.[23] Legitimacy of exercise should be distinguished from what the modern political theorist Daniel A. Bell has called "performance legitimacy," the success or failure of a government in providing order, peace, and material prosperity. Those are all goods but do not necessarily spring from the virtue of the ruler. Provision of such goods might indeed issue from a tyrannical impulse to cling to power. Such an impulse was the basis for Simonides' advice to the tyrant Hiero, in Xenophon's dialogue of that name, that he should do everything to benefit his people if he wished to remain in power. Aristotle gives similar advice to the tyrant in the *Politics.* Both texts influenced Machiavelli's analysis of the relationship between the exercise and the retention of power.[24] But the humanists rejected the instrumental use of benefits to retain power. For them such deceit violated a fundamental principle of ancient philosophical ethics: the summons to be, not to seem; *esse, non videri.*[25] Rule will not be morally legitimate unless it proceeds from the will of a moral individual. Legitimacy of exercise in the discourse of virtue politics must spring from the desire of a political leader both to *be* and to *do* good.

In humanist literature legitimacy of exercise contrasted above all with legitimacy in the most basic sense of the word: legitimacy of birth. In the Renaissance as in most premodern societies the primary mode of assigning legitimacy to rulers was through inheritance. Most power was patrimonial, the possession of a family or lineage, and most signorial power was acquired by right of birth corroborated by legal instruments. Most oligarchs in Renaissance republics also held power and influence at least in part because they had inherited it from their parents. There were exceptions, such as in the elections of popes and the Holy Roman Emperor, but the pope's or the emperor's virtue was not ordinarily the primary consideration of the College of Cardinals or the imperial electors in making their choices.[26] The custom of patrimonial inheritance of power was underwritten by a whole host of cultural memes and even deeper archetypal patterns (in the Jungian sense) such as the wise patriarch or the warlord. Most nobles traced their lineage to famous ancestors, real or imagined, and this could stand in for a claim to virtue. The idea of "breeding" was key. Renaissance Italy, despite its relative urbanization, was still overwhelmingly an agricultural society, and even city folk knew that the stock of plants and animals could be improved by breeding. It was hard for most people to resist the idea that the stock of human families and even whole descent groups or *nationes* could be improved by breeding as well, and many assumed that aristocrats enjoyed superior physical, mental, and even moral gifts. According to common belief, persons belonging to the lower orders were both physically and morally inferior by nature: they were "villains," "the vulgar," "the dregs." Doctors believed that the physical makeup of aristocrats was so different from that of ordinary folk as to justify different diets, cures, and rules for health. Oranges from the top of the tree were a fruit appropriate to aristocrats; peasants should feed on garlic dug up from the ground.[27] In Italy the commitment to patrimonial forms of power was somewhat less rigid than in northern Europe; Italian city-states lacked the social and legal practice of primogeniture, and the management of commercial enterprises, though normally kept within families, was regularly assigned to the most able member of the family rather than the eldest. Bastard children from prominent families were commonly legitimated by papal decree and often used as conduits to transmit a dynasty's claims on power. Nevertheless, since political rights were commonly treated as a form of property, the principle of hereditary power dominated all other forms of legitimation.

Thus the humanists, by making moral virtue the sine qua non, a necessary condition for the legitimate exercise of political power, were fighting a deeply rooted and well-defended cultural prejudice. To be sure, they were hardly the first in the Western tradition to challenge the principle of hereditary virtue. In the courtly love tradition of the Middle Ages it was common to make knightly virtue or *prowesse* a substitute for lineage in winning the hand of a fair lady. When that tradition was spiritualized by Dante, among others, a literature on "true nobility" emerged which commonly asserted that the real source of nobility was not parentage but a *cor gentil,* noble feelings—or in Dante's case, that it was ultimately a gift bestowed by God.[28] In another medieval tradition (based in great part on Seneca) philo-sophical wisdom was recognized as a source of nobility. Yet Dante and other me-dieval authors did not ordinarily apply the concept of true nobility to underwrite political legitimacy. In his *Monarchia* for example, Dante continued to consider the legitimacy of the Roman Empire as of divine origin. God rewarded Rome for its virtue, or perhaps providentially caused it, but Rome's empire was legitimate because God in his wisdom had made it so.[29]

The humanists made new use of the doctrine. They maintained that power can be legitimately exercised only by those who have "true nobility." This became a hu-manist term of art for a merit-based claim to belong to the ruling class. In making this connection between nobility, the acquisition of virtue and entitlement to rule others, the humanists were reviving claims made by what were, for them, the leading political authorities of the ancient world, Aristotle and Cicero. Texts from Aris-totle's *Politics* (especially 3.13, 1282a 31) and *Rhetoric* (1.9) and from Cicero's *De leg-ibus* (especially 3.4) were frequently cited in this connection by quattrocento lite-rati. It became a commonplace that the ancient Romans gained their empire thanks to their virtue and lost it through their vices.[30] "Virtue is the only and unique giver of true nobility," wrote the scholar-poet Cristoforo Landino: "[True] nobility is a kind of health-bringing planet and the highest support of the state. . . . All the greatest dignities and highest magistracies should be handed over and entrusted to those who are more noble; . . . and because the country itself especially belongs to the nobles, it should be committed to their care."[31] The country is the patri-mony, as it were, of those who are noble by virtue, a concept strikingly in contrast both with the idea of power as a legal inheritance and with the idea of the common good as the possession of the whole people, *res populi*.

In similar fashion Buonaccorso da Montemagno, the most popular quat-trocento writer on true nobility, writes that in an honorable republic nothing is owed to anyone by virtue of their family connections, even if their parents served the state well. Only those with learning, wisdom, and virtue deserve to rule.[32] Leon-ardo of Chios contrasts true and false nobility—that is, the humanist conception and the traditional, hereditary conception—as follows:

> Nobility is of two kinds: One is ostentatious, has a high opinion of itself, is (as often as not) possessed along with wealth, ancient lineage, pomposity, and he-reditary right. The other is a purer nobility, not to be judged by the common crowd, without contempt for poverty, replete with every virtue, and without

dishonor. The first kind, proceeding from ambition, encompasses the whole world. The second arises from the root of virtue, as though its strength had sprung from innate principles of nature, and it belongs most fittingly to those few who are strong in mind and dynamic in action. Whoever has *this* nobility, endowed as he is with wisdom and virtue, is better suited to govern the republic or to perform significant individual deeds.[33]

The humanist view, then, is that access to power should properly depend on meritocratic criteria. As the Florentine philosopher and humanist Giovanni Nesi writes in his *De moribus*, "[Distributive justice is satisfied] when honors, ranks and other rewards and signs of virtue are so divided up in a state that everyone receives his due share, and those who deserve more distinction for service to the commonwealth are marked out with rewards of higher distinction, and those who excel others in virtue also excel the rest in authority. Offices should be determined and ranks conferred in proportion to the merits and virtues of individual citizens."[34]

The wealthy and well-born may exercise power, but they only do so legitimately when they are also virtuous.[35] More radically, most humanists from Petrarch onward insist that even persons of humble birth can merit a place in the ruling class via the acquisition of virtue.[36] In his *De casibus virorum illustrium* Boccaccio insists that true, natural nobility can be found in all social ranks, from farmers and craftsmen to the rich and well born. He gives a litany of examples from Roman history—the *novi homines* Marius and Cicero, the soldier-emperors Vespasian and Aurelian, the farmers Regulus and Verginius, the defender of Roman liberty against the tyrannical Appius Claudius—all of whom achieved excellence as generals and statesmen despite their humble birth.[37] The list was often repeated in the quattrocento. Biondo Flavio in *Roma Triumphans* argues that ancient Roman greatness was to a large extent a result of Rome's readiness to accept into the ruling class virtuous men from the lower classes and from outside Rome, even outside Italy. Indeed, *Roma Triumphans* makes the innate virtue and piety of the Roman people, patricians and plebians working together in a Ciceronian *concordia ordinum*, the key to understanding the success of the greatest empire in history.[38]

The humanists of the quattrocento may indeed be credited with inventing a new form of equality not found in modern political theory—nor in ancient for that matter—which might be labelled "virtue egalitarianism." Modern political theorists recognize various competing conceptions of equality such as equality of opportunity, equality of economic outcomes, equality in "capabilities," or even "luck egalitarianism."[39] Ancient statemen like Pericles, in the famous funeral oration reported by Thucydides, praised the equal right of adult male citizens to participate in self-government, while Cicero praised equality of citizen rights under law as the basis of liberty.[40] The humanists champion another ideal of equality as well: equality in the capacity for virtue. The political writer and papal biographer Bartolomeo Platina writes:

> It is characteristic of nobility to follow the right, rejoice in duties, have command of desires and restrain avarice. Whoever does this, even if he were by some chance born from the lowest human condition, merits being called and regarded as noble. Is this not why we reproach Nature, the parent of us all (as certain perverse persons do), for making some of us noble and others ignoble [i.e., through heredity]? Assuming that Nature offers to all an equal [physical and mental] constitution, regardless of family, power, or wealth, the sons of private persons and the offspring of princes and kings, as far as the mind is concerned, are born the same way, though the latter be born in purple clothing and palaces, the former in rags and huts. . . . Seneca . . . says that Socrates was neither a patrician nor a Roman knight; philosophy did not find him noble but made him noble.[41]

Since virtue can be learned, any healthy, rational person of whatever origin can learn it, at least in principle. Virtue equality applied to women as well, and numerous humanists made the argument that women not only were capable of the same great deeds performed by men, but had in fact performed such deeds many times in the past.[42] Poggio Bracciolini even makes the striking claim—astonishing by the lights of ancient virtue ethics—that "virtue is ready to hand, and comes to all those who embrace it." For him, it is only the hereditary nobility, inclined as they are to rest on the laurels of their ancestors, who find it hard.[43]

This is not to say that humanist virtue politics can be construed as egalitarian in anything approaching the modern sense of that word. Like all premodern political thinkers, the humanists accepted that some degree of hierarchy in politics was natural and necessary. There always needed to be an elite, whether a republican political class, the *optimates,* with its magistrates or a monarch with his ministers. But the elite should be open, accessible to any persons of virtue and wisdom, whatever their social or national origin.[44] A political hierarchy should be able to justify itself in moral and rational terms, not rely merely on its inherited wealth and status.[45] Here the humanists differed from one of their basic authorities—Aristotle—who in the *Politics* reports without demur that people believe nobility *(eugeneia)* to depend in part on lineage and the long possession of wealth.[46]

The humanist conception of the *path* to virtue—*how* one acquires virtue—also stands in contrast with Aristotle's. Whereas Aristotle saw the acquisition of virtue as a matter of practice, philosophical reflection, and habit, and aided by good birth, wealth, good upbringing, and good friends, the humanists as a rule see liberal education—full stop—as the path to virtue. The path to virtue and thus to just political authority runs through the humanities or *studia humanitatis.* The humanities ennoble those who study them. As Pier Paolo Vergerio put it in the most famous of all humanist educational tracts, *The Mores of Gentlemen* (*De ingenuis moribus,* 1402 / 1403), if they are provided with an education in the humanities,

> children can usually overcome and bring distinction to obscure family origins and humble homelands. . . . Although it is fitting that everyone (and parents especially) desire to educate their children correctly, and that children be such that they may seem worthy of good parents,[47] it is particularly fitting that those of lofty rank, who cannot say or do anything in secret,[48] be instructed in the principal arts in such a way as to be held worthy of the fortune and rank they possess. For it is only fair that those who wish all the highest distinctions to be due themselves, be themselves obliged to show the highest distinction. Nor is there any more firm or solid ground for ruling than this: that those who rule be judged by all to be the worthiest to rule.[49]

This is the new and powerful justification for the study of classical literature offered by humanist educators in the fifteenth century, building on the new paideuma of Petrarch. They held that training in the classics, especially the language arts of grammar and rhetoric, plus poetry, history, moral philosophy, and other humane studies, would instill noble mores, *ingenui mores,* and practical wisdom, *prudentia*—all the qualities needed for excellence in government. Moral philosophy and history, precept and example, couched in the noble language learned from the ancient poets and orators, would give future citizens and rulers both the moral character to govern well and the eloquence needed for the finest form of leadership. "Those in charge of the state will take care, and at public expense, that each and every discipline may have the best teachers who may teach publicly."[50]

Educators who taught the humanities were thus performing a public service. By training the elite in the humanities, noble virtue would radiate down to the populace in general, who would benefit from and imitate the wisdom and moral excellence of their leaders.[51] The great humanist educator Guarino of Verona provides a vivid example of this kind of thinking. Writing to his disciple and countryman Gian Nicola Salerno, a humanistically educated *podestà,* or chief magistrate, whose superexcellent virtue (Guarino writes) had just reduced the rebellious Bolognese to order,[52] the famous schoolmaster declares that the judge should give credit to his education in the Muses, who have taught him the arts of ruling cities: "Hence you have demonstrated that the Muses not only govern stringed instruments and the lyre, but also republics. . . . How much should we value, how much should we praise that learning, those arts, in which he who is going to be a statesman is educated! Once provided with justice, goodness, prudence and modesty, he can share the fruit [of these virtues] with everyone, and their utility commonly spreads to everyone. Philosophical studies do not have the same utility when imbued in private persons." The liberally educated statesman is "nurtured by Jove" to prefer not his own advantage and benefits, but those of the people entrusted to him: "he rules empires not by violence and arms, as tyrants do, but with affability and mercy *(clementia),*" imitating the *duces* of the bees, who, themselve unarmed, require no stingers to govern the hive. "With good reason, then, did antiquity extol those who educated statesmen, since in this way they reformed the mores and customs of the many by means of a single person: as, for example, Anaxagoras taught Pericles, Plato Dion, Pythagoras the Italian princes, Athenodorus Cato, Panaetius Scipio, Apollonius Cicero and Caesar; and, even in this age, Manuel Chrysoloras, a great man and a great philosopher, educated many men."[53]

Such passages are easily multiplied. This is no surprise, given that the theme of moral rearmament via the study of literature and philosophy was a prominent one in the most famous text, *De officiis,* of the humanists' favorite ancient author, Cicero. We shall return to this point presently.

Political decline could by the same token be traced to the loss of humanistic disciplines. Niccolò Perotti seems to have drawn a parallel between the Roman civil wars and the late medieval decline of Christendom, since in the preface to his translation of Polybius' *Histories,* dedicated to Pope Nicholas V, he described how, after the fall of Rome, the destruction of the humanities *(optimae artes et disciplinae),* with their many examples of noble conduct, had resulted in laziness and self-indulgence on the part of Rome's leaders, and their torpidity had inevitably affected the whole citizen body:

> It is an established fact that such as are the city's leading men, such also is the rest of the city, and whatever moral alterations appear among leaders are always followed in the people. Since their leaders were illiterate, therefore, the rest were untaught and uneducated as well. [He goes on to complain that in medieval times there were no rewards or honor for anyone inclined to literary study.] For just as a temperate climate brings forth rich and plentiful fruit, so also the prince's humanity, honor and generosity produces the liberal arts and fine minds.[54]

So too the great humanist printer Aldus Manutius prefaced his edition of Plutarch's *Moralia* with an elaborate compliment to his friend Jacopo Antiquario, praising him for his saintly character and learning, qualities which his example had spread throughout his entire household:

> As your guest in Milan I saw you were endowed with every virtue; I admired not just your saintliness but also that of your young nephew Antiquario, your brother's son, who displayed such modesty and love of good literature—for he already knew Latin and Greek—that he looked to me as if he would soon be very expert and learned, just like you. I also admired your staff and the whole household, entirely modest and saintly, like its master. So I would affirm the truth of the saying: whatever the qualities of heads of families, masters, noblemen, princes, heads of state, such will be the qualities of a household, the staff and servants, the states and peoples themselves. This view is expressed elegantly, as always, by Cicero in his books *On the Laws*. . . . So I would wish all men who have command over others, "to whom peoples have been entrusted and such great affairs are a concern," to be of excellent character, my dear Antiquario, and very like yourself; certainly the whole of humanity would soon live a blessed existence, by general consensus crime and all vices would be banished.[55]

A perennial problem for all political meritocracies is inducing non-elite citizens to accept the authority of their presumed betters. A claim to superior wisdom and virtue is not so easily verified as a claim to be the legitimate heir or a magistrate duly elected in accordance with constitutional procedures. In humanist virtue politics, the solution to this problem looks to the force of example and eloquence. The commands of the ruling class are accepted because the ruled are imprinted in some way with the virtues of their betters, enough to recognize that what is being commanded is right and just and to their benefit. From a modern perspective this claim, or rather hope, might seem naïve, but the idealism that animates it is palpable.[56]

Classical Sources of Virtue Politics

It is obvious that the virtue politics of the Italian humanists has deep roots in the ancient world, and its inspiration is to be found not only in the sources so far mentioned, Aristotle and Cicero, but in Plato, Sallust, Livy, and the Roman Stoic writers as well.[57] Seneca was a pervasive presence in humanist literature on the prince.[58] In a sense the humanists were reviving and carrying on the work of the ancient philosophical schools, some of which, some of the time—like the early Academy, the Lyceum, and the Stoics—emphasized the reform of politics through philosophical study and training in moral virtue for rulers. They embraced the proverbial maxim of ancient statesmen that a man cannot rule others who cannot rule himself.[59]

All that being said, the role of Cicero in forming the humanist project was unique and foundational. The humanist project could even be described as a revival, continuation, and extension of Cicero's own program for the remoralization of Roman society. Cicero had presented his philosophical writings as a way of reawakening the moribund *mores et instituta* of ancient Rome—the native virtues that had made her great—after the moral and political disasters of the civil wars.[60] The humanists recognized parallels to the moral crises of their own time. Cicero's *De officiis,* based on Stoic teachings, was the most popular of all his philosophical texts, to judge from the number of editions and commentaries, and it is no surprise that quotations from that work pop up constantly in humanist writings. Particularly salient for virtue politics is book 2, where Cicero discusses how a leader can win the goodwill of the people by inspiring their love:

> Let us look first at good will and the rules for securing it. . . . The love of people generally is powerfully attracted by a man's mere name and reputation for generosity, kindness, justice, honour, and all those virtues that belong to gentleness of character and affability of manner. And because that very quality which we term moral goodness and propriety [*honestum decorumque*] is pleasing to us by and of itself and touches all our hearts both by its inward essence and its outward aspect and shines forth with most lustre through those virtues named

above, we are, therefore, compelled by Nature herself to love those in whom we believe those virtues to reside. Now these are only the most powerful motives to love—not all of them; there may be some minor ones besides.

Secondly, the trust [*fides*] of the people can be secured on two conditions: (1) if people think us possessed of practical wisdom combined with a sense of justice. For we have confidence in those who we think have more understanding than ourselves, who, we believe, have better insight into the future, and who, when an emergency arises and a crisis comes, can clear away the difficulties and reach a safe decision according to the exigencies of the occasion; for that kind of wisdom the world accounts genuine and practical. But (2) confidence is reposed in men who are just and true—that is, good men—on the definite assumption that their characters admit of no suspicion of dishonesty or wrongdoing. And so we believe that it is perfectly safe to entrust our lives, our fortunes, and our children to their care.[61]

Virtue creates a kind of charisma in a leader, making him loved and trusted by the people, whereas a tyrant rules by fear.[62] Practical wisdom, *prudentia* or knowledge of affairs, the quality most prized in modern "technical meritocracy," is necessary too but is not by itself enough.[63]

Of these two qualities, then, justice has the greater power to inspire confidence; for even without the aid of prudence, it has considerable weight; but practical wisdom without justice is of no avail to inspire confidence; for take from a man his reputation for probity, and the more shrewd and clever he is, the more hated and mistrusted he becomes. Therefore, justice combined with practical wisdom will command all the confidence we can desire; justice without wisdom will be able to do much; wisdom without justice will be of no avail at all.[64]

From Cicero too came the humanists' vision of how study of the humanities could benefit the state. Their favorite statement of the case came from his oration for the poet Archias, the *Pro Archia,* rediscovered by Petrarch in 1333, a text whose message the Italian poet trumpeted in various places in his writings.[65] Archias had been charged with claiming illegally the status of Roman citizen; Cicero's response was to argue that, whether or not he was legally a citizen, he deserved citizen status because of his contributions to the city's culture. Cicero then described how that literary culture had inculcated virtue and eloquence in himself and in other great Romans, and had made him a devoted and effective servant of the republic:

I have the better right to indulgence [in the study of literature], because my devotion to letters strengthens my oratorical powers, and these, such as they are, have never failed my friends in their hour of peril. Yet insignificant though these powers may seem to be, I fully realize from what source I draw all that is highest in them. Had I not persuaded myself from my youth up, thanks to the moral lessons derived from a wide reading, that nothing is to be greatly sought after in this life save glory and honor, and that in their quest all bodily pains and all dangers of death or exile should be lightly accounted, I should never have borne for the safety of you all the brunt of many a bitter encounter, or bared my breast to the daily onsets of abandoned persons. All literature, all philosophy, all history, abounds with incentives to noble action, incentives which would be buried in black darkness were the light of the written word not flashed upon them. How many pictures of high endeavor the great authors of Greece and Rome have drawn for our use, and bequeathed to us, not only for our contemplation, but for our emulation! These I have held ever before my vision throughout my public career, and have guided the workings of my brain and my soul by meditating upon patterns of excellence.

To the objection that there have been great servants of the state who lacked formation in letters, Cicero admits the point, but argues that great natural gifts, when developed by literary and philosophical learning, lead to a unique form of personal distinction, better than anything untutored nature can accomplish:

> Yet I do at the same time assert that when to a lofty and brilliant character is applied the ordering and moulding influence of learning *(doctrina)*, the result is often exceptional and unique distinction. Such a character our fathers were privileged to behold in the divine figure of Scipio Africanus; such were those patterns of continence and self-control, Gaius Laelius and Lucius Furius; such was the brave and venerable Marcus Cato, the most accomplished man of his day. These surely would never have devoted themselves to literary pursuits, had they not been aided thereby in the appreciation and pursuit of merit.[66]

Finally, Cicero's conception of the role of eloquence in public deliberation and especially its function of producing consensus—essential for achieving the humanist ideal of willing obedience and non-coercive government—was also decisive for humanist political thought. One of the key passages appears in what became a much-read humanist treatise on rhetoric, Cicero's *De inventione* 1.3:

> Consider another point; after cities had been established, how could it have been brought to pass that men should learn to keep faith and observe justice and become accustomed to obey others voluntarily and believe not only that they must work for the common good but even sacrifice life itself, unless men

had been able by eloquence to persuade their fellows of the truth of what they had discovered by reason? Certainly only a speech at the same time powerful and entrancing could have induced one who had great physical strength to submit to justice without violence, so that he suffered himself to be put on a par with those among whom he could excel, and abandoned voluntarily a most agreeable custom, especially since this custom had already acquired through lapse of time the force of a natural right.[67]

Eloquence could persuade powerful men to restrain their superior strength and subject themselves to reason and justice. Of course Cicero was only one voice in a long literary tradition stretching back to the Greek sophists that similarly stressed the social value of eloquence. His writings, above all the *De oratore,* were likely the humanists' first exposure to that tradition, but as they gradually recovered and studied other ancient writings on eloquence, first the full text of Quintilian (recovered by Poggio Bracciolini in 1417) and later the Greek orators and writers on education such as Isocrates, they came to appreciate how tightly ancient tradition had bound together moral goodness and the power of speech. From Quintilian above all they learned that, for their beloved ancient authors, the primary tool for the spread of virtue was the *vir bonus dicendi peritus,* the good man skilled in speaking.[68]

How Not to Reform a Republic

The humanists had strong views on the kind of solutions to corruption and tyranny that, they felt, did not work. They knew that prohibitions do not teach but good examples do. As Edmund Burke would later put it, "Example is the school of mankind and they will learn at no other." Abuse of power or tyranny, a perennial problem in all political communities, they saw primarily as a failure of human excellence and rationality. Instead of looking to the legal definitions of a Bartolus to determine when a ruler was behaving tyrannically, humanists read Tacitus to understand the psychology of political corruption.[69] The solution to the problem of rulers who abused their power was not to spin legal theories of consent or to elaborate arguments for legitimate resistance to tyranny. Tyrants could not be stopped by passing laws or quoting legal maxims. The humanist way of addressing tyranny was to surround the ruler with men of virtue whose charisma would influence him to do what was right, as Petrarch maintained in his *Invective against a Man of High Rank,* and as Baldassar Castiglione was still teaching a century and a half later in the *Courtier.*[70]

Above all, a corrupt ruling class could not be contained by popular agitation. Allowing the vulgar to influence government either through tumult, power sharing, or even the wrong kind of consultation only made things worse.[71] Nor could the problem be solved by bringing in a strong man, some *condottiere* who would enforce peace when civil order broke down—the preferred solution of fourteenth-century city-states in crisis. Coercion did not make men better. The humanists knew from their great textbook of political virtue, the *De officiis,* that society could not be knit together by brute power alone.[72] Any free man worthy of the name would not accept commands from a morally inferior person; to do so would be tantamount to slavery.[73] Moreover, the strategies of legitimation used by many Renaissance tyrants and oligarchs—managed communal elections, staged ceremonies of acclamation, loyalty oaths, the corruption and cooptation of guild leadership, the acquisition of imperial and papal vicariates, the purchase of titles of nobility, invented claims to high descent—all of these strategies were in the end transparently fraudulent; none would or could create a true community.[74]

Ultimately, for a stable political order to take root, fraud and force would have to be replaced by loyalty, trust, and mutual interest. It would require changing hearts; it would call for all the arts of persuasion. For the humanists, this required government by the wise and the good, men whose speech carried weight and whose lives compelled admiration. Virtue was the key; only the charisma of virtue gave a leader the power to change the human heart, to bring order, peace, and willing obedience.[75] Petrarch put it this way:

> It is [virtue] that has stormed the strongest and best-fortified cities, when hatreds have turned to love; that has often brought to an end the most deadly wars which warfare could not end, and has achieved a victory most welcome even to the defeated. This virtue opened the iron gates of the Faliscans to Camillus; this bound together by as much intimacy as was possible King Pyrrhus with brave Curius and stern Fabricius, the leaders of Romulus' people; virtue swiftly turned away the arrogant King Porsena of Etruria from his persistent siege; it bent down before the knees of Julius Caesar the petty Gaulish kings who might perhaps still have dared some grand revolt; virtue made Pompey the Great bow before the doorway of Posidonius and sent Alexander the Great to the barrel of Diogenes; virtue gave the most glorious name to the emperor Titus by the agreement of the human race and restored the principate taken from Germanicus to his admittedly undeserving son. Virtue subjected the peoples of the East and a mighty mass of men to the control of one widow

woman; recently it made Saladin king of Egypt not only mild but generous toward our men; and to touch on something from the histories of the Jews, it was for virtue that the queen of Sheba, that admirer of Solomon, came to Jerusalem from afar to see what she had heard tell of; and the embassy of Maccabaeus to cross the seas desiring Roman friendship.[76]

Men would not willingly obey magistrates who served their own interests rather than the common good. Rulers needed moral training that would make them other-directed and a grasp of history that would give them practical wisdom, *prudentia*. It is no accident that the most famous political quotation of the Italian Renaissance was Plato's famous dictum in the *Republic:* that states will not be happy unless philosophers ruled, or rulers become philosophers.[77] A close runner-up was another quotation from Plato, preserved in the *Letters* attributed to him (and reported by Cicero in the *De officiis*): that we are not born for ourselves alone, but for our family, our friends, and our country.[78]

Many city-states in the Renaissance tried to solve the problems of tyranny and corruption by passing more laws, insulating judicial processes from local influence, or setting up police magistracies concerned with public morals. But the humanists knew that this would not eliminate the real causes of vice. They had read their Tacitus: *corruptissima respublica plurimae leges* (*Annales* 3.27). "The most corrupt republic passes the most laws," but in vain. The laws were particularly useless in restraining the powerful. As an interlocutor in one of Poggio's dialogues says,

> Only the little people and the lower orders of a city are controlled by your laws. . . . The more powerful civic leaders transgress their power. Anacharsis justly compared the laws to a spider's web, which captures the weak but is broken by the strong. . . . Away then with these laws and rights of yours, that are . . . obeyed only by private persons and little folk who need their protection against the powerful! . . . Grave, prudent and sober men do not need the laws; they declare a law of right living for themselves, being trained by nature and study to virtue and good behavior. The powerful spit upon and trample the laws as things suited to weak, mercenary, working-class, acquisitive, base and poverty-stricken folk, who are better ruled by violence and the fear of punishment than by laws.[79]

Laws and legal coercion didn't work against the powerful: they either didn't need them, being already virtuous, or held them in contempt as paper barriers restraining only the weak. And laws made by tyrants and corrupt oligarchs could not be respected.[80] It is difficult, indeed, to exaggerate the disgust most humanists of the quattrocento felt toward contemporary legal culture; their attitude, if anything, was even more contemptuous than Petrarch's.[81] They respected Roman law as a repository of ancient prudence; they believed unreservedly in divine law and the *ius gentium;* but they treated the actual practice of law in their own time as desperately corrupt, a source of civil discord and inhumanity, a means of obscuring rather than revealing true justice. The law as practiced was a conspiracy against the public good, corrupted by money, indifferent to right and wrong, tying up true justice in webs of pettifoggery and useless technicalities. Humanists complained that the sheer multitude of laws and the procedural obstacles to applying the law fairly undermined moral freedom and humanity, ensured bad outcomes, and favored the wealthy and powerful. They rejected the premise that the law can dictate correct behavior by laying down specific rules. The law had no eyes, as Xenophon's ideal prince, Cyrus, said in the *Cyropedia* (a popular humanist text); just rulers could better see what should be done than blind law. Absent virtue, the list of rules would only get longer and longer, and the more numerous the laws, the more they would be flouted. Judges needed to have discretion and, as Aristotle taught, to possess the authority to temper the strict rigor of the laws with fairness.[82] *Summa ius, summa iniuria.* Justice taken to its extreme yields injustice. Like Plato and Aristotle, the humanists believed that the best judge was a wise and good man whom philosophy had trained to understand natural law and apply it in accordance with his discretion. For them, the Roman maxim that societies should be ruled by laws, not men, was conditional, not absolute. It depended on the laws, and it depended on the men.[83]

Eloquence and the "Virtuous Environment"

Since laws and institutions were inadequate safeguards against corruption, the only real bulwark against abuse of power in the ruling class was for that class to police itself, informally, via persuasion, not coercion.[84] The best members of the elite had to convince rulers and their fellow aristocrats to behave well. This could be done by education: by bringing up the next generation in the humanist tradition of moral self-cultivation, or by helping one's own children acquire virtue through study of the classics. But the humanist movement's ambitions went well beyond education of the young; they sought to colonize the symbolic environment of the adult world as well. Their ultimate goal was to forge a wider culture that celebrated classical virtue and shamed those who fell short of its ideals.

Here was another reason for the leading role played in humanist politics by eloquence and the arts of persuasion. Eloquence was not only the trumpet of an individual's own virtue; it was also the most important vehicle for the self-policing of the elite. The epideictic rhetoric of the humanists aimed to make men *want* to be virtuous by praising good conduct and character and blaming bad in the most lively colors.[85] Thanks to humanist influence in government and society, during the period from the 1390s to the 1430s occasions for public oratory gradually became more numerous.[86] Eventually it became the practice in quattrocento Italy to hold ceremonial orations, mostly in Latin but sometimes in Italian, at all the important junctures of public and private life: at weddings and funerals, on taking up public office, on beginning a course at a university, at the beginning of ambassadorial missions, even before battles in a military harangue. In Florence, for example, the practice began in 1415 for a member of the government to make a speech on justice, usually filled with classical and biblical authorities, whenever a foreign judge took up his six-month term of office in the city.[87] Humanists also engaged in "private rhetoric" in the form of familiar letters (often widely circulated) written to the mighty ones of the earth to advise them on matters of high moral concern. Petrarch, Francesco Filelfo, Marsilio Ficino, and many others produced such eloquent screeds. Humanist letters and speeches often praised members of the ruling class for their virtues, even when they had given little evidence of them—following Aristotle's advice in the *Rhetoric* that praising men above their merits was a way of motivating them to improve their behavior. But their larger purpose was to communicate the moral expectations of the community to people who were taking on new public and private responsibilities. Accountability—punishing those who fell below the standards expected of the elite—was left to literary invectives or to the pages of humanist histories. The ultimate punishment of those who abused power was social rejection by one's peers and eternal infamy.

To put this in modern terms, humanist eloquence was meant as a kind of social technology, incentivizing good behavior through the use of praise and blame—as opposed to repressing bad behavior by using the legal and coercive powers of government. To use Albert Hirschmann's analytic framework, the humanists aimed to neutralize corrupt passions and appetites, the desire for personal gain or for revenge, by stimulating a countervailing passion: the desire for honor and admiration from the community.[88] It involved replacing the existing honor code of the aristocratic classes, derived from feudal and chivalric sources, with a new honor code (or "honor world," to use Kwame Anthony Appiah's useful expression[89]), inspired by an idealized version of Graeco-Roman antiquity. Future statesmen were to be immersed in classical history, poetry, and moral philosophy—a moral universe where the highest praise and the highest rewards were lavished on public servants. The political class was to be exhorted to a Sallustian competition in virtue. The humanists understood that the classical ideal of virtue depended on cultivating a certain sense of self: that one is the kind of person who doesn't do certain things; that one's dignity and honor within a community depend on not acting, or not being seen to act, out of self-interest, catering to one's own appetites, but on serving the community. The humanists' aim was to build up a critical mass of true noblemen and noblewomen who in turn would create the presumption that meritorious behavior would be rewarded with high status and malicious behavior with shame and degradation.

To build up their honor world the humanists enlisted the arts in celebration of antique virtue. It became the goal of humanist culture to saturate the civic and courtly environment with images, inscriptions, theatrical productions, and music that kept the rewards of human excellence, and the consequences of bad behavior, continually before the senses and the minds of the elite.[90] Petrarch's custom of presenting rulers with ancient coins to remind them of great statesmen and emperors of the past was continued in the fifteenth century and transferred to the painted decoration of manuscripts.[91] The new, classicizing architecture of the quattrocento and the design of the built environment in general had the effect of bringing Rome alive again; to walk down a neoclassical courtyard lined with statues of the mighty dead was meant to inspire in the living a desire for similar deeds.[92] In the council chambers of kings and republics the humanistically educated man could read on the walls and ceilings inscriptions selected from his boyhood reading that would remind him of his obligation to act wisely and well; pictures, statues and architecture all reinforced the message. The inscriptional practices of the ancient world were renewed in the quattrocento, but with a difference: in addition to commemorating civic generosity, Renaissance inscriptions also taught political lessons. One quotation from Sallust, often found on the walls of Renaissance council chambers, gives the flavor: *Concordia res parvae crescunt, discordia maximae dilabuntur.* "Small states grow with concord; discord causes great ones to dissolve."[93] The lessons of Sallust's *Bellum Iugurthinum* were dramatized in Leonardo Dati's *Hiempsal* (1442), a humanist morality play on the superiority of natural virtue to inherited rank, combined with salutary warnings about the envy aroused by true virtue.[94] Most painting in the Renaissance continued to have religious subjects, but in the course of the quattrocento the representation of classical subjects, almost always with a moralizing message, became increasingly common.[95]

Even music was brought to bear on the project of classicizing the environment. Though humanists had little to do with the great polyphonic music we associate with the Renaissance today—Dufay, Josquin, Isaac and the rest—they did work out a new style of music criticism that celebrated the ancient ideal of moral music found in the last book of Aristotle's *Politics,* and they insisted that music had a proper civic function of supporting virtuous behavior. The humanists also championed a revival of the ancient singer of tales—a genre of musical literature now completely lost—which they reconstructed from their knowledge of ancient literature. We know of a fairly large number of musicians from the mid-quattrocento to the early sixteenth century who practiced the humanist art song—the performance of Latin poetry, classical or modern, often improvised, to the *lira da braccio.* As we learn from Raffaele Brandolini, the most famous of these singers, the goal was to reform and elevate the forms of entertainment used by civic and courtly elites. Such entertainments would no longer feature clowns, tumblers, mimes, and singers of love songs; there would henceforth be no drums and cymbals, trumpets and horns playing music of the hunt. These the humanists tried to stigmatize as vulgar or potentially immoral. Instead, the leisure hours of the upper classes would be transformed into occasions for the celebration of classical virtue.[96]

A New Way of Thinking about Politics

Virtue politics was thus never simply a program for the reform of political elites; it amounted to an entirely new way of thinking about politics. As we have seen, the humanist strategy for political reform was elaborated out of the new paideuma of Petrarch and involved, in the first instance, a revival of ancient character education. This was not mere *educatio* confined to schoolroom years, which in practice was concerned for the most part, and necessarily so, with learning to read, write, and speak Latin (and eventually Greek). It went far beyond that. It was *institutio,* the renewal of classical culture generally, in literature, history, philosophy, and the arts, with the aim of bringing to an end the degrading collapse of Italy into corruption, ignorance, impiety, and violence, and restoring the glory of Rome. Antiquity was now to be the treasure-house of civilization, and its preservation and enlargement became the proud duty of learned men. In political life the new *institutio* aimed to restore legitimacy to government by filling the courts of princes and the councils of republics with wise and virtuous human beings, inspired by the great deeds and great thoughts of classical antiquity. Making virtue the criterion of holding office meant opening the elite to persons of ability from all ranks of society, and even (as we shall see) to immigrants from other states. It meant dethroning heredity as the chief or only principle of legitimation. It also meant not relying on armed guards, oaths, and lawyers to impose order on society, but rather elevating to the apex of Church and state well-educated *principes* possessing practical wisdom and moral charisma. And it meant securing the obedience of the ruled not through force, but through justice and persuasion. The humanists recognized that the moral transformation they sought could not be achieved solely through the tongues of orators and the pens of literati, though both were sorely needed; it would also require social pressure from a new elite of influential leaders; it would require the reform of customs, laws, and mores;[97] and it would require Italians to bring the sublime majesty of ancient art, architecture, and music once more to bear upon the human soul.

Nearly all humanists shared a commitment to this strategy for political and civilizational reform. By the early fifteenth century that strategy had cemented itself into a kind of orthodoxy embraced passionately by humanistically educated men and women. That does not mean there was no room within the bounds of orthodoxy for disagreement and debate, as the rest of this volume will show clearly enough. Many humanists expressed strong preferences for one regime type or another—popular, aristocratic, monarchical, or a mixed regime. Some supported the Holy Roman Emperor, like Enea Silvio Piccolomini, others the spiritual empire of the pope, like Biondo Flavio and Lorenzo Valla. But virtue politics was in principle *supra partes,* a form of political prudence that all humanists could agree on. It promoted a form of political education adaptable to all forms of rulership and belonging to no political faction.[98]

The highest political commitment for humanists did not entail loyalty to a particular type of regime or to a faction. Francesco Patrizi of Siena, their greatest authority on politics, in the first chapter of his *De regno* relates approvingly numerous examples of ancient philosophers and statesmen who moved from republican to monarchical regimes and back again, sharing their wisdom with anyone who might profit from it.[99] As Petrarch and any number of fifteenth-century humanists were to show, even the rule of a tyrant, for a humanist, could present a matchless opportunity for virtue and wisdom to counsel vice and ignorance. The humanists generally saw open partisanship as unseemly and, like other passions, a threat to virtue and the rule of reason, quite apart from the damage it caused to the state in affairs domestic and foreign. It was precisely for partisan passions that Petrarch faulted his beloved Cicero in his famous letter to the ancient orator.[100] It was for factional zeal too that Boccaccio blamed Dante in his admiring biography of the great poet.[101] By the same token it was chiefly because he was seen as lacking partisan allegiances that Leonardo Bruni was chosen as chancellor of Florence in a time of bitter factional struggle.[102] The modern preference for republican government over monarchy has sometimes concealed this attitude from view and made historians read the easy mobility of humanists between signorial, oligarchical, and ecclesiastical regimes as signaling an absence of political conviction. This is to impose our own categories of what it is to be a man or woman of principle in politics—that is, a loyal member of a party, an *engagé* intellectual, or an exclusivist ideologue.[103] While it is not possible to exonerate many humanists of the charge of rhetorical insincerity (a fault they would hardly have recognized as such), it should be borne in mind that the goals of their political project operated on a plane higher than that of partisan conflict and regime loyalties.[104]

That is why a figure like Pier Candido Decembrio, secretary to the duke of Milan—regarded by many as a tyrant—could move smoothly into the position of secretary to the Ambrosian Republic after the duke's death. That is why no one thought the worse of Enea Silvio Piccolomini for leaving the service of the Holy Roman Emperor to enter that of the emperors' rivals for supreme authority in Christendom, the popes. Piccolomini eventually was able to become pope himself in the Roman obedience without being accused of ideological inconsistency, even though he had previously served as secretary to the anti-pope Felix V. That is why Leonardo Bruni could work for the ecclesiastical monarchy of four popes, then for the Florentine oligarchy, then continue in office when the Medici regime took over Florence in 1434, while simultaneously entertaining offers from other princes—all without being regarded as having betrayed the republican principles of the Florentine state that he served in the role of chancellor for seventeen years.[105] Bruni was not blamed by contemporaries for betraying a republican ideology because exclusive loyalty to a particular constitutional form was no part of what it meant to be a man of virtue and wisdom in the quattrocento.[106] The enemy of the Renaissance humanists was the tyrant, but, as both Plato and Pope St. Gregory the Great had taught them, tyranny was the universal temptation of the human race. It resided in the prideful soul, and tyrants could be found in republics no less than in principalities. "Where there are no tyrants, the people tyrannize," said Petrarch, and his mature solution to the problem of tyranny was to change humanity, not to substitute one regime type for another, or replace one party with another.[107]

That is why the humanist conception of politics differs so strikingly both from medieval and modern ones: because the humanists saw politics, fundamentally, as soulcraft. Their overriding goal was to uproot tyranny from the soul of the ruler, whether the ruler was one, few, or many, and to inspire citizens to serve the republic, whether it was a princely, oligarchical, or popular one.[108] This implied a transformation of political reform from a constitutional and legal mode to one emphasizing character and education. It led to a different way entirely of thinking about politics.

For example, humanists did not think of free speech as Americans do today, as a right guaranteed by law and protected in the courts. For them it was a virtue, speaking truth to power. For the statesman and diplomat Alamanno Rinuccini, free speech was closely related to the virtue of courage:

> No one would call free the man who either in the senate, the assembly, or the courts would be constrained by fear, cupidity or any cause you like from daring to say openly what he thought and to act on it, so that, as I said before, someone might claim without absurdity that freedom is part of fortitude, since the free man and the courageous man are best revealed in action. The brave man is praised for undergoing grave perils in accordance with reason; the free man is manifest more in speaking and giving counsel; yet the duty of the noble soul is revealed in both the brave and the free, since neither one gives way before dangers nor lives in fear of threats. It is an extremely useful thing in free cities when citizens, in giving counsel, give their undisguised views on what is best for the republic.[109]

To speak with freedom, to advocate what was right, especially before a tyrant or a howling mob, was a great virtue that required other virtues such as prudence and courage. It could proceed only from a strong soul that cared for the right. The distinction between a good man and a bad one was concealed by the communal practice of secret balloting, which meant that no person was held responsible for giving bad counsel.[110] To advocate what was the best course of action required a special kind of wisdom and a prudent understanding of human motivations, not merely knowledge of what one wanted for oneself. It required too a sense of the behavior appropriate to a free person. As Livy wrote, "The arrogant man has forgotten another man's *libertas;* the coward has forgotten his own."[111] Roman law stipulated that everyone affected by a decision should be consulted before the decision was taken, but without the virtue of free speech there was no guarantee that those consulted would speak their mind and not be intimidated by the powerful.[112]

Or take the question of citizenship. The issue of who counted as a citizen in a *civitas* was one that had preoccupied Roman lawyers and their medieval progeny for centuries, and there was a lively discussion of the subject as well among scholastic commentators on Aristotle's *Politics.* But citizenship was equally a matter of passionate debate in Italian city-states, especially those with traditional communal governments, since citizen status could confer the right to be entered in the lotteries to hold public office.[113] In general oligarchic parties favored restricting citizenship to taxpaying members of the more prominent guilds, wealthier men of several generations standing in the community, while popular factions favored granting lower guildsmen—artisans and shopkeepers—as well as recent immigrants from outside the city the right to enter their names in the lotteries for magistracies and citizen boards. This issue was among the most divisive in the politics of Renaissance republics.

The humanists in general opposed the popular method of choosing magistrates by lot, which they regarded as appallingly anti-meritocratic. But this does not mean they were acting merely as purveyors of a crypto-oligarchic ideology, as is sometimes supposed.[114] In Siena, for example, humanists like Andreoccio Petrucci, Barnaba Pannalini, and later Francesco Patrizi were sharp critics of party politics in general and the oligarchy that ran the city in particular.[115] Siena in the fifteenth century was moving toward a system of five hereditary castes—the "gentlemen," the Nine, the Twelve, the *Riformatori,* and the *populari*—membership in which determined citizenship and potential access to office.[116] Sienese humanists, who had a more cosmopolitan outlook than most of their fellow citizens and who disdained Siena's communal tradition as a relic of the corrupt medieval past, deplored the trend toward closed, hereditary citizenship. Hereditary citizenship for them was as inimical to virtue as hereditary lordship. It ignored the lessons of Roman history, which taught that openness to outsiders was what made Rome great.[117]

Andreoccio Petrucci, who came from a family of wealthy bankers and as magistrate and diplomat was a tireless servant of the city, nevertheless had nothing but

contempt for the moral character of the oligarchs who ran it. Writing to his friend
and political ally Barnaba Pannalini, later the humanist chancellor of Siena, he
vented his anger at the selfishness of the city's leading men in a time of crisis:

> The republic is still run by the same lot who were running it when you were
> here, and they haven't changed their moral character as we saw it then one bit.
> Almost none of them have the republic's interests at heart; all they care about
> is increasing their personal prestige (dignitas). That's what they all want, that's
> what concerns them, and they don't realize what the future of the republic is
> going to be, what the outcome will be, with this kind of behavior. My view is
> that *no* citizen has prestige in a republic that is wretched.[118]

Petrucci is afraid to write more since he doesn't trust the courier of his letter, but
in a later, franker message to the same correspondent he continues his thought.
He describes how depressed he is about the continuous conflict among the citizens, how obsessed they are with their status, how little concern they have for the
serious external threats facing them:

> What arrogant boasting, what damned insolence! These men claim that they
> are citizens, that their ancestors have lived in the city for ninety years, but there's
> no record that they've ever been of use to the republic in its worst times. Yet
> they reckon their country owes more to them than they owe to it. For me there's
> no difference between them and the four-footed beasts; both equally lack
> reason and judgment. The longer a man has lived in his city without being a
> useful citizen, the more swiftly he should be ejected from the assemblies of
> good men and from public life generally. Especially when they can't come up
> with a reason why they should be of any service to the state, any way they can
> be especially well deserving of the republic, which was [in antiquity] always
> dearer than life itself to all good men in every city![119]

So who then *is* the citizen? Who is worthy of that name? Is it the man who
is neglectful of the republic? Who looks on its tribulations with a mellow calm,
unmindful of how much he owes to it by nature? *He* is the citizen, *he* I say,
who, when it would be of benefit to the republic, would not hesitate to spend
his whole family fortune, undertake laborious tasks, endanger his life—*then*
he can think of himself as not just a citizen, but a fine citizen. All our affairs
would long since have turned out for us as we would wish if we were to have
citizens with an attitude like this.

If anyone should say to me that I'm following too strict a definition, let me
put it more crudely. If among mortals men of this kind are not easily found—for

how many men are there, in the end, who do something for the sake of the republic and are not reckoning that some great profit is going to come to themselves, or that they can't take a cut for themselves, or what is worse, that long and corrupt custom does not call them into the dock for unjustly taking something from the public till—if all that is true, what is the point of this long speech? Just so you can understand me when I say I find these people unbearable who think they are the most excellent of citizens simply because they have lived for a long time in the city, and haven't done a single thing in public life that we can say has earned them the slightest bit of praise, let alone admiration.[120]

From the point of view of virtue politics a citizen is not someone who holds a status based on residence and ancestry but is rather a man of high character and enterprise who has shown devotion to the city and has sacrificed his time and resources for its welfare.[121] Petrucci aims to transcend the whole debate about residence requirements and ancestry, which he sees as motivated by avarice and the desire for status, and to make virtue, public spirit, and concrete contributions to the common good the criteria of real citizenship.

Or take the principle of equality in free cities. In his book on ordering republics, *How to Found a Republic,* Francesco Patrizi devoted a whole chapter to civil equality (1.6), with the evident purpose of reforming practices in the city republics of his time.[122] In the popular communes of Italy since the thirteenth century, efforts to impose a form of civil equality had led to a great deal of turbulence and factional strife. Popular remedies for inequality included laws (like the Florentine Ordinances of Justice of 1293 / 1295), which excluded certain noble lineages permanently from holding office. Other measures inhibited members of political parties (such as Guelfs or Ghibellines) from participation in politics, sometimes making use of legal forms of intimidation and character assassination.[123] This was justified on the grounds that such groups were genetically or ideologically incapable of supporting peace and order on a basis of equality. Other laws instituted differential standards of evidence in criminal trials, making it (in principle) procedurally easier to convict persons of noble blood than commoners (even if the commoners were wealthier and more powerful, as they sometimes were). Punishments and taxes were often higher for citizens belonging to disfavored lineages. Communal governments were in effect partisan institutions that sacrificed equality under the law and due process in order to protect the rights of favored groups while disadvantaging others.

Patrizi was highly critical of these practices. He took a different approach to equality, one designed to secure harmony, liberty, and civic virtue. For him the over-riding purpose of civil equality was to maintain concord, a condition necessary to keep the republic strong and stable. Without internal concord, no amount of military power or wealth could save a state from destruction. To secure equality citizens should live *aequali iure,* with a sense of equal right, and treat each other justly, "directing all their acts to virtue, being content with what they have and not desiring what belongs to others." They should take turns holding office; all magistracies should be limited in time, and no one should hold more than one at a time. The principles governing prosecutions and punishments should be the same for all. Everyone should be industrious and have an occupation, and everyone should participate in public duties (with due account taken of age, ability [*virtus*], sex, and social status). Excluding selected families permanently from office (which certain cities of our time do, Patrizi says) is not a praiseworthy idea, even if some very learned men (Leonardo Bruni?) defend the practice.[124]

Patrizi's arguments rely above all on political psychology. Institutions should be designed to maximize concord, participation, and civic virtue. Excluding whole classes and families from power (a constant goal of partisan politics in Siena) was first of all unjust: those who bore equal burdens (meaning taxes) should have an equal opportunity to win honor (meaning communal offices). Patrizi makes the point, central to virtue politics, that sons of outstanding citizens, like the sons of Brutus, can go bad, while citizens from humble families can become distinguished servants of the state. But even more important, citizens who are permanently ex-cluded from power become *ignavi,* spiritless, resentful, ill-disposed to the city, living always in fear of punishment, without hope of reward. Useless as citizens, they become seditious and inclined to revolution. The man who has no hope of forgiveness will not try to redeem himself by acts of virtue, and the city needs virtue. Only those who have hope of serving in office will work to deserve well of their country. Serving in office is what liberty, in the sense of self-rule, is all about, and everyone wants liberty. The statesman should take advantage of that desire and direct it in positive ways by means of well-thought-out institutions. Let those who have been excluded participate in civic functions if their virtue and the support of their fellow citizens permits it; in this way no one will be afraid that he is suspect to his fellow citizens or think it risky to dwell in a free city. The best father treats all his children equally, as free born *(ingenui).* Thus everyone will be zealous for liberty, and one person will not think himself cut off from the *bonum commune* while another person believes he has inherited the patronage of the public by some kind of testamentary right. Both attitudes discourage civil virtue.[125]

The desire to instill virtue and to elevate the worthy was also why influential humanists like Leonardo Bruni and Biondo Flavio expressed a preference for the Roman system of electing magistrates, which they believed would produce more virtuous officials than the method of sortition.[126] They disapproved of secret balloting for the same reason.[127] The humanists broadly agreed with Tacitus that *sorte et urna mores non discerni* (*Histories* 4.7), moral qualities are made invisible through lotteries for office and secret ballots. In their (to us naïve) preference for elections and open voting in counsel they were largely channeling Cicero, who in his letters and in the *De legibus* flattered himself that the Roman people had chosen him as a magistrate because they respected his virtue and wisdom. Elections, for humanists, were not occasions to expose leaders to the accountability of the people, as they are for moderns, but an opportunity for leaders to impress their charismatic goodness on their followers. The people would make a choice not by calculating their interests but by conforming their wills to the moral leadership of *vir bonus dicendi peritus*. A number of humanist political thinkers on similar grounds favored elective or adoptive monarchies in the hope that monarchs would be chosen the way Hadrian chose Antoninus Pius, and Antoninus chose Marcus Aurelius as his successor: because of their surpassing virtue and wisdom.[128] In every case the humanists were convinced that wise legislators might seek to shape souls in external ways by laws and institutions, they might use law to corroborate and preserve what was good and fence out what was bad, but the real source of sound politics was the virtuous soul of political leaders and citizens. It was the same moral power that Plato had hoped to unleash through his Academy: the power of a dynamically balanced and ordered soul, in control of its passions and appetites, impelled to virtuous action by knowledge and love of the good.

CHAPTER 3

WHAT WAS A REPUBLIC
IN THE RENAISSANCE?

The Renaissance Concept of the State

It is not obvious that Italian humanist ideas about the state is a theme ripe for re-consideration. How the modern idea of the state emerged was, after all, the central theme of Quentin Skinner's great *Foundations of Modern Political Thought*, which dealt at length with humanist texts of the Italian Renaissance in its first volume. Skinner's book, living up to its title, has itself proved foundational: it is not too much to say that, in the English-speaking world over the last several decades, the work has continued to set the agenda for the history of early modern political thought. Work on the evolution of the concept of the state in Renaissance Italy, already the subject of a rich literature in Italian, has continued and even intensified since the publication of *Foundations,* with notable contributions by Skinner himself among others. Nevertheless, the central theme animating Skinner's work—the rise of the modern state—needs rethinking, particularly in relation to the political thought of the Italian humanists.

From its first appearance Skinner's *Foundations* drew criticism precisely for the way it formulated its central theme, the rise of the state. Many readers and reviewers noted the apparent contrast between the author's sophisticated methodological claims, which emphasized the dialogue of texts in a Weberian process of legitimation, and the conceptual framework of the work as a whole, which tended to the teleological and metahistorical. Critics pointed in particular to the "Conclusion" to volume 2, where Skinner summarized his work by specifying four "important preconditions for the acquisition of the modern concept of the State." These were (1) that "the sphere of politics should be envisaged as a distinct branch of moral philosophy, a branch concerned with the art of government"; (2) "that the independence of each *regnum* or *civitas* from any external and superior power should be vindicated"; (3) that "the supreme authority within each independent *regnum* should be recognized as having no rivals within its territory as a law-making power and an object of loyalty"; and (4) that "political society should be held to exist solely for political purposes."[1] Reviewers pounced on this apparent inconsistency between the conceptual framework of the book and its methodology. The political theorist Michael Oakeshott commented, "Is it not 'unhistorical,' anachronistic, to think of [the concept of the state] as a construction erected on 'foundations laid by Marsiglio, Bartolus, Machiavelli, Beza,' etc.? These writers were not laying foundations: they were casuistical moralists and lawyers fumbling for circumstantial arguments to support their clients."[2] Skinner himself eventually acknowledged, in 2002, that his hunt for the origins of the modern concept of politics and sovereignty had been methodologically flawed; he admitted that in the conclusion of the *Foundations* he was wrong to use

> a metaphor that virtually commits one to writing teleologically. My own book is far too much concerned with the origins of our present world when I ought to have been trying to represent the world I was examining in its own terms as far as possible. But the trouble with writing early-modern European history is that, although their world and our world are vastly different from each other, our world nevertheless somehow emerged out of theirs, so that there's a very natural temptation to write about origins, foundations, evolutions, developments. But it's not a temptation to which I would ever think of yielding in these post-modern days.[3]

Here Skinner may have granted too much to his critics. A conceptual framework motivated by present concerns may distort the past, but questions about origins and foundations are surely not a "temptation" but the lifeblood of historical inquiry. A methodology that cripples the ability to ask such questions needs rethinking. Historical questions and metahistorical questions are indeed different and should be kept separate, but this fact need not be taken as a source of epistemological despair.[4] Rather it is, or it should be, a call to exercise our imaginative understanding of human phenomena in relation to the entirety of past cultures, their *Lebenswelt,* the long-faded structures of practical constraints and inherited values that shaped those cultures and still renders them legible, with disciplined research, to an attentive mind. In practical terms this means exercising ceaseless vigilance against anachronism: something easier said than done. To see the past in its own terms goes against our naïve or interested desire to make use of the past for our own purposes. It also requires imagination, hard work, and (dare one say it) a certain kind of love. We want to root our own identities as individuals or groups in a glorious past, or (more often these days) we want to preen ourselves on our superiority to a benighted past, and this desire sometimes blinds us to difference, to anachronism, to moral universes other than our own. But sometimes we have to transcend our own needs in order to do justice to the reality of other persons and other times. And sometimes it is the truth we cannot see that is precisely the one we need.[5]

The point of relevance to the present study is simply to highlight that modern historiography, of the "Cambridge School" variety or otherwise, has not yet given us a contextual, non-teleological account of the state as it was conceived by the humanists of the Italian Renaissance.[6] The task of providing such an account requires us to look beyond the "mirror of princes" literature on which historians of political thought have hitherto tended to focus, and to take account of the humanists' own method, which was inherently moral and historical, seeking its inspiration in antiquity.[7] Humanists who thought about public affairs, the *ratio reipublicae,* resembled in certain respects the lawyer-antiquaries of seventeenth-century England who invented its "ancient constitution" with the aim of restraining what they took to be the tyrannical exercise of power in their own time. Italian humanists did not conceive of their task in legal-constitutional terms, quite the opposite, but they too looked to the past for guidance about present crises and did not think of state building as a process of moving toward or fulfilling abstract conditions, in the manner, say, of Francis Fukuyama's recent account of the origins of modern political order.[8] They had a different sort of historicism, a backward-looking one, constantly seeking out differences between modern degeneration and ancient flourishing, constantly looking for inspiration in the past. For them, "being on the right side of history," in the cant phrase, meant being on the side of the ancients. If modern historians are to deal in actors' categories and not modern definitions of the state, they will need to notice one elephantine fact hidden in plain view. For Italian humanists *did* have a remarkably consistent idea of the *civitas,* and they had a particular model of what a state should be. They did not, to be sure, express this idea as a set of analytical criteria in the manner of a Bodin or a Hobbes; they did not, before the time of Thomas More, elaborate ideal constitutions. Their idea of the best state was at once concrete and idealized: it was simply the historical Roman state, the *respublica romana* of the classical period, the way Romans managed public affairs in the time of their greatest flourishing.[9]

Here one must tread carefully. Using the word "state" to translate *respublica,* though correct from a lexical point of view, immediately threatens to hurl the historian on the rocks of anachronism. Rome in the ancient period could not be said to instantiate the *modern* concept of the sovereign state whose emergence Skinner aimed to trace in *Foundations* and whose difference from the ancient concept he has carefully analyzed in several important articles.[10] The concept the Romans had of their "state" or *respublica,* as Skinner shows, was not abstract and impersonal. There was for them no conceptual space between state and community; the magistrates' powers were entrusted to them on a temporary basis by the Roman people to conduct their business rather than alienated permanently to a sovereign entity. As Cicero put it, *res publica* was truly *res populi;* not the Senate, not some formal constitutional apparatus.[11]

There were, nevertheless, some concrete resemblances between Rome and modern sovereign states that set it apart from the nascent states of the Renaissance.[12] Rome did after all possess some notes of what today would be called sovereignty.[13] By the high imperial period, it had a conception of itself as a *civitas* having a single juridical identity and (after 212 AD) offered citizenship to all free men within the empire. By late antiquity Rome's emperor acted as the supreme military, administrative, and juridical authority within a certain geographical sphere, divided into provinces. Under the emperors there grew up a small but powerful imperial bureaucracy. But the important point for the Italian humanists of the early Renaissance was not these notes of sovereignty. It was that the Roman *respublica* in the classical period, apart perhaps from the relative chaos of Cicero's time, did not resemble *at all* the failed political order of the medieval centuries. The humanists thought, and with good reason, that the political order of Christendom in recent centuries represented both a military and a moral failure, a decline and fall in Biondo Flavio's influential phrase, the result of Rome's defeat by barbarians and its own internal moral decay. Two-thirds of the old empire had been lost to Islamic invaders; the various medieval revivals of the Roman Empire had failed to establish any strong or lasting authority even within Europe. The Papacy had preserved and refined Christian orthodoxy and by the fifteenth century had built, or rebuilt, a little state for itself in central Italy, but it had lost the spiritual authority that had brought the Roman emperors in the fourth century to embrace it as the one true religion, as a religion worthy of empire. The Crusades had essentially been lost with the fall of Acre in 1291, and the Ottomans were on the march in the southern Slavic lands, without effective or united opposition. Modern Italy was dreadfully disunited; its *signori* and free cities were politically corrupt; the ancient literary culture that used to inspire great men in Roman times had suffered grievous damage. In its current condition Italy offered no opportunities for true fame and glory.

We get a glimpse of contemporary attitudes at the dawn of the quattrocento from Leonardo Bruni, who in 1407 confessed to his friend, the arch-classicist Niccolò Niccoli, the writer's block he was experiencing while composing a funeral oration for his mentor, Coluccio Salutati. In this early period he still reflected the outlook of Petrarch, who saw modern polities as too weak and corrupt to ever approximate Roman glory:[14]

> You ask how I'm getting on with the *laudatio* of Coluccio. It's going rather brilliantly I think. I started off writing it like a funeral oration in the ancient manner. But I keep changing my mind whether it might not be better to alter the genre, avoid fictionalizing a serious matter and getting bogged down in the tears, lamentations, etc., appropriate to the ancient format. . . . I seem to have lost the thread, whether through poverty of the subject or poverty of invention I can't say. I now see clearly what you're always exclaiming, that we are all pygmies these days; we might have some greatness of soul, but we simply haven't the stuff whereof to enhance our names and our glory. Marcus Claudius Marcellus was made famous by the capture of Syracuse, the defense of Nola, the expulsion of Hannibal, numerous victories, five consulates, two proconsulates, a victory in single combat with an enemy general, spoils offered to Capitoline Jupiter, a Triumph and an Ovation. . . . But what can I write about today? . . . The only things left to praise are good behavior and humanity. But even with them, unless there have been some extraordinary deeds of liberality, humanity, prudence, self-control or constancy beyond common experience, there won't be much material for praise. Generalized praise isn't worth much unless it descends to particular instances.[15]

Ancient Rome, by contrast, was a success, the most successful polity in history, and it was, moreover, primarily an achievement of Italians. That is the most obvious reason why Italian humanists looked back to the *stans et integra respublica* to renew their models of political life.[16]

Furthermore, recent history, despite the young Bruni's pessimism, was beginning to provide some grounds to hope for the renewal of ancient virtue. In the late fourteenth century, hundreds of the tiny free towns and signories that had dotted the map of late medieval Italy had been absorbed—through conquest, purchase, or voluntary submission—by the five major states of Renaissance Italy. To the eyes of contemporary historians it seemed that Italy, after centuries of political atomization, was moving again toward unity; history had taken on a new direction, and the new genre of city-state history (led by the same Leonardo Bruni who had once despaired of modern pygmies) came into existence to celebrate great deeds.[17] The revival of Italy's political strength after a long *medium aevum* was eventually celebrated in the great (though, for a humanist, shamefully ill-written) history of Biondo Flavio, *Histories from the Decline of the Roman Empire* (1453).

By the early quattrocento educated and well-informed observers like Biondo had come to understand that the military competition among European powers had led to a rebirth of Italian *bellica virtus*. Between the pontificates of Martin IV and Gregory XI, Biondo wrote in his *Italia illustrata,* for one hundred years from the late thirteenth to the late fourteenth century, Italy had been terrorized by foreign mercenaries. Major towns had been cruelly sacked. In the vicinity of Rome alone, Biondo reported, more than sixty towns and castles had been destroyed. No one would hire Italian soldiers, and cities had to rely on inexpert citizen militias who were easily crushed by foreign professionals. But at the end of the fourteenth century things changed. The great condottiere Alberigo of Barbiano, in the employ of the Visconti rulers of Milan, succeeded in driving foreign soldiers out of Lombardy. Alberigo's well-trained and well-equipped professional army, the Compagnia di San Giorgio, established such dominance that "no one not born in Italy of ancestral stock dared to hawk their arms round the country." That was the beginning of Italy's military renaissance. All the famous captains of the early quattrocento came from the seedbed of Alberigo's army:

> I understand that about forty thousand foreign knights were then expelled from Italy, at a time when Alberigo had scarcely twelve thousand in his company, and those mustered in a hasty and confused fashion. And this was the tinder and wellspring, so to speak, of all the military captains who attained glory in fighting wars that I have heard of, or seen for myself: Braccio da Montone was in Alberigo's household and a familiar of his; and Muzio Attendolo Sforza, along with his kinsman Lorenzo Attendolo, took his first steps in soldiering under Brandolino's command in the army of Alberigo; Paolo Orsini, Mostarda da Forlì, Tartaglia da Lavello, and Tommasino Crivelli of Milan all likewise followed the profession of soldier under the command, leadership, and instruction of Alberigo da Barbiano.

Alberigo then went to fight for Ladislas of Naples, and if the latter had not died an early death, the twin "dignities" (meaning sources of respect), the Italian Kingdom and the Roman Empire, might have been brought back to Italy.

Once the foreigners had been expelled from Italy, he went over to the Kingdom of Naples, and worked to such good effect for King Ladislaus (by whom he was honored with the title of High Constable) that he not only got control of a realm occupied by many powerful invaders but even laid the foundations for the return to our land of the twin dignities, of the Kingdom of Italy and of the Empire—something that Ladislaus would clearly have brought about had he not been forestalled by his death, which followed that of Alberigo.

Ladislas' career, despite its untimely end, showed that political unity might be possible again for Italy in modern times, thanks to the recovery of its ancient military prowess. Now Italian soldiers were sought out in Northern Europe, even in France, the home of medieval chivalry. Italy as a result had experienced a great increase in its standard of living from its new status as a military power: "Since many Italians have taken to serving in the French and English armies as expensive mercenaries, money and spoils are being transferred from those countries to Italy. No one will convince me that the sumptuousness, elegance, and other magnificent paraphernalia of our buildings, dress, and decoration, and all the rest of the life we live in this world—surely pitched at a higher level than was customary in the past—originated from anything other than this sense of security and being protected."[18]

Biondo believed that this new golden age of Italian military virtue, which according to modern military historians lasted roughly from the 1380s to the 1490s,[19] provided the ground for all of Italy's other great cultural achievements of the early quattrocento: the rediscovery of lost ancient books in Latin, the humanists' mastery of the Greek language that had begun around 1400 with the teaching of Manuel Chrysoloras, the migration to Italy of the literary and scientific heritage of ancient Greece, and the renewal of ancient Roman eloquence that had begun (as both Biondo and Leonardo Bruni acknowledged) with Petrarch.[20] All these achievements were measured by the standard of Rome. Ancient military virtue had started to revive; ancient letters and eloquence were being revived; and the ancient symbiosis between Greek and Latin cultures, lost in the long *medium aevum,* was a reality once more.[21] A number of humanists had even begun to notice the remarkable efflorescence of the plastic arts and architecture that was occurring all around them, much of it inspired by antique models.[22]

But what of politics? What of the arts of government and empire? In the preface to the *Discourses,* Machiavelli remarked, with his habitual puckishness, that in his time ancient political virtue was more admired than imitated. In the case of law

and medicine—subjects humanists often ridiculed for their bad latinity and ignorance of antiquity—the leading authorities have constant recourse to the remedies prescribed by the ancients: "Nonetheless, in ordering republics, maintaining
states, governing kingdoms, ordering the military and administering war, judging
subjects and increasing empire, neither prince nor republic may be found that has
recourse to the examples of the ancients."[23] Machiavelli was clearly trolling his contemporaries here, especially his fellow humanists, whose universal boast was that
they imitated antiquity in every aspect of their lives. By saying his contemporaries
were not following the example of antiquity, he was laying down the premise for
his own very different, quasi-scientific way of analyzing the lessons to be learned
from ancient history. In fact, from the time of Petrarch to the time of Machiavelli
and beyond, humanist culture, when it came to politics, was one long, animated
seminar on the possibility of imitating ancient Rome. That meant asking, What
was it that made Rome great? And was it possible to revive the virtues of the Roman
respublica in modern times?

The weightiest (and certainly the longest) contribution to this seminar was the
Roma Triumphans of Biondo Flavio, a work that was to the Renaissance what the
Encyclopédie of Diderot was to the Enlightenment.[24] But Biondo's was just the most
detailed treatment of what was an incessant and passionate subject of discussion.
If the humanist concept of the state was "the subject of contestation and debate,"[25]
that debate took place within boundaries set by the defining humanist assumption that ancient Rome should be the model for modern Italy. In the course of the
fifteenth century, other ancient models were sometimes invoked—Sparta, Athens,
and the imaginary Persia of Xenophon's *Cyropaedia* were the commonest—but it
was ancient Rome that overwhelmingly occupied the political imagination of Renaissance Italians. It was their own ancient *respublica* that they set out to imitate;
it was the true *antiquam matrem* Vergil had urged Aeneas to seek out on his way
to Italy.[26]

What Is the Meaning of Respublica in the Italian Renaissance?

But what did humanists of the Renaissance mean by that word they used so often,
respublica? It is a matter of some surprise that, despite all the attention to political
vocabularies and discourses in recent Italian and Anglosphere scholarship, the
word *respublica* has been the subject of so little historical analysis.[27] Neglect of its
historical evolution has led to florid outbreaks of anachronism, especially among

scholars who write about a, or the, "republican tradition" in Renaissance and early modern Europe. Yet careful attention to the history of this word is essential to understanding what the modern terms "republicanism" and "civic humanism" might mean as applied to Renaissance political life, as well as Italian terms of the period such as *vivere civile* and *vivere politico*.

A major source of anachronism in modern writings about "the republican tradition" has to do with what may be called "exclusivism," a concept that spotlights the tendency to interpret republican government in the Renaissance in categories drawn from modern republicanism.[28] By "exclusivist republicanism" I mean the modern understanding of a republic, formalized in Rousseau's *Social Contract*, as a government based on the will of the people and therefore the only legitimate form of government. As a political movement to base all government on the will of the people, exclusivist republicanism *eo ipso* denies legitimacy to non-elective monarchies and, more generally, to any sort of hereditary or patrimonial political privileges. As a theory of legitimacy it was broadly opposed to the conception of political power as a piece of property typical of feudal and medieval civil law. Classic early statements of exclusivist republicanism in this sense would include those of American revolutionaries such as Tom Paine and Jacobins such as Robespierre in France and Georg von Wedekind in Germany.[29] In the premodern period, by contrast, *respublica* was a term applied to a wide variety of regimes, to kingship as well as to aristocracy and popular government, sometimes even to oligarchy.[30]

Nevertheless, the Italian humanists played a key role in the evolution of the word *respublica*. It was in the quattrocento that the new discursive practice arose of taking *respublica* to refer to popular or oligarchic governments—governments by a plurality of persons—and not to princely governments, that is, rule by *uno solo*, to use Machiavelli's expression.[31] Machiavelli was one of the authors who popularized this new discursive practice, but its history goes back deep into the previous century, long before its famous use in the first chapter of the *Prince*. We will need to explain how, why, and when Italian Renaissance humanists invented this new, non-monarchical sense of the word *respublica* that was to play such a key role in European political language.

It should be emphasized that Italian Renaissance political writers were not themselves exclusivist in the manner of republican ideologues during the eighteenth-century Age of Revolution. Italian humanists in general did not question the right of *signori* or other hereditary *principes* to rule; their criticism was of hereditary princes and oligarchic political leaders who lacked virtue, and they wished to open the elite to the virtuous, whatever their social rank. Like some of their classical authorities, they did not think that liberty or constitutional government was necessarily incompatible with monarchy. But the appropriation by some humanists of the word *respublica,* with its seductive historical associations and moral weight, to denote non-monarchical regimes turned out to be an important precondition for the later rise of exclusivist republicanism. Though this new discursive practice drew on a particular representation of the ancient Roman republic, in several key respects it was a new departure in the history of the republican tradition in the West. It led to the use of the word *respublica* (and its various cognates in the modern European languages) as *Staatsnamen,* in the formal, official titles of particular states such as the Republic of Venice and the Dutch Republic. It led in the eighteenth century to the use of "the Republic" as the regular name for the non-monarchical period of Roman history from the expulsion of the kings in 509 BC to the Battle of Actium in 31 BC.[32] Finally, it provided linguistic resources that helped enable the polarization of constitutional and absolutist governments that occurred in the early modern period—and ultimately, two centuries later, to the classing of autocratic governments as illegitimate *in se.*

The Renaissance transformation of the concept of a republic was not simply a matter of terminology, however. The transition from the premodern concept of a republic to modern exclusivist republicanism also implied a wider change in the character of formal political reflection. Before the time of John Milton and the English civil wars, republican thought tended to display a much lower ideological temperature than its modern counterpart. In premodern constitutional thought, the existence of popular and oligarchic regimes alongside kingdoms, tyrannies, and other forms of political organization tended to be taken, as Aristotle took it, as a natural fact. Nature produced peoples given to self-rule and others given to despotic rule or to looser tribal-nomadic forms of governance. Republics in the Renaissance might episodically favor other republics in their foreign relations and express solidarity with them, but they did not denounce kingdoms as illegitimate *in se* or try to spread popular government around the world.[33] There was nothing that could properly be called a republican *movement* during the Renaissance. Premodern republics did not see the world in terms of a binary opposition between good, legitimate republics and illegitimate despotisms and tyrannies, and—unlike the French and American revolutionaries of the eighteenth century (not to mention other political authorities in more recent times)—they did not claim the moral right to impose a republican regime on any non-republican regime.

To illustrate the point, consider Aristotle, the most important authority for the theory of polyarchic regimes (as well as of monarchy) in the premodern Western tradition. In his well-known analysis, there are six main types of constitution, which he sorts into sound and corrupt constitutions.[34] The criterion for distinguishing good and bad constitutions is a moral one: to judge a regime one must ask: Do the rulers govern for the sake of all or just a part of the community? Do they benefit the common good or are they out to favor their own private interests? This sounds at first blush like the basis for a polarizing discourse of good and illegitimate government, but in fact Aristotle undermines such a polarity in several ways. First of all, the division of his six constitutions into good and bad is overlaid by another gradation from best to worst. In order of moral value these are kingship, aristocracy, polity, democracy, oligarchy, and tyranny. Lest one plump immediately for kingship, Aristotle further explains that although monarchy is in principle the best constitution, it is the hardest to achieve in practice, whereas tyranny is the easiest. Aristotle's theory of constitutional degeneration, moreover, shows that monarchy is the constitution most likely to lead to tyranny, so the legislator has to balance the great advantages of monarchy against the great disadvantages of its degenerate form. To speak of an "ideal" constitution (*he aristê politeia*) is to speak of kingship and aristocracy, but these are only rarely possible. Most legislators will be better off aiming at polity or democracy, which are reasonably happy and stable arrangements as well as practicable for most polities, at least in the temperate regions of the earth. The particular constitutional form of a polity is ultimately less important than the virtue of its rulers; virtue can, however, be supported by good laws.

The second way Aristotle undermines any tendency to exclusivism is by what has been called his "circumstantialism" or "constitutional relativism": his view that some kinds of constitution fit some peoples better than others.[35] Aristotle describes the problem as a differential allocation of virtue that reflects different climates or different moral conditions resulting from concrete historical experiences. Societies in hotter regions of the world naturally gravitate to despotic forms of government, while colder regions tend to support looser forms of political organization. Only in temperate regions can one expect to find a proper Greek polity with citizens capable of broad participation in self-government.

Finally, Aristotle's analysis works against ideological polarization in a third way, through his doctrine of the mixed constitution. In his view, in addition to the simple constitutional forms of kingship, oligarchy, aristocracy, and so forth, there are also the mixed forms, empirically more common, and also more stable and therefore better. The kind of constitution that is best for the limited virtue of most states is one that mixes oligarchic and democratic institutions. In Polybius' version of Plato and Aristotle's regime theory, composed two centuries later, the mixed constitution (whose invention is ascribed to Lycurgus) is seen as a blending of royal, oligarchic, and democratic institutions.[36] It is this triple mixture—not Aristotle's double mixture—that most often recommended itself in the later constitutional tradition, thanks to its influence on Cicero. In Renaissance Italy, for example, humanists often praised Venice and Florence as well as Genoa, Lucca, and Siena for possessing mixed constitutions with royal, oligarchic, and popular elements.

As we shall see, Renaissance translations of Aristotle were to prove an important instrument used by Italian humanists to appropriate the word *respublica* for non-monarchical regimes. But to appreciate the significance of this move we shall need to go much further back, back to the ancient Roman orators, historians, and philosophers who shaped the humanists' understanding of the term's meaning.

Respublica Romana

A glance at the *Oxford Latin Dictionary* discloses a wide range of meanings for *respublica* in classical Latin. The one most germane for our purposes is its use as a translation for the Greek word *politeia,* attested in Cicero, Quintilian, Seneca, and other canonical authors.[37] Plato and Aristotle of course both use *politeia* also to mean constitution or regime—that is, the formal, constitutive characteristics of a polity, its organization.[38] Aristotle sees *politeia* in this sense as analogous to the *physis* or natural form of a living thing, its principle of growth and organization, as we might refer to someone's physical constitution as being strong or weak. In books 4–6 of the *Politics* he contrasts *politeia,* constitutional government restrained by law, with arbitrary and unstructured forms of political power such as tyranny, or the incipient tyranny signalled by hyperpartisanship. Cicero and the Romans, however, generally do not use the word *respublica* with the same range of meaning as is covered by the Greek *politeia.* In particular, they avoid the fatal equivocation in the use of *politeia* introduced in Aristotle's *Politics.* For Aristotle, in addition to using *politeia* in its generic sense of "constitution," also uses the term *politeia* of one specific constitution, one of the three "good" constitutions in his constitutional typology, inferior in principle to aristocracy but superior to democracy. It is sometimes translated as "constitutional government" in English or *Freistaat* in

German. "Polity" in this specific sense means the benign rule of the many, a constitution achieved by instituting laws and an arrangement of magistracies that Aristotle considered to be a mixture of oligarchic and democratic forms.

In this book I shall try to avoid Aristotle's equivocation by referring to these two meanings of *politeia* as "generic polity," that is, constitution or regime in general, and "specific polity," that is, the constitutional rule of the many, the hybrid democratic-oligarchic constitution.

In classical Latin the word *respublica* does not mean "the constitutional or benign rule of the many" or specific polity. When Cicero and other Roman writers want to stipulate a particular type of constitution, they are ordinarily compelled to qualify *respublica* in some way, and so they speak of the *status, forma,* or *species* of the *respublica.*[39] For the Romans the predominant meaning of *respublica* is "affairs of state," "the welfare of the state," "the public good," or simply "the state," often translated as *ta pragmata,* public affairs, by Greek historians writing about Roman history. *Respublica* is not a neutral analytical term like *politeia* in Aristotle but a word freighted with positive moral connotations. By extension it comes to mean a free state that respects the liberties of its citizens and the common good and that treats citizens as equal under law and not, despotically, as slaves. It can mean simply "the state" as a moral entity—more or less synonymous with *patria.* Its lexical opposite is tyranny or factionalism *(stasis),* not monarchy.[40] The Roman idea of *respublica* implies a society of persons linked together by a common law, a fair share of the commonweal for each citizen, and a government conducted on behalf of all the people. But it does not necessarily imply government by the people or power sharing among the aristocracy.[41] A dictator, or later the *princeps* (in the sense of "emperor"), can hold monarchical power in the *respublica* so long as he does so constitutionally, "as a magistrate and not as a potentate."[42]

Thus *respublica* can mean "constitution" in the generic sense, but its range of meaning does not exclude either monarchical or aristocratic constitutions. Livy for example regularly uses *respublica* to speak of the Roman state under the early kings, before Brutus founded what European writers since the eighteenth century have been pleased to call "the Roman Republic."[43] For Livy, what Brutus introduced was *libertas,* not *respublica,* a *libertas* that had been lost, not because the Roman kingship was by definition unfree, but because by his arbitrary actions Tarquinius Superbus had violated the conditions necessary for a free state.[44] Nor does Livy see the introduction of Augustus' principate as the end of *respublica.*[45] Hence Cicero's distinction between good and bad "royal republics." Scipio Africanus,

Cicero's model of political wisdom, in the dialogue *De republica* explicitly rejects the idea that kingship and *respublica* are incompatible: "We are not talking now about an unjust king, since we are inquiring about a royal *respublica*. So think about Romulus or Pompilius or King Tullus, and perhaps you won't be so dissatisfied with that (kind of) *respublica*."[46] In other passages of the same work, Cicero's Scipio makes it clear that *respublica* can refer to any of the "good" constitutions in the standard Greek analysis—kingship, aristocracy, or even popular government—so long as each respects the common good and does not decline into its corrupt form. In this respect *respublica* is identical with *res Romani populi*, the interests of the Roman people. "[Scipio] summed up by saying that a republic exists—that is, the welfare of the people—when it is conducted well and justly, whether by a single king or by a few optimates or by the people as a whole."[47] Since Cicero shares the wider Roman assumption that good government leads to the expansion and success of Roman interests around the world, *respublica* in some of his works comes close to meaning something like "Roman prosperity" or "strength" or "hegemony in the world."[48]

There were, to be sure, discursive practices found in canonical ancient Latin authors that tended to stigmatize some kinds of one-man rule. Since the expulsion of the Tarquins, said Livy, the Roman people hated the name *rex*, "king," and tended to see any king whatsoever as a tyrant. The Romans preferred to use the euphemism "dictator" when they were compelled during periods of crisis to resort to one-man rule. Yet by the first century BC the term "dictator" too had been poisoned by repeated abuse. The "perpetual dictatorship" of Octavian's adoptive father, Julius Caesar, was particularly controversial. This is presumably why Augustus chose to use the term *princeps*, "leading man," "civic leader," to describe his preeminence in the state. Naturally, the rule of the *princeps* (a word modern scholars translate as "emperor" when referring to the Roman head of state) in its turn came to be regarded by many in the disempowered Senate as a noxious constitutional development, hostile to *respublica*, to the public welfare. Tacitus, Suetonius and other figures in the so-called "philosophic opposition" to the Caesars in the first century CE thought gloomily that the Augustan Principate had put an end to *libertas* and had reduced the people, or at least the senatorial class, to a slavish condition. They believed that *respublica* (in the sense of Roman prosperity and public welfare) was endangered, owing to the moral failings of its rulers. The culprit, however, was not the monarchical principle as such but particular features of the Principate that undermined the possibility of free participation in government, especially the privatization of public deliberation—decision-making in the palace of the Caesars—and the pursuit of dynastic succession as opposed to the rule of the best. Both innovations worked against the interests of the senatorial class from which the critics of the Principate mostly came. In other words, the Principate was incompatible with *respublica* because it was a despotism, not because it was a monarchy.[49]

Those who did not agree that the Principate was despotic did not see it as the end of *respublica*. After the first century CE, the Tacitean interpretation of what had happened to *respublica* after Actium faded from view, and would not return until the Renaissance. It was replaced by what we might call the Augustan interpretation. This was most fully expressed in Augustus' own *Res gestae divi Augusti* (14 CE)—Augustus' funerary inscription, preserved in both Greek and Latin—and elaborated in works such as Seneca's *De clementia*, dedicated to Nero (54–55 CE), and Pliny the Younger's *Panegyricus* (100 CE).[50] In Augustus' account, the *respublica* of Rome had been "oppressed by the despotism of a faction," but he had restored liberty and constitutional propriety to the *respublica* and had become its guardian thereafter.[51] As triumvir he had been charged by the *populus* with *constituenda res publica,* with putting the state on a sound footing. This he proceeded to do through the acts then listed at length in the document, most of which describe his military services to the state, the offices he held, his reorganization of the Roman class system, his restoration of religion, his building program, his policy in the provinces, and so forth. At the end of the document, he transferred the *respublica* from his own control to the direction of the Roman Senate and People. In other words Augustus claimed that the *respublica* had continued to exist throughout his principate and that its existence was perfectly compatible with the quasi-monarchic power he had legally assumed. Whatever may be said of the constitutional propriety of Augustus' innovations, his use of the term *respublica* was entirely traditional.

Later imperial writers largely accepted the view that, whatever changes there had been in the mode of governing the *respublica* in the time of Augustus, the *respublica* itself had continued and flourished, and the emperors had continued to protect the liberty of the Roman people. In Seneca's *De clementia* the *princeps* is now the soul of the *respublica* (5.1), protecting its *summa libertas* and its peace by his virtue (1.8), which protects it from descending into tyranny (12.1). The *respublica* is not his, but he belongs to the *respublica* (19.8). The legitimacy of the mode by which he obtains power and the forms of the constitution are irrelevant so long as he behaves with virtue.[52] As the soul gives life and unity to the body, so the single rule of the *princeps* in the *respublica* guarantees peace and flourishing life (1.4.1–3, 1.5.4). The Augustan interpretation of the transition to the Principate is accepted at face value by later imperial historians.[53] No later Latin writers, for example the author(s) of the *Scriptores Historiae Augustae,* call into question the compatibility of monarchy and *respublica.*[54] The emperors continue to claim that their rule supports *libertas* and equality.[55]

The view of the transition between "republic" and "principate" of historians writing in Greek, who lacked a true equivalent or even a consistent translation for *respublica,* was notably different. Typically, they spoke of a transition from *democratia*—for them equivalent to social collapse—to the stable, ordered monarchy instituted by Augustus. But these writers—Dio Cassius, Appian, Strabo, Plutarch, Josephus—were largely unknown in the Latin West before the second half of the fifteenth century, when they began to be translated into Western European languages.[56]

Two final points about the ancient meaning of *respublica* require emphasis. First, the ancient Romans did not use *respublica* as the formal name of their state. When the Romans talked about their state as a political or legal entity or as a diplomatic actor, it was called "the Senate and People of Rome," or later the "Emperor and the Roman People," but never "the Roman Republic."[57] In treaties and other dealings with foreign nations their legal *persona* is the *Populus Romanus (ho demos ho Romaion* in Greek) or simply the *Romani (hoi Romaioi).*[58] Second, the Romans did not use *respublica* as the name of a historical period. For the overwhelming majority of ancient Latin authors the Roman *imperium* and *respublica* were coterminous: the empire went back to Romulus, and the *respublica* continued to the fall of Rome. The name for what we call the "Republican period" is either *libertas, leges* (in contrast with *reges*) or *consulatum* in the Roman historians writing in Latin.[59] The Roman revolution that took place in the time of Julius Caesar and Augustus is called a *mutatio* of the republic by ancient Roman historians, not the end of the republic.[60] Tacitus may seem to represent a partial exception to this rule, as he subversively suggests in several passages that the advent of the Principate spelled the end of *respublica.*[61] However, since the reason why it had come to an end, in his view, was the tyrannical behavior of the *princeps,* the theoretical possibility remained that it might be restored by a ruler or rulers who respected *libertas* and the common good. Tacitus never labels the period from the expulsion of the kings in 510 BC to the battle of Actium as "the Republic," and he never describes the period after the battle of Actium as "the Empire" or "the Principate."[62] In any case Tacitus was very little known before the fifteenth century, when Italian humanists first began to take notice of his view of Roman history, as we shall shortly see. The "Tacitean" distinction between the periods of the Roman Republic and the Roman Principate, common in history courses today, became common in modern languages only in the late eighteenth century.

Respublica *in Medieval Scholasticism*

Space does not permit us to survey the development of the term *respublica* from the Christianization of the Roman Empire through the twelfth century.[63] We shall instead skip down to the high scholastic period, the thirteenth and fourteenth centuries of our era. In this period, as in the earlier Middle Ages, the term *respublica* is only rarely used by philosophers and theologians in their discussions of the best regime, and never in the sense of "non-monarchical regime." This usage was only reinforced when Aristotle's *Politics* was translated into Latin in 1268. The translator, the Dominican friar William of Moerbeke, a close associate of Aquinas, generally preferred to transliterate Aristotle's Greek terminology rather than use their classical Latin equivalents.

Aristotle's Constitutional Scheme in *Politics* 3 (1279a), as Translated by William of Moerbeke in 1268

	good *politiae*	corrupt *politiae*
one	*regia potestas*	*tyrannia*
few	*aristocratia*	*oligarchia*
many	*politia*	*democratia*

Via Moerbeke's popular translation,[64] Aristotle's terminological ambiguity was transferred to the world of Latin scholasticism, and *politia* thus became a common equivalent both for Aristotle's specific polity and for generic polity. There are a few exceptions: authors such as Albert the Great and John Buridan, who follow the constitutional terminology in the Latin *Nicomachean Ethics* (8.10.1160a–b), avoid the ambiguity of the *Politics* by using *timocratia* as equivalent to specific polity.[65] Thomas Aquinas and his follower Engelbert of Admont, confusingly, use *democratia* for both good and bad forms of popular rule.[66] But Moerbeke's technical language became dominant, and his dual sense of *politia* is reflected in the terminology used for specific polity by most scholastic writers of the later Middle Ages, including Henry of Rimini *(politia populi)*, Giles of Rome *(gubernatio populi)*, John of Paris *(polykratia)*, Peter of Auvergne *(politicus status)*, Bartolus of Sassoferrato *(politia, regimen ad populum)*, Nicole Oresme *(timocracie* or *policie)*, Marsilius of Padua *(politia)*, and other scholastic writers on the *Politics*.[67] Even Ptolemy of Lucca (c. 1236–1327), the most radical republican thinker of the Middle Ages, who occasionally uses *respublica* in a sense that foreshadows Renaissance usage, generally preferred the term *politia* or *regimen populi* to describe the type of popular rule found in the Italian communes of his day.[68]

Ptolemy of Lucca is important for our story since his political vocabulary reflected the polarization of Italy into princely and communal governments and thus prefigured the situation in the fifteenth century, when the non-monarchical sense of *respublica* arose. Ptolemy's continuation of Aquinas' *De regimine principum* restricts the terms *regimen politicum, dominium politicum, principatus politicus,* and *rector politicus* (political regime, rule, leadership and magistrate) to regimes ruled by pluralities, that is, both oligarchic and popular regimes. Basing himself on a screamingly false etymology of *pluralitas* from *polis,* he states that the adjective *politicus* should be restricted to the kind of rule seen in the cities of Italy, that is, the popular commune.[69] Furthermore, he tends to associate "political" rule with the rule of law and tends to sees the rule of one man, *regimen regale,* as arbitrary, not restrained by law, and despotic.[70] This usage reflects Aristotle's in books 4–6 of the *Politics*.

Ptolemy's (admittedly extreme) case warns us against the persistent error that medieval scholastic writers on politics were all monarchists.[71] In fact it would do less violence to the facts to describe them as republican thinkers—but in the pre-Renaissance sense of the word *respublica,* meaning "constitutional government." Though many, perhaps most, scholastic writers favor monarchical regimes, they usually show some degree of approval of the popular city governments found in north and central Italy, even if their approval tends to be relativistic. Like Aristotle, they accept that communal governments are appropriate to some peoples in some times and places—not, as modern exclusivist republicans would insist, morally superior to monarchical regimes at all times and places. The word *respublica,* on the rare occasions when it is used at all, signifies any government that serves the common good or, in the discourse of civil law, an autonomous political association that does not recognize a superior, a variation on *civitas.*[72] Governments with a king or virtuous political class who rule constitutionally on behalf of all, not just a part of the citizen body, are numbered among the good polities, but that category can also include communal governments where there is some form of popular consent and participation. Most scholastic writers did not think there was anything strange about describing monarchical or aristocratic governments as republics; they saw no reason in principle why monarchies should not serve the *bonum commune* and allow a degree of consent and participation. In this sense all medieval political thinkers were republican. A major concern was the virtue of the ruler or rulers, as one may see from the scholastic "mirror of princes" literature beginning with Giles of Rome (c. 1243–1316), which is overwhelmingly concerned with how the prince (i.e., ruler) may acquire the moral and theological virtues needed to rule wisely. Most scholastics preferred some sort of mixed regime that included a monarchical element as well as aristocratic and popular elements.[73]

At the same time, it is hard to find among the scholastics unqualified approval of non-monarchical regimes *qua* non-monarchical. Ptolemy of Lucca is, arguably, the only exception. But even Ptolemy, as a papalist, preferred monarchy when it came to the ecclesiastical polity. Most scholastics preferred some kind of royal power, even if a figurehead king (like a doge) or a temporary ruler (like a consul). As these examples show, a number of scholastic theorists interpreted what we would consider "republican" magistrates, such as *podestà* or Roman consuls or Florentine priors, as monarchical elements in a constitution. This did not prevent them from upholding political ideals that moderns tend to associate with republican governments—values such as consultation, consent, participation, and virtue. But they did not associate these values with what moderns call the Roman Republic. They never call the period of Roman history from the expulsion of the kings to the battle of Actium "the Republic,"[74] they do not exclude monarchies from the class of states describable as *respublicae,* and they do not use the name *respublica* to identify Aristotle's specific polity or constitutional popular regimes.

Leonardo Bruni and Respublica *in the Fifteenth Century*

Political terminology evolved in new directions during the quattrocento. The main changes came about owing to the archaizing linguistic preferences of the Italian humanists as well as to the recurrent propaganda wars between Renaissance oligarchies and princes that marked the period from the 1390s through the 1440s.[75] The key figure in the emergence of the new meaning of *respublica* as "non-monarchical government" was the Florentine humanist and historian Leonardo

Bruni, apostolic secretary to four popes and later chancellor of Florence. He was the leading humanist in the first half of the fifteenth century, the best-selling Latin author in Italy before the invention of printing, and a key figure in the humanist reform of Latin.[76] Like most humanists he modelled his Latin primarily on Cicero, and his usage of *respublica* generally reflects this classicizing influence. Thus, though he uses the word often in his own literary and historical works, he does not use it in a way that forces us to read it as equivalent to "non-monarchical regime." Following Cicero, he uses *forma rei publicae* or *species gubernandi* as an equivalent for *politeia* in the generic sense of constitution or regime.[77] A *respublica* can be any regime that serves the common good and avoids tyrannical behavior.

In his historical writings Bruni contrasts the government of kings and other monarchical rulers with that of *populi*, not *respublicae*. He does so even in the revolutionary book 1 of his *History of the Florentine People*. In this work he discards the traditional scheme of the Four Monarchies found in Christian historiography. That scheme privileged the Augustan period of Roman history because it was the time of Christ, when the pax Romana was providentially established, enabling the spread of the Christian religion. Instead Bruni sees the Roman state before the time of the Caesars, when that state was ruled by the Senate and People, as Rome's golden age, the time when it acquired most of its empire and reached the pinnacle of its cultural development. The decline begins with the Julio-Claudians, and it is only a matter of time (a mere five centuries!) before the Roman order in the West was washed away by floods of barbarians. The period of senatorial and popular rule, between 509 and 44 BC, is clearly seen as a distinct period, a period of political freedom.[78] Still, Bruni never refers to what moderns would call the republican period as "the republic." Nor does he identify the evolving Roman form of government in the period from the end of the kingship to Actium as a republican constitution.[79] The period beginning with the Caesars is not called "the empire" or "the principate." Indeed, Bruni, as a champion of popular government, is eager to establish that the *imperium Romanum* was founded by the Roman people after the time of the kings (in 510 BC) and that its enlargement was the result of their own virtue and competition for glory. It is immediately after this passage that he refers to Rome as a *respublica*, clearly denoting the later imperial period, from Nerva to Augustulus, the last Western emperor.[80]

Hence in Bruni's original works, *respublica* maintains its ancient and medieval meaning of "any legitimate form of government serving the common good," or more neutrally as simply "the state" or "affairs of state."[81] His usage does not differ from that of his mentor, Coluccio Salutati, who also did not use the word *respublica* to specify either a regime or historical period.[82] So it is surprising that in his immensely popular Latin translations of Aristotle, Bruni uses *respublica* in a strikingly new, indeed revolutionary way.[83]

His first gesture in this direction came in his 1420 translation of and commentary on the pseudo-Aristotelian *Economics,* a work that was among the most popular of all humanist writings of the Renaissance.[84] Here Bruni, citing Cicero's authority, writes that *precepta circa rempublicam* (teachings about the republic) is the correct Latin translation of *politica,* understood as the branch of moral philosophy dealing with polities. But he then uses the authority of the pseudo-Aristotelian writer to make the sweeping claim that in *respublicae,* many people rule, whereas in families, one *paterfamilias* rules.[85] This would seem to distinguish *respublicae* from monarchies, but the thought is not developed. Much more important, however, is his famous translation of Aristotle's *Politics*—by far the most popular translation of this text in the Renaissance[86]—probably begun soon after he published his translation of the *Economics.*[87] With the advent of printing this became the standard version, as two-thirds of all editions before 1500 of the *Politics* printed Bruni's translation, and roughly 95 percent of sixteenth-century editions contained the Bruni version.[88]

It is in this work that Bruni introduced the novel constitutional terminology that must have played a large role in the acceptance of the modern meaning of the word *respublica.*

Aristotle's Constitutional Scheme in *Politics* 3 (1279a), as Translated by Leonardo Bruni

	Rectae formae rerum publicarum	*Transgressiones et labes*
Unum	*regia potestas*	*tyrannis*
Pauci	*optimatium gubernatio*	*paucorum potestas*
Multi	*respublica*	*popularis status*

Source: Aristotelis Politicor*um libri VIII interprete Leonardo Aretino,* Strasbourg 1469, [f. 118r].

Note that Bruni uses *respublica* to translate *politia* in both its generic and specific senses, though, surprisingly, when he finally published the translation in 1438, he retained the traditional medieval title *Politica* to translate the idea of politics as a branch of moral philosophy.[89]

Bruni today is famous as the archetypal "civic humanist" of Hans Baron's canonical study *The Crisis of the Early Italian Renaissance,* so the suspicion naturally arises that Bruni's choice of *respublica* to translate specific *politeia* sprang from ideological motives. Yet the stated reasons for his choice are philological rather than political, and given Bruni's avoidance of the usage outside of his translations, we should not be quick to assume that his new terminology was a conscious piece of republican propaganda. In his 1424 treatise *On Correct Translation,* in fact, he explicitly states that his concern was purity of language. The latter work was in effect a defense of his retranslations of Aristotle's moral philosophy against critics who preferred the medieval versions.[90] Bruni offers numerous penetrating criticisms of Moerbeke's translation of the *Politics,* but one of his chief objections is that Moerbeke creates obscurity by transliterating rather then translating:

> What shall I say of the words left in Greek, so numerous as to make the translation seem half in Greek? And yet there has never been anything said in Greek that cannot be said in Latin. Still, I will excuse him a few obscure and strange words if they cannot be translated easily into Latin. But it is certainly a very ignorant thing to leave words in Greek when we have perfectly good Latin equivalents. Why, tell me, do you leave *politeia* in Greek, when you can and ought to use the Latin word *respublica?* Why obtrude in a thousand places the words *democratia* and *oligarchia* and *aristocratia,* and offend the ears of your readers with outlandish and unfamiliar terms when we have excellent and widely used terms for all of them in Latin?[91]

Here Bruni's principal concern seems to be *proprietas verborum,* correct usage, and defending the implausible Ciceronian contention that Latin was a vehicle for philosophical expression equal to Greek. He does not discuss the obvious objection that by translating specific polity as *respublica* he not only perpetuates Aristotle's ambiguity but also puts the powerful moral authority of the word *respublica* into the hands of propagandists for Italian city-republics.[92]

Three years after publishing *On Correct Interpretation* Bruni himself took over the role of chief propagandist for the Florentine state, for in 1427 he became the chancellor of Florence and was put in charge of its public correspondence. In this period public correspondence was an important vehicle for Italian city-states to communicate a positive image of themselves and their actions, and Bruni inevitably found the ideological power of the word *respublica* a useful tool. Beginning in the time of Coluccio Salutati, his mentor and predecessor in the office of chancellor, the phrase *respublica nostra,* meaning the Florentine state, had frequently

appeared in state letters—many of which had a propagandistic function—as a classicizing synonym for the medieval terms *communis noster, populus noster, communitas nostra,* and *civitas nostra.*[93] Bruni continued this practice in the public letters he composed after becoming chancellor in 1427.[94] To describe Florence as a
respublica was in line with the late-medieval juridical understanding of the term
as "sovereign political association,"[95] and neither Salutati nor Bruni ever used the
word in such a way as to suggest that monarchies could not be republics. But the
humanists' need to find dignified classical terms to describe popular and aristocratic regimes meant that *respublica* came in the course of the fifteenth century to
be used almost by default for non-monarchical regimes such as those of Florence,
Venice, Lucca, and Siena. The day when such city-states would officially entitle
themselves "the Republic of Florence" or "the Republic of Venice" lay in the future,
in the sixteenth century, but the foundations for this usage were laid in the public
correspondence of the Italian city-states in the late fourteenth and fifteenth
centuries.[96]

The usefulness of the term *respublica* to humanist chancellors is undoubtedly one
reason why the new, non-monarchical sense of *respublica* caught on quickly in the
middle decades of the quattrocento. The new usage soon found a place in the semantic field of humanist Latin thanks in part to the contemporary political ter-
rain. For three decades begining in the 1420s, Italy was divided between the
Venetian-Florentine and the Milanese-Aragonese alliances. Despite many rapid
shifts in alliances and cross-cutting loyalties, it was possible to see the politics of
the Italian peninsula in those decades broadly as a competition between princely
and oligarchic blocs.[97] Since *oligarchia* and its Latin equivalent *paucorum potestas*
(the power of the few) were neither of them very complimentary terms; since *populus* and *popularis status* could not describe Venice and were increasingly implausible descriptions of Florentine government under the Medici (after 1434); and
since *commune, communitas,* and *dominatio politica* smacked of medieval usage, it
was natural that humanists who sympathized with (or at least worked for) oligarchic regimes should have tried to appropriate some term with positive moral and
historical associations to denote non-monarchical political entities. The word they
fixed on was *respublica.* The usage even began to filter into formal treatises on political theory in this period, as the example of the Venetian theorist Lauro Quirini
shows.[98]

A further reason why humanists favored the term is that it allowed those who served "republican" regimes to finesse the differences between popular and oligarchic government. In Florence's case, its political history in the fourteenth century had been essentially a long struggle between a narrow oligarchy and a more popular, guild-based government. By the late fourteenth century, the struggle was essentially over and the oligarchs had won. However, as John Najemy has argued, one of the victors' strategies was to appropriate the symbols and language of the popular commune, so that government was officially carried on in the name of the people and the guilds, though in practice the city was ruled by a small group of wealthy and powerful families.[99] The term *respublica,* which in its new, non-monarchical sense could apply either to a popular government or an oligarchy, could now do double duty, and allow the humanist chancellor or orator to rise above the grubby party politics of the day.[100]

This point is made explicit in the popular treatises of Francesco Patrizi da Siena on political education, *How to Found a Republic* (*De institutione reipublicae,* 1465 / 1471), where the word *respublica* comes to embrace a wider range of constitutional possibilities, including rule of the optimates (what Florentines later called *governo stretto*), rule of the *populus (governo largo),* and rule of the rich or oligarchy:[101] "We posit three forms of republican regime (as we've decided to say nothing of kings or tyrants). One is popular, the second is that in which the best men take the lead, and in the third rule is dispersed among the few."[102] It is striking that for the first time in the history of this word, a formal theorist is willing to use the term *respublica* to denote one of Aristotle's "corrupt" regimes: oligarchy. Patrizi makes this move not because he wishes to demoralize the concept of *respublica,* but because as a good humanist he regards the question of constitutional form as secondary to the issue of virtue in reforming the state. His advocacy in this text of a mixed constitution that included different social elements in the governance of the city-state—with leadership, as ever, provided by educated men of virtue—allowed him to propose this means of controlling factionalism while himself standing above party.[103]

Patrizi's understanding of *respublica* as government by a plurality of rulers, or polyarchy, rather than rule by one man (or by a mob) came to typify how the word was used by the one part of the early modern *orbis litteratus.* Patrizi himself was important for the adoption of this new usage, as his influence in the later Renaissance was considerable.[104] It was no doubt the wide circulation of Patrizi's treatises, combined with the success of Bruni's translation of Aristotle, that gave authority to the new Italian Renaissance meaning of "republic" as "non-monarchical regime." And one might add to Bruni and Patrizi the influence of Donato Acciaiuoli, who wrote the most important quattrocento commentary on the *Politics,* keyed to the Bruni version.[105] Acciaiuoli follows his mentor Bruni in using *respublica* both for generic and specific polity, but like Patrizi he broadens the meaning of *respublica* to cover aristocracy, oligarchy, and the virtuous popular regime.[106] Finally, surprisingly, Thomas Aquinas himself came to endorse the new usage. For in 1492 Bruni's translation of the *Politics* began to be printed with Aquinas' commentary on that text, which originally had accompanied Moerbeke's translation. The editor of this edition, Ludovicus Valentina, helpfully changed all the occurrences of specific *politia* in Aquinas' commentary to *respublica,* to match Bruni's version. Hence in the sixteenth century Bruni's translation of both generic and specific *politeia* by *respublica* came to be backed, though illicitly, by the authority of Aquinas.[107]

By the second half of the fifteenth century, then, *respublicae* and monarchies were commonly taken in Italy to be in binary opposition to each other, as competing modes of rule. This can be seen, for example, in Patrizi's contrasting treatises of civic education, *De institutione reipublicae* and *De regno et regis institutione,* or in Bartolomeo Platina's twin treatises *De principe* (1470) and *De optimo cive* (1474),[108] or in Aurelio Lippo Brandolini's dialogue *De comparatione regni et reipublicae* (1490 / 1491). The latter work makes explicit that the theoretical difference between a monarchy and a republic is the difference between a state ruled by one *(unum)* or by a plurality *(plures);* the latter term embraces both popular and oligarchic government. In Bartolomeo Scala's *Defense against the Detractors of Florence* (*Apologia contra vituperatores civitatis Florentiae,* 1496), the new terminology is taken for granted, though Scala feels the need to distinguish between popular republics (*respublica* without qualification) and *optimatum respublica,* or aristocratic republics:

> Three types of constitution are the least subject to criticism. In the first, which is called kingship, a sole ruler governs rightly. In the second, which is called a republic, all who enjoy the rights of citizenship govern. In the third, those whose conduct is best are chosen to rule. This kind of government the Greeks call *aristocracy,* and we imitate them by using our word for "best," and call it a republic of optimates. Our city has always hated kingship, thinking that it easily can and often does turn into tyranny, which is the worst of all constitutions.[109]

Hence by the time of Machiavelli and Castiglione,[110] the use of the term *respublica* to specify non-monarchical government had long been accepted in Italy as a valid secondary sense of the word, as one can see from the famous opening sentence of the *Prince,* which states flatly that there are really only two constitutions, the republican and the princely: "Tutti gli stati, tutti e' dominii che hanno avuto et hanno imperio sopra gli uomini sono stati e sono o republiche o principati." (All states and lordships that have had and have power over men were or are republics or principalities.) Machiavelli's enormous readership surely helped solidify the non-monarchical sense of *respublica* in the Renaissance lexicon, especially outside Italy.[111]

Next to the massive textual presence of Bruni's Aristotle, Patrizi's treatises, Aquinas' and Acciaiuoli's commentaries, and Machiavelli's political works, it seems unlikely, despite recent claims to the contrary, that a decisive role was played by the recovery of Tacitus' historical works. While it is certainly true that passages in his works can be read to authorize an opposition between *respublica* and *principatus,* Tacitus' influence was relatively feeble before the end of the sixteenth century, by which time the new discursive practice was long established. He was read carefully by some leading humanists such as Bruni, Biondo Flavio, and Lorenzo Valla, but a commentary was not written until 1517, and he was not a school author before the middle of the sixteenth century. The movement called by the name of "Tacitism" did not get off the ground until the commentary of Justus Lipsius was published in 1574. In any case, it was primarily a movement advocating a particular style of political prudence, and embraced monarchical as well as republican adherents.[112]

❧

Despite the Renaissance usage of *respublica* as a dignified name for oligarchies and popular communes, the ancient sense of the word, meaning any morally good, constitutional state that served the common good, persisted in the humanist lexicon. Since the lexical opposite of *respublica* in classical Latin is *tyrannis,* humanists who worked for princely regimes would naturally feel the rhetorical disadvantages of getting on the wrong side of that binary opposition. The humanist secretaries of the dukes of Milan in the first half of the fifteenth century, Uberto Decembrio and his son, Pier Candido, both insistently referred to the ducal government as a *respublica* in their official letters and in their literary works. Giovanni Gioviano Pontano, the humanist prime minister of the kings of Naples, regularly used the term in public correspondence to describe the Aragonese monarchy. Bartolomeo Platina tried to accommodate the new meaning in his *De optimo cive* (early 1470s) presented to Lorenzo de'Medici: there the Medici ascendency is spun so that members of the Medici party (which included the *Politics* commentator Donato Acciaiuoli) are presented as guardians of the *popularis respublica* against *domestici tyranni.*[113]

A fascinating text which reveals the semantic difficulties that such humanists found themselves in by mid-century is the *De vera republica (On the True Republic)*, written after 1452 by Michele Savonarola (c. 1385–1466), court doctor of Borso d'Este in Ferrara and grandfather of the more famous Girolamo. The title of the work (also called in the manuscript *De esse verae reipublicae*, or *On the Essence of the True Republic)* is already indicative of the changing semantic landscape. It is not an accident that Michele feels the need to qualify *respublica* with *vera*.

Michele begins by arguing that, according to his own definition of *respublica,* the Roman Republic *(Romanam rempublicam)* before the time of Julius Caesar was not a "true republic" but a *figmentum* of a true republic. In the same way, he argues, Venice should not be regarded as a true republic because it lacks a prince. Then he continues: "Perhaps you will be surprised at this expression of mine, since learned and grave men have hitherto described the Roman republic [*before Caesar*] as a true one, and you'll ask where this presumption of mine comes from that I dare oppose all these men. But it will have occurred to you [*the reader*] that a prince is an essential part of a true republic. [*Traditional monarchical arguments follow*]. And if I seem to deviate somewhat from the common view, I believe I have not deviated from the path of truth."[114] Michele Savonarola here advocates a definition of *respublica* that is exactly the opposite of the modern one: only a republic with a prince is a "true" one, so (paradoxically for us) the "true" Roman republic began with Julius Caesar. But at the same time he seems to recognize that his conception of the meaning of *respublica,* though it would have been perfectly orthodox in the fourteenth century, is no longer the *communis opinio* in the second half of the fifteenth. To deny the title of *respublica* to the Venetians and to the Roman republic before Caesar was going to be difficult, Michele realizes, yet by 1452 it was even more out of line with current Italian usage to use the term of a principality.

Despite this politicization of the term *respublica,* humanist writers generally avoid exclusivist claims outside the most highly charged of rhetorical situations. Many humanist writers on politics express a strong personal preference for one-man rule or for republican government, many are vitriolic in their criticisms of a particular regime or particular rulers, and some assert that one or the other form of government is best suited for the character of their own population. But none to my knowledge deny legitimacy to alternative forms of government as such. None yet believe that monarchy as such is an ungodly institution, as was argued in the seventeenth century by Milton and repeated in Thomas Paine's *Common Sense* in the eighteenth. No humanist thinker tries to argue that a "republican" constitution (in the modern sense) is the best constitution for all peoples at all times and in all places. Such an "exclusivist" attitude is far more likely to be found among monarchists than among republicans. In the fifteenth century the weight of Western tradition still favored monarchy, and it was popular government and oligarchy that had to struggle to establish their legitimacy and to overcome charges that they were inherently unstable and subject to factionalism.[115]

The typical attitude is prudential and relativistic. Patrizi, for example, explicitly denies any assertion that all republics are just and all kingdoms immoral.[116] He agrees with Aristotle that any well-ordered government of virtuous rulers is good.[117] Good government is ultimately about good rulers and not about ideal regimes. That is the conclusion too of Raffaele Lippi Brandolini's dialogue from the 1490s, *Republics and Kingdoms Compared*. In this text the chief interlocutor, King Matthias Corvinus, argues for the superiority of monarchy to the traditional popular commune inherited from medieval Italy, a form of government defended by a Florentine merchant at his court, Domenico Giugni. Giugni is finally convinced, after three days of argument, that royal government is vastly superior to "republican" government and declares his intention of leaving Florence and moving to some other country with a good monarch. But King Matthias, far from declaring Florentine government illegitimate, encourages Giugni to persevere in his loyalty to his native land and to act in it as a virtuous citizen. Thanks to its excellent laws and institutions, virtue is able to make republican Florence the equal of a kingdom: "And you, Domenico, although you should persuade yourself that one-man government is always the best, nevertheless, since there is a great lack now of excellent princes and your republic is governed by excellent laws and institutions and possesses a kind of image of that royal government, you should defend and respect your country and persuade yourself, if you shall live in it with the utmost goodness and rectitude, that you will have met with a form of government not worse than a kingdom."[118]

Respublica: *An Idealization of Ancient Government*

The purpose of the preceding discussion should by now be evident. Historians who for several generations now have been tunnelling into the past in search of a "republican tradition" have been led into anachronism by two false assumptions: that such a tradition could be identified by a commitment to popular self-government and liberty; and that this tradition drew mainly upon ideological resources provided by ancient republican thinkers such as Cicero. It is then but a step to celebrating this tradition as having laid the groundwork for our own splendid achievements in modern liberal democracies. But these assumptions about the nature of republicanism in the Renaissance cannot be so readily mapped onto the wider humanist project of virtue politics.

One form of distortion is the tendency in such literature to exaggerate the moral differences between Renaissance signories and the oligarchies that liked to call themselves *republicae*. Much specialized research in recent decades emphasizes rather the similarities in the experience of living under both forms of government—a signorial regime and the regime of a *Signoria* or town council dominated by wealthy oligarchs.[119] Tyrants since antiquity had been identified as such in part because they lived in fortified citadels surrounded by mercenary troops, but so did the *signori* of Florence, Siena and Lucca.[120] Princes and oligarchs maintained their power in the same ways: by tending systems of clientage, by foreign alliances, by displays of public devotion to religion, by magnificence and festivities, by surveillance, by the use of informers and secret denunciations, by prohibiting meetings to discuss politics outside the government palace, and by courting popular approval. Freedom of speech was strictly curtailed in both signories and oligarchies. Venice, for example, despite presenting itself as a modern defender of Roman liberties, did not permit the free circulation of political ideas, and prohibited criticism of its own, much-admired constitution.[121] *Signori*, on the other hand, however much the reality of their power might depend on armed men or on wealth, ordinarily assumed power by public, legal acts, with the formal approval of city councils. From this optic, the system of carefully managed sortition and apportionment of offices usually found in republics may appear more as a strategy for retaining popular approval than as marks of a genuine commitment to self-government. Both princes and republics promised to preserve the liberties of their subjects. Both princes and republics had court systems and laws served by the same circuits of itinerant judges trained at the same universities in Roman civil law. Both hired mercenary armies to conduct their wars. And both princes and republics were often accused of tyranny by their unwilling subjects.

Studies of provincial government under signories and "republics" also show similarities. John Law has written of governing "dyarchies" in subject towns, a system whereby a *signore* like Duke Giangaleazzo Visconti of Milan would take over a new town and appoint a governor but otherwise rule using the organs of the old communal government. The latter took care of ordinary business, especially extraction of taxes, the administration of justice, and maintenance of the city fabric, leaving the *signore* or his governor to be consulted only on major disputes, key appointments, and foreign relations.[122] The Florentine and Venetian republics showed a similar approach to governing their subject cities.[123] It is also worth noting that Florentine and Venetian oligarchs as a rule had extensive estates in the *contado* or *Terrafirma* where they acted as lords in their own domain and adopted signorial manners. The main difference as regards the locus of power between signories and oligarchies is that in the former, princes established a monopoly of public authority and resources, while in the latter they were shared informally among a small group of the wealthy and powerful.

This is not to say that there were no differences at all. In addition to princes who enjoyed a reputation for ruling with justice and obeying their own laws, the Renaissance certainly had its share of lawless and bloody tyrants, as well as legitimate princes who from time to time acted tyrannically. And republican governments in the Renaissance did display patterns of governance that can recommend them to those who prize political freedom today. The existence of regular, formal mechanisms for consulting the citizen body and building consensus was certainly one of these. Such mechanisms also made it harder for popular regimes to act in secrecy. The republican system of sortition acted as a brake on the arbitrary use of public power, since any abuse of office against a citizen was likely to lead to retaliation when that citizen or his friends in their turn were drawn for office. This practical form of accountability was not readily available in signories.

Most of all, Renaissance republics, thanks in part to the inspiration of Rome, had a cult of liberty—even if these were often "imaginary liberties" in Fabrizio Ricciardelli's phrase.[124] Citizens of Renaissance republics valued their freedom. It was a sign of their status as free men that they did not live under a single lord. They also were proud of living with their fellow citizens on a basis of equality, even if in practice they preferred to be equal to their social betters rather than to their inferiors. Their notion of liberty, as Quentin Skinner and Philip Pettit have pointed out, was likely to be a "non-domination" concept that emphasized freedom from arbitrary rule by other citizens. This contrasted with the usual idea of liberty cultivated in principalities, what may be called the "rational control" model drawn from Greek philosophy: that one was free so long as one obeyed a virtuous prince who maintained just laws. Obeying a just prince was on this model tantamount to obeying reason and the moral law. Yet the "rational control" model also could justify violent coercion of those deemed less rational, something harder to inflict on citizens under the "non-domination" model.[125] Citizens who tried to dominate in republics were restrained because their fellow citizens, raised in an egalitarian tradition, became envious and denied them honor.[126]

Nevertheless, though there were humanists like Leonardo Bruni and Bartolomeo Scala who composed stirring celebrations of republican liberty, especially in their role as official spokesmen for what were officially popular governments, humanist virtue politics was not fundamentally concerned with defending "republics" in the narrow, polyarchic sense, or even "republican liberty." When humanists praised service to the republic or the *patria,* when they advocated the education of *principes* in virtue and wisdom via the study of classical literature and philosophy, when they argued for moral legitimacy, or when they spoke of opening political elites to virtuous men from every social rank and from non-native populations, they did not intend to limit their political advice to the oligarchies of the Italian peninsula. As we have seen, humanists had been discussing these themes of virtue politics from the time of Petrarch, long before Leonardo Bruni popularized the use of the word *respublica* to signify the virtuous popular regime. For them, the ancient sense of *respublica*—with its reminder of the glorious Roman past, with its connotations of just government for the sake of the common good, of government by virtuous rulers on behalf of the people, of government that valued liberty and ensured it through observance of law and constitutional propriety—this idea of what a republic was became a kind of linguistic marker in humanist literature. The luminous word *respublica* all by itself evoked the great idealistic project of the Renaissance—bringing on a new golden age, bringing an end to the corrupt middle age—as it touched on matters political.[127] But that project was never confined to what we today refer to as the "republics" of the Italian Renaissance. The project of reviving republican government, the idealized political life of the ancients, was taken as seriously by Renaissance princes and prelates and their humanist courtiers as it was by humanists working in and for Renaissance oligarchies.

Is Civic Humanism Found Only in Non-monarchical Republics?

The considerations above raise the closely related question of whether the so-called civic humanism of the Renaissance should be seen as a phenomenon limited to Renaissance oligarchies. Answering this question requires a brief excursus into Renaissance historiography.

The term "civic humanism" was invented in the 1920s by the German historian Hans Baron.[128] At the time Baron coined this new term, one of his influences was the great historian and statesman Friedrich Meinecke, perhaps the most celebrated Machiavelli scholar of the early twentieth century. Meinecke embraced Machiavelli as the inventor of the doctrine of *raison d'état,* the idea that the needs of the state dictate their own criteria for action; these criteria are rooted in the state's natural drive to expand, and they transcend individual morality. He saw this *Machiavellismus* as a realistic tradition in modern thought, distinct from and preferable to the cosmopolitan moralism of neo-Stoic figures like Grotius, who tried to impose conventional classical and Christian ethical categories on inter-state relations.[129] Baron's conception of "civic humanism" in its original incarnation was intended in part to extend Meinecke's project by finding the intellectual roots of Machiavellian statism in the soil of Italian humanist thought. In order to show the relevance of the humanists to Machiavelli, Baron needed to correct a common misperception of humanism that prevailed in his time (derived proximately from Jacob Burckhardt): that the humanists were rootless literati, cosmopolitans who travelled from court to court, who had little interest in politics and were uncommitted to any political ideology or regime. It was common to dismiss them by saying that their affectation of imitating ancient authors made them unoriginal, unserious, and unread: "Having nothing to say, they said it endlessly" as one historian of the time sneered.[130] They were epigones of long-dead masters, out of history, *unpolitischen Menschen.*

Against this view, Baron argued—principally on the basis of his studies of Leonardo Bruni—that a central current of thought within the humanist movement was in fact highly patriotic and committed to a republican ideal. It was indeed the opposite of cosmopolitan.[131] It had elaborated a republican political ideology that made the state, not religious authority, the font of value. This "civic humanist" ideology represented a reversal of a feudal, otherworldly ideology supposedly inherited from the Middle Ages. Civic humanists like Bruni, by making the republic a source of value, accomplished a moral revolution. They now placed a positive value on wealth and commerce (as against a supposed medieval bias toward agriculture and monastic poverty), they praised family life (as against clerical belittling of the married state), and they found in the defense of the city-state a justification for citizen-soldiers (as against the chivalric ethos of the Middle Ages with its knights-errant, smiting the paynim in Outremer).[132] In general they valued participation in politics, the active life, and public service in this life, as against a "medieval" outlook that supposedly privileged the contemplative over the active life, subordinated the temporary to the eternal, and oriented politics to the salvation of souls. They represented therefore an important stage in the history of secularization (in the modern sense of secular as "non-religious").[133] Civic humanism was thus an agent of modernization.

As the repetition of the word "supposedly" indicates, however, much of this picture is no longer tenable in the light of research conducted in the second half of the twentieth century. In particular, Baron's presentation of the medieval *Denkwelt* as feudal and saturated by Franciscan theology is now recognized as seriously incomplete, and in general many of the civic humanist values he described are now seen to descend from the popular communes of the thirteenth century, not disinterred from antiquity by the humanists of the fifteenth.[134] What remains of Baron's picture is his salutary correction of the nineteenth-century caricature of humanists as *unpolitischen Menschen*. As the present work has been arguing, a political reform program is central to the humanist movement founded by Petrarch. But it is not a "republican" project in Baron's sense of republic; it is not an ideological product associated with a particular regime type. All of Baron's civic humanist ideals can be exemplified not only in the political writings of Italian humanists employed by oligarchies, but also in those of humanists working in the courts and chanceries of princes.[135] Baron was too learned a historian not to notice that this was sometimes the case, but he regarded signorial humanists as the servants of tyrants, merely aping in bad faith the "true" civic humanists. For him civic humanism had been invented at a precise historical moment—the military "crisis" of 1400 that threatened the continued existence of republican government in Florence—and he held it would be wrong, as a matter of method and conviction, to separate the ideals born at that time from their context.[136] Hence Baron never tried to demonstrate that civic humanist ideals were held with greater purity or sincerity by humanists in the service of commercial oligarchies, or to show that Florentine humanists held them earlier in a chronological sense than signorial humanists.

In fact such a project would have been impossible to carry out, as later chapters of this book will show, but it is worth offering some examples here that can illustrate precisely the point at issue.[137] Take the case of the Istrian humanist Pier Paolo Vergerio the Elder (1370–1444). Vergerio, like his friend and exact contemporary Leonardo Bruni, was a disciple of the Florentine chancellor Coluccio Salutati, as well as of Bruni's Greek teacher, the émigré Emmanuel Chrysoloras. Like Bruni, Vergerio wrote a famous educational tract that helped popularize the humanist ideal of education as the acquisition of virtue through study of the classics. Like Bruni he defended the active life of the citizen, admired military virtue in the service of the state, praised political commitment and participation, promoted the study of eloquence, and celebrated self-sacrifice for the *patria*. He lauded the Roman republic as a political arrangement for the promotion of virtue. He praised Cicero for defending the *respublica* against Caesar's demagoguery. He believed that a city's elite should always be free to express its political opinions, and that political structures should be devised that would enable free speech. He upheld the rule of law and opposed arbitrary power. Humanist orators and historians, he declared, should compose eloquent praise and blame of political figures so as to instill civic values and promote peace and good government.[138]

On the face of it, it seems hard to deny Vergerio the title of civic humanist, except for one circumstance: he was a monarchist and a lifelong servant of *signori,* including the Paduan "despot" Francesco Novello da Carrara, several popes, and the Holy Roman Emperor. Although he was capable of praising the Venetian republic for its mixed constitution, its aristocratic tone, and its public virtue, his considered view was that monarchy was the best form of government so long as the monarch was morally upright. Popular government at its best was able to accomplish little that was good; when corrupt it was the worst form of government. For him, the history of the Italian communes showed their inherent instability and the inevitability of one-man rule. But the real challenge of the times was not bringing about constitutional change but increasing the virtue of the ruling part of society, whether that part included one or a few men.[139] Good government ultimately came from good governors, not institutions, but *ceteris paribus* the best form of government is monarchy. This is because (and it became a classic argument of humanist monarchists) it is easier to find one good man than many.

Another significant example is offered by Uberto Decembrio of Vigevano, a long-time servant of the Visconti family. The Visconti dynasty was cast by Hans Baron in the part of tyrants who sought to impose their empire on Florence and the free cities of Tuscany during the "crisis of the early Italian Renaissance."

Decembrio was born and educated in Lombardy, and according to his son's testimony came under the influence of Petrarch as a young man in Pavia. Uberto served as humanist secretary to Giangaleazzo Visconti's son, Giovanni Maria, from 1404 to 1410 and was the father of Pier Candido Decembrio, secretary (1419–1447) to Filippo Maria Visconti, duke of Milan. Uberto is most famous today as having completed, with the help of his teacher Manuel Chrysoloras, the first translation into Latin of Plato's *Republic*. He also composed a political treatise of his own entitled *De republica libri IV*, which was dedicated in 1422 to Filippo Maria Visconti.

The work begins with a typical humanist call to revive the liberal arts of ancient Lombardy, those arts which had nourished the noble intellects of Virgil and Catullus, Ambrose and Augustine in antiquity. For Uberto, as for the so-called civic humanists, the republic is a product of nature, arising from mutual need and based upon justice. Everyone should be treated equally under the law, and the prince of the republic should promote university studies and sound forms of legal science. Since civic communities are not by themselves able to supply all their wants, there naturally arises a need for merchants and for money. Buying, selling, and banking are natural to society; even pawnshops are necessary to supply the needs of the poor. Luxury, however, is dangerous and leads to war and sedition. A class of professional soldiers like Plato's guardians, selected by the prince, is something every developed society needs, and the inculcation of warlike virtue is necessary in every city. The secret of a happy republic lies in its prince, its leading men, and its citizens possessing and exercising the classical virtues. A humanist education is necessary to inculcate these virtues. True nobility lies in virtue, not descent. Eloquence is proper to man and has the function of spreading the virtue of the speaker to his hearers. Like Bruni, Decembrio is a follower of Aristotle and Cicero who believes that marriage and the family are natural institutions, the building blocks of the commonwealth and necessary to its survival. Egoism is condemned: quoting a famous dictum of Plato, Uberto says that we are not born for ourselves alone but for our families, our friends, and our *patria*.

A substantial quotation is enough to give the flavor of Uberto's treatise. After noting our duty to worship God and honor religion, he continues:

> We should also devote ourselves with special love to our country where our parents, children, wives, relatives and friends dwell; no good man ever feared to die for his country. For the safety of one's country embraces the safety of all its inhabitants. [*Decembrio then cites from Livy several examples of Roman republican heroes who selflessly served the state.*] From this it follows that we should honor with the warmest love the governor and prince of our country,

whom we call its *pater patriae,* under whose rule subject peoples are governed with calm and quiet peace. We should also bind to us the affections of those guardians and soldiers to whom the protection of the city and the prince is committed, for by their vigils and scrupulous guardianship the whole people finds tranquillity and enjoyment of their goods when hostile calamity is driven entirely away. Moreover, every citizen should take care to live with his fellow citizens with a sense of right that is fair and equal; he should neither behave himself in a servile and abject manner so that he is held in contempt, nor should he get above himself so that he appears to oppress others. Also, he should desire for his *respublica* those things that are peaceful and honorable. Finally, he should so conduct himself that he be reputed a good man and a fair-minded [*aequus*] citizen by everyone. Let him be a cultivator of all the virtues, especially justice and moderation, both of which most cause a good man to find approval. Let him diligently observe the mores and customs of the commonwealth and never depart from them, even if it should perhaps seem otherwise to Socrates or Plato or another philosopher.[140]

Here again it is hard to deny Uberto Decembrio the title of civic humanist. Aside from his insistence that the best form of government is a regime headed by a virtuous prince, there is hardly a sentence of Decembrio's *De republica* with which Leonardo Bruni would have quarreled. Especially striking is his praise of equality, which in typical humanist fashion he sees not as a juridical status to be guaranteed by laws and institutions, but as a character trait, a habit of treating other citizens fairly and justly, as equals.[141]

It cannot be denied of course that the actual regime Uberto served was very far from the ideal painted in Decembrio's treatise. Indeed there is perhaps no ruler of the quattrocento to whom the name tyrant has more often been applied than Filippo Maria Visconti.[142] But similar criticisms could be made of the behavior of the oligarchies served by "republican" civic humanists. Florence's atrocities and acts of bribery during the siege of Pisa in 1406, for example, would not be easy to praise for their courage or humanity.[143] Civic humanism was inevitably an expression of political ideals, not a description of practice. It approached the reform of states in part by idealizing contemporary *principes,* not by describing the actual deeds of Renaissance rulers, who were no better than human rulers ever are. In this the humanists followed the advice of Aristotle to use praise and blame as a form of counsel.[144] To praise a prince or a city above its merits was an effective way of counseling them, holding up to them a finer standard of behavior. The rhetoric of praise and blame works because it makes people want to inhabit the characters for which they are praised.

Attitudes and values said to be characteristic of civic humanism eventually made their way into the standard humanist handbook of royal government, the *De regno et regis institutione* (1481 / 1484), one of the pair of treatises Francesco Patrizi wrote on the arts of government, the other being an earlier work, *De institutione reipublicae* (1465 / 1471). The twin treatises illustrate how ideals of civic humanism were not confined to republics. Even the language used in them is similar, for in the *De regno* the people of a kingdom are referred to as *cives,* or citizens, not as subjects, and the king's officials are called magistrates, not royal servants. In a good kingdom, the people's property, *res populi,* should be shared among all citizens who should be united in civil friendship and in common love for the *patria.* The life of involvement in politics is referred to as the *vita civilis* and is used without embarrassment of participation in the public life of a kingdom. The *vita civilis* is contrasted not with life in the court of a prince, but with private life, the life of literary retirement *(otium),* or with monasticism.[145]

Although Patrizi, like Bruni, acknowledges the traditional hierarchy of the contemplative over the active life, mental over bodily goods, he is also, like Bruni, at pains to praise the value and dignity of the active life. He even goes so far as to claim, invoking Cicero's *Dream of Scipio,* that the active life can make citizens blessed *(beati)* and through virtue can lead them to ultimate felicity, joining the inhabitants of the heavens.[146] In his praise of the active life Patrizi uses the same well-worn precepts and examples as republican civic humanists. The famous example of Socrates abandoning the useless speculations of natural philosophy to study the moral and civil life of mankind, beloved of Salutati and Manetti, is cited with approval, as is the equally well-worn dictum of Plato (now quoted directly from Bruni's translation of the pseudo-Platonic *Letters* rather than indirectly from Cicero's *Tusculans*) that we are not born for ourselves alone but for our family, our friends, and our country. In Italian humanist sources both these *topoi* are frequently cited to redress the traditional balance weighing in favor of the contemplative over the active life.

In the *De regno* we find that many themes associated in modern historiography with humanist republican thought are stressed equally by humanist writers on monarchy. Patrizi, for example, attacks the mercenary system, quoting a famous saying of the Emperor Galba in Tacitus that an *imperator* should love his troops, not buy them. The good ruler should have native, not foreign troops; it was when

Rome began to fill her armies with barbarians that she began her military decline. Like Machiavelli, Patrizi believes that a city's agricultural population is the best source of good soldiers, and that too much devotion to trade and commerce can weaken military virtue.[147] He is critical of the pursuit of gain—*neminem posse et opibus et virtuti simul indulgere,* no one can be fond of wealth and virtue at the same time—but commerce, so long as it is carried on licitly, benefits the *respublica.* Patrizi stresses that monarchs should obey their own laws and treat all citizens with equal justice. Citizens have a duty to obey the prince, but Patrizi calls for them to compete with each other in the display of virtue (9.10). They should be productive and hardworking (9.11). The prince should practice *libertas loquendi* but not *licentia;* his behavior, like that of his citizens, should be ruled at all times by moderation. The king's counselors should also cultivate free speech in the humanist sense, that is, the courage to speak freely. The prince should also foster the family, which is the building block of the state, and encourage fruitful marriages.

If the above arguments are accepted, the modern historiography of the Renaissance and early modern Europe faces a serious problem of terminology. If the expression "civic humanism" continues to be used, it will need to be glossed in such a way that historians and their readers are made aware that the political values this tradition promotes are not characteristic only of humanists associated with "republics" in the modern sense. This sort of redefinition ought to be possible within the discourse of the relevant historical fields.

The expressions "republicanism" and "the republican tradition" present more difficulties. The former is a modern term, a relic (along with many other "-isms") of Hegelian influence on historian's parlance. Even the adjective "republican" puts us at risk of anachronism, given that there is no adjectival form of *respublica* in Latin (unlike *politeia* in Greek, which generates *politikos,* from which we get "political" in English). It has been suggested in this chapter that humanist "republicanism" owes most of its inspiration to the ancient notion of *respublica,* which embraces several regime types (excluding only tyranny), and much less to the non-monarchical sense of *respublica* manufactured by Leonardo Bruni in the early fifteenth century. But to try to create a specialized sense of "republicanism" within the discourse of Renaissance studies or the history of political thought can only lead to confusion. To take just one measure, 149 states among the 191 member-states of the United Nations today refer to themselves as "republics," meaning by this term a legitimate sovereign state based on the will of the people.[148] The modern idea of a republic flows down from the powerful streams of Rousseauian and Kantian philosophy, and early modern historians cannot hope to swim against so strong a current of usage and still be readily understood.

There are other possibilities. Quentin Skinner, recognizing the importance of the monarchical republic in English thought, introduced the term "neo-Roman" in place of "republican" in his *Liberty before Liberalism* of 1998, though more recently he has returned to the terminology of republicanism and republican liberty. But "neo-Roman" focuses too much on definitions of liberty and would mislead by obscuring the formative impact of Greek philosophy and history on humanist political thought. In a stimulating book published in 2004 Eric Nelson argued that a "Greek tradition" can be discerned in early modern republican thought alongside Skinner's neo-Roman one. He saw Skinner's neo-Roman tradition as looking back to Cicero, Livy, and Sallust and as marked by its celebration of imperial expansion, glory, and private property as well as by its characteristic conception of liberty as "non-domination." Nelson's "Greek tradition"—which includes figures such as Thomas More, Tommaso Campanella, James Harrington, and Montesquieu—harks back to the Greek philosophers; is suspicious of glory, wealth, and empire; regards true liberty as living in accordance with nature; and above all, embraces a view of justice that permits the redistribution of property in the interests of political stability and civil happiness, construed as rational control of appetites and passions.

Nelson begins his "Greek tradition" with Thomas More and the northern humanists, so there is relatively little overlap with the figures discussed in this book, all Italian humanists of the period from Petrarch to Machiavelli. In my opinion, however useful the concept of a Greek tradition may be for the early modern period, it would not be easy to distinguish a neo-Roman from a Greek tradition in trecento and quattrocento Italian humanism. Though different humanists favored different sources and displayed a range of views on a wide variety of political issues, it is hard to think of a figure who could exemplify either a neo-Roman or neo-Greek tradition *in purezza* in the long quattrocento. Perhaps in the fifteenth century certain elements are still in solution that precipitate out into Greek and neo-Roman traditions in the sixteenth.

If one wished, nevertheless, to find a term that reflected the sources of humanist political thought in the early and high Italian Renaissance, one might consider a term like "neo-classical politics," which would at least acknowledge the deep and ongoing influence of both Greek and Roman sources and also avoid the implication that the Renaissance revival of ancient political thought and practice should be associated with any particular type of regime. But one hesitates to add yet another neo-classicism to the already-overflowing dossier of Western neo-classicisms. It would in any case be better to use a term that respects the creativity and coherence of humanist thought, which though reliant on ancient wisdom is not, in fact, reducible to it. In light of the discussion in this and other chapters of this book, I would suggest that the best solution is to open a new dossier for the political thought of Italian humanism, attaching to it a new label, the one used in the title of this book.

CHAPTER 4

TAMING THE TYRANT

Before the modern period, European civilization developed two principal understandings of the phenomenon of tyranny.[1] One understanding, or family of understandings, descended from the writings of ancient Greek philosophers and emphasized the role of character and intellect. The other emerged from the traditions of Roman law, which saw tyranny as a violation of *ius*: natural right or legality. Though Greek philosophical understandings of tyranny begin to blend with those of the Romans by at least the time of Cicero, and though considerations of legality and constitutional propriety are far from absent in ancient Greek analyses of tyranny, I shall nevertheless refer to the two understandings, for simplicity's sake, as Greek and Roman.[2] Neither understanding should of course be confused with either the reality of ancient tyranny, which remains highly controversial among historians of ancient Greece, or with what Nino Luraghi calls the ancient "discourse of tyranny," as reconstructed by modern historians of the ancient world.[3] In the course of the fifteenth century, as we shall see, Italian humanists gained access to many of the ancient Greek sources on tyranny known today, but—as in the case of the Spartan tradition—what they made of them often differed markedly from the way the same sources are interpreted by modern classical scholarship.[4]

Tyranny in Greek Philosophy

The most famous example of the Greek understanding of tyranny known to the Renaissance occurs in Plato's *Republic.* Among the book's principal concerns is the tyrannical character and how to explain and prevent it. Plato understood that, with the eclipse of traditional aristocratic morality in the generations before Socrates' time, the life led by tyrants, and even the tyrannical character, driven by a limitless desire for wealth and status, was immensely appealing to the young men of Greece.[5] The *Republic* is a thought experiment in which Plato tries to develop a model of education that would ground governing elites in moral realities, and this ontological awareness would prevent or at least slow the corruption of their characters. In his analysis, the tyrannical character is a disorder of the soul, a state wherein human beings, who should be ruled by the best thing in them—namely, the divine power of reason—are instead ruled by appetites and passions. Plato believed that most people in his time had disordered souls and therefore, given political power, were potentially tyrants. It was only by careful training in dialectic and other rational sciences, ordered in such a way as to achieve finally a vision of the Good, that a very few persons, the philosophers, would be able to resist the tyranny in their souls. The goal of politics was to ensure that such persons held power in the polis, or could imprint their wisdom and virtue on the laws sufficiently to restrain the ignorant and wicked.[6]

Aristotle also saw the causes of tyranny as rooted in bad character, especially inordinate desire, *pleonexia,* wanting more than one's share, wanting more than all the rest. Explaining in book 2 of the *Politics* why he thought mere mechanical reforms, such as redistributions of property, would not produce morally sound *poleis,* he writes, "It is not the possessions but the desires of mankind that need to be equalized, and this is impossible unless a sufficient education is provided by the laws."[7] Good laws and a good ordering of the polity are vital to prevent a city from slipping into factionalism *(stasis)* and ultimately tyranny; the laws should provide a form of moral guidance. In the case of "noble natures" who naturally desire to rule others, serious moral education, that is to say philosophy, is particularly vital: "Men always want more and more without end, for it is the nature of desire to be unlimited. The beginning of reform is not so much to equalize property as to train the nobler sort of natures not to desire more, and to prevent the lower sort from getting more."[8] Tyrannical power once achieved cannot and will not be restrained by law; indeed for Aristotle in the later books of the *Politics* a tyranny is no regime or *politeia* at all, but an absence of regime, an absence of stable political order, purely arbitrary rule responding only to the whim of the tyrant.[9] A tyrant by definition rules despotically for his own pleasure and treats his subjects as instruments to that end. There is no true justice or advantage in tyrannical rule "or any other form of perverted rule," because these are contrary to nature, the ground of justice.[10]

There can never be true justice in a tyranny, but this does not mean there cannot be relatively good government that, for bad reasons, serves the advantage of the governed. This form of tyranny, which I shall call "benign tyranny," appealed to some Renaissance humanists. In book 5 of Aristotle's *Politics* the philosopher describes the modes of tyranny in the context of a wider discussion of how different regimes can be made lasting. In chapter 9 he comes to tyranny and tells us that there are two ways that tyrants try to hold on to their power. One way is to use the familiar means of oppression and control perfected by the tyrant Periander of

Corinth and by the Persians. The first step is to put to death men of spirit who might oppose him, lopping them off "like overgrown ears of corn." The tyrant should then suppress what today would be called civil society, private clubs and associations, and outlaw humane education or *paideia*. He should be on his guard against anything that would build trust or courage among the political class, who should not be allowed to form friendships or even get to know each other. Everyone in his city should be forced to appear in large public spaces and before his palace to let them know who is boss; "if they are always kept down, they will learn to be humble." Aristotle continues: "A tyrant should also endeavor to find out what each of his subjects says or does, and should employ spies . . . and send eavesdroppers . . . to any place of resort or meeting; for fear of informers prevents people from speaking their minds, and if they do, they are more easily found out. Another art of the tyrant is to sow quarrels among the citizens; friends should be embroiled with friends, the people with the distinguished citizens *(gnorimoi),* and the rich with one another."[11]

The tyrant should keep his people poor and hard at work on building projects. He should multiply taxes, "after the manner of Dionysius of Syracuse, who contrived that within five years his subjects should bring into the treasury their whole property." The tyrant should also be continually embroiled in wars to keep his people occupied and in need of his services as a war leader. He should prefer bad men and foreigners to good citizens, as the former are more easily controlled. In short, the tyrant has to break the spirit of his citizens via various humiliations, create mistrust among them, and crush any signs of virtue; for good men "will not let themselves be ruled despotically and are loyal to one another and to other men." In other words, he has to make politics as the Greeks understood it impossible. Aristotle ends the passage by noting that the practices of the worst form of democracy, such as assaults on the natural family, are also all found in tyrannies. The worst democracies are consumed by factions seeking their own advantage, and this is the antechamber to tyranny.

But there is another τρόπος or "mode" by which tyrants can save themselves.[12] Aristotle says this other way proceeds from an almost opposite principle. As the way to *destroy* a kingship is to make it more tyrannical, the way to *save* a tyranny is to make it more like a kingship. The tyrant who wants to save himself should try good government, in other words. He should pretend a concern for the public fisc and not waste money; he should give careful accounts so that he seems to be a servant of the public: "He should be seen to collect taxes and to require public services only for state purposes." He should be dignified, not harsh, and cultivate the reverence of the people rather than fear. He should maintain the character of a military man to remind people of his most important function (like modern tyrants who like to appear among the people in uniform). He should live a temperate life and not abuse women or boys. He should "improve and adorn his city as though he were not a tyrant but the guardian of the state. Also he should appear to be particularly earnest in the service of the gods." In other words the tyrant should do everything a good ruler would do, except one: he should never give the people any form of political freedom or allow them to rule themselves. For if he does that, he will no longer be a tyrant.

Aristotle's discussion here, I believe, shows an awareness of the advice to tyrants given in Xenophon's dialogue the *Hiero,* written a few decades before. Set in 474 BC, the work purports to be a conversation between the tyrant Hiero of Syracuse and a member of his court, the famous poet Simonides. Hiero complains about the miseries of being a tyrant, and Simonides recommends, as a way of relieving himself from anxiety, an instrumental use of good government, which will allow him to hold on to power by winning the favor of the people. Many years ago Leo Strauss famously showed how this dialogue was absorbed and transformed by Machiavelli, who thereby invented one form of modern tyranny: the kind of tyranny that potentially can give the people everything they want except self-government. The people get peace, orderly government, and prosperity but are kept in tutelage, treated as children. The use of force is kept to a minimum. Material prosperity or military conquest is regarded as the most effective means to remove the desire for self-rule. The people may even be told that they are free and given some of the toys of freedom such as the vote, so long as they are kept from actual power.[13]

Xenophon and Aristotle present us, in other words, with a benign mode of tyranny that is not evil or oppressive, merely paternalistic. It is not a truly just regime, since its hidden purpose is to preserve the tyrant's power, but it presents a facsimile of justice, enough to keep the support of the people. As far as philosophers are concerned, the main damage done is to the soul, for without freedom and rational self-rule full human dignity is not possible. A healthy polity is built on rationality, sociability, and respectful cooperation among citizens, but benign tyranny prevents the actualization of those potencies of human nature. But most people don't care about that. By separating the principle of administration from the principle of the sovereign's legitimacy (as Jean Bodin was to do in the sixteenth century), this benign form of tyranny allows an illegitimate individual or ruling elite to short-circuit the whole question of who should rule.[14] Most people won't care about abstractions such as legitimacy or self-rule so long as their lives are secure and prosperous. As for philosophers, they can always gaze along with Plato at the best polity in the heavens; they can stay free in a world without freedom by maintaining true justice in their souls.

Cicero's Understanding of Caesar's Tyranny as Violation of Ius

What became, for the Renaissance, the most significant Roman debate about tyranny occurred in the late republic, in the period of the great warlords (*dynastai* or *hegemones* as the Greek historians of the period called them): Marius, Sulla, Pompey, and Julius Caesar. Most of what early Renaissance humanists knew about this debate came from Cicero; the historical background they gleaned from Sallust, Florus, Suetonius' *Life of Caesar,* Lucan's *Civil War,* and Caesar's own *Commentaries* with its continuation by Aulus Hirtius.[15] All of these writers lived in the shadow of the greatest constitutional change in Roman history: the transition from a mixed regime led by the Senate, under which Rome rose to dominate the Mediterranean, to the autocratic rule of the emperors. The latter regime, depending on one's political sympathies, could be described as a monarchical republic or as a despotism.

The character of this debate, however, differed sharply from the discussions of tyranny among Greek philosophers, and this difference was due above all to the role of the *ius civile* in shaping its terms. Roman civil law, which had begun to coalesce as a system of rules for settling court cases in the second century BC, had by Cicero's time assumed the character of an autonomous source of right set above the social and political struggles of Roman life, to which appeal might be made by all Roman citizens on a basis of equality. *Ius civile* was a positive interpretation of *ius gentium,* the law of nations, which itself was a manifestation of the law of nature.[16] As such, *ius civile* was in some measure natural and related to the divine management of the cosmos. The gatekeepers who determined the meaning and application of the Roman *ius civile* increasingly were jurisconsults, a body of experts in the law who advised judges and advocates. Most of the *ius civile* concerned issues in private law, and its function was largely "to preserve the long term material security of the existing social order" and protect it from the vicissitudes of politics, in part by enforcing what today would be called due process, limitations on the discretion of judges, and the supremacy of law.[17] This strong separation of law from politics was unexampled in the classical Greek world, as was the belief that justice consisted in fidelity to a system of rules authorized by a regular political process. As Cicero wrote, using what was to become a ubiquitous organic metaphor:

> You must concede to me that it is far more unworthy in a city bound by laws to depart from the laws. This is the bond of that [citizen] status *(dignitas)* we enjoy in the *respublica,* this is the basis of liberty, this is the font of equity. The mind *(mens)* and soul and purpose and judgment of the city are placed in the laws. As the body cannot use its sinews, blood, and members without its *mens,* so too the city without its laws. The magistrates are ministers of the law, the judges are its interpreters, and we are thus all slaves to the law so that we can be free.[18]

Roman citizens were subject to the law, not to persons, and if they became subject to persons they were *eo ipso* slaves or dependents, not *sui iuris,* directly under law.[19] The civil law of Rome had the authority of the Roman people behind it and was thus sovereign; the law was the expression of the historical experience of the people and its political norms and processes. Before the rule of the Caesars, that political process had evolved into a complicated system involving popular consent to senatorial advice and popular election of magistrates according to fixed procedures that guaranteed their legitimacy.

The exercise of power could also be radically simplified in times of war or extreme partisan division by appointing a dictator. The dictator, it is important to remember, was a constitutional magistrate. The office had been founded in the early republic to deal with moments of political paralysis or military emergencies. Dictators, chosen at times of crisis, were given full powers to command; their dictates could not be appealed through the judicial system *(provocatio).* The Greek historian Dionysius of Halicarnassus described the dictatorship as a voluntary (i.e., elective), legal tyranny, a description later borrowed by Machiavelli.[20] But the office also had strict limits: a dictator could only act within the remit of his appointment and had to resign his powers after six months. Even Roman dictators, in other words, had to yield to the sovereignty of the laws.

Dozens of figures are known to have held the office of dictator legally under the republic. Eventually, however, the office was abused and corrupted into tyranny during the last century of the republic, and in the time of Sulla the streets of

Rome ran with blood. Roman politics in Sulla's time displayed many of the features of tyrannical dysfunction: arbitrary, lawless use of power, the cowing of political opposition, incessant warfare, fear, proscriptions, confiscations, cruelty, and murder. Julius Caesar, however, when he came to power, seemed different to many. He was a war hero and a brilliant general who dispensed with constitutional proprieties when, as he claimed, his *dignitas* or personal honor had been injured; he had, shockingly, invaded his own country with Roman troops against the explicit command of the Senate. But his behavior in victory (and he nearly always won) appeared magnanimous and forgiving. He was reluctant to take the life of Roman citizens, and there were no cruel reprisals visited upon the defeated. He always seemed ready to make peace. He tried to make friends of his former enemies and even supported them for public office.[21]

When he finally did win the civil war he had started, he used his authority to have himself appointed dictator for life. This led instantly to accusations of tyranny. Some believed he was aiming to make himself king, and there is good evidence Caesar did in fact begin laying the foundations for a ruler cult of the Hellenistic type, later made a reality by the Julio-Claudian emperors.[22] Caesar was allowed to wear his triumphator's dress on all occasions, which recalled the purple of the old Roman kings, as did his gold chair in the theater with its gold crown. His statue was to be carried in procession along with that of the three Capitoline gods. So the fear that he aimed at a monarchy of the eastern type was a rational one for those who valued Roman tradition, and it was this that led to his assassination.[23]

To others his murder must have seemed reactionary. For those who looked outside the Roman tradition, it could seem that the story of the last three centuries, since the time of Alexander, was about the triumph of monarchy over city-state liberties. The Hellenistic kings, like Caesar, had been self-created monarchs who had built huge empires for themselves and established dynasties backed by military force.[24] What made them legitimate was a form of meritocracy—their ability to command an army and bring peace and prosperity—"performance legitimacy" in modern terminology. Greek political theory, well known in Rome, tended to see them, in contrast with tyrants, as supremely wise and virtuous rulers, and therefore as possessing moral legitimacy as well.[25] Such empires curtailed the liberties of the city-states they overshadowed, but on the other hand they put an end to their endless, debilitating factional struggles, something the old Roman constitution had resoundingly failed to do for nearly a century. A man like Tacitus, a century later, could regret the loss of the old citizen liberties and the enfeeblement of the Senate while still believing that monarchy was the inevitable destiny of so large an empire.[26]

It was in this context that Cicero charged Caesar with tyranny and justified his murder as tyrannicide. He did so most searchingly in his *De officiis,* a work that became the most popular textbook of political morality in the Renaissance. Cicero was the god of the humanists, so it is easy to forget that he was (unlike most of them) a trained lawyer who ordinarily showed great respect for law and legal expertise.[27] Cicero was certainly familiar with the psychological analysis of tyranny found in the Greek philosophers, and could apply it to Caesar in private.[28] But his published arguments against Caesar, overwhelmingly, pointed to his violations of the constitution and *ius.* The application of the law in Cicero's day was politicized in the extreme, and such an appeal must have fallen on deaf ears for many. But they were highly valued in that strand of the later republican tradition that saw laws and constitutions as the primary bulwark of liberty.[29] Proponents of virtue politics, on the other hand, found them less appealing, as we shall see.

Cicero's case for branding Caesar's rule as tyrannical is part of a larger argument in book 3 of *De officiis,* itself based in part on a work of similar name by the Stoic Panaetius. Cicero knew about the work through his own Stoic teacher, Posidonius. The Roman statesman maintains that everyone has duties to observe certain goods that are intrinsically beautiful and good, called *honesta,* "honorable goods," goods that bring honor to a human being. It is a matter of Stoic doctrine that everything honorable is beneficial, and everything truly beneficial is honorable. Therefore something that is dishonorable cannot be beneficial. To believe otherwise is destructive of human society: "No greater plague has assailed human life than the fancy of those who have separated the two" (3.34). There are some things that appear to be beneficial but not honorable, tyrannicide for example, when the tyrant is a friend and benefactor, but this is an illusion to be corrected by philosophical analysis. Caesar's tyrannicide, in fact, was judged by the Roman people to be "the fairest of all splendid deeds." Apparent conflicts between the honorable and the beneficial can be settled by establishing a "rule of procedure" or *formula* (analogous, in other words, to establishing a question of fact before a judge) and by following a *regula,* a correct precedent.

The basic principle of right *(ius)* in human societies is not to advantage oneself by harming another. For Cicero, what it is to be human is precisely the awareness that harming others and taking what is theirs by force is wrong.[30] Using coercion and violence to advantage oneself at the expense of others is by definition inhuman (3.26). The human race was given reason and language so that it could achieve common goods through voluntary consent. To take from others by force or fraud what is theirs destroys the bond of human society, *ius,* and makes the fellowship of the human race impossible. There is a law of nature, there is a universal law of nations *(ius gentium),* and there is a law regulating individual peoples, which in the case of Rome is the *ius civile.*

> The [civil] laws have as their object and desire that the bonds between citizens should be unharmed. If anyone tears them apart, they restrain him by death, by exile, by chains or by fines. Nature's reason itself, which is human and divine law, achieves this object to a far greater extent. Whoever is willing to obey it (everyone will obey it who wants to live in accordance with nature) will never act so as to seek what is another's, nor to appropriate for himself something that he has taken from someone else. . . . Therefore, all men should have this one object, that the benefit of each individual and the benefit of all together should be the same.[31]

It is impossible that a man can do wrong, harm someone else, and benefit either himself or the whole community. Benign tyranny is a contradiction in terms. That is why great Roman heroes of the past like Gaius Fabricius refused to do wrong things like engage in assassination plots, because there could be no true honor or glory, and no benefit to the community, from defeating an enemy through crime rather than through virtue.[32] Caesar claimed that he needed to do illegal things in order to defend his *dignitas,* his personal honor. Many Romans in Cicero's time accepted that argument, but Cicero's Stoic reasoning shows that this is an error, a contradiction. Breaking the law can never bring true honor or *dignitas.* Seeking power over others, taking freedoms guaranteed to them by civil right, is the act of a beast, not a man. The true nature of Caesar's actions was shown by what Cicero claimed to be the dictator's personal motto, drawn from Euripides: "If right *(ius)* must be violated for the sake of ruling, it must be violated; you may cultivate piety in other matters."[33] Caesar was prepared to dispense with *ius* when it got in the way of his personal lust for power. Since the law was sacred, such a violation was sacrilegious. Inhumane and impious acts were constant temptations to powerful, honor-seeking men, but they were wrong. Violating *ius,* the basis of the human community, for the sake of personal power is what made Caesar a tyrant.

It is important to grasp that in these passages Cicero is not claiming monarchy as such is an illegitimate form of government. There are plenty of other passages in Cicero's writings where he recognizes the legitimacy of monarchies elsewhere, even in some cases admires them. In his works on government, for example, *De republica* and *De legibus,* he discusses constitutions and makes it clear that kingship, like aristocracy and popular government, can be good or bad depending on the moral qualities of the king, that is, his virtues. Following Polybius, his best constitution, as presented in *De legibus,* is a mixed constitution that has an element of monarchy.[34] Cicero surely did not want to get into a debate about Caesar's virtues, both because they seemed great and evident to many, and because it was Stoic doctrine that a man who had one virtue had them all. He chose instead to declare him a tyrant on grounds of illegality. What he maintains in the *De officiis* is that Caesar is a tyrant because he violated the *ius civile* of the Roman people, which made citizens free and equal under law:

> Here you have a man who longed to be king of the Roman people and master of every nation; and he achieved it! If anyone says that such a greed is honorable, he is out of his mind; for he is approving the death of laws and liberty, and counting their oppression—a foul and hateful thing—as something glorious. But if anyone admits that it is not honorable to reign *(regnare)* in a city that has been free and ought to be so, but says that it is beneficial to the man who can do it—what reproach, or rather abuse, can I use to try to tear him from so great an error?[35]

To uphold liberty and equality required citizens and especially leading men to treat each other in a spirit of equity; it was that spirit which enabled friendship and mutual trust among citizens. Hence to aim at monarchy *within the Roman political tradition,* whatever the virtues of the prospective monarch, necessarily meant violating the liberties of others, thus destroying trust, creating fear, and destroying the natural bonds of benevolence between men. Rome's traditions of law and equity made it unjust for her citizens to accept subjection to a single man. Such a government could simply not be lawful in Rome.

Bartolus of Sassoferrato and Baldo degli Ubaldi

Cicero, as we know, lost this argument, at least in the short run, and the republican system he knew died out shortly after his death. Though a veneer of constitutional propriety was at first tacked onto the governing system that emerged under Augustus, by the time of Nero the justification of the *princeps'* rule had transitioned to a form of moral meritocracy, elaborated most famously by Seneca in his *De clementia*.[36] Government was legitimate when the ruler ruled well. Roman civil law, however, endured and continued to offer resources to theorists who wished to justify or to delegitimate regimes in terms of right and legitimate title. There is no need to trace this long history, which experienced a revival in Europe during the Investiture Crisis of the late eleventh and twelfth century, even were the present writer competent to do so. The most subtle analyses of tyranny in the civil law tradition, however—those of the great jurists Bartolus of Sassoferrato (1313–1357) and Baldo degli Ubaldi (d. 1400)—do require discussion in this chapter, both because their writings were used and criticized by Renaissance humanists, and because they illustrate the contrast between the legal tradition's solutions to the problem of tyranny and those of humanist champions of virtue politics.

Bartolus was known for his realism: for his willingness, when necessary, to dispense with the web of legal fictions that sustained the authority of the Holy Roman Empire, and for his recognition that institutions such as the popular *comune* needed an adequate legal basis for self-government. The latter he provided with his famous doctrine that a city refusing in practice to recognize a superior, whether the emperor or the pope or some regional authority, was *sibi princeps,* sovereign *de facto* if not *de iure.* A problem arose, however, in that the *ius proprium* or local law governing such communes was often heavily politicized by the dominant faction of the moment and did not enjoy the autonomy, prestige, and authority of Roman civil law. Bartolus was also painfully conscious, like Petrarch, of living in an age of tyranny.[37] He regarded with horror the collapse of dozens of free communes in north and central Italy in his day and the spread of *signorie,* lordships based on the power of wealth, status, and arms. Since the resulting regimes were often "dyarchies" or combinations of old communal institutions controlled manifestly or covertly by *signori,* the problem of defining tyranny arose in acute form. *Signori* had often imposed their rule by frightening the people or their leaders into an appearance of voluntary submission, and they were always eager to cloak their deeds under an appearance of legality. Bartolus' goal was to use the intellectual resources and prestige of Roman and canon law to expose tyrannical powers that relied on fear and to tear off their cloak of legality.[38]

Hence Bartolus' treatise *De tyranno* was meant to provide legal tools to fight the subtle forms of tyranny that had turned so many Italian cities into theaters of cruelty and oppression.[39] He began with a text of Gregory the Great excerpted in canon law that gave a theological definition of tyranny as an internal condition caused by pride. Tyranny was therefore potentially found in every human association and every human heart. But it did more damage the more powerful the tyrant was, so Bartolus concentrates on identifying concrete marks of tyranny in political societies that could become the basis for legal processes. His first principle was the very one so passionately rejected by Petrarch, namely, legitimate title.[40] The primary way a tyrant can be identified is by a defect in his title to rule: he has not been chosen by legitimate superiors, the emperor, or the pope, or by a city government with *de facto* legitimacy. He has illegally usurped a title to rule by force or fraud and is therefore guilty of *laesa maiestas* according the Roman *lex Julia maiestatis*.[41] Even if he rules well after illicitly obtaining a title to rule, he is still, legally, a tyrant.[42] Here the title to rule is understood as a piece of property like a benefice that lies in the gift of a higher authority and can be revoked for cause. But Bartolus realizes the principle of title is not enough to deal with the problem of tyranny. Since it is possible that a tyrant with an army has terrified a city into recognizing him under legal forms, he introduces the principle of *iustus metus* or *iustus timor*, legitimate or well-founded fear. There is a proper function for fear in enforcing the law: malefactors *should* be afraid of punishment. But it is also possible that good people can be cowed into accepting the rule of a tyrant through fear of violence, and this is (counterintuitively) called *iustus metus* or *iustus timor*, a sign of tyranny.[43] Such rule is no more valid than a contract one may be forced to sign with menaces.

Bartolus also recognizes that some tyrants have just titles to rule but nevertheless act tyrannically, and these are tyrants *ex parte exercitii*, because of the way they exercise power. They can be identified by the general principle that they aim at their private benefit rather than at the common good. This of course is the principle Aristotle invokes in the *Politics* to distinguish good and bad regimes, but Bartolus redescribes it as a violation of *ius:* "For [to rule solely for one's own advantage] is not rule by *ius*." He classifies such violations as infringements of the *lex Julia de vi publica*.[44] Bartolus recognizes, however, that this general principle will not be very useful in a legal process against a tyrant, so he "descends to more particular actions," identifiable harms that a tyrant commits against a political community. In order to specify the harms that mark out a tyrant, Bartolus turns to the same passage from Aristotle discussed above (*Pol.* 5.9), filtered through Giles of Rome's *De regimine principum* (3.2.10), where Aristotle had anatomized all the wrong ways a tyrant can protect his power. Bartolus makes a list of ten harms: (1) killing the city's leading men, (2) destroying its wise men, (3) abolishing education, (4) forbidding free association, (5) using spies and surveillance, (6) keeping the city divided, (7) impoverishing the citizenry, (8) provoking wars, (9) employing in his own guard foreign mercenary soldiers rather than citizens, (10) siding with one civic faction against another. Thus what in Aristotle had been advice to a tyrant on (bad) ways to maintain his power became in Bartolus grounds for legal action against a tyrant.

Remarkably, however, Bartolus believes that many of these "tyrannical" acts could be justifiably performed by good governments in the right circumstances; for instance, he says the use of spies could be legitimate when a judge needs spies "in order to correct delicts and other things which occur unjustly in a city." In fact, only three of the ten potentially tyrannical acts are always "without exception" tyrannical: numbers 6, 7, and 10. Number 8, causing wars, is only unjust without exception in the case of civil wars (and would thus be enough to convict Caesar of tyranny, though Bartolus does not say so). He calls on superiors to depose tyrants found guilty of any of these tyrannical acts. If an overlord refuses to remove a tyrant, there is no further remedy. "I say also that if those living under such a tyranny, in whatever way they plot publicly or secretly against a prince or his officials, they are rebels of the empire by the same law *(ius),* and they lose office (or rank: *dignitas*) according to the new law of the emperor Henry."[45] Tyrannicides, in other words, of the kind enacted in the assassination of Caesar, or conspiracies, or even public but illegal counter-coups, are wrongful acts. The process that removes a tyrant must follow proper legal forms.[46]

Bartolus also makes a distinction between manifest and hidden tyranny. He understands that there can be powerful people in a city (the fifteenth-century example would be the Medici) who do not hold any title to rule but nevertheless use their hidden power to cause tyrannical acts. In this case prosecution is more difficult, and use must be made of what today would be called circumstantial evidence. In general Bartolus is concerned to provide grounds for legally removing tyrants without undermining the Empire and other legitimate governments or rendering illicit what he considers legitimate tools of government. It is noteworthy, in light of the contrast with humanistic virtue politics, that for Bartolus one can never be a legitimate prince without a legitimate title to rule (whether *de iure* or *de facto*).

Bartolus' student, Baldo degli Ubaldi, the leading jurist of the later fourteenth century, also relies heavily on the concept of legitimate title to define the tyrant:

any ruler who seizes power over a people in defiance of that people's natural lord is *ipso facto* a tyrant, by usurpation. In the case of cities with *de facto* sovereignty, the criteria for identifying a tyrant are more stringent: a ruler has both to lack title *and* to exercise power tyrannically before he can be labelled a tyrant.[47] In contrast with Bartolus, Baldus allows that a ruler without a legitimate title *de iure* but who rules well and whose rule is tolerated by his superior is legitimate *de facto*.[48] But the superior's toleration of *de facto* rule has to be *propter bonum regimen,* because the regime is a good one, not simply because the superior, for example the emperor or the pope, lacks the power to depose the ruler. Baldus also makes more concessions to the principles of popular rule. He makes the silencing of free public deliberation a mark of tyrannical rule: "Every city is under a tyrant when the subjects cannot defend the public good with a free voice." He also emphasizes that, even under tyrannical rule, the people retain the right *(de iure)* to decide *(arbitrium)* in matters of public interest; it is only when the tyrant refuses to allow the people to assemble that its acts become invalid. If the tyrant lets political questions be decided by *pauci,* that is, by oligarchs, their acts are not valid. Whenever there is *iustus metus* there is tyranny; where there is tyranny there is no proper jurisdiction, and the tyrant's rule is simply invalid.

Like Petrarch, Baldus was a sometime client of *signori* whom certain contemporaries described as tyrants. He taught law for a time at the University of Padua, called to that post by Francesco I da Carrara, a *signore* by popular acclamation whose title to rule was regularized by the grant of an imperial vicariate. More dubiously, Baldus also served Giangaleazzo Visconti, who came to full power by engineering a coup against his uncle Bernabò but in 1395 acquired the title of Duke of Milan from the emperor. Baldus spent the last ten years of his career teaching at Pavia, the university town of the Milanese state (a state he referred to in his legal writings as a *respublica*).

Though in general supportive of legitimate princely power, Baldus was extremely uneasy with the prerogative of *plenitudo potestatis,* "fullness of power," that had been refashioned in the early fourteenth century from civil and canon law sources to justify the actions of *signori.* He recognized that the prerogative could, and very often was, abused in a tyrannical fashion. Invoked in legal cases it could overturn the autonomy of the law and effectively allowed the prince to become the judge in his own cause. It was difficult in such circumstances (and here Baldus was speaking of the pope) for the private passions of the holder of such power not to influence outcomes in his own favor. *Plenitudo potestatis* therefore needed to be corroborated in the ruler by *plenitudo honestatis,* fullness of moral worth. In other words the ruler needed to be morally good, a point with which the humanists would surely have agreed. But Baldus acknowledged that the law could not compel a sovereign ruler to be good. For him, the only real solution was for the ruler himself to maintain the autonomy of the law: "Decisions should not originate in the breast of the judge and the secrets of his heart, but from the womb and bosom of the law."[49] The law, not the character of the ruler, was the best criterion of just rule and tyranny, but the law did not have in itself the power to compel a ruler *legibus solutus* to exercise his power well. The law did not offer any way to make the ruler morally better.

Both Bartolus and Baldus display considerable subtlety and realism in their analysis of tyranny. Nevertheless, the legalistic approach to restraining tyranny, from a virtue politics point of view, had grave defects. It paid too little attention to the character of the ruler, the real source of tyrannical evil, and too much to his actions, which (as even Bartolus admitted) were often in themselves morally ambiguous and difficult to evaluate, let alone prosecute.[50] What if the practical choice was between a benign tyrant and a legitimate ruler who was incompetent, corrupt, or cruel? What about rulers like Bernabò Visconti of Milan, nephew of the tyrant Luchino Visconti, who acquired power by military conquest, was a sworn enemy of the pope, and was famous for his ruthlessness and cruelty? Was he to be considered a good ruler once the Emperor Charles IV had granted him the title of imperial vicar? Had his character been miraculously reformed by placing that title after his name? What about when that title was revoked in 1380? Should his previous acts be considered void now that he was a tyrant again? Wouldn't applying a merely legal principle of legitimacy in this circumstance cause social chaos? What about the Venetians, who liked to be authorized in their conquest of subject towns by summoning the population into the town square, surrounding them with troops, and staging an "acclamation by the people"?[51] This was surely an example of *iustus metus,* but how was that going to be proved in court? How could the philosopher's standard of ruling for the sake of the part rather than the whole be applied in practice? And if there were some court somewhere that would hand down an adverse judgment against a tyrant, how exactly would that be enforced, when the Empire was, militarily, the laughingstock of Europe? What if the emperor himself was corrupt?[52] Like the modern World Court, those who claimed jurisdiction often lacked any power of enforcement. It is no wonder that the humanists came to believe that the cure for tyranny did not lie in enforcement of the laws of Christendom, or in what Gabriele Pedullà called *la macchina probatoria escogitata dai giuristi,* the trial machine contrived by jurists. Rather, it lay in moral education and also, perhaps, in sounder, simpler laws and customs modelled on those of the ancients, laws that led both citizens and their rulers to virtue and did not simply seek to punish them after they had committed wrongs.[53]

Petrarch on Living with Tyrants

Petrarch, as we shall see in the following chapters, was always torn between the life of literary retirement he had invented for himself and a desire to counsel the rulers of his time, like Plato with the tyrant Dionysius or his beloved Seneca with Nero. His hope was that by associating with them he could improve their characters and in so doing encourage peace and relieve the sufferings of the poor and oppressed. The priors of Florence offered him the chance to teach young *principes* at the university there in 1348, during the worst ravages of the Black Death, and not surprisingly he turned them down, even though the offer had been made honorably through the hands of his devoted disciple Boccaccio.[54] The Florentines called him their fellow-citizen and even offered to restore his father's property, confiscated after his exile in 1303, but Petrarch was not tempted. Even so, it came as an enormous shock to Boccaccio in 1351 to learn from a mutual friend that Petrarch had accepted an offer of patronage from Archbishop Giovanni Visconti, the ruler of Milan, whom the Florentines called a tyrant.[55] If Petrarch had hoped to escape criticism for taking up this invitation, he was quickly disabused of his error.

Archbishop Visconti, who earlier in his career had been deposed from his prelacy and declared a heretic by Pope John XXII, then created a cardinal by antipope Nicholas V, had by 1351 been named archbishop again by a legitimate pope and had purchased from him, for 500,000 florins, the lordship of Milan, jointly with his brother Luchino. The latter was by any definition one of the cruelest tyrants of the fourteenth century. After his brother's death, the archbishop became sole ruler of Milan and began a program of territorial expansion that brought him into armed conflict with Florence, Petrarch's nominal *patria.* When Boccaccio heard the news that Petrarch had entered Visconti's service, he was stunned and wrote an allegorical letter to his idol in which he poured out his disillusionment and sense of betrayal. At first he could not believe the shepherd of Helicon had made himself into a Lombard swineherd, but eventually Simonides (their mutual friend Francesco Nelli) confirmed the report of Silvanus' (i.e., Petrarch's) "crime" (*facinus*) beyond doubt: "O the pain! Where has his moral gravity (*honestas*), his sanctity, his prudent counsel gone, now that he has made himself a friend of that cruel and inhuman (*immanis*) man whom he had once called Polyphemus and Cyclops? Once, almost sick with disgust, he condemned the insolence, pride, and tyranny of the one whose yoke he now bears of his own accord, neither pulled nor forced!" Boccaccio accuses Silvanus of having been seduced by the filthy whore Crisis (money). "I would have been less amazed to have heard him curse Cicero or Seneca!" *O me miserum!* Silvanus' fall into wickedness

has stained not only himself . . . , but you [Petrarch, the Petrarch addressed in the letter], me and the innocent others left behind that have exalted, loudly and with all our force, [Silvanus'] life, his habits, his song and his pen in every wood to every shepherd. Do you believe that those who will come to hear this wicked deed will suffer it in peace and not raise their voices against him? Indeed, they are already crying out and slandering his long-standing fame with shameful reproaches, saying that he is false, counterfeit, glittering with artificial splendor; and in the woods and in the streets they declare us to be adulators, falsifiers, liars, and perverts.[56]

The whole humanist movement has been disgraced and discredited, in other words, by Petrarch's association with a tyrant. Silvanus may claim that he was dishonored by the actions of the Florentine government in offering to restore his father's property, then rescinding the offer, but that is no excuse for becoming an enemy of the *patria*. Petrarch is now in the position of Caesar, who used an affront to his personal honor as an excuse to betray his country: "What will this lonely advocate and cultivator of solitude do, surrounded by the multitudes [in Milan]? And he who used to exalt with great praise the free life and honorable poverty, now that he has gone under a foreign yoke and embellished himself with ill-gotten riches— what will he do? What is left for this famous champion of virtue to celebrate, now that he has become a lackey of vice?" Boccaccio believes that Silvanus' closest friends—including Monico (his brother, the monk Gherardo), Socrates (Ludwig van Kempen), Idaeus (Giovanni Barili), and Phytias (Barbaro da Sulmona), all of whom have long admired him as an exemplar of moral goodness but are now filled with pain and anxiety—will now condemn him.[57] The only man who can bring Silvanus to his senses and tear him away from that most barbarous and inhuman of tyrants, *ab immanissimo homine,* is Petrarch himself, the true Petrarch, who alone by his wise moral counsel can return himself to "our common woods" (i.e., poetry) and become the beloved and delightful person he used to be.

This was a scalding denunciation, all the more so given Boccaccio's earlier adulation.[58] Even though he must have recognized a degree of rhetorical posturing in Boccaccio's letter, Petrarch knew that others shared his opinion and that he had to explain himself.[59] His admirers saw him as the leading literary man of Italy and, since the failure of Cola di Rienzo's revolution, an advocate of the solitary life of a scholar-poet, which meant living in close contact with nature apart from the moral contaminations of the city. Petrarch had now settled into a new role, that of counselor and willing servant of princes, and he needed to show how he could consort with bad princes and remain, himself, unspotted from the world. He needed to show why he now believed that "tyrants" could benefit from the counsel of literary men.[60]

Petrarch's response to his critics was laid out not in a reply to Boccaccio,[61] but in an invective of 1355, *Against a Man of High Rank with No Knowledge or Virtue*. The "man of high rank" has been identified by modern scholars as the French cardinal Jean de Caraman, a much less sympathetic adversary than Boccaccio.[62] Like Boccaccio, Caraman (according to Petrarch) could not find any personal faults of Petrarch to blame, so he blamed him for "frequenting evil men," for "intimacy and friendship with tyrants."

Petrarch constructs two lines of defense. His first line is to deny that men who held legitimate titles of dignity were necessarily any better than those who did not. The theme of the work as a whole, indeed, is the emptiness of rank and official titles if the holder of the title proves himself ignorant and vicious.[63] The other side of the coin is that rulers without titles are not necessarily tyrants. In fact Petrarch sees all regimes in his own day as morally defective and inclined to tyranny. Any form of lordship, whether of oligarchs or even of peoples in popular communes, is in some degree oppressive:[64]

> Hence, practically no one is free: slavery and prison and chains are found everywhere, unless some rare individual with heaven-sent virtue happens to break the bonds of human affairs. No matter where you turn on earth, you will find no place without tyranny. When there are no tyrants, the people tyrannize. So when you think you have escaped one tyrant, you fall into the hands of many, unless you can show me some place that is ruled by a just and benign ruler. If you can, I shall at once pack all my bags and move my home there. I shall not be hindered by my love of country, nor by Italy's grace and nobility.

I shall travel to the people of India, China, and the remotest Sahara to find such a place and such a ruler. But it is pointless to seek what exists nowhere. We may thank our age for making nearly all things equal and thus sparing us the trouble.[65]

Petrarch's claim of moral equivalence among modern regimes was an effective response not only to Caraman but also to Boccaccio's charge that he had discredited himself and his friends by serving a tyrant. Such a charge was really a claim that any kind of public service, whether to a prince or a commune, was morally tainted. In the dregs of time in which he lived, all governments were vitiated by tyranny, and all governments had their origins in tyranny. As he wrote in the *De remediis,* "What else are kingdoms but yesterday's tyrannies? Something bad by nature does not become good over time."[66] He brushes away as irrelevant the principle of *praescriptio,* beloved of civil lawyers, which counts as legitimate long-standing practices whose origins are lost in the mists of time. For Petrarch time doesn't make titles legitimate because titles can't by themselves confer true legitimacy, moral legitimacy. Only the virtue of the one who holds the title can do that. In other words he follows the Greek philosophers in seeing character, not lawfulness or right, as the wellspring of tyranny.[67] It is the *way* rulers rule and not their titles that makes them tyrants.

In fact, by the Greek philosophical definition of tyranny, the Visconti rulers in Milan he served were no tyrants, while the cardinal, for all his exalted titles as a prince of the Church, was precisely that. Caraman was the real tyrant, worse than Agathocles, Phalaris, Busiris, or any famous tyrant of antiquity, because he did not know how to love those over whom he was set in authority; he only knew how to exploit them for his own profit. He didn't know how to be a friend, to attract loyalty through mutual care and love. Instead he relied on his family distinction and his red beretta to overawe others. Caraman had made his own the motto of the tyrant-emperor Caligula: *oderint dum metuant.* Let them hate me so long as they fear me. But hate destroys society rather than binding it together. It makes the ruler feared, not loved. I at least, Petrarch says, do not fear the purple drapery "which covers both you and your horse." If the vulgar are impressed by his title and insignia, the good are not. The best, the philosophers, have the moral discernment to separate false from true authority.

Petrarch's second line of defense against the charge of serving tyrants is to argue that, even if he did live with wicked men, it was possible for him to do so without damaging himself morally. He could remain unspotted from the world even while living with sinners. The great philosophers of antiquity had all done the same: "You act as if people who live together must share everything, when in fact wicked people often live among the good, and good people among the wicked. Didn't Socrates live under the Thirty Tyrants of Athens? Didn't Plato live with Dionysius, Callisthenes with Alexander, Cato with Catiline, and Seneca with Nero? Virtue is not infected by the proximity of vice. Whereas trivial causes may disturb tender spirits, the contagion of evil character does not affect strong minds."[68] A counselor can be a friend, even an intimate friend of a tyrant without being stained by his evil; to claim the opposite is to accuse the prince's philosophical counselors of guilt by association, or worse, mental weakness: "Whereas trivial causes may shake tender spirits, the contagion of evil character does not lay a finger on strong minds."[69] The man of strong character will dominate the weak character, even if the latter happens to be a tyrant. The wise and virtuous man is truly subject only to other wise and virtuous persons to whom he is bound in love, whether those persons are humble or illustrious. In a higher sense he is subject to no one but Christ.[70] The friend of God is subject only to the sweet yoke of kindred souls.[71] His soul is free, but his body must "necessarily be subject to the lords whose lands it inhabits." Yet his subjection is freely chosen; he willingly submits only to those who deserve to be obeyed. He rejects the charge that he has ever been subservient to great men. His obedience has always been freely given both to the great and the humble, and was based on their merit:

> These included both the humble and the illustrious, and even kings and popes. Yet it was not their fortune and rank, but their virtue and love, that made me submit to them freely and completely, and to mourn them deeply when death released me from their service. This is why I often submitted to humbler persons: for I perceived in them less fortune, which I neither love nor revere, but more virtue, which I have always resolved to revere and love in others, if I could not in myself. Apart from these, there is no human being to whom my spirit is subject.

The young Visconti rulers he served (for by 1355 Archbishop Giovanni was dead) were no tyrants, but even if they were, that had nothing to do with him:

> They know as little of the tyrannical spirit as you do of equity and justice. Or at least until now: I can't predict their future. For the mind is changeable, especially in people whose happiness never changes and whose privileges are secure. But whether you falsely call them tyrants, or whether in the end time

makes true tyrants of them, or reveals what it has hitherto concealed—how does this affect me? I live with them, not under them; and I reside in their lands, but not in their houses. I have nothing in common with them, except for the benefits and honors that they continue to lavish on me, as long as I allow it. . . . For even now, they have promised in good faith that they require only my presence and my residence in this flourishing city and its charming quarters—a presence which, they say, glorifies both themselves and their realm. . . . In sum, recognize that they are not tyrants, and I am completely free.[72]

Petrarch never argues that a wise man has a strict duty to serve princes, even good ones; that ran counter to his constant assertion of the autonomy of the wise man.[73] Yet his life and writings offer a model of how a man of letters could act as a guide, philosopher, and friend of the powerful, and how that friendship could benefit princes inclined to tyranny and, through them, the whole community. The mature Petrarch came to see that the key to a fruitful philosophical friendship with princes was to maintain one's independence. A *literatus* should treat a prince respectfully, but as an equal, without subservience. While living in the orbit of a prince he should be content with little and not try to exploit his friendship with the prince to enrich himself or acquire titles of status.[74] If the prince should choose to grant them, they may be gratefully accepted, but they should not compromise his freedom. Most of all, he should remain *supra partes,* not engage in factional politics or be actively involved in the business of governing others: "Political deliberation and executive power, as well as the administration of public funds, are entrusted to others, who were born for this purpose. To me, nothing is entrusted but leisure, silence, security, and freedom. These are my concern and my business. While others at dawn seek great palaces, I seek my familiar woods and solitude. I feel the presence of such lords only because of their generosity and benefits."[75] His role is to set a moral tone, to be the voice of reason, informed by the wisdom of the ancients. The *literatus* who becomes a friend of the prince should not forget his own power, the power of his eloquence to influence the way that the prince will be seen by his contemporaries and by posterity. If the prince gave him security and the opportunity to influence the ruler's character, he gave the prince the things he sought above everything else: fame and glory. The wise man who kept his independence and had courage could use the promise of glory to shape his prince's conduct, especially if he were a young prince not yet set in his ways. The prince's humane friend could also offer him philosophical medicine for his sick soul, medicine that would bestow upon him tranquillity and freedom from anger and fear, and by so doing would curb his appetite for tyrannical behavior.

Petrarch left behind a model of how to counsel powerful men: the *Remedies for Fortune Fair and Foul,* which as we have seen already was by far his most popular Latin work.[76] Among many other things the work contains dialogues between Ratio—reason, the voice of philosophy—and lordly folk in states of elation or depression. In book 2 of this work Petrarch consoles a tyrant who has just lost his power. The dialogue shows that "consolation" on the Petrarchan model requires severity as much as sympathy.[77] Ratio's goal is to use the tyrant's downfall to educate him in the nature of vice and virtue. That moment of grief, insecurity, and rejection can be exploited to transform the tyrant's character and bring him to take a more rational and therefore more moral view of his past actions and present condition. Cheer up, says Petrarch's Ratio, you have been relieved of a terrible burden, and so have your subjects. You have only lost something you had no right to in the first place, namely, control over the liberty of your subjects. You should have served the people, but instead you enslaved them. Given your actions, it was only natural, it was inevitable, that you would lose your position. Nature decrees that when a ruler acts with arrogance, lust, and greed—greed above all—his subjects will hate him and depose him. Your downfall just restores the natural order. Citing the same passage of Aristotle's *Politics* (5.9) used by Giles of Rome and Bartolus in their discussions of tyranny, Petrarch shows the dejected lord that tyrannical acts caused his rapid downfall, whereas kingly acts could have preserved him in power. However, a lord should try actually to be, not merely seem to be, a good ruler: "Pretense, no matter how artfully and cleverly practiced, cannot last long under the gaze of so many people who are directly involved." Petrarch's analysis of the causes of tyranny is thus couched in the moral language of Greek philosophy and Seneca, not the legalistic language of Cicero and the academic jurists of his own time. His cure for the disease of tyranny is the same one embraced by the literary and philosophical movement he founded: moral education.

Was Caesar a Tyrant? Petrarch, Salutati, Guarino, Poggio

The figure of Julius Caesar presented a major challenge to virtue politics. The example of Caesar's life offered humanists a great proof of their beliefs about virtue, but also, potentially, undermined them. Whether he had been a tyrant or one of the noblest of Roman heroes remained a constant subject of debate.[78] The debate was an ancient one, to be sure. The ancient authorities most valued by the humanists disagreed sharply about his moral status. Sallust—a canonical author in the Roman literary tradition and later in the humanist school, who was himself a client and supporter of Caesar—praised him for his eloquence, generosity, and compassion. In his historical essay *The War with Catiline* he represented Caesar delivering a calm and noble speech before the Senate recommending clemency for Catiline and his co-conspirators. For Sallust, Caesar was an exemplar of far-seeing prudence and civic virtue.[79] Imperial Latin authors like Seneca and the whole Roman legal tradition were ranged on the side that upheld Caesar's legitimacy and beneficent rulership. Ancient Christian historiography saw Caesar as the founder of the dynasty under whose rule God sent Jesus Christ into the world, a kind of divine endorsement.[80] As the Greek historians and biographers of the Roman Empire became available in Latin in the course of the quattrocento, their writings, especially those of Plutarch, tended to reinforce the generally positive view of Caesar and the monarchy he established.

But there were important exceptions, one in particular. As we have seen, Cicero's voice, always a powerful one in humanist ears, had thunderously denounced Caesar as a tyrant in a canonical text of humanist political morality, the *De officiis*. The basis of his attack was Caesar's violation of *ius,* the legal norms of the Roman state, but these external, legalistic criteria of good rule were precisely what the virtue politics of the humanists sought to transcend. The poet Lucan too cast a negative vote against Caesar. In his epic poem, the *Pharsalia*—far more widely read in the Renaissance than today—he presented Caesar as a destructive military despot who struck fear into the hearts of good citizens.

In part because of these disagreements among his most revered authors, Petrarch became obsessed with Caesar and wrote what eventually became a small monograph on him, the *De gestis Cesaris,* a work that deserves to rank among the finest examples of Renaissance historiography. Petrarch was convinced that Caesar was the greatest general of all time and displayed magnificent virtues such as clemency, humanity, and moderation that were worthy of emulation, indeed desperately needed, by princes in his own time. The longest demonstration in Petrarch's writings of how the virtues conferred charismatic powers of leadership, in fact, comes in his discussion of why Caesar had been such a successful military leader, binding his troops to him with absolute loyalty.[81] One reason among many was that Caesar showed no respect for social status: "He did not value his soldiers based on their fine manners or good looks or their fortune, but on the basis of their physical and moral qualities."[82] Caesar's willingness to elevate the meritorious ob-viously chimed with the wider themes of virtue politics. His egalitarian attitude to merit allowed him, despite his noble descent, to bond with his troops, a skill his rival Pompey was said to lack.

On the dangerous question of whether Caesar had been a tyrant—dangerous because it threw into doubt the legitimacy of Rome's whole imperial system and its descendents—Petrarch sided firmly with Caesar and resisted Cicero's judgment. Petrarch was not writing panegyric, and he admits that Caesar did some things that were wrong and unjust. He privatized the teaching of military discipline, tra-ditionally a public exercise. He high-handedly raised legions on his own authority, and after his victory he seized, again on his own authority, the unconstitutional office of *dictator perpetuo.* The very worst thing he did was to take up arms against his own country, an act, says Petrarch, that can never be justified. Petrarch would not absolve him of blame for these actions: "He did things, I admit, which would confound a free city—indeed a city that was the mistress of nations—first with amazement *(stupor),* then anger."

The historian can, however, come to understand why a noble nature like Cae-sar's could be driven to such actions. Caesar was a great and noble man, and such men arouse envy in smaller minds. The envious were his fellow patricians, not the common people, who loved him. His opponents in the Senate, not excluding Ci-cero, were locked into a system of clientage and self-interest from which they could not escape and which led them to treat Caesar unjustly and to follow a mor-ally inferior man such as Pompey. There was no difference in legitimacy between Pompey and Cicero: both aimed at an autocratic form of rule similar to that which Sulla had employed a generation before. Both acted like kings and not generals of the Roman state. All rights human and divine in Rome had been turned upside down and perverted out of hatred for Caesar, and the political system was rigged against him. The tribunes of the people who had supported him had been treated with contempt and had left the city "either of their own free will or because they had been expelled." Caesar's choice was whether to follow the example of Scipio Africanus—Petrarch's other favorite Roman hero—and go voluntarily into exile when charged unjustly with crimes by his patrician enemies, or to fight for his rights. Caesar chose to fight. He crossed the Rubicon, having been encouraged to do so by a divine portent, then marched on Rome.

Caesar started a civil war for reasons that "perhaps had no small appearance of justice, if there can ever be any just cause for attacking your country, although other, less just reasons were adduced by others whose reliability is discredited by their manifest hatred of him."[83] But he was not a tyrant, because his actions were never those of a tyrant. Unlike Pompey, who promised only retribution against his enemies, Caesar showed great clemency and, after coming to power, ruled with generosity and justice. He always forgave his enemies and sought reconciliation. His victory in the civil wars brought hope to the people of Rome and to Italy; only Pompey and the Senate, the political elite in other words, were filled with fear. His civil virtue was shown by his manifest hatred of taking a fellow citizen's life. Above all—significantly for a Christian like Petrarch who valued the *pax romana* for religious reasons—he constantly sought to make peace. During the civil wars there had been a proposal for the rival generals to lay down their arms and return to practicing the virtues of restraint and moderation required for civil life (*ad aequam civilitatem*), which would at last make the city safe and free. Caesar wanted to make peace on these terms, but the supporters of Pompey could not bear to see anyone made equal to him. Over and over again Petrarch demonstrates—often relying on Cicero's own letters, which he had himself rediscovered—that Caesar was the man of peace, generosity, mildness, and virtue that Rome needed in the crisis of her republic. His assassination was thus an outrageous act of supreme wickedness. His assassins were all condemned to die violent deaths within three years: "some by shipwreck, others in battle; and certain ones fell by the very same sword they had used to stab Caesar, showing by clear proofs that his murder was pleasing neither to men nor to God."

The most important representative of Petrarchan humanism in the generation after the great poet's death was Coluccio Salutati, the chancellor of Florence and the mentor of numerous humanists, including major figures such as Leonardo Bruni, Pier Paolo Vergerio, and Poggio Bracciolini. By bringing the Byzantine émigré Manuel Chrysoloras to Florence, Salutati did as much as anyone to make a reality the dream of Petrarch to revive the study of ancient Greek. Salutati, however, had only a smattering of Greek himself, and this may help to explain his relatively conservative approach to the definition of tyranny, if not his attitude to Julius Caesar.[84]

It was his desire to defend Caesar against Cicero that drove Salutati's analysis of tyranny and led him, uncharacteristically for a humanist, to draw on contemporary legal theory to prove he was no tyrant and that his murder was therefore not justified.[85] He undertook this project in the treatise *De tyranno* (1400), his only formal work of political theory, composed when he was almost seventy.[86] The work was written primarily to defend Dante, Florence's famous and admired poet, for having placed the Roman republican heroes Brutus and Cassius in the lowest circle of hell, next to Judas Iscariot.[87] Defending Dante entailed repudiating the political principles of late republican Rome, the political judgment of the period's most famous statesman, Cicero, and defending the monarchical principle.

The interpretation of the *De tyranno* in modern scholarship has in general turned on resolving the apparent contradiction between Salutati's role as chancellor of Florence, the official spokesman for a "republican" regime, and his defense of monarchy in the treatise.[88] The work has been explained as a senile lapse into conservatism and piety, or as an insincere rhetorical exercise, or as a spasm of "medieval" sentiment provoked by the "hyperclassicism" of men like Niccolò Niccoli and Poggio Bracciolini in the younger generation. From the perspective of virtue politics, however, the work is readily intelligible. Salutati, like his disciple Leonardo Bruni, did indeed labor in his official writings as chancellor to defend the moral legitimacy of "political" (i.e., constitutional) government in city-states, including popular governments oriented to liberty, and like every political writer of the time he denounced tyranny. But none of this entailed a rejection of monarchy as a legitimate form of government. Like other humanists, Salutati was not an exclusivist.[89] To premodern ways of thinking the defense of civil republics was perfectly compatible with the argument that monarchy was the best form of government in the universal empire, that is, in the political order of Christendom, built on the foundations of the Roman Empire.[90] According to one typical view of the later Middle Ages, found for example in Tolomeo Fiadoni (Ptolemy of Lucca) and elaborated in the politico-legal thought of Baldus, the greatest jurist of Salutati's time, monarchy was the best form of universal government because, when functioning properly, it ensured internal peace within Christendom, provided a defense against barbarians, and imposed a legal structure for resolving interstate disputes. At the provincial or local level *civitates* were perfectly free to follow the forms of governance best suited to their traditions, moral character, and relative size, whether kingships, aristocracies, or popular governments.[91] Constitutional governments, whether of the one, the few, or the many, were always liable to degenerate into tyrannies, and tyrants should be resisted, but that unfortunate circumstance did not invalidate good regimes. In absolute terms, however, monarchy was the best form of government, provided the monarch possessed virtue and wisdom. Thus in *De tyranno,* Salutati writes (expostulating with his imagined interlocutor, Cicero):

> By the majesty of the everlasting God, is it not the case that one constitutional form of a commonwealth *(status reipublicae)* is to be found in monarchy? Was there no commonwealth at Rome while it was under kings? Was there to be none after Caesar under the rule of a single one of the holiest emperors? Is it not sound politics, approved by the judgment of all wise men, that monarchy is to be preferred to all other forms of government, provided only that it be in the hands of a good man who is devoted to wisdom? There is no greater liberty than obedience to the just commands of a virtuous prince.
>
> As there is no better or more divine rule than that of the universe under one God, so a human regime is better the more nearly it approaches that ideal. But no regime can be more like this than that of a unified leadership [*unico principante*]. For a polyarchic regime is nothing unless the multitude come together in one common will, and unless one commands and the rest obey, there will not be one regime but several. Why, Cicero, should you condemn what you have learned from Aristotle? You know that among the kinds of government, various both in their nature and in the order of time, considering the welfare of the subjects and natural necessity, monarchy has precedence over all the rest. It is a law of nature that, since some are born to serve and others to rule, in order that equality may be preserved among all in due proportion, government should be in the hands of the better [part].[92]

Here Salutati reminds Cicero that not only does monarchy count as a republican constitution *(status, condicio reipublicae)* and as non-despotic *(politicum),* but that the early Roman kingship and at least some of the emperors were also "republican" in this premodern sense. Equal justice, on the Aristotelian principle of "geometric justice" *(debitae proportionis aequalitas),* requires that the better sort rule.[93] In other words Salutati accepts the humanist meritocratic principle that the more worthy should rule the less worthy. He also defends the principle of unity in government and says it applies to a polyarchic government *(multorum regimen)* as well as to monarchies; this presumably includes both oligarchies and popular regimes. Such regimes imitate the divine principle of unity when they are backed by the unified will of the whole population *(in unam sententiam conveniat multitudo).* Salutati thus leaves open the possibility, as elsewhere in his writings, of legitimate polyarchic rule based on the popular will.

In the first chapters of the *De tyranno* we find an even stronger appeal to the legitimating function of the popular will. Salutati here makes use of Bartolus' treatise *De tyranno* but shows awareness as well of Baldus' writings on political questions.[94] Thus Salutati says that for a prince to be legitimate and not a tyrant, he must have just title to rule *and* he must rule justly and according to law: "We conclude, therefore, that a tyrant is one who usurps power, having no legal title to rule, and one whose governance is vitiated by pride or who rules unjustly or does not respect rights or laws; just as, on the other hand, he is a lawful prince upon whom governance is conferred by right, who administers justice and maintains the laws."[95] A tyrant may be lawfully resisted and even killed, so long as it is done lawfully by a legitimate political process:

> For, though a tyrant is the worst plague that can infect the people or the commonwealth, nevertheless no single person nor even several together may, of their own initiative and without the authority of the people or the prince, disturb that civil order, whether this is established by a decree of the people or else by the obedience or consent (express or implied) of the community. It would be a presumptuous, indeed, an arrogant act to rebel against a ruler while all the rest were willing to endure him, even if he were a Nero, an Ezzelino, a Phalaris or a Busiris.[96] And though it may happen that the overthrow of the tyrant is approved by the people, though the greatest happiness may be obtained by those who are set free, though the greatest praise may be heaped upon the liberator or liberators, with undying renown, still, if a valid procedure be lacking, the undertaking is unjust. But a successful and fortunate crime passes for a virtuous deed.[97]

That is why the murder of Caesar by Brutus and Cassius was wrong. Coups, conspiracies, and political murders are always wrong. And if it was wrong to kill any tyrant by an unjust process, in Caesar's case it was a heinous crime, because Caesar, by the time of his murder, had become a legitimate ruler; his case was therefore nothing like that of the famous tyrants of old.

Salutati cannot claim that Caesar came to power lawfully, for that was obviously untrue. Regarding Caesar's part in launching the civil war, he therefore adopts the tactic of maintaining moral equivalence between Caesar and Pompey. During their time, factionalism and the political corruption of the law was so extreme that there was no real lawful government to be defended. There was simply no way that Caesar could lawfully have come to power: "In view of this it seems to me that it was necessary for those two most praiseworthy leaders of Rome not to engage in partisan warfare but to strive with all their counsels, efforts and resources to prevent such a conflict and to avert civil war and bloodshed by lawful arms. The fact is, their struggle was not about whether some one man should rule and have supreme control of the state, but which of the two it should be."[98] Both Caesar and Pompey were at fault in pursuing factional struggles when they should have sought peace. Whoever won would inevitably have set up a monarchy. But "by the will of God" Caesar conquered and afterward sought to regularize his position lawfully and obtain just title. He also ruled justly, showing the virtues of clemency, magnanimity, and love of peace. As a result the people loved Caesar and accepted his rule, whereas the tyrannicides were deeply unpopular, were hounded out of the city, and were soon killed. For Salutati, the loving obedience of the people to Caesar conferred a *post hoc* moral legitimacy on him and indeed on the whole Roman monarchy that sprung from his line.

Salutati is aware that the principle of *iustus metus* invalidates acclamations of the people made under threat of violence, and he considers whether a tyrant may become legitimate by *praescriptio*. Perhaps his rule may be "purified" by the tacit consent of the people over time, after the fear and violence associated with usurpation have died down; perhaps his governance may then come to have the "semblance" of lawful rule.[99] Salutati takes no position on this question, but in the next paragraph he produces a robust defense of a people's right to legitimate a ruler when that right is expressed through the will of a majority:

> On this point I think it should be said that if a people is sovereign and neither has nor recognizes any higher authority [*si sit princeps populus qui superiorem nec habeat nec agnoscat*], the will of the majority validates their action [*quod maior pars populi fecerit ratum esse*]. And if, in a people having sovereign authority, the prince's confirmation ensues, then beyond all doubt the rule in question will be a lawful one. If, however, their consent is defective, as when the people do nothing lawfully, and if the person thus elected begins to govern without waiting for confirmation from the higher authority, then he is a tyrant. On the other hand, if the people acknowledge a prince, but are really without one because he does not rule but stays abroad [i.e., like the German emperor or the pope in Avignon], then perhaps the title may be just until the contrary be declared by the prince.[100]

This reasoning sets up a long historical argument to the effect that Caesar's rule was made legitimate by the will of the people. The people, it is shown, were not forced or cowed into acceptance of his rule but embraced it voluntarily. This key point is corroborated by prudential arguments showing that unity was needed after a long period of partisan strife and that the tyrannicides put the republic at needless risk by fomenting revolution. Their act only prolonged the civil war. Salutati also shows, quoting liberally from the Roman orator's own works, that both Cicero and the tyrannicides in effect recognized the legitimacy of Caesar's rule by accepting offices of state from him and, in Cicero's case, supporting him politically at other times during his rule.

In addition to these legal, historical, and prudential arguments, Salutati also offers what we have called "Greek" arguments based on character. At the very beginning of the treatise he cites (like Bartolus) the famous passage of Pope Gregory the Great, whose definition of tyranny linked both the legal and the ethical understandings of tyranny. In a "Roman" vein, Gregory says, "Properly speaking a tyrant is one who rules a common commonwealth without right [*or unlawfully*]." But then he cuts deeper and finds the roots of tyranny in the sin of pride. Tyranny, indeed, is found in every sinner's heart: "If outward power be lacking, he whose iniquity governs him inwardly is a tyrant at heart; for, although he cannot injure his neighbors outwardly, inwardly he desires to have power that he may injure them."[101] So there is inner and outer tyranny, and Salutati labors to show that Caesar was no more a tyrant inwardly than he was outwardly. This is done by showing in great detail that Caesar possessed the noble virtues of clemency and magnaminity and showed a love of peace and orderly, legal government. Quoting Cicero's own words he notes that "[Caesar] conquered, yet did not excite hatred in his good fortune, but rather allayed it by his leniency."[102] The quasi-royal honors that were heaped on him toward the end of his life, his perpetual dictatorship and the title of *pater patriae,* were conferred with the approval of a grateful citizenry. Salutati concludes:

> Was this title [of king] tyrannical or acquired by violence when it was offered him by a grateful state *(civitas)?* Can a man raised to power through his own merits, a man who showed such a humane spirit, not to his partisans alone but also to his opponents because they were his fellow citizens—can he rightly be called a tyrant? I do not see how this can be maintained, unless indeed we are to pass judgement arbitrarily. We may, therefore, conclude with this proposition: that Caesar was not a tyrant, seeing that he held his supremacy in the common commonwealth [i.e., the Roman Empire] lawfully and not by abuse of law.[103]

Both legal reasoning and the analysis of Caesar's character showed he was no tyrant. What made him legitimate by law was not adherence to Roman republican traditions—Cicero's version of legality—but winning the approval of the vast majority of Romans through beneficent government and charismatic virtue.[104] Salutati thus opens up a route to justified rule and the praise of posterity for Renaissance warlords and other *principes* who acquired power *ex post* by legally dubious means—the same route, what we might call "justified usurpation," that led Julius Caesar to glory. But to become legitimate they would need the virtues acquired through humane studies.

The question of Caesar's right to rule continued to be debated throughout the quattrocento. After Salutati's time the issue of legality was scanted, as one would expect in the discourse of virtue politics. The primary issue became Caesar's personal virtue and its charismatic power of eliciting voluntary, loving obedience from the people of Rome. A secondary issue was whether the rule of the Caesars had really led to the decline of humanistic culture in ancient Rome, as Leonardo Bruni had charged in his *Laudatio Florentine urbis* (1404) and repeated in more sober tones in book 1 of his *History of the Florentine People* (1415 / 1416) as well as in his biography of Petrarch (1436), written in the vernacular.

Thanks to Bruni, Caesar's virtues and the effect of the imperial monarchy on culture became a political issue between humanist partisans of republican and signorial rule. Bruni's friend Poggio took a characteristically extreme position and condemned Caesar's acts as tyrannical with far more vehemence even than Cicero.[105] Guarino of Verona, a humanist in the service of Leonello d'Este, prince of Ferrara, reproved Poggio for his partisanship and defended Caesar's right to rule in terms similar to Salutati's but with a far greater appearance of calm and even-handedness. Quoting Suetonius, he wrote, "Yet as for Caesar, how much he was supported by love and goodwill not just in the case of the people but also among the senatorial order is proven by the following: once, after he had restrained a multitude thronging around him, of their own free will, and uproariously promising their support in asserting his honor, 'the senate offered him thanks through its leading men and, after summoning him to the curia, praised him in the highest terms.'"[106] Guarino gives us more detail about how Caesar's virtue worked in practice to secure the support of the people and the Senate. He won support not only by his virtues of clemency and magnanimity and his readiness to make peace, but also through concrete benefits he bestowed on Rome as a magistrate and his program of adorning the city with beautiful new buildings, not to mention his services to the Latin language and Latin literature.

You [Poggio] seem either not to know or at least not to remember with how many types of liberality and munificence he earned the marvelous affection of the people, *since he understood that this was a not negligible help to those who want to partake in public life, and, as such, must of necessity be procured.* This end was served by the games, the spectacles and feasts, as well as the patronage he offered numerous people and the recommendations of candidates to this or that tribe or for judicial positions or magistracies, and likewise his dexterity, pleasant demeanor, and affability in shaking the hands of his elders, and his regard for and cultivation of the people in every way. It was on account of these virtues that the people, in turn, thought up new honors and magistracies for him, by which to repay such services to them.[107]

Here one glimpses already how the divine reason of the ancient philosophers, the reason that persuades us to virtuous conduct based on an analysis of human flourishing and excellence, blends into instrumental or Machiavellian reason that knows how to shape human conduct so as to bring about the desired political consequences.

Guarino also effectively disposed of Bruni's and Poggio's contention that Latin humanistic culture had flourished under the republic but had been crippled by the rule of the tyrannical Caesars.[108] Poggio in his response merely repeated Bruni's partisan view that the highest literary excellence could only be achieved in a climate of political liberty. He managed to avoid making an assessment of the literary value of patristic literature, all composed under the empire, which might have revealed his negative views about the effects of Christianity on culture.[109]

Poggio on Tyranny and the "Problem of Counsel"

The question whether humanistic literary culture was compatible with tyrannical rule, and more generally whether the humanities could fulfill their promise of civilizing corrupt men in public life, driven as such men were by a desire for wealth and status, became a burning issue in the 1430s and 1440s. This was, perhaps, the first real moment of doubt the humanist political project experienced since Petrarch's notional withdrawal from the world in his *De vita solitaria*.[110] Though this book explores the political teachings of the Italian humanists, it is well to remember that there remained a body of opinion among them that saw literary pursuits as fundamentally incompatible with political life. Such opinions called into question certain assumptions about human psychology central to virtue politics since the time of Petrarch.

The case for pessimism was put in its most uncompromising form in Poggio's dialogue *De infelicitate principum,* set in Florence in 1434 but not published until 1440.[111] The work is mostly devoted to laying out the interlocutor Niccolò Niccoli's extreme thesis that the exercise of political power is always incompatible with personal felicity. This could be demonstrated (he contended) of all *principes,* good or bad, whom Niccoli defines as "emperors, kings, dukes, and other persons who exercise lordship over others."[112] Cosimo de'Medici, one of the interlocutors in the dialogue, is himself described as *in nostra re publica egregium principem* (an eminent leader in our state), and in the course of the dialogue it is made clear that Poggio intends to include oligarchs and republican statesmen in the number of the *principes.*[113] The dialogue is therefore not about the failings of monarchy only but of power-seeking men in general. According to Niccoli, the principal speaker in the dialogue, most *principes* in this wider sense lacked virtue, especially prudence, and were only made worse by the exercise of power. They were therefore unhappy because virtue is necessary (though perhaps not sufficient) for happiness. It is possible, though unlikely, that there could exist a few virtuous princes, but even they won't be happy, because if a prince is truly virtuous, he won't allow himself the pleasures, palaces, and other trappings of wealth and power that most people regard as the prince's source of happiness.[114]

The real message of the dialogue, however, is much more radical. Niccoli, whom Poggio allows to dominate the debate, mounts a powerful argument that the things any lord has to do to maintain his sway over others—who by nature are his equals—are necessarily violent, coercive, and therefore evil. The nature of *principatus* or political domination itself corrupts and ultimately destroys virtue. Poggio makes no distinction between natural superiors and natural inferiors such as is typically found in the Aristotelian political tradition; his view is that all human beings of whatever class are equal in their capacity for virtue.[115] To try to dominate others on the pretext of a presumed superiority of natural character is to deny this form of equality that is characteristic of virtue politics. It is after all an axiom fundamental to virtue politics that human nature is dynamic, not static: it can be improved through education and a virtuous environment. But such education is not possible, for Niccoli, in the case of *principes.* Performing the violent and coercive acts a *princeps* must do to maintain his power has the effect of brutalizing his character and makes him impervious to prudent counsel and the humanizing effects of literature and philosophy. In other words there can be no real differences between good princes and tyrants: all rulers are forced by the nature of domination itself to be tyrants. For a good man to come to power in a principate of any kind is like a good rider attempting to control a wild horse: sooner or later he is going to be thrown.[116]

This radical view naturally raises protests from the other interlocutors in the dialogue, Cosimo de'Medici and his most loyal humanist follower, Carlo Marsuppini.[117] Carlo articulates the conventional distinction between good princes and tyrants. Surely history teaches us that there are many rulers who ruled for the sake of the common good with a power of judgment that is right and just? What about the rulers who were faithful ministers of the laws, sought peace, placed limits on their desires, and cultivated learned men, acting like parents to the peoples they ruled? Furthermore, Carlo argues, either God or nature has implanted within us a natural thirst for preeminence *(principandi appetitum)*: "The soul well instructed by nature, as our Cicero tells us, refuses to be subordinate and desires to lead."[118] This desire for glory and praise is best achieved through the exercise of leadership and power, which in turn brings out all our virtues and superior qualities. The highest forms of virtue require a wider sphere, that of politics, to flourish. To this Aristotelian argument Marsuppini adds the point that even we men of letters provide an example of this natural desire when we compete for preeminence in the humanities, "and indeed we are lifted up with a kind of glory when we excel the rest in prudence, good counsel, learning or artistic merit."

Impulses so natural cannot be evil, Carlo continues. We have natural desires for food, drink, and sex, and such desires are not vicious if enjoyed in the proper way. The fact that they can be abused does not make them wrong, and the fact that power can be abused does not make its exercise intrinsically wrongful. To pay attention only to abuses of power is to ignore all the good things that political power can do:

> What more useful, more desirable thing has God given us, what more conducive to the exercise of the virtues, than that power and capacity by which we are liberal, beneficent, magnificent, by which we are able to secure advantages for many men and to perform acts of piety towards both men and the gods? Through this power it is given us to protect the oppressed, raise up the afflicted, assist the needy, aid our friends, give rewards to the virtuous, and benefit as many people as possible. So, [Niccoli], stop saying that a position of leadership [*principatus*] is by nature evil, since it provides so great a capacity to do good, or that it is a cause of infelicity, [which is not the case] except when it is offered to evil men.[119]

Niccoli responds to this reassertion of conventional humanist wisdom by re-iterating the point made by Petrarch, that some with the title of king act like ty-rants, and some who are called tyrants act in a kingly way: "I don't know who these men are you are calling tyrants. We know this for sure, that some of them exer-cised a power that was better and more just towards their subjects than that of kings. A king is to be recognized not by the name, but by the deed."[120]

But Niccoli takes this observation, a staple in virtue politics, in a direction quite different from that of Petrarch. Petrarch had blurred the distinction between rightful rule and tyranny in order to dismiss the importance of legal titles and to demand virtue of those who aspired to political power. Niccoli uses it to claim that all princes who exercise power over others are no better than tyrants.[121] In ancient times, he says, the name of king was considered sacrosanct, so long as kings were content with what belonged to them, but over time corruption set in. The name kept its luster, but the reality disappeared and turned into tyranny. History and reason teach us that the possession of *principatus* makes its possessors wicked and *principatus* as such an evil thing.

Cosimo de'Medici protests this sweeping judgment, raising the issue of the good emperors like "the divine Augustus," Vespasian, Titus, and the Antonines. Were they not good princes? Niccoli in reply begins by conceding that some, though very few, among the emperors and other princes in antiquity (he refuses to discuss the princes of modern times) were good men. Yet even in those palmy times good princes were rarer than the phoenix or the Stoic wise man "who has never yet been found." A good prince is a "monstrosity" of nature, like reported cases of children born with the head of a dog or a cat. He then goes on to subvert even this slight concession by discussing concrete cases of "good" rulers. His strategy is to admit that historians classed them as good rulers but then to cast doubt on the veracity or sincerity of historians like Valerius Maximus, "the most sycophantic of all sycophants," who lied about Julius Caesar to curry favor with Tiberius. More-over, the so-called good rulers were often, in fact, not very good. Augustus, "cel-ebrated by all the ages," beloved of Petrarch as the ideal ruler, in his early career was unsparing in his cruelty, and as one of the Triumvirate "exceeded the mean in proscribing citizens." Some citizens he even took the trouble to name personally so that he could plunder their estates, "removing those who wanted to save the commonwealth and who stood in the way of his lusts." Together with Antony and Lepidus he took away Rome's freedom: "I shall pass over his betrayal of his country, by whom he was armed and raised to power through the efforts of Cicero [!], but turned both his arms and his power against its vitals to his country's destruction.

Then, removing one of his associates from power using the authority of the Senate and killing the other, he achieved sole power by wading through the blood of citizens."[122] Similar strategies are used to discount other examples of good rulers. Robert of Naples, the ideal modern ruler admired by Petrarch and Boccaccio, was "laudable in many ways," but Niccoli can't resist pointing out that he was also avaricious. Other famous rulers such as Alexander the Great and Julius Caesar were straightforwardly wicked, cruel, and bloody men. Good men like the Antonine rulers of Rome did come to power, but it made them miserable to be forced into wicked acts, and they longed to escape into philosophy and private life.

But what about Christian rulers? asks Carlo. Surely their Christianity made them better? What you say may be true of barbarians in our time, but "the faith of Christ has made our rulers more humane and more temperate, and distanced them from cruelty." Niccoli replies, "Such vices were common both to barbarians and to Latins and Greeks. In more recent times we see fratricidal strife among the Italians in pursuit of domination, and in France, Germany, Spain, and Britain there have been disastrous civil wars that spared no one, even those connected by ties of blood."[123] The implication, that Christians in recent times have behaved no better than pagans, goes unstated, but it is plain enough. Niccoli allows that history praises certain Hebrew and Christian rulers—slyly pointing out, however, that even King David was a rapist and a homicide—but when rulers such as Charlemagne have achieved *felicitas,* it is a gift of God and not the result of good rulership. If there is any good ruler, he is a slave *(mancipium)* of the state and not its master, and therefore not *felix. Principatus* is simply not compatible with *felicitas,* a concept variously assimilated to Aristotle's *eudaimonia* or the Stoic's *honestum.* Even moderately good men cannot flourish as lords; there are no compromises. The argument works both ways, going also to prove that no prince can be good, since felicity is an effect of virtue and felicity requires tranquillity of soul, which is unobtainable amid the turbulence, back-stabbing, self-promotion, fear, and hatred inseparable from court life, whether the formal court of a prince or the informal court of a powerful man and his hangers-on. There are just too many temptations to vice, and disordered desires are too easy to satisfy. Power corrupts. Human beings, like Gyges in Plato's *Republic,* are simply not built to resist the inflamed lusts made possible by the extraordinary power *principatus* gives them.

Poggio's dynamic view of princely personality and the way it is twisted by the court environment and the actions forced upon it by the logic of holding on to power raises in acute form what may be called "the problem of counsel." It is a problem that later, in the sixteenth century, will be at the heart of More's *Utopia* and Castiglione's *Courtier.* Given the atmosphere of court life, the prince can have no real friends who will tell him the truth and correct him when he is wrong. He attracts and embraces four sorts of men: toadies and flatterers, "fierce enemies of truth-telling" who corrupt the prince's mind to the point of insanity; ministers of pleasure and luxury who lurk in dark corners of his palace and give him counsels that cannot be spoken in the light of day; bankers, moneylenders, and tax-gatherers who lead the prince to despoil his people; and informers, *delatores,* who poison the prince's mind against good men.

What this means for Niccoli is that the whole project of humanist virtue politics is simply impossible. Princes have no use for the wise and the learned: "For the sake of the wise and learned I wish that princes *did* devote themselves to wisdom and obey its precepts. But since they have no concern for wisdom, they cannot even understand the virtues or make use of their help in their lives. Virtue flees ignorance and holds on to reason and wisdom. Since ignorance is the intimate companion of princes *(principum contubernalis),* they necessarily lack the virtues."[124] The wise and the good see too easily through the prince's mask of virtue, through the fine clothes and jewels and palaces and all the magnificence that impress the vulgar. *Non amant principes nisi suis moribus congruentes.* Princes only love men who fit their own mores, and these do not include the humanist educator. They hate truth and virtue, and they don't want wise counsel. They have never really favored learned men, despite the pieties of humanist educators. To the humanist educator's stock listing of the great men of antiquity who were advised by the wise and the good—Pericles by Anaxagoras, Dion by Plato, Alexander by Aristotle, Scipio by Panaetius, and so forth[125]—Niccoli juxtaposes his own anti-canon of rulers who persecuted men of wisdom and letters: Plato was sold into slavery by Dionysius, Callisthenes was murdered by Alexander, Zeno was cruelly tortured by Phalaris, Nero compelled Seneca and Lucan to take their own lives, Theodoric had Boethius put to death. Even Augustus, said by Petrarch to be the greatest of all patrons of literature, drove Ovid into exile. Niccoli goes so far as to claim, in defiance of well-known facts—recently documented in biographies by Leonardo Bruni—that Dante, Petrarch, and Boccaccio were neglected and insufficiently rewarded by the princes they served.

Niccoli's conclusion is that humanists should forget about counseling princes and avoid familiarity *(consuetudo)* with them. True virtue lives only among *privati,* private men who cultivate among themselves wise philosophy, the liberal arts, and humanity. As Petrarch recommends in the *De vita solitaria,* they should stay away from politics and cultivate the humanities. The virtues never enter the prince's door, but if by chance they do, they are compelled to flee at the sight of the vices they see within. The virtues dwell rather with private men among whom the desire for wisdom and learning remains vigorous, men who devote themselves to literature and whose souls are far from lust and ambition, men who are content with their own goods and do not desire those of others. Men of letters have taught us the arts of living a good life, have a true understanding of laws and polities, and provide remedies for us in fortune good and bad. They are the "priests of the virtues," lovers of peace and quiet, who alone have obtained felicity. "Thus if anyone should want felicity, he should understand that it is not to be found in political power *(in principatu)* but in virtue and the blessed life."[126]

Niccolò Niccoli was in real life a private man who avoided public office (and was blamed for it by Leonardo Bruni).[127] Poggio was not. He was the servant of a series of absolute princes, the seven popes from Boniface IX to Nicholas V, and he later became chancellor of Florence, a high minister of state under the Medici. He had, to be sure, a sentimental attachment to republican government, and a kind of egalitarianism underlies his political psychology. For him it is ultimately the natural equality of men that makes tyrants of those who try to dominate others. (Like Machiavelli, he avoids framing the issue as one of abstract justice or right.[128]) But Poggio was also a realistic observer of his times and understood who ran the city-states of Italy and the sort of people they were. In the *De infelicitate principum* he is certainly not defending republican government, even if at one point he remarks that philosophers and literary men preferred to live in free cities like Athens and republican Rome. (Florence, tellingly, is not mentioned.) As if to make the point that he is not defending republics, the interlocutor Niccoli is made to say that the one prince of modern times who truly supported men of learning was Giangaleazzo Visconti, the "tyrant" of Milan, officially hated by the Florentines as the enemy of their *libertas.*[129]

Thus the most devastating attack on princely and oligarchic government of the quattrocento was written not to promote the cause of popular government, but to justify and recommend the withdrawal of humanists from the councils of power. They should cultivate wisdom, virtue, and the disciplines as private individuals and pass them on to other private individuals. How much Poggio himself believed the case he made so powerfully through the mouth of Niccoli must be a matter of conjecture. The case was, after all, an extreme one, and the text betrays numerous signs of exaggeration for rhetorical effect.[130] But as we shall see, it was a case that nevertheless required refutation by those who believed that the humanities could be deployed to instill virtue and wisdom in the *principes* of republics. It became imperative for advocates of virtue politics to show why not all princes were necessarily tyrants.[131]

Pier Candido Decembrio on the Virtues of a Tyrant

The "Greek" view of tyranny embraced by the humanists involved various forms of realism. For Petrarch it meant realism about legitimate titles to power: a high-sounding title did not make you a good lord, and lack of one did not make you a bad one. For Salutati charismatic virtue made it possible for even a usurper like Caesar to acquire moral legitimacy. Salutati challenged the jurists' rejection of all forms of usurpation and their tendency to reduce legitimacy to mere legality. His recognition that virtuous rule could create its own legitimacy in the hearts of the people was another form of realism. Poggio's realism about the corrupting effects of power intrinsic to *principatus,* by contrast, was directed against the optimism of humanist virtue politics. The conviction of Petrarchan humanists that forming a prince's character through education in the humanities, then constraining him by a culture of noble examples—the spur of praise and the whip of blame—for Poggio's Niccolò Niccoli could never stand up to the structural reality of princely power. Power corrupts, and inordinate power would inevitably turn a prince into a tyrant. Even lesser forms of coercive power, when exercised unwillingly over equals, were corrupting as well.[132]

With Pier Candido Decembrio's *Life of Filippo Maria Visconti, Duke of Milan,* we encounter a fourth form of realism, one that points us forward to the view of tyrannical power adopted by Machiavelli. Decembrio's *Life,* the most remarkable portrait of a tyrant prince produced in the Renaissance, was written in the months following Visconti's death on August 13, 1447. It was the fruit of Decembrio's twenty-eight years of service in the duke's inner circle as secretary, diplomatic envoy, and literary factotum.[133] The work was an intimate biography that followed the example of Suetonius in portraying its subject "warts and all." Yet to use that cliché filters out the most striking aspect of the life, which is its refusal of the standard humanist economy of praise and blame. Decembrio attaches no value to the principle of *esse non videri,* of actually being what you pretend to be, a principle central to ancient virtue ethics. Nor does he distinguish between good fame and bad in the manner of Petrarch or Boccaccio. His presentation of Filippo Maria avoids drawing moral conclusions and is often almost clinically detached. Visconti is neither an ideal prince nor a wicked tyrant; morally speaking, he is something in between. His legitimacy is not moral legitimacy, at least not in the conventional sense, but is owed to his ancestry and military prowess. He has some virtues that can be imitated, but they are products of a deeply flawed personality that is difficult to admire. Some of his virtues express innate good qualities of character, but more often they are patterns of behavior instrumentalized to maintain his power and status. From the optic of power politics, his virtues are often hard to distinguish from the tyrannical arts of rule he deployed. And he has certain skills as a ruler, the products of his *ingenium,* that defy classification as moral qualities at all.

To begin with his virtues, Decembrio tells us that Filippo Maria had some good qualities of character that were reflected in his habits of rule. He had an inborn reverence *(pietas)* for his parents and relations, but this could lead him into extravagant acts of revenge when they were dishonored. He had a religious nature and cultivated the favor of the popes, and "although the logic of war forced him into a posture of hostility towards the Church, he placed personal advantage second behind his devotion to religious principle." Decembrio gives some dubious examples of how Visconti sacrificed his own interests to those of the popes. By nature he was kind and affable, but he was forced by paranoia to limit and control access to his person; it was hard to win his trust. He had a natural sympathy for the underdog, favoring the defeated and resisting the victorious. He seemed to be genuinely religious, though his religion was external, transactional, and superstitious— he liked to keep count, for example, of all the prayers he had said. His piety was not an expression of inner conviction or friendship with God. For the most part he controlled his anger and (as Seneca advised) never punished anyone when he was angry. He met his end bravely, despite having lived most of his life in terror of assassination.

Others among his virtues and princely arts Decembrio presents as strategems for maintaining and increasing power. Filippo Maria showed Caesar's most famous virtue, *clementia,* which won him fame and the admiration even of infidel princes. He was celebrated above all for his generous treatment of Alfonso of Aragon and his leading men after they were captured in the Battle of Ponza in 1435. Yet Filippo Maria soon afterward exploited his newly won favor with Alfonso to form an alliance with him against the house of Anjou, the Venetians, and the pope. His famous acts of clemency did not proceed from a fixed habit of virtue, since sometimes he ruled gently, sometimes harshly. He imitated Augustus to some extent in restoring churches, but his building projects seemed mostly to have been undertaken for his personal pleasure and were remarkable for their expense and elegance. Decembrio remarks that the duke did not take good care of his capital Milan because he did not personally spend much time within the city, but he at least paved the streets, sponsored public entertainments, and took measures against plague. He had real skill at winning people's goodwill *(benivolentia),* but this was not love inspired by charismatic virtue as in Cicero's *De officiis;* rather, it was engendered by respect for his good fortune and gratitude for concrete benefits. After his death, the people of Milan, "elated to see their prince taken from them," instantly held an assembly and reclaimed their liberty. This is the last line of the biography and underlines that, whatever the *benivolentia* Filippo Maria enjoyed, it did not extend beyond his person to his house or his regime. Decembrio tells us how the duke would bring the leading men of Milan into his council chamber and make a show of seeking their advice about his plans for war. "In this way he made his subjects more willing to foot the bill for war." This practice made almost a mockery of the Roman-law principle of the obligation to consult those affected by a decision.[134] Yet he also chose good officials and watched over them, punishing them when they indulged in any irregularities. However, Decembrio notes, sometimes, when under extreme financial pressure, he was willing to sell offices. The light of virtue, as always in this biography, is shaded by self-interest.

Filippo Maria lost a number of battles, but, all in all, considering that he had begun as a dispossessed prince reduced almost to the condition of private citizen, his military achievement in reconstituting the empire of his father Giangaleazzo was extraordinary. This was no accident but a result of his devotion to military affairs, which he considered the most important means of maintaining his power. He employed the best *condottieri* of his day and had some success in retaining their loyalty by offering ample rewards and even, in the case of Francesco Sforza, his daughter's hand in marriage. Like the Julius Caesar presented in Petrarch's biography, he paid no attention to the social origins of his captains and would elevate the worthy among them in accordance with their merit. In his earlier days he went into battle with his troops, a form of leadership always admired in the Western tradition, but as he grew older he withdrew to safety and relied on reports from the battlefield.

The limits of Filippo Maria's virtue and piety are nicely illustrated in an anecdote presented by Decembrio as an example of the duke's wit. As a practical joke,

Filippo wrote to Pope Eugene IV "pretending to be at death's door" and terrified of punishment in the afterlife. He asked the pope what act of restitution he might make to save his soul. The pope wrote back with the highly self-interested if not positively cynical suggestion that he might turn over to papal control some of his fortified towns. Filippo Maria responded, "Well might he value his body less than his soul, but he held the prestige of his lordship *(status dominatus sui)* to be far more important than the salvation of either body or soul." The anecdote provides a mocking contrast, perhaps intentional, with a famous story told about Cosimo de'Medici. The Florentine merchant prince too sought Eugene's advice on an act of restitution he might make for any usurious injustices he might have committed as a merchant banker. Eugene advised him to rebuild the ruined church of San Marco, which Cosimo duly accomplished with the greatest magnificence.[135]

In addition to these ambiguous examples of princely virtue, Decembrio's *Life* also presents features of Visconti's character and habits that were more straightforwardly those of a tyrant according to the ancient Greek conception. Filippo Maria made war for the sake of domination and never showed the slightest interest in peace except as another strategy of power. His settled view was that diplomacy was useless and the ends of power were best achieved by military force. In this he violated the sacred Ciceronian principle that war should be made only to secure peace.[136] Visconti also made regular use of treachery and fraud to achieve his ends. He would break a treaty whenever doing so was to his advantage. He was cryptic in his communications, leaving his meaning ambiguous—a well-known characteristic of ancient tyrants.[137] Another of the extraordinary skills that showed his *ingenium* was his mastery of dissimulation. No one could penetrate to his secret thoughts, but he knew the thoughts of others. He spied on everyone. He spied on his commanders, bribing their secretaries for information; he spied on his ministers; he spied on his wife; he spied on his mistress through her confessor; he even spied on his spies. Decembrio openly praises Filippo Maria for the effectiveness of his spy network. "Never did he trust any of his people so completely that he forgot to distrust them even more," he writes with seeming approval.

The duke, moreover, had little respect for legal processes and would imprison men secretly for years, even announcing that they had died when they were still alive. He was unbelievably paranoid and would sleep with constantly changing relays of guards and birds trained to chatter if anyone approached his bed. He controlled the marriages of his subordinates and monopolized the distribution of offices and benefices. Most shockingly to contemporary sensibilities was his family life and sexual mores. He had his wife tortured and killed for adultery—an act of supreme ingratitude, given that he owed his state to her—while he himself enjoyed the services of squadrons of young boys.[138] Some of these became favorites and were given positions of authority; some of them (according to Decembrio) even deserved those positions and performed well in them.

The duke's attitude to merit presents a marked contrast with the pieties of virtue politics and sometimes appears, from that perspective, to be utterly perverse. Filippo Maria had no respect, Decembrio said, for the possession of merit as such (*nullo meritorum habitu respectu*); virtue in a man could be useful, but so could vice. The problem for Visconti was to know whether a man's virtues—particularly the virtue of loyalty—were genuine or whether vices lurked under a cloak of hypocrisy. So he devised various tests of character:

> We know of no prince in history so skilled in assessing the loyalty of his dependents that he could outrank Filippo Maria in shrewdness and cunning. In this area the Duke truly perfected techniques of the most exquisite and refined kind imaginable. He was quite capable, in order to get to the bottom of someone's character, of thinking up some clever plan appropriate to the case. He used to say that there was no one in his entourage who could keep a secret from him, for anytime he wanted he could shake it out of them, or, to use his own words, he could force them "to cough up what was eating them." . . . He might for example pick out someone at court who had an outstanding reputation in some field of endeavor and demote him. He would then go around singing the fallen man's praises to the skies, leaving people to wonder at his saying one thing and doing its opposite. But in fact the whole show was calculated to torment his listeners into thinking that they might be next in line to lose his favor.
>
> There was one category of men for whom he devised a test with an entirely new twist, for he would take those who preached moderation and dangle the prospect of pleasure before their eyes, just to see whether they were really able to resist temptation. He might bring a man of this kind into contact with his harem of young boys, for example, on the pretext of getting him to educate one of the more lascivious among the bunch. The preceptor would be hived off with his pupil in some very private place, one most propitious for mischief. Then his dealings with the boy would be observed through a peephole by some of the duke's men, to see whether he tried any funny business, or made any nasty moves.[139]

Visconti's goal was not to promote merit as such but to know men's characters so that he could make the best use of them.

Men of letters were a special category, and here too Filippo Maria fits the norm neither of the virtuous prince nor the tyrant. "As for humanists and men of learning," Decembrio writes, "he neither held them in contempt, nor accorded them any particular place of honor at his court. He was more an admirer of their accomplishments than a patron or supporter of their work." He did not always appreciate their virtue or their services to him, as in the case of Decembrio's friend, the humanist friar Antonio da Rho. But sometimes his suspicion and neglect of them, as in the cases of Francesco Filelfo and Cyriac of Ancona (both Decembrio's own bitter enemies), was well founded.

Filippo Maria himself had not enjoyed the benefit of a humanist education, but Decembrio never remarks on that as an advantage or disadvantage (though in his other works, particularly his correspondence, Decembrio made due obeisance to the moral value of a humanist education). Visconti had some good men among his counselors, some of whom were interested in humanist culture, but Decembrio never connects their literary culture with the quality of their counsel. Filippo Maria's own diversions were typical of the princes of his day: hunting, gaming, banqueting, collecting curiosities, listening to stories. "He also enjoyed reading the French *chansons de gestes* that spin such tall tales regarding the heroes of old." His exposure to humanist culture, such as it was, came from Petrarch's sonnets and from Dante, as well as through vernacular translations of classical writers. His knowledge of Latin was limited: "He listened to readings from Livy as well, but in no particular order, preferring rather to select the highlights, and to home in on the passages he found to be most instructive. . . . He listened with great delight as well to histories relating the deeds of famous men, whether in their established vernacular versions, or as translated by humanists from the Latin."[140] We might like to postulate some positive moral influence of this reading on Visconti, despite the man's grievous defects of character, but Decembrio does not license us to do so. He never tells us that the duke's virtues were imitated from ancient examples found in his vernacular classics, nor that they were strengthened by heeding wise humanist counselors. His virtues, such as they were, seem strictly subordinated to the overriding goal of maintaining the *status dominatus sui.*

In short, Decembrio's portrait does not represent for us *in purezza* either a virtuous humanist prince or a tyrant. He admires his former master as a fine example of what modern political theorists might call transactional leadership. He does not inspire because of his vision or his virtues, but he has high levels of competence in matters of state and gets the job done. If he enjoys a measure of legitimacy, it is the contingent form known as "performance legitimacy"; it falls short of moral legitimacy.[141] Filippo Maria's principal mission in life was to reconstitute Visconti power and the Milanese state that had collapsed after the sudden death of his father Giangaleazzo in 1402. In this he was brilliantly successful, despite temporary failures and setbacks. That was a sort of *virtù* we can properly call Machiavellian.[142] Decembrio's *Life of Filippo Maria Visconti* thus presents us with the possibility that a ruler with grave moral defects, pursuing nothing but personal ends of power, might be good not only for his own *status dominatus* but for the state, considered more abstractly, and good not only for himself but also for his people.

The Recovery of Ancient Greek Sources on Tyranny

It took another two generations before a new kind of humanist advisor, exemplified by Niccolò Machiavelli, was ready to organize the techniques of power into a science of politics. What happened in Italy between the death of Filippo Maria Visconti in 1447 and the composition of the *Prince* around 1513 to open up this new, more realistic direction in political prudence? As we shall see in Chapter 19, Machiavelli's revolution in political thought was conditioned to a great extent by the political and military humiliation of Florence and Italy resulting from the invasions of the peninsula by foreign powers in the *calamità d'Italia* after 1494. But in the realm of intellect and letters as well there were developments that stimulated Machiavellian forms of realism about political power.

One development, undervalued in modern Anglophone scholarship on Machiavelli, was the ongoing recovery of the ancient Greek "discourse of tyranny" during the quattrocento.[143] The Greek sources that gradually became available in Latin tended to blur the distinction between monstrous and benign modes of tyranny sketched by Aristotle in that famous chapter (5.9) of his *Politics*. As the new sources began to give color and nuance to the bare outlines of Aristotle's account, both modes yielded more subtle colorings and a more refined sense of their moral dynamics—the inevitable result of their portrayal within complex historical narratives.

Some ancient sources, to be sure, presented little more than a caricature. The tyrant was often presented as a moral monster who came to power against the will of his subjects, typically by means of a military coup. He was an isolated outsider who ruled with the help of other outsiders and marginals. He paralyzed normal political life and favored no one faction; he was completely unaccountable and bound only by his lusts. He was distrustful of the people he ruled and took away their arms. He was cunning and deceitful, cryptic in his communications and a dissembler. He was transgressive when it came to traditional mores, particularly sexual and familial mores. He was sacrilegious as well, committing crimes in sacred places, plundering sanctuaries, violating the right of asylum. In numerous ancient accounts tyrants were seen as natural enemies of the gods and were ultimately punished by them, a satisfying outcome that provided their stories with an appropriate moral. Above all, tyrants were cruel and violent. They often put on spectacular shows of public cruelty to overawe their subjects. The most famous example in Graeco-Roman literature was the "bull of Phalaris," an instrument of torture said to have been employed by the sixth-century BC Sicilian tyrant of that name. It consisted of a hollow brazen bull with special pipes installed, built to order for the tyrant by the craftsman Perilaos. Phalaris, according to the legend, liked to shut a victim inside and burn him alive; the pipes would turn his screams, divertingly (for the tyrant), into the mooing of a bull. To show the arbitrary character of the tyrant's punishments, the story has Perilaos become, in defiance of the laws of gratitude, the first victim of his own art.

Humanists at the beginning of the fifteenth century were aware of this caricature of ancient Greek tyranny thanks to many scattered allusions to famous tyrants in Latin literature, particularly in the works of Cicero, Valerius Maximus, and Seneca. They had possessed since the late thirteenth century the key analyses of tyranny in Aristotle's *Politics,* translated by William of Moerbeke for Aquinas, and after 1438 they had Leonardo Bruni's far superior translation, which thereafter remained standard to the end of the sixteenth century.[144] Nevertheless, their view of the ancient Greek discourse of tyranny was vastly enriched in the course of the quattrocento by the importation of Greek texts from the Byzantine East and their translation into Latin. Plato's *Republic,* the philosopher's most profound if not his only attack on the tyrannic character, was translated four times in the fifteenth century, beginning with the Latin version of the Greek émigré Manuel Chrysoloras and his pupil Uberto December in 1402.[145] The humanists learned much more about the most famous ancient example of "monstrous" tyranny, Dionysius of Syracuse, from the collection of thirteen letters of Plato (probably pseudonymous, though not recognized as such during the Renaissance), translated by Leonardo Bruni between 1427 and 1434.[146]

But the most important new source, whose reception in the quattrocento has received scant attention from historians of political thought, was the *Histories* of

Herodotus. Though there was interest in this text from at least the 1420s, the first widely circulated translation into Latin was that of Lorenzo Valla, commissioned by Pope Nicholas V in 1453 and finished by 1455.[147] The recovery of Herodotus was epoch-making for Western understanding of ancient Greek tyranny. He provided European scholars with their first narrative accounts of archaic tyrannies, accounts which allowed humanists in the Latin West to move beyond the theoretical discussions of Plato and Aristotle and to form some notion of how tyranny had evolved historically within concrete social and political contexts.[148] Like Plato and Aristotle, Herodotus presented tyranny as a negation of normal city-state politics, incompatible with freedom and the rule of law. Like them, he was on the whole not concerned with questions of legitimacy. Unlike the fourth-century BC philosophers, however, Herodotus (like other writers before the fourth century) did not distinguish between "true" kingship and tyranny. For him, all forms of autocracy were debased and barbarous. Nor did he trace the cause of tyranny to the evil personality of the tyrant. Rather, more like Poggio, he saw the conditions and actions necessary to sustain absolute one-man rule, the violence and oppression inseparable from the exercise of great power, as the true source of tyranny. The tyrant wanted to hold onto power, and the tyrannical actions that followed from that objective were born of rational calculation and persuasion. Absolute rule lacked accountability (it is *aneuthunos,* 3.80) and isolated the tyrant from his people—even physically, in the form of the fortresses that protected him from the hostility of the populace (1.86–100). The fullness of a tyrant's power would drive even the best men out of their minds, says Otanes in the famous "debate on constitutions" (3.80.3). In general, however, Herodotus did not present the tyrant as a monster but as a talented individual motivated by selfish concerns. Once established, monarchical power led inevitably to the moral decay of the monarch. Its very nature forced him to become unjust, bloodthirsty, and wasteful. Herodotus emphasized "the tendency of powerful autocratic regimes to become more powerful still and to transgress more and more against the persons of those they rule[d] in the process." Such tyrannical regimes could include empires, even when the empire was controlled by a democratic regime, such as the Athenian empire under the fifth-century Athenian democracy.[149]

As Carolyn Dewald has pointed out, however, Herodotus' overall attitude of hostility to one-man rule is qualified by his descriptions of individual tyrants. For example, in the account of Deioces (1.96–100), who was "in love with tyranny," Herodotus explains the tyrant's rise to power as resulting from his reputation as an honest and just judge, which won him the support of the people. When De-ioces withdrew his services as a judge, the people of Media decided to make him their king, with the full understanding that the price of effective justice would be a harsher form of rule. Again, in his account of Pisistratus, the tyrant of Athens, Herodotus presented his tyranny as initially benign: "Pisistratus ruled the Athenians, disturbing in no way the order of offices nor changing the laws, but governing the city according to its established constitution and ordering all things fairly and well" (1.59). It was only on his second and third return to power that his actions became more tyrannical and began to undermine the Athenian spirit of freedom.

These more qualified accounts of tyranny bring us to the second mode of holding tyrannical power, referred to earlier as "benign tyranny." As discussed at the beginning of the chapter, the most important analyses of benign tyranny were found in Xenophon's *Hiero* and Aristotle's *Politics* 5.9. The *Hiero,* made available in a popular translation by Leonardo Bruni in 1403, argues that the tyrant should maintain his power by adopting selectively features of good rulership.[150] In addition, during the second half of the quattrocento, the idea that tyranny could take benign forms became more familiar thanks to the recovery of what has been called the "philotyrannical literature" of the Second Sophistic. The Second Sophistic refers to the revival of Greek higher education and literature, especially oratory, during the early imperial period of ancient Rome.[151] Philotyrannical writings, which formed a popular subgenre of imperial Greek literature, allowed the rhetor to display his cleverness by making a plausible defense of the indefensible. The infamous tyrant Phalaris was a popular subject for this sort of rhetorical tour de force. Lucian wrote two discourses entitled *Phalaris,* the more substantial of which purported to be a letter from the tyrant to the priests of Apollo in Delphi presenting them with his famous bronze bull as a gift offering. Phalaris explains that, despite its evil reputation, the bull can serve as a holy object since it was in fact only used once, to punish its wicked creator Perilaos. Phalaris then presents himself as an advocate of humane punishment and claims that the practice of spying on his subjects (which he was supposed to have invented) was done out of kindness and concern for their welfare.[152]

The most important philotyrannical text for the Renaissance was the *Letters of Phalaris,* a collection probably written around 190 AD under the influence of Lucian. The *Letters* were translated into Latin around the middle of the quattrocento by the humanist Francesco Griffolini of Arezzo and dedicated to the condottiere and enlightened *signore* of Cesena, Malatesta Novello (d. 1465), brother of the notorious Sigismondo Malatesta. They quickly became extraordinarily popular. They were copied in manuscript hundreds of times, translated into Italian, and had gone through thirty-two editions already by 1500. In the letters Phalaris emerges as a man of noble spirit and generosity, a just and benevolent ruler, a patron of poets and philosophers, as well as himself a lover of study and the Muses.

It is crucial to their reception that the translator Griffolini did not question the attribution of the letters to the real Phalaris, tyrant of Akragas (c. 570–554 BC).[153] In his preface to the collection he writes that Cicero and Valerius Maximus unjustly presented Phalaris as a cruel tyrant. In fact no Latin author had any idea who Phalaris really was, he says, and Eusebius' chronicle (in Jerome's excerpts) gave only the vaguest indication of the time when he lived. Griffolini claims he is publishing Phalaris' correspondence in Latin in order to set the record straight. He blames the "negligence and ingratitude" of earlier generations for unjustly reducing a fine ruler such as Phalaris to a mere byword for cruelty. It was a malignant judge who failed to balance the good with the bad and who did not consider the reasons why a ruler might use means that appeared cruel to those distant from the actual circumstances of his rule. Phalaris showed less cruelty toward those who had plotted against him than learned men had shown toward Phalaris in their writings. Possibly with Herodotus in mind, he claims that letters are the most trustworthy of genres *(scribendi genera)* and provide a clearer view of historical truth than histories do. The latter are inferior records of the past, being subject to the interests and partisanship of historians and the relative distance of the latter from events. By contrast, even if there can be dissimulation in personal letters, Griffolini says, a perceptive reader will be able to tell from the consistency of tone the sort of man their writer was; he can assess firsthand his *ingenium*. In the case of the Phalaris letters there can be no doubt that their author was sincere in his noble sentiments, a man of courage and independence, pious toward his country and the gods, full of prudence and wisdom. It is no wonder that the letters of Phalaris came to be read in the High Renaissance as a kind of "mirror of tyrants," a guide to the ways a tyrant can hold power well and remain respected, even loved.

Thus in the philotyrannical literature of the Second Sophistic we have a view of tyranny that virtually abolishes the distinction between good kings and tyrants. Unlike in the case of Machiavelli, however, the distinction is wiped out through rhetorical sleight of hand, without sacrificing the principle that no one can rule well without *virtus*—in the traditional understanding of that word. The *Letters of*

Phalaris went beyond the theory of benign tyranny in Xenophon and Aristotle, which made good rulership into a strategy of power. They suggested instead that a reputation for tyranny could be a mere matter of perception, a false judgment made by careless scholars imperfectly acquainted with the facts.

But the new Greek sources that helped blur the distinction between good and bad tyranny were not the whole story. The most prestigious Greek authorities on virtue politics in the Renaissance—Plato, Aristotle, Xenophon, and Isocrates—theorized instead a strong distinction between the arbitrary and immoral government of the tyrant and virtuous monarchy under a superior human being. As we shall see in Chapter 17, reflection on these authorities would lead the literati of the fifteenth and sixteenth centuries to propose a humanist version of what in later times came to be called absolutism.

CHAPTER 5

THE TRIUMPH OF VIRTUE

Petrarch's Political Thought

Francesco Petrarch is generally acknowledged to be a central figure in the cultural history of the West, the archetypal scholar-poet of the Renaissance, the *fons et origo* of humanism as a movement to reform education and transform culture. His central role in shaping the paideuma of Renaissance humanism has been described in Chapter 1. Petrarch does not, however, loom large in histories of political thought. To be sure, there is a considerable literature in Italian on *Petrarca politico,* but for the most part it is occupied with questions concerning the humanist's political engagement and its evolution over the course of his long career.[1]

Up to a point this neglect is understandable. Petrarch's own political thought hardly rises to the level of theory. The modern historian of political philosophy, used to his Aristotle or Hobbes, may find the great humanist's undulating periods, unrolling as they appear to do an endless tapestry of classical commonplaces and sonorous platitudes, unenlivened by analysis, to be unrewarding. In the passages where he seems to engage most with political ideas he may appear to act as little more than a transmitter of long-standing cultural memes, often seemingly contradictory, such as the *renovatio rei publicae Romanae* or the Senecan virtues of the *princeps.* As a political theorist, he was a fine poet, one is tempted to say. He was more original and more influential as a voice for Italian unity and patriotism, but his eloquence on the theme of *Italia mia* seems less a theoretical position than a utopian dream of the future, inspired by an idealized Roman past.[2] Yet Petrarch did think deeply about politics, and his political principles acquired a certain shape and consistency over the last decades of his life. His political philosophy, if we can give it so high a name, was never a mere ideology, a justification of partisan commitments and interests. It was, in a sense, as Albert Ascoli has written, a "private politics," a politics evolved from his personal loves and hatreds and convictions.[3] But it was also to become, in the quattrocento, the politics of the humanist movement as a whole.

In the standard account of quattrocento humanist political thought, going back to the writings of Hans Baron and Eugenio Garin in the 1930s and elaborated in the following decades by Baron's followers and later by the so-called Cambridge School, the emphasis on civic humanism, republicanism, the *vivere civile,* and popular liberty in some Italian city-states, principally Florence, left Petrarch's political thought in a kind of historical cul-de-sac.[4] He was acknowledged as among the founders of the humanist movement, but his political attitudes were held to be rooted in the medieval past.[5] His own mature politics were read as quietist, the opposite of the *engagé* civic humanists of the quattrocento, fiery partisans of republican government.[6] He did not utter the word "liberty" with nearly enough frequency or fervor to please modern students of republicanism. His failure to make a firm ideological commitment to non-monarchical regimes, his inability to shake off the spell of the universal authorities of the Middle Ages, the empire, and the papacy, and his quasi-monastic view of literary studies and praise of the *vita solitaria* combined to exclude him from what has long been presented as the central narrative of Renaissance political thought. There are important recent exceptions to this narrative, and Peter Stacey in particular has made a case for Petrarch's key role in the Renaissance transmission of Roman ideas about monarchy.[7] My aim here is to widen the project of recovering Petrarch as a Renaissance political thinker. I will argue that Petrarch's political thought floats comfortably in the mainstream of humanist political theory and indeed, to put the claim more strongly, that it should be considered the wellspring of humanist virtue politics.

Petrarch's Politics of Virtue

Petrarch's life and career in many ways set the pattern for humanist literati of the quattrocento. He alternated between living as a familiar of great churchmen, serving as an ornament of princely regimes, and enjoying a life of literary *otium* as a beneficed scholar in minor orders.[8] He never acted as a chancellor or humanist secretary, but like later humanists he did undertake a number of diplomatic missions for free cities and *signori.*[9] He made speeches on behalf of the princes whose patronage he accepted. Like his late medieval predecessors in Padua he promoted the idea of the ancient world as the standard for modern life and rejected cultural influences from the more recent past such as French chivalry and scholasticism.[10] He was concerned with the education of elites, and even though he never himself taught the young, he advised others how to do so.[11] He preferred to advise adult males who held power, and many of his letters and literary works, such as the *Rerum memorandarum libri* (Things Worth Remembering) and the *De remediis utriusque fortune* (Remedies for Fortune Fair and Foul) were created to package his historical and philosophical wisdom in accessible forms for the *principes* of Christendom. The classical literary genres he cultivated were continued and elaborated in the later humanist movement. He intervened on many occasions in the political life of his time through his widely circulated correspondence with great princes as well as through his poetry, including the *Canzoniere* in Italian, and *Bucolicum carmen, Metrical Epistles,* and the *Africa* in Latin. In his epistolary interventions, however—apart from his brief participation in the revolution of Cola di Rienzo— he adopted the stance of guide, philosopher, and friend, offering his wisdom *supra partes,* speaking truth to power.[12] Petrarch was always on the side of the angels, or wanted to be. This too was a stance regularly though not consistently adopted by humanists of the quattrocento.[13]

Petrarch's preference late in life for rising above partisanship was reflected in his attitude to laws, constitutions, and regime types. In general Petrarch, like later humanists, was conservative when it came to constitutional change. As he wrote in a famous letter-treatise directed to Francesco da Carrara, lord of Padua, probably in 1373, "on the sort of man one should be to govern a republic,"

> I consider those men as citizens who love the stable condition of the state *(respublica),* not those who aim at daily transformations of affairs; they should not be thought citizens but rebels and public enemies. Often this very topic naturally brings Augustus [Petrarch's favorite emperor] into the argument. That famous comment comes from him: "Whoever does not want the present condition of the state to be changed is a citizen and a good man." Hence the man who wants the opposite is undoubtedly bad, unworthy of the name or association with citizens or decent men.[14]

A state is made legitimate by justice, but any *form* of state, whether monarchic, oligarchic, or popular, can become just if its rulers or magistrates act with justice.[15] "Only justice distinguishes the king from the tyrant," he informed Cola di Rienzo.[16] This was the standard criterion of good government espoused by the Roman Stoics, contrasting in this respect with Plato and Aristotle, for whom constitutions enabled particular forms of moral formation. It was also the criterion of Cicero, as reported approvingly by Augustine in the *City of God* (2.21), who places in the mouth of Petrarch's hero Scipio Africanus the assertion that *respublica* only exists where there is justice, regardless of whether the state is governed by a king, a few aristocrats, or the people. For Petrarch, as for Cicero, the way to reform states is to educate and persuade both citizens and political elites to practice virtue. He is not an ideologue of the modern type, one who holds that states are illegitimate when democracy or human rights or other formal conditions are not legally guaranteed. Like most quattrocento humanists, he admires the jurisprudence of Roman antiquity. The *Corpus iuris civilis* is "the most holy temple of Roman justice," and he embraces the Stoic-Christian concepts of natural law and the law of nations *(ius gentium)* without question. But as we saw in Chapter 1, he regards the legal profession in his own day as nearing the nadir of its moral and historical cycle and hopelessly corrupt. Human laws of some kind are necessary, but like gold, they can be used for good or evil; whether they are good or evil for society depends on the moral quality of the men who interpret and enforce them:

> For the laws are not evil, although they are often twisted to bring ruin, despite being designed for the public welfare, just as gold too is not evil, although it has been the cause of sinning and of danger to many. . . . Indeed laws are good and often not only advantageous but even necessary for the world. Yet the men who busy themselves with the exercise of the laws can be both good and wicked, and the greater the number of the wicked, the greater the glory of good men.[17]

It is the *mens,* the moral disposition of the agent, that governs the moral quality of an act and determines whether a law, or an action governed by law, is praiseworthy; "it is the mind that turns what seem good actions to evil and evil to good." Petrarch's thinking here is deeply colored by the Stoic psychology of Seneca, an author in whose works he was steeped. The conclusion Petrarch draws is that the root cause of political evil is in the mind. Human character, therefore, must be the starting point as well as the sine qua non of political reform. From here it is an easy step to the standard quattrocento view that laws, offices, and political institutions in general depend for their moral legitimacy on the character of those who make and enforce them. When evil men make and enforce laws the outcome will always be unjust; laws can offer few protections to the weak when the powerful are not good.[18]

This belief is closely connected with another theme in Petrarch's moral writings that is close to being an obsession with him: the emptiness of titles, *tituli.* His world is full of people boasting of impressive titles—from the pope and Roman emperor on down—which are empty because they have been drained by historical change and human weakness of their true meaning, or because those who hold them do not deserve them.[19] Tyrants, including the Visconti of Milan whom Petrarch served, sought incessantly to acquire official titles from city councils or the pope or the emperor in order to shore up their illegitimate power. But titles are mere vanities and in themselves produce nothing of value: *Fecunda frondium est vanitas, sed inanis fructuum.* Vanity puts out many leaves but bears no fruit. To use a modern analogy, they are like the rows of medals on the uniform of a tyrant. Holders of such empty *tituli* use the disguise of the laws to proclaim their legitimacy, but fail in the simplest test of true legitimacy, which is virtuous devotion to the common good and willingness to sacrifice one's private interests to it.

In the letter to Francesco da Carrara already mentioned—one of two "mirrors of princes" he composed—he comments on the title *pater patriae:*

> At all events you should derive a great and honorable joy from this, feeling yourself so dear to your people that you are not the citizens' master but the father of your country. This was the title of almost all the ancient emperors, but quite justly in some cases, whereas for certain others it was so unjust that nothing could have been more so. Augustus was called "father of his country." Nero too was called father of his country, but the former was a true father, the latter the true enemy of both his country and of piety. But this title will fall to you in truth.

Petrarch's models of true legitimacy—the legitimacy that comes from possession of the virtues—were the Emperor Augustus and, in his own time, King Robert of Naples, the learned Guelf monarch who had conferred upon him the poet's laurel.[20] In a letter to his confessor, the Augustinian friar Dionigi da Borgo San Sepolcro, Petrarch praises Robert, invoking what the ancient historian Paul Veyne has called "the fundamental principle of almost all ancient political thinking": that only the man who has command of himself and who therefore knows how to impose *kosmos,* divine order, on the anarchy of human passion, is worthy of *imperium.*[21]

> Who in Italy, indeed who in Europe, is more glorious than Robert? And often when I think about him I have in mind not his diadem but his character, and I admire not his kingdom but his spirit. I would call him truly a king who rules and reins in not only his subjects but himself, who wields authority over his passions which rebel from the spirit, and would overwhelm it if it yielded. Just

as there is no more glorious victory than to be victor over oneself, so there is no loftier rule than to rule over oneself. . . . And to pass over the glittering names of virtues, who will tell me a man is free if he is weighed down beneath the multiple yoke of various desires? I shall stoop lower than that: with what countenance shall we call him a man whom we know to have nothing of a man except his bare likeness, disfigured with the behavior of wild beasts and terrible with the bestiality of savage creatures? So it is a strange, though common, madness to call a man "king" who is neither a king nor free and often not even a human being.

It is great to be a king, but insignificant to be called a king. Kings are more rare than common folk assume; this title is not a common one. Scepters would waste fewer jewels and less ivory, if only true kings carried them. True kings carry within them what makes them worthy of reverence; they are kings even when their attendants are removed and their emblems cast away; as for the others, it is their costume that makes them inspire fear.[22]

A title, jewels, a scepter, and fine clothing do not make someone a king, whatever the common people may think; indeed, if you are morally unfit you may not even deserve the rank of human being let alone that of king. By the same token, there are many rulers whom the world calls tyrants who are in fact fine rulers who benefit their people. What counts for Petrarch is the *way* power is exercised, the moral quality of the person who wields authority, not compliance with legal formulae, not whether the holder of power has just title to it or not. You are a king if you act in a kingly way.

In his other contribution to the "mirror of princes" genre, an extremely popular letter-treatise written to the powerful Florentine banker Niccola Acciaiuoli, grand seneschal of the king of Naples in 1352, Petrarch advises Niccola on how to educate young King Louis I, nephew of King Robert.[23] A key point for later humanist treatises on true nobility was Petrarch's contention that legal, hereditary succession does not make you truly legitimate unless you also possess the virtues. Justice is the sine qua non of true or moral legitimacy. The virtues are not merely "appropriate" to the prince, they are not mere "ornaments," as they might be to a potentate whose legitimacy derived from heredity or mere observance of law. That had been the doctrine of Giles of Rome, but Petrarch is more radical. A king *must act* justly to be legitimate. A state is not a state without justice, and a king is not truly a king unless he acts justly and makes peace, puts down tyranny and restores true freedom. Kingly acts give a king what is better than mere legality: they give him the trust of the people, who will obey him out of love and not fear.

> You have a king mature in spirit but youthful in years. . . . Show him the steps by which he has been carried to this summit of fortune and the arts he must use to stay there, striving henceforward not so much to climb higher but to show himself worthy of rising and to prove that his inherited scepter is due no less to his virtue than to his blood. Being a prince does not make a man but exposes him, and honors do not change our behavior and spirit but display it. Persuade him that it is less important to be born a king than to become a king by men's judgment; the first is a gift of fortune, the other of merit; teach him these things: let him worship God, love his country, observe justice, without which a kingdom, however sturdy and wealthy, cannot stand firm. Let him learn that nothing violent is long-lived, and it is much safer to be loved than to be feared; let him grow accustomed to desire nothing on earth except good sense, hope for nothing except a good repute, and fear nothing except disgrace. Let him reflect that the higher he is, the more clearly he is observed and so his actions can less easily be hidden, and the greater his power, the less his license. Let him know that a king is no more distinguished from his people by his clothing than by his behavior; shunning extremes equally, let him pursue the virtue which is a model to us all. . . . He should think himself fortunate and fulfilled and truly a king when he has driven off by his own virtue the wretchedness imported by other men's offenses; when he has compensated for losses, rebuilt ruins, reestablished peace, put down tyranny and restored freedom; let him persuade his mind to love those he rules, since love is earned by loving, and no monarchy is more sure than one in authority over the willing.[24]

Not only does virtue give the prince true, moral legitimacy, but it enables him to rule his people with love, not fear. Petrarch makes his own the teaching of the *De officiis* that coercion is dehumanizing and engenders hatred, while possession of the virtues, particularly justice, can alter the emotions a people feel toward their ruler, converting fear into love and willing obedience.[25]

Petrarch illustrates the effects of charismatic virtue in a speech written in 1358 for the restoration of Visconti power over the city of Novara. The poet had entered the service of the Visconti lords of Milan in 1353 under Archbishop Giovanni (denounced as a tyrant by the Florentines) and continued to serve Galeazzo II Visconti (later famous for the cruelty of his tortures) when the archbishop died in 1354.[26] In 1356 the city of Novara had been snatched from Visconti control by the marquis of Monferrato with the aid of rebels within the city, but Visconti lordship was restored in June 1358. On June 18 Galeazzo entered the city with a great retinue, but—significantly—without a military escort. A ceremony of restoration was held in the great cloister of the cathedral before an assembly of the people, and Petrarch delivered a thematic speech, or *arenga,* on the text *Convertetur populus meus hic,* from Psalm 72 (73):10.[27]

In the speech Petrarch describes the great virtue of Galeazzo, who has shown not just the *clementia* and *oblivio offensarum* (forgetfulness of offenses) that marked the fine behavior of Scipio and Caesar, but Christian *misericordia,* a divine and exemplary virtue that has elevated the people's *dignitas.* As a result, the people of Novara voluntarily surrendered to Visconti's virtue, "opening the doors not only of the city but of [their] hearts," thronging the unarmed ruler with a loving desire to see him with their own eyes. In total unity you have accepted his protection, Petrarch says, in the same way the Falisci surrendered to the Roman hero Camillus with the cry, "We are under your sway; send men to receive our arms and hostages, and our city, the gates of which stand open. Neither shall you be disappointed in our fidelity nor we in your rule." Petrarch then cites the famous line of Vergil, "Solvite corde metum, Teucri, secludite curas" (Free your hearts of fear, Trojans, shut out your cares)[28] and adds a legal gloss of his own: "And you, therefore, citizens of Novara, if because of rebellion—not voluntary but coerced—some fear of a lord has been bound to your hearts, if any cares have invaded your hearts, be free of fear, fence off your cares, and accept the security and trust you once knew."[29] Petrarch here alludes to the Bartolist doctrine of *iustus metus,* or legitimate fear, where consent is invalidated if tyrannical acts have been imposed on a people by the threat of violence or reprisals.[30] The people of Novara, in other words, have been victims of tyrannical violence under Monferrato, they never truly consented to his rule, and they are now returning voluntarily to the care of a loving and good prince, who has conquered them with benefits and with his virtue, just as Cicero had advised in the *De officiis.*

The allusion to the famous story of Camillus in Livy is laden with significance. This was a *locus classicus* for the fond humanist belief that the Romans had conquered the world by justice and virtue rather than through mere violence. In the story the Roman general Camillus has the chance to take the city of the Falisci, called Falerii, without bloodshed when a schoolmaster treacherously abducts the children of the Faliscan nobles and offers them to Camillus as hostages. The noble Camillus, however, refuses to take advantage of the schoolmaster's perfidy and returns the scoundrel and the abducted children to the besieged town, declaring that he will conquer the Falisci in the Roman way, "by virtue, toil and arms." The Romans had no formal covenant with the Falisci and owed them nothing, he says, but the *societas* which existed between all men by nature bound them to do what was right: "There are rights *(iura)* of war as well as of peace, and we have learnt to use them justly no less than bravely." (That is why the Romans were an imperial people, Dante said, because they obeyed the *ius gentium,* the sense of right that bound all nations into one.) When the Faliscans heard of what Camillus had done, they held a council, and "men underwent such a revulsion of feeling, that those who a short time before, in the fury of their hate and resentment would almost have preferred the doom of Veii to the peace of Capena, were now calling for peace, with the voice of an entire city."[31] Amazed at the Romans' sense of right, they surrendered to them, believing that "we shall be better off under your government than under our own laws." Here a splendid act of virtue works a profound transformation on the hearts of an enemy people and makes them voluntarily accept Roman rule. For Petrarch, the story was perfect: voluntary obedience, as we have seen, is the Holy Grail of humanist virtue politics.

Virtue also binds a society together in a second way, via political friendship. As Aristotle taught in both the *Ethics* and *Politics,* the basis of *politeia* in the sense of constitutional government was friendship and a sense of equality among the ruling class, ideally the middle class.[32] True friendship, he taught in the *Ethics,* was based on virtue. The same doctrines could be applied to monarchy. Just as virtue bound a people to a monarch in love, so it could bind to him his closest associates in loving friendship, whether the nobles of his court or magistrates. In the letter on kingship to Acciaiuoli Petrarch writes:

> Let that fine Sallustian concept of monarchy never leave the spirit of your king:[33] it is not armies nor treasures that are the guarantees of the kingdom but friends, and these are not coerced by force nor obtained by money but by dutiful behavior and loyalty. . . . After God and virtue he should have nothing dearer to him than friendship. If he has once thought a man worthy of friendship, he should always include him in his counsels; and following Seneca's advice, he should reflect over everything with his friend, but first deliberate about his friend.[34] Let him trust strongly but not in many and concentrate on distinguishing a true friend from a flattering enemy; let him welcome true praise as a goad to virtue but shun flattery like poison. Let him move slowly towards friendship and leave it more slowly, and if possible never; and he should

do it, not in headlong haste but step by step. As it says in the old proverb, let him unstitch a friendship, not tear it apart.[35] Let him hope to receive from others the same feelings he offers them, nor imagine he is loved by anyone whom he does not himself love. This is the blunder of the powerful; for men's emotions are completely free and do not endure a yoke or acknowledge a master: love is never compelled except by love, but never fails to be compelled by love.[36]

The choice of true friends was a ruler's most important decision. This doctrine too came from Cicero. His best friend will be a man who doesn't need him, a man of virtue for whom principle is more important than wealth or position, a man of wisdom whose prudence is informed by vast reading and understanding of human nature, a man of pure feeling who prefers unspoiled nature to the corruption of cities, a man fearless in his speech who will speak truth to power. He will be a man much like Petrarch, in other words. He will be the kind of man the "humanist advisor" of the quattrocento sought (or pretended) to be. The prince can reward him but not buy him. He should follow the example of "our Augustus"—for Petrarch the greatest ancient patron of literature—and foster men of excellence and learning, including jurists (provided they are "as expert in justice as in law"), doctors, and teachers of the liberal arts *(liberalium artium magistri):* "I mean by exceptional men those whom some excellence has detached from the herd of vulgar men and whom some distinguished traits of justice and holiness—which is alas very rare in our generation—or experience and learning with regard to warfare or a wealth of reading and knowledge of events has made unique."[37] The prince, again following the example of Augustus, should treat his philosophical friends as equals. "No man should feel shame at a plebeian friendship when intellect and learning make it noble." In return, the literati will offer "both advice in the present and a lasting name, showing you as well the right path to ascend to the gods and supporting you as you rise with the aid of their tongue and drawing you back when you stray."[38] By supporting the arts of civilization the prince ensures the longevity of his own name and glory. Augustus "was made no less glorious by this retinue of learned men than by all the Roman legions."

Particularly useful for preserving the prince's glory and strengthening the state was encouraging the "holy pursuit" of poetry. As we have seen, Cicero in the *Pro Archia*—a speech rediscovered by Petrarch himself—had praised how the art of poetry promoted virtue in the state and eloquence in its rulers. The example of Augustus' patronage, "who was both friend of poets and master of the world," shone out from the annals of literature.[39] In the speech Petrarch gave on the Capitoline when crowned with the laurel in 1341, he elaborated on the example of antiquity: "Once upon a time there was an age more auspicious for poets, when they were held in the greatest honor. This occurred first in Greece, then Rome, especially in the time of the emperor Augustus, under whom exceptional poets flourished: Vergil, Varus, Ovid, Horace and many others.... But today, as you see, all is changed."[40] The custom of crowning poets had died out 1200 years before, after the time of the Emperor Domitian, but Petrarch, "amidst the long senescence of the republic of the Romans," by God's will, was renewing "this loveliest custom of its flourishing youth." It was a straw in the wind, a sign perhaps of better times to come, that in recent years the Senate and leading men of Rome, the University of Paris, and good King Robert of Naples had competed to invite him to assume the laurel crown of poetry once more.

The decline of Latin poetry had gone *pari passu* with the decline of Rome, and in part explained it. Political flourishing required noble emotions. When a great poet, under divine inspiration and driven by his own love of study, has success in writing great poetry, that success is rooted in three psychological dispositions (*affectus animi*): to honor the republic, to burnish his own glory, and to spur other poets to emulate his example. All of these are good dispositions; even the desire for glory (despite Christian misgivings) was a good passion, felt by all wise and virtuous men. They were all dispositions little felt, alas, in recent times. But Petrarch hoped that his own glory would provide a spur to others to rise up and achieve excellence in letters. He knew there were already many learned men of genius in the Italy of his day, but they lacked a leader and were afraid to attempt the arduous pathway to Parnassus. He offered himself as their leader. And he promised *principes* and brave men everywhere that the poets of Italy, a new generation of Homers and Vergils, would celebrate their achievements and preserve their memory, so they would not have to lament, like Alexander at the tomb of Achilles, "O fortunate youth, who found such a herald of your virtue!" There was a symbiosis of great poetry and great deeds, a virtuous circle whereby each encouraged the other. This theme in Petrarch's work was later to be played with numerous variations by would-be humanist laureates in offering their services to Renaissance princes.[41]

The prince's duty to support literature and promote human excellence does not mean he can shirk the responsibility of devoting his own leisure hours to letters. Indeed, it is of capital importance, both to the prince's own happiness and to his capacity for rule, that he attain his full humanity through mastery of the humane studies, especially history. Augustus again, for Petrarch, was the ideal model, who according to Suetonius spent every spare hour listening to books and took great pains to be eloquent in his speech.[42] In the preface to *Remedies for Fortune Fair and Foul,* Petrarch explains to his dear friend and patron Azzo da Correggio, the reformed tyrant, how the ancient authors with their "great books" can act as sure guides on the voyage of life:

> Besides the efforts of a valiant mind ... and frequent discourse with wise men ... continued and diligent reading of the works of outstanding writers is of benefit, provided you have a mind receptive to the substance of their wholesome instructions. This, I am not afraid to state, is the only real source of sound advice in the world. Because of this ... I urge you to consider how much we owe to the brilliant and famous authors hundreds of years before our time, who still live and dwell with us, and talk to us with divine intellect in their great books. Amidst the perpetual turmoil of our minds, like so many bright stars fixed on the firmament of truth, like so many pleasant and favorable breezes, like so many eager and skilled sailors, they point us to the port of rest and guide the drooping sails of our hopes and the helm of our wavering thoughts until such time as our own judgments, battered by so many storms, shall find firm ground and government.[43]

The best "humanist advisors" of all, the surest guides to life, are the ancient authors.

Cola di Rienzo: Populism and Its Limits

Chapter 1 considered how the civilizational crisis of the fourteenth century led to a new paideuma, one largely of Petrarch's making, that reordered the fundamental orientation of Christendom to Graeco-Roman civilization, ultimately transforming its *institutio,* its modes of enculturation. The new humanistic paideuma produced a different kind of politics, virtue politics, that sought to rise above partisanship and combat the causes of political evil on a higher plane, through a program of moral reform directed at citizens and especially at civic elites. But the genesis of virtue politics can also be understood as a response by its principal inventor, Petrarch, to his own political experience. And no series of events left a deeper mark on Petrarch's political convictions than those set in train by the populist revolution of his beloved friend and onetime hero, Cola di Rienzo. A look at these events will help us understand why Petrarch in the end rejected populism, and partisan political conflict in general, as a path to reform.[44]

Cola di Rienzo at first sight was a humanist's dream come to life. It was an article of faith with humanists that even those of humble birth and fortune could and should rise to positions of political leadership, provided they were virtuous. Cola was just such a man. Born of peasant stock, son of an innkeeper and a washerwoman, he rose to be the leader of the Roman republic. His name, however resonant to our ears after Byron and Wagner, in Roman dialect just meant (as Mario Cosenza pointed out) something like "Nick, son of Larry." He had ennobled himself by self-education and a passion for antiquity: he was a keen student of Rome's history and monuments; he loved to collect and read the inscriptions that still lay in great numbers amid her ruins. Startlingly, it was he who had personally unearthed the most important inscriptional evidence for the history of the Roman imperial constitution, the *Lex de imperio Vespasiani*.[45] Cola yearned to revive the glory of ancient Rome and believed he was born to accomplish that glorious task. Like a good humanist ruler he had a learned advisor, Petrarch himself, ten years his senior, who tirelessly encouraged him to read and re-read the classics. (Touchingly, during his imprisonment in Avignon, Cola was allowed to read two books: his Livy and his Bible.) He was a man gifted with great natural eloquence who saw it as his duty to arouse languid Roma from her long slumbers. Like a good humanist ruler Cola used his eloquence as an instrument of peace. Rome had been shaken by violent factional struggles among baronial clans for decades; as in other Italian cities Guelfs and Ghibellines plotted and fought incessantly against each other. But Cola's eloquence seemed almost magically to put an end to factional strife on that glorious day in 1347 on the Capitoline—a little over six years after Petrarch was crowned poet laureate on the same spot—when by popular acclamation he was made ruler of the city and took the ancient title, thrilling in its revolutionary implications, of tribune.[46] He then embarked on a program of civic education, creating a "virtuous environment" by the means of painted murals, a *respublica picta,* by which he hoped to spark in the largely illiterate Roman populace an awareness of its ancient rights and glory.[47]

The Roman baronial families, by contrast, whose turbulent rule had tortured Rome before Cola's tribunate and who, after its failure, threatened to continue her sufferings, represented everything Petrarch detested about the politics of his own times. They claimed to be citizens by right of long residence, but in fact, Petrarch claimed (on the basis of medieval legends), their baronies had origins outside Rome and their bloodlines were Germanic, or at any rate not Roman. They were in other words barbarians and usurpers. They were tyrannical oligarchs (the Romans lived *sub paucorum infami tyrannide*); they were like the Thirty Tyrants of ancient Athens who had persecuted Socrates. They based their claims to power on pompous, inherited, empty titles, and on their wealth and power. But their power was not exercised for good because they lacked virtue and even reason; they were *rationis expertes,* devoid of reason, and their understanding of the past was shallow, built on fables. They were driven by pride in their titles and coats of arms but in fact were unworthy even of the title of humanity.[48] Thus they were obliged to use violent coercion to maintain their power. A sign of their ignorance, foreign origins, and malice was their lack of reverence for the ruins of Rome. They had even contributed to its ruination by despoiling "those eloquent memorials to ancient greatness" to build their own palaces.[49]

Thus Petrarch's reaction to the events of May 1347 was foreordained: it was nothing short of ecstatic. Already one of Cola's closest friends, he became a true believer. At his coronation with the laurel in 1341 Petrarch had been made a citizen of Rome, a reward for his poetic virtue and his devotion to the city, and as a Roman citizen and a commoner he saw Cola as his own *princeps.*[50] In his famous panegyric of the revolution, addressed to Cola and the Roman people in June 1347, Petrarch offers the new rulers of the city his pen. He will help them kindle the embers of old Roman virtue throughout Italy; he will celebrate Cola himself as the latest of Rome's great heroes. Cola is the new Scipio, the new Camillus, and as the latest savior of the republic, the third Brutus.[51] Petrarch even offers at the end of his panegyric to set aside his *Africa* and turn the prose of his letter-oration into shining verse; he will become the laureate of Roman liberty. At times his tone even acquires a prophetic strain as he announces a New Age of Rome.[52]

In this and other letters of the later 1340s it is not wrong to see Petrarch as something like a modern partisan ideologue. He owed his daily bread to the munificence of the Colonna family in the person of Cardinal Giovanni Colonna, its head, but he declares that in the end he was *amicus Johannes, sed magis amica Roma.*[53] He is willing to sacrifice personal loyalties and even his own interests for an idea.[54] In the panegyric of June 1347 he is as fiery a populist as any modern republican could want. Some of his statements about political liberty could be read as endorsing the "non-domination" concept of liberty that descends from the medieval Italian commune and was to become characteristic of early-modern republics. At one point he tells the Roman people, "[The barons] cannot be lords and you free men at the same time and in the same city": lordship and liberty are incompatible.[55] He reminds the Romans how they freed Rome from the kings and killed Caesars for the sake of liberty.[56] He tells how Cato the Younger committed suicide rather than live under the rule of Caesar (even though Caesar was "a remarkable and unique man," he adds).[57] In protecting liberty, the people are performing a task that rightfully belongs to them; they are not usurping anyone else's power. Only by being vigilant in the defense of liberty can they protect their happiness and way of life against the tyrannical barons, whether they are merchants, soldiers, farmers, religious, old men or young, maids or matrons.[58] It is the barons who revel in factional strife; the people want peace.

Eventually, however, political reality changed, and Petrarch changed too. It took only a few months. By the end of the summer of 1347 Cola's claims and ambitious were becoming ever more grandiose, and he began to challenge the power of the Church, which had hitherto supported him against the barons. He accepted a knighthood from the emperor, formed an alliance with the barbarous Hungarians, had himself crowned with the laurel (claiming it had been the custom of the Roman tribunes), and began to act like a prince: coining money, levying taxes, demanding obedience from lords and communes in the Papal State. In due course he even granted Roman citizenship to all Italians, in imitation of the *Lex Julia* of 90 BC, which Cola may have learned about from reading Cicero's *Pro Archia*. Petrarch heard about all Cola's doings from a reliable source, his dear friend Laelius, and began to lose heart and to regret the damage done to his own ties with the papal curia. Sometime in the fall of 1347 he wrote a pained letter to Cola, lamenting his former hero's moral decline. He wants to think of him as he once was, he knows Cola has been the object of many slanders, but now he has to credit reports that the tribune "no longer favors the whole people but only its worst element," and has become a traitor to Holy Church. By mid-December, isolated diplomatically, Cola had lost the support of the people, was driven from the Campidoglio by a riot, and was forced to flee: first to the Castel Sant'Angelo, then to Naples, then to a refuge of the Fraticelli high on Monte Maiella in Abruzzo. His revolution was over.

Petrarch's New Realism

We can trace the effects of Petrarch's disillusionment in his later writings on political themes. He remained at heart a kind of populist. He continued to believe that there were embers of ancient virtue still glowing among the Roman people, and he continued to denounce the powerful for their exploitation of the weak. In an invective of 1355 directed against Jean de Caraman, a cardinal of noble extraction, he answers the Frenchman's charge that he serves tyrants with a counter-charge:

> Indeed, you exclaim and often reiterate—for folly is the greatest chatterbox—you often repeat, I say, that I live under the sway (as you put it) of tyrants who subsist on the labors of paupers and widows. I might grant you this, but the charge would prove common to all rulers. Could anything but the sweat of peoples produce the great luxury, the great magnificence, and the great households of our princes? The most virtuous and innocent ruler—or, more correctly, the least harmful one—is the one who is most sparing and moderate in exploiting his privileges *(licentia)*. As in other matters, here too we must grant that, since no one is without fault, we may call best that person who is least evil.[59]

But worst of all are churchmen like Jean de Caraman, whose rich benefices were supported by extracting revenues from the mendicant orders.

> So the next time you decide to accuse others of living off the people's labors, remember that you do not live off the toils of merchants, the industry of craftsmen, or the revenues of the state, but off the backs and the squalor of beggars. Unless I am mistaken, others feed more honorably on the labor of the masses than you feed on the hunger of Christ's starvelings. What's more, none of the men you call tyrants hungers as avidly as you do for either plunder or gifts.[60]

Here Petrarch comes close to claiming that all rulership, even virtuous rulership, involves some degree of unjust exploitation. There is a kind of Rousseauian populism in the way he resented subordinating his will to another's. He had intimate experience of personal dependence thanks to his long years of service in the household of Cardinal Colonna. Even though the cardinal was the best of patrons, Petrarch still considered the role he had played to be one of "honorable enslavement," not to be compared with the freedom of being one's own master. After Colonna died of plague in 1348, Petrarch wrote to several members of his former household proposing that they pool their resources and set up a modest household together; in that way they would substitute for honorable slavery an even more honorable freedom: "Has the pursuit of slavery exercised more power over us than the love of liberty can obtain? Even if that slavery was more welcome than any freedom, as that excellent man's affection deserved, free of any arrogance in his condition, still, to be set under another, to obey another, to live on another man's support can seem part of a more honorable kind of enslavement, but these are surely not marks of freedom."[61]

Thus Petrarch remained a kind of moral populist, in the sense that he was someone who sympathized with commoners against oppressive lords—though it is well to remember that "the people" in his mind, as generally in Italian cities, meant the broad middle ranks of society and not the *infima plebs,* the very lowest members of society, uneducated wage laborers and servants. But a change becomes discernible in his attitude to political action after the collapse of Cola's revolution. At no point, of course, had Petrarch ever been an exclusivist republican in the modern sense: he had never claimed that only popular government was legitimate, or that all legitimate government rested exclusively on some form of authorization from the people.[62] But now, after the bitter experience of Cola's rise and fall, he became, reluctantly, more of a realist. He came to appreciate how difficult it was to change inveterate belief, how strong were the vested interests holding in place Europe's political order, how heavy was the weight of custom, wealth, and titles. It would not be enough to sound the trumpet for the people to rise up against injustice and reclaim the glory of their Roman ancestry.[63] He came to see that serious moral change would have to occur before any real political reform could take place. And he started to believe that the best way to begin the moral reformation he sought was not by setting aflame the embers of popular virtue in Rome but by educating and advising *principes* throughout Italy and Europe. His mission had changed, and with it the self-image he chose to present to the world.[64]

Already in 1351 we see signs of this new realism in a letter he wrote to the commission of four cardinals charged with reordering the Roman constitution after the restoration of the barons. It is a sign, perhaps, of the growing prestige of classical learning that the cardinals thought it appropriate to seek an opinion from Petrarch rather than a legal *consilium* from a famous jurist.[65] This long letter was the closest Petrarch ever came to writing what a modern scholar might think of as political theory. *Mutatis mutandis* the work might even be compared to the constitutions written by Rousseau for Sardinia and Poland. The letter makes clear that Petrarch still despised the Roman barons. Their origins, titles, wealth, and power still gave them no claim to rule. And he still believed the Roman people were capable of participation in government. The barons believed the opposite and had called for a restoration of the *status quo ante* where all civic offices and especially the Senate would remain exclusively under their control. In his response to the cardinals, Petrarch did not back the idea of a fully popular government, something like the popular communes that had emerged in thirteenth-century Italy, in which powerful families had been excluded from government. He did not approach the issue in terms of abstract right at all. Instead, his perspective was historical. He saw the whole conflict between the Roman people and the baronial families in light of the "Struggle of the Orders" in early Roman history as recorded by Livy.[66] There was, of course, no realistic hope of replacing the barons with virtuous patricians such as ancient Rome had once enjoyed. Such being the case, Petrarch was driven to rely on constitutional devices to deal with "the crooked timber of humanity." To restore the same families with the same vices to their former role, he told the cardinals, would change nothing; it would simply lead to more popular rebellions. The solution was to do what the ancient Romans had done, and give the *plebs* some share in office: "Since the spirits of the people did not calm down even then [after the creation of plebeian tribunes in the fifth century BCE], the goal that had long been frustrated by bloated patrician pride was ensured by the force of justice: that a plebeian consul should sit alongside a patrician and rule with equal majesty their common native land and empire won by common effort."[67] The commission of cardinals should take as its model the civic institutions of Rome in her glorious period, not those of corrupt modern times; it should

> follow the examples of that period when that city rose from nothing to the stars, not *this* period in which it is reduced from such a summit of fortune almost to nothing.... In this it will be right to recall Aristotle's statement that, like men straightening out crooked logs,[68] you should compel these nobles not only to share with others the dignity of senator and other offices, but to step back for a long time from the privileges they have so long usurped by means of their arrogance and the long-suffering of the people, until the republic bends back in the other direction and gradually returns to an appropriate state of equality.[69]

Here Petrarch defends the idea that different social ranks need to participate on a more equal basis for Rome to manifest again its ancient political virtues. The people might even take the lead in the state for a time until a constitutional balance could be restored of a kind similar to that which had obtained in antiquity. Petrarch's advice may reflect his practical judgment (which is also an Aristotelian principle) that rule is best entrusted to the most virtuous element in the republic, and that there was more virtue in the common people of Rome in his own time than in the nobility. But his advice assumes that in the normal course of affairs, there will always be nobles and commoners, patricians and plebs, and that both elements are legitimate elements in the Roman state.

For the fourteenth-century city, given its political reality, Petrarch advised a power-sharing arrangement modelled on the middle republic of Roman antiquity as described by Livy.[70] Elsewhere, however, for equally pragmatic reasons, he was an advocate of monarchy. Monarchy, indeed, had long been his default recommendation for most Italian city-states in his own time. Unlike Rome, most of them could not boast a people naturally capable of virtue.[71] In a letter subtitled *de optimo reipublicae statu,* addressed probably to Paganino da Bizzozzero, an advisor of Luchino Visconti, tyrant of Milan, Petrarch writes:

> Although I am well aware how much more the Roman state increased under the rule of many than under one man, I know many great men have thought that the happiest condition of any state was under one leader who was also just, so much do authority and experience seem in conflict. But this problem is too great to be analyzed in one short letter. Certainly, given the present condition of our affairs, amid such unappeasable discord of men's spirits, absolutely no doubt remains that monarchy is the best for recuperating and repairing the strength of Italy, which the long frenzy of civil wars has dissipated.[72]

Here Petrarch alludes to what was to become a major argument for popular government in the early Renaissance from Leonardo Bruni to Machiavelli—that Rome experienced its greatest expansion during the consular age of popular liberty and not under her early kings or her later emperors. In the end, however, Petrarch, like many other humanists, rejects Machiavelli's "republic for expansion" in favor of the peace and stability of a monarchical republic. Indeed, in the same letter, he urges Paganino to advise Visconti against undertaking imperialistic projects:

> So I am advising you, I say, to convince him that his territory is wide enough, whether he is aiming at wealth or glory. Nothing is enough for greed; let it not cheat him with vast promises. There is a golden moderation in every fortune, but human felicity, setting itself no limit and eager to advance, stretching out infinitely, contains the greatest anxiety and nothing solid, fixed and calm. . . . You see my mind, you know what I desire and what I fear.

I hear that he is attempting new initiatives;[73] I hope they may be fortunate if he persists, but I prefer him to stop, since this is the safer course. I beg you, oppose his undertakings.... You could easily protect a modest territory under your rule, but an unlimited empire is difficult to win and difficult to keep.[74]

Adopting monarchical government was a counsel of prudence in a time of bitter partisanship, and prudence and moderation should lead a prince to avoid military adventures abroad. Petrarch's objection to militarism was the same as Thomas More's in the *Utopia* would be: it risked unleashing uncontrollable passions of greed and ambition and neglecting tasks more within a prince's measure, such as defense of the realm.

Despite his new realism, virtue remained the guiding star of Petrarch's politics. That was why he could never bring himself to call Julius Caesar a tyrant. He could not excuse Caesar's attacks on his own country, and he admitted that Caesar had at times exceeded his constitutional authority. But the man had greatness of soul and showed magnificent virtues of moderation and clemency. He was a peacemaker while his senatorial opponents, though they wrapped themselves in notions of constitutional propriety, in fact constituted a *paucorum tyrannis,* a tyrannical oligarchy.[75] It is presumably no accident that he had branded the barons of Rome with the same phrase.

Ideally, a monarch would be chosen according to principles of virtue rather than heredity, which meant for Petrarch a form of elective kingship. Later humanists sometime admired Roman emperors like Trajan and Hadrian for choosing their own successors from among the most virtuous of their younger associates.[76] Petrarch, given his populist sentiments, had to look further abroad, even to ancient legend, for an example of a king chosen by the people for his virtue.[77] He might have turned to the early Roman kingship, which according to Livy was elective, involving a vote of the *comitia centuriata* and approval by the *patres,* a hereditary elite with control of religious rites. But to my knowledge Petrarch never appeals to this example; perhaps he was deterred by the name *rex,* which Livy states was hated by the Roman people after the expulsion of the tyrannical Tarquins.[78] Instead, he looked outside the Graeco-Roman world. In *De remediis* he held up for admiration the practice of the island of Taprobane (possibly modern Sri Lanka) in the Indian Ocean. Embroidering on Pliny's *Natural History* (6.89), he wrote a largely imaginary account of how this island people chose their king's successor:

The love of one's own son often turns the mind from the love of virtue. You must have read that in the great island of Taprobane, which lies far beyond India in the eastern ocean, diagonally across the diameter of the earth, directly opposite Britain, the king is elected by decision and consent of the people *(arbitrio populi consentientis)*. They choose the best of all their men, and neither blood nor wealth counts for anything. Only virtue leads to election, and favor never influences the decision. A blessed and beneficial way to choose, which I wish had come to our kings, so that the bad ones would not be succeeded by worse ones, and worse ones by the worst of men, and all the world would not have been corrupted by viciousness and arrogance handed down from father to son.

There in Taprobane, no matter how good and accomplished the man may be who is approved by the unanimous decision of all *(unanimi sententia omnium comprobatus)*, he cannot become king unless he is an old man, without a son, lest the fervor of youth or love for his son change him and prevent him from doing the right thing. He cannot assume the kingship if he has a son, and if a son is born to him after he becomes king, he is immediately removed from office. For even the wisest of men share the opinion that it is impossible for one man to care for both the people and a son.[79]

Even in his fiercest partisan moments, Petrarch showed no exclusivist loyalty to a particular type of regime or set of constitutional practices. He consistently condemned sources of authority that were entirely hereditary or patrimonial. A good state was one that aimed at peace, justice, and the welfare of all its citizens, and these aims could only be achieved when the state was served by wise and virtuous rulers. In some cases a people too, the citizen body, might be capable of virtue, and when actually virtuous should not be excluded from government. The people as such had no natural right to govern or to authorize a government, but among the Roman people at least, even in the dark age of the trecento, embers of virtue still burned that might justify their participation in some form of self-rule. In such cases a free state was desirable, but in most cases, especially when a city suffered from extreme factionalism, monarchy was best. The best republic, a republic modelled on ancient Rome, will be one where a true aristocracy and a virtuous people shared power on a basis of equality; the best monarchy will be elective, with a ruler chosen for his virtue.

CHAPTER 6

SHOULD A GOOD MAN PARTICIPATE IN A CORRUPT GOVERNMENT?

Petrarch on the Solitary Life

Petrarch's involvements in the politics of trecento Italy have often been the subject of criticism by later readers of his works—in effect, by that same posterity whose good opinion he so eagerly sought, and not just in his famous letter *To Posterity*. Indeed, almost all of Petrarch's literary interventions in the political life of his times come interlaced with pre-emptive apologias for his own stances. He knew that what he did and what he wrote would draw criticism, or was already drawing criticism. And his works certainly offer to hostile eyes what military tacticians would call a "target-rich environment." For there were many political Petrarchs: in approximate chronological order, there is Petrarch the Italian patriot, calling for the common defense of Italy against foreign powers, including the Holy Roman Emperor; there is Petrarch the admirer of Robert of Naples' enlightened monarchy; Petrarch the propagandist for Cola di Rienzo's popular revolt against Rome's baronial families; Petrarch the chastened critic of Cola's excesses; Petrarch the bitter opponent of the Avignon papacy; Petrarch the counselor and sometime spokesman for assorted north Italian *signori;* and the Petrarch who late in life urged Holy Roman Emperor Charles IV to invade and conquer Italy.[1] Since all of Petrarch's political projects, at least in the short run, ended in failure, one could add the charge of ineffectiveness to those more frequently heard, of inconsistency and an excess of moral flexibility.

There is one political Petrarch, however, who has drawn less attention from scholars than the rest, and that is the unpolitical Petrarch—at least if we follow the *marxisant* view that a refusal to take part in politics is itself a kind of politics. To be sure, even this Petrarch has found critics: it was the *unpolitisch* Petrarch, after all, who disappointed the great historian of Renaissance republicanism, Hans

Baron, and furnished the most important example of the key distinction he made between "politically quietist" trecento literati and the *engagé* civic humanists of the quattrocento—between the humanist movement before and after the putative "crisis" of the early Italian Renaissance.[2] Criticism is not necessarily analysis, however, and there is much about the unpolitical Petrarch that still merits study and discussion, especially in an age such as ours, where admirable examples of political engagement are hard to come by and alternatives to political life eagerly canvassed. Here too Petrarch has left us a preemptive apologia for withdrawal from the active life in his treatise *De vita solitaria* (hereafter *DVS*), written and rewritten and rewritten again between 1346 and 1372.[3] Whether a good man can or should participate in corrupt polities is a question worth considering as it bears directly on the crucial issue of whether the reform project of virtue politics is a real possibility or a utopian dream. It was a question that would often be raised in the 150 years separating Petrarch from Machiavelli.[4]

Though justifying his withdrawal from the active life is an intermittent concern with Petrarch throughout the *DVS,* this chapter will focus on one passage in particular, found in book 2 (2.9.19–22).[5] The passage stands out in the work as a kind of confession of his deepest convictions regarding the autonomy of the individual in the face of what present themselves as social and political obligations. It is also of considerable historical interest, as it throws light on how he strove to reconcile his aims as a humanist reformer with his *forma mentis* as a believing Christian. Petrarch in effect sets up a dialogue between the Augustine of the *City of God* and Seneca's *De otio* in order to resolve the tension between his hopes of reforming the political elite of his day and his desire to remain unspotted from the world. What comes out of this confrontation is neither Augustinian nor Senecan but Petrarchan, which is to say an attitude toward the self and its obligations that belongs more to the modern than to the ancient world.

The De Vita Solitaria: *An Ideal of Private Life for Literary Men*

A few words first about the project of the *DVS,* a far more radical one in the context of its time than is commonly appreciated.[6] The work was begun in the Lenten season of 1346, stimulated by a period of literary retirement Petrarch had enjoyed with his friend Philippe de Cabassoles (1305–1372). Philippe was a prominent papal diplomat from a noble family who in 1334 was appointed bishop of Cavaillon. As such he became Petrarch's spiritual and feudal lord when the latter acquired a country house in Vaucluse in 1337, a short walk from Philippe's castle. The two became intimate friends and exchanged many letters preserved in Petrarch's various letter collections. As was his habit, Petrarch continued to add to and revise the *DVS* long after 1346; though it was eventually declared finished in two books and sent to Philippe with a formal dedication in 1366, Petrarch continued to fiddle with it down to 1372. Contemporary evidence shows that the treatise was used as a devotional work by its early readers, which cannot have been quite Petrarch's intention.[7] In its wider historical context it might be regarded as an example of plague literature, as a work that carries the mental scars of the Black Death of 1347–1349. In the peroration ending book 1 Petrarch even compares flight from the moral contagion of cities with flight from the plague, which most people at the time regarded as the only effective prophylactic against the disease.

The work developed in tandem with another work on the retired life, *De otio religioso,* begun during Lent in 1347, a year after the inception of the *DVS*. It too was continually revised, at least until 1357, and possibly later.[8] This second work was dedicated to the Carthusian monastic community at Montrieux, about 150 kilometers southeast of Vaucluse, where Petrarch's brother Gherardo was a monk. The *De otio religioso* is a treatise that discusses religious retirement and the nature of monastic contemplation, a way of life described as the highest form of human life, the life closest to that of the angels. It is the life led by his brother Gherardo, whom Petrarch acknowledges to have taken a road through life higher than his own.[9] Though in this work, as ever, Petrarch introduces a fresh personal perspective inspired by his classical reading, it remains fundamentally a traditional work of monastic meditation, rooted in the theology of the Church Fathers. The monastic life Petrarch celebrates was of course a well-established form of life in his day, lived in thousands of monasteries across Europe. As a form of life it hardly required justification in a Christian world, at least in the fourteenth century.

This is not the case with the solitary life. In this work Petrarch introduces Christian civilization to a fundamentally new form of life, a life he has discovered for himself: the life of *otium litteratum,* or literary retirement.[10] He does his best to conceal its novelty by citing precedents for what he calls the life of the *solitarius* going back to Adam and the patriarchs, and including the Hebrew prophets, Church Fathers, popes, classical philosophers, poets, orators, Roman generals and emperors, and even "men outside the Christian religion," such as the "gymnosophists," Hindus, and Druids. His point is to show that the impulse to withdraw from normal social intercourse is universal, both historically and geographically. To show the universality of the impulse behind the solitary life was a necessary premise for someone whose aim was to defend it as a way of living; if the desire for such a life can be shown to be universal, it may be assumed to be natural, and therefore intended by the Creator. At the same time, true examples of the solitary life are rare. Only morally serious, pious men devoted to literature can live such a life: "It is not given to all men to excel by holiness of life or by literary achievement, or by noble use of leisure to earn the love and acknowledgement of posterity" (1.5.4). Without literature, the solitary life is sheer boredom and misery;[11] without good morals it can easily become depraved, like the Emperor Tiberius' life at Capri. Some women have been solitaries, but they cannot be part of the solitary life of a man as Petrarch envisages it (2.3.3). Solitary men are typically those who have a spiritual and even physical disgust for the crowd, the *vulgus,* which necessarily embraces the vast majority of mankind. To consort with crowds in city life is to endanger one's soul. Petrarch describes vividly his own disgust with the sights and smells and behavior of common men, fearing that among such unlovely specimens of humankind he will "unlearn humanity" (*humanitatem inter homines dediscere,* 1.4.9).[12]

What is most radical about the solitary form of life as Petrarch envisages it is its non-monastic character. It is intended for mature men who enter into it voluntarily, without taking vows. These men might be secular clergy living on sinecures or laymen of sufficient means, but they would not be "religious" in the canonical sense—that is, members of monastic orders who had taken formal vows of poverty, chastity, and obedience. They cannot be married, too young or too old, courtiers, merchants or artisans, office-holders in towns, or clerics too involved with careers in the Church hierarchy.[13] For Petrarch's solitaries there are no vows of silence (hardly imaginable for so voluble a man as Petrarch) and no rules about confinement within walls; Petrarch celebrates the wanderings of solitary men in the countryside, over rivers, meadows, and mountains; his *solitarii* are rustic gyrovagues. Solitary men should live outside cities, but a liminal situation at the edge of cities, within easy walk of the countryside, is acceptable. That is how Petrarch lived during his eight years in Milan (1353–1361), at what was then the edge of the city, near the basilica of Sant'Ambrogio, and during his various extended visits to Parma, although at other times he preferred to be somewhat more removed from city life, as at Vaucluse (thirty-five kilometers from Avignon) or Arquà (twenty-five kilometers from Padua).

The life lived by solitary men in Petrarch's conception is a life devoted to the study of literature and philosophy. It is explicitly contrasted with the mercenary studies of the medieval university, which Petrarch had experienced in Bologna as a young law student but rejected with disgust. "I saw Bologna but didn't take to it" *(Bononiam vidi et . . . non adhesi).*[14] Anticipating themes of his later invective *De ignorantia sui ipsius et aliorum* (1367 / 1371), Petrarch lays out a model of moral and intellectual self-cultivation that rejects the ethos of scholasticism. The latter for him represented a corrupt form of education, mere pre-professional training, oriented to power and money-making and transmitting expertise without concern for moral character. Scholasticism focuses on problem-solving in particular contexts; it is designed to train medical doctors or lawyers, future decision-makers in lay governments and in the Church. Petrarch's *otium litterarium* by contrast— revealing its Stoic inspiration—is designed to instill wisdom and virtue. It broadens the mind so that it adopts a universal perspective, the perspective of all of time and space. By ranging through past times and around the globe the *solitarius* is drawn out of the moment; he suppresses consciousness of those who work evil in the present by meditating on the fine deeds of great men in other times and places. By exchanging the company of the vulgar and the ugliness of the city for the company of the mighty dead and the beauties of nature, the soul is uplifted and purified. It enjoys an intimacy with God impossible in the city. A true literary life is really only possible for those who have withdrawn from the active life (1.4.10): "Exemption from life's duties is the source of arts and letters" *(vacatio litterarum atque artium fons est).* The solitary and his friends, by reading, writing, and quiet discussion, help preserve the collective memory of humanity and the work of the great authors to whom it owed so much *(traditio).* By honoring in our work the discoverers of literature and the noble arts, Petrarch says, we are "carving statues of illustrious men more enduring than brass or marble." Our writings

> pay to posterity the debt we cannot pay to the dead for the gift of their writings. [In this way we do not] remain altogether ungrateful to the dead but make their names more recognized if they are little known, restore them if they have been forgotten, dig them out if they have been buried in the ruins of time and hand them down to our grandchildren as objects of veneration, carry them in our hearts and as something sweet in our mouths, and finally, by cherishing, remembering and celebrating their fame in every way, pay them the homage that is due to their genius, even though it may not be commensurate with their greatness.[15]

The self-cultivation of men in literary retirement is conducted among equals: Petrarch rejects the idea that one can only learn, or best learn, from a master (1.5.1). That is for schoolboys, not adults. Adult solitaries learn from each other on a basis of equality. Titles to learning such as doctorates do not guarantee real learning, as Petrarch demonstrates with a certain zest in two letters attacking his former teacher, Giovanni d'Andrea, the famous Bolognese jurist, for his pretense of knowing the classics.[16] The life of the solitary man is also supremely free: free from the cares of the active life, free from family cares, free from the demands of social superiors *(vacatio)*. In the country, by oneself, there can be no pressures for conformity (which Petrarch calls *imitatio*) in morals or in mores, in dress or in manners. There one needs only modest means to support a simple life; there one can be authentically oneself, *integer vitae scelerisque purus*. Living unspotted from the world, warding off contamination from the *profanum vulgus,* unencumbered by the cares of this life, one can more easily prepare one's soul for the next.

Though the *solitarius* spends most of his time alone in study and writing, it is of the essence of the solitary life that he enjoy close friendships.[17] He should fly from crowds, not friends *(turbas, non amicos fugiendos dico);* his life is one of solitude, not inhumanity *(immanitas).*[18] "If I had the choice of doing without the one or the other, I should prefer to be deprived of solitude rather than of my friend" (1.5.4). Indeed, Petrarch's conception of the solitary life has a communal aspect: it is a virtual fellowship of learned men, bound by shared moral and spiritual values, sustained by moments of vivid personal contact but maintained also via a constant exchange of letters, books, and dedications—what the quattrocento would call the *commercium litterarum,* the commerce of letters (a phrase Petrarch would surely have detested). The solitary and his friends see themselves as belonging to a virtual society of philosophers and literary men, extended across time and space, who share a common devotion to truth and goodness, a common culture. From this point of view Petrarch's two great epistolaries, the *Familiares* in twenty-four books and the *Seniles* in seventeen, provide a collective portrait of the fellowship of men who shared his life of literary solitude.

A group of these letters in book 8 of the *Familiares* (8.2–5), written from Parma in May 1349, shows us that the ideal of living a solitary life with a few close friends was not a mere dream. After the Black Death had taken the life of his beloved patron, Cardinal Giovanni Colonna, Petrarch acquired sufficient means—thanks to another patron, Azzo da Coreggio, the ruler of Parma—to propose forming a community of solitaries (if the expression may be allowed) that would live in the house he had purchased in 1344 on the outskirts of Parma.[19] The community would consist of four former members of the cardinal's household: Luca Cristiani (Petrarch's "Olympius," a cleric in minor orders, holder of a modest benefice in Piacenza), the Florentine humanist Mainardo Accursio (a descendent of the famous jurist Accursius), Ludwig van Kempen (Petrarch's "Socrates," a well-known musician and musical theorist) and Petrarch himself. They would live a frugal life together as equals, without a lord, pooling resources, devoting themselves to the *bonae artes*, preparing their souls in what remained of life for the life to come. Social equality was a necessity, since inequality engendered pride and patterns of deference inimical to true friendship. Their former life as familiars of the cardinal, though he had been a good man without arrogance, had still been a kind of slavery:

> To be set under another, to obey another, to live on another man's support can seem part of a more honorable kind of enslavement, but these are surely not marks of freedom. Look now, freedom, hated as it may be, has fallen to our lot and we are our own men rather sooner than we desired. . . . We are not lords of sea and earth as Aristotle says, nor do we have to be to win a blessed life.[20] But we have a sufficiency for moderate spirits that accommodate themselves to nature. If that is enough for each, what do we expect will happen to us all, when each in turn will give a hand to the other and whatever need befalls us will be supplied by another's resources? We will be overflowing, believe me, and should perhaps fear envy rather than scarcity.
>
> So why are we waiting? Why are we kept apart by sea and mountains and rivers? Why doesn't a single house finally unite us, as unity of wills formerly united us, unless we are afraid of new and unfamiliar experiences and think it foolish to dismiss a hope that promises much and disregard a fortune that calls us to higher things?[21]

The solitary life is not one that can or should be undertaken by everyone, and Petrarch nowhere is so bold as to rank it as the highest kind of human life. Its rarity makes it fine (an Aristotelian principle), but other kinds of life are also admirable. Petrarch's realistic attitude to the choices of life is brought out in the letters of advice he was sometimes called upon to write to young men who had read his works and had as a result (no doubt to the alarm of their parents) developed moral scruples about entering the active life.[22] In one such case, writing perhaps around 1340 to a young man called Marco Portinari of Genoa, torn between monastic life and the life of politics, Petrarch warns the young man of the dangers to his soul inherent in a life seeking political power. But he does not counsel the "higher" life of monasticism, because wise counsel needs to take account of the circumstances and the bent of the individual as well as any fixed hierarchy of values. Petrarch advises the young man that many great men in the past have begun as solitaries and later entered the active life (like Pope Sylvester I) or have begun in the active life and ended up, after the storms of life, in the safe harbor of solitude (like Pope Celestine I). In any case the active life of serving one's country has divine approval; he should not fear that care for his fellow citizens disqualifies him for the saving grace of God. Sounding for all the world like a civic humanist of the quattrocento, Petrarch tells him he will not have been born in vain if he assists his fatherland with his labor and counsel,

> especially in these times when it needs you so badly and, as Plato indicates, rightfully demands a part of your birthright for itself. Heavenly is that saying of my [Scipio] Africanus in Cicero's work [*De republica* 6.13]: "For all those who have preserved, assisted and supported their fatherland, there is certainly a definite place in heaven where the blessed experience joy eternally." Well known is also what follows: "There is nothing that exists on this earth that is more acceptable to that supreme God who rules over all this world than the assemblies and meetings of men united by law and forming what are known as states."[23]

A decade or so later the same man, no longer young, wrote again to Petrarch to share his misgivings about the moral effects of studying law. Petrarch wrote back, warning him of the evils to which a life in the law would expose him, especially in corrupt modern circumstances. Yet given the serious commitment Marco had already made to his legal education, Petrarch in the end urged him to persevere in the life he had chosen, supplying him with a panoramic history of the law in antiquity in order to inspire him to embrace higher moral standards in his jurisprudence than were being taught in modern universities.[24]

The Defense of Private Life

In short, Petrarch in defending the solitary life was not trying to undermine other accepted forms of life. His ugly pictures of moral corruption in contemporary cities were not meant to imply that the active life could never be lived well or without endangering the soul. Clearly it could, given the right times and the right circumstances. Petrarch's concern was to establish the legitimacy of his own, novel form of life—a contemplative life for laymen and secular clergy in minor orders who did not have the care of souls—and to argue that, for those in his situation, such a life was morally preferable to other recognized forms of life in Christian society. He realized that the solitary life required defense against the accepted norms of sociability in his time; he had indeed heard "clamoring" and "mutterings" from hostile critics who challenged the premises upon which his notion of the solitary life rested. That was where Petrarch was compelled to dip a toe into the unfamiliar waters of political theory.

In a passage near the end of book 2 (2.10.7) he addresses three authorities whose conceptions of the ethics of sociability appear to challenge the moral worth of the solitary life. The first is Aristotle. The Greek philosopher famously defines man as a political animal who completes his nature and acquires virtue by ruling other men. In a striking passage, Aristotle declares that someone who tried to flourish outside the polis would not really be human; he would be either a beast or a god.[25] Petrarch's response is simply to translate Aristotle's definition of man as *zoon politikon* into *sociale animal;* whether this crucial mistranslation is intentional or not is difficult to say.[26] In any case the mistake, if that is what it is, allows Petrarch to claim that his solitary life comes under the definition of a society, since it includes friends and serves humanity. Much earlier, in book 1 (1.5.4), he had upended the Aristotelian association of full humanity with city life using one of his typical rhetorical paradoxes: it is urban dwellers who are bestial and solitaries who are god-like, or at least angelic. Thus he urges the solitary man to live in such a way that those who visit him "should have occasion to marvel that humanity, which is exiled from the cities, inhabits the wilderness, and that while he has found bears and lions in populous places, in solitude he has discovered angelic man."

As we have seen, Petrarch has already deployed the Stoic-Christian concept of spiritual equality to show the superiority of the solitary life to the life of ordinary men, most of whom must live in dependence on others. Implicitly he opposes Aristotle's view in the *Politics* that to have one's human potentiality fully realized, one must command not only one's own soul but other men. Aristotle argues that fully to develop prudence and other virtues, one has to exercise one's virtue within the wider arena of the *polis*.[27] His position reflects the perspective of a political elite, but Petrarch, the former retainer of a prelate, takes the view of a subordinate, a man for whom social hierarchy, even under a virtuous superior, inevitably imposes a kind of slavery.

Petrarch goes even further and claims that the solitary's struggle to master himself, in terms of its difficulty, its hazards, and its ultimate dignity, is a struggle equal to or greater than the corresponding struggle of a governor or a military commander to rule those placed under him:

> In respect of numbers I admit their problem may be greater, for they are entrusted with large populations and vast armies whereas we have but the care of a single soul. But as far as risks are concerned, I deny that there is any difference. . . . We too have to expel vice from our borders, put our lusts to flight, restrain our illicit propensities, chastise our wantonness, and elevate our mind towards higher objects. . . . Let some govern a popular city [*urbem populi*] and others rule the army. Our city is that of our mind, our army that of our thoughts. . . . We too are commanders of our own affairs and similar risks call for similar precautions. Why do I say similar? Both our risks and our reward [i.e., eternal life] are greater.

Petrarch then proceeds to argue that no ruler or general—the highest representatives of the active life according to the ancients—nor any system of law ever successfully mastered the untameable vices of the many, but the solitary has good hope of winning the battle for virtue in his own life against the passions. That alone makes his life superior to the statesman's. In effect he claims that what counts in developing the virtues is not the larger arena of the city, but success in actually acquiring virtue; this seems to be an original argument (dare one say it) and one not unworthy of consideration within an Aristotelian theoretical framework. Aristotle's contention that the exercise of mastery over men is necessary to the finest form of the active life is thus internalized, transferred to the sphere of the soul. The solitary does not need politics to acquire the active virtues; indeed politics, messing about with the recalcitrant multitude, is a positive hindrance to achieving mastery over oneself. Since the *solitarius* is able to acquire the active as well as the contemplative virtues, his is a complete way of life in itself, not epiphenomenonal to civic life, as is the contemplative life in Aristotle.

The second authority Petrarch needs to answer is Cicero. Petrarch complains that critics of the solitary life "mutter against me" Cicero's claim (in *De officiis* 1.44.158) that men are naturally sociable and would associate together from inclination even if necessity did not make them form communities. Cicero's argument runs like this: even if people could have all their necessities supplied without social cooperation, they would still seek social intercourse to complete their happiness. In response, Petrarch simply grants that this is so, which is why he insists that the *solitarius* must cultivate true friendship. He admits that the *solitarius* cannot really do without the city—the symbiotic relationship between city and wilderness is a theme that runs throughout the *DVS*. But he insists that someone following the solitary life must have the autonomy to choose when to interact with the city and when to avoid it. He has no categorical duty to participate in a corrupt community at all times and in all places, even if it is one's own *patria*.

This point leads to the third objection against the solitary life. For this objection no authority is given, though it presupposes an organic conception of the state similar to Aristotle's, where the community is naturally prior to the individual.[28] To modern ears the argument that advocacy of the solitary life is a threat to the state has an almost Kantian ring: "'What would happen,' they say, 'if you could persuade all men in general of your design? Who then would live in the cities? Beware lest you speak against the interests of the *respublica*.'" As an aside, it may be pointed out that civic humanists of the fifteenth century sometimes expressed similar views regarding monastic institutions, charging that they harmed the state by placing their vast resources, needed for the state's defense and flourishing, beyond its reach.[29] In any case Petrarch's response is simply that, even were he to preach such a message in the city (which he would not), it would have no chance of success. If the vulgar started to stream out from the city to the solitudes of nature in obedience to his urging, they would no longer be solitudes. (Think Lake Como on a Sunday in August.) But this is absurd. "The mores of mankind as a whole are not like this; the *vulgus* does not lend ears so alert and wide open to gentlemanly counsel" *(honestis consiliis)*. In general Petrarch rejects dogmatic forms of altruism; charity is a matter of personal choice that reflects one's circumstances, not a categorical imperative (*DVS* 1.3.4). Like Seneca he holds that love of mankind has to begin with love of the self. If one did not prioritize the good of one's own soul, one would never be able to enlarge one's sympathies toward others—toward family, friends, country, and ultimately toward the whole cosmos. Charity begins at home.[30]

Seneca versus Augustine: Political Obligation and Political Autonomy

These challenges to Petrarch's conception of the solitary life were relatively easy to answer. That is not the case with two other challenges presented in the long passage I promised to comment on earlier, which is given in full in Appendix A. These were challenges that came not from external critics but instead arose from internal conflicts among Petrarch's own deepest convictions.

The passage in question comes at the end of a long digression in book 2, which must have been inserted sometime after 1355, since it refers to Charles IV's quick passage through Rome in April 1355 to "snatch his imperial crown" (*rapto dyademate*, 2.4.3).[31] The passage begins with a discussion of Peter the Hermit, the solitary whose preaching, according to Petrarch, was really responsible for inspiring the Crusades. Petrarch then discusses the history of Christendom: how in antiquity the faith had spread through the whole world, even passing beyond the borders of the Roman Empire, but had afterward shrunk under pressure from the Muslim ("Egyptian") conquests; how the Crusades, initially a success, had more recently failed owing to the lack of commitment from cowardly, weak, and selfish Christian princes, among whom he includes the pope, the Holy Roman Emperor and the emperor of the Greeks in Byzantium. Blame for the relative collapse of Christendom since antiquity is thus placed squarely on the shoulders of the corrupt princes of Christendom. Given their failures, they have no right to despise the pagan heroes of ancient Rome. If Caesar were to return from the underworld today and acknowledge the name of Christ, "as he surely would" *(ut haud dubie faceret),* he could easily subdue Egypt as he had done in the first century BC as a gift for Cleopatra; in gratitude for his salvation he would surely make the same gift now to Christ. Petrarch then loses himself in a fantasy that the ancient heroes of Rome might come back from the dead as baptized Christians: "Would they suffer the name of Christ to be held in contempt in the regions associated with their glory? . . . If, wanting the light of true faith, they dared such great enterprises for an earthly country, what do you suppose they would have dared with Christ leading them to success?" That is what Christendom needs now: Christians with the virtue and zeal of the ancient Roman heroes. Such prodigies would certainly not behave like the princes of modern Christendom, who prefer to serve the interests of their own corrupt regimes rather than the interests of Christ and our one true homeland, the Heavenly Jerusalem.

This sets up the final passage in the digression, the passage which provides the focus, or pretext, of this chapter. It is as though Petrarch realizes almost too late that he has found himself praising pagan heroes of the active life while supposedly defending the solitary life. This involves a certain amount of backtracking and qualification. Two voices in his head have started a dialogue. One is his humanist voice, the trumpet voice that blares forth inspiring examples of noble conduct from classical antiquity with the aim of reforming trecento Christendom. The stench of corruption coming from that world has led to a crisis of legitimacy; it is careening toward the bottom of its historical cycle, but it might begin to rise again if ancient pagan virtue and early Christian faith can somehow be recovered and combined by modern Christians. Petrarch's first, naïvely political project of civilizational renewal had suffered an appalling setback with the sudden collapse of Cola di Rienzo's movement, but hope for such a renewal or rebirth never entirely faded in later life, though it gradually mutated into something like a cultural movement. In personal terms Petrarch's humanist voice opened up a fork in his own road: he could either continue in the solitary life, preserving and adding to the classical literary heritage for posterity, hoping for better times to come; or he could take another road, become a familiar and counselor of princes, with the temptations to wealth, status, and fame such a status involved, but also with the chance of effecting real moral change in the present.[32]

The other voice in his head is Augustine's, whose *City of God* he was meditating on as he wrote the passage under discussion. Augustine—the "philosopher of Christ" to whom Petrarch credited his personal reformation—presented him with a tragic view of the Christian's duty toward the state that Petrarch simply could not accept.[33] Augustine, writing after the Visigoths' sack of Rome in 410, believed the end times had come and that the world of time, the *saeculum,* was about to be rolled up into the scroll of eternity, making the possibility of political reform limited, not to say shortsighted—a bad investment of time that might better be spent on preparing one's soul for heaven. With his residual Neoplatonism, Augustine thinks of the temporal world, the world of history, as nothing but an inferior copy of the heavenly Jerusalem, the City of God, the eschatological society that will come into being at the Second Coming.[34] Owing to its inherent metaphysical inferiority, the temporal world of our experience never had a chance to achieve real virtue or true glory; the vaunted virtues of the old Romans were always vitiated by a false religion and by false motives: the love of glory rather than the love of God. Love of glory is an obstacle to spiritual progress; at best it can check the worst excesses of *libido dominandi,* the lust for lordship, but nothing more.[35] Since "an individual's true moral status consists in his inner disposition,"[36] not in the objective results of his acts (as Petrarch too believed), the value of the old Roman heroes as models for Christians was limited (which Petrarch did not believe). The Roman Empire, even at the apogee of its power, was always violent and corrupt. At best it provided peace and a semblance of order. It could not take credit even for its conquests: its power to rule had been given by Divine Providence.

But herein lies the tragedy. Despite the wickedness of the Roman Empire, the Christian cannot and should not refuse to serve in its offices when called upon to do so. The state provides peace and "a shadow of justice," and the benefits Christians derive from these goods generate a duty to participate in the state: "Human society constrains [the wise Christian] and sets him to perform his plain duty; to desert human society he considers unspeakable wickedness *(nefas)*."[37] Participation in rule unavoidably means participation in the administration of justice. However, such are the conditions of earthly justice that those who participate in government will inevitably commit some injustices owing to their inability to see into the hearts of others. Augustine gives as an example the Roman practice of obtaining evidence under torture: How is one to know whether to condemn someone based on evidence obtained by such means? One cannot. Doing injustice is unavoidably part of civil life, and the fact that the Roman Empire was now officially Christian has not changed that fact. One can hope for and expect some slight improvement in political justice from the participation of Christians in it, but the number of true Christians is too small, and comes too late in time, to alter the fundamental reality: our civic obligations sometimes force us to do evil, albeit unwittingly and unwillingly. We have to wage just wars precisely because they are just; if they were not we would be relieved of that duty, but the injustice of the opposing side lays on the wise man the duty of waging war, with the inevitable evils that follow. We cannot in this life truly remain unspotted from the world. We must not abandon our duty, even to an evil world.[38]

In *De vita solitaria* we see Petrarch negotiating between these two voices in his head. In the end he finds a way to cut through the fearful rigor of Augustine's logic: he simply denies that one has an unconditional duty to participate in the active life of politics and war.[39] Only a state ruled by justice and fair laws can deserve our allegiance. That is the inevitable corollary of his wider doctrine that virtue is a necessary condition of legitimate rule. Furthermore, he refuses to downgrade the virtue of the old Roman heroes in Augustine's way: by impugning the purity of their motives. The old Roman *respublica* was a good state, "as Sallust and Livy and many others have written," and worth fighting for, and the men who did so deserved the praise they won. Petrarch agrees with Cicero that the old Roman commonwealth was good, citing, via Augustine, a long passage from Cicero's *De republica* and another directly from the *De officiis*.[40] Even if the Romans were extremely violent and coercive in imposing peace (as Augustine had charged), "it was in the interests of those who were coerced to be coerced, however distasteful that might be, and in the interest of the world that it have a single head of affairs [i.e.,

Rome], provided it were the best and finest head." Or rather (he corrects himself), he might agree with Cicero—he is ready to grant the Romans' supreme justice and goodwill toward mankind—but (as a Christian) he has to register one strong caveat. They had to be faulted—and Petrarch admits it was a great fault—for refusing their obedience to the true God and for worshipping His enemies, the pagan gods, instead. He then refers the reader to Augustine's detailed *(curiose)* discussion of the passage from Cicero.[41]

This was a striking position to take. The upshot of Petrarch's tortured syntax was that the Romans had a good commonwealth but a bad religion. The good commonwealth can and should be a model for moderns, but not the bad religion. Petrarch's silence on the issue of what had motivated the Romans in their quest for glory—an issue fundamental for Augustine—is telling. In any case, the ancient Romans were right to serve their commonwealth because it was just, and we are right to refuse service to our corrupt modern commonwealths because they lack justice. No political obligation exists in a society where there is no justice. If things were to change, one's obligations would change as well. Petrarch's high appraisal of the ancient Roman republic and its moral foundations leaves open—as Augustine's does not—the possibility that modern Christian rulers might once again embrace classical virtue and wisdom. He leaves open, in other words, the possibility of a Renaissance.

Petrarch does not explain the source of this line of reasoning, but in fact, as all commentators have noted, it comes from Seneca's fragmentary treatise *De otio*. It is no doubt significant that, for once, he is silent about the source of his ideas. It would not do to follow a pagan philosopher in preference to "the philosopher of Christ."[42] For Petrarch goes on to argue (implicitly) against Augustine, that one need not fight for "an unjust country with evil customs, such as nearly all the ones we see today." If one were to shed one's blood for a corrupt *patria* one would in effect be trying to save its citizens from the justice of God, since (on Augustinian principles) defeat in battle is God's way of punishing wicked peoples. A man who fights for a corrupt country deserves no praise, no memorials. To indulge for a moment in the *reductio ad Hitlerum,* Nazis do not deserve our admiration, however selflessly they may have fought for the fatherland. The only country that deserves our unconditional loyalty is the Heavenly Jerusalem, for whose sake there would be nothing it would not be right to dare or to do.

The echoes of Seneca are important since they come from a famous passage in which the Roman philosopher discusses the very same issue, the morality of serving corrupt regimes. The Roman philosopher appeals to the principles of Stoic cosmopolitanism to find justifications, under some circumstances, for withdrawal from public life.[43] There are times when one's native commonwealth (*respublica*) is in such a bad condition that a good man cannot be of service, and under these circumstances the usual Stoic view that men should serve their fellow men by entering public life has to be relaxed. In this case a life of private leisure and philosophical study can be defended. Such a life observes the higher Stoic principle that governs the duty of political participation, namely, the good man's obligation to serve the whole of humanity. Someone who cultivates wisdom and the life of virtue in retirement (*otium*) is justified in that he is preparing himself to benefit others. He can do so, even when the state into which we are born is corrupt, or even when all states are corrupt, because Stoicism teaches us that as rational beings we belong to two commonwealths: that of our birth, and the greater commonwealth in which we are citizens together with all men and the gods. Moveover, nature has given us a natural desire for knowledge and contemplation, and "to employ the fruits of our contemplation in the service of humanity by writing and teaching satisfies the wider requirement."[44]

We can see from this summary how Petrarch has used Seneca to correct Augustine. As usual, he digests his authors without being mastered by them—a procedure he recommends in the sphere of literary imitation as well.[45] Seneca licenses Petrarch's withdrawal from civic life. But as a deracinated *literatus* Petrarch feels no real commitment to any state—certainly not to his own poor, long-abandoned Florence—except perhaps to the Rome he saw reborn in his dreams. He certainly does not share Seneca's reluctance to abandon service even to bad states.[46] But the great difference with Seneca, of course, is Petrarch's identification of the universal commonwealth of gods and men with the Heavenly Jerusalem. The difference is important. The Heavenly Jerusalem exists only in the future, in eternity, *in saeculum saeculorum*, and includes only Christians saved by the grace of God. No matter how cosmopolitan Petrarch may have been in his way of life, he was never a cosmopolitan in the sense that word was used in ancient Stoicism. For him Seneca's arguments lead to something more like the "negative" cosmopolitanism of the Cynics, a formula used to deny that the polis is the only possible focus of one's existence and loyalties.[47]

Petrarch's dissent from Augustine, anguished though it clearly is, has significant implications. The logic of virtue politics entails that states run by wicked men forfeit their right to command our obedience and service. States that lack justice—

either because their laws are unfair or they are ruled by evil men—are obeyed only out of fear; we need not sacrifice ourselves for them for the sake of duty. The roots of natural sociability, based in gratitude, have withered away. The wickedness of rulers trumps the fundamental loyalty one owes to one's country, or ought to owe to it. In virtue politics, the obligations of political obedience are always conditional. The injunctions of Jesus Christ and the Apostle Paul to obey the civil authorities is downgraded to a mere counsel of prudence. It is not a categorical endorsement of the legitimacy of present powers or a license for misrule. The structure of obligation is in effect the reverse of that common dilemma of modern utilitarian politics: Can one use unjust means to achieve just ends? That sort of dilemma can arise from a Machiavellian calculus of ends and means but is foreign to virtue politics, where ends and means are identical. In the tradition of virtue politics, acting unjustly to achieve justice is a self-defeating act. Justice is not mere adherence to positive law—mere legality—nor is it posterior to the acquisition or retention of political power. It is, precisely, acting justly—what Aristotle would call *eupraxia*.

In this respect Petrarch is a true representative of virtue politics. He sees no modern commonwealth that can command his loyalties and feels fully justified in removing himself from the trecento equivalent of public life: life in the court of a prince or prelate, or life as an officeholder in a city-republic. His violent distaste for the politics of his own time leads him to the radical conclusion—radical in his late-medieval context—that he has no categorical duty to serve the powers that be, whether they claim to be appointed of God or not.[48] Political obligation has to be mediated by an autonomous personal judgment that a given commonwealth is just or unjust, worthy or not worthy of our service. Like the Stoics and later humanists, to be sure, Petrarch does not deny that we are born with fundamental, inescapable duties to others; like later humanists he loves to quote the line of Plato reported in Cicero's *De officiis* (1.22): "We are not born for ourselves alone, but our friends and our country each claim a share in our origins." Seneca added all humanity to that list of innate, unchosen duties. But we have the autonomy to decide which of those duties deserve to be the focus of our moral benevolence. Political obligation is a two-way street: governments can claim our obedience, but they also have to earn it; obedience in some circumstances can licitly be refused. Petrarch has thus taken a step in the direction of the autonomous subject of modern politics, a subject who is free to enter into political contracts or to resist the authority of governments that do not take account of his own will. His ability to defend a degree of personal moral autonomy within the broader framework of the natural law tradition deserves more acknowledgment than it has found in histories of modern moral thought.[49]

Elsewhere in his writings Petrarch systematically cast doubt on the modes of legitimation used by medieval governments to justify their rule.[50] He expressed skepticism about the Papacy's right to transfer the empire from the Roman people; he questioned the right of the Germans to exercise imperial power. Following Sallust, he made the argument that the durable possession of empire depended, in the end, on the mores of those who exercised it. The *translatio imperii,* the movement of imperial power from one place to another, followed Fortune, who favored the virtuous, and could not be corroborated merely by the fictions of the lawyers or by appeal to Divine Providence.[51] Petrarch did not argue that the Donation of Constantine, the basis of the Papacy's claim to political power, was a forgery, as Lorenzo Valla later did, but he doubted its legal validity.[52] In general he dismissed legal titles to power in preference to an ancient, but in his day unfamiliar, criterion of justice: the virtuous exercise of power. Only those who have command of themselves and therefore know how to impose *kosmos,* divine order, on the anarchy of human passions are worthy of commanding others. The next century of humanism, from Salutati down to the time of Machiavelli, would undertake a great experiment to see if Italy, the ancient mother, could once again give birth to such extraordinary human beings.

CHAPTER 7

BOCCACCIO ON THE PERILS OF WEALTH AND STATUS

To anyone considering the enormous body of scholarship in several languages devoted to the life and work of Giovanni Boccaccio, the claim that he has never been taken seriously as a political thinker will seem surprising. Yet it remains the case, to take one indicator, that he has never merited sustained treatment in any modern history of political thought. There are only a couple of passing references to him in Quentin Skinner's canonical *Foundations of Modern Political Thought* and none at all in the relevant volume of *The Cambridge History of Medieval Political Thought.*[1] There seem to be no monographs or specialized studies on his relationship to the political thought of his time.

The reasons for this neglect are not hard to find. Boccaccio's political ideas are developed most extensively in the *De casibus virorum illustrium* (The Downfalls of Famous Men), a text written in awkward and often obscure Latin and deploying considerably less narrative charm than the *Decameron.*[2] Another obstacle is the persistent classification of Boccaccio as a "medieval" writer, most famously in Vittore Branca's classic biography *Boccaccio medievale.*[3] This classification has been reinforced by the modern historiographical tradition that emphasizes republican liberty as the most significant theme in humanist thinking about politics. That interpretation was first laid out by Hans Baron and Eugenio Garin in the middle decades of the twentieth century and was elaborated by Riccardo Fubini, J. G. A. Pocock, Quentin Skinner, and other scholars. It is still, broadly speaking, the consensus view. Baron saw the origins of Renaissance political thought in the "crisis" years around 1402, when republican Florence fought the Visconti "tyrants" of Milan for control of northern Italy. It was in the crucible of that struggle that the folklore of the popular medieval commune was fused, in Florence, with the erudite but politically quietist traditions of Petrarchan humanism, creating a new, hybrid political tradition he labelled "civic humanism." This understanding of Renaissance political thought, it will be seen, places Boccaccio on the "medieval" side of Baron's crisis date of 1402. My goal here will be to approach Boccaccio's political thought with a fresh eye and to test whether he can be considered, like his mentor Petrarch, as part of the tradition of humanist virtue politics, and thus, in this respect at least, more of a Renaissance figure than has hitherto been accepted.[4]

Boccaccio's Political Experience

Despite his well-known love of princely courts—above all, that of King Robert of Naples—and despite the frigid attitude to Florence expressed in his famous letter to Niccola Acciaiuoli, written just after his unwilling return to his native city in 1341, Boccaccio was, by the early 1350s, an active participant in Florence's public life.[5] He served frequently as a paid official of the republic. Indeed, it could be said that after his repeated failures during the 1340s to find a princely benefactor, the *comune* of Florence itself became, for some time in the 1350s, his most reliable patron.[6] Some of the relevant facts have been known for many years, but our understanding of Boccaccio's role in Florence's public life has recently been much enriched by the research of Laura Regnicoli for the exhibition *Boccaccio autore e copista,* mounted by the Biblioteca Medicea Laurenziana in 2013.[7] Among the offices held by Boccaccio were the following:

1348, tax collector (one of eight *Ufficiali delle Gabelle*)
1350, ambassador to the Romagna
1350, city treasurer *(Camarlengo della Camera)*
1351, one of the overseers of Florence's rural territory *(Difensori del contado)*
1351, ambassador to Emperor Ludwig of Bavaria
1352, emissary to Padua to invite Petrarch to lecture at Florence's university
1352, collector of the bread tax (the *Gabelle del pane*)
1353, member of the Overseers of Public Works *(Ufficiali di torre)*
1354, selected as candidate for the civic board in charge of Orsanmichele
1354, ambassador to Pope Innocent VI
1354, ambassador in the Valdelsa
1355, auditor of mercenary troops
1359, ambassador "to parts of Lombardy"
1364, proposed by the Guelf Party for selection to the *Tre Maggiori*—that is, the three highest civic boards: the town council (the *Signoria*), the

"Good Men" (an advisory body to the Signori), and the Standard-
Bearers of the civic militia, another advisory body

1364–1365, listed as one of the defense commissioners (*Ufficiali dei castelli*)

1365, credentialed to the Doge of Genoa

1365, ambassador to Pope Urban V

1367, member of a public arbitration committee evaluating the artist
Orcagna's work in Orsanmichele

1367, member of the board of overseers of Florence's hired troops (*Ufficiali della condotta*)

1367, ambassador to Pope Urban V

1368, second term on the Ufficiali della condotta

1373–1374, public lecturer on Dante

In this impressive record of civic involvement, a hiatus is noticeable between 1355 and 1364, during which time Boccaccio's only service to Florence was a brief embassy to Milan in the summer of 1359. This gap invites speculation as to its cause.[8] Boccaccio's disappearance from communal office may have been the result of his identification with the pro-Neapolitan party led by his boyhood friend and later patron, Niccola Acciaiuoli, the Grand Seneschal of the Kingdom of Naples. Acciaiuoli's visit to Florence in 1355, which ended by alienating Florentines from Neapolitan interests, could well have harmed Boccaccio's political career.[9] Florence's foreign policy became pronouncedly anti-Neapolitan in the later 1350s, and it is possible that Boccaccio's standing with the regime was damaged a second time by association with Acciaiuoli when the Grand Seneschal's return to Florence in 1360 again alarmed popular forces within the government. Acciaiuoli came to Florence from Bologna, basking in the new prestige that had come from his successful embassy on behalf of Naples, and his return gave new hope to the party of the self-proclaimed nobles. According to Leonardo Bruni's *History*, Acciaiuoli had helped to keep Bologna a papal state and to limit Milanese influence there, to the relief of most Florentines. Despite this success, he was prevented from holding office in Florence by anti-aristocratic sentiment in the Signoria and saddled with an enormous tax burden to hasten his departure.[10]

The later 1350s were years of bitter partisan strife in Florence, marked by the toxic politics of the conservative Parte Guelfa. As Stephen Milner has noted, Boccaccio's political connections were all on the side of the magnate and pro-Neapolitan houses—the Bardi, Rossi, Acciaiuoli, and Peruzzi houses, led by Lapo da Castiglionchio—who collectively sought to restore the *comune nobiliare* of the early fourteenth century.[11] Many of them benefitted from commercial relations with Naples. They were opposed by the more popular party, which was based in the guild community and more open to participation in government on the part of recent immigrants, the *gente nuova.* The patrician party lost the struggle for dominance, and just after Acciaiuoli's exit from the city, a group of malcontents, including Boccaccio's friend Pino de'Rossi, attempted to overthrow the popular regime. The leaders of the coup were executed or, in Pino's case, exiled. Around this same time Boccaccio received holy orders and the authorization to hold benefices *con cura d'anime.* Was this an insurance policy, brokered by friends in the Church, or a sign of a deeper change of heart?[12]

Nevertheless, despite all his glittering connections with Florence's rich and famous, in his famous consolatory letter to Pino de'Rossi, written just after his exile, Boccaccio seemed to be at pains neither to approve nor condemn the coup in which Pino had participated. His only supportive remark was to say that Pino himself did not deserve exile. Boccaccio's attitude to the politics of his noble friends, indeed, was by no means one of unquestioning support. A key principle of their political ideology was a kind of nativist opposition to *gente nuova,* but Boccaccio championed bringing men of low social station into government so long as they were virtuous. This is hardly surprising since his own father was an immigrant from the town of Certaldo in the Florentine countryside.

In his *Consolatory Letter to Pino de'Rossi* Boccaccio explicitly refused to blame *gente nuova* for the political corruption of Florence (as one might have expected a member of the Rossi family to do), finding plenty to blame among the *originali cittadini*:

> I am not going to blame those coming from Capalle or those from Celiaula or from the Sugana or Viminiccio, who were taken away from their ploughs and trowels [i.e. *gente nuova* engaged in manual labor] and elevated to our highest magistracy. In fact [Attilius Regulus] Serranus, led from sowing to the consulate of Rome, was perfectly able to hold the ivory scepter assigned to that magnificent office with hands used to breaking up hard clods in the field; and Gaius Marius, who grew up following his father's army and setting up tent poles, conquered Africa and dragged Jugurtha in chains back to Rome. And to avoid talking about those people any longer—since I for one am not surprised at [their rise to power], because souls are not poured into mortals by God in the same way as fortunes are [i.e., one can have a good soul despite

poverty]—even if we turn to whomever we want among the purest native citizens, these people, either because their souls are dominated by insatiable envy, or because they are swollen with pride or inflamed by unjustified anger, as they care about their own business rather than the public's, they have drawn this city into misery and keep drawing it into slavery—a city that we call ours today, and, if nothing changes, we'll one day regret being called its citizens. And in addition to that, we see (and to reduce our shame I won't mention the gluttons, the drunkards, the whoremongers, and similar scum) highly dishonest men, who, either by a most severe countenance, or by never uttering a word, or by scraping their feet against holy images [i.e., pretending to piety], or often by bloviating and presenting themselves as most loving fathers and defenders of the common good (though, if you inquire, they wouldn't be capable of counting how many fingers they have in their hands—and yet they are grand masters at stealing or bribery, whenever they have a chance for that), these men, since they are considered good men by the deceived people, are set at the steering wheel of so great a ship, a ship already worn out by so many storms.[13]

By the time he wrote his letter to Pino, Boccaccio was thoroughly disgusted with Florentine party politics. It seems clear that his experiences had lifted his thinking about government onto a more philosophical, non-partisan plane. It was a stance that resembled that of his mentor Petrarch, one that later humanists would often adopt. Boccaccio told Pino that he had exiled himself from Florence to Certaldo—and would have gone even further away had his poverty allowed it—to avoid the stench of the city's iniquity. In Certaldo he has begun to enjoy a new life in rough clothes, eating peasant food, and is happy to avert his eyes from the ambition and provocations of Florentine citizens. In exchange for anxious involvements with citizens, he sees trees with green leaves, fields dressed with bright flowers, things produced simply by nature. Where there are no citizens with their petty frauds, he sings sweet airs with a delight more than equal to the annoyance he used to feel listening all day to the tricks and treacheries of his fellow Florentines.[14]

The Need to Reform the Materia Prima of Politics: Human Nature

This biographical context is crucial for understanding Boccaccio's mature thinking about the problems of human government. The first drafts of the De casibus and the Trattatello in laude di Dante were begun around 1355, just as Boccaccio was ending his first period of civic involvement.[15] The consolatory letter to Pino de'Rossi was written most probably in 1361 / 1362, not long after the failure of the aristocratic coup.[16] These two writings are the most important sources for Boccaccio's political thought. They reveal not only his bitter disillusionment with Florentine politics but a strong conviction that involvement in the day-to-day passions of political life is bad for the soul.

Boccaccio's contempt is not just for the politics of Florence. Wherever he turns his gaze he finds corrupt political authorities. In the prologue of the *De casibus* he describes with satiric wit his search for someone to whom he might dedicate his treatise, someone with sufficient virtue to appreciate its contents. He looked first for a prelate, but all of them were armed to the teeth, eagerly spilling the blood of their fellow Christians. Then he thought of the emperor but realized he would be far to the North, swilling amid the snows of Germany *(inter nives et pocula),* ignorant of the great deeds of his Roman predecessors. He considered the Salian Franks, that is, the French, who presented themselves with rash daring as superior in ancestry and morals to other nations, but then he remembered that they were illiterate. He could think of no other European prince whose ignorance and vice would not make a mockery of his work's moral message. All of them filled him with nausea. That was when he decided that the best course would be to dedicate his work not to a powerful, corrupt, and heedless ruler, but to a trustworthy, loved, and generous friend, Mainardo Cavalcanti, a Florentine ennobled by his service to the Angevin court of Naples.

Boccaccio's contempt for the ruling elites of his time extended even to the wealthy *popolano* citizens of Florence. In *De casibus,* after contemplating the virtue of the ancient Roman heroes, he could not help drawing the contrast with the corrupt mores of modern times. In that connection,

> unless honor prohibits it, I would name also my own citizens. On undertaking any expedition, their first question, the one most holy to them, is about the prospect of profit, thievery and rapine; whether they can possess themselves of things both sacred and profane, even to the harm of the public, while they themselves remain immune from penalty. A man who understands the persuasiveness of avarice will understand well enough what reply they are going to make. I wish moreover that the men who want glory first and effort last would pay attention to what Attilius said in the [Roman] Senate for the public good against his own life and liberty—this man was willing to expose himself to torture for the slightest public benefit. But these men, [my fellow Florentines],

detestabile genus hominum, after they have taken over all honors and advantages through their wicked ambition, are not ashamed to lie in public that they are paupers—when in fact their private resources are abundant—in order to flee common burdens. It's hard to believe that these men would place their security and blood on the line for their country when they impudently deny it the slightest particle of their substance when necessity demands it. They have the resources to provide large dowries, hold magnificent wedding feasts—more like kings than citizens; they mount massive displays of finery but can't contribute to the public fisc.[17]

Spoken like a frustrated tax collector? Perhaps. But what is significant is that Boccaccio's bitter disillusionment about the exercise of political power in his own day drove him to draw the same conclusion drawn by Petrarch and all the leading humanists of the next century: that the inescapable preliminary to any rebirth of Roman glory lay in the revival of Roman virtue. And the only way to revive Roman virtue was to revive the lost disciplines of classical culture, especially philosophy and poetry, in which the noble ancients had been educated. This was Boccaccio's project in his last two decades. It may have had its root in the personal crisis that led him to embrace Petrarchan humanism sometime after the Black Death. But it was Boccaccio who understood, more clearly even than Petrarch, that no republic would ever be sound without morally sound men to govern it; that the reform of politics would require a new ethos of public service, a commitment to the common good and loyalty to one's family, friends, and country; that virtue and patriotism went together. In the current state of Christendom, moral corruption was planted too wide and deep to expect better government in the near term. Reflecting on the reasons for the greatness of Rome, filled with nostalgia for her lost glory, he understood that what counted in the end was not Rome's laws and institutions and military arts, but the quality of her human material.

De casibus makes a start on this project by driving home, again and again, that the false motives actuating the corrupt leaders of his own time would not and could not succeed in winning Fortune's lasting favor. Such motives need to be replaced by patriotism, public spiritedness, and sacrifice for the common good. At one point he states that "we are born first for our country, then for ourselves." This is a stronger version, because inverted in its emphasis, of the famous humanist commonplace taken from Plato via Cicero and so often cited by Petrarch, that we are born not just for ourselves but for our family, our friends, and our country.[18] The whole project of the *De casibus* clearly anticipates the quattrocento humanist program of moral rearmament: Boccaccio claims he is writing the book for the utility of the republic, *reipublicae utilitati,* to promote virtue by showing the inevitable consequences of vice. But since in his own time the virtuous were few and the tone of politics as a whole was set by men who were unable to detach themselves from perishable and worthless things, the strongest literary measures would be necessary to shake men out of their complacent selfishness and moral insensitivity. That is why Boccaccio filled nine books with an avalanche of moral exempla and denunciations and exhortations in the hope that, by sheer profusion, he might break through the hardened hearts of his contemporaries, just as dripping water eventually wears down stone.[19]

Boccaccio's sense of the depravity of his own times explains a great deal about his attitudes to Fortune, Virtue, Time, and Fame, those prime coordinates in the humanist moral geography.[20] In antiquity, when human virtue was strong, it was able to restrict the power of Fortune. *Ubi virtus sit, ibi nullas partes esse Fortune* (5.4): Fortune plays no part where there is virtue. No wonder that in Roman times the empire's only boundary was the Ocean Sea, given the immense reservoir of virtue on which it could call. But in modern times, virtue was no guarantee of good fortune. A central message of the *De casibus* is precisely this: Fortune brings low both the wicked and the virtuous, so long as men focus their desires on changeable things such as corrupt pleasures, wealth, power, and status. There is no one whose virtue and wisdom—or guile and perfidy, for that matter—is so effective as to guarantee Fortune's continuing favor. In fact, worldly success, however achieved, is intrinsically dangerous. It leads inevitably to your downfall, and its pursuit endangers the health of your soul. The only safe play for your soul is to remain humble and poor. That way a kind of happiness can be found. Personal virtue can aid the rise of someone focused on the wrong sort of goal—for example, a Pompey or a Zenobia—but since the goal itself is unstable, virtue alone won't save the ambitious man from disaster.

The wise man living in corrupt times must find a different goal and feed another sort of ambition: an ambition for Good Fame. The matter is most fully discussed at the beginning of *De casibus,* book 8.[21] There Boccaccio begins by questioning his own motives for writing, for seeking fame from the ashes of the past. He tells himself he is wasting his time, that seeking fame won't do him any good in the here and now; he should give up his efforts and spend what is left of his days seeking pleasure *pro qualitate temporis,* in proportion to what the evils of his time allow. Then Petrarch appears to him in a vision, wearing the laurel and dressed in a royal robe. Petrarch tells him that the desire for fame is natural; it is a good sought out by all mortals. Men seek virtue because they desire fame, so that if you condemn fame, you condemn virtue. Nature implants in everyone a kind of goad that day and night drives us through virtue to glory. The praise of fame is the only way the merit of mortals becomes immortal. Fame extends our life into the future, and knowledge that this is the case gives us satisfaction in the present. Petrarch goes so far as to claim that Jerome and Augustine and other holy men, although they desired eternal glory, were also drawn by an appetite for temporal fame when they wrote their divine works.[22]

The desire for good fame is thus a commendable motivation, transcending the present moment and therefore much more resistant to the power that Fortune wields over mere temporal goods. It is that desire which should drive the truly noble man, not wealth and status. To those who might object that a sincere Christian ought to fear pride and seek humility, Boccaccio replies that the love of good fame, like other human loves, can be justified if it is sought for the sake of God and for the good of others. The life beyond the grave offered by the Christian faith is ordered to mankind's eternal end, but there are lasting, if not eternal, things that require our care too in this human life of ours. The desire for good fame, for "separation from the herd," is natural and good. Its achievement is the reward of virtue. When virtue has good fame as its goal, it can succeed, and fame can survive far beyond the span of our lives. Seeking fame for oneself is good, because it fights against sloth (a deadly sin), because it recompenses God for the gifts he has given us, and because it serves others.

Fame for Boccaccio is already part of the social technology that encourages truly noble individuals to strive for virtue and by so doing to serve the state. That is most clearly seen in his proem to the *Life of Dante*, where he claims that what made ancient empires great, including both Greece and Rome, was their practice of celebrating great men with statues, triumphs, laurel crowns, funerals, and even deification. Dante had been deluded by popular favor, always unstable, and the belief that he could help so corrupt a city by participating in its civic life. He paid the price for this mistake. Florence's foul treatment of Dante shows how far the moderns have fallen from the ancients' respect for virtue. "If his deeds had been performed in a just republic," Boccaccio writes, "there is no doubt that they would have covered him in the highest merit." His own celebration of Dante's life will form some kind of recompense for what the city should have done; it will help save Florence from the charge of ingratitude. He (like Dante) writes in the *volgare* in order to lift up a city unable to appreciate Latin literature; perhaps by so doing he will begin to give it a proper respect for the liberal arts, the true foundation of a city's glory.[23]

Virtue, Education, and Tyranny

Though Boccaccio had no great hope for the revival of ancient virtue in his own times, he recognized, like later humanists, that virtue is the cement of every successful government, and vice its solvent. Rulers need virtue in order to keep the loyalty of their subjects. It is even the subject's duty, if his ruler is wicked, to commit tyrannicide. Remarking on the cruel and oppressive rule of Rehoboam, son of King Solomon, Boccaccio editorializes:

> I ask, when I see the man to whom I have turned over all honor, liberty, majesty, duty, and preeminence; to whom I have done obeisance, for whom I have sweated, with whom I have shared my substance, for whose safety I have poured out my blood—[when I see that man] spending all his time impoverishing me, cursing me and trying to ruin me; thirsting for blood, drinking, swindling, wasting his resources on lewd women and scoundrels—resources that should have been used to succour the needy and wretched—delighting in the worst counsel for the worst projects, and neglecting the public good—shall I call such a man a king? Shall I revere him as a prince, shall I keep faith with him as a lord? Perish the thought! He is an enemy. It is the work of the great-souled man to conspire against him, take up arms, form plots, and physically oppose him—it is a most holy and entirely necessary duty. There is no more acceptable offering to God than the blood of a tyrant. . . . Therefore let those who want to rule others learn, if they wish their reigns to be long ones and the people's trust to be stable, that they must suppress their appetites and rein in their lusts, and—the holiest rule of all—strive to be more loved than feared, so that they may seem to be fathers as much as commanders over the subject plebs.[24]

Apart from the vividness that comes from Boccaccio's exposing his own psychological state—his angry response to tyrannical vice—and the implication that a kind of informal moral contract exists between ruler and ruled, his advice here would be unsurprising in any medieval mirror for princes. But there is more. It is a constant theme of his that the best and most successful political leaders are those who possess true—that is, natural—nobility, and that this kind of nobility can be found in all social ranks, from farmers and craftsmen to the rich and well-born. It cannot be passed down by birth or hereditary right but is an acquired skill in right living that is transmitted as knowledge.[25] Therefore it belongs by right to the educated and not to those of high descent. Indeed, he goes further than most later humanists and claims that wealthy and powerful youths who have lived a soft life surrounded by sycophantic admirers are much less likely to end up as successful leaders than those brought up in humbler circumstances and a harder school of life. Commenting on the life of Marius, the Roman general and statesman, Boccaccio writes,

> True nobility does not live, as many stupid people believe, in royal households, nor does it delight in riches and splendid clothes; nor does it dwell in the *lares* of descendants because of the famous images of ancestors; it delights only in purity of mind in whomever and wherever it appears. Being persuaded of [this truth], Marius, a *novus homo,* purged the army that had been corrupted by the avarice of Metellus, a man thought noble by the foolish mob. Marius bested an enemy who had himself often bested slothful though noble generals; he bound a king who had very often bound the minds of noblemen with gold. When it will be obvious that *they* are ignoble, why then shall we not call *him* noble for his upright virtue? For those who wish to cultivate the virtues, to act with virtue—to condemn completely, repel and put to flight vice—must necessarily possess the most indisputable virtue, and not its shadow.[26]

The virtues of commoners, farmers, and even the urban plebs are praised by Boccaccio repeatedly throughout the *De casibus.* Commenting on Rehoboam's tyranny again, he writes, "Not even the least member of the plebs is to be regarded as worthless; each man, when driven by his own interest, carries a great soul beneath his breast."

All men of every class are capable of virtue, but they need the right kind of education. This education cannot be found in the universities, particularly the law schools. Boccaccio is writing a quarter century before the beginnings of the humanist school, but he shares Petrarch's prejudice (and that of later humanists) against legal education. Like Bartolomeo Scala in his *Dialogue on Laws and Courts,* Boccaccio recognizes that in antiquity there was a good, uncorrupted form of legal study, but that was only because ancient scholars learned in law already knew literature and philosophy before taking up jurisprudence.[27] But the present age, writes Boccaccio, snatches men away from their letters—indeed from their mothers' breasts—to "schools or rather brothels" in which holy laws are turned into wicked snares and that teach the young to pay court to avarice. Modern legal education doesn't provide any philosophical framework, it doesn't even lay out the parts of justice or say how the morals of men may be reformed. Instead, law professors "with filthy mouths and obscene vocabulary" say to their students, Let all that go; it's superfluous; it doesn't tell you how to earn your bread. The whole study of modern lawyers is to eviscerate the simple holiness of the laws and substitute litigiousness and pettifoggery. Assessors, judges, and patrons combine stony hearts with love of luxury and gold.[28]

It is easy to see from Boccaccio's denunciation of legal education how we arrive in the next generation at the movement to educate social and political elites in literature, eloquence, philosophy, and history—the humanities—prior to any professional training. Given Boccaccio's hostility to scholastic legal education, it is no surprise to see that his numerous discussions of tyranny in the *De casibus* anticipate the humanist emphasis on tyranny as the product of flawed character. This attitude contrasts with the legalistic attitude to tyranny exemplified by scholastic jurisprudence, most famously Bartolus of Sassoferrato, described in Chapter 4. How Boccaccio's analysis of tyranny differs from that of the jurists may be illustrated by his account in *De casibus* of the tyranny of Walter of Brienne in Florence. The following three paragraphs paraphrase Boccaccio's long-winded narrative.[29]

> Walter of Brienne was a French condottiere who acquired the signory of Florence from 1342 to 1343. He was noble of birth but morally degenerate. (*Degener* is a term of art in humanist discourse, denoting someone who lacks the virtue of his ancestors.) Having suffered a series of military disasters, the Florentine government, led by *popolano* elites (*primores populi*), was in a weakened condition. The city was deeply in debt, taxes were high, and nothing had come of the regime's effort to capture Lucca. Making common cause with the old magnate families, who hoped to repeal the Ordinances of Justice and recover their political rights, the regime called in Walter to save them from the mutinous plebs. They took care to turn over to him all the power of public arms, "basely choosing a foreigner's tyranny, a condition of which they were ignorant, rather than bearing the familiar yoke of the civil laws." They built support for themselves by forgiving and rescheduling the debt of the numerous citizens who were burdened by the consequences of their own improvidence. Then they started discussions to enslave their fellow Florentines to Walter's

lordship and to betray the birthright of liberty earned by previous generations. The Frenchman, setting aside honor and trust and aroused by a cruel desire for lordship, saw that he could take over the city gradually by deceit. He claimed the city was in imminent danger of destruction and that he needed greater executive power *(arbitrium)* in order to save it. This was granted by the weak and credulous. He used his power immediately to execute certain citizens (who perhaps deserved it, Boccaccio concedes), and meeting no resistance to his arbitrary deeds, soon made further demands for power *(imperium)*.

Then came a coup, abetted by the magnates, carried out with various theatrical shows of legality. The city government agreed to turn over power to Walter for one year on condition that he sign, on the True Body of Christ, a certain document. The city was summoned to a *parlamento* in the piazza before the Palazzo Vecchio and the magistrates processed out onto the *ringhiera*, the raised platform extending along the side of the Palazzo, fronting on the square. Walter arrived with squadrons of horse and foot and surrounded the citizens. Magnates concealing arms under their clothes supported him. He announced that his soldiers would set upon the unarmed if anyone made trouble. At the urging of the magnates he then occupied the highest seat. He addressed the people, and as soon as the subject of his year-long *imperium* was mentioned, the dregs of the common people *(vulgi fex)* began to shout that it should be made permanent. Then traitors opened the doors of the palace to him and the priors were shoved aside to make room for him in the seat of power, in violation of the oaths of loyalty he had taken.

Having thus broken his trust and having crushed it underfoot, and having made a mockery of his oath, he took possession of the citadel of Florentine liberty. As though what had been given him by the dregs of the plebs had been granted by the best citizens *(ab optimatibus)*, he accepted the lordship for life through a violent quasi-order *(ordine quodam violento)*.[30] Thus a city which we received free from our ancestors and which had never been subject to any persons other than the Roman emperors was subdued. By these devices utterly iniquitous citizens subjected it to the tyranny of an utterly wicked man.[31]

That was the beginning of Walter's downfall. He soon became swollen with hubris and turned the public palace into his private dwelling. He levied onerous taxes and embezzled public resources for his private use and those of his companions. He gave neither mercy nor favor. He and his ruffians committed every kind of crime and befouled all things human and divine. The citizens were at first beaten down, but before long they yearned to recover their lost liberty. They were inhibited, however, by discord, *desolationum urbium radix*. Eventually merciful God opened their eyes, "and with His virtue *(sua virtute)* strengthened their fearful hearts, composed their differences and gave them the courage to destroy their ruler." The magnates and the *populares* united against Walter and were on the point of attacking when he, coward that he was, surrendered himself tearfully to the people. Thus had it pleased God to demonstrate that his surrender had nothing to do with the merits of the Florentines and everything to do with Walter's iniquity, which had long grieved heaven and the divine spirits. After this it was only a matter of time before he was driven from the city. He died in exile, appropriately enough, by the hand of a Florentine avenger carrying out the justice of God.

There are a number of points worth noting in this account. First, Boccaccio clearly values Florence's tradition of civil liberties and regretfully observes the ease with which public liberty, when entrusted to corrupt leaders, may be lost. He shows no love for the magnates as a political force, despite his numerous friends among their families. Second, there are no heroes in his story. The regime leaders representing the *popolo,* the magnates, and the dregs of the lower classes all behave miserably. Noble birth does not lead to noble conduct; virtue is nowhere to be found. Tyranny is actively chosen by cowardly leaders to save themselves from the consequences of their own foolishness and injustice. It is rejected only when the tyrant reveals the full extent of his wickedness. The only social groups *not* blamed for the disastrous episode are the politically passive middle ranks of society, the *popolo;* but if they possessed any residual virtue it did not become active, owing to social divisions and the corruption of their leaders. Florence exits from Walter's tyranny only by the mercy and power *(virtus)* of God.

Tyranny in Boccaccio's account is the opposite of liberty and is caused by moral weakness. Ultimately, tyranny emerges from the tyrant's soul and the souls of those who allow themselves to be oppressed; it is superficial to regard tyranny simply as an illegitimate form of rule specified by legal criteria. By the lights of a Bartolus, Walter's tyranny would not have begun until the moment of usurpation in the piazza, when violence was used to extract consent. At that point Walter could have been identified as a tyrant *ex parte exercitii,* owing to an abuse of power—that is, a vote of the people passed under threat of violence, *propter metum.*[32] His oath breaking also would have delegitimated his power. Boccaccio's narrative, by contrast, makes it clear that Walter's tyranny had started much earlier, at the moment when the regime made the decision to sacrifice the city's liberty in order to secure its own hold on power. While the jurists were generally silent about the *causes* of tyranny, Boccaccio was eloquent, pointing his finger directly at human moral failure. The *cure* for tyranny required something more than the observance and enforcement of constitutional norms. For Boccaccio, law and liberty are worthless without virtuous citizens to defend them. There is even in his account the suggestion, made explicit by later humanists, that the real source of legitimacy is virtue. That is what this sentence seems to imply: "As though what had been given him by the dregs of the plebs had been granted by the best citizens *(ab optimatibus),* he accepted the lordship for life."[33] This seems to leave open the possibility that power might be handed over to a single ruler legitimately if those handing it over were themselves virtuous.[34] That Walter's public acclamation as *signore a vita* had been the work of the "dregs of the people" compromised its legitimacy, quite apart from the conditions of duress under which it was made.

Boccaccio and the Humanist Debate about Private Wealth and Economic Injustice

For Boccaccio, one of the chief causes of political corruption, leading ultimately to the loss of civic liberty and tyranny, was the unfettered pursuit of private wealth. He decries the malign influence of the thirst for gold on civic virtue frequently and passionately in his late works, not only in the *De casibus,* but also in the consolatory letter to Pino and in the *Trattatello.*[35] At *De casibus* 3.1 he stages a battle between Paupertas, a personification of voluntary poverty—described as the nurse of the Roman Empire—and an arrogant Fortuna, whom Paupertas defeats, causing Fortuna's child, Misfortune, to be put in chains. This literary victory, however, was far from being realized in his city of Florence. Despite Rome's example of noble frugality, as Boccaccio writes in his letter to Pino, his fellow Florentines, thanks to their "abominable avarice," had never in their centuries-long history produced figures exemplary for their indifference to wealth. Boccaccio knows of only one exception: the *popolano* leader Aldobrandino d'Ottobuono. Despite being a man of moderate means Aldobrandino refused an immense bribe offered him by the Pisans to secure his influence against the interests of his fellow citizens. Showing what was (for them) unusual gratitude, the Florentines granted him an "imperial" tomb after his death. "Thus it is not great palaces, ample possessions, or purple and gold clothes lined with fur that bring honor to a man, but a soul resplendent with virtue."[36]

For Boccaccio wealth was morally dangerous for the individual who possessed it and politically disastrous for states like Florence that valued it above virtuous frugality, as Rome's example showed: "As soon as riches with their weakening effect began to shape private lives, the empire declined more and more and finally fell into that state of decay in which it is today, when it exists in name only and not as a political reality. Thus no one should be so arrogant as to feel ashamed of being poor, inasmuch as the Roman Empire was founded on *paupertas.*"[37]

The dangers of private wealth is practically the only theme in Boccaccio's political thought that has drawn comment from modern scholars. Hans Baron, who first discussed these passages, ascribed Boccaccio's obsession with virtuous poverty to the influence of Franciscan spirituality and regarded it as exemplifying the "medieval" character of his thought. Baron contrasted Boccaccio's attitude with that of quattrocento thinkers such as Leonardo Bruni, Poggio Bracciolini, and Leon Battista Alberti. These "civic humanists" argued that wealth in the hands of private citizens, especially the rich with their "barns full of money," not only enabled the virtues of liberality and magnaminity but also embellished the state and supplied it with the sinews of war. Thanks to the private wealth of her great houses, Florence had been able to hire powerful armies to defeat her enemies. Baron saw the "positive attitude to wealth" among his civic humanists as prefiguring the ethos of capitalism that Max Weber had traced back to Calvinist moral theology of the sixteenth century.[38]

Quentin Skinner already in 1978 argued persuasively that Boccaccio's beliefs about the desirability of citizen poverty had their origins in Sallust, Livy, and the Roman moralists, not in the Franciscans. It was not Franciscan preachers who were Boccaccio's exemplars, but figures like the plebeian hero Manius Curius Dentatus—the Roman general who, when offered a great weight in gold by the defeated Samnites, replied that he did not believe it was glorious to possess gold but, rather, to command those who possessed gold.[39] Moreover, as Skinner also pointed out, a "positive evaluation of citizen wealth" could be found among Italian republican thinkers as far back as the thirteenth century. It was not something invented in the quattrocento by Leonardo Bruni.[40]

Some further points may be added to Skinner's critique. First, it is not clear that Baron correctly interpreted the texts in which he hoped to find a Renaissance spirit of capitalism adumbrating that of Weber's Calvinists.[41] The principle concern of quattrocento humanism with regard to wealth was not to endorse the commercial spirit of contemporary republics that were ruled in the interest of wealthy merchants and bankers. It was rather to regulate the insatiable desire for wealth typical of these societies by some standard of virtue, usually drawn (as Baron correctly saw) from the Aristotelian tradition of ethics and household management. If quattrocento humanists expressed "a positive attitude to wealth," it was because they recognized that a degree of wealth was needed to support virtue in civic life, and that states needed the resources supplied by wealthy citizens in order to flourish. For the humanists, wealth was legitimate only when subordinated to the needs of one's family, one's fellow citizens, and one's country. By acquiring wealth in a way that took account of social interests, one could redirect the acquisitive impulse away from purely selfish ends and elevate it to serve the nobler ends of human beings in political communities.

Leonardo Bruni, for instance, defended the acquisition of wealth for the purpose of augmenting one's patrimony. Wealth was a good needed to maintain a family and live a civil life. Relying on the authority of Aristotle and Plato, he asserted that wealth should not be sought for its own sake but as an instrument of virtue. Some "grander and more exalted" forms of civil life, those that require the virtue of magnificence, demand larger resources. Wealth should be acquired in an honorable way, without injustice to anyone, in order to sustain the good life in a city and to provide for the education of one's children. It should be preserved carefully and enjoyed without excess of luxury, in such a way as not to make us its slave.[42]

Poggio's *De avaritia* shows what happens when ethical modes of acquiring, maintaining, and spending are corrupted by the vices of avarice and luxury. The dialogue presents an argument for the restraint of avarice and the reform of characters disfigured by that monstrous vice. The damage can be repaired through the study of Greek philosophy and Greek patristic literature (in Latin versions newly made available by humanist translators). The messages of philosophy and ancient Christian teachings can be amplified through humanist eloquence, which was far more effective than the preaching of itinerant friars. A closer look at this dialogue will bring out more clearly the reforming aims of humanist soulcraft.[43]

The dialogue begins with a violent attack on the avaricious character, described as a supremely anti-social monstrosity that destabilizes all bonds of friendship and humanity in a city, destroying justice. Avarice is defined as "a boundless desire to possess, or better still, a kind of hunger to accumulate wealth." The speaker here, Bartolomeo da Montepulciano, claims that a man in the grip of avarice will always put private interest over public duty and become an enemy of the republic and the human race. Such men care nothing for their fellow man and "will walk right through those weeping in hardship in order to amass [their] fortune[s]."[44] The speech ends with a moralizing *explication de texte,* a passage of Vergil's *Aeneid* that paints in vivid poetical images the monstrous deformity of avarice.[45]

The second interlocutor, Antonio Loschi, takes the opposing view, arguing that avarice is natural to man and that all men necessarily put private above public interest. All men want more money and are driven by the profit motive. Even philosophers like Aristotle and kings like Robert of Naples (Petrarch's idol) were avaricious. Theology and law are really studied for the sake of gain. "Desire for money has grown, so that avarice is considered not a vice but a virtue; the richer a man is, the more he is honored." For Loschi that is all natural and good, for avarice makes the world go round; businesses and cities would collapse without the thirst for money. Cities could not defend themselves from attack without the barns of money filled by the wealthy: "Money is necessary as the sinews that maintain the state." Rome was driven to acquire its empire by avarice. Cities and churches were embellished by it. Echoing, but with the opposite intention, Augustine's famous comparison of unjust kingdoms to "large-scale robberies," Loschi asks, "What are cities, states, countries and kingdoms but workshops of avarice?" Far from being expelled from the city, as Bartolomeo had advised, avaricious men should be invited into it, as the wealth they create will add to its flourishing.

The third speaker, Andreas Chrysoberges, representing the divine wisdom of the Greeks, settles the debate decisively in favor of Bartolomeo. He begins by distinguishing the natural appetite of *cupiditas* (desire) from the settled vice of avarice. All men necessarily have a desire to preserve themselves, their families, and their communities, and they need some degree of wealth in order to do so. This is a natural impulse and free from blame. But *avaritia* represents a perversion of natural *cupiditas* that is neither innate nor good. It is a blind passion that seizes hold of a man and enslaves him. Men driven by avarice harm themselves and others. Worst of all is avarice in the hearts of *principes,* political leaders. They set a bad example which, as Cicero wrote in the *Laws,* "corrupts the entire city, for the sins of *principes* are not only evils themselves, but serve as examples to the many imitators of princes." Andreas continues:

The uneducated and ignorant consider that whatever they perceive has become an important concern of their princes must be good. So they imitate those customs that they think are fine and pleasing to princes. But while the avarice of private men does not harm many, the same avarice in a prince brings plague and public ruin with it. Under an avaricious prince no laws, no rights, no justice is preserved. Crimes go unpunished provided the rulers are paid off with gold. The innocent will be punished; the guilty will escape punishment. No crime will be so dark and hideous that the splendor of coin will not throw it into the shadows. Robbers, thieves and murderers will be free if they have the money to buy off the ruler. Everything will be sold off as though by the public crier.[46]

Loschi has pointed out all the benefits to cities that follow from the accumulation of wealth, but, Andreas responds, that does not make the man who has illicitly accumulated that wealth innocent. The rape of Lucretia brought freedom to the Roman people, but that does not excuse the rapist. Even if he does not commit actual crimes, the character of the small-minded, tight-fisted, selfish miser will lack the liberal, generous, and high-minded qualities necessary in public leaders. On civic councils he will always give self-interested advice, even if it means inveigling his fellow citizens into unjust and dangerous wars. He will not have the largeness of soul to reward true merit. He will lack the Christian virtue of charity, which according to the Greek church father John Chrysostom is what binds communities together in love; in its absence a community descends into tyranny.[47] Therefore—and this is proposed as a serious policy—all greedy and avaricious men should be expelled from the state. They should be ostracized for the same reason Plato wanted to expel immoral poets from his republic: because they corrupt public morals. There is no place for them in a republic that aspires to virtue.

Here we seem to find ourselves at some remove from the spirit of capitalism. Nor can we easily read Bruni's writings on the virtuous acquisition of wealth, or Poggio's passionate attack on the influence of greed in politics, as corroborating the claims of wealth and ancient lineage to rule republics—an "oligarchic ideology"—as some modern scholars describe it. An oligarchy that had been stripped of all its selfish and avaricious men would surely find it hard to keep its grasp on power. What we *can* find among humanists of the fifteenth century is something like the spirit of mercantilism. But we find the fullest expression of that spirit, not in commercial cities led by merchant-bankers like Florence or Venice, where Hans Baron expected to find the first stirrings of capitalism, but in the Kingdom of Naples.

It turns out that several humanist political writers in the Kingdom of Naples advised their prince to encourage mercantile and commercial activity as a bulwark of the state.[48] The most interesting of these, Diomede Carafa—a humanist, cavalry commander, art collector, and trusted minister of King Ferrante of Naples—devoted many pages of his treatise *On the Office of a King and a Good Prince* to that theme.[49] Dedicated in 1476 to Eleanor of Aragon, Duchess of Ferrara, the treatise explained *inter alia* the benefits of having wealthy subjects and decried as tyranny any attempt to strip them of their resources.

> If any citizen wants to work for mercantile profit and excels at it, it will not only be fitting to encourage him and show him favor, but even, if possible, help him with money. Business activity *(negotiatio)* is fruitful for sustaining states *(civitates)* and useful for supplying an abundance of the things you need.... Moreover, unless your citizens are brought up in this kind of activity, entrepreneurs *(institores)* from elsewhere will flock to your towns and will carry off the value they receive to their own countries, like wild pigeons.[50]

Carafa goes on to describe the wise measures taken by Eleanor's father, King Ferrante, to encourage commerce in Naples and the many benefits that had accrued thereby to the state. Ferrante had made loans to merchants, offered naval protection to their ships, maintained a sound currency, and also helped to develop agriculture, woolmaking, crafts, and natural resources such as alum mines. Thanks to Ferrante, Naples had seen a renaissance of trade and manufacturing unknown in earlier periods of its history, and its wares were now known all over the world. "A king cannot be weak who rules over wealthy subjects."

All this does not mean, writes Carafa, that the prince should favor the rich and powerful over other citizens. The law should be the same for rich and poor, and the prince should protect the weak, widows, and orphans from oppression by the powerful. It is also a mistake for the prince himself to seek profit. If he does so, he will crowd out the free mercantile activity of his subjects. They will either abandon commerce themselves or will be unable to buy or sell on an equal basis with him, since they will have to wait for his goods to clear the market first. He will fill his own treasury perhaps, but at the cost of damaging his own subjects, like a builder who believes his advantage lies in cutting costs on foundation stone, not realizing it will lead to the eventual collapse of the whole building: "The prince ought therefore to consider the resources of his subjects to be the foundation of his own kingdom. Let the civic leaders *(optimates),* merchants, craftsmen and farmers each exercise his own métier. The prince should not fail any of them. Let the king also stick to his own art [of rulership]. For just as it is not fit for a ruler's office to be encroached upon by citizens, so it is unbecoming for the citizens' businesses to be practiced by a king."[51]

One last amendment to Hans Baron's story about civic humanism and wealth deserves to be made. While there is certainly a positive view of citizen wealth in Italy long antedating the generation of Bruni and Poggio, as Skinner pointed out, it is also the case that fear of riches as a source of political corruption and praise of "political poverty"—preferring a wealthy state to wealth in private hands—by no means came to an end with the turn of the fifteenth century.[52] Strict limits on citizen wealth, habits of frugality, and a preference for public over private expenditure continue to be advocated in major humanist writings well into the sixteenth century. Bruni's contemporaries and fellow humanists Guarino of Verona and Pier Paolo Vergerio, for instance, both celebrated the Senecan value of virtuous *paupertas;* both held that a properly instrumental view of riches enabled the wise man to control the anti-social vice of avarice.[53] Biondo Flavio in book 5 of his *Rome in Triumph* wrote approvingly that the Roman people in its best period hated private luxury but loved public munificence: "Our ancestors had a mode of conduct arising from their greatness of spirit, such that in their private life they were content with very little and lived with few expenditures, while in government and in the dignity of public life they measured everything by the standard of glory and splendor."[54]

Francesco Filelfo, an outspoken critic of men driven by an uncontrollable thirst for riches—exemplified by the biblical figures Cain and Judas and also by his great enemy, Cosimo de' Medici—wrote in a speech on the theme of avarice that it was the vice most destructive of justice in cities; its opposite was liberality, the virtue of a gentleman. The avarice of one citizen could cause a mortal wound to the republic, as the example of Crassus showed.[55] He quoted the famous line of Vergil, "To what evils do you not compel mortal breasts, O accursed hunger for gold?"— already by his time a humanist commonplace.[56] Giovanni Nesi in his treatise on morality (dedicated to Piero de' Medici, son of Lorenzo the Magnificent) writes how the typical Florentine belief that money is the highest human good makes him sick to his stomach. To counter this destructive idea he gives a long list of classical figures who were rich but miserable, and claims that the rustic Scythians and Spartans were happier than the wealthy Athenians.[57] His older friend and mentor, the patrician Donato Acciaiuoli, in his standard commentary on Aristotle's *Poli-*

tics follows the Greek philosopher in condemning modes of acquisition that look only to profit and not to the good of the soul and of the republic. Money is not to be confused with true riches: the latter consist of resources licitly acquired that are not amassed to feed an insatiable appetite for more and more but that satisfy real, natural needs and supply the material basis for a life of virtue.[58]

Most striking of all, perhaps is the attitude revealed by Pietro Crinito, a poet and disciple of Poliziano, in his popular treatise on gentlemanly learning, *De honesta disciplina,* published in 1504. After a flood of quotations from Sallust and other authorities, Crinito writes that men of liberal temperament should take care to flee from the sort of republic where riches are more esteemed than virtue, quoting his friend Giovanni Canacci to the effect that excessively rich men are generally a curse to states. Plato too, he writes, condemned such states *(civitates),* "since where the wealthy have power, all the rest are not only held in contempt, but are generally wronged and insulted with extreme unfairness. For the rich have no respect either for equity or rational order, since they conduct themselves without such qualities when ruling and ordering the state, being driven rather by passion and lust." That is why it is prudent to impose limits on wealth by laws and decrees, "lest there be citizens who possess larger resources than would seem fair."[59]

The strand within Italian Renaissance thought that saw private wealth as a threat to the state had its greatest representative in Machiavelli, who famously declared that "properly ordered states must keep the community rich but the citizens poor." For Machiavelli, the idea of men like Bruni and Poggio that riches in the hands of individual citizens (such as the Medici) could promote virtue was one of the main causes of Florentine decline.[60] It was political poverty, expressed in the Roman virtue of frugality, that forced natural human selfishness into patterns of cooperation that in turn generated public spirit and love of country.[61] Thus Machiavelli's views on political poverty place him, like Boccaccio, comfortably in one stream of humanist thinking about wealth.[62] The tension in humanist thinking between those who valued private wealth in cities and those who saw it as a danger to civic virtue was one that persisted down into early modern times.

In the quattrocento, however, most humanists were united in excoriating avarice and luxury as ignoble moral weaknesses that turned men into monsters and ruined states. Most called for a revival of the traditional Roman virtue of frugality, echoing Sallust, Livy, and Lucan. To be sure, one man's frugality could be another's miserliness, but the debate over the difference served only to highlight how the humanists evaluated economic behavior in terms of moral purpose. That is why very few of them believed that the possession of wealth in itself was necessarily corrupting. Though the humanists shared the wider premodern prejudice that sudden increases in wealth could only come from criminal conduct, they generally agreed that increases in wealth issuing from diligence, careful planning, avoidance of luxury, and the licit use of capital were morally acceptable, even admirable.[63] It was bad character that turned a legitimate desire to accumulate wealth into a sickness damaging to self and society. Properly acquired and properly used—for the purpose of enabling virtue, serving others, or strengthening the state—private wealth could be a social good. The live questions for humanist political thinkers (as for us) were whether extraordinary stores of private wealth such as the Medici amassed were a benefit or a threat to the state; how, if at all, the commercial classes should participate in government—whether, for example, the Roman model of excluding moneymakers from politics should be followed; and how to prevent the interests of the wealthy from being accorded greater weight in the councils of government than those of poorer citizens.[64]

In these attitudes to wealth we can see a parallel to the way humanists redefined tyranny as corruption of character rather than as a violation of legal rights. A century before the humanist movement began, scholastic theorists had already begun to develop their own project of regulating the morals of commercial society, basing their reasonings on a conception of natural law. They elaborated a system of rules in theology and canon law to restrict usury, the illicit acquisition of property, and other forms of economic injustice. Their approach was to develop a body of case law to evaluate individual mercantile transactions and establish modes of restitution for economic injustices.[65] Individual cases were heard in episcopal courts or in the *forum internum,* the confessional. Scholastic jurists and theologians were no doubt actuated by a sincere desire to build a moral economy, yet, as humanists observed, an ideal that presents itself only as a series of legal prohibitions can never be very effective in changing conduct. As will be readily imagined, the Church's system for regulating economic behavior lent itself to constant abuse. There was endless legal gamesmanship to get around particular prohibitions as well as casual disregard of norms, and the stench of hypocrisy often rose from laity and clergy alike. The clergy, secular and religious, were themselves major economic actors in both the urban and rural economies, from the pope on down, and it was widely believed that the avarice of the clergy was no more restrained by canon law or the confessional than that of the laity. True moral leadership was hard to find.

The humanist approach to economic injustice was quite different, as will not surprise those who have followed the argument of this book so far. The strategy of humanist literati was to reform the character of civic leaders and men of wealth, to pull up the weed of avarice by its roots from the garden of the human heart. What made economic injustice hard to achieve was not the Church's inability to block usurious transactions, but the stubborn vices of avarice and luxury. Through their neo-classical *institutio* the humanists would try to change all that. They would mold the natural desire of human beings for economic security so that it would be disciplined and directed by the ancient philosophers' virtue of friendship and the Christian virtue of charity.[66] It would not be allowed to metastasize into the twin cancers of avarice and luxury, the source of all injustice and discord. Healthy forms of acquisition and expenditure that took account of the needs of others, especially the poor, would support the common good, preserve justice, and make the republic loved by its citizens.

Boccaccio and Virtue Politics

Given what has been said in this chapter, one might well ask whether there are *any* features of Boccaccio's political thought that are backward looking (to avoid the loaded term "medieval") and that might set him apart from the later humanist tradition of virtue politics. If one is forced to identify such features, two candidates present themselves.

First, it seems possible that Boccaccio was aware of and approved the teaching of some scholastic writers that the power of kings is derived from and limited by the express consent of the people. This is a doctrine that later humanists cared about little, if at all. Boccaccio says the following:

> Let kings resist it as much as they like, let them deny it a hundred times; nevertheless, they rule by the approval [or votes] of peoples [*suffragio populorum*], and it is the peoples' strength that makes them formidable.[67]

Nevertheless, he does not seem to have in mind here the sounding of popular sentiment via elections or popular acclamation or other formal means, for he goes on to say:

> If some [king] weakens that strength by unjust slaughter and injuries, he will immediately feel that his power is diminished, as is readily shown by the

example of Rehoboam and Shishak. [Peoples are thus not to be regarded as worthless, trodden under foot or disembowled.][68] But why should I say "people"? Not even the least member of the plebs is to be regarded as worthless. Every man impelled by his own interest bears great souls [*sic*] within his breast; and the life of kings, however much fortified by armed guards, cannot be reckoned longer than that man wills who is disposed to pour out his own life in return for the tyrant's death. . . . Individual men have dared to perform the greatest deeds and sometimes have achieved what they dared.[69]

In other words, if a ruler treats the people badly, they will lash out at him, and he is not safe from even the lowest of the plebs if that man is willing to kill a tyrant at the cost of his own life. Boccaccio is surely not calling for constitutional limits on royal power in this passage.

The second feature—and this must be taken much more seriously—is the general doubt and pessimism suffusing Boccaccio's accounts of the exercise of political power, especially its exercise by his own contemporaries.[70] There are a number of passages, both in the *De casibus* and in the letter to Pino de'Rossi, where he assumes that the desire for political power and the yearning to participate in politics is intrinsically corrupting, at least under modern circumstances, and dangerous to the health of our souls. A life spent in humility and poverty and virtuous literary retirement is better for us; it is less exposed to the giddy turns of Fortune's wheel. Boccaccio believes he lives in the dregs of time and that virtuous men are few. Could there be a Marcus Attilius Regulus today? Boccaccio has doubts. For him, Roman decline set in during the age of Cicero, when there was just enough virtue left in Rome's elites to recognize Cicero's merit despite his status as a *novus homo.* To expect virtuous governance on more than an episodic basis in modern Italy is foolish; one can only hope and pray for it. You might get a Robert of Naples once in a while, but most of the time, in this age, the exercise of political power will endanger our salvation, and the deck will be heavily stacked against the virtuous. In the present age Fortune is fickle, mortal things are unstable, happiness in this life is a false hope, glory is empty and fleeting.

Working toward a virtuous republic of the ancient type, powerful and free, happy and glorious, ruled by the best men—the agenda of later humanists—would for Boccaccio be unrealistic. In any case, what ultimately counts, he tells his exiled friend Pino, is one's personal reputation for virtue. To keep that good fame, it is often better *not* to exercise power than to exercise it. When you consider the foul crimes and shameful behavior of Florence's rulers, he tells Pino, you should be ashamed of not having exiled yourself earlier (as he, Boccaccio, had done). Boccaccio is speaking during a period of extreme bitterness in his own life, but his words also reveal a kind of secular pessimism. For that pessimism to change to optimism, for the humanist politics of virtue to become something like a real political agenda, Italy would have to await a later generation, one more attuned to the potential of the human species to reform its collective behavior.

CHAPTER 8

LEONARDO BRUNI AND THE VIRTUOUS HEGEMON

Why Florence Deserves to Be the Heir of Rome:
The Panegyric of the City of Florence

The present work has argued that the significance of Renaissance humanism for the history of Western political thought goes well beyond its role, highlighted by Hans Baron and Eugenio Garin toward the middle of the last century, in rejuvenating the Roman republican tradition. Baron's civic humanism (or the "neo-Roman" tradition, as Quentin Skinner later called it), gave new life to the folklore of popular government inherited from the medieval Italian commune and infused it with the authority of Rome and its great republican heroes from Brutus to Cicero. In so doing the humanists kept alive arguments for non-monarchical government and the love of liberty, handing them down to modern times. For these writers, Renaissance humanist political thought acquired significance as a chapter in a greater story: the prehistory of liberal democracy in the West.[1]

In Chapter 2 I argued that "virtue politics" provides an interpretive framework for humanist political thought that better saves the phenomena found in the primary texts. The promotion of virtue and wisdom in the political class, establishing morally justifiable hierarchies in society and moral legitimacy in government, replacing coercion with willing obedience to just rulers, the key role of humanistic culture and eloquence in the reform of elites—these are themes that in the period from Petrarch to Machiavelli are far more universal and pervasive in humanist political writing, broadly construed. They constitute the core of virtue politics. They are themes that transcend the partisan attitudes to "republicanism" or "tyranny" that have for so long engaged the attention of historians.[2] In contrast to virtue politics, the themes of republican liberty and the advocacy of popular government are relatively rare in humanist literature on politics, exemplified mostly in a few well-known texts associated with the oligarchic and Medici regimes in Florence.

Among these texts, the most well known is Leonardo Bruni's *Laudatio Florentine urbis* (Panegyric of the City of Florence), celebrated by Hans Baron and his many followers as a foundational text of civic humanism.[3] Bruni's *Laudatio* thus becomes a useful test case for the claim that promoting a wise and virtuous elite is the primary aim of humanist political thought. I maintain in this chapter that the *Laudatio* can and should be interpreted as an example of virtue politics, and indeed that Bruni uses virtue politics as the *Laudatio*'s central explanatory structure. Its "celebration of republican liberty," as Hans Baron described it, is subordinate to the text's advocacy of virtue politics. Liberty is valued above all because it produces virtue, and it is virtue that makes Florence worthy of leadership among peoples, perhaps even of empire. It is the virtuous rule of Florence that in turn guarantees liberty to other towns and cities within its sphere of influence.

In a wider sense, the speech represents an attempt on Bruni's part to negotiate between the claims of virtue politics in the tradition of Petrarch and Boccaccio and the inherited values and institutions of Florentine popular government. As an aspiring spokesman for the Florentine Signoria and a candidate to replace the aging Coluccio Salutati as its chancellor, Bruni aims to demonstrate how the ideology of the medieval popular commune can be appropriated and reinterpreted in terms of humanist virtue politics.[4] His unstated goal is to show that Petrarch's use of classical philosophy and ancient moral examples to educate and reform *principes* can be applied to the governance of republican regimes as well. From this perspective his "civic humanism" can be understood as an ad hoc, hybrid ideology, very much bounded by the rhetorical occasion, an adaptation of virtue politics to a particular political culture. Under this adaptive pressure Bruni explains how Florence's popular institutions promote virtue in the people—a new frontier in the evolution of humanist political thought, though not without parallels in Petrarch's praise of the Roman people.[5] The strategy of justifying Florence's hegemony in Tuscany by appealing to the virtue of the Florentine people displays both parallels and illuminating contrasts with Dante's arguments for the legitimacy of the Holy Roman Empire in his *Monarchia*. That comparison will be explored at the end of this chapter.

In the *Laudatio,* as has often been observed, Bruni makes a historical argument that Florence is the daughter of Rome and therefore the rightful heir to her power. He also makes a parallel case that has drawn less comment from scholars. This is an argument that, by proving her virtue, Florence has shown that she *deserves* to be the heir of Rome by moral as well as hereditary right. Her acts of virtue are the basis of her claim to preeminence, together with her Roman heritage. In making this claim Bruni was a faithful follower of Aristotle, who held that—though the descent and family resources of an individual helped to enable virtue—good examples, sound practical reasoning, and above all the habit of acting with virtue were of far greater importance.[6] Virtue was based in heredity and upbringing but actualized through practice and moral reasoning.

In the scholarly literature of the last quarter century it is commonly accepted that Bruni's *Laudatio,* written in the afterglow of Florence's successful defense of its liberty against Giangaleazzo of Milan, was intended to advertise Florence's potential to be the new imperial center of Italy.[7] There is much to agree with this position, though a qualification will be suggested later. At any rate, it is uncontroversial that the main theme of Bruni's speech is why Florence deserves to take the place of ancient Rome in modern Italy. Florence deserves hegemony because Rome, as the noblest of ancient peoples, surely deserved its empire, and Florence is the rightful heir of Rome.[8] Here is the key part of Bruni's argument:

> Indeed, if you are seeking nobility in a founder you will never find any people nobler in the entire world than the [ancient] Roman people; if you are seeking wealth, none more opulent; if you want grandeur and magnificence, none more outstanding and glorious; if you seek extent of dominion, there was no people on this side of Ocean that had not been subdued and brought under Rome's power by force of arms. Therefore, to you, also, men of Florence, belongs by a kind of hereditary right dominion over the entire world as though taking control of your parental legacy. From this it follows that all wars that are waged by the Florentine people are most just, and this people can never lack justice in its wars since it necessarily wages war for the defense or recovery of its own territory. Indeed, these are the sorts of just wars that are permitted by all laws and legal systems. Now, if the glory, nobility, virtue, grandeur, and magnificence of the parents can also make the sons outstanding, no people in the entire world can be nobler than the Florentines, for they are born from such parents who surpass by a long way all mortals in every sort of glory. Who is there among men who would not readily acknowledge themselves subjected to the Roman people? Indeed, what slave or freedman strives to have the same dignity as the children of his lord or master, or hopes to be chosen instead of them?[9]

This startling statement seems to license an endless series of offensive wars, since, after all, Florence would simply be reoccupying her hereditary possessions as the daughter of Rome if she should go on to conquer Italy and even the Mediterranean. Any wars of conquest she might engage in would therefore, by definition, be just.[10]

Of course we need to make allowances for the exaggerations of panegyric, and of course Bruni is dealing throughout the *Laudatio* with an idealized Florence.[11] But what one should notice here is that, alongside the argument for Florence's hereditary right to *dominium,* there is a moral argument that Florence *deserves* to have the same position in the modern world as Rome had in the ancient. Bruni is in effect answering the question, What moral conditions would have to obtain in order to justify Florence's hegemony over other peoples *(populi)*? Since a republic is by definition a just state that serves the people as a whole and not a tyranny, its hegemony over other states has to be justified in similarly organicist terms.[12] Bruni's answer is that republican hegemony can only be justified if the Florentine people, in addition to laying claim to its Roman inheritance, displays Roman virtue, a virtue that is superior to that of the other peoples that follow its leadership. Just as in Aristotle's *Politics* the dominance of a king or an aristocracy over other elements in the state is justified by a natural superiority in virtue,[13] so the rule of one state over another is justified by its superior virtue.

This is what stands behind the equally startling statement Bruni makes a little later in the speech, that the greater part *(maior pars)* of the Florentine citizenry—the majority—is also the better part *(melior pars):*

> Indeed, no city has ever been so well governed and established that it was completely without evil men. But just as the good qualities of a few men cannot really free the foolish and perverse mob from its infamy, so the perversity and evil of a few ought not to deprive an entire nation of being praised for its virtuous deeds. Now there are both public and private crimes, and there is a great difference between the two. A private crime derives from the intentions of the individual wrong-doer; public ones are the result of the will of the entire city. In the latter case it is not so much a question of following the opinion of one person or another as it is of following what has been hallowed by law and tradition. Usually the entire city follows what the majority of the citizen-body would like. While in other cities the majority often overturns the better part, in Florence it has always happened that the majority view has been identical with that of its best citizens.[14]

What Bruni in effect says here is that a key generalization Aristotle made about polities does not apply to Florence. In most polities, Aristotle claimed, there is a principle of *quantity* (i.e., the multitude of the people) and a principle of *quality* (i.e., the educated, noble and virtuous citizens, who by the rule of nature that excellent things are rare, tend to be a small minority). For Aristotle the key to good government is to arrange the constitution in such a way that the elements of quality in a city can guide the multitude who are less good and need direction. When the people rule, as they do in a "polity" or "constitutional government"—that is, justified rule by a people—the virtue of the people severally is generally of an inferior quality, but good institutions and education can compensate for the distributed character of popular virtue.[15] Bruni, by contrast, is saying that Florence is an exceptional community—that when it comes to public acts, the majority of Florentine citizens are noble and virtuous. In other words, in Florence's case, the quantity *is* the quality: the *maior* is the same as the *melior pars*.[16] Although there are evil men in any community, in Florence they are in the minority and do not affect her public decision-making and the behavior of the polity vis-à-vis other states. Florence's good laws and institutions also restrain the influence of individual bad actors and allow the good actors access to power. In saying this Bruni is making the same claim for the Florentines as Dante had made earlier for the Romans (and as Biondo Flavio would make for them later).[17]

In the passage just cited Bruni is claiming that individual virtue is scalable to states and that states have their own moral persona, which expresses that of the dominant element among the citizenry.[18] Among dozens of modern Italian states, there is one whose populace as a whole displays superexcellent virtue in its public acts, just as the ancient Romans naturally had more political virtue than other peoples in the ancient Mediterranean. Thus the actions of states can be judged by the standard of virtue, and morally good states deserve hegemony over the rest. In the case of states as well as in the case of individual human beings, the higher, more noble part should rule the lower. The superior virtue of the Florentine *popolo* guarantees that its hegemony will be benign.[19] Hence the Florentines are, and deserve to be, the new Romans, the new *princeps populus* of Italy.

So what are the political virtues of the Florentines in Bruni's understanding? The *Laudatio* has a long list of the virtues Florence has shown throughout her (idealized) history. Her actions in interstate affairs have manifested courage, steadfastness, loyalty, integrity, piety, largeness of counsel, justice and humanity, prudence, liberality, energy, loftiness of spirit, and contempt for danger. In short, the Florentine people as a whole possesses true nobility, not just noble descent. Florence has always been a peacemaker. Enemies of Florence tacitly acknowledge her *fides* when they commit their sons and property into the care of the city—they know Florence will keep her promises.[20] Even in victory, the city remains modest and gives God the credit for its good fortune. Florence is always on the side of the weak against the strong. She generously takes in exiles from all over Italy and treats them well, so much so that "there is no one in the whole of Italy who does not consider himself to possess dual citizenship *(duplex patria),* the one in the city to which he naturally belongs, the other in the city of Florence. As a result Florence has indeed become the common homeland *(communis patria)* and the most secure asylum for all of Italy."[21]

The language of the *duplex* or *communis patria* is one with a long and rich history in Roman imperial ideology. The concept of Rome as a *communis patria* for Italy goes back at least to Cicero's *De legibus,* where Cicero uses it to argue that, while one can have membership in several political communities at once, loyalty to the *communis patria,* Rome, has to take precedence.[22] Cicero's larger argument for the legitimacy of Rome's preeminence within her empire appeals to ideas of cosmic order and natural law.[23] In later Roman imperial ideology, as Clifford Ando has shown, Rome's efforts to make herself the *communis patria* were part of a conscious strategy to maintain loyalty in the provinces via institutions like law and citizenship and a program of material benefits as well as guarantees of peace.[24] Peace was so important that it justified Rome's use of force and coercion in certain cases. In modern theories of political legitimacy, this would count as a kind of "performance legitimacy."[25]

Bruni's use of the language of the *communis patria* reflects the influence of the *Laudatio*'s model: the *Panathenaicus* of Aelius Aristides (117–181 AD), an oration in praise of Athens. Aristides, though in other texts an apologist for Rome and a critic of Greek nativism, here makes an argument that Athens's generosity to other nations and her active support for liberty throughout the Greek world has deservedly made her the focus of loyalty, admiration, and affection for other Greeks.[26] Bruni's argument is that Florence displays courage, generosity, and selflessness not only when she succors the weak and exiled, but also when protecting smaller cities against tyrants, foreign and domestic. In other words, he uses a virtue argument to prove Florence's right to leadership in the community of city-states. Florence alone labors for the common good of all the states of Italy, and that noble pattern of behavior, on Aristotelian principles, proves her virtue and justifies her place at the head of the Italian state-system.[27]

It is worth emphasizing that Bruni seems here to be making a case for why other cities should accept Florence's leadership, not justifying expansionist military policies or claiming that Florence has sovereignty over other countries. That is why the views of Nicolai Rubinstein, Riccardo Fubini, Mikael Hornqvist, and a younger version of James Hankins, who saw the *Laudatio* straightforwardly as a justification of empire, need qualification.[28] In the passages discussed, Bruni is less a propagandist for Florentine expansionism and conquest and more the diplomat, persuading other cities why they should accept Florence as their *patrona,* why she should be allowed preeminence over them as the *princeps populus,* as first among equals—a phrase of Livian stamp.[29] This posture is in keeping with the general principle of virtue politics that the best form of submission is one that voluntarily recognizes the right of a superior to rule, and the best form of rule is one that creates affective bonds between ruler and ruled. Writing of Florence's role in leading the fight against Visconti imperialism, Bruni writes,

> Florence imitated its founders in every kind of virtue, so that in everyone's judgment the city seemed completely worthy of its great reputation and traditions. For Florence did not refrain from fighting until she had proven herself to be the protectress *(antistes)* of Italy. She gained for herself greatness *(amplitudo)* and glory, not by inaction and drowsiness, not by having recourse to crimes and fraud, but by largeness of counsel, by a willingness to face dangers, by keeping faith, integrity, steadfastness, and, above all, by taking on the protection of weaker peoples *(maximeque tenuiorum causa patrocinioque suscepto).*[30]

The language of *patrocinium* too has a rich history in Roman sources; to offer another state *patrocinium,* a protectorate, is to offer support on a voluntary basis within a context of justified hierarchical order and the *ius gentium,* as opposed to arbitrary lordship and oppression. The word *patrocinium,* indeed, points us to a text that likely was in Bruni's mind here, Cicero's *De officiis,* which (as we saw in Chapter 2) was a central text for humanist virtue politics.

> But as long as the empire of the Roman people was maintained through acts of kind service and not through injustices, wars were waged either on behalf of allies or about maintaining the prestige of power; wars were ended with

mercy or through necessity; the senate was a haven and refuge for kings, for peoples and for nations; moreover, our magistrates and generals yearned to acquire the greatest praise from one thing alone, the fair and faithful defence of our provinces and of our allies. In this way we could more truly have been titled a protectorate [*patrocinium*] than an empire [*imperium*] of the world.[31]

Here Cicero harks back with nostalgia to the period of the middle republic, when, he believes, Rome had an empire founded on justice and service to others, unlike the Rome of his own day, dominated by ambitious and corrupt generals. It was, in other words, a republican empire, resembling more a system of voluntary hegemony than a despotic empire based on sheer military force.

The contrast Bruni makes is with the tyrant empire of Milan. Under the late Giangaleazzo Visconti, Milan sought to dominate and oppress other cities. She used secrecy, cunning, and trickery, and she appealed to base, material profit. She sowed discord and division, and displayed the worst political vices: cowardice, moral degeneracy, sloth, crime, and oath breaking.[32] Bruni is at pains to distinguish Florence's leadership in Italy from Milan's. If Florence can be said to have an empire at all, it is a voluntary, liberal, organicist one that benefits her protégés and in which she enjoys deserved preeminence.[33] In his later writings, as we shall see, Bruni even chose to present Florence's preeminence among her allies as that of a *primus inter pares* within a federation of cities, like the pre-Roman Etruscan League. In the *Laudatio* Bruni emphasizes rather Florence's filial descent from the virtuous Romans. Florence most resembles the early republican empire of Rome, idealized by Cicero and Livy, whose wars were all defensive or undertaken reluctantly because of commitments to allies or intolerable threats to Rome's prestige and whose allies were glad to be clients of so virtuous a people as the Romans.[34]

Political Liberty as a Source of Virtue

Bruni's *Laudatio* not only gives us a virtue-based argument for why Florence, the rightful heir of the Roman republic, deserves a dominant position among modern Italian city-states; it also gives an account of how and why Florence had achieved a higher state of virtue than other cities. His first and most prominent explanation is her *stirps romulea:* Florence is virtuous because her people are of Roman descent, and the Romans were naturally—we might say "epigenetically"—superior to other nations in virtue. But Bruni goes further and offers proof of this assertion. Like most other humanists, Bruni believed that virtue was the criterion for true nobility and that only the truly noble—not those with mere hereditary claims to power—could be considered legitimate. Those who did have hereditary claims, as Florence did, had to demonstrate living virtue as well in order to validate those claims; they could not rely solely on the virtue of ancestors. And Florence's actions as a community had shown to everyone that she possessed Roman virtue and nobility of character. In every instance, Florence puts her liberty and the good of others above the mere accumulation of wealth, above status and titles, above expediency. These are signs that all writers on nobility for centuries, including Dante, had recognized as proving greatness of spirit above the common herd of humanity.[35]

With respect to the virtue of individuals too, Bruni explicitly invokes the principle that inherited nobility, to remain valid, has to maintain its luster by virtuous action in every generation. An example is found in the preface to his translation of Plutarch's *Life of Aemilius Paulus* (1407 / 1409), dedicated to the Venetian aristocrat Pietro Miani, a fellow disciple of Manuel Chrysoloras. After gently making fun *per ironiam* of Miani's claim to be descended from the ancient Roman clan of the Aemilii, Bruni changes his tone to a more serious register and says,

> In my view, all who allege a magnificent descent and put out images of their illustrious ancestors should be obliged by a kind of necessity to imitate the virtues of those from whom they say they are descended. Who is so dim as not to understand the utter shamefulness, who is so wicked as not to blush to degenerate from the virtue of his ancestors? Who doesn't see how much public utility this shame brings with it? Legislators and teachers of republics [*rerum publicarum magistri*] wish for nothing more than for an enlivening competition in the virtues to be poured into the spirits of citizens: unless I'm mistaken, it's that which principally creates nobility. It may be permitted to hide in other men of lower and less visible station, but the fame and glory of ancestors so shines with concentrated light upon all the affairs of their successors—it sets up, as though in a mirror, such expectations—that no wicked deed they may do can be kept hidden or dark. So you should frequently counsel with paternal exhortations Faustino and Giovanni, those outstanding young sons of yours— brothers of mine in love—not so much to swell with pride about their brilliant descent as to reckon it enjoined upon them by necessity to show themselves not unlike their distinguished ancestors in integrity, piety, goodness,

industry—in sum, in every form of probity both in public and private affairs, and to be zealous in the pursuit of the virtues, without which they cannot keep the rank of their ancestors.[36]

The desire to maintain one's nobility through living virtue is beneficial to the state because it sets off a competition in virtue among the citizens, a virtuous circle as it were, which inhibits selfishness and corruption while advancing merit.

In Florence's case, the virtuous circle of honor-seeking citizens is further enabled by political liberty; this too helps explain her preeminent virtue among Italian states. For Aristotle and other Greek philosophers, liberty is a reward of virtue and rational conduct rather than a natural right or inborn possession of mankind, as in modern rights theory. When reason controls the passions and appetites, when the virtues have been acquired, the soul becomes free and autonomous, able to actualize the good via its own agency. In the *Laudatio,* by contrast (and even more in his *Panegyric for Nanni Strozzi*), Bruni sees liberty and equality as conditions of political virtue.[37] Why is it that Florence's citizenry is of morally higher quality than those of other states? One reason is the *stirps romulea,* but another equally important one is that Florence's laws and free institutions stimulate and preserve her virtue. Her liberty is the school of virtue, corresponding to the element of training and habituation in Aristotle's theory of virtue acquisition. The case, implied throughout the latter part of the *Laudatio,* is put more concisely in Bruni's later *Panegyric of Nanni Strozzi* (1427), a parallel text which also contains an extended panegyric of Florence's institutions:

> The constitution we use for governing the republic is chiefly oriented towards liberty and fairness for all citizens. Since it is equal for all, it is called a popular constitution. We do not tremble beneath the rule of one man who would lord it over us, nor are we slaves to the rule of a few. Our liberty is equal for all, obeying only the laws, and is free from the fear of men. The hope of attaining distinction [or office] and of raising oneself up is the same for all, provided one applies industry, has talent, and follows a sound and serious way of life. Our city looks for virtue and probity in its citizens. Anyone who has these qualities is thought to be sufficiently well born to govern the republic. The pride and haughtiness of the powerful are so vehemently hated that more severe laws were enacted to penalize these kinds of men than for any other purpose, until the proud, finally mastered and, as it were, bound by the law's adamantine chains, were compelled to bend their necks and to humble themselves to a level

beneath even that of middling folk, so that it is held a great privilege to be allowed to transfer from families of the *grandi* to the status of commoner. This is true liberty, this is fairness in a city: not to fear violence or injury from any man, to have equality under the law for all citizens, and fair access to business affecting the public.[38]

Equality under law and Florence's "adamantine chains" on the powerful prevent the formation of a corrupt political elite made up of the *grandi,* wealthy men from old families, who despise and lord it over their inferiors. Instead, Florence's system ensures an elite of virtue drawn from the middle classes.[39]

Florentine liberty, which Quentin Skinner and Philip Pettit have well described as a "non-domination" concept of liberty,[40] is guaranteed, first, by the city's unwritten constitution: all citizens are forced to be equal by law and by the organs of state. The result, in principle, is that no individual has the prepotency to inflect the system in his own favor. Since powerful and rich citizens have the resources to look out for their own interests, it is the city's role to ensure that the weak are able to resist oppression by the strong. Liberty is, in other words, ensured by a form of political equality enforced by the state.[41] The same principle of preventing the dominance of one person or party is embedded in Florence's institutions, in particular the principle of Roman civil law that calls for consulting everyone affected by a law or decision. Everyone has a voice, no one is excluded; even the people have a veto over some measures via their councils.[42] Since no one has prepotency in government, Florence is free from the corruptions of power, and therefore, preeminent in virtue. The only way left for a citizen to distinguish himself is through virtue. There is no opportunity for a tyrant like Giangaleazzo Visconti to come to power. But by the same token, Florence's institutions cannot simply be copied by all other states, so that they too could enjoy *Florentina libertas.* As Bruni remarks in his *History of the Florentine People,* all peoples naturally desire liberty, but not all are capable of it.[43] *Virtus* is supported by institutions but transcends them. They are a necessary but not sufficient condition of Florence's greatness. The *stirps romulea* is still a sine qua non.[44]

Florence's virtue, in addition to being enabled by her egalitarian liberty, is also strengthened by two other institutions. Bruni's description of both is tendentious. Indeed, one institution is mostly imaginary: Bruni states that Florence's civil magistrates were elected, whereas in fact they were chosen by lot. "These men are not chosen by chance," he writes shamelessly. "They are men long approved by the judgement of the people and judged worthy of great honor."[45] Bruni no doubt wished Florence's magistrates *were* chosen by election, agreeing as he did with Cicero that open elections allow the virtuous candidate to triumph and with Aristotle that sortition disfavored virtue and talent.[46] Elsewhere, in the *History of the Florentine People*, Bruni criticizes the practice of sortition, comparing it unfavorably with the previous practice of voting, which followed ancient Roman practiced and encouraged virtue:

> But however much this procedure benefits the state, sortition harms it as much or even more, in that most of the time unworthy persons are assumed into the magistracy.... Moreover it extinguishes zeal for virtue, as men are much more careful in their behavior if there is a contest for votes and their reputation may openly be put in danger. I have no doubt, therefore, that the earlier practice [of voting] was much better and more useful to the state. It was also a practice that the Roman people always used in choosing its magistrates.[47]

There was also an element of fiction in Bruni's presentation of the Parte Guelfa as a magistracy that oversaw public morals. Employing hyperbolic comparison, he likens the political role of its Captains to that of Roman censors, the court of the Areopagus in Athens, and to the Spartan ephors:

> From its beginning, this magistracy has always had vast authority in Florence. It was founded to act as a kind of watchdog and guard to prevent the state from turning aside from the course followed by our ancestors and to block men who think otherwise from taking part in government. What the censors were to Rome, the Areopagites to Athens, and the ephors to Sparta, the Captains of the Parte Guelfa are to the city of Florence. This is to say that the leading men among those with correct views on the state are elected to protect the state.[48]

Bruni implies here that the role of the Parte was to act as constitutional guardians; it was meritocratic in that it was made up of *primari*, leading or excellent men, and its functions are compared to those of the censors in Rome and to what he takes to be similar institutions in Athens and Sparta. By analogy, the Captains were responsible for opposing corruption in Florence's political leadership.[49] In reality the Parte was a partisan political organization whose Captains had only a semi-official advisory role in the government of the commune. Its chief function was to enforce political loyalty to the Guelf cause and the oligarchy.[50] Whether Bruni's disingenuous claims regarding its function were more a matter of propaganda, as some scholars assume, or idealism is difficult to say. Bruni does seem to have been involved, more than a decade later, in efforts to reform the Parte in its role as a *societas militum,* a company of knights, charged with overseeing civic knighthood; his treatise *De militia* (c. 1420) laid out a new, meritocratic ideal for Florentine knights.[51] But at the time the *Laudatio* was written there was little substance to the claim that the Captains of the Parte formed a magistracy devoted to maintaining ancestral custom, the *mos maiorum,* and protecting Florence from moral corruption in its ruling class.[52]

Yet to dismiss such statements as flattery or propaganda, as is commonly done today, carries with it the danger that we might filter out the real idealism that stands behind Bruni's claims here, however exaggerated and even dishonest they might seem on their face to modern readers. In general, to regard the humanists only as professional rhetoricians and clients of the powerful, as modern scholarship tends to do, is to blind ourselves to their genuine convictions and even (dare one say it) to the lessons they might have to teach us. This is not to say that one may never doubt Bruni's sincerity, especially when in panegyrical mode. In particular one may well doubt the exclusivity of Bruni's commitment to republican government. It seems likely, despite the exclusivist rhetoric of his *Panegyric for Nanni Strozzi,* that he did not think monarchy and the rule of the few were necessarily illegitimate forms of government.[53] But given the ubiquity of these themes in his writings, it is hard to deny that Bruni and many other humanists were deeply sincere, indeed passionate, about reforming the political culture of their times, which for them meant improving the moral quality of their cities' princes and institutions using ancient models. This is one reason they were so drawn to Cicero and Livy, who were engaged in similar projects of re-moralizing corrupt elites through the study of philosophy and of history. Bruni and other humanists aimed to persuade ruling elites to embrace classical learning as a training in virtue. This they saw as the best way—perhaps, given the times, the only way—to restore concord, reverse the downward spiral of Italy, and return to the golden age populated by the noble Romans they so much admired. The *Laudatio* was surely part of this effort of reform, since Bruni knew well that one great function of epideictic rhetoric was to encourage men to virtue by praising them for already possessing it.[54]

The Etruscan Model: Leadership in a Federal Republic

A decade or so after writing the *Laudatio* Bruni ended his decade of service to the popes, who had been the first princes to make use of his literary talents. His master, John XXIII, had been declared an anti-pope by the Council of Constance, and as a result Bruni found himself unemployed. Returning to Florence where he had spent his youth, he began a new career as the city's official historiographer.[55] He had first floated the idea of writing a history of Florence in a letter of 1406 to his friend Niccolò Niccoli, in response to the latter's suggestion that he revise his *Laudatio* so as to celebrate Florence's recent conquest of Pisa. Bruni replied that the subject required too much elaboration to be included in the *Laudatio:* "That's why there is need of a history, and if your fellow-citizens were wise [Bruni himself was still a citizen of Arezzo at the time], they would entrust the task to some learned man."[56]

While assembling sources for book 1 of his *History* (completed in late 1415 or early 1416) he stumbled upon a second and even better ancient model for Florentine hegemony in Tuscany than the middle republic of Rome: the ancient, pre-Roman Etruscan League of free cities. Book 1 of the *History* proceeded to engraft Florentine history onto this far more ancient rootstock. Indeed, Bruni's sources told him that the Etruscans had been a flourishing nation long before the Trojan War. They were originally an Anatolian people allied with the Trojans who emigrated from Lydia to Italy hundreds of years before Aeneas founded Rome. At first the twelve Lydian tribes that settled in Etruria were governed by a king, but when the king's rule became too burdensome, the twelve cities of their league chose *lucumones,* or civil magistrates, to represent them in a common council. Eventually one of the *lucumones* achieved preeminence over the rest, not because of superior power but thanks to honor and authority. The league of free Etruscan cities proved to be highly successful and lasted almost a thousand years. Under their federal government the Etruscans proceeded to bring most of Italy under their sway between the Adriatic and the Tyrrhenian Seas, from the Alps to the Straits of Messina. Wherever they went they established colonies, such as Capua near Naples and Mantua on the other side of the Apennines. When Aeneas arrived in Italy he turned to the Etruscans for help in establishing a new center of Trojan power.[57] It was only after many hundreds of years that the Romans succeeded in subduing the Etruscans, who were in the end crushed between Rome and the rising power of the Gauls to the north.[58] Their besetting failure as a people was failure to unite their several cities in opposition to the Romans, allowing the latter to employ a strategy of *divide et impera*. Yet they were the superior culture, as was shown by the Romans' adoption of many Etruscan customs and religious practices. Before the Romans educated their children in Greek, it was the practice for them to be taught the (now lost) Etruscan authors.[59]

Bruni thus constructed a new model of interstate governance that was more egalitarian than the exploitative model of the Roman Empire, whose dominance from a single imperial center drained the periphery of its wealth, virtue, and opportunities for great deeds.[60] The Etruscans governed their empire as a federation of free cities with a common heritage that was ruled by a common council and led by the magistrate with the greatest prestige as *primus inter pares*. Its united federal government was a strength that gave it an advantage over other states.[61] It is surely no accident that this model of inter-state leadership was precisely the one promoted by humanist chancellors of Florence, Coluccio Salutati and later Bruni himself, to their Tuscan allies in the ongoing wars against Giangaleazzo and Filippo Maria Visconti of Milan from the 1390s through the 1430s.[62] Salutati and Bruni commonly presented Florence as the leader of an alliance of free city-states against the centralized, morally corrupt empire of the Visconti that sought only to dominate and exploit other cities.

We can illustrate how Bruni used the historical myth of Etruria in a concrete case by considering his short historical essay *De origine Mantuae* (On the Origins of Mantua).[63] This was written at the request of the ruler of Mantua, the young Gianfrancesco I Gonzaga (b. 1395). The latter was to become famous as a patron of humanist culture, hosting at his court the celebrated school of Vittorino da Feltre from 1423 to 1446.[64] Gonzaga was the nephew and (in his younger years) the ward of Carlo Malatesta, with whom Bruni had a close relationship.[65] Carlo and his brother Pandolfo Malatesta were military allies of Pope John XXIII, the former against the condottiere Braccio da Montone in the papal state, the latter in alliance with the Venetians against Sigismund of Luxembourg, later the Holy Roman Emperor.[66] Internal political forces in Mantua, however, favored Sigismund, and these in due course staged a coup (in 1414) against Gianfrancesco, which failed. Despite this, Gianfrancesco was not utterly alienated from the imperial cause since he was eager to acquire an imperial title for himself, something that could only be done if he maintained good relations with the future emperor.[67]

As ruler of a small buffer state, Gonzaga thus found himself constantly torn among competing interests, and before 1418 he had already been variously allied to, in the service of, or seeking favor from the Malatesta, the Venetians, Sigismund, the pope, and the Visconti. In the 1410s the Florentines had a strong interest in keeping him in the papal camp and alienated from that of Sigismund, whom they considered a threat to their Guelf entente. A few months after Bruni wrote his essay (dated April 27, 1418), the new pope elected by the Council of Constance, Martin V, briefly took up residence in Mantua (October 29, 1418–February 2, 1419), which afforded a further opportunity for cultural diplomacy. Bruni's essay might thus be seen as part of a Florentine campaign to deepen Gianfrancesco's sense of affinity for Florence and Tuscany.[68]

Bruni advances this agenda by emphasizing the ancient ties of blood and culture that united Mantua with the Tuscan city-states, led by Florence. In order to make the link between Mantua and the Etruscans, he was obliged to correct the authoritative account of none other than Dante.[69] In *Inferno* 20.52–99 Dante had stated through the mouth of his guide, Vergil—himself a native of Mantua—that the city had been named by the local inhabitants in honor of the Greek prophetess, Manto, daughter of Theban Tiresias, who had taken up residence on Lake Garda. Dante's Vergil closed his account by stating

Però t'assenno che, se tu mai odi
originar la mia terra altrimenti,
verità nulla menzogna frodi.

Therefore, I charge you, if you ever hear
other origin given to my city, let no falsehood
defraud the truth.[70]

Despite the admiring life of Dante that Bruni would compose later in 1436, in 1418 he was not about to let Dante get away with historical mythmaking, especially when it might undermine the interests of Florence and the pope.[71] In his essay on the origins of Mantua he deploys a wide range of sources, Latin and Greek, to show that Mantua was in fact an Etruscan foundation and had nothing to do with the Greek prophetess Manto.[72] Although his account drew upon book 1 of his *History,* Bruni is here far more explicit in identifying and quoting sources so as to refute beyond possibility of doubt Dante's poetic imaginings. Livy's history (5.33) is invoked to show that the Etruscans colonized the Po river valley, and Pliny the Elder's *Historia naturalis* (3.130) to identify one of these colonies as Mantua. Mantua was founded 300 years before Aeneas arrived in Italy and was thus far older than Milan, founded more than 450 years later (by the Gauls, according to Florentine propaganda, based on Livy 5.34) and more than 800 years before Cremona and Piacenza, both Roman colonies founded during the Second Punic War.

Thus Gianfrancesco should take it as "more than absolutely certain" *(plusquam certissimam)* that Mantua was founded in ancient times by the free Etruscan league of cities that dominated Italy before the Romans. Moreover, he should be proud of that fact, given that no nation before the Roman Empire was "more powerful in war, more noted for its wealth, or more glorious in the arts of peace." The Etruscans had defeated the autochthonous Pelagians and Umbrians and subdued three hundred other towns and cities; they even humiliated the Romans in battle repeatedly, and the Romans feared them more than any other nation. If origins are destiny, as most people in the Renaissance believed, then Gianfrancesco should consider that his city had been and remained by nature a Tuscan city. Bruni does not say so explicitly, but the implication of his historical essay is unmistakable: if Gianfrancesco embraces his Tuscan ancestry, he can expect to profit from a powerful alliance within which, among an equal confederation of noble cities related to his own by ties of blood, he can maintain the independence of his own city. The modern-day Tuscan confederation just over the Apennines, thanks to its wealth, its traditions of martial valor, and its reputation for virtuous dealings with other states, will be well able to defend him from the predatory powers surrounding him in the dangerous, war-torn Po Valley.

Dante and Bruni on the Legitimation of Empire

Before leaving the subject of Bruni's *Laudatio*, it will be instructive to compare its humanist project of legitimating multistate hegemony through virtue with Dante's arguments for accepting the authority of—or legitimating, or perhaps sanctifying—the Holy Roman Empire of his day, as laid out in book 2 of his *Monarchia*.[73] The contrast is indicative of how, over the course of a century, the humanist movement helped change modes of legitimation, moving Italy away from a sacral legitimacy, sustained by medieval theology and law, toward the moral legitimacy of virtue politics.[74]

Dante's *Monarchia*, to be sure, defends the legitimacy of the Holy Roman Empire as it existed in his own day—an empire that claimed continuous descent from ancient Rome. It defends the right *(ius)* of the successor of the old Roman emperors, Henry VII of Luxembourg, to rule Italy. Bruni's task is different: by his time, the Holy Roman Empire is too weak and discredited to be accepted by most Italians as a live option. For Bruni, as for Petrarch, the real Rome is ancient Rome, separated from the present by eight hundred years. It can serve as a model for modern times, but any political continuity was lost in late antiquity, in the period between the conversion of Constantine in the fourth century and the Lombard invasions of the sixth. All that is left is the *stirps Romulea,* Roman descent. For Bruni this appears to involve two elements. On the one hand Florence enjoys a kind of Lamarckian or "soft" (epigenetic) inheritance: Rome has passed on the moral characteristics it acquired in its long lifetime—exceptional virtue and nobility—to its offspring, Florence. On the other hand Florence inherits the legal right to Rome's empire, suspended as a result of the barbarian invasions; the city is like some remote, middle-class descendent who seeks to prove succession to a lapsed peerage held by a distant ancestor. Any lands over which it establishes its authority already belong to it by right.

These circumstances should make Bruni, as much as Dante, eager to prove ancient Rome's (or modern Florence's) right to rule other peoples, but here the contrast between the two political thinkers becomes sharp. What is noteworthy is how many of Dante's proofs of the legitimacy of Roman authority Bruni does not or cannot apply to Florence. In book 2 of the *Monarchia* Dante gives proofs based on reason and proofs from divine authority. Using rational proofs Dante shows that the founder of Rome, Aeneas, exceeded all other men in nobility since he was ennobled on all three of the continents (as then known) by descent or marriage. So Rome's origins are the noblest of all peoples. That nobility expressed itself in the extraordinary virtues of individual Romans such as Cincinnatus, Fabricius, Camillus, Brutus, Cato, and other heroes celebrated in Livy and Cicero's *De officiis.* Silently correcting Augustine, Dante claims the Romans were not driven by *libido dominandi* but by zeal for the common good, for which they even sacrificed their lives in the highest act of nobility. The extent and duration of her empire was in itself sufficient proof of Rome's nobility and its mastery of the arts of rule. It was as though Rome had won a series of trials by combat, proving her right to rule by always emerging the winner.

This last proof is linked with Dante's other set of proofs, those from divine authority. Dante has little use for the biblical model of the four empires popularized by Jerome: Babylonia, Persia, Greece, and Rome. For him, Rome towers over the rest; Rome was the final, eternal winner in the race for world domination; Rome's universal rule was part of the divine plan of salvation. Rome was in effect the Chosen Empire, providentially selected by God to bring peace and to unite all the peoples of the earth under a single power. God showed Rome's political power to be legitimate by signs and miracles, but above all by what may be called the "incarnational argument," elaborated by Dante from a passage in Orosius. Christ chose to be born in the time of Augustus, who restored monarchy to Rome, and to die in the time of Tiberius. By assenting to the legal right of the Romans to execute him, Christ showed the whole world that the Roman Empire was based on right. More bizarrely, Dante argues that for Christ's death to have legitimately counted as the price of our redemption, it required that the jurisdiction of Tiberius be both just and universal, representing the whole human race. This was the ultimate proof that Rome and her imperial system was chosen by God to rule the world.

Most of this highly elaborate argument was discarded by Bruni.[75] For Bruni, Rome ruled Italy and the Mediterranean simply by right of conquest in just wars: *ius ad bellum* yields *ius victoris super victos,* the right of a victor over the defeated. It was this right which Florence, the daughter of Rome, had inherited and whose underlying moral principles she endorsed and followed in her own life as a sovereign republic. Orosius' incarnational argument and Divine Providence could of course play no part in proving Florence's right to rule; the Florentines were not a Chosen People. In fact Bruni never invokes any kind of divine authority or law in justifying Florence's preeminence in Italy. Florence deserves to inherit Rome's empire just because the city was founded by Rome at the height of its power and glory and political liberty, and because Florence has proven through its behavior that it possesses the superexcellent virtue of Rome. In short, Bruni emphasizes hereditary and meritocratic forms of legitimation but largely excludes legal and sacral forms.

Where Dante and Bruni coincide is in recognizing the legitimating force of nobility and virtue. They agree that descent from noble ancestors is valuable only if each generation proves its nobility anew.[76] And they agree that supreme virtue and mastery of the arts of rule—practical wisdom or prudence—are sources of legitimacy. What this illustrates is a turning away in the humanist political tradition from the Christian religion and imperial Roman law as sources or modes of legitimation. Indeed, Bruni's moralized and secularized mode of legitimation pioneers a way of thinking found throughout fifteenth-century humanism.[77] In Bruni's *Laudatio* we can see, dimly ahead, the long-term consequences for political thought of the humanists' attempt to return to ancient patterns of thought and action: an assertion of the autonomy of politics as a realm distinct from religion; a greater willingness among educated elites to include virtuous men of humble condition in their ranks; and a renewed confidence in the power of leading men to reform and improve themselves and their societies through the acquisition of humane learning and the virtue it imparted.

CHAPTER 9

WAR AND MILITARY SERVICE
IN THE VIRTUOUS REPUBLIC

Late Medieval Civic Knighthood and the Context of
Leonardo Bruni's De Militia

In the comic tales of Franco Sacchetti, the trecento novelist, there is a story that shows with great vividness how Florentines of the early Renaissance viewed the knighthood of their time. A knight of the Bardi family has been chosen to serve as a foreign judge *(podestà)* in the city of Padua. He is a tiny man, unmilitary in his habits, and an indifferent horseman. To give himself a more impressive appearance, he decides to have a magnificent knightly crest attached to his helmet, painted with his arms, a bear rampant with drawn claws, and the couplet *Non ischerzare con l'orso, / se non vogli essere morso* (Don't play games with the bear if you don't want to be bitten). On his way to Padua, he passes through Ferrara, where in the main piazza next to the prince's castle he is accosted by a gigantic German knight. The German, who (following comic convention) is a bit tipsy, is incensed to see the diminutive Florentine bearing what he claims are his, the German's, own arms, and he challenges him to a duel. The Florentine, however, can see no point in coming to blows and arranges a deal through his seconds. "Let's settle this with florins and put honor aside," he says. "If you want me to go on my way as I came, I'll be off right now; if you mean that I shouldn't bear his crest, I swear by God's holy angels that it's mine and that I had it made in Florence by the painter Luchino and it cost me five florins; if he wants it, give me five florins and take the crest away." The German, "triumphant as though he'd conquered a city," paid up willingly. The Bardi knight went off with his five florins to Padua, where he was able to purchase a new crest for only two florins, making a clear profit of three.[1]

This little bit of buffoonery gives us a good idea of what knighthood had come to mean in the minds of many Italians by the late fourteenth century. For the Florentine judge, his knighthood was an honor that gave him the opportunity to dress up in a dazzling costume. It was a piece of merchandise he had purchased;

nothing more. He had no sense of shame at his lack of *bellica virtus*. Nor was this Bardi knight an isolated character, at least in the literary imagination. The theme of the decline of knighthood was a common one in the literature of the period. In Boccaccio's *Corbaccio* the knights of the time are depicted as "poltroons spangled with pearls and draped in ermine, decked with gold spurs and swords with gilded hilts, yet with as little appreciation of true knighthood as the devil has of the cross." The jurists were as acerbic as the novelists on the subject. Cino da Pistoia criticized "pseudo-knights who were immersed in their profits and scarcely knew how to gird on a sword."[2] They enjoyed the prestige and privileges of knights without having any of their military responsibilities.

The historical reality, so far as we can reconstruct it, seems to correspond to the literary image. In Florence we hear of four-year-old children or old men on their deathbeds being made knights. During the tumult of the Ciompi, the revolutionary uprising of Florence's workers in 1378, sixty-seven men were created knights by the revolutionary workers in a single day.[3] When the Ciompi revolt was put down and the oligarchy restored there was yet another orgy of knight-making: twenty-four new knights were created on January 20, 1382, at a single ceremony. Such mass creations were clearly political actions, not rewards for military virtue, as was shown many years ago by the eminent anti-fascist historian Gaetano Salvemini. The aim was to undermine or strengthen the power of the Parte Guelfa, a conservative political society in Florence that was also a *societas militum,* a fellowship of knights, to which knights automatically belonged by reason of their rank.[4]

A similar disregard for the military functions of knighthood is shown in the practice of awarding knighthood to men who were being sent on diplomatic missions. Here the motive seems to have been to permit Florentine diplomats to cut a better figure abroad when representing their city. As late as 1419 we hear of a mass creation of twenty knights, the sole purpose of which was to enrich the spectacle of welcome for the solemn entry of Pope Martin V into Florence. It seems that the desire to have twenty Florentines dress up in crowns of olive leaves, green tunics sewn with pearls, gold sword, spurs, and swordbelt, so as to welcome the Holy Father with greater splendor, was sufficient inducement for the Florentine government to debase the coinage of knighthood.[5]

But by 1419 things were changing; a reaction had set in. A movement was afoot in Florence to reform knighthood, and the Parte Guelfa was at the head of it. The Parte was an immensely wealthy and prestigious institution that occupied a curious semi-public, semi-private position in Florentine life. Unfriendly critics have compared its role to that of the Communist Party in the old Soviet Union, but this is to overstate its influence if not its aspirations. It is certainly true that its leadership overlapped to a surprising extent with the oligarchic leadership of Florence, especially in the period between 1382 and 1434, when that oligarchy was at the height of its power. Officially, the Parte's role was to guard against constitutional innovations. Less officially, it aimed to safeguard the position of old Florentine families and to minimize the influence of *gente nuova,* recent immigrants, in society and politics. It was also the institution charged with overseeing all activities relating to communal knighthood, that is, the *dignità cavalleresche* conferred by the *comune* of Florence on selected citizens. It had an important role, in other words, in conferring social status. On feast days it organized the part of civic processions that featured knights. Every year on July 28, the feast of St. Victor, it organized a horse race at San Felice in Piazza; on October 9, on the feast of St. Dionysius, it sponsored a joust in the Piazza Santa Croce. The latter two occasions celebrated Guelf victories over the Ghibelline city of Pisa. In addition, for citizens newly knighted by the commune, the Parte held lavish ceremonies in its own palace in Via delle Terme near Orsanmichele.[6]

By 1413 there were signs that the Parte was taking active steps to reform knighthood and to renew its own tarnished image. In typical fashion, the Parte saw its task as one of excluding the "Ghibellines and peasants," that is, *gente nuova,* who had infiltrated its ranks. The dignity of knighthood was to be ennobled by taking it out of the hands of the unworthy. The movement of reform culminated in March 1420 with the revision of the statutes of the Parte Guelfa. The new statutes were designed to ensure control over Parte affairs by the old Guelf families and to keep out *gente nuova.* They were also intended to prevent the indiscriminate creation of communal knights that had disfigured the institution in the past.[7] The statutes were revised by a commission of six Parte members, among whom was a man who had recently inherited a leading role in the Florentine oligarchy, Rinaldo di Maso degli Albizzi. The commission was aided in its work of drafting the new statutes by a former apostolic secretary to four popes, Leonardo Bruni, who had recently begun a new career in Florence as the official historian of the Florentine People. The original codex containing the revised statutes survives; it was written, significantly, in the new *littera antiqua* of the humanists decorated with a fashionable vine-stem initial. The hand is identifiable as that of the humanist scribe Antonio di Mario, who copied a number of Bruni's works for Florentine patrons, including the dedication copy of Bruni's translation of the pseudo-Aristotelian *Economics,* made for Cosimo de'Medici in that same year, 1420.[8]

The connection of Bruni and Albizzi is an interesting one. In December 1421, less than two years after the revision of the Parte Guelfa's statutes, Bruni dedicated to Albizzi a little treatise entitled *De militia*—a title best translated as *On Knighthood.* The coincidence of dates and persons as well as the topic of the treatise already suggest that Bruni's work should be linked to the Parte Guelfa's program to reform communal knighthood. What makes the work of more than antiquarian interest, however, is the surprising way Bruni realized that project. His aim in this political essay was nothing less than to co-opt the most glamorous of medieval ideals, the ideal of chivalry, and to reinterpret it through the lens of Graeco-Roman authorities on military service. In other words, he aimed to make the reform of knighthood into an aspect of the revival of antiquity, the great Renaissance movement which in those years was just beginning to sweep through Florence and other Italian cities. Bruni's goal was to exploit the Parte Guelfa's recent concern with its image to promote the cause of civic virtue.

It must be said that this interpretation of the *De militia* is by no means the accepted one. The most detailed study of the text, by C. C. Bayley, published in 1961, sees the work as "a link in a long chain of controversy, extending from the thirteenth to the sixteenth century, excited by the progressive displacement in Italy of citizen militias by mercenary troops."[9] Bayley, in other words, saw the text primarily as a critique of the condottiere system. His interpretation came under criticism in reviews by two famous Renaissance scholars, Paul Oskar Kristeller and Sergio Bertelli. Kristeller claimed that the contemporary meaning of the word *militia* was "knighthood," not "militia" in the sense of volunteer citizen soldiery. As a result, he claimed, the whole concept behind the book was flawed.[10] Bertelli added the suggestion that Bruni's treatise should be connected with the reform of the Parte Guelfa in 1420 rather than with the reform of the condottiere system.[11]

Not all of these criticisms were entirely fair. Bayley certainly knew that *militia* could mean "knighthood," and he speculated on the possibility of a connection between the *De militia* and the 1420 statues. Another possible translation of *militia* is to understand the word in its classical sense of "military service" or even "warfare," and it was not implausible to argue that Bruni's intention was to reform Florence's current military practices, broadly speaking, in the light of ancient models. Bayley for his part surely realized that the *De militia* was somehow related to contemporary criticisms of "carpet knights." The treatise, he admitted in passing, "lodged a discreet but unmistakable protest against the current decline of civic knighthood."[12] Nevertheless, Bayley's attempt to read the text primarily as a critique of the condottiere system inevitably skewed his interpretation and led to several false emphases in addition to the errors of fact and method pointed out by his critics.

Bayley's rather perverse view of Bruni's text—which after all never mentions condottieri or mercenaries—may be traced to the influence of Hans Baron's famous book, *The Crisis of the Early Italian Renaissance*.[13] This book, extremely popular in the 1960s and 1970s, understood Bruni to be a partisan ideologue promoting republicanism and civic humanism against the threat of monarchy, understood as tantamount to tyranny. Impressed by Baron's conception of civic humanism, Bayley was predisposed to read the *De militia* as a work that advocated replacing the mercenary system with citizen soldiers. In the context of the present work, which claims that virtue politics is the unifying theme of humanist political thought, it is worth reopening the question of the *De militia*'s meaning and purpose. The task is all the more pressing as the interpretation of Baron and Bayley has been endorsed by two leading Bruni scholars of the present day, Paolo Viti and Lucia Gualdo Rosa.[14] Moreover, the alternative interpretation of the *De militia*, as an attempt to reform communal knighthood in accordance with ancient models, has never been worked out in detail, beyond the passing suggestion in Bertelli's review. A careful reading of this text can help us understand more clearly, in a concrete social and political context—Florence in the 1420s—how humanists tried to turn their virtue politics into a practical program of reform.

Excursus: The Humanists and Partisan Politics

Humanist political thought in Florence is sometimes read today as an oligarchic ideology, or as the result of an ideological negotiation between popular and oligarchic parties.[15] In his classic work, *Corporatism and Consensus in Florentine Electoral Politics* (1982), John Najemy identifies two ideological poles within the ruling councils of Florence. One, based in the guilds, he calls "corporatism." Corporatists had an ethos of equality and participation in governance; according to Najemy they had "a vision of the Florentine republic as a sovereign federation of equal and autonomous guilds." In electoral politics they generally favored an egalitarian model of shared rule—choosing magistrates by lot, ruling and being ruled in turn—and were on balance more favorable to *gente nuova*, opening citizen rights to immigrants from Florence's territory and elsewhere. They were deeply concerned with establishing safeguards against the overwhelming power of great men in the state. Their egalitarian model of freedom required that the commune not be dominated by powerful individuals and their clientage groups. Indeed, it was guild republicanism that most closely approximated what Quentin Skinner and Philip Pettit have described as the "non-domination" model of liberty.[16] This concern with liberty and domination, still according to Najemy, was a response to the social group that formed the great rival of the guilds in Florentine politics, namely, the *grandi* or oligarchs. These were men who claimed the right to rule because of the long residence of their families in Florence over many generations, as well as because of their wealth, large clienteles, military experience, far-flung commercial relations, and great connections in the Church. Such men eventually, after 1378, established their dominance in government by promoting an ideology of "consensus": guildsmen would receive rewards and offices if they accepted the leadership in the republic of "prudent, wise, and expert men." Both groups would band together against the violence of the mob, whose destructive power was so vividly revealed by the Ciompi revolt.

In *Corporatism and Consensus* and a number of subsequent publications, Najemy has defended the view that civic humanism, particularly in the works of Leonardo Bruni, was an ideology that emerged to justify oligarchic power by manipulating the egalitarian ideals of guild republicanism. It integrated "the two cardinal points of consensus politics—the broad base of participation and the narrow pinnacle of elitist power—into a single coherent vision," thus helping to bury the political ideals of late medieval corporatism.[17] This view is surely correct insofar as it provides one explanation for why Florentine oligarchs were ready to embrace humanist ideals: they realized those ideals could serve to justify their own regime. But it needs to be pointed out that humanist political thinkers did not see their own role in this light, either in Florence or elsewhere. They saw themselves as serious reformers and not as "mere rhetoricians," talking puppets who produced ideological vehicles to maintain oligarchic power. Humanist virtue politics, as this book aims to show, was common to humanists all over Italy for well over a century and was promoted by literati with a wide range of political commitments, from populism to papal monarchy. It cannot be accounted for in terms of Florentine political rivalries alone.

Even in Florence it is clear that humanists usually tried to present themselves as non-partisan or above partisan politics. Sometimes they saw themselves as belonging to a party of virtue and philosophy that transcended ordinary partisan politics, driven by interests and passions. More often they understood partisanship as an obstacle to the kind of characters they wished to form. Partisanship could also be disadvantageous professionally. As Robert Black has pointed out, the humanist chancellors of Florence, until they were corrupted by the Medici after 1464, were chosen precisely because they were seen as non-partisan, and were expected to behave accordingly. They were meant, in other words, to embrace an ethos appropriate to civil servants who had to serve successive political masters and not to promote the interests of one party over another. They might advocate policies such as Machiavelli's plan for a civic militia, but they would be considered corrupt if they abused the organs of communal government to support or undermine particular politicians. Humanist chancellors were generally non-Florentine by birth—like Leonardo Bruni, Carlo Marsuppini, and Benedetto Accolti, all from Arezzo—or men from families with reduced prestige such as Machiavelli, who could be expected to have fewer political commitments to the republic's great men.[18]

The self-concept of civic humanists matched this non-partisan ethos of public service. Consider, for example, a passage from Matteo Palmieri's *Della vita civile*. Palmieri (1406–1475) was a student and disciple of Leonardo Bruni and has long been considered one of the authentic voices of Florentine civic humanism.[19] In this passage from book 3 he is discussing the theme of distributive justice, and asks how public honors, that is, offices, should be distributed. This depends, says Palmieri, on one's conception of dignity or worthiness.

> Public honors [*gl'honori publici*] should be distributed according to the worthiness [*degnità*] of the individual. It is a difficult thing in the republic to ascertain whose worthiness is greater, since people disagree about this subject. The nobles and the powerful say that worthiness consists in abundant resources and in noble and ancient families. Popular men [*i populari*] say it consists in the common humanity and benevolent intercourse of free and peaceful living. The wise [*i savi*] say it consists in active virtue. Those who have the task of distributing honors in the city who follow the most approved counsel always confer honors on the most virtuous. This is because honor ought to correspond to worthiness, and nothing is more worthy among men than the virtue of those who exert themselves for public utility. Those who seek glory [merely] through the virtue of their ancestors deprive themselves of all the merit of honor, and the man who destroys the reputation of his forefathers is certainly wretched.

Let him give proof of himself and not of his relatives who deserve honor; let him boast of his nobility only when his own virtues equal theirs. The wisest of the ancients who greatly enlarged their empires often elevated to the first offices of state foreigners, workers and men of low condition when they recognized in them signal excellences of virtue. [*Many historical examples follow.*] ... Let no one think it beneath him to be governed by the virtuous, even if they were born of low estate and unknown parentage.[20]

Palmieri presents himself here as dissenting from the views of both the *nobili e potenti* and of the *populari,* and as upholding the views of the *savi,* the wise, against what most people say.[21] The wise are, in other words, their own party. It is of course true that Palmieri is deeply influenced by Aristotle, and virtue in Aristotelian ethics is more easily achieved by the rich than by the poor. Persons of means are more likely to have a good upbringing and virtuous friends, both important part-causes or preconditions of virtue for Aristotle. Moreover, the rich have the time and means to get a humanist education, which all humanists believed indispensable to virtue. They have the wealth without which the virtue of magnificence cannot be displayed; even the lesser virtue of liberality is difficult for persons of slender means.[22] But all this is no guarantee that the rich and powerful will in fact achieve virtue; recent Florentine history was full of examples of elite members of society behaving badly. In any case the whole tendency of Palmieri's remarks is in one sense anti-Aristotelian: he aims to dismiss the idea that inherited wealth or descent makes you better and therefore entitles you to hold office.[23] In general the humanists were engaged in a project of justifying hierarchy, and a just political order for them was built upon the virtues of political leaders, including prudence and wisdom. The reforming message of the humanists to the powerful is that only virtue will justify your position of power. To those possessing few resources, their message is that virtue alone will enable you, or should enable you, to rise to a position of honor in the state.

This two-pronged message of reform is found all over humanist writings once one begins to look for it. Bruni, as we saw in the last chapter, disliked the principle of sortition and called for "prudent and experienced men" to rule the republic; he praised the election of magistrates as more likely to produce virtuous leaders. In his commentary on (pseudo) Aristotle's *Economics,* he even praised the accumulation of wealth as a service to the state. All that might seem to favor the *grandi,* but on the other hand he criticized trecento Florentines for giving up the practice of popular military service in favor of using mercenary troops, a practice he knew only increased the power of the wealthy and reduced Florence's *bellica virtus.* He could even praise Michele di Lando, the ringleader of the Ciompi revolt, for his *virtus et constantia,* even though he was born *ex minima plebe,* from the lowest of the low.[24] He counseled the nobility to restrain its desire for luxury, as it led to visible inequalities and impoverished the state, but the People were told that they should not let their zeal for equality lead them to abolish proper distinctions of merit. Like Palmieri, Bruni saw himself as an upholder of virtue and as a critic of both populist and oligarchic elements in the state. Like Palmieri too, and like most humanists in their treatises on true nobility, Bruni had as his goal one that humanists often identify, significantly, as "philosophical": to reduce the influence of wealth and family in politics and elevate the role of wisdom and virtue.

Bruni's De Militia: *A New Interpretation*

The *De militia* treats four main topics: (1) the origin and true nature of knighthood, (2) the question whether modern Italian knighthood conforms in its general pattern with ancient ideas about military service, (3) the question of how a knight should dress, and (4) the issue of what the duties of the knight should be during peacetime. The innovative nature of Bruni's approach becomes clear immediately in his treatment of the first topic. He ignores the usual view of his contemporaries that knighthood was a transalpine invention of recent centuries. Instead, he raises the question to a higher level of abstraction altogether by inquiring what the essence is of communal knighthood—that is, of military service to the state considered as a necessary social and political function. The question for him is as much a philosophical as a historical one. He begins from the Aristotelian proposition that man is a political animal. Since the *miles* is a man, it follows that an inquiry into the nature of the *miles* is fundamentally an inquiry into the nature of the state. "The city-state is the initiator and perfecter of our whole life and all human duties," he writes.[25] Following Macrobius' *Commentary on the Dream of Scipio* and Polybius' *Histories* (a text of which Bruni had published a paraphrase only the year before), he claims that there are two ways of investigating the nature of the state: the philosophical and the historical.[26] The philosophical way exists in the mind, as an analytical model, while the historical way is based on the experience of actual states. Both shed light on the origin of military service.

Bruni's philosophical guide to the essence of the *miles* is book 2 of Aristotle's *Politics.* This was a natural choice. He had just finished translating the *Nicoma-*

chean Ethics (1418) and the pseudo-Aristotelian *Economics* (1420) and would soon embark on a translation of the *Politics* that would eventually be published in 1436 / 1438.[27] He considered himself an Aristotelian, or as he put it, "a follower of Aristotle in matter, of Cicero in manner."[28] Despite his allegiance to the moral philosophy of Aristotle, however, Bruni uses Aristotle more as a historical source than as a philosophical authority. Aristotle himself had said little about the function of the *miles* in the state, but he reported the view of Phileas of Carthage, Hippodamus, and Plato that the protective function of the *miles* was "necessary and natural" to the state. *Milites* or *custodes* (guardians) should therefore be permanently constituted as one of the three orders or classes in the state with appropriate responsibilities and privileges. Bruni takes this to be the "philosophical" view of the *miles'* role in the state. He seems also to have consulted Plato's *Republic* itself, or the Latin translation by Uberto Decembrio, since he quotes a passage in *Republic* 2 (not found in Aristotle) where Socrates describes the ideal character of the guardian caste as similar to watchdogs, who combine ferocity against enemies with gentleness toward members of the household.[29]

As part of his "philosophical" consideration of the function of the *miles* in the state, Bruni investigates the etymology of the word *miles*. The results are not impressive. Bruni cites the derivation of *miles* from *malum arcendum*—the *miles* is one who wards off evil from the state—an embarrassingly close parallel to the notorious *lucus a non lucendo*. Here one is reminded of Voltaire's witticism that etymology is a science where the vowels count for nothing and the consonants for very little. But the digression shows that, in Bruni's mind, as in those of other humanists, there was a natural parallelism between grammatical and historical methods. Just as the meaning of a word was established by its derivation and current usage, so establishing the meaning of an institution had to take into account its original function as well as contemporary practice. This is precisely Bruni's approach in discovering the meaning of knighthood.

Bruni next turns to the historical part of his study of military origins. Here he relies chiefly on Livy and Cicero. In the best-constituted historical societies military service is treated very differently from the way it is treated in philosophers' republics. For Bruni (as for Macrobius), Rome is of course the best of all states that have actually existed. It is morally inferior to the philosopher's republic in that it makes concessions to human weakness, but it has the advantage of being possible.[30] According to Bruni, military service in the state founded by Romulus was a temporary condition, rigidly divided from civilian life by a religious oath. Soldiers did not form a caste apart but were citizens performing military duties on a temporary basis. The military oath, as Bruni learned from the *De officiis* (1.11.36), prevented the civilian from acting as a soldier and vice versa. In what was presumably a further concession to human weakness, Romulus also allowed for class distinctions among his *milites*. The Roman military consisted of both *pedites* and *equites*, foot soldiers and cavalry. The rank of *eques* was accorded to citizens of outstanding wealth, ancestry, or accomplishment. In time they formed the equestrian order and were (according to Bruni) considered noble. From thence they might rise further to consular or senatorial rank. This did not mean that the *pedites* were downgraded to servile status, as in the society of Gaul. "Romulus did not permit the plebs to be stripped of its right and dignity."[31] But he did give special honor and dignity to equestrian soldiers, and he allowed for a certain mobility between ranks—a principle that Bruni, himself a *novus homo,* heartily approves.

What Bruni is doing here is reinterpreting the meaning of communal knighthood, using the classical concept of the polis: a natural association of men under common laws organized for the purpose of realizing the good life. The military function of the state, whether temporary or permanent, is a necessary one and derives its value from its organic role in preserving other members of the state. We are now worlds away from the medieval concept of chivalry. Here are no divided loyalties to lord, lady, and church; no supranational code of conduct; no crusaders smiting the paynim in the Levant; no roving adventurers seeking the Holy Grail; no feats of *prowesse* to win the love of a fair lady. We would also seem to be at some distance even from the communal knights of late medieval Florence—those middle-aged merchants in fancy dress. So it comes as a surprise to hear Bruni assert, in the next section of his work, that it is possible to identify modern Italian knighthood with military service in ancient times.

By this statement Bruni does not mean that the ancient soldier or *eques* and the modern gentleman-*cavaliere* resemble each other in their way of life. Rather, the resemblance between ancient and modern knighthood is a formal one, seen mainly at the level of constitutional theory. According to Bruni, modern communal knighthood draws elements from both ancient philosophical theory and actual ancient practice. From Rome it adopts the practice of allowing mobility between the orders and the practice of requiring a military oath before a soldier could engage in warfare. From the philosophers it borrows the idea of a permanent caste of men dedicated to the military life. Bruni's analysis also reveals, implicitly, how inferior the French equestrian order is to both ancient and modern Italian forms of military service. French knighthood is a closed caste that, together with the priesthood, monopolizes all honor in the kingdom; by doing so it reduces the common people to servile status. The Florentine commune gave commoners the chance to compete with nobles for honor. As elsewhere in his writings, Bruni aims to bolster Italian pride in native institutions by assimilating them to ancient Roman ones, while contrasting them favorably with the ways of transalpine barbarians.[32] As elsewhere, he rejects the idea that commoners are unworthy of honor and leadership in the city-state.

In keeping with this aim, Bruni's analysis thus far has not breathed a word of criticism of Italian communal knighthood. Bruni accepts, indeed celebrates, the idea of a permanent order of men singled out for their ancestry, wealth, and accomplishments who follow a more honorable style of life devoted primarily to military affairs. It is, in short, the kind of life led by the dedicatee of *De militia*, Rinaldo degli Albizzi, whose public activity was devoted to diplomacy and military commissions.[33] This observation alone, it may be said, disproves the thesis that the *De militia* advocates the revival of the old Florentine civic militia, since militias by definition imply temporary military service by citizen-soldiers who follow different occupations in peacetime. It might be argued, to the contrary, that Bruni was unwilling to criticize communal knighthood openly because he could not afford to offend men such as Rinaldo, or his banker and close friend Palla Strozzi, or Michele di Vanni Castellani, the future father-in-law of his son, all of whom held the dignity of communal knights. To be sure, it seems likely that Rinaldo's own knighthood was given to him for ceremonial reasons, as it was conferred within ten days of his being appointed ambassador to Pope Martin V.[34] But while it is true that Bruni was never inclined, in this or other matters, to articulate sweeping criticism of the existing order, it cannot really be denied that his conception of knighthood was that of a permanent order of men dedicated to a life of honorable pursuits. It is quite impossible to make sense of the last section of the *De militia*, which deals with the peacetime occupations of the knight, on the assumption that Bruni favored instituting a trained militia of temporary soldiers—raised primarily from the peasant and artisan classes of the Florentine state and its territories—of the kind later advocated by Machiavelli. Such a theory would also contradict the ideal of military service enunciated in a parallel text, the *Oration on the Funeral of Nanni Strozzi*, discussed below.

In the first two sections of the *De militia*, then, Bruni is not so much a reformer of communal knighthood—someone who sought to change the institution fundamentally—as its panegyrist and champion. His aim is to refurbish communal knighthood, to ennoble it, to change the way people saw it by looking at it from the point of view of classical antiquity. Seen from the perspective of ancient history and philosophy, Italian civic knighthood could be viewed as a legitimate descendent of a classical institution that embodied, or could embody, classical virtues. In repackaging knighthood this way, Bruni was acting (as usual) as a political conservative, a faithful servant of the republic. To put it in anachronistic modern terms, the Parte Guelfa and knighthood had an image problem, and Bruni's treatise aimed to help remedy that by holding up before it an ideal of virtuous military service, a humanist mirror of republican knighthood. It is a fundamental misunderstanding of early quattrocento humanism to think of it in any way as interested in serious constitutional reform. What Bruni and other early Renaissance humanists wanted was not outward reform, that is, reform of laws or institutions. They wanted interior reform—reform of human nature. "Men, not walls, make a city," as the humanists delighted to quote from Thucydides. What made a city great was not its constitution, but the virtues of its citizens.

It is to the task of building knightly virtue that Bruni turns in the last two sections of the *De militia,* and it is here one can sense his true reforming fervor. His first goal is to discredit the vulgar view of many of his contemporaries that the essence of knighthood consists of dressing up in magnificent clothes. This view Bruni dispatches swiftly, citing various classical authorities to indicate that the dress of *equites* in Roman times was very simple: they distinguished themselves from the plebs only by the gold ring they wore. Even the olive crown was a later innovation, though Bruni considers it permissible to wear it, since it nevertheless had a good ancient pedigree.

In the last section of the *De militia,* on the peacetime functions of the knight, Bruni has to pick his way carefully. Having had the benefit of a legal education, he was no doubt aware of the legal maxim in the Justinianic Code that prohibited citizens from simultaneously exercising military and civic functions.[35] Moreover, he aimed to reform a social distinction existing in real time, and a number of influential figures who currently enjoyed that distinction were engaged in precisely the sort of activities Bruni believed were inappropriate for knights. Rejecting Justinian (and Cicero), Bruni thus argues that in the case of a permanent knightly caste, one has to allow the knight to have more than one persona: he can, while a knight, act as a judge or diplomat or senator or guardian or simply as a *vir bonus.* Though he is always a *miles,* he does not always act *qua miles.* But the fact that multiple activities are permitted to a person of knightly status does not mean that it is fitting for knights to engage in any and all activities.[36] It is most fitting for a knight to exercise functions wherein he makes use of his special virtue of fortitude. In peacetime this means protecting widows and orphans against wicked men. But it is, in Bruni's view—and here he recognizes that he is being controversial—absolutely wrong for a knight to engage in mercenary occupations, to "strive for profit." The good knight should already have sufficient wealth so that he can dedicate himself completely to public service. It is acceptable to be raised to the rank of knight because of one's wealth, but once one becomes a *miles,* the striving for "sordid profit" should cease.

Bruni underlines his point in the dramatic close of the treatise. The *De militia* ends with a stirring speech modeled on Plato's *Crito* (a text Bruni had translated years before)[37] in which a personified Patria addresses the aspiring knight. The knight, she declares, should be a man who seeks honor and glory rather than riches. His superior rank should imply a higher form of life, a more ample virtue, than that of merchants and tradesmen. It would be intolerable that one man should hold rank over another when he is indistinguishable in his way of life from others of lesser rank. Rank has responsibilities as well as privileges.

Thus Bruni's classicizing reinterpretation of communal knighthood accords perfectly with, and in effect provides a justification for, the reform of the Parte Guelfa in 1413 and 1420. Like the Parte reformers, Bruni envisages a form of knighthood restricted to those wealthy enough to engage in military and political activity without having to dirty themselves with actual moneymaking. Tradesmen and "peasants" need not apply. As we have seen, one theme in virtue politics is to decouple virtue from wealth, and this is a theme that Bruni himself invokes in different contexts in his writings. But in this case, in deference to the social realities of Florence, he is prepared to link knightly virtue with wealth. Wealth is the essential precondition for knightly status, and military virtue is effectively restricted to those of knightly status. Nevertheless, even this elite remains open since it is in principle possible for members of lower social groups who have earned sufficient wealth on their own to be raised to knighthood.

Further confirmation for this reading of Bruni's treatise can be found in another text which, surprisingly, is rarely cited by students of the *De militia*: the *Oration on the Funeral of Nanni Strozzi* (1428). Nanni Strozzi was a Ferrarese knight of Florentine extraction, a cousin of the great oligarch Palla Strozzi, who was killed at the battle of Ottolengo at the crisis of the Second Milanese War. Written only

a few years after *De militia*, Bruni's funeral oration for Strozzi was in part modelled on Pericles' Funeral Oration in Thucydides' *History of the Peloponnesian War*.[38]
The first part of the speech praises Florence and her free institutions as an introduction to the praise of Nanni himself, and it is this part of the speech which has
predictably received the most attention from modern scholars. In the second part,
however, there is a long passage in which Nanni is presented as the *beau ideal* of
Bruni's classicizing form of knighthood.[39] There are many explicit parallels with
and echoes of the *De militia*. We are told that Nanni, in order to devote himself
to the military life, gave up careers in commerce and farming. Unlike many others,
Nanni knew that what made a knight was not golden swordbelts and spurs, but
an honorable mode of life and brave deeds. He eschewed sartorial display and
luxury and lived his life according to an upright, simple, and noble plan of life
(*recta . . . et simplex et ingenua vivendi ratio*). When he was knighted, it was as
though he had received a sacrament; the military life, it is implied, is a special way
of life like that of the priesthood. Indeed, Bruni—like St. Bernard of Clairvaux
but with a wholly different intention—compares the profession of arms with the
monastic profession: Nanni was consecrated to "this perpetual vow of knighthood"
(*haec perpetua militiae religio*) "as though he was enclosing himself within the clois-
ters, as it were, of this great purpose" (*quasi intra claustra quaedam huius propositi
continere*). But the service to which Nanni was dedicated was not that of God, but
of his country:

> He held the welfare of his country so dear that he was judged to have been
> born for this one thing above all. His whole life showed this, which he con-
> ducted in such a way that everything he did seemed to have reference to his
> country. . . . Thus he inarguably preferred the affairs of war to the arts of
> peace. . . . His youthful battles, his study of military encounters, like his ath-
> letic exercises, were undertaken to achieve, through acts of courage, fame, glory,
> distinction and the enlargement of his reputation. But he believed his courage
> should be placed most of all at the service of his country, and he did so abun-
> dantly throughout his entire life.[40]

This passage surely demonstrates beyond question that Bruni's conception of
militia has nothing to do with citizen-levies, *scelte*, or the militia companies (*gon-
faloni*) of the *popolo*, either those Florence possessed in the thirteenth century or
those such as Machiavelli attempted to revitalize in the sixteenth. Rather, he was

inventing a new image for communal knighthood and the Parte Guelfa—the heart of the Florentine oligarchy—one that helped to justify its position of leadership in domestic and foreign affairs. At the same time, on the orator's principle that to praise someone for excellence is to encourage excellence, he hoped that his new ideal of *militia,* of military service to the state, would infuse the tawdry reality of Florentine knighthood with a fresh charge of classical virtue.

Excursus on the "Virtuous Environment": Donatello and the Representation of Classical Military Virtue

It is surely no coincidence that at the same time Bruni was inventing a new, more classical ideal for communal knighthood in his *De militia,* the Parte Guelfa, the custodian of communal knighthood, was endorsing in its artistic patronage the most radical form of artistic classicism available in early quattrocento Florence— namely, the classicism of Donatello and Filippo Brunelleschi. As Diane Finiello Zervas states in her study of the artistic patronage of the Parte, "These men [the Parte's leaders] . . . opted with surprising unanimity, and within the space of only a few years, for the explicitly *all'antica* style offered by Donatello and Brunelleschi and to a lesser extent by Ghiberti."[41] The great projects sponsored by the Parte Guelfa—Donatello's tabernacle and bronze statue of St. Louis for the Parte's niche on the exterior wall of Orsanmichele, and Brunelleschi's rebuilding of the palazzo of the Parte Guelfa—are remarkable visual correlatives to the ideological work of reconceptualizing knighthood and the Parte Guelfa being undertaken by Bruni. They illustrate a point made in Chapter 2, that humanist virtue politics aimed to promote a "virtuous environment" that would surround aspirants to true nobility with exemplary images and a classical stage, as it were, on which to enact great deeds.

A still more striking visual parallel is Donatello's famous statue of St. George, a work in stone created to adorn the niche of Orsanmichele assigned to the Guild of Armorers. Here we have what is certainly an idealized image of a knight, sculpted only a few years before Bruni's *De militia.* Obviously, it is not meant to invoke the standard image of the communal knight of the period—merchants in fancy dress, covered with pearls and gold. But neither is it meant to be an evocation of a medieval chivalric ideal. The point may not be evident, since the statue and imitations of it have, since the fifteenth century, become familiar icons of medieval knighthood, found frequently in Gothic settings. So it may be difficult to see at first sight how radically classical the image really is. Modern students of the work, however, have emphasized the antique sources for a number of motifs and decorative details in the statue, such as Roman military stelai, portrait-sculptures (especially portraits of the young Augustus), and Roman coins and gems. Some features of the military costume may be borrowed from the decoration of the Arch of Constantine. One scholar has argued that the drill holes around the head of the statue were not meant to hold a helmet, as was once thought, but rather an olive wreath—a striking suggestion in view of Bruni's view in the *De militia* that the olive wreath was one of the few appropriate ornaments a knight might wear.[42]

But in the end, the most impressive thing about Donatello's St. George is his countenance and bearing. Contemporary sources praise the face and physical attitude of the St. George for its effectiveness in communicating *prontezza* and *vivacità;* they marvel at Donatello's ability to combine beauty and martial valor. Modern critics describe "the focussing of the entire design of the statue upon a specific psychological state" as "a truly revolutionary achievement" in the art of sculpture.[43] But in looking at the statue through lenses provided by Leonardo Bruni and considering that countenance, assured and noble, determined without aggression, strong yet gentle, we might be tempted to see an image combining the austerity and martial spirit of the Roman military with the virtue and beauty of soul of Plato's guardians.

Do Humanist Teachings on Warfare Anticipate Machiavelli?

It is a principal theme of this book that Machiavelli's political thought cannot be considered part of the humanist tradition of virtue politics, and indeed that Machiavelli was the severest critic of that tradition.[44] But in comparing humanist writings on warfare with those of Machiavelli, above all his *Art of War* (1521), the historian is faced at once with a considerable challenge. Not only is there no comprehensive study of humanist literature on military matters, but the literature that does exist is distorted by a determination to find republican ideology in humanist writings on warfare. What is said to count as republican is praise of citizen militias and hostility to condottieri. The belief that such advocacy is typical of humanist military writing then allows the historian to link the humanists forward with Machiavelli's republican thought, also characterized by its commitment to citizen militias and hostility to condottieri. The most detailed evidence for this view was presented by the same C. C. Bayley whose work on Bruni's *De militia* was discussed above. Bayley devoted a chapter of his book to describing "The Survival of the Militia Tradition from Bruni to Machiavelli," which remains to this day the most sustained treatment of humanist military thought before Machiavelli.[45]

In the previous section a new interpretation of Bruni's *De militia* was advanced, rejecting the reigning view that the work in some way advocated a citizen militia and claiming instead that Bruni's intention was to create a new, neo-classical ideal for contemporary civic knighthood. The discussion in the next two sections extends this reappraisal of humanist thought on military affairs. A survey of humanist writings *de re militari* between Bruni and Machiavelli yields, indeed, a picture that is substantially different from the one painted by Bayley. The latter stressed that a hatred of condottieri and the advocacy of citizen militias was rooted in the humanists' admiration for republicanism and the military virtues of republican Rome. His analysis was infected by the same methodological vice that taints so much study of humanist political thought, namely, the belief that all roads must lead to Machiavelli. A reading of humanist writings on military matters that leaves the high road of teleology, however, and explores the towns and countryside of quattrocento humanism reveals a wider set of concerns. It discloses a more varied range of responses to the question of how the study of antiquity might (or might not) apply to the role of the military in contemporary life.

One of the first things one notices after leaving the Road to Machiavelli is that no small number of humanists expressed admiration for condottieri, beginning with Leonardo Bruni himself.[46] In 1409 he spent some months in Rimini living in the household of Carlo Malatesta, a mercenary captain who headed one of the major military clans of the quattrocento, a man later cultivated as an ally by Cosimo de'Medici. Carlo was an amateur student of literature who enjoyed disputing with Bruni about the ancient authors. In a later letter Bruni describes how, after the day's hunting was over, while the sun was going down, the two would engage in friendly shouting matches about the value of classical literature while riding back to town.[47] At the end of his sojourn in Rimini, Bruni wrote a gushing letter to his friend Niccolò Niccoli praising his new hero as a *pulcherrimum priscae antiquitatis specimen,* a lovely specimen of unspoiled antiquity.[48] Later he dedicated one of his most famous works, the educational treatise *On the Study of Literature* (1422 / 1426), to Malatesta's learned daughter Battista; this moral essay heaped fresh dollops of praise upon her father.

Bruni also wrote two speeches in praise of condottieri. The first, the *Funeral Oration for Nanni Strozzi,* was discussed in the previous section. The second, written in Tuscan dialect, was actually delivered by Bruni, in his capacity as chancellor of Florence, from the *ringhiera* or platform built outside the Palazzo Vecchio and used as a place for the city priors to address the populace. The occasion was the feast of San Giovanni Battista (June 24) in 1431, which also happened to be the beginning of campaigning season. The Florentine captain-general Niccolò da Tolentino had just been presented with the banner of the commune, a marshal's baton, a silver helmet, and a horse caparisoned with purple and gilt cloth. Bruni's speech praised Niccolò in the most extravagant terms, beginning with the declaration that Camillus and Marius had been far more useful to the Roman commonwealth than Plato and Aristotle had ever been to the Greeks: "The greatest philosopher must defer to the greatest captain, nor is Plato to be compared with Alexander, nor Aristotle with Caesar."[49] There survive a number of these ceremonial speeches by humanists in praise of mercenary captains and the military art, some of them containing important reflections on the role of warriors in civic life, such as Giannozzo Manetti's speech of 1453 presenting a marshal's baton to the new captain-general of Florence, the condottiere Sigismondo Malatesta.[50]

Humanists also wrote numerous Latin poems and biographies praising the deeds of condottieri. The most famous mercenary captain in the first quarter of the quattrocento, Braccio Fortebraccio da Montone, despite being the nemesis of the popes, had his epitaph written by Bruni, a short text that survives in dozens of manuscripts.[51] Braccio's biography was written in five books by Giovanni Antonio Campano, a humanist in the court of Pius II.[52] The son of Bruni's former colleague in the papal chancery, Jacopo di Poggio Bracciolini, wrote a popular biography of the famous Florentine soldier of fortune, Pippo Spano, whose portrait was painted by Andrea del Castagno.[53] Pier Candido Decembrio wrote the life of Braccio da Montone's most successful disciple, Niccolò Piccinino, the principal captain-general of the Visconti; his portrait medal was struck by Pisanello. A second life of Piccinino was composed by another of Poggio's sons, Giovanni Battista Poggio.[54] A kind of reportage of Piccinino's military exploits was composed by the Neapolitan poet Giannantonio de' Pandoni, known as Porcellio, in ten books of "commentaries" modelled on Caesar's *Commentaries.*[55] There were several humanist biographies of the most successful condottiere of the quattrocento, Francesco Sforza, who parlayed his military genius into political power and made himself the duke of Milan.[56] At the bidding of Lorenzo de'Medici, Francesco Filelfo wrote admiring *Commentaries on the Life and Enterprises of Federico Montefeltro of Urbino* about a condottiere prince celebrated for his fine library and literary knowledge as well as his military accomplishments.[57] The great condottiere who became captain-general of the Venetians, Bartolomeo Colleoni, had his life and virtues celebrated in six books by Antonio Cornazzano. A famous equestrian statue in bronze, designed by Andrea del Verrochio, was erected in the piazza of the Scuola Grande di San Marco in Venice to celebrate Colleoni's service to the state and to create a "virtuous environment" for citizens with military aspirations.

It would be too cynical to dismiss such celebrations of military virtue as mere power worship or as the perfunctory products of clientage. As we saw in Chapter 3, Italians such as Biondo Flavio with a sense of recent history were deeply grateful for the renaissance of Italian arms brought about in the 1390s (according to Biondo) by the condottiere Alberigo of Barbiano. Alberigo had put an end to a long period of helpless torment suffered by Italian cities at the hands of foreign freebooters and companies of adventure. Biondo went so far as to credit the greater prosperity Italy enjoyed in his lifetime to the virtue of her professional soldiers. A similar sentiment was expressed by the great humanist educator Guarino of Verona in a letter of 1446 to a young friend explaining why it was necessary to write history:

> Although there are many grievous aspects to the present age, my dear Toby, it does offer us one thing amid so many evils on which we may congratulate ourselves: it happens to have witnessed a revival of the long-buried art of warfare *(res militaris)*. At long last Italy has rid itself of foreign-born soldiers and boasts the abilities of more than enough military talent of her own. If she did not struggle against internal sickness and were to turn her sword on her enemies, she might take pride in this brilliant success and call these times blessed in which energetic captains and highly trained generals spring up on every side, as though from the fields of Thebes. When I see these men so devoted to glory and immortality as to make little of toil, sacrifice, danger, wounds and death to achieve them, I cannot but wonder at, and bitterly complain of their lack of foresight, deluded beliefs and frustrated hopes. For this recent glory, the news spread far and wide of these warlike transactions, will last but an instant and soon disappear should tongues be frozen and the living witnesses of their deeds pass from the scene.[58]

Guarino goes on to say, however, that there is a remedy against forgetfulness of present military glories. Fortunately, the military renaissance has occurred at the same time as the revival of letters and eloquence, and in the present age there are a great number of men with command of the Latin language. Through these faithful guardians of great deeds things that are old are given new youth, and things that are dying are brought back to life, as was done for the deeds of great commanders in antiquity. Young Toby should be afire to harness his literary talent and celebrate that modern rival of Alexander and Caesar, the condottiere Sigismondo Malatesta.

It is in fact relatively rare to discover among humanist writers anything resembling ideological opposition to condottieri, still less to the paid employment of non-native troops by free cities or princes. Most were proud to see their cities hire famous commanders from one of the renowned military clans of Italy. Humanists who advocated setting up native militias in preference to professional, paid troops were a small minority. Bruni, as we have seen, made no such recommendation in his *De militia,* nor did two of his closest followers, Stefano Porcari and Giannozzo Manetti.[59] Porcari, while serving as Captain of the People, one of Florence's foreign officials, in 1427–1428 made a speech in the vernacular before the Florentine priors in which he explicitly raised the issue "whether it is better to fight with the persons of one's own citizens or with one's own money to hire armies of foreigners and defend one's city with them."[60] While "many people" cite the *sentenzia* of the "glorious Romans" to argue that citizen armies fight better since they are fighting for their own families and interests, other nations believe that it is better to fight with your money. War is dangerous, outcomes uncertain, and it is not prudent to entrust a city's *libertas* to the fortune of a single battle. Even "those valorous Romans of ours" sometimes were forced to acknowledge this fact, for example after the military disaster of the Caudine Forks. The counsel of prudence prevailed with "the brave Carthaginians," who used their own people as military leaders but hired foreigners to fill their army's rank and file. "And that is why this opinion has always been to my mind more useful and more secure, and I highly commend your wisdom in this regard."[61] You [the priors of Florence] do not risk the persons of your citizens but have for a long time hired troops to defend "your triumphant republic."

Manetti too in his ceremonial speech addressed to Sigismondo Malatesta declared roundly that the citizen armies of the Romans could not be models for modern times. They were valid in antiquity but afterwards, after a long interval of many centuries, having considered minutely and better examined this practice, it appeared more useful for the safety of the republic and for the preservation of the city that they hire for a wage some outsiders and foreigners rather than conscripting soldiers from the citizenry. And this was well and wisely done so as not to subject the principal and more worthy part of the city to such great perils as the nature and condition of military service bring with them, and thus one understands from the old histories was done down to our times.[62]

Among the "many people" who did favor citizen militias was another follower of Bruni, the Florentine Matteo Palmieri, already mentioned above. Since Palmieri is the humanist whose views on militias most resemble Machiavelli's, they are worth discussing here, though they are far from typical.[63] Palmieri's *Vita civile* (1436 / 1438), however well known today, was written in Tuscan dialect and had a limited, local circulation in the quattrocento.[64] Its intended audience was future members of the Florentine governing class, and its primary inspiration came from Aristotle and Cicero's *De officiis*. In book 4 of the *Vita civile* Palmieri devotes two pages to comparing militias and mercenaries that read almost like a reply to Porcari.[65] He needs to touch on, he says, the *vulgare quistione* of whether citizen armies or mercenary troops are superior. There are views on both sides, he says, but the bottom line is that "in all past centuries one finds no city of the highest rank except those with *virtù* and arms in the hands of its own citizens." Citizen soldiers care for the honor, glory, and reputation of their republic and wish to see it safe and prosperous. Hired soldiers dishonor themselves by seeking only to be paid. They don't care about the people they are supposed to protect, and they flee from peril and change sides when they are offered better terms. Since their livelihood and reputation depend on war, they desire and seek out war. The ancients rarely hired troops, and only in times of grave danger. Their greatest conquests were made with their own citizen soldiers. The Florentines too, in their greatest period of expansion in the thirteenth century, relied on citizen soldiers. Some people object, says Palmieri, that it is unsafe to have powerful citizens drilling troops in your city, but this is an objection of weak-minded people who fail to consider that all great deeds involve risk. We can pray to God that He will respond to our desire for the felicity of our city by placing power in the hands of good men. Furthermore, to involve the people in military duties in wartime will pay two dividends in time of peace. First, by being involved in their own defense the people will become more united in common love, and second, the "less select" part of the people who are given over to mechanical labor (who thus rarely or never hold office) will have this way to exert themselves for the common good of the republic.

Readers now ready to enroll Palmieri among the Forerunners of Machiavelli might wish to pause, however, and consider his far longer discussion of military affairs in book 3 of the same work.[66] Here the resemblance to Machiavelli's political views is less straightforward. Book 3 as a whole discusses how to instantiate the virtue of justice in a city, and the passage in question shows how respect for justice bears on military affairs. Following Cicero and Livy, Palmieri idealizes the ancient Romans as his models of justice (and other virtues) in war. The Romans never engaged in war except for the sake of peace; they regarded war as justified only in response to injury or to defend themselves from attack. They observed strict moral principles in declarations of war, which was an act sanctioned by a college of priests, the *fetiales,* who also oversaw treaties and ceremonies restoring peace. The enemy was always given a chance to make peaceful restitution for injuries; surprise attacks were regarded as base. Soldiers were required to take an oath of loyalty to the republic, and faith was observed even with enemies. In the conduct of war the Roman soldiers were not allowed to indulge themselves with pleasures and looting, and any infractions of discipline were strictly punished: "In Marius' army one could not find even a cook or a woman; there were no dishonorable practices; it observed all due order and justice in its way of life." There are different modes of making war, depending on whether one is fighting for mere survival or for honor. Foreign wars are more honorable than civil wars. The Romans fought for honor and considered base the pursuit of riches in war. They regarded battles won through fraud to be dishonorable, and their goal at all times was to win glory through a reputation for noble conduct. The Romans understood that war involved risk and should be avoided unless honor or self-defense demanded it. But when sacrifice was demanded they were ready to make it out of a sense of *pietà,* religious obligation, toward their country. They fought only with enemies and avoided faction; the only competition among them was competition in virtue and in service to the state. When enemies fought well and honorably against them, the Romans not only treated them honorably but offered them citizenship. The gates of Rome were always open to the virtuous.

Palmieri's insistence that the conduct of war be regulated by the strictest application of traditional morality as modelled by the Romans is a far cry from Machiavelli's instrumental view of virtue in war, as we shall see in more detail in

Chapter 18. The humanist belief in the primacy of virtue also separates Machia-velli's views from those of Francesco Patrizi of Siena, the great humanist authority on politics and another humanist enemy of condottieri. In the ninth book of his treatise *De institutione reipublicae* (How to found a republic), which is entirely de-voted to military affairs, he begins by discussing the morality of different kinds of war. There is no difficulty justifying defensive war; if you are attacked, natural law gives you the right to defend yourself. Offensive war is much harder to justify. In the first place it is much riskier, since it requires the support of the common people, who are fickle and will turn on you (Patrizi is addressing republican magistrates) the moment the fortunes of war go against you. When a war goes wrong the senate will be divided and will not support you either, "since, as Plato writes in the *Laws*, truth is a splendid thing, but persuading people of it is not easy." You will make yourself unpopular with the wealthy too, because you will have to raise taxes, an inevitable source of ill will. Taxes are necessary because offensive war, a war for empire, requires you to hire mercenaries and gamble your liberty on "a mixed jumble of men of various national origins who are constrained by no *pietas* towards the country, no fear of God, no religious awe, but are attracted only by wages." Offensive war will also cause political instability because citizens with large armies under their control can become dangerous. Moreover, offensive war requires you to make a careful estimate of your own strength and that of your enemy, but even the best reckoning can go wrong, and Fortune can defeat good counsel as well as military expertise and virtue. Offensive war is bad for the moral health of city, as those who promote it must stir up passions of hatred and revenge, as happened among the warlords of the late Roman republic.[67]

Patrizi acknowledges the views of those who say that offensive war is the only way to enlarge one's territory and empire and achieve glory. Those who argue this way are following the view of Euripides (quoted via Cicero's *De officiis*): "If justice must be violated for sake of rule / Let it be so; you may preserve piety in other matters."[68] In other words, they (like Machiavelli) would abandon the splendid reputation of a good man in order to rule, a violation of right that Patrizi regards as base and unthinkable. Such men seem to be praising the Spartans, whose laws (he says) were designed for empire. The proponents of offensive war give exam-ples of cities that have escaped from imperialistic projects unscathed and have added to their empires and glory. A nation that seeks glory, they say, should be eager to engage in fighting; otherwise warlike virtue becomes rusty and the name of your city will die in base obscurity.

Patrizi's response to the champions of empire is to point out that many wealthy cities have been destroyed by war, and many preserved by peace. Furthermore, "the arts of peace are more worthy of admiration than those of war: it is in peacetime that humanistic studies *(bonarum artium disciplinae)* and true virtues find their theater of praise, while in war madness rules, and triumph proceeds from blood and slaughter." Patrizi admits that glory is not to be despised, that Rome, mistress of the world, earned greater praise than Athens, the mother of all disciplines. "Yet neither lacked the other's glory entirely. Rome was distinguished for all liberal studies too, and Athens did not lack glory in war; both cities venerated Minerva both armed and unarmed. We however follow more the arts of peace, and we want our citizens to be trained most of all in those arts, since they lead more securely to tranquillity of soul, and we [in this work] are describing the republic that follows the path of felicity." The desire for conquest is morally indefensible. It issues from a character disordered by a blind lust for praise and power. Quoting a famous speech of the Scythian legates to Alexander the Great, Patrizi declares that the thirst for conquest is unquenchable and leads in the end to utter insanity. It must be kept under control; it must recognize the inherent limits of the human condition: "O wretched condition of mankind, O deceitful hope of mortals, with what vehement desires are we seized, despite knowing that all our futile projects are transitory and that virtue should be our only desire!"[69]

A republic that aims at happiness and virtue must be content with its own borders and will refuse to make war without necessity. Its military establishment should reflect these principles. Patrizi calls for a small standing army—not a militia in the Renaissance sense—recruited from the citizenry and led by a magistrate. This magistrate (the second consul in charge of military affairs according to Patrizi's constitution) will recruit the bravest youths, who will dedicate themselves full-time to military service.[70] He will train them in arms, in peacetime as well as in time of war. The magistrate in charge of war should be competent in the *ars militaris* (9.2). His leadership is key to success in military affairs, and leadership rests on virtue, as Xenophon showed in the *Cyropaedia*. A commander cannot discipline others if he cannot discipline himself;[71] his first duty is to show himself to be a good man. He need not expose himself in the front lines, since, as the example of Cyrus the Great showed, the better part of prudence is to serve one's troops with *ingenium* rather than with physical force. The citizen army the military consul commands can be highly effective despite its small size, and its strength will be sufficient to repel brigands and discourage most potential attackers. A standing army will provide the city with a sense of security, without which no civil felicity is possible. A republic with its own armed force, if attacked by a large army, will also have the time to consider its options calmly and not be reduced to panic, make rash mistakes, or be forced into alliances that may threaten its liberty.

Virtue in Military Life

Here was a justification for a citizen army based on moral principles utterly different from those of Machiavelli. Patrizi's critique of imperialism alerts us to the existence of a much wider range of humanist reflection on warfare beyond the narrow issue of the advisability or otherwise of militias. Like Bruni, most humanist writers on war tended to see the problem of military service through a wider historical and philosophical lens. Their reforming zeal was directed not only at the cruelty and rapacity often displayed by Renaissance soldiery, men who killed for money, but also at the false values and misplaced loyalties of knights inspired by the chivalric ideal. For humanists in general, the only justified use of military power was in the service of a republic or prince. The profession of arms was natural, but its exercise was right only when it advanced the cause of peace, security, and the flourishing of the city. Absent this source of right, the desire for profit and fame was morally corrupt. Soldiers did not need to be natives of the state they served, but their actions were illegitimate and immoral if not obedient to the duly appointed magistrates or prince.[72] A speech in praise of Federico d'Urbino, probably written by the humanist poet Tommaso Baldinotti, declares, "The military art has no other end than to live in peace and quiet, and there is no other purpose in war than to live without injuries in peace. To this end he only may bear arms who is deputized to do so in some place and by some people (*natione*), assuming its deliberations have not been corrupted."[73]

The civic function of warfare is stated plainly in the most important humanist treatise on warfare, the *De re militari* of Roberto Valturio, dedicated to the condottiere prince Sigismondo Malatesta. Valturio defines *res militaris* as "a certain highly honorable part and function of civil life that preserves the other parts of the civil power by protecting them. It is natural, completely necessary, and made legitimate by historical example, by free choice, and by swearing an oath."[74] Valturio was doing no more than repeating what had become since Bruni's time a humanist commonplace. Manetti, in his speech on military affairs mentioned above, also stresses that military affairs should be subordinate to the realm of politics and that the proper role of captains is purely to execute the will of the magistrates, the *governo della repubblica*.[75]

Another issue of concern to humanists was the status of soldiers within the state. Any city-state, according to Bruni's *De militia* (following book 2 of Aristotle's *Politics*), has three natural classes: farmers, artisans, and soldiers. Soldiers were thus a class apart from other citizens. They should be free men and they should be distinguished by their sacred military oath and by simple but distinctive dress. Soldiers should take the military oath of their own free will.[76] It was their sacred oath that made them soldiers, not signing a contract with an employer. In ancient Rome, according to Manetti, the knightly class devoted itself exclusively to the practice of arms. Only in the corrupt late republican period, as Sallust noted, did *equites* begin "to thirst after sordid profit."

But where did the magistrates belong in this tripartite class scheme? Bruni's followers generally saw them as part of the military or knightly class, since like soldiers their function was to be concerned with the common good of the whole state, not just with their private interests. They served the state with their minds, the rank and file with their body, in an organic whole.[77] Since they formed a caste apart from the farmers and craftsmen, they should be accorded more honor. Having a special class of magistrates and knights in the city was perfectly compatible with hiring professional, non-native troops to carry out military policies.[78] The functional role of the warrior within society is satisfied if there is a class of citizens who occupy themselves chiefly with the direction of military affairs. It deserves high honor, whether its policies are executed by other citizens or by hired soldiers. The military defends peoples from injuries, it defends the faith, and it adorns justice and every virtue, writes Baldinotti. Without its special virtues, all cities would be reduced to violence and confusion.[79]

The humanists thus accorded the military or knightly calling high status within the city based on its public function and, remarkably, often ranked soldiers higher than members of the learned professions or philosophers. In Biondo Flavio's *Borsus* (1459 / 1460)—a treatise whose name comes from its dedicatee, Borso d'Este, duke of Ferrara—the learned papal secretary used the genre of the courtly *paragone* to argue that the true marker of social class should be virtue.[80] His account of the social rank of knights differs from the functional account of Bruni, which was based on Aristotle. The greatest expert of the age on Roman history, Biondo gave an account of the social position of *equites*, the Roman knightly class, that placed them correctly in a separate class below that of senators and magistrates, with distinct duties and privileges. This raised the question of their status compared to other professional groups in Roman history, particularly the jurisconsults. The issue had great resonance in Renaissance society, where judges and university professors of law were ordinarily considered to hold knightly rank. Biondo aims to settle the question by establishing the relative status of soldiers and jurists in the great age of Rome, then applying his results to contemporary society. Though both groups were respected in ancient Rome, Biondo says that *milites* had a higher status because the work they performed for the state was more fundamental: they guaranteed its survival. This means that in modern society, which (it goes without saying) should base itself on Roman principles, soldiers should also outrank *doctores legum*. Their status should be inferior only to high magistrates and prelates (and one must remember that Biondo was himself a papal official).[81]

However, in modern times, there were many who disgraced their calling: military captains by cowardice and jurisconsults by ignorance of literature. Among modern doctors of laws the great mass were an utter disgrace: "A few of the more worthy among them, friends of ours, are sorry and ashamed of their own doctorates on account of their fellow lawyers."[82] Biondo's conclusion, a typical expression of virtue politics, was that status in modern times could not rest on formal titles or membership in a social class, but only on virtue. Only knights who distinguished themselves for valor and other moral excellences should be held in the highest honor. The truth is that, ranked in terms of virtue, there are in both professions the best, the mediocre, and the worst, and their status in society should reflect those distinctions of merit. It is the prince that should make the judgment of rank, attending chiefly or only to the criterion of service to the republic: "Princes and whatever others have been given the regular or temporary role [of judging social rank] should assume this burden in such a way that the control of a superior reins in unsuitable and rash individuals, and that authority suppresses audacity."[83]

What then was military virtue, and how could a captain become virtuous? Manetti, following a passage of Cicero's speech in praise of Pompey, the *Pro lege Manilia*—much quoted in humanist military literature—lists four qualities necessary for the perfect captain: knowledge of warfare; virtue (courage, foresight, vigor); personal authority or *riputatione;* and "prosperity, that is, good luck." Knowledge, moral excellence, and personal authority are closely connected: together they impart the charismatic qualities a commander needs to win love, respect, and obedience from his troops. His virtue is amplified by his speaking ability. The leader of great virtue makes men want to obey him and fear being disobedient to *sì excelsa dignità imperatoria* (a commander of such supreme worth). His qualities put limits to the power of fortune.[84]

In discussing military virtue, humanists tended, as one might expect, to focus on the virtues of commanders and officers rather than troops, assuming that fine leadership was the key to good armies. As Biondo Flavio remarked, "The first and greatest foundation of military science and warfare is the choice of a good general."[85] That remark occurs in his extraordinary panorama of Roman civilization, *Rome in Triumph,* which devotes two of its nine books (6 and 7) to Roman military practices.[86] At the end of book 7, after quoting the same line of Cicero quoted above by Manetti, he inserts a long digest of a treatise *De optimo imperatore* (On the Best Military Commander) by the first-century military writer Onasander, which had recently been translated into Latin by Biondo's friend, the Greek émigré humanist and diplomat Niccolò Sagundino.[87] Onasander's work could only have been music to a humanist's ears. A philosopher in the Platonic tradition, Onasander insisted that the choice of a general should be based squarely on meritocratic principles. The best commander will be virtuous, eloquent, of good reputation, and married. He should not be chosen because he is wealthy, though he may be, but no merchant or banker should be chosen because such professions cannot form a noble character. Nor should a general be chosen for his ancestry, but only for his military accomplishments. Once in charge, he should always fight on the side of justice so that he will have the help of the gods, and he should prefer defensive to offensive war as more likely to stimulate the courage of his troops. If he does need to attack an enemy, he must announce clearly the reason for the attack and make reasonable demands, so that if the enemy refuses terms, it will appear that it is of necessity and not by preference that he takes to the field. "He should call heaven to witness that he is entering the war without offence, since he has not failed to consider the dangers that fall to the lot of combatants, and is not deliberately seeking, in every possible manner, to ruin the enemy."

Roberto Valturio on the Education of Soldiers

One way of summarizing what has been argued in this chapter so far might be the following: When most quattrocento humanists thought about using ancient teachings to improve contemporary military practice, their first idea was not to reintroduce the military organization of the ancient Roman republic with its citizen armies. Their principal concern was how to improve the moral qualities of military men, above all their commanders. The solution to corrupt condottieri who cared only about money and fame was not a citizen militia but rather virtuous condottieri who cared about true glory and the good of the republic they served.[88] The same moralizing strategy applied, as we saw in Bruni's case, to civic knighthood. The natural temptation of soldiers to be cruel and violent should be repressed, and ancient standards of virtuous military service should be held up for admiration and imitation. To the humanist mind, this inevitably meant classical education for the noble youths who would lead tomorrow's armies. Unlike Cicero and Onasander, many humanists expressed the conviction that commanders could acquire military excellence not only by precept and example in camp and on the battlefield, but through a specially tailored humanistic education.

That was the principal lesson of the most comprehensive humanist treatise on warfare, the twelve books of Roberto Valturio's *De re militari* (On military affairs), written around 1460 and first printed in 1472. It was also the most influential, circulating widely both in manuscript and in print.[89] Valturio, a former papal secretary turned military engineer, was for most of his career a humanist in the service of Sigismondo Malatesta, a condottiere prince whose principal residence was in the seaside town of Rimini.[90] Valturio's great work, synthesizing over a hundred ancient Greek and Latin authors, sought to recover the lessons of antiquity for those in the modern world who wanted to follow the profession of arms.[91] During those long winters between campaigns, future captains and officers should spend their time studying the classical authors and absorbing their practical and moral lessons. Valturio's treatise would be their guide. The practical lessons of ancient military history and lore could be found in the last seven books, covering every imaginable topic having to do with warfare, from the order of march, the order of battle, castellation and siege engines, to formulae for military oaths, punishments for desertion, types of arms, castrametation, spying and reconnoitering, army lingo, naval warfare, decorations and medals, flags and banners, triumphs, and military funerals. The first five books, however, which laid the moral foundation for military life, set out a program of humanistic studies for the future leaders of Italy's armies.

After an opening chapter on the origins of warfare, Valturio presents his argument for why military captains need a classical education (1.2–3). Fine leadership is based in the *ingenium,* which needs to be trained as much as does the body. Any commander knows that young, untrained troops, not knowing how to handle themselves, will scatter in flight at the first onset. Even if they are physically stronger than veterans, the latter will always acquit themselves better since they are used to blood and wounds and are long practiced in arms. The same applies to officers. Without education the chaos of battle will bewilder them. They too need to be trained in the necessary arts before going into battle and commanding others. The man who wants to be a general *(imperator)* and prove himself, like Achilles, better than all the rest, will not be able to justify his preeminence without mastery of all the relevant disciplines. He must know what to do, he must be aware of the finest examples of military action, before going into battle. This is the core aim of the *ars militaris.* But there is no discipline that does not require the knowledge of allied disciplines, and these the officer must also master, just as his troops need to master the use of a wide variety of weapons. So it should not seem strange to say that a military leader must devote himself to many of the liberal arts:

> Therefore let a commander, first of all, be able to read Latin,[92] and let him strive after the most salutary precepts of philosophy, let him commit manifold histories to memory, let him not be ignorant of the arts of oratory and poetry; let him have a knowledge of music, arithmetic, geometry and astronomy that is appropriate to his calling; let him have a firm grasp of the laws of diverse peoples and not spurn an understanding of healing; and let him devote himself entirely to gymnastics and military training both in times of peace and of war, and finally to all those other arts necessary to win laurels and triumphs.[93]

This summarizes the curriculum Valturio offers in the body of his work, but his argument for literary study does not end there. Military men should study literature not only because such studies civilize mankind, but because they help captains achieve glory and preserve forever the memory of their deeds. That prospect of immortality will inspire them on the battlefield. They need to affiliate themselves with the great traditions of ancient warfare in order to secure their legacy in literature. So they should not read "crude and barbarous writings in the vernacular" (Valturio probably means chivalric romances) but famous and finely wrought works filled with useful knowledge. This is why King Philip of Macedon brought in Aristotle to teach his son Alexander philosophy and Callisthenes to teach him eloquence. In a fine example of the *post hoc, propter hoc* fallacy, Valturio implies that Alexander's later conquests were a result of this training. Many other examples of ancient military leaders, Greek and Roman, who cultivated letters then follow, ending with Sigismondo Malatesta himself, who is praised not only for his own devotion to letters but also for his patronage of poets, scholars, and orators.

His fine library and beautiful church (designed by Leon Battista Alberti) and the citadel he has built (designed by Valturio himself) come in for particular praise.

Later books continue to explain the value of the humanities to military commanders. In book 2 we learn that history and philosophy both yield the greatest fruit for the military mind, and Valturio points out that some of the most famous generals of antiquity, such as Xenophon, the Emperor Claudius, and Julius Caesar himself, wrote histories. History is the light of prudence and a stimulus to great deeds. Philosophy sets out for its readers a *ratio vivendi,* a rational plan of life, teaching us about duty and honor as well as the seemly and the good. Philosophers teach us how to undergo suffering amid the crises of life, the importance of keeping faith with enemies as well as friends, and the duty to abide by our undertakings, such as those made in treaties. Philosophy also shows us the need for wise counsel, and Valturio asserts that all the greatest republics and kingdoms of the past pullulated with philosophers able to give good counsel.

History and philosophy are the future captain's master arts, but in book 2 we learn that he also needs to learn eloquence and poetry. All the old histories show commanders addressing their troops in the field, and the inspiration thus given them is said by Valturio to be a key to victory. The poets should also be studied for their glorification of great deeds, although Valturio has reservations about the morality of some poets, especially the satirists, and feels the need to respond to Plato's criticism of poets in the *Republic.* Liberal arts such as music also have military applications, as do arithmetic and geometry. All of book 3 is devoted to astronomy and astrology, said to be of great value to a general for predicting the future and choosing the best times for battle, a view underwritten by the authority of the poet Lucan. Book 4 presents an executive summary of the sort of things a commander needs to know about laws and constitutions, medicine and the arts of healing, and physical training. Book 5 treats the virtues a captain needs to acquire and presents him with a miscellany of *exempla* and wise maxims to help fix those virtues in his memory. The remaining seven books then present the other, more practical parts of a military captain's training as described above.

Valturio's treatise presents the humanities and allied branches of learning as a broad foundation of general knowledge upon which may be built specialized training appropriate to a particular *métier,* in this case, that of a professional soldier. He is thus the father of all those in later times who have called for a liberally educated officer corps. In the sixteenth century this hierarchy would become general in European education. All those aspiring to the class of gentlemen would of course need to be educated in the classics, but it came to be expected that lawyers, doctors, and churchmen would also need solid preparation in classical literature. Without it they could not discharge the duties of their several professions with humanity and due respect for religion and the norms of civil society. The old rivalry between the humanities and the professions stirred up in the letters and invectives of Petrarch and other early humanists would eventually be resolved into a more fruitful system of preparing the young for their roles in society.

CHAPTER 10

A MIRROR FOR STATESMEN

Leonardo Bruni's *History of the Florentine People*

History as Political Theory

It will perhaps seem odd to claim that Leonardo Bruni's *History of the Florentine People* has been neglected by students of Renaissance political thought. Written over the space of a quarter century, between 1415 / 1416 and 1442, it was the humanist's most important original work. When the famous Florentine chancellor died in 1444 he was laid out at his public funeral on a bier clasping a copy of the *History* against his breast, a pose later preserved by Bernardo Rossellini in a portrait sculpture for the Bruni tomb in Santa Croce.[1] The work was an official history, preserved in the chapel of the Palazzo Vecchio along with the *Pandects* of Justinian (captured at the conquest of Pisa in 1406), the banners of defeated foes, and other civic trophies.[2] It survives in some sixty manuscripts and was translated into Italian by command of Bruni's employer, the Florentine Signoria. The translation, by Donato Acciaiuoli, was also widely circulated in manuscript and was printed a number of times in the fifteenth and sixteenth centuries.[3] Then and now it was considered one of the greatest works of humanist historiography and was the model for an entire genre of city-state histories in the fifteenth and sixteenth centuries.[4]

Yet despite its importance as a monument of Renaissance civic humanism, the work *has* been neglected by historians of political thought. The most authoritative surveys in the field tend to rely on a handful of shorter texts such as the *Panegyric of the City of Florence*, the *Oration for the Funeral of Nanni Strozzi*, and the treatise *On Knighthood* when characterizing Bruni's political thought.[5] The *History of Florence*, on the other hand—when not dismissed as a Livian pastiche confected from vernacular chronicles—has been studied for its historical methodology; for its place in the history of humanistic historiography; as a work advocating republican liberty; as a work of imperialistic propaganda; as a rhetorical artifact; as a moment in the history of historical consciousness; and as a secularized account of historical development.[6]

While all these perspectives are illuminating in various ways, they miss one distinctive—indeed key—trait of Bruni's pioneering history: its didacticism. Bruni's history was intended as a work of moral education. It was meant to teach Florentine and Tuscan political elites how to behave with virtue, how to preserve and extend the power of their *respublica*. It showed them which policies and laws worked in the past and which did not work, and why. Its didacticism is sustained and explicit throughout. It is far more explicitly pedagogical than either its main source, Giovanni and Matteo Villani's chronicle, or its chief model, Livy. Bruni instructs his audience both in summaries and asides addressed directly to the reader or in the form of speeches delivered by admirable Florentines.[7] His didacticism is implicit as well, for Bruni surely knew Aristotle's view, expressed in *Rhetoric* 1.9, that praise could be deployed as a form of moral counsel. The *History of the Florentine People* is on the surface a celebration of the city's accomplishments, but Bruni is always counseling while he is praising: urging modern Florentines to live up to the accomplishments of their ancestors and not to repeat their mistakes.[8]

Attending to what Bruni takes to be the great lessons of Florentine history will greatly sharpen and in part correct our picture of him as a political thinker. In particular, it should change our view of his relationship to the Aristotelian tradition and to Machiavelli. Bruni is usually described as an Aristotelian in his political theory, and this seems plausible on its face given the many years of labor he devoted to translating Aristotle's *Ethics* and *Politics* as well as the pseudo-Aristotelian *Economics,* not to mention his own explicit statements that he was a follower of Aristotle.[9] But a closer study of the *History* shows that in certain crucial respects Bruni rejected Aristotle's political ideals in favor of goals that are at once more Roman and more realist.

Virtue in the Service of the Republic's Glory

Both Aristotle (*Politics* 7.2) and Plato (*Laws* 1.628b) criticize constitutions designed with a view to imperial expansion. Both see such constitutions as disordered, as enshrining a mistaken preference for the active over the contemplative life, for the life of the emotions and honor over the life of reason and self-mastery.[10] But Bruni's *History* passionately endorses the goal of glory and the acquisition of territory.

For example, in a speech put into the mouth of Pino della Tosa, who is advocating before the Florentine Signoria the purchase of Lucca in 1329, Bruni writes:

> And just think, too, how much your power will increase when you get control of this most beautiful and well-fortified city-state, with such a large territory and so many towns and citadels! Think how much the glory, fame and majesty of the Florentine People will grow if a city which has long been nearly our equal in wealth and power should be made subject to you! For my part, I confess, as one who practices the common life and moral customs of mankind, I am moved by the things that men hold to be goods: extending borders, enlarging empire, raising on high the glory and splendor of the state (*civitas*), assuring our own security and advantage. If we say that these are not desirable things, then the welfare of the republic, patriotism and practically this whole life of ours will be overthrown. If those who would dissuade you from taking Lucca despise such things and think them of no account, they are in their turn introducing new moral standards into life; if they approve of them and consider them goods, then they must necessarily believe that Lucca should be taken, for so many goods and advantages follow together therefrom. (6.5)[11]

There can be little doubt that this speech reflects Bruni's own views. He explicitly states, when Florence fails to take Pino's advice, that it was "an extremely bad decision on the city's part." Moreover, the speech occurs at the beginning of book 6, which is mostly devoted to Florence's failed attempt to take control of Lucca. The rest of the book in effect shows the high cost of this bad decision: enormous expense, loss of life, shame, military failure, and in the end, the tyranny of Walter of Brienne all result directly from this colossal error in political judgment.

Bruni's *History* reveals a civic humanism that is far less concerned with promoting classical virtues in the service of the good life, as presented by Graeco-Roman philosophers, and far more concerned with finding pragmatic solutions to pressing political and ethical problems threatening the welfare of the state. Bruni's central concern is with enabling a virtuous civil life so as to increase Florentine political and military strength. To some extent this means finding ways to inculcate classical virtues such as prudence, moderation, courage, love of country, and thrift. But Bruni's search for lessons in history takes him in new directions not explored by classical historians.[12] Thucydides, Livy, Sallust, and Tacitus all obviously expect their readers to acquire prudence from study of the past, but they do not develop a theory of political success or failure; success or failure is typically seen in moral terms without remainder. Polybius of course does have a theory of Roman success, but when elaborating it he has, in effect, to stop his narrative (at the end of book 5) in order to launch into a synchronic, abstract analysis of the Roman constitution, religion, and military customs in book 6.[13] Bruni's approach, by contrast, is both analytical and intrinsically historical; his explanations of Florentine success and failure both motivate and derive from the narrative. Prudence and imprudence are shown in action. A favorite maxim is that "time and experience, the mistress of affairs" reveal the truth. So, for example, the longevity of the institution of the Priorate shows that it was good and well designed (3.58–59).[14] Outcomes are one measure of prudence. To be sure, Bruni does not dissent from the basic assumption of ancient ethics, that practice of the virtues is the key to happiness, both private and public. But his understanding of political happiness as consisting in the wealth, strength, and imperial success of one's native city imports a Roman note that is alien to ancient Greek political theory.[15] It results in a strikingly different, proto-Machiavellian analysis of political virtue. For Bruni, virtue is already trending toward *virtù*.

The Primacy of the Popolo *and the Suppression of Factions*

Bruni's *History* gives his fellow citizens counsel in four broad areas: diplomacy, the conduct of war, the design of laws and institutions, and the nature of *vivere civile*, that is, the best forms of behavior for citizens to practice. Although these are all interrelated, I will focus on his lessons about citizen behavior and how such behavior is supported, or not supported, by laws and institutions.

Like Machiavelli—and most modern historians of Florence—Bruni identifies factionalism as the main obstacle to Florence's success. Factionalism had various causes.[16] There were foreign ones, such as the struggle between pope and empire, Guelf and Ghibelline; and domestic ones, such as rivalry between noble clans or class struggles between the nobility and the people. The term "People," or *popolo*, has a precise meaning for Bruni, as it did for his contemporaries, and signifies the broad middle ranks of society, excluding magnates or nobles on the one hand and the laboring classes, salaried workers, and household servants on the other.[17] In the thirteenth century the middle stratum of society had organized itself politically and formed a corporation for the purposes of self-protection, with its own statutes, offices, military organization, coats of arms, seals, and banners. From its earliest appearance in Florence the Popolo was aligned with the pro-papal Guelf Party against the Ghibellines. This well-defined corporate and ideological identity made Florence's middle classes quite unlike those of the ancient Greek city-states described by Aristotle. Again unlike Aristotle's middle class, members of the Popolo are not necessarily middling in economic means; as we shall see, the Popolo is distinguished from the magnate class primarily by its political culture. As the full title of the work suggests, *The History of the Florentine People,* the real hero of Bruni's history is the People of Florence—the People in this special, restricted sense.

Since the People in Florentine history act consistently to suppress the hereditary nobility, persecute Ghibellines, and exclude the poor from political power, it is also in Aristotelian terms the name of a faction, a *pars,* by definition opposed to the good of the whole. Given Bruni's Aristotelian commitments, therefore, one might expect from him a cool and critical analysis of the Popolo's factional behavior. But far from being a philosophical historian, above the fray, Bruni tells the story of the People as their partisan. Throughout the twelve books of the *History* he is an open partisan of the People against a lawless and unpatriotic nobility, against a passionate and dangerous mob, and against all Ghibellines. Bruni's partisanship is in aid of his larger goal, which is to encourage Florentines to put loyalty to their city above loyalty to faction, clan, class, or Church. His belief is that the Popolo can and should provide a focus for civic loyalty. By being victorious over all other sources of partisanship, it can transcend party.[18]

Bruni's patriotic partisanship is evident in his treatment of factional struggles in Florence. He describes a number of attempts to bring social peace to Florence and assesses their effectiveness. In 1266, during the Guelf restoration following the battle of Benevento, the Florentines attempted to pacify the parties by forcing intermarriage between Guelf and Ghibelline clans. They believed the old legend that the Guelf-Ghibelline split had its origins in a marriage dispute between the Buondelmonte and Amidei families, and reasoned that if a broken marriage had caused the problem, successful marriages would solve it—"a remedy of opposites," as Bruni called it. In fact, "the disease was too serious to be cured by such medicine," Bruni writes (2.110). The policy at the start offered hope but "was soon revealed as a wasted effort." It failed for two reasons. First, the inequality of power between Guelfs and Ghibellines meant that the strong and victorious party could not respect the defeated and weak one, so the weaker party was placed systematically in an inferior position in marriage negotiations. Each party regarded the other as traitors and enemies of the fatherland. Second, Ghibelline forces outside the city continued to threaten it, which generated suspicions within and made mutual trust between factions impossible.

Bruni also examines five attempts by the Church to make peace within the city, all of which failed. The peace of Gregory X (1273) failed because the pope, despite his holiness and good intentions, did not make a realistic assessment of the situation. He did not realize that memory could not be wiped out; he did not appreciate that partisans who had shown themselves wicked and deceitful in the past could not be trusted in the present; and he was mistaken in believing that intelligent citizens would not value their security above pious hopes for peace (3.24). Cardinal Latino's peace of 1279–1280, by contrast, showed more intelligence and understanding of the local situation. Latino was effective in persuading people that they would be more secure with both factions inside the city, and he designed institutions and legal procedures to protect both parties. He arranged formal reconciliations and marriages between factions, and even destroyed records of earlier partisan activities to wipe out the memory of mutual hatreds. His peace lasted a couple of years but was ultimately undone by the Sicilian Vespers of 1282, a successful rebellion against the ruling Guelf house of Anjou. A fragile balance of parties inside the city could not survive a major shift in the balance of power outside it (3.52, 3.58). Similar pressures and suspicions destroyed three later papal attempts at pacification of the quarrels between the White and Black factions in 1300, 1303, and 1306; the last two attempts, indeed, came apart owing to suspicions of the pope's own partisan agenda. In 1306 the papal peacemaker was not even admitted to the city on the grounds that the previous peacemakers had only made things worse (4.100). Bruni's conclusion is that whenever one party is stronger than another in the city—which will be practically all the time—any solution aiming at the peaceful coexistence of factions is doomed to failure. The implication is that exiles are better left outside the city. Piety and good intentions cannot abolish history or negate the influence of geopolitics.

Idealistic attempts at abstract social justice also fail to solve problems arising from antagonism between social classes. Bruni teaches this lesson with particular clarity at the beginning of book 7 while describing what happened after the expulsion of Walter of Brienne, the French tyrant who briefly dominated Florence in 1342–1343. In gratitude for the meritorious actions of the nobility in freeing Florence from the tyrant, the civic leaders, led by their bishop, Angelo Acciaiuoli, understandably but unwisely reversed the half-century-long policy of excluding the nobility from public life and allowed them to hold magistracies.

What was new, and of the greatest import to the republic, was their decision, against the example of earlier times, to accept the nobility into this and other magistracies of the republic. There were two principal reasons for this decision. One was concern for civic harmony. It was believed that the state would be tranquil and the spirits of its citizens quiet and peaceable if no part of the city were excluded from honors and thus driven to hate the present regime because of injustices to itself. The other reason was manifest merit, since the nobility had actively devoted its energies to expelling the tyrant. Their actions won still more approval in that the tyrant had granted many favors to their class, but they had preferred liberty and love of country to his acts of beneficence, which was a great proof of the sincerity of their public spirit. So for these reasons the nobility were allowed to share in the governance of the state. (7.3)

This innovation turned the ancient constitution *(antiqua gubernandi forma)* upside down and subverted the purposes of the old anti-magnate ordinances.

The latter [ordinances] had been wisely framed in the beginning and afterwards preserved in the state with salutary effect. But at this time, the body politic had been entirely equalized and through concord made as one; so with the sources of contention having lapsed, the safeguards against contention lapsed as well. (7.4)

The new situation in the abstract seemed just, but it was ineffective. "Although [the reforming magistrates] seemed to have good reasons for designing the constitution as they did," Bruni remarks, "it did not last very long" (7.6). The nobility soon began to be suspected of abuse of power, leading to unrest among the people. Envy and contention, "the usual civic diseases," returned to the city, and the *populares* began to think they had exchanged one tyrant for many. Eventually verbal contention turned to violence and civil war. Tranquillity was restored only when the People reasserted its military dominance over the nobility and restored the popular regime, excluding the nobles (7.10–14). Once again, abstract principles of justice had been undone by political reality. The nobility, being naturally prone to arrogance and power-seeking, were bound to abuse public power to achieve their ends; and the People, being more powerful militarily, was bound to reassert itself. History and the realities of power trumped ideals of political equality among classes.

Bruni's preferred solutions to the problems of partisanship and class struggle are institutional and moral. He praises the magistracy of the Priorate (3.59), in terms reminiscent of Aristotle, for empowering the middle classes against the nobility. Invoking his principle of the mean, Aristotle had written in *Politics* 4.11 that the middle class is the best class to rule because they are most likely to listen to reason and are therefore more likely to possess civil virtue. The upper classes are given to violence and great crimes, the lower classes to petty criminality, but the middle classes don't covet the goods of others. They know how to obey as well as command, unlike the other classes, and they are not consumed with ambition. They achieve what they want in a spirit of friendship, and a stable community depends on friendship; any good state aims at being as far as possible a society of equals and peers. Only in states with a large middle class, where there is rough equality of property, does the possibility of good government exist.

Bruni's analysis at first sight appears to echo this general sentiment. Writing of the foundation of the Priorate in 1282, he remarks,

> This form of administration was popular to the highest degree, as can be seen from its very name. Because there were certain powerful individuals who seemed inordinately given to civil discord, the government of the city was handed over to a quiet and peace-loving sort of person who was more inclined to carry on business in peacetime than to engage in war and strife. That is why they were called Priors of the Guilds. They enjoyed popular approval and preference because they were neither predatory nor seditious, but frugal and peace-loving persons, exercising each his own métier—for the lazy have to feed off the goods of others. (3.59)

But Bruni's emphasis here is not on the middling *economic* status of the magistrate—indeed he points out that one of the first priors, Jacopo de' Bardi, was from an immensely rich family—but on their moderate behavioral patterns. The distinction between magnate and *popolano* was for him (as for some modern historians of medieval Italy) a matter of political culture.[19] Magnates were men who admired and emulated the military, bucolic, and amatory ways of French chivalry, who rode horses in cavalcades through the city streets. They were given to violence and motivated principally by anti-social notions of personal honor.[20] For them, honor trumped the common good; they would tear the city apart out of misplaced loyalty to pope or emperor or clan or party. They lived off rents and could devote themselves full-time to military and political pursuits. They had no respect for the laws of the city, made by and for the powerless, and preferred private revenge to the use of the courts. A good guildsman, by contrast, was somebody who devoted most of his efforts to his own business and not to his political ambitions; whose business interests made him prefer peace to war; whose experience in trade and commerce made him prudent and far-sighted. He could rule and be ruled in turn because he had other things to do with his time. Not being able to rely for protection on an ancient and powerful clan, he looked to the city and its laws to defend him against his enemies, and therefore his first loyalty was to the city. He did not have a large clientele whose interests might compete with those of the city. It was obvious to Bruni that such a man would make a far better magistrate than a magnate would.

This is not to say that Bruni wanted his guildsman-citizen to be unmilitary. To allow the very lowest classes to take up arms was a capital error, as the Ciompi tumult had demonstrated (9.1–10). But the Popolo, ideally, should bear arms. Like most republicans, Bruni believed an armed and vigilant citizenry was necessary to defend its own prerogatives against powerful forces inside and outside the city. He believed the practice of bearing arms required institutional support, which is why he approved of the institution of militia companies to protect the Popolo against the domination of the magnates. The liberty of the people required them to be organized militarily (2.99). There was hardly anything Bruni deplored more in Florentine history than the custom that began in 1351 of allowing citizens to purchase exemptions from military service. Bruni roundly condemns this practice in a passage that offers a good example of his didactic manner:

> Many decisions were also taken that winter about raising funds for war. Among other blameworthy decisions, those with military obligations in Florentine territory were allowed exemption from military service if they paid money to the state for hiring foreign and outside soldiers. The only sure effect of this was to render the city's own population unwarlike, so that the citizens would look to others to defend their own fortunes, and would not know how to defend themselves or fight for their country. These and many similar mistakes of statecraft are committed by governors who lack experience, and though small in the beginning, such errors later give birth to massive harms. (7.101)

In Bruni's later *Constitution of the Florentines* (1439), a treatise in Greek describing the Florentine constitution in the manner of Aristotle, he remarked that it was this decision that had led to the emergence of oligarchy in Florence, since the predominant use of mercenaries put power into the hands of those who paid them.[21] Yet as Chapter 9 shows, Bruni was enough of a realist to accept that, in his own time, Florence's wars had to be managed by civilian commissioners (such as his friend, the knight Rinaldo degli Albizzi) who hired professional soldiers to fight for the city. Under modern conditions the best path to the reform of military life was to encourage civilians with knightly status and condottieri to embrace the highest ancient standards in the pursuit of their calling.

For Bruni, however, it was not enough that the People be able to defend their interests militarily; they also needed the support of the laws in their daily intercourse with the nobility. This is why he praises the institution of the Ordinances of Justice in 1293 and their sponsor, Giano della Bella, who is one of the great heroes of the *History* (4.26–40). Up to that time, says Bruni, the People had been in a relationship of "honorable servitude" *(honesta veluti servitute)* with respect to the nobility *(nobilitas)*. The nobility had never treated the People as an equal partner. As a result, the common people had suffered violence, arrogant contempt, seizure of goods, and injustices of every kind, and had been unable to enforce the laws. The Ordinances remedied this situation by placing the nobility under heavy political and legal disabilities. They were stripped of political rights and could not serve as magistrates. They were subject to heavier punishments and much looser standards of evidence in court cases. Clans could be punished for the misdeeds of individual members. The laws were enforced against them by a civic garrison of five thousand men commanded by the Gonfaloniere of Justice. A special magistrate, the Executor of the Ordinances of Justice, was established to deal with magnate offenses (4.99).

It is clear that no orthodox Aristotelian could or should have approved of the Ordinances of Justice. Aristotelian institutions in general and Aristotle's ideal mixed polity in particular were designed with a view to neutralizing partisanship. Aristotle's aim is to maximize virtue and wisdom in government and to ensure that governors rule in the interests of all. But everyone needs to see that his interests are being served, which means allowing each class of persons in the state—rich, middling, and poor—some voice in their own rule, some degree of participation in their own governance (*Politics* 6.4). This in turn requires a careful balancing of oligarchic and democratic elements in the design of the constitution. And however the interest of the rich and the poor are balanced, the predominant power in the state should be held by its wisest and most virtuous citizens, whom Aristotle identifies as the men of "free birth, wealth, culture, and nobility of descent." "Quality" should dominate "quantity," that is, the nobler sort should dominate the multitude (*Politics* 4.12). And the state cannot endorse formal injustices to particular classes because this leads only to further strife. Law is defined as reason free from passion (*Politics* 3.16) and should provide a check on partisanship by remaining a strictly neutral arbiter. Impartiality of the laws is of capital importance and should be characteristic of all constitutions (*Politics* 3.15).

Bruni's praise of the Ordinances, by contrast, shows that, like Machiavelli, he takes partisanship for granted; he regards it as an inescapable fact of political life. Bruni's *History* never argues that partisanship can be neutralized in the orthodox Aristotelian way, by a mixture of opposites.[22] Bruni instead endorses the Florentine solution, to ensure the victory of the best party by legal measures and force. In other words, he admires the Ordinances of Justice precisely because they give institutional support to the best party. They are explicitly designed to ensure that in any struggle between a *popolano* and a member of the nobility, the state will back the *popolano* and enable him to overcome the superior power of the nobleman. The laws have to be partial to the weak to protect the weak.

Bruni takes the same partisan view of the Guelf and Ghibelline factions. The Guelfs are the party of the popes, who are valued because (most of the time) they support the liberty of Italian cities. Historically, they had provided the ideological glue holding Florentine alliances in Tuscany and elsewhere together. The Ghibellines are an unpatriotic party consisting of potential traitors, a party which supports the German barbarians who have usurped the name of the empire. The Parte Guelfa—a semi-public patriotic society charged with neutralizing Ghibelline influence in the city—is praised by Bruni as a moral censor (2.117).[23] Although the Parte Guelfa is later criticized for a lack of moderation in persecuting Ghibellines, or supposed Ghibellines (8.19–20), Bruni strongly upholds the legitimacy of its role in suppressing pro-imperial partisanship.

Moderation in Politics as the Key to Social Concord

Thus guildsmen of the popular classes need to rule, and they need to make use of institutional partisanship—positive discrimination as one might say today—in order to enforce the laws against the nobility. And Guelfs need to be able to suppress Ghibelline power: a state can only have one foreign policy. At the same time, the People cannot do without the wide experience and expert military, diplomatic, and legal knowledge of the nobility. Ideally, the nobility and the People should cooperate. Magnates must learn to accept that political office is the exclusive possession of the People. They must learn to be good Florentines and put country ahead of private interests, even though public honors are largely denied them.[24]

Bruni offers in book 11 an example of a great man, Donato Acciaiuoli, who failed to be a good citizen. Acciaiuoli was a member of an extremely wealthy and powerful *popolano* family and a leading member of the regime. But he also had many friends and clients among the exile communities, nobles, and persons suspected of Ghibelline sympathies. At the end of 1395, in the middle of Florence's struggle with Milan, he made the mistake of putting the interests of his exiled friends above that of the city and began scheming secretly through his agents in the government to have them restored to political rights. His scheme was found out, and he was summoned before the Priors. Either from a sense of citizenship or from arrogance he did not appear with armed followers, as his friends were urging, and so he was taken captive and driven into exile (11.35–36). The following is Bruni's summation of his behavior. (It is worth keeping in mind that Bruni was composing this book of the *History* between 1439 and 1442 when serving on the Ten of War along with Donato's descendent Angelo Acciaiuoli and Cosimo de' Medici.)

> It was thought that two things most of all stood in the way of this great man: first, his excessive and unconstrained power, and second, his excessive liberty in censuring others. The former earned him envy, the latter, the ill-will of many men. Ambassadors sent to the city frequented his house, and all who had some business with the city took refuge with him as with a patron. Not even his friends approved of this behavior, and his enemies used to call him, calumniously, "duke" and "lord"—so vexing is all preeminence in a free city!
>
> His excessive freedom of censure was also an obstacle to him. Himself a man of blameless life, he could not bear vices in other men and often would criticize them. Such censures did not so much help the republic as they injured him; citizens in a free city should be advised and directed in a kindly way, not criticized insultingly. On these grounds Acciaiuoli was expelled and banished, and was deprived of his fatherland. Letters of state were written to his brother, a cardinal of the Roman church, explaining the reason for the banishments. They said the magistrates had driven this leading citizen into exile only with grief and reluctance, because at an extraordinarily difficult moment he had encouraged certain citizens to hope for a renewal of their political rights and restoration; and he had made preparations so that, if he could not obtain what

he wanted by public deliberation, he would set about accomplishing it by force of arms. (11.37)

The city needs great men, but they must learn to behave like citizens.[25] Yet the People too must learn to defer to the superior expertise of the nobility, especially in military and diplomatic affairs. The state needs the nobility as an "ornament" at home, it needs the wealth of the nobility to embellish the city, and it needs the nobility's guidance in matters of taste and letters; above all, however, it needs the nobility's advice in peace and war. Bruni demonstrates over and over again how failure to accept good advice from military experts led to disaster.[26]

This, indeed, is one of Bruni's chief messages in book 2, where the rashness and imprudence of a "fierce people"—its failure to take the wise advice of *illustres viri et rei militaris periti* (illustrious men experienced in war)—led directly to the greatest military disaster in Florentine history, the battle of Montaperti (2.36–51). "Plebeians ignorant of the art of war" ("the sort who tend to predominate in magistracies," he adds) were so eager for glory and plunder that they failed to appreciate the overwhelming advantages of the enemy's position and to see through the Ghibellines' disinformation campaign. So, foolishly, they decided to march out and face the enemy. At this point a group of *nobiles* led by Tegghiaio d'Aldobrandi de'Adimari tried to persuade the magistrates of their error, laying out carefully all the advantages and disadvantages of going to war—classic Florentine *ragione*. But it was all for naught. After Tegghiaio's speech there arose a *popolano* magistrate named Spedito, "the sort of person unrestrained liberty can sometimes produce."

> For some time he had barely been able to contain himself as he listened to this good advice. As soon as Tegghiaio had finished speaking, he shouted—his limbs and voice shaking with passion—"What are you after, Tegghiaio? Have you turned into a filthy coward? This magistracy isn't going to pay any attention to your fears and quakings. It's going to consider the dignity of the Florentine People. If you're paralyzed with fear, we'll let you off military service (2.48).

Tegghiaio defended himself with dignity, but the die had been cast.

> Then, when the rest of those present fell to grumbling and began to defend their decision, the magistrates fixed a fine for anyone who debated the matter further. The rashness of the magistrates was assisted by a fierce people, proud of its many victories. They wished to march out fearlessly and expose themselves

voluntarily to battle, not so much out of concern for their allies' perils, nor led by any particular goal, but simply to avoid the appearance of being afraid of their enemies. The best course having thus been shouted down, the expedition was prepared with resolve. (2.50–51)

The result, of course, was the disaster on the Arbia, the return of the Ghibelline exiles, and the temporary eclipse of the Popolo.

But here again, Bruni's Aristotelianism is less than orthodox. He does not take it for granted, as Aristotle did, that virtue is found predominantly among the rich and noble. He assumes that it is fairly widely distributed down the social pyramid. He is even able to praise the *virtus et constantia* of Michele di Lando, the ringleader of the Ciompi revolt, even though the latter is a man of the lowest origins. Indeed, he is frankly admiring of Michele's character, his "natural authority and not ungentlemanly appearance." Even though the man was from the lowest of the plebs, even from the working classes, he nevertheless showed a kind of virtue in restraining the worthless desires and malignant wills of the multitude.[27] It is hard to imagine Plato or Aristotle finding similar words for Cleon, the demagogue of late fifth-century Athens.

At the same time, Bruni does not mince words in describing the traitorous and wicked behavior of much of the nobility. Of course Florentine history provided him with numerous unavoidable examples of bad behavior on the part of the nobility. But this does not alter the fact that Bruni's beliefs about the distribution of virtue by classes reveal social prejudices quite different from those of Aristotle. His character descriptions in the *History* push against the Aristotelian assumption that nature divides mankind spontaneously into social pyramids, with virtue and wisdom found chiefly at the top among the wealthy and wellborn. Bruni himself manifests a prejudice in favor of the optimates on numerous occasions, to be sure, and in his personal life he was as deferential to noble families as any other upwardly mobile commoner and immigrant. There are numerous instances in the *History* where Bruni casts an admiring glance upward at rank and wealth and a contemptuous gaze downward at "the dregs" (*faex*) of Florentine society. Yet from an Aristotelian perspective it is still remarkable the extent to which Bruni is willing to praise the virtue of ordinary middle-class Florentines and criticize noble behavior. As far as the success of the Florentine state is concerned, the main usefulness of the nobility is not their moral virtue but their expert knowledge, wealth, and foreign connections.

For Bruni, in short, the great virtue of civic life is moderation, and it is a principal lesson of the *History* that all classes of citizens need to moderate their behavior. His prescription for civic harmony has far more to do with the Ciceronian concept of *concordia ordinum* than with Aristotle's careful apportionment of public powers among economic classes. For Bruni, the nobility need to accept the authority of the People and not attempt to exercise direct power through magistracies. They shouldn't behave like lords and soldiers when participating in civil society. Within the city they need to lay aside their signorial and military character— appropriate on their country estates and in wartime—and treat other citizens with equality and respect.[28] They should observe the laws and temper their desire for honor. If revenge is called for, they should seek redress through the courts, not by violence. They should restrain their desire for luxury as it leads to visible inequalities and impoverishes the state. The People, for its part, needs to defer to the experience, expertise, and tried loyalty of meritorious aristocrats and not be carried away by passion. It should not try to persecute the nobility to excess, as that only drives them into the hands of foreign enemies (6.93). It should not abolish proper distinctions for merit out of a misplaced zeal for equality (7.24). It should recognize that the nobility give *riputazione* to a city and help beautify it. The example to avoid is that of the French, a naturally uncivil people whose arrogant nobility treat the common people "almost like slaves" (6.112).

In sum, Bruni in his *History* often makes use of Aristotelian categories of analysis, but his conclusions and the beliefs that support those conclusions are foreign to Aristotle. Bruni uses Aristotle as a rhetorician would—as Cicero would— instrumentally, to strengthen his argument for a non-Aristotelian conclusion: that the historian can judge institutions and patterns of citizen behavior on the basis of their tendency to promote or inhibit the well-being and glory of the state. This is strikingly different from Aristotle's goal for political life. Although he states explicitly that ethics is a branch of politics and subordinate to it, ultimately Aristotle's state is meant to subserve human flourishing in both the active and contemplative lives. In the end, Aristotle sees a non-political activity, contemplation for its own sake, as the highest human activity. That is why he condemns any constitution designed with a view to expansion and empire (for example the Spartan), because it falsely privileges the honor-seeking part of our natures above the rational, knowledge-seeking part. In choosing between what Machiavelli would call "a republic for preservation" and "a republic for expansion," Aristotle sides with the republic for preservation (or longevity). Bruni resembles Machiavelli in wanting both longevity *and* expansion for Florence. He does not, to be sure, share Machiavelli's radical view that the rules of morality are fundamentally different from the rules of political success. But he does share his instrumentalized analysis of institutions and citizen behavior patterns.

An example from book 11 will help illustrate the point. The date is 1399, and Giangaleazzo of Milan is tightening the noose around Florence, taking control of one town after another in Tuscany until Florence is surrounded on all sides by enemies. The Florentines had an opportunity to break the chain of antagonists the previous year when the pro-Florentine ruler of Pisa, Gherardo d'Appiano, secretly offered them an alliance, via his representative Giovanni Grassolini, if only the Florentines would pay to send him a large bodyguard to protect his position in Pisa. Since Pisa was traditionally Ghibelline and anti-Florentine, Gherardo was in a weak position. The Florentines saw Gherardo's entreaty as a request to support tyranny and refused it. Instead of keeping the negotiations secret, they held a large public meeting where they concluded it would not be in keeping with the dignity of the Florentine People to buy friendship. As a result, Gherardo, whose position had become untenable, was bribed by Giangaleazzo to abandon the lordship of Pisa to him. The same thing happened when the Perugians offered an alliance in return for military support against the pope, who was trying to reassert his lordship over that city. The Florentines refused because they were much too good Guelfs to oppose the pope, but the result was that Giangaleazzo took control of another neighboring city. Thus the Florentines' misplaced sense of honor, exaggerated respect for the pope, and ideological opposition to tyranny blinded them to their true interests. It led them foolishly to refuse alliances that would have stopped Giangaleazzo in his tracks.

Bruni lets us know what he thinks of these actions in a speech of the oligarch Rinaldo Gianfigliazzi, another of his heroes, before a large political meeting, or *practica,* in the Palazzo Vecchio (see Appendix B). It effectively summarizes Bruni's views about the weaknesses of popular governments when engaging in military affairs as well as his ideas about how those weaknesses might be remedied.[29] What Bruni advocates in this passage is clearly a species of political realism. He is not recommending that the Florentines act with perfect honor like the Roman heroes Camillus or Fabricius. The existential threat of defeat in war requires that the Florentines place the good of the state first and that they shelve, at least temporarily, their traditional religious deference to the pope, their constitutional safeguards against overmighty citizens, and their folk prejudices in favor of popular decision-making and public debate of policy. Bruni observes a tendency for popular governments to manifest "sloth and negligence" and calls for vigor in the executive.

Thus Gianfigliazzi advocates constituting a war commission (presumably a *Dieci di Balìa* or Ten of War) consisting of wise and virtuous citizens to take charge of the state's foreign policy. Only such a magistracy can act with the swiftness and secrecy required for successful warfare, untrammelled by the usual cumbersome decision-making processes of the commune. Not coincidentally, this was a magistracy on which Bruni himself served three times in the period when he was writing the last three books of his *History*.[30] Like Machiavelli, Bruni sees the envy of small men as an obstacle to the emergence of great leaders and would like to see steps taken to prevent slander and judicial harassment. Above all, he manifests a respect for armed force and a certain contempt for citizens who always advocate peace, whether from religious or economic motives, and fail to recognize the need for strength in foreign affairs. His preference is for Florence to defend itself with professional soldiers led by a competent condottiere rather than with citizen levies. The good citizen should prefer peace, but when the state's interests are best preserved by war, he should be ready to support war.

Bruni's prescriptions for civic harmony and for acquiring strength and prestige internationally take him very far from the usual pieties of humanist educational thought, including those contained in his own *De studiis et literis* (On Literary Study). That work, like the majority of humanist educational treatises, belongs to the Isocratean tradition of cultivating one's abilities and virtues so as to achieve personal honor and distinction.[31] The state benefits indirectly, by possessing virtuous and educated political elites. The humanists' technique for acquiring distinction is study of the classics, which means emulating Roman linguistic and behavioral patterns, on the assumption that the ancients were better, more glorious, more wise, more powerful than the specimens of humanity found in the corrupt modern world. Ancient eloquence and shining examples of ancient virtue would of themselves inspire us to live better lives.

Bruni in the *History* is using a different economy of persuasion. He is urging his fellow citizens to act with virtue because their history shows that failure to do so leads to collective shame and disaster. (This is perhaps why he spends so much more time on Florence's failures than on her successes.) He does not promise that an individual's virtue will be rewarded with a flourishing life in every case—as, indeed, is shown by the fate of his hero, Giano della Bella, who was stripped of his property and expelled from the city by his ungrateful fellow citizens (4.40). But he does promise that the city whose ruling classes behave with virtue will be free, powerful, and glorious. Perhaps they will even prove themselves destined some day for universal empire, like ancient Rome. But that is the promise of a Roman statesman like Cicero, not a philosopher like Aristotle. And Bruni's mode of analysis, his subordination of private virtue to the glory of the state, and his attempt to establish loyalty to the state above all other loyalties to party, class, and even to the Church shows that his closest kinship as a political thinker is not with Aristotle, Polybius, Thomas Aquinas, or even with Ptolemy of Lucca, but with Machiavelli.[32]

CHAPTER II

BIONDO FLAVIO

What Made the Romans Great

The Roma Triumphans *and the Revival of Roman Civilization*

Modern scholarship tends to classify Biondo Flavio as an "antiquary"—indeed, as the true founder of the antiquarian tradition in the Renaissance, even though his work on classical and early Christian antiquities is not entirely without medieval precedents.[1] Yet for a scholar trying to assess the significance of his work, the word "antiquary" in English carries misleading associations. One might be led to imagine that what Biondo is doing is akin to the work of groups like the London Society of Antiquaries (meritorious as that body is); worse, the name "antiquary" might put one in mind of Sir Walter Scott's Jonathan Oldbuck, the principal character in his novel *The Antiquary*. Oldbuck is one of Scott's richest comic creations, an amateur gentleman-scholar, a trader in dubious antique curiosities, poking around in dusty old documents, his talk full of allusions to obscure authorities and far-fetched theories of interest only to his fellow antiquarians. Classical antiquity is his hobby, and he and his fellow antiquaries are depicted as slightly absurd *laudatores acti temporis,* marginal to the wider life of their time.

Biondo's scholarly activities, by contrast, whatever their superficial resemblance to later antiquarian studies, are far more central to the culture of his time, and spring from quite different motivations. What Biondo is doing in his vast, sprawling *Roma Triumphans* (ed. princ. 1473) is laying foundations for the whole Renaissance project as originally envisaged by Petrarch over a century before. His goal is to assemble and arrange the ancient sources needed to reconstruct what Rome was like in the period of its greatest flourishing in order to bring about civilizational reforms the humanists longed for. You can't model yourself on antiquity unless you know what antiquity was like, and the *Roma Triumphans* collects, sifts, and compares the ancient literary sources (as well as selected legal, archeological, inscriptional, and numismatic evidence) needed to understand what ancient Rome had to offer the modern world.[2] Biondo's reconstruction was encyclopedic in its scope, embracing the realms of religion, government, and military training *(disciplina)* as well as the arts and ceremonials of virtuous living in the ancient Roman family and in Roman society. According to Angelo Mazzocco, the foremost modern authority on Biondo, "The *Roma Triumphans* is the single most important rendition of classical civilization produced by fifteenth-century humanism."[3] The *RT* (as I shall abbreviate it henceforward) was thus a practical and highly effective research tool for realizing the aspirations of the humanists. Its key position among the texts produced by the Renaissance movement, in combination with Biondo's other works of classical research, may be compared to the position of the *Encyclopédie* of Diderot as an embodiment of Enlightenment values three centuries later. The *RT* bears on the history of political thought because it devotes three of its ten books to Rome's political institutions, always with the insistent question in mind: What was it that made Rome great?

It must be stipulated, of course, that Biondo was not a political theorist in anything like the modern sense. He does have a recognizable ideological profile that can be distilled from his many writings, to be sure, but the *RT* is not what a modern academic would recognize as a work of political theory. Nevertheless, though it is primarily a descriptive work, it does have a normative side that bears on political thought and is intended to convey lessons for humanist reformers. Biondo is not an indiscriminate admirer of ancient Rome, and there are a number of passages, especially in the books on Roman religion, where he warns that the ways of the Romans are not to be imitated. But there are also many occasions when he steps out of his role as a scholar to advise the men of his time to follow ancient Roman models. Ecclesiastical governors in the Papal States, to take but one example, are advised to follow the sound practices of Roman provincial governors.[4]

Indeed, the project as a whole is framed as a means to achieve the fondest political dream of Pius II, the work's dedicatee: motivating Christians to participate in a great crusade to recover formerly Christian lands in the East from the Turks. Biondo tells Pius in the dedication that when

> the mighty peoples of Italy, France, Spain and Germany whom you have roused to join the great and glorious expedition that you are preparing against the Turks—cruel and tyrannical oppressors of Greece, Constantinople and the Moesias [i.e., Bulgaria and Serbia]—will learn of deeds performed in earlier times, in other places, in similarly difficult circumstances, . . . imitation of the prowess of the ancients [will be] itself another factor likely to stimulate all noble

spirits with zeal to undertake the enterprise. You, meanwhile, while you read again and again of the triumphs of the ancient city of Rome, will anticipate the splendid triumph that our God in his goodness and piety will give you, Pius, first of all, for the destruction and annihilation of the Turks' power and the liberation of Europe, [and] after that, [for] the liberation of Jerusalem and the Holy Land adjoining it.[5]

At the end of work, in the eloquent peroration bringing book 10 to a close, Biondo declares that the modern Roman Church stands in the place of the ancient Roman state *(respublica)*—with the pope as its consuls, the Holy Roman Emperor as its *magister militum,* and the other Christian princes as its chief magistrates—and declares that if the princes of Christendom were to follow the authority of the pope as they ought, they would quickly retake the former provinces of the old Roman Empire. If they should resist his commands, however, they can anticipate that the Latin West will suffer the same fate as the Greeks and come under the power of the Turks, Saracens, and other infidels, losing their hope of eternal salvation in the bargain.[6] For Biondo, as for Petrarch, the Crusades should provide for modern Christians the ultimate motivation for reconstituting the old Roman Empire in all its power and glory.[7]

Thus the normative and descriptive purposes of the *RT* come together in the overarching questions that motivate the whole work. They are the same questions that obsess the whole humanist movement from Petrarch to Machiavelli: What was it that made Rome great? And how much of what made Rome great can be imitated in the modern world? Biondo has detailed and carefully considered answers to both questions. What makes his answers significant in a history of humanist political theory are his judgments in particular about the Roman *respublica.* The judgments made by historians about the successes and failures of the ancient Roman state were key to the fortunes of the republican tradition in the West, from Ptolemy of Lucca and Remigio de' Girolami to Machiavelli, Harrington, Montesquieu, and the founders of the American republic.[8] A positive evaluation of what scholars today refer to as "republican Rome," maligned as it was by Augustine and the tradition of Christian historiography, was vital to republican theorists who wanted to make the Roman republic a normative model for political institutions in their contemporary worlds. And Biondo's *RT* contained the most authoritative treatment of the Roman republic in the fifteenth century and continued to be consulted well into the sixteenth and seventeenth centuries.[9]

What Was the Respublica Romana *for Biondo?*

Before describing Biondo's reconstruction of republican institutions and mores, however, we must address the question of what the word *respublica* meant to him and his contemporaries. As discussed in Chapter 3, the word has often been misunderstood in the modern scholarly literature as referring to a republic in the modern sense, that is, a non-monarchical government hostile to hereditary privilege whose legitimacy stems from the express will of the people. This is an eighteenth-century conception that is far from Biondo's usage. His use of the term is more traditional but presents certain innovative features.[10] One sense in which Biondo uses *respublica* is fairly straightforward: it can simply mean "state" or "commonwealth" and is often used almost interchangeably with *civitas,* which in the Renaissance usually carries the meaning of a self-ruling state. This is the predominant ancient sense of *respublica,* as we have seen, and it is clearly the sense in which Biondo uses the word in the subtitles of books 3, 4, and 5 of *RT, de administratione rei publicae.* Since these books cover imperial institutions and those of the early kings as well as (what we moderns call) "republican" ones, we must conclude that Biondo is using here this broader, generic sense of *respublica.*

There is also a second sense in which Biondo uses the term *respublica,* essentially derived from a few famous passages in Cicero, Suetonius, and Tacitus. This use of the term is freighted with positive connotations, and also indicates a period of Roman history. But we have to be careful not to assimilate Biondo's usage entirely to the modern period concept of the Roman Republic. It is an error, though still a common one in modern English-language historiography, to believe that ancient sources themselves periodized Roman history into royal, republican, and imperial periods. It is only since the late eighteenth century, the age of republican revolutions, that the period concept of the word *respublica* has been elaborated from the aforementioned passages in Cicero, Suetonius, and Tacitus. In those passages one finds, on the modern reading of them, a sharp distinction, based on regime type, between the republican period—*stante re publica* in the famous phrase of Cicero in the *De officiis* (2.3)—and the imperial system of the Principate. The period concept of *respublica,* however, in humanist and early modern thought was not tightly linked to regime type. In the vast majority of ancient sources, including most of Cicero, Sallust, Livy, the *Scriptores Historiae Augustae,* and other imperial historians, *respublica* is not attached to any one period or regime in Roman history but is used simply to mean a good, constitutional government that protects citizen liberties under the rule of law. The same usage is found throughout most of medieval historiography and in scholastic political theory—with the partial exception of Ptolemy of Lucca, the scholastic author best informed about Roman history.

It would be less anachronistic to refer to Biondo's second sense of the word *respublica*—the early period of Roman history ending with the Caesars—as the "senatorial" understanding, reconstructed from various remarks revealing the hostile views of the Principate taken by some members of the senatorial class in the first centuries BC and AD. The more common premodern usage, which carries no periodic sense, we can call "Augustan," as it was first made explicit in the *Res gestae divi Augustae*. In this text—widely diffused in the Roman world in both Greek and Latin—the Emperor Augustus explains that the republic had been oppressed by the despotism of a faction, but that he had taken it under his personal protection until the time came to restore it to the Roman people. *Respublica* in this view is uncorrupt, traditional government, not a historical period.[11] This is the way Biondo uses *respublica* in book 1 of his great earlier work, the *Decades of History from the Fall of the Roman Empire* (1443–1453).[12] The Augustan periodization of Roman history that Biondo adopts there, following Florus and other imperial histories, divides Roman history into three periods, defined with respect to their principal magistracy—*sub regibus, sub consulibus, sub imperatoribus*—and admits only a *mutatio* of the republic in Octavian's time, not an end of the republic.[13] The Augustan usage implies, as one might expect, that the government of the Roman state under the emperors is still legitimate, constitutional, and protective of the liberties of Roman citizens. It is still good government and not tyranny—the lexical opposite of *respublica* before the fifteenth century.

Chapter 3 of this book has already discussed the change introduced into the meaning of the word *respublica* by Leonardo Bruni, who, unlike previous translators of Aristotle's *Politics,* used the word to translate *politeia* in Aristotle's "specific" sense of "legitimate (or constitutional) popular regime." Thus from the 1440s onward there is a strand in humanist political terminology that uses *respublica* to refer to any non-monarchical regime, whether popular or aristocratic. The new usage is also reflected in Biondo's *RT.* To be sure, Biondo never makes a tight link between *respublica* as a specific type of regime and the *respublica* as a period of Roman history. His understanding of the republican period, like that of Livy and Ptolemy of Lucca, includes the early monarchy in the history of the republic,[14] and this usage can be found in many later authors with republican sympathies, such as

Francesco Guicciardini and Carlo Sigonio. It must be allowed that in several places Biondo appears to use phrases such as *stans et integra respublica*—obviously of Ciceronian stamp—to specify what moderns would call the republican period and to distinguish it by regime type from the periods under the rule of kings or emperors. Another of his terms for the consular period is *libera civitas,* the free state of Rome, which also may connote a particular type of regime.[15] But from a variety of parallel passages it becomes clear that *stans et integra respublica* for him is really a kind of growth metaphor, meaning something like "when the republic (Roman state) was still sound and on its feet."[16] In using it Biondo does not mean to imply that only the period of consular rule was constitutionally valid, as certain passages of Cicero and Tacitus can be read to imply. The implied contrast is rather, as it was for Petrarch, with the modern, vastly reduced city of Rome. Like Livy, Tacitus, and Dionysius of Halicarnassus, Biondo sees the period of the early kings as embryonically republican but still primitive from the point of institutions.[17] Biondo praises, for example, the early kings' practice of proposing laws and magistrates to the people for their approval, a practice which "lasted afterwards as long as the republic was in existence" *(postea quamdiu respublica stetit).* In the same passage he reports Ulpian's opinion that Romulus and Numa founded the quaestorship and may have had the early quaestors popularly elected. The kings for Biondo were originally legitimate republican magistrates who eventually abused their power and were replaced by a magistracy that divided the royal power among two consuls in order to weaken it—though the consuls were still a very powerful magistracy that was effectively sovereign in time of war.

Biondo's Political Terminology

Constitutional Type

| *Sub regibus* | *Sub consulibus* | *Sub principibus et* |
| | *Libera civitas* | *Imperatoribus* |

Historical Development

Embyronic r.p.—*stans et integra respublica*—r.p. in decline (after the 4th c. AD)
aucta et florente r.p., ad summum florente r.p.

What made the kings something like republican magistrates and distinguished them from the later emperors was the fact that their constitutional powers were limited by the senators, the voice of patrician power, and by laws and magistrates. The senators themselves, after the death of Romulus, the first king, recognized a constitutional role for the people in selecting the next king. In fact they made over their supreme power to the people, decreeing that "once the people had designated a king it would be legitimate [*ratus*] provided it were supported by the patricians."[18] But as the republic / state grew stronger under the consuls, the people entered into open rivalry with the senatorial class for power and at times were able to check it effectively through the tribunate and the custom of *provocatio ad populum*—appeal of a magistrate's death sentence to the people as a whole—institutions about which Biondo (mirroring Cicero's judgments in the *De legibus*) expresses certain misgivings.

Yet what ultimately defines the republic for Biondo is the durable power of the people and the consequent inability, first of the kings, then the patricians, later the senatorial nobility, completely to control the polity in their own interest. Even the early emperors felt the need to court popular opinion. It was the struggle of the orders and the institutional frameworks it created, above all the tribunate, that made it possible to achieve something like observance of the common good and the rule of law. Biondo has a sophisticated awareness of the dynamic of power in the old republic and how various devices were used to control the popular classes: the Twelve Tables, the *cursus honorum* in which wealth was required to compete, the way the *comitia* were rigged, and the use of religion to curb popular violence. He is by no means an uncritical admirer of what we moderns would call "the Republic." He echoes, for example, Cicero's ambivalence in the *De legibus* about elections as a device for securing virtuous magistrates, and he understands that elections can be corrupt. But he recognizes that, nonetheless, an element of popular power had survived down to the time of Caesar and only disappeared completely after the early Principate. The early emperors still accorded a degree of respect to traditional Roman magistracies and institutions even while encroaching upon their powers. This only ended with the *lex de imperio Vespasiani,* the law of 69 AD, rediscovered in inscriptional form by Cola di Rienzo in 1347. Biondo believed, like much of early modern scholarship, that this was the very *lex regia* in which the authority of the Roman People had been delegated to the emperors.[19] For Biondo it documented the end of constitutional government and the beginning of absolutism, that distinction so fundamental to early modern political theory. In that period constitutionalism and absolutism came to distinguish the type of government advocated, respectively, by political Aristotelians, who advocated a mixed constitution and balanced powers, and by theorists such as Bodin and Hobbes, for whom sovereignty must be undivided and lodged in a monarchical power.[20] The dependence of this distinction on models drawn from Roman history has recently been explored in some detail, though its debt to Biondo's reconstruction has yet to be explored.[21]

Biondo's Virtue Politics, Republicanism, and the Greatness of Rome

At this point the reader might be tempted to conclude that Biondo was a closet republican. But he was not, at least not in the modern sense of the world "republican." He was not a proponent of either an aristocratic or popular republic. In fact, like most humanists, he does not regard non-monarchical republican government as necessarily and in all circumstances the best form of government, and he is certainly not what I have called in Chapter 3 an "exclusivist," someone who regarded a non-monarchical republic as the only legitimate constitution.[22]

In general, and again like the majority of humanists before Machiavelli, Biondo is agnostic about the influence of constitutional form *per se* on Roman greatness. In fact he was a firm believer in the virtue politics of his fellow humanists. Virtue politics, as we have seen, takes the legitimacy, success, and moral quality of government to be dependent above all on the virtue of its rulers. Other sources of legitimacy—constitutions and laws, hereditary right, popular participation or consent, divine sanction—are inadequate in themselves to secure good government. Virtue is the true, natural source of political right; its possession constitutes true nobility. Merit was a necessary condition, if not always a sufficient condition, of justified rank in society and government. Hereditary rule was either unjustifiable, or (some humanists allowed) could be justified only if the heir to a title was also virtuous. Yet humanists as a rule asserted that there was a fundamental equality among men in the sense that all were capable of virtue, no matter what their birth. Virtue was achieved primarily by the study of the humanities, "good letters"—the humane arts of literature, philosophy, and oratory—which provided training in the forms of excellence that were characteristic of free men and women. The humanities instilled the precepts and examples needed for good rulership and gave gifted young men and women access to an idealized world—the world of classical antiquity—which humanists assumed to be better than the corrupt contemporary world and therefore in some degree a model for moderns to imitate.

Biondo fully subscribes to humanist virtue politics, as can be seen above all in his analysis of Roman greatness. He isolates three factors as critical to Rome's success. One was religion and piety. In books 1–2 of *RT* Biondo carefully distinguishes, on the one hand, between awareness of and respect for the divine, the fundamental religious sense *(pietas)* possessed by all nations and, on the other, superstitious corruptions of religion (1.26). Biondo faults the Romans for their foolish and impious superstitions and the emperors for their persecutions of Christians, and he makes it clear that Christianity is the one true revelation to mankind of the way to salvation.[23] As secretary to the pope, he could hardly do otherwise. But he also makes it clear that, when it comes to piety and respect for the sacred, the Romans, despite their paganism, still had much to teach his own time. There were even real continuities between the forms of Roman pagan religion and the modern Church, for example in the election of religious leaders and the funding of priesthoods. The Romans gave the *ius sacrorum* precedence over the *ius magistratuum,* of which Biondo as a high papalist naturally approves, and all their acts of state and all the ceremonies of private life had a religious character.[24] Biondo also admires the effective use of Roman religion to restrain the natural tendency to violence, disorder, and sedition among the plebs.

The second great factor in Rome's success was her readiness to admit foreigners and men of talent to the citizenship, to magistracies, and even to the office of emperor. Their cosmopolitan sympathies and meritocratic practices illustrate the general Roman preference for virtue over birth. Biondo quotes Livy, Cicero's *Pro Balbo,* and the whole of the famous speech of Claudius in Tacitus' *Annales* 11 to demonstrate and to praise the Romans' readiness to promote foreigners and men of ignoble birth to leading positions in the state:

> Above, in a rather long passage, we have said much about the increase in the number of citizens of Rome, which we trust all, like us, are already well aware was the result of the citizenship having been given as wisely as generously, first to the Latins and the peoples surrounding the city itself, later to other communities of Italy, and finally to foreigners; so that now we may aptly repeat the judgment we quoted above from Livy, that the Roman empire grew as long as no class in which excellence might become illustrious was despised.[25]

In contrast with the Greek city-states, whose narrow nativism limited citizenship to men born of citizen parents, the Romans allowed men from all over the Roman world to enjoy citizen rights. This was a process that had begun already with Romulus and continued well into imperial times, when even emperors could be chosen from among men of provincial origins.[26] Like Petrarch, Boccaccio, and the humanist movement in general, Biondo lays great stress on the willingness of

Romans to accept as military and political leaders even persons of low status, so long as they demonstrated ability and loyalty to the state:

> From this source arose that splendid foundation of the administration of the commonwealth *(res publica),* a foundation which made the city of Rome into the commonwealth and native land of the whole world, as Cicero defending Aulus Cluentius says: "I say there were never greater rewards anywhere than here, where, if a man of ignoble birth lives in such a way that he is seen to be able to uphold the status of high rank through his excellence, he does arrive as far as the point where hard work allied with blameless character with goodness has brought him."[27] ... But to return to a surer and firmer support for the administration of the commonwealth, we shall adduce some from the almost infinite number of men, who though born in another country and in obscurity yet were raised by their excellence to be leading men among the Romans. [*A long list follows.*] Virtue was a great help to good administration of the commonwealth in the city of Rome itself, but the greatest benefit, in preserving and increasing the empire, was the virtue maintained in foreign parts by the magistrates. For this reason, in the period when the republic flourished [*stante re publica*], serious, good and honest men were sought and chosen to carry out the delegated powers and magistracies.[28]

This brings us to what is for Biondo the most important cause of Rome's greatness by far: the extraordinary private and public virtues of her leading citizens. He singles out in particular their integrity, moderation, frugality, sense of decorum *(pudicitia),* generosity, and the restraint and mutual tolerance that led to the high degree of political concord Rome enjoyed.

> When we have illustrated [these virtues], it will readily appear that neither the citizenship shared with the world, nor the supreme power of arms procured thence, nor the other arts of administering the state at home and abroad could, without [the virtues] just mentioned, either have established or preserved so great an empire. Moreover, this more certain proof will support the assertion I have made, that Roman power began to break down, collapse, and entirely fade away at the same time as did those very arts of virtuous living.[29]

Biondo spends many pages in the second half of book 5 illustrating all these virtues and showing how they made Rome great. It was virtue, piety, and inclusiveness that made Rome's rule attractive to the largest and best part of the world: successful empires are based on mutual interest, trust, and loyalty, not raw military power.[30] Biondo concludes that it was only when Rome lost its pristine virtues and the arts of holy living that it began its long decline. This took a long time: virtue began to decline well before the end of the republic; yet virtue's lamp remained lit, however fitfully, down to the very end of antiquity. Biondo thus ultimately dissociates Roman virtue from constitutional form.

It can, in short, be seen that there is nothing specifically republican in Biondo's explanation of Roman greatness. Unlike Bruni, who, following Sallust, had made the political freedom of republican Rome the cause of its greatness and the precondition of its cultural flourishing, Roman political liberty under the republic plays little or no role in Biondo's explanation of Rome's expansion and imperial successes.[31] Unlike Ptolemy of Lucca or Bruni, Biondo never says in the *RT* that participation in self-government was a cause or precondition of political virtue or military power. In a passage of his earlier *Decades,* indeed—surely aimed at Bruni— he demonstrated that the Roman state had become stronger and had continued to expand under the emperors (among whom he includes Julius Caesar). In the *RT* he expresses a good deal of admiration for Roman government under the emperors. He praises Roman provincial government, formed under the Caesars, whose justice and restraint helped cement loyalty to Rome. By contrast, in pre-Augustan times military action had often been necessary to control the formerly free cities. Military exploits were glorious, but the arts of peace more beneficial. The wise government of the Romans, their devotion to justice and useful public works, made their rule popular throughout the empire.

> Not only was there much justice in the Romans' government of the provinces but also, especially, great courtesy and generosity, with the result that their *principes* [i.e., either "leading men" or "princes"] and their peoples willingly bore their agreeable yoke. This was shown in the period of the emperor Valerian. [*Further examples of the munificence and generous rule of the emperors follow.*] . . . Undoubtedly, those deeds were splendid that the Roman *principes* [i.e., here, "emperors"] accomplished in the subjection of the provinces of Asia and of other provinces in the world, but it is pleasant and delightful to recall their good conduct in administering them and keeping their loyalty.[32]

Nor does Biondo accept Bruni's absurd view, prompted by a remark of Tacitus, that literary genius died out under the emperors.[33] As one of the great Renaissance masters of patristic literature, skillfully exploited in his *Decades,* Biondo could hardly dismiss the huge body of late antique Christian literature so cavalierly.

Moreover, in a long digression in praise of Roman letters in book 4 of *RT* Biondo gives what is in effect a potted history of pagan Roman letters, including patrons and readers as well as the cultivation of Greek letters within the Roman empire, from the First Punic War to the third century AD.[34] Implicitly responding to Bruni's charge, he pays particular attention to the emperors' patronage of literature and libraries as well as of rhetorical and philosophical education. Julius Caesar and the Emperor Augustus come in for particular praise.[35] Bruni's Whiggish view of Roman history that linked political freedom with a flourishing cultural life is firmly set aside.

Finally, Biondo never claims that the constitutional form Rome attained at the height of the republic had any bearing on the moral stature of its leading citizens. He does not claim that the monarchical regime of the Caesars offered less scope for virtue than the republican. His argument is that Roman success was the result of innate Roman virtue and piety, transmitted via customs and mores, and not of its free constitution under the republic. This would become the standard monarchist response to republican claims in the early modern debate between principalities and republics, as one can see already in the fourth book of Castiglione's *Courtier* or the *Comparison of Kingdoms and Republics* of Aurelio Lippi Brandolini.[36] The same claim, that the Romans had had a kind of epigenetic superiority in virtue, had been made by Dante and Petrarch and was admitted even by Bruni, who maintained that his Florentines had inherited the natural virtues of the *stirps romulea*.[37]

In fact Biondo is not so naïve or partisan or ill-informed that he tries to rank one period of Roman history over another. Virtue declined in the course of the Principate, but the decline had begun well before the end of the republic. Far from accepting Bruni's lurid, partisan account in the *Laudatio Florentine urbis* of the wickedness of the emperors, Biondo is unstinting in his praise of good emperors such as Augustus, Vespasian, Trajan, Antoninus Pius, and Marcus Aurelius, without concealing the faults of the bad ones. For him, Roman virtue did not begin to fade until after the time of Theodosius in the fourth century AD.[38] He admits that oratory declined somewhat under the Principate with the loss of freedom.[39] But he is far from being an uncritical admirer of republican institutions *tout court*. He criticizes the spread of the secret ballot, which (following Cicero in *De legibus*) he regards as undermining the role of virtue in public deliberation, and quotes the famous line of Tacitus, *Sorte et urna mores non discerni* (Moral qualities are not discerned in lotteries for office).[40] He reports with seeming sympathy

Cicero's view that the tribunes of the people were a necessary evil which allowed the plebs to believe (falsely) that they enjoyed equality with the nobles. Again following Cicero, he registers disapproval of Roman electoral practices that forced statesmen to debase themselves before the vulgar and were an open invitation to bribery; he credits Octavian with having stamped out bribery in Roman elections.[41] He approves of various imperial reforms of the Senate, even though they did nothing to enhance its power vis-à-vis the emperors.[42] From time to time he has disobliging things to say about the vulgar and displays the fear, shared by all Renaissance humanists, that the urban plebs, with its tendency to violence and unreason, might exercise political power. What is perhaps most surprising is that he does not to my knowledge anywhere play the trump card of traditional Christian historiography, still in common use during the Renaissance: the claim that the imperial period of Roman history must be ranked ahead of the violent and disorderly old republic because God had chosen to send his Son into the world in the time of Augustus, and that the *pax romana* introduced by Augustus Caesar was a precondition for the spread of Christianity.[43]

A Cosmopolitan Papalist

The reason why Biondo chooses not to play this card, no doubt, is that he was no more an imperialist than he was a republican. He was not interested in justifying imperial or monarchical government. Unlike Dante or Dino Compagni or Petrarch, he had no desire to see a restoration of the Roman Empire under a modern emperor. What he does show himself to be is a papalist and a cosmopolitan. Biondo's position on the revival of the Roman Empire, made explicit in the peroration of the *RT* mentioned above, resembles that of Lorenzo Valla in his famous first preface to the *Elegantiae linguae latinae* (1441). The revival of the Roman Empire that was the dream of some humanists is unnecessary, Valla wrote, since Rome's greatest achievement, the Latin language, lived on, its cultural triumph excelling and transcending the feats of arms performed by the ancient Roman generals or emperors. "What fair-minded man would not prefer those who won fame for cultivating the holy rites of literature *(sacra literarum)* to those who waged horrific wars?" Valla asks.[44] The latter were merely royal, the former divine; the latter as men enlarged the state and the majesty of the Roman People, but the former like gods brought salvation to the whole world. When the latter ruled, the conquered lost their liberty, but the victories of the former set men free.

For Biondo too, the revival of the Roman Empire is unnecessary because its role has been transcended and perfected by the spiritual empire of the Roman Church.[45] The Roman Church corrects old Roman superstitions while encouraging piety and true religion; the Church is like the ancient Roman state in that it is open to talent and takes the best from all over the world. Its universality and cosmopolitanism fight against the particularisms of human government and direct them to a higher purpose. You cannot be a successful king, magistrate, dignitary, or even a man if you oppose the Church's government, says Biondo, because the glory won by the ecclesiastical republic in granting eternal life is far more exalted than the glory the Roman state promised its champions.[46] (Missing, though perhaps implied, is the later claim of Roman Ciceronians that the Church has created a cultural empire by preserving the language of ancient Rome, Latin, the medium of civilization and the trumpet of virtue.)[47] For Biondo the ultimate triumph of Rome lies with the Roman Church, the only ancient institution surviving into the contemporary world, which spreads spiritual excellence in mankind and leads the whole world to salvation.

Biondo's position here represents a considered response to Augustine's *City of God,* a work of the highest authority, whose deflationary judgment of Roman virtue looms like a dark cloud over Biondo's—and humanism's—whole project. Ptolemy of Lucca (Tolomeo Fiadoni), a century and a half before, had experienced the same cognitive dissonance when praising Roman virtue but managed to adjust the claims of earthly and eternal glory by systematically misquoting and misrepresenting Augustine, as James Blythe has shown in a recent book.[48] Petrarch tries to save the greatness of Roman virtue by conceding the folly of Roman religion, as we saw in Chapter 6. Biondo is more honest and directly challenges Augustine's condemnation of the Romans' love for glory. In a remarkable passage of book 5, he tells the story of Isabel of Burgundy, whose crusading zeal, critics had suggested, had more to do with seeking personal glory than with the holy purposes of crusade. Isabel in response tells the story of a pilgrim to Santiago de Compostela who brought along a jewel to the famous shrine as insurance in case of extreme need. When in Santiago the pilgrim managed to sell the jewel for a higher price. The moral of Isabel's story is that the pilgrim's financial profit did not vitiate the profit to his soul. Biondo's message is that the rewards of earthly glory, which Augustine had condemned as morally corrupt, were a legitimate spur to virtue and fully compatible with higher spiritual purposes. Biondo observes, "The men of our times should learn that a Christian can win a reward and huge profit to his soul by allowing glory to stimulate his efforts in such a way that he devotes himself to works of virtue."[49] In short, Roman virtue and Roman glory, far from being sinful forms of the *libido dominandi* that drove the Roman engine of conquest, as Augustine had charged, was still to be admired and imitated. Indeed, the revival of Roman virtue and love of glory could be a cure for the ills of government in modern times. Biondo's argument illustrates how the new paideuma of Petrarchan humanism had succeeded in reorienting the Christian world in relation to its classical past, promoting a revaluation of Roman virtue that could inspire the governing elites of Italy and the Church.

Though Biondo was no republican, his *Roma Triumphans* offered plenty of materials that were to prove fruitful topics of reflection in the later republican tradition. One aspect of his work that proved prophetic was his interest in the Romans' use of pagan religion as an instrument of governance. Biondo was fascinated by how the rulers of Rome used religion, and the rites, auguries, and spectacles associated with it, as a tool for what we would today call "social control." In a number of passages he comments on how religion improved the behavior of the Roman plebs by helping to suppress their tendencies to self-indulgence, sedition, and tumults.[50] Numa Pompilius' institution of the *pontifex maximus,* he claims, helped cement Roman religious identity and prevented infection from foreign rites. By the tenor of his discussion, Biondo—perhaps unconsciously—objectifies religion itself as a cultural system and opens the door to comparison between religions in terms of their political usefulness. The influence of religious belief and practice on political health is of course a theme developed by Machiavelli, the French *politiques,* and various Erastian thinkers of the early modern period, and it would be interesting to ascertain to what extent these thinkers found stimulation in Biondo's work.[51]

Biondo also evinces great respect for old Roman traditions regarding the rule of law, particularly its principle that every Roman, no matter how powerful, wealthy, or well-deserving of the state, was subject to its authority. "The true excellence of Rome lies in the fact that no one could be exempted from a trial," he wrote in his discussion of Roman law in book 4.[52] This principle of the rule of law, if we are to believe the modern theorist Francis Fukuyama, was a sine qua non for the emergence of modern political institutions.[53] Biondo saw that principle as a benign result of the struggle of the orders in the early and middle Republic. Following

Cicero, Biondo declared that civil law was the ordering principle, the soul of the body politic, so that the exercise of arbitrary power without legal authority could only be interpreted as destructive to its health.[54]

One benign aspect of the rule of law, according to Biondo, is that it guaranteed an equal freedom, freedom under the laws, to all classes of Roman citizens— senatorial, equestrian, and commoner—so that each was contented in its proper status and protected from abuse by powerful persons. In early modern terms this constitutes a conservative definition of freedom in that it does not endorse popular participation in political decision-making, or to be more precise, it does not make participation a condition of freedom, as Bruni does in his famous orations in praise of Florence. Nevertheless, this conservative, legal, or "negative" understanding of the freedom of the subject or citizen had an important conceptual role to play in the aristocratic republics of early modern Europe such as Venice and the Dutch Republic, as well as in monarchical republics such as England. Biondo's great authority as an expert on Roman civilization surely contributed to the perception in early modern Europe that the rule of law belonged to the essence of the Roman state and was a condition of its successful imperial career.

To sum up: though Biondo is no populist, his understanding of the proper role of the people in a mixed constitution such as that of ancient Rome is akin to the one that was eventually accepted by many early modern republicans. For Biondo, the people have a legitimate role to play in a constitutional state, and even, occasionally—especially in the *provocatio ad populum*—a sovereign role. Individuals of popular origins are often, at least potentially, men of virtue who may deserve to be elevated to high public office. Popular men, like foreigners, supply new rivulets of virtue that can revive the polity's strength and refresh the stagnant waters of corruption to which all human states are subject. The collective power of the popular classes, duly constrained and limited by senatorial wisdom and guidance, good mores and customs, good law and good religion, can even be an important element in bringing about the harmony of purpose among the classes—Cicero's *concordia ordinum*—necessary to imperial success. Biondo was not a republican in the modern sense—and how could he have been?—nor did he endorse a popular republicanism such as that celebrated in Bruni's speeches. He expressed no preference that I can find for either a monarchical or aristocratic republic in lay government. But his *Roma Triumphans* nevertheless presents a positive and highly detailed image of the Roman mixed constitution, corroborated by Roman virtue, that would provide inspiration to republican theorists for centuries to come.

CHAPTER 12

CYRIAC OF ANCONA ON DEMOCRACY AND EMPIRE

A Short History of the Term Democratia

Intellectual history is full of key terms whose meanings have changed dramatically over time: words, for instance, like *respublica,* whose vicissitudes were discussed in Chapter 3 of this work. The history of the word *respublica* shows how radically a Latin word could change in meaning even in an age determined to model its linguistic usages as closely as possible on antiquity. Even more striking are the key terms that have not so much changed in meaning as undergone a complete reversal of their moral polarities. Well-known examples are words like *curiosity, innovation, ambition:* words that once, in premodern times, signified morally dubious phenomena but have come more recently to stand for positive qualities. Such changes in moral valence are often signals of what Kwame Anthony Appiah describes as "moral revolutions"—relatively sudden changes of heart about what constitutes ethical behavior.[1] In our own times, moral revolutions in attitudes to women and gay people have led to those rapid linguistic changes and reversals in the terms of moral approval and disapproval with which everyone is familiar— though the contemporary world has introduced the imprudent practice of trying to coerce such linguistic changes via legal, administrative, and political devices rather than through simple social pressure, as in earlier times.

However that may be, the present chapter aims to contribute to the history of a word that has both changed dramatically in meaning and also reversed its moral polarity: *democracy.* As is well known, the word has undergone a remarkable transformation in moral valence since the end of the eighteenth century.[2] A political constitution that was once widely regarded by the learned as rare, inherently unstable, and ill-advised suddenly, within the decade 1789–1799, acquired a positive significance, first for the Jacobins, and in due course for many radical friends of the French Revolution. Over the course of the following centuries, the word has come to signify a political system now regarded by many as the default setting of the human race, the form of government standing at the end of history, and the only legitimate form of government. What was an inkhorn term in the medieval and early modern periods became a battle cry in two world wars and is today on the lips of reformers in many parts of the world.

To grasp just how radical this change was, we will need to attempt an overview of attitudes to the word "democracy" and the democratic constitution since antiquity.[3] The desirability, practical and moral, of democracy was highly contested from the moment of its emergence in late sixth century BC Athens under the reformer Cleisthenes (who used the term *isonomia*, legal equality, rather than *democratia*). Though democracy had many defenders in Athens from the sixth to the fourth century BC, most famously Pericles in the "Funeral Oration" as related by Thucydides, political power in the hands of non-elite citizens was still widely regarded by many, even in the Greek classical age, as dangerous, destabilizing, and pernicious in its moral effects. It was regarded as such, unsurprisingly, by elites in rival regimes such as oligarchies, kingdoms, and tyrannies. But its most important enemies were the philosophers, especially Xenophon, Plato, Aristotle, and later the historian Polybius.[4] For Plato, democracy was a degenerate constitution, one that brought out the worst aspects of human character.[5] Aristotle regarded it as a bad constitution in its pure form but thought that certain democratic institutions like assemblies could be incorporated into his preferred constitution—what he called "polity"—in order to stabilize it. If oligarchic and democratic features could be balanced in this mixed constitution, the main classes in the state could be satisfied and their interests blended. With the help of good laws and virtuous magistrates—an aristocratic element—human political organization could reach its optimal state and thus maximize the prospects for happiness.[6]

Polybius' ideas were in some respects similar to Aristotle's.[7] Writing in the second century BC, he typologized constitutions following a similar sixfold scheme, agreed that corrupt popular government was bad, and argued that mixed constitutions were superior to their pure types. In his case the mixed constitution included monarchical, oligarchical, and democratic elements, not just oligarchic and democratic ones as in Aristotle's case.[8] This change reflected the revaluation of monarchy as a potentially ideal form of polity in the Hellenistic period.

However, Polybian constitutional theory displayed some crucial innovations that distinguish it from Aristotelian theory. First, Polybius introduced the idea of *anacyclosis,* the notion that there is a natural cycle of constitutional change, or rather degeneration and renewal.[9]

Polybius' Cycle of Constitutional Change

Monarchy (brute, pre-civilized one-man rule)
→ Kingship (improved monarchy, accepted as just by the people)
  → Tyranny (corrupted kingship)
    → Aristocracy (good rule by the few)
      → Oligarchy (corrupted aristocracy)
        → Democracy (good popular rule)
          → Ochlocracy (mob rule, bad popular rule)
            → Monarchy (which begins the cycle all over again)

Polybius believed this pattern was so regular as to have predictive value. Equally crucially, he used the term *democratia* where Aristotle had used *politeia* or *timokratia* for the uncorrupt popular regime.[10]

Polybius' Constitutional Scheme

Monarchia (Primitive Kingship)

	GOOD	CORRUPT
ONE	*basileia*	*tyrannis*
FEW	*aristocratia*	*oligarchia*
MANY	*democratia*	*ochlokratia*

This is the first and only surviving example we have from antiquity of the word *democratia* used in a positive sense by a political philosopher (as opposed to a historian or orator). Polybius specifies that this is "true" democracy, "a community where it is traditional and customary to reverence the gods, to honor our parents, to respect our elders, and to obey the laws, [and where] the will of the greater number prevails."[11] Democrats, he continues, "set a high value on equality and freedom of speech."[12] To distinguish true democracy from bad, he coined the term *ochlocratia,* or mob rule—that is, rule by lawless people who lack control of their appetites and passions and use government power to coerce others and unjustly to take their money. The term *ochlocratia* is used by Polybius himself only twice, both in book 6 of his universal history (6.4.7 and 6.57.9). It remained an extremely rare term. According to the *Thesaurus Linguae Graecae,* a modern electronic lexicon based on the totality of surviving ancient Greek texts and a vast number of Byzantine Greek texts as well, the word can be found only twenty-four times, almost always in obscure late ancient and Byzantine texts.[13]

Polybius was a major influence on Cicero,[14] but despite that, pure democracy never became a regime acceptable to educated Romans, and the word *democratia* itself was never naturalized in Latin the way that many Greek terms, *tyrannis* for example, were. It occurs in only a handful of cases in the Church Fathers, usually as a transliteration of an obscure Greek term, and never in a way that shows understanding of the concept of a democratic constitution.[15] Romans saw their own state or *respublica* as having a popular element, but the term *democratia* was only used to describe aspects of Roman political institutions by Greeks writing in Greek, such as Arrian, Dio Cassius, and Plutarch. All of these authors were hostile to democracy in its pure, direct form. It was regarded by most Hellenistic and later Greeks as a corrupt, failed constitution whose weakness and instability had led to the rapid downfall of Athens as a Greek power. Among the Byzantines, knowledge of the political history of Athens further declined, to the point where the most prominent meaning of the word *democratia* in medieval Greek came to be "a street riot."[16]

Active use of the term was not revived until the thirteenth century, when, following the translation of Aristotle's *Politics* by William of Moerbeke, the word entered the vocabulary of political Aristotelians in the scholastic tradition, beginning with Thomas Aquinas. Aquinas naturally used the term as Aristotle had, as the name of a corrupt or unjust regime conducted by the many, glossing it as *potentatus populi* or *principatus multitudinis*.[17] Aquinas regarded pure democracy as unjust but shared Aristotle's view that a democratic element in a mixed constitution could be a useful stabilizing device.[18]

A partial rehabilitation of the term appeared in Francesco Patrizi's *De regno et regis institutione* (1481 / 1484), a work which became a canonical expression of humanist political theory in the sixteenth century. This work registered a significant shift in the terminology for regimes from the ones Patrizi had used in his earlier work on republican statesmanship, *De institutione reipublicae* (1465 / 1471).[19] The earlier work had used *respublica* for all polyarchic regimes, excluding monarchy and tyranny, and had used the term *isonomia* (written in the Greek alphabet) or *respublica popularis* for the virtuous rule of the people, that is, Aristotle's *politeia* in the specific sense. In his later work Patrizi (1.3) accepted into Latin the transliterated word *politiae* to describe constitutions (also called *civiles administrationes*) in general. The expression *civilis societas* he used for all non-monarchical constitutions (thus providing a humanist equivalent for the scholastic term *regimen politicum*), and ἰσονομία (written in the Greek alphabet) or *popularis societas* to specify a good popular regime. However, Patrizi now felt the need to explain (reflecting, possibly, further study of Herodotus and Thucydides) that the word δημοκρατία was another term for popular rule and was a species of government "approved by philosophers." Implicitly criticizing Aristotle's terminology, he explains that δημοκρατία means rule by the people, not the plebs. The plebs are only a part of the people; the people as a whole includes also "patricians and senators." The rule of the plebs, *plebeium dominatum* or *plebeia gubernatio,* is always bad. Thus Patrizi, like Polybius, put δημοκρατία in the class of good regimes, but he did not endorse the use of the word *democratia* in Latin. To transliterate the word as a technical term was for him unnecessary and a solecism, since a correct Latin equivalent already existed. Someone who wished to write good Latin would thus be better off using *popularis societas* and would avoid the outlandish term *democratia.*

The word *democratia* remained for the most part a learned term down to the end of the eighteenth century, and democracy as a constitution, despite Patrizi, continued to be associated with rule by the common people. For that reason it was generally regarded as impractical and undesirable, except perhaps in certain very small communities in Switzerland and by clandestine followers of Spinoza.[20] The Founding Fathers during the American Revolution referred to themselves as republicans, not democrats, meaning that (after 1775) they rejected monarchy in favor of self-rule.[21] It was only later in the Age of Revolution that the word began to come back into wider use among the literate classes, to describe radical opponents of monarchical prerogative and aristocratic privilege. In America the Democratic-Republican Party came into existence in 1792, founded by James Madison and Thomas Jefferson, whose name announced popular opposition to the policies of Alexander Hamilton, deemed to be crypto-monarchical and aristocratic.[22] Thus a democrat, in late eighteenth-century usage, was an ideological enemy of aristocracy, monarchy, and inherited privilege. "Democracy" also changed in meaning, no longer signifying direct democracy but rather popular sovereignty and representative government. For Robespierre, in a famous speech, democracy had become identical with *la république.*[23] After the 1790s both the word and the thing it now denoted continued to be deeply contested and was not generally accepted in the Western world as a superior, "modern" form of government until the twentieth century. But by this time the term "democracy" meant something quite different from what it had meant for Pericles, Aristotle, or Polybius.[24]

Cyriac of Ancona's Attempted Rehabilitation of the Term Democratia

We are now in a position to appreciate the role played in the history of this word by Cyriac of Ancona (1391–1452).[25] Cyriac, the merchant-scholar now widely regarded as the father of classical archeology, came late (age thirty) to the study of Latin and even later to Greek (age thirty-seven). He never quite mastered either language, which did not prevent him, sometimes to the amusement of more accomplished humanists, from pouring out diaries, letters, speeches, and other compositions in idiosyncratic versions of both languages. Cyriac was a great *amateur* (in the best sense) of the classical world, παλαιόφιλος (a lover of antiquity) as he called himself, a tireless traveller, a civic dignitary in the town of Ancona, a protégé of Pope Eugenius IV, and a man who met and corresponded with many leading political and cultural figures of his time. Yet, though he had a number of followers in the later fifteenth century who carried on his work of collecting classical inscriptions and drawing the ruins of ancient buildings, he remained for the most part outside the mainstream of humanist activity, marginalized by his mercantile pursuits, his lack of a fine educational pedigree and the inelegance of his Latin style.[26]

The relevant point in the current context is that Cyriac was the one securely identifiable humanist of the fifteenth century to my knowledge who used the term *democratia* as a legitimate Latin word, and in a positive sense.[27] He is the one person who regarded democracy as a practical form of government and indeed praised it as the actual form of government enjoyed by his own hometown of Ancona, as well as by Florence and (oddly) the town of Recanati near Ancona.

The source of Cyriac's positive use of the word *democratia,* it seems almost certain, was his knowledge, apparently unique in his time, of book 6 of Polybius. The chief evidence for this is his use of the term *ochlocratia* in a short work written around 1440 called the *Six Constitutions.*[28] As we have already seen, the word was coined by Polybius and remained extremely rare. No later surviving source after Polybius used the term in an exposition of constitutional types, as we find it also used in Cyriac's *Six Constitutions.* It does not exist either in ancient or medieval Latin.[29] One can add that Cyriac's list of constitutions used the same Greek terminology and followed the same precise order as was found in Polybius' discussion of *anacyclosis* or the constitutional cycle.

Polybius' Constitutional Scheme in Book 6 of His History of Rome, with the Transliterations Used by Cyriac of Ancona in His *Six Constitutions* (c. 1440)

Μοναρχία (*Monarchia, Primitive Kingship*)

	GOOD	CORRUPT
ONE	βασιλεία	τυραννίς
	regnum	*tyrannis*
FEW	ἀριστοκρατία	ὀλιγαρχία
	aristocratia	*oligarchia*
MANY	δημοκρατία	ὀχλοκρατία
	democratia	*ochlocratia*

There are other signs as well in Cyriac's writings of a Polybian way of thinking about constitutional change that will emerge in due course.

This is a surprising discovery. In a classic article of 1974, the great émigré scholar Arnaldo Momigliano claimed that book 6 of Polybius was only recovered in the early sixteenth century and first entered the meme-pool of Western thought via Machiavelli's *Discorsi*.[30] Book 6, it should perhaps be explained, constitutes the most important surviving work of Hellenistic political theory and was well known as a key theoretical text during the early modern period, influencing not only Machiavelli but also thinkers like Guicciardini, James Harrington, Montesquieu, and the authors of the American Constitution. Its constitutional theory—its account of the Roman constitution and military organization as well as the explanation it offered for Rome's imperial success—quickly made it into a canonical treatment of the relationship between constitutional order and imperial power, once it finally began to be published and translated around the middle of the sixteenth century.[31]

Momigliano found no evidence that any Western scholar before Machiavelli knew of book 6, and the manuscript and early printed evidence seemed to bear him out. Books 1–5, to be sure, the only part of the text to survive in complete form, were known to have been available in Florence as early as 1419, and Leonardo Bruni produced in 1420 what proved to be an immensely popular adaptation of *Historiae* 1.7–2.34 called *De primo bello punico* (On the First Punic War), intended to fill a major gap in Livy's history.[32] When books 1–5 were first properly translated by Niccolò Perotti in 1454, Perotti stated explicitly in his preface to Nicholas V that to his knowledge only books 1–5 had survived.[33] Other manuscripts that we can connect with quattrocento humanists, men such as Antonio Corbinelli, Francesco Filelfo, and Cardinal Bessarion, also had only the five-book text.[34] Janus Lascaris (1445–1535) translated Polybius 6.3–18, a key passage for the historian's constitutional theory, at an uncertain date, probably around 1500, but the excerpt survives only in two manuscripts.[35]

Cyriac, however, judging by his demonstrable use of Polybius, must have had access more than a half century before Lascaris to one of the rather numerous manuscripts, mostly late, containing all or part of the so-called *excerpta antiqua,* in which long passages of book 6 and of some later books (7–18) were preserved.[36] It must have been his special access to Polybius, his disinterest in scholastic political literature, and his position out of the mainstream of humanist political discourse that led him to commit the linguistic barbarism of treating the transliterated words *democratia* and *democraticus* as Latin words, and even more disgracefully, using those words in a morally positive sense.

For most humanists of the Renaissance, such a usage would surely count as a barbarism in the strict grammatical sense of that word. As we saw in Chapter 3, Leonardo Bruni had attacked the medieval translator of the *Politics* on precisely this point in his treatise *On Correct Translation.*[37] Good taste, as humanists understood it, dictated that a writer make use of equivalents in his or her own language before importing an unfamiliar, odd-sounding foreign word, especially when there was no ancient authority for doing so. We can see what a stylistic faux pas this was if we look at another example of Polybian influence from the fifteenth century known to the present writer (also unknown to Momigliano), namely, the appearance of Polybius' theory of *anacyclosis* in a text from 1490 / 1491: Aurelio Lippo Brandolini's dialogue *Republics and Kingdoms Compared.*[38]

Polybius' Cycle of Constitutional Change (6.2–9) with Aurelio Lippi Brandolini's Latin Equivalents

Monarchy = *unius principatum*
→ Kingship = *rex, regnum*
  → Tyranny = *tyrannis*
    → Aristocracy = *optimatum gubernatio*
      → Oligarchy = *paucorum potestas*
        → Democracy = "*a Graecis* politice, *a nostris respublica*"
          → Ochlocracy = "*a nostris plebeius principatus, a Graecis* democratia"
            → Monarchy

Although Polybius is not named as the source of Brandolini's theory of *anacyclosis* in this passage (which is placed in the mouth of the dialogue's principal interlocutor,

King Mattias Corvinus), it is clear that Polybius must have been the source when we compare Brandolini's cycle with the accounts of constitutional degeneration in Plato and Aristotle.

Constitutional Degeneration in Plato's *Republic,* Book 8 (Unidirectional)

Aristocracy (the best, philosophical constitution, based on wisdom)
→ Timocracy (status based on honor and wealth)
  → Oligarchy (status based on wealth alone)
    → Democracy (equality and license)
      → Tyranny

Constitutional Degeneration in Aristotle's *Ethics* 8.10 and *Politics* 5 (Noncyclical)

Kingdom →	Tyranny	
Aristocracy →	Oligarchy	
Timocracy or polity →	Democracy →	Tyranny

Constitutional Degeneration in Aristotle's *Politics* 3.15.1286b (Noncyclical)

Primitive monarchy
→ Aristocracy
      → Oligarchy
        → Tyranny
          → Democracy

Here one may see that Brandolini, despite adopting Polybius' theory, had the good sense or good taste to use the standard Latin equivalents for Aristotle's constitutional terminology rather than the unfamiliar Polybian terminology, especially its outlandish use of *democratia* as the name for a good constitution.

Cyriac the Caesarian

It would be tempting to conclude that Cyriac was open to using *democratia* in a positive way because he himself had a preference for that kind of constitution. But in fact Cyriac was a democrat only in a very limited and idiosyncratic sense. It is true that another little-known work seems to show him as an enthusiastic democrat, but only after a fashion. This work, called *Anconitana Illyricaque Laus,* was a letter-treatise addressed to an ambassador from Ragusa (Dubrovnik), Marino de'Resti, dated June 18, 1440. It was designed as an introduction to the text of a treaty between Ancona and Ragusa.[39] In it Cyriac praises his native city for its ancient democratic constitution, which has allowed it to flourish with *unica et alma civium democratica libertas,* as a unique and gracious citadel of democratic freedom for refugees from tyranny going back to the Doric Greeks. Thanks to its fostering of liberty it has a political life marked by modesty, honor, tranquillity, peace, unity, concord, security, and piety. This description likely echoes Polybius' description of the citizen virtues present in a "true democracy." Yet Ancona is not a fully sovereign democracy like Athens but enjoys its liberty *sub alma Dei vicarii potestate,* "beneath the gracious power of the Vicar of God," that is, the pope. Here *libertas* comes close to one of its ancient senses: the enjoyment of a specified political privilege.[40] It is Ancona's liberty that makes it a natural sister-city of Ragusa, also distinguished for its liberty. Ragusa, however, enjoys an aristocratic constitution that Cyriac also praises for the great probity, resourcefulness, industry, and virtue of its citizens, as the uniquely honorable and best of the Illyrian polities, flourishing in aristocratic liberty through the dazzling power of its noble and optimate citizens.

Hearing this typically inflated praise one might suppose Cyriac to be a kind of minor Leonardo Bruni, praising his city's regime and its free institutions. In fact Cyriac shows himself (like Biondo Flavio) an opponent of the republican ideology elaborated by Salutati and Bruni in Florence as well as a critic of the republican narrative of Roman history the two Florentine chancellors had worked out decades before.[41] Unlike Bruni, who presents Florence in his political rhetoric as an independent, sovereign state, Cyriac sees his city-states in a more typically medieval way, as subject juridically to the authority of an emperor or a pope. The "democracies" of central Italy—Florence, Ancona, and Recanati—are protected and regulated by the pope. They are all, in a juridical sense, papal states. Monarchy is in principle universal. The supreme example of good monarchical power, defined as just kingship, is the Roman Empire under Caesar and Augustus. Cyriac regards the imperial expansion of Alfonso of Aragon in his own day as sanctioned by the approval of the "best and greatest" pontiff, Eugene IV, "who with great sanctity rules all Christians throughout the globe in the order of divine law."[42]

In general, Cyriac sees universal monarchy, exemplified by Rome, as the best form of government. His considered view is made clear in his longest work of political theory—if that is not too high a name for it—a letter-treatise in praise of Julius Caesar which he addressed to Leonardo Bruni in 1436, a couple of years after his visit to Florence.[43] In this treatise, known as the *Caesarea laus,* Cyriac defends Julius Caesar against the slurs of Poggio Bracciolini, who had compared the great dictator unfavorably with Scipio Africanus. In the *Laus* Cyriac gives us an explicit hierarchy of constitutions. Oligarchy and tyranny are set aside as bad forms of government; ochlocracy is not mentioned. This leaves Polybius' three "good" forms of government, which in ascending order of dignity are democracy, aristocracy, and monarchy. Following the usual argument, which goes back (at least) to Isocrates' *Ad Nicoclem,* monarchy enjoys the most esteem because it most resembles the government of God in heaven. And Roman monarchy was no arbitrary tyranny, dependent on the will of a single man, nor was it, in Cyriac's view, absolute monarchy. Julius Caesar's and Augustus' rule "used to take care to administer provinces and kingdoms throughout the world in accordance with law, senatorial decree or by resolution of the plebs and the tribunician power."[44] In other words, it was a constitutional monarchy, as that term was understood in the Renaissance and early modern period.

So Cyriac, like Polybius, considers democracy a good form of government, to be preserved in city-states with old traditions of democratic freedom. For Cyriac it is good in part because it is an inherently mixed form. It is not mixed in Aristotle's sense, that is, a mixture of institutional features taken from democracy and oligarchy, but is mixed in a somewhat novel sense—it consists of a mixture of a city's populace *(populus)* and other free townsmen *(municipes)*,[45] who on suitable occasions take the counsel of the Areopagites, which introduces an (informal) aristocratic element to the regime.

> Democracy: A mixed regime of the people *(populus)* and free townsmen *(municipes)* in a city-state *(civitas),* such as we learn the Athenians maintained, although they very often helpfully used to employ the excellent counsel of the Areopagites at suitable moments, just like an aristocratic regime. Today among the Italians, Florence in Tuscany, Ancona in Picenum and the colony of Recanati seem to maintain this [type of regime]. These indeed are protected and regulated beneath the fostering pontifical power of the vicar of God.[46]

In any case, in Cyriac's view, democracies had been sanctioned in recent times by the divine, universal authority of the Papacy and were therefore legitimate as a form of government. But they were still, in theory, inferior to aristocracies such as Venice and Dubrovnik and monarchies such as those in Germany, England, France, and the Kingdom of Aragon. We should note that Cyriac's limited defense of democracy is quite different from that found in the scholastic tradition of political Aristotelianism. The scholastics did not place any value on the pure form labelled democratic, but merely approved the inclusion of some democratic institutions and customs as part of a mixed constitution. Democracy for them was synonymous with mob rule. Cyriac sees a legitimate place for true democracy, with its commitments to equality and free speech, in the overall scheme of things, but equality and free speech are local privileges, justified by the customs and the virtue of local populations, rather than universal entitlements or natural rights. In this sense his position is rather similar to that of the scholastic republican Tolomeo Fiadoni (better known as Ptolemy of Lucca) in the early fourteenth century.[47]

Cyriac's preference for monarchy is in part influenced by the traditions of Christian historiography, which since the time of Eusebius had seen the *pax romana* instituted by Augustus as part of a divine plan to open the *oikumene,* the inhabited world, to Christian conversion. Caesar's monarchy was so pleasing to God, says Cyriac, that in the time of Caesar's son Augustus he sent his own son, Jesus, to mingle with the human race; and "just as though he held joint command with Caesar over heaven and earth, [Jesus] agreed in a sacred pronouncement that what is Caesar's should be given to Caesar, and what is God's, to God."[48] Here we have a position on the relationship between divine and human government very similar to that of Eusebius in his *Oration in Praise of Constantine.*

Yet Cyriac could be a critic of the first Christian emperor as well. We see this in the most historically and politically sophisticated part of the *Caesarea laus,* where Cyriac takes on Bruni's famous argument, stated in book 1 of his *History of the Florentine People,* that Roman power and culture declined after the fall of the republic, under the emperors and, moreover, directly as a result of their tyrannical rule.[49] For Bruni, republican government led to empire and cultural flourishing, while monarchy always threatened to decline into tyranny. Cyriac in response admits that the growth of the Roman empire was greatest under the consuls—in the period that we moderns anachronistically call "the Roman Republic"—and poses the question why that was the case if monarchy was the best form of government. The problem of the relationship between empire and constitutional form, we should notice, is the central problem raised by Polybius. Cyriac gives in effect *two* answers, a human and a divine one, which are not fully compatible. The divine or theological answer was that the fall of Rome was not the fault of constitutions, but of the Fates. The divine powers actively *willed* the fall of Rome, because if there should be any government that could last in perpetuity, there would then be no difference between the gods and men. The Emperor Constantine made things worse by transferring the capital from Rome to Constantinople, an action humanists generally deplored,[50] but the fundamental reason why Rome fell was that all human things are subject to decay. We are not gods, but men. We die, and our governments die too. The body politic is mortal.[51]

The second reason Cyriac gives for why Rome eventually collapsed under the emperors is much more Polybian in tone. Cyriac, in common with the tradition of Christian historiography, argues that Rome was suffering a terrible crisis during the civil wars of the late republic and in fact would have collapsed much more quickly under the rule of the consuls if Caesar had not overturned it and established a monarchy instead.[52] In other words, under the consuls in the late empire the natural cycle of constitutions had come to an end in civil war. Caesar's greatness was to begin the cycle anew, *da capo* as it were, with the best form of government, monarchy. Caesar himself was the proof that this was what had happened. Caesar displayed remarkable virtue, divine intelligence, foresight, military skill, and "inexpressible eloquence and mastery of the Latin language" in his literary works. Above all, there was his divine clemency, the royal virtue most needed to compose the quarrels of the age. If he had not been murdered by ambitious and envious fellow citizens, he would have adorned the city, enlarged the empire, subdued the Parthians, reformed the laws, built libraries, and patronized literature. His adopted son Augustus later brought all these projects to fulfillment.[53]

In other words, though Cyriac does not say this explicitly, Caesar was exactly the kind of man Rome needed to renew her constitution and begin her political life-cycle anew. Together with his son Augustus, Caesar embodied a rule that was therefore the best model for the revival of Italian greatness that Cyriac, like all Italian humanists of the Renaissance, longed to bring into being. In praising democracy, Cyriac may have been a voice crying in the wilderness, but when it came to the idea of the Renaissance, he was singing in chorus with the angels.

CHAPTER 13

LEON BATTISTA ALBERTI ON CORRUPT PRINCES AND VIRTUOUS OLIGARCHS

Leon Battista Alberti is among the most celebrated figures of the Italian Renaissance, taken by Jacob Burckhardt as the model for the "Renaissance man" in his *Civilization of the Renaissance in Italy*.[1] Nevertheless, like Petrarch and Boccaccio, he has not been much studied by historians of political thought. In part this is because such historians in recent times have had a rather narrow and anachronistic conception of what counts as political thought; and in part, one suspects, there exists among the academic brethren a certain lack of sympathy for Alberti's conservative political bent, described by Hans Baron as "reactionary." Then too there has been for a long time a well-founded understanding among Alberti scholars that he had a disgust for politics in general, which has no doubt inhibited examination of his political ideas. (Although contempt for politicians and their courtiers is by no means incompatible with serious thinking about politics, just as involvement in politics does not necessarily make one's political ideas worthy of attention.) To make matters worse, Alberti's views on politics are scattered unhelpfully through many works in Latin and Italian, often in the form of bizarre or cryptic narratives whose message can be elusive. Hence his works have been largely overlooked in general histories of political thought, especially in the Anglophone world, and it is fair to say that modern scholarship has provided no sustained, comprehensive analysis of his political thought.[2]

A short chapter such as this cannot fully supply this want. It will instead discuss just two texts in the enormous and varied corpus of Alberti's writings: his long Latin novel in four books, the *Momus*, a satire on court politics inspired by Lucian; and a late vernacular work, the dialogue *De iciarchia*, which espouses a political position that in some ways is unique among Renaissance humanists of the quattrocento. They might be seen as conceptually related, as diagnosis is related to cure. I will also look briefly at a short passage in Alberti's most famous work, his treatise *On Architecture,* which will help bridge the gap of almost three decades that separates the *Momus* from the *De iciarchia.* I shall argue that, though Alberti's mature position on the best form of government is an unusual one, it is perfectly possible to situate it within the broader stream of humanist virtue politics.

Why Virtue Is Incompatible with Court Life

The *Momus* is not a straightforward political treatise but a satire in the form of a long prose novel involving a large cast of historical and mythological figures.[3] Alberti clearly intends the work as some kind of humorous allegory, though whether one should go further and attempt to read it as a *roman à clef* is no easy question. He tells us in the preface and repeatedly throughout the work that his goal is to combine humor with moral instruction, *iocari serio*—a Lucianic strategy that was to became popular among humanists of the High Renaissance. The work presents notorious difficulties of interpretation, not least to the modern historian of thought who would like to extract political doctrines from it. The most serious of these difficulties is how one should read the statements of Momus himself, a morally repellent figure who nevertheless at times enunciates views that seem to align with those Alberti expresses elsewhere *in propria persona.* Also there is the question of Momus' "notebooks" or *tabellae* in which he digested for the use of Jupiter the political advice of the leading ancient philosophers. A summary of the contents of these *tabellae* is offered at the end of book 4, and here too we seem to encounter political teachings that can be paralleled in other works of Alberti. But why express your own moral teachings using the pen, as it were, of a thoroughly disreputable character such as Momus?

The interpretive problems presented by the text cannot here be treated in detail, but the view of Davide Canfora, that the *Momus* needs to be read in the context of the curial literature of the 1430s and 1440s, is persuasive. Canfora shows that the *Momus* must be placed alongside works such as Lapo da Castiglionchio's *De curiae commodis,* Flavio Biondo's account of Eugene IV's papacy in his *Histories,* and above all the *De infelicitate principum* of Poggio Bracciolini, of whose many parallels and common sources with the *Momus* Canfora offers a detailed inventory.[4]

This curial literature pays a great deal of attention to two issues in particular. Both involve the relationship of humanistic learning to political power. One is whether life as a prince or an advisor of princes is compatible with virtue and therefore happiness, or whether court life is necessarily destructive of moral character. The second issue revolves around what later comes to be known as "the problem of counsel," famously debated in the first book of More's *Utopia* and Castiglione's *Courtier.* If a prince lacks education and good judgment, how can a virtuous humanist advisor get him to accept good advice and keep him from being led by vicious and self-interested persons in his entourage who will play on his worst instincts? Both of these problems are standard issues in the theory of political meritocracy.

Canfora goes further and suggests that the Jupiter of the *Momus,* the well-meaning but lazy, ignorant, and impulsive ruler of heaven, should be identified with Pope Eugenius IV. By extension Alberti's Olympus should then be read as an allegory of the papal court. This too is an attractive suggestion, though one should be careful not to read the text as though it were addressed only to a particular milieu. Like most Renaissance humanists Alberti aimed at literary glory beyond the grave, and the work's message is surely meant to be of universal application. But the satire does seem to fit the immediate situation in which he found himself as a papal official and a holder of multiple benefices bestowed upon him by the same Pope Eugene.[5]

Nowadays most historians regard the pontificate of Eugenius IV as (on balance) a success, mostly because the pope managed, at the Council of Ferrara-Florence (1438–1443), to orchestrate a union with the Greek Church and other separated Christians; hence Eugenius has become for moderns "the pope of Christian union" as the historian Joseph Gill called him.[6] It is hard to keep in mind that for most of his reign he was regarded by many contemporary observers as a political naïf who ruined the papacy by alienating the Council of Basel, the Colonna family, and the Roman people, a weak ruler who allowed the papal state to fall prey to condottieri and who foolishly filled the curia with corrupt and evil men. The most scandalous of these was Giovanni Vitelleschi, a military prelate noted for his cruelty and greed, whom Eugenius made patriarch of Aquileia and then archbishop of Florence. Eugenius' own humiliating flight from Rome in 1434 disguised as a monk, pelted by the citizens with stones while being rowed down the Tiber, did not leave a high impression of his competence.[7]

Despite all this, in his *De infelicate principum* Poggio, who had spent thirty-four years in the papal curia, refuses to allow criticism of the pope on the grounds that to do so would be wicked *(iniquum).* In one of his few personal interventions in the dialogue, Poggio steps in to silence Niccoli, the main speaker, who had been about to launch into a critique of Eugenius, saying, "Let's let the pontiffs go, among whom there are more figures who have been found to be happy and acceptable to God than among other powers" (high praise indeed: they are better than your average prince!) "and turn our discussion to other princes who can be examined more respectably and freely."[8] So it is tempting to read the *Momus* as a work that dares, albeit in veiled form, to say what Poggio would not say about Eugenius' turbulent papacy. It would explain why Alberti chose the form of an allegorical novel whose anti-hero tries to subvert Jove and destroy the worship of the gods. Using this literary disguise Alberti can say all the things about the popes and their courtiers that Poggio could not allow himself to say in the *De infelicitate principum*. The disguise also allows Alberti himself to escape the charge of ingratitude, since, after all, he owed his decree of legitimation and several benefices to Eugenius' favor. At the same time Alberti provides a hilarious, mocking response to Lapo da Castiglionchio's sycophantic *De curiae commodis* of 1437. In this work, Lapo, an impoverished, would-be curial official, appears to praise the papal court as the capital of the holy Christian religion and also a paradise of pleasures, a fountain of wealth, and an academy welcoming scholars and men of learning—Alberti himself is given as an example—who cultivate literature, philosophy, and the arts.[9] This, needless to say, is not Alberti's view of the curia.[10]

The *De infelicitate principum*, as we saw in Chapter 4, sets out Niccolò Niccoli's extreme thesis that the pursuit and exercise of political power is always incompatible with virtue and the study of literature, and for this reason *principes* can never be happy. The dialogue allows Niccoli's pessimistic view of princes to triumph over the more measured assessments of Cosimo de'Medici and Carlo Marsuppini. Alberti's *Momus* makes a similar case for the moral dysfunction of courts, but Alberti's strategy is to show dramatically, rather than by argument, what happens when a ruler tries to please the people closest to him while lacking the knowledge and virtues that would enable him to rule well and happily. The *Momus* thus replaces argument with narration, a strategy that allows Alberti to show the consequences of ignorance, weakness, and vice in princes in real time, as it were.[11]

One strategy for extracting the political teachings of the *Momus* from their comic disguise might be to see the work as consisting of two interlocking narratives: one about Jupiter and a second one about the eponymous Momus; the prince and the courtier. Jupiter is a figure of enormous power who wants to be popular with the gods and loved by mankind, but he fails miserably because of his ignorance, imprudence, laziness, and self-indulgence—the vices Alberti most despises. He has no conception of justice and abuses his power arbitrarily. His rule is a tyranny, but a welcome tyranny to those of the gods who benefit from it. He makes the life of men wretched solely in order to allow the gods of his court to enjoy a greater sense of superiority. He rewards the bad and punishes the good. He realizes that Momus is seditious only thanks to informers, and the clumsy way he punishes Momus turns him into a formidable enemy. A poor judge of character, Jupiter is then fooled into taking Momus back into heaven, where the bloody-minded god works tirelessly to undermine him and Olympus itself. Momus does this principally by encouraging a foolish whim of Jupiter's: his absurd, utopian project of recreating the universe along new lines. Jupiter doesn't know what changes he would like to make, but he knows he wants to do something really big, new, and attention getting. But recreating the universe is a task so overwhelming that even Jupiter realizes he needs to take advice. He has heard that human philosophers might have the wisdom to guide such a project. He refuses to deify the philosophers—that is, admit them to his court—for fear that, once they enter heaven, they will insist on reforming his behavior and oppose his plan of radical change. So he schemes to tap their wisdom at a distance. All his schemes fail because the divine emissaries he sends to consult them lack the education in the *bonae artes* that would enable them to grasp philosophical teachings or discern the true ones from the false. *Nihil homini dignum nossent:* they lacked humane knowledge (3.10). Jupiter nevertheless calls a council to announce his plan for a new creation, but he is unable to come up with a serious plan in time for the meeting; furthermore, he mismanages the council by putting the worst possible person in charge, namely, Momus. Momus loses the support of the divine council, especially its female members, who know he has abused his divine power to get away with rape. He is expelled a second time from heaven, castrated, given a forced sex change, and finally punished by being chained to a rock like Prometheus. But this does not end Jupiter's travails.

In the fourth book the gods, led by Jupiter, are tempted by vanity to attend the mortals' religious festival, pretending to be statues in niches so they can watch the show. A high wind comes up, and the gods are exposed to the humans and humiliated. Alberti here steps outside the frame of the story to tell us, in his authorial persona, that he has breached decorum in presenting the gods in this undignified way but that he wants his readers to realize that "princes who are devoted to pleasure commit far more disgraceful acts than any we've recounted." We may note here that the gods are explicitly identified as *principes*. Alberti goes on to claim that in his previous writings he has always been careful not to violate decorum, "lest we hazard anything less grave and holy than religious or literary scruples would allow." These two statements taken together constitute a strong hint that the foregoing narrative has been a critique of ecclesiastical princes for their lack of learning, virtue, and piety. Their thirst for pleasure and popularity discredits them. It is only at the very end of the work that Jupiter finally, almost by accident, thinks to consult the humanist digest of political wisdom assembled for him by Momus. But by then it is too late.

The story of Jupiter thus illustrates the consequences of putting enormous, arbitrary power in the hands of a person without virtue or a proper education in the humanities.[12] The story of Momus, by contrast, shows just how much damage can be done by the presence of an unworthy and immoral person in the divine court. Momus in effect is the antitype of Castiglione's courtier, using all his knowledge and cunning to undermine the ruler and his regime: he is *cupidissimus rerum novarum,* a flaming revolutionary.[13] The combination of a feckless, lazy, ignorant prince and a bloody-minded, scheming, and subversive courtier proves to be disastrous, whether the courtier is banished from the court or raised to a position of honor in it. In exile, cast down into the human world, Momus takes his revenge on Olympus by perverting true piety. True piety is understood here in the traditional Roman way as a mean between irreligion and superstition, a deficit and an excess of piety.[14] First Momus tries to weaken piety by spreading tales about the gods' immorality as well as philosophical arguments questioning the gods' existence. Then he tries to undermine heaven by making mankind, and especially women, excessively pious, so superstitious that they overwhelm the gods with requests for trivial favors, like cosmetic changes to their appearance or "the return of a lost needle or spindle."

The gods, however, are too besotted with themselves to distinguish (at first) the humans' shower of votive objects raining down upon Olympus from true devotion, and Momus is received back into heaven in gratitude for the false benefit he has conferred on the gods. This time he decides to cement his position as principal advisor to Jove by schooling himself in the arts of hypocrisy. He learns how to appear virtuous, loyal, and public spirited, all the while secretly plotting to destroy heaven. Among his schemes to ruin heaven is a speech he gives at a banquet that aims to blacken the reputation of the *bonae artes* or humanities—the very studies that constitute the only hope Jupiter and the other gods have to improve themselves in the arts of government. To make the humans and their humanistic culture unpopular among the gods, Momus reports a long speech by an ambitious human orator (2.80–90). This false rhetorician is said to have attacked Jove for being a bad father to the human race and a bad patron of the gods as well. He makes humans hate the gods, which undermines the gods' divine status, since that status rests on human worship. The ambitious orator is then represented as having attacked the gods in general: they are supposed to be our fathers, but they take all the good things of earth for themselves and leave us humans more miserable than the beasts. They are unjust in that they reward the bad and punish the good. In fact, far from being our fathers, says the orator, the gods loathe the human race; they are poor administrators of human things and set a bad example for mankind owing to their moral license. In short, "either the gods do not exist at all, or if they exist, they are always hostile to wretched mortals, actively seeking to do them harm."

Alberti is extremely clever in this long passage of book 2. Momus is shown angering the gods by telling them the truth about themselves through the mouth of an orator who belongs to *illam omnem sceleratissimam familiam literatorum* (that most wicked of clans, literary men), also identified as *philosophi*. Momus is able to cast himself as the courageous defender of the gods against impious humanists, which furthers his own project of self-aggrandizement. Alberti as author is able to discredit such attacks by putting them in the mouth of the scheming Momus, while at the same time illustrating how the gods are unable or unwilling to see the truth about themselves. To underline his point, Alberti has Hercules, who had once been a human himself, rise to defend the human race and their wise men. In Hercules' words of praise for humanistic studies we hear again the genuine opinions of Alberti. Despite a few erroneous and absurd beliefs, says Hercules, the philosophers and literati have always investigated the true and the good; it is through the works of the philosophers that the human race has come to know itself and its fate; human rational faculties are a gift from the gods and come ultimately from the divine mind; *viri docti* educated in schools and libraries have worked so that mankind will understand and confess these facts. They have argued for the fair, the fitting, and the dutiful, and they have done this not to seek popular applause but to improve the human race. They promote *pietas, sanctimonia, virtus*. Their work is too laborious to be motivated only by a desire for glory. It is they who have done the most to support the gods among humanity. For humans, they open a pathway to the divine through reason, supported by virtue. As students of old books they have done everything they can to supply human needs and enable them to live well and blessedly, in ease and tranquillity, to provide "whatever conduces to the security, embellishment and honor of public and private affairs, whatever supports piety and observance of religion." We gods should therefore support the *viri docti,* the *studiosorum familia,* the *philosophi.*

This seems like a ringing endorsement of the humanities, even a call for patronage of the *bonae artes.* But again Alberti's fictional frame raises a question mark. Elsewhere in the novel Hercules is characterized as an insufferable braggart, a *miles gloriosus* who has fought his way into heaven under false pretenses: *assentando, blandiendo et sese iactando*—toadying, flattering, and boasting of his own accomplishments. This would tend to discredit his words for both the divine audience in the novel and Alberti's readers. As all students of rhetoric knew, the *ethos* or moral standing of the speaker affects the persuasiveness of his case. Presumably, Alberti wanted his humanistically trained readers to experience regret that the case for the humanities in the heavenly court cannot be made by a more impressive figure, and to reflect on the importance of good character to the defense of good causes.

Who Should Constitute the Political Elite?

Let me now summarize the main points of congruity between Alberti and the humanist tradition of virtue politics; I shall then try to highlight the distinctive ways in which Alberti inflects that tradition. Like all humanists before Machiavelli, Alberti accepts that there can be no just rule in human societies without virtuous rulers.[15] He shares the humanist prejudice that legal or constitutional bases for legitimacy are inadequate or irrelevant. He prefers to make legitimacy depend on virtuous government—what in Chapter 2 was described as moral legitimacy. Laws, lawyers, policing, and the paper walls of political institutions on their own are not enough to build a successful society. Contemporary jurisprudence, Alberti agrees, is driven by greed and lacks wisdom and learning. Lawyers are unable to advise princes well or imbue them with prudence and other virtues they need. Judges need to be philosophers to judge well: they should be guided by natural law, reason, and piety rather than mere textualism; they should avoid cruelty while promoting virtue and peace among men.[16]

Virtue in *principes* is charismatic and makes them loved rather than feared; virtue makes their rule willingly accepted, without need for dishonorable manipulation or coercion. Men spontaneously obey commands only when they are just and right. Like Petrarch, Alberti sees tyranny as the vicious exercise of power, which can be as easily exemplified in the actions of a formally legitimate king as in the acts of a condottiere who has seized power in a coup.[17] Societies need to be organic, ruled in such a way that the good of all, and not just the good of parties or favored elites, is considered. The interests of the weaker should never be subordinated to those of the stronger.[18] True nobility, the only real source of preeminence over others, comes from virtue, not heredity (or not just heredity), and in a good state the right to rule will not be seen merely as a patrimonial inheritance but as something to be earned by successful governance. Even those of lower social station (or those of illegitimate birth, like Alberti himself) have the capacity for virtue and hence for rule. The principal means through which virtue may be acquired is the study of the humanities. The study of literature, philosophy, and history makes men wiser and more virtuous, and thus more competent to rule.[19] Virtue can be spread through education, eloquence, morally improving literature (like the *Momus*), and the arts. It may be solidified by good laws and political institutions that promote virtue and wisdom, but these are secondary supports. What counts above all is what lies in the heart of a good *princeps.*

Alberti accepts all these premises, derived ultimately from the aristocratic cultural values of the ancients and common to nearly all Italian humanists before Machiavelli. But even though he agrees that virtue and humanity can be cures for corrupt polities, his pessimism about the possibility of exercising political power well inflects his virtue politics in a distinctive direction, as will be seen in the discussion below of *De iciarchia.* It leads him to look elsewhere than in the courts of princes for the sources of political renewal. It is worth taking a brief look, then, at another passage in Alberti's works that has been overlooked by historians of political theory, lurking unnoticed in his vast treatise on architecture and town planning, *De re aedificatoria.* Though it is only a few paragraphs long, Alberti presents in this passage a more hopeful view than elsewhere of what a well-ordered state with a virtuous political class might look like.

The twelve books *On Architecture* were by far Albert's most famous and influential work. They were written around 1452, more than decade after the *Momus* and a least a decade before the *De iciarchia.* In the first chapter of book 4, Alberti begins by explaining that in order to decide on the types of building that need to be constructed in a city, one needs to understand how nature divides men into classes, for each class of men requires its own building type. To find this out, he passes in review the opinions of ancient political philosophers about the main classes of citizens in a city; these are specified primarily according to their social function. The review ends with a brief account of the views of Aristotle and Plato, who recognized the need for a state to be led by the counsels of men distinguished for their high worth and rationality.

Alberti then offers his own view. If men are to be ruled by the best element in the political community, one needs to identify by strict observation of nature what that element is. This is accomplished by identifying the features of humanity that most distinguish it from the brutes. Those features, according to Alberti, are reason and the command of intellectual and material resources, namely, the *optimae artes*, the liberal arts, and an abundance of the goods of fortune. Men who best exemplify these faculties are human in the fullest sense and therefore constitute the natural elite whom others in society should obey. The passage presupposes the exposition in book 3 of Alberti's early treatise *Della famiglia* (On the family), where he links the acquisition of wealth with the bourgeois virtues and defends the idea that wealth can be used nobly if placed in the service of the city.[20] It is noteworthy that Alberti implicitly rejects the nearly universal view of ancient philosophers that the wealthy should not be allowed to influence political decision-making. The key passage is given here:[21]

> Now there is nothing by which men differ more from each other than by this one thing whereby they stand furthest from beasts: reason and understanding of the best arts [*optimae artes*, i.e., the humanities]—to which, if you wish, you may add prosperity and good fortune. There are few among mankind that stand out and excel in all these gifts at the same time. This then will open up to us our first division, so that we may select from the multitude as a whole a few whereof some are illustrious for their wisdom, good counsel, and intelligence; others tried and tested in practical affairs; and others who are renowned for their riches and abounding in the goods of fortune. Who will deny that these are the ones whom we must entrust with the principal roles in the commonwealth *(respublica)*?
>
> Thus the most excellent men, those most weighty in counsel, ought to be entrusted with the chief care and guidance of all affairs. These will order divine affairs with piety; frame laws with a due measure of justice and equity; and they will show the way to live a good and blessed life. They will keep close watch in order to protect and enlarge the authority and prestige of their fellow citizens. And when they have determined upon any convenient, useful or necessary actions—being perhaps themselves worn out with years and preferring

to devote themselves to contemplation rather than action—they will commit the execution of their plans to those with experience of affairs who are prepared to act with a view to deserving well of their country [i.e., competent, honor-seeking men with public spirit]. These others, having taken the business upon themselves, will faithfully perform their parts at home with skill and application and abroad with toil and endurance, giving judgment at law, leading armies, and exercising their own industry and that of those who are under them.

And lastly, since they know it is vain to try to bring anything to fulfillment without means, the next in place [to the two types of men already mentioned] will be men who back the former with the resources they have acquired from agriculture or mercantile activity. All the other orders of men ought to obey and be subject to these leading men as utility demands.[22]

In this passage we see that Alberti has chosen to blur the Aristotelian distinction between the "bad" constitution, oligarchy, in which the wealthy few rule in their own interest, and the "good" constitution of aristocracy, in which the virtuous and wise few rule in the interest of all. For Alberti, men of wealth have a key role to play in a state, supporting with their resources the intellectual elite and the men of practical experience. Alberti's indifference to traditional constitutional forms—his realism if one prefers—no doubt reflects his experience as an architect. Someone who had dealt with the practical difficulties of building important structures in cities as different and as differently ruled as Florence, Rimini, and Mantua will surely have realized the value of working with an educated elite possessing humane wisdom and practical experience, supported by enlightened men of abundant wealth.

The De Iciarchia *and the Regime of Virtuous "House-Princes"*

Alberti's distinctive version of humanist virtue politics is most fully disclosed in a late work, the *De iciarchia* (c. 1470), which elaborates further upon the political attitudes sketched out in the *De re aedificatoria* and in other works. The *De iciarchia* is a dialogue set in Florence and in present time. Despite its Latin title the work was written in Italian, and its tone and its survival in a single manuscript suggest that it was composed as an advice manual for a private readership, probably members of the extended Alberti clan and their affines.[23] Thanks to Luca Boschetto's well-documented study we may understand the work as an implicit critique of the Medici regime reflecting the political experience of the late 1460s, in the aftermath of an unsuccessful challenge to Medici dominance by rival oligarchs.[24] In form the work is a magisterial dialogue—that is, one in which a principal character, here Alberti himself, dispenses wisdom, prompted by questioning from disciples, or in this case from younger and less prominent members of the family. As in the case of the *Della famiglia* (1433 / 1434), the author's perspective is that of a man whose family had spent several generations in political exile. For that reason family members had learned to rely on each other and on personal ties of affection and mutual interest as well as their own personal virtue, gravitas, and enlightened cunning.[25] Their primary loyalty was to their clan, and they looked to it to secure their status and well-being rather than to political power in the *comune*. What is interesting about the *De iciarchia* is that Alberti is able to transform his commitment to the family into a kind of political theory of oligarchy.[26] Since the term "oligarchy" had a negative moral charge in the Aristotelian political terminology of the day, he invents the term *iciarchia,* combining the Greek words *oikos* (household) and *archia* (government) to designate the kind of rule exercised by the heads of families over their clans or *case*.[27] Such men, Alberti argues, were the best source of the virtue and wisdom needed to rule the republic, the moral opposites of the sort of men who were presently seeking advancement by controlling the comune in their own interest and in that of the Medici party.

For Alberti, political participation in the Florentine state was foreclosed by the nature of Medici ascendency, the informal regime that had controlled the Florentine government from behind the scenes since 1434.[28] Medici rule demanded servile behavior that Alberti thought unworthy of any man who aspired to moral excellence. It constituted a special case of his habitual pessimism about the possibility that virtue and therefore good governance could survive in courts, whether the curia of the popes or the informal court of the Medici. The ambitious competition for status and power in such environments inevitably corrupted character and led to tyranny and the desire for illicit dominance over others, often by bribery, force, or fraud. When princes or sovereign peoples were ignorant and vicious, virtue could be of no effect in politics, and the virtuous man had best keep himself out of government.[29] This was a familiar dilemma of Renaissance politics and had been theorized by Petrarch more than a century before in his *De vita solitaria,* a text Alberti seems to have read.[30] Alberti's view is similar to Petrarch's, but his recalibration of loyalties led him to make the family, not the cosmopolis or the Heavenly Jerusalem, the alternative focus of his duty and benevolent impulses. When the state is corrupt the best thing a virtuous man can do is to serve the narrower common good of the family, which means enabling the family to live in dignity and honor and helping its members to achieve moral excellence.[31]

Alberti supports his negative assessment of courts and other centers of political power by a theory of the passions, whereby those who seek excessive power over others "in almost every case" are corrupted by it. To seek power over equals only inflames passion on all sides and destroys the tranquillity that is the mark of true virtue:

> My sons, I tell you, power that exceeds the mean in anything whatsoever brings reckless license with it, causes desires to overflow beyond measure, and stimulates violent impulses in our actions. Since you can do what you want, you accordingly want everything in your power; you become rash and used to wanting more than is licit or appropriate. Thus it appears to me that uncontrolled desires are nearly always linked to unchecked license, and hence unexamined thoughts make our minds rash, impetuous, insolent and audacious.[32]

Yet Alberti would not accept Lord Acton's famous dictum that "all power corrupts, and absolute power corrupts absolutely." Alberti thinks that power over others, so long as it is contained within due order and measure, can not only be exercised in morally acceptable ways but can even nourish in a powerful person a sense of responsibility and thus a desire for virtue and honor. It is an aspect of Alberti's sovereign doctrine of moderation in all things that persons in a middle station in the republic, the "house-princes" or iciarchs, midway between would-be tyrants and the *moltitudine,* are best situated to acquire excellence of character.[33] The family or clan is the optimal site for the cultivation and practice of virtue; keeping one's ambition to authority over others within the bounds of the family is the best recipe for a life of happy tranquillity. Indeed, the intimacy of the family association and the bonds of affection that hold it together are natural sources of virtue. A man who loves his wife and children will naturally seek the best for them in a way that someone exercising political power over relative strangers will not.[34] Alberti was, to be sure, the last man to be naïve about family affections; he knew from bitter personal experience that families can be destroyed by factions and avarice just as city-states can. Nevertheless families are bound together with tighter hoops of love and mutual interest than any republic can ever hope to be, and this gives an iciarch a stronger motive to act for the common good of the family than any political actor can have to serve the public good. Thus the type of power a patriarch exercises over his family—with its households, properties, servants, and clients—provided he is of good character and follows Alberti's wise precepts, will be truly paternal, organic, and welcome to those placed under them.

To exercise power well the iciarch needs to understand which forms of rule are tolerable and which are not. As an aid to discernment Alberti elaborates a theory of natural and tyrannical rule, a theory that differs markedly from the justification of political hierarchy famously presented by Aristotle in book 1 of the *Politics*.[35] There Aristotle sets out three kinds of natural authority: that of parent over child, of husband over wife, and of master over slave. These three kinds of authority are subsequently taken to possess a natural isomorphism with the types of political authority exercised by the dominant element in kingdoms, polities, and despotisms, respectively. Alberti, by contrast, begins with a principle of human psychology: that all men naturally desire "to be inferior to no one" and would enjoy a mode of life that would let them be superior to everyone.[36] That is why, whenever they have the opportunity, they tend to reduce others to subjection so that they can usurp for themselves all the fruits of superiority. There are, however, tolerable as well as intolerable forms of subjection. Subjection to the laws is tolerable for the sake of living an honorable life *(onestà)*, subjection to the principle of equity is tolerable for the sake of reward *(premio)*, and subjection to love is tolerable because of the enticement of pleasure *(voluttà)*. In other words you will willingly obey a magistrate enforcing the law, an employer dictating actions in return for reward, or a beloved relative whom you want to please. Apart from the rational purpose of living a respectable life, the desire for just compensation, and the promise of gratification in love, all other kinds of obedience are "intolerable misery" and will be experienced as violent and tyrannical domination. Thus ambitious persons who aim to aggrandize themselves are mistaken and don't understand the real nature of civic preeminence: "I have said and I say again: the basis of a true preëminence is not in the servile obedience of someone who either through timidity or feebleness suffers the empty and tedious pretentiousness of insolent people."[37] Dancing attendance on tyrants does not make you worthy of respect. Virtuous iciarchs can enjoy true preeminence *(principato)*, but the creatures of tyrants cannot. And the tyrants themselves, those who try to exercise dominance in intolerable ways, can never do so without at least the threat of violence.

In effect, Alberti is arguing that the basis of good, noncoercive, natural hierarchy in society is not modelled on status relations such as parent or child, husband or wife, master or slave, as numerous scholastic Aristotelians maintained, but is rooted in the natural impulses of the will. Rule cannot be exercised over others without tyrannical injustice unless that rule is accepted by subordinates as lawful, profitable, or pleasurable. It will be noticed that Alberti's psychology-based theory of subordination, likely inspired by a passage of Aristotle's *Ethics,* is compatible with theories of natural equality and consent in a way that Aristotle's theory of subordination by status in the *Politics* is not.[38] Though Alberti follows the traditional view that virtue is empirically rare, he also embraces the humanist view that virtue is easy and open to all who understand what it is and care to acquire it, to subordinates as well as to house-princes, and indeed to anyone who seeks true preeminence.[39] True preeminence, real *principato,* is to be found in the realm of the spirit and not necessarily, or even primarily, in the exercise of formal political power.

Nevertheless, iciarchs, having natural opportunities to rule with virtue, will also make the best citizens and magistrates in the wider republic.[40] They are accustomed to use persuasion and loving authority rather than force, and they are better able to cooperate with other houses on a basis of friendship and goodwill. Alberti thus sees the noble household that does not try to exceed its proper bounds as the true site of virtuous power in the state, not the princely court (as Bartolomeo Platina held) or the councils of popular governments (as Leonardo Bruni argued). Under modern corrupt conditions, the leadership of virtuous iciarchs in the great *case* may be the only path to reform of the state.[41] And the virtuous iciarch, by moderating his desire for power, can win happiness and tranquillity for himself and his family, such being ever the reward of virtue in the classical tradition. As the story of Megalophos and Peniplusius in the *Momus* illustrates (4.92), a minor magistrate of small means has a better chance of virtue and genuine happiness than the "Big Man," the king or party boss who seems to the multitude to have everything.

Alberti understands that to refocus a young man's ambitions on the family rather than on politics will require transforming the vulgar understanding of what constitutes a successful life. This is the burden especially of book 1 of *De iciarchia,* where he tries to convince the young men of the Alberti family, eager for fame and glory, that true *principato* is not achieved by seeking political power and its rewards.[42] He admits that there is a natural desire for superiority over others in a noble heart, but he holds that reason, nature, and experience teach us that this desire should not be directed outwardly, toward the acquisition of wealth, status, political leadership, or popular acclaim, but inwardly. It should aim at superiority in virtue and knowledge and at fine public conduct or *buoni costumi.* In other words, true *principato*—which must here be translated "preeminence"—is moral and intellectual preeminence.[43] Thus, like others in this period such as Alamanno

Rinuccini or Marsilio Ficino—and indeed like Plato in the later books of the *Republic*—Alberti internalizes the concept of princely rule to mean in the first instance rule over oneself. Rule over oneself, the possession of justice in the soul, leads to natural authority over others. To his nephews eager to distinguish themselves in politics Alberti says this: First become persons of high character and behave well in public; first acquire eloquence, study history and your country's political traditions and the governance of foreign peoples, and you *will* win the best sort of influence over your fellow citizens; you will have "natural authority and preeminence indistinguishable from true power" *(autorità e preeminenzia nulla differente dal vero imperio).*[44] You will have the sort of power that doesn't come from truckling to Medicean power brokers, engorged like the Arno in flood with illicit and destructive power, or to an unworthy prince, but the sort that wins the respect of the best and brings the tranquil happiness of the truly superior man.[45]

Alberti's virtue politics is thus, in Florentine terms, conservative and backward looking. His idea of good government in a republic would seem to be modelled on a nostalgic, even idealized view of the pre-Medicean oligarchy. That was a system in which power and the fruits of office were shared among a restricted group of great families led by their *principes* or clan leaders, *capi di famiglia,* who cooperated on the basis of political alliances and personal friendships. For Alberti that was *il buon tempo antico* before 1434 when the Medici achieved a monopoly of political patronage. Alberti's contempt for the Medici regime leads him to imagine, *per repugnantiam* as it were, an alternative kind of republican government, a regime of mutually respectful power sharing among house-princes of sagacity and high character who would not overreach themselves or aim at personal domination. Such men would respect constitutional traditions and would be moderate and prudent in their use of power. They would consult together for the good of the country, constituting a kind of senate (as Alberti calls it in the *Trivia senatoria*). Unlike the Medici, they would not flood the republic with new laws, ordinances, and statutes, a practice which undermined respect for the laws and thus weakened the republic.[46] As Alberti acerbically remarks in book 3 of *De iciarchia*, Moses only needed ten commandments to rule the nation of Israel; the Romans had only the Twelve Tables of their law when they conquered the world; but modern Florentines had "sixty cabinets full of statutes" and every day produced new ordinances.[47] A regime led by house-princes would not mount vast, untried, ill-informed, and imprudent projects, like Jupiter's utopian project in the *Momus*. That would be a windmill too far. They would administer the laws, punish transgressors, provide for public quiet and tranquillity, and protect the republic's dignity and independence. And that was all.[48] Such a minimalist conception of the political would keep the republic under the rule of the best element in the state: its virtuous house-princes.

In sum, we can see the *Momus* and *De iciarchia* as different sides of an Albertian critique of contemporary governments, motivated by, or justified in terms of, virtue politics. In the *Momus* we find a critique of court life illustrating the moral causes underlying the failure of princely government. In the *De iciarchia* Alberti shows why the attempted dominance of a party over an aristocratic society made up of powerful, proud, and independent *case* leads inevitably to oppression and tyranny. Alberti's alternative is a government of wealthy aristocratic equals, what some political analysts might describe as an oligarchy, a negative classification Alberti implicitly rejects through his coinage of the inkhorn term *iciarchia*. Aristotle might have used the term "aristocracy" for the sort of regime Alberti admires, but Alberti is not an Aristotelian. He does not accept that man's higher nature can only be activated and fulfilled by political activity in the polis; he does not take Aristotle's view that only rulers of political communities can exercise the highest form of practical wisdom, securing the common good of the city-state. The function of the polis for Alberti is mostly to maintain public order and the prestige of the *populus* or political community, protecting it from its external enemies. The higher life, *bene beateque vivere,* tranquillity of soul, for him is realized not in the polis of the classical philosophers, but within the family. Or it is realized through the religious life.[49] In the end, the Florence of the old, pre-Medicean oligarchy, the Florence where the Alberti family in its greatest days had played a leading role, stands as the best model of a polity, triumphing over both Athens and Rome in Alberti's political imagination.

CHAPTER 14

GEORGE OF TREBIZOND ON COSMOPOLITANISM AND LIBERTY

George of Trebizond's name, it is fair to say, is unfamiliar to most students of Western political thought. The émigré humanist (Crete 1395–Rome 1472 / 1473) sometimes earns a footnote for his claim that the Venetian mixed constitution had its source in Plato's *Laws,* a text he was the first to translate into Latin.[1] But for the most part his political thought has been completely neglected. In part this may be because his most striking positions are hidden in a few chapters of his extended three-book rant against Plato, the *Comparatio philosophorum Aristotelis et Platonis* (Comparison of the Philosophers Plato and Aristotle, 1457 / 1458), available today only in a few manuscripts and in a single corrupt edition of 1523.[2] But even if this text were better known than it is, it seems likely that the ideas about cosmopolitanism and human liberty expressed in it would be too far out of the mainstream, or what has been perceived as the mainstream, of Renaissance political thought. Recent studies of liberty in the Renaissance emphasize the role of the "non-domination" model of liberty in Renaissance republics: liberty as equalization of political power among citizens.[3] Recent studies of empire focus on the dynamics of imperial expansion, the elaboration of imperial ideologies, and the justification of empire.[4] George's ideas about personal liberty are more reminiscent of classical liberalism or even modern libertarianism. His advocacy of cosmopolitan empire is founded on virtue arguments quite different from those of either ancient or modern theorists of universal government.[5] And no one could call mainstream the actual empire he envisaged, which involved a future, providentially destined alliance between an Ottoman universal monarchy and the Roman Catholic Church. Even in the Renaissance a dream like that was atypical, to use no stronger word. The argument of this chapter, however, is not that George was typical, but that he was prophetic.

George's Attack on Nativism and Defense of Cosmopolitanism

Let's begin with George's cosmopolitanism. The longest discussion of this subject occurs in book 3, chapter 11 of the *Comparatio*. There George is elaborating his obsessive theme that Plato, in both his life and his thought, always favored what was *contra naturam* and therefore morally wrong, destructive, or impossible.[6] Most of book 3 provides an extended refutation of Plato's *Laws*. Plato claims (according to George) that his ideal city, Magnesia, will be happy and eternal. George argues that it will in fact be miserable and short-lived if it follows Plato's prescriptions for a closed, authoritarian, hierarchical, static, inward-looking, and deeply conservative society. He prefers societies that are the opposite: open, meritocratic, dynamic, militant, cosmopolitan, and wealth producing.

What seems to have set George off in particular was a passage at the end of book 8 of the *Laws* where Plato declared that resident aliens may come to Magnesia and engage in trade but may not stay longer than twenty years. Children of resident aliens may only be craftsmen and also are limited to twenty years' residence after reaching their fifteenth year.[7] In other passages Plato prohibits them from engaging in politics, teaching, or intermarrying with the local population. Plato's legislation is meant presumably to prevent the citizen body from being infected with foreign ideas and to prevent foreigners from ever constituting a faction within the city.

George's praise of cosmopolitanism begins with an impassioned attack on these laws, an attack whose fervor surely springs from his own experience as an alien in foreign cities. Indeed he was doubly an alien, since his family had immigrated to Venetian Crete from Trebizond, and he himself later immigrated as a young man from Crete to Italy, where he had considerable difficulty overcoming prejudice against his Greek origins, even within the mainland Venetian empire.[8] George's attack on Plato's immigration laws took the line that they were simply impractical. People would not go to Magnesia as resident aliens if they were going to be prohibited from participating in political, military, and cultural life, no matter how long they lived there, and if they would not be allowed to put down roots, become citizens, and better themselves and the lives of their children. Furthermore, since native citizens of Magnesia would be prohibited from taking part in crafts and trade, all such business would be missing from the city. Who would do these jobs if there were no resident aliens to do them, especially as they had been branded by Plato as low-status jobs? How could a city survive without crafts, how could it prosper without foreign trade? Furthermore, Plato placed all agricultural labor on the backs of slaves; citizens were to engage in farming only in supervisory roles. This meant that Magnesian citizen-soldiers would not acquire the toughness and endurance that makes the best soldiers. Their military training wouldn't amount to more than field exercises, hardly more than play. They wouldn't be able to survive the rigors of real campaigning. There wouldn't be a Magnesian Regulus to leave his plow and fight in the legions; there would be no rugged farmer-soldiers like the Athenian hoplites in the city's phalanx. Magnesia would be impoverished, rustic, and unable to defend itself against rich and powerful predators.

George adds an interesting bioclimatological argument, derived ultimately from Hippocrates,[9] that it is environment, not genetics, that makes one truly belong to a particular place: "Everyone is by nature a citizen of the city where he was born." Those who are born and live for long periods in a country acquire corporeal complexions and a character from that country's physical situation and climate; their piety and their souls will have been shaped by the local religion. A resident alien born and bred in Magnesia will be as much a Magnesian as a child of citizen parents. This idea of "naturalized belonging" as we might call it, which he admits is contrary to the nativist prejudices of classical Greece—not just to Plato's *Laws*—is the basis of his argument for a kind of cosmopolitanism. Nativism—restricting citizen rights to the children of citizen parents—is unjust because it treats residents who naturally belong to a country as aliens, even those who have much to contribute to the commonwealth.

George uses his own experience as an example. Despite the fact that his great-grandfather had emigrated to Crete from Trebizond, a successor state of the Byzantine Empire in the Black Sea, he, George, never seemed to see that city in his dreams or "any Cappadocian monster," but he often dreamed, sleeping and awake, of the city of Crete where he was born (probably Venetian Candia), its walls, gates, forum, temples, port, and buildings. "Wouldn't he therefore be highly unjust if a person used his laws to push me out [of Crete] as though I were a Pontine and a barbarous man, or as a Scythian or Thracian, an alien to all virtue, as the proverb says?"[10] Whatever his family's remote origins, he was obviously now a man of high culture; he shouldn't be classed with rude barbarians from the Black Sea; he should be accepted anywhere because of his merits.

Here George gestures toward a virtue argument for cosmopolitanism, applying to a transnational context the standard humanist argument in favor of meritocracy and against hereditary right.[11] Virtue should be rewarded, whatever its origins. But the real focus of his argument for open societies and the free movement of talented individuals is a politically realist one. Cosmopolitanism is good because it makes states powerful. The great example from antiquity is Rome. Like Biondo Flavio, George praises the Romans for including ever-widening populations of foreigners within the ranks of its citizens. The practice goes back to Romulus, whom George contrasts favorably with Plato for his inclusiveness. While Plato kept foreigners at arm's length, Romulus was much wiser than *doctus Plato,* and much more successful:

> Witness the city of Rome and the Roman People itself, whose wealth equalled the wealth of the whole world, above all because they willingly gave foreigners citizenship. For Romulus, its founder, having laid its foundations, immediately opened it up as an asylum in imitation of the archaic Greeks, and summoned not only the innocent but the guilty. Then he did not abuse as slaves his neighbors that he had defeated in war, but destroyed their towns and compelled them to immigrate to Rome, where he offered them exactly the same rights as his own citizens. . . . [Romulus] not only had the humanity to grant liberty to defeated enemies, whom by the law of nations he might have reduced to slavery, but even with the utmost goodwill gave them citizenship.[12]

Hence it was that Romulus' laws subjected all the world to Rome, while Plato's had never held sway over even the smallest clod of earth *(ne glebula quidem).* Romulus' laws "made all of Italy into one city." This inclusive attitude to citizenship in the end made Rome wealthy and enduring. Indeed, by Augustus' time the Romans had "made all the world one city—and why? So that its wealth and resources might grow and so that its empire might last the longer, since everyone was well-disposed to the Roman Empire as to their own empire."[13] Because "no man felt himself to be a foreigner" in Rome, Rome attracted the loyalty necessary to maintain a great empire. Men found advancement in the Roman Empire based on their good fortune *(felicitas)* and their virtue *(virtus);* even men from far-off Spain could become emperors if they were worthy. Rome remained a great empire so long as virtue was rewarded without discrimination *(communiter).* Cosmopolitanism made the Romans great, but it was their tendency to nativism, their habit of closing the polis to foreign talent, that brought an end to the free city-states of Greece at the end of the classical era.[14] *A fortiori* Plato's even stricter nativist criteria for citizen rights would doom Magnesia to failure.

Even more striking is George's praise of the Ottoman Turks—Christian Europe's great geopolitical rival—for the cosmopolitan empire they had founded. The reason why the power of the Turks had grown so great so quickly, says George, is that they did not distinguish between Italians and Greeks and Scythians, or even between Thessalians and Epirotes or Thracians. They included even barbarians in their empire; they did not make distinctions of status between barbarians and those who claimed to be civilized. We Europeans, says George, talk obsessively about this one being born free, that one a slave; we say this one is of noble birth, that one of unknown origin; this one of citizen birth, that one of foreign origin. "Not so with the Turks: they say that all alike are human beings *(homines)*, and make no difference between man and man, except differences of virtue."[15] It's true they persecute Christians, but that is only because they consider the practice of their impious religion as a mark of virtue; that is why they persecute us Christians, for the vice of impiety, and this constitutes the only just reason for us to hate them. Thus the only limit on cosmopolitanism George recognizes is religious: the only persons rightly excluded from full participation in the state are those who participate in an impious cult. The Ottomans were mistaken in believing Islam the true religion but correct to regard the practice of a false cult *in se* as vicious and therefore grounds for exclusion from citizen rights.

This created a dilemma. George professed to admire the cosmopolitan Ottoman Empire more than any contemporary Western state. But of course the Ottomans were Muslims, followers of what George, like other Renaissance Christians, regarded as a heretical sect of Christianity. The only solution would be for them to convert to true, Roman Christianity, and this is precisely what George set about to accomplish. He had himself appointed a missionary to the Ottoman court and set out for Constantinople in 1466, hoping to convert the Sultan, Mehmed II, to Roman Christianity.[16] His apologetic tool would be Aristotelianism, the divinely inspired philosophy that had kept Roman Christianity from theological corruption and, as Thomas Aquinas had argued, was ideally suited to convert infidels to the truth. His task would be all the easier, as Mehmed was already an Aristotelian philosopher-king. Once the great Turk was a Catholic too, God would see to it that he would achieve world dominion and become the Autocrat of all Nations. The best of all human governments would then come at last, with the true religion, Roman Christianity, embraced by a just, cosmopolitan ruler steeped in the true philosophy of Aristotle.[17]

George's mission to the Turks will inevitably seem a lunatic project to us moderns, and it must have also aroused scorn or amusement in the court of the sultan. But although it is unlikely that he ever obtained the interview he sought with the Great Turk, the plan would not have seemed so impractical to contemporary Christians as it does to us today. The idea of converting a nation to Roman Christianity by converting its ruler had plenty of precedents in Christian history, beginning with Constantine the Great, the founder of the Christian empire, and continuing through Clovis the Frank, St. Stephen of Hungary, Recared the Visigoth, and others.[18] St. Francis of Assisi himself had been the model for attempts to convert Islamic rulers to Christianity. The Jesuits would follow the same strategy in China in the seventeenth century. And only a few years before George's abortive mission, Pope Pius II had famously written his *Letter to Mahomet,* in which the humanist pope too tried to argue the sultan out of his Muslim beliefs.[19]

It is clear that George's cosmopolitanism is a different animal from what moderns think of as cosmopolitanism. In fact it doesn't fit neatly into either ancient philosophical or modern political taxonomies of cosmopolitanism.[20] It does resemble superficially certain anti-establishment attitudes of the founder of Cynicism, Diogenes of Sinope,[21] who according to Diogenes Laertius used to "mock good birth and reputation and all such distinctions, calling them the cosmetics *(prokosmemata)* of vice. The only right polity was that bounded by the cosmos." Indeed, says Diogenes Laertius, "when asked what polis he came from, Diogenes answered that he was a citizen of the cosmos" *(kosmopolites).*[22] Diogenes emphasized that men were equal by nature and that status distinctions were purely a matter of *nomos,* artificial customs and laws. George's attempts to destabilize nativist prejudice and assert the claims of virtue, natural citizenship, and common humanity look a bit like Cynic positions, but he did not share the Cynics' aggressive primitivism, contempt for law and culture, and hostility to participation in politics and the economy.

Nor does his position appear to owe much to the cosmopolitanism of the Stoics. George does not appeal to moral universalism, natural law, cosmic citizenship, the transcendence of civic and ethnic boundaries by philosophic wisdom, or any of the usual Stoic arguments for cosmopolitanism. It is highly probable, to be sure, that he had encountered the famous cosmopolitan dictum, that the cosmos is a single city to which all gods and men belonged, in the pages of some Stoic writer or other.[23] But the more likely source for the cosmopolitan sentiments he expressed is one that is named explicitly in the *Comparatio* itself, namely, a speech of Aelius Aristides, the second-century AD sophist, known as the *Encomium Romae*.[24]

In this speech we find—worked out in much greater detail than in George's *Comparatio*—a theory of cosmopolitan empire that must have been his inspiration. Aristides praises the Roman Empire for "govern[ing] throughout the whole inhabited world as if in a single city." Rome manifests "a great and fair equality between the weak and powerful, obscure and famous, poor and rich and noble." The Romans had mastered the art of empire in ways the Greeks of the classical period had never managed to do. The latter had failed because they didn't know how to include their subject cities in the benefits of empire; instead they exploited and tyrannized them. "Although their possessions were minute, for example border lands and allotments, they could not preserve even these through their inexperience and inability in government, since they neither led their cities with generosity nor were able to hold them firmly, being at the same time oppressive and weak." But the Romans had acquired vast experience of rule because of the enormous size of their empire, and they understood that the way to preserve it was through equal justice for all and by giving Roman citizenship to the best element in each city: "Everywhere you have made citizens all those who are the more accomplished, noble and powerful people, even if they retain their native affinities, while the remainder you have made subjects and governed." "You Romans," continues Aristides, "knew that your empire would be the greater if you made the virtuous partners in government, 'giving freedom and self-rule to the best of them'" (94). "You classify no one as a foreigner in respect of any service which he is capable of performing and which needs to be done."

> And in your pride you have not made [Rome] admired by giving no one else a share of it, but you have sought a citizen body worthy of it, and you have caused the word "Roman" to belong not to a city, but to be the name of a sort of common race, and this not one out of all the races, but a balance to all the remaining ones. . . . Your governance is universal and like that of a single city . . . and [thus] there has arisen a single harmonious government which has embraced all men. (86–87)

George clearly derives from Aristides the concept of universal empire run by a transnational elite of virtue. Yet he does contribute a couple of elements of his own to the picture. One is to connect the growing wealth of Rome with the removal of trade barriers between cities. Aristides, by contrast, had attributed the universal splendor of the empire's cities to the generous distribution of Rome's wealth by the emperor. Another was the power-oriented, almost Machiavellian character of George's argument—that openness to merit, whatever its source, makes a country stronger and better able to compete among rival states than artificial social hierarchies or nativist prejudice. This instrumental style of argumentation is absent in Aristides, no doubt because, unlike George, he did not live in a world of fierce rivalry among city-states, principalities, and kingdoms.

George's argument from political realism is indeed one that would fit awkwardly in the toolkit either of the ancient Stoics or of Aristides. His ideal of a cosmopolitan empire also fails to fit neatly in the taxonomy of modern cosmopolitanisms. Modern theorists who advocate one-world government generally reject imperialism (at least in name), favoring consensual and democratic world institutions. Modern "moral" cosmopolitans focus on subjects like universal human rights and justice, the need for cooperation to prevent environmental disasters, or the nature and degree of one's duty to aid foreigners who are suffering.[25] Even so, he shares enough common ground with modern cosmopolitans, especially in his emphasis on inclusiveness, universal human nature, and equal treatment for persons of foreign origins, to be identified as their forerunner. Direct influence of George of Trebizond on later cosmopolitans is of course improbable. But his arguments and illustrations disclose the nature of the audience he appealed to: educated members of mercantile oligarchies, itinerant intellectuals, and international clerical elites. The discovery of a receptive audience in the commercialized world of the Renaissance for his vision of a less parochial international order, as well as his vivid demonstration of the incompatibility between Plato's illiberal politics and the dynamism of contemporary Italian city-states, surely qualifies George as some sort of prophet of modern cosmopolitanism.

A Renaissance Libertarian?

Nevertheless, it surely risks anachronism to apply the label of classical liberal or libertarian to George's brand of cosmopolitanism. This is not to say that there are no analogies with modern libertarian positions. Most contemporary libertarians advocate open borders and a free international labor market, prefer meritocracy to closed elites, and criticize governments that reserve economic privileges for favored groups or individuals. Modern libertarians would surely be sympathetic to George's view that the removal of political barriers to the economic activity of individuals and states leads to prosperity. One may be permitted to doubt, however, whether his grand solution to the problems of nativism, economic particularism, and closed elites—an Ottoman empire imposing Roman Catholic orthodoxy— would have been warmly embraced by a Friedrich Hayek or a Robert Nozick. In fact, as is well known, the rise of classical liberalism at the end of the seventeenth century was motivated in large part by an increasingly urgent need to separate religious and political authority.[26] Such attitudes lay beyond George's horizon.

The case is much stronger for placing his arguments for personal liberty under the rubric of classical liberal and libertarian positions. The key passage where he lays out his views on the subject is found in chapter 12 of book 3 of the *Comparatio*.[27] Here too he is criticizing the *Laws* for its hostility to social mobility and its prejudice against economic growth. Plato's Magnesia is designed to lock people and their descendents permanently into fixed economic classes, without the possibility of ever rising or falling from one's status. His polity is meant to be sustainable, in one sense of that word: its population is fixed at 5,040 hearths, and it is not allowed to become larger or wealthier. If growth begins to occur, steps are taken to control the population (a one-child policy?), or colonies are sent out so as to dispose of the excess citizenry, as in Thomas More's *Utopia*. Plato (and More) thought such measures would keep the city stable and happy. George disagrees. In his view, the larger, wealthier, and more powerful a city is, the better chance it has of surviving and flourishing, just as bodies survive the longest that try to achieve their maximum size. Plato's view that bigger cities have more civil unrest is historically uninformed, says George. And if money is the sinews of the state, where, my dear Plato (George asks) is that money going to come from, since you've forbidden your citizens to engage in commerce? It's commercial activity that generates private wealth and therefore public revenue. You won't be able to hire foreign soldiers (and we remember that George is writing in the great age of the condottieri), and your own soldiers will be too soft to fight, since they won't be allowed to go far from the city on campaigns and their training will be confined to gymnasia.

In fact, establishing permanent economic classes based on possession of fixed allotments of landed property, thus forbidding social mobility, will not make Plato's polity stable; it will have the opposite effect. It will lead to sedition and hostility among classes. Relationships of mutual help—the cement of social relations—and an ethos of public service cannot form unless there is some possibility of improving one's status:

When you [Plato] create great inequalities between income groups and make that inequality permanent and unchanging, you take away all good will both between the classes and towards the commonwealth. How could the lower class *possibly* embrace the higher in love, especially when it is quite certain that it cannot legally enrich itself by its labor and ascend to a higher class? How will an order that is rich in perpetuity not look down on and despise an order which is always poor, and always will be poor? And what man will serve the commonwealth when he knows he is prevented by law from rising to a higher station even if he is a man of great ability, even if he willingly undergoes perils, toils and vigils and other difficult tasks [for the state]?[28]

This passage exposes the underlying reason why, in George's view, Plato's legislation is bound to fail. Men have a natural disposition to social mobility. They will always try to improve their position in a polity, either by their wits *(ingenium)* or by rendering splendid services to the state. Plato's solution to this natural desire for recognition is to hand out public honors to the best citizens. But this, says George, just shows his ignorance of what human nature is really like. Plato says that the desire for wealth is foolish; the wise desire honor. George replies that the desire for wealth is simply human. Honors without emoluments are empty. Ambitious people want more than medals and magistracies; they want a real rise in status. "But you, [Plato,] allow no silver, no gold, no fine clothes or other precious things to be held by private persons." Public honors are all very well, but men seek security along with honor, and they seek to secure the future of their families too. Men are not worker bees, answering blindly the orders of superiors. They are fully rational, which means they think and plan for the future and for that of their families. They understand that wealth and status are ways to secure the future:

Men are driven by a kind of appetite to produce [or procure] wealth both for themselves and their children, and since man is an animal composed of body and soul, legislators will value bodily welfare too, if they are wise. Thus at nature's command the soul grows in newborn children and is made capable of handling affairs more effectively. But if we are not allowed to look after ourselves and our relations, if our labor brings us no private benefit, the soul is cast down and made effeminate, and ultimately is reduced to a mere counterfeit of its nature. This appetite must not therefore be pulled out by the roots. It is neither right nor possible to strip souls of considerations of private utility; nor is it in the least profitable. You [Plato] demand the impossible, and even if it were possible, it would not be expedient. These things must be tempered by reason, not entirely prohibited.[29]

The idea that human beings have a natural and legitimate desire to rise in wealth and status is an astonishing claim in a civilization that in general revered lordship, equated the pursuit of wealth with greed and dishonesty, believed social hierarchies to be natural, and regarded with suspicion and contempt anyone who tried to "rise above his station." This was true even in Renaissance Italy, of all Western societies the most open to rising talent and the most egalitarian in its mores. George's defense of the pursuit of personal wealth is to my knowledge the most radical of any humanist of the Renaissance. It goes well beyond the "civic humanist" defense of wealth as a precondition of a clan's prestige (as Alberti argued), or of civic virtue and military strength (as maintained by Bruni and Poggio). It might even be seen as prophetic of the new spirit of free enterprise that Max Weber thought was rooted in Protestantism but that Hans Baron, already in the 1920s, wanted to find in "the spirit of the quattrocento" and Italian humanism.[30]

No wonder George hated Plato's political thought, the polar opposite of all that is liberal. George had the insight to realize that Plato's politics was anchored in his psychology, which also needed to be exposed as false. In the passage above he alludes to one of his recurrent criticisms of Plato: that Plato understands human beings as souls dwelling in bodies. He believed falsely that bodies that are mere vehicles, distinct from a man's real self. Thus he tends to treat human nature as potentially angelic and to dismiss the legitimate needs of the body. George's own preferred authority, Aristotle, had a sounder view of human nature as a single substance, matter ordered by form, where the soul is the first actuality or form of the body, separable from it in thought but not *in re*—at least not in this life. Hence Aristotle's political philosophy was more sensible than Plato's in that it took account of bodily as well as psychic needs in defining happiness.[31]

Seeking wealth is not by this logic something below human nature; it is intrinsic to it. Just as man is a political animal, just as he is a material substance, just as he has by nature a desire to know, so also he is a *hoping* creature, a creature that thinks about and works to better his condition, in this life and the next:

For just as the brute animals live in the present by their imagination [*phantasia*], so man is sustained in life by hope of future things. And this is proper to him. It would be harder for you to make a man invisible or unpolitical or incapable of learning than it would be to take hope entirely from him: for whichever of these you [Plato] take away, you necessarily take away from him what it is to be human.[32]

Hope makes man seek wealth; hence it is natural and praiseworthy. But of course, like all other human desires, the desire to acquire wealth can become disordered; it needs to be moderated by reason and confined within the limits of what is honorable. Hence the legislator needs to establish a legal framework within which the individual can exercise his right to free economic activity, but this framework should be careful not to disincentivize hard work:

> Let the legislator, first, not only define in genus but spell out in species what is shameful or honorable, and let him encourage his citizens by honors and deter them by punishments so as to maintain, in word and deed too, their right as individuals *(ius singulorum)*. And [let him do so] with this stipulation, that they do not exceed unduly the wealth [appropriate to] individuals; for great wealth is not, as a rule, easily amassed without wickedness. But no one should ever be restrained by the laws from industriousness, which stimulates and enlarges human minds.[33]

What, then, of the common good, the principle that was the guiding light of medieval and Renaissance political thought and practice?[34] Here George makes some of his most interesting (and libertarian-sounding) remarks. In effect, he removes the common good from the sphere of human life in this world and transfers it to the afterlife. This means that the ancient pagan political theorists (including Aristotle!) who made observing the common good the measure of a healthy constitution were trying to do something impossible. They were trying to find a principle of happiness among mutable and fallen things. But owing to individual differences, it is never possible for human beings to agree on the nature of an earthly common good. Only Christians, thanks to the revealed teachings of Christ, know that in this life we have no abiding happiness:

> Why hope was planted in mankind is a matter of high speculation which you [Plato] and those like you could neither understand nor believe in, for in your [pagan] times, the Gentiles sensed not even the smallest spark of the True Hope. Your whole hope was placed in these fallen and mutable things. It could not be placed as a whole in a common thing [*res*], for there cannot be a common good or ultimate end for every person, unless everyone could share a single

judgment and a single will, a thing it is most foolish even to imagine could exist in this life.[35]

Human desires in this life are labile and restless; only in the next life (as Augustine taught) can they find rest in God, the real common good:

> For the human mind cannot in this life remain content with the same things unless, as has been said, it translates itself in faith to another life. This is something that in your times, [Plato], was not even understood; nowadays many understand it, but few believe it.[36]

Since it is impossible to establish a common good in this life, since our happiness lies in the life to come, human beings in the here-and-now are left only with proper goods, which everyone must be free to choose for himself. And here is where George begins to sound very libertarian indeed. Since there is no common good on which all can agree, coercion in the realm of licit private ends and private goods will not lead to happiness and cannot be justified:

> Necessarily then everyone who departs from the true end and the true good [which everyone does in this life, as George has argued] establishes each for himself according to his own judgment an end, and it is unfair and wicked for a legislator to remove him from this end unless it is a disgraceful one. He [the legislator] should not do so even if he adapts his laws to the true end. For that end is not to be chosen and obtained by force, but by freedom of the will. How much more iniquitous, then, is the man who uses laws to drag someone away from an end he has honorably set out for himself? I have established an end in literature, an end in medicine, an end in agriculture, an end in trade, and I hope therefrom merely that I shall have honor, income, peace, and eternal praise, and you [Plato] rob me of this hope by means of laws. You don't understand that if you take away my liberty, bringing despair instead, you are putting the noose around my neck.
>
> "But," you say, "I am offering you a better hope than the one you have fixed on for yourself." But why you, of all men? Isn't man free? What is this madness? Don't you see that judgments differ, that pleasures and pains differ? Perfectly honorable things which I find pleasant you snatch away from me and substitute things you find pleasant. You won't permit me to enjoy things I reckon as goods, even if they are honorable, and the things you imagine to be good you would force me to enjoy. But no one enjoys what

is forced upon him. Enjoyment is a sign of pleasure, but coerced enjoyment is not pleasant. Furthermore, there can be no pleasure where there is not liberty, but coercion and liberty are incompatible. Therefore coercion and pleasure are incompatible.[37]

To sum up, the ends of our spiritual nature are set by God and belong to the next life; those of our bodily nature in this life are legitimately set by the individual and can't be dictated by another. That end is the *iucundum*, what is agreeable or pleasant to our ensouled bodies, a term of art for George that embraces physical pleasure *(voluptas)* but also anything that our bodily nature finds attractive, such as security and recognition by others. We ourselves as individuals are the best judges of what is *iucundum* for us. This is the true basis of liberty, not an abstract principle of right. The ruler can constrain individual behavior only if it strays beyond the limits of what is right and honorable, but within those limits all attempts by government to control lives, to dictate what is *iucundum*—even in the name of high-sounding ideals—will be vain and unjust. Partly this is a question of the correct scope of law: legislators and rulers in matters that are morally indifferent have no standing to impose their preferences; in such matters human beings should enjoy a certain autonomy. But the main reason why legislators will fail in any attempt to coerce individuals toward a universal, philosophical ideal of happiness is the nature of coercion itself. Coercion is incompatible with happiness. You can't coerce someone into being happy; the *iucundum* is only *iucundum* when it is freely chosen. Liberty is therefore a necessary condition of achieving our ends in this bodily life. Plato's belief that happiness can be mandated by a ruler's command or a legislator's law is a philosophical delusion.

George's coercion argument, interestingly, bears a structural resemblance to Locke's liberal argument for toleration in the *Letter concerning Toleration*. Locke there makes the case that coercion is incompatible with true religion, because for religious belief to be genuine and vigorous, it has to be freely embraced. The mere act of coercion reduces the spiritual value of belief.[38] Coercion itself takes away the psychological state necessary to achieve the object of coercion. The liberalism of both Locke and George rests on fundamentally Christian ideas of free will. In George's case, it helps explain why virtue politics in the Renaissance could never become a "comprehensive doctrine" of the type advocated by some ancient philosophers and their modern imitators.[39]

George's liberalism carries with it certain implications, some of which show why he cannot be classed simply as an Aristotelian without qualification, as is often done in the modern literature. First, his denial that there can exist a common good acceptable to all who strive to flourish in this bodily life implies that there can be no basis for distinguishing good and bad constitutions on the Aristotelian model. George's position on the common good would thus seem to establish a premise for the simplified and demoralized constitutional analysis of Machiavelli. Second, his insistence on human freedom and autonomy within the limits of right presents a sharp contrast with the authoritarian character of Aristotle's own political theory.[40] By vindicating freedom as the ability to "live as you like" within moral and legal limits, he embraces what Aristotle and Renaissance theorists alike identify as the end of democrats under a popular constitution, an end that Aristotle regards as an inferior goal for a polity.[41]

Of course it needs to be emphasized that there are enormous differences between George's conception of liberty and that of classical liberals. In George's writings there is no trace of the harm principle so central to modern libertarianism even before it was codified by John Stuart Mill: that my freedom of action is limited only by the harm my actions might bring to others.[42] For George, as for most moralists of his time, one's freedom of action is bounded by natural law and natural right. Nor does George make any appeal to the libertarian idea of "self-ownership," a concept repugnant to Catholic ethics and incompatible with the Stoic belief in natural, unchosen duties owed by human beings to each other.[43] The Stoic principle, as we have seen, was foundational for humanist political thought. Moreover, George's praise of empires ancient and modern makes it unlikely that he would be sympathetic to the liberal thesis that the legitimacy of political authority rests on popular consent.

Despite these important differences, however, it is striking how successful George was in making an argument for personal autonomy and for limits on political coercion within a framework of Christian eudaimonism and virtue politics.[44] Whether that argument is fully coherent is another question. In any case, George's liberalism is to my knowledge both unique among Renaissance humanists and without any discernible influence on later thinkers. Its uniqueness no doubt stems from George's unusual self-positioning as the eternal outsider, the prophet of a future cosmopolitan empire, and an implacable foe of Plato's philosophy. Nevertheless, his example shows that the common view which sees liberalism as intrinsically modern, as a way of thought dependent on a particular *wirkungsge-schichtliches Bewusstsein* or historically determined consciousness, cannot be entirely correct. George clearly had an understanding of liberty, autonomy, and coercion distinct from those of the traditions he inhabited: distinct from ancient status-concepts of liberty; from freedom in the philosophical sense of rational control over passions and appetites; and from liberty in the Roman and Renaissance sense of "non-domination." George's concept of liberty as a personal freedom to set and pursue any morally licit end, free of direction or coercion from governments, shows that the horizons of premodern liberty are broader than our current narratives of the history of political thought might allow.

CHAPTER 15

FRANCESCO FILELFO AND THE SPARTAN REPUBLIC

Filelfo and the Recovery of the Spartan Tradition

In an essay first published in 1974, Arnaldo Momigliano said of the Latin translations of Greek historians made in the quattrocento that "the whole series of translations was potentially the most revolutionary event in historiography since Fabius Pictor introduced Greek historiography into Rome at the end of the third century BC. But nobody has yet discovered what happened as a consequence of this: Herodotus, Thucydides, Polybius, Strabo and Appian suddenly becoming available in the language of educated people."[1] Despite the size of this intellectual opportunity, however, there have been surprisingly few explorations since Momigliano's essay was published of how these and other Greek historical writings were received in the Latin West. Important exceptions exist: Mariane Pade's monumental two-volume study of the reception of Plutarch's *Lives* is surely a major advance in knowledge, and some basic research on the reception of Agathias, Arrian, Herodotus, Polybius, Thucydides, and Xenophon has been completed as well.[2] The work of Gabriele Pedullà on the presence of Dionysius of Halicarnassus in the early modern historical imagination, and especially Machiavelli's encounter with the Greek historian, brilliantly illustrates the profit historians of political thought can derive from reception studies.[3] But much remains to be done. In particular we lack as yet focused studies of how received understandings of key figures, events, political institutions, and other cultural phenomena of the ancient world were transformed by the humanist rediscovery of classical sources.[4] A great deal has been written, to be sure, about how ancient Rome, its history and culture, inspired the humanist revival of classical antiquity. But we are less well informed about how the memory of Athens and Sparta was reshaped by humanists as a result of their exposure to newly available sources in Greek. The narrative of Rome—its origins, the downfall of its kings, the vast expansion of its empire during the middle republic, the corruption and violence of the late republic, the monarchy of the emperors, and the eventual fall of the empire—was known to all educated people and haunted the Western political imagination down to modern times. But what of the narratives of other ancient states like Athens and Sparta? What lessons did humanist scholars draw from their histories? How did they weld together the historical materials at their disposal to buttress their moral and political teachings?

This chapter focuses on the ancient state of Sparta, whose story (or myth) has long been recognized as a powerful presence in the historical memory of the West.[5] Like Rome, Sparta, right from the beginning of the fifteenth-century Greek revival, provided a repertory of exemplary individuals, customs, and institutions that humanist writers and educators held up for admiration and imitation. Sparta influenced humanist political thought as well, particularly its subordination of private to public goods, its attitudes to wealth and the family, its respect for law and tradition, and its unique versions of monarchy and the mixed constitution. To deepen the study of how Spartan sources were recovered in the quattrocento and absorbed into Western political reflection, we can hardly do better than to focus on the humanist Francesco Filelfo (1398–1481), one of the finest Hellenists of the fifteenth century, who played the leading role in making the Greek sources for Spartan history available in Latin. Thanks largely to a flurry of recent editions by Jeroen De Keyser—of the forty-eight books of Filelfo's *Collected Letters* as well as his editions of the *Commentationes Florentinae de exilio,* the *Sphortias,* and three of Filelfo's translations of Spartan material—it is much easier to assess his role in forging some key themes of humanist Laconism.[6] It should go without saying that what Filelfo and the humanists made of Spartan sources is quite different from the critical reconstructions by modern scholars of ancient Spartan history and society, and different again from what modern scholars variously describe as the ancient "mirage," or myth, or legend, or image, or tradition of Sparta.[7] In this chapter the focus will be on the Sparta of Filelfo and his fellow humanists.

It has been a matter of debate to what extent Filelfo's translations of Spartan sources reflected his own personal and political agendas.[8] His early translations of three Spartan texts by Xenophon and Plutarch, dedicated in 1430 to Cardinal Niccolò Albergati, were perhaps motivated by no more than a desire for the patronage of an influential prelate everyone at the time regarded as highly *papabile.* Filelfo's comparison of Lycurgus' legislative prowess to Niccolò's wise management of factional conflict as bishop of Bologna and his peacemaking activities as legate *a latere* of Martin V have an odor of flattery all too familiar in humanist prefaces.[9] But in time, Filelfo became something of a champion of ancient Sparta. In a late letter (1476) containing his most detailed discussion of Lacedaemonian institutions, he stated flatly that the Spartans had the best-ordered of all republics from a moral point of view. This suggests a certain elective affinity.[10] In his time Filelfo was the leading humanist expert on Sparta and spoke admiringly of some—though by no means all—of its customs, laws, and institutions. Particularly useful rhetorically were Spartan laws preventing the state from being corrupted by the influence of wealthy men, which for Filelfo became a topos frequently deployed in his war of words against Cosimo de'Medici, his nemesis.[11] His insistence that the wise man should be indifferent to wealth may also have had something to do with neutralizing his own (undeserved) reputation for avarice.[12] In any case, the proper use of wealth and the defense of voluntary poverty were to become major themes in his moral writings. His worry about the influence of money on political life inevitably brought him back to the Spartans as the prime example of an ancient people whose military effectiveness and long-lived institutions he considered to be tightly linked to their rejection of personal wealth. Filelfo's fascination with the Spartans is shown by their frequent appearance in his correspondence down to the very end of his life and by his ongoing commitment to making Spartan sources available in Latin.

There is no doubt that it was the wider humanist project of translating Greek sources into Latin that brought Sparta—or at least the legends of Sparta that were known in antiquity[13]—back to prominence in the historical memory of the West, into its active memory as it were. Before the fifteenth century, the sources of information about Sparta available in the Latin West were few. Spartan history and institutions were known primarily from the second and third books of Aristotle's *Politics,* translated by William of Moerbeke in the late thirteenth century, and from scattered remarks in various writings of Cicero, Seneca, Justinus' epitome of Pompeius Trogus, and Valerius Maximus. Gross anachronisms abounded.[14] The fifteenth-century humanists changed this situation dramatically. They introduced a whole library of new Greek sources in translation, which collectively brought about a spectacular increase in available source materials concerning the Peloponnesian city-state. The new narrative sources that dealt extensively with Spartan history included Herodotus, Thucydides, Xenophon's *Hellenica,* and Diodorus Siculus 11–15.[15] An important treatment of the Spartan constitution was to be found in book 6 of Polybius, which (as shown in Chapter 12) was known to at least one humanist, Cyriac of Ancona, by the mid-fifteenth century. In addition there were the four important biographical essays of Spartan leaders in Plutarch's *Parallel Lives:*

- *Lycurgus,* first translated by Filelfo in 1430[16]
- *Lysander,* first translated by Guarino Veronese in 1435
- *Agis and Cleomenes,* a joint biography first translated by Alamanno Rinuccini in 1458
- *Agesilaus,* translated by Rinuccini in 1462[17]

Xenophon's Spartan writings, the *Agesilaus* and *The Spartan Republic,* were turned into Latin by Filelfo in 1430 and packaged with his translations of Plutarch's parallel lives of Lycurgus and Numa for presentation to Niccolò Albergati.[18] There was also a great deal of Spartan material in Plutarch's *Moralia,* especially in the various collections of apophthegmata (including aphorisms, maxims, and proverbs) and the *Instituta Laconica.* Filelfo translated the first of these, the *Apophthegmata ad Traianum,* in 1437 and the *Apophthegmata Laconica* in 1454; he also knew well and quoted a third important collection, the *Sayings of the Spartan Women.*[19] All of Filelfo's translations were extremely popular, both in manuscript and print forms, through the second half of the sixteenth century.[20] Plato's *Laws,* translated by George of Trebizond in 1451 / 1453 and later by Marsilio Ficino in 1484, contains extensive discussions of the Spartan constitution and Spartan customs.[21] The Greek orators, especially Demosthenes, often touched on Spartan history and customs, and these too were translated by Italian humanists, beginning with Leonardo Bruni in the first decade of the quattrocento.[22] The small body of poetry written by Spartans, chiefly Alcman and Tyrtaeus, began to be excerpted in fifteenth-century manuscripts, and many new details were provided by geographical writers like Strabo (translated by Guarino) and Pausanias.[23] So it can be said that by the end of the fifteenth century the West possessed in Latin the principal literary sources that are known to historians of Sparta today. One humanist, Cyriac of Ancona, even began to explore some of the inscriptional sources for Sparta on visits to its ruins.[24]

Filelfo and Humanist Adaptations of the Myth of Sparta

As the materials on Spartan history began to be recovered, certain patterns emerged in the way the humanists made use of this new information, and certain commonplaces were hammered out that became standard exempla in humanist moral and political thought. Some of these amounted to little more than restatements of ancient commonplaces about the Spartans, while others betrayed the new emphases and concerns of humanist virtue politics.

The Spartan sources, first of all, provided new material for humanist constitutional debates and raised new questions about the best ways to produce virtue in the ruling class. What is the best regime? Is it monarchical or non-monarchical, or should the best regime have a more limited monarchical element? Which is better: the rule of the best men or of a virtuous popular regime? Should the power of the prince be restrained by constitutional means, or should a virtuous prince be allowed the power to rule unencumbered by human laws and unchecked by the power of councils and magistrates?[25] Should a constitution be designed for long-term stability or to enable the acquisition of empire?[26] The Spartan sources, as Filelfo understood them, decisively supported the argument for limited monarchical power, for the rule of the best, for the strict control of wealthy and powerful men by laws and magistrates and good customs. More broadly, they provided an authoritative precedent for thinkers with statist inclinations, most famously Thomas More, who emphasized the claims of the collective over the individual and the subordination of private interests to the common good.

The new exposure to Spartan sources was disruptive of the status quo in several ways. When it came to constitutional theory, for example, even Aristotle had found it hard to classify the Spartan regime and fit it to his procrustean analytical bed of six constitutions.[27] New data about Spartan institutions thus led to deeper reflection on the question of what a republic was, and what kingship was. As was shown in Chapter 3, the concept of a republic in the Renaissance was not necessarily attached to a particular type of regime and could embrace monarchical as well as non-monarchical forms of government. The essential thing about a true republic for humanist writers on politics was its commitment to virtuous rule, preferably inspired by examples from classical antiquity. Hence in humanist sources *respublica* often implies little more than "good government" as opposed to tyranny.[28] This broader, moral conception of the republic found new sustenance in the freshly translated sources illustrating what humanists commonly called, following Filelfo's translation of Xenophon, the *respublica Lacedaemoniorum* or Spartan republic. The presentation of Sparta in ancient texts also emphasized virtue and the rule of the best as the marks of a *respublica,* but Spartan virtues sprang from mores and institutions differing sharply from those of Rome. Since the Spartans had two kings who played a powerful but limited role in their regime, it was easy for humanists to assimilate Sparta to contemporary republics with a monarchical element, such as Venice and Genoa, or to claim that monarchies restrained by laws and constitutional checks resembled the exemplary Spartan regime.[29]

Filelfo himself saw Spartan institutions as most resembling those of the Venetians, a high compliment—for the Venetians. In a late letter to the doge of Venice, Andrea Vendramin (ruled 1476–1478), Filelfo declared that the fine leadership the Venetians were offering in the crusade against the Turks was the result of the excellence of their constitution.[30] The philosophers tell us (he writes) that there are three good kinds of constitution or *respublica*—the popular *(populi)*, the aristocratic *(optimatium)*, and the royal *(regis)*—but that the royal corrupts easily into tyranny and the popular into factionalism. So the *administratio optimatium,* aristocracy, must be considered the best, because the word *optimates* signifies men of virtue. And "everyone agrees" that this is the form of constitution found in Venice.[31] The similarity of their senatorial rule to the Spartan constitution is evident. First, Filelfo pointed out, the two polities resemble each other in their longevity, stability, and greatness—both had flourished over many centuries, both enjoyed domestic harmony, and both had performed splendid deeds in war. Like Venice today, Sparta had been governed by a counsel of *optimates* led by a single person deemed worthy by their sagacious ballots.[32] He ruled the rest, and the function of his rule was to ensure obedience to the established laws: "Thus what Pausanias, son of Pleistoanax, is reported in the tradition to have said made sense, that the laws ought to dominate men, not men the laws. That the prince [of the optimates] would be subject to the laws is clear from the [institution of] six ephors, that is, examiners and preservers of the laws, who, being chosen by the same counsel of aristocrats, used to attend the same prince and see to it that he could order nothing against their will."[33] This is hardly adequate or accurate as an account of the Spartan regime—or of the Venetian one for that matter—but it shows an interesting independence from Aristotle's account of the Spartan constitution.[34] Aristotle saw Sparta as having a mixed regime in which the ephors formed the democratic element; he also criticized the Spartans for customs and institutions that did not promote virtue, such as their "childish" election procedures and the low social origins of the ephors. Filelfo's largely imaginary version of Spartan institutions emphasizes the constitutional check of the ephorate on the power of the king, who is said to be elected by the wise (the *gerousia?*), as well as the importance of the rule of law. The latter is a point he stresses many times in his writings, often citing the Spartans as exemplary in their respect for law. Filelfo's imaginary Spartan polity, unconstrained by careful consideration of even the sources he had himself translated, reveals more what he wanted the Spartans to be than the way they were presented in Xenophon, Herodotus, or Plutarch. Spartan customs and institutions, as presented by Filelfo, were exemplary for modern times because they built respect for the rule of law, because they trained the Spartans in the knowledge of how to rule and be ruled in turn, and because they embodied the wisdom of philosophers.[35]

Unlike George of Trebizond, Filelfo preferred the nativism of the Spartans to the cosmopolitanism of the Athenians. He praised the quasi-mythical founder of the Spartan regime, Lycurgus, for protecting the city's moral virtue from infection by foreign mores. Writing to King Ferrante of Naples in 1476, he declined to describe the laws of Lycurgus (which his royal correspondent might not have found attractive) but could not forebear to mention one aspect of them: Lycurgus' efforts to prevent corruption by excluding foreign mores. He likened these to Ferrante's laudable efforts to keep the coarse and uncultivated French out of Italy (unlike the ancient Romans, who, deplorably, had allowed these ungrateful barbarians into the peninsula). Just so, Lycurgus' laws kept anyone out of Sparta, including foreign merchants, who might deprave or corrupt it with soft and delicate ways: "That gravest of legislators understood that it was not the part of a temperate or just man to acquire the taste for anything base or effeminate, since men are driven to injustice most of all by temptations to lust and pleasure."[36] But they were happy to import men of wisdom. Filelfo praises the Spartan king Agesilaus II for inviting Xenophon, "that illustrious and reputable Socratic philosopher," to educate the boys of Lacedaemon in the old discipline, "which he judged to be the most beautiful of all the rest"—namely, the discipline of how to rule and be ruled.[37]

Agesilaus II could be described as the humanists' favorite Spartan. He owed this position to the adulatory biographical essay written by his own humanist advisor, Xenophon, for whom he was both the ideal king and the ideal citizen of a republic. In Agesilaus the humanists had their finest model of a great general whose successes never threatened the republic.[38] In other words, he was everything that the great Roman dictators, generals, and triumvirs of the first century BC were not—men like Marius and Sulla, Pompey, Mark Antony and Caesar, whose overwhelming power as military leaders was always threatening to turn them into tyrants, passing beyond the limits of constitutional government. The works of Cicero, canonical for humanists, were full of anxiety about how to restrain the power of such overmighty citizens, and this worry was also a central theme in humanist thought about tyranny.

Agesilaus the Spartan provided the perfect counterexample. Xenophon emphasizes that it was Agesilaus' brilliant military leadership and resourcefulness that brought large portions of Asia Minor under his control. His clemency in victory and wise governance were equally praiseworthy. Xenophon even suggests that the Spartan general might well have overcome the Great King of Persia himself had he been allowed to continue his victorious career. He could have set himself up as a kind of Alexander the Great and conquered Asia a century before the celebrated Macedonian. But instead, at the very peak of his success, at the moment when he was on the verge of establishing personal hegemony over Asia Minor, the richest part of the world at that time, he received a summons from Sparta's ephors to return to Greece and defend the homeland.

> His conduct at this juncture also merits unstinted admiration. Though ruler of countless cities on the mainland, and master of islands—for the state had now added the fleet to his command—becoming daily more famous and more powerful; placed in a position to make what use he would of his many opportunities; and designing and expecting to crown his achievements by dissolving the empire that had attacked Greece in the past, he suppressed all thought of these things, and as soon as he received a request from the home government to come to the aid of his fatherland, he obeyed the call of the state, just as though he were standing in the Ephors' palace alone before the Five, thus showing clearly that he would not take the whole earth in exchange for his fatherland, nor new-found friends for old, and that he scorned to choose base and secure gains rather than that which was right and honourable, even though it was dangerous.[39]

Unlike Julius Caesar, who returned from conquering Gaul and invaded his own country with an army, in defiance of the Senate and laws of Rome, Agesilaus returned home from his far greater conquests in Asia without hesitation, in willing compliance with the laws of Sparta and in obedience to its appointed magistrates.[40] Bringing his troops back across the Hellespont, he defeated the Athenians in the decisive battle of Coronea in 394 BC and saved his country.[41]

What this example signified to Filelfo and other humanists was that the Spartans had a uniquely social and civic form of virtue where personal excellence was always subordinated to the needs of the state. Merely private virtue was trivial and meaningless; all virtue had to have a civic dimension. Broadly speaking the humanists embraced the observation of Xenophon that the character of the state reflects the character of its leaders; that, indeed, was a key assumption in their schemes for political reform. In the preface to his translation of *The Spartan Republic,* Filelfo writes that through his institutions Lycurgus caused the citizens of his city-state to acquire his own virtues.[42] The institutions of Sparta in turn produced a series of fine leaders who set an example of good citizenship. That was why the city of Sparta needed no walls, because "men, not walls, make a city." (This Thucydidean aphorism was among the most famous humanist commonplaces.[43]) The great Spartan leaders lived as ordinary citizens, sharing the same food, clothing, and responsibilities as the rest when not ruling. In other words, they possessed the moral disposition, indispensable in republics, of knowing how to rule and be ruled in turn, and not seeking more than their just share. According to Filelfo, this was the secret of the Spartans' success.[44] They did not use their power to amass greater wealth than other citizens, nor did they claim unconstitutional authority, whatever their achievements and virtues. They put the good of the state before that of their families, an attitude most famously attested in the steely maxims attributed to Spartan women. Here are some famous ones:

> When a messenger came from Crete bringing the news of the death of Acrotatus, [his grandmother Gyrtias] said, "When he had come to the enemy, was he not bound either to be slain by them or to slay them? It is more pleasing to hear that he died in a manner worthy of myself, his country, and his ancestors than if he had lived for all time a coward.[45]

> Another [woman], as she handed her son his shield, exhorted him, saying, "Either this or upon this."[46]

> Another, when her son was being tried for some offence, said to him, "My child, either rid yourself of the charges, or rid yourself of life."[47]

In Sparta, the rule of law, backed by the divine authority of Lycurgus, was absolute.[48] Agesilaus, again, was here the ideal (and idealized) model of loyal deference to the laws, but the life of Lycurgus too supplied some key anecdotes.[49]

The humanists, like most Western political thinkers before the twentieth century, believed that the reason for the extraordinarily successful republican regime of the Spartans—its longevity, its military strength, its ability to restrain the ambitions of great men—lay in the institutions, laws, and mores put in place by its great legislator, Lycurgus. (The opposite case was tyranny, necessarily short-lived because a tyrant city was consumed by fear and hatred and not ordered by reason and loving respect.[50]) But they did not necessarily see what modern historians see when they look at Lycurgus' legislation. Some scholars today would see a legislator who prevented noble rivalry by insisting on a rough equality of landed property; who decentered the family's role in the education of youth in favor of the community's; who inspired the unusual gender regime of the Spartans, including polyandry and wife-sharing, that also gave women greater economic power and accorded them more dignity in the common task of strengthening the state. Women in the Lycurgan state, some modern scholars believe, were partners of their husbands in upholding civic virtue and were not mere servants of a paterfamilias.[51] The Spartans have also been described as hopeless philistines, militantly anti-intellectual and anti-philosophical. Their celebrated "laconic" speech stood in marked contrast to the Athenians' cultivation of the arts of eloquence. The Spartan army had difficulty holding territory outside the Peloponnese owing to its small numbers and to the constant danger of insurrection at home among the helots, Sparta's subject population—hence the Spartans' reluctance to involve themselves in imperial projects.

Quattrocento humanists did not necessarily take all that in, or want to. The aspects of Sparta less amenable to the humanist project were ignored or suppressed.[52] Their system of ritual pederasty, for example, could hardly commend itself to humanist moral thinkers. The gender regime of the Spartans, though it certainly piqued interest, was also difficult to adapt as a model, given contemporary mores. More commonly, as in Filelfo's case, the sources relating to Spartan women entered their commonplace books under the headings of the praise of marriage and the drawbacks of celibacy.[53] It is only in Thomas More's *Utopia* that we see, implicitly, a deeper understanding of how Spartan culture worked as a system to elevate public over private ends. More of this later.

A number of humanists were enthusiastic about the Spartans' military virtue, seeing a parallel to Roman patriotism in Herodotus' account, in book 7, of how the Spartans were willing to die for their country. Filelfo shared in the general admiration, but he also understood the difference between militarism and imperialism. The Spartans were a military people, undeniably, yet for him their militarism was motivated by the desire to display virtue and not by the desire for foreign conquest.[54] This accorded well with the ideal of Plato and Aristotle that a state should not seek to make conquests beyond its borders and should not allow the passion for honor to drive the state into imperialistic adventures.[55] The self-sacrifice of Leonidas at Thermopylae—for Greece and not just Sparta—was the ultimate example of this defensive but truly patriotic virtue.[56] The Spartans were defensive culturally too: they kept foreigners out and tried to prevent their influence from demoralizing their own carefully regimented citizenry. This meant that they were anti-cosmopolitan in one sense of that world; yet Spartan secrecy and isolation could be defended on the grounds that it created a valuable reserve of military virtue for all of Greece—the civilized world as the Hellenes saw it—and helped the country defend itself against barbarism. Uncorrupted by the soft customs found in the rest of Greece, they stood ready to act as a bulwark for their country when it was threatened by barbarian invaders.[57]

Filelfo and other humanists also brought the Spartans into their analysis of the causes of the corruption and fall of republics. The fall of Spartan virtue presented a parallel to Sallust's account of Roman republican corruption in the century before Augustus. Filelfo and other humanists laid the responsibility for Sparta's decline squarely with her navarch (i.e., admiral) Lysander. Lysander's rule was turned into a warning, even a morality tale, about four major causes of corruption: (a) departing from law and ancestral custom; (b) the corrupting effects of wealth; (c) the tendency of wealth to produce faction; and (d) the tendency of trade to corrupt mores via contact with foreigners. Above all Filelfo blamed Sparta's decline, following a famous passage in Xenophon, on the gradual weakening of Lycurgan mores through ambition and venality.[58] Nevertheless, the superiority of Sparta's virtue, its uniquely social and civic quality, guaranteed that the Spartan republic lasted longer than the polities of more selfish and greedy peoples like the Athenians and Carthaginians.[59] The Spartans' lack of interest in empire and in dominating other peoples (apart from the Messenians) also helped prevent corruption. Thus, for Filelfo and other humanist writers of the fifteenth century, Sparta had already become the archetypal "republic for preservation," contrasted with the "republic for expansion" in Machiavelli's famous analysis.[60]

Filelfo was particularly fascinated by the Spartans' refusal to enrich themselves through military conquest, a disposition they shared with the virtuous Romans of the middle republic like the plebeian hero Manius Curius Dentatus. The latter was the famous Roman general who, when offered a great weight in gold by the defeated Samnites, replied that he did not believe it was glorious to possess gold but to command those who possessed gold.[61] This attitude is sometimes called "political poverty," a conscious policy of keeping private citizens poor in order to make them identify more fully with the aims of the state. In Sparta (Filelfo believed) this took the form of prohibiting the military elite from engaging in trade and making mercantile exchange difficult by removing gold and silver from the city and adopting an iron coinage.[62] Contempt for private property was further inculcated in boys by encouraging them to practice theft as a kind of military exercise.[63] Spartan political poverty formed a contrast with the attitude of Florentine humanists such as Bruni, Poggio, and Matteo Palmieri, who held that numerous rich clans with their palaces and villas, were useful to the state as providing the sinews of war—an argument particularly compelling in an age of mercenary warfare. Filelfo's own position was more complex. Though he admired Spartan (and early Roman) frugality in principle, when advising princes and merchants, or discussing the matter on a more philosophical plane, he made careful distinctions. Riches are highly necessary to princes "as they are the sinews of war and the ornaments of peace."[64] Merchants who acquired their wealth licitly and used it well for public purposes, such as Vitaliano Borromeo, the dedicatee of *De exilio,* are to be admired. But those who acquired wealth by illicit means and put their own interests above those of the state, such as Cosimo de'Medici, rotted the moral fiber of the republic and would bring it to destruction.[65]

Filelfo's position is a moderate one in the wider quattrocento debate on the uses of wealth.[66] At the beginning of the sixteenth century, however, a more radical form of Laconism was invented by Thomas More and through him entered the bloodstream of Western utopian thought. It is well known that Lycurgus' Sparta was one of the chief elements in More's imaginative creation of an ideal society—and More's understanding of Sparta was surely formed, at least in part, by reading Filelfo's translations of Plutarch and Xenophon.[67] More's *Utopia* presented a society founded by a primitive legislator, Utopus, wherein the normal motives of human action in most societies—wealth, family status, empire, the hunger for domination—were stilled, and replaced by new, better motives that led individuals to subordinate themselves to the common good. The parallels between the institutions laid down by Lycurgus and by Utopus are striking. Through wise laws and customs Lycurgus was able to strengthen, to a far higher degree than in normal societies, common social bonds and loyalty to the state. Loyalty to the collective was enabled by customs inhibiting the desire and ability to seek wealth and by privileging agriculture above crafts and trade. Egalitarian customs—and even an egalitarian distribution of wealth—were secured both by law and by the example of great men like Lycurgus himself and the other great Spartan kings. Spartan custom emphasized toughness, unadorned speech, frugality, voluntary poverty—all to prevent the possibility that money could control the Spartans, as it did other nations. Lycurgan laws and customs brought about a higher, more virtuous, and more unified society.

Hence the history of Sparta—or what the humanists believed to be its history— showed that human beings did not have to settle for the corruptions of ordinary societies, for civic leaders ruled only by their passions and appetites. As Francesco Patrizi wrote in his classic work of humanist political theory, *How to Found a Republic* (1465 / 1471), Plato was wrong to say that all constitutions inevitably decline owing to the ineradicable moral weakness of humanity. Plato is wrong to be so pessimistic, says Patrizi, because

> if it can somehow be brought to pass that citizens act well in perpetuity, follow what is honorable and flee what is shameful, then the republic will be perpetual, provided that its leaders *(principes)* strengthen the unstable people. For just as the whole city is corrupted by their vices and lusts, so it is emended and corrected by their self-control—virtue being what can keep a constitution stable and lasting. The possession of the best morals as well as the best enactments on the part of those in charge of the people's business *(rem populi)* not only preserves but marvelously augments their status and power. This is a state which the same Xenophon shows by example when he writes of the Spartan republic. For he says that Sparta, despite its small population, had nevertheless grown in resources, power, population, status and empire in a short time, which aroused in him no small admiration. But when he contemplated Lycurgus' laws and holy institutions, he ceased to marvel.[68]

Human nature was plastic enough that properly designed customs and institutions could enlarge its capacity for moral goodness. Sparta was proof of that. There had existed once upon a time, in the glorious world of classical antiquity—the humanists' sourcebook for the reform of the modern world—social and political structures that could enable the dominance of reason and the common good. It was in this way that the Spartans provided intellectual resources and historical precedents for the tradition of utopian socialism that has played so important a role, if not always a benign one, in the political traditions of the modern West.[69]

GREEK CONSTITUTIONAL THEORY IN THE QUATTROCENTO

The "Second Wave" of Greek Constitutional Theory

Greek constitutional theory—the theories of ancient Greek thinkers about how polities naturally organize themselves, how they evolve over time, and how statesmen might optimize both their organization and evolution—arrived in Latin Christendom in two waves. The first came in the High Middle Ages, when Aristotle's *Ethics* and *Politics* were translated into Latin. The recovery of Aristotle's political thought stimulated a great deal of reflection among major theorists such as Thomas Aquinas, Giles of Rome, John of Paris, and Marsilius of Padua. These thinkers have been studied extensively by modern historians of scholastic political thought and their debts to Aristotle analyzed. Most authorities agree that the reception of Aristotle's *Politics* represents a major inflection point in the history of Western political philosophy.[1]

Less noticed by historians of political thought is the second wave in the reception of Greek constitutional thought. This occurred in fifteenth-century Italy, when philosophers, orators, and historians such as Plato, Xenophon, Isocrates, Demosthenes, Herodotus, Polybius, Appian, Plutarch, Diodorus Siculus, Dio Cassius, and Diodorus of Halicarnassus were translated for the first time into Latin. This second wave has been much less studied. Indeed, in some cases we still lack precise and comprehensive answers to basic questions: what texts were translated, by whom, when, and why; how widely diffused they were and who read them; and which were the commentaries and paratexts that escorted them into the Latin environment and governed how they were understood.[2] As yet there are only a few specialized studies of how and to what extent the reception in Latin of non-Aristotelian constitutional theory transformed the way Western political thinkers conceptualized their polities. There are some well-known analyses of Machiavelli's use of Polybius and Xenophon, but scholars have only begun to explore how those authors were understood and applied by earlier humanist writers.[3] For example, the

Hiero and the *Cyropaedia* of Xenophon were, in terms of manuscript diffusion, among the most popular Greek translations of the quattrocento, but no modern scholar to my knowledge has ever studied their reception in detail or their use by Renaissance writers on tyranny and empire.[4]

This is all the more remarkable as tyranny and empire were central concerns of humanist political theory. A common if unserious humanist view is that constitutions are irrelevant as long as rulers have virtue, but no one has so far documented what relationship this view might have to similar views in Isocrates (for example, *Panathenaicus* 132). The present writer and others have explored Uberto Decembrio's rethinking of Milanese signory with the help of Plato's *Republic,* and Leonardo Bruni's use of Thucydides and Aelius Aristides to conceptualize Florentine republican ideology.[5] Marianne Pade has provided a comprehensive study of Plutarch's reception in the early quattrocento and has done important work on the translation of Thucydides, but her work does not focus specifically on regime theory.[6] There is still to my knowledge no detailed study of how Plutarch's account of the Athenian and Spartan constitutions in the lives of Solon and Lycurgus were digested in Renaissance political thought. There are apparently no studies of Renaissance reactions to Isocrates' call for meritocratic reform of the Athenian constitution in the *Areopagiticus.*[7] An important article of 1979 by Thomas Africa showing Thomas More's debts to the myth of Sparta in the *Utopia* has never been followed up with detailed studies that might tell us, for instance, which texts and translations mediated More's understanding of Spartan institutions.[8] More surprisingly, despite the avalanche of Ficino studies in recent decades, there is still no adequate treatment of Ficino's presentation of Plato's political thought in the *Republic* and the *Laws.* The Greek historians of the Roman empire and their influence on Western constitutional thought have been almost entirely overlooked.

An exception to this last generalization are the detailed studies of Gabriele Pedullà on Dionysius of Halicarnassus's reception in early modern Europe and particularly his chapters on Machiavelli's encounter with Dionysius.[9] His work illustrates the potential profit historians of political thought can derive from reception studies of non-Aristotelian political thought. For modern scholars Dionysius hardly ranks among the leading political thinkers of antiquity—he is barely mentioned, for example, in the *Cambridge History of Greek and Roman Political Thought,* the standard reference work—but his *Roman Antiquities,* following Polybius, gave detailed attention to a question that obsessed Renaissance humanists: What had made Rome great and allowed the city on the Tiber to dominate the

Mediterranean? This question was at the center of humanist political reflection from Petrarch to Machiavelli and beyond. For Dionysius the question was linked with another: Why had Greece failed where Rome succeeded? This way of posing the question appealed to Machiavelli, whose *Discorsi* and *History of Florence* take a similar comparative approach: Why had the modern republic of Florence—the "daughter of Rome" according to her civic myths—failed even to defend herself from foreign conquest while the Roman republic had succeeded in conquering the world? What was it about Roman customs, religion, and institutions that had brought it universal dominion? As Pedullà shows in painstaking philological detail, at least four major elements in Machiavelli's explanation of Roman greatness were derived from his reading of Dionysius: his understanding of how Rome's mixed constitution worked, his judgment that nonviolent social conflict ("tumult") was essential to the health of a republic, his positive evaluation of the early republican dictatorship, and his conclusion that it was Rome's openness to the participation of non-Romans in its armies and citizen body that had given it a decisive advantage over the Greek city-states. In other words, Machiavelli used Dionysius to deepen and correct his reading of Livy. This he was able to do (since Machiavelli knew no Greek) by consulting the translation of Dionysius by Lampugnino Birago, commissioned by Pope Nicholas V but dedicated after his death to Paul II.[10] Earlier humanists had taken Livy, Sallust, and Cicero as their principal guides to Rome's rise and decline, but Dionysius prompted Machiavelli to ask a different set of questions and give a different set of answers, and this fresh, more detached, and historically aware approach helped sharpen the great Florentine's analytical understanding of Roman political institutions and customs.

This is just one example of what can be gleaned from studying the reception of non-Aristotelian political theory, and as with so much in classical reception studies, the fields are ripe unto harvest. A single chapter cannot explore the full range of texts and their transformations in Renaissance culture. What is offered here is rather a simple typology—an account of three modes in which the second wave of Greek constitutional thought was exploited by fifteenth-century humanists—with some examples of how those texts fed into Western conversations about political regimes inherited from the scholastics. I will call this typology's three modes or programs, with suitable theoretical pomp, Legitimation, Delegitimation, and Substitution. Like all typologies its categories risk being reductive and incomplete, but I offer it as an analytical tool that other scholars may find useful or may wish to revise and refine.[11] As we shall see, humanist interest in ancient Greek constitutional thought was frequently motivated by interest in the symbiotic relationship between regimes, virtue, and wisdom, discussed most profoundly in Plato's *Laws:* Might good laws and regimes act as a substitute for the active wisdom and virtue of living rulers? Or could regimes be constructed in such a way as to corroborate or even increase political virtue? By the same token, did overreliance on laws as a substitute for active virtue create a kind of moral hazard leading to the decay of virtue? Did too strict a legal regime place a straitjacket on the virtue and discretion of good rulers and prevent them from acting effectively for the good of the state? If so, how could that legal regime be modified without losing the advantages of a law-based society?[12]

Legitimation and the Republican Regime

By the program of Legitimation, I mean the use of Greek theory to render acceptable to educated people constitutional practices that before the quattrocento had lacked prestige or full legitimacy. In the Middle Ages Aristotle's regime theory had already been used to undermine Christendom's default setting in favor of absolute monarchy. When urban ("consular") communes first appeared in Italy during the twelfth century, they sometimes appealed to the memory of the old Roman republic as part of their strategies of legitimation, but their status remained juridically contested well into the thirteenth century—indeed, increasingly so, as the popular commune succeeded the consular. The recovery of Aristotle's *Ethics* and *Politics* by scholastic theorists such as Thomas Aquinas, Tolomeo Fiadoni (Ptolemy of Lucca), or Henry of Rimini, however, introduced a new way of thinking about polities outside the traditional framework of Roman imperial law or Christian theocracy.[13] Understanding different regime types as natural phenomena, conceptualizing them in descriptive as well as normative terms, resulted in an attitude of mind that James Blythe has called "circumstantialism."[14] In the circumstantialist way of thinking, several regime types might be regarded as equally legitimate. Hence the choice of one regime over another could be considered a matter of prudence rather than a binary choice between legitimate or illegitimate forms. This meant that a juridically awkward form of government such as the popular commune in Italy could be recognized as a natural regime type, analyzed by the great scholastic authority Aristotle, of which better and worse forms occurred in nature. The popular commune could now be validated as the type of regime called *politia* in Moerbeke's translation, or rather transliteration, of Aristotle's term for virtuous popular rule. The category of *regimen politicum,* or constitutional rule, could exist as a legitimate option alongside the category of *regimen regale.*

In the Renaissance this rehabilitation of constitutional government was enhanced by scholar-officials such as Leonardo Bruni, who decked out the popular government of Florence in a new vocabulary that had more positive historical associations.[15] Thus, in his translation of the *Politics* Bruni was the first to apply the splendid name *respublica* to Aristotle's virtuous popular regime, and *respublica* became the prevailing term used in Italy to distinguish popular from princely government.[16] Even more radical was the approach of Cyriac of Ancona. He too wanted to improve the prestige of popular government, especially that of his hometown, Ancona. This led him to rehabilitate the term *democratia,* a word that had denoted corrupt or defective popular rule in Aristotle's *Politics.* He accomplished this by consulting the constitutional analysis of Polybius in book 6 of his *History of Rome*—presumably in Greek, since the text had not yet been translated. There he found a constitutional analysis in some ways similar to Aristotle's, in that constitutions were analyzed along two axes. One axis was the familiar division by the quantity of rulers: the one, the few, and the many. The other was a moral division into good and corrupt regimes. In Polybius, however, the terms for good and corrupt rule by the many, respectively, were *democratia* and *ochlocratia,* mob rule. Polybius thus validated Cyriac in adopting the term *democratia* to describe the popular government of his hometown. In this way he became one of the first political thinkers since antiquity to use the term in a positive sense.[17]

This might well have become a useful terminological innovation. Cyriac was probably driven to use it because in a speech he was writing to ambassadors from the Republic of Ragusa (modern Dubrovnik), he needed to distinguish Ragusa's aristocratic republic from Ancona's popular one. But his example was not followed: the Aristotelian prejudice against the term *democratia*—and the humanist prejudice against neologism—ran too deep. So the term *respublica* retained its ambiguity. In the later fifteenth century it came to apply both to the virtuous regime of a few and the virtuous regime of many, and in order to make themselves clear, political writers had to specify whether they were describing a popular or an aristocratic republic. Furthermore, Cicero's *De republica,* in a famous passage quoted by Augustine, licensed the use of *respublica* to denote any good constitution, whether royal, aristocratic, or popular. Aristotle himself, to further complicate matters, had used the same term, *politia,* to denote constitution in general as well as using it as a term for the virtuous popular regime, which I called "specific polity" in Chapter 3. Bruni transplanted this ambiguity faithfully into Latin by translating *politia* both in the generic and specific sense as *respublica*.

Francesco Patrizi on Republican Constitutions

This riot of equivocation required some policing, which Francesco Patrizi of Siena set out to provide in his twin treatises on republican and royal statesmanship, *How to Found a Republic* (1465 / 1471) and *How to Found a Kingdom and Educate a Prince* (1481 / 1484). It is worth pausing to comment on these works, since they became canonical sources of humanist political terminology whose influence lasted far into the seventeenth century. Renaissance humanists liked to compile what they often called *artes,* reference works that collected and sifted as many ancient authorities as they could find on particular subjects, arranging them systematically under various headings. The object was to present ancient knowledge in a way that would be useful to contemporaries who shared in the great Renaissance project of reforming the corrupt present on the model of the noble past. Leon Battista Alberti wrote just such an *ars* on architecture (*De re aedificatoria,* 1452); Roberto Valturio on military matters (*De re militari,* 1450); Johannes Tinctoris on music (*De inventione et usu musice,* 1481 / 1483); Biondo Flavio on Roman religion, government, and customs (*Roma triumphans,* 1456); Marsilio Ficino on Platonic theology (*Platonica Theologia,* 1482); and so on.[18] Patrizi's twin treatises on politics were his contribution to this genre. *How to Found a Kingdom* might be seen as a humanist updating of Giles of Rome's *De regimine principum,* the most important scholastic mirror of princes of the later Middle Ages. But Patrizi's other *ars, How to Found a Republic,* was the more original work. It aimed to provide a comprehensive treatment, collected from ancient historians and political philosophers, of issues relating to the governance of republican regimes for the use of magistrates, counselors, and citizens. Both works were immensely popular. They were printed at least fifty-one times before 1608 and translated into all major West European languages. Epitomes based on them were printed twenty-four times in Latin and French. Before 1620, only the political works of Aristotle and Machiavelli were printed more often.[19]

In the present context, Patrizi's *artes politicae* are key texts because they aspired to bring together for the first time into a single systematic framework the constitutional observations and analyses of historians and philosophers both Greek and Latin. Patrizi knew Greek well, but he made use whenever possible of quattrocento

Latin translations. These included works of Herodotus, Thucydides, Xenophon, Polybius, Plato, Plutarch, and the Greek historians of the Roman Empire. These Patrizi integrated with more familiar Roman sources such as Cicero, Livy, Sallust, and Tacitus. The result was that Western regime theory burst out of its scholastic Aristotelian paradigms and was vastly enriched and historicized. Much more explicitly than in scholastic political theory, the lessons of antiquity were applied to contemporary problems of republican governance. In keeping with the general pattern of humanist political thought, regime analysis became more historical and prudential and decoupled itself from the formalism of Aristotelian political science. Patrizi's treatises crystalized a humanist style of political discourse that had begun with the letter-treatises of Petrarch and would last well into the early modern period, where its most famous exemplars would be Jean Bodin's *Les six livres de la republique* (1576), Justus Lipsius' *Politica* (1589), and Hugo Grotius' *De iure pacis et belli* (1625).[20]

Patrizi's discussion of constitutions in *How to Found a Republic* offers a fine example of how the newly recovered Greek sources enriched Renaissance analysis of regimes.[21] He begins by excluding kingship and tyranny from his discussion, reserving a treatment of them for his companion work on monarchy. Notice that he uses the word *respublica* here to denote polyarchic rule as opposed to monarchic. The latter usage differs from that of Bruni, who, as we have just seen, had used the term in two senses, as a translation of *politia* meaning regime in general (including monarchy and tyranny), and for *politia* in the sense of the virtuous popular regime.[22]

Having excluded kingship and tyranny, Patrizi proceeds to treat six polyarchic or republican constitutions in descending order of merit. The two best are the popular regime *(popularis respublica)* and the regime of optimates (or aristocracy).[23] Both of these are described in terms drawn explicitly from Herodotus' account of the debate on regimes between Otanes and Megabyzus at the Persian court (3.80–81). The terminology follows that of the translation of Herodotus by Lorenzo Valla, whom Patrizi surely knew personally from his time as Sienese ambassador to the court of Pope Nicholas V. Patrizi may have looked at the Greek text as well, as his name for popular government is *isonomia,* legal equality, which is written in Greek characters. Aristotle is also in the background, since Patrizi, without mentioning or citing him, alludes to Aristotle's judgment that the end *(finis)* of the popular regime is freedom, while that of the optimate regime is virtue.[24] The desirability of optimate government is further backed by quotations—violently wrenched from their context—taken from Homer and from Dio Chrysostom's *De regno.*[25]

Then Patrizi moves down a step and discusses the rule of the wealthy, the first of three kinds of oligarchy. This regime, which he says is close to tyranny, aims at wealth. Patrizi admits wealth can be useful to states; quoting Cicero he says that riches provide the sinews of war and the ornaments of peace. However, this kind of regime has grave moral defects: it enriches the few and reduces the plebs to the status of servants (Patrizi is careful to specify *famuli*, not the ambiguous word *servi*, which could mean slaves or servants). Furthermore, it is defective in that it doesn't value virtue; in support of this statement Patrizi cites a letter to the tyrant Periander from Thrasybulus, preserved in Diogenes Laertius, whose *Lives of the Philosophers* had been translated in 1431 by Ambrogio Traversari.[26] Thrasybulus states that bad rulers always need to cut down the virtuous like overgrown ears of corn; virtuous men just get in the way of those who would exploit others.

Patrizi then goes down yet another notch to two regimes that are even more defective morally. They not only exclude whole portions of the populace from the regime, but they treat the excluded portions even worse than wealthy oligarchs do. The wealthy merely make the poor their servants, but these two regimes are actively cruel and abusive toward the excluded. The first of the two bad oligarchies is a regime led by plebeians who rule in the interest of the lowest classes, artisans and farm workers. They persecute and rob the nobles and hold the virtuous and the learned in contempt. A plebeian regime like this might be able to last a short while, but it will ultimately be brought down by its own ignorance, inexperience and meanness of spirit. The second bad oligarchy is the rule of a junta. This too will be abusive and cruel. Patrizi's primary example here is the rule of Appius Claudius Crassus and the decemvirs, which the bishop knows from both Livy and Dionysius of Halicarnassus. A junta is made up of noblemen who use arbitrary violence against the plebs—Patrizi cites the example of Appius' rape of Verginia—and their aggressive spirit, unregulated by virtue, leads them into military adventurism. Sometimes, says Patrizi, this can lead to enlarging the state, but more often it leads to its collapse. Patrizi cites from Dionysius of Halicarnassus the example of the Spartans at Leuctra, and from Gemistus Pletho's compendium of Greek history, composed in Florence around 1440, he takes similar lessons about the fate of Thebes and Athens when under the control of aristocratic juntas.[27]

Having dealt with the five pure forms of polyarchic regime, Patrizi now reflects on the principle of inclusion and how it can be reconciled with the humanist preference for virtuous rulership. It seems unjust, he says, entirely to exclude from political power farmers and merchants. Civil society *(civilis societas)* can't survive without them, but their economic roles make them poor rulers; they don't have the leisure to devote to study or to politics. But in order that the weaker not appear to be entirely abandoned by the great, they should be included on less important civic committees. He then, following Cicero in the *De legibus,* speaks approvingly of the Roman *tribuni plebis,* and he commends Marcus Menenius Agrippa for defending the principle that the Senate and the People were one body, *unum corpus,* a speech he knows from Livy (2.33).

After invoking the organic principle that the best republic needs to act in concert like a single body, Patrizi alludes to the Aristotelian idea (again without mentioning Aristotle) that the middle class (the *mediocres*) are the class likeliest to rule *modestius,* in a more restrained, less self-serving way.[28] But if you have to choose between the rule of the plebs and the nobles, the nobles are better, because they are restrained by the reputation of their ancestors, or possibly by inborn virtue acquired from their ancestors, whereas the plebs are not. Patrizi thus adopts a pose of indifference to the issue, hotly debated among humanists, whether noble blood contributes to virtue. Diplomatically, he is careful to add, citing Livy's account of the Decii, that there are certainly some plebeians, even rustics and men of obscure origins, who have served the state well.

The potentiality for virtue in all social classes had been a standard humanist political meme since the time of Petrarch and Boccaccio. Here Patrizi uses it to introduce his final point, that the best polyarchic regime was one that mixed together popular and aristocratic elements: "I number myself with those who say the best polity is that which is mixed of every type of human being."[29] In proof of this contention he cites Plutarch's lives of Solon and Lycurgus. Solon advised including the *multitudo* in voting and the election of magistrates *(in suffragia electionesque magistratuum)* and also in *magna concilia,* presumably meaning something like the Athenian assembly. He then repeats Aristotle's argument (once again Aristotle is not named) in defense of democracy: that it can benefit from the pooling of knowledge in popular assemblies.[30] Just as the hive mind understands the arts better than individuals (here Patrizi adds painting to Aristotle's examples of music and poetry), so too in politics. Thus while the wise man is he who is aware of how much he doesn't know, the many jointly will be ignorant of fewer things *(coniuncti plures pauciora ignorabunt).* Patrizi's final position on polyarchic regimes is the same as Aristotle's: that the best practical regime is a mixture of popular government and government by the few. But he attributes this judgment not to Aristotle but to Lycurgus, whose constitutional arrangements he knows from Xenophon and Plutarch. Lycurgus made his state great, powerful, and enduring by blending the *paucorum potentia* with the *popularis status*. "He desired to constitute a society from the many to make it better and more stable."[31]

The total effect of Patrizi's analysis is to build a case for popular government, or rather for the inclusion of a popular element in a constitution that also values true nobility, learning, and virtue. The state will be stronger, more virtuous, just, and stable if the commoners and the plebs are included in the regime in prudent ways. The virtue argument for including the people in government is thus based on prudence, humanity, and active justice rather than on legalistic notions of legitimacy or right derived from popular consent. Prudence, it is implied, cannot be simply extracted whole from a single theoretical text such as Aristotle's *Politics* but has to be built up from careful study of a wide range of philosophers and historians. These, as Cicero claimed, extend the natural memory of humanity and thus contribute to practical wisdom. A good society is one that is organic, that recognizes the contributions of all classes to its welfare and shows its humanity by treating others with kindness and by avoiding war for the sake of war and conquest.

Patrizi's decision to avoid citing Aristotle, even when he is relying on well-known Aristotelian arguments, reflects a wider humanist methodology, descending from Petrarch, that regards reliance on a single authority as intellectually servile, whereas assembling and comparing the widest possible array of certifiably wise writers from antiquity frees and elevates the mind.[32] It may also reflect a desire to distinguish his humanistic treatment of political virtue from the *De regimine principum* of Giles of Rome, his most important scholastic rival.[33] Giles laid great emphasis on the Aristotelian pedigree of his ideas, though Aquinas' political thought exerts an enormous, unacknowledged influence.

Patrizi's treatise *How to Found a Republic* thus illustrates the first mode of reception in my typology: Legitimation. It is perhaps the most important mode in terms of its long-term consequences for European political thought. The translation of Aristotle's *Politics* in the thirteenth century opened up the theoretical possibility of justifying popular elements in a mixed constitution, and this is an avenue many scholastics from Thomas Aquinas to Marsilius of Padua exploited. Yet the majority of Aristotle's interpreters, including the enormously influential Giles of Rome, continued to regard him as a monarchist.[34] What the humanist recovery of ancient Greek political history and philosophy helped accomplish in this case was to make popular regimes more intellectually respectable, a task begun in a more polemical vein by Leonardo Bruni in the early quattrocento. By the 1460s humanists like Patrizi understood that the most famous city-states of the Greek world, Athens and Sparta, in their finest days had enjoyed, respectively, a popular regime and a mixed regime with a popular element. Thanks to Bruni, republican government, understood as a regime type, was already escaping the prejudice against the Roman republic transmitted by imperial and early Christian historiography. In time the humanists' study of Roman history brought them to a better appreciation for the Roman republican constitution.[35] The experience of the ancient Greek city-states provided them with further resources to explore how free institutions could be strong, effective, and lasting, so long as those who led them were virtuous and able to restrain the vicious.

As we saw at the end of the previous chapter, the Spartan regime in particular helped Patrizi demonstrate this point. The possibility that a polyarchic government could remain stable over centuries, that a republican constitution could be designed "sufficient to maintain itself," to use Machiavelli's words, was a key point in the defense of republics against their humanist critics. Pro-monarchical humanists such as Pier Candido Decembrio, Giovanni Pontano, and Aurelio Brandolini, like Dante before them, typically made the claim that republics were inherently unstable, and this was also a common view among political elites of the time. The idea that a free republic could be perpetual so long as it remained virtuous was one that was to have a long career in Western political thought, down to the time of the American Founding Fathers.

Delegitimation: Bruni and the Chivalric Ideal

The recovery of Greek constitutional thought in the quattrocento could also operate in a second mode, and indeed an opposite mode to that of Legitimation—namely, Delegitimation. By this I mean the use of Greek political thought to invalidate contemporary political mores and regimes that humanists held to be pernicious. An example will clarify the concept: Leonardo Bruni's use of Greek sources to delegitimate the medieval ideal of chivalry.[36]

This ideal enjoyed its greatest prestige in France but also had tremendous appeal in Italy as early as the thirteenth century, even in republican Florence. Francis of Assisi and Dante were only the most famous of the innumerable Italians inspired by the chivalric ideal. In late medieval Italy chivalry and knighthood were intimately connected with concepts of nobility—concepts humanists were determined to challenge with their insistence that true nobility came from virtue, acquired through the study of the classics. Bruni himself regarded the chivalric ideal as dangerous to civic life because it promoted transnational political commitments like crusading. It also compromised patriotism by creating loyalties to foreign potentates like the pope, the emperor, or the king of France, who distributed knighthoods to Florentine citizens. Such honors recognized no true military valor but merely gave the recipient the right to dress up in fancy clothes and lord it over his fellow citizens. Worse, chivalry taught powerful men that their private honor was more important than the common good.[37] Their feudal rivalries and misplaced sense of honor tore the city apart, as Bruni had demonstrated again and again in his *History of the Florentine People.* Chivalry also made a fetish of romantic love, a disordered passion which led to the weakening of families, the building blocks of the state, and to other types of civic discord.

As discussed in Chapter 9, Bruni in his treatise *On Knighthood* proposed an antidote to this dangerous nonsense spread by chivalric literature: a new ideal of civic knighthood suitable to Italian city-states, inspired equally by Greek philosophy and Roman history. In fashioning his ideal he showed an appreciation for the importance of mores and customs—taught primarily by the family and civil society—in the maintenance of political regimes. Ancient philosophers such as Plato and Aristotle and ancient historians such as Dionysius of Halicarnassus understood that a polity's way of life—its ways of earning a livelihood, its family life, its arts and music, its military organization, its religious observances and ceremonies—were far more important to the health of a regime than the formal, legal allocation of power among assemblies and magistrates that we tend to think of as "constitutions" today. It was in the daily life of citizens where true soulcraft occurred. This was an aspect of the polity virtually ignored by scholastic interpreters of Aristotle, with their focus on issues of justice, law, and the basis of *imperium* and *potestas.* The humanists brought it back once more into the spotlight.

Bruni also attacked the chivalric ideal in another way: by subjecting it to literary ridicule. This he did in his *Novella di Antioco, re di Siria* (1438).[38] Bruni composed this novel in the vernacular, basing it not on the anecdotal version of the story in Valerius Maximus but on the longer narratives of Plutarch (*Demetrius* 37) and Appian (*Syrian Wars* 59). It was written as a kind of companion piece to his Latin translation of the *Fabula Tancredi* from Boccaccio's *Decameron* (4.1). Bruni jokingly says that his novel represents compensation to the vernacular after his appropriation of the Tancred tale for Latin literature. In the latter tale, it may be recalled, Boccaccio recounts how the uncontrollable sexual jealousy of Tancred, prince of Salerno, leads him to kill his daughter's lover Guiscardo and to send her his heart in a goblet. His daughter, Sigismonda, adds poison to the cup and drinks it, dying pathetically in the approved Gothic manner. As an antidote to this tale of disordered passion, which he explicitly castigates as a modern "Italian" behavior pattern, Bruni tells the story of Antioco, son of King Seleuco of Syria.

In Bruni's novella, set like the *Decameron* in a villa outside Florence, the story of Tancred has just been told and has reduced all the women to tears. At this point a man, "whose name we shall hide for the present, but he is a man highly learned in Greek and Latin who has made a careful study of ancient history"—obviously Bruni himself—tells the ladies a tale "to restore their festive spirits, as though by means of a tale contrary to the previous one." The narrator starts by saying that he has always found the ancient Greeks far in advance of modern Italians when it comes to humanity and *gentilezza di cuore*. In Bruni's tale the king's son, Antioco, falls in love with the king's young wife, Stratonica, but conceals his passion out of decency and respect for his father. Under the influence of this unrequited love his health is ruined, and he is about to die when a wise physician learns the real cause. By a clever ruse, the physician leads King Seleuco to arrange for an amicable divorce and for the remarriage of his wife to his son. For Bruni this is a happy ending, showing eminently sensible behavior that leads to the prosperous continuance of the monarchy and the provision of grandchildren for the doting King Seleuco. The novel ends on a sentimental, bourgeois note: "And afterwards, when he cast his eyes upon his little grandchildren, certain to continue his lineage, he lived happily ever after." Bruni expects us to realize that rational behavior such as this would never be possible for someone immersed in chivalric traditions, where love and personal honor are inextricably intertwined. A man like Tancred will destroy his monarchy and kill his daughter to satisfy a pernicious notion of honor, but Seleuco saves his son *and* his monarchy by subordinating his private sense of honor to the common good. The ancient Greeks thus teach that love of family and loyalty to the state come before personal sexual honor.

Two could play at this game, and Bruni himself in the same decade became a target of a classic delegitimation ploy at the hands of Francesco Filelfo. As we saw in the last chapter, Filelfo was the most important humanist translator of Greek sources for Spartan history. Filelfo constantly used Spartan examples and the authority of Lycurgus, the most respected Greek lawgiver, to denigrate oligarchic regimes that gave too much power to the wealthy—above all the regime of his nemesis, Cosimo de'Medici. In so doing he was pushing back against the work of humanists like Bruni and Bruni's ally Poggio Bracciolini, both of whom had tried to defend the accumulation of private wealth as useful to the state. The principal work in which Bruni had taken this position was his translation and commentary on the pseudo-Aristotelian *Economics,* dedicated, unsurprisingly, to Cosimo de'Medici.[39] Marching out the Spartans against the Aristotelians brings us to our next program or mode of deploying ancient authorities: Substitution.

Substitution: Platonizing Venice's Constitution

By Substitution I mean using one ancient authority, or a set of authorities, to subvert or displace another. Probably the best-known example of (attempted) Substitution in Renaissance philosophy arose in the Plato-Aristotle controversy of the mid-fifteenth century. A party of Greek émigrés led by Cardinal Bessarion, a former student of the crypto-pagan philosopher Pletho, launched a campaign to reinstate in the West, after a long period when Aristotle had been the chief philosophical authority, the ancient and Byzantine hierarchy among philosophers, which had given the primacy to Plato. For them Plato was *theios,* godlike, Aristotle merely *daimonios,* or superhuman. Building on Petrarch's critique of scholastic culture in his famous invective *On His Own Ignorance and That of Many Others,* Bessarion's party aimed to re-establish Plato as the greatest ancient philosopher and the pagan philosopher closest to Christianity. They were opposed by George of Trebizond, a convert to Latin Christianity and therefore more Catholic than the pope. Trebizond believed one reason for Latin Christendom's superiority to Greek Orthodoxy was the former's reliance on Aristotle as its chief philosophical guide. To reintroduce Platonism as the handmaid of Christian theology would lead to its ruin, as it had (according to George) in the Greek East.

The controversy spilled over into the realm of political theory when George, in book 3 of his *Comparison of Plato and Aristotle* (1457 / 1458), brought his intimate knowledge of Plato's *Laws*—a text he had been compelled against his will to translate by Pope Nicholas V—to bear on the task of destroying Plato's reputation as a political philosopher.[40] Trebizond's savage review of the constitution of Plato's model city, Magnesia, attacked Plato just where one would expect a humanist to attack him. Magnesia was denounced for its rigid social classes and denial of civic rights to immigrants, even ones of long standing.[41] To humanist political thinkers, for whom it was a cardinal principle that political standing should rest on virtue, not heredity, this was a powerful argument. George's contemporary and colleague in the papal curia, the great antiquarian Biondo Flavio, had argued, with the authority of his immense learning, that a key reason for Rome's success in antiquity had been its openness to political and military participation from non-Romans and immigrants. When George presented Plato as a thoroughgoing restrictionist (as indeed he was), he was showing the Greek philosopher's incompatibility with the best Roman traditions.

Yet when under the compulsion of praising Plato, as he was in the second dedication of his translation of the *Laws* to the Venetian Senate (1460), George found himself able to employ the rhetorician's skill of speaking on both sides of a question. In this dedication George claims that the mixed constitution recommended by Plato in his *Laws* was the inspiration for the most perfect constitution the world had ever seen or ever would see, namely, that of the present-day Venetian state, a free city-state ruled with the greatest possible virtue. Indeed, he claims that the resemblance is so close that the original founders of Venice must have derived their mixed constitution directly or indirectly from the *Laws*:

> Plato believed that the only way the freedom of a city-state could be strong and lasting was for it to bear the image of the three most admired [kinds of] state: that which was governed by a single prince, that of the optimates, and that of the people. But he said these things in words that only the Venetians could truly understand and whose truth only they could demonstrate in reality. For they follow a single prince [the doge]; and optimates are chosen to deliberate on public business who are dazzling for their prudence, justice, and distinction, and they are in charge of all matters pertaining to war and peace. But they don't neglect the image of the popular state either, that is, the true power of the people itself, for they bring together in assemblies to elect magistrates all who have some share in public business.[42]

Trebizond goes on to itemize other Venetian offices and institutions that have parallels in Plato's *Laws,* speculating that the founders of Venice in the Dark Ages, Roman aristocrats fleeing from barbarian invasions, surely had a fine knowledge of Greek as well as Latin and could have read him in the original. But Venice's founders were greater than even Plato could have imagined. Plato believed that the only way his laws could be established was if some tyrant were to seize power and force the people to be free. That had not been necessary in Venice: "Plato plainly states that unless some well-behaved tyrant could be found, his laws would never be embodied in a state. Thus the men who founded Venice prevailed over all other men in the whole class of virtues and in civil science, so much so that, uncompelled by a tyrant, they themselves were led to turn the model of the Platonic state into a reality."[43] The Venetians, indeed, improved on the Platonic model, and George goes on to list the various ways in which they did so. He notes in particular that the Venetian senate was open to the virtuous, who might be elected for their knowledge of things human and divine, their piety, and for recognized qualities of affability and kindness. The Venetian citizenry who were summoned to the *comitia* were no seditious mob of vulgarians but men worthy to be compared with patricians and senators. Indeed, Venice was superior in its institutions to both ancient Athens and Sparta. Even Rome, great and long-lasting though its power had been, did not owe its greatness and longevity to its constitutional stability; in fact its constitution was unstable and changed often "in the manner of the chameleon." Its disunity was such that it hardly deserved the name of *civitas* or city-state. So unstable was it with sedition and civil war that many sought relative peace by engaging in foreign wars. "But the republic of Venice, home of justice, mistress of peace, never undertook war but for the sake of peace, and never substituted war for peace."[44] It has lasted more than a thousand years with a great empire on land and sea, growing in wealth and power through virtue and the favor of God, and has never shown a trace of faction, sedition, or even dissension. There is nothing left to say; one can only look on in silent wonder. The governors of Venice are truly like kings, and Venetian government more divine than human.

George of Trebizond's account of the Platonic origins of Venice thus presents us with two forms of Substitution. First, his grafting of Venetian institutions onto a Platonic rootstock gave the Venetian mixed constitution a Platonic rather than a medieval Aristotelian flavor. Earlier writers such as the Dominican Henry of Rimini, Benzo d'Alessandria, and the humanist Pier Paolo Vergerio had described Venice's constitution in vaguely Aristotelian categories mediated by Thomas Aquinas. George's mythologizing uprooted Venice's constitution from its medieval traditions and replanted it in more noble ancient soil.[45]

The second, more important form of Substitution is this: by tracing the inspiration of Venice's polity to a Greek source, George subverted the famous "myth of Venice" that presented her as a "New Rome," heir both to Rome's republican government and her empire, as well as the hazier myth of the founding of Padua and Venice by Trojan Antenor. These myths had been promoted by earlier humanists such as Vergerio, Lauro Quirini, and Paolo Morosini as well as in medieval sources.⁴⁶ Though the image of Venice as the New Rome was ultimately to prove the more dominant in Venice's imperial age, George provided *la Serenissima* with a substitute ancestry, a Greek constitutional ancestry, for those who might want it.

And indeed, some Venetian patricians, many of whom had enjoyed a fine education in the humanities, eagerly embraced the belief that the city's founders had learned from Plato how to maintain their civic liberty and majesty. Francesco Barbaro, a leading humanist and diplomat in the Venetian patriciate, wrote to George after receiving a first draft of the preface:

> Either love of country deceives me or this republic of ours, which has always lived by its own laws, was constituted with such pure morals, such just laws, such honorable decrees, that, as you say, our rivers appear to have risen from Plato's springs. . . . For the rest I urge you to dedicate to us these *Laws* of our Plato with a short preface, worthy of the author and the greatness of the subject, and I shall disseminate them among our citizens in such fashion that at some point you will receive no small recompense for your labors.⁴⁷

Yet the really fascinating part of George's description of Venice's Platonic origins lies in his assertion (perhaps fed in some way by his suppressed animus toward Plato) that Venice had surpassed and perfected Plato's political wisdom *ab initio*. In Plato's own judgment (according to George) his laws would have required tyrannical coercion to make them effective, but Venice had achieved an ideal mixed constitution without violent force, through the virtue and prudence of its founders. Unlike the Aristotelian or Polybian mixed constitutions that were counsels of prudence, directed at states trapped in cyclical crises, and unlike the makeshift institutions of Florence or Siena or Lucca that had emerged haphazardly through turbulent centuries, Venice's institutions were not improvised bulwarks thrown up in the course of historical struggles against tides of factionalism or corruption. They were a perfect achievement of human prudence guided by philosophical wisdom. They gave hope to the founders of other republics that it might be possible for societies of men "to establish good government from reflection and choice," that they were not "forever destined to depend for their political constitutions on accident and force," to quote Alexander Hamilton.

Venice had also surpassed the three great ancient states put forward by other humanists as models: Athens, Sparta, and Rome. Perhaps in George's case these claims came from the tongue of flattery, but they were to be repeated in the sixteenth century by the two leading authorities on the Venetian regime, Donato

Giannotti and Gasparo Contarini.[48] It thus came to be seriously debated among the learned whether the great but tumultuous and violent empire of Rome was really a better model for moderns than the more stable, peaceful, and prosperous empire of the Venetians. In other words Venice became the prime example of the capacity of modern societies to surpass the ancients in political wisdom—an aspect of that *querelle des anciens et des modernes* which helped defined the culture of the early modern period.[49]

Mario Salamonio Compares Florence to Athens

Another striking, though far less influential, attempt at Substitution appears in several orations before the Florentine Signoria delivered by the prominent Roman jurist Mario Salamonio degli Alberteschi when he was serving in Florence as a foreign judge (Captain of the People) for a six-month term in 1498 / 1499. Salamonio is best known today as a defender of popular sovereignty in the Bartolist tradition and an early contract theorist, a remarkable set of commitments for a Roman noble and papal official. He is often classified as a legal humanist thanks to his combination of scholastic and humanistic culture, a pairing increasingly common in the late fifteenth century.[50]

Salamonio came to Florence just after the execution of Savonarola when, by his own account, Florence was wavering in fear and desire between oligarchic, popular, tyrannical, and theocratic ("prophetic") forms of government. Salamonio compared his own situation to that of Plato when he was called in to bring order to Syracuse after the fall of the tyrant Dionysius I.[51] Like other foreign officials Salamonio was expected to deliver ceremonial speeches in the Palazzo Vecchio during his tenure of office, and these were apparently of sufficient distinction that he was later asked to have them copied out for interested parties. The seven orations were finally collected more than a decade later under the title of *Florentine Panegyrics.*[52]

In these orations Salamonio shows himself to be a passionate supporter of Florentine popular government and a student of its institutional development, something he has learned about from reading Bruni's *History of the Florentine People.* He gives an account of his own office of Captain of the People (or *Pretore*), which he presents (correctly) as a magistracy born of the popular struggle against magnates and nobles. He shows himself committed to the popular principles of liberty and equality and (like Bruni) believes that the function of the aristocracy is to advise and lead but not to share power on an equal basis with the

People.[53] More to the point, he shows considerable knowledge of Plato's *Republic* and *Laws,* quoting twice from book 7 of the latter in Ficino's translation of 1484. On the basis of Plato's authority he commends to his audience the need for *una pubblica disciplina,* an education in virtue that will bring up future citizens so that they will have no desire to do evil deeds. Plato's *Republic* is cited as a model for such a civic education. He sharply criticizes legislators who punish crimes but show no concern to abolish the causes of crime in the souls of citizens. He then lays out a whole program of Platonic-style education (for which he also cites Cicero and other authorities) designed to limit the exposure of youth to enervating luxury, demoralizing poetry, and libidinous forms of dress, while at the same time encouraging religion, sound letters, frugality, and virility.[54]

The oration that best exemplifies Substitution is the seventh and last, *De nobilitate Reipublicae Florentinae.*[55] Salamonio begins by addressing what the social historian Richard Trexler called the "honor deficit" of Florentine popular government: that it was a government run by tradesmen and merchants whose profits were widely believed to depend on *mendacio,* lying and deceit.[56] Salamonio stipulates that some famous ancient cities like Thebes, Roman statesmen like Cicero, and philosophers like Plato and Aristotle all agreed that men engaged in mercantile activities should be kept from public office. But Salamonio replies that, by Aristotle's own account (*Politics* 4.4.1291a), cities are defined by their ability to be self-sustaining, and that is not possible without farmers, artisans, and merchants. Hence they are organic parts of the state. Furthermore, trade and manufacture are not in themselves wicked *métiers* but can be carried on honorably. Citing Hesiod (via Plutarch's *Life of Solon* 2.3) he claims that commerce brings cities together with ties of friendship and helps them win the favor of kings. He then advises Florentines that the way to ennoble *(nobilitare)* commerce is to cultivate what in the early modern period came to be recognized as the bourgeois virtues: honesty, sincerity, simplicity, trustworthiness, sealing transactions of purchase and sale with a simple yes or no. Salamonio admits that it is *conveniente* to have a city governed by "mirrors of virtue" and that such men best represent the *maiestas* of the city to outsiders. Not all *populari* are suitable to participate in government for this reason. But as the *arti* or craft guilds are necessary to the city, their members cannot be excluded from city government; to do so would be to weaken the city and encourage sloth. That is why the ancients believed the *arti* were invented by the gods.

Then Salamonio begins a remarkable passage that compares Florentine popular government to the democracy of ancient Athens. This was an innovative comparison given the wider context. Since the thirteenth century Florence had based its civic myth on its foundation as a Roman colony. She was the daughter of Rome still, and the blood of Romulus continued to flow in the veins of her people. The Roman republican roots of the Florentine polity had been celebrated by the humanists Coluccio Salutati and Leonardo Bruni. Later Bruni decided to establish a different ancestry for Florence and traced her *gens* back to the Etruscans rather than to the Romans. Florence in this ideological refoundation was the leader of an Etruscan league and could reach out to cities like Mantua on the basis of a common Etruscan heritage.[57]

Salamonio will have none of this, perhaps because he is a Roman noble himself and is more interested in launching a new Florentine civic myth that will essentialize the city's populism. He asks his audience, What is the noblest of all republics? If you are inclined to answer, "The Roman!" you should first consider the many parallels between the Athenian and Florentine republics. Then you might be led to affirm instead, "The Athenian!" In fact the correspondences between Florence and Athens are so numerous, he claims, that it might appear that both cities were founded by Solon. Salamonio goes on to list nine parallels in proof of his contention, giving a dramatic example of what modern German reception theory refers to as *allelopoiesis*, that is, reshaping the meaning of an ancient text in the process of deploying it as an authority for contemporary practices. Most of these parallels were excerpted from his reading of Plutarch's *Life of Solon*, a text he undoubtedly knew in the translation of Lapo da Castiglionchio.[58] At least one detail comes from Herodotus, probably in Valla's translation.[59]

The parallels Salamonio noted are as follows: (1) Florence and Athens had a similarly infertile site, requiring them both to encourage crafts rather than agriculture. (2) Athens was composed of four tribes; Florence of four *quartieri*. (3) Both had popular governments. (4) Both had a similar class structure, except that Florence hired mercenaries to fight for her while Athens provided her own soldiers, who (according to Salamonio) formed a separate class of hoplites. (5) Both had similarly limited terms for their magistracies. (6) Both had two assemblies—a popular one and a more aristocratic one. (7) Both elected magistrates and council members by lot. (8) Both had systems that laid great emphasis on helping the weak to obtain justice from the strong, a consequence of their organic political ideal.

(9) Both cities valued work and celebrated *homo faber*. In Florence, guild membership was a condition of political participation, and the *scioperati,* those who lived on rents without working, were not only prohibited from holding public office but were also looked down upon as *otiosi et ignavi,* idle and spiritless—a far cry from the Ciceronian concept of *otium* as honorable leisure. Salamonio found a parallel to the Florentine concept of the dignity of work in Solon's legislation requiring fathers to teach their sons a craft and freeing sons not so taught from the obligation of supporting their fathers in old age.

Entering his peroration, Salamonio praises the law excluding from public office those who were not members of guilds as "the most blameless, useful and fruitful law, destroying idleness and lack of spirit, which are the root of, and the yeast for, all vice." He concludes:

> Thus, *signori miei,* when I consider these customs, institutions, and laws, I encounter a total similarity, and such that, if you were to take away the names, you couldn't tell what is Attic from what is Florentine. He who praises [Athens] must necessarily praise your state; he who admires and extolls the former has to hold the latter no less in veneration. And don't believe that your status is lower because of your popular government being subject to various uprisings and turbulence on the part of common people of obscure origins, who are credulous, suspicious, easily influenced, jealous and timid. Believe rather that you are more praiseworthy, because civic virtue has to do with hard and difficult things. Believe that the popular republic is the true republic, that is, the people's property *(id est res populi)*—not the royal or optimate republic. It is the republic where one lives naturally and everyone is born free, lives on a basis of equality with others, and dies free.[60]

Thus the recovery of Plutarch and other Greek historians and orators in the fifteenth century helped at least a few contemporaries form a more positive view of popular government by tracing its origins to the famous city of Athens, home of the Muses, fountainhead of philosophy and champion of democracy. The newly available Greek writers helped some Renaissance thinkers push back against the dominant humanist preference—reflecting the settled opinion of Aristotle and Cicero among others—for government to be guided by the hands of the *ingenui* and *generosi,* gentlemen who did not have to work for a living and had the leisure to study the liberal arts.[61] While most humanists continued to look to ancient Rome as the measure of a successful republic and as their inspiration for the renewal of civilization in general, the study of Greek literature presented the learned with other possible models, such as the polities of Athens and Sparta or the oligarchical republic of the Phoenicians or the monarchical empire of the Persians as idealized in Xenophon's *Cyropaedia*.[62]

It should by now be evident that the translation into Latin of non-Aristotelian Greek constitutional thought (and Greek political thought in general) in the course of the quattrocento vastly enriched Western political theory not only in the Renaissance but throughout the early modern period and beyond. In part this was because quattrocento humanist translations of the Greek theorists continued to be used and revised well into the seventeenth century, and new ones were made in the sixteenth century whose shelf life was even longer. Likewise, Italian humanist works of political literature, especially by authors such as Leonardo Bruni, Francesco Patrizi of Siena, Giovanni Pontano, Gasparo Contarini, Donato Giannotti, Francesco Guicciardini, and preeminently Machiavelli—all authors well informed about Greek political thought—continued to be part of the European conversation about the best regime down to modern times. More substantively, in a world where the vast majority of educated people favored monarchy, Greek regime theory helped to legitimate popular and aristocratic forms of government. Of course it would be wrong to say that Greek political theory as a whole favored polyarchic rule: as we shall see in the next chapter, a sizeable number of Greek theorists preferred monarchy or at least (like Isocrates) were prepared to consider its advantages. But in Western Christendom during the Late Middle Ages, republican regimes lacked cultural prestige, and this is what the Greeks gave them. Finally, the one principle Greek political theorists all did agree upon was the need for virtue in the ruling class. This was a principle they shared with the Romans of course, but the result was that all antiquity seemed to speak with one voice on the principle dearest to the hearts of humanist political thinkers: that only the good and wise deserve to rule.

CHAPTER 17

FRANCESCO PATRIZI AND HUMANIST ABSOLUTISM

In previous chapters we considered how the vast humanist project to recover the written heritage of ancient Greece and translate it into Latin—long the universal language of learned intercourse in the West—gradually enriched and transformed Western political thought during the Renaissance.[1] At the end of Chapter 4 I described the return to Italy of the ancient Greek "discourse of tyranny" in newly translated works by Xenophon, Plato, Herodotus, and various authors associated with the Second Sophistic. Chapter 15 discussed the recovery and use of sources concerning the Spartan regime, and Chapter 16 examined the assimilation of the "second wave" of Greek constitutional thought, as various non-Aristotelian sources of regime theory became accessible in the West. The present chapter examines Francesco Patrizi's theory of ideal kingship in his *De regno et regis institutione libri IX* (1481 / 1484), which elaborated a humanist version of royal absolutism based on principles of virtue politics. But as this theory was assembled primarily from ancient Greek discussions of ideal monarchy, and indeed is hardly imaginable without them, we shall need briefly to survey their recovery in the course of the quattrocento.

The Recovery of Ancient Greek Monarchical Theory

Greek theories of ideal monarchy began to appear in the fourth century BC and were principally the work of Athenian political thinkers. It will be less surprising that monarchical theory began in the home of democracy when one appreciates that the leading theorists were all followers of Socrates and were all in some degree alienated from Athenian democracy by its responsibility for the judicial murder of their spiritual master. It is to Socrates, indeed, that Xenophon attributes what counts as the first instance of a theoretical distinction made between tyranny and kingship in surviving Greek literature.[2] It occurs in his *Memorabilia,* a text first made available to the Latin West in Cardinal Bessarion's translation of 1442 under the title *De dictis et factis Socratis:*

> Kingship [βασιλεία, *regnum*] and despotism [τυραννίς, *tyrannis*], in his judgement, were both principles of government [ἀρχαί, *principatus*], but he held that they differed. For government of willing people in accordance with the laws of the state was kingship [ἀρχὴν βασιλείαν, *principatus regalis*], while government of unwilling subjects, not controlled by laws but imposed by the will of the ruler, was despotism [τυραννίς]. And where the officials are chosen among those who fulfill the requirements of the laws [*or* are guided by the laws], the constitution is an aristocracy; where ratable property is the qualification for office, you have a plutocracy; where all are eligible, a democracy.[3]

Here kingship and tyranny were distinguished by two criteria: willing subjects and legality.[4] Virtue does not make an appearance in this passage, though elsewhere in the *Memorabilia* Xenophon's Socrates makes it amply clear that good government cannot exist without wisdom and virtue.

Xenophon's most important contribution to the theory of kingship, however, was his *Cyropaedia,* an idealized (not to say fictionalized) tale describing the career of the great king Cyrus II, founder of the Persian Empire, who is presented as an ideal ruler governing his willing subjects with benevolence.[5] The work begins by deploring the pervasiveness of political instability and the inability of rulers to control the unruliness of their peoples. It raises the question, central to humanist theories of moral legitimacy, why it is that people willingly obey some rulers and not others. The answer, says Xenophon, can be found by looking to history, and outside the Greek world, for the finest examples of rulership:

> But when we reflected that there was one Cyrus, the Persian, who reduced to obedience a vast number of men and cities and nations, we were then compelled to change our opinion [that men are ungovernable] and decide that to rule men might be a task neither impossible nor even difficult, if one should only go about it in a knowledgeable manner. At all events, we know that people obeyed Cyrus willingly, although some of them were distant from him a journey of many days, and others of many months; others, although they had never seen him, and still others who knew well that they never should see him. Nevertheless they were all willing to be his subjects.[6]

Since Cyrus reduced many nations to willing obedience, study of his career should offer insight into this question. Cyrus' virtue, which included his competence as a ruler as well as his moral virtue, is the obvious answer, but behind that answer lies another question: How was that virtue acquired, and how was it deployed in practice? The rest of the *Cyropaedia* (called the *Cyri institutio* by humanists) gives the answer.

Cyrus had an education in moral action, especially just actions, that was prescribed by the laws of Persia (Xenophon says) but that (as modern scholars note) was in fact reminiscent of Spartan military education with its emphasis on service to the state. He learned that equal adherence to law is what distinguishes a king from a tyrant. From his father Cambyses he learned respect for the gods and the arts of rule, especially how to elicit willing obedience. Willing obedience requires not just praise and honor for the obedient, and blame and punishment for the disobedient, but wisdom, since people most willingly obey a person they think wiser than themselves, such as a doctor when they are sick or a pilot when they are at sea. People will love a ruler who acts as their benefactor.[7] His formation gave Cyrus the noble character that bred great deeds. He understood not only how to acquire empire but how to preserve in harmony the great multitude of nations that came under his hegemony. Like Biondo Flavio's Romans, Cyrus welcomed men of all nationalities into his empire and elevated to positions of responsibility all worthy persons without regard to their social or national origins.

The final book describes and analyzes the Persian ruler's exemplary political skills. Cyrus promoted virtue among the nobility by bringing them into his own court, where they would be given an example of fine character in his own person:

> In the first place, if any of those who were able to live by the labors of others failed to attend at court, he made inquiry after them; for he thought that those who came would not be willing to do anything dishonorable or immoral, partly because they were in the presence of their sovereign and partly also because they knew that, whatever they did, they would be under the eyes of the best men there; whereas, in the case of those who did not come, he believed that they absented themselves because they were guilty of some form of intemperance or injustice or neglect of duty. . . . But in those who did present themselves he believed that he could in no way more effectively inspire a desire for the beautiful and the good than by endeavoring, as their sovereign, to set before his subjects a perfect model of virtue in his own person.

Cyrus combined this personal training in virtue with a canny understanding of the weaknesses and desires of men of all stations. He formulated wise policies that channeled their self-interest into political support for the kingdom. He set up a centralized bureaucracy modeled on the army and personally took care to staff it with the ablest men. He rewarded virtue and devotion to the public good:

> He used to reward with gifts and positions of authority and seats of honor and all sorts of preferment others whom he saw devoting themselves most eagerly to the attainment of excellence; and thus he inspired in all an earnest ambition, each striving to appear as deserving as he could in the eyes of Cyrus.

He cultivated the friendship of the leading men through his munificence and through personal attentions. This was, in fact, the great key to his success. On his deathbed (in a speech already translated in Cicero's *De senectute*) Cyrus advises his heir Cambyses:

> As for you, Cambyses, you must also know that it is not this golden sceptre that maintains your empire; but faithful friends are a monarch's truest and surest sceptre. But do not think that man is naturally faithful; else all men would find the same persons faithful, just as all find the other properties of nature the same. But every one must create for himself faithfulness in his friends; and the winning of such friends comes in no wise by compulsion, but by kindness.

Cyrus was also known to have had "eyes and ears" everywhere in his kingdom. The same men who brought gifts to leading men were also expected to bring back reports of the state of the kingdom so that the king could know what was said of him and deal promptly with cases of malfeasance:

> For he thought he perceived that men are made better through even the written law, while the good ruler he regarded as "a law with eyes" for men, because he is able not only to give commandments but also to see the transgressor and punish him.[8]

He cleverly organized provincial government so that satraps would have civil jurisdiction and be backed by military force when necessary, but he himself kept direct command over the troops using his own commanders.

Some modern interpreters have seen proto-Machiavellian elements in Cyrus' statecraft, and Machiavelli certainly showed respect for Cyrus' political wisdom as presented by Xenophon.[9] But most Renaissance humanists tended to read Xenophon as a straightforward guide to virtuous rulership. The *Cyropaedia* was in fact among the most widely translated and circulated Greek texts of the Renaissance; parts or the whole of it were translated thirteen times into Latin before 1600, and it was the subject of no fewer than four commentaries in the sixteenth century. In the fifteenth century the two most widely circulated versions were those of Poggio Bracciolini and Francesco Filelfo. Poggio produced a condensed version of the text in six books (drafted by 1446), which formed the basis of Italian translations by his son Jacopo (c. 1476) and by the famous Ferrarese poet Boiardo (c. 1470). In his preface Poggio praises the value of the text as a model for the education of "all those who rule." Its usefulness for that purpose was shown by the examples of Scipio Africanus and Cicero, the greatest Romans in war and in peace, both of whom were said to have kept the book with them always.[10] If men in power today were to read the text, he says, "mortal affairs would be in a better place, and men would be less harassed by Fortune."

In the late 1460s a more complete, correct, and far more influential version of the *Cyropaedia* was made by Francesco Filelfo (who even named one of his sons Senofonte). Filelfo's long prefatory dedication of the work to Pope Paul II constituted an important document of humanist monarchical theory.[11] Whereas a few years later, writing to the Doge of Venice, Filelfo would describe the aristocratic as the best of the three "good" constitutions, in this text he asks, "Who can doubt that that regime is the best which is established by the wisdom and virtue of a single outstanding man?"[12] The need for unity even in aristocratic and popular constitutions, he writes, is shown by the existence of a doge in Venice and by the Florentines' ceremonial head of state, the Standard-Bearer of Justice. Even the Roman republican constitution had a *princeps senatus,* a position notably held by Scipio Africanus, who was chosen for this office by the censors. The Athenian, Carthaginian, and Roman Empires were all great, but all were riven by hatreds and factionalism so long as they were under popular or aristocratic governments. It was only when Julius Caesar, the most perfectly virtuous man nature ever created, founded the "royal empire" *(regium imperium)* of the Romans, "which still endures," that the ravages of civil war were pacified. This proves, says Filelfo, that government by one man is better than that by several. A unitary executive is the only long-term solution to the problem of political instability.[13]

Unlike Plato and Aristotle, not to mention his rival Poggio, Filelfo was confident that there could be wise and virtuous princes, and that numerous examples of such princes were to be found in history and even in the present day. Among the Romans after Julius Caesar there were the Antonine emperors and the first

Christian emperor, Constantine. Among the moderns the duke of Milan, Filippo Maria Visconti, King Alfonso the Magnanimous of Aragon, and his own prince, the "peacemaker" Duke Francesco Sforza, could all be described as good and wise. Among the recent popes, Filelfo mentions Eugene IV and Nicholas V (but not the humanist pope Pius II) and hints that he would include Paul II himself in their number were he not afraid of being charged with flattery. He then proceeds to flatter the pope for several more lines, saying that the pontiff is living proof that monarchy is the best form of government. All of which goes to show that the easiest way to become an ideal prince in the Renaissance was to hire a man like Filelfo to sing your praises.

Filelfo leavens this shameless adulation with more serious arguments, drawing on ancient Greek theories of monarchy. Many of these were to become stock analogies in later absolutist theory. The need for a principle of unity is shown in theology by God's rule over the cosmos, in mathematics by the generation of all number from unity, in physics by the prime mover, in psychology by the hierarchies of soul over body and mind over the other faculties of soul, in ethics by the queenship of Wisdom over the other virtues, in natural philosophy by the V-formations of flying geese, in economics by the authority of the paterfamilias over his family. Homer is pressed into service as an authority:

Multorum imperium mala res est, unicus esto
dux et rex unus, statuit quem rector Olympi.

Command by many men is an evil thing;
Be there but one, whom Jove makes king.[14]

Finally, the old "incarnational argument" used by Dante and many other imperial writers to legitimate the Holy Roman Empire is redeployed in support of the monarchical principle in general: "But what need is there of other examples or arguments when it is evident that best and greatest Christ, at once God and son of the high God—who first created man by a law that put him in charge of the other animals—willed to join himself to humanity at that very time when the single *princeps* Caesar Augustus ruled over the entire globe?" Beyond this, Christ himself was the single head of his apostles and, when he returned to heaven as the true king of mankind, he chose Peter to be the sole prince of the apostles after him. Thus, Filelfo concludes, "the gravest of philosophers, Xenophon, appropriately intends to teach us [about the principle of unity in politics, by] choosing one king,

[Cyrus], in whom he wanted there to be all the highest qualities which pertained to founding, enlarging, preserving and spreading an empire for posterity."

In neither Poggio's nor Filelfo's prefaces, it should be noted, was any doubt expressed about the historicity of Xenophon's life of Cyrus the Great, and even Machiavelli decades later appeared to accept the *Cyropaedia* as a historical work.[15] The only quattrocento humanist to cast doubt on the work's historical veracity, to my knowledge, was Francesco Patrizi, whose life and works will be introduced later in this chapter. Patrizi's doubts about the historicity of the text were aroused by his comparison of Xenophon's account with that of "other Greek historians." Of these he mentions Strabo, who presented Cyrus' father and teacher Cambyses as a monster who invaded Egypt unjustly and made war on the gods as well as on men.[16] Patrizi concludes that Xenophon used rhetorical embellishment to bring Cambyses back from the dead to teach virtue, or perhaps "that most erudite of philosophers" was not writing "in accordance with historical truth" but simply flattering the Persian kings.[17] Xenophon's works in his view were vitiated by fawning mendacity, qualities "alien to virtue." He cites Plato as an authority for his claim that "what is written about Cyrus is all fiction, said for the sake of winning good will rather than to be trustworthy," a judgment repeated by Cicero, "Plato's imitator in all things."[18] Patrizi could afford to be more critical of Xenophon because, as we shall see, he presents his own ideal king as a Platonic exemplar of kingship whose virtues could never be instantiated in any one historical figure. Humanists who believed that ideal conduct could be found exemplified in actual historical individuals could less afford the luxury of casting doubt on the veracity of their sources.

We can deal more briefly with the other Greek sources for ideal kingship that were recovered in the long quattrocento. In the first book of the *De regno* (1.4) Patrizi himself tells us that after the shipwreck of Greece (i.e., the fall of Constantinople in 1453) only two of the many known ancient Greek authorities on kingship managed to swim to Italy: the books Isocrates wrote for King Nicocles of Cyprus and the works on kingship by Dion of Prusa (usually called Dio Chrysostom or Dio Cocceianus today). If either of these authors had written at greater length, says Patrizi, he himself might have been spared the labor of writing the *De regno*.

Isocrates, one of the founders of humanistic education in antiquity, was an important authority for humanists generally in the quattrocento, and there has been some study of his influence on educational thought in the fifteenth and sixteenth centuries.[19] His reputation as an authority on kingship he owed to his so-called Cyprian speeches, which included a speech on kingship to King Nico-cles *(Ad Nicoclem),* another on kingship written for Nicocles and placed in his mouth *(Nicocles),* and a panegyric of Nicocles' father, King Evagoras *(Evagoras).*[20] These works contained many themes relevant to humanist virtue politics: the need for kings and princes to be persons of exceptional virtue; why they should be trained in literature, philosophy, and eloquence and be advised by wise and learned men; and why those with merit should rule the rest.[21] They were also important for monarchical theory since they contained arguments for why mon-archy is the best and most just form of government and why it is the form most consistent with virtue politics.

In the *Nicocles,* for example, the king claims to hold his office "not illegally or as a usurper, but with the just sanction of the gods and men," and through his own meritorious achievements and those of his ancestors. He is shown arguing that monarchy is the most just form of government because both kings and royal ser-vants easily identify their own interests with those of the state, while temporary office-holders in republics are forever looking out for their own interests, shifting responsibility for their failures onto others, and seeking to win credit for others' achievements. Monarchy is also the form of government friendliest to meritoc-racy. In an argument that resembles the case for meritocracy over democracy made by some modern Confucian political philosophers, Isocrates writes,

> Who, then, that is of sound mind would not prefer to share in a form of gov-ernment under which his own worth shall not pass unnoticed, rather than be lost in the hurly-burly of the mob and not be recognized for what he is? Fur-thermore, we should be right in pronouncing monarchy also a milder govern-ment, in proportion as it is easier to give heed to the will of a single person than to seek to please many and manifold minds. As for its other advantages, we can best appreciate how far monarchies excel other governments in plan-ning and carrying out any course of action required of them if we place their most important practices side by side and try to review them. In the first place, then, men who enter upon office for an annual term are retired to private life before they have gained any insight into public affairs or any experience in handling them; while men who are permanently in charge of the same duties, even though they fall short of the others in natural ability, at any rate have a great advantage over them in experience. In the next place, the former neglect many things, because each looks to the others to do them; while the latter neglect nothing, knowing that whatever is done depends upon their own

efforts. Then again, men who live in oligarchies or democracies are led by their mutual rivalries to injure the commonwealth; while those who live in monarchies, not having anyone to envy, do in all circumstances so far as possible what is best.[22]

The first humanists who took an interest in Isocrates' writings on kingship were associated with the famous humanist educator Guarino Veronese (1374–1460), whom we have already met as a defender of Caesar against Poggio.[23] Guarino's interest in the Cyprian speeches was hardly surprising, given the centrality of these texts in Byzantine culture of the Paleologan period, whose Hellenism he had inherited.[24] Guarino's former students, the Florentine Carlo Marsuppini and the Venetian Bernardo Giustiniani, made the first two translations of the speech *Ad Nicoclem* in 1430 and 1431 respectively, both dedicated to condottieri. But the text turned out to be generally popular among translators: more than a dozen additional Latin and Italian versions were made before the death of Machiavelli in 1527 (who borrows silently from its first paragraph in the first paragraph of his own *Prince*). One, made by the great Erasmus, was published in 1515 and was printed alongside Erasmus' own *Education of a Christian Prince*. The *Ad Nicoclem* circulated widely in hundreds of manuscripts and in printed editions, of which there were at least forty before 1600. Of the *Nicocles* Guarino himself made the first version in 1433, dedicating it to his patron Leonello d'Este, lord of Ferrara. Other versions followed by the Tuscans Lapo da Castiglionchio (1435 / 1436) and Lorenzo Lippi da Colle (c. 1464), by Carlo Valgulio of Brescia (1484 / 1492), and by the Hungarian scholar Michael Chesserius, a student of Filippo Beroaldo the Elder in Bologna (before 1506). There were some twenty-seven editions in Latin and seven in French printed in the sixteenth century. By the sixteenth century both the *Ad Nicocles* and the *Nicocles* were commonly read in humanist schools, both in Greek and in Latin, and a number of school commentaries on both were composed. The *Evagoras* was less fortunate in its reception than the other two Cyprian speeches, but thanks to Guarino's translation (c. 1434) the text was well known in manuscript. It circulated widely in print as well, owing to its inclusion in the corpus of Plutarch's *Lives* first printed in Rome in 1470 and reprinted many times.[25]

Dio Chrysostom's works on kingship had a much smaller profile in the quattrocento than those of Isocrates. Dio was an orator and moral writer of the Second Sophistic who claimed familiarity with the Emperor Trajan. His writings betray Stoic and Cynic influences, though he himself professed to have found his precepts on kingship in Homer. Dio's *Discourses* on kingship (numbers 1–4 of the eighty surviving discourses) were first brought to the attention of Western scholars in the 1430s by Francesco Filelfo in his *Commentationes de exilio.* Gregorio Tifernate, a student of Pletho, later made a translation of the four discourses under the title *De regno,* dedicated to Pope Nicholas V.[26] In the preface he claimed that no work was more appropriate and necessary for a prince's education, a judgment to his mind endorsed by Dio's friendship with Trajan: the two were so close "that they used to be carried together in the same chariot."

Another writer of the Second Sophistic who deserves mention alongside Dio was Philostratus, a courtier of the Emperor Septimius Severus.[27] He wrote no independent work on kingship, but in book 5 of his "novelistic biography" of Apollonius of Tyana—a contribution to the literary genre founded by Xenophon's *Cyropaedia*—Philostratus invents a dialogue on kingship said to have been conducted in the presence of the Emperor Vespasian in 69 AD. Two of the three interlocutors are philosophers, Euphrates and Dio, who are said to be partisans of "democracy" (*popularis gubernatio* in Alamanno Rinuccini's Latin translation). Both advise Vespasian to end the Principate, which had declined into a savage tyranny since the time of Tiberius, and to restore liberty and rule by the people. To restore popular government will be hard, they say, since the Romans had learned servility under the Julio-Claudian principate, but popular government, though not as good as aristocracy, is better than its alternatives, oligarchy and tyranny. This advice is criticized by the third interlocutor in the dialogue, Apollonius of Tyana, who is less a philosopher than a pagan holy man. Apollonius, a follower of Pythagoras, says that Euphrates and Dio err in giving advice that will only carry conviction with other philosophers. Vespasian is no philosopher but "a consular man" who faces ruin if he gives up power. He has fought hard for his power and is not going to give it up, any more than an athlete would give up a prize won in the Olympic Games. Besides, he has sons whom he loves and who expect to inherit his power.

This being the case, Apollonius advises Vespasian to retain power but to use it well, guided by wisdom and virtue. Debates about the form of the constitution are the sort of useless talk indulged in by philosophers. "To me no constitution matters, since I live as the gods' subject," he says. Vespasian is a man of exceptional virtue, and one good man with power can change everything. Real democracy is government not of the people, but government that serves the people: "Just as one man of exceptional virtue changes democracy so as to make it so appear the rule of one man better than the rest, so the rule of one man who is always looking out for the common good *is* a democracy."[28] Fundamentally, good rule is about virtue, not constitutions. True philosophers have overturned countless tyrannies in the past by teaching virtue. Philostratus then proceeds to give Vespasian the sort of advice standardly found in ancient *specula principum:* he should be temperate, just, and merciful, not abuse his power, avoid violence, and seek to cultivate the good-will of his people. He should choose the nobler of his two sons to rule after him, but they should not be allowed to assume they will inherit the empire from him. They must prove themselves honest and good, "and then they will think of the throne not as their birthright, but as a reward for virtue."[29]

Philostratus' *Life of Apollonius of Tyana* was translated by the Florentine humanist and diplomat Alamanno Rinuccini around 1473, and dedicated to Federico d'Urbino, a prince and condottiere much admired by humanists for his classical learning, his fine library, and his military virtue.[30] The work had some circulation in manuscript and was printed in 1502 in a translation revised by Filippo Beroaldo. In the sixteenth century the work was printed once in Greek, four times in Latin translations, and three times in Italian versions. Rinuccini was a friend and correspondent of Patrizi, but the latter does not seem to have used the text in his *De regno* (though in the absence of a critical edition it is difficult to be certain).[31]

So far no mention has been made of Plato or Aristotle. Both these writers were among the first Greeks to make strong theoretical distinctions between kingship and tyranny, yet Patrizi considered neither one to be an authority on monarchy. This is surprising in the case of Aristotle in particular, since (as we saw in the previous chapter) it was common in the Late Middle Ages and Renaissance to regard the Philosopher as a monarchist, and there are four theoretically dense chapters in *Politics* 3 devoted to the subject of absolute monarchy *(pambasileia).*[32] Despite Patrizi's love of parading his knowledge of ancient Greek sources, however, he does not often cite Aristotle in his *De regno,* and in both his treatises on government he often suppresses mention of Aristotle even when he is making use of Aristotelian analytical concepts and arguments.[33] Since one aim of his *De regno* was to provide a humanist substitute for Giles of Rome's *De regimine principum,* a thoroughly Aristotelian text, Patrizi may have simply regarded Aristotle as old hat, an authority too contaminated by scholasticism to excite enthusiasm among his readers. Then too, most of Aristotle's *Politics* is occupied with setting out his constitutional theory, which Patrizi (like Aristotle himself) regarded as an approach to political order fundamentally at odds with the theory of absolute monarchy.[34]

The reason for Patrizi's neglect of Aristotle's chapters on kingship in the *Politics* may simply be that he, like most modern interpreters, took the view that Aristotle in the end was a critic of absolute monarchy rather than an advocate of it.[35]

Patrizi's use of Plato in his theory of monarchy is more complex. Patrizi certainly knew the *Republic* well. In his time the text was available in three different Latin translations, all of which had some circulation in manuscript form.[36] He cites Plato's *Laws* as well, which he may have known in the translation of George of Trebizond, though this is less likely as that version did not circulate widely.[37] He does not appear to know the *Statesman,* which only became widely available in Latin when Marsilio Ficino's translation was published in 1484. He also read Diogenes Laertius' *Life of Plato,* presumably in the well-known translation (1431) by Ambrogio Traversari.[38] He undoubtedly values Plato as a major authority in moral philosophy. In a discussion of the human good in *De regno* 2.2, for example, he dissents from the Stoic view that excludes corporeal and "external" advantages from the class of goods, declaring himself to be a follower in this regard of the older Academic and Peripatetic schools, "and Plato before all, who in a wholly religious and pious way said that God was the highest good, and that through virtue alone we get to cleave to the source and end of all human goods, via similitude to God. Plato decided that divine justice was the universal law for everyone, which assigns rewards for the good and punishments for the bad." As we shall see, Patrizi also relies on Plato's theory of Ideas to theorize his own ideal king. Yet he did not regard Plato as himself an advocate of absolute monarchy or an authority on it as a regime. Tellingly, in the title he adopts for the work we call in English *The Republic,* he did not follow Pier Candido Decembrio, who translated the title as *The Celestial Polity.*[39] He calls it instead *De civili societate.* As we saw in Chapter 12, *civilis societas* was Patrizi's technical term for all non-monarchical constitutions, the opposite of government depending on the will of one person, whether monarchy or tyranny.[40] In the very first chapter of *De regno,* in fact, Patrizi explicitly describes Plato in his *De civili societate* as an authority on non-monarchical regimes, contrasting him with Xenophon, whom he presents as an authority on kingship in the *Cyropaedia.*

Since the essence of absolute kingship for Patrizi is placing all political decisions under the control of a single person, it seems likely that he regarded Plato's "Kallipolis," governed by "guardians," in the plural, as a form of aristocracy. Although there are passages in the *Republic* which suggest that a single philosophical ruler could impose ideal government, this possibility is explicitly rejected in the *Laws* on the grounds that any single individual entrusted with absolute power would never be able to resist temptations to moral corruption.[41] As has recently been emphasized by Julia Annas, the ideal regime envisaged in Plato's *Republic* is one where laws are an instrument of philosophical virtue.[42] Patrizi as a representative of the humanist tradition of virtue politics would surely have agreed with Plato's passionate affirmation that societies can never create an ideal polity full of virtuous and blessed citizens merely by improving laws and institutions.[43] He would have agreed that the basis of real political reform was the upbringing and education of *principes*. But the goal of Patrizi's program of royal education was not, like Plato's, a vision of the Good yielding scientific truths about an ideal political order, but rather the acquisition of moral goodness, eloquence, and political wisdom via the study and imitation of classical antiquity.[44]

Patrizi and His Project in the De Regno

That Patrizi late in life became an authority on absolute monarchy may seem surprising in view of his early life.[45] He was born in the republic of Siena in 1413 to a family prominent in communal politics, and himself participated in Sienese public life as a magistrate and diplomat well into his forties. He had enjoyed a fine humanist education and even learned Greek from Francesco Filelfo during the latter's sojourn in Siena in the mid-1430s.[46] After Filelfo's departure Patrizi set himself up as a teacher of Greek and humanities in the Sienese *studium*. In that quality he composed his earliest work on politics, a letter-treatise *De gerendo magistratu* (How to Conduct Oneself in a Civil Office), written for a former pupil, Achille Petrucci, who had been elected one of the priors of Siena in 1446.[47] The work gave powerful expression to humanist political ideals, urging Petrucci to leave the sand and oil of the palaestra, that is, the study of literature, and descend into the true field of battle for which the humanities had trained him—the battle of the citizen for virtuous government. As we saw in Chapter 2, Patrizi belonged to a group of Sienese humanists who, inspired by virtue politics, became critical of the commune's factional struggles, generated (in their view) by an obsession with wealth and status among the city's elite. When the Sienese commune came under the dominance of a popular faction after 1450, his alienation was complete, and in 1457 he was arrested and exiled for his part in a conspiracy of nobles to hand the city over to Alfonso of Aragon, King of Naples. For the next four years he tasted the bitter bread of exile as he traveled from place to place seeking a teaching post. It was during this time, while teaching in Verona, that he came in contact with Battista Guarino, son of the great humanist educator, who did not procure him gainful employment but at least composed for him a *consolatio exilii*. Between the school of Guarino and the activities of his teacher Filelfo, Patrizi would have had access to most of the new Greek writings about kingship discussed in the previous section.

Patrizi's fortunes changed in 1459, when his countryman and patron Aeneas Silvius Piccolomini became Pope Pius II. Patrizi promptly took orders and was given a benefice. In 1461 he was made bishop of Gaeta, and soon thereafter he was appointed governor of Foligno in the Papal States. Foligno was a pawn in the ongoing struggle between Pius and the tyrant prince and condottiere Sigismondo Malatesta, a man so hated by Pius that the pontiff declared him to be "canonized to hell." Patrizi's career as governor of Foligno (1461–1464) was brief but turbulent, and after being expelled from the city in a popular uprising he was tried (but exonerated) for malfeasance. Following this unhappy episode, Patrizi retired to his diocese in the seaside fortress and naval base of Gaeta, a part of the Kingdom of Naples, then ruled by the House of Aragon. Falling in love with the place, he remained there for most of the last thirty years of his life, devoting himself to his episcopal duties and to humanistic scholarship and poetry.[48] He found ways to make himself useful to the royal court in Naples as a diplomat, poet, and educator.

It was in Gaeta that he completed his two major works on political education. The *De institutione reipublicae* (How to Found a Republic) was begun during his exile but finished between 1465 and 1471. Though dedicated opportunistically to Pope Sixtus IV, it seems to have been composed with the intention of edifying his former fellow citizens in Siena. Its nine books represent the fullest expression of the ideals of humanist reformers in the Sienese city in the first half of the quattrocento.[49] The other treatise, the *De regno et regis institutione* (On Kingship and Royal Education), was completed between late 1483 and 1484 and was dedicated to Alfonso, Duke of Calabria, eldest son and heir of Ferdinando I, King of Naples and Jerusalem.[50]

The *De regno* was one of a number of humanist works on kingship and government written in the second half of the quattrocento, the so-called *trattatistica* of *umanesimo politico* that has received a good deal of attention in recent scholarship.[51] These works included Giovanni Pontano's treatise *De principe* (begun in the later 1460s, published in 1490); Bartolomeo Platina's twin treatises *De principe* (1470) and *De optimo cive* (1474); the Bolognese humanist Giovanni Garzoni's treatises *De eruditione principum* and *De principis officio*;[52] Diomede Carafa's

Memoriale sui doveri del principe (before 1476), twice translated into Latin but not published in Italian until 1668; Giuniano Maio's *De maiestate* (1492); Filippo Beroaldo the Elder's *Libellus de optimo statu* (first published 1497); and Giovanni Francesco Bracciolini's *De officio principis liber* (dedicated to Julius II and published 1504). Patrizi's treatises were by far the longest and most comprehensive in this group. They were also by far the most successful. As noted above, the work was in part intended as a humanist alternative to the most popular scholastic guide to princely education, Giles of Rome's *De regimine principum* (finished before 1281), and by the early sixteenth century it had successfully driven Giles' work out of the market.[53]

The contrast between Giles' treatise and Patrizi's provides an apt illustration of the differences between scholastic and humanist approaches to political counsel. Giles' work presents itself as a guide to the art of ruling for princes and is based on the moral philosophy of Aristotle (and pseudo-Aristotle), divided into ethics, economics (or household management), and politics; these constitute the three broad divisions of his work. Despite its incessant citation of Aristotle, modern scholarship has emphasized the work's debts to Giles' teacher, Thomas Aquinas, particularly the latter's *De regno.* The work derives its conclusions deductively from general principles or from the text of Aristotle, who is treated as the authority *par excellence* in politics. Prudential arguments are sometimes considered, but as a rule Giles prefers to settle questions about rulership by arguing from general principles of right. This is in keeping with Giles' view that the laws should do as much as possible and as little as possible should be left to the discretion of judges, a principle deeply at odds with virtue politics.[54] Giles takes the view that kingship is the best form of government, which is said to be the position of Aristotle. He spends a good many chapters refuting what is said to be Socrates' and Plato's regime of "excessive unity." What is judged excessive are the notorious doctrines of the *Republic,* prescribing that possessions and wives be held in common, doctrines he knew only from the unreliable reports of them in *Politics* 2.[55] Giles' work is formally absolutist in that it maintains that the king is subject only to natural law but above civil (or positive) law, which he has the right to change.[56] He is accountable only to God. The work avoids any discussion of the relationship between the lay and the spiritual power, in this respect resembling Patrizi and most other humanist political thinkers.

The differences between Giles' scholastic approach to politics and Patrizi's humanist one may be brought out by comparing two chapters where both writers explain the distinction between kingship and tyranny.[57] Giles lists four differences between kings and tyrants that he claims to be extracting from Aristotle's *Politics*.[58] Kings respect the common good, tyrants their own. Kings seek a good that produces honor, a *bonum honorificum;* tyrants want a *bonum delectabile,* something they can personally enjoy. The tyrant wants money, the king virtue; the tyrant is guarded by foreigners, the king by his own citizens. All this is set out in clear if plodding scholastic prose.

Patrizi gives us a far more spacious and ruminative comparison that draws on a variety of classical sources, most prominently Plato's *Republic* and Isocrates' Cyprian orations. His principal interest is not establishing analytical categories for identifying tyranny, but in understanding and combatting the psychology that underlies tyranny. The weapons for combatting tyranny are the virtues, particularly prudence, that the future king will acquire through his study of classical authors. Patrizi wants his reader to understand why it is both prudent and desirable to be a good king, and why tyranny is both dangerous and repulsive. Patrizi's prose is not exactly sparkling, but his language is elegant, and he constantly enlivens his prose with historical examples and memorable aphorisms from great writers. He criticizes sharply philosophers (his example is the Stoics) who try to compel assent through logical arguments alone: "They may extort agreement but they do not win assent." Such philosophers need to take account of the way people actually live their lives, and offer a form of counsel that recognizes the legitimacy of a proper degree of wealth, friends, family, country, and other human goods, "as the Academics and Peripatetics taught."[59]

There are, to be sure, underlying analytical distinctions in Patrizi's comparison of tyranny and kingship, but they function primarily as topics for persuasion. The tyrant rules unjustly, measuring every act by his own utility, whereas the purpose of the king, "as Socrates says in Plato," is to lead his citizens to felicity, which he can only do through his virtue. The tyrant's end is to force those he dominates to serve his own will. Thus the king uses virtue and reason, the tyrant force and power. The king ought to model in his own person and actions a law common to all, he should embrace all citizens not only with benevolence but also piety, he should show himself humane and accessible *(facilis),* and he should delight in his people's company. The tyrant is afraid of his own people. The rule of a king is accepted voluntarily when it is just, and just rule requires meritorious rulers. Quoting the *Nicocles,* Patrizi asserts that the king should reward people in accordance with their moral worth: "Virtue indeed ought to be the measure of all things." Hence the king should show himself to love the better citizens, have affection for the moderately virtuous, and not neglect the rest; he should hate no one among the citizenry but constantly seek to make them better. "Thus let him imitate that civil precept of Plato when he said, 'We are not founding the republic with an order that makes only one genus in it happy, but the whole city, which achieves beatitude by justice alone.'"[60] The king should promote a blessed life for his citizens, "so that the city is honored by virtue, great in its glory, rich in numbers and strong in resources." The tyrant is the opposite: he hates those of his citizens who are wise or virtuous, distinguished or rich or popular. He treats his citizens like slaves. His violence makes citizens hate and fear him, and as a result he drives out every liberal instinct, like a schoolmaster who uses the rod too much and makes his students hate literature. The king is thus safe and happy and surrounded by those to whom he is bound by mutual esteem, the conferral of benefits and loyal service, while the tyrant's rule is weak and full of plots and scheming. Kings liberate; tyrants enslave. Kings are secure in the love of their people, and they win fame in this life and glory hereafter; tyrants are hated, and their rule is solitary, fearful, miserable, and short.

It was noted in Chapter 3 that Patrizi was not an "exclusivist" in the sense of regarding one type of regime as the only legitimate form of government. As a follower of Petrarchan humanism he does not espouse the view of any one philosophical school, and the same principle applies to politics. Lack of dogmatism is a general feature of his political writings, which are measured in their judgments and avoid the extremes of panegyric when describing historical figures. Characteristically, he rejects Pliny the Younger's statement that one should only praise the *optimus princeps,* and that it would be arrogant to teach him.[61] Patrizi responds dryly that he regards adulation as a far more serious crime than teaching the doctrine of Greek philosophers. He notes that certain men (thinking, perhaps, of Pier Candido Decembrio in his *Life of Filippo Maria Visconti*) have been criticized for praising qualities they should have kept silent about, "either because [those qualities] seemed to be too trivial or because they were entirely repellent, almost shameful, and unworthy of a free man." In any case, he is remarkably independent in his judgments about the great monarchs of history. Unlike Petrarch, for instance, his judgment on Augustus (whom he prefers to call Octavian) is frigid. Octavian was a cruel man in his youth, and for Patrizi there was no quality so ugly, impious, and inhuman as cruelty. Octavian's later good fortune veiled the wickedness of his youth, and once he had achieved supreme power he became milder and more forgiving.[62] He and his successors were accepted only because Rome was sick of civil war, not because they were virtuous. Clearly influenced by his reading of Plutarch's biography, Patrizi found Julius Caesar worthy of the greatest admiration and imitation: he was the model general, the best in history; he was a man of extraordinary civil virtues; he was an elegant writer and speaker; he was never cruel or tyrannical. But he had vices as well, such as prodigality and an unhealthy thirst for popular favor *(ambitio),* and he could not be excused for attacking his own country. His ruling passion (which he shared with Pompey) was for personal domination, a goal to which he subordinated the *salus et dignitas* of the Roman people.

In general Patrizi's position is that he is describing in his treatise what an ideal prince would do and be. The ideal prince is a mental picture, which he compares to a Platonic Idea, like the ideal image of Jove in the mind of Phidias the sculptor. Patrizi does not expect that any one historical figure or state will provide an adequate model in every respect. That is why the ideal is necessary. Plato did not look to the Athenians or Spartans for a model, but "he devised a new and imaginary perfect city, gazing at that idea I spoke of just now, a city that never was and never shall be."[63] Patrizi's method was explicitly modelled on Cicero's *Orator,* an attempt to paint a portrait of the ideal orator, which itself looked to Plato's theory of ideas for inspiration. Patrizi even quotes the following passage from the work:

> "But I am firmly of the opinion that nothing of any kind is so beautiful as not to be excelled in beauty by that of which it is a copy, as a portrait is a copy of a face. This ideal cannot be perceived by any human sense; we grasp it only in mind and thought." *And when a little bit later he talks about Phidias, he says,* "In the mind of that artist there dwelt a surpassing vision of beauty; at this he gazed and all intent on this he guided his artist's hand to produce [the god's] likeness."[64]

In *The Prince* Machiavelli famously ridiculed previous political theorists who "have imagined republics and principalities that have never been seen or known to exist." The image of an ideal prince for Machiavelli was no more than a blind alley and a distraction from the *verità effettuale*—from what really works for those who want power: "How men live is so different from how they should live, that a ruler who does not do what is generally done, but persists in doing what ought to be done, will undermine his power rather than maintain it."[65] But the paradox of Patrizi's idealism is that it enables a kind of realism, albeit one foreign to Machiavelli's understanding of political reality. The Sienese humanist's mental vision of an ideal prince gave him an independent moral standard to decide which actions of great figures in the past were worthy of emulation and which were not. It was therefore not an ideal theory in John Rawls's sense, outlining a best possible state that will then be enforced by political institutions with a view to its eventual realization. It was something more like a Kantian regulative idea, a standard for judging existing political actions and practices that can never be fully achieved but can guide rulers and their advisors in the present.[66] Using his standard it was possible for Patrizi to consider figures like Julius Caesar and Augustus and even Xenophon's idealized Cyrus not as plaster saints of politics, as other humanists too often did, but as real human beings who had accomplished great deeds despite their faults and mistakes and mixed motives. Machiavelli's realism, and the whole basis of his political science, started from the assumption that human beings could be counted on to do the self-interested action, and that appeals to moral principle or religion were either manipulative or delusional. Readers may decide for themselves whether a "realism" that excludes the influence of ideals on rulers and ruled alike provides an adequate account of "how men live."

Virtuous Royal Legitimacy and Humanist Absolutism

Patrizi's idealistic realism can be illustrated by his position on the sources of royal legitimacy. Here he differs somewhat from the classic humanist view, which privileges moral legitimacy above all other kinds. At the beginning of book 2 of *De regno*, Patrizi defines the king as "a good man to whom it has been given to rule states and peoples because of his high birth or through lawful election."[67] He explains that this definition has been modelled on Cato's definition of the orator as *vir bonus dicendi peritus*, a good man skilled in speaking, and Strabo's understanding of what a true poet was, "as though without virtue an orator has no power to speak nor a poet to sing."[68] The force of his definition, in context, is to emphasize that the legitimacy of a king does not depend just on ancestry or some constitutional process but on virtue as well. Nevertheless, the need for just title is recognized. Legitimacy comes from two sources, both necessary but neither in themselves sufficient: lawfulness and virtue.

Patrizi thus holds a humanist mirror to the criteria of trecento jurists like Bartolus and Baldus, who had insisted that legitimacy rested both on lawful title and on the lawful exercise of power. Patrizi, however, has detached the question of just title from the web of legal fictions that for late medieval jurists sustained the authority of the Holy Roman Empire and the Papacy. He lived, after all, in an age when European kings were abandoning their traditional deference to pope and empire. So it is no surprise that for Patrizi, title has nothing to do with the Holy Roman Emperor. It is either simply inherited like a piece of property or proceeds from an unspecified process of lawful election, which might be anything from popular acclamation to the vote of an aristocratic counsel. Or it might conceivably be a cross between the two, such as the process, used in the glorious days of the Antonines, by which virtuous emperors chose their own successors via adoption. In place of the jurists' conception of just exercise, usually presented as adherence to law or respect for inveterate rights and due process, Patrizi substitutes the idea of virtue as a source of legitimacy. An act that proceeds from a just king is *eo ipso* just, and his acting justly is a condition of his legitimacy. Though piety is one of the virtues, and the overall guidance of Divine Providence is acknowledged, neither the king's legitimacy nor that of his dynasty is said to come from divine right. Nor is appeal made to Plato's teaching that true legitimacy comes from a scientific (in the sense of certain) knowledge of the Good.[69] Indeed, Patrizi explicitly excludes the study of theoretical subjects from the prince's education, advocating instead a literary curriculum that educes moral and civil virtues and also provides the practical knowledge (like geography or calculation) needed for effective princely rule.[70]

Patrizi gives an example of how to adjust the claims of virtue and lawfulness in his discussion of how the royal succession should be managed.[71] Unlike some humanists (such as Petrarch), he does not declare a preference for elective monarchy. But the principle of virtue should not be entirely overlooked either. When the king who has lived a life of virtue is old, he should give due thought for who shall succeed him, like a wise father who plans for the good of his family after his death. He will have already seen to it that his sons have had a good education and training in rulership, "so that they may be similar to him not only in appearance but in virtue and mores, that the king may seem not to have departed, but to have been made younger." Nature and custom demand that the oldest son inherit the title. But it might happen that the eldest son is a wicked man, like Commodus, son of the philosopher-emperor Marcus Aurelius. In such a case the king should think of what Alexander the Great said when asked on his deathbed who should succeed him. "The worthiest" was his reply. Heeding this advice the king should follow the example of great kings who chose someone other than their eldest sons to succeed them. It might also happen that the king's sons are too young to rule, and in this case the king should weigh the example of Phraates, king of the Parthians, who chose his brother Mithridates to occupy the throne after him. A king might also consider the example of the Egyptians, who (according to Diodorus Siculus) in questions of succession treated bastard children on an equal basis with legitimate children, even ones born of slave mothers, thus enlarging the pool of available children from whom to choose the best. (It may be remembered that Ferrante of Aragon, who ruled the Kingdom of Naples in Patrizi's time, was the son of King Alfonso by his mistress.) In short, the stability provided by the usual rules of legitimate succession should be the first consideration, but the king should be prepared to set these aside when the virtuous exercise of power might be compromised: "When a successor will be unworthy, the interests of the kingdom must be consulted rather than the order of nature or one's descendants."

Laws of succession such as the Salic Law in France were regarded as fundamental law in most European monarchies, beyond the power of kings alone to abrogate or modify.[72] Patrizi's counsel to set aside the rules of succession when necessary on prudential grounds in the interests of virtuous government thus spotlights another characteristic of his theory of kingship: its thoroughgoing absolutism. Patrizi's king is constrained by no constitutional apparatus of parliaments or noble councils or independent courts. Whom he takes as his counselors is entirely a matter of his own choice. No one has a right to be consulted, and there is no one except God to whom he is accountable. The standard list of monarchical analogies, already deployed by Filelfo (as discussed earlier in this chapter), reinforce the point. For a king's subjects to call him to account over his actions would be as unjust and unthinkable as the universe calling its Creator to account, or the body seeking a check on the power the soul, or the passions and appetites exercising a veto over reason. Thus it is right that "the king contains all magistracies in himself alone, and is considered a law over all persons."

This does not make his rule unlawful or arbitrary. In book 8, chapter 6, Patrizi discusses "how the king should act with respect to the laws." He should obey good laws himself in order to set an example; it is wrong and undermines justice for him to command others to obey a law he does not himself observe. He should not be like a parent who says, "Do what I say, not what I do." The king has power over all law, but that does not mean he should rush into reforming programs. In fact he should respect the historical achievements of Roman law. Isocrates taught that the king should repair the laws and make new ones for the sake of concord, for the utility of citizens, and to stop incessant lawsuits. This was sound advice in Isocrates' time, says Patrizi, when the world was not so full of vice and greed. But in later times, as morals declined, laws improved: "Good laws arise from bad morals, as the proverb has it."[73] Eventually the Romans brought civil law to a high state of perfection: "As they conquered the world with their arms, they emended it with their laws, with courts of justice, and with good moral conduct." There is no need to look to the Greeks when it comes to law, since "everybody agrees" that the books of "our Roman jurisconsults" excel those of the Greek philosophers in gravity, eloquence, learning, and wisdom.

This means that kings need not labor to write new laws or reform old ones since they can simply enforce Roman law, the law of the *populus Romanus,* victor over all nations and all kings, which prescribed a legal code of civil wisdom for the whole world, the faithful image of divine and natural law. Roman law is universal and eternal. It has lasted far longer than laws of Lycurgus, which endured a mere five hundred years. Kings are advised simply to endorse this law and direct their energies to choosing the most virtuous and learned men to interpret it.[74] Magistrates should be required to observe the laws themselves, there should be equality under law, and in every courthouse there should be inscribed the words *Whoever decides what is right for another should adopt that same rightness in his own case.*[75] Innovation is sometimes needed when new crimes and outrages are invented by human wickedness, but in general, Patrizi advises his king, the application of the law is best left to lawyers and jurists.

What should limit a king's power, for Patrizi, is not law or constitutional devices but his own prudent consideration of what functions he can best perform and the practical limits imposed by his own knowledge and energies. For this reason he should leave sacred things and ceremonies to the high priests *(pontifices)* and civil legislation to the senators. He should, however, exercise oversight of the senators to make sure that when they pass laws they are not opening more avenues to litigation than to justice. They should be discouraged from unnecessary innovation. In matters of law kings are urged to exercise moral discernment so that the rigor of the law is not confused with cruelty, or prudence with low cunning. Royal justice should always be high-minded and noble in its ends, marked with mildness, humanity, and clemency.

In general, since the king has no constitutional or legal limits to what he can command, his need for prudence is all the greater. Outcomes always have to be considered, though Patrizi is far from embracing the consequentialist calculus of Machiavelli, in which principles of action are retrofitted to the desired outcomes.

Princely prudence should feed on the nourishing bread of history rather than the thin gruel of lawyers. History will teach him which authorities are to be followed, or not followed, in given circumstances. For example, Greek authorities like the legislator Lycurgus and the philosopher Plato prescribed equalization of property for their polities, and even Aristotle taught that healthy cities should take steps to reduce income inequality. Patrizi thinks such measures are inadvisable, not only because Roman law protects property but because history shows they are impractical. He advises against measures that would equalize either property or honor, since they will run up against natural differences in ability and so force the legislator who tries to preserve those measures into acts of manifest injustice or malfeasance. In an argument that sounds almost Nozickian, he says that forced redistributions of property have been tried in the past but have always failed because in a short time the industrious became rich again and the lazy poor; at that point it will have seemed grossly unfair to divide patrimonies a second time, "making the lazy equal to the industrious." The same principle is applied to *isotimia,* the Greek name for the practice of equalizing rewards.[76] A regime where all must have prizes cannot well be preserved by law, since "one person will seem suitable through virtue and industry for any and all offices, while another has to be entirely excluded from all public duties because of carelessness and disgraceful behavior." For a ruler to defy the principle of merit results inevitably in injustice and incompetence.[77]

The Argument for Monarchy

That absolute kingship was more compatible with meritocratic principles than republican government was a lesson Patrizi had learned from Isocrates.[78] In the second book of *De regno,* alluding to and adapting Isocrates' *Nicocles,* Patrizi praises kings as permanent magistrates who can master the arts of rule over the course of their lives, unlike constitutional magistrates who only have a short term of office to learn their jobs.[79] Republican magistrates carry their private interests with them into office, knowing they will soon return to private life, and this makes it harder for them to serve the common good and practice the virtues of justice and equity. It is wrong for the worse to rule the better, and a wise king will always be better placed than any polyarchic government to make merit the basis of his administration. He can command the resources of the best counselors. Private men are fortunate when they have a few friends of learning and distinction, but the king's munificence will attract the very best scholars and philosophers into his service, even from beyond the borders of his kingdom.[80]

Patrizi's principal argument for monarchy, however, has to do with the relative stability of regimes. It is a matter of constant emphasis in the *De regno* that there should be only one supreme decision-maker in the kingdom, a single individual with final *arbitrium*. The unitary power of decision became known as sovereignty in the early modern period *(summum ius),* and theorists like Hobbes alleged that it could reside in collectivities such as the English Parliament or the Venetian Senate as well as in monarchs. In modern times sovereignty or supreme authority is often said to reside in the people.[81] This abstract way of thinking about sovereignty did not exist within Patrizi's horizon. It required a strong view of the autonomy of law to which humanist virtue politics was inherently hostile. For Patrizi as for his Greek sources the problem to be solved by monarchy was the problem of political discord, leading in extreme cases to factionalism, sedition, tyranny, or civil war. There were ways to keep discord in check in constitutional republics, many of them discovered by the ancients, but to expect more than a transient unity of wills in a state governed by the few or by the many was an expectation that, for Patrizi (at least in *De regno*), could find no support in the pages of history. Those who favored republican government were willing to tolerate discord for the sake of freedom, and a virtuous citizenry was a safeguard against injustice, the main source of discord. But there would eventually be a reckoning. The study of history revealed that republics didn't last, and monarchy was nature's remedy for the inherent instability of polyarchic rule.

In his earlier work on constitutional government, *How to Found a Republic,* Patrizi had taken the view that a republic might continue indefinitely so long as its leaders continued to offer examples of virtue to the people and acted to suppress vice. In *De regno* Patrizi presents republican or polyarchic government (a *societas civilis* in his new terminology) as inherently unstable. The positions are not necessarily incompatible. Within a shorter time scale, the tendency to monarchy may be countered by the underlying disposition some peoples have for freedom. Different peoples have different customs, Patrizi writes, and the *varia gentium consuetudo,* the varied customs of nations, means that some peoples are used to obeying a prince while others are used to annual magistrates, civil equality, and ruling by turns.[82] Each type of people, being content with its own ways, spurns and hates the ways of the other. This was why ancient Athens kept reverting to a popular regime throughout its classical period, despite attempts by tyrants and oligarchs to dominate it.[83] Intelligent and virtuous statesmen learned ways to prolong the life of popular government. But eventually Athens too, in the wider sweep of history, had to yield to the monarchy of Alexander the Great.

The same pattern played out in Roman history, Patrizi's prime example of the inevitability of monarchy. At the end of book 1, after some general considerations showing why any decision made on behalf of many requires some kind of unity, Patrizi gives us a potted history of the Roman republic.[84] It began when the corrupt tyranny of Tarquin the Proud made the name of "king" *(rex)* hateful to the Romans. The Romans tried to rule themselves constitutionally, sharing power between classes, but whenever a crisis arose they took refuge in the monarchical principle in the form of a dictator.[85] Patrizi admits that Rome conquered the world in its consular period, but in the typical fashion of monarchical theorists he ascribes her success to innate Roman *virtus* rather than to her free constitution (as Bruni had done). But eventually, in the first century BC, from the time of Sulla onward, the competition for glory among warlords, each aiming at tyranny, led to continual sedition and bloody factional strife, and the people yearned for peace. Finally it was recognized that peace could only come from the rule of a single person. Even Cicero, "whose continual care was for the best condition of the state *(respublica),*" recognized that it would be better to be "well tyrannized" than to continue in a state of violence and disorder.[86] Thus Roman history showed the necessity of Caesar's unification of power for the continuance of the Roman state. Caesar was killed by misguided tyrannicides, but the imperial system established by Augustus brought Rome lasting peace, concord, prosperity, and good government. If so great and virtuous a people as the Romans had chosen monarchy after a long and unhappy experience with polyarchy, that could only add to the weight of history's verdict.[87]

Questions of geographical as well as chronological scale also pointed to the need for monarchy.[88] Absent universal empire, a single city did not have the resources to defend itself against predatory neighbors, some of whom could draw on the resources of an entire region. Effective warfare required manpower and territory. This showed that a kingship must be a territorial state encompassing the resources of many cities and lands in order to defend itself. (No doubt Patrizi was holding before his mind's eye the territorial kingdom of southern Italy in which he resided and to whose future king his book was dedicated.[89]) Patrizi takes for granted the view of his Greek sources that democracies and oligarchies were city governments not appropriate to large territories. In a rare quotation from Aristotle's *Politics* he cites the Philosopher's dictum that a king must be sufficient to himself and so excel everyone in all goods that he does not require anyone's help in securing the utility of the people. Patrizi explains why a territorial monarchy will always provide a more effective defense of the region than a city-state. Experience and common sense show that a city-state cannot resist a determined royal army. To escape their weakness cities sometimes band themselves into confederations. But Patrizi argues that a confederation of city-states—his example is the Etruscan League, celebrated by Leonardo Bruni—will be subject to the same conflicting interests and factions that beset any polyarchic form of government.[90] They are like parts of a body lacking any single mind or heart. Thus a confederation of city-states will also be unstable and short-lived, and could end in the tyranny of a single city over the rest.[91] Such a confederation of city-states would be better ruled and better defended if it submitted to the rule of a king: "At that point all of them will be allowed to act in accordance with virtue, a condition which seems to be, as it were, the goal of human society and of an allied multitude of human beings." Life in a city is mere life; life in a territorial kingdom is the good life—a dramatic revision of Aristotle.

A final argument for the superiority of kingship is that, historically, the office of king was of divine origin.[92] God gave primitive men reason, which led them to form societies for mutual aid and to develop their powers of speech. But corruption set in; everyone began to seek their own good and neglect common needs. This prepolitical society realized the only way to settle disputes and guide the human flock toward common purposes was to have a single shepherd. They chose the man who was most outstanding in virtue, speech, and courage to rule them and provided him with the resources to support his life and office so that he would not have to engage in illiberal, banausic tasks. This figure came to be regarded as divine, and authorities such as Homer recognized that no one could rule well without divine power. Patrizi shows that it was common among ancient peoples from all three continents (no distinction is made among Greeks, Romans, Persians, and Egyptians in this respect) to regard their kings as having divine sanction and divine qualities. In illustration of this point he relates a story from Herodotus describing how Darius had been acclaimed king of the Persians thanks to a divine sign.[93] (Patrizi's version leaves out the scheming of Darius' groom to manage the auspices.) In short, Patrizi rejects Aristotle's developmental model of political institutions, which saw kingship as primitive and democracy as the inevitable future, given the multiplication of large, wealthy urban centers in Greece.[94] Patrizi shows the same reverence for the holy, uncorrupted, primaeval government of humanity that his contemporary Marsilio Ficino showed toward the primordial sources of religious knowledge, the ancient theology.[95] And the primaeval government of mankind, founded under divine auspices, was royal government. Patrizi's argument for the divine character of the kingly office is thus exquisitely historical; it is a humanist argument distinct from juristic claims that the rule of individual emperors or kings was rightful owing to divine approval.

Can Monarchical Power Be Virtuous?

The voice of doubt, however, is not so easily stilled. Even were it granted that monarchy in principle was the best form of government, and that its advantages were worth the sacrifice of city-state liberties, the question still remained whether that good prince, without whom there could be no true monarchy, could ever really exist. Poggio, as we saw in Chapter 4, made the extreme case that political life was inevitably dominated by men who sought power for the sake of wealth and status. Men of virtue who wandered into the courts of princes would be ignored, mocked, or corrupted. If by some fate a good man were allowed to ride the wild horse of the state, he would soon be thrown from the saddle. Literature and philosophy had no effect on power-seeking men, and only *privati* who did not seek to control or despoil others could hope to achieve virtue and true felicity.

Patrizi was well aware of Poggio's arguments, although, in keeping with his uniform practice of not identifying modern authors, he never mentions Poggio's name.[96] By the nature of his response, nested among several chapters of book 1, the Sienese humanist seemed to understand that Poggio's critique involved at least four interrelated issues. One was whether political power was compatible with virtue.[97] A second was whether nature had so constituted human society that the retention of political power inevitably required immoral behavior (an assumption Machiavelli would later use as his starting point in *The Prince*). Or in other words, is virtue reliably rewarded and vice punished in the political sphere, in this life? This was a question Plato had answered in the negative at the end of the *Republic*. The third issue was whether the tendency of all human things to undergo moral decay, a tendency of both individuals and states, could be arrested or even reversed by human wisdom and virtue. The fourth issue, fundamental to ancient political thought, was whether it was possible via education to produce in political leaders the degree of virtue and wisdom necessary for benign rule, or at least to instill in them sufficient appreciation for political wisdom that they would be willing to take good advice from the wise.

The first issue is confronted in a chapter entitled "Whence the pattern of fine living that leads to felicity, and whether a king or a private individual is more fitted to fine and blessed living."[98] Patrizi repeats the gist of Poggio's argument, laying out a contrast, taken from Isocrates' *Ad Nicoclem*, between how a private citizen's way of life prevents his doing evil, and how the life of a prince encourages bad morals and tyrannical conduct.[99] Worse, the depraved prince corrupts his own people, who will follow his example more than his words. Few have access to princes and kings, and those few are afraid to speak freely. Instead they flatter and corrupt and make impossible the task of offering a prince wise counsel. But there is an answer to such pessimism:

> Generally led by such reasoning, the best men think private life is safer and more excellent and far more suited to fine and blessed living than the life of a man who exercises power from his earliest age amid such delights. Such a dilemma, thus simply enunciated, has a solution that is not hard to find. For who has so feeble and dark an understanding *(ingenium)* that he doesn't prefer to be Socrates and not [the corrupt oligarch] Critias, or Brutus rather than Tarquin, the man who brought down the Roman monarchy by his tyrannical abuse of it? Come, compare Brutus to Numa Pompilius: who then is not going to prefer the royal dignity to private life?

Patrizi then goes on to describe how Numa (in an account derived from Livy and Plutarch) was a wise and holy private citizen called reluctantly to the kingship by the Roman people, who then distinguished himself in that role above all others. By his justice and moderation he led the fierce Roman clans to gentleness and a love of peace; he promoted agriculture rather than the pursuit of riches, and he gave the Romans religious fear and taught them to honor the gods.

What the example of Numa Pompilius shows for Patrizi is the possibility of nullifying the noxious moral effects of absolute power by holding out to the prince the greatest reward of all. It is the reward that comes to all who rule justly: "the honor and glory and imperishable fame peoples will bestow upon them in every age." The virtue of a just king gives him a kind of divinity, a power that is more than human to bring blessings to his people. Unjust kings and tyrants, by contrast, are despised in life because of the foul cruelty and injustice they inflict on others;

after death they are held in perpetual execration by the living and suffer terrible torments among those below. The tyrant is a repulsive figure, a lump of foul deformity. In between is the virtue of the *privatus,* real but limited in its effects and in the honor it confers. A noble thirst for true fame and glory, a love of the superexcellent goodness that benefits mankind, can be stimulated by a humanistic culture of praise and blame. But Patrizi insists that the thirst for goodness and felicity is rooted in human nature, even if the desire for good must be cultivated and directed:

> Nature begets human beings who are neither good nor bad; it renders them fit for goodness yet inclined to what is bad. Reason persuades us of this, intelligence reveals it, experience teaches it, and Aristotle, basing himself on proofs of the Old Academy, bears witness to it. Nature herself has sown in us little celestial fires and seeds, as it were, of the virtues, which if allowed to grow quickly bring forth the finest fruit, as Plato says. From these are born a pattern of acting well and living with rectitude, which represses all turbulent affections, orders the human faculties and strengthens habits of virtue. These paths lead us to felicity, desirable for its own sake, supplying us with everything we need, lacking nothing.[100]

It is harder for a prince to be a good man because of his environment, but the rewards for success are correspondingly greater, and in the end far overbalance the sacrifice of his lower impulses. Nor will divine help be lacking to princes who rule with justice.

In the course of the *De regno* Patrizi offers the king two broad incentives to follow the path of virtue. One is the honor argument outlined above: to be a good king is necessary to his honor, and the felicity or infelicity of his kingdom is an expression of his own moral status, as the royal regalia are the signs of his legitimate title. Goodness, to be effective, has to be real, not a lie or a fiction. Lies will out, as Cambyses taught his son Cyrus, and their discovery will make a king distrusted by his friends and his people. The worst sort of lie is self-deception.[101] Honor cannot live without truth; the harmony in the king's soul can only be maintained by truthfulness and integrity. It is a sign of tyranny when a king's court is filled with lies, calumny, dissimulation, flattery, adulation, and other forms of dishonesty. The worst dishonesty is when the king inflates his own achievements by boasting, which makes him unlovable: "He who loves himself too much will have no rivals." It is precisely the dishonesty involved that would foreclose for Patrizi any consideration of benign tyranny, as presented in Xenophon's *Hiero*. A prince who has been brought up to care about things like honor and nobility would never, should never, want to do what is right for his people only for his private benefit, concealing his true motive. Cunning is not the mark of a king, as Xenophon taught in the *Agesilaus,* but sincere goodness and moral excellence.[102] To rule well for no other reason than to cling to power would be a base and shameful idea. It would mean enslaving oneself to a passion. Such an idea could only appeal to someone of corrupt, tyrannical character, and would violate the true prince's sense of self-worth. It would take away the dream of virtue politics, the return to the Golden Age, when power and virtue and wisdom dwelt in the same house, a condominium whose stupendous effects still echoed in human memory as the glory that was Greece and the grandeur that was Rome.

But can a king be confident that his virtue will be rewarded in the sphere of politics, and that his kingdom will be made happy by his virtue? That question leads to the other argument or incentive for royal virtue: the nature argument. Was Nature herself ordered in such a way that acting with virtue would lead to felicity in this life, for states as well as for individuals? To answer in the affirmative, Patrizi understood that he had to clarify the relationship of nature to the human will, which he attempts in 1.12, a chapter on fortune, fate, and chance. It cannot be said that Patrizi's flood of quotations, many from Homer, rises to the level of argument, but his intent is clear enough. He admits that ruling well is the hardest human act and that no amount of virtue will help the king retain popular favor without good fortune. "Not only for barbarians does trust depend on outcomes." Yet Fortune is the companion of the virtues and should not be called a goddess. She is not omnipotent over human affairs. Fortune is merely a sudden and unexpected event whose effects, when malign, can be limited by good counsel and the king's perseverance in virtue. Patrizi prefers to think of Fortune in the manner of the Greek tragedians, as Nemesis striking down the proud. Homer was wise to speak of Fate rather than Fortune in his poems. He understood it, "not straying from true theological reason," as the divine will. Even so, fate was not inexorable in the Stoic manner; fate did not govern all human affairs with an iron will. It merely struck down rash mortals who blamed the gods for their adversities, when in fact the true cause lay in their own folly and cowardice. The point of Patrizi's discussion is evidently to carve out a space for human virtue in the world of nature and to combat Poggian fatalism about politics and power. The courts of princes are not impregnable fortresses of corruption that can never be conquered by royal virtue, guided by prudent counselors. *Principes* were not evil of necessity. As Patrizi's contemporary Marsilio Ficino wrote against astrological fatalism, "The wise man shall dominate the stars."

That the cultivation of human excellence could alter what might seem to be fixed patterns of decadence was a bedrock principle of Renaissance culture. But whether it was truly possible to do so was ultimately a theological question. On this question Patrizi (and one often has to remind oneself that he was a bishop) was a confirmed Pelagian, or perhaps semi-Pelagian. But he was careful to confine his Pelagianism, in the Petrarchan manner, to the present life. Salvation in the next life is not at issue, but only what humanity can do for itself in this life. Patrizi is careful to specify that he is only discussing human felicity, the *finis humanarum rerum,* the end of human affairs in this life, or what Aristotle in the *Ethics* called the specifically human good *(to anthropinon agathon)*.[103] The human good is not wealth or status, nor is it eternal felicity beyond the grave—the sphere of religion—but virtuous activity in accordance with reason, here and now. We depend on God for salvation in the next life but on our own capacities in this one. To be sure, our capacity for virtue comes from God operating in nature, is helped invisibly by God, and is potentially godlike, returning us to God, but it depends on our free will.[104] Without some commitment to a doctrine of free will, there can be no possibility of virtue politics, of political reform enabled by the explosive power of human virtue.

How the King May Become Virtuous

God helps those who help themselves, and to help himself the king has to know how to acquire the virtues, especially prudence, and to quell the passions that will lead him astray, blackening his honor. That is the task that occupies the bulk of *De regno.* Like all Renaissance literati Patrizi takes it for granted that the humanities provide an indispensable training in virtue. He lays out the king's curriculum in the second half of book 2. It is stipulated that his teachers must be moral men and that his companions be decent and respectable boys. His studies must of course begin with grammar, that is, learning Latin. Grammar is the artisan of speech, the interpreter of poets and historians, the commander and chariot of all other disciplines. He should then go on to read poetry, especially Homer among the Greeks and Vergil from among "our Latin authors": "This heroic reading *(heroica lectio)* is of great use to princes and kings, whose minds will be lifted up by the sublimity of heroic song." It will show them what nobility and virtue look like in action and will motivate them to imitate such actions. He should then go on to the other poets, lyric poets like the Spartan Tyrtaeus, the tragedians Euripides and Sophocles, and the comic poets too—but selectively, heeding Plato's warnings in the *Republic* to read only poets with a strong moral message. (Patrizi provides an example of selective reading himself by failing to mention Plato's doubts about the moral value of Homer.)

After the poets he should read history, the school of princely prudence, which Cicero called "the witness of time, the mistress of life, the life of memory and the messenger of truth." All kings and political leaders and commanders of troops need to read history, for all examples of virtue are found in its pages. Patrizi introduces an elaborate *paragone* showing why the reading of history is more inspiring for a king than having sculpted images of great men in his palace: "For if the likenesses of bodies and images made with the hand of artisans are wont to stimulate the minds of youth to the imitation of those whose images they are, how much more will histories accomplish this and the records of great deeds, which express the mind and soul, not the lineaments of the body and the outward appearance of its form? History excels the image by as much as the mind excels the body."[105] The "virtuous environment" is useful, but history more useful still. (Patrizi, whose interest in the plastic arts appears frequently in the *De regno,* helpfully recommends that sculptors represent heroes with togas or armor like the Romans rather than naked like the Greeks, because the hero's mind is more fully expressed in the Roman way.)[106]

The reading of history should be followed by study of the orators, particularly Demosthenes and Cicero, who excelled all others not just in eloquence but *in morali sapientia.* And as Cicero himself taught, eloquence is vain without the study of moral philosophy. At the end of book 2 Patrizi explains the virtues of royal speech and recommends that the prince memorize maxims and sayings that are salted with prudence. Socratic irony, however, verges on untruth and should be employed by private men only. The prince should never speak anything but the naked truth.[107]

Beyond these core disciplines of the *studia humanitatis*—Latin grammar, poetry, history, oratory, moral philosophy—there are other liberal disciplines worth studying for their practical utility, such as mathematics, geometry, music, and astronomy. These are surveyed in book 3. Geography and travel literature deserve the king's particular study, and it is recommended that he scrutinize painted pictures of the world, especially those parts of it where wars might be conducted. But he should avoid purely theoretical and abstruse studies, instead concentrating on more evident matters that treat of civil life and fine conduct, and studies that perfect his powers of reasoning and speech. These should all be appropriately adapted to royal education. For example he should not seek models for the virtue of liberality, which befits private men, but rather magnificence, which befits a king. Patrizi also provides a list of appropriate and useful outdoor activities such as riding, hunting, fowling, swimming, and playing ball. The study of agriculture is useful for every citizen and paterfamilias, but also for princes, as the examples of Cyrus and Lysander show.

Nevertheless, the best way to spend his leisure is to frequent the company of learned men. This is what Isocrates recommended in the *Ad Nicoclem,* Patrizi notes. The king should avoid flatterers and yes-men, and also men whose only recommendation is their lively talk and easy ways. He should prefer accomplished, well-mannered men whose writings and counsel will help him perform great deeds. His religious advisors should recommend true religion and worship of the divine and not retail superstitions, foolish fears, and old wives' tales. Quoting Terence, Patrizi advises the king to consort with men from whose company he will not depart without having learned something of value.

Above all (and this advice fills the first half of book 4) the king should avoid those who speak evil and untrue things, flatterers, adulators, and dealers in gossip and calumny. The fable of Ulysses and the Sirens warns allegorically against the effects of such bad company. Informers *(delatores)* too should be regarded with extreme suspicion, but not entirely disregarded. Those who lie should be punished by law, but sometimes such men give information that is true and salutary: Caesar should have paid attention to the tale-bearers who warned him about the plan to murder him in the Senate. In general the king should cultivate an atmosphere where people feel able to criticize him in his presence. *Regium esse bene agere et male audire:* the royal way is to listen to the evil but do what is good. Following the pattern of Xenophon's Cyrus, the king should do his best to become aware of how he is regarded by his people. This will create in him a healthy incentive to avoid even the smallest shameful acts lest they be spread about and grow in the telling. It is natural for those who spread evil rumors about kings to be regarded as lovers of the multitude, zealous in the cause of liberty and virtue, while those who praise the king will inevitably be considered flatterers or persons corrupted by promises of profit. But princes need to know what the people are saying about them to prevent self-deception and self-indulgence. Patrizi recommends the practice of the painter Apelles, who according to Pliny hid himself behind his paintings so he could hear what people said about them.[108] If he does all this he will solve the "problem of counsel" and not open his ears to evil advice while closing it to the admonitions of the wise and the good.

The rest of book 4 and all of book 5 are consumed with a description of the passions the king should expel or control, such as anger or laziness, and the damage they can do to him and to his kingdom. The order and list of passions track to some extent their treatment in Giles of Rome's *De regimine principum,* revealing the presence of that work on Patrizi's desk. Books 6–8 treat the kingly virtues, beginning with fairness and equanimity, the monarchical analogue to the republican virtue of equality.[109] A Greek text not yet mentioned, Plutarch's *Moralia,* makes a frequent appearance in these pages.[110] Fortitude and justice are singled out for extended treatment, and five whole chapters of book 8 are devoted to a treatment of friendship, relying on Cicero, Plato, Aristotle, and examples drawn from Roman history. In particular Patrizi praises what he calls civil (or social) friendship, not without a certain nostalgia for city life, reminding the reader that the author was himself an exile. Civil friendship is a concept said to be taken from Plato and is a kind of mutual goodwill that comes from rubbing shoulders with one's fellow citizens inside city walls, sharing a climate, diet, mores, and speech. Patrizi says that this kind of friendship "between many" is more appropriate to a king than the philosopher's preferred form of friendship among the virtuous few. Epicurus, remarkably, is here cited as an authority against Aristotle's privileging of friendship based on virtue. (Aristotle's name, as so often, is suppressed.) Patrizi compares the royal kind of civil friendship to a paterfamilias' affections, which should extend to the whole family and not just to his wife. The prince can support civil friendship by allowing the poor to earn their living and preventing magistrates from oppressing the people. As far as his personal circle is concerned, the king should have friends but not favorites.

One virtue in particular deserves comment, as it is central to the theme of this study: *humanitas.*[111] As is well known, Aristotle in the *Politics* distinguishes good from corrupt constitutions by the criterion of whether the rulers serve their own interests or the common good. He does not, however, explain the affective basis for a commitment to the common good on the part of an individual ruler or ruling part *(politeuma),* beyond a general disposition to the virtues, meaning above all a disposition to be law-abiding (general justice) and a disposition not to take more than one's share and give to everyone what they deserve (particular justice). In the broader context of Aristotelian ethics these dispositions might seem to be mainly actuated by a desire for personal distinction and therefore a form of self-love. Christian interpreters since Lactantius saw such dispositions as inadequate to the new Christian age of grace. The new age had released an overflowing of the heart with love toward God and one's fellow humans, a new exchange of mercy and forgiveness among mankind. The scholastics sometimes appealed to a notion of "love for the common good," explained in terms of Augustine's *ordo caritatis,* an ordered benevolence toward others rooted in the Christian's love of God.[112]

Patrizi, by contrast, finds the affective basis of good rulership in natural sympathy between human beings. We possess an *affectio generalis,* a natural sentiment inclining the mind to love of and benevolence toward others, even people we don't know. By nature we rejoice with others in their successes and feel for them in their sufferings. Hence we offer help to the indigent, water to the thirsty, directions to travellers, all out of a sense of right action toward our kind instilled in us by natural affection. It is the part of a free or noble man *(ingenuus)* to love his fellow human beings, while narrow and perverse wits hate their own kind. Such men the Greeks called *misanthropes,* identified by their lack of humor. Patrizi's *affectio generalis* bears some resemblance to early modern notions of universal benevolence such as Leibniz's *philanthropia* or natural love of mankind, or David Hume's conceptions of natural sympathy and benevolence—conceptions informed, like Patrizi's, by Cicero's understanding of the social virtues.

When strengthened by habit and reflection the general disposition to benevolence becomes the virtue of *humanitas.*[113] This is a virtue we must acquire if we are to be truly human. The man who obeys nature can never harm another man, and indeed nature instructs us that human beings must go further than merely avoiding harms: we must always do good to each other. When we refrain from harming others, we thereby excel those beneath us in the order of nature, the animals, and when we benefit each other we imitate God, the giver of all gifts. The essence of being human is to be humane. Thus the noble or free man will help others freely; if he demands repayment he is a mere usurer.[114]

But how is *humanitas* acquired, this virtue so basic to a good polity? Humanity (or *philanthropia,* "an elegant word used by the Greeks") is greatly aided by education ("or *paideia*"), and that is why the ancients used *humanitas* to mean instruction and training in the "good arts" and called the liberal disciplines *humaniores literae,* the literature that makes one more fully human.[115] This was appropriate, because this kind of education belongs only to the human species, with its higher rationality and moral sense. And that most pleasant form of companionship, the companionship of humane letters, though appropriate to all mortals, is so in the highest degree to kings and princes, who are the supreme givers of benefits to their citizens, the most godlike of human beings. For Patrizi, the education of *principes* in the humanities is thus a fundamental condition of good government.[116]

In Patrizi's *De regno* we witness in extreme form the faith in the reforming power of education that is characteristic of virtue politics. To modern political thinkers, Patrizi's book will inevitably seem hopelessly inadequate on the level of theory. To claim a king's legitimacy depends in part on his virtue and wisdom may be true as a statement of fact but is hard to regularize as a principle of government. Failures of virtue and wisdom are difficult to correct even when there exist constitutional processes of accountability.[117] General admonitions that the king should know the minds of his people and be counselled by the wise will seem a feeble substitute for fixed institutions that require consultation of parties affected by government decisions. Patrizi also describes no mechanisms for resisting unjust power. Book 9 of the *De regno,* which discusses the duties of the citizen to the king, mentions no duties to resist him when he does wrong. For our age, with our painful memories of what happens when unlimited power is put into the hands of a single individual, Patrizi's faith that absolute monarchy can be made benign through humanistic education can only seem terrifyingly naïve.

In the Italian Renaissance, however, absolute, unaccountable power was political reality over most of the peninsula. Apart from the four republics of Venice, Florence, Siena, and Lucca, rule was signorial and usually backed by the signore's troops. When the condottiere Francesco Sforza marched into the starving city of Milan in February 1450, the day after a coup had removed the last vestiges of republican government, the leaders of the coup who proclaimed him their duke were not in a position to constrain his power with constitutional devices.[118] Aristotle's famous question, whether it was better to be ruled by a good king or by good laws, did not present them with a live option. In Patrizi's second home, the Kingdom of Naples, the king regularly dealt with baronial challengers to his authority by laying siege to their castles or by summary execution; no Magna Carta emerged from Southern Italy in the Renaissance.[119] Unloved rulers such as Galeazzo Maria Sforza were removed by conspiracies or poison. Most of the marcher states were ruled by condottieri, effectively as military dictatorships. Even in the stable principalities of Ferrara and Mantua, whose dynasties were accepted as legitimate through long custom, the power of the ruler was limited only by the feeblest of civic institutions. Under these circumstances it was hardly irrational to believe that the best hedge against tyranny might be the good character of the ruler. When the spiritual leader of the Catholic Church was also an absolute ruler with a sizeable territorial state, competing with other Italian states for control of the peninsula, it was unlikely that elite educators could appeal persuasively to religious authority when seeking to bridle a prince's will; hence the appeal of literary and philosophical authorities from pagan antiquity—revered but remote. As we have seen many times in this book, pagan antiquity offered numerous models for education as a tool of political reform, beginning with Plato's *Republic* and Xenophon's *Cyropaedia.* Character education of *principes* based on the study of classical literature was something the age believed in deeply, and although Patrizi's treatise remained the most detailed and most popular work in the genre, new humanist treatises on the best prince or the duties of princes or the education of a Christian prince continued to pour from the presses for well over a century after his death.[120]

The ideal humanist king, to be sure, was a kind of utopian dream. It was occasionally teased to waking reality when a prince like the young Henry Tudor seemed responsive to the message of his humanist educators. As that example shows, it was a dream doomed to constant disappointment, as any dream must be that is dependent on a single, fallible human will. Henry VIII, after all, ended up, in the judgment of one recent historian, "the most contemptible human specimen ever to sit upon the throne of England."[121] Yet princely education must have had its successes too, which, given the secret workings of the human conscience, remain largely hidden from historical research. The Renaissance produced no work like the *Meditations* of Marcus Aurelius that allows us access to the moral struggles of a ruler who tried to remain true to his philosophical convictions. But the example of Marcus Aurelius shows that sometimes, in some places, it may be possible for a state to possess rulers who govern with humane wisdom and virtue.

CHAPTER 18

MACHIAVELLI

Reviving the Military Republic

The Calamità d'Italia

The humanist tradition of virtue politics had its origins in the civilizational crisis that gripped medieval Christendom in the mid-fourteenth century. The effects of that crisis on the intellectual plane were above all to bring into question the legitimacy of Christendom's highest authorities—political, spiritual, and educational. Petrarch sought a remedy for the crisis in a new paideuma, a new way of understanding the relationship between the comprehensive doctrines of Christianity and the forms of moral and intellectual formation inherited from pre-Christian civilizations. Adapting ideas of Christian *reformatio* worked out by the Church Fathers, Petrarch thought of his new paideuma as a way to revive human character in its uncorrupt ancient form, including the humanity of primitive Christianity.[1] The decline of Christendom could be reversed, he hoped, by reconstituting the moral and political order of the ancient world, its *institutio.* Its decaying body needed to be rejuvenated with fresh infusions of virtue and wisdom recovered from the classical past. Reform could not be achieved through violent changes in the political or legal order, but only through a slow process of reconstituting the *materia prima* of society, human nature itself. Petrarch's new paideuma was elaborated into a reforming movement by his humanist followers, and by the second half of the fifteenth century that movement had achieved its zenith. By the end of the century it had acquired the status of conventional wisdom.

Eventually, however, that wisdom in its turn was challenged by a new generation of thinkers. These men had themselves enjoyed a humanistic education but no longer believed in the promise of virtue politics. Like Petrarch, they had been taught by events to doubt received wisdom—but by then, the received wisdom was Petrarch's. The events to which the men of the early cinquecento were responding did not, to be sure, amount to a vast civilizational crisis like that of the mid-trecento, though such a crisis would come soon enough with the Reformation. Instead, their political outlook was molded by the astonishing military and political collapse of Italy that occurred in the four decades following 1494, the series of events labelled by the great historian Francesco Guicciardini the *calamità d'Italia*.[2] The outcome of this calamity was that the Italian peninsula would be dominated by non-Italian powers for the next 350 years. It is no accident that the deadliest missile fired against the edifice of humanist virtue politics was let fly by Niccolò Machiavelli (1469–1527), the thinker who meditated most deeply on the lessons to be learned from Italy's loss of political independence.

Italy's calamity was sudden and unexpected. In the forty years between the Peace of Lodi in 1454 and Charles VIII's invasion of Italy, the peninsula seemed to many observers to have achieved the highest level of prosperity and power it had enjoyed since classical antiquity. It was still divided among five main powers,[3] but those powers for the most part—with only a few, relatively brief intervals of warfare—were kept in peaceful balance by what seemed, in retrospect, the exceptional prudence of their leaders. The age-old threats to Italy represented by the "barbarians" of northern Europe were in abeyance for a variety of reasons: weakness and division in imperial Germany, the War of the Roses in England, the French crown's entanglements with the Duchy of Burgundy, the all-consuming devotion on the Spanish peninsula to the *Reconquista*. But to Italians it appeared to be the Italic League—a mutual defense pact formed in 1455 among the five leading powers of Italy—that had secured them against invasion from the north. The threat of an Ottoman invasion was for most Italians far more real, and the Peace of Lodi was brought about primarily by the shock administered to Christendom by the fall of Constantinople, the capital and last bulwark of the Christian empire of the east, to Sultan Mehmed II in 1453. The threat from the east fostered an increasing sense of common *italianità*. The perpetually warring powers of Italy realized they could not hope to defend themselves individually against what was believed to be an imminent threat unless they acted in concert. Yet the Ottoman attack, when it did at last arrive in the southern Italian seaport of Otranto in 1480—terrifying though the capture of the town and the slaughter of its inhabitants was—was nevertheless easily turned back, in hardly more than a year, by Neapolitan troops under the command of Alfonso, Duke of Calabria, the heir to the Aragonese throne.[4] This success, and the distraction of the non-Italian powers of Christendom, led Italians to enjoy a false sense of security, a certain feeling even of superiority to the non-Italian world. Was the cycle of history turning upward again? Was it possible that Rome could be reborn? Many humanists had begun to believe that this was the case. If ancient Roman virtue and eloquence was being reborn, could a revival of Roman power be far behind?[5] At the very least, the trope of rebirth after a Dark Age of defeat and disgrace, dreamed of by Petrarch, enunciated with increasing confidence from the early decades of the quattrocento, had by the second half of the century become ubiquitous in speeches, dedicatory prefaces, and histories.[6]

By the second half of the fifteenth century, indeed, humanists who had worked to reform the governments of Italy by means of classical education and the recovery of ancient virtue could gaze upon their achievements with a measure of satisfaction. Their movement had had real successes. The hero of Otranto himself, Alfonso of Calabria, had been personally educated by the great humanist poet and statesman Giovanni Pontano. It will be remembered that Alfonso was also the prince to whom Francesco Patrizi had dedicated his *De regno,* and he was the recipient as well of many other dedications by humanists who invested in him their hopes for virtuous kingship. His father, Ferrante, the reigning king of Naples from 1458 to 1494, could hardly be regarded as a light of virtue, but he at least continued the policies of supporting literature and the arts put in place by his own father, Alfonso the Magnanimous. Ferrante had also made Pontano his prime minister, a foreigner raised from obscurity thanks to his mastery of ancient literature, thus a luminous example of "elevating the worthy." In Rome the Papacy itself had been occupied by an illustrious humanist, Pius II (r. 1458–1464), and the papal curia and the households of cardinals were filled with humanist literati. In Florence, the greatest center of humanist learning, three generations of the Medici family—all classically educated, all great patrons of humanist literature and classicizing art—managed to maintain stability and relative prosperity in the city despite dark mutterings about lost freedoms from marginalized aristocrats. The other great Italian republic, Venice, had long been penetrated by humanist culture, and by the late fifteenth-century most of its aristocratic ruling class enjoyed a classical education.[7] The great Renaissance principalities of Milan, Ferrara, Mantua, and Urbino could all boast princes trained by famous humanist teachers such as Guarino Veronese, Vittorino da Feltre, and Francesco Filelfo.[8]

The classical revival and virtue politics had transformed the material world as well as the realm of the spirit. Under the leadership of classically educated princes and patrons, the built environment of Italian towns was gradually being ennobled by the classical language of architecture, redeployed to suit contemporary building types. Guided by humanists such as Alberti and Filarete—whose very name means "lover of virtue"—whole cities were planned *all'antica* where, in imagination at least, the glory of Rome and the genius of the Hellenes could find physical expression. Leading collectors such as Lorenzo de'Medici, Federico d'Urbino, Alfonso of Aragon, and a succession of popes had assembled great libraries where the literary heritage of Greece and Rome, along with the now considerable body of modern Latin literature, was opened up to rising generations. Painters and sculptors were filling the palazzi and villas of Italian princes and statesmen with images meant to inspire them to embrace virtue and wisdom, to regard themselves as true heirs to the Roman Empire. Italians of the period were considered the finest soldiers in the world, and humanists claimed part of the credit. Roberto Valturio's *De re militari*—the most popular work on the military art in Machiavelli's lifetime—systematically collected ancient texts with a view to reviving the lost military prowess of the ancients. There were even attempts to renew ancient forms of sociability with the spread of informal academies, symposia, and a new, nobler form of musical performance modeled on the practice of the ancients.[9]

Quant' è bella giovanezza, che si fugge tuttavia! The moment was all too brief. The extraordinary cultural self-confidence and political independence of Italy in the late quattrocento was dealt a swift and stunning blow by a series of events—the *calamità d'Italia*—that began with the invasion of Italy in 1494 by Charles VIII, the "barbarian" king of France. The first foreign intervention in Italy in over half a century was not, to be sure, especially bloody or destructive, not at least compared to later wars of the period. Italians were bewildered by the power of the French king's mobile artillery to knock down their defensive walls, many of them constructed only recently and at great expense. It was only a few small towns and fortresses that were reduced by French military power—Rapallo and Mordano in the north, Fivizzano in Tuscany, Montefortino and Monte San Giovanni in the Regno. Nevertheless, the terrifying cruelty toward the defeated of the transalpine soldiery, especially the Swiss mercenaries—the slaughter of the wounded and of innocent townsmen, the rape of women—was something Italy had hardly experienced for the better part of a century. Adding to the emotional shock was the sense of utter humiliation at the hands of foreign barbarians. The warlike virtue of the ancient Romans and patriotic devotion to the *respublica,* it seemed, were nowhere to be found. Nor did the French pay the least attention to the humanist doctrine that virtue and care for the common good were necessary conditions of legitimacy. The French invasion was predicated on traditional claims to lordship, based on the principle that rulership was simply a piece of property that could be handed down to one's heirs. French claims to rule Milan and the Regno were based *prima facie* on the feudal law of succession, which justified the invasion of Italy as a necessary application of violence in pursuit of a legal title to rule.

The sheer speed of Italy's collapse added to the humiliation. The French army had burst through the Alps at the end of August, reaching Asti on September 9, 1494. The "invasion" soon turned into a royal progress as one city after another opened its gates unresistingly to the conquering army. The king's troops marched swiftly down the peninsula to the Kingdom of Naples, arriving in February 1495. King Alfonso II, the hero of Otranto and the humanists' great hope, had already hastily abdicated in favor of his twenty-four-year-old son, Ferrantino; he himself fled to Sicily where he entered a monastery. By February 20, after minimal resistance, the Kingdom of Naples had capitulated to Charles. The keys to the king's palace, the Castel Capuano, were formally handed over to Charles's forces by none other than the leading humanist statesman of the quattrocento, Giovanni Pontano. The old poet, crushed by the ruin of all his hopes, composed an angry Sapphic ode addressed to goddess Good Faith or Trustworthiness.

To Good Faith

Whither do you flee, O Fides, goddess of Nature,
Nurse of the gods? The high seas refuse you shelter,
in wicked league with the earth itself. The citadels
drive you away, as do forums, temples, camps;
both Kings and High Priest, alas! put you to flight.
Lest Aër block your path to heaven's height—
you who now are everywhere cast out—
or the very winds seal off your starry home,
go! flee to the spirits below, flee to the depths
even of Tartarus, in the world beneath.
For the Manes will receive you companionably there:
they cultivate the just and venerate what is right;
rising up, they shall give you the holy seat deserved—

On condition you drag the pope, bound in chains,
drag him like a criminal by a hook!
Stand him before that fearful altar-throne,

he who fouls holy things with monstrous deeds,
he who faithlessly gave Italy to the Gauls,
he who sold our southern kingdom for gold
that he might becrown his offspring, fruit of crime,
and place those infamous creatures on a throne,
still gory with unexpiated blood!
Drag him, goddess, drag him by a hook,
and drown him—and them—in Tiber's watery flood!
Thrust him—and them—in Erebus' yawning jaws![10]

Pontano was especially bitter that the pope, the nominal overlord of the Aragonese kingdom, had sold out to the French, but he was hardly the only prince to have broken faith in this year of shock and sorrow. Italian virtue was humiliated by innumerable betrayals that had collectively made possible the French conquest. Ludovico Sforza, the *de facto* ruler of Milan, received much of the blame for summoning the French into Italy in the first place. He used the occasion to poison his nephew Gian Galeazzo, the legitimate heir of the duchy, and proclaim himself duke. The French made it clear, once in Italy, that they were ready to betray their ally Ludovico and press the claims of Louis d'Orleans to Milan. The latter was even prepared to make a deal for King Alfonso to retain Naples in return for supporting the French claim to the duchy. Gian Giacomo Trivulzio, a leading condottiere in exile from Milan, was allied first with the invaders, then with Alfonso of Aragon, then, betraying him, returned to the service of Charles VIII. Alfonso II of Naples was betrayed by one of the Regno's greatest noblemen, Antonio di Sanseverino, Count of Marsico, Prince of Salerno, and formerly grand admiral to Alfonso's father, Ferrante. Even before the invasion Cardinal Giuliano della Rovere, the future Pope Julius II, had allied himself with Charles against his enemy, Pope Alexander VI, and when Charles made his triumphal entry into Rome on New Year's Eve 1494, the cardinals della Rovere and Ascanio Sforza rode in with him on either side. Pope Alexander himself, after telling Charles that he should be crusading, not attacking fellow Christians, wrote to the Ottoman Sultan Bayezit urging him to intervene in the defense of Naples against the French. After Charles occupied Rome, the pontiff shifted allegiance again, siding with the French against Alfonso. Piero de'Medici, son of Lorenzo, betrayed his own city of Florence by surrendering to Charles, without consulting the city government, the great strongholds of Sarzana and Pietrasanta, and promised him a subsidy of 200,000 ducats.

The port city of Pisa, the jewel of the Florentine dominion since 1406, whose loyalty to Florence Lorenzo il Magnifico had labored for many years to cement, surrendered rapturously to her new French overlords. The hated Florentines did not get control of the city back until 1509. Everywhere, noble Italians with fine humanistic educations used the French invasion to advance their own interests and settle old scores.

When Italy at length roused itself to expel the French, she was betrayed by the Florentines, now bankrolling the French in exchange for commercial privileges. The new Holy League against the French was forced to rely on foreign help from the Spanish and from the Holy Roman Empire. Even so, the first major battle of the Italian Wars, the battle of Fornovo outside Parma on July 6, 1495, was on balance a victory for the French, even though the "Gauls" were outnumbered two to one by the largely Venetian forces and could not use their cannon owing to rainfall.[11] Thus the two most powerful states of Italy had failed to defeat the barbarians, and the classically educated began to wonder whether the new birth of Rome they had long hoped for had turned into a new decline and fall. In any case, the presence of the Spanish and Germans in the Holy League against France showed that Italians had lost control of their own destiny, and that political loyalty to *italianità* was dead. And the fault lay above all, contemporaries like Machiavelli believed, with the leaders of Italy. After a century of humanistic character education and virtue politics, when the time came to defend Italy against barbarian invaders, the *principes* of Italy, with very few exceptions, had displayed only cowardice, pragmatism, and self-serving opportunism.

Machiavelli and Humanist Literary Culture

Machiavelli was twenty-four years old when Charles invaded Italy.[12] At the time he was finishing his education, probably hearing lectures at the Florentine Studio. His father, Bernardo, a lawyer tainted by opposition to the Medici, had given him a good Latin education under a succession of grammar masters "of some distinction" in Florence.[13] He learned the elements of Latin from Maestro Matteo da Rocco San Casciano, the official grammar master of the Florentine Commune; from Ser Battista di Filippo da Poppi, who taught at a small private school near the classrooms of the Studio; and from Benedetto Riccardini, known as Philologus, who was a student of the great classicist Poliziano and later an editor of classical texts for the Giuntine Press. Machiavelli also studied briefly at an "abacus" or business school, where he would have learned commercial arithmetic, accounting, the workings of the monetary system, and how to write business letters. His last known teacher of grammar, Ser Paolo Sassi da Ronciglione, held a communal teaching post and, later, positions as grammar master at the church school of San Lorenzo, a Medici foundation, and at the Florentine cathedral. Robert Black has recently discovered documents showing that Sassi was a notorious pedophile who was dismissed from his post at the cathedral school in 1495 for violating a pupil or pupils.[14] William Connell and Black have speculated that Sassi's behavior with pupils was alluded to in a letter of 1515 to Machiavelli from his intimate friend, Francesco Vettori, who had also been at Sassi's school.[15] If Machiavelli was indeed molested at school, as was common enough at the time, it might help explain why in later life he displayed skepticism toward the more extravagant claims made by his contemporaries about the power of a humanistic education to impart virtue and nobility.

Given the amount of scholarly labor that has gone into studying Machiavelli's education and the ancient sources of his thought, it is all too easy to exaggerate his mastery of the classics. The best-known of his letters, the letter of 1513 on the composition of *The Prince* to Francesco Vettori, with its memorable description of how Machiavelli in exile spent his evenings in "the venerable courts of the ancients," inevitably leaves the impression of a deep, lifetime devotion to classical literature.[16] In some measure, to be sure, the impression is justified. After his elementary study of Latin grammar and composition, he probably did hear lectures at the Florentine Studio in the 1490s from Marcello Virgilio Adriani, Poliziano's successor as professor of humanities. It may well be Adriani who encouraged him to study Roman comedy, particularly Terence, and introduced him to Lucretius' *De rerum natura*, a didactic poem in hexameters on Epicurean philosophy.[17] Roman comedy was to be the chief inspiration for his later plays, *Mandragola* and *Clizia*, and his study of Lucretius was foundational for his mature attitudes to nature and culture.[18]

Machiavelli certainly lived in a bookish environment and was surrounded by amateurs of humanism. He shows familiarity with the standard Latin authors of the time. But as a scholar he does not deserve to be mentioned alongside leading contemporary authorities in classical studies: men such as Marsilio Ficino, Giorgio Merula, Filippo Beroaldo, Aldo Manuzio, and Giorgio Valla. He ranks far below Poliziano, who, mining the riches of the Medici library, vastly extended the West's familiarity with classical Greek and Hellenistic literature. He made no contribution to the revival of antiquity remotely comparable to that of Marsilio Ficino, who almost single-handedly recovered the heritage of ancient Platonism for Western Christendom.[19] He had nothing like the deep learning in ancient political thought displayed by Francesco Patrizi of Siena. Machiavelli knew little or no Greek; in his later study of authors such as Xenophon, Herodian, Polybius, and Dionysius of Halicarnassus, he relied entirely on translations. He discovered no classical texts, copied few, and edited none. His sole translation, of Terence's *Andria,* was into Italian and was never published.[20] He shows little knowledge of ancient law, science, or medicine. He had little or no exposure to classical rhetoric, a cornerstone of humanist culture, whose revival was considered one of the humanists' greatest accomplishments.[21] As far as we know, he never attempted to write Latin verse. His Latin prose style remained unpolished. He could never rival the elegant Latinity of the celebrated secretaries of Leo X, Pietro Bembo and Jacopo Sadoleto.

Machiavelli today is considered, and rightly so, as one of the finest minds produced by the Italian Renaissance, and he is unquestionably the most widely read of its literary figures. This makes it hard to remember that to most contemporaries he must have seemed during his lifetime a man of limited accomplishments, judged by the standards of humanist culture. His education, insofar as it can be reconstructed from the surviving documents and from the evidence of his works, was utilitarian. It barely qualified him for employment as a chancery official, which by this date required a good command of Latin and some familiarity with the classics, but nothing more. In terms of educational pedigree and literary accomplishments, he could never rival his teacher Adriani, who had studied with Cristoforo Landino and Poliziano, who later became Machiavelli's supervisor in the Florentine chancery.[22] He could never have succeeded Adriani in the post of principal chancellor, since that position from the time of Coluccio Salutati had ordinarily required great distinction in Latin literature and an international reputation. It may indeed be that his failure to find employment with the Medici in the 1510s had less to do with his political unreliability than with his lack of literary prestige. Machiavelli's brilliance was known to and appreciated by his closest associates, but his private reputation was built on his wide experience of military and diplomatic affairs and his powerful analytical intelligence.

It was only after the return of the Medici in 1512—after he had been dismissed from his post as second chancellor, publicly humiliated, imprisoned, and tortured— that Machiavelli took serious steps to enhance his reputation as a man of letters.

Up to that point his literary output had consisted mostly of official reports, practical policy proposals, and poetry written in the *volgare*. In the 1490s, during the Savonarola years, while waiting for a post in the chancery to open up, he saw himself primarily as a vernacular poet, and he continued to write in non-classical genres such as *capitoli,* sonnets and burlesques rooted more in popular Florentine culture than in the latinate culture of humanism. The bulk of his vernacular poetry was written before 1512.[23] His first major work after his disgrace, *The Prince,* was meant to showcase his practical expertise in government and had only a slight patina of classical learning. As Robert Black writes, "The most significant role of the ancients and the humanists in the *Prince* was to reject their heritage."[24] When Machiavelli at last achieved fame as a writer in the last few years of his life, it was as a writer of comedies in the vernacular. Though this fame was well deserved, it did not place him among the greatest writers of his age, or even of Florence, in the opinion of contemporaries.

In the latter part of the 1510s, owing in part to the stimulus of the classical enthusiasts he encountered at the famous gatherings in the Rucellai Gardens, and also, perhaps, because he wanted to improve his credentials as a writer on politics, Machiavelli made a far more careful study of ancient historical, military, and political writers. The effects of that encounter are manifest throughout his mature political works, the *Discourses* and *The Art of War.* Yet Machiavelli, unlike most of his educated contemporaries, never worshipped at the altar of the ancient authors. In a period when it was standard practice for humanists to make a great parade of their classical sources, Machiavelli rarely cited and often concealed his. In the *Discourses,* nominally a commentary on Livy, he does not begin the way any humanist commentator would, with praise of the author. In fact neither Livy nor any other ancient authority is ever praised in *The Prince,* the *Discourses,* or *The Art of War,* either as a source of wisdom or as a practical guide to politics or war. It is Rome that is great, not Livy. We learn about the reasons for Rome's greatness by sifting Livy with our own understanding, not by absorbing Livy's own authorial wisdom. We should imitate the practices of the ancients when they are admirable, but the advice of ancient authors, couched as it generally was in moralizing terms, may mislead and should be received with skepticism. No prominent writer of the Italian Renaissance showed less interest than Machiavelli in promoting the moral authority of ancient authors.[25]

Even more remarkably—and in violent contrast with virtue politics—the superiority of ancient to modern history as a source of political prudence, as far as

Machiavelli was concerned, could not be assumed.[26] Unlike Francesco Patrizi, who carefully avoided mentioning contemporary events or authors in his political treatises, Machiavelli's mature works on politics and war blended ancient and modern examples with no sense of hierarchy.[27] Indeed he regarded his contemporaries' preference for the past over the present as an irrational bias caused by the influence of the passions on reason. In the preface to the *Discourses,* book 2, he explained why people wrongly believe that things used to be better in the past. History is written for the victors, and writers who seek reward will celebrate the winners' deeds and conceal their infamy. Our passions are involved when we observe the actions of our contemporaries because they affect us; not so with actions in the past. News of current events makes us angry and fearful by turns, while we view the past through a golden mist of memory. The great men of the past are safely dead and do not threaten us. In fact, says Machiavelli, human behavior is a constant, and there has always been about the same amount of goodness and wickedness in the world. It may well be that things are now getting better (or worse) for us than they were in the past, but we can't tell that. In retrospect we can see that first the Assyrians had *virtù*, then the Medes, then the Persians, then Rome. If we lived in one of those empires on the rise and believed the past was better, we would be wrong; if we lived in a time of decline and held the same opinion, we would be right. But in the present we are unable to tell where we are in the cycle. Machiavelli confesses that even his own firm conviction that he lived in a time of decline might be mistaken. (Since he in fact lived in a period when Europe was on the brink of dominating the rest of the world, one has to concede his point.)

Machiavelli makes the further point, however, that our ignorance of where we are in the cycle of history does not mean we cannot learn from the past. Some people might think that to claim all times are equally happy or unhappy means there is nothing to be learned from the past. Machiavelli disagrees. Even though roughly equal quanta of goodness and wickedness have always existed in the world, they have always been unevenly distributed. Some peoples are better at some things than others, and for longer periods of time. The Romans were good at domination, for example, and they dominated for a long time.[28] It is worth studying the causes of human excellence so that we can try to replicate them and perhaps improve our own political life. The modern world, given the relative corruption of its politics, is more likely to present us with examples of what to avoid than what to imitate, but failure as well as success can inform our prudence. As Machiavelli wrote later in the *Florentine Histories,* "It is perhaps as useful to observe these things [the corrupt behavior of princes, soldiers and heads of republics, *i capi delle republiche*] as to learn ancient history, because if the latter kindles free spirits to imitation, the former will kindle such spirits to avoid and get rid of present abuses."[29] The Romans could not and should not be imitated in every respect. We first need to assess what the Romans did well before trying to be like them. What we can take from them is laid out by the interlocutor Fabrizio Colonna in *The Art of War*: "To honor and reward excellence, not to despise poverty, to esteem the methods and regulations of military discipline, to oblige the citizens to love one another, to live without factions, to esteem private less than public good, [are elements of Roman political culture that] could easily fit in with our times."[30]

Machiavelli's attitude to the lessons of history and the wisdom of classical authors shows his rejection of basic assumptions underlying virtue politics. A number of places in his writings even reveal a certain contempt for the "softness" and "idleness" induced by literary study and imply that too great a devotion to letters among *principes* (as opposed to the manly arts of war) is a sign of corruption. At the same time, an excessive interest in literature and philosophy are an unavoidable consequence of military success and peace, leading in a Sallustian cycle to the ruin of a polity. Wise princes will guard against such softening of manners. In the preface to book 5 of the *Florentine Histories* Machiavelli writes:

> Usually countries [*provincie*][31] go most of the time, in the changes they make, from order to disorder and then pass again from disorder to order, for worldly things are not allowed by nature to stand still. As soon as they reach their ultimate perfections, having no further to rise, they must descend; and similarly, once they have descended and through their disorders arrived at the ultimate depth, since they cannot descend further, of necessity they must rise.... For virtue gives birth to quiet, quiet to leisure [*ozio*], leisure to disorder, disorder to ruin; and similarly, from ruin, order is born; from order, virtue; and from virtue, glory and good fortune. Whence it has been observed by the prudent that letters come after arms and that, in countries and cities, captains arise before philosophers. For, as good and orderly armies give birth to victories and victories to quiet, the strength of well-armed spirits cannot be corrupted by a more honorable leisure [*onesto ozio*] than that of letters, nor can leisure enter into well-instituted cities [*città bene institute*] with a greater and more dangerous deceit [*inganno*] than this one. This was best understood by Cato when the philosophers Diogenes and Carneades, sent by Athens as spokesmen to the Senate, came to Rome.[32] When he saw how the Roman youth was begin-

ning to follow them around with admiration, and since he recognized the evil that could result to his fatherland from this honorable leisure, he saw to it that no philosopher could be accepted in Rome. Thus countries come by these means to ruin.[33]

Here the study of letters and philosophy are a "dangerous deceit" that undermines a city's *institutio,* the disciplines of civic life that buttress warlike virtue; and the softening of manners that result from literary study ultimately brings the state to ruin. Greek philosophy is singled out for its seductive corruptions, substituting competition in words for rivalry in active virtue. There is an electric charge of sarcasm running through the phrase *onesto ozio,* meant surely to recall Cicero's famous political slogans *cum dignitate otium* or *otiosa dignitas.* These phrases, whose significance has been the object of some debate among classicists, meant in their political sense an absence of civil strife and tumult, domestic tranquillity, combined with preservation of the established republican forms, and a deferential relationship between the people and the ruling optimates such as would preserve the preeminence of the latter. For Cicero personally *otium cum dignitate* came to mean something like an honorable compromise with adverse forces in politics, licensing him to withdraw and get on with literary studies beneficial to the state; in other words it was an *otium* that is not mere repose and pleasure.[34] It is this literary *ozio* that Machiavelli sees as a source of corruption and a "dangerous deceit" leading a country to ruin. Indeed, for him the study of the humanities is, from the point of view of a statesman, a kind of fraud on the public (another meaning of *inganno*) that corrupts warlike virtue under the cloak of an honorable pursuit.[35]

In another passage, this time in *The Art of War,* Machiavelli gives a satiric portrait of a prince all too immersed in literary activities, a vice he correlates with other moral weaknesses as well as poor judgment in governing the court and army. This is the sort of prince, Machiavelli writes, who flourished before the Italian wars and the *calamità,* and whose softness and poor judgment led directly to the collapse of Italy in 1494.

Our Italian princes believed, before they tasted the blows of the oltramontane wars, that it was enough for a prince to know how to think up a sharp response in his study, to write a beautiful letter, show quickness and cleverness in his words, know how to weave a deception, dress himself in gems and gold, sleep and eat with greater splendor than others, to be surrounded with wanton pleasures, to deal with subjects avariciously and proudly, to decay in laziness [*ozio*], to give positions in the army by favor, to despise anyone who showed them any praiseworthy course, and to expect their words to be taken as the responses of oracles. It did not enter the minds of these wretches that they were preparing themselves to be the prey of whoever attacked them. From that came in 1494 great terrors, sudden flights and astonishing losses; and thus three of the most powerful states in Italy have been many times spoiled and plundered. What is worse is that those who are left continue in the same error and live by the same bad system, and do not consider that those who in antiquity wished to keep their states did and caused to be done all those things that I have discussed, and that their effort was to prepare the body for hardships and the mind for perils. . . . These things [the stories about how Alexander and Caesar fought in the front line of battle], if Italian princes read and believed them, it would be impossible for them not to change their form of life and for their countries not to change their fortune.[36]

Machiavelli here again dwells on two of his constant themes: the need for action, not mere talk, in political life, and the failure of his classically educated contemporaries to take the right lessons from history.[37] A number of his strictures, to be sure, echo traditional humanist attitudes: the enervating effects of luxury and avarice, the need for military leaders to be chosen on the basis of merit and not favor, the need for captains personally to lead their troops. But traditional humanists would never do what Machiavelli does here: staple the vices of contemporary princes to an effete and unwarlike character resulting from fancying themselves as literati and spending too much time at their *scrittoi,* their writing desks. If they really wanted to imitate the ancients, if they took the right lessons from their ancient books, Machiavelli says, they would toughen up: they would be out on the field of battle like Caesar and Alexander, sweating in their armor in the front lines, risking their lives. That was the only way they could expect to keep their *stato.* One needs to resist the temptation to turn Machiavelli's argument here into a static ranking of arms over letters, in the manner of contemporary courtly *paragoni.* The historical dimension he introduces makes it rather an assertion about the dynamic relationship between military and literary cultures. When a military culture is dominant, a prince can expect to maintain his *stato;* once a soft, effete literary culture is allowed to take precedence, a country risks slipping a notch down the historical cycle and into ruin.[38]

Machiavelli's Political Education and The Art of War

Machiavelli's real education, the education that taught him how to think about war and politics, was his formation as a civil servant, diplomat, and close observer of political and military failure. He acquired his position as second chancellor of the Florentine Signoria in 1498, a few weeks after Savonarola's execution for heresy outside the Palazzo Vecchio. The relatively popular regime that followed the one controlled by that fanatical preacher was determined to put an end to the almost unimaginably violent factionalism that followed the expulsion of the Medici in 1494. There was a concerted effort to purge the Florentine bureaucracy of partisan elements. Machiavelli was chosen to replace a Savonarolan official precisely because he himself seemed to be a blank slate politically. He came from a family that had not enjoyed the favor of the Medici, and though privately hostile to Savonarola he had taken no part in the factional politics of the previous four years, devoting himself instead to literary pursuits. Like his humanist predecessors in the chancery of the early quattrocento, he continued to steer clear of partisan politics while in office, never allowing himself to become a mere political operative of the Soderini regime that came to power in 1502. Like Coluccio Salutati, Leonardo Bruni, and other humanist officials before him, his attitude to office was that of a permanent undersecretary in modern parliamentary systems, bidden to discharge the policies of his political masters without intruding any private or factional interests of his own.[39] He continued to present himself as an expert on government and war with analytical skills and experience that could profitably be exploited by any person with *stato.* After losing his post as second chancellor in 1512, he offered himself to the Medici, newly returned to power, on that basis. He believed that they would understand his readiness to subordinate any private political loyalties to their interests. Eventually, after almost a decade, he persuaded them of his value and became their informal advisor. By the 1520s he had established a position as a political wise man, above partisan politics, liked and respected by both Mediceans and republicans. Though his sympathies remained republican, though he had a lifelong hostility to aristocrats, and though his advice to the Medici was meant to nudge them toward an eventual republican restoration in Florence,[40] the advice he gave in his mature political writings remained coolly analytical, designed to profit political *principes* of all stripes, whether republican or monarchical. He never presented himself to outsiders as a republican ideologue.

Machiavelli's self-positioning above (or behind) partisan politics is shown above all in the two areas of policy contemporaries rightly associated with him, namely, his military doctrine and his study of ways to eliminate factionalism. Chapter 20 will take up Machiavelli's analysis of cures for hyperpartisanship and will show how that analysis led him to call for a mixed regime, balancing aristocratic and popular humors.[41] The rest of the present chapter will discuss his military doctrine, the doctrine for which he was most famous in his lifetime and the root of all his later political thought.[42]

For a chancery official, Machiavelli acquired impressive credentials as an expert on the military art and its sister art of diplomacy. In part because his superior in the Florentine chancery, Adriani, was frequently more engaged with his literary than his public career, many responsibilities of the first chancellor fell on Machiavelli's shoulders. That meant Machiavelli often filled the role of Florence's secretary of state and secretary of war combined, and he acquired much wider experience as an official envoy than a second chancellor of the republic would normally receive.[43] Legations on behalf of Florence took him all over Italy and into France and Germany, where he met and observed in action the leading princes and generals of his time. He was a firsthand witness to the failures of political and military leadership. In Florence he had seen with his own eyes, already before 1498, the effects of the *calamità*: the collapse of the Medici regime, the city's descent into religious fanaticism, the paralysis induced by factional strife, the loss of Pisa, and the rebellions within Florence's little empire in Tuscany. Once he entered the Palazzo Vecchio as secretary to the Florentine government, he came to appreciate how Florence's sclerotic institutions and its political culture of endless debate, delay, and indecision prevented effective action to recover its lost territories.[44]

Machiavelli found himself on the staff of Florence's military commissioners during the siege of Pisa in 1500, when Florence spent vast amounts of treasure on foreign professional troops and condottieri, only to see them repulsed by Pisa's relatively small garrison of citizen soldiers. Travelling abroad as a representative of Florence he observed rulers whose decisions were made with far more speed and effectiveness, and he learned to see Florence's status as a power through the eyes of foreigners: as a city that was absurdly weak and vacillating, a bazaar of soft, unwarlike merchants trying to buy military protection. With his own eyes he saw the stunning rise and fall of the cardinal-turned-condottiere, Cesare Borgia. With his own eyes he witnessed the shocking audacity of Pope Julius II who, violating existing treaties, risked his own life to gain control of Perugia and then high-handedly "reformed" the government of Bologna, sweeping away existing laws and institutions. With his own eyes he witnessed the indignities of Milan's subjection to its new French viceroys.[45] With his own eyes, while on a mission to Mantua in 1509, he saw with horror the atrocities and devastation wrought by French, Swiss, and Albanian soldiers after the battle of Agnadello, and he marvelled at the swift collapse of the Venetian empire in its *Terraferma,* "where in one day's battle Venice lost what she had acquired with the utmost labor over the course of eight hundred years."[46]

It is no wonder that from his earliest days in the chancery, Machiavelli came to see the fundamental challenge of his time, both for Florence and for Italy, as a military one. If the main cause of Florence's internal weakness was factionalism, its main weakness as a power among other powers lay in its inability to address security issues with a reliable armed force drawn from its own people. He became the leading advocate within the Florentine government for a native-born and native-led militia[47] as well as the leading opponent of reliance on professional soldiers and mercenaries. In advocating this policy he was decidedly in a minority among contemporaries, for all the armies of his day, including the great French army that had humiliated Italy in 1494, relied heavily on mercenary soldiers.[48] Almost all leading military authorities for a century had regarded professional armies as an unquestioned necessity of modern warfare. It is a measure of Machiavelli's powers of persuasion within the councils of Florentine government—and of the Florentines' desperation after two decades of military failure—that he was able to convince the government of Florence to allow him to reorganize its native levies into a proper army. He himself drafted the legislation establishing the new force in 1506, and he personally supervised its recruitment, training, and provisioning, acting as *de facto* military commissioner of the Signoria. And he himself received a great deal of credit, at least from some observers, when in 1509 he oversaw its most glorious success, the recapture of the city of Pisa, the chief object of Florentine foreign policy since 1494. He accompanied the ambassadors of the defeated to Florence and signed their capitulation, just below the name of the first chancellor, Adriani. Two days after the victory he received a letter from Agostino Vespucci describing the bonfires and jubilation in Florence and declaring that the Secretary deserved "not the least portion" of the glory. His friend Filippo Casavecchia wrote to him a week later with equal joy to say, "I wish you a thousand benefits from the outstanding acquisition of that noble city, for truly it can be said that your person was cause of it to a very great extent, although I do not blame thereby any of those very noble commissioners [i.e., those officially in charge of military operations] concerning either their wisdom or indeed their efforts."[49] The letter's tone of irony tells us that Casavecchia believed other, more noble citizens would get credit for the conquest, but those who understood what had gone on behind the scenes would know that the Florentine militia had been Machiavelli's idea and its greatest victory was really his. The recapture of Pisa remained without question his greatest achievement as a man of action.

Machiavelli was thus a highly experienced man of action with real successes to his credit when he was driven from office in 1512 after the fall of the regime headed by the ineffectual Piero Soderini, who had been elected "gonfaloniere for life" by the Florentines in 1502. The Medici restoration, however, was enabled by the easy victory of professional Spanish troops over elements of Machiavelli's militia at Prato, and this defeat continued to cast a shadow over his reputation as a military theorist.[50] All the same, he never wavered in his conviction that well-trained and well-led native militias could and must replace professional soldiers if Florence and Italy were to exit their downward spiral and recover the glory of Roman arms. Machiavelli continued to promote this idea for the rest of his life and especially in *The Art of War* (1521).

This dialogue, distributed in seven books, deserves to be considered as a full member of his trio of political treatises, alongside *The Prince* and the *Discourses*. Today military doctrine as a rule is studied in isolation from political theory, but during the Renaissance it was ordinarily treated as a vital part of a complete political education, being included for example in Giles of Rome's *De regimine principum* and in Francesco Patrizi's treatise on republican government.[51] Nevertheless, the emergence of *res militaris* as a distinctive "art" that required specialized treatment began with the humanist treatise of Roberto Valturio *(De re militari)* and Antonio Cornazzaro's *Dell'arte militare*, a popular work written in terza rima.[52] Specialization was no doubt encouraged by collections of ancient treatises on military matters offered by the printing houses, such as the one containing Frontinus, Vegetius, (pseudo) Modestus, Aelianus Tacticus, and Onasander entitled *Scriptores rei militaris*, edited by the Roman humanist Giovanni Sulpizio da Veroli and published in Rome in 1494.[53] Machiavelli's *Art of War* can be considered a contribution to this growing genre.[54] It was the only one of his political works to be published during his lifetime and can also stake a claim to be his most popular work among Renaissance readers. Although editions of the work in Italian are slightly less numerous than editions of the *Discourses, The Prince,* and the *Florentine*

Histories, its popularity in French translation vastly outstripped that of the other three works in that language.[55]

This success, however, does not necessarily mean that Machiavelli's advocacy of native militias was being enthusiastically embraced by his readers. Nor would it necessarily have been seen as a "republican" work, given that its advice was explicitly addressed to ruling elites both in republics and monarchies. The most detailed studies of the work's reception indicate that its chief attraction to Renaissance readers was its project of adapting ancient military science to modern conditions.[56] As Machiavelli himself says (in the voice of the principal interlocutor, Fabrizio Colonna), the subject of the work as a whole is how to win wars.[57]

In terms of contemporary military doctrine, however, Machiavelli's advocacy of native militias as a substitute for professional soldiers must have been perceived by most informed contemporaries as eccentric.[58] It is true that the loyalty of mercenary troops was seen as an ongoing problem by most governments of the time, and the need to hire subjects of other potentates for one's own army was deplored as complicating military alliances. The mounting size and cost of military establishments in the fifteenth and sixteenth centuries drove many governments to regularize the training and equipping of native levies. Sudden military threats could also focus attention on improving the preparedness of local forces, as when Turkish raids across the Isonzo into Friuli in the 1470s drove Venice to create a comprehensive military ordinance for its territories in the *Terrafirma*.[59] Only a year after Machiavelli's militia legislation of 1506, Venice reorganized its own militia yet again in response to threats from French armies. Other Italian cities and regions eventually followed suit: Urbino in 1533, Ferrara in 1560, Piedmont in 1566. Such forces could help keep order, perform garrison duties, and man defensive works at less cost to cities and princes than professional armies. But arming rural populations and relying on native generals also carried risks. In cities suffering from intense partisanship, the presence of armed *contadini* could easily turn faction into civil war. The Florentines had not forgotten that both the Medici and their oligarchic rivals had been backed by armed peasants from their estates during the crisis of 1433–1434 that brought the Medici to power. A state that armed its rural population and relied on domestic military forces had to be confident of its own stability, which is surely why the insecure Spanish governments in Milan and Naples during the later Renaissance never tried to organize militias.[60] The Medici showed the same reluctance to trust local levies. Cosimo de'Medici's power in quattrocento Florence had been guaranteed by personal alliances with various foreign condottieri, above all Francesco Sforza, and the Medici restoration of 1512 relied on professional soldiers as well, several of whom were members of the Medici family. Such considerations help explain why containing factionalism for Machiavelli was so central a concern of his political theory and also why, as the principal champion of native militias in Florence, he had difficulty persuading the Medici to accept his services.

But the real problem with militias, in the eyes of most contemporaries, was simply that they were militarily irrelevant.[61] The invasion of Italy by the French in 1494 wrought tumultuous changes in Italian military doctrine, and the French success with mobile field artillery in particular required Italian commanders to adapt quickly their modes of fortification and siegecraft as well as their equipment, infantry drills, tactics, and strategy.[62] Amid all this turmoil, the restructuring of militia forces, among professionals, was not a high priority. The gradual ratcheting up of the size of armies during the Renaissance meant that by the second decade of the Italian Wars many field armies were larger than the entire male population of Florence. Even if one added rural levies it would be difficult for a militia to match, simply in numbers, the French army that had invaded Italy in 1494, some 25,000 strong. The growing expense of war was rapidly making it impossible for smaller states to pay the costs even of short, defensive wars. Defenders of citizen militias liked to make the argument that their superior devotion to country and their own interests made them fight better, but this argument too was unrealistic. The decisive units in the field armies of the new era tended to be the artillery and the *arquebusiers,* both of which required intense training to be effective. As Charles de Gaulle once remarked, "All the virtue in the world was useless against firepower."[63] The infrequent training imposed haphazardly on rural militiamen, often distracted by their own agricultural tasks and often equipped with primitive and ill-assorted arms, put them at a crippling disadvantage when faced with well-trained and well-equipped professional troops. No sane captain would risk putting militia troops in the line against properly trained, regular forces. Though contemporary military doctrine recognized a limited role for local levies, it is hard to find a military expert other than Machiavelli himself who believed that militias led by citizen generals and officers could win wars. As J. R. Hale commented, "In professional eyes, [militiamen] remained cyphers, necessary to line coasts and walls and look like soldiers in defensive campaigns but all too often, as a Venetian administrator put it, 'like farmyard dogs, fearless of death in the yard, fleeing at the least alarm outside it.'"[64]

Why Princes and Republics Should Follow
the Ancient Way of Warfare

The Art of War is what is known to literary historians as a "magisterial dialogue" in that it presents a single figure, the main interlocutor, as an authoritative source of doctrine whose knowledge unfolds under questioning from friends or disciples.[65] The magisterial figure Machiavelli used to present his own views in *The Art of War* was Fabrizio Colonna, a choice that has puzzled numerous interpreters. If your intention is to argue for the superiority of militias to professional troops, why choose a professional soldier and a famous condottiere as your mouthpiece? Various answers have been suggested. It has been argued that Colonna was picked for the role because of his politics: he was an eminent captain known to be friendly to republican interests. Piero Soderini tried to recruit him to lead Florence's troops under the republican regime, on this hypothesis, because the Colonna were inveterate rivals of the Orsini family, themselves long allied with the Medici.[66] It has been pointed out that he was safely dead by the time Machiavelli finished the dialogue and therefore could not contradict the views attributed to him. It is moreover quite possible that the historical Fabrizio Colonna did visit the Rucellai Gardens and meet Machiavelli and his friends in 1516, the dramatic date of the dialogue. This fact may have been known well enough among Machiavelli's earliest readers to fool some of them into thinking that the real Colonna favored citizen militias.[67]

These observations, however, do not quite get to the bottom of the way Machiavelli uses Colonna in the dialogue. In Florence the failure of Machiavelli's militia to defend the republic against the mercenary forces of the Medici in 1512 was taken by most observers as definitive proof of their ineffectiveness and of the impracticality of Machiavelli's own military ideas.[68] Moreover, like every student of classical literature, Machiavelli knew the story of Phormio, the Aristotelian philosopher, who, presuming to give an oration on military matters before Hannibal, was dismissed by the celebrated general as an old fool who had no idea what he was talking about.[69] To make the case for his ideas in the 1520s, Machiavelli needed to find a man of action with a high reputation in military affairs who would be acceptable to those who might still harbor republican sentiments. Colonna is thus presented as a man who is well read in ancient history but does not learnedly cite authors like a humanist.

Machiavelli gives fictional (and probably fraudulent) authenticity to Colonna's views, furthermore, by representing him as a reluctant condottiere. Colonna's principal questioner in book 1, Cosimo Rucellai, recognizes the incongruity of the professional soldier's advocacy of militias and asks him to explain himself. This leads to a sort of confession on Colonna's part that a professional soldier cannot expect to be a good man because the nature of his calling forces him to be a greedy warmonger. The question of why Colonna continued to work as a professional soldier despite his (supposed) private belief that Roman-style citizen armies were militarily superior is left hanging until the last book of the dialogue. At the very end of book 7 Colonna finally reveals his true convictions. He returns again to Rucellai's question why his admiration for Roman citizen armies is not belied by his own career as a professional general-for-hire. He excuses the inconsistency in his behavior by claiming that, despite his eminence, he has never had the power to institute the sort of radical change that would be necessary to return to Roman ways. The change is perfectly possible, but it would have to be made by sovereign princes "of such great states that they can assemble from their subjects at least fifteen or twenty thousand young men." This is a figure that excludes the petty domains of condottiere princes, based in rural lands or hill towns like Urbino or Camerino, but would include populous city-states like Florence or Milan.[70] To create such a new army inspired by classical examples would be a great accomplishment, worthy to stand next to the achievement of King Cyrus of the Persians, and doing so would guarantee glory and conquest to whoever could do it. This was never in the realm of possibility for Colonna himself, whose troops' loyalty was based on their pay, but another prince of a larger state might accomplish it with loyal subjects. Colonna goes on to explain that the failure of Italian states in the disastrous period after 1494 had nothing to do with the valor of Italian soldiers themselves, but only with their leaders. Italy simply lacked *principi savi* who possessed real understanding of how to imitate the ancients.

This is the central issue of *The Art of War*, as of Machiavelli's mature political thought in general: how best to imitate the ancients. In *The Art of War* the question takes the form of asking why modern military establishments are so inferior to those of the Romans. That of course is an assumption, but Machiavelli is not interested in the hypothetical of whether a modern army could defeat a Roman army. He takes it as obvious that the Romans were supreme in warfare: they had a long-lived, successful empire; modern Italians did not, and had lost the ability to defend themselves even against barbarians. The military failures of modern Italy could not be reversed simply by reconstructing Roman strategy, tactics, training, and weaponry. Valturio had done that already in 1460, but his antiquarianism had not changed any outcomes during the Italian Wars. Nor had the humanist emphasis on the literary and moral education of commanders resulted in more powerful field armies or strengthened the defense of cities. When a foreign army threatened to sack your city, burn your country estates, and rape your wife and daughters, human beings were going to do whatever was necessary to save the things dearest to them, whether or not they lived up to finest standards of ancient virtue. That is how necessity became Machiavelli's watchword and the basis of his political science. Power, *virtù* in Machiavelli's sense, is the condition of all other goods. The only way to recover ancient virtue in its root meaning of manly strength and competence was to find a different approach to imitating the ancients. That approach meant not sitting at the feet of ancient authorities seeking their wisdom, but analyzing the written records of the past to find out the secrets of the ancients' success. It meant finding out why—*di necessità* in Machiavelli's recurring phrase—the Romans were virtuous. What were the laws and customs that had made them so, and could they be reproduced in the modern world?

Machiavelli's answer to this question was a firm yes: a renaissance of Roman military effectiveness was possible. Italians should not be dismayed or terrified by Italy's parlous condition, "because this land seems born to raise up dead things, as she has in poetry, in painting, and in sculpture."[71] The extreme toughness and indifference to hardship the Romans displayed in their best period could not be brought back in soft modern times, but "judging from what I have seen and read," as Machiavelli wrote in the dedication of *The Art of War*, "it is not impossible to bring military practice back to ancient methods and to restore some of the forms of earlier excellence *(virtù)*."[72] The main obstacle is "damaging opinions" and "errors" that make most people abhor the mere thought of military life. Book 1 of *The Art of War* begins with Machiavelli deploring the divorce of civil and military affairs in modern life. In contemporary Italy even the grooming, dress, and behavior of soldiers differed from that of ordinary citizens. It was not that way in the ancient Roman republic, where all adult male citizens shared military duties and had experience of war. It is the intimate relationship between civil and military affairs in ancient Rome that is the real secret of the Romans' success in war. Rome was a society whose *modi* or forms of civic life were ordered for war by custom, religion, and law. It was this aspect of ancient Rome, the free Roman state of the consular period, that modern Italian cities and princes who wanted to be militarily successful would do well to imitate, to the degree possible in the corrupt societies inherited from the feudal and Christian past.

Machiavelli, in other words, is calling for the partial militarization of Italian principalities and city-states, reordering their military ordinances to resemble those of the Roman republic before the time of the Gracchi, when the Romans were still well governed.[73] This radical way of imitating antiquity goes far beyond the bookish proposals of Bruni and his followers to reimagine civic knighthood as a closed, dedicated class of military experts. Though Machiavelli advised recruiting infantry for his neo-Roman armies preferentially from the countryside (as the Romans had done), he also would include manual workers from minor guilds (arti) in the city: "After these [countrymen, the authorities should recruit] the smiths, carpenters, farriers, masons, of whom it is useful to have plenty because their skills can be applied to many things."[74] He also expected to recruit cavalry from citizens inside the walls—presumably the more prosperous ones who could afford horses and armor—as Florence had done in the days of its greatest victories such as the Battle of Campaldino (1289). Machiavelli did not share the humanist snobbery about the unsuitability of certain professions for military recruitment (the delectus); he excluded no trade or calling as too ignoble to produce good soldiers. By recruiting young men at the age of seventeen, he expected to mold them in the ways of virtù before they could be spoiled by other influences. All young men in the state would potentially be part of Machiavelli's neo-Roman army. Colonna notes that the class system of early Rome under its kings is "nothing else than an ordinance permitting the rapid assembly of an army for the defense of the city."[75]

Thus Machiavelli expected a great part of the popular classes in the city to be involved in military life, leaving their daily work for voluntary, unpaid service in the ranks during wartime and returning gladly to their occupations once the war was over. His new laws and ordinances would break down prejudice against the soldier's life. Defending one's city from attackers was an admirable task that could only grow in status as new armies on the Machiavellian model were formed and won new victories. Citizen soldiers would train in times of peace as well as in wartime, as Roman youths used to do on the Field of Mars, where they assembled in their assigned military formations.[76] There would be marching in the streets; there would be flags and banners and medals and military exercises in the piazzas, as in the time of Machiavelli's ill-fated militia. Machiavelli did not go so far as to suggest enrolling all male citizens in military formations, but whatever recruits the prince or city did select should be chosen from among the best young men in the prince's or the city's own domains, without regard to social class or calling.

Machiavelli's proposal requires the abolition of professional soldiering and condottieri. The reasons for this are put in the mouth of Colonna, who has the authenticity to denounce them. Colonna's objection is not that it is dishonorable for soldiers to fight for money. The problem is that professionals are at it all the time: they need to be fighting in order to make a living. This is morally bad for the individuals involved and disastrous for cities.[77] A professional military man does not get paid in peacetime, so he will always counsel war; condottieri who counsel princes are thus unlikely to give disinterested advice. A free-floating, international caste of professional soldiers is hard for political authorities to control, and powerful foreign captains will always be potential tyrants or tools of tyrants.[78] What Machiavelli wants instead are military ordinances, laws, and, eventually, customs and religious rites ensuring that soldiers are part of society, or rather *are* the society in its military expression. This would be a radical change for Renaissance Italian cities, with their lax inhabitants and laxer laws, their soft artistic pursuits and *ozio,* but the desperation of the times gives the lawmaker an opportunity. Desperation lays bare the law of necessity, and necessity is the only force that can bring a city or a prince to make the radical changes in laws and customs needed for survival. The only way the citizens of a modern state can acquire *virtù* is if they are compelled by the laws to be virtuous.[79]

Machiavelli's military reform, unlike that of the humanists before his time, thus focuses on soldiers, not commanders. Where humanist military writers tended to deliver themselves of great gusts of eloquence describing the virtues and accomplishments of the ideal general—their *optimus imperator*—Fabrizio Colonna expends only a single paragraph on the subject, after six books of advice on the practical details of military science.[80] Unprompted by his interlocutors he inquires whether anyone wants to hear him talk about the qualities of a general, and without waiting for an answer he remarks merely that they should know how to do all the things he has just described. In other words, the general's education in military science can be purely technical. There is not a word about the general's moral qualities or his need to study classical literature.[81] Colonna adds that all the things discussed in the previous books the good commander should be able to find out for himself. This a clear slap at writers like Valturio with their learned reconstructions of ancient warfare. The remark is also thoroughly disingenuous, since the information about Greek and Roman warfare that fills the previous books was in fact extracted by Machiavelli from his own wide reading in ancient sources, none of which are explicitly acknowledged.[82] In any case, Colonna then goes on to comment that a great commander will be tactically creative, have *invenzione,* like Alexander the Great, whom he credits only with a new signalling technique and a new way of kneeling on the left knee so as to withstand a charge. The humanist image of the legendary conqueror is thus deflated with a single prick of the pin. Francesco Patrizi in a similar context had quoted the orator Demades to the effect that Alexander's army without Alexander was like the Cyclops without his eye.[83] Machiavelli thus turns upside down the humanist contention that the moral and intellectual qualities of the commander are the most important element in warfare.[84] For him, the Roman army was great because of the virtues of the Roman citizen-soldier. If modern Italy wants to produce such soldiers again, it will need to reorder profoundly its polities in imitation of Roman modes and orders.

The militarization of Italian societies will also be highly beneficial, for someone of Machiavelli's popular sympathies, because of its political effects. Though Machiavelli does not quite say so in *The Art of War*, he surely expects that forcing large parts of the urban and rural population to engage in military service will empower them politically against the aristocrats he hated. Like any student of Greek and Roman history he was aware that the participation of the common people in warfare went hand in hand with their right to participate in politics. During the Struggle of the Orders in early Roman history, the plebs were able to enforce its claims to political power because of the indispensable role they played in Rome's wars.[85] Hoplite warfare had similarly enhanced the political weight of farmers and craftsmen in the Greek polis during the classical period. Machiavelli was doubtless aware that armies dominated by native infantry rather than cavalry amplify the popular voice in a republic, given that the rich and noble ordinarily served in the more prestigious equestrian units. This was surely one reason why he consistently championed the use of infantry and attacked condottieri for their overreliance on mounted knights.[86] Engaging in military exercises makes the common people tougher, more self-reliant, and harder to dominate. Moreover, military training teaches the people respect for religion, the right kind of religion that keeps them disciplined and devoted to duty.[87]

This is what Machiavelli means when he declares in *The Prince* that good laws depend on good soldiers.[88] It is not just that a state will fall victim to more powerful neighbors unless it is protected by its military forces. At a deeper level, the laws will not be good unless they are made by a state, or for a state, in which a warlike people is frequently called upon to defend itself against all enemies foreign and domestic.

CHAPTER 19

MACHIAVELLI

From Virtue to *Virtù*

Machiavelli's Prince *and Renaissance Conceptions of Tyranny*

Machiavelli's *Prince* is commonly read as a manual for tyrants, and the prince of its title is usually taken to be synonymous with the tyrant.[1] This understanding goes back to the Renaissance itself. The political theorist Giovanni Botero, for example, interpreted Machiavelli's prince as an embodiment of Aristotle's malign tyrant as described in a famous chapter of the *Politics*.[2] Accepting the equation of prince and tyrant ties scholars up in hermeneutical knots when they collate descriptions of tyranny in the *Discourses* with the doctrine of *The Prince* and try to reconcile the republican hatred of tyranny on display in the *Discourses* with advocacy of tyrannical behavior in the *Prince*.[3] Did Machiavelli have a change of mind in the years between the composition of *The Prince* and the *Discourses,* as Hans Baron believed?[4] Or was he simply a cynic, a man willing to write whatever would find him employment, regardless of ideological inconsistencies? Or was he the prototype of the modern political scientist, as Friedrich Meinecke argued, a man who sets aside commitments to any particular regime to analyze dispassionately the nature of political power? Was *The Prince* just a satire, as Garrett Mattingly maintained, or was it really, as Cardinal Pole believed, a poison pill intended to destroy any ruler who tried to carry out its precepts?[5] Does Machiavelli aim to disgust his fellow republicans—or perhaps even his prospective Medici employers—by showing them the sort of cruel and shameful behavior that would be required to impose a new prince on a city with republican traditions? Such interpretations are belied, as Robert Black and others have pointed out, by the continuity of political assumptions and amoral advice between *The Prince* and the *Discourses.* Yet many inconsistencies remain, some of them no doubt due to inconsistencies in Machiavelli's own thinking and use of terms.[6] Amid so much disagreement and uncertainty, historians can only pick their way with caution and humility.[7]

The approach taken in this chapter starts by situating Machiavelli's new prince in relation to earlier Renaissance conceptions of tyranny, outlined in Chapter 4. My argument in general will be that Machiavelli's prince is not a tyrant in any traditional sense but a prudent ruler who appreciates the limits of Greek philosophy as a guide to statecraft. He understands that the counsels of humanist moral philosophy are incompatible with the *necessità* imposed by human weakness and political reality. He therefore must sacrifice any personal aspiration to moral integrity of the Stoic or Ciceronian kind in order to save the power and prestige of his regime—its *stato*—and achieve glory. He must be guided by a realistic art of political power based on experience, not moral theory. If he is, he will have the potential to be a great ruler, even the savior of Italy. Machiavelli's new kind of prince represents one model that can be followed to make any monarchical *stato* powerful enough to protect itself from hostile neighbors, invaders, and local barons. It was a practical model designed for men of action, not theorists. We know in fact that Machiavelli intended his work for the private use of the Medici brothers Giuliano and Lorenzo, who ruled Florence in the 1510s but were well known to be seeking principalities of their own, probably in the semi-rural region of the Romagna.[8]

The strategy of power outlined in *The Prince* is not, however, the best strategy for a city that wants to achieve great and long-lasting security and empire. That strategy, revealed in the *Discourses,* was to revive the modes and orders of the middle republic of Rome, Livy's Rome, in the belief that "the moral health and political vigor of a free nation [was] the ultimate source of power."[9] The two strategies, princely and republican, were perfectly compatible because Machiavelli, unlike modern republican ideologues, was not an exclusivist. He was, writes Robert Black, "a political, sociological, geographical and historical pragmatist—like Montesquieu—not a monochromatic apologist for any particular political regime."[10] The model of the Machiavellian prince, a new and more astute incarnation of Cesare Borgia, though potentially of wider application, was the right model for men aiming to control an inland signory whose cities were hardly more than market towns with a few churches, public buildings, and baronial residences attached, towns with small experience of free political institutions.

Chapter 4 laid out two broad ways that tyranny was understood in the Western tradition down through the early Renaissance. Both were concerned above all with identifying reasons why tyrants should not be accepted as legitimate rulers. The Roman republican tradition saw the tyrant as a political or military figure who violated *ius,* the civil order of the state, which was derived from the laws of nature and the gods and was therefore sacred. By violating *ius* the tyrant took away the liberties of the people and reduced them to slavery. The Greek philosophical tradition found the sources of tyranny in corrupt character and thus made legitimate statesmanship depend on virtue and wisdom. Those human perfections would impart charisma to a ruler and cause his subjects to bestow upon him their willing obedience. They would do this ultimately because the behavior of the tyrant made them miserable, whereas that of a good ruler brought felicity. Nature was designed, as Plato, Aristotle, and the Stoics believed, to reward goodness with happiness.

The Greek tradition made a further distinction between oppressive and benign tyranny. Aristotle referred to these in Greek as two *tropoi* of tyranny, a word Bruni's Latin translation of the *Politics* rendered as *modi*.[11] In the first mode, the oppressive tyrant instinctively used his unlimited power to fulfill his every desire and force others to do his will. Drunk with power, driven headlong by his appetites, he would soon be shipwrecked by the violence of his own passions, despised and hated by his subjects. But a tyrant that would accept advice from a wise man, like Simonides in Xenophon's *Hiero* or Aristotle in the *Politics,* could follow a better mode, which would allow him to extend the duration of his regime and live a more secure life. Those sages advised the tyrant to act as much as possible in the way a good king would act. Doing so would make his people happy and content. His actions would in fact proceed from a base desire to hold on to power rather than from a good will, but insofar as they had the same effects as those of a good king, he could take advantage of Nature's disposition to reward good governance by longevity. He would be a kind of moral parasite, a pretender to virtue, but he would avoid being hated and might even die safely in his bed.

Machiavelli's new prince does not fit anywhere in this paradigm. He follows a new mode undreamt of by the ancient philosophers or their modern epigones, a path as untrodden as the one laid out at the beginning of the *Discourses.*[12] Machiavelli is, first of all, utterly unconcerned with whether his prince meets any criteria of legitimacy, juridical or moral. His prince is imagined as unconstrained by respect for law; when he comes to power in a city that used to have free institutions, his first task is to subvert them.[13] Whether or not a people dominated by a new prince should be allowed to live under its own laws is purely a question of expediency, not of right. As for moral legitimacy, Machiavelli recognizes that a reputation for virtue, honor, and piety can be useful to a ruler, but such considerations cannot guide his policies. His prince is not therefore a benign tyrant, since by Xenophon's and Aristotle's logic, the more virtuously the tyrant behaves, the more long-lived and pleasant his regime will be. Machiavelli does not believe that. What should guide a ruler's policies is the logic of necessity, which belongs to a different register entirely from the laws of morality.

Educated by humanists, the prince already knows how to be good; now he must learn from Machiavelli how *not* to be good. He can be good most of the time, and his *stato* can benefit from a reputation for goodness, but a policy of consistent goodness will fail.[14] When necessity dictates, he must be willing to act with sudden violence and cruelty; he will lie, commit fraud, use trickery of the lowest kind, violate any and all laws. Thus, unlike Simonides and Aristotle, Machiavelli the advisor of princes counsels the use of tyrannical tactics where necessary. After these sudden, well-chosen bursts of evil designed to neutralize threats to his power, he should return quickly to the norm of princely behavior.[15] The brevity or imperceptibility of his departures from the conduct expected of princes will ensure that he is feared but not hated. He still holds power, so it will be in the interest of others to pay him respect, and his unpredictability will make him feared. He should, however, maintain as far as possible the façade of virtuous government. A consistent policy of manifest evil, as we shall see, is as dangerous to a prince as a consistent policy of goodness.

All this is in sharp contrast with humanist educational theory, based to a large extent on Aristotle's *Ethics* and Cicero's *De officiis*. The humanists tried to build up consistent habits of moral behavior, inspired by the finest examples of ancient virtue. Virtue should be internalized; it should become second nature. Machiavelli teaches his prince that following habits of behavior, whether good or bad, as though on a kind of moral autopilot, will bring him to ruin. He must learn moral flexibility, strategic inconstancy, selective clemency, and cruelty. Goodness must become the servant of *necessità,* the logic of power. The humanists, by contrast, like most ancient philosophers, believed rationality was inseparable from traditional morality. The virtues were Nature's directions for living a happy life, and that applied to states as well as individuals. Machiavelli does not believe that the rules of traditional morality, however successful they might (or might not) be in achieving personal happiness, were scalable to states. Sometimes virtue got in the way of *virtù*, and there were other forms of reasoning besides moral reasoning. The humanists wanted to leverage character education of *principes* in the classics to bring about political reform in the state. Machiavelli thinks that too great a devotion to the humanities and to the virtues of philosophers is an obstacle to the prince's pursuit of power.

As always, however, Machiavelli's relationship to previous traditions of humanism remains complex, and this applies as well to his ideas about tyranny. There are some teachings of Machiavelli's *Prince* that look like radicalizations of attitudes already present in humanistic writers and in the Greek sources they had made available to the Latin world. Machiavelli's prince was not a benign tyrant of the kind described by Xenophon's Simonides or Aristotle, but his inspiration for the new prince nevertheless owes much to those writers. As we shall see, Machiavelli could use a "Simonidean" voice where appropriate to counsel a prince-turned-tyrant. The principle that virtue and beneficent government should be instrumentalized in the interests of the prince's security was assumed in all of Machiavelli's counsels. From Leonardo Bruni he learned *raison d'état:* that a student of history can judge institutions and patterns of citizen behavior on the criterion of their tendency to promote or inhibit the well-being and empire of the state. Bruni and Poggio also espoused a limited form of political realism in foreign relations, which Machiavelli would take much further.[16] Poggio, Alberti, and other critics of courtiers had no doubt reinforced his skepticism about the ability of virtuous *principes* to transform the dynamics of courts and other milieux filled with power-seeking nobles. The virtuous prince who tries to ride the wild horse of politics will quickly be thrown. Like Herodotus' tyrant, Machiavelli's prince is possibly a good man with a good purpose; he is not merely selfish, but the form of his power is incompatible with civic liberty and is apt to become corrupt. Like Decembrio in his portrait of Filippo Maria Visconti, Machiavelli does not attach any value to the humanist ideal of actually being what you claim to be. He too holds that the prince's selfish pursuit of dynastic success can bring benefits to the state and win him the support of his people. If he ever read Decembrio's biography of Visconti he must have nodded his head in agreement with the duke's conviction that power and empire were best acquired through military force, and that fraud, treachery, and dissimulation were acceptable means to compass the ends of power.[17] Like the writers of the Second Sophistic translated by the humanists, Machiavelli was fully aware that whether one was called a tyrant or not was in large measure a question of perception, and perceptions can be managed.

The problem of perception is one that modern interpreters of Machiavelli have struggled with as well, and, as noted above, it is all too easy to identify the subject of *The Prince* with the tyrant *simpliciter.* Interpreters convinced that Machiavelli's prince was just a tyrant under another name have naturally sought out parallel passages in the *Discourses* where he discusses tyrants, then used those passages straightforwardly as a kind of commentary on *The Prince*. The *Discourses* are thus claimed to reveal Machiavelli's "real" republican beliefs and hatred of tyranny, or taken as evidence of a conversion experience during the 1510s from monarchist to republican, or as conclusive proof that Machiavelli was a man without deep ideological loyalties, a political operative offering himself to the highest bidder. If one begins, however, without the presumption that *The Prince* advises a *signore* how to be a tyrant, a different picture emerges. Many students of Machiavelli have noted that the prince of *The Prince* is never referred to as a tyrant, but this fact is usually taken as evidence that Machiavelli wanted to conceal his true feelings about tyranny from readers of his tract—and it needs to be remembered that the *Prince* was intended for a select private readership in manuscript and not for print publication. Similar false preconceptions bedevil scholarly commentary on the *Discourses*. Thanks to the widespread but mistaken belief that the *Discourses* is a work about republics, interpreters have tended to dismiss its teachings about kingship, princes, oligarchies, and dictatorships as marginal.[18] Hence it has not been fully appreciated that Machiavelli continues to use the term *principe* in the *Discourses* too, and that in the later treatise the term's range of reference is wider.

A summary view of the usage of the words *principe* and *tiranno* (and *principato* and *tirannide*) in the *Discourses* in fact discloses relatively stable patterns if not perfectly consistent ones. *Principe* and *tiranno* are not synonymous. Princes are those who dominate in a state. There can be one, few, and many *principi*. Sometimes the prince is the whole people.[19] Sometimes the members of an oligarchic junta are the *principi*. And sometimes a single individual, *uno solo,* will achieve dominion over all the rest. This prince will sometimes be a *principe della repubblica,* an individual who is formally granted quasi-monarchical power, either temporary like a dictator's or permanent like that of the early Roman emperors.[20] Such a mode is akin to the *principato civile,* a term that in Machiavelli indicates a principate cloaked in the forms of republican government, like the rule of the early Medici in fifteenth-century Florence.[21] This is a conception distinct from an elective or constitutional monarchy, a form of principate Machiavelli also fears as likely to lead to tyranny.[22] Princes can also be hereditary monarchs, like the kings of France and Spain, and their rule can be compatible with *vivere politico,* some forms of constraint or power-sharing imposed by their subjects.[23] A prince can lead a state informally, like Pericles in Athens or Dion in Syracuse. Some are figurehead princes like the doges of Venice and Genoa. Others will be sovereign *signori* or despots in cities and countries that lack effective institutions of self-government. This sense of *principi* was the commonest in ordinary Italian discourse. They are the kind of princes chiefly addressed in the *Prince*.

Not all princes are tyrants. The Roman emperors can either be good princes or tyrants. Most Roman dictators were good until the very end of the republic, when the institution was corrupted and produced tyrants. Nor are all those who from time to time use devices labelled as tyrannical by lawyers and moralists to be considered tyrants. A tyrant, properly so called, for Machiavelli in the *Discourses* is almost always a weak or failed prince. Like the oppressive tyrant of antiquity he is someone ruled by his appetites who does not take good counsel. To satisfy his lust for power he takes away others' freedom and makes himself hated. His lack of self-control makes him weak, and his rule is short-lived and miserable. The logic of his position and his own appetite for power makes him act in the worst possible way.[24] He earns infamy rather than glory, and deserves contempt.[25] Tyrants, being insecure, are rarely able to conquer new territories, Machiavelli's test of a virtuous state. The insecurity of their power explains why the early Medici added little to Florentine territory. Just as princes who try to be consistently good will fail because they refuse to perform the necessary evil acts to stay in power, so tyrants will fail who refuse to do the good acts necessary to preserve their *stato*. In the *Prince* Machiavelli addresses the former in what one may call his "Machiavellian" voice, the voice that whispers to good men that they must sometimes do evil, while in the *Discourses* Machiavelli addresses tyrants in his "Simonidean" voice, counselling them to govern well if they want to save themselves from ruin.[26] Tyranny, in short, is a tactic, not a strategy.

There are only few examples in history of tyrants who become accepted as princes. The greatest of these, Julius Caesar, succeeded in founding a dynasty that sanitized his reputation after the fact. A virtuous tyrant—a tyrant of Machiavellian virtue who has learned how to be a competent ruler—is possible, though rare.[27] On the other hand, merely being a prince does not make you a tyrant. What counts is how you exercise your power. Princes who act immorally do not *eo ipso* become tyrants. If their immoral acts are done with lucid intelligence, as tactics necessary to keep their *stato,* they may not be good *qua* men but *qua* princes they will be successful—*virtuosi* in Machiavelli's sense. A prince of Machiavellian virtue can win glory and can establish a dynasty that can have a long life. If successful princes allow their might to be constrained by law like the French kings, if they do not "break the bridle that can correct them," their dynasties can be powerful and last for centuries.[28] Sovereign princes unconstrained by law are those most at risk of becoming tyrants, just as peoples unconstrained by laws are most at risk of becoming violent mobs. But properly ordered, both republics and principalities can be successful in Machiavelli's sense of success: minimally, achieving stability and security, and maximally, acquiring empire and glory.

To sum up, the prince of Machiavelli's *Prince* is not a tyrant—either in the traditional sense of the word or in Machiavelli's own usage. He is a new prince, thus relatively weak. He has probably had a humanist education, which will lead him to believe that he can become a good prince by consistent exercise of the virtues, especially justice, and by following the advice of wise counselors trained in philosophy and literature. Giuliano de'Medici and Lorenzo de'Medici, successively intended as the dedicatees and principal readers of the tract, had both had just such an education. As son of Lorenzo the Magnificent, Giuliano (aged thirty-four in 1513) a boyhood companion of Machiavelli had studied with the humanists Bernardo Michelozzi (an associate of the Platonist Marsilio Ficino) and Gregorio da Spoleto. Along with his brothers Piero and Giovanni, the future Leo X, he may have had lessons with Poliziano and the émigré Hellenist Demetrius Chalcondyles. Lorenzo or Lorenzino (aged twenty-one in 1513), the eventual dedicatee of the *Prince,* studied with Guarino Favorino, the distinguished Hellenist and disciple of Poliziano.

With such training, both Giuliano and Lorenzo would need to disabuse themselves of any inclinations they might have had to be good humanist princes and to behave in a consistently honorable way. They would need to learn from Machiavelli, the man of action with vast experience of the real world, how not to be good, and this would mean using tyrannical tactics when necessary to maintain their *stato.* Such tactics need not make them tyrants, failed princes of the sort Machiavelli describes in the *Discourses.* If the use of tyrannical tactics is enough to make a prince into a tyrant, then we have to accept that Machiavelli's republic is also tyrannical, since he recommends the same tactics to its *principi.*[29] Machiavelli's prince, the prince who takes his advice, will be smart and successful, a good transactional leader who knows how to deploy the tools of moral government and the tools of tyranny as needed to achieve his goals. Just as Machiavelli's virtuous republic requires maintaining a dynamic balance between the *popolo* and the nobles in such a way that neither can dominate or destroy the other, so the *ingenio* of his *virtuoso* prince needs to be balanced between his desires for *onore e riputazione* on the one hand and for the security of his *stato* on the other. To maintain this balance he will need a Machiavellian voice in his ear, advising him how to negotiate the logic of power.

The Machiavellian Revolution in Political Thought

Machiavelli's new political science required setting aside the (for him) failed counsels of virtue politics, championed both by classical writers and by the most prestigious authorities of his own time. It meant setting aside the teachings of Greek philosophers that the humanists sought to appropriate in order to instill moral integrity in citizens and rulers. The rest of this chapter explores the significance of the Machiavellian revolution in political thought, whose effects are still with us today.

Machiavelli's political counsels were certainly revolutionary. Before his time, it was shameful and vanishingly rare, at least in the literary record, to advise princes to employ immoral methods to maintain their power. Princes and cities that acted without virtue or justice were condemned by orators and philosophers and shown to be preparing their own ruin by historians. Even Thucydides—an author for whom Machiavelli had deep affinities—though able to articulate what is today called a realist perspective on power, ultimately condemns it as psychologically naïve and self-destructive.[30] After Machiavelli's time, and under his direct influence, it became common, if not quite respectable, to recommend to princes the use of immoral tactics, defended as *arcana imperii* or traditional secrets of statecraft.[31] Nowadays many consider it obvious and uncontroversial that states need to use means to protect themselves that would be considered immoral in private citizens and are in fact prohibited to them by law. We have debates about the morality of secret surveillance, torture, "black ops" (i.e., political assassination), "disinformation" campaigns (i.e., fraud and deceit), "collateral damage" (i.e., the intentional murder of innocent noncombatants), and destabilization of foreign governments, but such debates have hardly altered the behavior even of democratic governments or popular attitudes.[32] Machiavelli's key argument, that one cannot adopt a consistent policy of goodness among so many who are not good, is taken as unanswerable. Modern academics are hardly aware that older moral traditions exist which hold states to the same moral standards as individuals.[33] Typically, political realism in international relations theory is contrasted with liberalism, which emphasizes cooperation among nations based on mutual interest, or utopian idealism, which holds that human nature can be made morally perfect only in a perfect world state, to be achieved on the Greek Kalends.[34] Many such "idealists" do not regard it as a contradiction to work toward the perfect state through violent revolution, the planned murder of millions, and forms of oppression far beyond the imagination of any ancient tyrant.

It is no accident that Machiavelli himself has become a much-admired figure in our time and that his *Prince* has been frequently adapted as a self-help book for ambitious politicians, businessmen, and bureaucrats. His worship of power appeals to many academics too, already drawn to the cult of Nietzsche and Foucault. Machiavelli's tendency to pontificate has been matched by the tendency of all too many of his readers to treat him as infallible. He was in fact a rather poor prophet and on salient issues predicted the exact opposite of what turned out to be the case. For example, he prophesied the inevitable reversion of Florence to republican government, the imminent liberation of Italy from foreign invaders, and the inability of Christians to shake off the corruptions of church government. For a man believed to have extraordinary powers of observation and analysis, it remains astonishing that he seems to have lived through the Reformation without noticing it.[35] He condemned Christianity as a source of military weakness at the very moment when it was transforming itself into an ideology of empire and European world dominance. He wrote in *The Prince,* with his usual dogmatism, that subjects of ecclesiastical princes can never get rid of their rulers; three decades later a third of Europe had rid itself of ecclesiastical princes.[36] His contemptuous dismissal of the "weak and womanish" nature of Catholic Christianity ignored the popes' role since the late eleventh century in inspiring the Crusades, some of whose greatest triumphs were to come later in his own century.[37] Most of his predictions about the future of military tactics and strategy were proved wrong.[38] Even his own career as a political advisor was crippled by a persistent inability to back the right horse.

Machiavelli's goal was to break the spell cast by ancient philosophical ethics over political decision-making, but his own work has turned out to have its own deep powers of enchantment. The tradition of virtue politics as taught by humanists from Petrarch in the mid-fourteenth century to Francesco Patrizi in the late fifteenth may provide the sharp contrast needed to break the spell of Machiavellian political realism and bring into higher relief the limitations of his political science. At the very least it may remind moderns that other ways of thinking about political leadership and state action have existed and can exist.

The humanists of the Renaissance who advocated some form of virtue politics were convinced that human nature and human government could be improved. Human beings had a natural desire for goodness and wisdom that could be cultivated through education and encouraged through a variety of social technologies, including public eloquence, historical writing, and the arts. Like most ancient philosophers, they believed there was a divine element in human nature giving it access to an intelligible moral order in nature. Stoic and Christian authors called this conscience.[39] Divine rationality could order the souls of rulers and, through them, civil society. Human beings in society had a natural desire for good rulers and would willingly obey those who ruled with justice and promoted the common good. Laws and their coercive enforcement were not sufficient to achieve the good life, *bene vivere,* the full flourishing of human nature. Humanist political thinkers were thus perfectionists, in the sense that word is used by modern political philosophers.[40] Like Plato, Aristotle, and the Stoics they had a conception of the good life that was at least in part realized through politics. But unlike them they were *moderate* perfectionists: they did not have what Rawls called a "comprehensive doctrine" of the good, since they excluded the highest ends of human life, which belonged to the domain of religion.[41] Their perfectionism was also in principle noncoercive, since they did not imagine using the state to require people to adopt valuable ways of life or abandon worthless ones. That sort of coercion, in the Renaissance, was still the business of confessors (the *forum internum*) and ecclesiastical courts. The state (or republic, as the humanists preferred) was a source of value, and service to the state could be a measure of virtue, but the state did not take the lead in promoting the good life in the secular world. That was primarily the work of educators and other literati, who appealed to the precepts and examples of antiquity to authorize their ideals of the good life.

Most humanists were well aware of the large gap between ideals and practice in the ancient world, but they valued classical ideals as articulating aspirations for political leadership they felt were missing in their own time: virtue, nobility, equality (rightly understood), and wisdom. They believed that ancient polities—above all Rome, Athens, Sparta, and the (semi-mythical) Persia of Cyrus the

Great—had in their best periods achieved a greatness of which only flickers remained in their own world. They believed that the study of classical literature and philosophy written in Latin and Greek could rekindle a love of lost ideals and lost greatness. Like the Confucian scholars of imperial China, they believed (to vary the metaphor) that antiquity was the eternal spring from which all civilization and good government flowed.

Machiavelli also believed in the possibility of improving human behavior and government under the right conditions, but his background assumptions, methods, and goals were completely different from those of virtue politics. He believed, first of all, that good character and moral integrity in rulers were potential threats to their power.[42] His overriding concerns, as we have seen, are power and freedom—freedom of the sort that depends on political power. Power was necessary to survival and to glory, the minimal and maximal goals of Machiavellian political science. Glory was an ideal of a sort but was based on what was fundamentally an Epicurean view of human nature. Human beings were nothing more than a stream of selfish and insatiable desires that ended only in death. Some (the people) wanted pleasure, and some (the nobles) wanted power, but unlike for Plato, Aristotle, and the Stoics there was for Machiavelli no third element in human society (the philosophers) that was motivated principally by the desire for truth and goodness. Machiavelli thus rejected the humanist project of justifying hierarchies in human society on grounds of merit. The existence of hierarchies in the state was a phenomenon based on natural "humors," without moral significance. This does not mean that merit went without reward in popular republics. When a polity enjoyed a free way of life, those with merit were rewarded "through certain honorable and determinate causes" *(mediante alcune oneste e determinate cagioni)*—naturally, in other words, without need for a meritocratic political system.[43] Hence the goal of politics was not to elevate the worthy or to form a hierarchy wherein the higher could regulate the lower in the interests of the good life. The goal of politics was simply to satisfy as many human desires as possible. To satisfy one's desires securely, one had to live in a well-ordered state, of which the two main types were the principality and the republic. The most successful, glorious states were the ones that enabled their citizens to dominate other states over a long period of time.[44]

A well-ordered state was one strong enough to protect its citizens from predatory foreigners and from domination by the more powerful among their fellow citizens. Both goals were best achieved by a dynamic balance of forces in a republic. This balance was maintained by the continuous, low-level, nonviolent conflicts between nobles and peoples Machiavelli referred to as *tumulti*. These and other customs such as public trials allowed the people to vent their passions before they metastasized into toxic factionalism.[45] Unless the people were enabled by carefully designed institutions such as the popular tribunate to stand up for themselves against the nobles, they became servile and the state itself became weak and prey to enemies.[46] This belief was the chief premise of Machiavelli's argument in favor of popular liberty. In this he pioneered modern "mechanical and reductive" forms of liberalism, as distinct from the transcendent forms that seek to realize a higher human self.[47] The love of liberty for Machiavelli was not a noble aspiration but was motivated by a fear of domination and the desire for riches and empire.[48] Liberty was also intrinsically pleasant, but without proper constraints of law and custom it would produce license, which was dangerous, leading to political corruption.[49]

A mixed regime designed to balance the people against the nobles produces virtuous citizens. The best historical example of such a regime, Machiavelli thought, was what modern historians refer to as the "middle republic" of Rome, lasting roughly from the outbreak of the First Punic War (264 BC) to the time of the Gracchi in the late second century BC.[50] In this period of a little less than a century and a half the Romans extended their power over most of the Mediterranean world. The history of this glorious period, or most of it, was described in the surviving portions of Livy's history, the work on which Machiavelli's *Discourses* provided an idiosyncratic commentary.[51] Approximately the same period was covered by Polybius' history, translated into Latin by Niccolò Perotti in the mid-fifteenth century. Polybius also provided in his book 6 an analysis of the Roman mixed regime and Roman military organization with a view to explaining the city's extraordinary success as the first world empire since that of Alexander the Great. Machiavelli in addition used Dionysius of Halicarnassus to deepen and correct his study of Livy and Polybius.[52]

From his careful reading of these sources Machiavelli concluded that the same aggressive spirit or *virtù* that kept the Roman people from being dominated by patricians and the senatorial landowning class also perfected its constitution and made Rome's armies invincible. Rome did not follow the "normal" cycle of regimes via periodic corruptions and revolutions, as laid out by Polybius in his theory of anacyclosis. Machiavelli knew this theory and summarized it in *Discourses* 1.2, but he did not apply it to Rome. Rather, following Dionysius of Halicarnassus, he believed Rome's constitution had evolved from a basic pattern, a mixed regime *in nuce,* laid down by its founder and first king Romulus.[53] No one social element had ever completely dominated the other in Roman history, but each constitutional innovation left behind it a residue of previous "orders" *(ordini).* The Roman constitution was thus in the end more a product of chance than design, yet it had reached a state of perfect balance in the third and second centuries BC. Perfection was attained thanks to the *tumulti* or political agitation of its virtuous plebs, who insisted on a place in government commensurate with their military contributions to the state. That same aggressive spirit, when turned outward toward rival states, built Rome's empire. Foreign powers reliant on mercenary troops or levies driven into battle by the whip could not rival an army of citizen-soldiers totally identified with the *patria,* thanks to their active political role in its public affairs, its *res publica.*

Moreover, Rome's citizen armies continually grew because, unlike the nativist regimes in ancient Sparta or modern Venice, Rome was willing to include foreigners in the ranks of its citizens and accord them citizen rights.[54] This policy seems to echo humanist cosmopolitan thinkers like Biondo and George of Trebizond, but the moral calculus behind Machiavelli's version of cosmopolitanism was different. Quattrocento humanists praised Rome's cosmopolitanism for embracing the virtuous no matter where they had been born. For Machiavelli, Rome's apparently friendly attitude to foreigners was in reality a kind of fraud, since by welcoming the most virtuous foreigners to Rome, by creating a kind of "virtue drain" to the imperial center, the Romans destroyed the prosperity and power of other cities.[55] The apparently benign relationships Rome cultivated with its allies were a ruse to become more powerful than they, and the deceit was maintained only until Rome was in a position to dominate them. At that point Rome's allied states turned into her provinces.[56]

Thus if modern Italians wanted to repel the transalpine invaders who had reduced Italy to shame and misery, if they wanted to climb out of the abyss of their historical cycle, they could do no better than to reconstitute the type of aggressive, self-seeking military republic that had made the Mediterranean an Italian lake in the second century BC. Since Italy was now in an advanced state of corruption, it would need new modes and orders laid down by a farsighted modern legislator who understood the virtuous dynamic of Roman republican *ordini.* Although the *Discourses* presents itself as offering advice to kings, princes, military captains, and even tyrants as well as republican leaders, its ill-concealed subtext was that the most powerful kind of state Italians could institute was a mixed regime of the ancient

Roman type.[57] The *ordini* of this regime would force its people to be martial and to participate in their own government. Equally ill-concealed was the suggestion that the best candidate for legislator of the new regime was Machiavelli himself.[58] Those who pondered the direction of his reasoning would come to realize the deceptive character of his positioning *supra partes*. They would see that he was not so much above partisan politics as behind them, an ideological puppet master every bit as skillful as the great political puppet master of the quattrocento, Cosimo de'Medici. In his hunger to legislate for future ages Machiavelli also reveals his own self-interested drive for power, which by his lights was an ambition to exercise his own special brand of virtue.

Machiavelli's Virtù

Every reader of the *Prince* and the *Discourses* notices that Machiavelli redefines the meaning of *virtù* as effectiveness, a kind of manly competence equal to all circumstances.[59] The full consequences of this demoralizing redefinition are not always recognized, however, and the contrast with traditional humanistic conceptions of virtue may help bring them out. In the traditional conception, worked out theoretically in Aristotle's *Ethics*, human life may be lived at a pre-political and subhuman level, at a political and fully human level, or at a godlike level—in the polity but not of it. To move from the subhuman (or potentially human) to the human is to move from physical survival in villages to the good life in cities—from *vivere* to *bene vivere* as the Latins put it—or from mere existence to flourishing existence, also called *eudaimonia* or felicity. To achieve *bene vivere*, the fully human or active life requires formation of habits or fixed dispositions or habits of virtue, including courage, temperance, prudence, and justice, that lie in a mean between excess and defect. Those citizens who acquire these mean dispositions (as clarified in the *Politics*) make the best magistrates.[60] To achieve the godlike or contemplative life requires further perfections, the intellectual virtues. The sort of deep or scientific wisdom that would be necessary to found a new polis or reorder a failed one, the wisdom that recognized the best patterns in human polities and had the prudence to apply them to particular cases, would have to come from the contemplatives, also called philosophers.

Machiavelli's political science has no room for philosophers, whom he considers *oziosi*, armchair emperors, and impractical, corrupting influences.[61] States should be reordered by experienced men of action who are also students of history and have the analytical skills to take the correct lessons from history and experience. Machiavelli also has no interest in rising from mere survival to a life where higher and finer human capacities are actualized by the virtues. Instead of *vivere* and *bene vivere,* he offers—as alternative ends of human government—survival and glory. The divine life of the mind is reduced to entertainment. Fixed habits of virtue, as we have seen, are for him foolish and lead to ruin: the good prince must learn how to be bad when the situation calls for it, and the tyrant must learn to use the arts of good government tactically to hold on to his *stato.* Instead of fixed dispositions to virtue, Machiavelli recommends a tool kit full of *modi,* some traditionally associated with good government and others with tyranny. The wise prince or republican leader should learn to set aside whatever moral attitudes he has been educated to have toward these *modi* and to use them as circumstances dictate, in the interests of power.

The Aristotelian mean, the "golden mean" of moralists, which Machiavelli calls the *via del mezzo,* the middle course, is one of his bugbears. It is recommended only by witless people, unfortunately numerous in civic and princely counsels, who lack understanding of politics. The middle course, according to Machiavelli, is almost always the wrong one. In *Discourses* 3.9, for example, he raises the question of whether a general should act in an impetuous or a cautious "mode." Aristotle saw this as a moral problem concerning the virtue of courage, and counseled those who wished to form a fine character to develop a mean disposition between rash audacity and fearful hesitation. Machiavelli says that in military affairs the mean (which he ironically calls "the true way") cannot be followed, and that one has to be either impetuous or hesitant as circumstances dictate.[62] Fabius Maximus (known as Cunctator for his delaying tactics) was hesitant and cautious by nature, but in the circumstances in which Rome found herself after her initial defeats at the hands of Hannibal, Fabius' risk-averse modes matched the times. He won glory as a result, but in other times his hesitant modes would have brought disaster. By the same token, the impetuosity of Caesar was the right mode in his circumstances. Cautious modes have their time and place, but Machiavelli on the whole favors bold, audacious, risky enterprises over half-measures and defensive thinking. Cautious modes are represented by the use of fortifications, which Machiavelli thinks are sometimes necessary but in general are overrated.[63] Real power is won on the field of battle.

Another example that allows comparison with virtue politics may help bring out the blind spots in Machiavelli's realist assumptions about power and virtue.

In Chapter 5 we encountered the famous story of Camillus and the Falisci in Livy, where the Roman general's noble refusal to profit from betrayal by the Faliscan schoolmaster induces them to submit to Rome as to a morally superior polity. For humanists this was an archetypal example of charismatic virtue, showing how the Romans built their empire as much by the noble way they conducted themselves abroad as by their military prowess. Machiavelli discusses the case of Camillus in *Discourses* 3.20 while addressing the celebrated Ciceronian question of whether it is better to be loved than feared. Machiavelli chooses to take the Camillus story at face value as a "true example of how much more a humane act full of charity is sometimes able to do in the spirits of men than a ferocious and violent act." The key word is "sometimes," signaling that for Machiavelli, humanity is just another tactic. Like the liberality of Fabricius and the chastity of Scipio, it was successful only because of the circumstances. In the next chapter (3.21) Machiavelli goes on to explain why Hannibal, "using modes contrary to these," that is, "cruelty, robbery, violence, and every type of faithlessness," had as much success in Italy attracting the loyalty of allies as Scipio with all his virtues had in Spain. Circumstances were different, so different modes were required. Leaders who became fixed in their modes would fail. Those who tried to stick to the golden mean would fail, because that mode is simply unnatural: "He who desires too much to be loved becomes despicable, however little he departs from the true way [i.e., the golden mean]; the other, who desires too much to be feared, becomes hateful, however little he exceeds the mean *(modo)*. One cannot hold exactly to the middle way *(via del mezzo)* for our nature does not consent to it, but it is necessary to mitigate excessive conditions with an excessive virtue, as did Hannibal and Scipio."[64] Machiavelli then comments that Scipio's generosity to the Spanish population made his troops cease to fear him, so he was forced to move to the opposite extreme and treat them with "part of the cruelty he had fled from" before.

Here Machiavelli's realist analysis seems to fall short, and he provides no answers to questions that might, hypothetically, have been put to him by a humanist in the tradition of virtue politics such as Francesco Patrizi.[65] How could behavior so inconsistent be a basis for mutual trust, and how could allies who distrusted each other work together effectively? And how can one expect to make new allies after betraying old ones? Changing modes implies the power to change modes, but what if the very act of changing modes undermines that power? Trust in leadership comes from constancy and goodwill. How could a prince make effective use of the mode of Camillus if he was obliged to change modes when his circumstances changed? If the Falisci had submitted to Rome because they admired noble behavior in a Roman leader, wouldn't that change once his nobility was revealed to be a sham? Wouldn't that justify the Falisci in rebellion? And how can we know what our true circumstances are and how long they will last? Are the prince's advisors really so cunning that they can see which way the wind will blow tomorrow?[66] Given his Epicurean view of nature as radically subject to chance, how could Machiavelli, or any other political advisor, claim to know what necessity dictates from moment to moment? Machiavelli advises the tactical use of virtues and vices where appropriate, cloaking vice in virtue as much as possible, but those who observe the prince closely over time will hardly be unaware that he follows a different rule and consistently chooses his own *utile* over the *bonum*.[67] That will make him predictable rather than unpredictable; perhaps not hated, but despised. Others will treat him instrumentally as he treats them: serving him when it is to their advantage, abandoning him when it is not.

Furthermore, lack of *fides* casts a shadow on all the prince's other virtues and doubt on all his achievements. Faithlessness makes it impossible for a king to be admired, something all kings and other honor seeking *principes* desire. The way of trickery, deceit, and rash arrogance was the way of the barbarous Parthians, not the Romans.[68] Even Machiavelli admits that the desire for *onore e riputazione* motivates political elites, but are mere titles and empty honors enough to earn princes the admiration they seek? Did Caesar with all his power and that of his dynasty succeed in blotting out the memory of his crimes? Another humanist might add to Patrizi's critique that just as law is insufficient to motivate good behavior in the absence of a good will, so shared interests, however sealed by contracts and treaties, are incapable of motivating cooperation in the absence of *fides*. Where there is no trust, force will have to take its place. Where there is no guidance from conscience, there can only be calculation, which in a world of shifting circumstances is bound to go wrong. Corrupt laws corruptly enforced by persons without virtue are morally indistinguishable from mere force and will restrain only the weak and gullible, those caught in the spider's web of Anacharsis.[69] Machiavelli presents himself as a champion of the people, but his emphasis on law inevitably empowers the interpreters of the law, who will always side with the powerful individuals who pay them.

Refounding laws, customs, and institutions—not improving individual human character—was Machiavelli's principal avenue to the reform of Italian government in his time. It is good *ordini* that strengthen *virtù* in individuals. People by nature are selfish and weak and have no morality at all in their pre-political state. Machiavelli thus anticipates Hume's position that the genesis of morality is the self-interest of men in communities, and Hobbes' view that moral preferences are ineffectual without a political order to enforce them.[70] A polity's *modi e ordini* give it its character, which can be good or bad. Polities with bad character are quickly destroyed. *Modi e ordini* include not only institutions, magistracies, and laws but customs such as those ordering marriage and family life, the upbringing and military training of youth, the interpretation of oaths and auguries, priesthoods, ceremonies, and funerals. According to Machiavelli, Rome's fundamental *modi e ordini* were laid down by its first kings, Romulus and Numa Pompilius, and these were what gave the Roman people their extraordinary virtue and prevented corruption, not any genetic or epigenetic qualities.[71] Corruption, which Machiavelli equates with weakness and servility, came only six hundred years later, as a result of wealth and empire—a view that builds on Sallust's famous analysis of the decline of Rome.[72] After the Romans had beaten all their enemies they inevitably went slack, having no use for their former virtue, and began fighting among themselves. What maintained Roman virtue for so long, and the only prophylactic against corruption for states generally, was rigorous laws, rigorously enforced, especially laws against extremes of wealth.[73] But once the citizens of any republic become corrupt, no laws can save it. Laws made for an uncorrupt republic do not work in a corrupt one. The only recourse is new modes and orders laid down by a legislator, backed by extreme force.[74]

In this respect the character of a people differs from that of an individual. The character of individual *principes* in modern times was mostly bad, and humanist attempts to improve it, according to Machiavelli, had failed and must fail in most cases. The few successes were self-defeating. Rigid moral dispositions in personal behavior lead princes to adapt badly to changing circumstances and can be a source of weakness and error. But the character of a people is different. Men on their own easily become corrupted when their circumstances change, but the iron chains of good laws can force them collectively to be virtuous.[75] Good laws constrain and channel in beneficial ways the passions that, unchecked, can lead to hyperpartisanship.[76] The force of the laws thus builds upon and mimics the necessity of nature. Where humanists had made classical precept and example the sources of virtuous behavior, Machiavelli makes law, free assemblies, and the experience of political struggle ("tumults") the citizens' best teachers. Moral behavior is downstream from good laws, not a condition of them, as the humanists held. Once good orders are in place, however, they generate a feedback mechanism whereby good laws and (Machiavellian) virtue become mutually reinforcing.[77] Good laws also protect the state against changing circumstances and the power of fortune. Fortune may or may not favor the brave individual, but she always favors the virtuous republic.

Of all the *modi e ordini* that discipline a people in virtue, the most important are its religious customs. Like Polybius, Machiavelli sees the Romans' religion as the real key to their power: "Whoever considers well Roman history sees how important religion was in commanding armies, uniting the people, keeping men good and making the wicked ashamed."[78] By contrast, the Catholic Church and the Christian religion as practiced in his time were for Machiavelli major sources, perhaps *the* major sources, of political corruption and weakness in Italy. Here again Machiavelli's views stand in sharp contrast with those of humanist champions of virtue politics. Humanists of the early Renaissance were often outspoken critics of clerical corruption and ignorance, despite the patronage they themselves so often enjoyed from the Church. They often contrasted the decayed spirituality of the modern Church with the fervent belief and practice of ancient Christianity. But they did not challenge the Church as an institution or its teachings about the eternal destiny of the human soul. They saw their own classical lessons as supplementary to those of the Church, preparing the young and supporting adults in their earthly roles in this life, including their roles as members of the political elite.[79] Humane letters could in addition lay the moral foundation necessary for an authentically Christian spiritual life, as Basil of Caesarea had taught. The *studia humanitatis* and the *studia divinitatis* could work in harmony to build a city of virtue in this world as the Christian awaited his translation to the next.

Machiavelli rejects this beautiful dream, this Christian humanist utopia, in favor of his own more realist dream of ancient Rome, when the Campus Martius echoed to the sound of marching youth and the altars of the gods swam in blood. He wanted a new Rome that would be strong, united, and martial, and such a republic could not be built by steeping the young in ancient literature and philosophy. The humanities could not fill the educational gap created by an otherworldly religion. Only a this-worldly religion could, quite literally, put the fear of God into the hearts of citizens, enough to make them observe their *modi e ordini* and obey without question the commands of their military leaders. The only politically effective *educazione* comes from good *religione*.[80] The particular strength of the Roman religion lay in its ability to reinforce social bonds and patriotism with oaths—precisely the function that Christian oaths had so spectacularly failed to perform in the period of the Italian Wars. Whether Machiavelli believed the Christian religion could ever be reformed to fulfill this vital function in modern republics is a controversial question among Machiavelli scholars, to which an answer will be attempted below.

Despite the opinion of some authorities, it remains hard to believe that Machiavelli was a faithful Christian in any meaningful sense, though sometimes social duties compelled him to pretend otherwise.[81] Apart from extensive contemporary evidence of his indifference to religious practice, the radically instrumentalized view of Christianity in his writings is hardly compatible with belief in it. His view of the corrupt state of Christianity in his times was, to be sure, hardly without precedent. Indeed, it was taken as a deplorable given by most writers of the period. And humanist writers before Machiavelli had analyzed Roman religion in an instrumental way, like Biondo Flavio, who explored the relationship between Roman power and Roman religion in books 1 and 2 of his *Rome in Triumph*.[82] Some had gestured toward a civil religion that was not specifically Christian, inspired above all by Cicero's vision of the eternal rewards for civic virtue in the *Dream of Scipio*.[83] Many humanists, like Francesco da Fiano or Poggio Bracciolini, reveal an attitude similar to that of Cicero in the *De natura deorum,* where popular superstitions have to be tolerated and managed for the benefit of the state, while the religious convictions of the educated are few and based in philosophy. Humanist theologians such as Marsilio Ficino and Pico della Mirandola had tried to situate Christianity in the family of world religions, a reform project that involved a certain objectification of religion as an analytic category.[84] From Ficino (godfather of his friend Francesco Guicciardini) or from Ficino's unacknowledged source, Gemistus Pletho, Machiavelli might also have taken his belief that all religions are subject to the influence of the heavens and have natural cycles of birth, corruption, and renewal.[85] Many humanists from the time of Petrarch sought to reform modern Christianity on the model of classical Christianity, and the Protestant Reformers of the sixteenth century built their own rebellion against the Catholic Church on foundations laid by humanists.

Machiavelli too was a reformer, but in several respects he was unique. He wanted to reform modern Christianity, not on the model of classical or evangelical Christianity, but on the model of the religious practices of the Roman republic.

He wanted to reform religion for the sake of politics, not politics for the sake of religion. And most shocking of all, he did not believe in the religion he wanted to reform. He thought all religion was at best a popular superstition, at worst a fraud, but no state could be successful without a good religion.[86] A good religion did not mean a true one that provided a way to salvation, but one that gave rise to *buoni ordini* and strengthened a state's *virtù*.

Machiavelli's criticism of contemporary Christianity was directed above all at its embodiment in the Catholic Church.[87] His ferocious polemic operated on three distinct levels.[88] At the most basic level, the leadership of the Catholic Church was so morally corrupt and so openly hypocritical that it could exercise no spiritual authority. Its moral stench meant it could not perform the task of transforming behavior that was the proper role of a good civil religion. If it had not been for the unexpected support it received from credible holy men such as St. Francis and St. Dominic and the orders they founded, it would surely have collapsed long ago.[89] Machiavelli did not, however, follow the view of many of his contemporaries that religious virtue had become rarer in modern times owing to astrological or other natural causes. In his own youth in Florence there had appeared a prophet and holy man—Savonarola—who convinced even sophisticated Florentines to change radically their accustomed lax behavior, rekindle their lukewarm belief, throw off the yoke of the Medici, and refound the popular republic. This astonishing phenomenon demonstrated the power of religion, even in corrupt modern times, to remake a state's *modi e ordini*.[90] Savonarola's success was brief, however, and he ultimately failed for the same reasons the republic of Florence had failed to recapture Pisa for so many years. He had no arms of his own; he was an "unarmed prophet." His greatest weapon, his prophetic interpretation of Scripture, could not withstand the institutional authority of the pope—even so corrupt a pope as Alexander VI—who declared him a heretic, thus crippling his power to lead the city. Eventually Savonarola lost the support of the magistrates too, and his miraculous reformation of Florence came to an end. Unlike Numa Pompilius, the founder of Roman religion, he was not a king. Unlike Moses, he was not a prince with unquestioned authority to make and interpret Scripture.

Savonarola's failure points to the second and third levels of Machiavelli's critique of the Church: the malign political influence of the Church within Christendom, and its doctrinal control of belief and praxis among Christians. The Church's position in Christendom could hardly be other than destructive given its anomalous political status.[91] It was a power in its own right in the Italian state-system but also played the role of a super-state in legitimating the rule of other powers and controlling the operation of their ecclesiastical courts. In disputed cases it remained the highest court of appeal, and this power could cripple the freedom of action of a prince, as the dramatic case of Henry VIII of England's marriage to Catherine of Aragon demonstrated. A number of European states since the thirteenth century had taken steps to limit the Church's powers of patronage—its control of church benefices and appointments—but its residual powers throughout Europe and especially in Italy remained enormous. All this meant that there could be no stable alignment between the interests of European states and those of the Church. Machiavelli deplored this situation. Florence, like other Guelf cities in Italy, had traditionally regarded the Papacy as a protector of its liberties, and Leonardo Bruni, formerly secretary to four popes, in his *History of the Florentine People* had presented loyalty to the Guelf party as an essential element of Florentine patriotism. Machiavelli, however, in the review of medieval history in book 1 of his *Florentine Histories,* presents the Church's politics as more destructive even than the barbarian invasions of late antiquity, guaranteeing that Christendom would continually be engulfed in civil war.[92] In the Europe of his day, Machiavelli thought that the Church's own political interests as a state discredited it as a source of legitimacy for other states, as was illustrated by its highly interested inconsistency in supporting the houses of Aragon and Anjou in their rival claims to the Kingdom of Naples. Its own military weakness led it to betray *italianità* by inviting foreign powers in to prop up the unstable Papal State. The result was that the Church was not able to establish political and military dominance in its own right, though it retained enough power to prevent other states in Christendom from doing so. Its spiritual battalions made it impossible for modern European states to use religion the way the Romans did, to cement loyalty to the state, impose virtue in political life, and, above all, to motivate troops in battle.

Even worse, the institutional church, thanks to its authority over the interpretation of doctrine, had turned Christianity into a "weak and womanish" religion focused on the afterlife. It encouraged a monkish attitude of withdrawal from politics and made Christians tolerant of "beatings," which were too often understood as God's condign punishment rather than injuries to be avenged. This false piety made Christian armies militarily ineffective, thus "disarming Heaven."[93] Machiavelli claimed, perhaps ironically, that such an outcome was far from the intention of Christianity's founder, who wanted Christian republics to enjoy felicity through genuine religion. The Florentine thus asserted a distinction, reminiscent of the Protestant reformers, between the original piety of Jesus Christ and the elaborations of doctrine and praxis imposed by "the princes of the Christian republic," that is, the popes.[94] This extended to the *ordini* under which religious interpretation occurred, which in the Roman republic were kept subordinate to the needs of the state and its magistrates and generals. The right way to manage the natural piety and devotion of the people—their respect for oracles, auspices, and priests—was shown by the example of the consul Lucius Papirius Cursor, who through skillful interpretation of auspices and rituals was able to direct his soldiers' religious devotion in ways that strengthened their virtue.[95] This was "religion well used."[96]

Machiavelli's critique of the institutional Church in his day adds up to an implicit proposal for reform, but one which had to be disguised, given his desire to serve and influence the Medici princes who controlled the papacy for most of his later life.[97] What Machiavelli seems to have wanted was a relationship between religion and the state akin to what later in the century came to be called Erastianism. Erastianism was named for Thomas Lüber (Erastus in Latin), who wrote a treatise in 1589 which, citing the example of the Hebrew commonwealth in the Old Testament, recommended that the power of excommunication should reside with the magistrates and not with independent church authorities. Erastianism thus came to stand for the position that the civil magistrate was and should be the ultimate and exclusive source of valid religious law.[98] Versions of Erastianism were already implicit in the Anglican settlement of the Church of England in the 1530s and would influence the Gallican church in the seventeenth century.[99] Machiavelli, as Gennaro Sasso put it, wanted the power of interpreting religion taken out of the hands of the Church, where it served only the *ozio ambitioso* of prelates, and returned to the magistrates of the republic, where it could become once more "the proud essence of a people and its customs."[100]

A crucial issue for intellectual historians is whether that popular religion would still be Christianity, or whether Machiavelli thought some other religion, a version of ancient paganism or a new religion of the state, must take its place.[101] Here, it seems, the stronger arguments have been marshalled by those who hold that he wanted to reform Christianity. Though a realist, Machiavelli was not always sensible, but even he could not seriously have contemplated a revival of Roman paganism in the early cinquecento.[102] He does not comment on the use of high pagan theological language by humanists in the papal court, but he could not have regarded such playacting with anything but scorn.[103] He himself states that men who destroy religions, states, and the arts of virtue are the worst of men, infamous and detestable.[104] He lays constant emphasis on the need to conceal substantive changes in government by preserving existing forms and rituals. But any attempt to restore pagan rituals or auguries would violate that rule and likely meet with the same furious reaction that broke on the head of Pletho when he tried to compose a new pagan liturgy.[105]

Machiavelli admires the kings of France and Spain for subjecting the church establishments in their kingdoms to their will, contrasting them favorably with the unruly prelates of Italy. This implies that he believed state control of Christianity was possible and could be beneficial. In any case, to believe that Machiavelli thought Christianity was intrinsically weak and womanish overlooks his understanding of religion as a historical phenomenon whose political effectiveness can change depending on how it is interpreted and practiced. Religious belief for him is not a given, an unchanging truth which remains undiminished in its essence through all historical vicissitudes, but is intrinsically historical; it exists only through interpretation and praxis. The interpretation and praxis of "our religion" can change if the *ordini* authorizing interpretation and practice change. Machiavelli criticizes "the vileness of the men [i.e., churchmen] who have interpreted our religion according to *ozio* and not according to *virtù*," exploiting its wealth to support their own leisure and not to strengthen the state. He goes on to say that "if those [same] men would consider that it [i.e., our Christian religion] permits the exaltation and defense of the *patria,* they would see that it wants us to love and honor our country, and to prepare ourselves to be the kind of men who can defend it. It is these *educazioni* and these *interpretazioni*—so false!—that have caused there to be so many fewer republics today than in antiquity."[106] The problem with the corrupt modern Church is that it constitutes a transnational religious aristocracy, and like all forms of aristocracy, in Machiavelli's view, it is based on an idea of exploitation and self-interest and not of service. Christian belief too needs to be democratized, and the way to do this is to place it under the control of a republic. What the resulting form of Christianity would look like is hard to say, but it would certainly no longer be a Christianity ordered by the power and authority of the Roman Church. It would no longer, with Augustine, reject the earthly city of the Romans but reconstitute it as a virtuous amalgam of a country, its people, and their God.[107]

Machiavelli's attitudes to virtue, law, and religion thus present a striking contrast with those of the humanist advocates of virtue politics. The humanists inherited from the ancients the paradox of philosophical politics. This was exposed most clearly by Plato in the *Republic*. The Greek philosopher had a vision of an ideal order in the state, but ultimately it was an order that could never be realized in the world of time and change, thanks to human ignorance and vice. Political philosophers had to be content with approximations of the ideal in states, or live the ideal in their own lives, awaiting a rectification of moral accounts in the afterlife. This was the paradox of the ancients. Machiavelli was the first to explore the paradox of the moderns: that evil must be done in order to safeguard the good. This is a paradox of statesmen, not of philosophers, and it acquires moral gravity because, even in democracies, statesmen must choose not only for themselves but for others. Humanist statesmen in the tradition of virtue politics were required "to take a vow of goodness in every circumstance" because of their commitment to the classical ideal of virtue.[108] They believed, or hoped, that virtue and the good life, *bene vivere,* once achieved by individual *principes,* would lead to happiness for states. Machiavelli sees *bene vivere* as the enemy of *vivere,* the survival of the state. Statesmen cannot aim at nobility and personal integrity but must be ready to choose baseness in order for the state to survive. For Machiavelli that is another reason to prefer a popular regime, because its *ordini,* properly formulated, demand *virtù* but not nobility in its leaders.

The belief that power is necessary for the survival of the state is not of course false or morally wrong. Aristotle knew that military power was a condition of the higher flourishing of the polis, just as health, wealth, and standing in one's community were for an individual. But these were "external goods," preconditions of *eudaimonia,* not constitutive of it. External goods existed to enable higher human flourishing in the soul. Through politics those living the active life could achieve the full human good, and those following the contemplative life could approximate the gods. Machiavelli had no such perfectionist aspirations in politics: for him a successful republic was one that was rich, powerful, glorious, and long-lived. The gap between the humanists and Machiavelli is thus a gap between ancients and moderns: a gap between two visions of a good state, and between two ways of using the past. The humanists admired the Romans because at their best they were noble and godlike. Machiavelli admired them because they were powerful and dominated other peoples for a thousand years. As Leo Strauss noted long ago, Machiavelli's brand of politics implies a certain declension in the moral aspirations of states and statesmen. Machiavelli preferred being a live dog to a dead lion, forgetting that in the long run we are all dead. He believed that a powerful dog could win glory, even become top dog, forgetting that a glorious dog was still a dog.

CHAPTER 20

TWO CURES FOR HYPERPARTISANSHIP

Bruni versus Machiavelli

There cannot a greater judgment befall a country than such a dreadful spirit of division that rends a government into two distinct peoples, and makes them greater strangers to one another, than if they were actually two different nations. . . . A furious party-spirit, when it rages in its full violence, exerts itself in civil war and bloodshed, and when it is under its greatest restraints naturally breaks out in falsehood, detraction, calumny and a partial administration of justice. In a word, it fills a nation with spleen and rancour, and extinguishes all the seeds of good-nature, compassion and humanity.

THE SPECTATOR, JULY 24, 1711

Two Competing Narratives of Florentine History

The differences between virtue politics and Machiavelli's political science may be further illustrated by comparing him to an earlier historian who in Machiavelli's time was the most famous and widely read of Florentine historians: Leonardo Bruni. In Chapter 10 it was argued that Bruni's analysis of Florentine history led him away from Aristotelian models of the good state and toward a more "Machiavellian" attitude to state power. This chapter will survey the great gulf that still separated the two historians in their aims, moral outlook, and conclusions.

The titles of their respective histories, Bruni's *History of the Florentine People* (1415 / 1416–1442) and Machiavelli's *Florentine Histories* (*Istorie fiorentine,* 1520–1525), already signal their deeper divergences and point to one of the principal fault lines separating the two historians. Both are constructing "narratives" in the sense used by modern political journalists: readings of the past designed to influence the actions of statesmen in their own day.[1] Both are concerned to improve their city's performance in internal governance and foreign relations. Both regard factionalism as the major obstacle to Florence's success throughout its history. But the solutions to the problem of factionalism that each proposes are incompatible, even mutually contradictory.

Bruni, as the chancellor of the Florentine Signoria, representing the Guilds and People of Florence, saw the *popolo*—the broad middle ranks of society—as the key to the city's stability and strength. He wrote not only as the official historian of the People but as their champion. He wanted the middle-class party, represented above all by the institution of the Priorate, to be empowered to govern the state. Magnates and the lowest of the plebs should be excluded from office. The former were too arrogant and lawless to rule well, the latter too passionate and ignorant. Virtue and moderation were likeliest to be found in the middle ranks of society. Magnates who refused to moderate their behavior were rightly exiled. The Ordinances of Justice—a foundational measure of popular government that excluded the magnates from government—was a wise institution that should be preserved at all costs. Powerful *popolani* should participate in the regime only if they were capable of living civilly as equals with their fellow citizens.

Machiavelli did not side with any one social element in his *Histories*. Even if his analysis of regimes in the *Discourses* disclosed a preference for popular rule, he endeavored to appear nonpartisan and above the petty political struggles for power. His Florence, and indeed his times, were trending strongly in the direction of monarchy and aristocratic power. That required him to make the case for popular participation in government all the more strongly, but he was under no illusion that the power of the aristocracy could ever be eliminated in politics. At best it could be balanced by a vigorous popular voice. He famously saw all republics, and Florence in particular, as divided into two humors, the nobles and the people: the one wanted to command, the other not to be commanded. For him the moral differences Bruni observed between the magnate families excluded by the Ordinances and the powerful *popolani* of later times were superficial; they shared the same lordly humor. The prospect of inducing nobles to behave in a more egalitarian fashion was to his mind unrealistic, a violation of the laws of political physiology. In his later political writings, above all in the *Histories* and the *Discursus Florentinarum rerum* (1520), his proposed constitution for Florence, Machiavelli maintained that the only way to end the toxic factionalism of Florence and channel the energies of class conflict in a positive direction—imitating the Roman republic and its salutary *tumulti*—was to introduce a radical change of constitution. The new constitution would break entirely with Florentine republican traditions. It would be designed to include every social class in the city's government and disperse power among them in such a way as to defuse violent conflict, resolving clashes of interest through institutional devices. In this way the city would achieve a higher degree of unity and *virtù* than it had ever had. It would be a true republic, for the first time in its history.[2]

Bruni and Machiavelli thus had completely different advice for Florentine statesmen, advice they justified each by his own interpretation of the same sources. Books 2 through 7 of his narrative Bruni constructed from a careful selection and adaptation of materials from vernacular chronicles, principally Giovanni Villani's.[3] Machiavelli, in order to tell a different story with a different moral, was forced to go back to those same chronicles, make a different selection of materials, and interpret them differently.[4] The Florentine chroniclers of the fourteenth century were thus present, subterraneously as it were, in the histories of the two great Florentine political thinkers. In going back to the chroniclers, Machiavelli was carrying on a silent historiographical debate with Bruni, a dialogue with the dead, questioning the older historian's choices as to what details were most pertinent, the real motivations of the historical actors, the near and long-term consequences of decisions made by those actors, and above all, the real lessons to be drawn from Florence's history. Machiavelli's wrestling match with Bruni is far fiercer and more extensive than one might suppose from the one passing criticism he makes of him in the preface to his own *Histories*.[5]

Machiavelli's *Istorie* also differed from Bruni's *History* by having a much narrower target audience. Bruni's primary audience was the *popolano* statesmen who held the major civic offices (the *Tre maggiori*) and the men who advised them, a few hundred leading citizens.[6] Machiavelli's history was initially intended for private manuscript circulation and was not printed until 1532, years after his death. It was dedicated to the Medici pope, Clement VII, who held *de facto* hegemony over the city-state of Florence. The dedication was no mere formality; the work was addressed to the pope in his capacity as head of the Medici clan. It was part of Machiavelli's campaign to persuade the pope and the leaders of the Medici party to impose on Florence his proposed constitutional reform of 1520, the *Discursus Florentinarum rerum*.[7] He promised the pontiff that if he would only allow the political theorist to whisper in his ear, he would have the opportunity to make himself into a new Solon or a new Lycurgus, refounding the city of Florence on sounder lines.[8]

Machiavelli's *Florentine Histories* are in effect an extended meditation on the problem of factionalism in Florentine political history. They are intended in part to answer the many influential critics of republics who argued that all republican government by nature is subject to factionalism and so unstable that any republican constitution would sooner or later end in anarchy, ultimately requiring a monarch to restore order. This was the dominant view of republics in the Europe of Machiavelli's day, based on a monarchist reading of Roman history. Machiavelli's counterargument also pointed to Rome, which for centuries had maintained a consular republic with a positive balance of political "humors," punctuated by benign *tumulti*. These were nonviolent struggles between the nobles and the people that left the *respublica* stronger—so strong, indeed, that it was able to conquer the Mediterranean world. There were, in other words, good forms of political conflict as well as bad, virtuous competition for power as well as factionalism, which might in more current political language be called hyperpartisanship.[9]

The kind of *tumulti* Rome experienced between the fifth and the second century BC exemplified the good kind of political conflict. They showed that the people were vigorous in standing up for their rights, forcing the nobles to respect their common utility, winning military victories to enhance their bargaining power with the rich and powerful. But when "sects" *(sette)* appeared under the control of ambitious nobles and dynasts in the first century BC—when they were transformed into the clientage groups under the protection of great men—Rome suffered from violent and destructive factionalism.[10] What Machiavelli was trying to do was to show why Florence's political conflicts had always, in the past, degenerated into factionalism. His goal was to demonstrate via historical narrative the need for a new, more permanent kind of constitution, the "well-ordered republic" he had proposed to the Medici in the *Discursus*. The *Istorie* diagnosed the disease, and the *Discursus* prescribed the cure. This, in a nutshell, is what has recently been called Machiavelli's "realist republicanism," characteristic of his final years and based on his careful study of Florence's republican experience.[11]

It was to accommodate this new theory, I believe, that Machiavelli was forced to change his original design for the *Istorie*. In its initial conception it was to have begun with an introductory book, setting Florence's modern history in the wider context of Italy from the fall of the Roman Empire. There would then have followed, in book 2, a much slower-paced narrative of the Medicean period from the rise of Cosimo in 1434. In other words the book would have been a vernacular sequel to Bruni's history. But eventually Machiavelli must have realized that if he were to instrumentalize the *Istorie* to promote his theory of faction in Florentine history, he would have to rewrite Bruni's narrative, as it carried quite a different set of lessons. So after his original book 1 he added a second introductory book, now book 2, which began (after a single brief chapter on Florentine history from her founding to 1215) with the legendary *fons et origo* of factionalism in Florence, the feud between the Buondelmonte and the Amidei in 1215 over a broken marriage contract. The eventual books 2 and 3 then proceeded to rewrite Bruni's account, above all with regard to factionalism.[12]

Machiavelli alludes to this change of plan in his preface, where he explains why he has chosen to devote particular attention in his narrative to Florence's domestic politics. He claims that Bruni and Poggio are excellent on foreign affairs but either silent or too brief on civil strife and internal hostilities.[13] As regards Bruni, this criticism is simply false. Bruni often deals at great length with internal discord, sometimes at even greater length than Machiavelli does when describing the same events. Machiavelli's real objection is to *what* Bruni says, not his failure to say it.

The problem is that Bruni's account of the causes of factionalism and his advice about how to avoid it are at odds with Machiavelli's analysis and prescriptions. Bruni's approach is straightforwardly moralistic; he regards human vice as the ultimate cause of factionalism. The highest and lowest classes in the state are naturally uncivil and immoderate, while the broad middle classes—the *popolo*—have the greatest capacity for civic virtue. It is only the middle classes that have a real interest in observing the common good and are capable of governing on a basis of friendship—another Aristotelian argument—because (unlike the aristocracy) their sense of honor is not bound up with their standing as the heads of clientage systems.[14] They can identify their own interests more closely with those of the state. Like Poggio, who believed that wealthy persons driven by avarice should be exiled to prevent them from corrupting the body politic, Bruni approved the People's actions in excluding from the councils of government arrogant magnate families who had proven to be sources of conflict in the past. Exceptions could be made, to be sure. Certain individuals of proven virtue, men such as the nobleman Tegghiaio degli Aldobrando de'Adimari on the one hand and Michele di Lando, leader of the

Ciompi, on the other, could, under certain conditions, make notable contributions to the state. It was a principle of humanist virtue politics that any individual from whatever class, even the lowest, who proved his merit should be worthy of inclusion in the ruling class. For Bruni as for other humanists, true nobility, the quality that should mark out a republic's leadership class, was not based on inherited wealth and rank, but on education, experience, and virtue.[15]

The issues of leadership and inclusion in politics were at the heart of Machiavelli's disagreement with Bruni. In his late political thought, as in his great writings of the 1510s, Machiavelli always thought in terms of the *verità effettuale*: what flawed human beings were necessarily going to do, not what they should do. Good government for him was not a matter of moral struggle in the breast of a statesman, as it was for fifteenth-century humanists. For Machiavelli, individual virtue was enabled by culture, laws, and political institutions, not vice versa. Solving a city's problems required, therefore, a wise legislator to improve its institutions, not a humanist educator to teach virtue to its elites. Since any political organism was always going to have the two opposing humors, it would never be possible or desirable to exclude whole classes of citizens from political power. *Naturam expellas furca, tamen usque recurrit,* as Horace wrote: you can cast out Nature with a pitchfork, but she will keep coming back nonetheless. For him, the Soderini regime fell because, after the expulsion of the Medici in 1494, "the city decided to resume the form of a republic, but did not apply herself to adopting it in a form that would be lasting, because the ordinances then made did not satisfy all the parties among the citizens. . . . The reason why all these regimes [since 1393] have been defective is that alterations in them have been made not for the fulfillment of the common good, but for the strengthening and security of a party."[16] The fundamental humors of all political societies would always need to be "contented" or satisfied in some way, and malign *sette* or factions would inevitably form if one or another humor were suppressed or excluded from power. The city itself needed the distinctive contributions that the different social classes could make: the honor and military skill of the nobles, the warlike power of a loyal and virtuous multitude. Moreover, if all the humors were not contained within the state, there would be no occasion for those benign *tumulti* or political conflicts that allowed the people to "vent" and kept the aristocracy from oppressing them.

It would be possible to give many instances of how Bruni selected from and reshaped vernacular chronicles in order to illustrate moral and political lessons, and how Machiavelli returned to the same sources to help him construct his own narrative against the grain of Bruni's account. I will give only three characteristic examples.

The Ordinances of Justice

In order to strengthen support for his new constitution, Machiavelli knew that he would have to undermine reverence for the Ordinances of Justice (1293 / 1295), regarded by many Florentines as a founding document of the republic. This was the legislation that, after a long struggle with the magnates, put the People definitively in charge of the state and prevented it from being ruled by powerful magnate clans. Bruni had celebrated the passing of the Ordinances of Justice in book 4 of his *History* as a triumph of popular courage and sound politics, and had praised the Ordinances' champion, Giano della Bella, as the greatest of Florentine statesmen.[17] Machiavelli by contrast presents the late duecento attempts of the People to exclude the magnates from power as ineffective, because their institutions remained too weak to prevent them from being influenced by the wealth and power of the *grandi*. The lesson he draws is that *grandi* were going to be part of the political equation whether they held formal power or not. Bruni tended to see the *magnati* as a defined group of thirty-eight malevolent families who had been deservedly expelled from civic offices because of their violent and selfish behavior, while Machiavelli saw them as simply one incarnation of a permanent political humor, those *soi-disant* nobles who had a need to lord it over others. Having lived the first twenty-five years of his life under the Medici, he understood, better than the immigrant Bruni could, that actual office-holding was not the only or even principal way that the wealthy and powerful exercised influence.

For Bruni the story of Giano della Bella was a tragic one, a tale of civic ingratitude toward the People's noblest hero. For Machiavelli, Giano's self-exile counted as proof that the institutional structures he had created in the Ordinances of Justice were badly thought out and inadequate to constrain either humor in the city. The anti-magnate harshness of the Ordinances in fact soon revealed their poor design: almost immediately they had to be softened in view of the violent resistance of the nobles. The latter series of events, documented in Villani, is omitted by Bruni but highlighted by Machiavelli.[18] Machiavelli ends the chapter by inserting an indirect-discourse speech purporting to summarize the view of a group of wise mediators.[19] The speech warns the nobility that they should moderate their arrogance; their nobility could not by itself defeat the People owing to the latter's superior numbers and wealth. The People are warned not to try to exclude the nobles entirely from participation in the city or pass laws against them that would make them desperate. They should remember that, in the past, the nobility had done honor to the city in its wars. The speech of the mediators is found in neither Villani nor Bruni; it is surely the voice of Machiavelli, telling Florentines that their political system has to find a different way to contain and regulate all its humors or risk dissolution.

Walter of Brienne and the Instability of Tyranny

In 1342–1343 Florence experienced an overt, formal tyranny, following upon a military coup, for the first and only time in its history. Both Bruni and Machiavelli were eager to turn this famous episode into an object lesson to demonstrate their respective views of history's lessons.

The two historians differ as to who was responsible for the tyranny of Walter of Brienne. For Bruni it was the nobility who "raised Walter up" but he himself who, sensing an opportunity in the regime's weakness, plotted to make himself a tyrant; the logic of Walter's plot is told from the Frenchman's point of view.[20] Bruni leaves out Villani's report of secret meetings between the nobles, the *ottimati* (leaders of the people), and the tyrant. Machiavelli by contrast, building on a phrase or two in Villani, constructs a picture in which alienated nobles and corrupt, debt-ridden *popolani grassi* conspire from the beginning to make Walter a tyrant.[21]

Bruni, like Boccaccio before him, tries to exonerate the *medius populus*—for him the true source of civic virtue—from responsibility for the tyranny.[22] At the beginning of Walter's rule, the *medius populus,* leaderless, had been overawed by the summary executions of Florentine optimates. That, indeed, had been Walter's intention: he could not induce the People as a whole to support his tyranny, so his only recourse was to intimidate them. Later, during the coup of September 8, magnates and certain great *popolano* clans had brought Walter in and supported him during the coup; the *faex plebis,* the dregs of the plebs, had acclaimed him as their lord forever, *signore a vita,* with enthusiasm. The rest of the Florentines had been subdued by the threat of violence from Walter's men-at-arms and magnates who concealed weapons under their clothing. The People had thus never endorsed the legitimacy of Walter's rule, which was an illegal tyranny (to use Bartolus' terms) *ex parte exercitii,* because it was only accepted under duress, *propter metum.*[23]

Machiavelli, surprisingly for those who think of him as a democrat, is far less protective of the People's reputation.[24] It was the incompetence of the Twenty, who had botched the Lucca campaign, that led *il Popolo di Firenze* to become angry with their rulers and led the Twenty in turn to bring in Walter "either to check or remove the causes for slandering themselves."[25] The executions, fines, and exiles that Walter meted out to the leaders of the Lucca war frightened *i mediocri cittadini*—a phrase that seems modelled on Bruni's *medius populus*. But Machiavelli goes further and describes how the middling citizens had painted Walter's arms on their houses to show their allegiance to him. This detail, based on Villani but omitted by Bruni, shows that the People was not just passively frightened, but intimidated into positive actions to show their solidarity with the duke's rule.[26] Most revealing of all, Machiavelli directly blames the People—not just the *faex populi* as Bruni (and Boccaccio) had done—but the whole of the People without qualification, for consenting via acclamation to Walter's tyranny, thus granting it at least a veneer of legitimacy. Villani had made it clear that the acclamation had come from the lower orders (at the instigation of Walter and his elite supporters)—"wool-carders, the rabble, thugs who work for certain great men."[27] Machiavelli, by contrast, says baldly that the cry of acclamation came from the People, and that Walter was elected perpetual *signore* "with the consent of the People."[28] He nowhere explains that Walter was accompanied (according to Villani and Bruni) by his own men-at-arms and by magnates with concealed weapons who implicitly threatened violence against opponents of his signory. Thus, in Machiavelli's version of events, the People could not even disclaim responsibility for Walter's tyranny *propter metum*. Nothing he had done to that point would have counted by the lights of a Bartolus as a tyranny *ex parte exercitii*. That came only later, when he began to abuse his new signorial power.

Bruni and Machiavelli differ, finally, on the causes of Walter's downfall. Bruni in typical fashion explains the tyrant's evil fate as a failure of prudence and personal morality. Walter's tyranny was unstable because of the "errors" he had made: his personal behavior was overbearing and uncivil; he showed disrespect for the Priors; he nullified honors and magistracies; he was untrustworthy in his alliances with various social groups; he was greedy, cruel, and raised taxes; he treated citizens like slaves because, being French, he came from a culture where the common people were not respected. In short, he behaved as any magnate would and worse. He did not know how to behave like a magistrate who respected Florence's civic traditions, as Charles, the duke of Calabria, had been able to do in 1326 under similar circumstances.[29]

Machiavelli analyzes the reasons for Walter's downfall in the form of a speech placed in the mouths of the Priors who came to him the night before the coup of September 8.[30] Like Bruni, he paints the Priors as good men who courageously speak truth to power. They tell him frankly that they know he wants to seek illegal power, but being unable to oppose him by force, they hope to convince him by argument that his coup will ultimately prove unsuccessful. The Priors present a classic Machiavellian decision tree to calculate the consequences of his seizure of power. The speech is in effect a prophecy of what will in fact happen later in Walter's reign.

I. A city with a long tradition of liberty will never willingly give that up. "Have you considered how important and how strong in a city like this is the name of liberty, which no force crushes, no time wears away, and no benefit counterbalances?" So the city will have to be enslaved, its liberty will have to be taken from it by force.

II. (a) Large forces are necessary to enslave a large city. (b) These can come from outside the city or from within. (b1) Those from outside, foreigners, will not be enough at every moment, and (b2) of those who support you from within the city (b2α) the powerful will discard you once they have used you to overcome their enemies, and (b2β) the common people *(plebe)* are fickle. So (c) eventually the whole city will be against you, and (d) nothing can protect a *signore* when an entire population opposes him: "he who fears all men cannot secure himself against anybody." (e) If you try an exemplary punishment of part of your opposition, the rest will just become more filled with hatred and the desire for vengeance.

III. The reign of one *signore* is not enough time to stamp out liberty. The memory of liberty, even when lost, is powerful and hard to eradicate. It will be passed down lovingly through the generations, and if liberty is ever regained, it will be held onto all the more tenaciously. Even if the city fathers forget it, "the public palaces, the official venues of the magistrates, and the symbols of free institutions will bear the memory of liberty, and these things will be recognized by the citizens with the greatest longing."

IV. You cannot win over the Florentines either by military conquests or good government (you cannot achieve performance legitimacy, to use modern terms). (a1) The glory of military triumphs will count as yours, not theirs;

(a2) more peoples conquered by you will only increase the number of the Florentines' fellow-slaves, because subject cities will be subject to you, not to them. (b) Good, pious, just government will not be enough to make you loved, because "to someone used to living unfettered, every chain has weight and every bond cuts." (c1) Good government and violence are inconsistent with each other. (c2) Since you can't hope to please people by good government, you will have to use the utmost violence (a possibility already disproved in II) or you will have to be content with the constitutional power we, the Priors, have already given you.

The speech of the Priors shows in the clearest possible terms the lessons Machiavelli hoped his Medici readers might draw from the story of the Duke of Athens. The Duke failed—as by inference the Medici would fail—because he did not understand the deep attachment of republics to liberty. The usual humanist solutions to the problem of obedience—military glory and good governance based on the assumptions of virtue politics—is dismissed as ineffective in the case of free peoples; the desire for freedom trumps even the best signorial or aristocratic governments.

Walter is not convinced, and Machiavelli allows him to make a reply (2.35), which, again, is found in neither Villani nor Bruni. Walter advances in response what had for centuries been the standard monarchical idea of liberty, an idea that was embraced by the majority of quattrocento humanists: that a virtuous order was tantamount to liberty, and a factionalized, disorderly city was already in a condition of slavery. He omits only the usual corollary, derived from Stoic sources, that true liberty lay in obedience to a virtuous prince. Perhaps that addition, placed in the mouth of Walter, would have strained even Machiavelli's loose standards for suspension of disbelief.[31]

The Restoration of Popular Institutions in 1343

A key feature of Machiavelli's later political thought is his emphasis on including in appropriate ways *all* elements in society—the nobles, the middle classes, and the poor—within the constitutional order. Failure to do so would only continue the destructive cycle of factional struggle, exiles, coups, and restorations. Machiavelli had in his earlier, "Roman" period of republican theory held views of the relative worth in government of the *grandi* and the *popolo* not unlike those of Bruni. In his later, "Florentine" period, however, he came to reassess his views of both social groups: he was now more willing to recognize the contributions the great families could make to Florence's prestige and military strength, while casting a more jaundiced eye on the actions of the People when deprived of the balancing influence of the nobles.[32]

Bruni's narrative of the restoration of popular institutions following the tyranny of Walter of Brienne thus represented a major obstacle to the lessons that Machiavelli wished to be drawn from Florentine history. After Walter was expelled, in Bruni's account, the magnates had been able to insist on the restoration of their political rights. They had been a key force in the Fourteen, the conspiratorial countergovernment set up by the bishop of Florence, Agnolo Acciaiuoli, to take power away from Walter. After Walter's expulsion the Fourteen was temporarily the only magistracy upholding public authority, and the magnates used their influence on this board to shape the new form of government. The regime that was eventually set up in late 1343 effectively overturned the Ordinances of Justice. Bruni's account of the events relied on Villani, but he added a further explanation of the motives for reintegrating the magnates into the new government.[33] The statesmen of the time wanted civic harmony and believed that they would get it by including the formerly excluded magnates in the system of public honors. They also felt that the manifest merit of the magnate class in helping to expel the tyrant deserved some reward, even though they had benefited from the tyrant's rule. Nevertheless, Bruni insisted it was a mistake to restore the political privileges of the magnates, since it meant overturning the Ordinances of Justice, the constitutional safeguard against magnate violence: "The [Ordinances] had been wisely framed in the beginning and afterwards preserved in the state with salutary effect. But at this time [1343], the body politic had been entirely equalized and through concord made as one; so with the sources of contention having lapsed, the safeguards against it lapsed as well."[34] Bruni then illustrated his point that restoring political rights to the nobles was a mistake by showing how it led immediately to a renewal of factionalism and, eventually, to open and violent class warfare between the People and the *grandi*.[35] The People could not tolerate sharing office with the rich and powerful:

> For scarcely had the new priors been installed when the people were stirred up by this unaccustomed state of affairs; by that time the sharing of offices with the nobility was no longer in favor and was a cause of fear for the future. For it seemed likely that noblemen, leaders of great families, who were already formidable by themselves without any public power, would become intolerable if they acquired a magistracy as well, and people reckoned that they would not

restrain themselves from acts of injustice. This reason was advanced as a pretext, and there was something to it.[36]

Bruni is repeating here the arguments earlier put in the mouth of his hero, Giano della Bella. He then states that, with the breakdown of the Ordinances, "envy and contention, the usual civic diseases, . . . returned to the city together with liberty."[37] Civil war broke out, ending in victory for the People. The Ordinances were restored, and with them, a measure of civic tranquillity. Some noble families were degraded to *popolano* status, while others left for foreign courts, where they continued to plot against the city's security. Thus, the brief period during which nobles were included in the regime was shown to be a terrible mistake; only rule by the People, buttressed by the Ordinances of Justice and the restoration of militia companies, could guarantee a virtuous magistracy whose interests were fully aligned with those of the *respublica*.

This was precisely the view of republican government that Machiavelli could not accept. Countering Bruni's narrative led Machiavelli to introduce his weightiest critique of the traditional Florentine constitution and the reason why it had led to the crippling factionalism that had characterized its history from the beginning. This appears at the beginning of book 3 as a kind of summing up of Florentine history up to 1343. The previous book ended with the defeat of the nobility in the civil war of late 1343 that followed upon the expulsion of the tyrant. In contrast with Bruni's satisfaction at the defeat of the magnates, Machiavelli expressed regret for the military power and greatness of spirit that had been lost with the ruin of the nobles: "This was the reason why Florence was deprived not only of arms, but of every noble sentiment."[38] Bruni had complimented the People on their restraint in punishing the nobles, and blames the *multitudo infima,* the urban mob, for sacking and burning their houses.[39] Machiavelli ignores the mitigating remarks of Villani and Bruni and roundly condemns the action of the People "and its most ignoble part": "Meanwhile the People, and of these the most ignoble part, thirsting for booty, looted and sacked all their houses, pulled down and burned their palaces and towers with such rage that the cruelest enemy to the Florentine name would have been ashamed of such ruin."[40] Even Florence's worst enemies, in other words, would have felt shame for having acted as its own People had done.

Machiavelli then opens book 3 with what appears to be a digression, comparing the enmity between the nobles and the people in ancient Rome and medieval Florence. This highly original analysis of good and bad partisanship refines his previous discussions of *tumulti* in the *Discourses*.[41] Strife between nobles and the common people, Machiavelli claims, exists in all cities and is natural. Strife cannot be prevented, but it can have good or bad effects depending on how it is channeled by institutions, and depending on the ends sought by the contending parties: "For the enmities between the people and the nobles at the beginning of Rome that were resolved by disputing were resolved in Florence by fighting. Those in Rome ended with a law, those in Florence with the exile and death of many citizens; those in Rome always increased military virtue, those in Florence eliminated it altogether; those in Rome brought equality among citizens to a very great inequality, those in Florence reduced it from inequality to a miraculous equality."[42] In other words, Rome's political contentions had good effects, and in particular they had made it strong militarily. It is noteworthy that Machiavelli here does not seem to regard Florence's "miraculous equality" in 1343 as a desirable trait; the adjective *mirabile* is probably meant to suggest that its extreme equality was something unnatural. The explanation for the difference between good Roman and bad Florentine partisanship was precisely the issue of inclusive institutions. The Roman people wanted, justly, to share power with the nobles, so the conflict never became existential; the Florentine people wanted unjustly to ruin the nobility or make them conform to *popolano* ways. Roman partisanship thus led to positive effects, since the victories of the people made Rome stronger *(più virtuoso)* and gave the common people experience with magistracies and military commands; this enlarged the pool of talent that Rome could draw upon, another source of strength. The Florentine people by contrast became weaker by excluding the nobles and ruining them. The strife between the classes resulted only in "blood and the exile of citizens"; laws became the expression of popular injustice, benefiting only the popular power and neglecting the common utility. Worse, the People's demand that nobles should pretend to act like *popolani* ended by destroying the special gifts nobles could bring to a city: "From this arose the variations in coats of arms, and the changes of family titles that the nobles made so as to appear as popolani. So the virtue in arms and the generosity in spirit that were in the nobility were eliminated, and in the people, where they had never been, they could not be kindled; thus did Florence become ever more humble and abject." The consequences produce a typically Machiavellian paradox: "And where Rome, when its virtue was converted into arrogance, was reduced to such straits that it could not maintain itself without a prince, Florence arrived at the point that it could easily have been reordered in any form of government by a wise lawgiver."[43]

The great virtue of the Roman republic could only end in the vice of pride, which in turn meant that its political life had necessarily to be suppressed by a prince. But Florence, since its institutions had failed so miserably, left an opening for a wise legislator to introduce radical reforms of the type Machiavelli was recommending in his *Discursus,* and indeed throughout his mature political writings.

Two generations before, Francesco Patrizi had written in his treatise *How to Found a Republic* that a republic might hope to be perpetual so long as its rulers continued to set an example of virtue and restrain the vicious desires of the people. Machiavelli had no such faith in the preservative power of virtue as traditionally understood. All the virtue of Rome's republic was brought low by the arrogance and corruption of its leaders, and in the end the city's power could only be maintained by instituting an autocracy. Even a virtue so extraordinary as the Roman republic possessed could not preserve it against ruin when the end of its cycle arrived, and indeed its superexcellent virtue might even be said to be the cause of its ruin. But the collapse of the Florentine republic gave it the chance to begin its cycle anew and aim for a future of *virtù,* power, and success, so long as it listened to the words of a wise legislator—Niccolò Machiavelli.

Two Cures for Hyperpartisanship

To modern ears it is inevitable that Machiavelli's solutions to the evils of factionalism will seem more applicable to our own times than those of Leonardo Bruni. Bruni's belief that bad actors can simply be excluded from politics, and institutions designed to promote competition in virtue, seems, at least at first sight, naïve and impracticable. From a modern pluralist perspective, any attempt to limit political participation to the virtuous will look like an invitation to the most arrogant form of elitism, incompatible with dignitarian accounts of equality fundamental to liberal democracy. The legalistic forms of modern egalitarianism, in any case, are deeply incompatible with moral hierarchies.[44] In foreign affairs, the idea that a state should side with the forces of liberty and virtue against tyranny is less plausible to present generations than it was to the generations that fought in the Second World War and lived through the Cold War. We would all like to see a more civil and moderate citizenry, but where standards of civility can be found in pluralistic societies, deeply divided over values, is hard to imagine. How our societies, increasingly polarized by wealth and culture, could succeed in relocating political power in the middle classes, and how the middle classes could summon up the civic virtue necessary to rule, seems even more challenging now than it did two or three decades ago during the heyday of communitarianism. In the understanding of most academics in the modern university, the humanities and the arts are "enriching" and enjoyable, but the moral formation of citizens and political elites lies outside their vision. Those academic humanists who are interested in molding the political values of students seem most interested in making them into partisans of their own favored causes. The Renaissance humanists' attempt to brand partisanship not only as counterproductive but personally shameful, an unjust form of political action, would be incomprehensible today; we still live in a world that admires ideologues and sees them as models for committed intellectuals.[45] Bruni, like other humanists, believed that one cure for factionalism lay in morally serious leaders, possessed of a practical intelligence that had been trained in eloquence, poetry, history, and moral philosophy; but those subjects are rapidly vanishing from our schools. Without soulcraft of some kind all statecraft must fail, but of all the insights of Greek philosophy and Renaissance humanism, that is the one most opaque to contemporary political scientists.

Machiavelli's solutions to factionalism appear more viable in the world of modern politics. After all, there is a direct line between the healthy "conflictualism" championed by Machiavelli and the adversarial party system used in most modern democratic societies. Machiavelli rejects the holistic tendencies of virtue politics and accepts a pluralism of interests as part of politics. More worrisome, but still attractive to many, is the line from Machiavelli's acceptance of inevitable conflict to modern advocates of violent revolution.[46] It is in keeping too with our low expectations of politics that Machiavelli does not believe in the possibility of a virtuous political elite. For him there are two permanent political humors in all polities, the elites and the people, and the *grandi* will always try to oppress weaker citizens. The only question for a man of popular sympathies like Machiavelli is how to prevent that from happening.

As we have seen, Machiavelli had three solutions to the problem. The first was the remilitarization of the Florentine people. A polity whose military power depends on its citizens cannot exclude them from politics, as Roman republican history showed. A strong people, aware of its "horizontal" class interests, was a prophylactic against the formation of "vertical" clientage groups (or *sette*) that could weaken its solidarity. Second, religion should be subordinated to the state, and the influence of the transnational elite that ran the Catholic Church should be eliminated. With no divided loyalties to external powers, a major source of factionalism would be removed. The third solution was a redesign of institutions in such a way as to diffuse power among different social elements and break up systems of clientage such as that which maintained the Medici in power. Exclusion of seditious elements from the city, such as Bruni proposed, would not work, because exile communities would continue to be a source of instability. Since, for Machiavelli, it was futile to expel the *grandi* from the republic, and the project of making them prefer justice and the common good via humanistic soulcraft was a proven failure, a certain amount of conflict must be allowed and could be exploited by the wise legislator. Conflict could be "vented" though assemblies, popular trials, and tribunes of the people. Conflicts could be kept from exploding into violent factional strife by sound laws and institutions—including laws against calumny—ferociously enforced.

Machiavelli is admired by some today because of his commitment to equality and popular power and his hatred of oppressive elites. He surely deserves credit for understanding the importance of good laws and institutions in maintaining a well-functioning civil order. That is something the tradition of virtue politics, thanks to its distrust of legalism, did not always fully appreciate. It is not really true, as Isocrates glibly remarked, that regime types do not matter so long as rulers are virtuous.[47] Laws and political institutions do matter. Paper walls do not protect polities from corruption by evil rulers, but evil rulers can be hedged in by laws and institutions so long as there are virtuous people (in Machiavelli's sense) to defend them. This was something Machiavelli understood better than many champions of virtue politics did.

But the ultimate judgment on Machiavelli's political counsel must be clouded with a kind of historical foreboding when we consider the effects that his demoralized form of realism has had in later times. Conflict in Machiavelli is tolerated within the state because only through conflict can the people make themselves free from oppression and feel that their will is represented in the actions of the state. That is what makes them willing to fight *for* the state, to defend it against enemies, to conquer them and expand the state's borders. In other words, the chief purpose of his brand of republicanism is not to achieve social harmony or peace or justice, as in the philosophical republicanism of virtue politics, but to enforce greater equality among citizens and make the state into a military power able to defend itself and expand its territory.

That purpose exposes what is the real problem with Machiavelli: he was willing to countenance almost any degree of wickedness to maintain and increase the power of the state.[48] His view of the Roman Empire is precisely the opposite of Biondo Flavio's. Biondo thought Rome was great because of its virtue and openness to talent. Machiavelli believed Rome was great because it would do anything, up to and including genocide, the razing of cities, and the enslavement of whole populations, in order to preserve and enlarge its empire. It smilingly embraced its free allies, then stripped them of their most talented citizens and reduced them to provinces under the rule of Roman governors. It carried out these monstrous acts under both republican and monarchical forms of government. Machiavelli never condemns such acts. His view is that they were necessary for Rome's survival and glory. The secret of Roman success, what set Rome apart from soft modern nations, was that the Romans were cruel, deceptive, violent, and inhuman when they needed to be. The clear implication of Machiavelli's political teaching is that modern states, to be successful, must imitate the selfish inhumanity of the Romans.[49] Far too many in later times have taken his advice, and are taking it now, using arguments similar to his.

The question is not whether Biondo or Machiavelli was right about the Romans. Both were right. Any historian can find numberless things to admire and to despise in the Romans, as in all historical societies. The question is how we use the past. Historians these days tend to be cynics. Seeing ourselves as social scientists, we tend to believe that the most selfish explanations for human behavior must be the true ones—just as, in modern political life, we believe malign gossip about individuals if it suits our prejudices. We find it hard to believe that any public figure can act from disinterested motives, for the common good. But if we are honest, we will recognize that Machiavelli's realistic explanation for Roman power, like the idealizing account of Biondo, is only a partial truth. Laws matter, but ethical ideals matter too. Modern academic historians shrink from creating heroes out of flawed human beings; we fear our colleagues will think us sanctimonious or naïve. But all human societies need heroes, or at least decent, well-educated people of goodwill who can serve as models for later generations. There are ways of finding political ideals exemplified in history, as Francesco Patrizi argued, that do not require the historian to turn a blind eye to the flaws of individuals and states. Machiavelli's use of the past falsifies it fully as much as Bruni and Biondo do, but in the opposite way, by excluding from consideration or deflating the value of the numberless good and selfless acts human beings have done for their communities and their countries in the past, and still do, every day. His version of history, in which political actors, to be successful, are driven by necessity to perform evil acts, has been praised by some as giving birth to the modern science of politics. Others may conclude that the humanists did more for the moral formation of citizens and rulers by reviving the prudential history of the ancients: history as a teacher of virtue.

CHAPTER 21

CONCLUSION

Ex Oriente Lux

One who rules through the power of Virtue is analogous to the Pole Star: it simply remains in its place and receives the homage of the myriad lesser stars.

CONFUCIUS, ANALECTS 2.1

I transmit but do not innovate; I believe in and love antiquity.

ANALECTS 7.1

Sometime in the late 1590s the Jesuit missionary Matteo Ricci, then living in the Chinese city of Nanchang, paid a visit to the famous Confucian scholar Zhang Huang. A few years earlier Ricci had exchanged his garb as a Buddhist monk, his initial disguise in China, for the robes of a Confucian scholar. He had come to the conclusion that the best way to advance the Christian faith in China was to present it as a religious philosophy compatible with Confucian teaching. His Confucian dress reflected this new conversion strategy. So when he met Zhang Huang, to casual observers the occasion might have seemed like a meeting of two Confucian scholars.

The two men hit it off immediately. Ricci's reputation for high moral virtue and recondite learning in astronomy and mathematics had preceded him, and Zhang Huang admired his mastery of the Confucian classics. The meetings continued, and the two became friends. Ricci in his turn admired the elder man's virtue and literary accomplishments. The Chinese scholar was a Confucian but not a mandarin. He had refused to serve as a government official in order to distance his commitment to learning from charges of careerism. But he was highly respected, the teacher of many mandarins and Confucian philosophers at his academy on the banks of East Lake in Nanchang. As a man of the Renaissance Ricci sympathized with Zhang Huang's efforts to disentangle the original wisdom of Confucius from later corruptions imported from Buddhism and Daoism. Thanks to the

495

Jesuits, Ricci had himself enjoyed a fine humanistic education in Latin and Greek literature and philosophy, and the *forma mentis* those studies had imparted only strengthened his affinities with Zhang Huang's scholarly world. The two discussed whether Christian social ethics could be harmonized with Confucianism, and whether there might be room for the Christian message of revelation and redemption in a Confucian culture. Much as humanist scholars of the Italian Renaissance sought to harmonize Graeco-Roman philosophy with Christian faith, using the wisdom of the former to guide the present life while reserving the message of Christ's salvation for the next, so Ricci came to understand Confucianism as a kind of Stoic philosophy that anchored public life in ancient philosophical wisdom, leaving the higher life of the spirit open to the light of Christianity. Just as Greek philosophy, according to Church Fathers like Eusebius, had prepared the Roman Empire for Christianity, so Confucianism might serve as the *praeparatio evangelii* for China.[1]

Ricci's admiration for Confucian scholars like Zhang Huang was bound up with his wider respect for Chinese government and administration. The way China was ruled seemed to him a dream of Renaissance virtue politics come true. In a report of 1584 sent back to his Jesuit superior, Ricci wrote, "I only wish that Your Grace judge the Chinese through their statecraft, into which they have put all their effort and achieve such brilliance that they leave all other nations behind."[2] His account of the Jesuits' China mission, published in Latin translation in 1615, included two chapters filled with praise for Chinese attainments in the liberal arts and the arts of government.[3] The first of these began with an allusion to Plato's famous *sententia aurea,* claiming that "even if philosophers do not rule in this kingdom, it nevertheless must be said that its kings are themselves ruled by philosophers."[4] Philosophers on Ricci's account were the dominant element in the Chinese governing elite, much more important than military men. They were trained in literature, including poetry, history, and above all moral philosophy. Their philosophical learning was based on the works of Confucius, who had lived five hundred years before Christ. His wisdom was "equalled by few of our pagan philosophers and superior to most of them." Confucius inspired others to a life of virtue through both precept and example.[5] Though the Chinese were excelled by the West in the exact sciences and in military skills, the Chinese far surpassed the West in the arts of government. Their examination system, which Ricci describes in minute detail, was designed to promote moral men distinguished for their wisdom and practical skill in governance:

Furthermore, only those holding doctorates or licentiates officially announced in the examinations are appointed to rule the state and guide the whole Kingdom, nor do they need any influence with either the magistrates or even the King himself for this purpose. Every office of their republic depends on their proven science, virtue, prudence, and astuteness, whether they are taking office for the first time or are already experienced magistrates. This practice moreover is so prescribed by the law of Hongwu [founder of the Ming dynasty], and for the most part it is observed—except in the case of sinning against justice and the laws on a daily basis thanks to human evil coming from the lack of religion among the Gentiles [i.e., non-Christians].

Like the classically trained administrators of the British Empire two centuries later, the mandarin philosophers of China were all-rounders, and their education in Confucian ethics made them "competent to pass judgment on any subject, however far distant it was from their own calling."[6]

The Chinese from time immemorial had followed a monarchical form of government and had never even heard of other constitutions such as aristocracy, democracy, or any forms of polyarchy or power sharing. There were no dukes, marquises, or counts who could challenge royal power. Their emperors came to the throne via hereditary succession, though "it happened not infrequently that a man who ruled incapably might be ejected from the throne by the people, impatient of their yoke, and replaced, thanks to popular favor, by a man eminent for his competence and virtue, who would thereafter be accepted with reverence as their legitimate emperor."[7] Though there were no formal constitutional limits on the emperors' powers, they were in practice restrained by their need to rely on customary rites and the goodwill of the mandarin class. Their magistrates in some respects resembled, said Ricci, the Spartan ephors and Roman censors, and possessed the gravitas to oppose bad behavior even in the emperors themselves. The Chinese suffered no civil tumults thanks to wise government, but they were weak militarily owing to their peaceful ways and lack of interest in conquest. The absence of a militaristic spirit, Ricci writes approvingly, was due above all to the influence of the mandarin class (referred to throughout as "the philosophers"), who are described as possessing *merum mixtumque imperium,* full discretionary power:[8]

All military affairs are governed by the philosophers, who take an active role in them, and their advice and counsel has more weight with the emperor than that of military leaders, who by custom are but rarely admitted to deliberations concerning war. Hence it is that among nobler spirits, few are drawn to the things of war, and they would rather aspire to the lowest rank in the philosophical senate than to the greatest magistracies of war; for it seems to them that the philosophers far exceed them in gainful employment as well as in the esteem of mankind. But what appears most wonderful in the eyes of foreigners is that these philosophers, when it comes to nobility of soul, loyalty to the state and to the king, and contempt for danger and death in the cause of their country, doubtless take the palm from those who profess arms as their trade. The origin of this trait is perhaps that the mind of man is ennobled by the study of literature, or that from the very origins of this kingdom letters always brought gentility to more people than did the profession of arms, among a nation little given to expanding their empire.[9]

In general, Ricci reported, the Chinese disliked arms and (like Plato in the *Laws*) distrusted resident aliens, who might bring into the kingdom corrupting foreign ideas and customs.

Thanks to Ricci's influential presentation of China as an ideal monarchy governed by philosophers, many of his early modern readers came to take a utopian view of the Chinese state. The groundwork had already been laid in the late 1580s by the political theorist Giovanni Botero, who had expressed his admiration of China for bringing order and prosperity to a population he estimated at sixty million, four times that of Europe.[10] Ricci's fellow Jesuit Adam Contzen inserted Ricci's laudatory description of Chinese government whole cloth into book 7 of his *Politicorum libri X* (1621), a work which became the standard political textbook for Catholic Europe in the seventeenth century.[11]

To writers brought up in the humanist literary tradition, the admiration for China is readily understandable. China in the Ming dynasty was by far the largest and most populous state in the world. It was ruled by an emperor in Beijing, a hereditary monarch, but all other high offices of state were occupied by mandarins, men trained in classic Confucian texts, who had passed examinations on those texts qualifying them to hold office. The mandarinate was arranged in a hierarchy of nine ranks, and higher rank was won through meritorious service and fine literary accomplishments. Mandarins ruled with great pomp and ceremony, and were carried through the streets on litters, "like the pope," as Ricci noted. The common people dropped to their knees to do them reverence. Ricci was deeply impressed that these mandarins, "these *laoye* [venerable lords] are sons of farmers and artisans who rise to their status because of their studies of letters." The system reminded him of the Catholic Church, which he, like Biondo Flavio before him, thought of as a meritocratic hierarchy, elevating a lettered elite to high rank above the common crowd.

The resemblances between Confucianism and virtue politics go much deeper than this, however, beginning with the origins of both movements. Confucius' thought was shaped by a period of political and moral turmoil in the Spring and Autumn Period, a time when China was dominated by warlords and petty princes, illegitimate rulers whose power was based on military force and guile. This was a time when the peace, order, and virtue of the early sage-kings and of the Shang and Western Zhou dynasties was a distant, idealized memory. Confucius' philosophy was thus a response to war, misrule, and social chaos that looked back to a lost golden age for moral guidance. Both Confucius and Petrarch drew similar conclusions from the disorders and sufferings of their times. What the times required was not new laws and institutions, but a renewal of humanity itself. Restoration of the ancient political and social order depended on a prior ordering in the souls of rulers, on moral self-cultivation.[12] And both Confucians and Italian humanists discovered similar means to recover those traditions and revive the virtue of the ancients: the study and imitation of ancient authors. Those who studied the ancient texts would constitute a new nobility, based on merit and not heredity; they would deserve their places because of their moral training and knowledge of the classics. Hierarchies of power were to be justified by the possession of superior virtue. Even the textual practices of the Confucian scholar-officials, such as memorization and commentary on classical texts, combined with original compositions in the style of ancients, written in beautiful literary hands, resemble those of the humanists.[13]

The humanists' "ethicization of nobility" and their belief that political hierarchies had to be justified by virtuous rule forms a close parallel to the beliefs of the early Confucian movement in the Spring and Autumn Period and the Warring States Period, as reconstructed by scholars such as Yuri Pines.[14] The Senecan motto of *detur digniori*, "let it be given to the more worthy," had its counterpart in the Confucian ideal of "elevating the worthy." In China too the "superior man," the *junzi* or gentleman, had to earn the right to govern through moral self-cultivation. This included study of the *Odes*, the *Analects of Confucius*, and other classic works; practicing benevolence or humanity *(ren)*; and cultivation of the rites or right patterns of behavior.[15] The Confucian tradition, like humanist virtue politics, defended the idea that all human beings possessed at least the capacity to acquire virtue, and that this capacity was not limited to persons of high birth.[16] Confucius, Zengzi, Mengzi, and Zisi in the *Four Books,* especially as interpreted by the standard neo-Confucian commentator Zhu Xi, believed, like the humanists, that the man of virtue possessed a special charisma that came from his harmonious relationship to *dao,* a concept analogous to natural law.[17] Confucian sources also taught that the ruler's virtue generated love among the people and true friendship among the ruling class; as a result, obedience was freely given and coercion unnecessary, since the ruled would grasp that their ruler was benevolent and acting in their higher interest.[18] The parallels of Confucian *dezhi,* virtuous rule, with virtue politics are numerous and remarkable.[19]

There is, however, one enormous difference between Confucian governance in China and humanist virtue politics: the success of the former and the relative failure of the latter. Confucian ideals of government lasted in imperial China for close to 1800 years, from the Han dynasty, approximately coeval with the Roman Empire, to the end of the Qing dynasty in 1905. Confucianism was enshrined institutionally via the examination system, introduced during the Sui dynasty (coeval with the Merovingians in medieval Gaul), and its influence was diffused widely over law, mores, state rituals, and the arts during the Song dynasty. In the West, by contrast, virtue politics reached its apogee in Italy during the Renaissance. After the Renaissance it continued to exercise great influence on education, mores, and the arts for another three hundred years, but its ways of thinking about political power fell out of favor in the seventeenth century. Virtue politics was replaced by constitutional, rights-based, and contractarian approaches to the justification and ordering of political power. To put the difference far too simply, virtue politics aimed primarily to bring to power rulers who were good and wise; constitutional thought aimed primarily to limit the damage that might be done by bad and foolish rulers. The master values of Renaissance political meritocracy were virtue and practical wisdom; the master values of constitutionalism were an ordered freedom and the rule of law. In its medieval origins Western constitutionalism sought to buttress forms of legitimacy based on religion, custom, and the hereditary principle, but eventually, in the later eighteenth and nineteenth centuries, it came to be believed that a regime could only be legitimated by the popular will.[20] Following Rousseau's and Kant's definitions, such a regime became known in the parlance of international relations as a republic. The merit of rulers was almost completely eliminated as a criterion of legitimacy in formal political writings. One of the few meritocratic elements in the U.S. federal constitution of 1787, for example, a senate to consist of senior statesmen appointed by state legislators, was abolished by the Seventeenth Amendment (1913), which provided for direct election of senators.[21] The many admonitions of the American Founders that no form of government can succeed without virtue in the people could not withstand the democratic impulse to abolish distinctions, as Tocqueville observed in *Democracy in America.*

An explanation for the relative failure of virtue politics in the West is not hard to find. The Italian Renaissance was in some respects a unique moment in the history of European civilization. In the Late Middle Ages, models of political order still appealed to the edifice of legal rights and theological doctrines supporting, and supported by, the Roman Church and the Holy Roman Empire. These rights were elaborated and defended by scholastic jurists and theologians in the universities. When Italy was brought under the domination of foreign powers in the early sixteenth century, a new legal order was imposed, based in the kingdoms of France and Spain as well as the Holy Roman Empire based in Germany. In the period in between, from the mid-fourteenth to the early sixteenth centuries, from Petrarch to Machiavelli, Italians lived in a society where prelates and lawyers, and the sciences of canon and civil law that sustained them, did not enjoy anything like the moral prestige they had enjoyed in the high medieval period. Roman law and jurisprudence were studied for their educational value but had little relevance to the legal codes actually in use in most Italian cities. Legal documents were dated by the reign of an emperor whose rule, for Italians, was a fiction.[22] Ruling elites and institutions lacked legitimacy. Italy was free from imperial dominance, but political sovereignty was dispersed among many small states anxious to manufacture a legitimacy of their own. Italian republics such as Florence, Siena, and Lucca were dominated illicitly by wealthy oligarchs whose power was cloaked under forms of popular rule. Many signories were in the hands of men whose dubious titles to rule were backed mainly by military force. This turned out to be an ideal soil for ideas of political meritocracy to take root, since one of the things virtue politics offered was legitimacy, and legitimacy in Renaissance Italy was in short supply.

The comparison with the status of Confucianism in imperial China throws into high relief the reasons for the relative failure of humanist meritocracy in the West before modern times. The Spring and Autumn and Warring States Periods in Chinese history gave way to the Qin, Han, and later dynasties, when China was ordinarily unified under a single emperor, and rival forms of nobiliary and patrimonial power were vastly reduced in importance. The emperor had extensive authority over the legal system, and there was no independent legal profession, no

professional jurists or advocates. The only specialists were the scribes or legal secretaries who advised magistrates, who had no independent power.[23] At the local
level, law was "judge's law," where a magistrate was able to exercise wide discretion
following the Confucian principle that bringing social order to the infinite variety
of human interactions must rely ultimately on the judgment of good men.[24] Priestly
power did not take the form of centralized institutions that competed with the
imperial bureaucracy for political power.

In European civilization the situation was almost the opposite. After the time
of Charlemagne no Roman emperor, Holy or otherwise, was ever able to dominate all of Western Christendom. After the thirteenth century the Holy Roman
Emperors were, with few exceptions, absurdly weak. In the High Middle Ages they
fought with the popes for ideological and political hegemony. Neither side won.
In the early modern period both Empire and Papacy went into terminal decline,
and rivalrous territorial states, the future nation-states of Europe, grew in size and
power. Still, no European power ever succeeded in establishing complete hegemony
over the rest. Incessant warfare between European states had the effect, socially,
of allowing those who could help the kings win their wars to accumulate prestige.
These included nobles with their retinues and military skills, financiers with their
monetary resources, and technical experts such as scientists, geographers, and en-
gineers who had knowledge that could be converted to military uses. The humanists, whose main sphere of influence was quickly reduced to education, were never
able to compete successfully for political influence with these other professional
groups. The Renaissance tradition of humanist chancellors, bureaucrats, and
statesmen did not survive the sixteenth century.[25] The Jesuit order, the greatest
champion of humanistic education within Catholic Europe, was only a partial, and
ambiguous, exception.[26] The Renaissance ideals of the humanist scholar-official
or the humanist advisor to princes did not, except vestigially, outlive the
Renaissance.

The professionals who did end up staffing the governments of early modern
Europe, by and large, were lawyers. Here is where the contrast with China is particularly sharp. In the West, as long ago as the Roman republic, the legal system
developed a comparatively large degree of independence from political authorities. Roman civil law had by Cicero's time assumed the character of an autonomous source of right set above the social and political struggles of Rome, to which
appeal might be made by all Roman citizens (in principle) on a basis of equality.
Law was regarded as ultimately of divine origin, a claim that was never made for

law in China. Throughout European history courts, judges, and legal education maintained their relative independence from the state. In Renaissance Italy the higher courts were ordinarily run by foreign judges appointed for fixed terms who were (in principle) insulated from local political influences. The strong separation between law and politics in the West, embodied today in principles such as the independence of the judiciary and the separation of powers, had no parallel in imperial China. The art of designing constitutions to restrict the power of rulers was not a Chinese art. Nor did there ever take root in Confucian societies the principle that justice consisted primarily in fidelity to a system of rules authorized by legislation and regular judicial processes. The supremacy of law over politics, the rule of law as it is called, is generally regarded in the West as an unalloyed good, an absolute and unquestioned precondition of civilization and modernity.[27] That was never the case in China and is still not the case.

This is not to imply that the merit of rulers and law are mutually exclusive forms of legitimation. Indeed, the dominance of jurists and lawyers in Western and particularly Anglo-Saxon societies could be defended as itself a type of meritocracy. From the twelfth century into the early modern period the principal product of Western universities was lawyers, and admission to and graduation from medieval universities was arguably no less (or more) open to non-elites than the examination system of imperial China.[28] Legal expertise and proven administrative ability provided a pathway to climb the social ladder for at least some Europeans, however corrupt the processes promising to "elevate the worthy" might be in practice. It is striking how many church officials, for example, and even popes began life in humble circumstances but rose through the study of canon law.

Nevertheless, the humanist movement may be said to represent a protest against the progressive lawyerization of Western governments, which vastly exceeded (and still exceeds) in scope that of any other historical civilization, even Islamic civilization. Many humanists denounced not only the corruption of the law as practiced, its tendency to serve the interests of the powerful, but also the effects of legal education on the *ingenium,* its tendency to wither the soul, depriving it of the wider moral and civilizational nourishment it needed. Legal education, many humanists believed, led to a perception of justice as a morally empty positivism, the mere enforcement of rules, as though all rules were good no matter what sort of persons made them, or who interpreted and enforced them. The legalistic idea of justice stood in sharp contrast to the belief of Confucian and Renaissance literati alike that justice was a virtue exercised by rulers and could only be effective when rulers possessed a deep and humane culture and were permitted the discretion to make their virtues effective. Such was the case in China, at least as early modern men of letters imagined it. Renaissance literati, by contrast, never succeeded in completely displacing lawyers at the apex of European governments, even in High Renaissance Italy, and had only limited success thereafter in humanizing Europe's lawyerly heart. The enchantments of the law were too strong. Thanks to the universities, the tradition of Roman law lasted all through the Middle Ages, through the Renaissance and into modern times. The *Corpus of Civil Law* remained the backbone of legal education in the West down to the nineteenth century. This meant that Roman law principles entered into the legal codes of all European states to varying degrees, and legal expertise was needed to apply and interpret them. In Western states, the apparatus of the law, not the prudence of magistrates, was the primary tool of governance, and this was no doubt the principal reason why, after the Renaissance, the ideal of a scholar-official failed to establish itself as a reality.

The purpose of the elaborate comparison presented above between virtue politics and principles of Confucian governance in imperial China should by now be evident. This book has argued that the virtue politics of the Italian humanists represents not just a core set of beliefs about the reform of states widely shared among literati of the Renaissance, but a distinctive way of thinking about politics that amounts to a lost tradition of political prudence. That Ricci and so many other early modern literati trained in humanist schools admired Chinese meritocracy highlights the deep elective affinity between it and the ideals of virtue politics.[29] Moreover, the reality of Confucian governance in China over two millennia shows that to organize a polity on meritocratic principles is not a utopian dream. It is a real alternative. This is not to say that such principles can or should be revived, translated into constitutional form, and turned into a model for polities generally, as has been proposed by some modern Confucian political theorists.[30] Indeed, study of humanist virtue politics shows that it is possible to conceive of meritorious governance as an ideal independent of regime type. Meritorious governance can be distinguished from regimes of political meritocracy, whether historical or theoretical.[31] Debates about the best regime are intrinsically difficult to separate from partisan politics, and to design constitutional forms for real societies inevitably involves bargaining among concrete sectional and economic interests. Advocacy of meritorious governance and the reform of elites, by contrast, need not involve partisan commitments and is best advanced by rising above them. Neither Confucianism as a politico-ethical tradition nor Western virtue politics is necessarily committed to a particular form of constitution, and it is indeed debatable whether the system of governance used in imperial China can be characterized as a constitution at all.[32]

It would be a mistake, of course, to idealize too much the governing elite of premodern China, which like all human institutions had its moral weaknesses and limitations. In particular, it seems that the mandarinate was much more of a closed elite than one might suppose from reading the canon of Confucian texts. Confucian elites all too often displayed the vices typical of elites, beginning with arrogant contempt for the people they notionally served.[33] Nevertheless, the relative success of imperial Chinese governance over long periods shows the potential value of considering rulership from the point of view of virtue, education, and the recognition of merit. The type of prudence formed through an education in literature, history, and moral philosophy was once a possession of Western elites too, from the Renaissance into the modern period, and it has not exhausted its usefulness. In fact it may be more necessary today than it has ever been.

If virtue politics represents a distinctive way of looking at political questions, how may that outlook be characterized in general, and what contrasts does it offer with more familiar forms of political thought? One way of understanding virtue politics is as a regimen for strengthening and maintaining the health of polities, analogous to the approach of "positive psychology" to mental health. While traditional psychology deals with mental disorders after they manifest themselves— typically treating them with talking cures or (more commonly today) drugs— positive psychology, inspired in part by ancient virtue ethics, aims to resist mental disease before it occurs by forming healthy character traits that enable *eudaimonia* and a well-lived life.[34] It is preventive medicine for the psyche. Virtue politics can also be conceived as a kind of preventive medicine for the body politic. Just as virtue ethics tries to escape from the rule-making mentality of modern ethical traditions and concentrates instead on the kind of person one ought to become, virtue politics focuses on the moral character of the state, its magistrates, and its citizens.[35] On this analogy, constitutions, guaranteed civil rights, legislation, and regulatory bureaucracies will be seen as negative and reactive ways of containing disorders in the body politic. They are necessary guardrails, but they are not sufficient on their own to prevent corruption and ensure the healthy functioning of the state. Human beings who occupy offices and who staff institutions have to possess a certain character for those institutions to be successful. If those in charge of institutions have good character, they will be followed willingly by their subordinates and their actions will be accepted by the public. In short, as Plato, Aristotle, and Confucius already saw, soulcraft is prior to statecraft.[36]

In this book virtue politics has been presented in contrast with what I have called legalism, or the practice of trying to compel obedience or solve social problems via the proliferation of laws or by strengthening the apparatus of surveillance and enforcement. During the Renaissance such negative measures were on the rise in many republics and principalities.[37] The humanists in general thought coercive tactics were futile, even a sign of corruption. They liked to repeat Tacitus' maxim: *Corruptissima respublica innumerae leges,* "The state at its most corrupt will have innumerable laws."[38] To be sure, their prejudice against legalism was rooted in the long rivalry in Italy between literary and legal cultures stretching back into the Middle Ages. But literati after Petrarch began to elevate their distaste for legal education into a serious critique of contemporary law. In constructing this critique they often made use of resources mined from classical Greek philosophy that emphasized the role of good character in the state. Of course no Italian humanist ever said that states could dispense with legal systems, any more than the Greek philosophers had, and many praised the rule of law—the equal sovereignty of law over all citizens—as a shining achievement of the Roman state. Francesco Patrizi thought that Roman law should be assumed as the legal basis for the rule of an ideal king. No one questioned that wicked people needed to be restrained and injustices rectified. Nevertheless, humanists made a strong distinction between the wise legislators of antiquity, the *prisci legum latores,* and the corrupt legal systems that had been created by contemporary rulers and jurists. The law as written and enforced in their Italy was excoriated as irrational and hopelessly venal. It favored the strong, permitted the worst crimes, and was a source of discord and inhumanity. Its practitioners were learned in the law but ignorant of humanity. And when the human beings charged with making laws were tyrants, and those charged with interpreting them were corrupt, law became arbitrary and thus morally indistinguishable from violence. The law itself became a tyrant.[39]

The humanists recognized the rule of law as an immensely valuable civilizational achievement, but it was not enough. That a country should be ruled by laws and not men is the doctrine of societies that have learned the hard way that human virtue is not to be trusted. This is one reason why that doctrine became dominant in the era of religious warfare, when the contrast between rulers' professions of piety and their appalling actions was particularly sharp. The humanists were pushing in the other direction, responding to what they saw as the dysfunctional institutions of their time. They wanted political and legal systems to be more responsive to human virtue and prudence; they feared their manipulation by the powerful, who benefited from the costly mystifications of legal science. For them, the solution to the corruption of the legal system could not be merely to pass more laws and double down on enforcement. More basic changes would be needed that would restore the confidence of citizens in the motives of those who made, construed, and enforced the law.

Rulers, first of all, had to display good character and they had to be able to communicate their practical wisdom or prudence. The principal way the good character and wisdom of rulers could become evident to the ruled was through the arts of eloquence, what today would be called communication skills. The good man skilled in speaking, the *vir bonus dicendi peritus,* could build consensus by appealing to common moral principles and shared goals. True eloquence was not mere mastery of the tricks of rhetoric. The ancient art of rhetoric, as humanists learned from Isocrates, Cicero, and Quintilian, was a powerful tool that should never be abused or put to evil purposes. It could strengthen true eloquence but was not its real source, which was the speaker's character or *ethos.* Through true eloquence rulers revealed their *ingenium,* their inner intentions, which could not as easily be hidden from an audience as sophists (and their modern imitators) might suppose. That was why the maxim of *esse, non videri*—being, not pretending—was crucial: it supported what today would be called authenticity. Authenticity built trust. Trust between ruler and ruled, in other words, was built on confidence in the moral quality, sincerity, and consistent conduct of rulers.

Virtue politics thus provided its own solution to what political theorists call the "principle-agent" problem: the tendency in most societies for the interests of political elites or their agents to diverge from those of the people they are supposed to serve. Modern technical solutions to the problem emphasize performance measurement, reducing asymmetries of information between agent and principal, or obtaining "feedback" from principals. The humanist solution was a moral one: shaming elites into good behavior and offering psychological rewards for meritorious action. This meant inculcating shared standards of behavior in elites via education and the arts, and strengthening incentives to meritorious action via a culture of praise and blame. In that way the natural desire of elites for honor (or status) could be channeled in socially useful directions.[40] As Rémi Brague has written, "Praise is the nourishing source of all art and culture," and a society that wants to flourish spiritually must learn how to praise.[41] Livy's Romans were valuable models because their collective standards of behavior were admirable and, precisely because they were admirable, led to just government and justified hegemony over other states.

Punishment for self-interested actions, on the other hand, lay in the realm of reputation and informal, collective enforcement. A critical mass of civic leaders committed to virtuous rule was a necessary precondition. Since Italian cities of the era were led by very small groups of men, the project of creating such an elite was not as infeasible as it might appear, and damage to one's reputation could act as a very real sanction. Renaissance *principes* who fell short of the expected standard disgraced others of their class and would be punished by losing the friendship of the best. In particular, members of the elite who promoted the unworthy—their unworthy friends and relatives for example—delegitimated the system as a whole. The elite had to be visibly open to talent and merit in order to avoid corruption. So too, the culture of praise and blame needed to be carefully calibrated to avoid flattering the unworthy and unfairly blaming the meritorious. There was a fine line between praising someone above their merits as a form of encouragement and the kind of flattery that discredited both speaker and subject. Seneca's moral treatise *De beneficiis* provided humanists with invaluable guidance as to how one might confer benefits in a way that preserved the honor of both giver and receiver, and served the state and the human race as well.[42]

Virtue politics thus entailed a view of political life that was in some measure perfectionist. It was not compatible with an Augustinian view of the state that reduced the role of rulers to keeping order and punishing crime. On the other hand, thanks to the hierarchy built into Christianity between the goods of the present life and those of the next, humanists could hardly embrace a perfectionism of the Aristotelian type, where all human goods were contained within and realized by the *bios politikos*.[43] The Christian commitments of Renaissance societies (paradoxically for some) thus inoculated humanist literati against the sort of "comprehensive doctrines" in Rawls's sense—specific and interconnected beliefs about nature, virtue, religion, the state, social norms, family life, and personal values—that may threaten liberty and pluralism in modern societies.[44] The *institutio* engendered by their paideuma aimed instead to elaborate an "independent political ethic" similar in some respects to the one advocated by Hugo Grotius in the seventeenth century.[45] Theirs was a public morality abstracted from dogmatic religion and built upon foundations independent of religious belief. Humanist public morality was grounded in nature, reason, and antiquity. Nature, above all, the source of true law, had to be the statesman's guide to public morality. As Patrizi wrote in *How to Found a Republic,*

> Let the legislator in his laws imitate Nature, which provides a principle of virtue and honorable utility, so that he may look to what is fair or good, and consult the utility of all citizens if possible, or at least the majority. Let the legislator see to it, first of all, that the laws correct vices and commend the virtues, so that teaching about a [good] way of life may be educed from them. Philosophy will provide rich material for this, as Cicero plainly teaches in the *De legibus*. Let all law be for the well-being of the citizens, the preservation of human society, the protection of the state *(civitas)*, and the quiet and happy life of individuals. Persuasion causes fair-minded people to accept all these principles consciously, even those that seem to some extent prejudicial to the liberty of individuals. Let the law defend and protect the good and punish the wicked, but on the principle that it prefer to improve rather than destroy citizens.[46]

The state itself, however, should not be in charge of soulcraft. In general Renaissance literati set aside the passages at the end of Aristotle's *Ethics* that appear to give the polis the coercive authority and responsibility for leading its citizens to virtue. For the humanists, soulcraft, moral education, should be promoted by the prince or republic and deducible from the laws, but not required or imposed by fiat. In his treatise on republics, Patrizi issues what may well be the first call in world history for universal literacy in the citizen body—a visionary reform usually credited to the utopian society imagined by Thomas More.[47] Patrizi writes:

> If possible, everyone should learn their letters. . . . Not only should letters be learned, but I hardly think, in a free city, that anyone deserves the title of a free-born citizen *(ingenuus civis)* who is illiterate. For without letters, how can we master or preserve even the smallest of the arts, to say nothing of the liberal disciplines? Neither mercantile nor agricultural activities may be kept sound without letters. They preserve historical memory, instruct posterity, link the past with the future, and compel us always to consider our lives as a whole. For this reason it is well done to imbue youth with literature before setting them to other studies if we wish at some point to turn them into men and count them as citizens. It will therefore be the duty of the best paterfamilias to see

with the utmost care to the education of his sons, or at least to their basic literacy.[48]

The study of literature will make them better and more productive citizens. (Patrizi leaves in the air the suggestion that unlettered men do not deserve to be citizens.) Nevertheless, he places responsibility for educating children in the hands of the paterfamilias. The city should give prizes for accomplishments in arts and letters, and it should establish public professorships in each of the disciplines. But that is all.[49] To be sure, humanists encouraged princes as well as republics to take an interest in education. In the paradigmatic case of the famous humanist educators of the early quattrocento—Guarino Veronese, Vittorino da Feltre, Gasparino Barzizza—the prince promoted virtue by establishing schools in his court or city that noblemen and noblewomen were invited to attend. Places were also regularly offered to talented individuals of lesser social rank. *Principes* have an interest in rewarding virtue, but they should not seek to indoctrinate the citizenry in comprehensive doctrines.

What princes should do, above all else, is to set an example for their subjects. Humanist educators often repeated the admonition that everything the prince does is visible to the people, as though he were placed in a high tower or on a stage.[50] In their political acts, princes needed to consider the moral personality of their *stato* and the effect on the character of those who were subject to those acts. Virtue, like the good, was *diffusivum sui* and radiated from the higher ranks of society to the lower. The good prince made his people good too, and the same was true, or should be true, of political elites generally. Moreover, in successful polities people take pride in the way their rulers act at home and abroad, and they are more likely to support rulers whose actions are morally admirable and can be defended by some form of public reason. Rulers must provide moral leadership at home and interact with other states in principled ways. The authority of one state over another was justified when the hegemon behaved in morally superior ways and benefited other states. Moral leadership was more important even than good laws. In Florence, as Leon Battista Alberti observed, good government would not come from the ambitious men who had filled sixty cabinets with new laws, but from a natural civic aristocracy.[51]

Virtue politics thus requires rulers and citizens to think differently about the principles and ends of government. The ruler's task is not merely to protect citizens from exploitation by the powerful, defend them against external enemies, and promote their material welfare. A degree of perfectionism is necessary to the health of the state. Rulers and elites can promote the good life—a civic life in which men and women are able to flourish and live well in a moral sense—by promoting a different understanding of political values. Free speech for them was not a right hedged about with legal protections, as for moderns, but the courage to speak truth to power or the integrity to reject bad counsel that might be in one's personal interest. Free speech, in other words, was a form of moral courage. What we call "transparency" the humanists moralized: the good ruler does not fear the sight of others; he does not conceal his actions in the shadows.[52] The good citizen will not be the one who meets residence requirements or who inherits citizen status from parents, but one who selflessly serves the city. Tyranny is a problem of character, not merely a matter of violating rules laid down by jurists. Equality is not a legal status or a political right but a fixed habit of treating others fairly, respecting them as equals. Political liberty cannot simply be declared; it has to be deserved. Titles to power elicit real respect and willing obedience only when conferred upon the meritorious. Conferring honors on the unworthy cheapens the currency of those honors. The highest form of accountability is one that puts the magistrate's own reputation on the line. Wealth is only to be admired when licitly acquired and used well, above all in the service of the republic. The military calling is honorable only when exercised in the service of one's fellow citizens. To be just is not (or not only) a matter of following legal rules. It is to treat others justly, to possess the disposition to place another's good in equal balance with one's own, even when the other person is less powerful than oneself. Laws mechanically applied, without the exercise of humane discretion, are brittle and cruel. *Dura lex, sed lex,* said Justinian's *Digest:* the law is harsh but still the law. Such a maxim makes the state hated as well as feared. That is why the humanists placed so much emphasis on *aequitas,* or fairness. They knew the maxim *summum ius summa iniuria*—rigorous enforcement of the law can cause the greatest injustice. They knew the prudence and discretion of those in authority was needed to temper the rigor of the laws if the rule of law was to be made bearable to the ruled.[53]

If there is a master value anywhere in humanist virtue politics it is the Stoic and Ciceronian conviction that the best government does not need to surveil and coerce the good citizen. The attention to the psychological health of princes and citizens typical of virtue politics led humanists to judge governments, at least in part, by the passions they aroused in the ruled. Governments that were feared and hated by good citizens were by definition bad. Just rulers who could use moral argument or personal example to persuade those they ruled to obey the laws voluntarily were good rulers. That was why virtuous rule did not compromise the liberty of the ruled.[54] Voluntary obedience to good rulers and good laws was thus a criterion of political happiness both in republics and principalities. Selfish, unjust rule had the opposite tendency. Ambitious members of the political class who voluntarily obeyed unworthy rulers would become servile and lose their humanity. Hence, when governments became hopelessly corrupt, the good should consider their own psychic health and withdraw from political life.[55] Freedom was not tantamount to consent or the possession of rights or adherence to a social contract, as in modern Western democratic polities. Ultimately, freedom—and servility—were traits of character. Just as Lycurgus imprinted his own character on the Spartans through his legislation, so virtuous rulers would imprint their own character on the states they ruled.

Whether or not the humanist tradition of political prudence still has something to offer modern societies is not a question that a mere historian, perhaps, is best situated to address. One might at least counsel educators, political thinkers, and those set in authority over us to consider the need for a virtuous elite in the light of history, east and west, and our shared traditions of moral reflection. Those traditions are not neutral with respect to the good life, but neither are they oppressive comprehensive doctrines. They can be taught in ways that are appropriate to free and pluralistic societies and that improve the performance of their institutions. And some agreement about what constitutes decent and moral behavior is surely necessary to build the trust required for personal freedom and moderate rule in large-scale, multi-ethnic societies.[56] The rule of law is not a solution to all problems in a state and may itself become corrupted, as appalling abuses of prosecutorial powers, police powers, and judicial review in contemporary American politics show.[57] Moreover, all states are governed by elites, and in the absence of a hereditary aristocracy elites will always have to justify their preeminence on some grounds other than inheritance or the favor of the powerful. In modern liberal democracies, elites ordinarily claim to merit their positions by appeal to educational credentials or technical expertise rather than moral excellence or commitment to the common good. When their errors harm their fellow citizens, they rarely accept responsibility or expose themselves to democratic accountability. Modern ideological autocracies have become surveillance states where merit is assigned using a complex algorithm. Status is awarded and privileges granted on the basis of perceived obedience to the state's ruling elite. The question in modern societies is not whether there will be meritocracy, but what kind of meritocracy it will be.

In the United States, Europe, South America, India, and China the economic and ideological gap between elites and the rest of the population has widened dramatically in recent decades, in the Western world to the point where so-called populists (or nationalists) are in open revolt against governing elites. Among Western elites the typical response to this situation is to blame the common people for their ignorance, paranoia, and moral failings. It is less usual for elites to ask themselves whether they truly deserve their status, wealth, and power over others, and why they are hated by so many of those they seek to govern. As Michael Sandel has said, when meritocracy diminishes the capacity to see ourselves as sharing a common fate, when it leaves little room for solidarity between ruler and ruled, it becomes a kind of tyranny.[58] The humanist tradition of virtue politics was rich in reflection on precisely this question: the psychology of tyrannous rule. A bestial, power-hungry character, a soul without sympathy or a sense of decency, would lead to cruelty and inhumanity. Virtue politics also considered, more deeply than Aristotle or Cicero, the psychic diseases at the root of factionalism. Humanist literati believed that those deprived of a humane education and the shared values and understandings it imprints on hearts would be much readier to dehumanize political rivals, the deepest source of partisan hatreds. Like the Confucian scholars of imperial China, Italian humanists believed that the study of literature, history, and moral philosophy was a training in humanity in the full sense of that word, the most effective form of soulcraft. For them the humanities were a prophylactic against the beast in human nature and a reminder of the goodness of which it was capable.

And today? To believe that the humanities as taught in contemporary universities could recover something of their former role in moral and civilizational reform would surely be a triumph of hope over experience. But the history of Renaissance Italy and the struggle of its literati to reform their governing elites may still have, nevertheless, something to contribute to political prudence in modern times. Their ideals have not yet lost their moral power. The humanists, like the Greek philosophers of antiquity, taught that effective statecraft depended on soulcraft, and that the purpose of education and culture was not to control minds but to free them. The liberal temper that allows a citizen to rule and be ruled in civilized societies must be formed by rigorous training in the use of reason and speech and actuated by just praise for merit and fine examples of conduct. An education in "more human letters," *literae humaniores,* decenters the here and now and reaches out to understand other times and places. As Renaissance literati recognized, the twin dangers facing all societies, tyranny and factionalism, cannot be restrained merely by constitutional protections and law enforcement. Those in power need to be shaped by education and culture to understand, respect, and even love their political opponents as well as powerless people under their care. When dealing with other nations, governments need to consider not only what is in their own interest but what moral principles should guide their actions. In short, they need *humanitas.* The best advice the humanists can give us—the same advice Plato gives us—is that good leaders are those who make their people good. A rebellious people is a symptom of bad government. And the best warning we could take from the humanists is that political authority cannot in the long run be maintained without moral authority, and moral authority cannot be acquired without nurturing society's rulers in the best traditions of the peoples and civilizations they aspire to serve.

Appendixes

Notes

Bibliography

Acknowledgments

Index of Manuscripts and Archival Documents

General Index

Petrarch on Political Obligations:
De vita solitaria 2.9.19–22 (Chapter 6)

The translation is mine, though some phrases have been borrowed from the version of Jacob Zeitlin.

19. Not for any country whatever are all things to be dared, although those who have died are exalted to the skies with much praise. Among the men who have shed blood for our country praise has been won by Brutus, Mucius, Curtius, the Decii, the Fabii, and the Cornelii. Foreigners are praised too, for a like virtue deserves like praise. Athens praises Codrus and Themistocles, Sparta Leonidas, Thebes Epaminondas, Carthage the brothers Philenus, and other cities praise other citizens.

20. If you ask my view about all this, it is the heavenly republic that is to be loved, which is not roiled by the tumults of tribunes, secessions of the plebs, the arrogance of the senate, envy and feuding, civil and foreign wars. Whoever gives his blood for the heavenly republic is a good citizen and sure of reward. Not that I think on that account that this temporal and earthly country should be forsaken; if circumstances demand it, we are bidden to fight for it too, but in the end only if it is ruled by justice and lives by fair laws—the sort of country that the Romans' republic was at one time, as Sallust and Livy and many others have written.

21. Cicero in his books *On the Republic* argues this point acutely and at great length. I might readily agree that, at that time, it was just even when it was imposing force on the whole world and appeared to be extremely violent, because it was in the interests of those who were coerced to be coerced, however distasteful that might be, and in the interest of the world that it have a single head of affairs, provided it were the best and finest head. Except that what I shall now say would represent a strong objection to that argument. Namely this: that although they may have preserved justice among men, rendered to each his due, imposed through those Roman arts of peace described by the poet a habit of peace, "sparing the defeated and subduing the proud";[1] although, as the same Cicero elsewhere splendidly says, "The empire of the Roman people *may have been* maintained [or, to

use the archaic English subjunctive, 'were maintained'] through acts of service, not injustice, though its wars *may have been* waged on behalf of allies or for supremacy; though victory *may have been* accompanied by gentleness or only such force as necessity demanded; though the senate *may have been* a refuge and a harbor for kings, peoples, and nations; though our magistrates and generals *may have* sought to win the highest praise only for having defended our provinces and allies with fairness and loyalty"; and allowing it to be utterly true that "their empire over the whole world could have more truthfully been described as a protectorate than as an empire"[2]—although, I say, I might agree that the empire of the Romans of that time was conducted with the highest justice and goodwill toward mankind, still, there can be no doubt that they were unjust toward God, for they deprived Him of something not insignificant, namely of themselves, in the manner of fugitive slaves making theft of themselves from their master, and, what is the most serious form of theft, offering to His enemies [i.e., the pagan gods] the worship due to Him, which is doubtless a much greater injustice than if some ancestral estate or property were seized from a neighbor. The passage [from Cicero] is examined and discussed in detail by Augustine in his books *On the Heavenly Republic*.[3]

22. But suppose someone happens to be born in an unjust country with evil customs, such as nearly all the ones we see today? Shall he be praised for shedding blood for such a country? Not at all! Are you really telling me that a man who sacrificed his life to ensure that the deeds of wicked men and bad citizens *not* receive public punishment deserves praise and memorials?—although we read this has in fact happened in such cases to many.[4] Are you telling me that this man lives on in glory? I say that the man was doubly prodigal, of both his life and his death, and has thrown away his body *and* his soul at the same time, both this life and eternal life. On the other hand, not to wander too far, if there is any piety or justice in us, what would it not be right to dare and do on behalf of the Heavenly Jerusalem, for that lasting country which assures us of a blessed dwelling-place without end, without toil, without anxiety, without fear, without any vexation, in which there dwells nothing disgraceful, nothing impious, nothing unjust?

23. Truly I have now journeyed as far from my beginning as Peter [the Hermit] did from his home. The encounter of a single solitary old man gave me the courage to rebuke the princes and peoples of the West with our reproach in relation to the East [i.e., for its failure to protect Jerusalem from the "Egyptians"]. Would that my right hand [i.e., his writings] were as effective in this as was Peter's tongue! That

this wish is vain I am not at all sure;[5] my greater fear is lest I should be thought to have spoken with too much insistence and boldness by those who regard freedom of mind as recklessness, truth as madness, and every exhortation as an insult.[6] But however the matter may be received, being now by these words and this digression eased of the heavy and distressing load of my grievances, I return to the path of the original narrative with greater alacrity.

Speech of Rinaldo Gianfigliazzi before the Florentine Priors, 1399, from Leonardo Bruni's *History of the Florentine People*, 11.75–78 (Chapter 10)

Translation from Bruni, *History,* ed. Hankins, 3: 242–247.

We must all give you the greatest thanks, most excellent Priors, that, in this most difficult time, when everything is awash in uncertainty and suspicion and dangers manifest themselves on all sides, you have resolved to consult your citizens about the security of the republic. For when magistrates neglect dangers and take no counsel, they generally allow scope for irreparable ruin. I shall give my view faithfully and I ask you to forgive me if some things I say are said with excessive freedom, for the truth must not always be silent. For my part I confess that the dangers now besetting the city are great, but I am afraid not so much on account of those dangers themselves as on account of our own character. For as long as I can remember I have always seen us, because of our sloth and negligence, feebly losing the opportunity in every enterprise to take provident action. The reason for this evil is that the people and the mob do not look to the future and do not sense dangers until they actually occur; and outstanding men, if there are any among us involved in governing the state, although they may foresee dangers, nevertheless dare not and cannot forestall them. For so great is the freedom to calumniate in this city of ours that no sooner does someone explain the danger and advise taking action against it than many people start shouting that he is a warmonger and can't bear peace, and they hedge him in with malicious laws and tie him up with a thousand difficulties and prohibitions. So even if someone wants to take precautions for the security of the republic, he is left no way to do it! Thus it happens that we flee from opportunities and do nothing. But when dangers are at the doorstep and cannot be avoided, then—finally!—do we become alarmed and take advice, then we summon the Council of Two Hundred and the Council of One Hundred and Thirty together to discuss a matter and a business from which there is no escape.

I should not be so upset if our struggle was with another popular regime, for then the positions of both parties would be equal, or nearly so. But our present struggle is not with another popular regime but with a tyrant, who is ceaselessly awake to his own interests, does not fear slanderers, is not held back by malicious laws and does not wait upon the decree of the mob or the deliberations of the people. So it is not to be wondered at if he strikes first in conducting his affairs, while we are still pondering remedies when our affairs are already lost. Certain of our citizens took extremely poor advice and rejected the Pisan Giovanni Grassolini when he offered us alliance and confederation with the Pisans, spurning the advice of those who pointed out the danger of that city coming into Giangaleazzo's power. If that danger had been blocked then, we would not be beset with dangers as we are now. Recently, too, certain men took equally bad advice and rejected the Perugian envoys who came to us to inform us of the dangers they were in and asking to join our confederation and alliance. They shouted that the men who thought they should join were trying to start a new war against the pope. The Perugians then turned to Giangaleazzo and have now, I believe, been caught in his net.

Now we are at last starting to think about the danger threatening us from that source. We should blame no one but ourselves; nothing has made the Duke of Milan's power in Tuscany grow more than our own sloth and weakness. But what has been done up to now cannot be changed. In future, however, if you do not rein in calumnies of this sort and excessive license in belittling others and the impediments that stand in the way of quick action, you may expect no remedy for your condition. But if you wish to correct behavior of this sort and take correct counsel from us, there is still good hope that we may preserve not only our liberty, but our prestige (status) as well. For we do have a large and wealthy city, a wide dominion, many towns besides, a large and strong population and almost innumerable fortified citadels. Our adversary will come to realize that it is a harder matter to crush us than he thinks, if we have the will to act as men and protect the position and the liberty left us by our forebears.

But above all it is necessary to remove now the evils I have just enumerated from the city. Let there be some vigilant persons in the state who have the power to act without being compelled to refer every single thing to the multitude and wait upon their decree. State affairs generally require swiftness and secrecy, things which are very much at odds with mass decision-making. Let the slanders and indictments of calumniators against great men cease. Let everyone understand the grave perils that threaten us and the great virtue and industry and expense it will require to ward them off. Only after these steps have been taken at home, I think, should we make provision for foreign affairs; let us provide ourselves with soldiers and a captain-general who may stand ready for our expeditions. We shall be more respected by both friends and enemies if they see we have sufficient power about us; if we lack such power, everyone will despise us. This is my general advice.

Renaissance Editions, Translations, and Compendia of Francesco Patrizi of Siena's Political Works (Chapter 16)

Comparative data compiled from the *Universal Short Title Catalogue (USTC)* and other bibliographic repertories listed below shows that Machiavelli's *Prince* and *Discourses* were the most popular political treatises of the sixteenth century, there being some 82 imprints, half in Italian. The Latin translations of Machiavelli's treatises were printed 12 times. Patrizi was more frequently printed in the more prestigious, international scholarly language, Latin (34 times), not counting 14 printings of the Latin epitome. Machiavelli was printed in French twice as often as Patrizi (29 printings), but if one adds the popular French epitome of Patrizi the two authors are nearly equal (24 printings). Aristotle's *Politics,* by contrast, was published only 26 times (24 in Latin) and Jean Bodin's political works 40 times (27 times in French, 8 times in Latin, 5 times in other languages). The first edition of Bodin's *De la république,* however, appeared in 1577; the more authoritative Latin version in 1586.

I EDITIONS OF PATRIZI'S LATIN TEXT

De institutione reipublicae	*De institutione regni et regis*
Prato 1514	Paris 1519
Paris 1518	Paris 1520
Paris 1520	Paris: Galiotus à Prato, 1531
Paris 1534	Paris: Jacobus Parvus, 1531
Paris 1569	Paris: Gilles Gourbin, 1567 = *USTC* 139755
Paris 1575	Paris: Gilles Gourbin, 1567 = *USTC* 158227
Paris 1577 (in *Opera*)	Paris 1567
Paris: Jean de Bordeaux, 1578	Paris: Jean de Bordeaux, 1578
Paris: Michel Julien, 1578	Paris: Jean Hulpeau, 1578
Paris: Jean Hulpeau, 1578	Paris: Marc Locqueneulx, 1578
Paris: Guillaume Julian, 1578	Paris 1582
Paris: Marc Locqueneulx, 1578	Montbéliard 1594 = *USTC* 110230

Paris 1585
Montbéliard 1594
Strasbourg 1594
Strasbourg 1595
Torgau 1599
Strasbourg 1608

Montbéliard, Strasbourg 1594 = *USTC* 658063
Strasbourg 1594 = *USTC* 658064
Torgau 1599
Strasbourg 1608

2 FRENCH TRANSLATIONS

Paris 1520
Paris 1528
Paris: Regnault, 1534
Paris: Cousteau, 1534
Lyons 1574
Paris 1584
Paris 1589
Paris 1590
Paris 1600

Paris 1577
Paris 1600

3 TRANSLATIONS INTO ITALIAN

Venice 1545

Venice 1547
Venice 1553
Venice 1569

4 OTHER VERNACULAR TRANSLATIONS

German: Mainz 1573
Spanish: Madrid 1591

5 EPITOME OF BOTH WORKS, IN LATIN

Paris 1520
Paris: Arnoul L'Angelier, 1543
Paris: Jean Fourcher, 1543
Paris: Charles L'Angelier, 1543
Paris: Oudin Petit, 1549
Paris: Jean Fourcher, 1549
Paris 1552
Paris 1559
Paris 1560
Paris 1566

Paris 1570
Paris 1574
Paris 1577
Cologne 1591

6 EPITOME OF BOTH WORKS, IN FRENCH

Paris 1544
Paris 1545
Paris 1546
Paris: Etienne Groulieau, 1549
Paris: Oudin Petit, 1549
Paris: Charles L'Angelier, 1549
Paris 1550 (in two parts)
Paris: Jean Ruelle, 1553
Paris: Madeleine Boursette, 1553
Paris: Guillaume Thibaut, 1553
Paris 1554
Paris 1584
Paris 1600

7 EPITOME OF BOTH WORKS, IN ENGLISH

London 1576

SOURCES

Edit16. Censimento nazionale delle edizioni italiane del XVI secolo (Istituto Centrale per il Catalogo
    Unico delle biblioteche italiane e per le informazioni bibliografiche)
Incunabula Short-Title Catalogue (British Library), online *(ISTC)*
Universal Short-Title Catalogue (University of St. Andrews), online *(USTC)*
WorldCat = Online Computer Library Center (OCLC), First Search (union catalogue)
Karlsruhe Virtueller Katalog (KVK), Karlsruhe Institut für Technologie

NOTES

NOTE ON SOURCES AND TRANSLATIONS

When quoting Renaissance texts I have in general not given the Latin or Italian text of quotations when these may be found in modern editions, but I have made exceptions in particular cases when terminology was of the essence. I do provide the Latin when quoting from manuscripts or early printed books that are not currently or easily available online. In these cases the capitalization and punctuation have been silently modernized. Modern text editions are referred to in the notes by author, short title, and editor(s); Renaissance text editions are referred to by author, title, and date; manuscripts by city, library, collection, and shelfmark. Fuller references are supplied under "Texts and Translations" in the Bibliography. Texts dated in the form "1346 / 1352" (for example) mean that, according to the best available evidence, the text was begun, completed, or published sometime between the two dates indicated.

All translations are my own, except where otherwise noted. For the convenience of the reader I have translated into English quotations from modern scholarly literature written in foreign languages. In translating Renaissance texts, when the original text uses masculine nouns, pronouns, or adjectives, I have not sought to make the source sound more feminist than it is by translating substantives or relative pronouns in masculine cases with "he or she," "a person," etc., or by altering singular persons to the plural number, or similar shifts. I have usually translated *vir* by "man" but *homo* in more gender-neutral ways. When describing or paraphrasing the views of Renaissance authors I have followed the same principle.

ABBREVIATIONS

The titles of classical texts when abbreviated follow those of the digital *OCD*.
ASF = Florence, Archivio di Stato
AW = Machiavelli, *The Art of War*
BAM = Milan, Biblioteca Ambrosiana
BAV = Vatican City, Biblioteca Apostolica Vaticana
BLF = Florence, Biblioteca Medicea Laurenziana
BNCF = Florence, Biblioteca Nazionale Centrale

BRF = Florence, Biblioteca Riccardiana

Cortesi-Fiaschi = Mariarosa Cortesi and Silvia Fiaschi. *Repertorio delle traduzioni umanistiche a stampa: Secoli XV–XVI.* 2 vols. Florence: SISMEL Edizioni del Galluzzo, 2008.

CTC = Paul Oskar Kristeller, F. Edward Cranz, Virginia Brown, and Greti Dinkova-Bruun, eds. *Catalogus Translationum et Commentariorum: Medieval and Renaissance Latin Translations and Commentaries, Annotated Lists, and Guides.* 11 vols. to date. Washington, DC: Catholic University of America Press; Toronto: Pontifical Institute of Mediaeval Studies Press, 1960–2016.

DBI = *Dizionario biografico degli italiani.* Rome: Treccani, 1960–. Cited from the unpaginated online version at treccani.it.

DH = Dionysius of Halicarnassus, *Roman Antiquities*

Disc. = Machiavelli, *Discourses on the First Decade of Titus Livy*

DL = Diogenes Laertius, *Lives of the Philosophers*

DVS = Petrarch, *De vita solitaria*

ed. princ. = *editio princeps,* first edition

Fam. = Petrarch, *Epistulae familiares*

FH = Machiavelli, *Florentine Histories*

Gilbert, *CW* = Niccolò Machiavelli. *The Chief Works, and Others,* translated by Allan Gilbert. 3 vols. Durham, NC: Duke University Press, 1965. Reprint, 1989.

Hoven = René Hoven. *Lexique de la prose latine de la Renaissance.* 2nd ed. Leiden: E. J. Brill, 2006.

inc. = *incipit*

ISTC = British Library. *Incunabula Short Title Catalogue.* Online at bl.uk /catalogues/istc/.

ITRL = I Tatti Renaissance Library

LSJ = Henry George Liddell and Robert Scott. *A Greek-English Lexicon,* revised and augmented throughout by Sir Henry Stuart Jones, with the assistance of Roderick McKenzie. 9th ed., with revised supplement, edited by P. G. W. Glare with the assistance of A. A. Thompson. Oxford: Clarendon Press, 1996.

MS, MSS = manuscript, manuscripts

New Pauly = *Brill's New Pauly Online: Encyclopedia of the Ancient World,* edited by Hubert Cancik and Helmuth Schneider (Antiquity) and Manfred Landfester (Classical Tradition). Leiden: E. J. Brill, 2005–.

OCD = Tim Whitmarsh, ed. *Oxford Classical Dictionary.* Online at classics .oxfordre.com.

OLD = P. G. W. Glare, ed. *Oxford Latin Dictionary.* Oxford: Clarendon Press, 1982.

PhE = Francesco Filelfo [Philelphus]. *Epistolae,* as referenced in the 48-book edition of his letters edited by Jeroen De Keyser (see the Bibliography).

PL = Jacques-Paul Migne, ed. *Patrologiae cursus completus, series latina.* 221 vols. Paris: J.-P. Migne, 1844–1891.

Pr. = Machiavelli, *The Prince*

Ramminger = Johann Ramminger. *Neulateinische Wortlist: Ein Wörterbuch des Lateinischen von Petrarca bis 1700.* Online at www.neulatein.de.

Rem. = Petrarch, *De remediis utriusque fortune*

Rezasco = Giulio Rezasco. *Dizionario del linguaggio italiano storico ed amministrativo.* Florence: Le Monnier, 1881. Reprint, Bologna: Forni, 1982.

RT = Biondo Flavio, *Roma Triumphans*

Sen. = Petrarch, *Res Seniles*

SEP = Edward N. Zalta, ed. *Stanford Encyclopedia of Philosophy.* Online at https://plato.stanford.edu.

SESL = Members of the Language Department, School of Economic Science, London, the anonymous translators of Marsilio Ficino's *Letters* (see the Bibliography)

SHA = *Scriptores Historiae Augustae*

SVF = Hans Friedrich August von Arnim, ed. *Stoicorum veterum fragmenta.* 4 vols. Leipzig: Teubner, 1903–1924. Reprint, Stuttgart: Teubner, 1978–1979.

TLG = *Thesaurus Linguae Graecae: A Digital Library of Greek Literature.* University of California, Irvine, 2001–, with updates. http://stephanus.tlg.uci.edu.

TLL = *Thesaurus linguae latinae.* Leipzig: Teubner, 1900–. Online edition, Berlin: de Gruyter, 2006. https://www.degruyter.com.

TOGB = *Tutte le opere di Giovanni Boccaccio,* edited by Vittore Branca. 10 vols. Milan: Mondadori, 1964–1994.

USTC = *Universal Short-Title Catalogue,* directed by Andrew Pettegree, hosted by the University of St. Andrews. https://www.ustc.ac.uk.

PREFACE

1 For a similar judgment, see Cappelli 2014a, 91, and note.

2 See Philip Jones in Law and Paton 2010, 5: "The argumentation on both sides was predictable and simple. The republicans' theme was liberty.... The monarchists' theme was order, peace and unity."

3 For the centrality of Latin to humanist culture, see Celenza 2004, 2018.

4 One finds this sentiment even in major historians such as Eric Cochrane; see Cochrane 1981, xiv–xv. The effect on Renaissance studies caused by the modern neglect of its Latin literature is discussed by Celenza 2004.

5 A deflationary account of humanist political education is given in Black 1998, 273–274. A Renaissance answer to the already common view that the wise did not act wisely was offered in Richard Pace, *De fructu qui ex doctrina percipitur,* ed. Manley and Sylvester, 15–19.

6 Baker 2015. For an example of eloquence understood as equivalent to civilization, see Chapter 1, page 23.

7 Grafton and Jardine 1986. For a resumé of the debate, see Black 2001, 12–33. Black 2007, 297–298, emphasizes the indirect moral benefits of schooling. Black shows in great empirical detail that there was little new (at least in Tuscany and at least before the later quattrocento) about the methods of humanist schoolmasters in their grammar teaching; see ibid., 46–52, 164–165, for a summary of his results. Yet this was never claimed to be a point of originality by the humanists themselves, who emphasized the recovery of eloquence (through study of the ancient art of rhetoric), the revival of Greek studies, the rediscovery and emendation of ancient books, and the formation of libraries. See for example Biondo Flavio's famous account of the Renaissance of letters in *Italy Illuminated* 6.25–31, ed. White, 300–309. These innovations of the humanists are acknowledged in Black 1998.

8 The celebrated printer Aldus Manutius in the preface to his own Latin grammar (1501, in Manutius, *Humanism and the Latin Classics,* ed. Grant, 194–201), addressed to grammar school teachers, gave a clear statement of priorities: "And so we must strive with all our strength to see to it that our young are taught virtuous behavior at the same time as they are being taught good letters *(bonae litterae),* since in no way can one of these be done without the other. But if one were to fall short in one area, I think that how to live an honorable life is more important than even how to acquire learning in the best possible way. For I prefer upright youths who know nothing of literature to immoral persons who know everything . . . but are as wicked as can be." Teachers are thus "the prime cause of all the good and bad things that are done in the world," and parents should be aware, in choosing teachers, of "how much good or harm teachers contribute to their cities *(civitates)."* *Civitates* could also be translated as "communities" or "states."

9 Platina writes of grammar in his oration *De laudibus bonarum artium,* ed. Vairani, 110, "for it contains the stone, the wood and the cement for building the edifice of the humanities." The wider point was already made by Seneca in *Epistulae Morales* 88.20.

10 A metaphor used by Marsilio Ficino when describing the riches of the Platonic corpus; see Hankins 2003–2004a, 201–202.

11 Cicero, *Pro Archia* 16: "These studies nurture adolescence, delight old age, embellish good times, offer refuge and solace in bad, are delightful at home and no obstacle in public life, they accompany us through the night-time, when travelling and in the country." For the importance of the *Pro Archia* in the humanist conception of education, see Chapter 2, page 46.

12 For humanist moralizing of the dinner party following ancient models, see Hankins, forthcoming. It may be noted that the commonest translation of the Greek *paideia,* culture, was *institutio* (for example in the title and preface to Filelfo's translation of the *Cyropaedia*).

13 For my special sense of the expression "classic music," see Hankins 2015b.

14 The evidence that elites persist and perpetuate themselves even in societies explicitly committed to egalitarianism such as Soviet Russia or American higher education is overwhelming: see Howard and Gaztambide-Fernández 2010.

15 See Marianne Pade in Ramminger, s.v. *humanitas* (2010). Baker 2015, 238–240, discusses the terms used for humanists and humanistic studies in contemporary writings.

16 Hankins 2005, 2017d.

17 See Witt 2000, 2011.

18 Hankins 1995a, 1996, 2000b; Cappelli 2008, 2009.

19 That the best regime was the central question of ancient political philosophy may well be an anachronistic assumption motivated by modern preoccupations. My own impression as a non-specialist is that the focus of modern scholarship on regime type in ancient political thought tends to obscure the equally important emphasis among the ancients on political education.

1. A CIVILIZATION IN CRISIS

1 Frobenius 1921. For Frobenius the term referred to the core modes of absorbing, expressing, and applying comprehensive beliefs in African societies. It described the relationship between the creative inner realm of belief, *Seelenraum,* and the environment those beliefs aimed to control, *Lebensraum.*

2 I take *paideuma* to be related to *paideia* in the realm of culture as in politics *politeuma* is related to *politeia* in Aristotle. A *politeuma* for Aristotle is the authoritative *(kurios)* element in a regime that governs it via deliberation; see Aristotle, *Politics* 3.1279a25–28. This passage is restated by Ober 1993, 131, to mean "The polis is a *koinonia* [community] of citizens whose practices and norms are arranged in respect to the beliefs and powers of the dominant subsociety [*politeuma*]." (The closest relevant sense of the ancient Greek word παίδευμα means simply "a thing taught.").

3 Appiah 2010. Appiah gives as examples the moral revolutions that brought about the end of slavery in the Atlantic world, foot-binding in China, and dueling in Europe.

4 See Voice 2014: "A comprehensive doctrine is a set of beliefs affirmed by citizens concerning a range of values, including moral, metaphysical, and religious commitments, as well as beliefs about personal virtues, and political beliefs about the way society ought to be arranged. They form a conception of the good and inform judgments concerning 'what is of value in life, the ideals of personal character, as well as ideals of friendship and of familial and associational relationships, and much else that is to inform our conduct, and in the limit to our life as a whole.'" Rawls contrasts comprehensive doctrines with a "political point of view," which may draw on reasonable comprehensive doctrines but is "freestanding," independent of them and capable of negotiating between them.

5 "It is my belief that it is not religion or culture at the root of human conflict but the way in which groups use religion or culture to dominate one another. Let me hasten to add that if it were not religion or culture that people used as a stick with which to beat others, they would just use something else" (Jean Vanier, *Becoming Human* [1998]).

6 On comprehensive doctrines see my comments on humanist public morality in the Conclusion, page 508. The term *paideuma* I believe to be useful in analyzing how comprehensive doctrines relate to elements in a civilization that may not share its conception of the good. In the modern world it might apply to dogmatic religions such as radical Islam or to contemporary progressivism. A *paideuma* will experience severe stress when it gains or loses political power, and what counts as the shared public culture and the autonomy of the secular

(or the exopaideumic) will become matters of intense contestation. The advantage of the term paideuma is that it enables us to speak dynamically and historically about the life of belief systems and to ask the question how and why some make themselves into comprehensive doctrines, while others may transform themselves (or be forcibly transformed from without) from comprehensive doctrines into benign, mutually tolerant elements in civil society, as in the "denominationalism" of American religions. For the latter, see Taylor 2002, 73–75.

7　In conceptualizing the relationship between Christianity and its secular political and cultural inheritances, I have found illuminating the studies of R. A. Markus, particularly Markus 1988, 1991, and 2006. See also Marenbon 2015 for the wide range of attitudes among Christian philosophers and theologians to the questions of whether pagans could be virtuous and wise and could merit salvation in the next life.

8　Brown 1997, 26.

9　See esp. St. Augustine's *De doctrina christiana,* quoted in note 65 below.

10　I simplify a complex reality that includes the destructive impact of barbarian invasions on educational institutions. I also pass over revivals of classical studies in the Carolingian and Ottonian Empires, which did not produce comprehensive paideumata of the Petrarchan type. For a full account of the survival of classical culture in this period, see Riché 1999. For the limits of medieval literary humanism, see Jaeger 1994.

11　The most insightful account of the nature and goals of scholasticism remains Southern 1995–1999.

12　The classic studies on the Renaissance conception of the humanities were written by Paul Oskar Kristeller; see for example Kristeller 1990a. The phrase *studia humanitatis et litterarum* is modeled on Cicero, *Pro Archia* 3. Kristeller's definition of the *studia humanitatis* was extended and given a diachronic dimension in Kohl 1992; it was related to the humanists' own image of their movement in Baker 2015. In this book I will use the term "humanities," in this sense, to signify the *studia humanitatis*—the direct ancestors of the modern humanities—rather than in the meta-historical, quasi-scientific, and demoralized sense confected by Bod 2013. On Bod's conception of the humanities and its limits, see Malcolm 2014.

13　See Falkeid 2017 for reactions to the long "Babylonian Captivity" of the Church in Avignon.

14　The Italian rejection of French culture in the fourteenth century in part reflected the failure of French knights not only in the Crusades but also in the Hundred Years' War; by Petrarch's time they were no longer the admired and feared warriors of the crusading legends. See Petrarch, *Fam.* 22.14, tr. Fantham 4.14.

15　*Sen.* 10.2, tr. Fantham 9.1.135.

16　*Sen.* 17.2, tr. Fantham 2.17.29.

17　Dante, *Purgatorio* 6.76–77, 88–89 (tr. Hollander, modified slightly). The "harness" is of course the *Corpus iuris civilis,* Roman civil law, codified under the Emperor Justinian.

18　*Fam.* 20.4, tr. Fantham 3.14, to Marco Portinario of Genoa, written 1355 / 1359. Petrarch's view of Roman law in this period is shaped by his reading of Cicero's *Pro Caecina,* esp. 65–78.

19　Petrarch also expounds on the senescence of Roman law in his *speculum principis* in the form of a letter-treatise to Niccola Acciaiuoli, discussed in Chapter 5. He is here perhaps gesturing toward the new conception of law as autonomous and jurists as mere technicians that appears in the early empire, for which see Frier 1985, esp. 184–185. Petrarch and the humanists are consistently hostile to the idea of legitimation through mere legal procedure, a central legacy of Roman legal thinking under the empire. For the significance of Petrarch's historical understanding of the development of Roman law, see Orestano 1987, 188–189. On Petrarch's considerable attainments as a student of Roman law, see Lupinetti 1999.

20 The text is found in Petrarch, *Invectives,* ed. Marsh, 222–363.

21 Cicero, *Tusculan Disputations* 5.4.10. The story of Socrates' "conversion" to moral philosophy was well known in antiquity and descends from Plato's famous account in *Phaedo* 96a–c.

22 Hankins 2007d, 2008b, 2010b.

23 Petrarch, *Invectives* 108, ed. Marsh, 317. As David Marsh points out in his note to this passage, "a peddler of morality" is a mistranslation of Aristotle, *Metaphysics* 1.6, 987b1–2. The alleged enmity between Aristotle and Socrates is based on faulty readings in Cicero, *De officiis* 1.1.4, which alludes to the enmity between Aristotle and the orator Isocrates.

24 Petrarch, *Invectives* 109, ed. Marsh, 317. See Cicero *De officiis* 1.5.15, citing Plato, *Phaedrus,* 250D. The whole passage about the need for an eloquence that will move the audience is doubtless inspired by passages in Cicero's writings such as *Brutus* 131 or *De optimo genere oratorum* 1.3, perhaps also by Cicero's criticisms of the Stoics for excessive detachment and use of technical language in expounding the teachings of philosophy, e.g., at *De finibus* 4.3.7. Luke 24:32 may not have been absent from his thoughts.

25 Petrarch, *Invectives* 110, ed. Marsh, 317.

26 *Fam.* 6.3 (from the 1340s).

27 *Rem.* 2.39, tr. Rawski 2:101.

28 Romans 13:1–5: "Let every soul be subject to higher powers: for there is no power but from God: and those that are, are ordained of God. Therefore he that resisteth the power, resisteth the ordinance of God. And they that resist, purchase to themselves damnation. . . . For he is God's minister to thee, for good. But if thou do that which is evil, fear: for he beareth not the sword in vain. For he is God's minister: an avenger to execute wrath upon him that doeth evil. Wherefore be subject of necessity, not only for wrath, but also for conscience' sake" (KJV).

29 On Ockham's doctrine of resistance, see Miethke 2004; on St. Thomas Aquinas', see *Summa theologiae* 1–2 q. 96, a. 4, and 2-2, q. 104, a. 5.

30 *Fam.* 18.1.

31 Petrarch, *Sine nomine* 4.63, ed. Cascio, 72.

32 Petrarch, *Metrical Epistles* 3.33, to Francesco Nelli, 1351 / 1353, ed. Schönberger, 322. The whole letter, rarely cited, is highly revealing of Petrarch's attitude toward his times.

33 *Sen.* 7, tr. Fantham 7.6. The letter plays on the dual sense of wander, *errare,* to mean aimless physical movement but also error of thought. See also *Fam.* 18.1.

34 Petrarch, *Africa* 9.453–457 (lines 635–641 in the Bergin and Wilson translation). This passage of book 9 was probably drafted in the early 1350s, after the death of King Robert and the Black Death.

35 Petrarch, *Africa* 9.458–461 (lines 642–647 in the Bergin and Wilson translation).

36 *Fam.* 12.2, tr. Fantham 5.5, to Nicola Acciaiuoli, discussed further in Chapter 5, page 158. On the popularity of Petrarch's works in the Renaissance, see Hankins 2007–2008b.

37 *Fam.* 13.6, tr. Fantham 5.5.32. The passage is inspired by Cicero's *Pro Archia,* for whose influence see Chapter 2, page 46.

38 McClure 1991. See also the important study of Panizza 1991.

39 Petrarch, *De viris illustribus,* pref. 6, ed. Ferrone, pp. 2–4.

40 Witt 2000. Petrarch's most important predecessors in terms of virtue politics are Albertano of Brescia, Brunetto Latini, and Albertino Mussato: see Witt 2011, 438–485. The Renaissance

humanists themselves regarded Petrarch as the real founder of their movement: see Mazzocco 2006; Hankins 2007–2008b; Baker 2015.

41 For Petrarch's personal charisma, see the remarkable description of how Petrarch affected others in Boccaccio, *Trattatello in laude di Dante* 7, ed. Ricci, esp. caps. 21–23, where Petrarch's speech is compared to that of the Sirens.

42 For an example of a humanist formally challenging the precedence of lawyers to (humanist) secretaries at the papal court, see Bruni, *Epistolae* 5.5 (November 1426, to Pope Martin V), ed. Mehus 2: 25–29.

43 An informed sketch of the development of the movement is given in Kohl 1992, 201–202, who regards the key moment in the movement's self-consciousness as having occurred in 1415, when Guarino of Verona and Francesco Barbaro of Venice visited the scholars of Florence. A far more detailed and elaborate narrative of early Italian humanism from the late thirteenth through the early fifteenth century is given in Witt 2000. Closer to the view presented here of the genesis of Renaissance humanism as a movement is Revest 2013, 2014.

44 A standard point of reference for the meaning of the liberal arts as those worthy of a free person was Seneca, *Epistulae morales* 88. Seneca requires teachers of the liberal arts to reshape the soul like philosophers before their teaching can be counted as truly liberal; he condemns mere antiquarianism as frivolous.

45 Kallendorf 2002. The enlarged role of humanist oratory in social and civic rituals from the 1390s on is stressed by Witt 2000, chapter 8, and Maxson 2014, passim.

46 Brucker 1977, 290–293, traces this process in the *Consulte e practiche*, the records of public debate in Florence.

47 See Dionisotti 1984 and Kristeller 1974 for the involvement of members of religious orders in the humanist movement.

48 Grendler 2002; Davies 1998; Rummel 1995.

49 Petrarch, *Invectives* (*De ignorantia* 92), ed. Marsh, 302: "Summum enim ingenii et scientie argumentum claritas."

50 How well the ordinary Roman could understand formal Latin was a matter of debate among humanists in the quattrocento, however; for this debate, see Celenza 2018, chapters 5 and 9.

51 Murphy 1983.

52 See Francesco Patrizi's standard work of humanist political theory, *De inst. r.p.* 2.4, 1534, f. XXIr–v, where eloquence is described as medicine for the soul, repressing vice and arousing the torpid; the mistress of public affairs, providing the people with leadership. "Et si recte iudicare volumus, ex omnibus disciplinis nulla magis congruat civitati quam oratoria" (And rightly considered, of all the disciplines, none is more appropriate to the state than the oratorical discipline). For the praise of eloquence as an art that imparts to a whole civilization the ability to communicate its most sublime wisdom, see Pontano, *Aegidius* 24, ed. Gaisser. For eloquence defined as "civilized refinement," see below. For the belief that the only true purpose of eloquence was moral transformation, see Bracciolini, *De avaritia*, 3–5, tr. Kohl, 245–247.

53 Horace, *Ars poetica* 333–334, 343–344. The idea is also found in Aristotle's *Poetics*.

54 Bruni, *Epistolae* 6.6, ed. Mehus, 2: 48–51; tr. Griffiths, Hankins, and Thompson, 251–253, which contains a typical pitch for why a young man should study the humanities rather than law. Only the former studies will make him a better man, even though the latter is more saleable (*vendibilis*). For Poggio's critique of law, which went much deeper than Bruni's, see Krantz 1987, and for the humanist critique of the modern discipline of law in general, see Chapter 2, page 50.

55 Barbaro, *Preface to Themistius' Paraphrase of the Physics,* dedicated to Antonio de Ferrariis (il Galateo): "Nihil aeque pernitiosum in omni republica est quam ista persuasio, nihil tota vita incommodius indignius foedius quam perversio haec et depravatio studiorum. Addicerem hoc necessariis rebus et testibus, sed nolo esse longior in re non dubia. Illud non possum tacere, hoc quod vulgo creditur, philosophos non esse rebus gerendis aptos nanosque, non aliunde habuisse ortum quam quod ex his plurimi, dum se totos ponunt in una illa cui addicti sunt artes, aspernantur et deserunt cetera, eloquentiam abdicant, idest cultum et elegantiam vitae, historiam negligunt, idest magistram et ducem bene ac beate vivendi, de qua et usus rerum omnium provenit et peritia tota reipublicae administrandae constituendaeque paritur. Hi cum legati ad externos mittuntur, cum praetores iuridicundo sedent, cum in senatu sententiam rogantur, mirum non est si aliquando presentibus risum excutiunt, si fatua, si delira, si extrema deblaterant, si tota eorum non plus incompta quam imprudens oratio est. Et Hercules nullum hominum genus visitur tam abhorrens a sensu communi, tam distorto et corrupto iudicio, quam qui aut philosophiam aut ius civile sine literis cultioribus adierunt. Sed mittamus (obsecro) hos qui non verbis sed ferula commonendi essent." For Barbaro's own public eloquence, see Cappelli 2010c.

56 For the defense of Aristotle's eloquence as a humanist theme, see Griffiths, Hankins, and Thompson 1987, 263–265, 289–291 (Bruni's *Life of Aristotle*); Botley 2004, 41–62.

57 Botley 2004.

58 See Bruni's letter to Niccolò Niccoli of 1404 / 1405 describing the thrilling experience of translating Plato's *Phaedo:* "Although I had already, my dear Niccolò, a strong love for your Plato (for such I like to call him for whom you are always contending against the ignorant mob), when I began to translate him, so great was the increase of goodwill I experienced, that it seems to me that I have come to love him now for the first time, and that before I had merely had affection for him. You can't imagine anything more wisely or eloquently written. I understand this so much better now since for my task of translating I am compelled to examine intensely from every side and exhaust the several sayings of the man. . . . Before, I had merely met Plato; now, I believe, I know him. If I shall ever finish his books, translating them the way I should like, even you, dear Niccolò, will despise everything you have yet read in comparison with the majesty of this man. He has the utmost urbanity, the finest method of disputation, and the deepest subtlety; his fruitful and divine sentiments are conveyed with a marvelous pleasantness on the part of the interlocutors, and with extraordinary verbal power. In his discourse there is the greatest facility, and much admirable χάρις [gracefulness] as the Greeks say. There is nothing labored, nothing violent. All is said as though by a man who has words and their laws at his command, that best and richest of natures expressing all the sentiments of his mind with the greatest facility and beauty." See Hankins 1990a, 1: 42.

59 Hankins 2003–2004b.

60 Hankins and Palmer 2008. The *CTC* is the principal reference work devoted to documenting this movement. A cursory examination of the eleven published volumes discloses that the vast majority of translations were made during the Renaissance rather than in the Middle Ages. See also Maillard, Kecskeméti, and Portalier 1995, and Cortesi-Fiaschi for a sense of the enormous scope of the secular civilizational project of transferring Greek literature, science, and philosophy into the Latin language.

61 Annas 2017.

62 The inclusion of Greek philosophy in the curriculum of the humanities might be taken as an implicit answer to Seneca's criticism of the liberal arts in *Epistulae morales* 88 (see note 44 above)

that they were trivial and had no moral effect by comparison with philosophy. By adding philosophy to the liberal arts and forging the *studia humanitatis,* literary studies would acquire a deeper moral purpose than they had usually enjoyed in ancient Rome or medieval Italy. A similar philosophical prejudice against "grammarians" is expressed by Seneca's younger contemporary Epictetus in his *Enchiridion* (cap. 49), a text which first became available in Latin in Niccolò Perotti's translation of 1450 and was later (1479) translated by Poliziano for Lorenzo de'Medici. See Hankins and Palmer 2008, 40–41.

63 Platina, *De laudibus bonarum artium,* ed. Vairani, 110–111. Bartolomeo della Fonte borrowed extensively from Platina's oration in his own academic prolusions for courses held in Florence; see Trinkaus 1983.

64 Ronconi 1976; Marenbon 2015.

65 St. Augustine, *De doctrina christiana* 40.60. He goes on: "In the same way all branches of heathen learning have not only false and superstitious fancies and heavy burdens of unnecessary toil, which every one of us, when going out under the leadership of Christ from the fellowship of the heathen, ought to abhor and avoid; but they contain also liberal instruction which is better adapted to the use of the truth, and some most excellent precepts of morality; and some truths in regard even to the worship of the One God are found among them."

66 Giovanni d'Andrea, *Commentary on the Liber sextus,* "De regulis iuris," *ad* 2: "Nam subiectum scientiae iuris canonici est homo dirigibilis non solum in bonum commune, sed in Deum … sed in materia non concernente periculum animae, leges sunt servanda in foro suo et ius canonicum in suo. Nam Papa non potest tollere leges quoad iudicium seculare nisi in iis in quibus vertitur periculum animae, cum potestates sint distinctae, videlicet ecclesiastica a potestate seculari." It may be noted that Giovanni d'Andrea's view of the scope of papal power was rather narrow by the standards of most papalists. On Petrarch's studies with him, see Lupinetti 1999, 30–31.

67 Particularly illuminating is Markus 1988, who revises his earlier views somewhat in Markus 2006. For the distinction between canon and civil law, see Brague 2007, chapter 9.

68 See Chapter 7, page 199.

69 See D'Elia 2016, esp. the conclusion. Sigismondo's rebellious pagan spirit was in part motivated by his hatred of the humanist pope, Pius II, who famously "canonized him to hell." Cappelli 2017c sees the humanist movement in general as preparing the ground for the modern idea of the autonomy of human culture from religion, a view of their movement that would probably have surprised and distressed most humanists of the Renaissance.

70 The text is in the Loeb Library, vol. 270, 378–436, tr. Roy J. Deferrari. Bruni's Latin translation was by far his most popular work, preserved in over 440 MSS and printed well over 100 times before 1650; see Hankins 1997 and Fedwick 1993–2004 (vol. 2, part 2, of Fedwick contains a list of manuscripts and editions containing Bruni's translation and other translations of the work).

71 Patrizi, *De inst. r.p.* 3.4, 1531, f. XXXIXr–v. On Patrizi, see further in Chapters 2, 16, and 17. It should be noted that Patrizi held the office of bishop of Gaeta, though his education was humanistic rather than clerical. By contrast, in a dialogue by the schoolmaster Tito Livio Frulovisi, which survives in only two manuscripts, including the dedication copy for Leonello d'Este, the humanist calls for the clergy of a *respublica* to be subject to the prince in matters relative to civic life (Frulovisi, *De republica,* ed. Previté-Orton, 357), a position reminiscent of the Erastian attitude of Machiavelli and some sixteenth-century Protestant political writers. (For the second manuscript—Seville, Biblioteca Capitular y Colombina MS 7-2-23, which documents

the date of composition as 1435—see Kristeller 1963–1997. The latter codex is possibly the presentation copy for Humfrey, Duke of Gloucester.)

72 In Giovanni Pontano's dialogue of 1501, *Aegidius* 31–32, the interlocutor Tristano, called upon to address the subject of the afterlife in *sermo Christianus,* discusses the difficulty of using humanistic Latin, "more appropriate and applicable to the discussion of human matters," to treat of sacred matters. Among Roman humanists it became the practice to translate ecclesiastical and theological terms into classical Latin, thus arousing the mockery of non-Roman humanists such as Erasmus; see DellaNeva 2007.

73 This is not to say there was no criticism from clerical conservatives such as Bruni's nemesis, Giovanni Dominici, and later St. Antoninus of Florence. See Hay and Law 1989, 294–297.

74 Platina, *De laudibus bonarum artium,* ed. Vairani, 111. Lapo da Castiglionchio in his *De curiae commodis* (1438), edited in Celenza 1999, 152–153, distinguishes *studia haec humanitatis* from theology, mathematics, natural philosophy, astronomy, music, and law.

75 Hankins 2007a, 2017d.

76 See Chapter 18 for the impact of the *calamità d'Italia.*

77 Quirini, *De republica,* ed. Seno and Ravegnani, 161. The interesting substitution of liberty for the traditional fourth virtue, courage, shows the close connection in humanist minds between liberty and virtue, for which see further Chapter 2, page 57.

78 Hankins 2007a. On the efforts of Italian universities of the period to teach ethics, increasingly influenced by humanism, see Lines 2003.

2. VIRTUE POLITICS

1 For the "legitimacy deficit" of Renaissance Italy, see Cappelli 2016b, 7–9.

2 See Stacey 2000; Roick 2017, 163–166.

3 See Chapter 4 and note 81 below.

4 Black 2009.

5 Annas 2017.

6 See Rawls 2005, where the liberal political project is also justified by appeal to the Kantian notion of public reason. The argument that republican government is superior because it reflects the will of a larger number of persons was, however, known to the Renaissance; see Brandolini, *Republics and Kingdoms* 3.47, ed. Hankins, 202. For a more primitive version, see Frulovisi, *De republica,* ed. Previté-Orton, 316, where one of the interlocutors (Ottino Caracciolo, count of Nicastro) defends popular rule on the grounds that it looks out for the utility of the citizens better than other forms of rule, which look more to the utility of the rulers. Ottino personally is a royalist and in the dialogue defends popular government merely for the sake of argument; at the end of the book the royalist arguments are allowed to carry the day.

7 See Macedo 2013 for the presence of meritocratic elements in the U.S. constitution.

8 *Digest,* praef. 1 (*Constitutio "Deo auctore"*): "Deo auctore nostrum gubernantes imperium, quod nobis a caelesti maiestate traditum est."

9 See Quaglione 2012b, 67–68, for the constraints imposed by the necessity for a sovereign not to undermine his own sovereignty, as expressed in the law *Digna vox* (in the *Codex* of Justinian 1.14.4, under *De legibus*).

10 *Digest* 1.3.32.2 (Julianus): "Inveterata consuetudo pro lege non immerito custoditur, et hoc est ius quod dicitur moribus constitutum; nam, cum ipsae leges nulla alia ex causa nos teneant, quam quod iudicio populi receptae sunt, merito et ea, quae sine ullo scripto populus probavit,

tenebunt omnes." Brunt 1977, 116, writes: "Even in the late empire the emperor was in principle elective, just as the kings had been, and at his election the people, eventually the senate as its representative, invested him with all its own sovereignty."

11 *Digest* 1.4.1, pr. (Ulpian): "Quod principi placuit, legis habet vigorem: utpote cum lege regia, quae de imperio eius lata est, populus ei et in eum omne suum imperium et potestatem conferat."

12 Canning 1996, 7–9; Lee 2016, chapters 1 and 2.

13 Marsilius of Padua, *Defensor Pacis* 44–49, 61–63, 65–72, 88–90.

14 See Spade and Panaccio 2015.

15 See Langston 2015.

16 See Finnis 2017.

17 For the influence of this text, see Chapter 17.

18 Giles of Rome, *De regimine principum* 3.2.5, ed. 1607, 461–465, says hereditary succession is better for kings, on patrimonial grounds, so that it can be transmitted like our other goods and rights. This judgment is echoed by Bartolus in his *De regimine civitatis* 2, ed. Quaglione, 167.

19 McAleer 1999, 34.

20 Hendrick 2009; Stadter 2009.

21 For an overview, see Hursthouse 2013. For a more extended treatment, see Annas 2011. This is not to say that MacIntyre would describe himself as an exponent of virtue ethics in its current form. My term "virtue politics" overlaps a good deal with the concept of "political meritocracy" in modern political science, where it is associated with Chinese political Confucianism (see note 63 below). Ancient Chinese philosophical terminology even has a term correlative to "virtue politics," i.e., *dezhi;* see Schwartz 1985, 40–55; for its use in modern political Confucianism, see Kim 2018, 8, 200, 241.

22 The ancient source most in evidence in this way of understanding legitimacy is Seneca's *De clementia;* for its influence on the Renaissance genre of the "mirror of princes" see Stacey 2007.

23 The *locus classicus* for this form of legitimacy comes in Petrarch's *Invective against a Man of High Rank with No Knowledge or Virtue,* in Petrarch, *Invectives,* ed. Marsh, 180–222. For discussion, see Chapter 4, page 120, and Roick 2017, 163–166.

24 See Chapters 4 and 19.

25 See *Rem.* 2.80, tr. Rawski 3: 187. After advising the tyrant that his immorality explained why he had lost power, and citing Aristotle's advice to the tyrant (*Politics* 5.11) how he can retain power by benefitting the people, Petrarch writes, "Observation of these and similar things, endorsed by Aristotle and myself, makes ruling a more stable business. However, a lord should sincerely try actually to be what Aristotle would have him appear to be. Pretense, no matter how artfully and cleverly practiced, cannot last long under the gaze of so many people who are directly involved." On moral sincerity as a source of authenticity, see Conclusion, page 507.

26 See for example Pope Pius II's vivid account of his own election in his *Commentaries* 1.36, ed. Meserve and Simonetta, 177–203.

27 Grieco 1987, 2003, forthcoming.

28 Dante, *Purgatorio* 7.121–123: "How seldom human worth ascends from branch / to branch, and this is willed by Him who grants / that gift, that one may pray to Him for it!" (tr. Mandelbaum). For Dante's views on the sources of nobility, see Santagata 2016, 176–181.

29 For the medieval background of the theme of true nobility, see Robiglio 2006 and 2015. Dante considers the Romans' virtue a proof of their legitimacy rather than a cause of it; see Chapter 8, page 234.

30 For example, Platina, *De laudibus bonarum ariium,* ed. Vairani, 111: "Non te latet, beatissime pater, Kartaginem foedifragam et crudelem corruisse, Corinthum petulantem et superbam incendio consumptam, urbem Romae, imperio orbis terrarum potitam, auaritia et libidine ciuium suorum eo loci redactam, ut quae ante caeteris nationibus imperitare consueuerat, nunc omnibus cum dedecore et turpitudine pareat." (It doesn't escape you, most blessed father, that Carthage came to grief for its cruelty and faithlessness, that Corinth was consumed by fire in its proud petulance, that the city of Rome, having attained empire over the whole world, was reduced by the avarice and lust of its own citizens to the place where she, once accustomed to command other nations, now exposes her shame and disgrace before all the world.) See Chapter 11 for Biondo's argument to the same effect.

31 Landino, *De vera nobilitate,* ed. Liaci, 49; tr. Rabil, 212. Landino mentions Plato as the source of his idea of true nobility.

32 Buonaccorso, *On Nobility,* tr. Rabil, 40–52 (speech of Flaminius). The text was generally (but falsely) attributed to Leonardo Bruni, which could only have increased its authority; it was widely circulated in the original Latin as well as in Italian, German, French, and English. The statement quoted above is put in the mouth of the interlocutor Flaminius, whose opinion is plainly the one endorsed by Buonaccorso himself.

33 Rabil 1991, 118–119. Rabil's translation is based on the Latin text in *Caroli Poggi De nobilitate liber disceptatorius, et Leonardo Chiensis De vera nobilitate tractatus apologeticus cum eorum vita et annotationibus Abbatis Michaelis Justiniani* (Avellino: heredes Camilli Caballi, 1657), which I was not able to consult.

34 Nesi, *De moribus,* cited from BLF, MS Plut. 77.24, f. 113v: ". . . cum honores, dignitates ac cetera praemia insigniaque virtutum ita in civitate dividuntur, ut ad unum quemque sua debitaque portio deferatur, et qui de re publica praeclarius quodammodo meritus est, praeclarioribus etiam praemiis afficiatur, et qui ceteros virtute excellit ceteros quoque excellat auctoritate; pro singulorum enim civium meritis virtutibusque decernendi sunt honores dignitatesque conferendae."

35 For humanist efforts to adjust the claims of heredity and virtue, see Cappelli 2016c and Chapter 17 in this volume. Tito Livio Frulovisi (*De republica,* ed. Previté-Orton, 298–299) considers the virtue of the prince, his adherence to law, and the love and voluntary obedience of the people all to be signs of legitimacy, and whether he comes to power via a hereditary claim or via election by the people is a matter of indifference. Venetian patrician Lauro Quirini, the humanist author most inclined to defend the role of heredity in forming a noble character, still makes the virtue of rulers the *principalissimam causam* and goal of the ideal state in his *De republica* (ed. Seno and Ravegnani, 136, 139–140).

36 *Fam.* 4.7, tr. Fantham 3.5.5; *Fam.* 11.16, tr. Fantham 6.6.20–23; *Rem.* 1.16. This view presents a sharp contrast with the view of both Plato and Aristotle that banausic work is incompatible with the acquisition of virtue; see Aristotle, *Politics* 7.8, 1328b–1329a. The humanists identified more with the opinion of the *novus homo* Cicero, who naturally approved of social mobility for the virtuous.

37 See Chapter 7, page 202.

38 See Chapter 11.

39 See Gosepath 2011. Unsurprisingly, equality in the capacity for virtue is not among the varieties discussed. The concept of equality in the capacity for virtue can, however, be paralleled in ancient Confucianism; see Chan 2014, 11, 78, 145.

40 Raaflaub 2004; on the Roman conception of liberty in Cicero's time see Wirszubski 1954. The idea that all humans have an equal capacity for virtue—by no means held by all humanists—probably reflects Christian anthropological conceptions; see Waldron 2002 on Christianity and modern ideas of equality.

41 Platina, *De vera nobilitate,* ed. 1529, 172; tr. Rabil, 282 (translation modified): "Nobilitatis enim proprium est recta sequi, gaudere officio, cupiditatibus imperare, auaritiam coercere. Hoc qui facit, etiam si ex infima sorte hominum natus fuerit, is merito suo nobilis haberi et dici potest. Neque est cur parentem rerum omnium naturam (ut quidam improbi faciunt) reprehendimus, quod hos nobiles, illos uero ignobiles faciat? Aequalem siquidem omnibus temperamentum praestat, non genus, non potentiam, non opes inspiciens, eadem [enim], quoad animum pertinet, nascendi ratio in privatorum hominum filiis est quae in principum ac regum natis, licet ii in purpura et magnis domibus, illi in centonibus et casulis plerunque nascantur.... Seneca... philosophus insignis... 'Non fuit,' inquit, 'Socrates patricius, non eques Romanus, quem tamen philosophia non accepit, sed nobilem reddidit.'" The Senecan quotation is from *Epistulae morales* 44.2. Seneca is the likeliest Stoic source for the virtue egalitarianism of the humanists: see *De beneficiis* 3.18.2, where Seneca writes, "Virtue closes the door to no man; it is open to all, admits all, invites all, the freeborn and the freedman, the slave and the king, and the exile; neither family nor fortune determines its choice—it is satisfied with the naked human being" (Loeb translation).

42 This was a major theme of Boccaccio's *Famous Women.* Mario Equicola's *On Women* makes the argument on psychological and physiological grounds.

43 Bracciolini, *De vera nobilitate,* ed. Canfora, 36; tr. Rabil, 86. Elsewhere in the same dialogue (84) Poggio claims that nobility, which is "the radiance of virtue," "belongs to us through our own will and power and cannot be withdrawn or taken from us against our will." A similar view, that virtue and nobility are easily acquired by anyone who desires them, is found in Alberti, *Della famiglia,* prologue (*Opere volgari,* ed. Grayson, 1: 9), and in his *De iciarchia* (ibid., 2: 222). See Chapter 13.

44 For Cicero's classic praise of an elite "open to the industry and virtue of all citizens," see his *Pro Sestio* 137.

45 Luscombe 1998.

46 Aristotle, *Politics* 5.1, 1301b. Compare 4.8.1294a, where Aristotle seems more dismissive of "gentle birth" as an element in true aristocracy. Aristotle is even more explicit about the role played by good birth in achieving happiness in his *Rhetoric,* also a well-known text in the Renaissance. What Aristotle's real views were is debated in Poggio's *De nobilitate,* where an effort is made to defend the self-sufficiency of virtue in Stoic terms and to devalue Aristotle's contrary opinion on the importance of external goods. The interlocutor who defends the humanist view claims that when Aristotle said that nobility depended on *externa* (listed as "divitias, genus, patria, corporis et fortune adiumenta"—riches, ancestry, homeland, and aids to the body and fortune) he was merely following the opinion of the crowd, and that this was not a real philosophical opinion. Bartolomeo Platina in his *De principe* (c. 1470), ed. Ferraù, 73, expresses astonishment that Aristotle, "the wisest of men," could think nobility could have anything at all to do with the virtue of one's ancestors or riches, "since true nobility stems from no other source than from a man himself, that is, from virtue." For Francesco Patrizi's more nuanced interpretation of Aristotle on this point, see *De inst. r.p.* 6.1, ed. 1534, f. LXXXIr–v.

47 See pseudo-Plutarch, *De educatione puerorum* 11.

48 See Seneca *De clementia* 1.8.1.

49 Vergerio, *De ingenuis moribus* 2, in Kallendorf 2002, 5 (translation slightly modified). See also Rinuccini, *De libertate*, ed. Adorno, 67, who claims that there is a natural desire for true, inner freedom which is the fruit of virtue and wisdom, but it must be brought to actuality by education in the humanities ("bonarum artium studiis et recta educatione").

50 Patrizi, *De inst. r.p.* 2.1, ed. 1534, ff. XIX*v*–XX*r*: "Curabunt qui reipublicae praesunt, et publica quidem mercede, ut singulae quaeque doctrinae optimos praeceptores habeant, qui publice instituant." See Conclusion, page 509, for Patrizi's advocacy of literary education for all citizens of free cities and principalities.

51 By the same token, criminal deeds performed by those in power are imitated by those subject to them; see Francesco Filelfo's speech to the leaders *(Oratio ad principes)* of the Ambrosian Republic in Milan (July 1, 1448) "on the administration of the state," in BAM, MS F 55 sup., ff. 31r–33v: "Quo fit, ut paucorum plerumque facinora qui potestatem habent, reliquos omnes quibus praefecti sunt in exitium secum agant. Ut enim capitis imperio corpus reliquum obtemperans et melius et deterius habet pro imperantis aut ratione aut temeritate, ita in civitatibus usu venire consuevit." (Thus it happens that the misdeeds of a few men in power generally drive all the rest over whom they have charge, along with themselves, to destruction.)

52 It is worth noting that one of Salerno's accomplishments was helping the pope to disband the communal organs of consultative government there.

53 Letter of Guarino to Gian Nicola Salerno (1419), in Guarino, *Epistolario,* ed. Sabbadini, 1: 263–264 (*Ep.* 159). See also Guarino's letter to the same correspondent on the latter's assumption of the office of *podestà* of Mantua, ibid., 1: 107–108 (*Ep.* 50). The passage is possibly inspired by an essay in Plutarch's *Moralia* (776a–779c), "That a philosopher ought chiefly to converse with great men." On this theme see also Cappelli n.d., who notes that the idea of *imitatio* is a reflection in politics of the humanists' literary methods. The devaluing of the contemplative life in comparison with the active life reflects Cicero, *De officiis* 1.28.

54 Perotti, *Preface to Polybius,* 13. Perotti is surely following here Cicero, *Laws* 3.14: "Quaecumque mutatio morum in principibus extiterit, eandem in populo secutam." (Whatever moral changes appear in princes are followed by the people.) The same passage of Cicero is echoed, to the same effect, in Aldus Manutius' preface to his 1513 edition of Plato's complete works; see Manutius, *The Greek Classics,* ed. Wilson, 234. On this theme in Pontano see his *De principe,* ed. Cappelli, 52–54.

55 Manutius, *The Greek Classics,* ed. Wilson, 201, quoting Cicero, *De legibus* 3.31–32 and Homer, *Iliad* 2.25.

56 The question is explicitly posed by Cicero in *De officiis* 2.20 and leads to his famous discussion of why it is better for a ruler to be loved than feared.

57 In general, see Hendrick 2009.

58 Stacey 2007.

59 "Absurdum est ut alios regat qui seipsum regere nescit," a proverbial saying, frequently quoted by humanists. My late colleague Richard Pipes, a profound student of totalitarianism, makes the opposite point: "Power provides psychological compensation: it impels a person who cannot rule himself to rule others." See Pipes, *Vixi: Memoirs of a Non-Belonger* (New Haven: Yale University Press, 2003), 210. For the Renaissance debate about the effects of power on character, see also Chapters 4 and 17.

60 See Long 1995. Vasaly 2015, 127, finds a similar purpose in Livy.

61 Cicero, *De officiis* 2.32–33.

62 Another classic passage for the charisma of virtue is the *De officiis* 2.31–32, where Cicero says that nature compels the masses to love men who have the virtues. Thus far Cicero's notion is consistent with Max Weber's definition of charisma as authority "resting on devotion to the exceptional sanctity, heroism, or exemplary character of an individual." According to Weber, charismatic *Herrschaft* is free of compulsion and thus the opposite of bureaucratic / legalistic authority and traditional authority. But Cicero's idea differs from Weber's since the latter regards charisma as irrational, temporary, and characteristic of demagogues, whereas Cicero sees it as a habit of virtue born of reason and characteristic of the true statesman; see Weber 1976, 124–130.

63 I take the term "technical meritocracy" from modern Confucian political theory, where it is used to describe demoralized forms of meritocracy that emphasize technical qualifications rather than moral virtue. The analogy is not precise, since prudence is a moral virtue in the ancient understanding, "the knowledge of what to seek and what to avoid" (*De officiis* 1.153)." Cicero here, however, as the Loeb editor remarks, is probably thinking of prudence as knowledge of the law and the management of practical affairs.

64 Cicero, *De officiis* 2.32–33 (Loeb translation with slight modifications). The whole passage from 2.12 to 2.32 is relevant, and Cicero also applies the lesson of being loved rather than feared to the problem of how to retain the loyalty of provinces in the empire.

65 De Keyser 2013. For the importance of this discovery, see Reeve 1996, 20–26. Petrarch seems to have been personally responsible for almost all the early circulation of the text in humanist circles.

66 Cicero, *Pro Archia* 13–16 (Loeb translation with adjustments).

67 See Andreas Brentius' elaboration of this passage of Cicero in his *Oratio,* ed. Müllner, 76, lines 4–8.

68 Gualdo Rosa 1983. For information about the humanist recovery of Greek oratory, see Cortesi-Fiaschi, ad indices. In *Fam.* 19.18 (tr. Fantham 6.13) Petrarch attacks Fr. Giacomo Bussolari OESA, the tyrant of Pavia, who for Petrarch is *not* a good orator precisely because he is not a good man, in that he is opposed to the public weal; he is a disgrace to true piety as well since he is a monk who is also a man of war. This may reflect the view of Quintilian, *Institutio oratoria* 12.1.3 (who reports Cato's definition of the orator as a *vir bonus dicendi peritus*) that "no one can be an orator *unless* he is a good man" (Loeb translation). The arguments for why the orator / statesman must be a just man were first laid out by Plato in the *Gorgias,* a text translated into Latin by Leonardo Bruni around 1410. For Renaissance critics of the Catonian and Quintilianic idea that powerful speech depends on good character, see Monfasani 1992 and Cox 1999, esp. 274; for the influence of the *vir bonus* idea in the Middle Ages, see Ward 1995.

69 See Chapter 4.

70 Chapter 4 and, for *The Courtier,* Hankins 2002a, 2003–2004a, 1: 493–509.

71 This sentiment, often implicit, is made explicit in the first paragraph of Platina's *De principe* (ed. Ferraú, 53). For reflections on how the plebs might be consulted without compromising the wisdom of the deliberative process, see Guicciardini's *Discorso di Lograno,* discussed in Moulakis 2000, 211–216.

72 See esp. Cicero, *De officiis* 2.21–35, a key passage for virtue politics. At 2.23 he writes, "Fear is a poor watchman even in the short run, but benevolence keeps faithful guard forever."

73　This is the argument of book 1 of Alamanno Rinuccini's *On Liberty* (1479): see Rinuccini, *De libertate,* ed. Adorno, esp. 63–69. A free man can also enslave himself by servility toward unworthy rulers, in this case the Medici.

74　For such strategies, see Law and Paton 2010. On Bartolus' legalistic definition of nobility as a principle target of humanist polemics concerning "true nobility," see Landino, *De vera nobilitate,* ed. Liaci, 45–46.

75　See for example Petrarch's remarks in *Rem.,* praefatio and 2.190, explaining how the virtues, especially courage, automatically inspire respect and love in good men, bewilderment in evil ones. A similar description of how virtue inspires obedience may be found in Pontano, *De principe,* ed. Cappelli, 2–6.

76　*Fam.* 9.11, tr. Fantham 4.5.

77　Plato, *Republic* 5.473d.

78　Cicero, *De officiis* 1.22.

79　Bracciolini, *Historia tripartita,* ed. Fubini, 1: 48–49.

80　In general, see Black 2009. This does not mean that the humanists were necessarily the most effective opponents of the corruption of laws, and Black's book suggests that the more able opposition to the arbitrary power of tyrants came precisely from the jurists.

81　For the humanists' critique of contemporary law and the legal profession, the fundamental work is Maffei (1956) 1972; more recent approaches are illustrated in Gilli 2014. The most radical critique is that of Poggio in the *Historia tripartita,* for which see Krantz 1987. For Valla's attack on Bartolus and on Tribonian as the editor of the *Corpus iuris,* see Regoliosi 1997, Rossi 2008, and Rossi 2015b. The *De iure* of Alberti, a philosophical critique of contemporary judicial practice, is discussed in Quaglioni 2004, 97–104; see also the articles cited in Chapter 13, page 603n16. For Enea Silvio Piccolomini, see Gar 2015; for Benedetto Accolti and Niccolò Tignosi, see Black 1985, 80–83. On Scala's *De iudiciis* as intended to vilify the entire medieval legal profession, see Fredona 2008. Cappelli 2016b, 101, describes Pontano's hostility to jurists. Other texts of interest are Salutati, *De nobilitate legum et medicinae* (for which see Witt 1983, 331–345); Rinuccini, *De libertate,* ed. Adorno, 83, for criticism of the corruption of Florence's once-famous mercantile courts under the Medici; and PhE 0319, a letter of Filelfo to Federico Correr.

82　In Donato Acciaiuoli's commentary on book 3 of the *Politics* (cited from BLF, MS San Marco 67, f. 49r–v) he states that Aristotle prefers laws to men so long as discretion is permitted to living rulers in particular matters, and so long as the laws are made by *rectae respublicae,* not corrupt ones, since the goodness or badness of the laws reflects the type of regime.

83　See for example, aside from Poggio's devastating critique, the debate in Scala, *De legibus,* tr. Marsh, 158–231, esp. §29. For Boccaccio's hostility to contemporary legal education, see Chapter 7, page 202.

84　In line with Stoic doctrine, the coercion of innocent men is regarded by Cicero as inhuman; see *De officiis* 3.26: the man who relies on force to get what he wants "takes the human out of a human" *(qui omnino hominem ex homine tollat).* At 3.46 he writes that cruelty is "extremely hostile to the nature of man, which we ought to follow."

85　In general, see the acute remarks in McManamon 1989, chapter 2.

86　Witt 2000, chapter 8.

87　See Neumahr 2002.

88 Hirschman 1977.

89 Appiah 2010, 19–22.

90 For the role of the plastic arts in the moral reform of politics, see Cappelli 2017b.

91 For Cyriac of Ancona's gift of a coin of the emperor Trajan to the Holy Roman Emperor Sigismund III, presumably to remind him of Trajan's virtue, see his *Life and Early Travels,* ed. Mitchell et al., 91; for examples of coins of emperors used to decorate manuscripts, see De la Mare 2009.

92 Patrizi, *De inst. r.p.* 1.9, 1534, ff. XV*r*–XVI*v*.

93 See Pedullà 2018, chapter 1, for the importance of this *sententia* in humanist writings on political concord. For the use of inscriptions as forms of political indoctrination, see Gionta 2015. Among many other places, the quotation can be found painted on the walls of the chapel of the Signoria in the Palazzo Vecchio of Florence.

94 Dati, *Hiempsal,* ed. Grund, 188–243. For the reception of Sallust, see Osmond and Ulery 2003 and Osmond 2015 (with references to her numerous earlier articles).

95 Patrizi, *De inst. r.p.,* 1534, f. XVI*v*, describes the moral usefulness of painting: "Quinetiam legendo picturas, in quibus praeclara facinora exprimuntur, excitamur ad studium laudis et ad magna negotia obeunda, veluti si alicuius historiae monumenta volverimus. Locum igitur habeant in republica pictores et honestum quidem, ut studio gloriae incendantur, et ad parem laudem adolescentulos invitent. [Then he lists famous men of antiquity who painted.] . . . Quocirca non erit verendum ne manus adolescentulorum coloribus inquinentur, cum proxima doctrinae accedat pictura. [Then he describes the honors accorded to the great artists of antiquity.]" (Indeed, by looking at pictures in which famous deeds are depicted we are aroused to desire praise and to undertake great affairs, as though we were reading historical accounts. Let painters therefore have a place in the republic, and an honorable one, that we may be set aflame with the desire for glory, and induce the young to seek equal praise. . . . On this account we ought not to fear staining the hands of youths with colors, since painting comes right after learning.) The importance of creating a "virtuous environment" in educating princes was later (1516) recognized by Erasmus in *The Education of a Christian Prince,* ed. Jardine, 10.

96 See Hankins 2015b.

97 The reform of manners, to become a major theme of sixteenth-century humanism, was pioneered in the fifteenth by Pontano in his treatises on the social virtues.

98 Even a humanist like Lauro Quirini, who argues explicitly (within a circumstantialist framework) for the superiority of the virtuous popular regime the Renaissance called *respublica* (see Chapter 3), couches his critique of kingship, tyranny, oligarchy, and democracy in terms of their relative virtue, while ultimately preferring *respublica* to aristocracy on the grounds that the popular consent characteristic of *respublica* guarantees liberty, also conceived as a virtue; see his *De republica,* ed. Seno and Ravegnani, 140–143. For "circumstantialism," see Chapter 3, page 73.

99 Patrizi, *De regno* 1.1, 1567 ed., 6–8. In the *De inst. r.p.,* preface to book 6 (1534 ed., f. LXXIX*v*), Patrizi remarks that whether a state is ruled by one or many is irrelevant to the best customs and laws, which remain the same under both kinds of regimes: "Nihil enim refert unus ne an plures imperent; de ratione siquidem vivendi deque optimis legibus nihil mutatur." (It makes no difference whether one or many rule; there is nothing to change either in [customary] patterns of life or the best laws.)

100 *Fam.* 24.3, tr. Fantham 8.2.

101 See Chapter 7.

102 Kent 1978, 227n; Field 2017, 57, 131, 170.

103 Lilla 2001. For the view of Petrarch as soft on tyrants, see Chapter 4, page 118. For exclusivism—the view that constitutions are artificial creations of willing parties to a contract, not naturally occurring varieties of human community, and that some constitutions are illegitimate *in se*—see Chapter 3, page 71. One suspects that this was a reason why Petrarch suppressed his name as the author of the letters *Sine nomine,* as they show him at his most nakedly and passionately partisan, siding with the Italian party in the Church against the French, whereas he wanted to project a wholly different image in the *Familiares* and *Seniles.*

104 For an example of easy movement between a preference for aristocracy and for monarchy, compare Filelfo's declaration in favor of aristocracy in Chapter 15, page 356 (writing to the doge of Venice), and of monarchy in Chapter 17, page 390 (writing to Pope Paul II).

105 Hankins 1995a, 1996, 2007–2008a, and below, Chapter 9.

106 See Field 2017, 173–179, who believes that Bruni's sympathies were with the oligarchic party and that he was kept in office under the Medici only because the latter feared sacking so eminent a literary figure. The difficulty of assessing exactly where Bruni's political loyalties lay (and the contrary view of Ianziti 2012 should also be considered) helps underline the point, made also in Black 2013 (see Chapter 18, page 437), that it was not to the advantage of high government functionaries to align themselves with political factions.

107 For Plato's and St. Gregory the Great's psychological analyses of tyranny, and humanist ideas of tyranny, see Chapter 4.

108 See Chapter 3.

109 Rinuccini, *De libertate,* ed. Adorno, 70–72. On 82 and 85 Rinuccini describes how free speech and free deliberation are compromised by fear of the powerful. This attitude found its way into public speeches made in Florence. For example, an anonymous Latin speech *de libertate* (*inc.* Rimabar mecum ipse) to the Florentine Signoria, delivered during the chancellorship of Leonardo Bruni (1427–1444) and surely written under his influence (or even by him), states, "Quid igitur melius utilius atque sublimius civibus esse potest quam in contione et aliis plerisque locis posse rei publicae commodum libera voce proponere? Certe nihil." (What can be better, more useful and more elevated for citizens than to advocate the good of the republic in the assembly and other many other places with a free voice? Surely nothing.) The speech is preserved in BNL MS Plut. 90 sup. 47, ff. 87v–90v.

110 Brandolini, *Republics and Kingdoms* 1.56–63, ed. Hankins, 68–76.

111 Livy, *Ab urbe condita* 23.12.9.

112 Fasolt 2014.

113 In general, see Costa 1999; Kirshner and Mayall 2002.

114 See Chapter 9.

115 On Patrizi, see further below and Chapters 16 and 17.

116 Hicks 1960.

117 See Chapter 11.

118 Petrucci, *Epistole* 1, ed. Pertici, 40.

119 See Cicero, *De officiis* 1.7.22

120 Petrucci, *Epistole* 7, ed. Pertici, 51–52. Petrucci's friend, the far more influential Francesco Patrizi, defines the citizen in *De inst. r.p.* 5.2, 1534 ed., f. LXVI*v,* as "a good man who is useful to the *respublica,*" who keeps before his eyes the dictum of Plato that we are not born for

ourselves alone, but for our family, friends, and country. At 6.1, 1534 ed., f. LXXXI*v,* he says that long residence in the community should be respected only where there is virtue and good conduct; at 6.4, 1534 ed., ff. LXXXV*v*–LXXXVI*r,* he says a city should welcome foreigners for the economic benefits they bring, but recommends offering citizenship only in a few cases where foreigners have proven themselves well deserving of the republic.

121 For a parallel sentiment in classical antiquity, possibly known to Petrucci, see Xenophon's *Memorabilia* 4.6.13 (where it is placed in the mouth of Socrates). The work was translated into Latin by Bessarion in 1442. Patrizi's *De regno,* book 9, takes the same view. The view of the Sienese humanist reformers may be contrasted with the definition of citizenship in modern democratic republics, for example in the Seventeenth Amendment to the U.S. Constitution, where citizenship is understood (in Hannah Arendt's phrase) as "the right to have rights."

122 For more on this work of Patrizi, see Chapter 17.

123 For example the laws of *ammonizioni* of 1359, which licensed leaders of the Parte Guelfa to "warn" political unreliables not to accept office, which in effect turned into a system of depriving political opponents of office; see Brucker 1962, 170–172.

124 See chapters 8, 10, and 20 for Leonardo Bruni's defense of these practices using virtue arguments. The Florentine Ordinances of Justice actually listed the names of thirty-eight magnate families that were henceforward deprived of full political rights.

125 Patrizi explains why the practice of assigning magistracies in accordance with virtue and merit is not inconsistent with civil equality at *De inst. r.p.* 6.1, 1534 ed., ff. LXXXII*v*–LXXXIII*r*): "It is not possible that there be equality with respect to individual [magistracies], since it must be stipulated in advance what I have often said, that magistracies are the reward of virtue, not of power or ancestry." [See ibid., book 5 passim.] "Citizens are equal in matters where they can be, so that in passing laws, wealth, power and ancestry should not prevail. . . . But the weak, humble and those without a reputation for virtue should not take it ill that more outstanding citizens are preferred to them in choosing magistrates, so long as they can use what is rightfully theirs and suffer no injury in private matters but are defended by the laws and the magistrates, so that they are preserved without harm, and may acknowledge that they have obtained their due portion from the *respublica.* They ought to confess that they have been dealt with satisfactorily in accordance with their deserts." Honors should be proportionate to the capacity of citizens to serve their country well (a principle common to both Plato and Aristotle). Patrizi goes on to warn citizens against the natural tendency to overrate one's own merits and deserts.

126 For Bruni and Biondo, see Chapters 8 and 11. A more nuanced position can be found in Francesco Patrizi, *De inst. r.p.* 3.3, 1534 ed., f. XXXVIII*v.* Discussing the form of selection to be used in the case of senators, Patrizi states that sortition as used by the Florentines and Sienese has the advantage of inhibiting the influence of wealthy and powerful men driven by ambition but is dangerous because the eligibility lists become full of unworthy and unsuitable candidates who are unequal to the tasks of government in its times of peril. "Hence free election of the Senate seems superior." As an advocate of virtue politics Patrizi stipulates that senators should be chosen from among men of mature years with proven records of public service, distinguished for their virtue and education. To elevate such men to office he approves of what he describes as the Venetian mode of selecting magistrates in the Maggior Consiglio (a kind of electoral college, in Patrizi's time a closed hereditary body of patricians), which employed a combination of sortition and election designed to prevent electioneering by the ambitious. Alamanno Rinuccini (*De libertate,* ed. Adorno, 87), on the other hand, approves the ancient Florentine

practice of sortition, but only because he sees the practice as fairer than the cronyism of the Medici regime.

127 See for example Brandolini, *Republics and Kingdoms* 1.58–63, ed. Hankins, 70–76.

128 See Chapter 5, page 172, for Petrarch's praise of elective kingship. Machiavelli too praises the elective monarchy of the Antonines as superior to the hereditary mode used by the Julio-Claudians in *Disc.* 1.10. Erasmus in the *Complaint of Peace* opposes hereditary monarchy and dynastic marriage as causes of war, and (as frequently in his political writings) he has a position on royal succession similar to that of Patrizi. In his *Institutio Christiani principis* (1517) elective monarchy is preferable, but if succession is to be hereditary, the country's best hope lies in the prince's tutor, whose instruction can keep him from tyranny.

3. WHAT WAS A REPUBLIC IN THE RENAISSANCE?

1 Skinner 1978, 2: 350–358.

2 Oakeshott 1980, 452, quoted by Goldie 2006, 11.

3 Ibid., 12 (quoting Skinner). See also Skinner 2009, 325–326 and notes, which emphasize instability and inconsistency in modern ideas of the state, "the impossibility of showing that it has any essence or natural boundaries." For a recent overview of historians' theories of state-formation in the seventeenth century with a sharp critique of the same, see the introductory chapter in Friedeburg and Morrill 2017.

4 Schiera 1996, 17: "We are all aware that some form of teleology is inevitable in any attempt to understand the state as a unitary phenomenon developing according to a single dynamic from the Middle Ages to our own time."

5 This is in no way meant as a criticism of Skinner's own work, to which all historians of political thought owe gratitude; in fact it offers us a model of how to avoid anachronism while introducing a fruitful element of historical contingency into modern debates about political values.

6 The problem is addressed, however, in Cappelli 2016b.

7 For studies of this literature, the so-called *trattatistica,* see Cappelli 2016b, and Chapter 17, page 399.

8 Fukuyama 2011.

9 A particularly clear example is provided by Lauro Quirini's *De republica,* described by its editors as promoting a *politica militante* and using an analytical framework provided by Aristotle's *Politics.* Yet the optimal polity that emerges from his analysis turns out to model its constitution explicitly on the middle republic of Rome. See Quirini, *De republica,* ed. Seno and Ravegnani, esp. 136–139. In Chapter 18 I shall argue that the military and religious reforms advocated by Machiavellian statecraft and often said to prefigure the early modern state were modelled on Roman institutions of the middle republic.

10 Skinner 1989. See also idem, "From the State of Princes to the Person of the State," in Skinner 2002a, 2: 368–414; and more recently Skinner 2009. On the distinction, see also Schofield 1999b, 181: "In truth, the emergence of the concept of the state is a topic for historians of Renaissance and early modern, not ancient, political thought."

11 It is significant that modern lexicography, to make sense for moderns of the way *respublica* is used in ancient sources, has devised secondary or tropical senses of both *respublica* and *civitas* as "state" (see *OLD* s.vv.), though there are no explicit ancient definitions that authorize this translation. The fundamental sense of *respublica,* as Cicero tells us, is "the affairs of the people,"

res populi, public affairs, while the basic sense of *civitas* is "citizenry." The translation "state" can sometimes be misleading. For example, since Forcellini's lexicon (1771), the basis of Lewis and Short's dictionary, it has been common to cite *Pro Sestio* 46 as defining *respublica,* though in context it is no more than a list of items with which statesmen need to concern themselves when they are interested in producing *otium cum dignitate,* honorable peace; it is not a "constitution" in our sense. For *otium cum dignitate* as Cicero's political ideal, see Chapter 18, page 435.

12 See Straumann 2016a.

13 On the evolution of the popular state as sovereign, see Quaglione 2003 and Lee 2016. The expression *summum ius* in the sense of the location of ultimate sovereignty, an authority beyond legal appeal, is not found in ancient sources; and Cicero's phrase *summum ius, summa iniuria* (*De officiis* 1.33) tells us why.

14 Bruni acknowledged the inspiration of Petrarch in his *Memoirs* 16, ed. Hankins, 3: 312.

15 Bruni, *Epistolae* 2.1, ed. Mehus 1: 27–30.

16 See Chapter 1. *Stans et integra respublica,* despite the Ciceronian origins of the phrase, in Biondo means "the ancient Roman state," including the empire; see Chapter 10. In Patrizi's *De inst. r.p.,* whose importance is discussed in Chapters 16 and 17, the Roman state of the classical period is constantly in the background as an example and criterion of political excellence.

17 Cochrane 1981, chapter 1.

18 Flavio, *Italy Illuminated* 6.49, ed. White, 1: 324 (translation altered). By "Kingdom of Italy" Biondo means the kingdom set up by Charlemagne after his defeat of the Lombards. Part of the Roman Empire, it included most of north and central Italy except for Venice.

19 Pieri 1971; Mallett 1974.

20 Flavio, *Italy Illustrated* 6.26–31, ed. White, 1: 300–308.

21 Hankins 2002b, 2002–2003.

22 The earliest example of which I am aware, from 1406 / 1409, appears in the preface to Jacopo Angeli's translation of Ptolemy's *Geography,* edited in Hankins 2003–2004c.

23 *Disc.* preface, tr. Mansfield and Tarcov, 6. Machiavelli criticizes his contemporaries again for their failure to imitate the grand strategy of Rome at *Disc.* 2.4. At *AW* 7, tr. Gilbert, *CW,* 2: 724–725, he also complains about his contemporaries' failure to draw the correct lessons from antiquity. On this theme in Machiavelli, see Chapters 18 and 19.

24 See Chapter 10.

25 Skinner 2009, 360.

26 Vergil, *Aeneid* 3.96: "Antiquam exquirite matrem."

27 See Wootton 2006; Hankins 2010a.

28 I coined this term as applied to the theory of regimes in Hankins 2010a, and it was adopted, with suitable acknowledgment, in Nelson 2010, 151. See Straumann 2018, 29n20.

29 On the radicalization of the republican tradition after the French Revolution, see Mager 1984, 596–600. Mager discusses here the development of terminology in Robespierre (who in the early stage of his career used *république* in a more traditional way) and Wedekind. For Tom Paine's exclusivism, see *The Rights of Man,* part 1, chapter 16. *Republicanism* is of course a modern term, first attested in 1788 according to Mager 1984, 603–604.

30 The description of the English monarchy as a republic seems to have drawn the attention of students of English republicanism only recently; see McDiarmid 2007.

31 Mager 1984, 580–589. See also Rubinstein 1968, 447; Rubinstein 1990b, 4; and Wootton 2006.

32 For Renaissance periodizations of Roman history, see Chapter 11.

33 For an apparent exception in the writings of Leonardo Bruni, see Hankins 2014a.

34 This is the model in book 3; there are in fact several constitutional schemata in the *Politics,* for which see Hansen 2013. The six-constitution model, however, was by far the most familiar to Renaissance political writers, in part because of Cicero's adoption of Polybius' analysis, and also because of its use in Giles of Rome's *De regimine principum.* I use "polyarchic" here and elsewhere as a neutral term to indicate regimes ruled by more than one person, or power-sharing arrangements, whether oligarchies or popular governments.

35 See Aristotle, *Politics* 4.1 and 4.12. I take the term "constitutional relativism" from Blythe 1992, chapter 10. More recently Blythe has adopted the term "circumstantialism"; see Blythe 2009, 151.

36 Polybius 6.10.

37 *OLD,* 1635–1636. In conducting research for this chapter, with the help of Ada Palmer, I surveyed the several thousand occurrences of the word *respublica* found in the Packard Humanities Institute database of classical literature. For an analysis of the ancient usage of the word, see Suerbaum 1977 and Hodgson 2017. For the ancient historians' perception of the republic and principate as historical periods, see Sion-Jenkis 2000, 19–53.

38 In general, see Harte and Lane 2013.

39 Merguet 1905, 633–634; compare Quintilian, *Institutes* 5.10.63; Tacitus, *Annales* 4.33.1.

40 See esp. Cicero, *De republica* 3.43. The semantic change in the term during the Renaissance may be illustrated by two quotations from Cicero and Valla. Cicero writes (*De republica* 3.43), "Ergo ubi tyrannus est, ibi . . . dicendum est plane nullam esse rem publicam." (Where there is a tyrant, then, it must be said that there simply is no republic.) Valla, by contrast, in his famous oration *On the Donation of Constantine,* cap. 50 (ed. Bowersock, 87), writes "Ubi rex est, ibi res publica non est." (Where there is a king, there is no republic.)

41 Wirszubski 1950, 14–15.

42 Mager 1984, 553.

43 For example at 1.28, 1.30, 1.35, 1.49, 1.59.

44 Thus the historian Florus (2nd century CE) describes the acts of Brutus and Collatinus as having brought about a *mutatio reipublicae,* not an *instauratio* (1.3).

45 Sion-Jenkis 2000, 20–21.

46 *De republica* 3.47. At 1.42, Cicero explicitly states that *regnum* is a *status reipublicae,* i.e., a constitutional form.

47 See Augustine, *De civitate Dei* 2.21, where Augustine paraphrases a speech of Scipio from a now-lost portion Cicero's *De republica,* book 1. See also *De republica* 1.41–43, where Cicero states (through his interlocutor Scipio) that kingship is the best of the "simple" constitutions, though a mixed government containing royal, optimate, and popular elements is the best constitution of all. That this passage was known to humanists is shown by Salutati's allusion to it; see Chapter 4, page 129.

48 Mager 1984, 552.

49 In the same way, Cicero believed that there had been no republic under the rule of the Decemvirs (450–449 BC)—during what we would call "the Republic"—because they had behaved tyrannically; see *De republica* 3.47. It is noteworthy that both Suetonius and Tacitus continue to use the word *respublica* often to refer to the Roman state under the Caesars. See for example Tacitus, *Histories* 1.5, 11, 13, etc. Suetonius, *Caligula* 22.1, distinguishes between Caligula's

legitimate *principatus* and his immoral slide toward a tyrannical *regni formam.* Tacitus usually prefers an expression like *dominatio,* lordship, or *Caesaribus fastigium,* the superior rank enjoyed by the Caesars (e.g., *Annales* 3.27), to describe the princely position of the Caesars in the state.

50 See Griffin 2005, 535–543; Stacey 2007, chapter 1.

51 On the meaning of the document, see Augustus, *Res gestae,* ed. Cooley, with her introduction and commentary. For the debate about the meaning of *respublica* in the imperial period, see Millar 2000, 1–38, with discussion. For modern anachronistic readings of the famous statement in Suetonius, *Augustus* 28, "De reddenda respublica bis cogitavit," see ibid., 6–7.

52 Griffin 2005, 536, 538.

53 For example Velleius Paterculus (1.14–15, 2.89), Sextus Aurelius Victor (*De Caesaribus* 1), and Eutropius (7.8, 10).

54 For example *SHA* Hadrian 8.3.

55 Wickert 1949 collects a mass of evidence for emperors' claims to support *libertas.*

56 The earliest example I have seen of the late republic described in a Renaissance Latin author as a *democratia* is in Polydor Vergil, *On Discovery* (*ed. princ.* 1499) 2.3 ("On Three Ways of Ruling the Roman State," ed. Copenhaver, 210–216), where Rome's constitutions are traced from a monarchy or "royal power" ("monarchiam, hoc est regium imperium"), to the early republic ("aristocratia idest optimatum principatus"), followed by the dictatorial *decemviri* who were more like oligarchs than aristocrats, followed by "democratia, idest popularis principatus." Then, thanks to Julius Caesar, Rome turns back to "monarchia, idest ad unius imperium."

57 Mager 1984, 550–551.

58 For many examples of Roman treaties, see those collected in Sherk 1969.

59 Sion-Jenkins 2000, 25–30.

60 Ibid., 27, citing Suetonius and Seneca. In *Annales* 1.1 Tacitus says that Rome in the beginning had kings but that Brutus instituted *libertatem et consulatum.* In his account of the history of the Roman constitution (3.27) he never uses the term *respublica* to indicate either the Roman constitution after the expulsion of the Tarquins or as a period of Roman history. In his *De officiis* and other writings, Cicero frequently described the *respublica* as lost owing to the actions of various military dictators, but these claims were not interpreted as a statement about historical periodization but rather as describing a loss of respect for traditional political principles.

61 See esp. Tacitus, *Annales* 1.3; *Histories* 1.50.

62 See *OLD,* 1438, s.v. *principatus.* Tacitus uses "principate" for the Augustan system of government and for the period of rule of individual *principes* (e.g., *principatum divi Nervae*) but not of the period after Actium as a whole; see Suerbaum 1977, 83.

63 The subject has in any case been adequately surveyed in the existing literature; see esp. Mager 1984, 554–563, and Schütrumpf 2014 for further references.

64 Aristotle, *Politica,* Moerbeke translation, ed. Susemihl, 178–179. Moerbeke is followed closely by Giles of Rome in his *De regimine principum,* 3.2.2 (ed. 1607, 453): *regnum, aristocratia, politia* are the sound forms; *tyrannides, oligarchia, democratia* are the corruptions.

65 For Albert's terminology, see Kempshall 1999, 44. For Buridan, see Blythe 1992, 193.

66 Aquinas had used the term *regimen politicum* as distinct from *regimen regale* to indicate the difference between the power of a ruler constrained by law and the unrestrained power of a monarch; see Blythe 1992, 43–46. He may also have been influenced by the typology in Aristotle's *Rhetoric* 1.8.1365b, which lists *monarchia, aristocratia, democratia,* and *oligarchia* as four

forms of government. The latter passage seems to have been decisive for Engelbert of Admont; see his *De regimine principum* 1.4.15–17.

67 Blythe 1992, Henry (281), Giles (67), John (146), Peter (86), Bartolus (172–173), Oresme (215). For Marsilius of Padua, see the *Defensor pacis* 1.8.

68 Blythe 1992, chapter 6; Mager 1984, 582–583.

69 See also Rubinstein 2004b, 317–333.

70 This may seem to make Ptolemy an "exclusivist" *avant la lettre;* for an argument to the contrary, see Hankins 2010a. The considerations of Straumann 2018, 49–53, have not changed my mind on this issue; see the discussion of Blythe 2009, chapter 6, for a detailed study of the relevant passages.

71 See Blythe 1992, chapter 1, as well as Blythe 2000; the same point is made in Black 2006 and Black 2010.

72 See Mager 1984, 559–563; Mager calls this the "corporate" concept *(der körperschaftliche Begriff)* of *respublica.* Thus Bartolus of Sassoferrato, the leading jurist of the fourteenth century, defines republics broadly as any corporate political entity. The jurist Baldus sees sovereignty as the keynote: republics are "universitates quae superiorem non recognoscunt" (collectivities having a legal persona which recognize no superior). See Chapter 4 on Bartolus and Baldus.

73 See Blythe 2000, 34–35; for the "mirror-of-princes" tradition, see Bejczy and Nederman 2007.

74 Ptolemy of Lucca divides Roman history according to regimes in the modern way, even if he does not use the word *respublica* to describe the period of popular/aristocratic rule.

75 On the propaganda wars, see Baron 1966; Lanza 1991; Griffiths 1999.

76 On Bruni, see Hankins 2003–2004a, 1: 9–239, and Chapters 8–10 in this volume.

77 See Hankins 2014a.

78 Bruni says the period of free rule lasted for 465 years after the downfall of the kings (*History* 1.70, ed. Hankins, 1: 86).

79 In his vernacular *Life of Petrarch* (*Opere,* ed. Viti, 554), Bruni distinguishes a culturally healthy period that existed during the *buon stato della repubblica* and says that liberty was lost with the *signoria degli imperadori,* but he never refers to the period from the expulsion of the kings to the Battle of Actium as "the republic" *simpliciter.*

80 Bruni, *History* 1.69–71 (ed. Hankins, 1: 86–91).

81 See for example ibid. 2.13 and 4.17 (ed. Hankins 1: 120, 348).

82 See Chapter 4, page 129.

83 Schütrumpf 2014, 49–55, criticizes Hankins 2005 for claiming that Bruni invented the new, non-monarchical sense of *respublica.* He unfortunately was not aware of Hankins 2010a, where my case was refined and presented in much greater textual detail. He is of course correct that a shift occurs in the meaning of *politeia* in the later books of the *Politics,* where the term is used to mean "constitutional government" and sometimes contrasted with monarchy. It is difficult to see, however, how this affects my point about the history of the Latin word *respublica.* I think it likely, in fact, that Bruni's revolutionary use of *respublica* as equivalent to non-monarchical regime was influenced by the sense of *politeia* developed by Aristotle (and other fourth-century-BC writers like Demosthenes, whom Bruni also translated), where the word is used in contrast with disordered governments like tyranny or factionalized governments that are not restrained by law. Schütrumpf draws attention to the telling gloss Bruni silently introduces in his translation of *Politics* 3.15.1286b5–13: "The contrast of monarch *(rex)* and *respublica,* which in Aristotle is only implied, is actually created in Bruni's translation, because he added the

object *regem,* king, to the verb "tolerated," which in the Greek text is used without an object." Note that Salutati in *De tyranno* 6 had followed medieval usage and referred to constitutional government as *principatus politicus* (as opposed to monarchy, *dominium regale,* and despotism). See Chapter 4, page 129.

84 The work survives in at least 260 MSS and fifty-five printed editions before 1600; see Hankins 2003–2004a, 1:191; a list of known manuscripts is found in Hankins 1997.

85 Since the many early editions (there is no modern edition) descend from corrupt copies, I cite the dedication copy for Cosimo de'Medici, BLF, MS Plut. 79.19, f. 3r *(Proemium).* The manuscript may be consulted online via the website of the Biblioteca Medicea Laurenziana ("Plutei online").

86 There survive 120 MSS, and sixty-eight editions of it were printed before 1600. See Hankins 1997.

87 For the date of composition and publication, see Hankins 2007–2008a.

88 Hankins and Palmer 2008, 21.

89 It seems he originally planned to call his translation of the *Politics* "De republica," as one passage in his *Economics* commentary suggests.

90 Hankins 2003–2004b.

91 Bruni, *De interpretatione recta,* ed. Viti, 120, cap. 43.

92 On Bruni's "Romanization" of Aristotle, see Schütrumpf 2014, 44–45.

93 See Langkabel 1981, ad indices, s.v. *res publica.*

94 Some samples are published in Viti 1992 and in Griffiths 1999.

95 See note 72 above.

96 In formal documents such as treaties and legislation, and in the addresses of public correspondence, the medieval terminology continues to be used down to the early sixteenth century in Florence and Venice, though humanists (e.g., Piero Paolo Vergerio the Elder) refer to Venice informally as the *Respublica Veneta* as early as 1400 / 1403. The term *Respublica Ambrosiana* for the restored communal government in Milan in 1447–1449 was not the official *Staatsname* of the city government. According to Jane Black (private communication) the official name of the so-called *Respublica Ambrosiana* was usually the *Communitas libertatis Mediolani,* and the term *Respublica Ambrosiana,* beloved of modern Renaissance historians, is not found before the seventeenth century. The earliest references I have found in Florentine public correspondence in which Florence is officially styled a republic are from the late 1540s, under the Medici dukes, where Cosimo I and his counselors, addressing foreign powers, write as "Cosmus Medices dux et consiliarii Reipublicae Florentinae (1546)" or "Cosmus Medices Reipublicae Florentiae dux et eius consiliarii." See ASF, Archivio della Repubblica, Missive Ia Cancelleria 58, ff. 132v, 170v.

97 In general, see Allmand 1998, 547–587.

98 In his *De republica* of 1449 / 1450 (in Branca et al. 1977, 131), Lauro Quirini, a cordial enemy of Bruni, uses *politia* for generic constitution but *respublica* for specific. By contrast, the humanist Tito Livio Frulovisi in his treatise on the state dated 1434 (Frulovisi, *De republica,* ed. Previté-Orton) generally uses the term *populus* for a popular regime.

99 Najemy 2000.

100 Leon Battista Alberti, since he preferred oligarchy to popular government, felt compelled to invent a new term, *iciarchia,* to avoid the negative connotations of *oligarchia* and the vaguer denotation *respublica;* see Chapter 13.

101 On Patrizi's constitutional analysis in the *De institutione reipublica,* see Chapter 16. His later and rather different terminology (where polyarchic government is called *civilis societas*) in the *De regno* is discussed in Chapter 17.

102 Patrizi, *De inst. r.p.* 1.4, 1534 ed., f. VII*v*: "Statum rerumpublicarum (siquidem de rege et tyranno nihil dicere constituimus) triplicem principaliter ponimus. Una namque popularis est, altera in qua optimates agunt, tertia quae in paucos diffunditur."

103 See Chapter 16.

104 See Appendix C.

105 Composed in 1472, the versions circulated in manuscript until the *ed. princ.* of 1566.

106 See Acciaiuoli, *In Politica,* 1566 ed., ff. 124v, 128v.

107 Mager 1984, 566; see also Schütrumpf 2014, 59, 64.

108 See Rubinstein 2004c.

109 Scala, *Apologia* 17, ed. Watkins, 252–254.

110 See especially book 4 of Castiglione's *Il Cortegiano,* where the contrast between *repubbliche* and *signori* is assumed. Castiglione's work also had an enormous readership in the sixteenth century.

111 It is noteworthy, however, that in *Disc.* 1.2.10 (ed. Bausi, 1: 19), Machiavelli reverts to the traditional sense of *repubblica* as a public power capable of three forms, or *stati*—namely, "principato, ottimati e populare." There are also (according to "others" who "according to the opinion of many are wiser") three *ragioni governi* that represent corruptions of the three good forms: *tirannico, stato di pochi, licenziosi.*

112 For an interpretation emphasizing the importance of Tacitus, see Wootton 2006. For the reception of Tacitus, see Ulery 1986. Ulery writes: "The interest in Tacitus was, after Bruni, not Florentine and not political, and it was limited to the contents of the Second Medicean [codex] (*Annales* XI–XVI and *Historiae*)."

113 Rubinstein 2004c, 268–269. Of course there were many others, like Alamanno Rinuccini in his *De libertate* and Leon Battista Alberti (see Chapter 13), who took the opposite view of the Medici.

114 The text, whose full title is *De vera republica et digna seculari militia* (On the True Republic and Worthy Military Service in This Age) is unpublished but is preserved in Modena, Biblioteca Estense, MS Est. lat. 114 (α W 6 6); the passage cited is on ff. 1v–2r. On Michele Savonarola, see Samaritani 1976 and Remy Simonetta in *DBI* 91 (2018).

115 See Chapter 16 for the role played by non-Aristotelian Greek theory in breaking down this prejudice.

116 Patrizi, *De inst. r.p.* 1.1.

117 Patrizi, *De regno* 1.1.

118 Brandolini, *Republics and Kingdoms* 3.106, ed. Hankins, 259.

119 Kohl 1998, esp. xvii; Najemy 2004, 189; Law and Paton 2010, esp. the essays of Jones and Kohl; Zorzi 2010 (with a review of the historiography, 1–10); Ricciardelli 2015. This tendency in current historiography may be traced back to Jones 1965. Zorzi 2010, x, writes, "In reality, throughout the thirteenth and fourteenth centuries, citizens considered the two forms of government, the communal and the signorial, as alternative resources to which they could have recourse as necessity or circumstances dictated," and notes that signorial power (as in the case of Cola di Rienzo) was not infrequently deployed in defense of the *popolo* against oligarchic forces in cities. On Petrarch's view of Cola, see Chapter 5.

120 See Aristotle, *Politics* 3.14.1285a: "For the same reason [that kingships are hereditary and legal], their guards are such as a king and not such as a tyrant would employ, that is to say, they are composed of citizens, whereas the guards of tyrants are mercenaries" (trans. Everson). See Rubinstein 1995 for the Palazzo Vecchio as a fortress. Patrizi in *De inst. r.p.* 8.9, 1534 ed., ff. CXIv–CXIIr, inveighs against the custom of building citadels in free cities, arguing on the basis of many historical examples that they are an invitation to tyranny and sedition.

121 See Carlo Seno and Giorgio Ravegnani in Branca et al. 1977, 110–112.

122 Law 2010. The article discusses the use of the term *diarchia* in Italian historical literature.

123 Connell and Zorzi 2000, 6: "The only true end of the territorial order was to preserve the political, military and economic might of Florence" (Zorzi).

124 Ricciardelli 2015, 158–169.

125 For the non-domination model of liberty, see Pettit 1999 and Skinner 1998.

126 This observation is made in Pietro Marsi's popular commentary on Cicero's *De officiis* (1484, f. 75), commenting on 3.32. A similar point is made repeatedly in Alberti's *De iciarchia;* see Chapter 13. Machiavelli later takes it for granted that citizens used to a free regime will be more difficult for *signori* to dominate. Quentin Skinner and Philip Pettit rightly point out that the non-domination concept of liberty is not as morally vacuous as modern liberal "negative liberty," since on the pre-modern understanding to maintain liberty and equality requires a form of citizen virtue.

127 Petrarch, quoted in Cosenza and Musto 1996, 108: "No words strike a more responsive chord in the human heart than these: *Respublica Romana.*" For Petrarch the words "Roman republic" signified the virtuous polity of ancient Rome, which was opposed in his mind to the modern city of Rome, governed by tyrannical barons of foreign extraction. See Chapter 5.

128 See Fubini 1992 (in Fubini 2001 in expanded form), Schiller 2000, and Hankins 2000a, introduction, on the evolution of Baron's concept of *burgerliche Humanismus.* As Donald Kelley once remarked (in a private comment to the author), it is unlikely that Baron's concept would have had the success it enjoyed in America had he chosen to translate it as "bourgeois humanism."

129 Meinecke 1957, 208–210. On Baron and Meinecke, see Fubini 2001, 288, 309, 327. On Meinecke as an advocate of reason of state, see Werner Stark's introduction in Meinecke 1957.

130 Monnier 1924, 1: 228.

131 See Chapter 14 on humanist cosmopolitanism.

132 In his studies of humanist attitudes to wealth, Baron aspired to revise Weber's account of the origins of capitalism in a "Protestant ethic," pushing those origins back into the Italian Renaissance. See Chapter 7.

133 See Chapter 1, page 4.

134 Hankins 1995a.

135 Cappelli 2016b, 10, 66, 98. For humanist ideals of marriage in the courts of princes, see D'Elia 2004.

136 Baron 1966, 458–462.

137 For examples of Petrarch and Boccaccio espousing "civic humanist" values, see Chapters 5 and 7.

138 For all of the above, see McManamon 1996, esp. 55–59, 65–70, 116–119.

139 Vergerio, *De monarchia,* ed. Smith, 447–450.

140 Decembrio, *De republica,* cited from Milan, Biblioteca Ambrosiana, MS B 123 sup., ff. 93v–
94r: "Aliud est, ut patriam, in qua nos ipsi parentes, liberi nostri, coniuges affines et amici de-
gunt, potissima caritate colamus, pro qua nullus bonus unquam mori timuit. Salus enim patriae incolarum omnium salutem amplectitur. . . . Ex hoc necesse est, ut illius gubernatorem et
principem, quem ipsius patriae patrem dicimus, amore benignissimo prosequamur, sub cuius
regimine placida quietaque pace subiecti populi gubernantur. Custodes etiam illos et milites,
quibus tutella urbis cura<que> principis est commissa, plurimum diligere coartamur, illorum
etenim vigilia exactaque custodia universus populus requiescit bonisque suis fruitur, hostili pro-
tinus calamitate depulsa. Unicuique praeterea civi curae esse debet, aequo et pari iure cum civibus reliquis vivere, neque submissum et abiectum se gerere, ut habeatur contemptui, neque
se efferentem, ut alios videatur opprimere. Tum in re publica illa velle quae tranquilla et honesta sunt. Postremo taliter se habere, ut bonus vir et aequus civis ab omnibus reputetur, cultor
sit virtutum omnium, potissime iustitiae et moderationis, quibus duabus vir bonus maxime com-
probatur. Leges, mores, et consuetudines rei publicae diligenter observet, nec ab eis declinet,
etiam si Socrati vel Platoni aut alteri philosopho fortassis aliter videretur" [i.e., even if the laws
and customs of the commonwealth do not agree with philosophical positions such as the infamous *communio mulierum et bonorum* of Plato's *Republic*]. On this text, see Hankins 1995a,
328–329; Ferraù 2005.

141 See Chapter 2, page 60.

142 See Chapter 4, page 141.

143 See Ross and Ericksen 1909, 81, for the Florentine siege of Pisa: "Since March 1406 the Florentine army had lain before Pisa. In June the commissary, Gino Capponi, ordered an attack, which
was repulsed. But the Pisans were starving. They drove out the useless mouths, whereupon the
Florentines hung the men, cut the women's clothes off at the waist, branded the women on the
cheek with the lily of Florence, and drove them back to the gates of the city. Women being still
expelled by their starving fellow-citizens, the besiegers cut off their noses." The passage is based
on Minerbetti's *Chronicle,* ed. Bellondi, cap. 8, probably via Capponi 1876, 2: 106–107.

144 Aristotle, *Rhetoric* 1.9.

145 Compare Pocock 2003, 57: "*Vivere civile* became a technical term for a broadly based civic
constitution." But other passages in the *De regno* show the term *vita civilis* contrasted with
villa life, with contemplative life, or with a retired, scholarly life. Even Machiavelli uses *vivere
politico* and *vita civile* (as opposed to the absolute rule of a tyrant) in *Discorsi* 1.25–26 to apply
to kingdoms as well as republics. "Civil life" is impossible only in tyrannies. This broad sense
of *vita civilis* is the one adopted in the canonical work of the monarchist Justus Lipsius,
Politica 1.1: "I define civil life as the life we enjoy in community with other people, to the mutual benefit or profit" (tr. Waszink, 261). In Frulovisi, *De republica,* ed. Previté-Orton, 316–317,
one interlocutor claims that citizens can have leadership roles, act as judges, and give counsel
under the rule of a king; another replies that it can't be called a monarchy if citizens dominate;
and a third, Frulovisi himself, remarks that princes *(principes)* seem to rule no less in kingdoms
than in popular or oligarchic governments—in other words, that all forms of government
have political elites.

146 Patrizi, *De regno* 9.21, 1567 ed., ff. 422r–423v. Bruni had made a similar claim at the end of his
Panegyric of Nanni Strozzi.

147 See Chapter 9, page 262.

148 A listing of the official names currently used by the 195 countries of the world may be found in United States Central Intelligence Agency 2016–2017.

4. TAMING THE TYRANT

1 In the modern period there has emerged a third variety of tyranny, called by Newell "millenarian tyranny" (I would prefer "ideological tyranny"). See Newell 2013. Newell's book is stimulating, but as a survey of Western ideas on tyranny it contains some large gaps, such as the Roman Empire, the Roman legal tradition, the Middle Ages, and the Renaissance before Machiavelli. The same lacunae appear in Boesche 1996. The overview by Robert von Friedeburg in the *New Pauly,* s.v. Tyrannis, executes a less drastic leap, merely from Thomas Aquinas to Luther, while the far more detailed work of Turchetti 2001 manages to devote only a dozen or so pages to Petrarch, Boccaccio, Bartolus, Salutati, and the Renaissance debate about Julius Caesar. For the historical phenomenon of tyranny in the Italian trecento Zorzi 2013 is of great value. Also relevant is Villard 2008, which argues for a general change during the high and late Renaissance from the concept of tyranny as a corrupt constitution (as in Aristotle's *Politics*), to tyranny as a pattern of behavior marked by greed, cruelty, and licentiousness.

2 Greek sources beyond Plato and Aristotle in general understand a tyrant to be a ruler who imposes his rule on unwilling subjects without any basis in law and for his own benefit rather than that of the population as a whole. See the standard work of Berve 1962, who notes that by the time of the Hellenistic kings "tyrant" had become hardly more than a term of censure, condemning the moral quality of a ruler.

3 Luraghi 2015, summarized on page 147 in this chapter. While acknowledging that most of the discourse of ancient Greek tyranny focused on the character-type of tyranny, Luraghi sees the motivation of this discourse as political. For the uncertainties of modern scholars about archaic tyranny, see Dewald 2003 and Luraghi 2013.

4 For the Renaissance interpretation of the Spartan tradition, see Chapter 15.

5 On Greek tyranny as a problem of psychology, see Luraghi 2013, 136, and more fully in Luraghi 2015.

6 The latter strategy is pursued in Plato's *Laws;* see Annas 2017.

7 Aristotle, *Politics* 2.7.1266b. A similar position is adopted by Plato in the *Laws,* outlined by Annas 2017, 72–119.

8 Aristotle, *Politics* 2.7 1267b; see also 1267a: "If any desire [inordinate] pleasures which depend on themselves, they will find the satisfaction of their desires only in philosophy" (tr. Everson).

9 Aristotle, *Politics* 4.2.1289b, 4.4.1292a. But see also 4.10.1295a, where Aristotle seems to say that tyranny is among the *politeiae,* unless we should read ἐπειδὴ καὶ ταύτην τίθεμεν τῶν πολιτειῶν τι μέρος to mean not that tyranny is a form of government but a part of the study of polities. Aristotle is often slippery about what forms of government are polities and even whether particular regime types are good or bad; note his statement at 4.8.1293b that aristocracy and "polity" (constitutional government) are perversions (παρεκβάσεις) relative to the absolutely best form of government, kingship, exercised by a superior man. For this sort of "relativism" in Aristotle, see Chapter 3, page 73.

10 Aristotle, *Politics* 4.10.1295a and 3.17.1287b.

11 Aristotle, *Politics* 5.11, 1313b.

12 Aristotle's τρόποι is translated into Latin as *modi* by Bruni—interestingly, in light of Machiavelli's later use of the Italian equivalent in the *Prince*. See Chapter 19, page 451.

13 Strauss 1958, 2013.

14 Tuck 2015. Hoekstra 2012–2013 regards the doctrine of sovereignty as essentially a renaming of the ancient idea of (benign) tyranny. For the history of the idea that absolute sovereignty and tyranny are identical, see Quaglione 2012b. It is a persistent delusion of Western juristic thought to believe that constitutional restraints can by themselves compensate for lack of virtue in rulers and citizens, as though laws could be just or even effective without the inclination to justly interpret, enforce, and obey them.

15 As Greek sources began to be recovered and translated in the fifteenth centuries, the humanists were able to read the Greek historians of Rome—Dionysius of Halicarnassus, Plutarch, Appian, and (by the sixteenth century) Dio Cassius—who in general were far more pro-imperial than the surviving Latin sources. See Chapters 16 and 17.

16 For their relations, see Cicero, *De officiis* 3.69.

17 Frier 1985, 187.

18 Cicero, *Pro Cluentio* 53 (my trans.). The dramatic notion of slavery to the law as a protection against the arbitrary power of individuals may well come from Plato, *Laws* 4.715c–d.

19 A view endorsed in the *Digest of Roman Law;* see Skinner 1998.

20 Pedullà 2018, 198–203. In fact dictators had been known to execute individuals who aspired to kingship; see Smith 2006. Machiavelli could also have taken his understanding of dictatorship from Patrizi, *De regno,* 1.13, where Patrizi compares the *aesymnetas* to the Roman dictator. DH assimilates dictatorship to *aesymnetas,* described by Aristotle as elective tyranny, and says the office shared features of kingship and tyranny; see *Politics* 4.10.1295a15.

21 The historical reality was, as always, quite different: see Ernst Badian's relentlessly critical account of Caesar's life in Badian 2014, describing Caesar's genocide in Gaul and massive venality and corruption. Badian accepts Suetonius' claim that the real reason why Caesar invaded Roman territory was to avoid conviction and exile for previous misdeeds.

22 Weinstock 1971. Caesar had spent most of the decade of the 70s in the East, where he would have had ample exposure to Greek ideas of kingship. He wanted the title of god but not of king, because the title of Caesar with his godlike and political powers and ancestry was better than that of king. See Rawson 1975.

23 Cicero, *Philippics* 2.85.

24 See Glinister 2006.

25 Rawson 1975, 151.

26 Tacitus, *Histories* 1.1.1, 1.16; *Annals* 4.33.2. This view was endorsed also by the Roman jurist Pomponius (*De origine iuris* l.2 *novissime*), and in this way it became the conventional wisdom of the Middle Ages. See for example Giles of Rome, *De regimine principum* 3.2.3–4, ed. 1607, 456–460, who is cited by Bartolus, *De regimine civitatis* 2, ed. Quaglione, 153–168.

27 When the needs of his case required it, Cicero could sound a different note, for example in *Pro Murena* 13, where, atypically, he derides law as a science for petty minds.

28 In his private correspondence with Atticus he kept up a frequent invocation of Plato and Greek models of tyranny; see especially *Att.* 7.11.1, from 49 BC: "And he says he is doing all this for honor's sake *(dignitatis causa)!* Where is honor without moral good *(honestas)?*" But then he immediately reverts to legal arguments: "And is it good to have an army without public

authority, to seize Roman towns by way of opening the road to the mother city, to plan debt cancellations, recall of exiles and a hundred other villanies," all "for that greatest of gods, the possession of tyranny?" See Gildenhard 2006 (his trans., with slight modifications).

29 Straumann 2016a.

30 Høgen 2015, 41–67.

31 Cicero, *De officiis* 3.23, 26.

32 Cicero, *De officiis* 3.86. See also Chapter 5.

33 Cicero, *De officiis* 3.92, quoting Euripides' *Phoenician Women* lines 524–525.

34 See Chapter 3, page 73.

35 Cicero, *De officiis* 3.83.

36 Discussed in detail by Stacey 2007, 23–72. See esp. *De clementia* 3.11–12 (the differences between the tyrant and king are purely moral) and *De beneficiis* 2.20 for Seneca's summary of the reasons why the republic could not have continued in the time of Julius Caesar (whom Seneca does not admire; see ibid., 4.43). Compare Petrarch, *Fam.* 4.2.7–12, quoting Seneca's *Thyestes* 344–349 and 380–388. One should note the parallel theme in Renaissance religious thought prioritizing a person's interior state or will over the mere observance of external forms. The theme is ultimately Pauline (see Romans 7–8) and Augustinian. See also Chapter 17 for meritocratic justifications of absolutism based on the same Greek sources that fed Seneca.

37 Bartolus, *De tyranno* pref., ed. Quaglione, 175. On the new trecento perception of *signori* as *tiranni*, see Zorzi 2010, 145–148.

38 The classic work is Quaglione 1983; see also the important essay of Ryan 2000. The term "dyarchy" for a mixture of communal and signorial power goes back to Ercole 1910; see also Chapter 3, page 92. For the category of the *tiranno velato*, or veiled tyrant, in the trecento, see Pio 2013.

39 Sometimes reflected in actual theatrics, as in Mussato, *Ecerinis* (ed. Grund).

40 For Petrarch's hostility to *tituli*, see Chapter 5.

41 *Digest* 48.4.3; Quintilian, *Institutes* 4.18.

42 Bartolus, *De tyranno* 6, ed. Quaglione, 187.

43 Ibid., 186–187. Bartolus, as often, is applying to political life an edict of Roman private law commented on by Ulpian in the *Digest* 4.2.6–7, where *iustus metus* means well-founded fear as opposed to the fear displayed by someone not of good character. Bartolus adds that sometimes the *maior pars*, meaning the better people, are cowed into accepting a tyrant by the *maior pars numero*, the numerically greater part (i.e., the majority), and this too counts as legitimate fear because "vile persons of low condition" have no business deciding for a city.

44 *Digest* 48.6.

45 Bartolus, *De tyranno* 9, ed. Quaglione, 203–204; the "new law of Henry" is *Extravagantes Henrici VII, 2, Qui sint rebelles,* according to Quaglione.

46 This may be contrasted with Aquinas' position that in cases of tyranny, it is the tyrant who offends against the common good and is seditious, not a people who rises up against him, and therefore a popular rising against a tyrant is justified when performed to restore the orientation of the political community to the common good. See Kempshall 1999, 125–126 and page 130 in this chapter, on Salutati's use of Bartolus.

47 On Baldus, see Pennington 1997 and Canning 1987; for Baldus on tyranny, see ibid., 225–226.

48 Baldus, *Tractatus de tyranno*, ed. Quaglione, 78–83.

49 Quoted in Black 2009, 28.

50 Tito Livio Frulovisi (*De republica,* ed. Previté-Orton, 295–318, composed in 1435) and his interlocutors discuss throughout book 1 the difficulty of fitting actual historical regimes (including modern regimes) into Aristotle's sixfold analysis of one, few, and many / good and bad, distinguished by their devotion to the common good or to private goods. Sometimes bad kings successfully conceal their evil deeds and are loved by the people: Should the love of the people then be trusted as a criterion of legitimacy? Sometimes a king, intending to benefit himself, also benefits the people: Should he be called a *semirex* or *medius rex?*

51 See O'Connell 2017 on the subject of "voluntary submission" (following military conquest) to Venice's imperial rule.

52 Baldo himself raises this possibility (Canning 1987, 90–92) and states that a people who resist a tyrannical emperor, one who has violated the principle of *utilitas publica,* would not be in violation of natural reason, though he does not say their actions would be legal. In general, however, medieval theory had difficulty accepting the possibility that a legitimate ruler could be evil; see Nederman 2018. When wrong acts issued from a monarchy the standard response was to blame the ruler's counselors or ministers and not the sovereign.

53 See Black 2009 on the attempts of lawyers to reform arbitrary power in the Visconti state, which had some limited success. Humanist lawyers—most famously, perhaps, Andrea Alciati—regularly called for the reformation of modern laws on the model of antiquity. The quotation from Pedullà is from the introduction to his edition of Machiavelli's *Prince,* XLII.

54 Boccaccio, Letter VII, as from the Priors of Florence to Petrarch, but undoubtedly composed by Boccaccio.

55 On the move to Milan and the "tempesta di polemiche" aroused by his decision to accept the protection of the Visconti, see Fenzi 2005.

56 Boccaccio, Letter X.

57 They were also all men of Guelf sympathies, who would surely have been appalled at Petrarch's agreement to serve the leader of the Ghibelline cause in Italy.

58 For example, in his *De vita et moribus Francisci Petracchi de Florentia,* begun in 1341, while Petrarch was still living with Azzo da Carreggio (see note 59).

59 It is noteworthy that in Boccaccio's life of Petrarch he sees no stain in the poet's close personal friendship with Azzo da Correggio, with whom Petrarch had a relationship similar to the one he later had with Cola di Rienzo. Azzo, whom Giorgio Montecchi (*DBI* s.v. Correggio, Azzo da) describes as "the greatest of the brigands of the period," began life as a cleric and came to power with his brothers in Parma in 1336 without legal title, as part of a Ghibelline alliance with the Visconti and Mastino della Scala. When Azzo reconquered Parma from the della Scala in 1341, he was accompanied in his triumphal entry by Petrarch, fresh from his crowning as poet laureate in Rome. Azzo presented himself as the liberator of Parma from the tyrant Mastino and was supported in this ideological self-presentation by Petrarch, as is witnessed by a *Canzone ad Azzo da Correggio* (*Rime,* ed. Neri et al., 619–624), which celebrates Azzo as a modern Cato. The poem was originally part of the *Canzoniere* but was later suppressed and replaced with the famous canzone *Italia mia.* This was an editorial decision that, as Steinberg 2009, 91, notes, amounted to replacing a partisan "republican" political poem with a nonpartisan one. In his letter *Posteritati* Petrarch mused that Azzo's rule had failed because of dissension among brothers. Azzo is the Gillias of *Bucolicon carmen* 8 and the dedicatee of *De remediis* (as a man who had experience both good and bad fortune). After losing Parma in 1346 he became essentially a condottiere.

60 See Chapter 6, page 184, for Petrarch's argument that literary men had no duty to serve bad governments.

61 Though there are echoes of Boccaccio's criticism in *Sen.* 17.2, tr. Fantham 2.17 (from 1373), written just before Petrarch's death, where, to Boccaccio's remark that he has wasted much time "in service to princes," Petrarch responds firmly: "Here, so you do not go astray, read the truth. I was with the princes in name but in fact they were with me. Their councils never held me and their dinners most rarely. I never gave approval to any restriction which would keep me even a little from my freedom and my studies. So when they all made for the palace, I went to the woods or remained quietly with my books in my chamber." He did not want to be seen as a courtier. A similar concern to present himself as independent of princes is found in *Posteritati,* his letter to posterity, in *Sen.* 18, tr. Fantham 9.2.

62 Petrarch, *Invectives,* tr. Marsh, 180–202. Like Boccaccio, Jean had once idolized Petrarch and eagerly sought out his friendship (see §§ 9–12).

63 An obsessive concern with Petrarch; see Chapters 5 and 6.

64 See *Fam.* 3.7.3, tr. Fantham 5.4.3, for the tyranny exercised by oligarchs. Petrarch cites the tyranny of the Thirty in ancient Athens as an example of a tyrannical oligarchy. Even Bartolus, the great definer of legitimacy, writes (*De tyranno* 12) that all governments are sometimes tyrannical. Petrarch takes a darker view. In *Rem.* 3.39, tr. Rawski 2: 100, he says of his times, "Who can enumerate all the tyrants of old, and of the present? Today there are so many of them, so securely entrenched and supported by wealth and the power of the people, as well as by custom and madness, that they cannot be counted or eradicated." In *Rem.* 1.85, the matter is put even more strongly, such that being a *dominus* and a good man are mutually exclusive. Even the oppressed themselves are not let off the hook, for in *Rem.* 2.30 Petrarch points out the responsibility citizens bear for allowing themselves to be ruled by tyrants. On these points, see also Cappelli 2016a.

65 Petrarch, *Invectives,* tr. Marsh, 212–213.

66 *Rem.* 2.78: "Nam quid sunt aliud regna quam vetuste tyrannides? Non sit bonum tempore, quod natura est malum," perhaps an echo of Augustine's "Quid sit regna nisi magna latrocinia?" (*De civitate Dei* 4.4). See also *Rem.* 2.81, tr. Rawski 2: 183: "As I said before when we talked about a king without a son, nearly all kingships were once tyrannical lordships. Yet in the course of time they gained strength and, due to the forgetfulness of the people, they hide now behind a veil of justice, so that today lordships are hateful because they seem unlawful and unusual." At *Rem.* 1.85 Petrarch implies that even good lords are tyrants because they necessarily take away from their subjects the best thing they have, namely, liberty.

67 See the previous note for the origins of "nearly all kingships" in tyranny; compare 1.96, where the figure of Ratio claims the Greeks did not distinguish between a king and a tyrant (Petrarch's source is probably Augustine, *De civitate Dei* 2.21).

68 Petrarch, *Invectives,* tr. Marsh, 209.

69 Ibid., 209–211. His independence of powerful persons is also a theme of the *Letter to Posterity* (*Sen.* 18, tr. Fantham 9.2). In practice, maintaining independence was difficult; Petrarch acknowledges his own struggles for liberty as a dependent of Visconti in *Fam.* 17.10.9, tr. Fantham 4.16.9.

70 Petrarch, *Invectives,* tr. Marsh, 211.

71 Compare Philostratus' presentation of Apollonius of Tyana in book 5 of the *Life:* "Apollonius: 'To me no constitution matters, since I live as the gods' subject, but I do not think that the

human herd should perish for lack of a just and reasonable herdsman. Just as one man of exceptional virtue changes democracy so as to make it so appear the rule of one man better than the rest [an allusion to Thucydides' judgment on Pericles], so the rule of one man who is always looking out for the common good is a democracy'" (Loeb translation). The work was unknown to Petrarch but was translated in the fifteenth century by Alamanno Rinuccini, after which it enjoyed considerable popularity; see Chapter 17, page 395.

72 Petrarch, *Invectives,* tr. Marsh, 212–215.

73 See Chapter 6.

74 A similar point is made later by Giovanni Pontano, humanist prime minister to five kings of Naples, in his dialogue *Aegidius,* cap. 52 (ed. Gaisser), where he claims that by controlling his greed and not taking opportunities to enrich himself, he attained greater influence over the kings he served.

75 Petrarch, *Invectives,* tr. Marsh, 215.

76 Chapter 1, page 18.

77 *Rem.* 2.81. On Petrarch's concept of consolation, see McClure 1991.

78 For the figure of Caesar in the Middle Ages, see Witt 1969; Panou and Schadee 2018.

79 In his speech (Sallust, *Bellum Catilinae* 51) Caesar is, crucially, made an eloquent spokesman for the rational control model of morality as it applies to public deliberation.

80 On what might be called the "incarnational argument" for the legitimacy of the Roman Empire, see Davis 1957, 57–68.

81 Petrarch, *De gestis Cesaris,* ed. Ferrone, 3: 231–233.

82 Ibid.

83 Probably referring to Cicero's and Suetonius' belief that Caesar invaded Italy to save himself from debt and charges of criminal activity; see Badian 2014.

84 See Hankins 2010b on Salutati's limited knowledge of Plato.

85 In his *De nobilitate legum et medicinae* (see Garin 1947) Salutati saw medicine as a dubious application of unreliable natural philosophy while showing a Ciceronian appreciation for law as the bond of human society and a sphere for eloquence. Nevertheless, like Petrarch he saw modern legal practice as a corruption of a noble aspect of Roman moral greatness.

86 Witt 1969; Witt 1983, 368–386.

87 Dante, *Inferno* 34.61–67.

88 See Quaglione 2012a for an overview of the historiography. For the historical context of Salutati's willingness to defend monarchy in this treatise, see Black 1998, 992–993.

89 For "exclusivism," see Chapter 3, page 71.

90 The use of *communis respublica* to mean the Roman Empire comes from Baldus. Salutati in general uses the term *respublica* to mean constitutional or legitimate government and may be avoiding the term *imperium* for Christendom because Florence was a Guelf city that recognized a spiritual overlord, the pope, but exercised *de facto* sovereignty *(sibi princeps)* with respect to the empire.

91 Blythe 1992. For this conception in Baldus, see Canning 1987; in Salutati's *De tyranno,* see Witt 1983. See also Chapter 12. Quaglione 2012a, 345, gives a useful summary of this conception: "The survival of a strong imperial tradition in the thought of the medieval jurists, almost in contradiction to the weakness of the Empire, has often occasioned surprise. In reality, the faith in the Empire among the medieval jurists is faith in a principle that validates every other process of power, a universal ordering principle, a "sovereign" guarantee of a juridical order turning

on the idea of *iurisdictio* and the exercise of justice, one that manifests itself in a more open manner precisely in an age when universalism was in crisis and when new forms of power seeking legitimation were making their appearance." For the premodern conception of sovereignty, see Quaglione 2004, 2007, and 2012b.

92 Salutati, *De tyranno* 4.16–17, ed. Baldassarri, 128–130 (translation modified).

93 See Aristotle, *Nicomachean Ethics* 5.3.1131a–1131b, where arithmetical and geometrical principles of distributive justice are distinguished.

94 Witt 1983; see also the notes to Baldassarri's edition.

95 Salutati, *De tyranno* 1.9, ed. Baldassarri, 79.

96 Nero and Phalaris were famous ancient Roman and Greek tyrants, respectively. Ezzolino III da Romano (1194–1259), tyrant of Padua, was the eponymous subject of a tragedy by Albertino Mussato (1261–1329), edited in Grund 2011, 2–47. Busiris was a mythological tyrant implicated in the Hercules legends, about whom Salutati writes in *The Labors of Hercules* 3.20.

97 Salutati, *De tyranno* 2.15–16, ed. Baldassarri, 101.

98 Ibid., 113.

99 Ibid., 95.

100 Salutati, *De tyranno* 2.10, ed. Baldassarri, 95. Salutati is relying here on language and arguments used in Bartolus' *De tyranno* and Baldus' *Commentary on the Codex* 1.2.16: see Baldassarri's apparatus.

101 Gregory the Great, *Moralia* 12.38. Compare Bartolus, *De tyranno* 2, ed. Quaglione, 177–178. A "common commonweath," *communis respublica,* in Gregory's text simply means a state, not the empire, as in the fourteenth-century jurists (see note 84 above). I owe this clarification to the late Paul Meyvaert. Bartolus assumed the phrase meant the *respublica Romanorum*.

102 Cicero, *Pro Marcello* 10.31.

103 Salutati, *De tyranno* 3.12, ed. Baldassarri, 115.

104 Nederman 2018, 150: "Salutati thus approaches, if he does not explicitly endorse, a conception of benevolent despotism that challenges the usual bases for the medieval distinction between king and tyrant."

105 On Poggio's career and thought, see Celenza 2018, 138–156. For his role in the Scipio-Caesar controversy, see Pedullà 2010–2012.

106 Guarino, *De praestantia*, in Canfora 2001, citing Suetonius, *Julius* 1. I make use of a provisional translation (slightly adjusted) by Hester Schadee, forthcoming in the I Tatti Renaissance Library.

107 Ibid. (emphasis added).

108 Guarino's line of argument was later elaborated in much greater detail by Biondo Flavio; see Chapter 11.

109 Exposed and deplored by his teacher Salutati in an earlier dispute about literary style and religious belief. See Hankins 2007–2008b, 913–915.

110 See Chapter 5. On the 1430s, see also Canfora 2005, who (following Garin) connects the new mood with the rise of the Medici to power in Florence and the fading of republicanism.

111 See Canfora's introduction to Bracciolini, *De infelicitate principum;* the work survives in about 50 MSS, a considerable circulation in the last age of the manuscript book.

112 The ambiguous Latin word is *duces,* which in classical Latin means "commander" but in medieval Latin could mean "duke" in the sense of "territorial ruler."

113 They are explicitly included at caps. 93–94; wealthy men at cap. 86.

114 See Schadee 2018, 172–190. In addition to the sources listed in Canfora's edition, the sentiment probably also reflects Aristotle's *Politics* 5.11, 1313a34–1314a29, translated by Leonardo Bruni in 1438.

115 See Chapter 2, page 40.

116 Bracciolini, *De infelicitate principum* 32, ed. Canfora, 20–21.

117 Field 2017, 276–319, classes Poggio himself as a "Medicean intellectual," but the argument of the dialogue as a whole, especially the paragraph on how acquiring riches destroys felicity (cap. 86), would seem to contain an implicit critique of Cosimo, the wealthy oligarch. For those given to sniffing out subtexts and esoteric messages, the dialogue might even be read as a warning to Cosimo, the would-be humanist *princeps,* not to assume princely power or to seek to distinguish himself in the ways described in cap. 36 (quoted below). Using an indirect form of counsel was a well-known humanist strategy. I do not mean to suggest that Poggio was not closely identified with Cosimo's party, as the circumstances of his dismissal from office in 1456 show; see Black 1985, 88–93.

118 Cicero, *De officiis* 1.4.13.

119 Bracciolini, *De infelicitate principum* 36, ed. Canfora, 23.

120 Ibid., 37, ed. Canfora, 24.

121 The idea that all earthly government is simply a wicked tyranny, an inevitable outcome of the orientation of the "earthly city" to corrupt ends, has clear Augustinian antecedents, and one can find such views as well among medieval critics of the empire such as Pope Gregory VII, who in 1081 wrote, "Who does not know that kings and dukes had their rulership from those who, not knowing God, strove from blind greed and intolerable presumption to dominate their equals, namely mankind, by pride, rapine, perfidy, murder, and crimes of all sorts, urged on by the ruler of the world, that is, the devil?" (Gregory VII in 1081, cited by Poole 1920, 201n5, my trans.). But Poggio does not appeal explicitly to Christian principles in the *De infelicitate* and even expresses skepticism (as did Augustine for that matter) that Christianity could make any difference to the moral quality of earthly government.

122 Bracciolini, *De infelicitate principum* 41, ed. Canfora, 26.

123 Ibid., 79, ed. Canfora, 49.

124 Ibid., 47, ed. Canfora, 29–30.

125 For one example, see Chapter 2, page 43. The list, first assembled by Petrarch, was commonly quoted by educators in the quattrocento.

126 Poggio may well be conscious here of a similar point about the incompatibility of real virtue and political life made by Plato's Socrates in the *Apology* 32a, a text translated twice by his friend Leonardo Bruni.

127 See Bruni's invective against Niccoli, *In nebulonem maledicum,* in *Opere,* ed. Viti, 333–370. See Field 2017, 233–275, on Niccoli's politics.

128 Bracciolini, *De infelicitate principum,* ed. Canfora, cap. 66. When explaining in cap. 48 why princes necessarily lack the virtues, Niccoli uses rather the language of virtue politics: he explains that princes cannot be just men *(iusti),* "because this virtue has to do with distributing rewards and punishments, and they confer punishments on the principle of maintaining their own position *(status).* They don't punish the guilty but very often exalt them for acknowledged wickedness. They by no means reward the good, but those whom their lusts persuade them to reward, usually reprobates and scoundrels."

129 See BRF, MS Ricc. 784 (s. XV ¼) for a collection of speeches by various Milanese literati in praise of Giangaleazzo Visconti's virtues. The attitude of withdrawal was common among humanists in the time of Eugene IV and in Medicean Florence. See Chapter 13 on Leon Battista Alberti, Alamanno Rinuccini's *De libertate,* as well as the letters of Niccolò della Luna in BRF, MS Ricc. 1166.

130 In the *De avaritia* 20, tr. Kohl, 270, the speaker Andreas Chrysoberges, who seems to represent Poggio's point of view, describes the corruptions to which princes are subject in less Manichean terms: though most rulers are bad, some are good, and it is not impossible for them to possess wisdom, though most do not. See Chapter 7, page 208.

131 See Chapter 17 for Francesco Patrizi's response to Poggio.

132 Chapter 17 discusses yet another form of realism, a kind of moral realism that consists in understanding just how bad a prince or a state is by comparing him, or it, with an ideal standard.

133 Jacob Burckhardt wrote, "The picture of the fifteenth century would be incomplete without this unique biography, which is characteristic down to its minutest details" (Burckhardt 1958, 242, cited by Gary Ianziti in his introduction to the I Tatti edition of the text (ix), who adds in a note, "Burckhardt's thumbnail sketch of Filippo Maria Visconti . . . is entirely dependent on Decembrio's biography."

134 See Fasolt 2014.

135 Decembrio, *Life of Visconti* 44, ed. Ianziti and Zaggia, 77. For the story about Cosimo de'Medici, see Kent 2000, 172.

136 Cicero, *De officiis* 1.34. Compare Machiavelli, *FH* 6.1, tr. Banfield and Mansfield, 230: "It has always been the end of those who start a war—and it is reasonable that it should be so—to enrich themselves and impoverish the enemy. For no other cause is victory sought nor for anyone else are acquisitions desired than to make oneself powerful and the adversary weak."

137 See Decembrio, *Life of Visconti* 62.2, ed. Ianziti and Zaggia, 125: "There was just one thing that was truly peculiar to him alone and quite typical of his style, and this was his never wanting to write anything that was clear and transparent. Rather, having laid out beforehand what was to be said, he would add an observation at the end that would strike a note of ambiguity, throwing into confusion everything that had come before." For the love of ancient tyrants for cryptic communication, see Luraghi 2015, 74.

138 That contemporaries found the inclusion of such details shocking and unseemly is shown by correspondence with Leonello d'Este published in Decembrio, *Life of Visconti,* ed. Ianziti and Zaggia, 250–255; see also xiii–xiv.

139 Decembrio, *Life of Visconti* 41, ed. Ianziti and Zaggia, 67.

140 Ibid., 62 (Ianziti and Zaggia, 125). Ianziti notes, "Throughout the 1430s Decembrio was directly involved in the production of vernacular versions of ancient historians at the Visconti court. During this time he personally translated the *Historia Alexandri* of Curtius Rufus and the *Commentarii* of Julius Caesar. His friend and fellow humanist Antonio da Rho translated the *De vita Caesarum* of Suetonius."

141 See Chapter 2.

142 For the possibility that Machiavelli read Decembrio's *Life of Visconti,* see Chapter 19, note 17.

143 For that discourse, see Turchetti 2001; Luraghi 2013, 2015. The most comprehensive list of ancient sources for Greek tyranny to my knowledge is to be found in Berve 1962, vol. 2.

144 Hankins 2007–2008a, 20–33; Hankins and Palmer 2008, 20–23.

145 For the four translations, see Hankins 1990a. Another important Platonic text on tyranny was *Gorgias* 466d–481b, translated in 1405 / 1409 by Leonardo Bruni.

146 For the date of Bruni's translation, see the addenda to the second impression (1991) of Hankins 1990a, 849. For questions about the authenticity of some letters (but not the crucial Seventh and Eighth Letters), see Hankins 1990a, 1: 79–80, 306–307. The latest attempt to disprove Plato's authorship of the Seventh Letter is Burnyeat and Frede 2015.

147 Pagliaroli 2006, with further bibliography; the *ed. princ.* is undated but datable to "before 1474." There are also three later incunable editions. Giovanni Pontano claimed that Valla began the translation at the request of Alfonso of Aragon and left it at his death in 1459 without the *ultima manus;* see Percopo 1907, 25–26. A translation by Mattia (not Matteo) Palmieri, completed certainly before 1463 (but more probably in the 1440s), survived in four manuscripts, on which see Pagliaroli 2012, who published an edition of the proemium on 39–43. The *ed. princ.* of the Greek text was published by Aldus in 1502; the preface is edited and translated in Manutius, *Greek Classics,* ed. Wilson, 106–112. It should be noted that Valla (unlike some modern English translators) consistently renders the various substantive, verbal, and adjectival forms of τυραννίς with their Latin cognate. On the reception of Herodotus, see Gambino Longo 2012 and Priestley and Zali 2016, esp. the articles by Adam Foley, Dennis Looney, and Benjamin Earley. Guarino had translated much of book 1, and an Italian translation by Boiardo was undertaken for the Estense court.

148 Dewald 2003. A fine example of how Herodotus came to inform the historical consciousness of Latin humanism is found in chapter 1.3 of Patrizi's *De regno* (1481 / 1484), where a summary of Athens's political history is given, including an extended account of Pisistratus' tyranny that relied also on the supposed correspondence of Solon and Pisistratus preserved in Diogenes Laertius. For Patrizi's use in the *De inst. r.p.* of the "debate on constitutions" in Herodotus 3.80–82, see Chapter 16, page 370.

149 Dewald 2003, 32. Thucydides was translated by Lorenzo Valla in 1448 / 1452 (see Pade 2003, 120). Thucydides claims through the mouth of Pericles that the empire of democratic Athens is "like a tyranny, which is deemed wrong to take, but dangerous to let go" (2.63.2–3). In 1.13 Thucydides makes increasing wealth the cause of the transition from "hereditary kingship based on fixed prerogatives" to tyranny. The *ed. princ.* of Thucydides in Greek was published by Aldus in 1502; the preface is edited and translated in Manutius, *Greek Classics,* ed. Wilson, 98–103.

150 The text circulated widely: there survive over 200 manuscripts, and there are translations from Bruni's Latin into French, German, and Spanish; see Hankins 1997. For the eight incunable editions of Bruni's translation, see *ISTC.* For its influence in the early quattrocento, see Maxson 2010.

151 For orientation, see Richter and Johnson 2017.

152 Lucian's *Phalaris* speeches were (unusually) published in Greek first (*ed. princ.* Florence 1496, ed. Janus Lascaris), but the first translation to my knowledge was that of Vincentius Opsopoeus (d. 1539) from c. 1530. Lucian also wrote *The Downward Journey or the Tyrant (De navigatione vel tyranno),* which was translated by Cristoforo Persona (Rome: Georgius Lauer, 1470 / 1472, *ISTC* il00320400). It contains a more conventionally moralizing presentation of the tyrant as not being as happy as most people think; his misery is exposed on the downward journey to Hades. See Marsh 1998, 51–55. Lucian's *The Tyrannicide* does not hold much interest for historians of political theory. Another text of the Second Sophistic is the fifth discourse of the Cynic

philosopher Dio Chrysostom, on the misery of tyrants, which was not published in translation until 1545.

153 Their authenticity was still being defended in the seventeenth century. The pseudonymous character of the letters was proven by Richard Bentley. Poliziano, *Letters* 1.1, ed. Butler, 1: 4–5, shrewdly attributed them to Lucian in a letter to Piero de' Medici written in 1494 and first published in 1498.

5. THE TRIUMPH OF VIRTUE

1 For Petrarch's politics, see Ascoli 2011; Bayley 1942; Bejczy 1994; Bernardo 1980; Bigalli 2002; Cosenza and Musto 1996; Dotti 2001; Fenzi 2005, 2005–2006; Feo 1992–1993, 1994; Ferraù 2006; Furlan and Pittalunga 2016; Kölmel 1970; Lázar, Coroleu, and Steiner-Weber 2012; Luciani 1985; Manselli 1976; Mazzotta 1993 (esp. 102–128 and 181–192); Mazzocco 2006b; Melczer 1975; Ponte 1997; Santinello 1974; Stacey 2007, esp. chapters 3 and 4.

2 See Mazzocco 2006.

3 Ascoli 2011.

4 Hankins 1995a.

5 Petrarch is ignored in Carlyle and Carlyle 1950, Burns 1988, and Canning 1996. Skinner 1978 treats him as a founder of humanism but not as a political thinker in his own right. Witt 2000 does not treat his political thought, but he thinks it significant that Petrarch had "no direct experience of communal life" and was the first major humanist to be a cleric (231), and he casts him as a monarchist (288n) who grew up "in the monarchical environment of Avignon" (287).

6 For Petrarch as politically quietist and a typical "Trecento intellectual," see Baron 1966, 9; Skinner 1978, 1: 108 agrees. The impression is based on works such as the *De otio religioso* and the *De vita solitaria* (see Chapter 6) and letters such as *Sen.* 17.2 (tr. Fantham 2.17.19), where Petrarch protests angrily against Boccaccio's charge that he wasted his time dancing attendance on princes (see Chapter 4, page 118), as well as on Petrarch's famous attack on Cicero for his involvement in politics (*Fam.* 24.3, tr. Fantham 8.2).

7 Stacey 2007, chapters 3 and 4. Other exceptions to the rule include Ferraù 2006, who sees Petrarch as founder of the "signorial tradition" of Renaissance humanist political thought. Dotti 2001 in general sees Petrarch as a forerunner of a modern *engagé* intellectual, exploring "the exact mission of the intellectual in relation to political life" (188). He emphasizes a "transgressive" Petrarch who challenges the "establishment," including "the Christian point of view." Bigalli 2002 offers a measured critique of Dotti. A note similar to Dotti's is struck in Fenzi 2005–2006. Feo 1992–1993 and 1994 emphasize Petrarch's engagement in the political life of his times and his internationalism; Cosenza and Musto 1996 emphasizes his Italian patriotism.

8 See Dotti 2001, 181, 208–212, and Ferraù 2006, passim, who argue that Petrarch's relationship with princely patrons foreshadows the "humanist advisor" relationship of the later Renaissance. On the differences between Petrarch's way of life and that of quattrocento humanists, Baron 1988, 1: 185–90, is well worth re-reading, despite the rather artificial distinction between the mentalities of trecento and quattrocento humanists. Through his direct influence Petrarch seems mainly to have inspired a plague of poetasters; see *Fam.* 13.7, tr. Fantham 3.11, where he engages in some humblebrag about the ill effects of his poetic example, how his example has led members of the Curia to desert Gratian and Galen for Homer and Hesiod, etc. (No work

of Hesiod was available in Latin in Petrarch's time.) One should also not underestimate the influence of his attractive portrait of the solitary life, for which see the next chapter.

9 Fenzi 2005. Petrarch was offered the position of apostolic secretary to the pope but evaded the offer by claiming *per ironiam* that he was unable to adapt his high-flown manner to the humble style of the papal chancery. See *Fam.* 13.5.11–20. The role of the quattrocento humanist as diplomat is emphasized in Maxson 2014.

10 Witt 2000, 2011.

11 For example in the letter to Niccola Acciaiuoli, discussed below, and *Fam.* 1.9, 6.4, 7.17, tr. Fantham 5.1–3.

12 Ascoli 2011. Another outburst of partisanship, tinged with Guelf loyalties, is heard in Petrarch's canzona *Quel ch'a nostra natura in sé più degno,* which was suppressed from the *Canzoniere,* as Giacomo Ferraù suggests, precisely because it presented a partisan image of himself that Petrarch wanted to efface; see Ferraù 2006, 43–44.

13 A good example is provided by humanist crusade literature, for which see Hankins 1995b. The *Collected Letters* of Filelfo, often directed to Christian princes, provide numerous parallels.

14 *Sen.* 14.1.28, tr. Fantham 5.6.28. The quotation from Augustus comes (with a slight change) from Macrobius, *Saturnalia* 2.4.18. The letter circulated as a separate treatise in numerous manuscripts.

15 Feo 1992–1993, 120. Petrarch is able to ignore Augustine's view that Rome was not really a republic precisely because he thinks it obvious that *ancient* Rome was capable of justice. See *Fam.* 3.7, tr. Fantham 5.4, and Chapter 6 in this volume. The emphasis on justice ultimately goes back to Cicero's famous definition of *civitas* as "concilium coetusque hominum iure sociati," justice as the social bond of the citizenry.

16 *Fam.* 3.7.3, tr. Fantham 5.4.3.

17 *Fam.* 20.4, tr. Fantham 3.14.21–29 (translation modified).

18 Petrarch may well have been influenced by the outrageous corruption of civil law during his time there by the theory of *plenitudo potestatis;* this in effect legalized tyrannical acts on the part of the *signore;* see Jane Black 2009, esp. 8–35; see also Lupinetti 1999 for Petrarch's critique of the law of his time.

19 In particular, the *Invective against a Man of High Rank without Knowledge or Virtue* (i.e., a man who doesn't deserve his high rank), e.g., cap. 40 (tr. Marsh), where an unworthy man who holds an inherited rank is in essence committing an act of theft from his ancestors, stealing their virtue. On this text, see Chapter 4, page 120.

20 Petrarch links them in a letter to Robert on his coronation (*Fam.* 4.7, tr. Fantham 3.5.5), above all for their support of literature. Later in the same letter he claims that Robert consciously imitates Augustus in his governing practices.

21 Paul Veyne, quoted in Bigalli 2002.

22 *Fam.* 4.2, tr. Fantham, 6.1.7–11 (translation modified).

23 Of this text Feo writes (1992–1993, 127), "The Florentines loved this work, they translated it twice and gave it an extraordinary diffusion; indeed it is absolutely the best-known work of Petrarch in Florence, precisely because it posed the problem of the union of power and justice." A commentary on the work (Paris, Bibliothèque Nationale de France, MS Par. lat. 14845) was composed by Petrarch's friend and follower Barbato da Sulmona, an official at the Neapolitan court, who had earlier been a sympathizer of Cola di Rienzo. See Augusto Campana's entry on Barbato in *DBI.* For further discussion of Petrarch's treatise, see Stacey 2007, 138–144.

24 *Fam.* 12.2, tr. Fantham, 5.5.9–13. Petrarch elaborates these ideas further in *Rem.* 1.96.

25 See also Chapter 1, page 18; Chapter 2, page 45; *Sen.* 14.1, tr. Fantham 5.6.27; and Schofield 2009, 204.

26 Wilkins 1958; Dotti 2004. In *Invective against a Man of High Rank* (tr. Marsh, 209) Petrarch defends the young Visconti rulers—Bernabò, Matteo, and Galeazzo—who inherited their power from Archbishop Giovanni as "the best of lords" *(optimi domini),* whereas his accuser is the worst of tyrants. Elsewhere he insists they are "rectores patrie, non tyranni" (their country's guides, not tyrants). "They know as little of the tyrannical spirit as you do of equity and justice." He speculates that time may make tyrants of them, but he cannot be certain of their destiny.

27 The ceremony resembles in many respects those used in the Venetian empire to demonstrate the "voluntary" submission of the subject cities often following military conquest; see O'Connell 2017.

28 Vergil, *Aeneid* 1.562.

29 *Arenga,* ed. Hortis, 341–358: "Et vos ergo cives novarienses, si ex rebellione non voluntaria sed coacta metus aliquis domini cordibus vestris annexus erat, si que cure in animos adivissent, solvite metum, secludite curas et securitatem pristinam fiduciamque recipite."

30 See Chapter 4, page 114. For many more examples of Petrarch's use of legal concepts in his writings, see Lupinetti 1999.

31 Livy 5.27.

32 Aristotle, *Nicomachean Ethics* 8.1.1155a: "Friendship also seems to keep cities together, and lawgivers seem to pay more attention to it than to justice. For like-mindedness seems to be similar, in a way, to friendship, and it is this that they aim most at achieving, while they aim most to eliminate faction, faction being enmity; and there is no need for rules of justice between people who are friends" (tr. Rowe).

33 Compare Sallust, *War against Jugurtha* 10.4 and 6.

34 Seneca, *Moral Letters* 3.2.

35 Cicero, *On Friendship* 76.

36 *Fam.* 12.2, tr. Fantham 5.5.14. The emperor is Domitian; see Suetonius, *Life of Domitian* 9.3.

37 *Sen.* 14.1, tr. Fantham, 5.6.98 (to Francesco da Carrara).

38 Ibid. This is a classic passage on the benefits to princes of acting as a patron of letters. See also *Fam.* 4.7, tr. Fantham 3.5, to King Robert of Naples. At *Rem.* 1.49 Petrarch takes a darker view of the relationship between the prince and the *literatus,* including "the problem of counsel," i.e., the difficulty of getting the prince to take good advice and the dangers of doing so (see Chapter 4, page 134). On Petrarch's relationship to the humanist advisor of the quattrocento, see Ferraù 2006 and Dotti 2001, 208–212. On Augustus as "the best of emperors," see *Fam.* 24.6, tr. Fantham 8.5.24.

39 *Fam.* 13.6, tr. Fantham 6.5.22–24.

40 Petrarch, *Collatio laureationis,* ed. Maggi, cap. 4. Boccaccio in his letter inviting Petrarch to teach in Florence (*Epistole* 7, dated 1351) alludes to this speech and to the political duty of the poet. Varius is Lucius Varius Rufus, an Augustan poet whose works do not survive.

41 Marrasio, *Poems,* ed. Chatfield, 203. In general this volume of ITRL documents the wave of interest among princes around 1430 in acquiring humanist poet laureates, including men such as Francesco Filelfo, Enea Silvio Piccolomini, and Antonio Panormita.

42 Suetonius, *Divus Augustus* 78–79.

43 *Rem.* praef., tr. Rawski, 1: 3.

44 The relevant texts are usefully collected and translated in Cosenza and Musto 1996, with introductions and notes.

45 See Lee 2016, 25–28, on the importance of this discovery. The inscription was taken as recording the original text of the *lex regia* mentioned in the *Digest* (see Chapter 2) and therefore documenting the moment when the Roman people authorized the emperor to exercise its power. Hence Biondo Flavio and many later historians dated the end of the republic to the reign of Vespasian rather than, as today, to the Battle of Actium.

46 Later he calls himself the "Tribune of liberty, peace and justice and deliverer of the Holy Roman Republic." He claims to have put an end to partisanship and the exile of citizens (Cosenza and Musto 1996, 86). The fact that Cola takes the title of tribune, not consul (as more commonly in medieval Italian communes), is indicative of his populism.

47 Cosenza and Musto 1996, xxiin17.

48 Noble coats of arms were a common object of humanist mockery. The chancellor of Florence, Bartolomeo Scala, a *novus homo,* sent up noble pretension by adopting as his coat of arms a ladder, with the motto, "Gradatim," step by step.

49 Petrarch, *Variae* 48 and *Fam.* 11.16–17.

50 Petrarch addresses a number of his letters to Cola as to the *Princeps Romanorum,* the prince or leader of the Romans. The diploma of citizenship Petrarch received in 1341 mentions his excellence as a poet: see Cosenza and Musto 1996, 120–121. Barbato da Sulmona, Petrarch's friend at the Neapolitan court, wrote a letter-treatise for Cola, *Romana respublica urbi Rome,* in which he recommends that the city of Rome be ruled as a dyarchy between the mind of Petrarch and the strong arm of Cola, "ut scilicet quecumque Laureatus consulit, Tribunus exequatur" (so that whatever the Laureate advises, the Tribune executes). See Augusto Campana's entry on Barbato in *DBI* (1964).

51 On Petrarch as a propagandist, see Feo 1994.

52 See Petrarch, *Sine nomine* 2, tr. Zacour, 38: "Wait a brief moment; you will see great events in the world, and you will be amazed that what you would have earlier thought impossible is now happening."

53 Not Petrarch's but my adaptation of Aristotle's famous line about Plato; see Cosenza and Musto 1996, 109, translating *Fam.* 11.16: "In fact I wish to state here that none of the princely families of this world have been dearer to me than [the Colonna family]. Nevertheless, the public welfare *(respublica)* is even dearer to me. Dearer is Rome, dearer is Italy, dearer the peace and security of the upright."

54 His relations with Colonna grew troubled during and after the experience with Cola, particularly after Giovanni Colonna died in the Black Death; see Chapter 6, page 179.

55 Petrarch, *Variae* 48: "In eadem urbe illos simul dominos et vos liberos esse non posse."

56 Ibid.: "Ausos pro indignis dominis et pro obscena servitute tam grandia audere aliquid pro vobis et pro libertate dignum est, pro qua inventus est et qui Urbe reges et qui vita Cesares spoliaret."

57 See Chapter 4, page 125, for Petrarch's opinion of Caesar.

58 Petrarch, *Variae* 48.

59 Petrarch, *Invectives,* tr. Marsh, 203. See also Chapter 4.

60 Ibid., 207.

61 *Fam.* 8.4. See further, Chapter 6, page 179. The letter was written in 1349.

62 On the limits of Petrarch's "republican" sentiments, see Ferraù 2006, 49–50n11.

63 Despite continuing rumors of popular sympathy for Cola. See for example Cosenza and Musto 1996, 67 and 158. The latter passage suggests that Petrarch as late as 1352 thought a popular or patriotic Italian uprising was possible.

64 A sign of Petrarch's new self-concept as a political advisor to princes and leading men can be glimpsed in the revisions he made to his correspondence: *Variae* 48, the populist panegyric of June 1347, as well as other letters in support of Cola were suppressed, not only from the canonical collection of the 350 *Familiares* finished in 1366, but even from the more politically radical and anonymous *Sine nomine* (finished by 1361). The suppression of this and similar letters was a signal that by the time he was collecting (and rewriting) his letters in the 1360s, they no longer reflected his state of mind or the image of himself he wished to project.

65 *Fam.* 11.16, tr. Fantham 6.6. Feo 1992–1993 points out that this letter had been part of an official dossier, in principle to be kept secret, but was in effect made public by Petrarch when he published it in his *Familiares*. Cosenza and Musto 1996, 105–125, contains useful commentary.

66 *Fam.* 11.16, tr. Fantham 6.6.

67 *Fam.* 11.16.32, tr. Fantham 6.6.32.

68 See Aristotle, *Nicomachean Ethics* 2.9, 1109b7. The passage is the origin of the famous phrase "the crooked timber of humanity."

69 *Fam.* 11.16.34–35, tr. Fantham 6.6.34–35.

70 It is noteworthy that Machiavelli too sees the middle republic as the model for the reform of modern republics; see Chapter 19, page 461. See Flower 2010 for historiographical discussion of the term "middle republic."

71 Petrarch might have found the idea that the Roman people had a genetic superiority to other peoples in Cicero's *Philippics* 4.13: "Virtus propria est Romana generis et seminis" (Roman virtue is a property of its race and seed); see also *Verrines* 2.4.81. For Leonardo Bruni's use of this idea, see Chapter 8.

72 *Fam.* 3.7, tr. Fantham 5.4, datable to 1347 / 1349, four years before Petrarch took up residence in Milan as an ornament of the Visconti court. See also *Fam.* 17.4, to Guido Sette: "It is well established and determined by the wise that the best constitution *(optimum reipublicae statum)* is to be under the just rule of a single person." The same opinion is given in *Sine nomine* 4.

73 Probably an allusion to Luchino Visconti's planned invasion of Piedmont, and possibly the attack on Genoa planned in 1348, according to Ugo Dotti's commentary on this passage.

74 *Fam.* 3.7.4–7, tr. Fantham 5.4.4–7. Ferraù 2006, 48–53, suggests not implausibly that Petrarch had a degree of sympathy with and supported the Visconti ambition to re-establish the old Lombard Kingdom, citing among other documents his poetic *laudatio* of Luchino Visconti *(Metrical Epistles* 3.6). I would note only that it does not follow from Petrarch's approval of Genoa's submission to Visconti lordship that he favored Visconti ambitions in general; he may well have made a pragmatic judgment that Genoa, a famously unstable city, would in its current circumstances benefit from being subject to an external power. In the *Arenga super pace tractanda* (1353) he asserts that Genoa's submission to Milan was voluntary *(sponte sua)* and not forced. For more on the diplomatic situation, see Fenzi 2016.

75 Petrarch, *De gestis Cesaris,* composed in the late 1460s at the request of Francesco da Carrara. For more on Petrarch's view of Caesar, see Chapter 4, page 125.

76 See Tacitus, *Histories* 1.16, where Galba renounces the dynastic principle of succession, claiming he is trying to make the principate less despotic. Galba's speech advocates choosing a successor

henceforward on grounds of merit and not on dynastic grounds; this new practice will be *loco libertatis,* it will give a space for (or possibly "be a substitute for") liberty. Dynastic succession for Tacitus is the mark of despotism. Thus to choose a *princeps* on the basis of merit, a *princeps* who rules not like a master over slaves but allows a modicum of liberty, will prevent the principate from being a tyranny. The ambiguous phrase *loco libertatis* may allude to the common Stoic view that true freedom is to obey just laws and need not imply self-government or freedom from domination. In Polybius 6.6–7, a passage not known to humanists until the mid-fifteenth century (see Chapter 12), primitive kings are said to have been elected for merit and were modest, humble figures. Bartolus too in his *De regimine civitatis* 2 (ed. Quaglione, 166) says that the election of rulers is better than hereditary succession because the former practice more resembles that of the Church and is therefore more divine.

77 Coluccio Salutati implicitly prefers elective kingship in the *De tyranno,* cap. 1, but prefers the election to be made by the good citizens *(inter bonos)* and not by *popularis ambitio,* i.e., by seeking the favor of the people; see Chapter 4, page 128. Salutati says this was the custom in the case of the original Roman kings, as reported in Justin's *Epitome* of Pompeius Trogus (2.1). Later in the same text he claims that Julius Caesar's monarchy had the consent of the vast majority of Romans. See also Chapter 11, pages 293–294, for Biondo's understanding of early Roman kingship as a legitimate form of constitutional government.

78 Glinister 2016. Cicero, *De officiis* 2.41 also presents early Roman kingship as elective.

79 *Rem.* 2.78, tr. Rawski 2: 178. Note that Brahman and Hindu societies are also idealized in Petrarch's *DVS;* see Chapter 6. Some of Petrarch's information about the *Brachmani* came from a treatise of pseudo-Ambrose, *De moribus Brachmanorum (PL* 17: 1131–1146), whose Latin style, as Petrarch already recognized, "did not smack of Ambrose."

6. SHOULD A GOOD MAN PARTICIPATE IN A CORRUPT GOVERNMENT?

1 For modern literature on Petrarch's political thought and action, see Chapter 5, note 1.

2 The most mature statement of Baron's views on Petrarch is found in Baron 1988. For an overview of Baron's interpretation of the early Renaissance and its reception, see Hankins 1995a. For the context of Baron's disdain for the *unpolitisch Mensch,* see Schiller 2000, 99–173.

3 See Dotti 2004, 140–141. In his edition of book 1 of the *DVS,* 8, Enenkel was the first to find evidence of revisions as late as 1372. Wilkins 1961, 182, 232, noted additions in 1362 and 1371.

4 In addition to Poggio (Chapter 4) and Alberti (Chapter 13), other humanists who discussed whether men of virtue needed to withdraw from corrupt polities were Alamanno Rinuccini in his *De libertate* (1479) and Francesco Guicciardini in the *Dialogo del reggimento di Firenze* (1521 / 1526).

5 In what follows I shall be citing the edition of Carraud, which is based on Enenkel (see note 3 above) for book 1 and the edition of Guido Martellotti for book 2, with minor changes. There is a reasonably accurate English translation by Zeitlin that I follow, with modifications as necessary.

6 For the older literature on the *DVS,* see Enenkel's edition, 635–654; for more recent work, see Maggi 2009. Celenza 2017 provides a sensitive portrait of the interplay between Petrarch's personality (at times verging on the misanthropic), his literary world, and his writings.

7 See Wilkins 1961, 204, 208.

8 On the date, see Goletti's remarks in his edition of *De otio religioso* 7. However, in 1.2.62 (ibid., 30) Petrarch refers to the *DVS* "quam nuper edidi" ("which I have recently published"); its publication is usually dated to 1366. On the other hand, in *Fam.* 19.3.20, dated to February 25, 1355, in reporting to his friend Laelius a conversation with the Emperor Charles IV, Petrarch also claimed to Charles to have "recently published" *(nuper ediderim)* the *DVS*. On the relationship between the *De otio religioso* and the *DVS,* see also the remarks of Witt in the introduction to Scheurer's translation of the *De otio religioso,* vii–xxv.

9 The confession is made allegorically in the famous letter *On the Ascent of Mt. Ventoux (Fam.* 4.1, tr. Fantham 2.1). The superiority of Gherardo's way of life is also a frequent theme in their correspondence, for example in *Fam.* 10.3.1–4 (tr. Fantham 7.2) and 10.5.1–3.

10 The model of life was not absolutely new because such ideals had existed in the ancient Greek world, as Petrarch may well have known from his Roman sources; see Brown 2009. He may also have had in mind the example of Augustine's retreat at Cassiciacum or Cassiodorus' Vivarium. Marsilio Ficino discusses the *vita solitaria* in a letter to Gregorio Befani: *Lettere* 1.10, ed. Gentile, 55.

11 Petrarch echoes *De tranquillitate animi* 2.9–10, one of his favorite works by Seneca, and a constant presence in the *DVS*.

12 The phrase echoes Seneca in the *Moral Epistles* 7.3, where he states that he comes home from popular spectacles "inhumanior, quia inter homines fui" ("less human, because I was among humans").

13 *Fam.* 8.4, tr. Fantham 4.11. *Fam.* 19.3.20, tr. Fatham 6.11 (also discussed below) shows that the solitary life and the life of a courtier are also mutually exclusive.

14 *Fam.* 4.16, tr. Fantham 3.8. Petrarch attacks the moral vacuity of scholasticism in the *DVS* at Praef. 9–10, ed. Carraud, 32–36. A more generalized attack on the learning of his day as morally and religiously defective is found in *Fam.* 10.5; see also Chapter 1.

15 1.4.9. Translation adapted from Zeitlin, 151.

16 *Fam.* 4.15–16, tr. Fantham 3.7–8 (the letters may be dated to 1442).

17 On Petrarch's wider views of friendship, see Lafleur 2001. Cf. Seneca, *De tranquillitate animi* 7.3–6.

18 In humanist literature of the fifteenth century, *immanitas* is the lexical opposite of *humanitas,* often meaning something like "cruelty" or "barbarism."

19 Dotti 2004, 94–95. Like Vaucluse, the house permitted easy escape to the countryside, especially to Azzo's castle of Guardasone, twenty-four kilometers to the south, from which Petrarch could wander through the wooded hills of Selvapiana. It was in Selvapiana that he took up anew his writing of the *Africa,* begun in Vaucluse.

20 See Aristotle, *Nicomachean Ethics* 10.8.1179a.4–5. Petrarch alludes to a famous passage that makes his point very well, where Aristotle argues that only moderate resources are necessary for happiness in the contemplative life.

21 *Fam.* 8.4, tr. Fantham 4.11.23–25. The letter reports Petrarch's encounter with Charles in which he defends the solitary life against Charles's hope of having him become his courtier.

22 It should be noted that Petrarch, unlike his ancient Greek sources, includes among those practicing the active life not only soldiers and statesmen but also lawyers and courtiers, temporal and spiritual lords and their superior servants. See *DVS* 1.2.4–9.

23 *Fam.* 3.12.6. The translation is Bernardo's (1: 146). The passage from Cicero's *De republica* (preserved in Macrobius' commentary on the *Somnium Scipionis*) was the most famous passage cited in support of civic religion in the quattrocento. Petrarch cites it again in his famous "mirror of princes" directed to Francesco da Carrara, included in his correspondence as *Sen.* 14.1.28, tr. Fantham 5.6.28. See Chapter 5, page 157.

24 *Fam.* 20.4, tr. Fantham 3.14, discussed in Chapter 1, page 9. Petrarch's advice to Marco Portinari tracks the advice given by Seneca to the non-philosophical man who is already embarked on public life in *De tranquillitate animi* 2.9–3.1.

25 Aristotle, *Politics* 1.2.1253a.

26 Ed. Carraud, 382: "Deinde Aristotelicum illud obiciunt, ubi ait, vel quod naturaliter sociale animal est homo, vel quod, qui aliis non comunicat, aut bestia est aut deus." (Then they throw out the statement of Aristotle where he says either that the human being is naturally a social animal, or that the man who has no dealings with others is either a beast or a god.) The slippage from *animal politicum* to *sociale* was a common one in medieval political literature, going back at least to Aquinas (e.g., *De regimine* 1.1.3). See Blythe 2000, 59–60.

27 Aristotle, *Politics* 3.4.1277b; see Schofield 1999a, 103.

28 E.g., Aristotle, *Politics* 1.2.1252a–b. Elsewhere, when describing in idealized terms the government of Francesco da Carrara in Padua (*Sen.* 14.1.26, tr. Fantham 5.6.26), he chooses to employ the organic metaphor of the body politic: "So you must love your citizens like sons, or rather, so to speak, like the limbs of your body or parts of your soul, since the community is one body, and you are its head." In general, however, Petrarch prefers familial metaphors to describe signorial rule.

29 For example, Bracciolini, *Contra hypocritas*.

30 For the sources of the proverb "Charity begins at home," to which Petrarch alludes, see *DVS*, ed. Carraud, 404n149. For the Stoic doctrine of *oikeosis*, how the wise man following reason expands his sympathies from himself to his family, friends, country, and the cosmos, see Nussbaum 1997. The opposite of Petrarch's Stoic view would be represented by the recent work in the utilitarian tradition of Singer 2015, for whom, *ceteris paribus*, your sick mother has no greater claim on your charity than a baby in Bangladesh, and quite likely less.

31 Petrarch had urged him to take up permanent residence in Rome, thus re-establishing the empire as Roman, and was disgusted when Charles stood by his agreement with the pope to leave immediately after his coronation: see *Fam.* 19.12.

32 Dotti 2004, 277–278.

33 Petrarch, *De otio religioso* 2.7; for Augustine as "philosopher of Christ," see ibid. 2.5, and *Fam.* 17.1.11, tr. Fantham 7.4.11.

34 On Augustine's notion of the secular, see Markus 1988, 1991, and 2006.

35 The point often goes unrecognized by modern historians of political theory who fail to consider the metaphysical rationale behind Augustine's refusal of political action for the betterment of society; for example, in the otherwise illuminating article of Burnell 1995. It would be absurd to pretend that Petrarch had a metaphysics, of time or anything else, but prolonged, receptive reading of Cicero and Seneca gave him something like the *forma mentis* of a Stoic and thus a very different, more hopeful attitude to the world of time and change.

36 O'Daly 1999, 79.

37 Augustine, *De civitate Dei* 19.6.

38 Burnell 1995, 40: "One must do one or the other, for of the three logical possibilities— cooperating, opposing or abstaining [from participation in unjust regimes]—abstaining is not an option: while not necessarily refusing all excuses, Augustine has refused the permanent ubiquity of social injustice as an excuse for permanent retreat from public life."

39 For another example of Petrarch expressing disagreement with Augustine, see *Fam.* 15.9.5–14, tr. Fantham 6.7.5–14, where Petrarch vigorously rejects Augustine's description of Rome as the "new Babylon," a term he liked to reserve for Avignon.

40 Augustine, *De civitate Dei* 19.21; Cicero, *De officiis* 2.8.26.

41 Both editors of the *DVS*, Martellotti and Carraud, refer us to *De civitate Dei* 19.21, where Augustine specifically denies that there ever was a Roman republic answering to the description of Rome in the *Somnium Scipionis*. Augustine, however, also argues that Roman rule might be considered minimally just on the grounds that coercion of the unjust was necessary to maintain order. See Markus 1988.

42 Petrarch's claim at *DVS* 1.6.2 ("I shall never tire of citing Seneca to you") evidently admitted of exceptions. The importance to Petrarch of some Senecan themes in *De otio* is discussed by Stacey 2017.

43 See the discussion by Griffin 2005, 555–558. Griffin remarks that the question of whether or not one should abstain from public life is a persistent theme in Seneca's writings. The *De tranquillitate animi* is highly relevant in this context; see esp. caps. 3–4.

44 Griffin 2005, 556.

45 *Fam.* 22.2, tr. Fantham 3.18, to Boccaccio.

46 Seneca, *De tranquillitate animi* 4.8–5.3.

47 See Moles 1996; and Konstan 2009; for more on humanist cosmopolitanism, see Chapters 11 and 14.

48 In this sense Petrarch might be said to be reverting to the position of the early Christians, that one is obliged to obey the authorities constituted of God but not necessarily to serve them, especially when they command the Christian to act against his or her religion. See Markus 2006, 11–30.

49 According to the standard work on the subject, Schneewind 1998, modern ideas of autonomy depend on "setting religion aside" and abandoning the framework of the natural law tradition, a process that for him only begins with Machiavelli.

50 My thinking on these matters was stimulated by an unpublished graduate seminar paper by Daniel Jacobs, "Petrarch and the *Populus Romanus*" (2017).

51 See *Fam.* 22.14, tr. Fantham, 4.14.6, citing Sallust, *Bellum Catilinae* 2.5–6 (quoted by Jacobs, "Petrarch and the *Populus Romanus*," 14–15).

52 Especially but not only in the *Sine nomine* letters (esp. 4 and 19). On the validity of the Donation in Petrarch's time, see Black 2011b. In *Sine nomine* 4 he rejects the *lex regia* as authorization for the emperors to ignore the will of the Roman people, and in *DVS* 2.4 he contests the right of the popes to perform *translatio imperii*, the legal fiction on which the German empire of the Middle Ages rested. The effect of Petrarch's analysis was to historicize and naturalize the concept of the Roman Empire, leaving open the possibility that its universal authority might be reborn in modern times. On Petrarch's conception of the empire, see Lee 2018, passim.

7. BOCCACCIO ON THE PERILS OF WEALTH AND STATUS

1 Skinner 1978; Burns 1988. Even the standard Italian surveys of humanist political thought, Pastore Stocchi 1984 and Treccani's online *Il contributo italiano alla storia del pensiero,* make only passing mention of Boccaccio.

2 Boccaccio, *De casibus.* In his long review of this edition, Manlio Pastore Stocchi refers to the work as "almost forgotten"; see Pastore Stocchi 1984. The situation is not much better in the present decade; see Marchesi 2013. The abridged translation (often in fact a paraphrase) by Lewis Brewer Hall, in addition to rendering only about half of the text, is often misleadingly inaccurate. The translations of the *De casibus* in this chapter are my own.

3 Branca 1996. It is perhaps owing to Branca's influence that the now-standard work of Witt 2000 places so little weight on Boccaccio's role in the humanist movement. For the historiography, see Gittes 2015. Zaccaria in the introduction to his edition of *De casibus* (xxiv) also classifies Boccaccio as a pre-humanistic thinker.

4 For Boccaccio as a Renaissance figure and his ongoing presence in quattrocento and cinquecento literature, see Eisner and Lummus 2019. Pastore Stocchi 1984, 429–430, remarks in passing on some themes common to Boccaccio and the humanist movement: "una certa passione civile," exhortations to concord and good government, horror of the tyrant, and an apologia for tyrannicide. A kinship between Boccaccio's *De casibus* and the values of Renaissance readers is further suggested by its surprisingly wide diffusion in the fifteenth and sixteenth centuries: seventy-two manuscripts of the complete text, twenty more containing various parts of the work, and nine incunabula, including translations into English, French, and Spanish.

5 Boccaccio, *Epistole* V, ed. Auzzas and Campana, 542–543, dated Florence, August 28, 1341.

6 It was during this period (July 1453) that Boccaccio wrote to Petrarch (*Epistole* X, ed. Auzzas and Campana, 574–583) and criticized him for becoming a subject of the Visconti tyrants and thus becoming a passive enemy of his own *patria.* See Chapter 4, page 118.

7 Regnicoli 2013a. The first part of a more complete and detailed presentation of these documents may be found in Regnicoli 2013b. For Stephen Milner's parallel discoveries, see Armstrong, Daniels, and Milner 2015, 9–12, from which some of the information below comes. The number of known documents has more than doubled, and further documents are likely to emerge from Regnicoli's ongoing research.

8 For the details of Florentine party politics in this period, see Brucker 1962, esp. chapter 4; see also Najemy 2006, 124–151.

9 Brucker 1962, 147.

10 See Brucker 1962, 147, and Bruni, *History* 8.39, ed. Hankins, 2: 433.

11 Armstrong, Daniels, and Milner 2016, 9.

12 The authorization could be taken as evidence that Boccaccio had influence with the clerical party in Florence, which was generally aligned with the older clans against the more popular forces in the city; see Brucker 1962, 172–183.

13 Boccaccio, *Consolatoria,* ed. Chiecchi, caps. 35–37. It should be noted that Boccaccio's letter to Pino circulated widely in literary manuscripts of the fifteenth century.

14 Compare Boccaccio's attack on the Florentines in the *Trattatello in laude di Dante* 7, ed. Ricci, cap. 7, where he sarcastically describes them as having "many ancestors but no virtue" and as being consumed with seeking office "by robbery, treachery and falsehood."

15 The linkages among these three works are extensive. The *De casibus* leaves the strong impression that portions of the *Trattatello* may have originally been part of book 9 before it evolved into an independent work; see note 23 below. The *De casibus* was begun in 1355 and finished through book 7 by 1359; the first redaction in nine books was finished around 1360, and a second redaction was ready in 1373. See Pastore Stocchi 1984, 421–422.

16 Boccaccio, *Consolatoria,* ed. Chiecchi, 296–297.

17 Boccaccio, *De casibus* 5.4.

18 Ibid., 5.4, ed. Ricci and Zaccaria, 398: "Non aspiciunt cives huiusmodi, imo aspicere nolunt, quod primo patrie nascimur, inde nobis." (Citizens like these don't realize, indeed they refuse to realize, that we are born first for our country, then ourselves.) This is an allusion to Cicero's famous version of the Stoic formula *non nobis solum* in *De officiis* 1.22, itself based on [pseudo] Plato, *Letters* 9.358a. In the *Consolatoria,* ed. Chiecchi, cap. 117, Boccaccio admonishes "every good citizen [to] lay out not only his own property, but even his blood and his life for the common good and the exaltation of his own city."

19 Boccaccio, *De casibus* 2, prohemium.

20 Pastore Stocchi 1984, 430, writes of the "overlooked fact" that Poggio Bracciolini's treatises, *De varietate fortunae, De miseria humanae conditionis,* and *De infelicitate principum,* are in effect rewritings of the *De casibus,* "explicating and enriching their most evocative themes with a more felicitous moral inspiration and a more nimble style." For a different view, emphasizing the "medieval" aspects of Boccaccio's view of Fortune, see Marchesi 2013, esp. 247–248.

21 A parallel but shorter discussion is found in the *Consolatoria.* Boccaccio's concept of Good Fame is close to Petrarch's of mortal fame in the *Secret,* ed. Mann, 3.15.4, 3.15.10, 3.17.1–4.

22 A similar statement is found in Petrarch's speech on receiving the laurel, the *Collatio laureationis.*

23 Boccaccio, *Trattatello,* Proem, I, IV, VII, XV. TOGB 3, ed. P. G. Ricci. The passage should be placed next to *De casibus* 9.23, where Boccaccio in a vision espies the shade of Dante among a crowd of unfortunates. Boccaccio offers to tell Dante's story, but the latter denies that he himself is among those struck down by the blows of Fortune (presumably because of his good fame). Instead, he has entered Boccaccio's vision in order to urge him to tell the story of another of Fortune's victims, Walter of Brienne, "to make it clear to posterity what sort of persons your citizens expel, and what sort they accept."

24 Boccaccio, *De casibus* 2.5.

25 Ibid. 6.3: "My view, indeed, is that nobility is nothing other than a kind of splendid distinction, resplendent for its correct behavior and affability in the eyes of those who regard it correctly, arising from a well-trained will in a given soul and committed, to the best of its ability, to executing its work of spurning vice and imitating virtue; it is something which can be left to posterity, not by hereditary right or by right of a legatee, but only as knowledge and intelligence may be left." This view may be contrasted with that of Dante, who regards true nobility as simple human goodness, which in the end is a gift of God; see *Convivio* 4.1, 4.16, 4.20. On Dante's larger context, see Robiglio 2006.

26 Boccaccio, *De casibus* 6.3. The doctrine that anyone, even a slave, can become virtuous and that wealth and lineage (*pace* Aristotle) do not confer advantages in that regard is of Stoic prove-

nance; see Lactantius (*SVF* 3.253) and Ps. Plutarch (*SVF* 3.350). Boccaccio would also have known Seneca, *De beneficiis* 3.28 (*SVF* 3.349). See also Chapter 2, page 40.

27 See Boccaccio, *De casibus* 3.10. For an English edition of Scala's *De legibus,* see David Marsh's translation.

28 In the *Trattatello* Boccaccio uses Dante as a moral example of a great man who embraced the liberal rather than the lucrative studies and sought eternal fame, not transitory wealth.

29 See Chapter 20 for the interpretation of Walter's tyranny by Bruni and Machiavelli.

30 The sense is not clear, but Boccaccio seems to be suggesting that Walter employed a form of order that resembled just order but was backed by the threat of violence.

31 Boccaccio, *De casibus* 9.24.

32 Bartolus, *De tyranno* 6, ed. Quaglione, 185–187; see also ibid., 5, ed. Quaglione, 184: "The tyrant of a city is he who does not rule the city by right." Boccaccio follows instead the teaching of Seneca's *De clementia* 12.1: "What distinguishes a tyrant from a king are his actions, not his name." See Chapter 4.

33 The phrase is mistranslated in Zaccaria's Italian version: he translates *ab optimatibus* by *dai magnati,* but Boccaccio is clearly using *optimates* in the Ciceronian sense of the morally best citizens in the state, the defenders of what is best in the state.

34 Boccaccio here might be thinking of legitimate transfers of power such as that made by the Florentine regime to Charles of Calabria, son of King Robert of Naples, in 1326, for a period of ten years. Najemy 2006, 122–123, believes that Charles might have suffered the same fate as Walter had he not died in 1328.

35 These passages are discussed in detail in Baron 1988, 1: 197–198, and 205–210. Chapters 7–9 in the same volume are still the best overview of humanist economic thought.

36 Boccaccio, *Consolatoria.* On Aldobrandino, see Giovanni Villani, *Nuova cronica* 7.42, under the year 1256, who describes him only as a *franco popolano da San Firenze,* a free commoner from the parish of San Firenze.

37 Boccaccio, *Consolatoria,* quoted in Baron 1988, 1: 207.

38 Baron 1988, 1: 237, points to the influence of Xenophon's *Oeconomics,* brought to Italy in the 1420s and translated into Latin in the mid-quattrocento by Lampugnino Birago. This was "of all classical works probably the most kindly disposed toward economic acquisition and the closest to the capitalistic spirit." On Baron and Weber, see Fubini 2001, 399, and Schiller 2000. In general Baron's views of the history of capitalism were more influenced by Werner Sombart than by Weber. Garin 1964 (tr. Munz, 1965, 44), and Garin 2009, 221, 228–229, are more explicit about the role of the humanists in preparing the ground for Weber's spirit of capitalism. Yet both ignore the one humanist who (to my knowledge) really does seem to have put a positive value on the accumulation of wealth, George of Trebizond: see Chapter 14, page 343.

39 Cicero, *De senectute* 16.55; Plutarch, *Vita Catonis maioris* 9.

40 Skinner 1978, 1: 43. Skinner was criticizing the original formulation of Baron's views in an article published in 1938. Later, in a vastly expanded and far more nuanced form of this article (Baron 1988, chapters 7–9) Baron silently revised his treatment to take account of Skinner's criticisms and the medieval sources he cited, though without mentioning Skinner. He continued to defend the point, however, that Boccaccio's attitude to wealth was "medieval."

41 Baron's lead was followed by Garin 1964, 54–55, and Bec 1967, 379–382, in interpreting Bracciolini's *De avaritia.*

42 Bruni, *Epistolae* 5.2, ed. Mehus 2: 8–15. The letter defends his translation and commentary on the Aristotelian *Economics* dedicated to Cosimo de'Medici, in whose preface he had described riches *(divitiae)* as goods. His correspondent, a Ferrarese lawyer named Tommaso Cambiatore, denied that riches were goods *(bona),* using Stoic arguments. For the proper acquisition and use of money *(pecunia),* see also the passages from Bruni's preface to and commentary on the pseudo-Aristotelian *Economics,* translated in Griffiths, Hankins, and Thompson 1987, 305–317. The latter text was a humanist "best-seller," circulating in hundreds of manuscripts and in seventeen incunabular editions.

43 Bracciolini, *De avaritia;* I make use of Kohl's translation. On the dialogue, composed in 1428, see the rich discussion in Bausi 2009 and Field 2017, 308–315. Unlike Field I think both Bruni and Poggio were not supporting oligarchic values but seeking to reform them. I agree with him that the words put in Poggio's mouth by his enemy Filelfo in the dialogue / invective *De exilio* cannot be trusted as evidence of his real views (Field 2017, 225). Bausi's article definitively rebuts the views of earlier interpreters (e.g., Garin 1964 and Fubini 1990b, 189–219) who saw Antonio Loschi as the mouthpiece of Poggio's own views. Baron himself, surprisingly, ignores the *De avaritia,* basing his account of Poggio's ideas about wealth on his dialogue *De vera nobilitate;* see Baron 1988, 1: 247–251.

44 In the dialogue, following Bausi and Field, I take the Dominican theologian Andreas Chrysoberges of Constantinople to be representing the position of Greek philosophy and thus expressing Poggio's considered view. Antonio Loschi's outrageous, almost neo-liberal defense of avarice—described as an "academic" speech, that is, a case made by a skeptic for the sake of argument—represents rather a common but morally debased opinion that is expressed here only for the purpose of refutation. No humanist of the quattrocento to my knowledge expresses transgressive opinions like those of the interlocutor Loschi. The views closest to his might be those of George of Trebizond (see Chapter 14, page 343), who is far from typical, but even he insists on moral and legal constraints on money-making and would never characterize the deadly sin of avarice as natural. The next closest would be Lapo da Castiglionchio's defense of the wealth of curialists (probably ironic), for which see Celenza 1999, 27, 71–80, 83–84, and the interlocutor Poggio's drunken outbursts in Filelfo's dialogue *De exilio* (undoubtedly parody). It should be noted that the points of view expressed in the *De avaritia* do not resemble those of the several speakers in real life. It is a well-known feature of Poggian humor to put opinions in the mouths of living interlocutors that they would personally have found embarrassing or repugnant. Thus Bartolomeo was known for extravagance (Bruni criticized him for planning a magnificent marble tomb for himself in Montepulciano), Antonio Loschi was a Ciceronian and a Stoic in ethics, while Andreas Chrysoberges (according to Field) was known for his avarice. The dialogue's perspective on the dangers of an immoderate desire for wealth is similar to that of Plato's *Laws* 5.728e, but the text was unavailable to Latin readers in this period.

45 Vergil, *Aeneid* 3.214–218.

46 Bracciolini, *De avaritia,* 21, tr. Kohl, 271 (slightly modified).

47 St. John Chrysostom, a writer prized for his eloquence, was reportedly a favorite author both of Niccolò Niccoli, Poggio's "spiritual guide," and of Cosimo de'Medici. This suggests that the moral message of the *De avaritia* may have been intended in particular for Cosimo (see Bausi 2009, 43–45). For another possible attempt to influence Cosimo in the *De infelicitate principum,* see Chapter 4, page 565n117.

48 On this political literature, the so-called *trattatistica,* see Chapter 17, page 399.

49 On Carafa, see the article of Franca Petrucci in *DBI* 19 (1976).

50 Carafa, *Memoriale,* tr. Guarino, 76. The treatise, written in Neapolitan court dialect, was translated into Latin twice, once by Battista Guarino (son of the famous educator and a courtier of Eleanor), who gave it the title *De regis et boni principis officio* (On the Duty of the King and the Good Prince). I translate from Guarino's version here. See also Brandolini, *Republics and Kingdoms,* 2.19–35, which has a fascinating and highly relevant discussion of the morality of protectionism and free trade in international commerce, analyzing under what circumstances merchants could licitly enrich themselves and how international trade might inflame worthless desires and undermine virtue. The arguments put into the mouth of King Matthias Corvinus in this passage seem almost like responses to Carafa's defense of commerce. Brandolini and Carafa were probably acquainted with each other while both were at the Neapolitan court in the 1470s.

51 Carafa, *Memoriale,* tr. Guarino, 66–67. Carafa's advocacy of royal support for industry and commerce is similar to the line of thought later elaborated by mercantilist thinkers such as Giovanni Botero. For George of Trebizond's positive attitude to wealth-creation as increasing the power of the state and social cohesion, see Chapter 14, pages 341, 344.

52 The expression "political poverty" is Baron's; see Baron 1988, 1: 208.

53 Guarino of Verona, *Epistolario* 1: 7–11 at 9–10. Vergerio, *Epistolario,* 28–30, responds to a letter from his friend Santo de' Pellegrini (ibid., 26–28) who quoted Lucan's line "Poverty is the mother of manhood" from a passage (*Bellum civile* 1: 158–174) illustrating how wealth had caused the decline of Rome in the late republic. Santo goes on to comment that "the necessity [imposed by poverty] drives men to virtue," a sentiment reminiscent of Machiavelli.

54 Biondo, *RT* 5, 1530 ed., 119, citing Cicero's *Pro Murena* 74–76.

55 Filelfo, *De avaritia* (in Italian), cited from BNCF MS Magl. VIII 1440, ff. 99v–101v, and BRF, Ricc. 1200. Book 3 of Filelfo's *De exilio* is devoted to the theme of the correct use of wealth; see Chapter 15 below.

56 Vergil, *Aeneid* 3.56–57: "Quid non mortalia pectora cogis / auri sacra fames!"

57 BLF MS Plut. 77.24.

58 Acciaiuoli, *In Politica,* 1566 ed. (on book 1), f. 14r.

59 Crinitus, *De honesta disciplina* 25.9.

60 See Clarke 2018, chapter 4.

61 See for example *Pr.* 16 and *Disc.* 1.55, 3.28. The classic work on the humanist distrust of commerce and private wealth is Pocock (1975) 2003. Among the more trenchant critiques of Pocock, which discusses a range of humanist opinion on private wealth, is Jurdjevic 2001.

62 Another example of a humanist who called for private frugality and public riches was the papal biographer Bartolomeo Platina; see his *De principe* 132, a passage clearly inspired by Sallust; discussed by Baron 1988, 1: 253–254.

63 See, among other texts, Bruni's commentary on the pseudo-Aristotelian *Economics,* Leon Battista Alberti's *Della famiglia,* and above all, Filelfo's dialogue *De exilio,* book 3 ("On Poverty"), where the issue is examined entirely in categories drawn from ancient Greek philosophy. See in particular the comparison of the virtuous merchant-banker Vitaliano Borromeo (the dedicatee of the work) with the corrupt and vicious Cosimo de'Medici, who is used to exemplify the destructive effects of avarice on the body politic. According to Filelfo, Florence during the exile of Cosimo (1433–1434) experienced a golden age of tranquillity, social harmony, and virtue (*De exilio* 8–11).

64 See Nelson 2004 for Renaissance attitudes to private property; on Machiavelli, see McCormick 2018, chapter 2. The moral attitude to wealth as something to be sought in a spirit of moderation is captured in Pontano's motto, *Egere nolo, opulentus esse recuso* (I don't want to be in need, but I reject opulence).

65 A useful point of entry to this literature is Langholm 1992.

66 On friendship as a virtue and the basis of political society, see Aristotle, *Nicomachean Ethics* 8.11, 9.8–9.

67 Boccaccio, *De casibus* 2.5.

68 The bracketed phrase is preserved in one of the oldest MSS and is clearly needed to complete the sense. Zaccaria (931) states that the phrase should be inserted after paragraph 1, rather than paragraph 11; I suspect this is a typographical error in the Ricci and Zaccaria edition.

69 Boccaccio, *De casibus* 2.5: Boccaccio, like Bruni, distinguishes between the *popolo,* the broad middle ranks of society, and the *plebs,* the poor.

70 I would align this pessimism with what Zaccaria in his introduction to the *De casibus* calls Boccaccio's *moralismo tragico.* This is not to say that no later humanists shared Boccaccio's pessimism about the possibility of reforming political life.

8. LEONARDO BRUNI AND THE VIRTUOUS HEGEMON

1 For a recent overview of the literature on civic humanism, see Moulakis 2011. Quentin Skinner's early work on Renaissance republicanism is usefully collected in Skinner 2000a.

2 For a criticism of such views as they apply to Renaissance signory, see Cappelli 2009 and Kohl 2010.

3 Principally in Baron 1955, 1966. In what follows I cite Bruni's *Panegyric of the City of Florence (Laudatio florentine urbis)* according to the paragraph numbers of Baldassarri's edition. My translation is adapted from that of Benjamin Kohl in Kohl and Witt 1978, 135–175.

4 On the circumstances of composition, see Hankins 2000b. Bruni's reinterpretation of popular liberty in the medieval commune in terms of virtue politics runs parallel to his reinterpretation of medieval chivalry in his treatise *De militia,* for which see Chapter 9.

5 *Fam.* 11.16, tr. Fantham 5.6; see also Chapter 5, page 166.

6 Aristotle's theory of virtue acquisition is discussed in Cooper 2012, 117–122.

7 See Bruni, *Laudatio,* cap. 18. For this view of the *Laudatio,* see above all Rubinstein 1990a; Fubini 1990a; Brown 2000; Hornqvist 2004; see also note 28 below.

8 Bruni's promotion of Florence as the new leader of Italy in succession to Rome should be taken together with his denigration of the modern Roman people in letters written shortly after the *Laudatio* while he was in the service of Innocent VII; see Bruni, *Epistolae* 1.4–5, ed. Mehus, 1: 6–11.

9 Bruni, *Laudatio,* caps. 31–32. For the humanist view that the nobility stemming from virtue legitimates rule, see Chapter 2, page 39.

10 Given the date of the *Laudatio,* Bruni's justification of offensive war may be intended to defend Florence's ongoing attempts to conquer the former Roman city of Pisa, which it finally accomplished in 1406. See further below.

11 By Bruni's own account (*Epistolae* 8.2, ed. Mehus, 2: 111–112, from 1440), his *Laudatio,* belonging as it did to the panegyrical genre, required rhetorical exaggeration. See my discussion of this passage in Hankins 2000b, 160–161.

12 For Cicero's understanding of *respublica,* which is close to Bruni's, see Schofield 1999b. For service to the common good in general as a criterion of the good polity in medieval thought, see Kempshall 1999. I take the term "organicist" from Cappelli 2016b, 10, who describes the legitimacy of the quattrocento prince as stemming from his role in maintaining a cohesive, organic whole, "a body [*corpus*] that reflects the natural order of the world, in which each part discharges its proper role, a complex system inspired by justice and oriented to the *bonum commune,* in which *virtus* flows, circulating from top to bottom throughout the body, and that therefore includes a precise series of reciprocal obligations between *caput* and *membra* of the metaphorical organism: [this is] political organicism." Cappelli sees the humanist form of organicism, though rooted in medieval political theology, as naturalistic and free from religious presuppositions, independent of juristic means of legitimation, and "in large measure independent of the contingent institutional form of government," i.e., indifferent to the form of the regime.

13 See Aristotle, *Politics* 3.17.1288a.

14 Bruni, *Laudatio,* cap. 51.

15 For the language of quantity versus quality, see Aristotle, *Politics* 4.12.1296b; see also 2.2.1261a. For elements of political meritocracy in Aristotle, see *Politics* 3.9.1281a1–4, 7.9.1329a, and his accounts of the Spartan, Cretan, and Carthaginian constitutions in 2.9–11.1269a–1273b. In Aristotelian terms, Florence is even better than the good popular regime Aristotle calls "polity" (and Bruni translates as *respublica*); the latter is Aristotle's best practical state, which distributes equal political power to the people, who have been nurtured and improved by good institutions and education. Again, we must remember that Bruni is writing panegyric, which by his own account operates on a plane *supra veritatem.*

16 Aristotle also seems to hold out the theoretical possibility that the entire citizen body, in the "polis of our prayers" in book 7, could become virtuous in a city with optimal laws and institutions; see Ober 2005. One may contrast Lauro Quirini's updating of Aristotle's *Politics,* his *De republica* (ed. Seno and Ravegnani, 142), a passage criticizing popular government: "In multitudine praeterea maior pars meliorem vincit." (In [a regime of the] many, the greater part overcomes the better.)

17 See Chapter 11 for Biondo and the end of this chapter for Dante.

18 The isomorphism between person and state here is based on Aristotle, not Plato; see *Politics* 7.1.1323b30–35. The key passage is quoted as an epigraph to this book.

19 It should be noted that the *popolo* is constituted by the broad middle ranks of society and does not include the urban plebs. See Chapter 10.

20 The point echoes Cicero's *De officiis* 2.27, a passage important for understanding the *Laudatio;* see page 597n32.

21 Bruni, *Laudatio,* caps. 55–56. In cap. 69, Bruni reverses the relation and writes that Florence treats other states as though they belonged to her own homeland.

22 Cicero, *De legibus* 2.5. In a letter to Stefano Colonna (*Fam.* 15.7.1, tr. Fantham 2.13.1) Petrarch calls Rome the "communem patriam, matrem nostram." See also *Fam.* 23.2.34, tr. Fantham 6.12.34, where Rome is "communis omnium . . . patria, rerum caput, orbis atque urbium regina" (the common country of everyone, the head of [public] affairs, the queen of the world and of cities).

23 See Straumann 2016b, who reconstructs Cicero's argument from the fragments of *De republica* 3, to which Bruni would not have had access, although he would have known the argument in the *De officiis;* see esp. the passage quoted below.

24 Ando 2000, esp. 10, 15, 65.

25 Bell 2016, 81. In Chapter 2, page 37, I distinguish Bell's performance legitimacy from "legitimacy of exercise," a species of moral legitimacy. The latter is typical of Renaissance humanist political thought; see also Cappelli 2016b, 10, 102.

26 For George of Trebizond's appropriation of Aristides to criticize the Greek cities as too nativist and to praise Rome as cosmopolitan, see Chapter 14. The praise for Florence's willingness to take in exiles as testimony to her generosity is inspired by Aelius Aristides' similar praise of Athens in the *Panathenaicus*, ed. Behr: "[All of the Greeks] each privately called his original land his country, but all named [Athens] their common home" (1: 49); and "Although Athens is the oldest of Greek cities, it is as it were the country and common hearth of the race by its admission of those from everywhere rather than its precedence in time" (1: 53). For a detailed study of Bruni's use of Aristides, see Santosuosso 1986.

27 Bruni, *Laudatio*, caps. 43–46.

28 Fubini 1990a, esp. 30, 39, and Hornqvist 2004, esp. 74–75. I also took this view in Hankins 1995a and Hankins 2000b. The evidence presented in Hankins 2000b indicates that the audience for the work was probably intended to be as much international as local.

29 Bruni, *Laudatio*, cap. 91. The phrase *princeps populus* is an echo of Livy, pref. 3: "Utcumque erit, iuvabit tamen rerum gestarum memoriae principis terrarum populi pro virili parte et ipsum consuluisse." (However this may turn out, it will gratify me that I have done my part, to the best of my abilities, to relate the annals of the foremost nation in the world.) On the meaning of this phrase in Livy, see Vasaly 2015, 22. The phrase *princeps populus* was also used in Salutati's *De tyranno* to mean a sovereign state; see Chapter 4, page 131. For passages invoking Florence's *patrocinium* of other states, see *Laudatio*, caps. 44–47.

30 Bruni, *Laudatio*, caps. 43–44. *Amplitudo* here seems to be a diplomatic way of referring to Florence's own expansionism.

31 Cicero, *De officiis* 2.26–27 (Loeb translation). The same passage about *patrocinium* is quoted in a key passage of Petrarch's *De vita solitaria* (2.9), which I describe as Petrarch's "political testament" in Chapter 6. On *patrocinium* in Florentine political thought, see Woodhouse 2018.

32 Bruni, *Laudatio*, caps. 17, 70.

33 Bruni's ekphrastic description of Florence in *Laudatio*, caps. 2–29, as the most beautiful, wealthy, populous, and central of Italy's cities, a mean between a port and a mountain citadel, admirable for its culture, is also part of his justification of Florentine leadership.

34 For the "republican" justification of the Roman Empire, see Harris 1985. The just and benign nature of the Roman Empire is also taken as a given in Biondo's *Roma Triumphans;* see Chapter 11.

35 Robiglio 2006. An important text for humanists, including Bruni, on the nature of nobility is Aristotle's *Rhetoric* 1.9.1366b–1367a, which may be in the background here. Aristotle makes a tight connection between noble qualities and the genre of panegyric. See also note 54 below.

36 Pade 2007, 2: 96 (my trans.).

37 The analogy with Confucian ideas of equality and justified hierarchy is striking; see Bai 2012, 30–35, and the Conclusion of this volume.

38 Bruni, *Panegyric of Nanni Strozzi*, ed. Daub, 285 (cap. 19): The translation is revised from Gordon Griffith's version in Griffiths, Hankins, and Thompson 1987, 124–125. As is well known, this part of the speech imitates Pericles' Funeral Oration in Thucydides; the relationship is analyzed in Daub's commentary on the passage.

39 For Bruni's version of Aristotle's view that the middle classes should be the basis of the best regime, see Chapter 10, page 278. For Bruni's presentation of the Florentine political system as a meritocracy see Najemy 1982a, 308–309.

40 See Pettit 1999 and, for analysis of this concept in Machiavelli, Skinner 2002b.

41 Bruni, *Laudatio,* cap. 76. This in Bruni's mind is compatible with the existence of social ranks *(ordines),* which are described in Ciceronian fashion as acting in concert thanks to Florence's equally harmonious political institutions.

42 Ibid., cap. 81: "Quod enim ad multos attinet, id non aliter quam multorum sententia decerni consentaneum iuri rationique iudicavit." (A matter affecting the many is judged conformable to right and to reason only if it is decided by the many.) The sentence is clearly elaborated from the well-known formula in Justinian's *Codex* (5.59.5.2; also invoked in canon law in the *Liber Sextus* 5.12.29)—"Quod omnes tangit debet ab omnibus approbari" (What affects everyone should be approved by everyone)—commonly cited in communal debates when seeking to broaden consultation of (not necessarily voting by) the citizen body. For the history of the so-called "QOT principle," see Fasolt 2014.

43 Bruni, *History* 7.48, ed. Hankins, 2:327. The principle is derived from Livy; see Vasaly 2015, 53–55. Bruni echoes a remark of Petrarch in *Sine nomine* 4, where the poet says that all *gentes* naturally desire *libertas* but often do so in a manner *inconsultus et praeceps,* when by nature they should remain subordinate to a superior, such as the Roman people.

44 This is a material point in Florence's propaganda wars against Milan, where Bruni and other defenders of Florence like to point out that Milan was founded by the Insubres, an uncivilized Gaulish people inferior in virtue to Rome. See Lanza 1991 and the discussion below of Bruni's letter-treatise *On the Origin of Mantua.*

45 Bruni, *Laudatio,* cap. 79 : "Urbe igitur in regiones quatuor divisa, ne cui illarum suus unquam deesset honos, ex singulis partibus bini viri eliguntur, nec ii quidem fortuiti sed iudicio populi iam dudum approbati et tanto honore digni iudicati." The *suggestio falsi* here is cleverly put, since the root meaning of *eligo*—from which the word "election" is also derived—is "to extract": the process of sortition in Florence worked by extracting names from leather bags. But the so-called scrutiny *(scruptinio)* for inclusion in the bags was not made with the intention of elevating the most worthy to office; the most important criteria were that one not be in arrears in one's taxes and that close family members should not recently have held office.

46 For Cicero's criticism of secret balloting in *De legibus* 3, see Vishnia 2012, 129–134. In his *De lege agraria* (2.4), Cicero regards it as an endorsement of his own superexcellent virtue that the people chose him openly "by universal acclamation" rather than by taking advantage of a written vote that "protects their silent liberty." Aristotle took the view that election to office was aristocratic, sortition popular, and undesirable; see *Politics* 2.11.1272b32–40. On the other hand, like Cicero, he regarded the type of election where candidates canvassed openly for popular support as potentially corrupt; see *Politics* 2.9.1271a10–19. Plato in the *Laws,* a text Bruni is not known to have read, also prefers election to sortition on meritocratic grounds; see Morrow 1993, chapters 5 and 6.

47 Bruni, *History* 5.81, ed. Hankins 2: 73. Bruni implicitly prefers election to sortition also in his *Vita di Dante,* where his wording implies that Dante's career of public service deserved more honor because it occurred at a time when Florence still elected its magistrates: "Et finalmente, pervenuta alla età debita, fu creato de' priori, non per sorte, come s'usa al presente, ma per eletione, come in quel tempo si costumava fare." (And finally, having come to the appropriate age,

he was chosen as one of the priors, not by lot, as is done now, but by election, as used to be done in that time.) See the text in *Opere,* ed. Viti, 542.

48 Bruni, *Laudatio,* cap. 87 (my trans.).

49 Bruni could have known about the censors from Livy or from Cicero's proposal for the magistracy in *De legibus* 3.7; about the Areopagus from his model, Aelius Aristides' *Panathenaicus,* caps. 46–47 (ed. Behr, 14), or Plutarch, *Life of Solon* 20; and about the ephors from Aristotle's *Politics.* If Bruni did take his account from Aristotle, it would be another case of his "reading against his sources" (see Ianziti 2012, passim), since Aristotle's account of them in *Politics* 2.9.1270b7–35 is sharply critical. Another possible source for the ephors available to Bruni was Plutarch's *Life of Lycurgus* 7, which presents the ephorate as a post-Lycurgan attempt to control the defects of oligarchy. At 29.6, Plutarch further claims that the ephorate strengthened Lycurgus' civil polity and that "though it was thought to have been done in the interests of the people, it really made the aristocracy (τὴν ἀριστοκρατίαν) more powerful" (Loeb translation). For further remarks about humanist uses of the Spartan myth, see Chapter 15.

50 See Brown 1992.

51 See Chapter 9. In his *History* 9.2, ed. Hankins, 3: 2, Bruni takes a more realistic and critical view of the Parte's activities in the period after the Ciompi uprising.

52 For other examples of Bruni fictionalizing Florentine history in his civic panegyrics, see Hankins 2000b.

53 Hankins 2014a.

54 See Aristotle, *Rhetoric* 1.9.1368a, where he writes that to praise a man is akin to urging a course of action in accordance with his ascribed virtue. A relevant text from one of Bruni's followers on the capacity of praise and blame to spur men on to great achievement is Lapo da Castiglionchio the Younger's proemium to Demosthenes' *Funeral Oration,* datable to 1434 / 1438 (ed. Luiso, 296–297). After alluding to Herodotus, Thucydides, and Pindar, Lapo writes, "For what is there that ought to have been desired more by these [ancient Greek statesmen and soldiers]— since death naturally puts a limit to all things—than to be granted the ability to die with glory and not perish beyond all knowledge like the beasts? Nowadays those arts which were held in the highest honor by the ancients lie deserted and uncultivated, without rewards, and almost no one thinks they are worth pursuing, being arts that bring nothing apart from labor. If any just or brave man is discovered he is now regarded as a prodigy. Different rewards are effective with different people, but in the case of the greatest spirits and most excellent minds the gravest proof of their virtue lives in hope of commendation from a famous city or the most eloquent of men, that they might be rescued from silence and oblivion and from mortal men be made immortal."

55 His appointment as such began in June 1416, when Bruni was granted Florentine citizenship and an exemption from taxes to pursue his historical work (an admirable custom). For Bruni's *History,* see Chapter 10.

56 Hankins 2008a, 3, and note.

57 A detail (along with others in Bruni's account) based on Dionysius of Halicarnassus, *Roman Antiquities* 2.37, 42–43. (Dionysius refers to the Etruscans as Tyrrhenians.)

58 Bruni notes (1.17), "The Etruscans behaved very differently toward the Romans than they did toward the Gauls. Against those barbarian and savage peoples they waged implacable war. Against the Romans, they never fought with hatred and bitterness; in fact, from time to time they were more Rome's friends than her adversaries." Compare Cicero, *De officiis* 1.38.

59 On Etruscanism in Renaissance Florence, see Cipriani 1975 and 1980. For the influence of Bruni's Etruscanism on Andrea Biglia and the lessons to be drawn from Etruscan history, see Meserve 2008, 183–185.

60 Compare Machiavelli's analysis, discussed in Chapter 19, page 462.

61 Bruni's view thus contrasts with Strabo's (5.2.2), who states that the Etruscans were weakened by giving up monarchy for federal government. Patrizi in the *De regno* (see Chapter 17, page 411) also regards federations of city-states as intrinsically weak and unable to stand up to a centrally organized regional monarchy. For the reception of Strabo, see Chapter 17, page 392, and 619n16. See also Servius, *Commentary on the Aeneid* 2.278, 8.475.

62 See Cipriani 1975, 258–259; Witt 1983, 75–76, 153–154, 166–167, 247–249; Griffiths 1999. Bruni's *History* also provided numerous examples of cooperation among Tuscan city-states, under the leadership of Florence, in the thirteenth and fourteenth centuries; see above page 222 for Bruni's use of Livy's term *princeps populus*. Witt 1969, 462, notes that the pattern of Florence's alliances in the Second Milanese War of the 1390s did not permit Salutati to emphasize an ideological contrast between republican liberty and monarchical forms of government, a point also emphasized in Black 1986, 992–993.

63 Bruni, *De origine Mantuae,* ed. Mehus, 2: 217–229. Mehus inserted the text into his edition of Bruni's letters as *Ep.* 10.25, but the text was written originally as an independent historical essay and was never included in either the eight- or nine-book Renaissance collections of Bruni's letters. See Gualdo Rosa 1993–2004. The work was quite popular both in the original Latin (twenty-seven MSS) and in a fifteenth-century Italian translation (forty-three MSS); see Hankins 1997. I have found useful the essay of Mazzocco 2012a on this text.

64 Goeing 2014; on Gianfrancesco, see the article by Isabella Lazzarini in *DBI* 54 (2000). For some of the many future princes trained in Vittorino's humanist school, see Chapter 18, page 425.

65 See Chapter 9, page 255.

66 Bruni probably met Gonzaga either in 1413 when the latter came to meet his employer, Pope John, in Bologna, or certainly in January-February 1414 when the papal court sojourned in Mantua at Gonzaga's invitation. Gianfrancesco fought as a condottiere under the papal banner in 1412 and 1417.

67 Gianfrancesco eventually achieved this goal on May 6, 1433, during Sigismondo's imperial progress in Italy and was given the hereditary title of Marquess of Mantua.

68 Viti 1992, 368n, hypothesizes, but without evidence, that Bruni's aim in writing the treatise was to find employment for himself at the Gonzaga court in Mantua. It is possible, however, that Bruni, as a former papal secretary, was acting in Pope Martin V's interest. Later, during Martin's residence in Florence, Bruni maintained close relations with him and even composed a few letters for him, though he seems to have had no official status as his secretary. See Bruni, *Memoirs* 64–71, ed. Hankins, 3: 354–363; and Griffiths, Hankins, and Thompson 1987, 35.

69 There were likely other voices besides Dante's promoting different versions of Mantua's origins. See *De origine Mantuae,* ed. Mehus, 2: 225, where Bruni says, "For those who say that Mantua was founded in the beginning by the Etruscans, but in later times began to be inhabited by Gauls and Venetians along with its Tuscan founders, are not giving a very satisfactory account." Bruni remarks that even if Venetians and Gauls (read: Milanese) populated Mantua in later times, they came there "in such a way that the Tuscans ruled and remained preëminent in the city." At 226, Bruni says he is compelled to admire Dante, "since [Dante] was himself a Tuscan," but he was simply mistaken about Mantua's origins since he was unacquainted with the sources;

no other authority agreed with Dante, and his views on the subject should be dismissed along with other *poetarum deliramenta puerilia* (childish delusions of the poets).

70 Trans. Charles Singleton.

71 As Singleton points out in his note to the passage (352), Dante's Vergil disagrees with what Vergil himself says in *Aeneid* 10.298–300, where the founder of Mantua is Ocnus, son of Manto, who is herself represented, not as a Greek prophetess, but as the mate of the River Tiber. Bruni points out the discrepancy at *De origine Mantuae,* ed. Mehus, 223. At 223–225 he dismisses Vergil's account as a poetic fiction as well but observes that if there was truth behind it, it would indicate that Ocnus too was a Tuscan (since the Tiber is called the "Tuscan river" in Vergil).

72 Bruni's impressive account of the Etruscans, which went far beyond that of his predecessors Villani and Salutati (see Cipriani 1980), is informed not only by his reading of Latin authors such as Vergil, Horace, Livy, Servius, and Pliny the Elder, but also by Dionysius of Halicarnassus, Plutarch, and Plato's *Phaedrus.* A critical edition of the text might well reveal other sources.

73 I use the text in Kay's edition.

74 The classic work is Kantorowicz 1957. This is not to claim that the humanist movement was the only such motor of desacralization; such was also the broad tendency of scholastic political thought in the late thirteenth and fourteenth century (not excluding Aquinas), for which see Canning 1996, chapter 4.

75 Bruni had surely read the *Monarchia* by 1436 when he wrote his *Vita di Dante,* but whether he knew it in 1404 / 1405 when he wrote the *Laudatio* is not clear.

76 Dante had been more dismissive of lineage as a source of nobility in *Convivio* 4; see Santagata 2016, 176–181.

77 See Chapter 2; Cappelli 2016b, 101; and Roick 2017, 163–165.

9. WAR AND MILITARY SERVICE IN THE VIRTUOUS REPUBLIC

1 Sacchetti, *Trecentonovelle* 150, ed. Puccini, 472–475.

2 Bayley 1961, 206.

3 Acciaiuoli, *Cronica,* ed. Scaramella, 25.

4 Salvemini 1972, 113.

5 Ibid., 189 (no. 77).

6 Brucker 1977; Zervas 1988; Brown 1992, esp. 104–108 on the attempted revival of the Parte in the period 1423–1434.

7 ASF, Capitani della Parte Guelfa *rosso,* vol. 3, f. 2r.

8 On Bruni's role, see De Angelis 1990. On Antonio di Mario's copies of Bruni's works, see De la Mare 1985, 1: 483. For another contemporary humanist attack on the decay of military ideals that reflects Bruni's, see Lapo da Castiglionchio's long letter to Simone di Simone di Boccaccino Lamberti (c. 1434), discussed in Fubini 1979. A more measured judgment on *res militaris* is found in Lapo's unpublished *Comparatio inter rem militarem et studia litterarum,* essentially a defense of the dignity of humanistic studies, which I consulted in Rimini, Biblioteca Civica Gambalunga, MS 47 (4.A.II.25), ff. 52r–76v. Both dedications of this work, to Gregorio Correr and Duke Humfrey of Gloucester, have now been published in Gualdo Rosa 2018, 96–99.

9 Bayley 1961, vii.

10 Kristeller 1963.

11 Bertelli 1964. More technical criticisms of the edition were made in Goldbrunner 1966. Similar criticisms of Bayley are found in Hale 1964 and Rubinstein 1963.

12 Bayley 1961, 208.

13 Baron 1955, 1966. For Baron's view of the relationship between civic humanism and advocacy of citizen militias, see Baron 1966, 430–440 ("The Ideal of a Citizen Army").

14 Gualdo Rosa 1990; Viti in Bruni, *Opere,* 651–653; Bayley's interpretation is followed also by Verrier 1997, 45, and Pincelli in Flavio, *Borsus,* XV. The Baron / Bayley view of the *De militia* also lives on among historians of political theory, for example Lukes 2004, 1093. By contrast, Bayley's interpretation is rejected by Böninger 1995, 204–209, whose reading is closer to the one advanced here. For the historical phenomenon of civic knighthood in general, see Gasparri 1992.

15 The best recent examples of this understanding are found in the work of John Najemy (see note 17 below) and Arthur Field (see Field 2017, passim); Hankins 1995a and Hankins 2000b also took this view. Najemy's work seems to represent an application to Florentine history of Barrington Moore's thesis on elites; see Khan 2012, 366.

16 Skinner 1998; Pettit 1999.

17 Najemy 1982a, 314–315. See also Najemy 2000; Najemy 2004, 200–210.

18 Black 1985, 101–108; Black 2013, 32–34.

19 Palmieri was the son of a druggist and an amateur man of letters; he supported the return from exile of Cosimo de'Medici in 1434 and was rewarded with a lifetime supply of political offices. On him see Elena Valeri in *DBI* 80 (2014), with bibliography, and the detailed study of Mita Ferraro 2005.

20 Palmieri, *Vita civile,* book 3 (1429), ed. Belloni, 136–137 (my trans.).

21 For a similar self-positioning of Sienese humanistic reformers as a "third force," a nobility of knowledge, between rich *popolani* and hereditary nobles, see Ascheri 1986, 29.

22 See Aristotle, *Nicomachean Ethics* 10.8.1178a.

23 See Chapter 2, page 42, for humanist dissent from Aristotle on this point.

24 It is significant that Bruni rejects the face-saving theory reported by his chief source for the Ciompi uprising, written by the oligarch Alamanno Acciaiuoli, that Michele di Lando was descended of French nobility; see *History* 9.5, ed. Hankins, 3: 7.

25 "Civitas enim totius vite cunctorumque humanorum munerum princeps est et perfectrix." For the text with an Italian translation, see Bruni, *De militia,* ed. Viti (quoted passage on 656); for an English translation, see Griffiths, Hankins, and Thompson 1987, 127–145 (quoted sentence on 128).

26 Macrobius, *Commentary on the Dream of Scipio* 1. The comparison of philosophical and historical republics is most fully worked out in book 6 of Polybius' *Histories,* the surviving fragments of which did not become known in Italy until the middle of the fifteenth century (see Chapter 12). But the principle is implicit throughout the first five books (paraphrased by Bruni in his *De primo bello punico* of 1419 / 1422), for example at 1.1–3.

27 See Hankins 2007–2008a, 22–35, where it is argued that Bruni likely began work on the *Politics* version already in the mid-1420s but did not finish the final version until 1436 and only published it in 1438.

28 Bruni, *Epistolae* 9.4, ed. Mehus, 2: 147–149.

29 See Plato, *Republic* 2.375c, and Hankins 2003–2004a, 1: 84.

30 Bruni's view mirrors Cicero's own: see Atkins 2013, chapter 2. Aristotle also distinguished between a state that was the best absolutely and one that was the best in practical terms.

31 Bruni, *De militia,* ed. Viti, 672; Griffiths, Hankins, and Thompson 1987, 134.

32 Böninger 1995, 205, identifies as the likeliest target of Bruni's work the *Liber gentilis militiae* of Gentile d'Adeguardo de' Mainardi (after 1396), a tractate which places Italian knighthood in the chivalric tradition of medieval French knighthood.

33 Extensively documented in Guasti 1867–1873. In his *History* 8.44, ed. Hankins, 2: 439, Bruni is critical of professional soldiers who took advice from civilian military commissioners: "For knowledge of military affairs is unusual enough in men who spend their whole lives doing nothing else, let alone in commoners who are used to leisure and mercantile activities." See also 8.80, ed. Hankins, 2: 472–475, for the disastrous results of following civilian military advice.

34 Guasti 1867–1873, 1: 294–295.

35 Bruni's source according to Bayley 1961, 212. A more obvious source is Cicero, *De officiis* 1.36–37.

36 The point is possibly derived from Aristotle, *Politics* 7.9.1328b.

37 See Hankins 1990a, 1: 51–53, 73–74; 2: 379–387. Bruni translated the text a second time shortly after finishing the *De militia.*

38 For a full analysis of the speech, see Hankins 2000b, 159–167, and the commentary of Susanne Daub in her edition of Bruni, *Panegyric of Nanni Strozzi.*

39 Bruni, *Panegyric of Nanni Strozzi,* ed. Daub, 291–295, with commentary on 337–342.

40 Ibid., 294–295.

41 Zervas 1988, 94.

42 Greenhalgh 1982, 49–63, esp. 51–54, correcting Janson 1963, 29.

43 Janson 1963, 29.

44 See Chapter 19, passim. For a similar conclusion, though arrived at for different reasons, see Cappelli 2017a.

45 Bayley 1961, chapter 5. Bayley's account of humanist ideas on *res militaris* is followed, for example, by J. R. Hale and Michael Mallett, the foremost English-language authorities on Renaissance warfare; see Hale 1985, 73, and Mallett 1974, 208–211. See also Verrier 1997, 45–46, and Anglo 2005, 538n64. Anglo 2005, 520, goes still further and regards Bayley's account as showing that "it is difficult . . . to regard Machiavelli as anything other than a traditional military platitudinist." Rubinstein 1963, in contrast, remarks that Bruni's treatise "connects with Machiavelli's projects of military reform by way of contrast rather than affinity."

46 Hankins 2003–2004a, 1: 123–136, 169–174.

47 Bruni, *Epistolae* 6.7, ed. Mehus, 2 : 51–52. See also Bruni's *Memoirs,* included in the third volume of my edition of Bruni's *History,* 3: 343 (cap. 47).

48 Bruni, *Epistolae* 3.9, ed. Mehus, 1: 76–83.

49 Bruni, *Orazione per Niccolò da Tolentino,* ed. Viti. It was the most popular of Bruni's *volgare* compositions after the *Vita di Dante.* Hankins 1997 lists seventy-nine surviving manuscripts of the text, although it did not reach print until 1759. On this and other ceremonial speeches of humanist orators to condottieri, see Maxson 2015, who discusses also the Manetti speech (below) and surviving speeches by Bartolomeo Scala and attributed to Cristoforo Landino.

50 Manetti, *Oratione,* ed. Donati; see below. Another such speech that bears on political theory is an anonymous speech in praise of the much-admired condottiere Federico d'Urbino, in

BNCF MS Magl. VII 1095, 90r–93v. The speech occurs in a collection containing works of the Pistoiese humanist Tommaso Baldinotti, who may be the author. Other *ringhiera* speeches such as that of the podestà and Roman hothead, Stefano Porcari, address military matters on other ceremonial occasions, such as the entrance of the new priors into the Palazzo Vecchio; see Porcari, *Orazioni,* ed. Manni, 188. On Porcari, see D'Elia 2009; on Sigismondo Malatesta, see D'Elia 2016.

51 Hankins 1997.

52 Campano, *Opera* (folios unnumbered, signatures irregular).

53 Also known as Filippo de' Scolari. See Bracciolini, *Vita di Filippo Scolari,* ed. Polidori.

54 See the entry on him by Giancarlo Schizzerotto in *DBI* 13 (1971).

55 O'Brien 2009.

56 For the two lives by Decembrio, see *Lives of the Milanese Tyrants,* ed. Zaggia and Ianziti, and Chapter 4, page 141. For those by Giovanni Simonetta and Leodrisio Crivelli, see Ianziti 1988.

57 Filelfo, *Commentarii.*

58 Guarino, *Epistolario,* letter 796, ed. Sabbadini, 2: 458–460.

59 Nor did at least one of his successors as Florentine chancellor, Benedetto Accolti, who also defended condottieri and contemporary military practice. See Black 1985, 204–205.

60 On Porcari, see D'Elia 2009, 53–67.

61 Porcari, *Orazioni,* ed. Manni, 192–194. The idea that the Carthaginians hired the bulk of their army comes from Bruni's epitome of Polybius' *Histories,* books 1–5, called *De primo bello punico.*

62 Manetti, *Oratione,* ed. Donati, 807.

63 For Bruni's views on the regrettable decline of the Florentine militia in the fourteenth century and the consequent empowerment of the wealthy, see Chapter 10, page 279.

64 The critical edition by Belloni lists eighteen manuscripts, almost all of Florentine provenance, and the work was not printed until the sixteenth century: in Florence by Giunta in 1529 and in an extremely rare second edition from around the same time. The popularity of the work as a source for Florentine republican thought dates only from the nineteenth century.

65 Palmieri, *Vita civile,* ed. Belloni, 185–186.

66 Ibid., 115–131.

67 Patrizi's contemporary, Diomede Carafa, a humanist counselor of King Ferrante and something of a war hero, took a similarly negative view of offensive warfare, advising his prince to beware of anyone telling him that war was necessary. He adds to Patrizi's arguments the claim that whoever attacks first in a war will likely be at a disadvantage owing to God's disfavor: "For it is well known from ancient and contemporary experience that the one who is the first to cause discords will be, almost miraculously, the one who is not only defeated in battle, but also suffers the graver losses and the more bitter disasters. This can be considered an evident proof that this type of injustice [causing wars] is unpleasing to the Divine Majesty" (*De regis et boni principis officio,* 74).

68 Cicero, *De officiis* 3.82; Cicero quotes Euripides' *Phoenician Women,* lines 524–525. Those who knew their Cicero would remember that these lines were "always on the lips" of Julius Caesar.

69 See Quintus Curtius Rufus, *History of Alexander* 7.12.

70 For the consulate in Patrizi's republic, see *De inst. r.p.* 3.5, 1534 ed., ff. 39v–40r.

71 Quoting Cicero, *Pro lege Manilia* 38.

72 A special case was the issue of serving in crusades against the Turks, which the humanists considered well justified if the service was approved by the pope and by the proper lay authorities; see Hankins 1995b and 2003–2004a, 1: 293–424. The humanist pope Pius II was the most fervent advocate of holy war in the fifteenth century.

73 [Baldinotti], *Oratio.*

74 Valturio, *De re militari,* 1535 ed., 1.2.

75 Manetti, *Oratione,* ed. Donati, 803.

76 See Valturio, *De re militari,* 1535 ed., 6.5.

77 Porcari, *Orazioni,* ed. Manni, 195: "Ma pare che alcuna dubitatione nascere possa in sententia philosophica, pero che nelle numerate tre parti non si contiene alcuna cosa dell'ordine nel governo de' publici magistrati, la quale pare essentiale et principale parte della republica. Ma certo a questo si risponde per che in quel membro de propulsatori delle battaglie si contiene tacitamente l'ordine de magistrati, e'quali posto che con l'armi et colle spade attualmente di fuori alla patria non difendano. Non di meno la difendono con la parte migliore, sedendo nella cicta cioè collo ingengno et colla industria." (There appears to arise some doubt in philosophical opinion, because in the three numbered parts nothing is included about the order of public magistrates in the government, which seems an essential and principal part of the state. But surely one responds to this [doubt] that the order of magistrates is tacitly included in the class of the guardians, despite the fact that the former are not placed outside the country with armor and swords to defend it. Nonetheless they defend it, stationed inside the city, with the best part [of the soul], namely with intelligence and industry.)

78 Ibid.: "Vedete addunque, Magnifici Signori et prudentissimi cictadini, essere verificata la sententia del philosopho ponente le ymagini della perfectamente instituta re publica, cioè artefici, coloni et propulsatori di battaglie, e'quali possono essere o di exerciti proprii o vero condocti." (Thus you see verified, magnificent lords and most prudent citizens, the conviction of the Philosopher, who laid down the image of the perfectly founded republic, namely, artisans, farmers and guardians, who can either be in an army of your own or hired.)

79 [Baldinotti], *Oratio.*

80 Flavio, *Borsus,* ed. Pincelli. See Rossi 2013.

81 Flavio, *Borsus,* ed. Pincelli, 29 [XX.112]. He remarks, "If we shall imitate the ancients in every part of life as superior to us in their integrity, continence, trustworthiness, liberality, beneficence and other virtues, I shall reckon that [*milites*] should be worthy of all honor among our fellow citizens and fellow tribesmen and placed above them, with the exception of the higher magistracies and church prelacies." It should be noted that papal secretaries saw themselves as the social rivals of canon lawyers; see Bruni, *Epistolae* 5.5, ed. Mehus, 2: 25–29, who argues to Pope Martin V that secretaries should have precedence over jurists in the papal court. See also Gilli 2014. Biondo's mention of "fellow tribesmen" may be intended to include other Italians outside the city-state, since in antiquity Italians who were given citizenship in Rome were enrolled in Roman tribes.

82 One may compare Bruni's remark in a letter to a young student of the humanities, Niccolò Strozzi (6.6, ed. Mehus, 2: 48–51; tr. Griffiths, Hankins, and Thompson, 252–253) from 1431 / 1434: "Again, it is not seemly for great and distinguished men to intermeddle themselves in the mercenary business of quarrels and litigation. This is why the rich and noble take pride in the honor of knighthood, but regard the doctorate [of laws] as low and dishonorable."

83 Flavio, *Borsus,* ed. Pincelli 2009, 31 [XXIII.127]. In humanist discourse, *audacia* was a vice, not the term of praise it became later, probably through Machiavelli's influence. Rossi 2013, 26, points out a text by Bartolomeo Cipolla, a Ferrarese jurist influenced by humanism, *On Choosing a General* (1453 / 1454), which also argues that it should be up to the prince to decide on the greater or lesser noble status of condottieri based on their service to the state.

84 Manetti, *Oratione,* ed. Donati, 817. See Cicero, *Pro lege Manilia* 28, also quoted in Patrizi, *De inst. r.p.* 9.2.

85 Flavio, *RT,* book 7, 1531 ed., 152. Patrizi in the *De inst. r.p.* 9.1 speaks of military leadership as the sine qua non of military success.

86 See Chapter 11. On the relationship between the *Borsus* and the *Roma Triumphans,* see *Borsus,* ed. Pincelli 2009, XIX–XXV.

87 Στρατηγικός *sive de imperatoris institutione.* Later dedicated to Alfonso of Aragon (1455 / 1456). The *ed. princ.* of Sagundino's translation was printed in Rome in 1494 by Eucharius Silber. On Sagundino, see Christian Caselli in *DBI* 89 (2017).

88 This may be considered an aspect of what Michael Mallett called "the domestication of the condottiere" (Mallett 1974, 257–258), the noticeable increase in the civility and loyalty of condottieri by the late fifteenth century. See also Chapter 15, page 360, on the virtuous, defensive militarism of the Spartans.

89 There were six Latin editions between 1472 and 1535, an Italian translation by Paolo Ramusio (1483), and two printings of a French translation by Loys Meigret, both published in 1555. There is no modern critical edition and no census of manuscripts, but Kristeller's *Iter Italicum,* which ordinarily registers somewhere between 20 and 25 percent of surviving copies of humanist manuscripts, lists a dozen manuscripts.

90 On Valturio, see D'Elia 2016, *ad indices;* and Delbianco 2006. A facsimile edition of the 1472 edition was published along with this volume, edited by Paola Delbianco and Agostino Contò. There are also a number of studies of Valturio's military machines, which unsuspecting students of Leonardo da Vinci have sometimes taken as the artist's own inventions; see Delbianco 2006. To my knowledge there is no study of Valturio's educational thought.

91 Preface to Sigismondo Malatesta in Valturio, *De re militari,* 1535 ed., *sign.* a iv v). After a long apology for himself, a soft literary man without experience of war engaging in a study of ancient arms, he writes, "I am seeking only this: that these writings of mine be reckoned, not as having been composed to teach or show anything new, but rather as restoring what has been lost, the memory of famous men, so that we may follow in the footsteps of our ancestors."

92 Valturio, *De re militari,* 1535 ed., 1.2: "Sit itaque in primis litteratus dux." To be *litteratus* in the period meant being able to read Latin; the ability merely to read Italian did not count as a claim to be literate.

93 Ibid.

10. A MIRROR FOR STATESMEN

1 Griffiths, Hankins, and Thompson 1987, 43–44, 52.

2 Fubini 2003, 113–115.

3 Hankins 1997. On Acciaiuoli's translation, see Bessi 1990.

4 Cochrane 1981, 3–9.

5 See for example Skinner 1978, 1: chapter 4; Skinner 2002a, 128–135; Black 1992, 129–135; Burns 1988, 605–606; Pastore Stocchi 1987, 9–17.

6 Baron 1955, 1:52–54, 143–144, 324; 2: 618–623, 630–632; Baron 1988, chapters 3–4; Cabrini 1990; Fubini 2003, chapters 5–7; La Penna 1968; Santini 1910; Ullman 1955; Wilcox 1969; Struever 1970; and Chapter 20 in this volume.

7 Nancy Struever's view that Bruni's speeches were rhetorical displays meant to show both sides of an issue has been rightly criticized by Pedullà 2003, 223 (citing Struever 1970, 129).

8 On this point, see Mansfield 2000, 230–232.

9 Griffiths, Hankins, and Thompson 1987, 259–262.

10 For a humanist who shares the view of Plato and Aristotle about military aggression, see the discussion of Francesco Patrizi in Chapter 9, page 261.

11 Bruni's *History* will be cited throughout by the book and paragraph numbers of my edition; the translations are also taken from my edition.

12 For the teaching of political morality in the Roman historians, see Balmaceda 2017.

13 Bruni apparently did not know book 6. See Chapter 12 for the recovery of book 6 in the fifteenth century.

14 Bruni chose not to draw this conclusion when discussing the institution in 1323 of voting by lot—of which he disapproved—though he admitted that it had lasted down to the present time, "maintained in the state by a measure of popular favor" (5.81).

15 For the tension or rivalry between Greek and Roman republican theories in the early modern period, see Nelson 2004.

16 For a detailed comparison of Bruni and Machiavelli on the causes and cures for factionalism, see Chapter 20.

17 For this definition, see Najemy 2006, 35: "When Florentines spoke of the popolo in specifically political contexts, they usually understood it as synonymous with the large majority of guildsmen who did not belong to elite families." Bruni himself frequently distinguishes (as does Machiavelli) between the *populus* and the *plebs,* the latter term usually indicating the urban poor, *sottoposti,* and the serving classes.

18 For Bruni's conversion of the consensus politics practiced by the oligarchic leadership of Florence, with its various exclusions and co-optations, into a civic ideology, see Najemy 1982a, 301–317.

19 See Lansing 1991.

20 For Bruni's criticism of the medieval French chivalric ethos, see Chapter 9, page 248, and Chapter 16, page 374.

21 Bruni, *Constitution of the Florentines,* ed. Viti. The work was written for Greek visitors attending the Council of Florence in 1439. On the context, see Hankins 2007–2008a, 35–36.

22 In his *Constitution of the Florentines* Bruni states that Florence's constitution has a mixture of democratic and oligarchic elements, though power remains predominantly in the hands of the oligarchy (ed. Viti, 776, 784).

23 See Chapter 8, page 229.

24 Bruni does approve the practice of awarding to magnates "ornamental" offices such as ambassadorships and civic knighthoods. But he insists that the nobility should never have other than an advisory role in making policy. An example of a nobleman behaving with appropriate moderation, patriotism, and deference to popular power is the Pisan noble Franceschino Gambacurta (7.70–75), who lays aside his feudal obligations to the archbishop of Milan in order to oppose the prelate's tyrannical designs on Pisa.

25 Bruni comes to similar conclusions in summing up the mistakes of another great man, Corso Donati, at 4.104.

26 See for example, Bruni, *History* 8.44 and 8.80, where citizens ignorant of war are again criticized for overruling military experts, in this case professional condottieri.

27 Bruni, *History* 9.7–10. The phrases used to describe Michele di Lando in Latin are "homo ex minima plebe . . . auctoritas quaedam nativa et forma viri non illiberalis . . . etsi ex infima plebe ex ipsoque opificio prognatum." *Liberalitas*, nobility of character and education, is a regular humanist substitute for ascribed nobility or nobility of descent.

28 See Chapter 9.

29 ASF, Archivio della Repubblica, Consulte e practiche vol. 34, which preserves the political debates of the Signoria and its advisors for the period, reports no speech of Rinaldo Gianfigliazzo on which Bruni's imaginary oration might notionally be based, though many of the views expressed are broadly consistent with Rinaldo's statements and those of other members of the optimate regime as they are preserved in the documents. See the documentation for the period cited in Bruni, *History*, ed. Hankins, 3: 424–428 (notes to the translation for book 11).

30 See *Memoirs*, caps. 110–118, in Bruni, *History*, ed. Hankins, 3: 391–397. Bruni's three terms on the Ten of War began on June 1 in 1439, 1440, and 1441; the last three books of his *History* were written between February 1439 and January 1442. For the intricate chronology of Bruni's *History* and *Memoirs*, see Hankins 2007–2008a.

31 Bruni, *De studiis et literis,* ed. Viti, 243–279, tr. Griffiths, Hankins, and Thompson 1987, 240–250. One must take into account, to be sure, that the treatise was addressed to a woman, Battista Malatesta (daughter of the condottiere Carlo Malatesta), and advanced a program of education for aristocratic women.

32 For the important differences that still separate Bruni's political thought from that of Machiavelli, see Chapter 20.

11. BIONDO FLAVIO

1 Momigliano 1990, 70: Biondo's works "became the prototype of all later antiquarian research on ancient Rome." The literature on Biondo as an antiquarian is reviewed, with an extensive bibliography, in Mazzocco 2014–2015. Mazzocco points out that Biondo himself never used the term *antiquitates;* the term, modelled on the usage of Varro, only seems to have come into common use among humanists in the late fifteenth century (126–127). Elsewhere, against Momigliano, Mazzocco points out that Biondo in the *RT* makes little use of Varro and does not take him for his model: "It is Cicero, rather than Varro, who emerges as the author's leading literary authority" (136; see also 140).

2 Mazzocco 2014–2015, 139n79: "Emulation of classical civilization by modern society constitutes the leitmotif of the *Roma Triumphans.*"

3 Ibid.

4 In what follows I shall cite the *RT* from the 1531 Basel edition for books 3–10. For books 1–2, I shall cite the edition of Maria Agata Pincelli and the translation of Frances Muecke in ITRL. Frances Muecke kindly allowed me to see her draft translation of books 3–5, which I have sometimes adapted in quotations below.

5 *RT,* ed. Pincelli and Muecke, 5, with slight alterations.

6 *RT,* 1531 ed., 216–217. Biondo's summons to crusade was a popular theme in humanist literature; see Hankins 1995b and 2003–2004a, 1: 293–424.

7 See for instance Petrarch's letter to Urban IV (*Sen.* 7, tr. Fantham 7.6). In *Fam.* 12.1 to Charles IV (dated to 1352), Petrarch similarly links the reconstitution of Rome's ancient power with the need for a crusade and the defense of Christians beyond Europe.

8 The relevance of historical writing to political theory has long been a theme in the work of J. G. A. Pocock; for a theoretical perspective, see Pocock 2009.

9 See the chapters by Pincelli and Stenhouse in Campanelli and Muecke 2017 for the textual history and reception of the *RT.*

10 On the changing significance of the word *respublica* between antiquity and the early modern period, see Chapter 3.

11 Augustus, *Res gestae,* ed. Cooley, 58 (cap. 1), 98 (cap. 34).

12 Flavio, *Histories,* 1531 ed., 3.

13 Cf. Florus 13 and Hankins 2010a, 460; for period terminology see also Tacitus, *Annales* 1.1.

14 Blythe 2009, 189. Note that "political rule" is Ptolemy's term for what moderns call "constitutional rule." The usage follows Livy 1.28, 30, 35, 49, etc., and contrasts with "despotic" rule, the absolute rule of a monarch unconstrained by institutions or any division of power.

15 *RT,* 1531 ed., 59, 64, 76, 112; in the last passage Biondo includes the period of Augustus' conquests as belonging to the *floruit* of the Roman republic.

16 See book 4 (1531 ed., 98), where Biondo uses the phrase *ad summum florente republica* to date the flourishing of Latin literature, which clearly is not restricted to the republican period as conceived by modern Roman historians, since the passage discusses republican and imperial literature alike. At the beginning of book 5 of *RT* (1531 ed., 112) he uses the parallel phrase *aucta et florente respublica,* which in context means the mature Roman state, including the early Principate. Some of the variation in usage between the *Histories* and the *RT* may be due to Biondo's evolution as a historian: Mazzocco notes that Biondo began his career as a humanist scholar under Bruni's influence but gradually developed independent views; see Mazzocco 2014–2015, 138n76.

17 *RT,* 1531 ed., 55, 58. The same view, that the early kings belonged to the republican period of Rome, was held by Ptolemy of Lucca; see Blythe 2009, 189 (but see also the quotation at 197, which seems to say the opposite). Compare Tacitus, *Annales* 3.27. For Machiavelli's similar view of Rome's constitution as developing from an embryonic republic under the kings, see Chapter 19.

18 *RT,* 1531 ed., 55: "Summa potestate populo facta, decreveruntque ut cum regem populus iussisset, id sic ratum esset si patres auctores fierent."

19 See Brunt 1977. For the later significance of the *lex regia,* see Chapter 2.

20 See Hoekstra 2012–2013.

21 See Lee 2016 and Straumann 2016a, neither of which discusses Biondo's work.

22 See also Hankins 2010a, which dates republican exclusivism to the writings of Milton in the seventeenth century.

23 The argument of book 1 of the *RT* is in fact that the Romans, despite being pagans, which they inevitably were before the time of Christ, were *less* superstitious than other ancient peoples and practiced a purer form of religion—even, under their holy King Numa (1.28–29, ed. Pincelli and Muecke, 56–65), a kind of monotheism that eschewed making statues of the gods. This is part of Biondo's argument for the natural superiority of the Romans to other peoples (see below).

24 See *RT* 1.26 (ed. Pincelli and Muecke, 53), where Biondo, quoting Livy (*Periochae* 17.1), approvingly states that with the Romans "religious right prevailed over that of the magistrates" (*sacrorum quam magistratuum ius potentius est*). The parallel to the relative rank of civil and canon law in the Renaissance world would hardly have required flagging.

25 *RT,* 1531 ed., 72, citing Livy 4.3.13.

26 For example, see *RT,* 1531 ed., 149: "Trajan, who was born of Spanish forebears, equalled or exceeded all of Rome's greatest leaders in the magnificence of his accomplishments and in virtue, glory and praise of every kind."

27 Cicero, *Pro Cluentio* 110; also quoted in Flavio, *Borsus,* ed. Pincelli, 44.

28 *RT,* 1531 ed., 123–124.

29 Ibid., 115.

30 Ibid., 71 (cited in note 32 below) and ibid., 119: "But was it not a very fine and excellent way of administering the commonwealth when its men of the first rank so fostered and protected the confederated allies and men from the whole world, who had been accepted into friendship and subjection, that they thought nothing in life more delightful, more sweet or secure than being under Roman rule?"

31 Biondo is more explicit about the connection of liberty and greatness in his earlier historical work, the *Histories* (1531 ed., 4). There Biondo briskly rejects Bruni's theory (Bruni of course is not mentioned by name) that imperial decline was linked to the loss of freedom and virtue; the continued expansion of the empire under the Caesars disproved that theory according to Biondo. On the question of why Rome ultimately succumbed to the barbarian invasions, which for him is a different question, Biondo reports three theories. One is Bruni's theory that the triumph of the Caesars over liberty was responsible for the loss of vigor; this Biondo describes as "by no means absurd." A second theory (which resembles the views of Cyriac of Ancona and is opposed implicitly to Dante's view that the Roman Empire is of divine institution) merely holds that empires are human things and all human things are subject to decay; this Biondo describes as a theory "not to be scorned." Biondo appends to this theory an allusion to Orosius' view that the transition from republic to monarchy was inevitable. The third theory, which Biondo considers the best "because it is the most pious," blames the fall of Rome on the neglect of religion and particularly on Rome's persecution of Christians, whom God punished when Constantine transferred the imperial capital to Constantinople. See Mazzocco 1984. On Cyriac of Ancona's theory of Roman greatness and decline (derived from Polybius), see Chapter 12.

32 *RT,* 1531 ed., 68, 71–72. The passage recalls Cicero, *De officiis* 2.27, where Cicero praises the Roman people's "fair and faithful defense" of her allies and provinces before the time of Sulla; the implication of Biondo's remarks here and elsewhere is that such benign *patrocinium* returned in the early empire after the period of the civil wars of the late republic. On the concept of *patrocinium* in Bruni, see Chapter 8, page 224.

33 Tacitus, *Annales* 1.1. For Bruni's view, see Griffiths, Hankins, and Thompson 1987, 96 *(Life of Petrarch).*

34 His account is based on Cicero's letters and orations (especially the humanists' favorite, the *Pro Archia*), both the Elder and the Younger Pliny, Tacitus, Aulus Gellius, the *Scriptores Historiae Augustae,* and Augustine's *City of God,* among other sources.

35 *RT,* 1531 ed., 96–100. It will be remembered that Petrarch considered Augustus the greatest of all Roman patrons of literature.

36 See Hankins 2002a. See also Brandolini, *Republics and Kingdoms,* ed. Hankins, esp. 14–38, which reflects a number of Biondo's ideas about the causes of Rome's rise and decline.

37 See Chapter 8.

38 *RT,* 1531 ed., 68. Compare *Histories* (ibid., 5), where Biondo says that the time of Theodosius in fact represented the *culmen ipsum et tamquam verticem* (the very summit and peak) of Rome; this is of a piece with Biondo's insistence throughout the *Histories* that there was no connection between the spread of Christianity and the fall of Rome.

39 *RT,* 1531 ed., 94: "It is not now my task to set out how the power of the orators' eloquence was at its greatest in the free city, but we see that it kept its standing to a small extent in the Principate" (my translation). Biondo then proceeds to give examples of the use of eloquence in imperial society drawn from Pliny the Younger and Tacitus; his point is that, *pace* Bruni, eloquence did *not* die out under the emperors.

40 Tacitus, *Histories* 4.7.

41 *RT,* 1531 ed., 79, drawing heavily on Cicero's *De legibus* 3.33–39. Octavian's suppression of bribery (*RT,* 1531 ed., 80) is based on Suetonius, *Augustus* 40.2.

42 *RT,* 1531 ed., 81, based on the *SHA* and Aulus Gellius.

43 Ibid., 149 (book 7). Biondo merely mentions the fact that Christ "willed to be born" in the third year after Augustus closed the doors of the temple of Janus (AUC 571), but this fact is not used to deploy the "incarnational argument" for the superiority of monarchy over the traditional Roman constitution, as is done by Orosius (1.1), Dante (*Convivio* 4.5, *De monarchia* 2.10) and many later Christian writers, including contemporaries such as Petrarch, Aeneas Silvius Piccolomini, and Cyriac of Ancona (see Cyriac of Ancona, *Life and Early Travels,* ed. Mitchell, Bodnar, and Foss, 209). On the incarnational argument in Christian historiography, see Mommsen 1959.

44 Valla, *Praefatio,* 594.

45 On this theme in Biondo, see Mazzocco 2014–2015, 135–136, with the literature cited there; Mazzocco himself emphasizes the ambiguities in Biondo's supposed Christian triumphalism. See also Mazzocco 2012b.

46 *RT,* 1531 ed., 117.

47 In his prooemium Biondo emphasizes the *mission civilisatrice* of ancient Rome, spreading good arts and mores, uniting all the varied nations of the Mediterranean world into one and the same state *(civitas)* by sharing the Latin language and common magistracies (ed. Pincelli and Muecke, 6).

48 Blythe 2009, 179–185.

49 *RT,* 1531 ed., 117–118.

50 On the Romans' instrumental use of religion, see esp. *RT* 1.27–28 (ed. Pincelli and Muecke, 54–56). Gabriele Pedullà comments on the importance of Biondo's *Roma Triumphans* for Machiavelli in Pedullà 2011 and 2018.

51 For Machiavelli's views on this subject, see Chapter 19, page 472.

52 *RT,* 1531 ed., 91: "Vera autem fuit virtus Romana in qua nullus a iudiciis eximi potuit."

53 Fukuyama 2011.

54 *RT,* 1531 ed., 88–90, a collage of quotations from Cicero and other sources that theorize the supremacy of laws over personal authority in Rome, including Cicero's famous lines in the *Pro Cluentio* 146 about all citizens being slaves of the law in order to be free (cited in Chapter 4, page 108). See also *RT,* 1531 ed., 55.

12. CYRIAC OF ANCONA ON DEMOCRACY AND EMPIRE

1 Appiah 2010.

2 See the classic article of Palmer 1953. For the clandestine advocates of "democracy" (i.e., radical egalitarians) before the mid-eighteenth century, see Israel 2006, 249–263.

3 For more detailed accounts, see Meier and Reimann 1972 and Nippel 2010.

4 For the political and philosophical opposition to democracy in Greek antiquity, see Roberts 1994, chapters 3 and 4.

5 See esp. book 8 of the *Republic* and *Gorgias* 515b–519d, but anti-democratic sentiment is found scattered throughout Plato's dialogues.

6 Hansen 2013, esp. chapter 1, with further references.

7 On Polybius as a political thinker, see Hahm 2006 and Hahm 2009, esp. 190–196.

8 Plato's mixed constitution, combining monarchy and democracy as opposites (see *Laws* 3.693d), had few if any followers in the later Western tradition.

9 That Polybius invented this concept is argued by von Fritz 1954.

10 Polybius 6.3–10.

11 Polybius 6.4.4–5 (Loeb translation).

12 Polybius 6.9.4 (Loeb translation).

13 See *TLG*. An exception is an occurrence of the word in Philo's *On the Confusion of Tongues* 23.108, a text that was not known in the Latin West until the mid-sixteenth century; the Greek *ed. princ.*, edited by Turnèbe, appeared in Paris in 1553. Pseudo-Plutarch, *On Monarchy, Aristocracy, and Democracy* also uses *democratia* in a positive sense. Its idiosyncratic terms for the standard six constitutions in Greek are *monarchia, oligarchia, democratia* (good constitutions), and *tyrannides, dynasteiai, ochlokrateiai* (bad constitutions). The work survives in fragmentary form, handed down with Plutarch's *Moralia* (see 826b–827c). The text was printed in Greek in Aldus' 1509 edition but was unavailable in Latin before the translation of Gisbertus Longolius (1507–1543) from the 1530s.

14 See for example *De republica* 1.41–43, where Cicero states (through his interlocutor Scipio) that kingship is the best of the "simple" constitutions, though a mixed government containing royal, optimate, and popular elements is the best constitution of all.

15 For example, Jerome's *Interpretatio* of the chronicle of Eusebius in *PL* 29: 6c. For the handful of other occurrences, see *TLL* 5: 498 (Servius on *Aeneid* 1.21) and *TLL Onomasticon* 3: 101 (inscriptions).

16 Roberts 1994, 120.

17 Thomas Aquinas [pseud.?], *De regimine principum (De regno ad regem Cypri)*, 1.2: "Si vero iniquum regimen exerceatur per multos, democratia nuncupatur, id est potentatus populi" (But if an unjust regime is conducted by the many, it is called democracy, that is, the people in power). Elsewhere, in his commentary on the *Ethics* (*In librum* 8, *lectio* 10) Aquinas gives the more correct translation "principatus multitudinis" (the many in power). Aquinas however shares Aristotle's view that democracy is the least bad of the "bad" regimes; see *De regno* 1.4.

18 Blythe 1992, chapter 3. On political Aristotelianism, a tradition lasting well into the modern period, see Horn and Neschke-Hentschke 2008.

19 See Chapter 16.

20 For the interesting though rare cases of *democratia* and the adjective *democraticus* used by Catholics as negatives to describe churches with Protestant tendencies in the early Reformation, see

Hoven, 154; to the citations there one may add the letter to Erasmus from Conrad Heresbach (1534 / 1536), where it is used negatively to describe radical Protestants; see Erasmus, *Epistolae* 11: 157, 160. Spinoza uses the term (*Tractatus theologico-politicus* 16.8) to mean the sovereignty (*summum ius*) of the people, in a manner similar to the way *république* is used by Rousseau and *republikanisch* by Kant, to denote a legitimate government stemming from the endorsement of the popular will. See also Spinoza's unfinished *Tractatus politicus* 2.17, 3.1, 7.5, where *democratia* is used in a more traditional way as a constitutional form. On Spinozistic "democratic republicanism" (which rarely employs the *term* "democracy" and its cognates in European languages before the latter half of the eighteenth century), see Israel 2006, chapter 10.

21 Nelson 2014.

22 Wood 2009, 718: "But increasingly in the years following the Revolution, the Republicans and other popular groups, especially in the North, began turning the once derogatory terms 'democracy' and 'democrat' into emblems of pride. Even in the early 1790s some contended that 'the words Republican and Democratic are synonymous' and claimed that anyone who 'is not a Democrat is an aristocrat or a monocrat.'"

23 Palmer 1953, 214–216.

24 For a comparison of ancient and modern concepts of democracy, see Liddel 2009. For the further development of positive ideas about democracy in modern times, see Kloppenberg 2016.

25 For the literature on Cyriac of Ancona, see the bibliographies in Cyriac of Ancona, *Later Travels,* ed. Bodnar, and *Life and Early Travels,* ed. Mitchell, Bodnar, and Foss.

26 See, for example, the letter of Poggio to Bruni mocking Cyriac's learning and eloquence in *Life and Early Travels,* ed. Mitchell, Bodnar, and Foss, letter 6.

27 For an exception, see Hankins 2014a, 80–82. There I discuss an anonymous text, possibly an early work of Bruni, where *popularis status,* said to be the Latin equivalent of the Greek *democratia,* is treated as the constitutional form of contemporary Florence and is classified as a "legitimate" (as opposed to corrupt) constitution. If the text is by Bruni, it is an early work and Bruni later abandoned both the use of the transliterated word *democratia* and the meaning assigned to it of "virtuous popular constitution." For the text, see Hankins 2003–2004a, 1: 26–29. I am more doubtful that the work is by Bruni than formerly. To the reservations expressed in ibid., 23–25, one may add that, unusually for Bruni, none of the three MSS can be dated to before 1445.

28 Cyriac of Ancona, *Life and Early Travels,* ed. Mitchell, Bodnar, and Foss, appendix 4. In the *De republica* of Tito Livio Frulovisi (ed. Previté-Orton, 298), dated 1435 (see chapter 1, note 54), the humanist uses the corrupt, unaccented term ὀχλαρχια as a description of a *principatus* ruled by the people: "Patriam aut regit unus qui dicitur principatus, a Graecis ἡ μοναρχία; aut pauci, et hunc principatum τὴν ὀλιγαρχίαν uocant; aut uniuersus populus, et hic est ἡ ὀχλαρχια siue ἡ δημοκρατία." Frulovisi was a former student of Guarino Veronese and had acquired a smattering of Greek; it is possible that he too either encountered Cyriac in the 1430s or had independent access to a copy of the *excerpta antiqua* of Polybius (see below), which could account for his confused memory of the term ὀχλοκρατία. Ὀχλαρχια is not attested in LSJ or dictionaries of Byzantine Greek.

29 It does not occur in the *TLL* 9.2 or in the online Brepols database of medieval Latin dictionaries; nor does it appear in any searchable database of medieval and Latin texts such as that based on *PL* or the online *Library of Latin Texts* published by Brepols.

30 Momigliano (1974) 1977. For more recent work on Machiavelli and Polybius, see Guelfucci 2008; Pedullà 2011, 419–430; Monfasani 2016; Nederman 2016. Momigliano 1977, 87, follows Carlo Dionisotti in stating that the first known reference to book 6 occurs in the *De urbe Roma* of Bernardo Rucellai, which he dates to "before 1505" on the grounds that it is mentioned by Petrus Crinitus, whose death he places in 1505 (correctly July 5, 1507), in the latter author's *De honesta disciplina* (4.9). A better *ante quem,* however, would be 1503 / 1504, when the *De honesti disciplina* was completed and published; see Roberto Ricciardi, "Del Riccio Baldi, Pietro," in *DBI* 38 (1990). From internal references, however, it is clear that the composition of the book must have begun in the mid-1490s.

31 See De Keyser 2016 (Fortuna). For the wider significance of its recovery, see Nederman and Sullivan 2012.

32 For the manuscripts, see Hankins 1997.

33 Quoted from De Keyser 2016, 11. For the twenty-two manuscripts and nine editions of this translation, and for further bibliography, see De Keyser's discussion.

34 J. M. Moore 1965.

35 De Keyser 2016; Monfasani 2016.

36 J. M. Moore 1965, part 2.

37 Bruni, *De interpretatione recta,* ed. Viti, 120, cap. 43; the relevant passage is quoted in Chapter 3, page 84.

38 Brandolini, *Republics and Kingdoms* 3.85–86, ed. Hankins, 238–240. Brandolini also takes his "constitutionalist" explanation for why Rome was able to subdue Carthage from Polybius 6.51. See the discussion in Nederman 2016, 467–472.

39 The text was published in Praga 1932–1933.

40 Another possibility is that Cyriac is using *libertas* in the sense in which Dante uses the word in the *De monarchia* 1.12.8–10, as a type of autonomy belonging only to those regimes that exist under a just universal monarchy; for Cyriac's debts to Dante, see Schadee 2008.

41 For Salutati's underappreciated contribution to this narrative, see Salutati, *Reply to a Detractor,* ed. Baldassarri and Bagemihl.

42 Cyriac of Ancona, *Six Constitutions,* in *Life and Early Travels,* ed. Mitchell, Bodnar, and Foss, appendix 4: "But today Alfonso, the king of Italy, with great fame and distinction, rules as his own supremely famous kingdom Tarraconensian Spain (i.e. Aragon), Sicily, the Balearic Islands and Italy, with the approval of Eugene, best and greatest of pontiffs, who with great sanctity rules all Christians throughout the globe in the order of divine law."

43 Cyriac of Ancona, *Caesarea laus,* in *Life and Early Travels,* ed. Mitchell, Bodnar, and Foss, 197–221 (letter 4). The work was previously edited (with commentary) by Mariarosa Cortesi in 1998 and independently by Hankins in Gualdo Rosa 1993–2004; see Bibliography.

44 Cyriac of Ancona, *Six Constitutions:* "Monarchy: a single good emperor in the world, like Caesar or Augustus, who used to take care to rule provinces and kingdoms throughout the world in accordance with law, senatorial decree or by resolution of the plebs and the tribunician power, under good magistrates."

45 It is far from clear what Cyriac means by *municipes.* Most likely it translates *demos,* "people of a country district," or commoners, since the *demos* in Athens included both city-dwellers and those who worked estates near the city and enjoyed citizen rights. It is also possible Cyriac is thinking of Roman imperial citizenship and thus wishes to specify, in addition to Roman

citizens who lived in Rome itself, the free citizens of other towns in the empire and who enjoyed Roman citizen rights; see Aulus Gellius' essay on the word *municipes* in *Attic Nights* 16.13.

46 Cyriac of Ancona, *Six Constitutions*. Recanati was in origin a colony of the Roman city of Helvia Recina, founded after that city was devastated by the Goths under Radagaisus in 406 AD.

47 See Blythe 2009.

48 Cyriac of Ancona, *Caesarea laus,* in *Life and Early Travels,* ed. Mitchell, Bodnar, and Foss, 208–209.

49 Bruni, *History* 1.37–40, ed. Hankins, 1: 49–55.

50 See Osmond de Martino 1988.

51 Cyriac of Ancona, *Caesarea laus,* in *Life and Early Travels,* ed. Mitchell, Bodnar, and Foss, 212–213.

52 Ibid.

53 Ibid., 214–217.

13. LEON BATTISTA ALBERTI ON CORRUPT PRINCES AND VIRTUOUS OLIGARCHS

1 Burckhardt 1958, 149–150. On Burckhardt's portrait of Alberti, based on Alberti's autobiography, see McLaughlin 2006, 3–18. On Alberti's life and work, see Grafton 2000.

2 Skinner 1978, 1: 92–100, engages only briefly with the *Della famiglia,* mostly to flesh out his account of humanist conceptions of virtue. In Burns and Goldie 1991 Alberti is virtually ignored. Baron 1988, 1: 258–288, on Alberti's relationship to Florentine civic humanism, is almost the only treatment of his political thought worth reading in English. (The characterization of Alberti's politics as "a socially and politically reactionary kind of romanticism" is found on 283–284; see also Paoli 2007). Pastore Stocchi 1987 devotes only a few pages (57–60) to the *De iciarchia,* and those are rather wrong-headed ones. Catanorchi 2012 offers a judicious assessment of key issues in the interpretation of Alberti's political thought; see also Catanorchi 2005. In the journal *Albertiana* and in the research tools and conference papers emerging from the *ambito* of the Edizione Nazionale delle Opere di Leon Battista Alberti there have appeared useful studies of various works wherein Alberti discusses political themes. Particularly relevant are Boschetto 2000b, Martelli 2000, and Paoli 2007. Canfora 2005, a short but stimulating monograph on quattrocento political thought, situates Alberti as part of an anti-political generation of humanist thinkers of the mid-quattrocento; see also Canfora 2007.

3 Alberti, *Momus,* ed. Brown and Knight. I shall quote from this translation, using the book and paragraph numbers of the I Tatti edition. Kircher 2012 offers guidance on negotiating Alberti's decidedly unpropositional style of argument in the *Momus.*

4 Bracciolini, *De infelicitate principum,* ed. Canfora, xxix–xlv. For further discussion of this text, see Chapter 4.

5 Less convincing is the thesis of Tafuri 2006 and others identifying Jupiter with Nicholas V. I find unpersuasive the argument of Albanese 2012 identifying Pope Pius II as the dedicatee of the *Momus* and the character of Hercules in the novel as a personation of him.

6 Gill 1961.

7 For the negative views of Eugenius' pontificate shared by many humanists and the humanist critique of the saintly image of the pope his defenders tried to construct, see Fubini 2003, 211–248, and above all Boschetto 2012.

8 Bracciolini, *De infelicitate principum,* ed. Canfora, 17. As Boschetto 2012 points out, Poggio was much more ready to criticize Eugenius after he was safely dead.

9 Lapo da Castiglionchio, *De curiae commodis dialogus,* edited in Celenza 1999, 102–227. Celenza makes the case (as does Partner 1990, 114–118), no doubt correctly, that much of Lapo's praise of the curia is ambiguous and should be taken as satire or as a demonstration of his rhetorical skill in praising the indefensible. (The initial position of his interlocutor and advocate, Angelo da Recanate, on the moral turpitude of the curia more closely resembles Alberti's.) This however does not make Lapo into less of a sycophant, as can be seen most obviously in his willingness to praise the military prelate Giovanni Vitelleschi and defend the cardinal's use of military force; see Fubini 1979.

10 Particularly vivid is Alberti's savage picture of life in the court of Pope John XXIII in book 4 of *Della famiglia,* ed. Grayson, 1: 279–282. See also Celati 2019 for Alberti's disguised critique *per ironiam* of the papal curia in his epistolary account of the Porcari conspiracy.

11 A parallel passage is found in Alberti, *Della famiglia,* book 4, in *Opere,* ed. Grayson, 1: 265–266.

12 Throughout the dialogue Alberti employs the common quattrocento terms for the figures modern scholars call "humanists": *literati, studiosi, philosophi,* and *viri docti;* see Preface, page xx.

13 Catanorchi 2012 discusses the interesting contrast between the character Momus and Piero di Bartolomeo Alberti in book 4 of the *Della famiglia,* as "due modelli opposti ma entrambe esemplari" (two opposed but equally exemplary models) of the life of the courtier.

14 See Hankins 2011a.

15 Cf. Alberti, *De iciarchia,* book 3, in *Opere,* ed. Grayson, 2: 271: "And if, in the task of governing, that man is most worthy who towers above the rest in the most excellent things, then certainly the good and the virtuous will be the most suited [for office]. Nothing is more excellent than virtue, and that is why it was the practice in several of the most honored republics of the past that the highest magistracy and command was limited to the men of virtue and integrity, and they were compelled to discharge it. The reason why the people consented to remain under the jurisdiction of their ruler was to live together without injustice and to enjoy their property in quiet liberty."

16 The principle text is Alberti, *De iure,* ed. Banchi. See esp. cap. 22 (ed. Banchi, 826–827) for an example of Alberti's organicism: "In fact what a citizen possesses belongs to the state, since he is a member of the state, and what belongs to a member necessarily belongs to the whole body." This means fraud on an individual is a fraud on the state. "It follows that the private interest cannot derogate from the public, such that what is approved by everyone cannot be invalidated by the few, and what concerns everyone should be approved by everyone" *(quod omnes tangit, omnes comprobent).* The principle effectively moralizes Alberti's preferred regime of "good oligarchy" or *iciarchia* discussed below. For discussion of the *De iure* and Alberti's other scattered comments on law, see Rossi 1999; Rossi 2000; Quaglione 2003, 97–104; Rossi 2007. A similar attitude to the inadequacies of contemporary jurisprudence is found in Poggio: see Krantz 1987. For the "QOT" principle *(quod omnes tangit),* see Fasolt 2014. On the concept of "organicism" as characteristic of humanist political thought, see Cappelli 2016b, quoted on page 583n12.

17 Poggio Bracciolini's chief interlocutor in the *De infelicitate principum* takes a similar view; see Bracciolini, *De infelicitate principum,* ed. Canfora, 24: "I don't know whom are you are calling

tyrants. We know this for sure, that some of them exercised a power that was better and more just towards their subjects than that of kings. A king is to be identified not by the name, but by the deed."

18 Alberti, *De re aedificatoria* 4.1.

19 Kircher 2012 argues that Alberti adopted a stance of critical irony toward his contemporaries' tendency to equate humanistic learning with virtue, emphasizing instead the need for concrete moral experience. In *De commodis,* however, Alberti takes the standard humanist view that literary study is, unlike studies such as law and medicine, free and honorable, as well as productive of wisdom and good character in its devotees—despite being, in these decayed modern times, poorly remunerated and often engaged in for mercenary reasons. In the same way, he states, with his customary pessimism about politics, that in corrupt modern times, literary men should avoid public office, having no knowledge that will be recognized as useful to the state (*De commodis,* ed. Regoliosi, 45–46). In antiquity, however, human and divine knowledge was not only a guide to good conduct and to true glory, but also "governed the state *(respublica)* and accustomed the whole world to act in an orderly way and in accordance with the highest law" (ibid., 47).

20 See Baron 1988, 1: 276–278, and Chapter 7. The view that virtue is needed for the *acquisition* of wealth, and that the mere inheritance of wealth made by others is potentially harmful to character, is in stark contrast to the view reported in Aristotle's *Politics* that nobility or good birth *(eugeneia)* comes from "ancient wealth and excellence"; see *Politics* 4.8.1294a. It also constitutes a rejection of Dante's view in *Convivio* 4.11–12 that the acquisition and enlargement of personal wealth are always morally suspect.

21 The political import of this passage to my knowledge has been discussed only by the historian of architecture Alberto Giorgio Cassani; see Cassani 1996.

22 Alberti, *De re aedificatoria* 4.1. My translation is based on the *ed. princ.* of 1485, sign. h i *v*–h ii *r.* I have emended *proximierunt* to *proximi erunt.*

23 On the circulation of Alberti's works in general, see Bertolini 2004.

24 Boschetto 1991; Paoli 2007 speculates that Alberti's drafts of *De iciarchia* may go back to the early 1460s.

25 A key passage for understanding the "familial" perspective—the instrumentalization of politics in the service of the family—is the speech of Piero Alberti on how to win the friendship of princes in book 4 of *Della famiglia,* ed. Grayson, 1: 270–282.

26 Cf. Boschetto 2000b and Paoli 2007, 538.

27 Alberti, *De iciarchia,* book 3, ed. Grayson, 2: 273: "How shall we call this man of ours? Let's give him a name taken from the Greeks, *iciarch,* which means the supreme man and foremost leader of his family—his office, in short, will be to take care individually of each person, and understand his abilities and how much he can achieve, both on his own and with others, and on that basis to provide for the security, tranquillity and honor of the family."

28 For the character of Medici rule, see Black and Law 2015.

29 This is also the central theme of Alberti's *Theogenius:* One might desire that magistracies and the government of the republic be reserved to good men and that the counsels of the wise might prevail, but "I have often seen how the pestilential opinion and open rashness of one very insolent fellow can be more favored by the multitude than the good advice of a most wise and excellent citizen"; see Alberti, *Opere,* ed. Grayson, 2: 78. On this theme, see also Boschetto 1993.

30 See Chapter 6. Canfora 2005, 57, 63, claims that Alberti's *Theogenius* is dependent on Seneca via Petrarch's *De vita solitaria*. See also Chapter 17 for Francesco Patrizi's response to Poggio Bracciolini's *De infelicitate principum.*

31 Alberti, *De iciarchia,* book 3, in *Opere,* ed. Grayson, 2: 283: "Your goal in this enterprise will not be to strive to command, so that your commands are obeyed in every way as if to satisfy yourself alone, but the goal that combines all your cares will be to promote integrity in everyone you love, and thereby to strengthen the dignity of the whole family."

32 Alberti, *De iciarchia,* book 1, in *Opere,* ed. Grayson, 2: 188.

33 Ibid., 2: 189: "Let us then enjoy this moderation, my sons, which is the friend of quiet, the bond of peace, the nurse of happy tranquillity in our soul and our blessed repose in all of life."

34 Alberti, *De iciarchia,* book 3, in *Opere,* ed. Grayson, 2: 266.

35 See Schofield 1999c. The doctrine of the "modes of rule" based on the three types of rule within the family was widely appropriated in scholastic political writings of late medieval Europe, including the most influential of them, Giles of Rome, in his *De regimine principum;* see Blythe 1992, 11–12, 19, 42, 63–65 (on Giles of Rome), 69, 86, 95–97, 122–124.

36 Alberti, *De iciarchia,* book 3, in *Opere,* ed. Grayson, 2: 263–264.

37 Ibid., 2: 264.

38 This does not mean that the iciarch who exercises power in a family should ignore the different relations within a family or that he should not adjust his manner of rule to different relations such as parent, child, brother, etc.; see ibid., 2: 274. For the debt of Alberti's theory of natural subordination to Aristotle, compare *Nicomachean Ethics* 2.3.1104b30–31, where, in the context of discussing the relation of pleasure and pain to virtue, the three objects of choice (or goods) are said to be the noble *(to kalon),* the useful *(to sumpheron)* and the pleasant *(to hedu).*

39 On the easiness of virtue, see Alberti, *De iciarchia,* book 2, in *Opere,* ed. Grayson, 2: 222: "It often happens that I wonder how proper it is to man, how easy, how ready to hand it is to acquire virtue, a thing so necessary in all of life, goodness being a thing that is so worthy, esteemed and loved, something you acquire with such pleasure, from which you receive such profit and such marvelous rewards—I say, I wonder why it is that such a great number of men refuse it and indeed cut themselves off from it." Compare Alberti, *Della famiglia,* Prologo, in *Opere,* ed. Grayson, 1: 9: "It can hardly be doubted that, of whatever kind it is, when you seek it out and love it, nothing is easier for you to have and obtain than virtue. The only man who lacks virtue is the one who doesn't want it." On the "easiness" of virtue in humanist thought, see Chapter 2, page 41.

40 Alberti, *De iciarchia,* book 2, in *Opere,* ed. Grayson, 2: 229, 256. On this theme, see esp. Boschetto 2000b, 175.

41 Alberti, *De iciarchia,* book 3, in *Opere,* ed. Grayson, 2: 273: "Paulo: O blessed is that city where such a man were found in every family! Niccolò: And how blessed it would be if this republic of ours should have so great a number of similar men, even ten, even six . . . I say no more." This affords a striking, perhaps conscious contrast with the usual humanist commonplace from Plato's *Republic* (5.473c11–d6) that states will be blessed when rulers are philosophers or philosophers rule.

42 The whole book reads like a reply to the speech of the interlocutor Lionardo degli Alberti in book 3 of *Della famiglia* defending the value of participation in public life and its rewards of fame and glory (*Opere,* ed. Grayson, 1: 182–185).

43 Alberti, *De iciarchia,* book 1, in *Opere,* ed. Grayson, 2: 195: "Let the maxim that I have stated convince you that true preeminence lies in being superior to others in virtue, good conduct, prudence and a vast knowledge of the arts and in good things." The passage reprises a theme of the *Theogenius:* whether the public or the private life is superior.

44 Alberti, *De iciarchia,* book 3, in *Opere,* ed. Grayson, 2: 224; on this passage, see the illuminating remarks of Baron 1988, 1: 285–286.

45 For the Arno in flood as an image of Medici power, see Boschetto 1991, 187. It is worth noting that same image of a river in spate is used to describe the effects of popular rule in Herodotus' famous constitutional debate in *Histories* 3.81. For Herodotus in the Renaissance, see Chapter 4; for Alberti's interest in Herodotus, see Grafton 2000, 276–278.

46 Alberti, *De iciarchia,* book 3, in *Opere,* ed. Grayson, 2: 261: "New opinions teach disobedience to old laws. There is nothing so pernicious to the republic than diminishing respect and fear of the laws." This is a frequent theme in Alberti. See also Celati 2019, for Alberti's horror of any attempt to overturn the established political order, any *cupiditas rerum novarum.* See also the *Lacus* and *Bubo* in book 10 of the *Intercenales* for Alberti's condemnation of new laws that spoil existing social relationships, relationships that would be perfectly harmonious but for meddling politicians; the effect of new laws for him is to unsettle the social order, a situation that inevitably empowers tyrants.

47 Alberti, *De iciarchia,* book 3, in *Opere,* ed. Grayson, 2: 262–263: "Ten laws and no more, after Moses, ruled the whole Hebrew nation for several hundred years in the veneration of God and in the observance of honor, equity and love of country. Only twelve very brief tables sufficed for the Romans to enlarge their republic and establish their preeminence. We have sixty cabinets full of statutes and every day we produce new ordinances."

48 Alberti, *De iciarchia,* book 2, in *Opere,* ed. Grayson, 2: 193: "Thus it follows that preeminence does not grant discretion to impose new servitude on others, but imposes on him who rules it the civil obligation to preserve the liberty and prestige of his country and peace among private citizens."

49 In the *De iure* 23 (ed. Banchi and Coppini, 827), Alberti declares that the care of divine things should be left to God and that in assigning rewards and punishments human judges should consider only human things, stipulating that they be mindful of God and utterly devoted *(amantissimus)* to justice.

14. GEORGE OF TREBIZOND ON COSMOPOLITANISM AND LIBERTY

1 See Monfasani 1976, 102–103; Monfasani 1984, 744–747; Hankins 1990a, 1: 174–184; and Chapter 16, page 377, for George and the Venetian constitution.

2 For the manuscripts and the 1523 edition, see Monfasani 1984, 600–602, and Monfasani 2007. The 1523 edition is accessible online via the Hathi Trust Digital Library (original from the Universidad Complutense de Madrid). John Monfasani is preparing a critical edition.

3 See Pettit 1999; Skinner 1990; Skinner 1998.

4 Recent studies of Renaissance political thought regarding empires include Pagden 1995; Lupher 2003; Hornqvist 2004; Stacey 2007; Meserve 2008; O'Connell 2009; Kingsbury 2010; Dandelet 2014; and Lee 2018.

5 The Renaissance period has not attracted much interest from historians of cosmopolitanism. There are a few remarks in Heater 1996, 48–52 (chiefly on Erasmus and Lipsius).

6 George of Trebizond, *Comparatio,* 1523 ed., sign. Q8*v*–R4*v*.

7 Plato, *Laws* 850b–c. For an overview of Plato's late political theory, see Klosko 1986 and Laks 2000; for more recent perspectives, see Bobonich 2010.

8 Monfasani 1976.

9 See esp. his treatise *On Airs, Waters, and Places* for many observations about the effects of climate on a person's complexional nature and character.

10 George of Trebizond, *Comparatio,* 1523 ed., sign. R1*r*–*v*. Pontines are peoples from the Black Sea, part of the region northeast of classical Greece which the Greeks imagined to be populated by barbarous peoples such as the Scythians and Thracians. George perhaps thought his dream probative because of the ancient medical doctrine that a "synkrimatic" dream revealed one's true nature. So the dream shows that George is really a Cretan, not a Pontine; the detail that George had not seen a "Cappadocian monster" (Typhoeus?) indicates that his dream was healthy, not diseased. See Oberhelman 1987.

11 For a useful anthology of texts, see Rabil 1991. Andrea Robiglio is writing a monograph on this tradition of thought.

12 George of Trebizond, *Comparatio,* 1523 ed., sign. R1*v*–R2*r*. Among George's sources for these ideas are Livy, Plutarch, Dionysius Halicarnasseus, and Aelius Aristides.

13 Ibid., sign. R2*v*. Compare Aelius Aristides, *Encomium Romae,* tr. Behr, 2: 80: "You Romans govern throughout the whole inhabited world as if in a single city." For Trebizond's debt to Aristides here, see below.

14 The comparison between Rome's mastery of the art of empire and the Greeks' failure is again based on Aristides' *Encomium Romae,* tr. Behr, 2: 81–85.

15 George of Trebizond, *Comparatio,* 1523 ed., sign. R3*r*.

16 See Monfasani 1976, 131–132, 184–194.

17 On George's mission, see texts CXLIII–CXLV in Monfasani 1984, 491–574. Of course there are plentiful resources within early Christianity to support cosmopolitan sentiments (e.g., Acts 17:26 and Galatians 3:28).

18 George himself, addressing Mehmed II in *On the Eternal Glory of the Autocrat,* (Monfasani 1984, 495), discussed how the Goths had converted to Christianity (in its heretical Arian form) and were rewarded by Providence with the conquest of Rome. But, warned George, when they failed to convert to Roman Catholicism they were quickly wiped out.

19 See Hankins 1995b, reprinted in Hankins 2003–2004a, 1: 293–424, esp. 319–320.

20 For ancient cosmopolitanism in general, see Long 2008, and, in the Second Sophistic, Richter 2017. For a detailed account of Cynic cosmopolitanism, see Moles 1996 and 2005. For typologies of modern ideological cosmopolitanism, see Kleingeld and Brown 2013.

21 Sinope, interestingly, is a port city on the Black Sea, only about 500 kilometers west of Trebizond. Like Trebizond, it was a place where Greeks mingled with "barbarian" peoples; Diogenes too lived as a resident alien in more civilized cities such as Athens and Corinth.

22 Diogenes Laertius, *Lives of the Philosophers* 6.72 and 6.63 (my translation).

23 Possible sources for the dictum are Cicero's *Laws* 1.7.23 and *De finibus* 3.62 (Cicero is writing as a Stoic in both passages); less plausible is Philo, *On the Creation of the Universe* 3, or Plutarch, *On the Fortune of Alexander* (*Moralia* 329a–b).

24 See notes 13–14 above. The translations below are Behr's; the passages quoted or alluded to may be found on pp. 80–87 of his translation. For a Greek text and commentary, see Fontanella 2007. On Aristides' *Encomium Romae,* see Pernot 2008.

25 For an overview of issues and concerns in modern cosmopolitanism (a huge academic industry), see Appiah 2006; Brown and Held 2010.

26 Especially insightful is Marshall 2006.

27 George of Trebizond, *Comparatio*, 1523 ed., sign. R4*v*–R8*r*.

28 Ibid., R6*r*.

29 Ibid., R6*v*.

30 Baron 1988, esp. essays 7–9 in volume 1. See also Jurdjevic 2001, and Chapter 7.

31 See my discussion in Hankins 2003–2004a, 1: 214–215.

32 George of Trebizond, *Comparatio*, 1523 ed., sign. R7*r*.

33 Ibid., R6*v*.

34 Kempshall 1999. I have been unable to find a position similar to George's in this very thorough and precise study.

35 George of Trebizond, *Comparatio*, 1523 ed., sign. R7*r*.

36 Ibid., R7*v*–R8*r*.

37 Ibid., R7*r*–*v*.

38 Locke, *Letter concerning Toleration,* ed. Shapiro, esp. 219–232.

39 See Waldron 2002 on the Christian background of Locke's ideas of free will and egalitarianism. For virtue politics and Rawlsian "comprehensive doctrines," see the Conclusion, page 508.

40 For a sobering account of the limits of Aristotle's toleration for personal freedoms, see Barnes 2005.

41 See Aristotle, *Politics* 3.7–8. Francesco Patrizi of Siena, the great humanist authority on political theory, similarly identifies the end of popular republics as the desire of the multitude to live as it wishes *(vivere ut vis),* provided what one wants to do is not constrained by force or right *(nisi quod vi aut iure prohibetur);* see his *De inst. r.p.* 1.4, 1534 ed., f. VIIIr–v. (The definition of liberty is attributed to Cicero and to the second-century Roman jurisconsult Florentinus.) The end of popular republics is distinguished from that of aristocratic republics (virtue) and of oligarchies (wealth).

42 John Stuart Mill, *On Liberty,* ed. Collini, 13: "The sole end for which mankind are warranted, individually or collectively, in interfering with the liberty of action of any of their number, is self-protection. That the only purpose for which power can be rightfully exercised over any member of a civilised community, against his will, is to prevent harm to others. His own good, either physical or moral, is not a sufficient warrant." But there does exist a premodern harm principle expressed in terms of right; see Chapter 4, page 111.

43 See the section on self-ownership in Vallentyne 2012. For a discussion of the incompatibility of libertarian self-ownership with Catholic / Christian conceptions of natural law, see Feser 2010.

44 Compare Petrarch's argument for autonomy in Chapter 6, page 184.

15. FRANCESCO FILELFO AND THE SPARTAN REPUBLIC

1 Momigliano 1980, 1: 131.

2 Pade 2007. Detailed information about the Renaissance reception of the various Greek historians mentioned above can be found in *CTC:* Agathias (10: 239–272), Arrian (3: 1–20), Polybius (11: 1–60), Thucydides (3: 103–181), and Xenophon (7: 75–196 and 8: 341–344).

3 Pedullà 2010, 2011 / 2018.

4 Models for such studies, mostly having to do with transalpine humanism, may be found in Helmrath, Shirrmeister, and Schlelein 2013.

5 There is a useful sketch in Rawson 1969, esp. 130–157 on the Renaissance. Rawson discusses the influence of Sparta on education in the fifteenth century and on political thought in the sixteenth, beginning with Machiavelli; she does not, however, discuss the Laconism of Filelfo or Thomas More. Marsh 1991 discusses and edits Lilius Tifernas' translation of Xenophon's *Lacedaemoniorum respublica* (Constitution of the Spartans). In general the Italian fifteenth century is neglected in the reception history of Sparta. See, e.g., Losemann 2003, which covers the Renaissance reception of Sparta in a single paragraph. Paul Cartledge's entry on Sparta in Grafton, Most, and Settis 2010, 898–901, has one sentence on the fifteenth century and a paragraph on Thomas More's Laconism; see also Cartledge 2006 for a page on Pletho and Sparta. Vlassopoulos 2012 starts his discussion of early modern Laconism with Machiavelli. An exception to the general neglect of Sparta in the quattrocento is Humble 2012, 2018.

6 Filelfo, *Traduzioni;* Filelfo, *De exilio,* ed. De Keyser, tr. Blanchard; Filelfo, *Sfortiae, De Genuensium deditione, Oratio parentalis,* ed. De Keyser; Filelfo, *Collected Letters,* ed. De Keyser.

7 For modern reconstructions of Spartan society, history, and culture, see Cartledge 2001, 2002; Cartledge and Spawforth 2002. A recent textbook approach is Kennell 2010. Rahe 2016 provides an analysis of the Spartan constitution and Sparta's "grand strategy"; a more contextual approach is explored in Cartledge 2001, 9–67. For the "mirage" of Sparta, the classic work is Ollier (1933–1943) 1973.

8 For the presumed political context and motivation of Filelfo's translations, see Resta 1986, 20–21; Viti 2005; De Keyser 2006–2007; Fiaschi 2007; Pade 2007, 1: 262.

9 Filelfo, *Traduzioni,* ed. De Keyser, 3. It is worth noting that Cicero praises Xenophon's life of Agesilaus in *Fam.* 5.12.1, 7, a recommendation that may well have encouraged interest in the text. For an analysis of this preface, see Humble 2012, 2018.

10 PhE 46.01, in Filelfo, *Collected Letters,* ed. De Keyser, 4: 1850, to Ferdinand, King of Sicily. Filelfo's elective affinity for Sparta may have to do with his wider attraction to Stoicism. As Schofield 1999a, 35–42, argues, Zeno of Citium's political thought was deeply influenced by the example of Lycurgus' Sparta.

11 See Filelfo, *De exilio,* book 3, passim, and Cao 1997. For Filelfo's attitude to "political poverty," see also below.

12 Robin 1983, esp. 204–212.

13 For an assessment of the reliability or otherwise of ancient sources on Sparta, a constant concern in the scholarly literature of the last half century, see Tigerstedt 1965–1978, vol. 1; Ollier 1973.

14 Morris 2012 gives a good sense of what little could be known in the late medieval period before the translation movement of the fifteenth century.

15 Herodotus and Thucydides were both translated by Lorenzo Valla; see Chapter 4, page 149. Xenophon's *Hellenica* was epitomated by Bruni under the title *Commentaria rerum graecarum* (1439) but not properly translated until Willibald Pirckheimer did so in the early sixteenth century. See *CTC* 7: 80 (David Marsh) and Hankins 2007–2008a. Diodorus Siculus 11–15 was first translated by Iacopo da San Cassiano (a translation falsely attributed to George of Trebizond) for Nicholas V in 1453 but was never printed; see Monfasani 1976, 105n152, and the fuller information in Monfasani's article on Diodorus for *CTC* 11: 105–115.

16 On the date, see Pade 2007, 1: 260–263, and De Keyser in Filelfo, *Traduzioni,* XVI–XVII. It seems likely that Filelfo presented the dedication to Albergati during the latter's visit to

Florence, January 17–30, 1430, which was also the occasion on which Bruni presented to the prelate his *Vita Aristotelis;* see Hankins 2007–2008a, 18n5.

17 Pade 2007.

18 Another translation of *Agesilaus* was made by Battista Guarino in 1457 / 1458 (printed with Ulrich Han's 1470 Roman edition of Plutarch's *Lives*). A second quattrocento version of *The Spartan Republic* was made by Lilius Tifernas. For both versions, see Marsh 1992.

19 On the "Spartan tetralogy" of 1430 and Filelfo's other translations of Spartan sources, see Filelfo, *Traduzioni,* ed. De Keyser. Filelfo mentions the translations in PhE 02.18, 02.84, 04.18, 05.37, 11.49, 30.02, 34.06, 42.29, 43.01, 47.01 (all in Filelfo, *Collected Letters,* vols. 1–4). On the patriotism of Spartan women, see *De exilio,* 2.70, ed. De Keyser, 231, and book 4 of *De morali disciplina,* 1552 ed., 68–69, and page 359.

20 The numerous manuscripts and editions of Filelfo's Xenophon translations are listed in Marsh 1992; for the popularity of Filelfo's translations in print, see Cortesi-Fiaschi. The timocratic regime in Plato's *Republic* 8 is sometimes thought to be modelled on Sparta, but I know of no Italian Renaissance humanist who made this connection.

21 Hankins 1990a, 1: 180–192 and 1: 300–318.

22 On Bruni's translations of Demosthenes, see Hankins 2002b; Hankins 2003–2004a, 1: 243–271.

23 For Pausanias and Strabo, see *CTC* 2: 215–220 and 2: 225–233, respectively; on the Spartan poetry in the Greek anthology, see Hutton 1935. Filelfo quotes Tyrtaeus in *De morali disciplina* (1552 ed., 69, 70), remarking that Spartan poetry was morally sound and could not come into the class of poetry condemned by Plato.

24 Cyriac, *Later Travels,* ed. Bodnar, 299–305, 329–337 (Diary V.1–11, 55–65).

25 It may be noted that as early as 1404, Leonardo Bruni compared the Parte Guelfa to the ephors of Sparta in his *Laudatio Florentine urbis* (see Chapter 8, page 229). In general, however, as Rawson 1969, 137–138, notes, Bruni preferred to compare Florence with Rome or Athens; see also Chapter 16, page 383. By contrast Francesco Patrizi saw the ephors as having a function similar to the *tribuni plebis* of the Roman republic in his *De regno* 1.3. His account is informed by his reading of Herodotus 6.51–76 as well as Aristotle's *Politics.*

26 The question is raised in Polybius 6.10 and 6.50. See also Plutarch, *Lycurgus* 31.1–3, which praises Sparta for aiming at virtue and harmony within itself rather than seeking hegemony over other cities. Either source could have been known to Machiavelli, who in *Disc.* 1.4–6 expresses his preference for ordering a state for empire rather than for stability.

27 Aristotle's discussion of Spartan kingship is in *Politics* 3.14.3–5.1085a. On other classifications of constitutions in the *Politics,* aside from the famous sixfold analysis in book 3, see Hansen 2013.

28 Hankins 2010a; Schofield 1999a, chapter 10.

29 For instance, writing to the Venetian patrician Federico Corner, Filelfo says, "The doge holds that place of authority among you that the king used to hold among the Spartans"; see PhE 03.19. Cyriac of Ancona also regards Venice as having preserved into modern times the aristocratic constitution of the Spartans; see Chapter 12, page 315. Patrizi, *De regno* 1.13, takes the Spartan kingship to be a form of constitutional monarchy.

30 PhE 47.01, in Filelfo, *Collected Letters,* ed. De Keyser, 4: 1877–1883. The need to mount a crusade against the Ottoman threat was a constant refrain in humanist literature in this period; see Hankins 1995b, reprinted with corrections in Hankins 2003–2004a, 1: 293–424.

31 Filelfo makes the same point in PhE 03.19 (dated 1439) to Federico Corner that the Venetian constitution was aristocratic, modelling in its relations with non-elites the father-son relationship in the family, and thus resembled Sparta.

32 Filelfo ignores the fact that the Spartan kings ruled in pairs (possibly misled by Xenophon's *Agesilaus* where the other *basileus* is never mentioned) and that their office was hereditary.

33 PhE 47.01, in Filelfo, *Collected Letters,* ed. De Keyser, 4: 1880.

34 Aristotle, *Politics* 2.9. For a modern scholarly account of the Spartan regime, see Kennell 2010, 97–114.

35 Theoretically speaking, this counts as an example of "allelopoesis," a reuse of an ancient source that changes thereby the understanding of the source text; see Helmrath, Hausteiner, and Jensen 2017. The surprising idea that the Spartans were skilled in philosophy may come from Plato, *Protagoras* 342a9–10.

36 PhE 46.01, in Filelfo, *Collected Letters,* ed. De Keyser, 4: 1850.

37 PhE 47.01, in Filelfo, *Collected Letters,* ed. De Keyser, 4: 1880.

38 The humanists generally followed Aristotle, *Politics* 3.14.1285a, in understanding the chief function of Sparta's kings to be military leadership; the life of Agesilaus reinforced that impression. For modern accounts of Spartan kingship, see Cartledge 2001, 55–67; Kennell 2010, 93–192. Plutarch's presentation of Agesilaus' behavior was more equivocal than Xenophon's, but the humanists, ever in search of examples of ancient virtue, preferred the latter's panegyrical version of the great commander's life.

39 Xenophon, *Agesilaus* 36 (Loeb translation). Filelfo translates "he obeyed the call of the state" (*polis* in Greek) as *reipublicae paruit* (*Traduzioni,* ed. De Keyser, 25).

40 For humanist criticisms of the actions of Julius Caesar, and attempts to defend them, see Chapter 4.

41 See the summary of Agesilaus' career in PhE 47.01, in Filelfo, *Collected Letters,* ed. De Keyser, 4: 1880–1881.

42 Filelfo, *Traduzioni,* ed. De Keyser, 4: "It is a most beautiful thing, by the god of truth, to live an honorable life, but it is far more beautiful and divine to be able to make others as like as possible to one's own outstanding virtue. We read that Lycurgus was person like this, who not only prepared himself for uprightness, honor and glory, but indeed turned all his care, zeal and effort to making his citizens the kind of men he himself was reckoned to be at that time by nearly the whole world. Thus he founded a city through legislation, established a state and built a power that was both feared by barbarians and respected by all of Greece."

43 The ultimate source is the speech of Nicias in Thucydides 8.77, though there are numerous intermediate sources as well.

44 PhE 47.01, in Filelfo, *Collected Letters,* ed. De Keyser, 4: 1880: "Thus king Agesilaus, having subdued a great part of Asia, being summoned back to his country by the ephors, did not dare oppose them, saying that a good leader *(principem)* ought to obey the laws. And when he had returned home, in order that he might benefit from his company, he saw to it that Xenophon, that illustrious and upright Socratic philosopher, should be offered honorable rewards to educate the boys of Sparta, training them in the discipline he judged to be the most beautiful of all: to rule and to endure the rule of others." The point is repeated in a letter to Ercole d'Este (1471); see PhE 33.25 (to Ercole d'Este, dated 1471), ibid., 3: 1444, along with the standard list of famous rulers of antiquity counseled by learned men. On the divine inspiration of Lycurgus' laws: PhE 08.08 (to Andrea Alamanno, dated 1450), ibid., 1: 414. On civil

behavior and rejecting partisanship: PhE 40.05 (to Federico d'Urbino, dated 1474), ibid., 3: 1671.

45 Plutarch, *Lacaenarum Apophthegmata* (*Moralia* 240f), no. 2 (Loeb edition, 3: 459).

46 Ibid., 241f, no. 16 (Loeb edition, 3: 464). The verses mean "Bring this shield back, or be brought back (dead) on it."

47 Ibid., 2241e, no. 12 (Loeb edition, 3: 465).

48 PhE 47.01, in Filelfo, *Collected Letters*, ed. De Keyser, 4: 1880.

49 PhE 48.01 (to Ludovico il Moro, a. 1477), in Filelfo, *Collected Letters*, ed. De Keyser, 4: 1907, discusses how Lycurgus willingly gave up his power as regent in favor of the legitimate heir, even though the latter was a baby. The anecdote is based on Plutarch's *Life of Lycurgus* 3.1–4 but is reported also in Justin 3.2. Morris 2012, 23–24, shows how this anecdote was twisted by Humfrey, Duke of Gloucester, to justify his own claim to the regency on behalf of the young Henry VI.

50 PhE 04.03 (to Cosimo de'Medici, a. 1440), in Filelfo, *Collected Letters*, ed. De Keyser, 1: 243–249.

51 Aristotle, by contrast, railed against the license of Spartan women; see *Politics* 2.9.1269b. For modern disagreements about the position of women in Sparta, see Cartledge 2001, 106–126. Rawson 1969, 135–136, discusses Renaissance responses to Spartan women.

52 Filelfo mentions equality as a Spartan virtue, but it is *morum aequalitas,* everyone following the same customs. Spartans were equal because they did not seek wealth and cultivated frugality (PhE 07.37; see also PhE 04.02). Lycurgus' land equalization scheme, a kind of distributism, is faithfully reported in Filelfo's translations, to be sure, but Filelfo does not comment on it in his own works. Contrast the positive treatment of this Lycurgan institution in the medieval *Liber de vita et moribus philosophorum*, discussed by Morris 2012, 8. Aristotle, whom Filelfo follows in many matters of public morality, criticized the effectiveness of Lycurgus' land legislation as a mode of securing equality in *Politics* 2.9.13–16, 1270a. For a modern interpretation of Spartan ideas about equality, see Cartledge 2001, 68–75. For early modern appeals to the Spartan regime as justification for an "equal agrarian," see Nelson 2004.

53 See for example PhE 11.51 (to Niccolò Ceba, dated 1454), in Filelfo, *Collected Letters*, ed. De Keyser, 2: 573 (that the celibate life brought infamy among the Spartans), and PhE 28.34 (to Francesco Griffolini, dated 1468), in Filelfo, *Collected Letters*, ed. De Keyser, 3: 1230 (the laws of Lycurgus disapproved of men who maintained celibacy into old age).

54 PhE 16.05 (to Pasquale Malipiero, dated 1460), in Filelfo, *Collected Letters*, ed. De Keyser, 2: 787–788 (factionalism and contempt for law are inversely proportional to the durability of empire; the Spartans and Venetians are compared to each other).

55 Plato, *Laws* 1.624a-642d; Aristotle, *Politics* 1.8–11, 1256a–1259a.

56 PhE 19.13 (to Ludovico Foscarini, dated 1463), in Filelfo, *Collected Letters*, ed. De Keyser, 2: 930. Filelfo quotes the example of Leonidas at Thermopylae in the context of a letter encouraging the Venetians to take up the crusade against "the tyrant" Mehmed II; he uses Thermopylae to show that Western virtue can defeat *mollis ignavaque barbaria* (soft and base barbarian lands), assimilating the ancient Persians to the Turks. See also Filelfo's *De morali disciplina,* book 4, 1552 ed., 68, which quotes Leonidas as saying that virtue can always overcome sheer numbers. "Leonidas understood that every danger is to be borne for the liberty of one's country, and that death should be considered most lovely by which public salvation is compassed through the deaths of a few men." Filelfo's knowledge of the battle of Thermopylae seems to come

directly from Herodotus; see PhE 22.23 (to Alberto Parisi, dated 1464) in *Collected Letters,* ed. De Keyser, 2: 1022–1023 (where he translates *Histories* 1.81–82), and PhE 23.01 (to Pope Paul II, dated 1464), in Filelfo, *Collected Letters,* ed. De Keyser, 2: 1030.

57 PhE 46.01, in Filelfo, *Collected Letters,* ed. De Keyser, 4: 1850.

58 On Lysander and Spartan decline: PhE 16.05, 32.23, 33.25, 46.01, 47.01. *De morali disciplina,* book 4, 1552 ed., 55, explicitly draws the parallel between Roman and Spartan decline. Xenophon, *The Spartan Republic* 14, registers the fact of Spartan moral decline since Lycurgus' day, but blames uncontrolled ambition outstripping virtue.

59 PhE 16.05: "The state of the Spartans alone lasted longer. So long as they obeyed the laws of Lycurgus, so long as they were zealous of praise, so long as they put honorable behavior before all external goods, they remained famous and triumphant in all of Greece for up to five hundred years."

60 Machiavelli, *Disc.* 1.5–6, based on Polybius 6.10.

61 Cicero, *De senectute* 16.55.

62 PhE 25.07.

63 Noted in PhE 26.01; *De morali disciplina,* book 4, 1552 ed., 70.

64 PhE 39.01.

65 See *De exilio,* book 3, where this view is put ironically in the mouth of Leonardo Bruni, whose own position on the wealth debate was quite different (see Chapter 7, page 208). Book 3 of *De exilio* contains Filelfo's most extensive discussion of the moral uses of wealth.

66 Jurdjevic 2001; and see also Chapter 7, page 206, for a broader discussion of humanist attitudes to wealth, avarice and luxury

67 *Africa* 1979.

68 Patrizi, *De inst. r.p.* 6.5, 1534 ed., f. LXXXVIv: "Nam si qua ratione fieri potest, ut cives perpetuo bene agant, sequantur honesta, fugiant autem turpia, perpetua erit respublica, dummodo principes labantem populum firment. Ut enim eorum cupiditatibus a<c> vitiis tota civitas inficitur, sic emendatur et corrigitur continentia—virtutem siquidem est quae civilem societatem stabilem ac diuturnam praestare potest. Et optimi mores optimaeque constitutiones eorum, qui praesunt rem populi, non modo conservant, verum dignitatem ac imperium mirum in modum augent, quod quidem exemplo idem Xenophon ostendit, cum de Lacedaemoniorum republica scribit. Dicit namque Sparten, quae civium frequentiam habebat exiguam, eam tamen parvo tempore opibus, potentia, multitudine, dignitate, et imperium plurimum crevisse, quae res eum in admirationem non mediocrem adducebat." Patrizi's selective reading of Xenophon to support the possibility of a polity's avoiding corruption is all the more remarkable in that Xenophon says precisely the opposite in *The Spartan Republic* 14. Perhaps Patrizi is inferring the permanence of the Spartan state from the longevity of its kingship, noted in Xenophon, *Agesilaus* 5.

69 For Rousseau's view of Sparta, for whom Sparta was "something of a utopia," see Cartledge 2006, 43–44.

16. GREEK CONSTITUTIONAL THEORY IN THE QUATTROCENTO

1 Skinner 1978, 1: 49–51; Burns 1988, 360–361; Flüeler 1992; Canning 1996, 125–134. The view that the medieval reception of Aristotle's political thought constituted a theoretical watershed between the medieval and the modern world was stated in its strongest form in Ullmann 1965; for a critique of this view, see Nederman 2009, 5–9.

2 Only some of these authors are so far treated in the reference work devoted to such problems, *CTC* (Diodorus Siculus, vol. 11; Polybius, vol. 11; Thucydides, vol. 8, Xenophon, vol. 7).

3 Polybian influence on Machiavelli and via Machiavelli on the later republican tradition was a major theme of Pocock 1975 (2003); for more recent analyses of Machiavelli's use of Polybius, see the literature mentioned above on page 601n30. For Xenophon and Machiavelli, see Newell 2013, 228–270 (chapter 5: "Machiavelli, Xenophon and Xenophon's Cyrus"), who builds on the work of Leo Strauss.

4 For Xenophon's Spartan writings in the Renaissance, see Chapter 15. For the *Cyropaedia* and the reception of ancient monarchical theory, see Chapter 17. For the reception of the *Hiero,* a beginning is made in Maxson 2010.

5 On Decembrio and Plato, see Hankins 1990a, 1: 105–117; Vegetti and Pissavino 2005. On Bruni and Thucydides, see Susanne Daub's introduction and commentary on Bruni, *Panegyric of Nanni Strozzi;* on Bruni and Aelius Aristides, see Santosuosso 1986.

6 Pade 2003, 2007, 2017.

7 The work seems not to have been translated before Juan Luis Vives' version was published in his *Declamationes sex . . . item Isocratis orationes duae, Areopagitica et Nicocles, eodem Lodovico Vive interprete* (Basel: Robert Winter, 1538). The work illustrated his polemic against "the present state of Europe" and the failure of Europeans to fight the Turks.

8 Africa 1979. Neither the Yale edition of More's *Utopia* edited by Hexter and Surtz (1965) nor the more recent Cambridge edition (1995) edited by Logan, Adams, and Miller address the issue of which translations More might have used in consulting classical sources.

9 Pedullà 2010, 2011 / 2018.

10 The work was begun in 1449 / 1460, and the *ed. princ.* was printed in Treviso in 1480. The preface to Pope Paul links the pontiff's restoration of modern Rome with Dionysius' account of Rome's founding and praises Paul's homeland, Venice, for its greatness and longevity and the virtues of its rulers.

11 Scholars interested in more elaborate theorizing of the processes of reception and transformation may consult Helmrath, Hausteiner, and Jensen 2017.

12 Annas 2017 addresses some of these issues in Plato, Cicero, and Philo of Alexandria.

13 Blythe 1992: 161–179; Skinner 2002a, 10–38. The principal exception was John of Salisbury, whose *Policraticus* drew on Cicero and Valerius Maximus, while his knowledge of Greek philosophy was mostly indirect.

14 Blythe 2009, 151. Earlier, in Blythe 1992, chapter 10, he referred to this attitude as "relativism."

15 This paragraph and the next summarize developments in political terminology treated in more detail in Chapters 3 and 12.

16 See Chapter 2.

17 See Chapter 12.

18 On Valturio's treatise, see Chapter 9; on Tinctoris, Hankins 2015b; on Biondo's *RT,* Chapter 11.

19 See Appendix C, where it is shown that Patrizi's treatises were more popular in Latin, the international language of learning in early modern Europe.

20 Grotius emphasizes in the Prolegomena to *De iure pacis et belli* (40) that "to prove this [law of nature] I have made use of the testimonies of philosophers, historians, poets, finally also of orators, not that these are to believed indiscriminately, for they customarily serve to support sects, arguments and cases, but that where many [authors] affirm the same thing as certain across many

times and places, that must be related to a universal cause." Patrizi's methodological approach, canvassing the most prestigious ancient authorities before formulating one's own opinion, is similar, an application to politics of the humanist approach to literary imitation. On Patrizi's method in general, see Rossi 2015a.

21 Patrizi, *De inst. r.p.* 1.4, 1534 ed., ff. VII*v*–VIII*v*.

22 See Chapter 3.

23 Patrizi does not here use the term *democratia* to mean popular rule, but see Chapter 17 for his discussion of regimes in the *De regno;* see also Chapter 3.

24 Aristotle, *Politics* 4.8.1294a and 6.2.1217a.

25 For Dio Chrysostom's *De regno* (= *Discourses* 1–4) in the Latin translation of Gregorio Tifernate (*ed. princ.* Venice, 1471), see Chapter 17, page 394.

26 DL 1.7.

27 DH 2.17; Pletho, *Opuscula de historia*, ed. Maltese. Pletho's *E Diodoro et Plutarcho de rebus post pugnam ad Mantineam gestis per capita tractatio,* with its *Adnotationes,* seems to have been intended as a continuation of Leonardo Bruni's compendium of Xenophon's *Hellenica,* entitled *Commentaria rerum graecarum* (1439); see Hankins 2007–2008a, 36.

28 Aristotle, *Politics* 4.11.4–11.1295b.

29 Patrizi, *De inst. r.p.,* 1534 ed., f. VIII*v*: "Ego autem in eorum numero sum qui optimam rem publicam dicant quae per omni genere hominum commixta sit."

30 Aristotle, *Politics* 3.11.1281a.

31 In the dedication of *De inst. r.p.,* book 6, 1534 ed., f. LXXIX*v,* Patrizi seems to contradict his earlier position, stating that the *modus* of royal and aristocratic republics is one ("It makes no difference whether one or many rule, since nothing changes regarding the way of life and the best laws"). The Spartans recognized this and combined both elements in their constitution: "They put a king in charge, who differed very little from private citizens, and drew their civil institutions from the memoranda of Lycurgus."

32 Hankins 2007b, 39–46.

33 See Chapter 17, page 400, for the eclipse of Giles' treatise by Patrizi's work in the sixteenth century.

34 Flüeler 1992; Nederman 1996; Flüeler 2002, 5. In *De regimine principum* 3.2.3 Giles of Rome states (relying on Aquinas' *De regno*) that Aristotle supported monarchy as the best form of government; see Lambertini 1995. Giles also argues (*De regimine principum* 3.2.5) that hereditary succession is better than election of rulers, an anti-meritocratic principle that was anathema to humanist political writers.

35 See Straumann 2018 and Chapter 11.

36 For an overview of the historiography on chivalry in late medieval Tuscany and Florence, see Sposato 2018.

37 Sposato 2018: "The privileged practice of violence, especially when personal and familial honor were in question, was central to chivalric identity in medieval Europe."

38 Hankins 2006a.

39 Skinner 1978, 1:74. The preface to Leonardo Bruni's version of the *Economics* is in Viti 2004, 262–263. For Bruni's defense of private wealth as a human good compatible with virtue see Chapter 7, page 208.

40 On the circumstances of the dedication to Nicholas V, see Monfasani 1984, 198–199, 744–745.

41 See Chapter 14.

42 My translation. The Latin text is in Monfasani 1984, 200. An English translation of the entire preface, with introduction and notes (by John Monfasani), can be found in Kraye 1997, 128–134.

43 Ibid., 200–201. For the "well-behaved tyrant" as the favored instrument of political reform, see Plato, *Laws* 4.710d.

44 Ibid., 201.

45 Robey and Law 1975 (with an edition of Vergerio's *De republica veneta* at 38–49); Skinner 1978: 1: 140. A translation of portions of the Vergerio text (by Ronald G. Witt) may be found in Kraye 1997: 117–127. Not all humanist writers agreed that Venice had a mixed constitution; Francesco Filelfo for example, writing in a letter to Doge Andrea Vendramin, said "no one disagrees" that Venice's constitution was aristocratic; see Chapter 15, page 356.

46 Chambers 1970, 12–30, for Venice as the New Rome. Morosini's *De rebus et forma reipublicae Venetae* is in Valentinelli 1868–1873, 3: 231–264; for Venice's foundation by Trojan Antenor, see 3: 232.

47 My translation; text in King 1986, 45nn221–222. A more critical Venetian reader of Plato's *Laws* was Domenico Morosini, who in his treatise *On the Well-Ordered Republic* (begun in 1497 at the age of eighty) admires Plato's elitist and meritocratic measures but believes his restrictions on commerce were too harsh. They were inapplicable to the situation of Venice, which needed to have mercantile interests represented in government and could not afford Platonic poverty, given the need to hire soldiers to defend itself from warlords and tyrants. Like Patrizi, Morosini disapproved of expansionism, believing empire and the wealth generated by empire to be a threat to liberty and likely to lead to moral decline. See Morosini, *On the Well-Ordered Republic*, 98, 111, 216–217 ("Whether a republic should rule other cities or be content with its own territory").

48 Gaeta 1961.

49 Bouwsma 1990. Donato Giannotti in his *Dialogi de republica Venetorum* (written in 1526 / 1527, published 1540) explicitly argues for the superiority of Venice to Rome. For John Adams's admiration for Venice, see his *Defense of the Constitutions of Government of the United States of America,* chapter 2, "Venice," in vol. 4 of his works, edited by Charles Francis Adams (1851).

50 On Salamonio, the basic work is D'Addio 1954, 3–115; see also Skinner 1978, 1: 148–152 and 2: 131–134. A more recent bibliography may be found in the excellent study of Baldassarri 2018.

51 D'Addio 1955, 82. Salamonio's information about Plato came from the pseudo-Platonic letters (most of which were believed in the Renaissance to be genuine), translated by Leonardo Bruni after 1427.

52 They survive in a single manuscript of the early sixteenth century, BLF, MS Plut. 51.19, and were not published until modern times. I use the problematic edition of D'Addio 1955 but have checked his text against the MS. The MS could not have been written before the pontificate of Leo X (1513–1521), since Salamonio in the dedication of the collected speeches to the Florentine Signoria styles himself by his titles of Count Palatine and *cavaliere,* awarded to him by Leo.

53 See Chapters 10 and 20. By way of contrast, a contemporary Medici partisan, Petrus Crinitus, in his *De honesta disciplina* 1.4 (1504), attacks this division of responsibilities, citing a *Anacharsis Scythae sententia,* derived from Plutarch, that Athens could not long survive a popular government: "O rempublicam brevi perituram in qua viri principes consultant, populus autem et

imperita rerum plebecula decernat." (O short-lived republic in which the principal men give advice, but the people and the ignorant little plebs decide!")

54 D'Addio 1955, 92–95 (fifth oration).

55 D'Addio 1955, 99–102.

56 Trexler 1980, 17–19.

57 For Bruni's Etruscan refoundation of Florence see Chapter 8, page 231. I am reminded by Marianne Pade that there is an implied comparison between Athens and Florence already in Bruni's work, for example in his translations of Demosthenes' orations and Plutarch's life of Demosthenes, in his (silent) use of Aelius Aristides' encomium of Athens as a model for his own *Laudatio*, and in his use of Pericles' funeral oration from Thucydides as a model for his *Oratio in funere Nanni Strozzae*. See Hankins 2002b; Pade 2007: 252–254; Bos 2018; and Bruni, *Panegyric of Nanni Strozzi*, ed. Daub. Alamanno Rinuccini claims that the sound Florentine practice of exiling turbulent citizens, of which he gives several examples drawn from Bruni's *History*, had a classical precedent in Athens's practice of ostracism; see Rinuccini, *De libertate*, ed. Adorno, 91. Tito Livio Frulovisi notes a similarity between classical Athenian democracy and Florentine popular government in the first book of his *De republica*, ed. Previté-Orton, 309.

58 Pade 2007, 1: 275–280 and 2: 33–35. The translation was made around 1433 / 1434 for Pope Eugenius IV and printed six times in Latin during the incunabular period and once in an Italian translation based on Lapo's Latin. Among the details excerpted by Salamonio from Plutarch's *Life of Solon:* Solon believed in adapting the laws to the city and not the city to the laws (22.3; cf. Aristotle, *Politics* 4.1.9.1289a, where the saying is not attributed to Solon); Athenian social classes (17.1–2, 23.4); Athens's two assemblies (19.1); Solon's concern that the weak be able to defend themselves against the strong (18.5); Solon's insistence that citizen fathers were responsible for their sons being taught an *arte* (22.1). The latter customary practice established by Solon was also praised by Pico della Mirandola according to Crinitus, *De honesta disciplina* 1.12.

59 From Herodotus, *Histories* 2.177, Salamonio draws the detail that Solon put the Areopagus in charge of verifying that all citizens followed a just way of life, "seguitando in ciò la politica de Egiptii" (following in this the political practices of the Egyptians). Plutarch's *Moralia* 154E *(Septem sapientium convivium)* is probably the source of Solon's dictum that what most effectively perpetuates democracy is when the uninjured as well as the injured aid in the prosecution of criminals.

60 I have corrected D'Addio's text against BLF, MS Plut. 51.19, f. 40v: "Hora, signori miei, quando contemplo questi costumi, instituti, legi, rescontro una omnimoda conformità et tale *quod si substuleris nomina* non discernerai la Atthica dalla Fiorentina—chi lauda quella, è neccessario commendi la vostra; chi admira et extolle quella, è necessaria non meno habia questa in veneratione. Né reputate sia in inferior grado per esser gubernation populare, subiecta ad varii moti et turbulentie per lo incerto et obscuro uulgo, facile, credulo, suspecto, geloso, timido, ma pero più laudabile, quia *virtus civica circa difficilia et ardua*. Et la populare e vera republica, *idest res populi, non regia, non optimatum,* dove se vive secondo primi termini naturali, tucti nascono liberi, tucti in conversatione aequali, tucti morono liberi." The famous definition of *respublica* as *res populi* comes from Cicero, *De republica* 1.39, *apud* Augustine, *De civitate Dei* 2.21.

61 Cf. Aristotle, *Politics* 3.5.5.1278a: "No man can practice virtue who is living the life of a mechanic or laborer."

62 See Lapo da Castiglionchio's *De curiae commodis,* edited in Celenza 1999, 103. Lapo says that while "most honor the empire of Rome with praise and even veneration," there were others

who praise Athens for its civil and military institutions, or Sparta, "founded on the most holy laws of Lycurgus," or "the republic of the Carthaginians, powerful on land and sea" (tr. Celenza). Among the new Greek sources that provided the humanists with information on Phoenician and Carthaginian government and military institutions were Polybius, Appian, Plutarch, and Dio Cassius, though Aristotle's *Politics* remained their principal source in the quattrocento.

17. FRANCESCO PATRIZI AND HUMANIST ABSOLUTISM

1 For an overview of the recovery of Greek philosophy between 1400 and 1600, see Hankins and Palmer 2008.

2 According to Luraghi 2013, 140.

3 Xenophon, *Memorabilia* 4.6.12, following the Loeb translation, with modifications (the Loeb translates ἑκόντων τε τῶν ἀνθρώπων, "with men willing it," as "willing consent," but this rendering imports the false implication that Xenophon is endorsing popular sovereignty). Bessarion's terminology is in brackets following the Greek term. For Bessarion's translation, see Marsh 1992, 7: 166. It appears the translation was less well known than other works of Xenophon, as Marsh reports only nine MSS and no incunabular editions; the first edition of the translation was printed only in 1521.

4 Bessarion's interesting gloss "with men willing it *and not resisting it" (volentibus et non repugnantibus hominibus)* might be read to make room for a theory of tacit consent, especially in societies with graded citizenship, i.e., virtuous and non-virtuous, or informed and uninformed.

5 On the Renaissance career of this text, see Biasiori 2017. Xenophon was not the only follower of Socrates to admire Cyrus; see Plato, *Alcibiades* 105d, the more critical *Laws* 3.694a–696b, and the works by Antisthenes listed by DL 6.16, 18.

6 Xenophon, *Cyropaedia* 1.1.3 (Loeb translation, but I have changed ἐπισταμένως from "in an intelligent manner" to "in a knowledgeable manner"); see also 3.2.2.

7 For the dialogue between Cyrus and Cambyses, see Nadon 2001, 164–174.

8 Xenophon, *Cyropaedia* 8.1.39.

9 See Nadon 2001, following Strauss 1958, 137–138, and Biasiori 2017. As Biasiori shows, Machiavelli read the *Cyropaedia* in Jacopo Bracciolini's Italian translation of Poggio's Latin version. Biasiori also demonstrates that the use made of the *Cyropaedia* by Machiavelli is much more extensive than one would at first suspect from the few explicit references in *The Prince* and the *Discourses.*

10 The text of the preface is given in Marsh 1992, 118–119. Poggio is mistaken: the Scipio of the anecdote was Scipio Aemilianus, not the great Africanus. Poggio might have added that Alexander and Caesar were also reported to be diligent readers of the text. There are some thirty MSS but no printed edition of Poggio's translation. Scipio's devotion to the text is also noted by Patrizi in his preface to book 5 of the *De regno.*

11 Marsh 1992, 121–123. The translation was drafted by 1467 and dedicated to Pope Paul II in 1469. It survives in seventeen MSS and twelve printed editions, the *ed. princ.* being c. 1477. The excerpts from the preface in Marsh 1992 exclude the monarchical theory, which can be found in Filelfo, *Traduzioni,* ed. De Keyser, 101–106.

12 Ibid. See Chapter 15, page 356. In a speech of 1448 *(Oratio ad Mediolanenses principes de administratione reipublicae)* to the leaders of the revolutionary regime in Milan, the so-called Respublica Ambrosiana, Filelfo, in search of employment, finds himself able to praise the new

regime while attempting to redescribe it (in a fine example of "persuasive definition") as an aristocracy of virtue. For the text, see Adam 1974, 2: 337.

13 This argument—that constitutional, polyarchic governments were inherently unstable and would inevitably end up as monarchies—was first made in the West by Darius in the "debate on constitutions" in Herodotus 3.80–82. The argument would later be repeated by Appian, who in his preface claimed that the divinity *(ho theos)* had guided Rome from the chaos of the republic into "harmony and monarchy." Appian was a Greek historian of Rome who lived in the second century of our era and wrote a *Roman History* originally in twenty-four books, including five surviving books on the civil wars, strongly pro-monarchical in tone. Most of the surviving portions were translated by Pier Candido Decembrio in 1452 / 1454 for Nicholas V and for King Alfonso I of Naples. The *ed. princ.* of Decembrio's version appeared in 1472. The Augustinian historian Orosius later Christianized Appian's positive interpretation of Rome's transition to autocracy. For another Renaissance example of the "Appianic" view that the unstable polyarchic government of the republic could only end in monarchy under a single prince, see Aeneas Silvius Piccolomini (the later Pius II), *De ortu,* ed. Wolkan, 8; tr. Izbicki and Nederman, 98.

14 Homer, *Iliad* 2.204–205 (my translation); Luraghi 2013, 135: "In any case, the Greeks themselves do not appear to have seen in these lines a statement in favor of monarchy." The quotation cannot come from Aristotle, *Politics* 4.1292a11 because Aristotle only quotes the first line and in any case is not using the quotation in support of monarchy.

15 Strauss 1958, 137, 161, 322n assumes that Machiavelli knew the *Cyropaedia* was fiction but offers no convincing textual proof of that judgment. On the other hand, Machiavelli's *Life of Castruccio Castracani,* described by R. Black 2013, 225, as "a piece of romantic fantasy," bearing "only an occasional relationship to historical fact," suggests that he was aware of the ancient genre of historical romance that poses as history in order to increase its rhetorical effect.

16 The historical geographer Strabo, who lived in the era of Augustus and Tiberius, advocated the study of geography for statesmen and generals and all those "who bring together cities and peoples under a single empire and political management." This advice was repeated by Patrizi in *De regno* (3.14). Patrizi cites Strabo frequently in the *De regno.* Like other authors of the Principate, Strabo regarded monarchy as the only practical form of government for a large empire. See 6.4.2 (286–287): "But it were a difficult thing to administer so great a dominion otherwise than by turning it over to one man, as if to a father; at all events, never have the Romans and their allies thrived in such peace and plenty as that which was afforded them by Augustus Caesar, from the time when he assumed the absolute authority" (Loeb translation). This passage is summarized by Patrizi at *De regno* 1.13. A Latin translation of Strabo was commissioned by Nicholas V from Guarino, who finished it after the pope's death, dedicating it to the Venetian patrician Giacomo Antonio Marcello in 1458. The first Latin edition (Rome, 1469 / 1470) published a composite translation, half by Guarino and half by Gregorio Tifernate. See Gino Pistilli on Guarino Guarini in *DBI* 60 (2003).

17 Patrizi, *De regno* 2.4, based on Strabo 17.5, 27, 46, 54. Cambyses is also denounced for his impiety at *De regno* 8.15.

18 In fact Patrizi's claim must be mediated by DL 3.34. Plato at *Laws* 3.694c states that "Cyrus was a fine general, a patriot, but lacked any grasp at all of correct education, and never having given a moment's thought to how his household was run" (tr. Tom Griffith). As Malcolm Schofield points out in his notes to this passage, Xenophon's account of Cyrus was also

contradicted by Herodotus 1.136.2; and Isocrates (Plato's rival) at *Nicocles* 23 had denied that wisdom played any role in the growth of Persian power. See Plato, *Laws,* ed. Schofield, 126–127.

19 Gualdo Rosa 1983, 2017.

20 On Isocrates' use of biography to teach political ethics, see Hendrick 2009.

21 Isocrates also called for meritocratic reform of the Athenian constitution in his *Areopagiticus,* but this text was apparently unknown, at least in Latin, before 1538. The (pseudonymous) *Ad Demonicum,* a particularly sententious educational tract with a royalist tincture, is sometimes also associated by modern scholars with the Cyprian tracts (as in the Loeb edition). This text too was extremely popular; see Gualdo Rosa 1983.

22 Isocrates, *Nicocles* (Loeb translation). For a similar argument by a modern political Confucian that meritocracy allows for continuity and the accumulation of experience in political offices more than democracies do, see Bell 2015, chapter 2. The argument is repeated by Patrizi at *De regno* 2.3 (see page 408 below).

23 Chapter 4, page 133.

24 Gualdo Rosa 1983, 12–14.

25 For details, see Gualdo Rosa 1983, passim. Gualdo Rosa's data for translations and editions have been supplemented from Cortesi-Fiaschi 1: 796–836. For Lapo da Castiglionchio's translations of *Ad Nicoclem, Nicocles,* and *Ad Demonicum,* with a critical edition of the texts and prefaces, see Gualdo Rosa 2018. For the key 1470 edition of Plutarch, edited by Giovanni Antonio Campano and published by Ulrich Han in Rome, which also contained a number of lives of ancient figures not by Plutarch, such as Bruni's life of Aristotle and Guarino's of Plato, see Pade 2007, 1: 385–388.

26 Filelfo, *De exilio,* ed. De Keyser, 448, 458, 466. Tifernate's translation was accompanied in the two incunabular editions (1471 and 1492) by a preface (dated 1469) written by Cardinal Francesco Piccolomini (later Pope Pius III) to the young prince Maximilian, the future Holy Roman Emperor. See Malta 1990, 182. For Dio Chrysostom, see Jackson 2017, 217–232. See also Chapter 4 for Dio's discourse(s) on tyranny (which were not, however, available in Latin before the mid-sixteenth century).

27 Omitted here is Plutarch's (or pseudo-Plutarch's) fragmentary essay on constitutions, handed down among the *Moralia,* which was first translated into Latin in 1542 by the Dutch scholar Gijsbert van Langerack (Gibertus Longolius, 1507–1543), a friend of Melanchthon, under the title *De tribus reipublicae generibus, monarchia, democratia, et oligarchia, hoc est regia, populari et paucorum potestate* = *Moralia* 826–827). He also produced a Greek edition of Philostratus' *Life of Apollonius of Tyana* (1532). One may also mention two other texts. One is from Plutarch's *Moralia* and was translated by Niccolò Sagundino under the title *Politicorum seu de civili institutione opus ad Traianum imperatorem.* This in fact consists of the *Praecepta gerendae reipublicae* (Precepts of Statecraft = *Moralia* 798–825), with a dedicatory letter to the Venetian patrician Marco Donato. To this genuine work of Plutarch was prefaced a pseudo-Plutarchan text known as the *Institutio Traiani.* This was an alleged letter from Plutarch to Trajan, which was probably composed originally in Latin during late antiquity and was preserved in John of Salisbury's *Policraticus* (see Desideri 1958). The two texts were printed together, first in Milan 1500 and then Venice 1501, later as part of complete editions of the *Moralia* such as that printed by Ascensius in Paris (1521). According to Bevagni 1994, 79, there were two other quattrocento versions of the *Praecepta gerendae reipublicae,* by Giovanni Lorenzi and Carlo Valgulio.

28 Philostratus, *The Life of Apollonius of Tyana*, 5.35.4 (tr. C. P. Jones). The "one man of exceptional virtue" who changes democracy alludes to Pericles; see Thucydides, 2.65.9.

29 Philostratus, *The Life of Apollonius of Tyana*, 5.36.2–5.

30 On Rinuccini, see Lorenz Böninger's article in *DBI* 87 (2016). For the *Preface to Apollonius of Tyana*, see *Lettere e orazioni*, ed. Giustiniani, 104–116, which contains Rinuccini's famous evocation of the Renaissance. Rinuccini also made a translation of Isocrates' *De regno* around 1471 with two dedications, one to Federico d'Urbino and a second to Alfonso, duke of Calabria, the heir to the Aragonese throne (also the dedicatee of Patrizi's *De regno*).

31 The need for a critical edition is even more urgent in light of the variations among the manuscript witnesses identified by De Capua 2014, 219–220. Since Patrizi was among other things a Catholic bishop, he may have been reluctant to cite Philostratus' life as an authority, given its presentation of Apollonius as a pagan holy man and miracle-worker rivaling Jesus Christ.

32 Aristotle, *Politics* 3.14–18.

33 See Chapter 16 for several examples. In the *De regno*, Aristotle's *Ethics* is cited far more frequently than the *Politics*.

34 See, among many passages, *Politics* 3.13.1284a, 3.16.1287a. But Aristotle is not always consistent on this point; compare 3.15.1286a. Patrizi observes at *De regno* 1.1 that despite being an authority on constitutional government in the *Politics*, Aristotle also gave advice on kingship to Philip of Macedon. He is perhaps thinking of the pseudo-Aristotelian *Secreta secretorum*, where Aristotle is represented giving advice to Alexander the Great, not Philip. For the popularity of the latter work, see Hankins and Palmer 2008, 24.

35 See in particular *Politics* 3.15.1286a1–4, where Aristotle stages a debate between a defender of absolute monarchy ("you") from the point of view of a defender of constitutional government ("we"). In 3.16.1287a he appears to be criticizing an argument from analogy in Plato's most monarchical work, the *Statesman*, while 3.16.1287b, 25–35 may be directed against what is said to be a valuable political tool of Cyrus in Xenophon's *Cyropaedia* 8. I share with other modern readers the suspicion that the apparent exception at 3.17.1288a for the individual or family of superexcellent virtue may represent a political accommodation to the Macedonian monarchy. In contrast with the Greek writers of the early Roman Empire, Aristotle seems to believe that, thanks to the increasing size of cities, his time has seen an "end of history" in the democratic regime (*Politics* 3.15.1286b20, further explained at 4.6.1293a1–10).

36 Chrysoloras-Decembrio (1402), P. C. Decembrio (1438 / 1439), and Antonio Cassarino (before 1447); Ficino's translation did not circulate outside of Florence before its publication in 1484. For all of these translations, see Hankins 1990a. Patrizi's most extensive engagement with the *Republic* is his paraphrase of the Myth of Er at the end of *Republic* 10 in *De regno* 9.21.

37 The *Laws* is cited at *De regno* 1.13, a brief description of Cretan monarchy, and again at 9.18, on offerings to the gods. For George of Trebizond's version of the *Laws* (1450 / 1451), see Hankins 1990a. Patrizi cites the *Phaedrus* at 4.11, probably from Leonardo Bruni's partial translation (1424), which circulated widely in manuscript. His references to the *Symposium* at *De regno* 5.1 and 7.9 may also depend on the (heavily censored) version of the Speech of Alcibiades in Bruni's *Epistulae* 7.1, ed. Mehus, 2: 70–76. For Bruni's version, in addition to Hankins 1990a, 80–81, see Hankins 2007c.

38 A story from Diogenes Laertius, for example, is cited in 2.4. Another possible source for this story could have been Guarino's *Life of Plato*, partly based on Diogenes Laertius, which was

included in the 1470 Roman edition of Plutarch edited by Giovanni Antonio Campano and in later editions. For Guarino's life of Plato, see Hankins 2003–2004a, 62–77.

39 Hankins 1990a.

40 In *De regno* 2.6, Patrizi even renames his own previous work, the *De institutione reipublicae,* as *De civili societate.*

41 See Plato, *Republic* 499b1–d6 and 502a–c7, and *Laws* 874c7–875d5.

42 Annas 2017, chapter 2.

43 Plato, *Republic* 472d4–473a2.

44 See page 416 below. For extended treatments of the differences between virtuous monarchy and tyranny in Latin literature, one can mention, apart from Seneca, only Pliny the Younger's *Panegyricus,* composed in 100 AD, which contrasted Trajan as the ideal of the good emperor with the tyrant Domitian. For the reception of this work in the quattrocento, which begins with Giovanni Aurispa at the Council of Basel, see Lucia Ciapponi Stadter in *CTC* 9: 96–97. The *ed. princ.* was printed at Milan in 1482. For Patrizi's use of Pliny, see page 402 below.

45 See Matteo Maria Quintiliani's article on him in *DBI* 81 (2014). The richest source for Patrizi's biography are his letters, extensively summarized and excerpted with commentary in De Capua 2014. There is no comprehensive study of Patrizi's political thought, but the English reader may find scattered comments in Skinner 1978 and Pedullà 2011 / 2018.

46 Whether he learned Greek well enough to read the language easily is another question. My own unsystematic study of Patrizi's sources suggests that he relies on Latin translations whenever he can; of the sources he quotes in Greek he seems most familiar with Homer.

47 The work survives in at least eight manuscripts but was never published; a summary is given in De Capua 2014, 42–44. See also the summary in Petrucci, *Epistole,* ed. Pertici, 9n. Among other things, the work stresses that a good magistrate must possess knowledge of *optimae artes* and the canons of physical beauty.

48 For Patrizi's love of Gaeta, see the letter excerpted by De Capua 2014, 201, where the humanist says that a great part of Gaeta's appeal for him, apart from its fine weather and welcoming people, was his knowledge that Scipio Africanus and his friend Laelius were in the habit of taking their leisure there, picking up shells on the beach.

49 De Capua 2014, 193–213. In the proemium to book 6 (cited in De Capua 2014, 215, from a Vatican manuscript) Patrizi remarks that some will consider it odd to dedicate a work on republican government to an absolute monarch such as the pope, and he himself admits that it would have been more correct to dedicate a treatise on kingship to him. But "if [his critics] will considered the matter rightly, they would understand that these two disciplines [i.e., the arts of founding republican and royal regimes] are interrelated and have very many precepts in common that are mutually supportive."

50 Ibid., 213–219. De Capua speculates that the work might have been begun even before the republican work was in the hands of its dedicatee.

51 See Skinner 2002a, 136–138. The recent literature in Italian may be accessed through Delle Donne 2015 and Cappelli 2016b. See also the introduction to Pedullà's edition of the *Pr.,* XVIII–XXVIII, where he lists authors of political *trattati,* reviews the historiography, and discusses Machiavelli's innovations with respect to the earlier tradition.

52 Both appear in an edition edited by Alessandra Mantovani (2014).

53 For the remarkable success of Patrizi's treatises, second only to Machiavelli's in the sixteenth century, see Appendix C. Giles of Rome's *De regimine principum* survives in more than three

hundred Latin manuscripts and was translated into several vernaculars. It was published three times in Latin, twice in Catalan, and once in Spanish during the incunabular period. After that, the next (and the last) edition to appear was published in 1607. Patrizi's treatises survive in only a handful of manuscripts but proved remarkably popular after the first edition of 1518.

54 Giles of Rome, *De regimine principum* 3.2.20: "Quod quantum possibile est, sunt omnia legibus determinanda, et quam pauciora possunt, sunt arbitrio iudicum committenda" (Everything should be decided by law as much as possible, and as little as possible committed to the decision of judges).

55 For humanist responses to these doctrines, see Hankins 1990a, passim.

56 Giles of Rome, *De regimine principum* 3.2.29.

57 Ibid., 3.2.20 and Patrizi, *De regno* 2.1.

58 The same chapter, *Politics* 5.10, figures importantly in the theory of tyranny, discussed in Chapter 4.

59 Patrizi, *De regno* 2.2.

60 Patrizi, quoting Plato, *Republic* 519e1–520a4.

61 Patrizi, *De regno* 2.5, quoting Pliny's *Epistles* 3.18.3–4, in which Pliny excuses the sycophantic tone in his *Panegyricus* (see note 46 above). I have found no allusions to the *Panegyricus* itself in the *De regno*—not surprisingly, in view of Patrizi's oft-expressed horror of flattery and adulation.

62 Patrizi, *De regno* 8.6 and 4.20. Patrizi's judgment of Augustus reflects Seneca, *De clementia* 3.11.

63 For the status of Plato's ideal constitutions and the question whether they could serve as practical blueprints in Renaissance polities, see Hankins 1990a, 228–230.

64 Patrizi, *De regno* 2.4, 1567 ed., 71: "'Ego enim sic statuo, nihil esse in ullo genere tam pulchrum, quo non pulchrius id sit unde illud ut ex ore aliquo quasi imago exprimitur, quod nullis humanis sensibus percipi potest; mente tantum et cogitatione complectimur.' Et quum de Phidia paulo post loqueretur, dixit: 'Insidebat in mente illius artificis species quaedam pulchritudinis eximia, quam intuens, in eaque defixus, ad illius similitudinem artem et manum dirigebat.'" The quotation varies from modern texts of *Orator* 8–9 in ways that suggest quotation from memory.

65 *Pr.* 15 (tr. Price).

66 Rawls 1971, 245. On Rawls's distinction between ideal and non-ideal theory, see Simmons 2010, esp. 27: "The ideal is not so much a condition to be achieved (like the Rawlsian ideal of perfect institutional justice), but rather a personal or institutional value to be always taken seriously in any practical deliberations." Compare Kant, *Critique of Pure Reason,* tr. Guyer and Wood (Cambridge, 1998), 552, on the Stoic sage, who may not exist in reality, but by existing in thought provides "no other standard for our actions than the conduct of this divine human being, with which we can compare ourselves, judging ourselves and therefore improving ourselves, even though we can never reach the standard." Joseph Chan has made interesting use of Kantian regulatory ideas in adapting Confucian political thought to modern conditions, a project in some way similar to that of virtue politics. See Chan 2014.

67 Patrizi, *De regno* 2.1: "Rex est vir bonus cui per generis dignitatem vel per legitimam electionem concessum sit ut civitates populosque regat." *Civitates* might also be rendered as "cities" or "city-states."

68 Patrizi must mean this passage at Strabo 1.2.3: "Eratosthenes contends that the aim of every poet is to entertain, not to instruct. The ancients assert, on the contrary, that poetry is a kind

of elementary philosophy, which, taking us in our very boyhood, introduces us to the art of life and instructs us, with pleasure to ourselves, in character, emotions, and actions. And our school [the Stoics] goes still further and contends that the wise man alone is a poet. That is the reason why in Greece the various states educate the young, at the very beginning of their education, by means of poetry; not for the mere sake of entertainment, of course, but for the sake of moral discipline. . . . You may hear this contention made not merely by the Pythagoreans, but Aristoxenus also declares the same thing. And Homer, too, has spoken of the bards as disciplinarians in morality" (Loeb translation).

69 The contrast between Plato's philosophical and Patrizi's humanist idea of legitimacy is evident when one considers *Statesmen* 292, which argues that *basilike* or kingship is a science: "It is, then, a necessary consequence that among forms of government that one is preeminently right and is the only real government, in which the rulers are found to be truly possessed of science [*episteme*], not merely to seem to possess it, whether they rule by law or without law, whether their subjects are willing or unwilling, and whether they themselves are rich or poor—none of these things can be at all taken into account on any right method. . . . All other forms must be considered not as legitimate [*gnesias*] or really existent, but as imitating this; those states which are said to be well governed imitate it better, and the others worse" (Loeb translation).

70 Patrizi, *De regno* 3.1: "Non enim acuta illa quae a dialecticis subtilius disputantur regi convenire videntur. Neque etiam ea quae praeter communem hominum opinionem sunt et a Stoicis ἄσκοπα vocantur, neque abdita Democriti aut obscuriora illa Pythagorae, quae multorum annorum silentium desyderabant, sed clariora quaedam, quae de civili vita tractantur deque optimis hominum moribus praecipiuntur et rationem orationemque perficiunt, redigenda sunt ad regiam institutionem." (Those subtle matters of which the dialecticians argue with such fine discrimination do not seem appropriate to the prince. Nor are the matters that go beyond the common views of mankind, called "off target" by the Stoics, nor the esoteric subjects of Democritus or the dark secrets of Pythagoras, which require many years of silence. The things that should be set in order to educate the prince are those that treat of civil life and teach the best behavior and perfect our reason and our speech.)

71 Patrizi, *De regno* 9.22.

72 Giles argues in favor of hereditary succession and against any form of election by merit in *De regimine principum* 3.2.5.

73 Patrizi does not name his source, which is Macrobius' *Saturnalia* 3.17.10.

74 The view that Roman law had already been brought to perfection by the Roman jurists and did not need further codification is also stated in *De inst. r.p.* 1.5, 1534 ed., f. Xr.

75 Patrizi, *De regno* 8.6: "Quod quisque iuris in alterum statuerit, ipse quoque eodem iure utatur."

76 This rare word is used in Xenophon's *Hiero* 8.10 but may be a corruption there, and the sense in any case is not germane; also in Lucian's *Phalaris* 1.3, where it means impartiality (as between rich and poor). But the probable source is Patrizi's beloved Strabo, at 8.5.4, where in a passage describing early Spartan history it seems to mean an equal right to hold office. The same sense of the word is found in Dionysius of Halicarnassus's *Roman Antiquities* 10.30 (a speech opposing a grant of political rights to the plebs), which could have been available to Patrizi in the Latin translation (before 1469, *ed. princ.* 1480) made for Pope Paul II by the Milanese humanist Lampugnino Birago.

77 Patrizi, *De regno* 4.10.

78 See ibid., 2.3 and 4.10, where it is emphasized that the king's magistrates should live on their own income and not make profits from governing the people.

79 Ibid., 2.3. Patrizi here contradicts Giles of Rome in *De regimine principum* 3.1.13 (1607 ed., 433), who favored term limits for magistrates.

80 Patrizi, *De regno* 3.13, 4.9.

81 On modern and premodern forms of sovereignty, see Quaglione 2003, 2007.

82 Patrizi, *De regno* 1.1.

83 Ibid., 1.3. Patrizi's sources for Athenian history include Herodotus, Plutarch, and the pseudo-correspondence of Pisistratus and Solon preserved in DL.

84 Patrizi, *De regno* 1.13. Needless to say he does not use the word "republic" to describe the historical period we moderns call "the Roman Republic"; see Chapters 3 and 11.

85 Patrizi helpfully informs us that Greek cities, according to Dionysius of Halicarnassus, had the same institution of *aesymnetes*.

86 Patrizi cites a letter from Cicero to Atticus, which must be *Ad Atticum* 2.14, where the Roman orator wittily employs (or possibly coins) the Greek word εὐτυραννεῖσθαι, to be "well tyrannized" (some less witty modern editions give ἐντυραννεῖσθαι, to be tyrannized over).

87 Patrizi's judgment echoes that of Herodotus and Appian (see above). For Patrizi, those who assassinated Caesar "under the pretense of defending liberty" were fighting against the natural pressure of circumstances that were already trending toward monarchy, and their act merely opened the way to the second triumvirate, marked by the savage cruelty of Octavian, worse than any tyrant's (*De regno* 4.4).

88 Patrizi, *De regno* 2.3.

89 In this chapter Patrizi sometimes directly addresses his royal reader as "you," presumably meaning his dedicatee, Alfonso, duke of Calabria, who is also addressed in the prefaces to books 2–6 as well as in the preface to the work as a whole. For Patrizi's very different idea about the best kind of army for a city-state, see Chapter 9, page 262.

90 See Chapter 8 for Bruni's praise of the Etruscan League as a city-state confederation.

91 Patrizi, *De regno* 2.3. Patrizi might have been thinking of Pericles' speech in Thucydides 2.60, where the Athenian empire is described as a tyranny. In his early treatise *De gerendo magistratu*, Patrizi had described Siena as the home of Etruscan liberty, a citadel of defense against the tyrannical hegemon, Florence.

92 Patrizi, *De regno* 1.10–11.

93 Herodotus 3.85–86. The image of the primitive king as a shepherd of the human flock may come from Homer, *Iliad* 2.243, etc.; Xenophon, *Cyropaedia* 1.1.2; or Plato, *Statesman* 265b–268d, 274e–277a.

94 See note 37 above.

95 Walker 1972, 10–21. See also Hankins 1990a, 1: 283–285, and 2: 459–463, on how Ficino's Platonism reverses Aristotle's developmental account of the history of philosophy, privileging the pure source over downstream corruptions. For Patrizi's awareness of and respect for ancient theology, see *De regno* 8.15, on piety, where Patrizi claims that Homer and Hesiod learned their theology from the Chaldaeans and Egyptians.

96 For other humanist critics of Poggio's "anti-politics," see Roick 2017, 163–165, which discusses Bartolomeo Facio and Panormita (Antonio Beccadelli).

97 It is worth noting that neither Poggio nor Patrizi consider the possibility that one might do wrong things to accomplish good ends, a view incompatible with virtue ethics. In fact it is a

modern dilemma that begins with the new moral universe of Machiavelli, who famously taught that the prince "must learn how not to be good." This question is known in modern political theory as the "dirty hands" problem after a famous article by Michael Walzer (1973).

98　Patrizi, *De regno* 1.7.

99　In *De regno* 1.5, Patrizi responds to Poggio's argument (again without naming him) that princes have never favored liberal studies and have even persecuted wise and learned men. Patrizi says in reply that it may be all too true that support today for the *studia humanitatis et bonarum disciplinarum artes* is rare, but that was not the case in antiquity. Patrizi then proceeds to drown Poggian skeptics in dozens of counterexamples, noting especially the support of Roman emperors for liberal studies. In return, the *docti viri* gave their patrons prestige in life and preserved their memory in death, which showed that solid interests tied *docti viri* and patrons to each other.

100　Ibid., 1.7. The theme of seeds of virtue in humanist literature has been explored in Horowitz 1998.

101　Patrizi, *De regno* 4.1.

102　Ibid., 3.13.

103　Ibid., 1.9.

104　Those familiar with the Catholic theology of grace may recognize here a naturalized version of the concepts of antecedent, habitual, and consequent grace, though Patrizi as far as we know had no formal theological training and very rarely quotes Christian authorities in his political works.

105　Ibid. 2.10.

106　For the importance of historical study in princely education in general in the period, see Grell, Paravicini, and Voss 1998.

107　Patrizi, *De regno* 2.11–12. The question of whether princes should use Socratic irony (understood as self-deprecation) was considered with similar concerns but rather more nuance by Pontano (*De sermone* 6.4.31–33, ed. Pigman, 398–401).

108　Pliny the Elder, *Natural History* 35.36.

109　Giles of Rome, *De regimine principum* 1.3; see also Chapter 2, page 60.

110　For the reception of this collection of moral essays in the Renaissance, see Hankins and Palmer 2008, 14–15. On quattrocento Latin translations of the *Moralia* in general, see Bevagni 1994. In addition to the moral essays printed in the sixteenth century (see above), Bevagni lists three quattrocento translations of *Ad principem ineruditum* (To an uneducated prince = *Moralia* 779d–782f), a collection of commonplaces about virtuous rule; a translation by Theodore Gaza of *Maxime cum principibus philosopho esse disserendum* (That a philosopher ought to converse especially with men in power = *Moralia* 776b–779c), a plea for philosophers to involve themselves in political life; and three translations of *Regum et imperatorum apophthegmata* [= *Apophthegmata ad Traianum*] (Maxims of kings and emperors = *Moralia* 172a–208a).

111　Patrizi, *De regno* 8.17–18.

112　Kempshall 1999, esp. 145–146, 216–218, 297–299, 312–313.

113　For *humanitas* as a virtue in Roman antiquity, see Høgel 2015, 34, 45n, 53, 71, 77.

114　See Seneca, *De beneficiis* 4.3.

115　Patrizi relies here silently on Aulus Gellius, *Noctes Atticae* 13.17.

116　For more on Patrizi's concept of *fides* or trustworthiness, see Chapter 19, page 465.

117　The usual constitutional remedy in Anglo-Saxon constitutional republics is impeachment, but the rarity of this procedure shows its impracticality. Prince Shotoko Taishi's "Seventeen-Article

Constitution" of 604 AD, inspired by Confucianism and Buddhism, provides an interesting parallel case in classical Japan; the "constitution" attempted to reduce virtue politics to legal form, but it too, unsurprisingly, is silent on the subject of sanctions against corrupt rulers.

118 Sforza continued to present himself, however, as being legitimated in part by popular acclamation. Though this was a mere "pretence," according to J. Black 2015, Slorza's backers felt the danger, later in his reign, that "the [popular] foundations of his reign could be used against him."

119 For some particularly grisly examples of royal justice, see Porzio, *La congiura,* ed. Pontieri, first published in 1565.

120 On this literature, see Mühleisen, Stammen, and Philipp 1997. For its medieval predecessors, see Bejczy and Nederman 2007. For Renaissance literature on character education in general, see Quondam 2010, 75–248.

121 See Bradshaw and Duffy 1989, 15. For the great hopes humanists invested in the young Prince Henry at his accession, see Bainton 1969, 89–90; Erasmus, *Epistolae,* ed. Allen, Allen and Garrod, 1: 436–437, 569–570. Pace, *De fructu qui ex doctrina percipitur,* 138–141, was still praising in 1517 a letter written (supposedly) by Henry in 1507 at the age of fifteen.

18. MACHIAVELLI: REVIVING THE MILITARY REPUBLIC

1 See the Conclusion. For patristic ideas of *reformatio,* and the special character of Christian ideas of reform, see Ladner 1967.

2 Guicciardini, *History of Italy* 1.prol., tr. Alexander, 3. The observation that a general change in political outlook occurred among the generation of thinkers that came to maturity after 1494 is hardly new. In the English-language literature it goes back at least to Gilbert 1965. For an updated version see Jurdjevic 2014, for whom it was the experience of Savonarolan Florence that was above all dispositive for Machiavelli and Guicciardini.

3 The use of the term *potentiae,* or powers, to designate the five signatories to the Italic League in 1455 and their *amici* (or allies) may be the first instance of this term being used in the modern diplomatic sense. It signalled a new, nonhierarchical sense of transnational order distinct from the late Roman and medieval models of empire and Papacy.

4 Hankins 1995b, reprinted with corrections in Hankins 2003–2004a, 1: 295–424.

5 As an example of this kind of buoyant thinking, one may cite a letter of 1452 from Gian Pietro da Lucca to Lorenzo Valla (*Correspondence,* ed. and tr. Cook, 261). After praising Valla's restoration of pure Latinity, he goes on to describe Valla himself as "a man sent down from heaven. A man, that is, who is an omen and a prophecy, so to speak, of empire renewed. For now that he has restored our native tongue and reestablished the Latin language, can this be the moment when empire and worldly power will return to Italy at last?"

6 Ferguson 1948, chapter 1, gives numerous examples. For the use of the trope of rebirth or revival of antiquity in music, see Hankins 2015b; in the arts, see the classic work of Panofsky 1972.

7 King 1986; see also Ross 2016 for aspirational Renaissance culture among the Venetian middle classes.

8 The tyrannical Galeazzo Maria Sforza (r. 1466–1476) was educated by Guiniforte Barzizza (son of the famous educator Gasparino Barzizza). Ludovico Gonzaga (r. 1444–1478) was taught by Vittorino da Feltre "for the sake of the commonwealth," and his son Federico (r. 1478–1484) went to school with Ognibene da Lonigo. The princes of Ferrara were educated by Guarino

Veronese and his son Battista. Federico da Montefeltro of Urbino, the very model of the humanist condottieri, frequented for two years the school of Vittorino da Feltre, who admired the youth's "divine gifts."

9 See Hankins 2015b, forthcoming.

10 See Kidwell 1991, chapter 11, for context. The poem appears in Pontano, *Carmina,* ed. Oeschger, 374–375 (*Lyra* 14):

Ad Fidem

Quo fugis, rerum dea, quo, deorum
o Fides, nutrix? Maria alta tete
hospitem pellunt, fugat ipse iniquo
    foedere tellus,
te fugant arces, fora, templa, castra
te fugant reges; fugat et sacerdos
summus, heu! Ne te undique iam fugatam
    arceat aer,
quo minus coelum repetas et ipsae
denegent aurae in patriam regressum.
I, fuge ad manes, fuge ad ima et atri
    Tartara mundi;
comiter namque accipiere Manes;
et colunt iustum et venerantur aequa;
hi tibi assurgent meritae piaque
    sede locabunt,

si modo et tu Pontificem catenis
traxeris vinctum. Hoc age, diva, et unco
protrahens tracta soliique ad aram
    siste tremendam,
foedat incestu sacra qui nefando,
qui fide fracta Italiam Rutenis
prodidit, quique Ausoniam repenso
    vendidit auro,
quo suos natos (scelus ah supremum!)
ornet insigni diademate, alto et
ponat infames solio pianda
    caede cruentos.
Hunc trahe, hunc unco, dea, merge et illos
amne mactatos Tiberino; et una
hinc patrem, hinc natos Erebi profundos
    trude ad hiatus.

11 See Mallett and Shaw 2012, on whom my account of the invasion is largely based. Both sides claimed victory. Guicciardini's verdict, "The general consensus awarded the palm to the French," is cited by Mallett and Shaw. Machiavelli's view of this period of Italian history is first revealed in his two *Decennali,* translated in Gilbert, *CW* 3: 1444–1462; these were chronicles of Florentine history in vernacular verse covering the years 1494 to 1509.

12 The classic biography in modern times has been the adulatory *vita* by Roberto Ridolfi (1954 and later editions), which still dominates Italian scholarship; I use the reprint (2014) of the last (eighth) edition. Of the recent biographies, I have found most useful R. Black 2013 for its understanding of the historical and educational context and its expert assessment of the documentation, and Bausi 2005, who authoritatively situates Machiavelli in Italian literary history. Historians of political thought have long consulted Quentin Skinner's short but masterly biography (1981), which highlights Machiavelli's relationship to the Roman republican tradition. The studies of John P. McCormick (2011, 2018), useful also for assessments of recent work on Machiavelli's political thought, interpret him as a democrat. Godman 1998 is valuable for its analysis of Machiavelli's relationship to humanism. Capponi 2010 is the most authoritative on Machiavelli's military expertise and its limits, and succeeds brilliantly in explaining Machiavelli's Florentine sense of humor and the attractions of his company. For Machiavelli's debts to classical sources, the foundational work is Sasso 1987. Additions and corrections to Sasso may

be found in the 2013 edition of *Il Principe* by Pedullà *(Pr.)*, with extensive commentary, invaluable for historians of political thought; in Bausi's critical edition (2001) of the *Discorsi (Disc.)*; and in Marchand, Fachard, and Masi's 2001 edition of *L'Arte della guerra (AW)*. In general I follow R. Black's view that Machiavelli's thought represents a genuine revolution in political morality in the Western tradition, against various modern attempts to sanitize him (Machiavelli as a moment in the republican tradition), banalize him (Machiavelli as a typical representative of humanism or as a faithful Christian), or trivialize him (Machiavelli as a mere conduit of classical political thought).

13 R. Black 2013, 17.

14 R. Black 2015, 112–113.

15 Machiavelli, *Lettere,* ed. Gaeta, 486–488, tr. Atkinson and Sices, 310, letter 246. The hypothesis that Machiavelli was molested at Sassi's school was originally put forward by Connell in an interview for *Corriere della Sera,* published on November 11, 2005. Vigorous disagreement with this interpretation was expressed in Bausi 2016. As Black notes, there can be no doubt that Sassi was a pedophile; what is in dispute is whether he molested Machiavelli (and Vettori).

16 Machiavelli, *Lettere,* ed. Gaeta, 438, tr. Atkinson and Sices, 262–265, letter 224. Some read the letter as an ironic response to Vettori's parade of classical learning. Inglese 1987 defends the contrary view that Machiavelli possessed a deep classical culture, a view restated even more emphatically in the "Avvertenza" to Inglese 2006. See also the considerations of Cappelli 2017e.

17 See Bausi 2005, 270, on Adriani's role in encouraging Machiavelli's early career as a writer of vernacular comedies.

18 On Machiavelli's Lucretian studies, see Rahe 2008; Brown 2010a, chapter 4; Palmer 2014, esp. 81–93. R. Black 2013, 18–19, expresses more doubt about the extent of Lucretius' influence on Machiavelli. On Machiavelli's early career as a writer of comedies and his later *Mandragola* (c. 1518) and *Clizia* (staged in 1525), see Bausi 2005, chapter 9.

19 Hankins 1990a; Robichaud 2018.

20 Bausi 2005, 270–274. The translation seems to have been made for private performance, probably for an audience in the Rucellai Gardens. Bausi writes (273): "Machiavelli was not a faithful translator nor a particularly accurate one, and we might say that the version of the *Andria* confirms the limits of his classical education and of his knowledge of the Latin language that emerges in clear terms in all the Secretary's [literary] productions. . . . It is extremely indicative of Machiavelli's working method and at the same time of his modest humanistic culture" (my translation).

21 Since Machiavelli lived in a literary world soaked in the conventions of classical rhetoric, his mature works frequently show marks of rhetorical patterns of construction and style, but we have no evidence that Machiavelli ever formally studied rhetorical textbooks or examples of ancient oratory such as Cicero's speeches; such study was a regular part of literary education at the more prestigious humanist schools.

22 Adriani did not treat the post quite as a sinecure, but thanks to his teaching duties in the Studio he left many of his responsibilities in Machiavelli's capable hands; on him, see the entry by Giovanni Miccoli in *DBI* (1960); Godman 1998, esp. 144–150 and 239–242; Brown 2010a, chapter 3. Godman is less confident that Machiavelli studied formally with Adriani than Brown.

23 On Machiavelli's relationship to Florentine poetic traditions, see Bausi 2005, chapter 4, and R. Black 2013, 23. On the superficial classical learning of *The Prince,* see R. Black 2013, 159–160. On the limits of Machiavelli's literary culture, see also Bausi's discussion in his introduction to Machiavelli, *Discorsi* (2001), 1: xxx.

24 R. Black 2013, 160.

25 Pedullà 2018, 7, labels Machiavelli's attitude as "political classicism," that is, a rejection of the teaching of the ancients accompanied by an attempt "to recover the actual political prudence of the Romans through a hermeneutics of the ancient historical narratives (beginning with Livy)." Celenza 2018, chapter 6, discusses a parallel tendency in Alberti, ever the outsider, to be critical of his fellow humanists' excessive veneration of ancient authors to the neglect of the achievements of contemporaries.

26 This is stated explicitly in *FH* 5.1.12–14, ed. Montevecchi and Varotti, 451–452; tr. Gilbert *CW* 3: 1233; tr. Banfield and Mansfield, 186.

27 This is not to say that the humanists thought no modern persons or polities worthy of imitation; their virtues, however, are usually presented as the fruit of imitating the ancients. Patrizi's only mentions of contemporary events in the *De regno,* for example, appear in the several prefaces praising its dedicatee, Alfonso, Duke of Calabria, where the latter is said to be inspired by or to exemplify ancient virtue.

28 For the belief that antiquity was not comprehensively better than the present but could be corrupt in some respects, see *AW* 1.16–17, ed. Marchard et al., 35; tr. Gilbert, *CW,* 2: 570.

29 *FH* 5.1.14, ed. Montevecchi and Varotti, 452; tr. Banfield and Mansfield, 186.

30 *AW* 1.33, ed. Marchand et al., 38; tr. Gilbert, *CW,* 2: 572.

31 *Provincie,* translated by Banfield and Mansfield as "provinces," in contemporary usage means something closer to *paesi,* countries inhabited by peoples of the same descent; see Rezasco, 885.

32 Machiavelli refers to an embassy of three philosophers (not two)—Carneades, Critolaus, and Diogenes—sent by Athens to Rome in 155 BC, representing, respectively, the Academic, Peripatetic, and Stoic philosophical traditions. Machiavelli's source for the anecdote must be Plutarch's *Life of Cato* 22.1–4. Plutarch explains further why Cato was horrified: "But Cato, at the very outset, when this zeal for philosophical debate came pouring into the city, was distressed, fearing lest the young men, by giving this direction to their ambition, should come to love a reputation based on mere words more than one achieved by martial deeds."

33 *FH* 5.1.1–5, ed. Montevecchi and Varotti, 449–450; tr. Banfield and Mansfield, 185. See also the comments of Godman 1998, 289–290.

34 For the political slogan, see Cicero, *Pro Sestio* 96–100, with the commentary of Wirszubski 1954. It is worth remembering, in evaluating Machiavelli's attitude, that we owe to Cicero's *otium* the preservation of much of what we know about Hellenistic philosophy. Alamanno Rinuccini in *De libertate,* ed. Adorno, 36 (pref.), uses the phrase in this sense of honorable leisure. It is hard to find a use of the word *ozio* in Machiavelli that does not carry its load of contempt. In his writings it often occupies the same semantic area as *scioperato,* a word that in communal Florence indicated contempt for those who do not work but live on the labor of others. See Chapter 16, page 384, where Mario Salamonio links *scioperati* with *otiosi et ignavi.*

35 Machiavelli's belief that humanistic studies can enervate republican virtue may be linked to the frequent mockery in his political works of "the wise of our times," *i savi de' nostri tempi;* see Hornqvist 2004, 108–110.

36 *AW* 7.236–239, ed. Marchand et al., 287–288 (my translation). *Oltramontane guerre* means "wars having their origins beyond the Alps," or "wars with transalpine powers."

37 On the failure of the latter to read *sensatamente,* see Rahe 2008, 57 and 99.

38 This is of a piece with Machiavelli's statement in *Pr.* 14 that "a prince should have no other object, nor any other thought, nor take anything as his art, but that of war and its orders and discipline; for that is the only art which is of concern to one who commands" (tr. Price). In Francesco Patrizi's *De regno,* by contrast, the prince is advised (2.1) that the proper role of a king is not to fight but to rule with justice.

39 On this see the excellent pages in R. Black 2013, 32–48. See also Chapter 9, page 242, on attitudes of humanists to partisan politics. In addition to Black's account of Machiavelli's election to the office of second chancellor, see Godman 1998, 145.

40 Jurdjevic 2014.

41 For Machiavelli's revolutionary teachings on factionalism in the *Discourses,* especially his positive assessment of nonviolent political conflict (his "conflictualism") and the contrast between his views and traditional humanist teachings about the importance of concord, see Pedullà 2011 / 2018.

42 On Machiavelli's military teachings, see Denis Fachard's introduction to the edition of *AW* by Marchand et al., and Colish 1998. Gilbert 1985, 11, remarks, "It hardly goes too far to say that Machiavelli became a political thinker because he was a military thinker." Mallett 1990, 173, says that Machiavelli's military doctrine "lies at the heart of his whole thinking" in his political works.

43 The office of second chancellor was invented in the time of Leonardo Bruni to relieve the chancellor of his less vital bureaucratic duties. The second chancellor's chief diplomatic role, in principle, was to oversee relations with subject communities within Florentine territory; see Marzi (1910) 1987, 1: 196–197; R. Black 2013, 36.

44 The fullest accounts of Machiavelli's diplomatic activities are in Ridolfi 2014, 85–218; Dotti 2003, 41–221; and Marietti 2009, 59–161. A shorter but critically valuable account is R. Black 2013, chapter 4; there is also an illuminating discussion of the relation between Machiavelli's diplomatic experience and his political thought in Skinner 1981, chapter 1.

45 Gagné 2008.

46 *Pr.* 12.

47 The phrase "citizen militia," so often used to describe Machiavelli's military ideal, is a misnomer, since Machiavelli expected to recruit much of the infantry from the agricultural population of the Florentine territorial state, most of which would not have had citizen rights in the city of Florence. For the composition of Machiavelli's militia, see further below, page 446.

48 Potter 2008. For contemporary military ideas, see Hale 1985 and Mallett 1974.

49 Machiavelli, *Lettere,* ed. Gaeta, 360; tr. Atkinson and Sices, 180–182, letter 169.

50 Note Machiavelli's defensiveness about his militia's "one defeat" in *AW* 1.169, ed. Marchand et al., 60–61 and note; tr. Lynch, 23–24; with comments by R. Black 2013, 216; Bayley 1961, 268–276.

51 The third part of the third book of *De regimine principis* is devoted to "how a city or kingdom is to be ruled in time of war," with much practical information on the military organization of the polity, based on Vegetius; see Wisman's article on Vegetius in *CTC* 6: 176. A long section in book 3 of Matteo Palmieri's *Della vita civile* is dedicated to military matters, and Patrizi's *De inst. r.p.* devotes book 9 to military affairs (see Chapter 9, page 261). Biondo Flavio in *RT,*

book 6, 1531 ed., 225, underlines the intimate connection between civil and military administration. Biondo himself devotes books 6–7 of *RT* to *res militaris.* On the military teachings of Palmieri, Patrizi, and Biondo, see further Chapter 9.

52 For the popularity of Valturio's treatise, see Chapter 9, page 267. According to *USTC,* there were fourteen editions of Cornazzano's work before 1600. Francesco Patrizi also intended to write a separate work on warfare (see *De inst. r.p.,* 1534 ed., f. 40r) but never completed it as far as is known.

53 On the reception of Vegetius and Aelian see *CTC.* The work attributed to Modestus (called Modestinus by Biondo) is actually an extract from Vegetius. Two of the four works were written in Greek and were translated into Latin for the first time during the fifteenth century. Aelian's treatise on military tactics was translated both by Giovanni Aurispa and by Theodore Gaza; Gaza's far superior translation became standard. Onasander's work *De optimo imperatore* was translated by Niccolò Sagundino, whose version was excerpted by Biondo in *RT* 6; see Chapter 9, page 266. See Formisano 2009 on the idea of military science in antiquity and the formation of a corpus of writings on the military art in the Renaissance.

54 The original title of the work was more traditional: *De re militari;* see Bausi 2005, 226–227, who comments on Machiavelli's penchant for giving Latin titles to works and chapters written in Italian.

55 A survey of editions of Machiavelli before 1600 in *USTC* yields 16, 18, 18, and 22 Italian editions, respectively, of *The Art of War, Prince, Histories,* and *Discourses,* but the 26 printings of French versions of *The Art of War* far outnumber those of the other major works (six of *The Prince,* five of the *Discourses,* and one of the *Histories*). On the other hand the work was never translated into Latin, unlike the *Discourses* (eight printings) or *The Prince* (six printings). All four works were also printed in the eleven sixteenth-century editions of Machiavelli's complete works. This accounting does not include plagiarisms and reworkings by other authors, for which see Anglo 2005.

56 For example, the preface to Gabriel le Veneur, Bishop of Eureux, found in many of the French editions, emphasizes its value for civilian students of the military; the dedication of the English translator, Peter Whitehorne, to Princess Elizabeth (the future Queen Elizabeth I) makes no mention at all of Machiavelli's doctrine of the militia. On the reception of *The Art of War,* see Procacci 1995 and Anglo 2005 (who emphasizes the distinct avenues through which *AW* was received as compared to Machiavelli's political works; see esp. 17–41, 477–513, 517–572). Machiavelli's defense of native troops (in both *AW* and *Disc.*) did, however, become a debating point in sixteenth-century discussions of war; see Anglo 2005, 96–97, 501–502, 537–538.

57 *AW* 1.115, ed. Marchand et al., 54; tr. Gilbert, *CW,* 2: 581.

58 On Machiavelli's failure to appreciate the military realities of his time, see Mallett 1974, esp. 87–97, 196–197, 257–259; Mallett 1979; Hale 1985; Mallett 1990; Mallett 1994. The military historian Niccolò Capponi (2010, 245) writes, "The book itself [*The Art of War*] demonstrates Machiavelli's ignorance about military matters, despite his experience as an administrator of soldiers."

59 Bayley 1961, 235–236, who mentions similar ordinances in Ferrara and Lucca in the same period.

60 Hale 1985, 52, 201–202.

61 Mallett 1974 makes this argument; see also Mallett 1990, 173–180, where he writes that the *AW*'s military doctrine "had little impact on the development of specialist thinking about war" (174).

See also 178–179, where, while allowing that Machiavelli's ideas were based on military thinking of the time and not on classical or republican illusions, he describes them as nevertheless "founded on certain anachronistic assumptions."

62 Mallett and Shaw 2012, 177–216.

63 Jackson 2018, 34.

64 Hale 1985, 203.

65 Hirzel 1895.

66 Colish 1998.

67 See Bausi 2005, 234; Capponi 2010, 244–245; R. Black 2013, 215.

68 In *AW* 1.153–157, ed. Marchand et al., 58–59; tr. Gilbert, *CW,* 2: 583–584, Machiavelli puts this common opinion in the mouth of Cosimo Rucellai, which is then refuted by Colonna.

69 Told in Cicero, *De oratore* 2.75, who remarks, "And upon my word he was right, for what better example of prating insolence could there be than for a Greek, who had never seen a foeman or a camp, or even had the slightest connexion with any public employment, to lecture on military matters to Hannibal, who all those years had been disputing empire with the Roman people, the conquerors of the world?" (Loeb version). In the preface to his *De re militari,* Valturio recalled this story, embarrassing for a humanist, in trying to explain what qualified him to give military counsel to Sigismondo Malatesta.

70 This remark chimes with the comments about the weakness of condottieri princes made by Machiavelli *in propria persona* in *FH* 1.39.

71 *AW* 7.247, ed. Marchand et al., 289; tr. Gilbert, *CW,* 726.

72 *AW* Pref.10, ed. Marchand et al., 29, tr. Gilbert, *CW,* 567. As has often been noted, the meaning of *virtù* in Machiavelli's works often slips back and forth between its traditional sense, indicating above all the moral virtues of the ancient philosophers, and *virtù* in Machiavelli's new sense (for which see the next chapter).

73 *AW* 1.74, ed. Marchand et al.; tr. Gilbert, *CW,* 576. On the middle republic of Rome as Machiavelli's model, see further in the next chapter. In *FH* 2.5, Machiavelli also presents the *primo popolo,* Florence's first popular government of 1250 (which he admires much more than the city's later governments), as defended by a military *ordine,* a militia in which were enrolled "all the young men" under twenty banners in the city and seventy-six in the countryside. Florence continued to expand its empire in Tuscany so long as this order remained in existence; its expansion came to a halt soon after Florence began to employ mercenaries. At 2.6 he summarizes, "On these military and civil orders the Florentines founded their freedom" (tr. Banfield and Mansfield, 58).

74 *AW* 1.194, ed. Marchand et al., 64; tr. Gilbert, *CW,* 587.

75 *AW* 1.190, ed. Marchard et al., 64; tr. Gilbert, *CW,* 587 (modified). Machiavelli's remark is based on Livy 1.48.

76 DH 4.22.1–2, 5.13.2; Horace, *Carmina* 3.73.25–28; Vegetius 1.10; Livy 1.44.1–2. The same locale, significantly, was used to assemble the Roman popular assembly for voting in their centuries, as Machiavelli surely knew.

77 It is well to remember that Machiavelli tends more to follow conventional morality in the *AW,* a work intended for publication, than in *The Prince* and the *Discourses,* which were intended for a private readership; see R. Black 2013, 218, who points out several places in *AW* where Machiavelli seems to contradict amoral pronouncements in his other political writings. The *FH,* a public commission and dedicated to a pope, also approximates conventional morality.

78 Compare also Machiavelli's comments in *FH* 1.39.7–10.

79 See page 467.

80 *AW* 7.190, ed. Marchand et al., 281–282; tr. Gilbert, *CW,* 721.

81 At *Pr.* 14, however, Machiavelli says that the prince should study history in order to learn about war.

82 See the apparatus of the Marchand edition and Burd 1897. Machiavelli's wide range of sources includes Thucydides, Caesar, Livy, Suetonius, Josephus, Diogenes Laertius, Plutarch, and the *Scriptores Historiae Augustae,* though most of the technical details of Roman warcraft come from Vegetius and Frontinus; the original elements in Machiavelli's treatment are mostly owing to his use of book 6 of Polybius, a hitherto unexploited source. But most of what Machiavelli says about training, tactics, and strategy is unoriginal. The precepts for warfare in book 7 were taken more or less whole cloth from Vegetius. Machiavelli surely knew Valturio, but students of Machiavelli have not to my knowledge studied in detail his possible role as an intermediate source. Gabriele Pedullà has shown the importance of Dionysius of Halicarnassus for Machiavelli subsequent to the composition of *The Prince* (ed. Pedullà, ad indices; Pedullà 2011, capitolo 5; Pedullà 2018, chapter 6) but does not detect his presence in the military chapters of *The Prince* (12–14); he shows him to be a major but unacknowledged intertext in the *Discourses.* It remains to be seen whether Machiavelli considered Dionysius in *The Art of War.*

83 Patrizi, *De inst. r.p.* 9.1.

84 See Chapter 9, page 266.

85 *Disc.* 1.47 shows Machiavelli's awareness of this as a factor in the Roman plebs' claim to political participation.

86 *Disc.* 2.18, the third of three military chapters in that work, where he blames Italian military weakness after 1494 on the neglect of infantry in armies led by condottieri.

87 *AW* 2.302–309, 4.141–146, 6.125, ed. Marchand et al., 122–123, 185–186, 230; tr. Gilbert, *CW,* 623, 661, 691.

88 *Pr.* 12.

19. MACHIAVELLI: FROM VIRTUE TO *VIRTÙ*

1 R. Black 2013, 99: "It is clear that the new prince for Machiavelli is synonymous with the tyrant." Black's argument rests on parallels between discussions of tyrants in the *Pr.* and *Disc.* and the supposition that "new prince" is a euphemism for tyrant, chosen so as not to offend the Medici. On the expression "new prince," however, "a euphemism but not a neologism," see Pedullà's introduction (XLII) to his edition of *Pr.* (2013). Pedullà's discussion of the disjunction *principe / tiranno* in Machiavelli (XXXIX–LVII) and its relationship to Bartolist definitions of tyranny is particularly valuable.

2 Aristotle, *Politics* 5.9, discussed in Chapter 4. Botero in R. Black 2013, 117–118; *Pr.,* ed. Pedullà, XLV, who mentions similar judgments of Agostino Nifo, Innocent Gentillet, Descartes, and Hermann Conring. For numerous other examples of Renaissance readings of the *Pr.* as a handbook for tyrants, see Anglo 2005.

3 See Baron 1988, 2: 101–151, esp. 101–108 for a history of this problem in the interpretation of Machiavelli.

4 Modern studies of the dating of both works have made this argument less tenable, for there is good evidence that the composition of the *Pr.,* begun in 1513, lasted into 1516, while the *Disc.*

developed out of an early treatise on republics, already mentioned in the latest revision of the *Pr.*, datable to late 1515 or early 1516. The *Disc.* were certainly finished by 1519. See R. Black 2013, 96, 138.

5 Mattingly 1958; for Pole's view, see R. Black 2013, 125, and Anglo 2005 (ad indicem).

6 R. Black 2013, 145–148; the opposite view, emphasizing the differences between the doctrines of *Pr.* and *Disc.*, is taken in Baron 1988, 2: 101–151.

7 As recommended by Baron 1988, 2: 101.

8 R. Black 2013, 85. Lorenzo eventually did acquire the principality of Urbino but was unable to keep it. Hence the *Pr.* could have had for Machiavelli, with his republican sympathies, the added function of encouraging the hated Medici scions to find some place other than Florence to impose their rule. That would explain why Machiavelli repeatedly highlights the difficulties of a new prince ruling a city with republican traditions (see also Chapter 20, page 485). As Black points out, if Machiavelli did intend to counsel the Medici princes how to acquire states in the Romagna, it would help to account for why he chose Cesare Borgia, backed by Pope Alexander VI, as his model for the new prince. With Machiavelli's advice, Giuliano and Lorenzo might succeed where Cesare failed.

9 The phrase is Hans Baron's, in Baron 1988, 2: 111.

10 R. Black 2013, 176; on Machiavelli as non-exclusivist, see 117: "Machiavelli was not a republican in the sense that he thought princely government was never appropriate." On exclusivism, or the lack of it, in Renaissance constitutional thought, see Chapter 3, page 71, and Hankins 2014a; on the origins of republican exclusivism in the seventeenth century, see Hankins 2010a. At *Disc.* 1.55 Machiavelli says that lands which have a great many gentlemen, men who live in leisure from their rents, cannot be made into republics because inequality of incomes makes a truly political life impossible. The only way to reform such places is via a monarchical system.

11 See Chapter 4.

12 For Machiavelli's use of the word *modo* to describe both individual and collective behavior patterns, see Pedullà 2018, passim.

13 *Pr.* 5.

14 *Pr.* 15.

15 *Pr.* 8, ed. Pedullà, 100–101, with commentary.

16 See Chapter 10. For Poggio's realism, see Chapter 4, page 141.

17 For a sign that Machiavelli may have read Decembrio's life of Filippo Maria Visconti, see *FH* 1.39.6, ed. Montevecchi and Varotti, 1: 186, which may be compared with Decembrio, *Life,* cap. 26, ed. Ianziti and Zaggia, 34. Compare also *FH* 3.7.8, ed. Montevecchi and Varotti, 1: 312, whose probable source in the diaries of Gino di Neri Capponi is indicated in their notes, but the passage provides an interesting parallel with Visconti's similar declaration in Decembrio, *Life,* cap. 44, ed. Ianziti and Zaggia, 77.

18 See *Disc.*, ed. Bausi, 2: 858–860. In the notes Bausi points out that the friends who gathered in the Rucellai Gardens while Machiavelli was composing the *Disc.* did not constitute "a coven of republicans or anti-Mediceans." This is not to say that the work does not defend good republics, which it does, but to believe that the main subject matter of the work is republican government is simply false.

19 *Disc.* 1.58.17, ed. Bausi, 1: 282: *i popoli quando sono principi.* Bausi comments, "when they hold power; thus a republican regime"; *Disc.* 1.58.29, ed. Bausi, 1: 284: *le città dove i popoli sono principi.* See Chapter 8, page 224, for Bruni's use of the term *princeps populus,* based on Livy's preface.

But Bruni uses the term differently, to mean a people that acts as a virtuous hegemon or the leading member of a city-state federation, a principal state.

20 *Disc.* 1.10.16, ed. Bausi, 1: 71, with his note.

21 *Pr.* 9, ed. Pedullà, 104–119, with commentary.

22 R. Black 2013, 116.

23 *Disc.* 1.25–26, where Machiavelli grants that kingdoms can have *vivere politico,* a political life, and are not equivalent to tyrannies. It is only a man who wants to establish absolute power who is a tyrant. Hence it is not the case, as is often said, that *vivere civile* or *vivere politico* is equivalent to republican government for Machiavelli. The same is true of the humanist usage of these terms; see Chapter 3, page 99. A constitutional monarchy where the prince is constrained by law and there are participatory institutions may be considered to have a political life. Machiavelli as a republican sympathizer does not discuss whether the people could act as tyrants, although the possibility had sometimes been raised by humanists, Petrarch for example; see Chapter 2, page 57. At *Disc.* 1.58.4 he does say that a licentious people unshackled by laws can give rise to a tyrant; at 2.2.1 he describes with satisfaction the cruel treatment meted out to nobles who threatened the people's freedom. Oligarchs can of course be tyrants; for example, at 3.6.19 he speaks of a revolutionary junta that "seized the tyranny" of Thebes with the help of a Spartan army.

24 *Disc.* 1.16, 1.26. At *Disc.* 1.25–26 Machiavelli seems reluctant to label an absolute prince a tyrant *simpliciter* using his own words, saying instead (1.25.5, ed. Bausi, 1: 117) that "quello che vuole fare una potestà assoluta, la quale dagli autori è chiamata tirannide, debbe rinnovare ogni cosa" (the man who wants to take absolute power, *called by the authors* tyranny, should change everything [my translation]). A weak prince coming to power cannot choose civil forms of power, either kingship or republic, but must become an absolute tyrant to survive and must use such extremely cruel means, up to and including ethnic cleansing, that any human being should flee them (1.26.4, ed. Bausi, 139) "e volere piuttosto vivere privato, che re con tanta rovina degli uomini" (and would rather live as a private citizen than as a king with such ruin to mankind [my translation]).

25 See Machiavelli's remarks on Agathocles (*Pr.* 8, ed. Pedullà, 92–96, with commentary), a tyrant whose consistent recourse to evil means deprives him of glory. In *Disc.* 1.26–27 the only person worse than the tyrant, from the point of view of the arts of power, is the prince who tries to be half-good, not in a smart Simonidean way but because of a weakness for *vie del mezzo* and half-measures. See page 464 below for Machiavelli's condemnation of the doctrine of the golden mean.

26 Above all, *Disc.* 1.10. See also *Disc.* 1.16.5, a discussion of the tyrant Clearchus of Heraclea, in which Machiavelli's voice is again Simonidean.

27 At *Disc.* 2.2.16, ed. Bausi, 1: 313, Machiavelli raises the possibility that there could be a virtuous tyrant, meaning a tyrant competent enough to conquer new lands; possibly he is thinking of Caesar or Augustus. He goes on to say, however, that if this should happen, the conquests would benefit the tyrant and not the state, citing Xenophon as his authority.

28 *Disc.* 1.58.9, ed. Bausi, 1: 279.

29 For moral continuities between *Pr.* and *Disc.*, see R. Black 2013, 145–148. Examples of tyrannical behavior recommended to republics: *Disc.* 1.9 (constructive fratricide at Rome's founding), 1.16.5 (killing ambitious citizens if necessary), 1.44 (deceptive bargaining). A republic's way of interacting with its rivals is inherently fraudulent (2.2–4), and a successful republic is bad for its neighbors, *contra* Bruni (2.13). For Machiavelli's view that Rome's success was based on

defrauding its allies, see below. Seneca, *De clementia* 3.11, is not an exception to the rule that advising immorality was not approved by philosophers in antiquity, since Seneca as a Stoic sees cruel necessity not as a violation of natural law but as part of a prince's duty in unhappy circumstances. Given that for Stoics everything Nature does is good, so too is what the prince does of necessity.

30 See Ahrensdorf 1997. For Machiavelli's relationship to Thucydides, see Reinhardt 1960, Sasso 1987, Canfora 1997, Simonetta 1997, and Murari Pires 2015. For Machiavelli's appropriations of Thucydides in *FH,* see Portogallo 2017. In moral terms, the figure from Greek philosophy who most resembles Machiavelli is Callicles, as presented in Plato's *Gorgias* (translated into Latin by Leonardo Bruni in 1411 and printed in Bologna in 1475). Callicles, who is more radical even than Machiavelli, attacks conventional morality as the morality of the weak, while outlining a meritocracy of the strong and a realist theory of international relations; see *Gorgias* 483d, 488c–d, 491a–d, 492a–c.

31 See Meinecke 1957; Donaldson 1989. The realist tradition in politics and international relations from Thucydides and Machiavelli to the present is treated in the rich collection of Campi and De Luca 2014. Machiavelli was, to be sure, not the only or even the principle source of realism in the early modern period. The usual form in which realism came down to the nineteenth century was not via unfiltered Machiavelli, who could not be endorsed because of his open advocacy of immoral means, but via Giovanni Botero and Justus Lipsius, whose realism (labelled *prudentia mixta,* or "mixed prudence") was more palatable because it was moralized. See the introduction to Jan Waszink's edition of Lipsius, *Politica,* 98–102, and *Politica* 4.13. I exclude of course claimed examples of realism from non-Western cultures, such as Kautilya's *Arthashastra* (India, second to third centuries AD) or Sun Tzu's *Art of War* (China, fifth century BC) or Han Feizi (China, d. 233 BC).

32 For an entry point into the modern debate, see Coady 2018.

33 On the possibility of applying virtue ethics to international relations, see Ainley 2017. She writes, "There is virtually no literature on virtue in international relations—no body of work that systematically or otherwise applies the insights of virtue ethics to the international realm."

34 Boucher 1998, for example, takes the prehistory of modern international relations to be a dialogue between realism and legalism.

35 I have not been able to find a single reference to Martin Luther in Machiavelli's literary works or correspondence, for example.

36 *Pr.* 11: "They [the subjects of ecclesiastical princes] cannot get rid of these rulers, nor even think about doing so [because of their religious beliefs]. Only these principalities then, are secure and successful" (tr. Price).

37 Housley 1992.

38 Oman (1937) 1999, 94: "[Machiavelli] thought that artillery was going to continue [to be] negligible, that the day of cavalry in battle was quite over, that infantry was going to continue in huge units, like the legion, and that the pike was destined to be put out of action by short weapons for close combat, like the sword of the ancient Romans or of the Spanish footmen of Gonsalvo de Cordoba. In every case his forecast was hopelessly erroneous."

39 On the Greek roots of this concept, see Sorabji 2014.

40 See Chan 2000.

41 See Chapter 1, page 25. This does not mean, especially in the High Renaissance, that humanists believed the humanities could not be a support to religious belief and observance; see

page 27. For further thoughts on the humanist form of moderate perfectionism, see the Conclusion.

42 This belief appears most famously in chapter 18 of the *Prince,* where the ruler is advised not to observe *fides* when it is to his advantage, and in general to set aside the moral standards of humanity and instead act in a subhuman way, like a fox or a lion. "Indeed, I shall be so bold as to say that having and always cultivating [the virtues] is harmful, whereas seeming to have them is useful" (tr. Price, 62). Machiavelli is consciously inverting a fundamental maxim of ancient moral philosophy: "One should *be,* not seem" (μὴ δοκεῖν, ἀλλ' εἶναι; *esse, non videri*).

43 *Disc.* 1.16.8, ed. Bausi, 1: 101–102.

44 The highest purpose of politics is glory: see R. Black 2013, 101–103. Augustine in the *City of God,* of course, condemned the Roman state precisely because it was driven by love of glory.

45 *Disc.* 1.7–8: The ability to accuse malefactors in public is good, but calumnies that are allowed to fester without evidence being presented as to their truth are noxious; see also the next chapter. Machiavelli's theory of *tumulti* was a direct challenge to the Roman republican traditions of *concordia;* see Pedullà 2018 for discussion of Machiavelli's "political conflictualism."

46 See *Disc.* 1.4 for Machiavelli's hearty approval of the popular tribunate, an institution about which Cicero and most humanist commentators such as Biondo had misgivings (Chapter 11, page 295).

47 See Dunn (1979) 1993, 35.

48 *Disc.* 2.2.9, ed. Bausi, 1: 312. The free way of life leads to riches and dominion. *Disc.* 1.29.16, ed. Bausi, 1: 149: A city that lives free has two ends, one to acquire, the other to maintain itself free.

49 *Disc.* 1.16.9, ed. Bausi, 1: 102, on the pleasure and utility of freedom: "being able to enjoy one's things freely, without any suspicion [i.e., anxiety], not fearing for the honor of wives and that of children, not to be afraid for oneself" (tr. Banfield and Mansfield, 45).

50 On the periodization of the Roman republic, see Flower 2010.

51 The apogee of the Roman republic is described in Livy's books 21–45. Books 41–45 were not discovered and published until 1531. Books 1–10 and 21–40 were assembled from various manuscript sources by Petrarch. Machiavelli's "commentary" of course only extended to the first decade (i.e., books 1–10), though later books are occasionally mentioned. For the commentary genre of the *Disc.,* see Dionisotti 1980, 258–259, who says it was without models; its unique characteristics as a commentary are also acknowledged by Bausi in his edition of the *Disc,* 1: xxxi, who, however, points out works by Giovanni Cavalcanti and Jacopo Bracciolini as possible forerunners and models. For the Renaissance recovery of book 6 of Polybius, see Chapter 12, page 310.

52 See page 634n82.

53 That Machiavelli's account of Rome's constitutional development here follows DH rather than Polybius is shown in Pedullà 2011, 430–460.

54 *Disc.* 1.6. Compare Biondo in Chapter 11, page 297.

55 *Disc.* 2.3–4. This echoes the judgment of Bruni in *History* 1.10, ed. Hankins, 1: 16–17, about the effects of the dominance of Rome over other cities in the empire, though Bruni does not attribute this to fraudulent scheming on the part of Romans; see Chapter 8, page 232. Machiavelli states that the Romans' political dominance gave them a monopoly on military virtue as well; see *AW* 2.302–303, ed. Marchand et al., 122.

56 *Disc.* 2.13. Here again, Machiavelli radicalizes an idea already found in Bruni's *History* (1.11, ed. Hankins, 1: 16–19): how the hegemony of Rome made it impossible for lesser cities to flourish.

57 This often presents itself as a traditional Florentine defense of republics against an assumed preference for monarchy, for example, at *Disc.* 1.58, where Machiavelli argues against the conventional wisdom that a prince is wiser and more constant than the multitude.

58 The mask slips most visibly in *Disc.* 1.58. Machiavelli's self-promotion as a suitable legislator for a refoundation of Florence is a theme of *FH* and his later political thought in general; see Jurdjevic 2014.

59 See R. Black 2013, 103–107, for Machiavelli's *virtù* and further references.

60 For Aristotle's concern with meritocratic governance in the *Politics,* a neglected side of his teachings, see 2.9.1270b–1271a ("The worthiest should be appointed whether he chooses or not"), 2.11.1273a, 3.4.1277a ("The good *ruler* is a good and wise man, but the good citizen need not be wise"; "the excellence of a ruler differs from that of a citizen"), 3.13.1283a, 4.4.1292a, 7.9.1329a.

61 See Chapter 18, page 435.

62 For "the true way" as Machiavellian code for the *via del mezzo* or the Aristotelian mean, see also *Disc.* 3.21.12 (ed. Bausi, 2: 670), quoted below, where he says that the middle course is impossible to maintain because it is unnatural.

63 *Disc.* 2.24. See Hale 1985, 189–209. Machiavelli's attitude to urban fortifications is colored by the traditional hatred of republicans for signorial castles within the walls of the city. In *Pr.* 20 he writes that the prince's best fortress is not to be hated by the people.

64 Following Bausi's commentary (2: 670n20) I take *modo* here to mean "measure" or "mean" rather than Mansfield and Tarcov's "mode," i.e., I take it as an elegant variation balancing *la vera via* in the first colon of the period. Bausi lists the parallel passages in the *Prince.*

65 I reconstruct what might have been Patrizi's interrogation of Machiavelli mostly from *De regno* 8.20, a chapter on trustworthiness *(de fide).* The exercise is not wholly speculative given that Patrizi and Machiavelli rely on many of the same examples from Roman history, and Patrizi's account of *fides* is implicitly meant to persuade a prince who is inclined to prefer his own *utile* to the *bonum* to be steadfast in his commitments. A moral realism synthesizing virtue politics and Machiavellian realism was later elaborated in Giovanni Botero's *Della Ragion di Stato* (1589). Botero makes some of the same criticisms of Machiavellian realism that I make here, arguing for example that a prince's behavior has to be consistent if he is to maintain his *riputazione,* the key element in his political success.

66 Patrizi notes that prudence without *fides* is merely "a sly and shrewd cunning" *(vafra quaedam versutaque calliditas).*

67 For Petrarch's view that a pretense of virtue is easily exposed, weakening a prince's power, see page 540n25. It seems not a little perverse that Machiavelli makes so much of the "cloak of religion" in cases like that of Ferdinando II "the Catholic" of Aragon, living as he did at beginning of the Reformation, when that cloak was being so roughly stripped from the backs of popes, ecclesiastical princes, and bishops in Northern Europe.

68 Patrizi, *De regno,* 1567 ed., 383: "Among the Parthians, however, there was no trust in words or promises, for they were all arrogant, seditious, scheming, deceiving, tricky and over-bold. They said that violence was a man's way, and that kindness was for women. They conducted all their counsels in wondrous silence and were always prepared to attack their enemy with trickery and deceit. But the Romans carefully observed a *fides* that was holy, steadfast and elevated among all nations, and defeated their enemies with true virtue and not with tricks and deceit."

69 See Chapter 2, page 50.

70 *Disc.* 1.2.14–23, ed. Bausi, 1: 20–25, with commentary.

71 On the epigenetic explanation for Roman virtue, entertained by Dante, Bruni, and Biondo, see Chapter 8, page 235, and Chapter 11, page 300. (I use the word "epigenetic" in the sense used in developmental psychology.)

72 On Machiavelli and Sallust, see Osmond 1993, Fontana 2003, Kapust 2007, and the article on Sallust by Patricia J. Osmond and Robert W. Ulery in *CTC* 8 (2003): 183–326.

73 Hence Machiavelli's insistence on laws against excessive wealth, with the goal of keeping the public rich and the citizens poor; on this see McCormick 2018, 45–68. He parted ways from most previous humanist thinkers by taking a relatively positive view of the Gracchi's agrarian laws, whose underlying intention he accepted as good; see Nelson 2004, 77–86. Patrizi praised the *tribuni plebis* (see Chapter 16, page 372) but opposed redistribution as impractical (Chapter 17, page 408). For humanist attitudes to wealth generally, see Chapter 7, page 206.

74 *Disc.* 1.17–18. This leads to the Machiavellian paradox that only a bad man can become prince in a republic, but only a good prince can reform a republic.

75 *Disc.* 1.43.

76 *FH* 4.1, ed. Montevecchi and Varotti, 1: 374–375; see also Chapter 20.

77 *Disc.* 1.4.7, ed. Bausi, 1: 34–35: "For good examples arise from good education, good education from good laws, and good laws from those tumults which many inconsiderately damn" (tr. Mansfield and Tarcov, 16). Later in the same chapter Machiavelli underlines the surprising ability of an "ignorant" people to discern truth when advised by good men in assemblies. At 3.1.18, ed. Bausi, 2: 527, he writes that, apart from external "accidents" such as the foreign invasions, the rebirth of states can take place through either farsighted legal reforms or the influence of charismatic virtue: "from a good man who arises among them who with his examples and his virtuous works produces the same effect as the [law]" (tr. Mansfield and Tarcov, 210). He goes on to say that the legal orders of a state need to be kept alive by the virtue and spirit of citizens who defend them against transgressors. But "virtue" turns out to be tantamount to a readiness to conduct exemplary "executions" at frequent intervals of those who threaten its *ordini*.

78 *Disc.* 1.11.8, ed. Bausi, 1: 78–79 (my translation); compare 3.33.7. For Polybius' judgment on the role of religion in Roman success, see his *History* 6.56, and compare Augustine, *De civitate Dei* 4.32.

79 See Chapter 1, page 27.

80 *Disc.* 2.2, with the comments of Najemy 1999, 667–668, to whom my understanding of Machiavelli's religious thought is indebted. Since, as I will argue below, he was not a believer, controlling the people by means of religion implied a certain contempt for the people's understanding, despite Machiavelli's supposed democratic sentiments and despite his praise of the multitude's political prudence.

81 The *Esortazione della Penitenza,* the most important textual evidence for those who hold that Machiavelli was a Christian, in my view falls into this category of compliance with social duties; see also the examples given by Brown 2010b, 164–165. The chief and most extreme defender of the view that Machiavelli was in some sense a Christian is Ridolfi, who is followed by De Grazia 1989, Colish 1999, Nederman 1999, Viroli 2010, and others. Capponi's characterization of Machiavelli's religious feeling as "shallow," at best, seems sensible; see Capponi 2010, 30–35, 252–253, 285–286. Najemy 1999, 664, emphasizes his ambivalence and the unresolved tensions in his attitudes to religion.

82 See Chapter 11, page 296.

83 See for example the invocation of civil religion at the end of Bruni's *Oration for Nanni Strozzi,* cap. 86, ed. Daub, 302, with Daub's comment.

84 See Hankins 2006b.

85 See *Disc.* 2.5.2, ed. Bausi 1: 339–340, where religious *sette* are said to undergo periodic obliterations from celestial or human sources ("parte vengono dagli uomini, parte dal cielo"); for Ficino's views about the historicity of religions, see Hankins 1990a, 1: 283–285, 302–304; 2: 460–464.

86 *Disc.* 1.11, 3.1.

87 On these issues, see Sullivan 1996; Cutinelli Rèndina 1998; Najemy 1999; Couzinet 2001; Rahe 2008; Brown 2010b.

88 I have found clarifying the observations of Celenza 2015, 124–133.

89 *Disc.* 3.1.32–33, ed. Bausi, 2: 532.

90 Machiavelli also cites the case of Joan of Arc and the exploitation of her religious virtue by the king of France.

91 In general, see Hay 1977.

92 See esp. *FH* 1.9, 1.23.

93 *AW* 4.141–146, 6.125, ed. Marchand et al., 185–186, 230; tr. Gilbert, 661, 691. For "il Cielo disarmato," see *Disc.* 2.2.35, ed. Bausi, 1: 318–319.

94 *Disc.* 1.12.12, ed. Bausi, 1: 86: "La quale religione se ne' príncipi della republica cristiana si fusse mantenuta, secondo che dal datore d'essa ne fu ordinato, sarebbero gli stati e le republiche cristiane più unite, più felici assai, che le non sono" (tr. Mansfield-Tarcov, 37: "If such religion [*religione,* i.e., piety] had been preserved by the princes of the Christian republic in accordance with the way its founder established it, Christian states and republics would be more united and happier than they are"). The term *respublica christiana* was widely used by humanists to denote the Church since at least the days of Pius II. Bausi's note 27 to this sentence interprets *i principi della repubblica christiana* as the popes, citing a parallel passage from *FH* (1.9). Machiavelli's account of the ordinances of Christianity's founder hardly accords with Christ's admonitions at Luke 6:27–36 to be passive in the face of injury, but then he was no biblical scholar. He also chooses to ignore that interpreting political failure as a sign of divine punishment is a common feature of many religions, including Greek and Roman pagan religion.

95 *Disc.* 1.14–15; see the close reading in Najemy 1999.

96 Najemy 1999, 675. Najemy summarizes: "This is the crux of Machiavelli's view of Roman religion: complete respect for the ceremonies, prayers, and rituals, not out of cynical concern for appearances, but because that respect was the foundation of obedience to the laws, of *educazione,* of loyal and disciplined armies—in short, of *civiltà;* and, at the same time, skillful interpretation, as necessity requires, of the strictures and demands of religion."

97 The first Medici popes were Leo X (1513–1521) and Clement VII (1523–1534).

98 See Nelson 2010, 92.

99 The Erastian position was defended by Richard Hooker in *The Ecclesiastical Polity,* book 8. Hooker requires the consent of the laity through Parliament to legislate on ecclesiastical matters. For Gallicanism, see Parsons 2004.

100 Sasso 1980, 510–517.

101 For the view that Machiavelli opposed Christianity for its implicit political morality and aimed at a revival of paganism, see Prezzolini 1954. Sullivan 1996 sees Machiavelli's brand of republicanism as anti-Christian; Rahe 2008, 96–100, takes Machiavelli to be hostile to monotheistic religion as such. Israel 2001, like the Enlightenment and proto-Enlightenment radicals he

studies, takes Machiavelli to be saying that religion is nothing but "a political device contrived to discipline and control the people utilizing their ignorance and credulity" (176), and that to found a just and free commonwealth requires curtailing the power of organized religion.

102 Berlin 1972 argues that Machiavelli wants to revive the morality of the pagans in order to stiffen the womanish morality of the Christian world. Berlin takes a romantic view of pagan morality and thus sees Machiavelli as a forerunner of Rousseau and Nietzsche.

103 See Monfasani 1999.

104 *Disc.* 1.10.7, ed. Bausi, 1: 68–69. In the previous sentence he declares that the founders of religions are the most esteemed of men. That the founders of new religions must destroy old ones is an unexplored paradox.

105 Hankins 1990a, 1: 193–217.

106 *Disc.* 2.2.35–37, ed. Bausi, 1: 318–319 (my translation). Bausi's philological notes are critical for interpreting this famous passage.

107 Fontana 1999, 657.

108 For the meaning of *fare . . . professione di bontà* as "take a vow of goodness," analogous to a monastic vow, see Rezasco, 874 IV.

20. TWO CURES FOR HYPERPARTISANSHIP

1 Ianziti 2012, chapter 6; Jurdjevic 2014. On Bruni as historian, in addition to Ianziti 2012, see Fubini 2003, chapters 5–7; on Machiavelli as historian, see Gilbert 1965; Anselmi 1979; Martelli 1992. For a comparison of Bruni and Machiavelli as historians that reads Bruni as favoring oligarchy and preparing the ground for Medici dominance, see Clarke 2018.

2 See *Disc.* 1.49, where Machiavelli states that Florence has never been a true republic because it was born in servility under the Roman Empire and all of its reformers have been partisans rather than statesmen seeking the common utility.

3 For Bruni's sources, which in the later books of the *History* included extensive materials from the Florentine chancery's archives, see my introduction and notes to the third volume of the *History*.

4 See Cabrini 1990, 275–276.

5 See Clarke 2018, chapter 2.

6 For the data, see Hankins 1997, analyzed in Hankins 2008a.

7 For editions and translations of the *Discursus,* see the Bibliography. For analysis, aside from Jurdjevic 2014, see R. Black 2013, 231–238.

8 For the audience of the *FH,* see Najemy 1982b; R. Black 2013, 242–244; Jurdjevic 2014.

9 See Geuna 2005 and Pedullà 2011 / 2018 for Machiavelli's political vocabulary for benign civil conflict. Among the terms he uses for the latter, in addition to *tumulti,* are *disunioni, controversie, dissensioni, differenzie,* and *rumori.* These he distinguishes from factionalism or hyperpartisanship, for which he uses expressions like *civili discordie, intrinseche inimicizie,* and *guerre civili* to describe the formation and actions of *fazioni* and *sette.*

10 On the criteria separating good political conflict from bad factionalism, see Pedullà 2011 / 2018, whose analysis, though focused principally on the *Disc.,* also discusses passages in the *FH.*

11 Jurdjevic 2014, chapter 1. The contrast is with the earlier republicanism of the *Discorsi,* based on Machiavelli's study of Roman history. For criticism of Jurdjevic on this point, see McCormick 2018, 69–105. R. Black 2013 generally agrees with Jurdjevic that Machiavelli in the *Istorie* put aside the populism of the *Discourses.*

12   *FH* 2.2, ed. Montevecchi and Varotti, 1: 191–195, the chapter on early Florentine history, swiftly dispatches many of Bruni's critical conclusions. The burden of book 1 was to show that Italy's divisions from the fall of Rome to the fifteenth century had been the fault of the Papacy's political ambitions; in a fashion similar to his treatment of Bruni, Machiavelli relies on Biondo Flavio's *Historiarum decades* (1453) for historical information but reverses Biondo's broadly positive portrait of the Papacy. Clarke 2018, chapter 2, notes that Machiavelli's focus on the Buondelmonte-Amidei feud as the origin of Florentine factionalism displaces Bruni's emphasis on the wider sources of factionalism in Italy, the Guelf-Ghibelline struggle.

13   *Proemio dell'autore,* in Machiavelli, *FH,* ed. Montevecchi-Varotti, 1: 89–90.

14   See Aristotle, *Nicomachean Ethics* 8.10–11 and 9.8–9. Aristotle holds that concord in the state is built on relationships of mutual regard among those who rule and a virtuous egoism that links the goods of others with one's own good. See Cooper 2005.

15   Francesco Patrizi explicitly follows Aristotle and also endorses the rule of the middle classes in *De inst. r.p.* 6.1., 1531 ed., f. LXXXII—always provided that "they excel in moderation and virtue, having either won distinction in learned disciplines or made themselves useful in some honest trade."

16   *Discursus* 12, 14, ed. Marchand, Pachard, and Masi, 627; tr. Gilbert, *CW* 3: 103.

17   Bruni, *History* 4.26–34, ed. Hankins, 1: 358–373.

18   Villani, *Cronica* 9.12.

19   *FH* 2.14, ed. Montevecchi and Varotti, 1: 219–221.

20   Bruni, *History* 6.112, ed. Hankins, 2: 265.

21   *FH* 2.33, ed. Montevecchi and Varotti, 1: 262–265.

22   See Chapter 7, page 203, for Boccaccio's account of Walter of Brienne's tyranny.

23   Bruni, *History* 6.113–116, ed. Hankins, 3: 264–268. See Bartolus, *De tyranno* 5–6, ed. Quaglione, 184–187, discussed in Chapter 4, page 112, for the terms *ex parte exercitii* (because of the way power was exercised) and *propter metum* (owing to fear).

24   This is a general characteristic of Machiavelli's late republicanism according to Jurdjevic 2014, chapter 4, who sees a moderating of Machiavelli's populism in the *Discorsi.*

25   *FH* 2.33, ed. Montevecchi and Varotti, 1: 264.

26   *FH* 2.34, ed. Montevecchi and Varotti, 1: 266.

27   Villani, *Cronica* 13.3.

28   *FH,* 2.35, ed. Montevecchi and Varotti, 1: 271.

29   Bruni, *History* 6.121–122, ed. Hankins, 2: 272–274. While Bruni admires the Guelf commander Charles, Machiavelli opines that Charles would have become a tyrant just like Walter had he not died shortly after his election.

30   *FH* 2.34, ed. Montevecchi and Varotti, 1: 265–270.

31   On the logic of Walter's speech, see Stacey 2013, 187.

32   Jurdjevic 2014, chapters 3 and 4; the periodization of Machiavelli's political thought into "Roman" and "Florentine" periods is Jurdjevic's.

33   Villani, *Cronica* 13.18.

34   Bruni, *History* 7.3, ed. Hankins, 2: 285–286; see also Chapter 10.

35   Bruni is careful to blame the actual outbreak of violence on the *plebs* and not on the *popolo* (*History* 7.10, ed. Hankins, 2: 292). Machiavelli (*FH* 2.39, ed. Montevecchi and Varotti, 1: 280) blames the *popolo* without qualification.

36   Bruni, *History* 7.6, ed. Hankins, 2: 289.

37 Ibid., 7.7, ed. Hankins, 2: 289.

38 *FH* 2.42, ed. Montevecchi and Varotti, 1: 291 (my translation).

39 Bruni, *History* 7.13, ed. Hankins, 2: 295, based on Villani, *Cronica* 13.21.

40 *FH* 2.41, ed. Montevecchi and Varotti, 1: 290; tr. Banfield and Mansfield, 104.

41 Pedullà 2011, chapter 1.

42 *FH* 3.1, ed. Montevecchi and Varotti, 1: 292–293; tr. Banfield and Mansfield, 105 (translation slightly altered).

43 *FH* 3.1, ed. Montevecchi and Varotti, 1: 294; tr. Banfield and Mansfield, 106 (translation slightly altered).

44 Hankins 2017e; Nelson 2019.

45 Lilla 2001.

46 See Pedullà 2018, chapter 7. Pedullà writes, "Through the radical Enlightenment, the French Revolution, nineteenth-century liberalism, and the doctrine of the class struggle, conflict has long enjoyed complete legitimacy in political theory (in parallel with a progressive marginalization of the concept of the 'common good')" (250). He goes on to analyze six aspects of Machiavelli's conflictualism that sets it apart from later variants. For "holism" in the sense of moral opposition to the legitimacy of political parties, see Rosenblum 2008.

47 Isocrates, *Panathenaicus* 132.

48 An apparent exception is any act so wicked that it diminishes the glory of the actor; see Machiavelli's remarks about the tyrant Agathocles in *Pr.* 8. Pedullà's commentary on the passage (96–97) argues that what made Agathocles inglorious was that his wicked actions did not serve the common good. I would add only that Machiavelli's debased ideal would be better described as the common utility than the common good.

49 Clarke 2018, 65–78.

21. CONCLUSION

1 Hsia 2010, 2016; Marenbon 2015, 258–262. It is worth noting that Ricci's understanding of Confucianism as a kind of Stoicism occurred during an important revival of Stoicism in the late sixteenth century, traditionally dated from the publication of Justus Lipsius' *On Constancy* in 1584. For Confucianism as an ancient theology in late seventeenth-century European thought, see Walker 1972, chapter 6.

2 Hsia 2016, 55.

3 The original Italian text, called *Commentari della Cina,* was not published until 1911–1913. The work first became known in the Latin translation of Nicolas Trigault, S.J. (1615), from which translations into French, German, Italian, and Spanish were made within the space of six years. Trigault's account was eventually absorbed into the mammoth historical description of China published by Jean-Baptiste Du Halde (1735), which became the basis of Enlightenment accounts of China such as the idealizing account of Voltaire, who praised China as a uniquely humane civilization, and Montesquieu, for whom China was the archetypal example of oriental despotism.

4 Ricci, *De Christiana expeditione* 1.5, tr. Trigault, 1615 ed., 25 (my translation): "Ac tametsi huic regno Philosophi non imperent, dici tamen debet Reges ipsos a Philosophis gubernari." Ricci then goes on to compare Chinese writing with Egyptian hieroglyphics and praises the philosophers of China for writing only in the learned tongue and not that of the people.

5 Ibid. 1.5, 29.

6 Ibid. 1.6, 46–47 (my translation).

7 Ibid. 1.6, 44. Ricci uses the word *rex,* king, for emperor. Compare to the humanist preference for elective kingship discussed in Chapters 5 and 17.

8 The expression comes from the Roman jurist Ulpian (*Digest* 2 tit. 1 s3) and came to mean the full discretionary powers a magistrate possesses by law to protect private and public interests.

9 Ricci, *De Christiana expeditione* 1.6, tr. Trigault, 1615 ed., 59–60 (my translation).

10 Botero, *Delle cause della grandezza delle città* (1588), cited in Bireley 1990, 47–48, and *Della ragion di stato* (1589).

11 Contzen, *Politica,* 7.31, 1621 ed., 538–544, "De regno Sinensi," is based on Trigault's Latin translation of Ricci's *De Christiana expeditione.* On Contzen, a standard political authority in the seventeenth century, see Bireley 1990, chapter 6.

12 The reform of human nature starts from within: *Four Books,* tr. Gardner, xxiii, 112. On the Confucian tradition of moral self-cultivation and its conception of humanity, see Wei-ming 1998.

13 On Confucian political thought, see Bai 2012.

14 See Yuri Pines in Bell and Li 2013, esp. 164–165. The phrase "ethicization of nobility" is Pines's.

15 Rites *(li)* are correct forms of behavior authorized by tradition and in conformity with *dao,* analogous in some respects to the "small morals" or etiquette that became an important part of humanist education in the sixteenth century.

16 Mencius, in *Four Books,* tr. Gardner, 6–7.

17 See the *Zhongyong,* chapters 22 and 26, in *Four Books,* tr. Gardner, 124, 127, for the metaphysical sources of the superior man's charisma.

18 The Stoic concept that a good ruler can dispense with coercion, at least among the most rational of his subjects, is paralleled in the Confucian understanding of *wu wei* (effortless action) as governance without coercion; see *Analects* 2.1, 2.21, 8.18–19, 12.19, 13.6, 15.5, 17.19. The contrast in Neo-Confucianism is with *youwei,* activist government; see Bol 2018. The modern Confucian political theorist Jiang Qing writes that "the essence of the Kingly Way [in early Confucianism] is to rule by virtue rather than coercion." See Fan 2011, 165, and the *Zhongyang,* in *Four Books,* tr. Gardner, 112.

19 See Sandel 2018 for a modern dialogue between Confucianism and a major Western political theorist whose thought emphasizes civic participation and virtue.

20 Lee 2016.

21 See Macedo 2013.

22 Francesco Corte, a quattrocento professor of civil law at the University of Pavia, wrote of the Holy Roman Emperor's power in Milan, "The emperor can do nothing in the Duchy of Milan, except insofar as he is given permission by the duke, any more than he can in the lands of the Turkish sultan" (quoted in J. Black 2015, 87.)

23 Bodde and Morris 1967. In the *De Christiana expeditione,* tr. Trigault, 1615 ed., 44, Ricci notes that "in this [Chinese] empire there are no ancient laws, like the laws of the Twelve Tables and the law of Caesar [i.e., the Justinianic Code] by which the republic is governed in perpetuity," but each emperor makes his own laws or chooses to enforce those of his predecessors.

24 Bodde and Morris 1967.

25 On the humanist chancellors of Florence, responsible for running the departments of state and war, see Garin 1979; Brown 1979; Witt 1983; and R. Black 2013. On the humanist (Giannozzo Manetti) as provincial governor, see Connell 2015, chapter 6.

26 See O'Malley 1993 for the deep debt of Jesuit education to humanist culture. As an example of the ambiguity of Jesuit influence, one may note the case of Adam Contzen, S.J., whose *Politicorum libri X* was mentioned above. His *Methodus doctrinae civilis seu Abissini regis historia* (A Plan of Political Instruction, or the Story of King Abyssinus, 1628)—a fictional biography of an ideal Coptic Christian prince, set vaguely in late antiquity and modelled on Xenophon's *Cyropaedia*—provided a perfect adaptation of virtue politics to the form of a novelistic mirror of princes. (I owe this reference to Katharina Rilling, who is preparing a dissertation on Contzen's *Methodus* at the University of Freiburg i.B.) Yet Contzen's anti-Machiavellian *Politicorum libri decem* was regarded with deep suspicion (not without reason) as an ideological tool of Jesuits to undermine Protestant princes.

27 Fukuyama 2011.

28 Ridder-Symoens 1992, shows that the number of lawyers produced by the higher faculties of medieval universities vastly outnumbered the theologians and medical doctors.

29 The admiration for the Chinese examination system would eventually find expression in the West in the age of democratic revolutions; see Teng 1943.

30 Jiang 2013; Bell 2015; Hankins 2017e.

31 I owe this distinction between political meritocracy and meritorious governance to Joseph Chan, who made it in a paper given at a roundtable at the University of Hong Kong in June 2018. See Hankins 2018b. Chan distinguishes between political meritocracy, which is a regime type, and meritorious governance, which is a kind of political excellence to which any regime may aspire. The regime of political meritocracy is defined as "the idea that a political system should aim to select and promote leaders with superior ability and virtue." It thus differs from democracy, which chooses its leaders via popular elections, and monarchy, which ordinarily invokes the principle of heredity. Meritorious government, by contrast, is not necessarily present in the regime of political meritocracy—its forms of selection and promotion may not work well—and not necessarily absent from democracy or monarchy.

32 The only premodern attempt I am aware of to express Confucian meritocracy in constitutional form is Prince Shotoko Taishi's *Seventeen Article Constitution* in seventh-century-CE Japan. Scholars question whether this list of rules for meritorious governance can really count as a constitution in the Western sense of a system to constrain arbitrary power and factionalism. A Vietnamese scholar, Bui Ngoc Son, has recently argued the controversial thesis that Confucian emperors were in effect constitutional rulers with real constraints on their power, citing the example of imperial Vietnam; see Bui 2016. Matteo Ricci would have agreed, as he gives many examples of customary limits on the powers of the emperor in his *De Christiana expeditione* 1.6.

33 Bol 2008, 34–42; see Robert Hymes in Chaffee and Twitchett 2015, 621–664, for the social origins of the literati class in Sung China. The Qing dynasty cases discussed by Bodde and Morris 1967 reveal some shocking (though presumably atypical) abuses of power by authorities at various levels of Chinese society.

34 Christopher Peterson, "What Is Positive Psychology, and What Is It Not?," *Psychology Today* (May 2008), https://www.psychologytoday.com/us/blog/the-good-life/200805/what-is -positive-psychology-and-what-is-it-not: "Positive psychology is the scientific study of what makes life most worth living. It is a call for psychological science and practice to be as concerned with strength as with weakness; as interested in building the best things in life as in repairing the worst; and as concerned with making the lives of normal people fulfilling as with

healing pathology." *Eudaimonia* has acquired the status of a technical term in positive psychology. An early advocate of positive psychology, Jonathan Haidt, explored parallel teachings in ancient Greek philosophy in *The Happiness Hypothesis* (2006). See also the website of the Positive Psychology Center at the University of Pennsylvania, https://ppc.sas.upenn.edu.

35 For the Confucian view that *li*, or patterned guidance in accepted forms of behavior, is preventive, while *fa*, law, is punitive, see Bodde and Morris 1967, 20.

36 Or, as Erasmus says in *Education of a Christian Prince* (ed. Jardine, 11)—a work with heavy, unacknowledged debts to Patrizi's *De regno*—"It is fruitless to attempt advice on the theory of government until you have freed the prince's mind from those most common, and most truly false, opinions of the common people" (i.e., that wealth and status are the chief goals of life).

37 An example from Florence is the Officials of the Night, an office founded in 1432 to stamp out sodomy, prostitution, and other practices viewed as social vices; see Rocke 1996. For other examples of legal crackdowns on social and moral problems, see Brundage 1987; Zorzi 1988; and Stern 1994.

38 The proto-Confucian writer Shu-hsiang, in a letter of protest to Tzu-ch'an, prime minister of the state of Sheng, who had just published (in 536 BC) China's earliest known legal code, predicted that doing so would lead to endless litigation and commented, "I have heard the saying that, 'When a state is about to perish, there will be many new enactments in it.'" See Legge 1861–1872, 5.2: 610.

39 For Poggio Bracciolini's view that modern law was a tyrant, see Krantz 1987.

40 For a similar strategy in Confucian culture, see Bai 2012, 70. The second half of Bacon's maxim *detur digniori,* "let it be given to the more worthy," is *qui beneficium digno dat omnes obligat,* "he who benefits the worthy creates an obligation in everyone," because everyone benefits when the worthy rule.

41 Brague, "From What Is Left Over," *First Things* (August 2017), https://www.firstthings.com /article/2017/08/from-what-is-left-over.

42 Griffin 2003. The younger Pliny's letters, especially those to Trajan, gave more practical examples of how the exercise of grace and favor could be regulated by moral ideals.

43 The demands of Aristotelian perfectionism are often underestimated, but see Barnes 2005. For further remarks about the humanists and perfectionism, see Chapter 19, page 459. For the limits of perfectionism in Aquinas, motivated by his distinction between the natural and supernatural ends of man, *beatitudo imperfecta* and *beatitudo perfecta,* see Finnis 1998, chapter 7, passim.

44 Voice 2014; see Chapter 1, page 3. Even More's Utopia, intolerable though it is, allows for some pluralism in religion, and its institutions aim merely at a moderate perfectionism, stopping well short of indoctrination.

45 See Taylor 1998. Grotius' view bears some resemblance to Rawls's (2005) idea of "free-standing" justificatory modes of political argument.

46 Patrizi, *De inst. r.p.* 1.5, 1534 ed., f. Xr: "Naturam igitur imitatur in legibus suis legumlator quae virtutis et honestae utilitationis rationem habet, ut aequum aut bonum spectet, et utilitati omnium civium, si fieri potest, vel complurium saltem consulat. Videat imprimis ut leges suae emenditrices sunt vitiorum commendatricesque virtutum, adeo ut ab illis vivendi disciplina ducatur. Cuius rei materiam uberam philosophia praestabit, ut Cicero in libris, quos de legibus scribit, manifeste docet. Sit lex omnis ad salutem civium, conservationem humanae societatis, incolumitatem civitatis, vitamque singulorum quietam ac beatam. Quae persuasio efficit ut populi

aequo animo scita illa accipiant, quae etiam aliqua ex parte libertati singulorum obesse videntur. Defendat ac tueatur bonos, malos autem supplicio afficiat, ea tamen ratione ut malit cives emendare quam interimere."

47 More, *Utopia,* 1965 ed., 159, 229, 432–433 (where the commentary notes the parallel with Patrizi). In general, the editors of the Yale edition, Surtz and Hexter, remark (clxxvi–clxxvii) on the "countless parallels" between the *Utopia* and Patrizi's political treatises. In Utopia, however, education is in the hands of priests, not the paterfamilias or the city. Patrizi's call for citizen education may reflect Plato, *Laws* 7.809e. Grendler 1989, 21–22, writes that Italian city governments of the Renaissance established publicly supported schools in recognition of the value of literacy to lay society, but never aimed or could aim at educating the citizenry as a whole. See also R. Black 2007, 295–306, on the more limited goals of civic education in the fourteenth century.

48 Patrizi, *De inst. r.p.* 2.1, 1534 ed., ff. XIX*r*–XX*r:* "Literas imprimis ab omnibus, si fieri potest, ediscendas esse.... Eas igitur non modo ediscendas esse censeo, sed vix arbitrari possum in libera civitate quenquam sine literis ingenui civis nomen mereri. Qui enim sine literis non solum liberales disciplinas, sed minimas quasque artes ediscere aut tueri possumus? Nec mercatura ipsa aut agricultura sine eis satis tuta esset. Hae nanque memoriam rerum conservant, posteritatem instituunt, praeterita futuris connectunt, et ratiocinationem totius vitae nostrae perpetuo agunt. Idcirco optimum quidem factum eis pueros imbuere priusquam aliis literis incumbunt, si eos viros aliquando evadere volumus aut in civium numero censeri. Erit igitur officium optimi patrisfamilias summa diligentia curare ut filios saltem his primis literis eruditos habeat." The word *ingenuus* can also carry the sense of "liberal" or "gentlemanly."

49 Salutati, *De tyranno,* preface 1, ed. Baldassarri, tr. Bagemihl, 65, makes the moral education of citizens a general human obligation: "[We have an obligation to instruct others] not only in things that relate to our final end or direct us towards that final end, given that we are all bound by the community of faith, but also in those which distinguish the good citizen or, more broadly, the good man. Faith, citizenship, and nature unite humanity; the first regards our final salvation; the second political society; the third the human community and the perfection of mankind." Baldassarri's note points out the continuity with the medieval tradition in this respect, indicating parallels in Giles of Rome, *De regimine principum* 2.1.6, 3.2.32, and Marsilius of Padua, *The Defensor pacis* 1.3.

50 Three examples among many: Alberti, *Momus,* ed. D'Alessandro and Furlan, 17; Maio, *De maiestate,* ed. Gaeta, 220; Machiavelli, *Disc.* 3.29; see Cappelli 2016b on this theme in Pontano.

51 See Chapter 13, page 333. One can only imagine what Alberti would have made of the contemporary federal government of the United States, with its (estimated) 4,500 laws and 300,000 regulations.

52 See Seneca, *Ad Lucilium* 97.12; Cicero, *De officiis* 2.44, and compare Petrarch, *Rem.* 1.42. The lack of transparency between "il palazzo e la piazza" was famously criticized by Guicciardini (*Ricordi,* ed. Spongano, 153), who remarked that the people had less knowledge of what was done by the Florentine government than they had of what was done in India.

53 Cicero, *De officiis* 1.33. *Aequitas,* the principle that law had to be interpreted *ex bono et aequo,* in accordance with the fair and good, is praised in Bruni's *Isagogicon moralis disciplinae,* the most influential humanist text of moral philosophy, frequently printed in editions of Aristotle's *Ethics,* and in many other humanist texts—for example Pontano's *De principe,* ed. Cappelli, cap. 57, and Carafa, *De boni principis officio,* 1668 ed., 44 ("The king ought to differ from

the laws most of all in that they, being deaf and merciless, allow of no relaxation or pardon. But it is the duty of royal humanity *(humanitas)* to take into account the times and the malefactor's age and to reckon the danger, amid so many human errors, of living a blameless life.") The moral hazards of legal micromanagement and limiting the discretionary powers of officials and judges in modern America is discussed in Howard 2009 and 2014.

54 On this theme in Pontano and other Neapolitan political writers, see Cappelli 2016b, 106–107, 122–125.

55 In addition to the discussion in Chapters 4, 6, and 13; see Rinuccini, *De libertate,* ed. Adorno, 63–69; both Alberti and Rinuccini were responding to the corruptions of Medici rule.

56 A detailed argument to this effect is made in Rose 2019.

57 See Waldron 2006 for a democratic critique of judicial review in the United States.

58 Michael Sandel, "The Tyranny of Merit: Why the Populists Have a Point," paper for the Harvard Political Theory Colloquium, October 4, 2018.

APPENDIX A

1 Vergil, *Aeneid* 6.852–853.

2 Cicero, *De officiis* 2.8.26–27. In the original text the verbs are in the indicative; Petrarch changes them to the imperfect subjunctive, not to throw doubt on Cicero's statements but because the whole thought is rendered in a conditional form. Such future-less-vivid constructions are a persistent stylistic tic of Petrarch's moral writing, symptomatic of his wider scepticism about absolutes in politics.

3 Augustine, *De civitate Dei* 19.21.

4 The argument assumes that defeat of one's country is God's punishment for wickedness, or God's testing of the virtuous, an assumption found throughout Augustine's *De civitate Dei.* To the extent that one fights for the victory of a morally depraved country, one is fighting the judgment of God.

5 Is Petrarch expressing hope in this backhanded way that his counsels will be heeded and Christendom renewed?

6 This is possibly an allusion or echo of Seneca, *De tranquillitate animi* 6.2, where Seneca justifies withdrawal from public life in the case of persons excessively prone to freedom of speech who might bring harm upon themselves in the normal circumstances of court life.

BIBLIOGRAPHY

TEXTS AND TRANSLATIONS

Acciaiuoli, *Cronica.* Alamanno Acciaiuoli. *Cronaca.* In *Il tumulto dei Ciompi: Cronache e memorie,* ed. Gino Scaramella, 13–34, with the "aggiunte anonime," 35–41. Fascicule 1. Bologna: Zanichelli, 1917. (Rerum Italicarum scriptores, 18.3).

Acciaiuoli, *In Ethica.* Donato Acciaiuoli. [*Commentary on Aristotle's* Nicomachean Ethics.] In Aristotle, *Ethicorum ad Nicomachum libri decem, cum commentariis.* Geneva: Jacob Stoer, 1588.

Acciaiuoli, *In Politica.* Donato Acciaiuoli. [*Commentary on Aristotle's* Politics.] Cited from *Donati Acciaioli in Aristotelis libros octo Politicorum commentarii.* Venice: Vincentius Valgrisius, 1566.

Alberti, *De commodis.* Leon Battista Alberti. *De commodis litterarum atque incommodis,* ed. Mariangela Regoliosi. In Alberti, *Opere latine,* 19–87.

Alberti, *De iciarchia.* Leon Battista Alberti. *De iciarchia.* In volume 2 of Alberti, *Opere volgari.*

Alberti, *De iure.* Leon Battista Alberti. *De iure,* ed. Maila Banchi and Donatella Coppini. In Alberti, *Opere latine,* 821–844.

Alberti, *Della famiglia.* Leon Battista Alberti. *I libri della famiglia.* In volume 1 of Alberti, *Opere volgari.*

Alberti, *De re aedificatoria.* Leon Battista Alberti. *L'architettura (De re aedificatoria),* ed. and tr Giovanni Orlandi, introd. and notes by Paolo Portoghesi. Milano: Edizioni il Polifilo, 1966. English translation in *The Ten Books of Architecture: The 1755 Leoni Edition.* New York: Dover Publications, 1986.

Alberti, *Momus.* Leon Battista Alberti. *Momus,* ed. with commentary by Paolo D'Alessandro and Francesco Furlan. Pisa: Fabrizio Serra, 2016. English translation with Latin text in Leon Battista Alberti, *Momus,* ed. Virginia Brown and Sarah Knight, tr. Sarah Knight. Cambridge, MA: Harvard University Press, 2003. (ITRL 8.)

Alberti, *Opere latine.* Leon Battista Alberti. *Opere latine,* ed. Roberto Cardini. Rome: Istituto poligrafico e zecca dello Stato, 2010. (Centro di Studi sul Classicismo di Prato).

Alberti, *Opere volgari.* Leon Battista Alberti, *Opere volgari,* ed. Cecil Grayson. 2 vols. Bari: Laterza, 1960–1973.

Alberti, *Philodoxeos.* Edited and translated in Grund 2005, 70–169.

Alberti, *Theogenius.* In volume 2 of Alberti, *Opere volgari.*

Anon., *Oratio de libertate.* Anonymous. *Oratio de libertate coram dominis Florentinis.* Unpublished. Cited from BLF, MS. Plut. 90 sup. 47, ff. 87v–90v.

Aristides, *Encomium Romae.* Greek text and commentary in *Elio Aristide: A Roma,* ed. Francisca Fontanella. Pisa: Edizioni della Normale, 2007. English translation in volume 2 of *P. Aelius Aristides: The Complete Works,* tr. Charles A. Behr. 2 vols. Leiden: E. J. Brill, 1981–1986.

Aristides, *Panathenaicus.* In Aristides, *The Complete Works,* volume 1, as above.

Aristotle, *Politica,* Moerbeke translation. Aristotle. *Politicorum libri octo cum vestusta translatione Guilelmi de Moerbeke,* ed. Franz Susemihl. Leipzig: Teubner, 1872.

Augustus, *Res gestae.* Augustus [Octavian Caesar]. *Res gestae divi Augusti: Text, Translation, and Commentary,* ed. Alison E. Cooley. Cambridge: Cambridge University Press, 2009.

[Baldinotti], *Oratio.* [Tommaso Baldinotti]. *Oratio.* Unpublished. Cited from BNCF MS Magl. VII 1095, ff. 90r–93v. (For the attribution to Baldinotti, see Chapter 9, note 50.)

Baldus, *De tyranno.* Baldus de Ubaldis. *Tractatus de tyranno,* edited in Quaglione 1983, 78–83.

Barbaro, *Preface to Themistius' Paraphrase of the Physics.* In *Paraphraseos libri in Posteriora Aristotelis . . . interprete Hermolao Barbaro,* f. 13v. Venice: Giunta, 1530.

Bartolus, *De regimine civitatis.* In Diego Quaglione, *Politica e diritto nel Trecento italiano: Il* De Tyranno *di Bartolo Sassoferrato (1314–1357),* 147–170. Florence: Leo S. Olschki, 1983.

Bartolus, *De tyranno.* In Quaglione, *Politica e diritto,* as above, 171–213.

Biondo. *See* Flavio

Boccaccio, *Consolatoria.* Giovanni Boccaccio. *Consolatoria a Pino de' Rossi,* ed. Giuseppe Chiecchi. In *TOGB,* vol. 5.2: 615–687 (1994).

Boccaccio, *De casibus.* Giovanni Boccaccio. *De casibus virorum illustrium,* ed. Pier Giorgio Ricci and Vittorio Zaccaria. In *TOGB,* vol. 9 (1983). Abridged English translation by Louis Brewer Hall: *Giovanni Boccaccio: The Fates of Illustrious Men.* New York: Frederick Ungar, 1965.

Boccaccio, *De mulieribus claris.* Giovanni Boccaccio. *Famous Women,* ed. and tr. Virginia Brown. Cambridge, MA: Harvard University Press, 2001. (ITRL 1.)

Boccaccio, *Epistole.* Giovanni Boccaccio. *Epistole,* ed. Ginetta Auzzas and Augusto Campana. In *TOGB,* vol. 5.1 (1974).

Boccaccio, *Trattatello.* Giovanni Boccaccio. *Trattatello in laude di Dante,* ed. Pier Giorgio Ricci. In *TOGB,* vol. 5.1 (1974).

Bracciolini, *Contra hypocritas.* Poggio Bracciolini. *Contra hypocritas dialogus* (1448). In Bracciolini, *Opera omnia,* ed. Fubini, 2: 39–80.

Bracciolini, *De avaritia.* Poggio Bracciolini. *De avaritia.* In Bracciolini, *Opera omnia,* ed. Fubini, 1: 1–31. Translated in Kohl and Witt 1978, 241–289.

Bracciolini, *Defensio.* Poggio Bracciolini. *Defensio de praestantia Caesaris et Scipionis ad Franciscum Barbarum virum clarissimum.* In Canfora 2001, 141–167.

Bracciolini, *De infelicitate principum.* Poggio Bracciolini. *De infelicitate principum,* ed. Davide Canfora. Rome: Edizioni di Storia e letteratura, 1998.

Bracciolini, *De praestantia.* Poggio Bracciolini. *De praestantia Scipionis et Caesaris.* In Canfora 2001, 111–118.

Bracciolini, *De vera nobilitate.* Poggio Bracciolini. *De vera nobilitate,* ed. David Canfora. Rome: Edizioni di Storia e letteratura, 2002. English translation in Rabil 1991, 63–89.

Bracciolini, *Historia tripartita.* Poggio Bracciolini. *Historia tripartita.* In Bracciolini, *Opera omnia,* ed. Fubini, 1: 32–63.

Bracciolini, *Opera omnia.* Poggio Bracciolini. *Opera omnia,* ed. Riccardo Fubini. 4 vols. Turin: Bottega d'Erasmo, 1964–1969. (Vol. I is a photoreprint of the edition of Basel, 1538.)

Bracciolini, *Vita di Filippo Scolari.* Jacopo di Poggio Bracciolini. *Vita di messer Filippo Scolari, cittadino fiorentino per sopranome chiamato Spano, composta e fatta da Jacopo di messer Poggio, e di latina in fiorentina tradotta da Bastiano Fortini.* In F. Polidori, "Due vite di Filippo Scolari, detto Pippo Spano." *Archivio storico italiano* 4 (1843): 119–184, at 163–184.

Brandolini, *Republics and Kingdoms.* Aurelio Lippi Brandolini. *Republics and Kingdoms Compared,* ed. and tr. James Hankins. Cambridge, MA: Harvard University Press, 2009. (ITRL 40.)

Brentius, *Oratio.* Andreas Brentius. *Oratio in disciplinas et bonas artes Romae habita.* In Karl Müllner, *Reden und Briefen italienischer Humanisten: Ein Beitrag zur Geschichte der Pädagogik des Humanismus,* 71–85. Vienna: Alfred Hölder, 1899.

Bruni, *Constitution of the Florentines.* In Bruni, *Opere,* 771–787. Translated in Griffiths, Hankins and Thompson 1987, 171–174.

Bruni, *De interpretatione recta.* In Leonardo Bruni, *Sulla perfetta traduzione,* ed. Paolo Viti, 73–220. Naples: Liguori, 2004. Translated in Griffiths, Hankins, and Thompson 1987, 217–228.

Bruni, *De militia.* In Leonardo Bruni, *Opere,* 649–701. Translated in Griffiths, Hankins, and Thompson 1987, 127–145.

Bruni, *De origine Mantuae.* In Bruni, *Epistolae,* 2: 217–29 (*Ep.* 10.25).

Bruni, *De studiis et literis.* In *Opere,* 243–279. Translated in Kallendorf 2002, 92–125.

Bruni, *Epistolae.* Leonardo Bruni, *Epistolarum libri VIII,* ed. Lorenzo Mehus. Florence: Bernardus Paperinius, 1741. Photo-reprinted as *Epistolarum libri VIII, recensente Laurentio Mehus (1741),* ed. with an introduction by James Hankins. 2 vols. Rome: Edizioni di Storia e letteratura, 2007.

Bruni, *History.* Leonardo Bruni. *History of the Florentine People (Historiarum Florentini populi libri XII),* ed. and tr. James Hankins. 3 vols. Cambridge, MA: Harvard University Press, 2001–2007. (ITRL, 3, 16, 27.)

Bruni, *Laudatio.* Leonardo Bruni. *Laudatio Florentine urbis* [Panegyric of the City of Florence], ed. Stefano Ugo Baldassarri. Florence: SISMEL, Edizioni del Galuzzo, 2000. Translation in Kohl and Witt 1978, 35–175.

Bruni, *Memoirs.* In Bruni, *History,* 3: 300–397.

Bruni, *Opere.* Leonardo Bruni, *Opere letterarie e politiche,* ed. Paolo Viti. Turin: UTET, 1996.

Bruni, *Oratio* (to King Alfonso the Magnanimous). In *Opere,* 844–845.

Bruni, *Orazione per Niccolò da Tolentino.* In *Opere,* 813–823.

Bruni, *Panegyric of Nanni Strozzi.* Leonardo Bruni. *Laudatio clarissimi viri Iohannis Stroze equitis florentini.* In *Leonardo Brunis Rede auf Nanni Strozzi: Einleitung, Edition, und Kommentar,* ed. Susanne Daub. Stuttgart and Leipzig: B. G. Teubner, 1996. Partial translation in Griffiths, Hankins, and Thompson 1987, 121–126.

Bruni, *Proemium* to his translation of the ps.Aristotelian *Economics.* Cited from BLF, MS Plut. 79.19, f. 3r–v, online at the website of the Biblioteca Laurenziana ("Plutei online:" see teca.bmlonline. it). Translated in Griffiths, Hankins and Thompson, 305–306.

Bruni, *Vita di Dante e del Petrarca.* In *Opere,* 531–560. Translated in Griffiths, Hankins, and Thompson, 85–100.

Buonaccorso, *On Nobility.* Buonaccorso da Montemagno. *Trattato di Nobiltà.* In *Prose e rime de' due Buonaccorsi da Montemagno* [etc.], ed. Giuseppe Manni, 2–97. Florence: Stamperia di Giuseppe Manni, 1718. Translation in Rabil 1991, 32–52.

Campano, *Opera.* Giovanni Antonio Campano. [*Opera omnia*]. Venice: Eucharius Silber, 1495. Reprint, Westmead, Farnsborough, UK: Gregg International Publishers, 1969.

Carafa, *Memoriale.* Diomede Carafa. *Memoriale sui doveri del principe.* In idem, *Memoriali,* ed. Franca Petrucci Nardelli. Rome: Bonacci, 1988. The Latin translation of Battista Guarino was published under the title *De regis et boni principis officio.* Naples: Castaldus, 1668.

Castiglione, *Courtier.* Baldassarre Castiglione. *The Book of the Courtier: The Singleton Translation: An Authoritative Text, Criticism,* ed. Daniel Javitch. New York: W. W. Norton, 2002.

Contzen, *Politica.* Adam Contzen, S. J. *Politicorum libri X, in quibus de perfectae reipublicae forma, virtutibus, et vitiis; institutione civium, legibus, magistratu ecclesiastico, civili, potentia reipublicae; itemque seditione et bello, ad usum vitamque communem accomodatè tractatur.* Mainz: Ioannes Kinckius, 1621.

Cortesi, *De hominibus doctis.* Paolo Cortesi. *De hominibus doctis dialogus,* ed. Maria Teresa Graziosi. Rome: Bonacci, 1973.

Crinitus, *De honesta disciplina.* Petrus Crinitus. *Commentaria de honesta disciplina.* Florence: Filippo Giunti, 1504.

Cyriac of Ancona, *Caesarea laus.* "La *Caesarea laus* di Ciriaco d'Ancona," ed. Mariarosa Cortesi. In *Gli umanesimi medievali: Atti del II Congresso dell'Internationales Mittellateinerkomitee, Firenze, Certosa di Galluzzo, 11–15 settembre 1993,* ed. Claudio Leonardi, 37–65. Florence: SISMEL Edizioni del Galuzzo, 1998. Also edited by James Hankins, "Addenda to Book X of Luiso's *Studi su l'Epistolario di Leonardo Bruni,*" in *Censimento dei codici dell'Epistolario di Leonardo Bruni,* ed. Lucia Gualdo Rosa, 2: 396–406. 2 vols. Rome: Istituto Storico Italiano per il Medio Evo, 1993–2004. Also in *Life and Early Travels,* as below, 197–221, with English translation.

Cyriac of Ancona, *Later Travels,* ed. and trans. Edward W. Bodnar with Clive Foss. Cambridge, MA: Harvard University Press, 2003. (ITRL 10.)

Cyriac of Ancona, *Life and Early Travels,* ed. and tr. by Charles Mitchell, Edward W. Bodnar, and Clive Foss. Cambridge, MA: Harvard University Press, 2015. (ITRL 65.)

Dante, *Inferno, Purgatorio.* In Dante Alighieri, *Divine Comedy,* tr. with text and commentary by Charles S. Singleton. 3 vols. Princeton: Princeton University Press, 1970.

Dante, *Monarchia.* Dante Alighieri. *Monarchia,* tr. with Latin text and commentary by Richard Kay. Toronto: Pontifical Institute of Mediaeval Studies Press, 1998.

Dati, *Hiempsal.* Leonardo Dati. *Hiempsal.* Edited and translated in Grund 2011, 188–243.

Decembrio, *De republica.* Uberto Decembrio. *De republica libri IV.* Unpublished. Cited from BAM, MS B 123 sup.

Decembrio, *Life of Visconti.* Pier Candido Decembrio. *Life of Filippo Maria Visconti, Third Duke of Lombardy.* In *Lives of the Milanese Tyrants,* ed. Max Zaggia and tr. with introduction and notes by Gary Ianziti, 1–149. Cambridge, MA: Harvard University Press, 2019. (ITRL 88.)

Decembrio, *Life of Francesco Sforza.* Pier Candido Decembrio. *A Record of the Deeds of the Most Illustrious Francesco Sforza, Fourth Duke of Milan.* In *Lives of the Milanese Tyrants,* as above, 150–247.

Equicola, *On Women.* Mario Equicola. *On Women (De mulieribus).* In Mario Equicola, *Selected Works,* ed. and tr. Bernard Schirg. Cambridge, MA: Harvard University Press, forthcoming. (ITRL 100.)

Erasmus, *The Complaint of Peace.* Desiderius Erasmus. *A Complaint of Peace (Querela Pacis).* In *Literary and Educational Writings,* vol. 5, ed. and tr. A. H. T. Levi. Toronto: University of Toronto Press, 2000. (Selected Works of Erasmus 27.)

Erasmus, *Epistolae. Opus Epistolarum Desiderii Erasmi Roterodami,* ed. P. S. Allen, H. M. Allen, and H. W. Garrod, with Barbara Flower. 12 vols. Oxford: Clarendon Press, 1906–1958.

Erasmus, *Education of a Christian Prince.* Desiderius Erasmus. *The Education of a Christian Prince,* ed. Lisa Jardine. Cambridge: Cambridge University Press, 1997.

Ficino, Marsilio. *Lettere I: Epistolarum familiarium liber I,* ed. Sebastiano Gentile. Florence: Leo S. Olschki, 1990.

Filelfo, Francesco. *Collected Letters,* ed. Jeroen De Keyser. 4 vols. Alessandria: Edizioni dell'Orso, 2015. (Cited as PhE, by book number and letter number.)

Filelfo, *Commentarii.* Francesco Filelfo. *Commentarii de vita et rebus gestis Federici comitis Urbinatis ligae italicae imperatoris.* Edited in G. Zannoni, "Vita di Federico d'Urbino, scritta da Francesco Filelfo, pubblicata secondo il cod. Vaticano Urbinate 1022," *Atti e memorie della Reale Deputazione di Storia Patria per le Provincie delle Marche* 5 (1901): 263–420.

Filelfo, *De exilio.* Francesco Filelfo. *On Exile,* ed. Jeroen De Keyser, tr. W. Scott Blanchard. Cambridge, MA: Harvard University Press, 2013. (ITRL 55.)

Filelfo, *De morali disciplina.* Francesco Filelfo. *De morali disciplina libri quinque* [etc.], ed. Francesco Robortello. Venice: Gualterus Scottus, 1552.

Filelfo, *Oratio ad principes.* Francesco Filelfo. *Oratio ad principes civitatis Mediolanensis de administranda reipublicae.* Cited from BAM, MS F 55 sup., ff. 31r–33v. Published in Adam 1974, 2: 337.

Filelfo, *Orazione della avaritia.* Cited from BNCF, MS Magl. VIII 1440, 99v–101v.

Filelfo, *Sfortiae, De Genuensium deditione, Oratio parentalis.* In *Francesco Filelfo and Francesco Sforza: Critical Edition of Filelfo's* Sphortiae, De Genuensium deditione, Oratio parentalis, *and His Polemical Exchange with Galeotto Marzio,* ed. Jeroen De Keyser. Hildesheim: Olms, 2015.

Filelfo, *Traduzioni.* Francesco Filelfo. *Traduzioni da Senofonte e Plutarco: Respublica Lacedaemoniorum, Agesilaus, Lycurgus, Numa, Cyri Paedia,* ed. Jeroen De Keyser. Alessandria: Edizioni dell'Orso, 2012.

Flavio, *Borsus.* Biondo Flavio. *Borsus,* ed. Maria Agata Pincelli. Rome: Istituto storico italiano per il Medio Evo, 2009. (Edizione nazionale delle opere di Biondo Flavio 2.)

Flavio, *Histories.* Biondo Flavio. *Historiarum ab inclinatione Romanorum imperii decades III* (Histories from the fall of the empire of the Romans in thirty books). Basel: Froben, 1531.

Flavio, *Italy Illuminated.* Biondo Flavio. *Italy Illuminated,* ed. Jeffrey White. 2 vols. Cambridge, MA: Harvard University Press, 2005 and 2016. (ITRL 20, 75.)

Flavio, *RT.* Biondo Flavio. *Rome in Triumph,* ed. Maria Agata Pincelli, tr. Frances Muecke (books 1–2 only). Cambridge, MA: Harvard University Press, 2016. (ITRL 74.) Biondo Flavio. *De Roma triumphante libri decem* [etc.] (books 3–10). Basel: Froben, 1531.

Four Books. In *The Four Books: The Basic Teachings of the Later Confucian Tradition,* tr. Daniel K. Gardner. Indianapolis: Hackett, 2007.

Frulovisi, *De republica.* In Tito Livio Frulovisi, *Opera hactenus inedita,* ed. C. W. Previté-Orton, 287–389. Cambridge: Cambridge University Press, 1932.

Garzoni, *De eruditione principum.* Giovanni Garzoni. *De eruditione principum—De principis officio, prima edizione,* ed. Alessandra Mantovani. Roma: Edizioni di storia e letteratura, 2014. (Temi e testi 131.)

George of Trebizond, *Comparatio.* George of Trebizond. *Comparatio phylosophorum Aristotelis et Platonis,* ed. Augustinus Claravallis Montefalconius. Venice: Iacobus Pentius de Leuco, 1523. Reprint, Frankfurt am Main: Minerva, 1965 (unpaginated; cited by signatures).

George of Trebizond. *On the Eternal Glory of the Autocrat,* ed. and tr. John Monfasani. In Monfasani 1984, 492–563.

Giles of Rome, *De regimine principum.* Giles of Rome (Aegidius Columna Romanus). *De regimine principum libri III,* ed. Hieronymus Samaritanius. Rome: Bartolomaeus Zannettus, 1607.

Giovanni d'Andrea (Johannes Andreae), *Commentary on the Liber sextus.* Johannes Andreae. *In sextum decretalium librum novella commentaria.* . . . Venice: Franciscus Franciscius Senensis, 1581. Online at Harvard University Library via hollis.harvard.edu.

Giovio, *Notable Men and Women.* Paolo Giovio. *Notable Men and Women of Our Time,* ed. and tr. Kenneth S. Gouwens. Cambridge, MA: Harvard University Press, 2013. (ITRL 56.)

Guarino, *De praestantia.* Guarino Veronese. *De praestantia Scipionis et Caesaris.* In Canfora 2001, 119–140.

Guarino, *Epistolario. Epistolario di Guarino Veronese,* ed. Remigio Sabbadini. 3 vols. Venice: A spese della Società, 1915–1919. (Miscellanea di storia veneta, ser. 3, 11.)

Guicciardini, *Dialogue.* Francesco Guicciardini. *Dialogo del reggimento di Firenze,* ed. Gian Mario Anselmi and Carlo Varotti. Turin: Bollati Boringhieri, 2006. English version: *Dialogue on the Government in Florence,* tr. Alison Brown. Cambridge: Cambridge University Press, 1994.

Guicciardini, *History of Italy.* Francesco Guicciardini. *The History of Italy,* tr. Sidney Alexander (abridgement). Princeton: Princeton University Press, 1969.

Guicciardini, *Ricordi.* Francesco Guicciardni. *Ricordi,* ed. Raffaele Spongano. Florence: Sansoni, 1951. English version: *Maxims and Reflections of a Renaissance Statesman,* tr. Mario Domandi, introd. Nicolai Rubinstein. Gloucester, MA: Peter Smith, 1970.

Kant, *Critique of Pure Reason.* Immanuel Kant. *Critique of Pure Reason,* tr. Paul Guyer and Allen W. Wood. Cambridge: Cambridge University Press, 1998.

Landino, *De vera nobilitate.* Cristoforo Landino. *De vera nobilitate,* ed. Maria Teresa Liaci. Florence: Leo S. Olschki, 1970. English translation in Rabil 1991, 190–260.

Landino, Cristoforo. *Poems,* tr. Mary P. Chatfield. Cambridge, MA: Harvard University Press, 2008. (ITRL 35.)

Lapo da Castiglionchio, *De curiae commodis.* Lapo da Castiglionchio. *De curiae commodis dialogus,* ed. and tr. Christopher Celenza. In Celenza 1999, 102–227.

Lapo da Castiglionchio, Proemium to his translation of Demosthenes' *Funeral Oration.* In F. P. Luiso, "Studi su l'epistolario e le traduzioni di Lapo da Castiglionchio juniore," *Studi italiani di filologia classica* 7 (1899): 205–299, at 296–297.

Leonardo of Chios. *On True Nobility, against Poggio (De vera nobilitate contra Poggium, tractatus apologeticus),* tr. Albert Rabil Jr. In Rabil 1991, 112–143.

Lipsius, *Politica.* Justus Lipsius. *Politica: Six Books of Politics or Political Education,* ed. and tr. with introd. by Jan Waszink. Assen: Royal Van Gorcum, 2004.

Locke, *Letter concerning Toleration.* In John Locke, *Two Treatises of Government and A Letter concerning Toleration,* ed. Ian Shapiro. New Haven: Yale University Press, 2003.

Machiavelli, *AW.* Niccolò Machiavelli. *L'arte della guerra. Scritti politici minori,* ed. Jean-Jacques Marchand, Denis Fachard, and Giorgio Masi. Roma: Salerno Editrice, 2001. (Edizione Nazionale delle opere di Niccolò Machiavelli, Sezione 1, Opere politiche, vol. 3.) English translations: Gilbert, *CW*, 2: 561–726. Also *Art of War*, tr. Christopher Lynch. Chicago: University of Chicago Press, 2003.

Machiavelli, *Disc.* Niccolò Machiavelli. *Discorsi sopra la prima deca di Tito Livio,* ed. Francesco Bausi, with commentary. 2 vols. Roma: Salerno Editrice, 2001. (Edizione nazionale delle opere di Niccolò Machiavelli I / 2.) English version: *Discourses on Livy,* tr. Harvey Mansfield and Nathan Tarcov. Chicago: University of Chicago Press, 1996. Also translated in Gilbert, *CW*, 1: 175–529.

Machiavelli. *Discursus.* Niccolò Machiavelli. *Discursus florentinarum rerum post mortem iunioris Laurentii Medices.* In Machiavelli, *L'arte della guerra. Scritti politici minori,* ed. Marchand, Fachard, and Masi, 621–641, as above. Translated in Gilbert, *CW*, 1: 101–115.

Machiavelli, *Pr.* Niccolò Machiavelli. *Il principe,* ed. with modern Italian translation by Carmine Donzelli, introd. and commentary by Gabriele Pedullà. Rome: Donzelli, 2013. English translation: *The Prince,* ed. Quentin Skinner and tr. Russell Price. Cambridge: Cambridge University Press, 1988.

Machiavelli, *Lettere.* In Niccolò Macchiavelli, *Opere,* ed. Alessandro Montevecchi, vol. 3, *Lettere,* ed. Franco Gaeta. Turin: UTET, 1984. English translation: *Machiavelli and His Friends: Their Personal Correspondence,* tr. James B. Atkinson and David Sices. Dekalb: Northern Illinois University Press, 1996. (Abbreviated as Atkinson-Sices.)

Machiavelli, *FH.* Niccolò Machiavelli. *Istorie fiorentine.* In *Opere storiche,* ed. Alessandro Montevecchi and Carlo Varotti (1: books I–IV; 2: books V–VIII). 2 vols. Rome: Salerno, 2010 (Edizione nazionale delle opere di Niccolò Machiavelli II). English translation: *Florentine Histories,* tr. Laura F. Banfield and Harvey C. Mansfield Jr. Princeton: Princeton University Press, 1988. Also translated in Gilbert, *CW*, 3: 1034–1425.

Maio, *De maiestate.* Giuniano Maio. *De maiestate, inedito del sec. XV,* ed. Franco Gaeta. Bologna: Commissione per i testi di lingua, 1956.

Manetti, *Oratione.* Giannozzo Manetti. *Oratione . . . facta in Domenica, adì XXX di Septembre MCCCCLIII, quando e' dierono . . . il bastone . . . al . . . Gismondo de Pandolfo de' Malatesta.* In Donati 2010, 802–822.

Manutius, Aldus. *The Greek Classics,* ed. Nigel Wilson. Cambridge, MA: Harvard University Press, 2016. (ITRL 70.)

Manutius, Aldus. *Humanism and the Latin Classics,* ed. John N. Grant. Cambridge, MA: Harvard University Press. (ITRL 78.)

Marrasio, *Poems.* Marrasio Siculo. *Angelinetum and Other Poems,* tr. Mary P. Chatfield. Cambridge, MA: Harvard University Press, 2016. (ITRL 73.)

Marsi, Petrus. [*Commentary on Cicero's* De officiis.] Venice: Bernardinus Rizus and Bernardinus Celerius, 1484.

Marullus, Michael. *Poems,* tr. Charles Fantazzi. Cambridge, MA: Harvard University Press, 2012. (ITRL 54.)

Mill, *On Liberty.* John Stuart Mill. *On Liberty, with The Subjection of Women and Chapters on Socialism,* ed. Stefan Collini. Cambridge: Cambridge University Press, 1989.

More, *Utopia.* Thomas More. *Utopia,* ed. Edward Surtz, S.J., and J. H. Hexter. New Haven: Yale University Press, 1965. (Complete Works of St. Thomas More 4.)

Morosini, *On the Well-Ordered Republic.* Domenico Morosini. *De bene instituta republica,* ed. Claudio Vita-Finzi. Milan: Giuffré, 1969.

Morosini, *On the Venetian Republic*. Paolo Morosini. *De rebus et forma reipublicae Venetae*. In Valentinelli 1868–1873, 3: 231–264.

Mussato, *Ecerinis*. Albertano Mussato, *Ecerinis*. Edited and translated in Grund 2011, 2–47.

Nesi, Giovanni. *De moribus*. Unpublished. Cited from BLF, MS Plut. 77.24.

Pace, Richard. *De fructu qui ex doctrina percipitur*. Edited by Frank Manley and Richard S. Sylvester. New York: Ungar 1967. (Renaissance Society of America, Renaissance Text Series, 2.)

Palmieri, *Vita civile*. Matteo Palmieri. *Vita civile*, ed. Gino Belloni. Florence: Sansoni, 1982.

Patrizi, *De inst. r.p.* Francesco Patrizi of Siena, *De institutione reipublicae libri novem, historiarum sententiarum varietate refertissimi* [etc.]. (How to Found a Republic, in nine books stuffed with a variety of stories and maxims.) Paris: Galeottus Pratensis, 1534.

Patrizi, *De regno*. Francesco Patrizi of Siena. *De regno et regis institutione . . . ope vetustussimorum librorum manuscriptorum et cura ac diligentia doctorum quorundam virorum ab innumeris paene mendis perpurgati*. (How to Found a Kingdom and Educate a King . . . utterly purged of almost innumerable errors with the help of very old manuscripts and through the careful attention of certain learned men.) Paris: Aegidius Gorbinus, 1567. [Edited by Jean Charron, with a preface by Denys Lambin.]

Perotti, *Preface to Polybius*. Niccolò Perotti, [Dedicatory preface to Pope Nicholas V of his translation of Polybius' *Histories*.] In De Keyser 2016, 11–14.

Petrarch, *Africa*. Francesco Petrarch. *Africa*, tr. with a Latin text by Thomas G. Bergin and Alice S. Wilson. New Haven: Yale University Press, 1977.

Petrarch, *Arenga*. Francesco Petrarch, *Arengna facta per dominum Franciscum Petrarcham poetam laureatum in civitate Novarie coram populo eiusdem ciuitatem et presente magnifico domino Galeaz de Vicecomitibus de Mediolano dum dicta ciuitas fuisset rebellis ipsi domino reducta ad obedienciam dicti domini Galeaz MCCCLVI, XVIIII Junii*. In *Scritti inediti di Francesco Petrarca*, ed. Attilio Hortis, 341–358. Trieste: Tipografia dell Lloyd Austro-Ungarico, 1874.

Petrarch, *Collatio laureationis*. Francesco Petrarca. *La collatio laureationis: Manifesto dell' Umanesimo europeo*, ed. Giulio Cesare Maggi with Italian translation. Milano: La vita felice, 2012.

Petrarch, *De gestis Cesaris*. In Petrarch, *De viris illustribus*, ed. Ferrone, vol. 3.

Petrarch, *De otio religioso*, ed. Giulio Goletti. Florence: Le Lettere, 2006. English version: *Petrarch on Religious Leisure*, tr. Susan S. Scheurer, introd. Ronald G. Witt. New York: Italica Press, 2002.

Petrarch, *De viris illustribus*. Francesco Petrarca. *De viris illustribus*, ed. Silvano Ferrone, with Italian translation. 4 vols. Florence: Le Lettere, 2006–2012.

Petrarch, *DVS*. Francesco Petrarca. *De vita solitaria*, ed. K. A. E. Enenkel with commentary (book 1 only). Leiden: E. J. Brill, 1990. *De vita solitaria = La vie solitaire, 1346–66*, ed. Christophe Carraud (cited for book 2) with a French translation and commentary. Grenoble: Éditions Jérôme Millon, 1999. English translation: *The Life of Solitude*, tr. Jacob Zeitlin. Urbana: University of Illinois Press, 1924.

Petrarch, *Fam*. Francesco Petrarca. *Le familiari*, ed. Vittorio Rossi and Umberto Bosco. 4 vols. Florence: Sansoni, 1933–1942. English translations: *Selected Letters*, tr. Elaine Fantham. 2 vols. Cambridge, MA: Harvard University Press, 2016. *Letters on Familiar Matters*, tr. Aldo S. Bernardo. 3 vols. New York: Italica Press, 2005.

Petrarch, *Invectives*. Francesco Petrarch. *Invectives*, ed. and tr. David Marsh. Cambridge, MA: Harvard University Press, 2003. (ITRL 11.) Contains *On His Own Ignorance and that of Many Others* and *Invective against a Man of High Rank with No Virtue or Wisdom*.

Petrarch, *Metrical Epistles*. Francesco Petrarca. *Epistulae metricae: Briefe in Versen,* ed. with a German translation and notes by Otto and Eva Schönberger. Würzburg: Königshausen & Neumann, 2004.

Petrarch, *Rem*. Francesco Petrarch, *Les remèdes aux deux fortunes = De remediis utriusque fortune, 1354–1366,* ed. Christophe Carraud with a French translation and commentary. 2 vols. Grenoble: Éditions Jérôme Millon, 2002. English version: *Petrarch's Remedies for Fortune Fair and Foul,* tr. Conrad H. Rawski with commentary. 4 vols. Bloomington: Indiana University Press, 1991.

Petrarch, *Rime*. Francesco Petrarch. *Rime,* ed. Natalino Sapegno. In *Trionfi e poesie latine,* ed. Ferdinando Neri et al. Milan and Naples: Ricciardi, 1951.

Petrarch, *Secret*. Francesco Petrarch. *My Secret Book,* ed. Nicholas Mann. Cambridge, MA: Harvard University Press, 2016. (ITLR 72.)

Petrarch, *Sen*. Francesco Petrarch. *Res Seniles,* ed. Silvia Rizzo with Monica Berté. 4 vols. Florence: Le Lettere, 2006–2017. English translations: *Selected Letters,* tr. Elaine Fantham. 2 vols. Cambridge, MA: Harvard University Press, 2016. *Letters of Old Age,* tr. Aldo S. Bernardo, Saul Levin, and Reta A. Bernardo. Baltimore: Johns Hopkins University Press, 1992.

Petrarch, *Sine nomine*. Francesco Petrarch. *Liber sine nomine,* ed. with an Italian translation by Giovanni Cascio. Florence: Le Lettere, 2015. English translation: *Book without a Name,* tr. Norman P. Zacour. Toronto, CA: Pontifical Institute of Mediaeval Studies, 1973.

Petrarch, *Variae*. Francesco Petrarch. *Lettere disperse: Varie e miscellanee,* ed. Alessandro Pancheri. Parma: Fondazione Pietro Bembo, 1994.

Petrucci, *Epistole*. *Tra politica e cultura nel primo Quattrocento senese: Le epistole di Andreoccio Petrucci, 1426–1443,* ed. Petra Pertici. Siena: Accademia Senese degli Intronati, 1990. (Monografie di storia e letteratura senese 10.)

Piccolomini, *De liberorum educatione*. Enea Silvio Piccolomini [Pius II]. *De liberorum educatione.* In Kallendorf 2002, 126–259.

Piccolomini, *De ortu*. Enea Silvio Piccolomini [Pius II]. *De ortu et auctoritate imperii Romani.* In *Der Briefwechsel des Eneas Silvius Piccolomini,* ed. Rudolf Wolkan, in *Fontes rerum austriacarum,* vol. 62 (Vienna: A. Holder, 1912), 6–24. English translation in *Three Tracts on Empire: Engelbert of Admont, Aeneas Silvius Piccolomini, and Juan de Torquemada,* tr. Thomas M. Izbicki and Cary J. Nederman, 95–112. Bristol: Thoemmes Press, 2000.

Pius II. *Commentaries,* vol. 1, *Books I–II.* Edited by Margaret Meserve and Marcello Simonetta. Cambridge, MA: Harvard University Press, 2003. (ITRL 12.)

Platina, *De laudibus bonarum artium*. Bartolomeo Platina. *Oratio de laudibus bonarum artium.* In *Cremonensium monumenta Romae extantia,* ed. Tommaso Agostino Vairani, 109–118. Rome: Generosus Salomonius, 1778.

Platina, *De vera nobilitate*. In Bartolomeo Platina, *De vita et moribus summorum pontificum historia* [etc.]. Cologne: Gottfried Hittorp and Eucharius Cervicornius, 1529. Translation in Rabil 1991, 267–298.

Platina, *De principe*. Bartolomeo Platina. *De principe,* ed. Giacomo Ferraù. Palermo: Edizioni Il Vespro, 1979.

Plato, *Laws,* ed. Malcolm Schofield, tr. Tom Griffith. Cambridge: Cambridge University Press, 2016.

Pletho, *Opuscula de histora*. Georgius Gemistus Pletho, *Opuscula de historia graeca,* ed. Enrico V. Maltese. Leipzig: Teubner, 1989.

Poliziano, *Letters.* Angelo Poliziano. *Letters,* vol. 1, *Books I–IV,* ed. Shane Butler. Cambridge, MA: Harvard University Press, 2006. (ITRL 21.)

Pontano, *Aegidius.* Giovanni Gioviano Pontano. *Dialogues,* vol. 2, *Actius, Aegidius, Asinus,* ed. and tr. Julia Haig Gaisser. Cambridge MA: Harvard University Press, 2020. (ITRL 91.)

Pontano, *Antonius.* Giovanni Gioviano Pontano. *Dialogues,* vol. 1, *Charon and Antonius,* ed. and tr. Julia Haig Gaisser. Cambridge, MA: Harvard University Press, 2012. (ITRL 53.)

Pontano, *Carmina.* Giovanni Gioviano Pontano. *Carmina, ecloghe, elegie, liriche,* ed. Johannes Oeschger. Rome and Bari: Laterza, 1948. (Scrittori d'Italia 198.)

Pontano, *De principe.* Giovanni Gioviano Pontano. *De principe,* ed. Guido M. Cappelli. Rome: Salerno Editrice, 2003.

Pontano, *De sermone.* Giovanni Gioviano Pontano. *The Virtues and Vices of Speech,* ed. G. W. Pigman III. Cambridge, MA: Harvard University Press, 2019. (ITRL 87.)

Porcari, *Orazioni.* Stefano Porcari. *Orazioni.* In *Prose e rime de' due Buonaccorsi da Montemagno* [etc.], ed. Giuseppe Manni. Florence: Stamperia di Giuseppe Manni, 1718.

Porzio, *La congiura.* Camillo Porzio. *La congiura dei baroni del Regno di Napoli contro il re Ferdinando,* ed. Ernesto Pontieri. Naples: Edizioni scientifiche italiane, 1964.

Quirini, *De republica.* Lauro Quirini. *De republica libri II,* ed. Carlo Seno and Giorgio Ravegnani, in Branca et al. 1977, 123–161.

Ricci, *De Christiana expeditione.* Matteo Ricci. *De Christiana expeditione apud Sinas suscepta ab Societate Jesu, ex P. Matthaei Ricii eiusdem Societatis commentariis libri V.* Latin translation by Nicolas Trigault. Augsburg: Christophorus Mangius, 1615.

Rinuccini, *De libertate.* Alamanno Rinuccini. *La libertà perduta = Dialogus de libertate,* ed. Francesco Adorno. Italian translation by Giuseppe Civati. Monza: Vittone, 2002.

Rinuccini, *Preface to Apollonius of Tyana.* Alamanno Rinuccini. *Lettere ed orazioni,* ed. Vito R. Giustiniani. Florence: Leo S. Olschki, 1953. (Nuova collezione di testi umanistici inediti o rari 9.)

Sacchetti, *Trecentonovelle.* Franco Sacchetti. *Il trecentonovelle,* ed. Davide Puccini. Turin: UTET, 2004.

Salutati, *De tyranno.* Coluccio Salutati. *De tyranno.* In idem, *Political Writings,* ed. Stefano Ugo Baldassarri and Rolf Bagemihl, 64–143. Cambridge, MA: Harvard University Press, 2014. (ITRL 64.)

Salutati, *Reply to a Detractor.* Coluccio Salutati. *Reply to a Slanderous Detractor of Florence.* In *Political Writings,* as above, 174–395.

Savonarola, Michele, *De vera republica.* Unpublished. Cited from Modena, Biblioteca Estense, MS Est. lat. 114 (α W 6 6). Also called in the MS *De esse verae reipublicae* and *De vera republica et digna seculari militia.*

Scala, *Apologia.* Bartolomeo Scala. *Apologia contra vituperatores civitatis Florentiae.* In idem, *Essays and Dialogues,* tr. Renée Neu Watkins, 232–279. Cambridge, MA: Harvard University Press, 2008. (ITRL 31.)

Scala, *De legibus.* Bartolomeo Scala. *De legibus et iudiciis (On Laws and Courts),* tr. David Marsh. In *Essays and Dialogues,* as above, 158–231.

Traversari, *Epistolae.* Ambrogio Travesari. *Latinae Epistolae,* ed. Petrus Cannetus. Florence: Ex Typographio Caesareo, 1759. Reprint, Bologna: Forni, 1968.

Valeriano, *De litteratorum infelicitate*. In *Pierio Valeriano on the Ill Fortune of Learned Men: A Renaissance Humanist and His World,* tr. with introd. by Julia Haig Gaisser. Ann Arbor: University of Michigan Press, 1999.

Valla, Lorenzo. *Correspondence,* ed. and tr. Brendan Cook. Cambridge, MA: Harvard University Press, 2013. (ITRL 60.)

Valla, Lorenzo. *On the Donation of Constantine,* ed. and tr. Glenn W. Bowersock. Cambridge, MA: Harvard University Press, 2007. (ITRL 24.)

Valla, *Praefatio.* Lorenzo Valla. *In sex libros elegantiarum praefatio.* In *Prosatori latini del Quattrocento,* ed. Eugenio Garin, 594–600. Milan: Ricciardi, 1952.

Valturio, *De re militari.* Roberto Valturio. *De re militari libri XII, multo emaculatius ac picturis elegantioribus expressum.* Paris: Chrestien Wechel, 1535.

Vegio, Maffeo. *Short Epics,* tr. Michael C. J. Putnam with James Hankins. Cambridge, MA: Harvard University Press, 2004. (ITRL 15.)

Vergerio, *De ingenuis moribus.* Pier Paolo Vergerio the Elder. *De ingenuis moribus et liberalibus adulescentiae studiis liber.* In Kallendorf 2002, 2–91.

Vergerio, *De monarchia.* Pier Paolo Vergerio the Elder. *De monarchia sive de optimo principatu (1399).* In Vergerio, *Epistolario,* ed. Smith, 447–450.

Vergerio, *De republica veneta.* Pier Paolo Vergerio the Elder. *De republica veneta.* In Robey and Law 1975, 38–49. Partial translation by Ronald G. Witt in Kraye 1997, 117–127.

Vergerio, *Epistolario.* Pier Paolo Vergerio the Elder. *Epistolario,* ed. Leonardo Smith. Rome: Istituto storico per il Medio Evo, 1934. (Fonti per la storia d'Italia 74.)

Vergil, *On Discovery.* Polydor Vergil. *On Discovery (De inventoribus rerum),* ed. Brian P. Copenhaver. Cambridge, MA: Harvard University Press, 2002. (ITRL 6.)

Verino, *Carlias.* Ugolino Verino. *Carlias: Ein Epos des 15. Jahrhunderts,* ed. Nikolaus Thurn. Munich: Fink, 1995.

Villani, *Cronica.* Giovanni Villani. *Nuova cronica,* ed. Giuseppe Porta. 3 vols. Parma: Fondazione Pietro Bembo, 1990.

SECONDARY LITERATURE

Adam, Rudolf Georg. 1974. "Francesco Filelfo at the Court of Milan, 1439–1481: A Contribution to the Study of Humanism in Northern Italy." Ph.D. diss., University of Oxford.

Africa, Thomas W. 1979. "Thomas More and the Spartan Mirage." *Historical Reflections / Réflexions Historiques* 6(2): 343–52.

Ahrensdorf, Peter J. 1997. "Thucydides' Realistic Critique of Realism," *Polity* 30(2): 231–265.

Ainley, Kirsten. 2017. "Virtue Ethics." In the *Oxford Research Encyclopedia of International Studies.* DOI: 10.1093 / acrefore / 9780190846626.013.107.

Albanese, Massimiliano. 2012. "Pio II nel Momus di Leon Battista Alberti, datazione e dedicatorio dell'opera." *RR, Roma nel Rinascimento,* 159–179.

Allmand, Christopher, ed. 1998. *The New Cambridge Medieval History.* Cambridge: Cambridge University Press.

Ando, Clifford. 2000. *Imperial Ideology and Provincial Loyalty in the Roman Empire.* Berkeley: University of California Press.

Anglo, Sidney. 2005. *Machiavelli: The First Century; Studies in Enthusiasm, Hostility, and Irrelevance.* Oxford: Oxford University Press.

Annas, Julia. 2011. *Intelligent Virtue.* New York: Oxford University Press.

———. 2017. *Virtue and Law in Plato and Beyond.* Oxford: Oxford University Press.

Anselmi, Gian Mario. 1979. *Ricerche sul Machiavelli storico.* Pisa: Pacini.

Appiah, Kwame Anthony. 2006. *Cosmopolitanism: Ethics in a World of Strangers.* New York: W. W. Norton.

———. 2010. *The Honor Code: How Moral Revolutions Happen.* New York: W. W. Norton.

Armstrong, Guyda, Rhiannon Daniels, and Stephen E. Milner. 2015. "Boccaccio as Cultural Mediator." In *The Cambridge Companion to Boccaccio,* edited by Guyda Armstrong, Rhiannon Daniels, and Stephen E. Milner, 3–19. Cambridge: Cambridge University Press.

Ascheri, Mario. 1986. "Siena nel primo quattrocento: Un sistema politico fra storia e storiografia." In *Siena e il suo territorio nel Rinascimento: Renaissance Siena and Its Territory,* vol. 1, edited by Mario Ascheri and Donatella Ciampoli, 1–53. Sicna: Il Leccio.

Ascoli, Albert R. 2011. "Petrarch's Private Politics: *Rerum Familiarium Libri.*" In *A Local Habitation and a Name: Imagining Histories in the Italian Renaissance,* by Albert R. Ascoli, 118–158. New York: Fordham University Press.

Atkins, Jed W. 2013. *Cicero on Politics and the Limits of Reason: The* Republic *and* Laws. Cambridge: Cambridge University Press.

Badian, Ernst. 2014. "Julius Caesar." In *The Oxford Companion to Classical Civilization,* ed. Simon Hornblower, Anthony Spawforth, and Esther Eidinow. http://oxfordreference.com.

Bai, Tongdong. 2012. *China: The Political Philosophy of the Middle Kingdom.* London: Zed Books.

Bainton, Roland H. 1969. *Erasmus of Christendom.* New York: Scribner.

Baker, Patrick. 2015. *Italian Renaissance Humanism in the Mirror.* Cambridge: Cambridge University Press.

Baldassarri, Stefano U. 2018. "La *Oratio de Nobilitate rei publicae florentinae* di Mario Salamoni degli Alberteschi." *Rivista di letteratura storiografica italiana* 2: 79–100.

Balmaceda, Catalina. 2017. *Virtus Romana: Politics and Morality in the Roman Historians.* Chapel Hill: University of North Carolina Press.

Balot, Ryan, ed. 2009. *A Companion to Greek and Roman Political Thought.* West Sussex, UK: Wiley-Blackwell.

Barnes, Jonathan. 2005. "Aristotle and Political Liberty." In *Aristotle's Politics: Critical Essays,* edited by Richard Kraut and Steven Sculety, 185–202. Lanham, MD: Rowman and Littlefield.

Baron, Hans. 1938. "Franciscan Poverty and Civic Wealth as Factors in the Rise of Humanistic Thought." *Speculum* 13: 1–37.

———. 1955, 1966. *The Crisis of the Early Italian Renaissance: Civic Humanism and Republican Liberty in an Age of Classicism and Tyranny.* 2 vols. Princeton: Princeton University Press. Revised edition in one volume, Princeton: Princeton University Press, 1966.

———. 1988. *In Search of Florentine Civic Humanism: Essays on the Transition from Medieval to Modern Thought.* 2 vols. Princeton: Princeton University Press.

Battaglia, Felice. 1935. "Il trattato *De republica* di Tito Livio Frulovisi." *Rivista internazionale di filosofia del diritto* 15: 487–505.

Bausi, Francesco. 2005. *Machiavelli.* Roma: Salerno Editrice.

——. 2009. "La *mutatio vitae* di Poggio Bracciolini: Ricerche sul *De avaritia.*" *Interpres* 28: 7–69.

——. 2016. "Povero Machiavelli fra grammatici e pederasti (per non parlar degli storici)." *Interpres* 34: 286–314.

Baxandall, Michael. 1971. *Giotto and the Orators: Humanist Observers of Painting in Italy and the Discovery of Pictorial Composition, 1350–1450.* Oxford: Oxford University Press.

Bayley, Charles Calvert. 1942. "Petrarch, Charles IV, and the *Renovatio Imperii.*" *Speculum* 17(3): 323–341.

——. 1961. *War and Society in Renaissance Florence: The* De militia *of Leonardo Bruni.* Toronto: University of Toronto Press.

Bec, Christian. 1967. *Les marchands ecrivains: Affaires et humanisme à Florence, 1375–1434.* Paris: Mouton.

Beck, Hans, ed. 2013. *A Companion to Ancient Greek Government.* Chichester, UK: Wiley-Blackwell.

Bejczy, István. 1994. "The State as a Work of Art: Petrarch and His *Speculum principis* (*sen.* XIV, 1)." *History of Political Thought* 15(3): 313–321.

Bejczy, István, and Cary J. Nederman, eds. 2007. *Princely Virtues in the Middle Ages, 1200–1500.* Turnhout: Brepols.

Bell, Daniel A. 2015. *The China Model: Political Meritocracy and the Limits of Democracy.* Princeton: Princeton University Press.

——. 2016. "Political Legitimacy in China: A Confucian Approach." In *East Asian Perspectives on Political Legitimacy: Bridging the Empirical-Normative Divide,* edited by Joseph Chan, Doh Chull Shin, and Melissa S. Williams, 78–106. Cambridge: Cambridge University Press.

Bell, Daniel A., and Chengyang Li, eds. 2013. *The East Asian Challenge for Democracy: Political Meritocracy in Comparative Perspective.* Cambridge: Cambridge University Press.

Berlin, Isaiah. 1972. "The Originality of Machiavelli." In *Studies on Machiavelli,* edited by Myron Gilmore, 149–206. Florence: Sansoni. (An extended version of this paper is available online via the Isaiah Berlin Virtual Library, at berlin.wolf.ox.ac.uk.)

Bernardo, Aldo S. 1980. "Petrarch on the Education of a Prince: *Familiares* 12.2." *Medievalia* 6: 135–150.

Bertelli, Sergio. 1964. Untitled review of Bayley 1961. *Rivista storica italiana* 76(3): 834–836.

Bertelli, Sergio, Nicolai Rubinstein, and Craig Hugh Smyth, eds. 1979–1980. *Florence and Venice: Comparisons and Relations; Acts of Two Conferences at Villa I Tatti in 1976–1977.* 2 vols. Florence: La Nuova Italia.

Bertolini, Lucia. 2004. "Come 'pubblicava' l'Alberti: Ipotesi preliminari." In *Storia della lingua e filologia: Per Alfredo Stussi nel suo sessantacinquesimo compleano,* edited by Michelangelo Zaccarello and Lorenzo Tomasin, 219–240. Florence: SISMEL, Edizioni del Galuzzo.

Berve, Helmut. 1962. *Die Tyrannis bei den Griechen.* 2 vols. Munich: Beck.

Bessi, Rosella. 1990. "Un traduttore al lavoro: Donato Acciaiuoli e l'elaborazione del volgarizzamento delle *Historiae.*" In Viti 1990, 321–338.

Bevagni, Claudio. 1994. "Appunti sulle traduzioni latine dei *Moralia* di Plutarcho nel Quattrocento." *Studi umanistici piceni* 14: 71–84.

Biasiori, Lucio. 2017. *Nello scrittoio di Machiavelli:* Il Principe *e la* Ciropedia *di Senofonte.* Rome: Carocci.

Bigalli, Davide. 2002. "Petrarca: Dal sentimento alla dottrina politica." In *Motivi e forme delle Familiari di Francesco Petrarca: Gargano del Garda, 2–5 ottobre 2002,* edited by Claudia Berra, 99–118. Milan: Cisalpino.

Bireley, Robert. 1990. *The Counter-Reformation Prince: Anti-Machiavellianism or Catholic Statecraft in Early Modern Europe.* Chapel Hill: University of North Carolina Press.

Black, Anthony. 1992. *Political Thought in Europe, 1250–1450.* Cambridge: Cambridge University Press.

Black, Jane. 2009. *Absolutism in Renaissance Milan: Plenitude of Power under the Visconti, 1329–1535.* Oxford: Oxford University Press.

———. 2015. "Medici and Sforza: Breeds Apart?" In Black and Law 2015, 85–99.

Black, Robert. 1985. *Benedetto Accolti and the Florentine Renaissance.* Cambridge: Cambridge University Press.

———. 1986. "The Political Thought of the Florentine Chancellors." *Historical Journal* 29: 991–1003.

———. 1998. "Humanism." In *The Cambridge Medieval History,* vol. 7, *c. 1415–c. 1500,* edited by Christopher Allmand, 243–277. Cambridge: Cambridge University Press.

———. 2001. *Humanism and Education in Medieval and Renaissance Italy: Tradition and Innovation in Latin Schools from the Twelfth to the Fifteenth Century.* Cambridge: Cambridge University Press.

———. 2006. "Republicanism." In *L'Italia alla fine del medioevo: I caratteri originali nel quadro europeo,* vol. 2, ed. Federica Cengarle, 1–20. Florence: Firenze University Press.

———. 2007. *Education and Society in Florentine Tuscany.* Leiden: E. J. Brill.

———. 2010. "Communes and Despots: Some Italian and Transalpine Political Thinkers." In Law and Paton 2010, 49–59.

———. 2011a. *Studies in Renaissance Humanism and Politics.* Farnham, UK: Ashgate Variorum.

———. 2011b. "The Donation of Constantine: A New Source for the Concept of the Renaissance?" In Black 2011a, essay 2.

———. 2013. *Machiavelli.* London: Routledge.

———. 2015. "The School of San Lorenzo, Niccolò Machiavelli, Paolo Sassi, and Benedetto Riccardini." In Frazier and Nold 2015, 107–133.

Black, Robert, and John E. Law. 2015. *The Medici: Citizens and Masters.* Florence: Villa I Tatti. Harvard University Center for Italian Renaissance Studies.

Blythe, James M. 1992. *Ideal Government and the Mixed Constitution in the Middle Ages.* Princeton: Princeton University Press.

———. 2000. "'Civic Humanism' and Medieval Political Thought." In Hankins 2000a, 30–74.

———. 2009. *The Worldview and Thought of Tolomeo Fiadoni (Ptolemy of Lucca).* Turnhout: Brepols.

Bobonich, Christopher. 2010. *Plato's Laws: A Critical Guide.* Cambridge: Cambridge University Press.

Bock, Gisela, Quentin Skinner, and Maurizio Viroli. 1990. *Machiavelli and Republicanism.* Cambridge: Cambridge University Press.

Bodde, Derk, and Clarence Morris. 1967. *Law in Imperial China: Exemplified by 190 Ch'ing Dynasty Cases with Historical, Social, and Juridical Commentaries.* Cambridge, MA: Harvard University Press.

Bod, Rens. 2013. *A New History of the Humanities: The Search for Principles and Patterns from Antiquity to the Present.* Oxford: Oxford University Press.

Boesche, Roger. 1996. *Theories of Tyranny from Plato to Arendt.* University Park: Pennsylvania State University Press.

Bol, Peter K. 2008. *Neo-Confucianism in History.* Cambridge, MA: Harvard University Press.

———. 2018. "The Literati, Talent, and Virtue in the Middle Period." Unpublished paper from the conference *Political Meritocracy in Comparative Historical Perspective,* Harvard University, November 1–2.

Böninger, Lorenz. 1995. *Die Ritterwürde in Mittelitalien zwischen Mittelalter und Früher Neuzeit.* Berlin: Akademie Verlag.

Bos, Jacques. 2018. "Renaissance Historicism and the Model of Rome in Florentine Historiography." In Velema and Weststeijn 2018, 20–39.

Boschetto, Luca. 1991. "Note sul *De iciarchia* di Leon Battista Alberti." *Rinascimento,* n.s., 31: 163–217.

———. 1993. "Ricerche sul *Theogenius* e sul *Momus* di Leon Battista Alberti." *Rinascimento,* n.s., 33: 3–52.

———. 2000a. "Tra politica e letteratura: Appunti sui *Profugiorum libri* e la cultura di Firenze negli anni '40." *Albertiana* 3: 119–40.

———. 2000b. *Leon Battista Alberti e Firenze: Biografia, storia, letteratura.* Florence: Leo S. Olschki.

———. 2012. "Les humanistes et le portrait d'Eugène IV." In *Humanistes, clercs e laïcs dans l'Italie du XIIIe au début du XVIe siècle,* ed. Cecile Caby and Rosa Maria Dessì, 297–318. Turnhout: Brepols.

Botley, Paul. 2004. *Latin Translation in the Renaissance: The Theory and Practice of Leonardo Bruni, Giannozzo Manetti, and Desiderius Erasmus.* Cambridge: Cambridge University Press.

Bots, Hans, and Françoise Waquet. 1997. *La République des Lettres.* Paris and Berlin: De Boeck, 1997. Italian translation: *La repubblica delle lettere.* Bologna: Il Mulino.

Boucher, David. 1998. *Political Theories of International Relations.* Oxford: Oxford University Press.

Bouwsma, William. 1990. "Venice and the Political Education of Europe." In *A Usable Past: Essays in European Cultural History,* by William Bouwsma, 266–291. Berkeley: University of California Press.

Bradshaw, Brendan, and Eamon Duffy, eds. 1989. *Humanism, Reform, and the Reformation: The Career of Bishop John Fisher.* Cambridge: Cambridge University Press.

Brague, Rémi. 2007. *The Law of God: The Philosophical History of an Idea.* Chicago: University of Chicago Press.

Branca, Vittore. (1956) 1996. *Boccaccio medievale e nuovi studi sul Decameron.* 2nd ed. Florence: Sansoni.

Branca, Vittore, et al., eds. 1977. *Lauro Quirini umanista.* Florence: Leo S. Olschki.

Brett, Annabel, and James Tully, eds. 2006. *Rethinking the Foundations of Modern Political Thought.* Cambridge: Cambridge University Press.

Brown, Alison. 1979. *Bartolomeo Scala, 1430–1497, Chancellor of Florence.* Princeton: Princeton University Press.

———. 1992. "The Guelf Party in Fifteenth Century Florence." In *The Medici in Florence: The Language and Exercise of Power,* by Alison Brown, 103–150. Florence: Leo S. Olschki; Perth: University of Western Australia Press.

———. 2000. "The Language of Empire." In *Florentine Tuscany: Structures and Practices of Power,* edited by William J. Connell and Andrea Zorzi, 32–47. Cambridge: Cambridge University Press.

———. 2010a. *The Return of Lucretius to Renaissance Florence.* Cambridge, MA: Harvard University Press.

———. 2010b. "Philosophy and Religion in Machiavelli." In Najemy 2010, 157–172.

Brown, Eric. 2009. "False Idles: The Politics of the Quiet Life." In Balot 2009, 485–500.

Brown, Garrett Wallace, and David Held, eds. 2010. *The Cosmopolitan Reader.* Cambridge: Polity Press.

Brown, Peter. 1997. *Authority and the Sacred: Aspects of the Christianization of the Roman World.* Cambridge: Cambridge University Press.

Brucker, Gene A. 1962. *Florentine Politics and Society, 1343–1378.* Princeton: Princeton University Press.

———. 1977. *The Civic World of Early Renaissance Florence.* Princeton: Princeton University Press.

Brundage, James. 1987. "Sumptuary Laws and Prostitution in Late Medieval Italy." *Journal of Medieval History* 13: 343–355.

Brunt, P. A. 1977. "Lex de imperio Vespasiani." *Journal of Roman Studies* 67: 95–116.

Bui, Ngoc Son. 2016. *Confucian Constitutionalism in East Asia.* London: Routledge.

Burckhardt, Jacob. 1958. *The Civilization of the Renaissance in Italy,* tr. Samuel G. C. Middlemore. 2 vols. New York: Harper and Row.

Burd, L. Arthur. 1897. "Le fonti letterarie di Machiavelli nell' *Arte della Guerra.*" *Atti della R. Accademia dei Lincei, Classe di scienze morali, storiche e filologiche,* ser. 5, 4(1): 187–261.

Burnell, Peter. 1995. "The Problem of Service to Unjust Regimes in Augustine's *City of God.*" In *The City of God: A Collection of Critical Essays,* ed. Dorothy F. Donnelly, 37–49. New York: Peter Lang.

Burns, J. H., ed. 1988. *The Cambridge History of Medieval Political Thought, c. 350–c. 1450.* Cambridge: Cambridge University Press.

Burns, J. H., with Mark Goldie, eds. 1991. *The Cambridge History of Political Thought, 1450–1700.* Cambridge: Cambridge University Press.

Burnyeat, Miles, and Michael Frede. 2015. *The Pseudo-Platonic Seventh Letter.* Edited by Dominic Scott. Oxford: Oxford University Press.

Cabrini, Anna Maria. 1990. "Le *Historiae* del Bruni: Risultati e ipotesi di una ricerca sulle fonti." In Viti 1990, 247–319.

Campanelli, Maurizio, and Frances Muecke, eds. 2017. *The Invention of Rome: Biondo Flavio's* Roma triumphans *and Its Worlds.* Geneva: Droz. (Travaux d'humanisme et Renaissance 576.)

Campi, Alessandro, and Stefano De Luca. 2014. *Il realismo politico: Figure, concetti, prospettive di ricerca.* Soverio Mannelli: Rubbettino, 2014.

Canfora, Luciano. 1997. "Tucidide e Machiavelli." *Rinascimento,* n.s., 37: 29–44.

Canfora, Davide. 2001. *La controversia di Poggio Bracciolini e Guarino Veronese su Cesare e Scipione.* Florence: Leo S. Olschki.

———. 2005. *Prima di Machiavelli: Politica e cultura in età umanistica.* Rome: Laterza.

————. 2007. "Leon Battista Alberti: Modello di letteratura politica in età umanistica." In *Alberti e la cultura del Quattrocento: Atti del Convegno internazionale del Comitato Nazionale VI centenario della nascita di Leon Battista Alberti, Firenze, 16–17 dicembre 2004,* edited by Roberto Cardini and Mariangela Regoliosi, 699–717. Florence: Edizioni Polistampa, 2007.

Canning, Joseph. 1987. *The Political Thought of Baldus de Ubaldis.* Cambridge: Cambridge University Press.

————. 1996. *A History of Medieval Political Thought.* London: Routledge.

Cao, Gian Mario. 1997. "Tra politica fiorentina e filosofia ellenistica: Il dibattito sulla ricchezza nelle *Commentationes* di Francesco Filelfo." *Archivio storico italiano* 155: 99–126.

Cappelli, Guido. 2008. "Sapere e potere: L'umanista e il principe nell'Italia del Quattrocento." *Cuadernos de filología italiana* 15: 73–91.

————. 2009. "Conceptos transversales: República y monarquía en el Humanismo político." *Res publica. Revista de Filosofía política* 21: 51–69.

————. 2010a. "Prolegomena al *De obedientia* di Pontano." *Rinascimento meridionale* 1: 47–70.

————. 2010b. "Aristotele veneziano: Il *De republica* di Lauro Quirini e la tradizione politica classica. *Parole rubate / Purloined Letters* 1 (online journal). www.parolerubate.unipr.it.

————. 2010c. "Debutto napoletano: Un'ignota orazione ufficiale di Ermolao Barbaro." *Humanistica: An International Journal of Early Renaissance Studies* 5(1): 111–124.

————. 2011a. "Vida y muerte del humanismo político." *Claves de Razón práctica* 212: 40–47.

————. 2011b. "*Exemplar mundi*: El príncipe renacentista como espejo del mundo." *Despalabro: Ensayos de humanidades* 5: 129–37.

————. 2012. "Umanesimo politico: La monarchia organicista nel IV libro del *De obedientia* di Giovanni Pontano." *California Italian Studies* 3(1): 1–20. http://escholarship.org/uc/item /6ct9b8w1.

————. 2014a. "Il castigo del re: Bartolo, Pontano e il problema della disubbidienza." In *Bartolo da Sassoferrato e il pensiero giuridico e politico tra Medioevo e Rinascimento,* edited by Giancarlo Abbamonte. Special issue of *Studi umanistici piceni* 34: 91–104.

————. 2014b. "La realtà fatta dottrina: Sarno e dintorni nel pensiero politico aragonese." *Bullettino dell'Istituto storico italiano per il Medio Evo* 116: 91–104.

————. 2016a. "*Italia tota est plena tyrannis*: Petrarca e l'Impero alla luce della teoria giuridico-politica." In *Petrarca politico,* edited by Francesco Furlan and Stefano Pittaluga, 9–25. Milan: Ledizioni.

————. 2016b. *Maiestas: Politica e pensiero politico nella Napoli aragonese, 1443–1503.* Naples: Carocci.

————. 2016c. "E tutto il resto è dottrina: Sangue e virtù nella caratterizzazione dottrinale di Alfonso." In *L'immagine di Alfonso il Magnanimo tra letteratura e storia, tra Corona d'Aragona e Italia,* edited by Fulvio Delle Donne and Jaume Torró Torrent. Florence: SISMEL, Edizioni del Galluzzo, 2016.

————. 2017a. "Prima di Machiavelli? Fisionomia (e autonomia) dell' umanesimo politico." In *El conflicto y el consenso: Reflexiones de filosofía política sobre* El Príncipe *de Maquiavelo,* edited by Guido Cappelli and Juan Varela-Portas. Special issue of *Res publica: Revista de historia de las ideas políticas* 20(1): 81–92.

————. 2017b. "*Maiorum imagines*: Politica e visione nel pensiero del Rinascimento." *Engramma* 150 (online journal). http://www.engramma.it/eOS/index.php?id_articolo=3232.

———. 2017c. "Una modernità (im)possibile: L'umanesimo italiano come fenomeno storico." *Quaderns d'Italià* 22: 21–38.

———. 2017d. "La *fides* di Machiavelli tra volgare e dottrina umanistica." In *Problematizing 'Il principe,'* edited by Mario Barbuto, 183–198. Barcelona: Edicions de la Universitat de Barcelona.

———. 2017e. "*Voltare la reputazione:* Machiavelli 'populista' e altre variazioni su *Principe* IX." *L'Illuminista: Revista di cultura contemporanea* 17(49–51): 45–72.

———. n.d. "Lo stato umanistico: Organicismo e Umanesimo politico del Quattrocento." Conference paper downloaded from Cappelli's page on academia.edu.

Capponi, Gino. 1876. *Storia della Repubblica di Firenze.* 3 vols. Florence: G. Barbèra.

Capponi, Niccolò. 2010. *An Unlikely Prince: The Life and Times of Machiavelli.* Cambridge, MA: Da Capo Press.

Carlyle, R. W., and Alexander James Carlyle. 1950. *A History of Mediaeval Political Theory in the West.* 6 vols. New York: Barnes and Noble.

Cartledge, Paul. 2001. *Spartan Reflections.* Berkeley: University of California Press.

———. 2002. *Sparta and Laconia: A Regional History, 1300 to 362 BC.* 2nd ed. London: Routledge.

———. 2006. "Spartan Traditions and Receptions." *Hermathena* 181 (Winter): 41–49.

Cartledge, Paul, and Anthony J. S. Spawforth. 2002. *Hellenistic and Roman Sparta.* London: Routledge.

Cassani, Alberto Giorgio. 1996. "*Tabulae civitatis:* Il governo della città secondo Leon Battista Alberti." In *Forme della città,* edited by Marco Biragi et al. Special number of *Paradosso: Quadrimestrale di filosofia,* n.s., 1: 113–121.

Catanorchi, Olivia. 2005. "Tra politica e passione: Simulazione e dissimulazione in Leon Battista Alberti." *Rinascimento,* n.s., 45: 137–177.

———. 2012. "Leon Battista Alberti." In *Il Contributo italiano alla storia del pensiero: Filosofia, Ottava appendice.* Rome: Treccani (online at treccani.it).

Celati, Marta. 2019. "Ironia, storiografia, critica politica: La *Porcaria coniuratio* di Alberti." Proceedings of the conference *Alberti Ludens: In Memory of Cecil Grayson,* to be published in the journal *Albertiana* 22(4).

Celenza, Christopher S. 1999. *Renaissance Humanism and the Papal Curia: Lapo da Castiglionchio the Younger's* De curiae commodis. Ann Arbor: University of Michigan Press.

———. 2004. *The Lost Italian Renaissance: Humanists, Historians, and Latin's Legacy.* Baltimore: Johns Hopkins University Press.

———. 2015. *Machiavelli: A Portrait.* Cambridge, MA: Harvard University Press.

———. 2017. *Petrarch: Everywhere a Wanderer.* London: Reaktion Books.

———. 2018. *The Intellectual World of the Italian Renaissance: Language, Philosophy, and the Search for Meaning.* Cambridge: Cambridge University Press.

Chaffee, John W., and Denis Twitchett. 2015. *The Cambridge History of China,* vol. 5, Part Two: *Sung China, 960–1279.* Cambridge: Cambridge University Press.

Chambers, David Sanderson. 1970. *The Imperial Age of Venice, 1380–1580.* London: Thames and Hudson.

Chan, Joseph. 2000. "Legitimacy, Unanimity, and Perfectionism." *Philosophy and Public Affairs* 29(1): 5–42.

———. 2014. *Confucian Perfectionism: A Political Philosophy for Modern Times.* Princeton: Princeton University Press.

Chiecchi, Giuseppe. 1979. "La lettera a Pino de' Rossi: Appunti cronologici, osservazioni e fonti." *Studi sul Boccaccio* 11: 295–331.

Cipriani, Giovanni. 1975. "Il mito etrusco nella Firenze repubblicana e medicea nei secoli XV e XVI." *Ricerche Storiche* 5(2): 257–309.

———. 1980. *Il mito etrusco nel Rinascimento fiorentino.* Florence: Leo S. Olschki.

Clarke, Michelle T. 2018. *Machiavelli's Florentine Republic.* Cambridge: Cambridge University Press.

Coady, C. A. J. 2018. "The Problem of Dirty Hands." In *SEP.*

Cochrane, Eric. 1981. *Historians and Historiography in the Italian Renaissance.* Chicago: University of Chicago Press.

Colish, Marcia. 1998. "Machiavelli's *Art of War:* A Reconsideration." *Renaissance Quarterly* 51: 1151–1168.

———. 1999. "Republicanism, Religion, and Machiavelli's Savonarolan Moment." *Journal of the History of Ideas* 60(4): 597–616.

Connell, William J. 2015. *Machiavelli nel Rinascimento italiano.* Milan: FrancoAngeli.

Connell, William J., and Andrea Zorzi, eds. 2000. *Florentine Tuscany: Structures and Practices of Power.* Cambridge: Cambridge University Press.

Connolly, William E. 1993. *The Terms of Political Discourse.* 3rd ed. Oxford: Blackwell.

Cooper, John M. 2005. "Political Animals and Civic Friendship." In Kraut and Skultety 2005, 65–89.

———. 2012. *Pursuits of Virtue: Six Ways of Life in Ancient Philosophy from Socrates to Plotinus.* Princeton: Princeton University Press.

Cosenza, Mario, and Ronald Musto. 1996. *Petrarch: The Revolution of Cola di Rienzi.* 3rd ed. with new introduction, notes, and bibliography by Ronald G. Musto. New York: Italica Press.

Costa, Pietro. 1999. *Civitas: Storia della cittadinanza in Europa,* vol. 1, *Dalla civiltà comunale al Settecento.* Rome: Laterza.

Couzinet, Marie-Dominique. 2001. "Sources antiques de l'irréligion moderne chez Machiavelli: Crise religieuse et imitation des Anciens." In *Sources antiques de l'irréligion moderne: Le Relais italien, XVIe–XVIIe siècles,* edited by Jean-Pierre Cavaillé and Didier Foucault, 47–67. Toulouse: Presses Universitaires du Mirail.

Cox, Virginia. 1999. "Ciceronian Rhetoric in Italy, 1260–1350." *Rhetorica* 17(3): 239–288.

Cutinelli Rèndina, Emanuele. 1998. *Chiesa e religione in Machiavelli.* Pisa: Istituti editoriali e poligrafici internazionale.

D'Addio, Mario. 1954. *L'idea del contratto sociale dai sofisti alla riforma e il De principatu di Mario Salamonio.* Milan: A. Giuffré.

———. 1955. *Marii Salamonii de Alberteschis: De principatu libri septem nec non Orationes ad priores Florentinos.* Milan: A. Giuffré.

Dandelet, Thomas. 2014. *The Renaissance of Empire in Early Modern Europe.* New York: Cambridge University Press.

Davies, Jonathan. 1998. *Florence and Its University during the Early Renaissance.* Leiden: E. J. Brill.

Davis, Charles Till. 1957. *Dante and the Idea of Rome.* Oxford: Clarendon Press.

De Angelis, Laura. 1990. "La revisione degli statuti della Parte Guelfa del 1420." In Viti 1990, 131–156.

De Capua, Paola. 2014. *Le lettere di Francesco Patrizi*. Messina: Centro internazionale di studi umanistici.

De Grazia, Sebastiano. 1989. *Machiavelli in Hell*. New York: Harvester Wheatsheaf.

De Keyser, Jeroen. 2006–2007. "Per la *Respublica Lacedaemoniorum* e *l'Agesilaus* di Francesco Filelfo." *Sandalion* 29–30: 187–213.

———. 2013. "The Descendents of Petrarch's *Pro Archia*." *Classical Quarterly* 63(1): 282–328.

———. 2016. "Polybius." *CTC* 11: 1–60.

De la Mare, Albinia C. 1985. "New Research on Humanistic Scribes in Florence." In *Miniatura fiorentina del Rinascimento: 1440–1525; Un primo censimento*, vol. 1, by Annarosa Garzelli, 395–600. Florence: La nuova Italia.

———. 2009. *Bartolomeo Sanvito: The Life and Works of a Renaissance Scribe*. Paris: Association nationale de bibliophile.

Delbianco, Paola, ed. 2006. *Roberto Valturio, De re militari: Umanesimo e arte della guerra tra Medioevo e Rinascimento, Saggi critici*. Rimini: Guaraldi; Milan: Y Press.

D'Elia, Anthony F. 2004. *The Renaissance of Marriage in Fifteenth Century Italy*. Cambridge, MA: Harvard University Press.

———. 2009. *A Sudden Terror: The Plot to Murder the Pope in Renaissance Rome*. Cambridge, MA: Harvard University Press.

———. 2016. *Pagan Virtue in a Christian World: Sigismondo Malatesta and the Italian Renaissance*. Cambridge, MA: Harvard University Press.

DellaNeva, Joann, ed. 2007. *Ciceronian Controversies*. Translated by Brian Duvick. Cambridge, MA: Harvard University Press. (ITRL 26.)

Delle Donne, Fulvio. 2015. *Alfonso il Magnanimo e l'invenzione dell'umanesimo monarchico: Ideologia e strategie di legittimazione alla corte aragonese di Napoli*. Rome: Istituto storico italiano per il Medio Evo.

Desideri, Saverio. 1958. *La "Institutio Traiani."* Genua: Istituto di filologia classica.

Dewald, Carolyn. 2003. "Form and Content: The Question of Tyranny in Herodotus." In *Popular Tyranny*, edited by Kathryn A. Morgan, 25–58. Austin: University of Texas Press.

Dionisotti, Carlo. 1974. "Fortuna del Petrarca nel Quattrocento." *Italia medievale e umanistica* 17: 92–94.

———. 1980. Carlo Dionisotti. *Machiavellerie*. Turin: Einaudi.

———. 1984. "Chierici e laici." *Geografia e storia della letteratura italiana*. Turin: Einaudi.

Donaldson, Peter S. 1989. *Machiavelli and Mystery of State*. Cambridge: Cambridge University Press.

Donati, Andrea. 2010. "L'immagine vittoriosa di Sigismondo Pandolfo Malatesta e l'orazione di Giannozzo Manetti per la consegna del bastone di comando dell'esercito fiorentino (Vada, 30 settembre 1453)." *Studi Romagnoli* 61: 773–840.

Dotti, Ugo. 2001. *Petrarca civile. Alle origini dell'intellettuale moderno*. Rome: Donzelli Editore.

———. 2003. *Machiavelli rivoluzionario: Vita e opere*. Rome: Carocci.

———. 2004. *Vita di Petrarca*. Rome-Bari: Laterza.

Dunn, John. (1979) 1993. *Western Political Theory in the Face of the Future*. 2nd ed. Cambridge: Cambridge University Press.

Eisner, Martin, and David Lummus, eds. 2019. *A Boccaccian Renaissance*. Notre Dame, IN: University of Notre Dame Press.

Ercole, Francesco. 1910. *Comuni e signori nel Veneto: Scaligeri, Caminesi, Carraresi; Saggio storico-giuridico.* Venice: Istituto Veneto di arti grafiche.

Falkeid, Unn. 2017. *The Avignon Papacy Revisited.* Cambridge, MA: Harvard University Press.

Fan, Ruiping, ed. 2011. *The Renaissance of Confucianism in Contemporary China.* Dordrecht: Springer.

Fasolt, Constantin. 2014. "Quod omnes tangit ab omnibus approbari debet: The Words and the Meaning." In idem, *Past Sense: Studies in Medieval and Early Modern European History,* 222–267. Leiden: E. J. Brill.

Fedwick, Paul. 1993–2004. *Bibliotheca Basiliana Universalis: A Study of the Manuscript Tradition of the Works of St. Basil of Caesarea.* 5 vols. Turnhout: Brepols (Corpus Christianorum, Claves, Subsidia 1).

Fenzi, Enrico. 2005. "Petrarca a Milano: Tempi e modi di una scelta meditata." In *Petrarca e la Lombardia, Atti del Convegno di Studi, Milano, 22–23 maggio 2003,* edited by Giuseppe Frasso, Giuseppe Velli, and Maurizio Vitali, 221–265. Padua: Antenore.

———. 2005–2006. "L'intellettuale e il potere. Il potere dell' intellettuale." *Petrarca, l'Umanesimo e la civiltà europea* 1: 169–229. Special issue of *Quaderni Petrarcheschi* 15–16.

———. 2016. "Petrarca politico e diplomatico tra Genova e Venezia, 1351–1355." In Furlan and Pittalunga 2016, 63–108.

Feo, Michele. 1992–1993. "Politicità del Petrarca." *Quaderni petrarcheschi* 9–10: 115–128.

———. 1994. "Epistola come mezzo di propaganda politica in Francesco Petrarca." In *Le forme della propaganda politica nel Due e nel Trecento: Relazioni tenute al convegno internazionale organizzato dal Comitato di studi storici di Trieste, dall'École française de Rome e dal Dipartimento di storia dell'Università degli studi di Trieste (Trieste, 2–5 marzo 1993),* edited by Paolo Cammarosano, 203–20. Rome: École française de Rome.

Feo, Michele, ed. 2003. *Petrarca nel tempo: Tradizioni, lettori e immagini delle opere.* Pontedera: Bandecchi e Vivaldi.

Ferguson, Wallace K. 1948. *The Renaissance in Historical Thought: Five Centuries of Interpretation.* Boston: Houghton Mifflin.

Ferraù, Giacomo. 2005. "Esemplarità platonica ed esperienza viscontea nel *De republica* di Umberto Decembrio." In Vegetti and Pissavino 2005, 431–464.

———. 2006. "Petrarca e la politica signorile." In *Petrarca politico: Atti del convegno, Roma-Arezzo, 19–20 marzo 2004,* 9–23. Roma: Istituto storico italiano per il Medio Evo. (Also published in Ferraù, Giacomo. 2006. *Petrarca: la politica, la storia.* Messina: Centro interdipartimentale di studi umanistici.)

Feser, Edward. 2010. "Classical Natural Law Theory, Property Rights, and Taxation." *Social Philosophy and Policy* 27(1): 21–52.

Fiaschi, Silvia. 2007. "Filelfo e 'i diritti' del traduttore: *L'auctoritas* dell' interprete e il problema delle attribuzioni." In *Tradurre dal greco in età umanistica: Metodi e strumenti, Atti del seminario di studio, Firenze, Certosa del Galluzzo, 9 settembre 2005,* edited by Mariarosa Cortesi, 79–138. Florence: SISMEL, Edizioni del Galluzzo.

Field, Arthur. 2017. *The Intellectual Struggle for Florence: Humanists and the Beginnings of the Medici Regime, 1420–1440.* Oxford: Oxford University Press.

Finnis, John, 1998. *Aquinas: Moral, Political and Legal Theory.* Oxford: Oxford University Press.

———. 2017. "Aquinas' Moral, Political, and Legal Philosophy." In *SEP.*

Flower, Harriet I. 2010. *Roman Republics.* Princeton: Princeton University Press.

Flüeler, Christoph. 1992. *Rezeption und Interpretation der Aristotelischen* Politica *im späten Mittelalter.* Bochumer Studien zur Philosophie 17. Amsterdam: B. R. Grüner.

———. 2002. "Politischer Aristotelismus im Mittelalter: Einleitung." *Vivarium* 40(1): 1–13.

Fontana, Benedetto. 1999. "Love of Country and Love of God: The Political Uses of Religion in Machiavelli." *Journal of the History of Ideas* 60(4): 639–658.

———. 2003. "Sallust and the Politics of Machiavelli." *History of Political Thought* 24(1): 86–106.

Formisano, Marco. 2009. "La tradizione dell'arte della guerra antica nel Rinascimento." In *Andrea Palladio e l'architettura della battaglia, con le illustrazioni inedite alle* Storie *di Polibio,* edited by G. Beltramini, 225–239. Venice: Marsilio.

Frazier, Alison, and Patrick Nold. 2015. *Essays in Renaissance Thought and Letters in Honor of John Monfasani.* Leiden: E. J. Brill.

Fredona, Robert. 2008. "Carnival of Law: Bartolomeo Scala's dialogue *De legibus et iudiciis.*" *Viator* 39(2): 193–214.

———. 2011. "Baldus de Ubaldis on Conspiracy and *Laesa Maiestas* in Late Trecento Florence." In *The Politics of Law in Late Medieval and Renaissance Italy: Essays in Honour of Lauro Martines,* edited by Lawrin Armstrong and Julius Kirshner, 141–160. Toronto: University of Toronto Press.

Friedeburg, Robert von, and John Morrill, eds. 2017. *Monarchy Transformed: Princes and Their Elites in Early Modern Western Europe.* Cambridge: Cambridge University Press.

Frier, Bruce W. 1985. *The Rise of the Roman Jurists: Studies in Cicero's* Pro Caecina. Princeton: Princeton University Press.

Fritz, Kurt von. 1954. *The Theory of the Mixed Constitution in Antiquity: A Critical Analysis of Polybius' Political Ideas.* New York: Columbia University Press.

Frobenius, Leo. 1921. *Paideuma: Umrisse einer Kultur- und Seelenlehre.* Munich: Beck.

Fubini, Riccardo. 1979. "Lapo da Castiglionchio, detto il Giovani." In *DBI.*

———. 1990a. "La rivendicazione di Firenze della sovranità statale e il contributo delle *Historiae* di Leonardo Bruni." In Viti 1990, 29–62.

———. 1990b. *Umanesimo e secolarizzazione da Petrarca a Valla.* Rome: Bulzoni.

———. 1992. "Renaissance Historian: The Career of Hans Baron." *Journal of Modern History* 64: 541–574.

———. 2001. *L'umanesimo italiano e i suoi storici.* Milan: FrancoAngeli.

———. 2003. *Storiografia dell'umanesimo in Italia da Leonardo Bruni ad Annio da Viterbo.* Rome: Edizioni di Storia e Letteratura.

Fukuyama, Francis. 2011. *The Origins of Political Order: From Prehuman Times to the French Revolution.* New York: Farrar, Straus, and Giroux.

Furlan, Francesco, and Stefano Pittaluga, eds. 2016. *Petrarca politico.* Genoa: Univesità di Genova, Scuola di Scienze umanistiche.

Gaeta, Franco. 1961. "Alcune considerazioni sul mito di Venezia." *Bibliothèque d'Humanisme et Renaissance* 23: 58–75.

Gagné, John Edmond. 2008. "French Milan: Citizens, Occupiers, and the Italian Wars." Ph.D. diss., Department of History, Harvard University.

Gambino Longo, Susanna, ed. 2012. *Hérodote à la Renaissance: Etudes réunis.* Turnhout: Brepols.

Gar, G. 2015. "Enea Silvio e la polemica umanistica contro la scienza del diritto." In *Pio II nell'epistolografia del Rinascimento, Atti del XXV Convegno Internazionale (Chianciano Terme-Pienza, 18–20 luglio 2013),* edited by Luisa Rotondi Secchi Tarugi, 599–618. Florence: Franco Cesati.

Garin, Eugenio. 1947. *La disputa delle arti nel Quattrocento.* Florence: Vallecchi.

———. 1964. *L'umanesimo italiano: Filosofia e vita civile nel Rinascimento.* Bari: Laterza. (First published as *Der italienische Humanismus.* Bern: Francke Verlag, 1947. English translation by Peter Munz: *Italian Humanism: Philosophy and Civic Life in the Renaissance.* New York: Harper and Row, 1965.)

———. 1979. *La cultura filosofica del Rinascimento italiano.* 2nd ed. Florence: Sansoni.

———. 2009. *Interpretazioni del Rinascimento,* edited by Michele Ciliberto. 2 vols. Rome: Storia e letteratura.

Gasparri, Stefano. 1992. *I milites cittadini: Studi sulla cavalleria in Italia.* Rome: Istituto storico italiano per il Medio Evo.

Geuna, Marco. 2005. "Machiavelli ed il ruolo dei conflitti nella politica." In *Conflitti,* edited by Alessandro Arienzo and Dario Caruso, 19–47. Naples: Libreria Dante e Descartes.

Gilbert, Allan. 1938. *Machiavelli's* Prince *and Its Forerunners:* The Prince *as a Typical Book de regimine principum.* Durham, NC: Duke University Press.

Gilbert, Felix. 1965. *Machiavelli and Guicciardini: Politics and History in Sixteenth-Century Florence.* Princeton: Princeton University Press.

———. 1985. "Machiavelli: The Renaissance of the Art of War." In *Makers of Modern Strategy from Machiavelli to the Nuclear Age,* edited by Peter Paret, with the collaboration of Gordon A. Craig and Felix Gilbert, 11–31. Princeton: Princeton University Press.

Gildenhard, Ingo. 2006, "Reckoning with Tyranny: Greek Thoughts on Caesar in Cicero's *Letters to Atticus* of Early 49." In Lewis 2006 (unpaginated online edition).

Gill, Joseph. 1961. *Eugenius IV, Pope of Christian Union.* London: Burns & Oates.

Gilli, Patrick. 2014. *Droit, humanisme et culture politique dans l'Italie de la Renaissance.* Montpellier: Presses universitaires de la Méditerranée.

Gionta, Daniela. 2015. "Epigrafia antica e ideologia politica nell'Italia del Quattrocento." *Studi medievali e umanistici* 13: 115–156.

Gittes, Tobias Foster. 2015. "Boccaccio and Humanism." In Armstrong, Daniels, and Milner 2015, 155–170.

Glinister, Fay. 2006. "Kingship and Tyranny in Archaic Rome." In Lewis 2006 (unpaginated online edition).

Godman, Peter. 1998. *From Poliziano to Machiavelli: Florentine Humanism in the High Renaissance.* Princeton: Princeton University Press.

Goeing, Anja-Silvia. 2014. *"Summus mathematicus et omnis humanitatis pater": The Vitae of Vittorino da Feltre and the Spirit of Humanism.* Dordrecht: Springer.

Goldbrunner, Hermann. 1966. "Leonardo Brunis *De militia:* Bemerkungen zur handschriftlichen Überlieferung." *Quellen und Forschungen aus italienischen Archiven und Bibliotheken* 46: 478–487.

Goldie, Mark. 2006. "The Context of the Foundations." In Brett and Tully 2006, 3–19.

Gosepath, Stefan. 2011. "Equality." In *SEP.*

Grafton, Anthony. 2000. *Leon Battista Alberti: Master Builder of the Italian Renaissance.* New York: Hill and Wang.

Grafton, Anthony, and Lisa Jardine. 1986. *From Humanism to the Humanities: Education and the Liberal Arts in Fifteenth- and Sixteenth-Century Europe.* Cambridge, MA: Harvard University Press.

Grafton, Anthony, Glen Most, and Salvatore Settis. 2010. *The Classical Tradition.* Cambridge, MA: Harvard University Press.

Greenhalgh, Michael. 1982. *Donatello and His Sources.* London: Duckworth.

Grell, Chantal, Werner Paravicini, and Jürgen Voss. 1998. *Les princes et l'histoire du XIVe au XVIIIe siècle: Actes du colloque organisé par l'Université de Versailles-Saint Quentin et l'Institut historique allemand, Paris/Versailles, 13–16 mars 1996.* Bonn: Bouvier.

Grendler, Paul F. 1989. *Schooling in Renaissance Italy: Literacy and Learning, 1300–1600.* Baltimore: Johns Hopkins University Press.

———. 2002. *The Universities of the Italian Renaissance.* Baltimore: Johns Hopkins University Press.

Grieco, Allen. 1987. "Classes sociales, nourriture et imaginaire alimentaire en Italie (XIVe–XVe siècles)." Thèse de doctorat, Ecoles des Hautes Etudes en Sciences Sociales, Paris.

———. 2003. "Lebensmittel und soziale Hierarchen im spätmittelalterlichen und frühneuzeitlichen Europa." In *Die lange Weg in den Überfluss: Anfänge und Entwicklung der Konsumgesellschaft seit der Vormoderne,* edited by Michael Prinz, 37–46. Münster: Aschendorff.

———. Forthcoming. *Food, Social Politics, and the Order of Nature in Renaissance Italy.* Milan: Officina Libraria.

Griffin, Miriam. 2003. "*De beneficiis* and Roman Society." *Journal of Roman Studies* 93: 92–113.

———. 2005. "Seneca and Pliny." In Rowe and Schofield 2005, 532–558.

Griffiths, Gordon. 1999. *The Justification of Florentine Foreign Policy Offered by Leonardo Bruni in His Public Letters, 1428–1444.* Rome: Istituto storico italiano per il Medio Evo.

Griffiths, Gordon, James Hankins, and David Thompson, trs. 1987. *The Humanism of Leonardo Bruni.* Binghamton, NY: Center for Medieval and Early Renaissance Studies and the Renaissance Society of America.

Grund, Gary R., ed. 2005. *Humanist Comedies.* Cambridge, MA: Harvard University Press. (ITRL 19.)

Grund, Gary R., ed. 2011. *Humanist Tragedies.* Cambridge MA: Harvard University Presss. (ITRL 45.)

Gualdo Rosa, Lucia. 1983. *La fede nella paideia: Aspetti della fortuna europea di Isocrate nei secoli XV e XVI.* Rome: Istituto storico italiano per il Medio Evo.

———. 1990. "L'elogio delle lettere e delle armi nell'opera di Leonardo Bruni." In *Sapere e/è potere: Discipline, dispute e professioni nell'università medievale e moderna ; Il caso bolognese a confronto, Bologna 13–15 aprile 1989,* vol. 1, *Forme e oggetti della disputa delle arti,* edited by Luisa Avellini, 103–113. Bologna: Istituto per la storia di Bologna.

———. 1993–2004. *Censimento dei codici dell'Epistolario di Leonardo Bruni.* 2 vols. Rome: Istituto storico per il Medio Evo.

———. 2017. *La paideia degli umanisti: Un'antologia degli scritti.* Rome: Edizioni di storia e letteratura.

———. 2018. *Lapo da Castiglionchio il giovane e la sua versione delle prime tre orazioni di Isocrate, con in appendice l'edizione critica dei testi.* Rome: Istituto storico italiano per il Medio Evo.

Guasti, Cesare. 1867–1873. *Le Commissioni di Rinaldo degli Albizzi per il comune di Firenze dal MCCCXCIX al MCCCCXXXIII.* 3 vols. Florence: Cellini.

Guelfucci, Marie-Rose. 2008. "Anciens et Modernes: Machiavel et la lecture Polybienne de l'histoire." *Dialogues d'histoire ancien* 34: 85–104.

Hahm, David E. 2006. "Kings and Constitutions." In Rowe and Schofield 2006, 457–476.

———. 2009. "The Mixed Constitution in Greek Thought." In Balot 2009, 178–198.

Hale, John R. 1964. Review of Bayley 1961. *English Historical Review* 79(311): 405–406.

———. 1983. *Renaissance War Studies.* London: Hambledon Press.

———. 1985. *War and Society in Renaissance Europe, 1450–1620.* London: Fontana.

Hankins, James. 1990a. *Plato in the Italian Renaissance.* 2 vols. Leiden: E. J. Brill.

———. 1990b. "The Latin Poetry of Leonardo Bruni." *Humanistica Lovaniensia* 39: 1–39. (Reprinted in Hankins 2003–2004a, 1: 137–175.)

———. 1995a. "The Baron Thesis after Forty Years: Some Recent Studies on Leonardo Bruni." *Journal of the History of Ideas* 56: 309–338.

———. 1995b. "Renaissance Crusaders: Humanist Crusade Literature in the Age of Mehmed II." *Dumbarton Oaks Papers* 49: 111–207. (Reprinted with minor revisions in Hankins 2003–2004a, 1: 293–424.)

———. 1996. "Humanism and the Origins of Modern Political Thought." In *The Cambridge Companion to Renaissance Humanism,* edited by Jill Kraye, 118–41. Cambridge: Cambridge University Press.

———. 1997. *Repertorium Brunianum: A Critical Guide to the Writings of Leonardo Bruni.* Vol. 1. Rome: Istituto storico italiano per il Medio Evo.

———. 1998. "Unknown and Little-Known Texts of Leonardo Bruni." *Rinascimento,* n.s., 38: 125–161. (Reprinted in Hankins 2003–2004a, 1: 19–62.)

———, ed. 2000a. *Renaissance Civic Humanism: Reappraisals and Reflections.* Cambridge: Cambridge University Press.

———. 2000b. "Rhetoric, History, and Ideology: The Civic Panegyrics of Leonardo Bruni." In Hankins 2000a, 143–178.

———. 2002a. "Renaissance Philosophy and Book IV of *Il Cortegiano.*" In *Baldesar Castiglione: The Book of the Courtier,* edited by Daniel Javitch, 377–388. New York: W. W. Norton. (Reprinted in enlarged form in Hankins 2003–2004a, 2: 493–509.)

———. 2002b. "Chrysoloras and the Greek Studies of Leonardo Bruni." In *Manuele Crisolora e il ritorno del greco in occidente, Atti del Convegno Internazionale (Napoli, 26–29 giugno 1997),* edited by Riccardo Maisano and Antonio Rollo, 175–203. (Reprinted in Hankins 2003–2004a, 1: 243–271.)

———. 2002–2003. "Greek Studies in Italy: From Petrarch to Bruni." In *Petrarca e il mondo greco: Atti del Convegno internazionale di studi (Reggio Calabria, 26–30 nov. 2001),* edited by Michele Feo, Vincenzo Fera, Paola Megna, and Antonio Rollo, 329–339. 2 vols. Special issues of *Quaderni petrarcheschi,* vols. 12–13.

———. 2003–2004a. *Humanism and Platonism in the Italian Renaissance.* 2 vols. Rome: Edizioni di Storia e Letteratura.

———. 2003–2004b. "The Ethics Controversy." In Hankins 2003–2004a, 1: 193–239.

———. 2003–2004c. "Ptolemy's Geography in the Renaissance." In Hankins 2003–2004a, 1: 457–468.

———. (1992) 2003–2004d. "Cosimo de'Medici as a Patron of Humanistic Literature." In *Cosimo 'il Vecchio' de'Medici, 1389–1989: Essays in Commemoration of the 600th Anniversary of Cosimo de'Medici's Birth,* edited by Francis Ames-Lewis, 69–94. Oxford: Clarendon Press. Reprinted in Hankins 2003–2004a, 1: 427–456.

———. 2005. "Renaissance Humanism and Historiography Today." In *Palgrave Advances in Renaissance Historiography,* ed. Jonathan Woolfson, 73–96. New York: Palgrave Macmillan.

———. 2006a. "Humanism in the Vernacular: The Case of Leonardo Bruni." In *Humanism and Creativity in the Renaissance: Essays in Honor of Ronald G. Witt,* edited by Christopher S. Celenza and Kenneth Gouwens, 11–29. Leiden: E. J. Brill.

———. 2006b. "Religion and the Modernity of Renaissance Humanism." In *Interpretations of Renaissance Humanism,* edited by Angelo Mazzocco, 137–153. Leiden: E. J. Brill.

———, ed. 2007a. *The Cambridge Companion to Renaissance Philosophy.* Cambridge: Cambridge University Press.

———. 2007b. "Humanism, Scholasticism, and Renaissance Philosophy." In Hankins 2007a, 30–48.

———. 2007c. "Teaching Civil Prudence in Leonardo Bruni's *History of the Florentine People.*" In *Ethik—Wissenschaft oder Lebenskunst? Modelle de Normenbegründung von der Antike bis zur Frühen Neuzeit,* edited by Sabrina Ebbersmeyer and Eckhard Kessler, 143–57. Berlin: Lit.

———. 2007d. "Socrates in the Italian Renaissance." In *Socrates, from Antiquity to the Enlightenment,* edited by M. B. Trapp, 179–208. Aldershot: Ashgate.

———. 2007–2008a. "The Dates of Leonardo Bruni's Later Works." *Studi medievali e umanistici* 5–6: 11–48.

———. 2007–2008b. "Petrarch and the Canon of Neo-Latin Literature." In *Petrarca, l'Umanesimo e la civiltà europea. Atti del Convegno Internazionale, Firenze, 5–10 dicembre 2004,* edited by Donatella Coppini and Michele Feo, 2: 905–922. Florence: Le Lettere. Special issue of *Quaderni petrarcheschi* 17–18.

———. 2008a. "Notes on the Composition and Textual Tradition of Leonardo Bruni's *Historiarum Florentini populi libri XII.*" In *Classica et Beneventana: Essays Presented to Virginia Brown on the Occasion of Her Sixty-Fifth Birthday,* edited by Frank T. Coulson, 87–109. Turnhout: Brepols.

———. 2008b. "Manetti's Socrates and the Socrateses of Antiquity." In *Dignitas et excellentia hominis: Atti del Convegno Internazionale di studi su Giannozzo Manetti,* edited by Stefano U. Baldassarri, 203–219. Florence: Le Lettere. .

———. 2010a. "Exclusivist Republicanism and the Non-Monarchical Republic." *Political Theory* 38(4): 452–82.

———. 2010b. "Salutati, Plato, and Socrates." In *Coluccio Salutati e l'invenzione dell'Umanesimo, Atti del Convegno internazionale di studi, Firenze 29–31 ottobre 2008,* edited by Concetta Bianca, 283–293. Rome: Edizioni di Storia e letteratura.

———. 2011a. "Monstrous Melancholy: Ficino and the Physiological Causes of Atheism." In *Laus Platonici philosophi: Marsilio Ficino and His Influence,* edited by Stephen Clucas, Peter J. Forshaw, and Valerie Rees, 25–43. Leiden: E. J. Brill.

———. 2011b. "Humanist Academies and the "Platonic Academy of Florence." In *On Renaissance Academies: Proceedings of the International Conference "From the Roman Academy to the Danish Academy in Rome," 11–13 October 2006*, ed. Marianne Pade, 31–46. Rome: Edizioni Quasar.

———. 2012. "Modern Republicanism and the History of Republics." In *Nuovi maestri, antichi testi: Umanesimo e Rinascimento alle origini del pensiero moderno: Atti del Convegno internazionale di studi in onore di Cesare Vasoli, Mantova, 1–3 dicembre 2010*, edited by Stefano Caroti and Vittoria Perrone Compagni, 109–126. Florence: Leo S. Olschki.

———. 2013. "Machiavelli, Civic Humanism, and the Humanist Politics of Virtue." *Italian Culture* 32(2): 98–109.

———. 2014a. "Leonardo Bruni on the Legitimacy of Constitutions (*Oratio in funere Johannis Strozze* 19–23)," in *Reading and Writing History from Bruni to Windschuttle: Essays in Honour of Gary Ianziti*, ed. Christian Thorsten Callisen, 73–86. Farnham, UK: Ashgate.

———. 2014b. "Civic Knighthood in the Early Renaissance: Leonardo Bruni's *De militia* (ca. 1420)." *Noctua: International On-line Journal on the History of Philosophy* 1(2): 260–282.

———. 2015a. "George of Trebizond: Renaissance Libertarian?" In *Essays in Renaissance Thought and Letters in Honor of John Monfasani*, edited by Alison K. Frazier and Patrick Noll, 87–106. Leiden: E. J. Brill.

———. 2015b. "Humanism and Music in Italy." In *The Cambridge History of Fifteenth-Century Music*, ed. Anna Maria Busse-Berger and Jesse Rodin, 231–262. Cambridge: Cambridge University Press.

———. 2016. "Europe's First Democrat? Cyriac of Ancona and Book 6 of Polybius." In *For the Sake of Learning: Essays in Honor of Anthony Grafton*, ed. Ann Blair and Anja-Silvia Goeing, 2: 692–710. Leiden: E. J. Brill.

———. 2017a. "Leonardo Bruni's *Laudatio Florentine urbis,* Dante, and 'Virtue Politics.'" *Bullettino dell' Istituto Storico Italiano per il Medio Evo* 119: 1–25.

———. 2017b. "Biondo Flavio on the Roman Republic." In *The Invention of Rome: Biondo Flavio's Roma Triumphans and Its Worlds*, edited by Frances Muecke and Maurizio Campanelli, 101–118. Geneva: Droz.

———. 2017c. "Leonardo Bruni and Machiavelli on the Lessons of Florentine History." In *Le cronache volgari in Italia: Atti della VI Settimana di studi eedievali (Roma, 13–15 maggio 2015)*, edited by Giampaolo Francesconi and Massimo Miglio, 373–395. Rome: Istituto storico italiano per il Medio Evo.

———. 2017d. "Marsilio Ficino and Christian Humanism." In *Re-envisioning Christian Humanism: Education and the Restoration of Humanity*, edited by Jens Zimmermann, 55–76. Oxford: Oxford University Press.

———. 2017e. "Reforming Elites the Confucian Way." *American Affairs* 1(2) (Summer).

———. 2018a. "Filelfo and Sparta." In *Francesco Filelfo, Man of Letters*, edited by Jeroen De Keyser, 81–96. Leiden: E. J. Brill.

———. 2018b. "Confucianism and Meritocracy: Light from the East." *American Affairs* 2(3) (Fall).

———. Forthcoming. "Vocal Music at Literary Banquets in the Italian Renaissance." *Basler Jahrbuch für historische Musikpraxis*.

Hankins, James, and Ada Palmer. 2008. *The Recovery of Ancient Philosophy in the Renaissance: A Brief Guide*. Florence: Leo S. Olschki.

Hansen, Mogens H. 2013. *Reflections on Aristotle's Politics.* Copenhagen: Museum Tusculanum Press.

Harris, William V. 1985. *War and Imperialism in Republican Rome, 327–70 BC.* Oxford: Oxford University Press.

Harte, Verity, and Melissa Lane, eds. 2013. Politeia *in Greek and Roman Philosophy.* Cambridge: Cambridge University Press.

Hay, Denys. 1977. *The Church in Italy in the Fifteenth Century.* Cambridge: Cambridge University Press.

Hay, Denys, and John E. Law. 1989. *Italy in the Age of the Renaissance, 1380–1530.* London: Longman.

Heater, Derek. 1996. *World Citizenship and Government: Cosmopolitan Ideas in the History of Western Political Thought.* New York: St. Martin's.

Helmrath, Johannes, Albert Schirrmeister, and Stefan Schlelein. 2013. *Historiographie des Humanismus: Literarische Verfahren, soziale Praxis, geschichtliche Räume.* Berlin: De Gruyter.

Helmrath, Johannes, Eva Mariene Hausteiner, and Ulf Jensen. 2017. *Antike als Transformation: Konzepte zur Beschreibung kulturellen Wandels.* Berlin: De Gruyter.

Hendrick, Charles W., Jr. 2009. "Imitating Virtue and Avoiding Vice: Ethical Functions of Biography, History, and Philosophy." In Balot 2009, 421–439.

Hicks, David L. 1960. "Sienese Society in the Renaissance." *Comparative Studies in Society and History* 2(4): 412–420.

Hirschman, Albert O. 1977. *The Passions and the Interests: Political Arguments for Capitalism before Its Triumph.* Princeton: Princeton University Press.

Hirzel, Rudolf. 1895. *Der Dialog, ein literarhistorischer Versuch.* Leipzig: S. Hirzel.

Hodgson, Louise. 2017. Res Publica *and The Roman Republic: "Without Body or Form."* Oxford: Oxford University Press.

Hodkinson, Stephen, and Ian Macgregor Morris, eds. 2012. *Sparta in Modern Thought: Politics, History, and Culture.* Swansea: Classical Press of Wales.

Hoekstra, Kinch. 2012–2013. "Early Modern Absolutism and Constitutionalism." *Cardozo Law Review* 34: 1079–1098.

Høgel, Christian. 2015. *The Human and the Humane: Humanity as Argument from Cicero to Erasmus.* Taipei: National Taiwan University Press.

Horn, Christoph, and Ada Neschke-Hentschke, eds. 2008. *Politischer Aristotelismus: Die Rezeption der aristotelischen Politik von der Antike bis zum 19. Jahrhundert.* Stuttgart: J. B. Metler.

Hornqvist, Mikael. 2004. *Machiavelli and Empire.* Cambridge: Cambridge University Press.

Horowitz, Mary Ann. 1998. *Seeds of Virtue and Knowledge.* Princeton: Princeton University Press.

Housley, Norman. 1992. *The Later Crusades, 1274–1580: From Lyons to Alcazar.* Oxford: Oxford University Press.

Howard, Adam, and Rubén A. Gaztambide-Fernández, eds. 2010. *Educating Elites: Class Privilege and Educational Advantage.* Lanham, MD: Rowman and Littlefield.

Howard, Philip K. 2009. *Life without Lawyers: Restoring Responsibility in America.* New York: W. W. Norton.

———. 2014. *The Rule of Nobody: Saving America from Dead Laws and Broken Government.* New York: W. W. Norton.

Hsia, Ronnie Po-chia. 2010. *A Jesuit in the Forbidden City: Matteo Ricci, 1552–1610.* Oxford: Oxford University Press.

———. 2016. *Matteo Ricci and the Catholic Mission to China, 1583–1610: A Short History with Documents*. Indianapolis, IN: Hackett Publishing Company.

Humble, Noreen. 2012. "The Renaissance Reception of Xenophon's Spartan Constitution: Preliminary Observations." In *Xenophon: Ethical Principles and Historical Enquiry,* edited by Fiona Hobden and Christopher Tuplin, 63–88. Leiden: E. J. Brill.

———. 2018. "Erudition, Emulation, and Enmity in the Dedication Letters to Filelfo's Greek to Latin Translations." In *Francesco Filelfo, Man of Letters,* ed. Jeroen De Keyser, 127–173. Leiden: E. J. Brill.

Hursthouse, Rosalind. 2013. "Virtue Ethics." In *SEP.*

Hutton, James. 1935. *The Greek Anthology in Italy to the Year 1800.* Ithaca: Cornell University Press.

Ianziti, Gary. 1988. *Humanistic Historiography under the Sforzas: Politics and Propaganda in Fifteenth-Century Milan.* Oxford: Clarendon Press.

———. 2012. *Writing History in Renaissance Italy: Leonardo Bruni and the Uses of the Past.* Cambridge, MA: Harvard University Press.

Inglese, Giorgio. 1987. "Per una discussione sulla 'cultura di Machiavelli.'" *La cultura* 25: 378–387.

———. 2006. *Per Machiavelli: L'arte dello stato, la cognizione delle storie.* Roma: Carocci.

Israel, Jonathan I. 2001. *Radical Enlightenment: Philosophy and the Making of Modernity, 1650–1750.* Oxford: Oxford University Press.

———. 2006. *Enlightenment Contested: Philosophy, Modernity and the Emancipation of Man, 1670–1752.* Oxford: Oxford University Press.

Jackson, Clair Rachel. 2017. "Dio Chrysostom." In Richter and Johnson 2017, 217–232.

Jackson, Julian. 2018. *De Gaulle.* Cambridge, MA: Harvard University Press.

Jaeger, C. Stephen. 1994. *The Envy of Angels: Cathedral Schools and Social Ideals in Medieval Europe, 950–1200.* Philadelphia, PA: University of Pennsylvania Press.

Janson, Horst W. 1963. *The Sculpture of Donatello.* Princeton: Princeton University Press.

Jiang, Qing. 2013. *A Confucian Constitutional Order: How China's Ancient Past Can Shape Its Political Future.* Translated by Edmund Ryden, edited by Daniel A. Bell and Ruiping Fan. Princeton: Princeton University Press.

Jones, Philip J. 1965. "Communes and Despots: City States in Late Medieval Italy." *Transactions of the Royal Historical Society,* fifth series, 15: 71–96.

Jurdjevic, Mark. 2001. "Virtue, Commerce, and the Enduring Florentine Republican Moment: Reintegrating Italy into the Atlantic Republican Debate." *Journal of the History of Ideas* 62(4): 721–43.

———. 2014. *A Great and Wretched City: Promise and Failure in Machiavelli's Florentine Political Thought.* Cambridge, MA: Harvard University Press.

Kallendorf, Craig W. 2002. *Humanist Educational Treatises.* Cambridge, MA: Harvard University Press. (ITRL 5.)

Kantorowicz, Ernst. 1957. *The King's Two Bodies: A Study in Medieval Political Theology.* Princeton: Princeton University Press.

Kapust, Daniel. 2007. "Cato's Virtues and *The Prince:* Reading Sallust's *War with Catiline* with Machiavelli's *The Prince.*" *History of Political Thought* 28(3): 433–448.

Kempshall, M. S. 1999. *The Common Good in Late Medieval Political Thought.* Oxford: Oxford University Press.

Kennell, Nigel M. 2010. *Spartans: A New History*. Chichester, UK: Wiley-Blackwell.

Kent, Dale V. 1978. *The Rise of the Medici: Faction in Florence, 1426–1434*. Oxford: Oxford University Press.

———. 2000. *Cosimo de' Medici and the Florentine Renaissance: The Patron's Oeuvre*. New Haven: Yale University Press.

Khan, Shamus. 2012. "The Sociology of Elites." *Annual Review of Sociology* 38: 361–377.

Kidwell, Carol. 1991. *Pontano: Poet and Prime Minister*. London: Duckworth.

Kim, Sungmoon. 2018. *Democracy after Virtue: Towards Pragmatic Confucian Democracy*. Oxford: Oxford University Press.

King, Margaret L. 1986. *Venetian Humanism in an Age of Patrician Dominance*. Princeton: Princeton University Press.

Kingsbury, Benedict, ed. 2010. *The Roman Foundations of the Law of Nations: Alberico Gentili and the Justice of Empire*. Oxford: Oxford University Press.

Kircher, Timothy. 2012. *Living Well in Renaissance Italy: The Virtues of Humanism and the Irony of Leon Battista Alberti*. Tempe: Arizona Center for Medieval and Renaissance Studies.

Kirkham, Victoria, and Armando Maggi, eds. 2009. *Petrarch: A Critical Guide to the Complete Works*. Chicago: University of Chicago Press.

Kirkham, Victoria, Michael Sherberg, and Janet Lavarie Smarr, eds. 2013. *Boccaccio: A Critical Guide to the Complete Works*. Chicago: University of Chicago Press.

Kirshner, Julius, ed. 1996. *The Origins of the State in Italy, 1300–1600*. Chicago: University of Chicago Press.

Kirshner, Julius, and Laurent Mayall. 2002. *Privileges and Rights of Citizenship: Law and the Juridical Construction of Civil Society*. Berkeley: Robbins Collection.

Kleingeld, Pauline, and Eric Brown. 2013. "Cosmopolitanism." In *SEP*.

Kloppenberg, James T. 2016. *Toward Democracy: The Struggle for Self-rule in European and American Thought*. New York: Oxford University Press.

Klosko, George. 1986. *The Development of Plato's Political Theory*. London: Methuen.

Kohl, Benjamin G. 1992. "The Changing Concept of the *Studia Humanitatis* in the Early Renaissance." *Renaissance Studies* 6: 185–209.

———. 1998. *Padua under the Carrara, 1380–1405*. Baltimore: Johns Hopkins University Press.

———. 2010. "The Myth of the Renaissance Despot." In Law and Paton 2010, 61–73.

Kohl, Benjamin, and Ronald G. Witt, eds., with Elizabeth B. Wells. 1978. *The Earthly Republic: Italian Humanists on Government and Society*. Philadelphia: University of Pennsylvania Press.

Kölmel, Wilhelm. 1970. "Petrarca und das Reich: Zum historisch-politischen Aspekt der *studia humanitatis*." *Historisches Jahrbuch* 90: 1–30.

Konstan, David. 2009. "Cosmopolitan Traditions." In Balot 2009, 473–484.

Krantz, Frederick. 1987. "Between Bruni and Machiavelli: History, Law, and Historicism in Poggio Bracciolini." *Politics and Culture in Early Modern Europe: Essays in Honor of H. G. Koenigsberger,* edited by Phyllis Mack and Margaret W. Jacob, 119–152. Cambridge: Cambridge University Press.

Kraut, Richard, and Steven Scultety, eds. 2005. *Aristotle's Politics: Critical Essays*. Lanham, MD: Rowman and Littlefield.

Kraye, Jill, ed. 1997. *Cambridge Translations of Renaissance Philosophical Texts.* 2 vols. Cambridge: Cambridge University Press.

Kreyszig, Walter Kurt. 1993. "Franchino Gaffurio als Vermittler der Musiklehre des Altertums und des Mittelalters: Zur Identifizierung griechischer und lateinischer Quellen in der *Theorica musice.*" *Acta musicologica* 65(2): 134–150.

Kristeller, Paul Oskar. 1963. Review of Bayley 1961. *Canadian Historical Review* 44: 66–70.

———. 1963–1997. *Iter Italicum: A Finding List of Uncatalogued or Incompletely Catalogued Humanistic Manuscripts of the Renaissance in Italian and Other Libraries.* Leiden: E. J. Brill. (Cited from the unpaginated online version at *Iter, Gateway to the Middle Ages and Renaissance,* https://www.itergateway.org)

———. 1974. "The Contribution of the Religious Orders to Renaissance Thought and Learning." In *Medieval Aspects of Renaissance Learning: Three Essays,* edited by Edward P. Mahoney, 95–158. Durham, NC: Duke University Press.

———. 1990a. *Renaissance Thought and the Arts: Collected Essays.* Expanded ed. with a new afterword. Princeton: Princeton University Press.

———. 1990b. "Humanist Learning in the Italian Renaissance." In Kristeller 1990a, 1–19.

Lafleur, Claude. 2001. *Pétrarque et l'amitié.* Paris: Vrin.

Ladner, Gerhardt. (1959) 1967. *The Idea of Reform: Its Impact on Christian Thought and Action in the Age of the Fathers.* New York: Harper and Row.

Laks, André. 2005. "The *Laws.*" In Rowe and Schofield 2005, 258–292.

Lambertini, Roberto. 1995. "The Prince in the Mirror of Philosophy: About the Use of Aristotle in Giles of Rome's *De regimine principum.*" In *Moral and Political Philosophies in the Middle Ages, Proceedings of the Ninth International Congress of Medieval Philosophy, Ottawa, 17–22 August 1992,* edited by Bernardo Carlos Bazán, Eduardo Andújar, and Léonard G. Sbrocchi, 3: 1522–1534. New York: Legas.

Langholm, Odd. 1992. *Economics in the Medieval Schools: Wealth, Exchange, Value, Money, and Usury according to the Paris Theological Tradition, 1200–1350.* Leiden: E. J. Brill.

Langkabel, Hermann. 1981. *Die Staatsbriefe Coluccio Salutatis.* Cologne: Böhlau.

Langston, Douglas. 2015. "Medieval Theories of Conscience." In *SEP.*

Lansing, Carol. 1991. *The Florentine Magnates: Lineage and Faction in a Medieval Commune.* Princeton: Princeton University Press.

Lanza, Antonio. 1991. *Firenze contro Milano: Gli intellettuali fiorentini nelle guerre con i Visconti, 1390–1440.* Rome: De Rubeis.

La Penna, Antonio. 1968. "Il significato di Sallustio nella storiografia e nel pensiero politico di Leonardo Bruni." In idem, *Sallustio e la "rivoluzione romana,"* 409–431. Milan: Feltrinelli.

Law, John E. 2010. "Communes and Despots: The Nature of 'Diarchy.'" In Law and Paton 2010, 161–176.

Law, John E., and Bernadette Paton. 2010. *Communes and Despots in Medieval and Renaissance Italy.* Farnham, UK: Ashgate.

Lázar, István Dávid, Alejandro Coroleu, and Astrid Steiner-Weber. 2012. "Petrarca e la tirannide." In *Acta conventus Neo-Latini Upsaliensis: Proceedings of the Fourteenth International Congress of Neo-Latin Studies (Uppsala 2009)* 2: 605–611. Leiden: E. J. Brill.

Lee, Alexander. 2018. *Humanism and Empire: The Imperial Ideal in Fourteenth Century Italy*. Oxford: Oxford University Press.

Lee, Daniel. 2016. *Popular Sovereignty in Early Modern Constitutional Thought*. Oxford: Oxford University Press.

Legge, James. 1861–1872. *The Chinese Classics: With a Translation, Critical and Exegetical Notes, Prolegomena, and Copious Indexes*. 7 vols. in 5. Hong Kong: Lane, Crawford and Co.

Lewis, Sian, ed. 2006. *Ancient Tyranny*. Edinburgh: Edinburgh University Press. Published by Edinburgh Scholarship Online (March 2012). DOI: 10.3366 / edinburgh / 9780748621255.001.0001.

Liddel, Peter. 2009. "Democracy Ancient and Modern." In Balot 2009, 133–148.

Lilla, Mark. 2001. *The Reckless Mind: Intellectuals in Politics*. New York: New York Review of Books.

Lines, David. 2003. *Aristotle's Ethics in the Italian Renaissance, ca. 1300–1650: The Universities and the Problem of Moral Education*. Leiden: E. J. Brill.

Long, A. A. 1995. "Cicero's Politics in the *De officiis*." In *Justice and Generosity: Studies in Hellenistic Political Philosophy*, edited by Andrew Laks and Malcolm Schofield, 213–240. Cambridge: Cambridge University Press.

———. 2008. "The Concept of the Cosmopolitan in Greek and Roman Thought." *Daedalus* 137(3): 50–58.

Losemann, Volker. 2003. "Sparta. 1. Bild und Deutung." In *Der Neue Pauly: Enzyklopädie der Antike, Rezeptions- und Wissenschafts-geschichte* 15.3, 153–171. Stuttgart-Weimar: J. B. Metzler.

Luciani, Evelyne. 1985. "Théodore, idéal du prince chrétien dans la correspondance de Pétrarque: Sources augustiniennes." *Revue des études augustiniennes* 31: 242–257.

Luiso, Francesco Paolo. 1980. *Studi su l'Epistolario di Leonardo Bruni,* edited by Lucia Gualdo Rosa. Rome: Istituto storico italiano per il Medio Evo.

Lukes, Timothy J. 2004. "Martialing Machiavelli: Reassessing the Military Reflections." *Journal of Politics* 66(4): 1089–1108.

Lupher, David. 2003. *Romans in a New World: Classical Models in Sixteenth-Century Spanish America*. Ann Arbor: University of Michigan Press.

Lupinetti, Mario Quinto. 1999. *Francesco Petrarca e il diritto*. 2nd ed. Alessandria: Edizioni dell' Orso.

Luraghi, Nino. 2013. "One-Man Government: The Greeks and Monarchy." In *A Companion to Ancient Greek Government,* edited by Hans Beck, 131–145. Chicester, UK: Wiley-Blackwell.

———. 2015. "Anatomy of the Monster: The Discourse of Tyranny in Ancient Greece." In *Anti-Monarchic Discourse in Antiquity,* edited by Henning Börm, 67–84. Stuttgart: Franz Steiner.

Luscombe, David E. 1998. "Hierarchy in the Later Middle Ages: Criticism and Change." In *Political Thought and the Realities of Power in the Middle Ages,* edited by Otto Gerhard Oexle and Joseph Canning, 113–126. Gottingen: Vandenhoeck and Ruprecht.

Macedo, Stephen. 2013. "Meritocratic Democracy: Learning from the American Constitution." In Bell and Li 2013, 232–256.

Maffei, Domenico. (1956) 1972. *Gli inizi del umanesimo giuridico*. 2nd ed. Milan: Giuffré.

Mager, Wolfgang. 1984. "Republik." In *Geschichtliche Grundbegriffe: Historisches Lexicon zur politisch-sozialen Sprache in Deutschland* 5: 549–651. Stuttgart: E. Klett.

Maggi, Armando. 2009. "'You Will Be My Solitude': Solitude as Prophecy *(De vita solitaria).*" In Kirkham and Maggi 2009, 179–195 (notes on 409–414).

Maillard, J.-F., J. Kecskeméti, and M. Portalier. 1995. *L'Europe des Humanistes (XIVe–XVIIe siècles)*. Turnhout: Brepols.

Malcolm, Noel. 2014. "Masters of What?" [Review of Bod 2013.] *Times Literary Supplement*, no. 5801 (June 6, 2014), 3–4.

Mallett, Michael. 1974. *Mercenaries and Their Masters*. Totowa, NJ: Rowman and Littlefield.

———. 1979. "Preparations for War in Florence and Venice in the Second Half of the Fifteenth Century." In Bertelli, Rubinstein, and Smyth 1979–1980, 1: 149–164.

———. 1990. "The Theory and Practice of Warfare in Machiavelli's Republic." In Bock, Skinner, and Viroli 1990, 173–180.

———. 1994. "The Art of War." In *Handbook of European History, 1400–1600: Late Middle Ages, Renaissance, and Reformation*, edited by Thomas A. Brady, 535–561. Leiden: E. J. Brill.

Mallett, Michael, and Christine Shaw, 2012. *The Italian Wars, 1494–1559*. New York: Pearson.

Malta, Caterina. 1990. "Per Dione Crisostomo e gli umanisti: I. La traduzione di Giorgio Merula." *Studi umanistici* (Messina) 1: 181–201.

Manselli, Raoul. 1976. "Petrarca nella politica delle signorie padane alla metà del Trecento." In *Petrarca, Venezia e il Veneto*, edited by Giorgio Padoan, 9–22. Florence: Leo S. Olschki.

Mansfield, Harvey C. 2000. "Bruni and Machiavelli on Civic Humanism." In Hankins 2000a, 223–246.

Marchesi, Simone. 2013. "Boccaccio on Fortune *(De casibus virorum illustrium)*." In Kirkham, Sherberg, and Smarr 2013, 245–254 (notes on 442–446).

Marenbon, John. 2015. *Pagans and Philosophers: The Problem of Paganism from Augustine to Leibniz*. Princeton: Princeton University Press.

Marietti, Marina. 2009. *Machiavel: Le penseur de la nécessité*. Paris: Payot & Rivages.

Markus, Robert A. 1988. *Saeculum: History and Society in the Theology of St. Augustine*. Cambridge: Cambridge University Press.

———. 1991. *The End of Ancient Christianity*. Cambridge: Cambridge University Press.

———. 2006. *Christianity and the Secular*. Notre Dame, IN: University of Notre Dame Press.

Marsh, David. 1991. "Sparta and Quattrocento Humanism: Lilius Tifernas' Translation of the *Spartan Constitution*." *Bibliothèque d'Humanisme et Renaissance* 53(1): 91–103.

———. 1992. "Xenophon." In *CTC* 7: 75–196 and 8: 341–344.

———. 1998. *Lucian and the Latins: Humor and Humanism in the Early Renaissance*. Ann Arbor: University of Michigan Press.

Marshall, John. 2006. *John Locke, Toleration, and Early Enlightenment Culture: Religious Intolerance and Arguments for Religious Tolerance in Early Modern and "Early Enlightenment" Europe*. Cambridge: Cambridge University Press.

Martelli, Mario. 1992. "Machiavelli e la storiografia umanistica." In *La storiografia umanistica: Convegno internazionale di studi, Messina, 22–25 ottobre 1987*, edited by Anita di Stefano et al., 1: 113–52. Messina: Sicania.

———. 2000. "*Motivi politici nelle* Intercenales *di L. B. Alberti*." In *Leon Battista Alberti, Actes du Congrès international, Paris, 10–15 avril 1995*, edited by Francesco Furlan et al., 1: 477–489. 2 vols. Turin: Nino Aragno; Paris: J. Vrin.

Marzi, Demetrio. (1910) 1987. *La cancelleria della Repubblica Fiorentina*. 2 vols. Florence: Le Lettere.

Mattingly, Garrett. 1958. "Machiavelli's *Prince:* Political Science or Political Satire?" *American Scholar* 27(4): 482–491.

Maxson, Brian Jeffrey. 2010. "Kings and Tyrants: Leonardo Bruni's *Hiero* in Early Renaissance Florence." *Renaissance Studies* 24(2): 188–206.

———. 2014. *The Humanist World of Renaissance Florence.* Cambridge: Cambridge University Press.

———. 2015. "Humanism and the Ritual of Command in Fifteenth Century Florence." In *After Civic Humanism: Learning and Politics in Renaissance Italy,* edited by Nicholas Scott Baker and Brian Jeffrey Maxson, 113–129. Toronto: Center for Reformation and Renaissance Studies.

Mazzocco, Angelo. 1984. "Decline and Rebirth in Bruni and Biondo." In *Umanesimo a Roma nel Quattrocento: Atti del Convegno su umanesimo a Roma nel Quattrocento, New York, 1–4 dicembre 1981,* edited by Paolo Brezzi and Maristella de Panizza Lorch, 249–266. Rome: Istituto di Studi Romani.

———. 2006a. "Petrarch: Founder of Renaissance Humanism?" In *Interpretations of Renaissance Humanism,* edited by Angelo Mazzocco, 214–242. Leiden: E. J. Brill.

———. 2006b. "Un idea politica italiana in Petrarca?" In *Petrarca politico: Atti del convegno, Roma-Arezzo, 19–20 marzo 2004,* 9–23. Roma: Istituto storico italiano per il Medio Evo.

———. 2012a. "Dante, Bruni, and the Issue of the Origin of Mantua." *Modern Language Notes* 127(1): 257–263.

———. 2012b. "A Glorification of Christian Rome or an Apology of Papal Policies? A Reappraisal of Biondo Flavio's *Roma Instaurata* III 83–114." In *Roma e il papato nel Medioevo: Studi in onore di Massimo Miglio,* vol. 2, *Primi e tardi umanesimi: Uomini, immagini, testi,* edited by Anna Modigliani, 73–88. Rome: Edizioni di Storia e Letteratura.

———. 2014–2015. "A Reconsideration of Renaissance Antiquarianism in Light of Biondo Flavio's *Ars Antiquaria.*" *Memoirs of the American Academy in Rome* 59–60: 121–159.

Mazzotta, Giuseppe. 1993. *The Worlds of Petrarch.* Durham NC: Duke University Press.

McAleer, Graham, 1999. "Giles of Rome on Political Authority." *Journal of the History of Ideas* 60: 21–36.

McClure, George M. 1991. *Sorrow and Consolation in Italian Renaissance Humanism.* Princeton: Princeton University Press.

McCormick, John P. 2011. *Machiavellian Democracy.* Cambridge: Cambridge University Press.

———. 2018. *Reading Machiavelli: Scandalous Books, Suspect Engagements, and the Virtue of Populist Politics.* Princeton: Princeton University Press.

McDiarmid, John F., ed. 2007. *The Monarchical Republic of Early Modern England: Essays in Response to Patrick Collinson.* Aldershot, UK: Ashgate.

McLaughlin, Martin. 2016. *Leon Battista Alberti: La Vita, l'umanesimo, le opere letterarie.* Florence: Leo S. Olschki.

McManamon, John M. 1989. *Funeral Oratory and the Cultural Ideals of Italian Humanism.* Chapel Hill: University of North Carolina Press.

———. 1996. *Pierpaolo Vergerio the Elder: The Humanist as Orator.* Tempe: Arizona Center for Medieval and Renaissance Studies.

Meek, Christine. 2010. "'Whatever's Best Administered Is Best': Paolo Guinigi *signore* of Lucca, 1400–1430." In Law and Paton 2010, 131–143.

Meier, Christian, and Hans Leo Reimann. 1972. "Demokratie." In *Geschichtliche Grundbegriffe: Historisches Lexikon zur politischen-sozialen Sprache in Deutschland,* edited by Otto Brunner, Werner Conze, and Reinhart Koselleck, 1: 821–899. Stuttgart: E. Klett.

Meinecke, Friedrich. 1957. *Machiavellism: The Doctrine of* Raison d'État *and Its Place in Modern History.* London: Routledge and Kegan Paul. English translation by Douglas Scott of the next item.

———. (1924) 1963. *Die idee der Staatsräson in der neueren Geschichte.* 3rd ed. Munich: R. Oldenbourg.

Melczer, William. 1975. "Cola di Rienzo and Petrarch's Political Solitude." *Explorations in Renaissance Culture* 2: 1–13.

Mercer, R. G. G. 1979. *The Teaching of Gasparino Barzizza with Special Reference to His Place in Paduan Humanism.* London: Modern Humanities Research Association.

Merguet, Hugo. 1905. *Handlexicon zu Cicero.* Leipzig: Dieterich.

Meserve, Margaret. 2008. *Empires of Islam in Renaissance Historical Thought.* Cambridge, MA: Harvard University Press.

Miethke, Jürgen. 2004. "The Power of Rulers and Violent Resistance Against an Unlawful Rule in the Political Theory of William of Ockham." *Revista de ciencia política* 24(1): 209–226.

Millar, Fergus. 2000. "The First Revolution: Imperator Caesar, 36–28 BC." In *La révolution romaine après Ronald Syme: Bilans et perspectives; Sept exposés suivis de discussions, Vandœuvres-Genève, 6–10 septembre 1999,* edited by Fergus Millar et al., 1–38. Geneva-Vandœuvres: Fondation Hardt.

Mita Ferraro, Alessandra. 2005. *Matteo Palmieri: Una biografia intellettuale.* Genoa: Name.

Mitchell, Charles, Edward W. Bodnar, and Clive Foss. 2015. *Cyriac of Ancona: Life and Early Travels.* Cambridge, MA: Harvard University Press. (ITRL 65.)

Moles, John L. 1996. "Cynic Cosmopolitanism." In *The Cynics: The Cynic Movement in Antiquity and Its Legacy,* edited by Robert Bracht Branham and Marie-Odile Goulet-Cazé, 105–120. Berkeley: University of California Press.

———. 2005. "The Cynics." In Rowe and Schofield 2005, 419–434.

Momigliano, Arnaldo. (1974) 1977. "Polybius' Reappearance in Western Europe." In *Polybe: Neuf exposés suivis de discussions,* edited by F. W. Walbank, 347–372. Vandoeuvres-Genève: Fondation Hardt. Republished in *Essays in Ancient and Modern Historiography,* 79–98. Middletown CT: Wesleyan University Press.

———. 1980. *Sesto contributo alla storia degli studi classici e del mondo antico.* 2 vols. Rome: Edizioni di Storia e Letteratura.

———. 1990. "The Rise of Antiquarian Research." In idem, *The Classical Foundations of Modern Historiography,* 54–79. Berkeley: University of California Press.

Mommsen, Theodor E. 1959. *Medieval and Renaissance Studies,* edited by Eugene F. Rice. Ithaca: Cornell University Press.

Monfasani, John. 1976. *George of Trebizond: A Biography and a Study of His Rhetoric and Logic.* Leiden: E. J. Brill.

———. 1984. *Collectanea Trapezuntiana: Texts, Documents, and Bibliographies of George of Trebizond.* Binghamton, NY: Medieval and Renaissance Texts and Studies.

———. 1992. "Episodes of Anti-Quintilianism in the Italian Renaissance: Quarrels on the Orator as a *vir bonus* and Rhetoric as the *scientia bene dicendi.*" *Rhetorica* 10(2): 119–138.

———. 1999. "The Ciceronian Controversy." In *The Cambridge History of Literary Criticism*, vol. 3, *The Renaissance,* edited by Glyn P. Norton, 395–401. Cambridge: Cambridge University Press.

———. 2007. "A Tale of Two Books: Bessarion's *In Calumniatorem Platonis* and George of Trebizond's *Comparatio Philosophorum Platonis et Aristotelis.*" *Renaissance Studies* 22(1): 1–15.

———. 2016. "Machiavelli, Polybius, and Janus Lascaris: The Hexter Thesis Revisited." *Italian Studies* 71(1): 39–48.

Monnier, Philippe. (1901) 1924. *Le Quattrocento: Essai sur l'histoire littéraire du XVe siècle italien.* Paris: Perrin.

Moore, John B. 1966. *Social Origins of Dictatorship and Democracy: Lord and Peasant in the Making of the Modern World.* Boston: Beacon Press.

Moore, John M. 1965. *The Manuscript Tradition of Polybius.* Cambridge: Cambridge University Press.

Morris, Ian Macgregor. 2012. "Lycurgus in Late Medieval Political Culture." In Hodkinson and Morris 2012, 1–41.

Morrow, Glenn R. (1960) 1993. *Plato's Cretan City: A Historical Interpretation of the* Laws. Princeton: Princeton University Press.

Moulakis, Athanasios. 2000. "Civic Humanism, Realist Constitutionalism, and Francesco Guicciardini's *Discorso di Logragno.*" In Hankins 2000a, 200–222.

———. 2011. "Civic Humanism." In *SEP.*

Mühleisen, Hans-Otto, Theo Stammen, and Michael Philipp, eds. 1997. *Fürstenspiegel der frühen Neuzeit.* Frankfurt am Main: Insel.

Murari Pires, Francisco. 2015. "The Thucydidean Clio between Machiavelli and Hobbes." In *A Handbook to the Reception of Thucydides,* edited by Christine Lee and Neville Morley, 141–157. Chichester, UK: John Wiley and Sons.

Murphy, James Jerome, ed. 1983. *Renaissance Eloquence: Studies in the Theory and Practice of Renaissance Rhetoric.* Berkeley: University of California Press.

Nadon, Christopher. 2001. *Xenophon's Prince.* Berkeley: University of California Press.

Najemy, John M. 1982a. *Corporatism and Consensus in Florentine Electoral Politics, 1280–1400.* Chapel Hill: University of North Carolina Press.

———. 1982b. "Machiavelli and the Medici: The Lessons of Florentine History." *Renaissance Quarterly* 35(4): 551–576.

———. 1999. "Papirius and the Chickens." *Journal of the History of Ideas* 60(4): 659–681.

———. 2000. "Civic Humanism and Florentine Politics." In Hankins 2000a, 75–104.

———, ed. 2004. *Italy in the Age of the Renaissance, 1300–1550.* Oxford: Oxford University Press.

———. 2006. *A History of Florence, 1200–1575.* Malden, MA: Blackwell.

———., ed. 2010. *The Cambridge Companion to Machiavelli.* Cambridge: Cambridge University Press.

Nederman, Cary J. 1996. "The Meaning of 'Aristotelianism' in Medieval Moral and Political Thought." *Journal of the History of Ideas* 57(4): 563–585.

———. 1999. "Amazing Grace: Fortune, God, and Free Will in Machiavelli's Thought." *Journal of the History of Ideas* 60(4): 617–638.

———. 2009. *Lineages of European Political Thought: Explorations along the Medieval/Modern Divide from John of Salisbury to Hegel.* Washington, DC: Catholic University of America Press.

———. 2016. "Polybius as Monarchist? Receptions of *Histories* VI before Machiavelli, ca. 1490–1515." *History of Political Thought* 37(3): 461–79.

———. 2018. "There Are No 'Bad Kings': Tyrannical Characters and Evil Counsel in Medieval Political Thought." In Panou and Schadee 2018, 137–156.

Nederman, Cary J., and Mary Elizabeth Sullivan. 2012. "The Polybian Moment: The Transformation of Republican Thought from Ptolemy of Lucca to Machiavelli." *European Legacy: Toward New Paradigms* 17(7): 867–881.

Nelson, Eric. 2004. *The Greek Tradition in Republican Thought.* Cambridge: Cambridge University Press.

———. 2010. *The Hebrew Republic: Jewish Sources and the Transformation of European Political Thought.* Cambridge, MA: Harvard University Press.

———. 2014. *The Royalist Revolution: Monarchy and the American Fouding.* Cambridge, MA: Harvard University Press.

Neumahr, Uwe. 2002. *Die* Protestatio de Iustitia *in der Florentiner Hochkultur: Eine Redegattung.* Hamburg: Lit.

Newell, Waller R. 2013. *Tyranny: A New Interpretation.* New York: Cambridge University Press.

Nippel, Wilfried. 2010. "Democracy." In Grafton, Most, and Settis 2010, 256–259.

Nussbaum, Martha. 1997. "Kant and Stoic Cosmopolitanism." *Journal of Political Philosophy* 5(1): 1–25.

Oakeshott, Michael. 1980. Review of Skinner 1978. *Historical Journal* 23(2): 449–453.

Ober, Josiah. 1993. "The Polis as a Society: Aristotle, John Rawls, and the Athenian Social Contract." In *The Ancient Greek City-State,* ed. Mogens H. Hansen, 129–160. Copenhagen: Royal Danish Academy of Sciences and Letters.

———. 2005. "Aristotle's Natural Democracy." In Kraut and Scultety 2005, 223–243.

Oberhelman, Steven M. 1987. "The Diagnostic Dream in Ancient Medical Theory and Practice." *Bulletin of the History of Medicine* 61(1): 47–60.

O'Brien, Emily. 2009. "Arms and Letters: Julius Caesar, the *Commentaries* of Pius II, and the Politicization of Papal Imagery." *Renaissance Quarterly* 62(4): 1037–1097.

O'Connell, Monique. 2009. *Men of Empire: Power and Negotiation in Venice's Maritime State.* Baltimore: Johns Hopkins University Press.

———. 2017. "Voluntary Submission and the Ideology of Venetian Empire from History to Myth." *I Tatti Studies in the Italian Renaissance* 20(1): 9–39.

O'Daly, Gerard. 1999. *Augustine's* City of God: *A Reader's Guide.* Oxford: Clarendon Press.

Ollier, François. (1933–1943) 1973. *Le mirage spartiate.* 2 vols. Paris: Les Belles Letters, 1933–43. Reprinted in one volume. New York: Arno Press, 1973.

O'Malley, John W. 1993. *The First Jesuits.* Cambridge, MA: Harvard University Press.

Oman, Charles William Chadwick. (1937) 1999. *A History of the Art of War in the Sixteenth Century.* Mechanicsburg, PA: Stackpole Books.

Orestano, Riccardo. 1987. *Introduzione allo studio di diritto romano.* Bologna: Il Mulino.

Osmond de Martino, Patricia. 1988. "The Idea of Constantinople: A Prolegomenon to Further Study." *Historical Reflections / Réflexions Historiques* 15(2): 323–336.

Osmond, Patricia. 1993. "Sallust and Machiavelli: From Civic Humanism to Political Prudence." *Journal of Medieval and Renaissance Studies* 22: 407–438.

———. 2015. "Pomponio Leto's Life of Sallust: Between *vita* and *invectiva*." In *Vitae Pomponianae: Lives of Classical Writers in Fifteenth-Century Humanism,* edited by Marianne Pade. Special issue of *Renaessanceforum: Tidsskrift for renaessanceforskning* 9: 36–62.

Osmond, Patricia, and Robert W. Ulery. 2003. "Sallustius." In *CTC* 8: 183–326.

Pade, Marianne. 2003. "Thucydides." In *CTC* 8: 103–181.

———. 2007. *The Reception of Plutarch's Lives in the Fifteenth Century.* 2 vols. Copenhagen: Museum Tusculum Press.

———. 2017. "Popular Government Revisited: New Texts on Greek Political History and Their Influence in Fifteenth-Century Italy." *Neulateinisches Jahrbuch* 19: 313–338.

Pagden, Anthony. 1995. *Lords of All the World: Ideologies of Empire in Spain, Britain, and France, c. 1500–c. 1800.* New Haven: Yale University Press.

Pagliaroli, Stefano. 2006. *L'Erodoto del Valla.* Messina: Centro interdipartimentale di studi umanstici.

———. 2012. "Il Proemio di Mattia Palmieri alla traduzione latina delle storie di Erodoto." In Gambino Longo 2012, 23–43.

Palisca, Claude V. 1985. *Humanism in Italian Renaissance Musical Thought.* New Haven: Yale University Press.

Palmer, Ada. 2014. *Reading Lucretius in the Renaissance.* Cambridge, MA: Harvard University Press.

Palmer, R. R. 1953. "Notes on the Use of the Word 'Democracy.'" *Political Science Quarterly* 68(2): 203–226.

Panizza, Letizia A. 1991. "Stoic Psychotherapy in the Middle Ages and Renaissance: Petrarch's *De remediis.*" In *Atoms, Pneuma, and Tranquillity,* ed. Margaret J. Osler, 39–65. Cambridge: Cambridge University Press.

Panofsky, Erwin. (1960) 1972. *Renaissance and Renascences in Western Art.* New York: Harper and Row.

Panou, Nikos, and Hester Schadee, eds. 2018. *Evil Lords: Theory and Representations from Antiquity to the Renaissance.* Oxford: Oxford University Press.

Paoli, Michel. 2007. "Battista e i suoi nipoti: Il 'conservatorismo' albertiano nel *De iciarchia* e le ultime opere." In *Leon Battista Alberti umanista e scrittore: Filologia, esegesi, tradizione, Atti del Convegno internazionale del Comitto Nazionale VI centenario della nascita di Leon Battista Alberti, Arezzo, 24–25–26 giugno 2004,* edited by Roberto Cardini e Mariangela Regoliosi, 2: 523–540. Florence: Edizione Polistampa.

Parsons, Jotham. 2004. *The Church in the Republic: Gallicanism and Political Ideology in Renaissance France.* Washington, DC: Catholic University of America Press.

Partner, Peter. 1990. *The Pope's Men: The Papal Civil Service in the Renaissance.* Oxford: Oxford University Press.

Pastore Stocchi, Manlio. 1984. "Il Boccaccio del *De casibus.*" *Giornale storico della letteratura italiana* 161(515): 421–430.

———. 1987. "Il pensiero politico degli umanisti." In *Storia delle idee politiche, economiche e sociali,* vol. 3, *Umanesimo e Rinascimento,* edited by Giuseppe Alberigo et al., 3–68. Turin: UTET.

Pedullà, Gabriele. 2003. "Il divieto di Platone: Niccolò Machiavelli e il discorso dell'anonimo plebeo (*Ist. Fior.* III, 13)." In *Storiografia repubblicana fiorentina, 1494–1570,* edited by Jean-Jacques Marchand and Jean-Claude Zancarini, 209–266. Florence: F. Cesati.

———. 2010. "Giro d'Europa: Le mille vite di Dionigi di Alicarnasso." In *Dionigi di Alicarnasso: Le antichità romane,* edited by Francesco Donadi and Gabriele Pedullà, lxxxiii–cxi. Turin: Einaudi.

———. 2010–2012. "Scipione e i tiranni." In *Atlante della letteratura italiana,* ed. Sergio Luzzatto and Gabriele Pedullà, 1: 348–355. Turin: Einaudi.

———. 2011. *Machiavelli in tumulto: Conquista, cittadinanza e conflitto nei* Discorsi sopra la prima deca di Tito Livio. Rome: Bulzoni.

———. 2018. *Machiavelli in Tumult: The* Discourses on Livy *and the Origins of Political Conflictualism.* Cambridge: Cambridge University Press. (Translation of Pedullà 2011 with reduced documentation but with revisions and expansions of the text.)

Pennington, Kenneth. 1997. "Baldus de Ubaldis." *Rivista internazionale di diritto comune* 8: 35–61.

Percopo, Erasmo. 1907. *Lettere di Giovanni Pontano a principi e amici.* Naples: Francesco Giannini.

Pernot, Laurent. 2008. "Aelius Aristides and Rome." In *Aelius Aristides between Greece, Rome, and the Gods,* edited by William V. Harris and Brooke Holmes, 175–201. Leiden: E. J. Brill.

Pettit, Philip. 1999. *Republicanism: A Theory of Freedom and Government,* Oxford: Oxford University Press.

Pieri, Piero. (1934) 1971. *Il Rinascimento e la crisi militare.* 2nd ed. Turin: Einaudi.

Pio, Berardo. 2013. "Il tiranno velato fra teoria politica e realtà storica." In Zorzi 2013, 95–118.

Pocock, J. G. A. (1975) 2003. *The Machiavellian Moment: Florentine Political Thought and the Atlantic Republican Tradition.* Princeton: Princeton University Press.

———. 2009. "The Politics of Historiography." In idem, *Political Thought and History: Essays on Theory and Method,* 257–269. Cambridge: Cambridge University Press.

Ponte, Giovanni. 1997. "I consigli politici del Petrarca a Francesco da Carrara (*Sen.* XIV, 1)." In *Petrarca e la cultura europea,* edited by Luisa Rotondi Secchi Tarugi, 121–127. Milano: Nuovi orrizonti.

Poole, Reginald Lane. 1920. *Illustrations of the History of Medieval Thought and Learning.* New York: Macmillan.

Portogallo, Claudia Rammelt. 2017. "A Greek in the City: Thucydides between Leonardo Bruni and Niccolò Machiavelli." Ph.D. diss., Yale University.

Potter, David. 2008. *Renaissance France at War: Armies, Culture, and Society, ca. 1480–1560.* Woodbridge, UK: Boydell Press.

Praga, Giuseppe. 1932–1933. "Indagini e studi sull'umanesimo in Dalmatia: Ciriaco de' Pizzicolli e Marino de' Resti." *Archivio storico per la Dalmazia* 13: 262–280.

Prezzolini, Giuseppe. 1954. *Machiavelli, anticristo.* Rome: G. Casini.

Priestley, Jessica, and Vasiliki Zali, eds. 2016. *Brill's Companion to the Reception of Herodotus in Antiquity and Beyond.* Leiden: E. J. Brill.

Procacci, Giuliano. 1995. *Machiavelli nella cultura europea dell'età moderna,* Rome-Bari: Laterza.

Quaglione, Diego. 1983. "Un *Tractatus de tyranno:* Il Commento di Baldo degli Ubaldi (1327?–1400) alla *Lex Decernimus,* c. De sacrosanctis ecclesiis (C. 1, 2, 16)." *Il Pensiero Politico* 13(1): 64–83.

———. 2003. *La sovranità,* Roma-Bari: Laterza.

———. 2004. *La giustizia nel Medioevo e nella prima età moderna.* Bologna: Il Mulino.

———. 2007. "Sovranità: Un paradigma premoderno." In *Filosofia del diritto: Concetti fondamentali,* edited by Ulderico Pomarici, 551–561. Turin: Giappichelli.

———. 2012a. "'A Problematical Book': Il *De tyranno* di Coluccio Salutati." In *Le radici umanistiche dell'Europa: Coluccio Salutati cancelliere e politico,* edited by Roberto Cardini, 335–350. Florence: Edizioni Polistampa.

———. 2012b. "Sovereignty versus Tyranny in Medieval and Early Modern Political Thought." In *In the Footsteps of Herodotus: Towards European Political Thought,* edited by Janet Coleman and Paschalis Kitromilides, 65–76. Florence: Leo S. Olschki.

Quondam, Amadeo. 2010. *Forma del vivere: L'etica del gentiluomo e i moralisti italiani.* Bologna: Il Mulino.

Raaflaub, Kurt. 2004. *The Discovery of Freedom in Ancient Greece.* Chicago: University of Chicago Press.

Rabil, Albert, Jr., ed. 1991. *Knowledge, Goodness, and Power: The Debate over Nobility among Quattrocento Italian Humanists.* Binghamton, NY: Medieval and Renaissance Texts and Studies.

Rahe, Paul A. 2008. *Against Throne and Altar: Machiavelli and Political Theory under the English Republic.* Cambridge: Cambridge University Press.

———. 2016. *The Spartan Regime: Its Character, Origins, and Grand Strategy* New Haven: Yale University Press.

Rawls, John. (1971) 1999. *A Theory of Justice.* Revised edition. Cambridge, MA: Harvard University Press.

———. 2005. *Political Liberalism.* Expanded ed. New York: Columbia University Press.

Rawson, Elizabeth. 1969. *The Spartan Tradition in European Thought.* Oxford: Clarendon Press.

———. 1975. "Caesar's Heritage: Hellenistic Kings and Their Roman Equals." *Journal of Roman Studies* 65: 148–159.

Reeve, Michael D. 1996. "Classical Scholarship." In *The Cambridge Companion to Renaissance Humanism,* edited by Jill Kraye, 20–46. Cambridge: Cambridge University Press.

Regnicoli, Laura. 2013a. "Documenti su Giovanni Boccaccio." In *Boccaccio: Autore e copista; Firenze, Biblioteca Medicea Laurenziana, 11 ottobre 2013–11 gennaio 2014* (exhibition catalogue), edited by Teresa De Robertis, Carla Maria Monti, Marco Petoletti, Giuliano Tanturli, and Stefano Zamponi, 385–402. Florence: Mandragora.

———. 2013b. "Codice diplomatico di Giovanni Boccaccio: I. I documenti fiscali." *Italia medioevale e umanistica* 54: 1–80.

Regoliosi, Mariangela. 1997. "L'*Epistola contra Bartolum* del Valla." *Filologia umanistica per Gianvito Resta,* edited by Francesco Fera and Giacomo Ferraú, 2: 1501–1572. Padua: Antenore.

Reinhardt, Karl. 1960. "Thukydides und Machiavelli." In *Vermächtnis der Antike,* edited by Carl Becker, 184–218. Göttingen: Vandenhoeck und Ruprecht.

Resta, Gianvito. 1986. "Francesco Filelfo tra Bisanzio e Roma." In *Francesco Filelfo nel quinto centenario della morte, Atti del XVII convegno di studi maceratesi, Tolentino, 27–30 settembre 1981,* edited by Rino Avesani, Giuseppe Billanovich, Mirella Ferrari, and Giovanni Pozzi, 1–60. Padua: Antenore.

Revest, Clémence. 2013. "La naissance de l'humanisme comme mouvement au tournant du XVe siècle." *Annales. Histoire, Sciences Sociales,* 68 / 3 (July–September): 665–696.

Revest, Clémence. 2014. "L'émergence de l'idéal humaniste de la *Roma instaurata* dans le contexte curial de la fin du Grand Schisme," in É. Crouzet-Pavan, D. Crouzet et P. Desan (eds.), *Cités humanistes et cités politiques (1400–1600). Actes du colloque international (Paris, 27–28 mai 2011),* 123–138. Paris: PUPS.

Ricciardelli, Fabrizio. 2015. *The Myth of Republicanism in Renaissance Italy.* Turnhout: Brepols.

Riché, Pierre. (1979) 1999. *Écoles et enseignement dans le Haut Moyen Age: fin du Ve siècle—milieu du XIe siècle.* 3rd ed. Paris: Picard.

Richter, Daniel S. 2017. "Cosmopolitanism." In Richter and Johnson 2017, 81–98.

Richter, Daniel S., and William A. Johnson. 2017. *The Oxford Handbook of the Second Sophistic.* Oxford: Oxford University Press.

Ridder-Symoens, Hilde de. 1992. *Universities in the Middle Ages.* History of the University in Europe 1. Cambridge: Cambridge University Press.

Ridolfi, Roberto. (1954) 2014. *Vita di Niccolò Machiavelli.* Reprint of 8th ed., edited by Giuseppe Cantele with an introduction by Maurizio Viroli. Rome: Castelvecchi.

Roberts, Jennifer Tolbert. 1994. *Athens on Trial: The Antidemocratic Tradition in Western Thought.* Princeton: Princeton University Press.

Robey, David, and John Law. 1975. "The Venetian Myth and the *De republica veneta* of Pier Paolo Vergerio." *Rinascimento,* n.s., 15: 3–59.

Robichaud, Denis. 2018. *Plato's Persona: Marsilio Ficino, Renaissance Humanism, and Platonic Traditions.* Philadelphia: University of Pennsylvania Press.

Robiglio, Andrea A. 2006. "The Thinker as a Noble Man *(bene natus)* and Preliminary Remarks on the Medieval Concepts of Nobility." *Vivarium* 44(2 / 3): 205–247.

———. 2015. "La nobiltà di spada in Dante: Un appunto su *Il Convivio* IV xiv 11." In *Il Convivio di Dante,* edited by Joannes Bartuschat and Andrea Robiglio, 191–204. Ravenna: Longo.

Robin, Diana. 1983. "A Reassessment of the Character of Francesco Filelfo (1398–1481)." *Renaissance Quarterly* 36: 202–24.

Rocke, Michael. 1996. *Forbidden Friendships: Homosexuality and Male Culture in Renaissance Florence.* New York: Oxford University Press.

Roick, Mattias. 2017. *Pontano's Virtues: Aristotelian Moral and Political Thought in the Renaissance.* London: Bloomsbury.

Ronconi, Giorgio. 1976. *Le origini delle dispute umanistiche sulla poesia (Mussato e Petrarca).* Rome: Bulzoni.

Rose, David C. 2019. *Why Culture Matters Most.* Oxford: Oxford University Press.

Rosenblum, Nancy L. 2008. *On the Side of the Angels: An Appreciation of Parties and Partisanship.* Princeton, NJ: Princeton University Press.

Ross, Janet, and Nelly Ericksen. 1909. *The Story of Pisa.* London: J. M. Dent.

Ross, Sarah G. 2016. *Everyday Renaissances: The Quest for Cultural Legitimacy in Venice.* Cambridge, MA: Harvard University Press.

Rossi, Giovanni. 1999. "Un umanista di fronte al diritto: A proposito del *De iure* di Leon Battista Alberti." *Rivista di storia del diritto italiano* 72: 77–154.

———. 2000. "Intorno al *De iure* di Leon Battista Alberti." *Albertiana* 2: 221–248.

———. 2007. "Alberti e la scienza giuridica quattrocentesca: Il ripudio di un paradigma culturale." In *Alberti e la cultura del Quattrocento: Atti del Convegno internazionale (Firenze, 16–17–18 dicembre 2004),* edited by Roberto Cardini and Mariangela Regoliosi, 59–121. Florence: Edizioni Polistampa.

———. 2008. "Valla e il diritto: *L'Epistola contra Bartolum* e le *Elegantiae,*" in *Pubblicare il Valla: Percorsi di ricerca e proposte interpretative,* edited by Mariangela Regoliosi, 507–599. Florence: Edizioni Polistampa, 2008.

———. 2013. "Il *Borsus* di Biondo Flavio: *Militia* e *iurisprudentia* a confronto dall' antica Roma all'Italia delle corti rinascimentali." *Historia et ius: Rivista di storia giuridica dell'età medievale e moderna* 4 (paper 4), 1–26 (online only at www.historiaetius.eu).

———. 2015a. "L'umanista senese Francesco Patrizi e la lezione etico-politica degli antichi: Il trattato *De institutione reipublicae* (ante 1471)." In *Acta Conventus Neo-Latini Monasteriensis: Proceedings of the Fifteenth International Congress of Neo-Latin Studies (Münster 2012),* edited by Astrid Steiner-Weber and K. A. E. Enekel, 440–449. Leiden: E. J. Brill.

———. 2015b. "Sulle orme di Lorenzo Valla: Una rilettura del trattato *De insigniis et armis* di Bartolo. In *Bartolo da Sassoferrato nella cultura europea tra Medioevo e Rinascimento,* edited by Victor Crescenzi e Giovanni Rossi, 63–96. [Sassoferrato]: Istituto Internazionale di Studi Piceni "Bartolo da Sassoferrato."

Rowe, Christopher, and Malcolm Schofied. (2000) 2005. *The Cambridge History of Greek and Roman Political Thought.* Cambridge: Cambridge University Press.

Rubinstein, Nicolai. 1963. Review of Bayley 1961. *History* 48: 211–214.

———. 1968. "Florentine Constitutionalism and the Medici Ascendency in the Fifteenth Century." In *Florentine Studies: Politics and Society in Renaissance Florence,* edited by Nicolai Rubinstein, 442–462. London: Faber.

———. 1990a. "Il Bruni a Firenze: Rhetorica e politica." In Viti 1990, 15–28.

———. 1990b. "Machiavelli and the Florentine Republican Experience." In Bock, Skinner, and Viroli, 3–16.

———. 1995. *The Palazzo Vecchio, 1298–1532: Government, Architecture, and Imagery in the Civic Palace of the Florentine Republic.* Oxford: Clarendon Press.

———. 2004a. *Studies in Italian History in the Middle Ages and the Renaissance,* vol. 1, *Political Thought and the Language of Politics.* Rome: Storia e letteratura, 2004.

———. 2004b. "The History of the Word *politicus* in Early-Modern Europe." In Rubinstein 2004a, 317–333.

———. 2004c. "The *De optimo cive* and the *De principe* by Bartolomeo Platina." In Rubinstein 2004a, 259–271.

Rummel, Erika. 1995. *The Humanist Scholastic Debate in the Renaissance and Reformation.* Cambridge, MA: Harvard University Press.

Ryan, Magnus. 2000. "Bartolus of Sassoferrato and Free Cities." *Transactions of the Royal Historical Society* 10: 65–89.

Sabbadini, Remigio. 1928. "L'ortografia latina di Vittorino da Feltre e la scuola padovana." *Rendiconti della R. Accademia Nazionale dei Lincei* 4: 209–221.

Salvemini, Gaetano. 1972. *La dignità cavalleresca nel Comune di Firenze e altri scritti,* edited by Ernesto Sestan. Milan: Feltrinelli.

Samaritani, Antonio. 1976. *Michele Savonarola riformatore cattolico nella corte Estense a metà del secolo XV.* Ferrara: SATE.

Sandel, Michael. 2018. *Encountering China: Michael Sandel and Chinese Philosophy.* Cambridge, MA: Harvard University Press.

Santagata, Marco. 2016. *Dante: The Story of His Life.* Cambridge, MA: Harvard University Press.

Santinello, Giovanni. 1974. "Il pensiero politico e religioso del Petrarca." *Studia patavina* 21(3): 586–601.

Santini, Emilio. 1910. *Leonardo Bruni Aretino e i suoi* Historiarum Florentini populi libri XII. Pisa: Nistri.

Santosuosso, Antonio. 1986. "Leonardo Bruni Revisited: A Reassessment of Hans Baron's Thesis on the Influence of the Classics in the *Laudatio Florentinae Urbis.*" In *Aspects of Late Medieval Government and Society: Essays Presented to J. R. Lander,* edited by J. G. Rowe, 25–51. Toronto: University of Toronto Press.

Sasso, Gennaro. (1958) 1980. *Niccolò Machiavelli: Storia del suo pensiero politico,* Bologna: Il Mulino.

———. 1987. *Machiavelli e gli antichi e altri saggi.* Milano: R. Ricciardi.

Schadee, Hester. 2008. "*Caesarea Laus:* Ciriaco d'Ancona Praising Caesar to Leonardo Bruni." *Renaissance Studies* 22(4): 435–449.

———. 2018. "'I Don't Know Who You Call Tyrants': Debating Evil Lords in Quattrocento Humanism." In Panou and Schadee 2018, 172–190.

Schiera, Pierangelo. 1996. "Legitimacy, Discipline, and Institutions." In Kirshner 1996, 11–33.

Schiller, Kay. 2000. *Gelehrte Gegenwelten: Über humanistische Leitbilder im 20. Jahrhundert.* Frankfurt am Main: Fischer.

Schneewind, J. B. 1998. *The Invention of Autonomy: A History of Modern Moral Philosophy.* Cambridge: Cambridge University Press.

Schofield, Malcolm. 1999a. *Saving the City: Philosopher-Kings and Other Classical Paradigms.* London: Routledge.

———. 1999b. "Cicero's Definition of the *res publica.*" In Schofield 1999a, 178–194.

———. 1999c. "Equality and Hierarchy in Aristotle's Thought." In Schofield 1999a, 100–114.

———. 2009. "Republican Virtues." In Balot 2009, 199–213.

Schütrumpf, Ekart. 2014. *The Earliest Translations of Aristotle's* Politics *and the Creation of Political Terminology.* Paderborn: Wilhelm Fink.

Schwartz, Benjamin I. 1985. *The World of Thought in Ancient China.* Cambridge, MA: Harvard University Press.

Sherk, Robert Kenneth. 1969. *Roman Documents from the Greek East:* Senatus consulta *and* Epistulae to the Age of Augustus. Baltimore: Johns Hopkins Press.

Simmons, A. John. 2010. "Ideal and Non-Ideal Theory." *Philosophy and Public Affairs* 38(1): 5–36.

Simonetta, Marcello. 1997. "Machiavelli lettore di Tucidide." *Esperienze letterarie* 22(3): 53–68.

Singer, Peter. 2015. *The Most Good You Can Do: How Effective Altruism Is Changing Ideas about Living Ethically.* New Haven: Yale University Press.

Sion-Jenkis, Karin. 2000. *Von der Republik zum Principat: Ursachen für den Verfassungswechsel in Rom im historischen Denken der Antike.* Stuttgart: Franz Steiner.

Skinner, Quentin. 1978. *Foundations of Modern Political Thought.* 2 vols. Cambridge: Cambridge University Press.

———. 1981. *Machiavelli.* Oxford: Oxford University Press.

———. 1989. "The State." In *Political Innovation and Conceptual Change,* edited by Terence Ball, James Farr, and Russell L. Hansen, 90–131. Cambridge: Cambridge University Press.

——. 1990. "The Republican Ideal of Political Liberty." In Bock, Skinner, and Viroli 1990, 293–309.

——. 1998. *Liberty before Liberalism.* Cambridge: Cambridge University Press.

——. 2002a. *Visions of Politics,* vol. 2, *Renaissance Virtues.* Cambridge: Cambridge University Press.

——. 2002b. "The Idea of Negative Liberty: Machiavelli and Modern Perspectives." In Skinner 2002a, 186–212.

——. 2009. "A Genealogy of the Modern State." *Proceedings of the British Academy* 162: 325–70.

Smith, Christopher. 2006. "*Adfectio regni* in the Roman Republic." In Lewis 2006 (unpaginated digital publication).

Sorabji, Richard. 2014. *Moral Conscience through the Ages: Fifth Century BCE to the Present.* Chicago: University of Chicago Press.

Southern, Richard W. 1995–1999. *Scholastic Humanism and the Unification of Europe.* 2 vols. Oxford: Blackwell.

Spade, Paul Vincent, and Claudio Panaccio. 2015. "William of Ockham." In *SEP.*

Sposato, Peter. 2018. "Chivalry in Late Medieval Tuscany and Florence: Current Historiography and New Perspectives." *History Compass* (June). DOI: 10.1111 / hic3.12458.

Stacey, Peter. 2000. "Imperial Rome and the Legitimation of Political Authority in Renaissance Naples." Ph.D. diss., University of Cambridge.

——. 2007. *Roman Monarchy and the Renaissance Prince.* Cambridge: Cambridge University Press.

——. 2013. "Free and Unfree States in Machiavelli's Political Thought." In *Freedom and the Construction of Europe,* ed. Quentin Skinner and Martin van Gelderen, 1: 176–194. Cambridge: Cambridge University Press.

——. 2017. "The Image of Nero in Renaissance Political Thought." In *The Cambridge Companion to the Age of Nero,* edited by Shadi Bartsch et al., 290–304. Cambridge: Cambridge University Press.

Stadter, Philip A. 2009. "Character in Politics." In Balot 2009, 456–470.

Steinberg, Justin. 2009. "Petrarch's Damned Poetry and the Poetics of Exclusion." In Kirkham and Maggi 2009, 85–100.

Stern, Laura I. 1994. *The Criminal Law System of Medieval and Renaissance Florence.* Baltimore: Johns Hopkins University Press.

Straumann, Benjamin. 2016a. *Crisis and Constitutionalism: Roman Political Thought from the Fall of the Republic to the Age of Revolution.* Oxford: Oxford University Press.

——. 2016b. "*Imperio sine fine:* Carneades, the Splendid Vice of Glory, and the Justice of Empire." In *International Law and Empire: Historical Explanation,* edited by Martti Koskenniemi, Walter Rech, and Manuel Jiménez Fonseca, 335–358. Oxford: Oxford University Press.

——. 2018. "The Roman Republic as a Constitutional Order in the Italian Renaissance." In Velema and Weststeijn 2018, 40–61.

Strauss, Leo. 1958. *Thoughts on Machiavelli.* Chicago: University of Chicago Press.

——. (1961) 2013. *On Tyranny.* Corrected and expanded ed., including the Strauss-Kojève Correspondence, edited by Victor Gourevitch and Michael S. Roth. Chicago: University of Chicago Press.

Struever, Nancy S. 1970. *The Language of History in the Renaissance: Rhetoric and Historical Consciousness in Florentine Humanism*. Princeton: Princeton University Press.

Suerbaum, Werner. 1977. *Vom antiken zum frühmittelalterlichen Staatsbegriff: Über Verwendung und Bedeutung vons* res publica, regnum, imperium *und* status *von Cicero bis Jordanis*. 3rd ed. Muenster: Aschendorff.

Sullivan, Vickie B. 1996. *Machiavelli's Three Romes: Religion, Human Liberty, and Politics*. Dekalb: Northern Illinois University Press.

Tafuri, Manfredo. 2006. "*Cives Esse Non Licere*': *Nicholas V and Leon Battista Alberti*. In idem, *Interpreting the Renaissance: Princes, Cities, Architects*, tr. Daniel Sherer, 23–58. New Haven: Yale University Press; Cambridge, MA: Harvard University Graduate School of Business.

Taylor, Charles. 1998. "Modes of Secularism." In *Secularism and Its Critics*, edited by Rajeev Bhargava, 31–53. New York: Oxford University Press.

———. 2002. *Varieties of Religion Today: William James Revisited*. Cambridge, MA: Harvard University Press.

Teng, Ssu-yü. 1943. "Chinese Influence on the Western Examinations System." *Harvard Journal of Asiatic Studies* 7(4): 267–312.

Thurn, Nikolaus. 2002. *Kommentar zur Carlias des Ugolino Verino*. Munich: Fink.

Tigerstedt, Eugène Napoleon. 1965–1978. *The Legend of Sparta in Classical Antiquity*. 3 vols. [Stockholm]: Almqvist and Wiksell.

Trexler, Richard C. 1980. *Public Life in Renaissance Florence*. Ithaca: Cornell University Press.

Trinkaus, Charles E. (1960) 1983. "A Humanist's Image of Humanism: The Inaugural Orations of Bartolomeo della Fonte." *Studies in the Renaissance* 7: 90–147. Reprinted (without appendices) in idem, *The Scope of Renaissance Humanism*, 52–87. Ann Arbor: University of Michigan Press.

Tuck, Richard. 2015. *The Sleeping Sovereign: The Invention of Modern Democracy*. Cambridge: Cambridge University Press.

Turchetti, Mario. 2001. *Tyrannie et tyrannicide de l'antiquité à nos jours*. Paris: Classiques Garnier.

Ulery, Robert W. 1986. "Tacitus." In *CTC* 6: 87–174.

Ullman, Berthold Louis. 1955. "Leonardo Bruni and Humanist Historiography." In idem, *Studies in the Italian Renaissance*, 321–344. Rome: Edizioni di Storia e Letteratura.

Ullman, Walter. 1965. *A History of Political Thought: The Middle Ages*. Harmondsworth, UK: Penguin.

United States Central Intelligence Agency. 2016–2017. *The World Factbook*. Washington, DC: Central Intelligence Agency. Online only: cia.gov/library/publications/the-world-factbook.

Valentinelli, Giuseppe. 1868–1873. *Bibliotheca Manuscripta ad S. Marci Venetiarum*. 6 vols. Venice: Ex Typographia Commercii.

Vallentyne, Peter. 2012. "Libertarianism." In *SEP*.

Vasaly, Ann. 2015. *Livy's Political Philosophy*. Cambridge: Cambridge University Press.

Vegetti, Mario, and Paolo Pissavino, eds. 2005. *I Decembrio e la tradizione della* Repubblica *di Platone tra Medioevo e Umanesimo*. Naples: Bibliopolis.

Velema, Wyger, and Arthur Weststeijn, eds. 2018. *Ancient Models in the Early Modern Republican Imagination*. Leiden: E. J. Brill.

Verrier, Fréderique. 1997. *Les armes de Minerve: L'humanisme militaire dans l'Italie du XVIe siècle*. Paris: Presses de l'Université de Paris-Sorbonne.

Villard, Renaud. 2008. *Du bien commun au mal nécessaire: Tyrannies, assassinats politiques et souver-ainté en Italie, vers 1470–vers 1600.* Rome: École française de Rome.

Viroli, Machiavelli. 2010. *Machiavelli's God.* Princeton: Princeton University Press.

Vishnia, Rachel Feig. 2012. *Roman Elections in the Time of Cicero: Society, Government, and Voting.* London: Routledge.

Viti, Paolo, ed. 1990. *Leonardo Bruni Cancelliere della Repubblica di Firenze.* Florence: Leo S. Olschki.

———. 1992. *Leonardo Bruni e Firenze: Studi sulle lettere pubbliche e private.* Rome: Bulzoni.

———. 2004. *Sulla perfetta traduzione.* Naples: Liguori.

———. 2005. "Traduzioni 'repubblicane' e traduzioni 'signorili': Sul rapporto fra storiografia clas-sica e storiografia umanistica." In *Il Principe e la storia, Atti del convegno Scandiano 18–20 settembre 2003,* edited by Tina Matarrese and Cristina Montagnani, 535–563. Novara: Interlinea.

Vlassopoulos, Kostas. 2012. "Sparta and Rome in Early Modern Thought: A Comparative Approach." In Hodkinson and Morris 2012, 43–69.

Voice, Paul. 2014. "Comprehensive Doctrine." In *The Cambridge Rawls Lexicon,* edited by Jon Mandle and David A. Reidy, 126–129. Cambridge: Cambridge University Press. doi:10.1017 / CBO978 1139026741.041.

Waldron, Jeremy. 2002. *God, Locke, and Equality: Christian Foundations of John Locke's Political Thought.* Cambridge: Cambridge University Press.

———. 2006. "The Core of the Case against Judicial Review." *Yale Law Journal* 115(6): 1346–1406.

Walker, Daniel Pickering. 1972. *The Ancient Theology: Studies in Christian Platonism from the Fif-teenth to the Eighteenth Century.* London: Duckworth.

Walzer, Michael. 1973. "Political Action: The Problem of Dirty Hands." *Philosophy and Public Af-fairs* 2: 160–180.

Ward, John O. 1995. "Quintilian and the Rhetorical Revolution of the Middle Ages." *Rhetorica* 13(3): 231–284.

Weber, Max. 1976. *Wirtschaft und Gesellschaft,* edited by Johannes Winckelmann. 5th ed. Tübingen: Mohr-Siebeck.

Wei-ming, Tu (1978) 1998. *Humanity and Self-Cultivation: Essays in Confucian Thought.* Boston: Cheng and Tsui.

Weinstock, Stefan. 1971. *Divus Julius.* Oxford: Clarendon Press.

Wickert, Lothar. 1949. "Der Prinzipat und die Freiheit." In *Symbola Coloniensia Josepho Kroll sexa-genario A.D. VI. Id. Nov. a. MCMIL oblata,* 113–141. Cologne: B. Pick.

Wilcox, Donald. 1969. *The Development of Florentine Humanist Historiography in the Fifteenth Century.* Cambridge, MA: Harvard University Press.

Wilkins, Ernest Hatch. 1958. *Petrarch's Eight Years in Milan.* Cambridge, MA: Medieval Academy of America.

———. 1961. *Life of Petrarch.* Chicago: University of Chicago Press.

Wilson, Blake. 2009a. *Singing Poetry in Renaissance Florence: The "Cantasi come" Tradition (1375–1550).* Florence: Leo S. Olschki.

Wirszubski, Chaim. 1950. *Libertas as a Political Ideal during the Late Republic and Early Principate.* Cambridge: Cambridge University Press.

———. 1954. "Cicero's *Cum Dignitate Otium:* A Reconsideration." *Journal of Roman Studies* 44: 1–13.

Witt, Ronald G. 1969. "The *De tyranno* and Coluccio Salutati's View of Roman Politics and History." *Nuova rivista storica* 53(3–4): 434–474.

———. 1983. *Hercules at the Crossroads: The Life, Works, and Thought of Coluccio Salutati*. Durham, NC: Duke University Press.

———. 2000. *In the Footsteps of the Ancients: The Origins of Humanism from Lovato to Bruni*. Leiden: E. J. Brill.

———. 2011. *The Two Latin Cultures and the Foundations of Renaissance Humanism in Medieval Italy*. Cambridge: Cambridge University Press.

Wood, Gordon S. 2009. *Empire of Liberty: A History of the Early Republic, 1789–1815*. Oxford: Oxford University Press.

Woodhouse, Adam. 2018. "Subjection without Servitude: The Imperial Protectorate in Renaissance Political Thought." *Journal of the History of Ideas* 79(4): 547–569.

Wootton, David. 2006. "The True Origins of Republicanism: The Disciples of Baron and the Counter-example of Venturi." In *Il repubblicanesimo moderno: L'idea di repubblica nella riflessione storica di Franco Venturi,* edited by Manuela Albertone, 271–304. Naples: Bibliopolis.

Zervas, Diane Finiello. 1988. *The Parte Guelfa, Brunelleschi, and Donatello*. Locust Valley, PA: Augustin.

Zippel, Giuseppe. 1979. "Il Filelfo a Firenze (1429–1434)." In *Storia e cultura del Rinascimento italiano,* edited by Giani Zippel, 215–253. Padua: Antenore.

Zorzi, Andrea. 1988. *L'amminstrazione della giustizia penale nella repubblica fiorentina*. Florence: Leo S. Olschki.

———. 2010. *Le signorie cittadine in Toscana: esperienze di potere e forme di governo personale (secoli XIII–XV)*. Milan: Mondadori.

———, ed. 2013. *Tiranni e tirannide nel Trecento italiano*. Rome: Viella.

Acknowledgments

CHAPTERS 1, 4, 5, AND 6: Based in part on seminars given in the Facoltà di lettere e filosofia, Università degli Studi di Firenze (2017). I thank Prof. Concetta
Bianca and the participants in the seminars for various suggestions.

CHAPTER 2: A shorter version of the middle sections of this chapter was first given
in lecture form at Amherst College (Classical Legacy Lecture, 2013); at the XXIV°
Congresso Internazionale di Studi Umanistici in Sassoferrato, Italy (2013); at the
American Academy in Rome (2014); and at a conference in Berlin sponsored by the
Sonderforschungsbereich 644: Transformations of Antiquity, based at Humboldt
University (2015). An edited version of the original paper has now been published as
"The Virtue Politics of the Italian Humanists," conference proceedings for *Beyond
Reception: Renaissance Humanism and the Transformation of Classical Antiquity,*
Humboldt-Universität zu Berlin, 23–24 (March 2015), ed. Patrick Baker, Johannes
Helmrath, and Craig Kallendorf (Berlin: De Gruyter, 2019), 95–114. The portions of
the chapter based on the paper have been revised and considerably expanded.

CHAPTER 3: The first section is based in part on a paper given at the "Recent
Trends" panel at the Renaissance Society of America at its National Meeting in
Berlin, 2015. The middle sections evolved from a short paper at the conference *La
Repubblica di Platone e la sua tradizione,* sponsored by the Dipartimento di Filosofia, Università degli Studi, Pavia (2000), and published as "*De republica:* Civic
Humanism in Renaissance Milan (and Other Renaissance Signories)," in the proceedings of the conference *I Decembrio e la tradizione della* Repubblica *di Platone
tra Medioevo e Umanesimo,* ed. Mario Vegetti and Paolo Pissavino (Naples: Bibliopolis, 2005), 485–508. In my study of the history of the word *respublica* I received invaluable help early on from Ada Palmer. Later versions of the paper were
given to the Committee on Social Thought, University of Chicago (Nef Lecture);
the American Academy in Berlin (Anna-Marie Kellen Lecture); at the Institut für
Philosophie, Seminar für Geistesgeschichte und Philosophie der Renaissance,
at the Ludwig Maximilians Universität, Munich; at the Scuola Normale Supe-
riore, Pisa; at the Seminar in Political and Moral Thought at The Johns Hopkins

University; at a conference at the CUNY Graduate Center, New York; and at a seminar at the Humanities Center, Princeton University. The paper was eventually published as "Exclusivist Republicanism and the Non-Monarchical Republic," *Political Theory* 38(4) (August 2010): 452–482. Those sections of the chapter appear here in revised and extended form.

CHAPTER 4: Some portions were given as an address to the annual conference of the Center for Ethics and Culture, University of Notre Dame (2017) and as a La Motta Chair lecture at Seton Hall University (2018). I thank William Connell for the latter invitation.

CHAPTER 6: First published in substantially the same form under the title "The Unpolitical Petrarch: Justifying the Life of Literary Retirement," *Et amicorum: Essays on Renaissance Humanism and Philosophy in Honour of Jill Kraye,* ed. Anthony Ossa-Richardson and Margaret Meserve, Brill's Studies in Intellectual History, vol. 273 (Leiden: Brill, 2017), 7–32. Copyright © 2018 by Koninklijke Brill NV, Leiden, The Netherlands. The chapter omits the Latin texts included in the earlier version.

CHAPTER 7: Based on a paper given at the conference *A Boccaccian Renaissance* sponsored jointly by University of California at Berkeley and Stanford University (2013). An edited version of the original paper was published as "Boccaccio and the Political Thought of Renaissance Humanism," *A Boccaccian Renaissance,* ed. Martin Eisner and David Lummus, Devers Series in Dante and Medieval Italian Literature (Notre Dame, IN: Notre Dame University Press, 2019), 3–35. The version published here has been substantially revised and extended. Copyright © 2019 by the University of Notre Dame.

CHAPTER 8: An earlier version of this chapter was given at the conference *Potenza nella cultura moderna* in Florence, sponsored by the Scuola Normale di Pisa and the Istituto Nazionale di Studi sul Rinascimento (2011). A version much closer to the present chapter was delivered at a conference in Rome in honor of Prof. Lucia Gualdo Rosa; it was later delivered in Italian as an *oratio magistralis* at the Scuola di Dottorato in Scienze Umanistiche, Università degli Studi di Verona. I would like to thank Paolo Pellegrini for his hospitality on that occasion and to the learned audience on both occasions for their comments. The paper was published as "Leonardo Bruni's *Laudatio Florentine urbis,* Dante, and 'Virtue Politics,'" *Bullettino dell' Istituto Storico Italiano per il Medio Evo* 119 (2017): 1–25. The version published here has been substantially revised and extended.

CHAPTER 9: The first and third sections were based on papers given in 1995 for the University of Copenhagen's Faculty Lecture Series and in 1999 at the conference *The Transformations of the Medieval Knight in Renaissance and Early Modern Europe,* sponsored by the Forum for Renaissance Studies, University of Copenhagen. A version of the same sections was published as "Civic Knighthood in the Early Renaissance: Leonardo Bruni's *De militia* (*ca.* 1420)," *Noctua: International Online Journal of the History of Philosophy* 1(2) (2014): 260–282.

CHAPTER 10: A shorter version based on a conference paper was published as "Teaching Civil Prudence in Leonardo Bruni's *History of the Florentine People,*" in *Ethik—Wissenschaft oder Lebenskunst? Modelle de Normenbegründung von der Antike bis zur Frühen Neuzeit,* ed. Sabrina Ebbersmeyer and Eckhard Kessler, Pluralisierung und Autorität 8 (Berlin: Lit Verlag, 2007), 143–157. Copyright © Lit Verlag, Dr. W. Hopf, Berlin, 2007.

CHAPTER 11: An earlier version based on a conference paper was published as "Biondo Flavio on the Roman Republic," *The Invention of Rome: Biondo Flavio's Roma Triumphans and Its Worlds,* ed. Frances Muecke and Maurizio Campanelli, Travaux d'humanisme et Renaissance 576 (Geneva: Librarie Droz, 2017), 101–118. Copyright © 2017 Librairie Droz S.A., 11, rue Massot, Genève.

CHAPTER 12: The chapter was published in substantially the same form as "Europe's First Democrat? Cyriac of Ancona and Book 6 of Polybius," *For the Sake of Learning: Essays in Honor of Anthony Grafton,* ed. Ann Blair and Anja-Silvia Goeing, 2 vols. (Leiden: Brill, 2016), 2: 692–710. Copyright © 2016 by Koninklijke Brill NV, Leiden, The Netherlands.

CHAPTER 13: Based on a paper given at *Alberti ludens: A Conference in Memory of Cecil Grayson,* University of Oxford, June 26–27, 2017. The revised conference paper will be published as "Alberti on Corrupt Princes and Virtuous Oligarchs," *Albertiana* 22(2) (2019), a special issue entitled *Alberti ludens,* edited by Francesco Furlan and Martin McLaughlin. Copyright © 2019 Leo S. Olschki Editore, Florence, Italy.

CHAPTER 14: First published as "George of Trebizond: Renaissance Libertarian?" *Essays in Renaissance Thought and Letters in Honor of John Monfasani,* ed. Alison K. Frazier and Patrick Noll, Brill Studies in Intellectual History 241 (Leiden: Brill, 2015), 87–106. Copyright © 2015 by Koninklijke Brill NV, Leiden, The Netherlands. The version in this chapter has been revised and corrected.

CHAPTER 15: Reprints and slightly expands on "Filelfo and the Spartans," *Francesco Filelfo, Man of Letters,* ed. Jeroen De Keyser, Brill Studies in Intellectual History 289 (Leiden: E. J. Brill, 2018), 81–96. Copyright © 2018 by Koninklijke Brill NV, Leiden, The Netherlands.

CHAPTER 20: Reprints most of and expands on "Leonardo Bruni and Machiavelli on the Lessons of Florentine History," *Le cronache volgari in Italia: Atti della VI Settimana di studi medievali (Roma, 13–15 maggio 2015),* ed. Giampaolo Francesconi and Massimo Miglio, Nuovi Studi Storici 105 (Rome: Istituto storico italiano per il Medio Evo, 2017), 373–395. Copyright © 2017 Istituto storico italiano per il Medio Evo, Rome.

CONCLUSION: Various papers and seminars given at Peking University, Tianjin University, Shandong University, Sichuan University, Shanghai Normal University, Fudan University, Hong Kong University, and the Chinese University of Hong Kong have provided opportunities to develop comparisons between Confucian and Italian humanist political thought. I would like to thank my kind hosts, especially Tongdong Bai, Daniel Bell, Wu Fei, Lin Guo, Stuart McManus, and Liang Zhonghe for those opportunities, as well as the many Chinese scholars who have tolerated my inexpert generalizations and improved my understanding of Confucian meritocracy.

The author of a book that has been gestating for almost a quarter century and actively in composition for nearly a decade will have many debts, and though history may be the *vita memoriae,* this historian fears that his own memory may overlook some who deserve acknowledgment here. It impossible to forget, however, the immense gratitude I owe to the electors of the Carlyle Lectureship in the Faculty of History at the University of Oxford, especially George Garnett. Equally unforgettable was the hospitality and kindness I experienced at All Souls College in

2010 and again as a Visiting Fellow in 2014, particularly from Noel Malcolm, Ian Maclean, Keith Thomas, Margaret Bent, Justin Stover, and George Woudhuysen. Elsewhere in Oxford I found wonderful interlocutors in Bonnie Blackburn and Leofranc Holford-Strevens, Myles Burnyeat, Caroline Elam, Matthew Kempshall, Martin McLaughlin, David Rundle, and Nigel and Hanneke Wilson.

At Harvard, Eric Nelson has been a constant interlocutor and generous reader, as was, until his early death in 2015, my dear friend Mark Kishlansky. I have learned much about civil conversation in republics from my friendship over three decades with Harvey Mansfield, a gentleman of the most humane virtue. For many years I have enjoyed the delightful intellectual companionship of Theo Theoharis, and it was in conversation with him that the title of this book emerged. Other Harvard colleagues have generously shared their learning with me, especially Dimiter Angelov, David Armitage, the late Ernst Badian, Ann Blair, Peter Bol, Joe Connors, Emma Dench, C. P. Jones, Cemal Kafadar, Jim Kloppenberg, Jenny Mansbridge, Michael McCormick, Lino Pertile, Michael Sandel, and Dan Smail.

From outside Harvard I am grateful for information, help, and support of various kinds from Michael J. B. Allen, Alberto Ascoli, Patrick Baker, Stefano Baldassarri, Francesco Bausi, Concetta Bianca, Rémi Brague, Shane Butler, William Caferro, Guido Cappelli, Michele Ciliberto, Michelle Clarke, Brian Copenhaver, Jeroen De Keyser, Anthony D'Elia, Arthur Field, Clive Foss, the late Riccardo Fubini, Julia Gaisser, Ken Gouwens, Anthony Grafton, Allen Grieco, Lucia Gualdo Rosa, Johannes Helmrath, Kinch Hoekstra, Ferenc Hörcher, Gary Ianziti, Mark Jurdjevic, Craig Kallendorf, Tim Kircher, Jill Kraye, John Law, David Lines, David Marsh, Angelo Mazzocco, John P. McCormick, Massimo Miglio, John Monfasani, Frances Muecke, Lodi Nauta, Cary Nederman, Monique O'Connell, Patricia Osmond, Marianne Pade, Ada Palmer, Gabriele Pedullà, Maria Agata Pincelli, Paul Rahe, Silvia Rizzo, Andrea Robiglio, Hester Schadee, Quentin Skinner, Benjamin Straumann, Jan Waszink, and David Wootton. My old undergraduate teacher Ronald G. Witt passed away in May 2017, and it is among my keenest regrets that he was not able to see a book that has benefited so much from his learning and humanity.

At Harvard University Press I am grateful to Ian Malcolm, who convinced me of the virtues of dealing locally. Above all I would like to thank Joy de Menil, my peerless editor at the Press, who read every word of my manuscript, red pencil in hand, and helped reduce the thickets of academic prose to allow easier access to non-specialists. My readers for the Press have all been outed in various ways beyond their control, but this mild violation of academic protocol at least allows me to give them the warmest thanks for the generous terms of their approval and for many valuable suggestions: Robert Black, Christopher Celenza, and Peter Stacey. The Department of History at Harvard generously provided a subsidy to defray the editorial costs of publishing this volume.

This book would not have been finished but for a term of free time in 2018 afforded me as a Visiting Research Fellow at the Center for Ethics and Culture of the University of Notre Dame. I would like to express my warmest thanks to my former student Gladden Pappin and to the Center's director, O. Carter Snead, for making possible that blessed respite from the burdens of teaching at Harvard.

I have dedicated the book to the memory of my beloved companion of thirty years, who embodied *humanitas* in every sense of that word.

Index of Manuscripts and Archival Documents

Florence, Archivio di Stato
Archivio della Repubblica, Capitani della Parte Guelfa *rosso,* vol. 3: 588n7
Archivio della Repubblica, Consulte e practiche vol. 34: 585n29
Archivio della Repubblica, Missive Ia Cancelleria, vol. 58: 554n96

Florence, Biblioteca Medicea Laurenziana
Plut. 51.19: 616n52
Plut. 77.24: 541n34, 581n57, 617n60
Plut. 79.19: 554n85, 653
Plut. 90 sup. 47: 547n109
San Marco 67: 545n82

Florence, Biblioteca Nazionale Centrale
Magl. VII 1095: 591n50
Magl. VIII 1440: 581n55

Florence, Biblioteca Riccardiana
Ricc. 784: 566n129
Ricc. 1166: 566n129
Ricc. 1200: 581n55

Milan, Biblioteca Ambrosiana
B 123 sup.: 557n140
F 55 sup.: 543n51

Modena, Biblioteca Estense Universitaria
Est. lat. 114 (α W 6 6): 555n114, 660

Paris, Bibliothèque Nationale de France
Par. lat. 14845: 569n23

Rimini, Biblioteca Civica Gambalunga
47 (4.A.II.25): 588n8

Seville, Biblioteca Capitular y Colombina
7-2-23: 538n71

General Index

Abelard, xvii

Abruzzo, 167

absolutism, xxii, 400, 406–407. *See also* monarchy, absolute

Academics, 397, 401, 630n32

Academy, 45, 62

Acciaiuoli, Alamanno, 589n24

Acciaiuoli, Angelo (Agnolo), 276, 282, 487

Acciaiuoli, Donato, 87, 89, 212–213, 271, 545n82

Acciaiuoli, house of, 194

Acciaiuoli, Niccola, 18, 158, 193, 194–195, 534n18, 535n36, 569n11

Accolti, Benedetto, 244, 545n81, 591n59

accountability, 52

Accursio, Mainardo, 180

Actium, 82, 552n62

Actium, battle of, 72, 77, 79, 81, 553n79, 571n45

active life, 95, 99, 183

Acton, John (Dalberg-), Lord, 330

Adams, John, *Defense of the Constitutions of Government of the United States of America,* 616n49

Adimari, Tegghiaio d'Aldobrandi de', 283–284, 480

Adriani, Marcello Virgilio, 430, 431, 438, 439, 629n17, 629n22

Adriatic Sea, 231

Aelian, 632n53

Aemilii clan, 226

Aeneas, 231, 235

Africa, Thomas, 365

Agathias, 351, 608n2

Agathocles, 636n25, 644n48

Agesilaus II, 357, 358, 609n9, 611n38, 611n41, 611n44

Agnadello, battle of, 439

Agrippa, Marcus Menenius, 372

Alamanno, Andrea, 611n44

Albanzani, Donato, 11

Albergati, Niccolò, 352, 354, 609–610n16

Alberigo of Barbiano, 68, 257

Albertano of Brescia, 535n40

Alberti, Leon Battista, 207, 269, 318–334, 345, 425, 453, 510; *De commodis litterarum atque incommodis,* 604n19; *De iciarchia,* 318–319, 326–327, 328–334, 542n43, 556n126, 602n2, 603n15, 604n24, 604n27, 605n31, 605n33, 605n39, 605n41, 606n43, 606nn46–48; *De iure,* 545n81, 603n16, 606n49; *Della famiglia,* 327–328, 329–330, 542n43, 581n63, 602n2, 603n10, 603n13, 604n25, 605n39, 605n42; *De re aedificatoria (On Architecture),* 319, 326–328, 369; *Intercenales,* 606n46; *Momus,* 318–319, 320, 321–324, 326, 332, 333–334, 602n3, 602n5; *Theogenius,* 604n29, 605n30; *Trivia senatoria,* 333

Albert the Great, 79

Albizzi, Rinaldo degli, 240, 249, 280

Alciati, Andrea, 561n53

Alcman, 354

Aldobrandino d'Ottobuono, 206, 579n36

Alexander the Great, 109, 122, 138, 139, 163, 262, 358, 405, 410, 436, 447, 448, 461, 618n10, 621n34

Alexander VI, pope, 428, 470, 635n8

Alfonso I, King of Naples, 142, 314, 391, 398, 406, 425, 426, 427, 428, 429, 567n147, 593n87, 619n13

Alfonso, Duke of Calabria (Alfonso II, King of Naples), 399, 424, 425, 621n30, 625n89, 630n27

allelopoiesis, 383, 611n35

Ambrose, saint, 97

707